S0-AXJ-149

SENSATION AND PERCEPTION

SIXTH EDITION

SIXTH EDITION

SENSATION AND PERCEPTION

STANLEY COREN

LAWRENCE M. WARD

JAMES T. ENNS

JOHN WILEY & SONS, INC.

ACQUISITIONS EDITOR *Tim Vertovec*
ASSISTANT EDITOR *Lili DeGrasse*
MARKETING MANAGER *Kate Stewart*
SENIOR PRODUCTION EDITOR *Norine M. Pigliucci*
SENIOR DESIGNER *Kevin Murphy*
PHOTO EDITOR *Lisa Gee*
PHOTO RESEARCHER *Teresa Romito*
PRODUCTION MANAGEMENT SERVICES *Pine Tree Composition*
COVER ART *Norm Christiansen*

This book was set in Times Roman by Pine Tree Composition and printed and bound by Donnelley Willard. The cover was printed by Lehigh Press.

This book is printed on acid free paper.

Library of Congress Cataloging in Publication Data:
Coren, Stanley.
Sensation and perception / Stanley Coren, Lawrence M. Ward, James T. Enns.—6th ed.

p. cm.
Includes bibliographical references and index.
ISBN 0-471-27255-8 (cloth)
1. Senses and sensation. 2. Perception. I. Ward, Lawrence M. II. Enns, James T. III. Title.

BF233. C59 2003
153.7—dc21

2003049725

ISBN 0-471-27255-8
WIE ISBN 0-471-45147-9

Printed in the United States of America

10 9 8 7 6 5 4 3 2 1

PREFACE

Take away the sensations of softness, moisture, redness, tartness, and you take away the cherry. Since it is not a being distinct from these sensations; a cherry, I say, is nothing but a congeries of sensible impressions or ideas perceived by various senses; which ideas are united into one thing. . . .

George Berkeley, 1713

Virtually everything we know about our world entered our minds in some form through our senses. We all realize that if even some of our senses were missing, our experiences would be incredibly limited. Consider the impossible problem of explaining the difference between the color blue and the color green to a person who has been blind since birth. Or how you would explain to a person who has no taste buds how the taste of chocolate and vanilla differ from each other? Such aspects of the world will never exist for these individuals. For the blind person, salt and pepper differ only in taste. For the person with no ability to taste, salt and pepper differ only in color or texture. For those of us who have senses of sight, hearing, taste, touch, and smell, our world is a rich and continuous flow of changing percepts. Each new sensation carries with it information about our world.

This book provides an introduction to the study of sensation and perception. This sixth edition of *Sensation and Perception* has not only moved to a new publisher but it also represents a revision and a substantial reorganization of the material in the fifth edition. First, the text has been updated with more than 600 new research citations, making this, we believe, the most up-to-date textbook available at this level. These changes incorporate many of the recent findings that have emerged, or coalesced into meaningful patterns, since the completion of the fifth edition, plus new insights provided by some cutting-edge methodologies, such as the various methods of human brain imaging.

The book has been shortened and streamlined, with an eye toward readability. We have rewritten all of the chapters, with some sections revised "from the ground up." We have retained the general structure and organization of the fifth edition so that the book will still feel familiar to our previous users, although there are new chapters and we have reduced the number of chapters to 16. This has required a reorganization of the material that we present, so that now color and brightness are combined in one chapter, and music and speech are included in the hearing chapter. We have a new chapter on patterns and edges, another on objects and scenes, and yet another on consciousness. These chapters reflect the new directions and emphases that are emerging in the field of perception.

We have also retained those features that instructors felt made the previous editions such a useful teaching tool. For instance, we use concrete examples throughout the text in order to make the subject matter "come alive" for students. Whenever possible, we describe common or natural instances of perceptual phenomena during the discussion of the concepts underlying them. Each chapter is preceded by an outline, which serves as a preview to its contents. These outlines also provide a structure that can guide students as they review the chapters. We have added a set of study questions at the end of each chapter.

One special feature of our text is the inclusion of over 100 Demonstration Boxes. Each box describes a simple demonstration designed to allow the students to experience many of the perceptual phenomena described in the text. Most require only the stimuli in the box itself or commonplace items that can be found in most homes and dormitory rooms. The majority of these demonstrations require only a few moments of preparation, and we feel that this is time well spent in improving understanding of the concepts under discussion and in maintaining student interest. Some instructors report that having students perform the demonstrations in class has been very useful. In such cases, the demonstrations may also serve as the focal point for a lecture or for classroom discussion. There are also four special Demonstration Boxes that allow individuals to screen their own sensory capacities without the use of special equipment. A test for color vision is found in Chapter 4, for visual acuity in Chapter 8, for uncorrected stereopsis in Chapter 9, and for hearing sensitivity in Chapter 15. These are behaviorally validated screening tests that allow for quick testing of these abilities and may prove useful in a variety of research projects; moreover, they provide students with useful information about their own sensory capacities.

A new addition to this text is the inclusion of several Biography Boxes in each chapter. Although we want the text to be as current and up to date as possible, we do not want students to lose the sense of history for the sake of modernity. The Biography Boxes allow us to briefly introduce some people who have made significant contributions to the field. Some are founders of the field, such as Helmholtz, but others are still active today. This allows the student to get some idea of the continuity of scientific progress, and the fact that the advances and applications are made by real people often with their own interesting histories, while at the same time not impending the presentation of the most current scientific findings.

This text is designed to survey the broad range of topics generally included under the heading of "sensation and perception." The reader will notice that we champion no single theory of perception. In general, we attempt to be as eclectic as possible, describing various viewpoints in areas of controversy and attempting to present a balanced viewpoint so that instructors of different opinions will be comfortable using the text.

In order to keep the book to a manageable size, we have occasionally been selective in our coverage. It is our first priority to cover the central concepts of each topic in enough detail to make the material clear and coherent. If it had been our goal to include all the topics ever classified as part of the field of sensation and perception, we could have only presented a "grocery list" of concepts and terms, each treated superficially. Such an alternative was unacceptable to us.

Each of the chapters has been written so that it is relatively self-contained and independent of the other chapters. When this is not possible, such as when material from other chapters is used in a discussion, the location of that information is always cited at the relevant place in the text. This has been done to provide instructors with maximum flexibility in chapter sequence presentation. By altering the sequence in which chapters are presented, an instructor can impress his or her orientation on the material. Generally speaking, the first half of the book covers topics usually associated with sensation, while the second half of the books is more oriented toward issues associated with perception. This separation, however, is blurred in the book, as it is in the field itself, so there is real overlap between the two halves of the book.

Finally, the reader might notice that there is no dedication page. This is not to say that we do not wish to dedicate the book to anyone; it merely reflects the fact that there are too many people who have been important in our personal and professional lives to list on any single page, no matter how small the print. Perhaps it is best simply to dedicate this book to all of those researchers who have provided the knowledge that we have attempted to organize and review between these covers, and to all of those researchers who will provide further insights into sensation and perception for future authors to collate, review, digest, wonder at, and learn from.

S.C.
L.M.W.
J.T.E.

CONTENTS

CHAPTER 1

SENSATION AND PERCEPTION

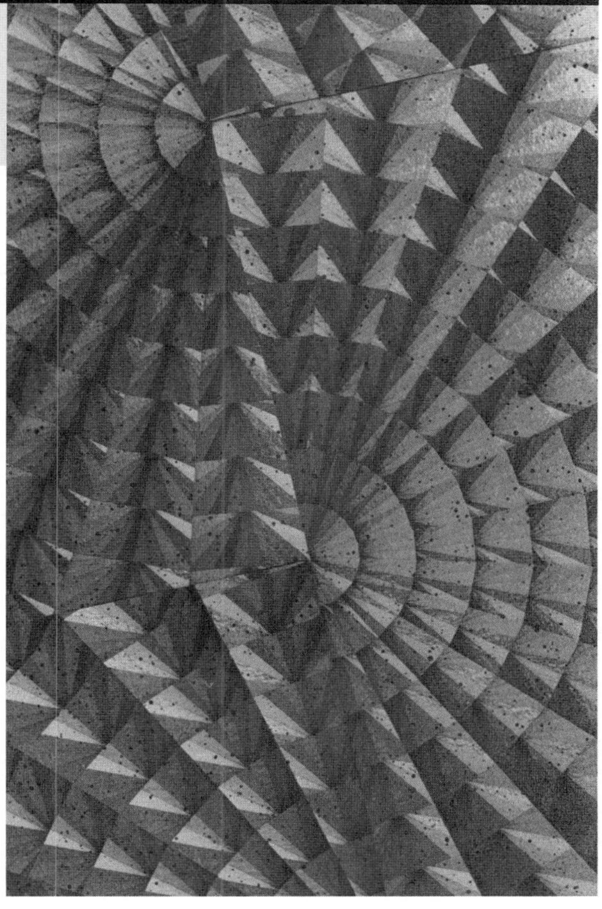

CHAPTER SUMMARY

Can you answer the following questions? What color is the sky? Which is warmer—fire or ice? Which tastes sweeter—sugar or vinegar? Which has a stronger smell—burning wood or burning rubber? Which sounds louder—the chirp of a bird or the crack of a rifle? Such questions probably seem trivial and the answers obvious. Perhaps we should phrase the questions differently. How do you know what color the sky is? How do you know how hot fire is relative to ice? How do you know that sugar is sweet? Again, you might feel that the answers are obvious. You see the color of the sky, you feel the temperatures of a flame and an ice cube, and you taste the sweetness of sugar—in other words, the answers come through your senses.

Let us push our questioning one step further. How do you know anything about your world? You might say that you learn from books, television, radio, films, lectures, or the actual exploration of places. And how do you obtain the information from these sources? Again, the answer is through your senses. In fact, without your senses of vision, hearing, touch, taste, and smell, your brain, the organ that is responsible for your conscious experience, would be an eternal prisoner in the solitary confinement of your skull. You would live in total silence and darkness. All would be a tasteless, colorless, feelingless, floating void. Without your senses, the world would simply not exist for you. The philosopher Thomas Hobbes recognized this fact in 1651 when he wrote, "There is no conception in man's mind which hath not at first, totally or by parts, been begotten upon the organs of sense." The Greek philosopher Protagoras stated the same position around 450 B.C. when he said, "Man is nothing but a bundle of sensations."

You may protest that this is a rather extreme viewpoint. Certainly, much of what we know about the world does not arrive through our eyes, ears, nose, and other sense organs. We have complex scientific instruments, such as telescopes, that tell us about the size and the shape of the universe by analyzing images too faint for the human eye to see. We have sonar to trace out the shape of the sea bottom, which may be hidden from our eyes by thousands of feet of water. We have spectrographs to tell us about the exact chemical composition of many substances, as compared to the crude chemical sensitivity of our noses and tongues. We have magnetic resonance imaging (MRI), X-rays, and CAT scans to tell us about how the internal parts of our bodies work.

Although such pieces of apparatus exist and measure phenomena not directly available to our senses, this does not alter the fact that it is the perception of the scientist that constitutes the subject matter of every science. The eye of the scientist presses against the telescope, examines the photograph of the distant star, inspects the X-ray or print out of the CAT scan. The ear of the scientist listens to the sound of sonar tracing out the size and distance of objects, or his eyes read the sonograph. Although the tongue of the scientist does not taste the chemical composition of some unknown substance, her eye, aided by the spectrograph, provides the data for analysis. Really, the only data that reach the mind of the scientist come not from instruments but rather from the scientist's senses. The instrument he or she is looking at can be perfectly accurate, yet if the scientist misreads a digital readout, misses a particular shadow on the X-ray, or does not notice a critical shift in the operation of a measurement device, the obtained information is wrong and the resulting picture of the world is in error. The minds of the scientist, the nonscientist, our pet dog sniffing about the world, or a fish swimming about in a bowl—in fact, the minds of all living, thinking organisms—are prisoners that must rely on information smuggled in to them by the senses. Your world is what your senses tell you. The limitations of your senses set the boundaries of your conscious existence.

Because our knowledge of the world is dependent on our senses, it is important to know how our senses function. It is also important to know how well the world that is created by our senses corresponds to external reality (i.e., the reality measured by scientific instruments). At this point, you are probably smiling to yourself and thinking, "Here comes another academic discourse that will attempt to make something that is quite obvious appear to be complex." You might be saying to yourself, "I see my desk in front of me because it is there. I feel my chair pressing against my back because it is there. I hear my phone ringing because it contains a tone generator that makes sounds. What could be more obvious?" Such faith in your senses is a vital part of existence. It causes you to jump out of the way of an apparently oncoming car, thus preserving your life. It provides the basic data that cause you to step back from a deep hole, thus avoiding a fall and serious bodily harm.

Such faith in our senses is built into the very fabric of our lives. As the old saying goes, "Seeing is believing." Long before the birth of Christ, Lucretius stated this article of faith when he asked, "What can give us surer knowledge than our senses? With what else can we distinguish the true form from the false?" Perhaps the most striking example of this faith is found in our courts of law, where people's lives, freedom, and fortunes rest solely on the testimony of the eyes and ears of witnesses. A lawyer might argue that a witness is corrupt or lying, or even that his memory has failed, but no lawyer would have the audacity to suggest that her client should be set free because the only evidence available was what the witnesses saw or heard. Certainly no sane person would charge the eye or ear with perjury!

The philosophical position that perception is an immediate, almost godlike knowledge of external reality has been championed not only by popular sentiment but also by philosophers of the stature of Immanuel Kant (1724–1804). Unfortunately, it is wrong. Look at the drawings shown in Figure 1.1. Clearly, they all are composed of outlined forms on various backgrounds. Despite what your senses tell you, A, B, and C all are perfect squares. Despite the evidence of your senses, D is a perfect circle, the lines in E both are straight, and the lines marked x and y in F both are the same length.

The ease with which we use our senses—seeing, apparently through the simple act of opening our eyes, or touching, apparently by merely pressing our skin against an object—masks the fact that perception is an extremely sophisticated activity of the brain. Perception calls on stores of memory data. It requires subtle classifications, comparisons, and myriad decisions before any of the data in our senses become our conscious awareness of what is "out there." Contrary to what you may think, the eyes do not see. There are many individuals who have perfectly functioning eyes yet have no sensory impressions. They cannot perceive because they have injuries in those parts of the brain that receive and interpret messages from the eyes. Epicharmus knew this in 450 B.C. when he said, "The mind sees and the mind hears. The rest is blind and deaf."

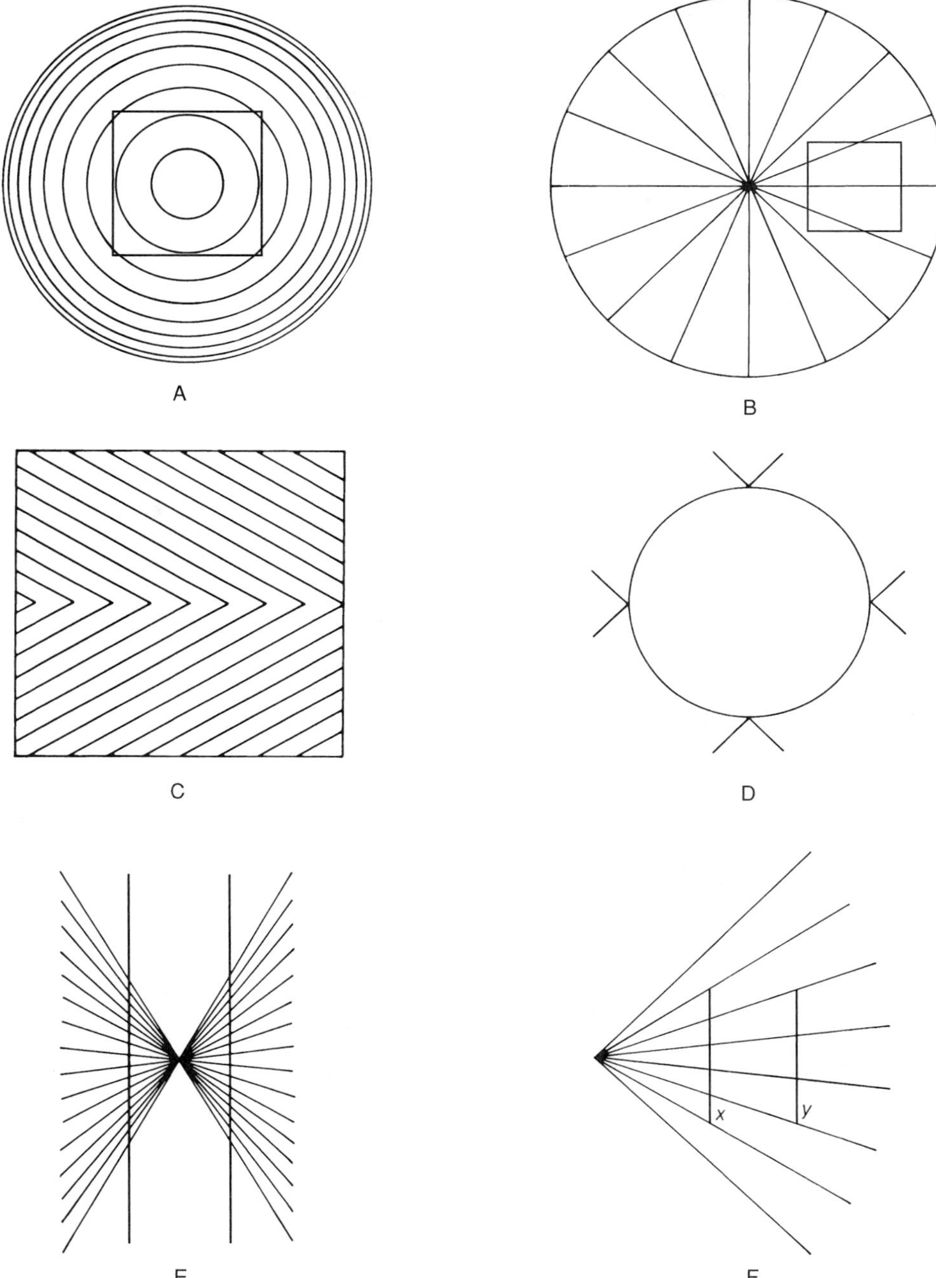

FIGURE 1.1 Some instances where the senses tell lies.

"So what?" you mutter to yourself. "So sometimes we make errors in our perceptions; the real point is that the senses simply carry a picture of the outside world to the brain. The picture in the brain represents our percept. Of course, if we mess up the brain we will distort or destroy perception." Again, this answer is too simple. If we look outside and see a car, are we to believe that there is a picture of a car somewhere in our brains? If we notice that a traffic light is green, are we to believe that some part of the brain has turned green? And suppose that there were

DEMONSTRATION BOX 1.1

THE FRASER SPIRAL

Look at the figure here. It clearly looks like a spiral, converging toward the center. How much would you be willing to bet that it is a spiral? On the basis of your perception alone, would you ever believe that it is actually a set of concentric circles? It actually *is* a set of circles, which you can verify for yourself. Place one finger on any line making up the "spiral." Place a finger from the other hand beside it, and carefully trace the line around with this finger while not moving the first finger. Eventually the moving finger will come back to the stationary one because the lines that appear to spiral are all part of a set of concentric circles (see Fraser, 1908; Stuart & Day, 1988; Taylor & Woodhouse, 1980, for variations of this illusion). This shows that no matter how convincing a perception might be, because it is based on a hypothesis or conclusion used to interpret stimuli reaching us, our conscious interpretation may be wrong!

such images in the brain, carried without distortion from the senses; would this help us to see? Certainly, images in the brain would be of value only if there were some other eyes in the head, which would look at these pictures and interpret them. If this were the case, we would be left with the question of how these internal eyes see. Thus, we would eventually be forced to set up an endless chain of pictures and eyes and pictures and eyes because the question of who is perceiving the percept, and how, still remains.

If we are to understand perception we must consider it in its natural context. Sensation and perception are some of the many complex processes that occur in the continuing flow of individual behavior. There is no clear line between perception and many other behavioral activities. No sensory impression gives direct knowledge of the outside world; rather, such knowledge of the outside world is the end product of many processes. The wet-looking black spot on the edge of a desk could be the place where ink was spilled. Of course, this percept could be wrong. The ink may be dry, or the spot might not be there at all. The desk that is seen and touched might not really exist. We might be dreaming, drugged, or hallucinating. Too extreme, you say? Consider the following example that actually happened to one of the authors. One night he walked across the floor of his darkened home. In the dim gloominess of the night, he saw one of his dogs resting on the floor, clearly asleep. When he bent to touch the dog, he found that it was a footstool. He stepped back, somewhat startled at his stupidity, only to bump against the cold corner of a marble-topped coffee table. When he reached back to steady himself, he found that the corner of the table was, in fact, his dog's cold nose. Each of these perceptions—dog, stool, table, and dog again—seemed, when first received in consciousness, to be accurate representations of reality. Yet sensory data are not always reliable. Sometimes they can be degraded or not completely available. There seems to be no sudden break between perceiving or sensing an object and guessing the identity of an object. In some respects, we can say that all perception of objects requires some guessing. Sensory stimulation provides the data for our hypotheses about the nature of the external world, and it is these hypotheses that form our perceptions of the world. What's important about what we have been discussing is that no matter how convincing a percept may be, it still may be wrong, as is shown in Demonstration Box 1.1.

Many human behaviors have been affected by the fallible and often erroneous nature of our percepts. For example, the most elegant of the classic Greek buildings, the Parthenon, is bent. The straight clean lines, which bring a sense of simple elegant grandeur, are actually an illusion. Figure 1.2A shows the east wall of the building as it appears. It looks quite square, and the columns look quite vertical. Actually, the Parthenon was built in a totally distorted fashion in order to offset a series of optical illusions. There is a common visual distortion in which we find that placing angles above a line (much as the roof is placed over the architrave) causes the line to appear slightly bowed. One form of this illusion is shown as Figure 1.2B, where the ends of the horizontal line appear

FIGURE 1.2 (A) The Parthenon, looking square and elegant; (B) an illusion that should cause the Parthenon to appear as (C); (D) the way the Parthenon is built to offset the illusion.

DEMONSTRATION BOX 1.2

GEARS AND CIRCLES

The pattern shown in this box should be viewed in motion. Move the book around so that the motion resembles that you would make if you were swirling coffee around in a cup without using a spoon. Notice that the six sets of concentric circles seem to show radial regions of light and dark that appear to move in the direction you are swirling the book. They look as though they were covered by a liquid surface tending to swirl with the stimulus movement.

A second effect has to do with the center circle that seems to have gearlike teeth. As you swirl the array, the center gear seems to rotate, but in a direction opposite to that of the movement of the outer circles. Some observers see it moving in a jerky, steplike manner from one rotary position to another, and other observers see a smooth rotation. Of course, there is no physical movement within the circles, and the geared center circle is also unchanging, despite your conscious impression to the contrary.

slightly higher than the center. If the Parthenon were built physically square, it would appear to sag as a result of this visual distortion. This is shown in an exaggerated manner in Figure 1.2C. The sagging does not appear because the building has been altered to compensate for the distortion. Figure 1.2D illustrates what an undistorted view of the Parthenon would look like. The upward curvature is more than 6 cm on the east and west walls and almost 11 cm on the longer north and south walls.

The vertical features of the Parthenon (such as the columns) were inclined inward in order to correct for a second optical illusion in which the features of rising objects appear to fall outward at the top. Thus, if we projected all of the columns of the Parthenon upward, they would meet at a point somewhat less than 2 km above the building. Furthermore, the corner columns were made thicker because it was found that when these columns were seen against the sky, they appeared to be

DEMONSTRATION BOX 1.3

A SUBJECTIVE COLOR GRID

The figure in this box consists of a series of thinly spaced diagonal black lines alternating with white spaces. Study this figure for a couple of seconds, and you will begin to see faint, almost pastel streaks of orange-red and other streaks of blue-green. For many observers, these streaks tend to run vertically up and down the figure crossing both white and black lines; for others, they seem to form a random, almost fishnet-like pattern over the grid. These colors are not present in the stimulus; hence they are subjective, or illusory, colors.

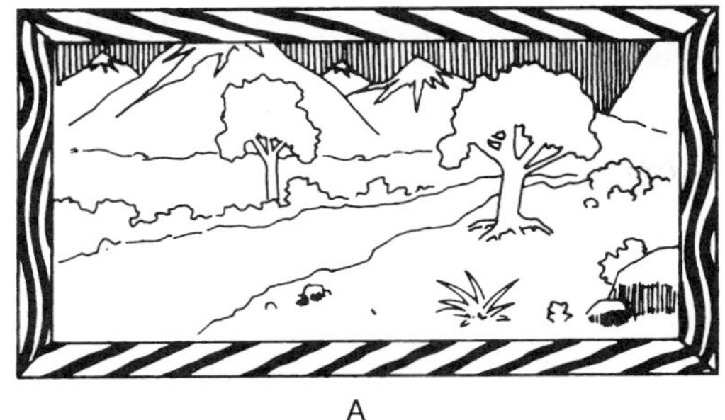
A

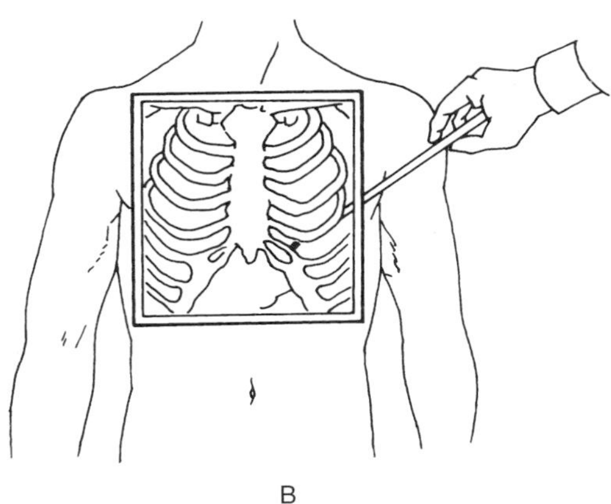
B

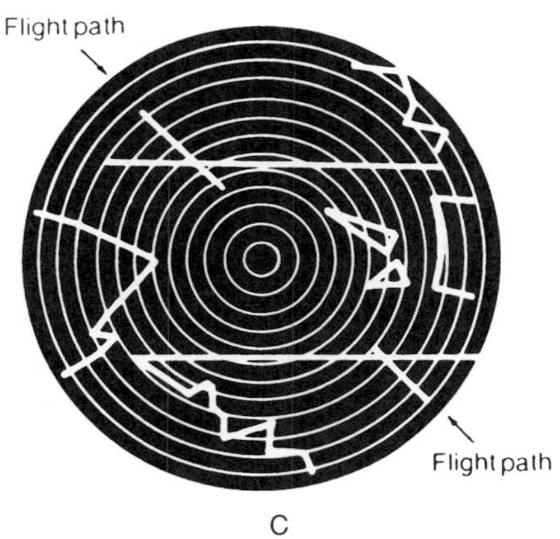

C

FIGURE 1.3 Some perceptual distortions in common situations.

thinner than those seen against the darker background formed by the interior wall.

These were conscious corrections made by the Greek architects. To quote one of them, Vitruvius, writing around 30 B.C., "For the sight follows gracious contours, and unless we flatter its pleasure by proportionate alterations of these parts (so that by adjustment we offset the amount to which it suffers illusions) an uncouth and ungracious aspect will be presented to the spectators." In other words, the Parthenon appears to be square, with elegant straight lines, because it has been consciously distorted to offset perceptual distortions. If it were *geometrically* square, it would not be *perceptually* square.

It is amazing to discover the degree to which our conscious experience of the world can differ from the physical (scientific) reality. Although some perceptual distortions are only slight deviations from physical reality, some can be quite complex and surprising, such as that shown in Demonstration Box 1.2.

Such distortions, in the form of disagreements between percept and reality, are quite common. We call them **illusions,** and they occur in predictable circumstances for normal observers. The term *illusion* is drawn from the Latin root *illudere*, meaning "to mock," and in a sense illusions do mock us for our unthinking reliance on the validity of our sensory impressions. Every sensory modality is subject to distortions, illusions, and systematic errors that misrepresent the outside environment to our consciousness. There are illusions of touch, taste, and hearing, as well as of vision. Virtually any aspect of perception you might think of can be subject to these kinds of errors. For instance, such basic and apparently simple qualities as the brightness of an object or its color may be perceptually misrepresented, as shown in Demonstration Box 1.3.

Many perceptual errors are merely amusing, such as those in Demonstration Boxes 1.1 and 1.2, whereas others may be thought provoking, as in Demonstration Box 1.3. Others may lead to some embarrassment or annoyance, such as might have been felt by the artisan who created the picture frame in Figure 1.3A. Although his workmanship is faultless, he appears to be a sloppy craftsman because the grain of the wood is too prominent. Despite the fact that the picture is perfectly rectangular, it appears to be distorted. Unfortunately, some perceptual errors or illusions are quite serious. In Figure 1.3B, we have shown a surgeon probing for a bullet. She is using a fluoroscope, which presents the outline of the patient's ribs, and her probe is positioned so that it is exactly on line with the bullet lodged below the rib. As you can see, it appears that she will miss and that her probe will pass above the bullet despite the fact that the probe is angled perfectly. Figure 1.3C shows an even more disastrous occurrence of an illusion. It represents a radar screen with various flight regions marked across its face.

The two oblique streaks represent jet aircraft approaching the control region, both flying at about 950 kph. The information displayed is similar to that which an air traffic controller might use. From it he might conclude that if these two aircraft continue in the same direction they will pass each other with a safe distance between them. At the moment represented here, however, these aircraft are traveling toward each other on the same line. If they are flying at the same altitude, it is very likely that they will collide.

These examples illustrate how important discrepancies between perception and reality can be. Therefore, it becomes important for us to know how our perceptions arise, how much we can rely upon them, under what circumstances they are most fallible, and under what conditions our perceptions most accurately represent the world. An exploration of these questions is the purpose of this book.

ASPECTS OF THE PERCEPTUAL PROCESS

The study of perception is diverse. This is partly because perceptual problems have been studied for a long time. The Greek philosophers, the pre-Renaissance thinkers, the Arabic scholars, the Latin scholastics, the early British empiricists, the German physicists, and the German physicians who founded both physiology and psychology considered issues in sensation and perception to be basic questions. When Alexander Bain wrote the first English textbook on psychology in 1855, it was titled *The Senses and the Intellect,* with the most extensive coverage reserved for sensory and perceptual functions. The major portion of both the theorizing and the empirical work produced by Wilhelm Wundt, who is generally credited with the founding of experimental psychology, was oriented toward sensation and perception. In addition to the diversity caused by a long and varied history, perception has been affected by many "schools" of thought. Each has its own major theoretical viewpoint and its own particular set of methodological techniques. Thus we encounter psychophysicists, gestaltists, functionalists, analytic introspectionists, transactionalists, sensory physiologists, sensory-tonic theorists, "new look" psychologists, efferent theorists, artificial intelligence experts, and computational psychologists, to name but a few. There are even theorists (such as some behaviorists) who deny the existence of, or at least deny our ability to study, the conscious event we call perception. Despite this chorus of diverse voices, there seems to be a consensus about the important aspects of perceptual study.

Before we look at the major areas of emphasis in the study of the perceptual process, let us first offer a disclaimer. We recognize that it is difficult, perhaps impossible, and most certainly unwise to attempt to draw sharp lines separating one field of inquiry from another. However, there are certain problem areas, or orientations, that characterize certain groups of investigators, and these seem to be definable. The study of **sensation,** or sensory processes, is concerned with the first contact between the organism and the environment. Thus, someone studying sensation might look at the way in which electromagnetic radiation (light) is registered by the eye. This investigator would look at the physical structure of the sense organ and would attempt to establish how sensory experiences are related to physical stimulation and physiological functioning. These types of studies tend to focus on less complex (although not less complicated) aspects of our conscious experience. For instance, this investigator might study how we perceive brightness, loudness, or color; however, the nature of the object having a given brightness, sound, or color would not make much difference to the investigator.

Someone who is interested in the study of **perception** is interested in our conscious experience of objects and object relationships. For instance, the sensory question might be "How bright does the target appear to be?" whereas the perceptual questions would be "Can you identify that object?" "Where is it?" How far away is it?" and "How large is it?" In a more global sense, those who study perception are interested in how we form a conscious representation of the outside environment and in the accuracy of that representation. Those of you who have difficulty in distinguishing perception from sensation, rest easy. Since Thomas Reid introduced the distinction in 1785, some investigators have championed its use, and others have totally ignored the difference, choosing to treat sensation and perception as a unitary problem.

Cognition is a term used to define a very active field of inquiry in contemporary psychology. The word itself is quite old, probably introduced by St. Thomas Aquinas (1225–1274). He divided the study of behavior into two broad divisions: cognition, meaning how we know the world, and affect, which was meant to encompass feelings and emotions. Today's definition of cognition is as broad as that of Aquinas. Although many investigators use the term to refer to memory, association, concept formation, language, and problem solving (all of which simply take the act of perception for granted), other investigators include the processes of attention and the conscious representation and interpretation of stimuli as part of the cognitive process. In other words, cognition tends to be somewhere between the areas that were traditionally called perception and learning, and it incorporates elements of both. The similarity between many of the problems studied by cognitive psychologists and those studied by perceptual psychologists is best seen by the fact that both often publish in the same journals and on similar topics.

Information processing is a relatively general term but is used to emphasize the whole process that finally leads to identification and interpretation of stimuli. This approach focuses on how information about the external world is operated on (processed) to produce our conscious percepts and guide our actions. Information processing is typically assumed to include a registration or sensory phase, an interpretation or perceptual phase, and a memoric or cognitive phase. Thus, rather than being a separate subdiscipline, the information processing approach attempts to integrate sensation, perception, and cognition within a common framework. It relies on a **levels-of-processing** analysis in which each stage of sensory processing, from the first registration of the stimulus on the receptor to the final conscious representation entered into memory, is systematically analyzed.

None of these labels should be taken as representing inflexible, or completely separate, areas of study. At a recent professional meeting one well-known psychologist lamented, "When I first started doing research, people said I studied perception. After a while, they said I studied cognition. Now they say that I am studying human information processing. I don't know what is going on—I've been studying the same set of problems for the last twenty years!"

THEORIES OF PERCEPTION

In the same way that there are many aspects of perception, there are also many theoretical approaches to perceptual problems. One important approach may be called **biological reductionism.** It is based on the presumption that for any given aspect of the observer's sensation there is a corresponding physiological event. According to this approach, the main goal of the perceptual researcher is to isolate these underlying physiological mechanisms. The search for specific neural units, pathways, or processes that correspond to specific sensory experiences is common to such theories. One example is the work of Margaret Livingstone and David Hubel (1988), who view the visual system as a set of channels, each containing neural units that process or extract specific aspects of incoming information.

The newest variation of biological reductionism involves belief in the **modularity of perception**. This viewpoint was first offered by Jerry Fodor (1983) and it views the mind as a set of distinct units or modules, each of which is complete in itself and has a specific function with dedicated neural hardware. This allows the processing to be quick but does not require any conscious intervention. Perception, made up of the output of many modules, is then passed on to higher centers where cognitive processes can come into play.

Other theoretical approaches are often less bound to a specific class of mechanism. For example, **direct perception** begins with the premise that all the information needed to form the conscious percept is available in the stimuli that reach our receptors. Even though the image in our eye is continually changing, there are certain aspects of the stimulation produced by any particular object or environmental situation that are invariant predictors of certain properties, such as the physical size, shape, or distance of the object being viewed. These perceptual **invariants** are fixed properties of the stimulus even though the observer may be moving or changing viewpoints, causing continuous changes in the optical image that reaches the eye. This stimulus information is automatically extracted by the perceptual system because it is relevant to survival. Invariants provide information about **affordances,** which are action possibilities afforded or available to the observer, such as picking up an object, going around it, and so forth. The label of direct perception was given to such theories by J. J. Gibson (e.g., 1979), who argued that this information is directly available to the perceiver and is not based on any higher-level cognitive processing or computation, although it might involve the integration of several aspects of the stimulation.

A number of perceptual theorists, whose thinking has been influenced by developments in artificial intelligence systems, have adopted an alternative approach. Their theories are usually presented in the form of computer programs or computational systems aimed at allowing machines to directly interpret sensory information in the same manner that a human observer might. The precursor of such theorists is David Marr (1982), who began with the general presumption made in direct perception that all of the information needed is in the stimulus input. This approach differs from direct perception in that it describes the piecing together of information based on some simple dimensions in the stimulus, such as boundaries and edges, line endings, particular patterns where stimuli meet, and so forth. This process of interpretation or synthesis is believed to require a number of computations and several stages of analysis that can be specified as mathematical equations or steps in a computer program. This added requirement of calculating features of objects or aspects of the environment from aspects of the stimuli reaching the observer has resulted in the label of **computational theories** for this approach. Certain aspects of such computational theories often involve fairly difficult mathematics.

A much older (but still active) theoretical approach begins with the recognition that our perceptual representation of the world is much richer and more accurate than might be expected on the basis of the information contained in the stimuli available at any one moment in time. Theories to explain this fact often begin with the suggestion that perception is much like other logical processes. In addition to the information available to our sense organs at the moment, we can use information based on our previous experience, our expectations, and so forth. This means that, for example, a visual percept may involve other sources of information, some nonvisual in nature, some arising from our past history and cognitive processing strategies. The similarity of some of these mechanisms to reasoning leads us to refer to this type of theory as **intelligent perception.** This approach probably originated with Helmholtz in 1867 and continued in the work of researchers such as Irvin Rock (1983), who have a more cognitive orientation. These theories are also called **constructive theories** of perception because our final conscious impression may involve

APPLICATION BOX 1.1

AGING AND REDUCED INTELLECTUAL FUNCTIONING

How many times have you heard your parents or grandparents say something like "I just don't remember as well as I did. I must be getting old" or "Do you want to add these numbers for me? Now that I am older my mind just doesn't work as well as it used to"? The idea that our cognitive and intellectual functioning diminishes with age is a well-accepted concept in folk psychology, which is a collection of beliefs that the average person has about the way the mind works. In this case, the scientific evidence seems to support these findings. There seems to be lots of evidence that older people do poorly on a variety of cognitive tests. Some have said that this is evidence that the older brain just doesn't work as well—proof of the saying that "you can't teach an old dog new tricks." However, we now know that these conclusions may be wrong.

When we look at the way in which perceptual ability changes as we grow older, we usually find a decline with age for both our visual acuity (the ability to see fine details) and our auditory sensitivity (the ability to hear faint sounds and to discriminate the differences between tones). These age changes are shown in Figure A, plotted in relative scores (where the average is 50 and each standard deviation away from the mean is 10). Until recently, very few researchers considered the possibility that the apparent decline in mental functioning may be related to the decline in perceptual abilities. There is a reason, however, why you might expect a relationship. People with poor sensory ability don't register all of the details of what is in their environment, and some of what they do register is distorted or incomplete. In the end, this sensory restriction reduces the quality of information they have to think about. In some instances people with poor perceptual abilities may simply stop processing a lot of what is going on because it is often unreliable or difficult to interpret. Imagine what this might do to a person's thinking ability over the course of many years. To take just one example, people with poor auditory sensitivity would process less verbal information; hence their verbal skills would get "rusty" through disuse. Then, when they were called on to solve verbal problems, they would simply no longer be as good, and we would conclude that their verbal intelligence had dropped. This is what actually happens with age.

Figure B shows a typical experimental result, where people aged 25 to 103 years of age were tested on five different cognitive tests commonly used to measure intelligence, such as a test of reasoning or of memory. The test scores were then averaged into a composite "intellectual functioning" score (Baltes & Lindenberger, 1997). Notice the usual decrease in overall mental ability with age. However, when we statistically remove the effects of the decreasing visual and hearing abilities of older people, the picture changes dramatically. Now we find only a very small decline in mental ability with age, as is shown in the figure.

combining a number of different factors to "construct" the final percept.

It is likely that each of these approaches is useful in describing some aspects of the perceptual process (see Coren & Girgus, 1978; Uttal, 1981); however, different orientations tend to lead researchers in different directions, searching for different types of mechanisms. Each approach is likely to be valid for some parts of the problem and irrelevant to others. This is a common occurrence in many areas of endeavor. For instance, a metallurgist might look at a bridge and consider its material components, whereas a civil engineer might look at the load-bearing capacity of the entire structure, and a city planner might look at the same bridge in terms of traffic flow. At first glance there may seem to be very little overlap between the various views because the city planner does not care about the specific shape of the bridge structure, and the engineer cares only about the structural aspects of the beams, not their specific alloy constituents. Yet each level of analysis is valid for some specific set of questions. This book addresses the problem of how people build a conscious picture of their environment through the use of information reaching their senses. We follow the lead of many contemporary theorists and try to use data from all levels of the perceptual process—and discussions in terms of several different theoretical positions—in order to give an integrated picture of the process of perception. After all, the label that we apply to our approach is of considerably less importance than the answer itself.

Perceptual factors are important, not only for theories of perception but also for other theories. Many times in science perceptual contributions have been ignored, and the result has been an inadequate, or perhaps wrong, explanatory theory. One important example concerns the effect of aging on intelligence and cognitive functioning. This story is told in Application Box 1.1.

The first moral of this story is that you can "teach an old dog new tricks" but only if the old dog can see and hear well enough to know what is required to perform the tricks. The quality of our thinking depends on the quality of the sensory information we have to think about. It is not so much that the aging mind is less intelligent but, rather, that the aging sense organs are not allowing the aging mind to perform at the level of which it is capable. The second moral is that failure to consider possible perceptual factors has led people to reach the wrong conclusions about aging for many years.

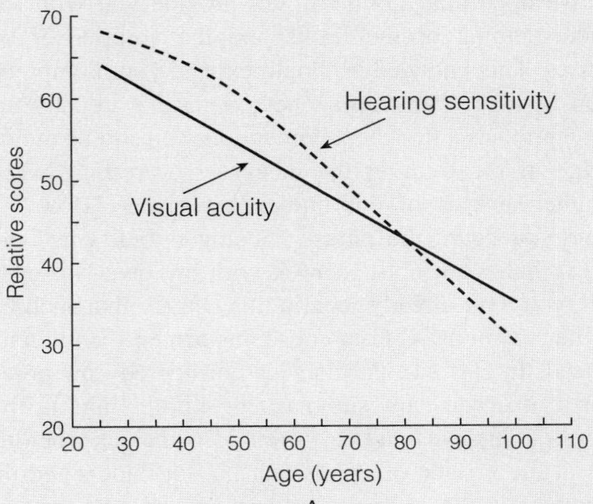

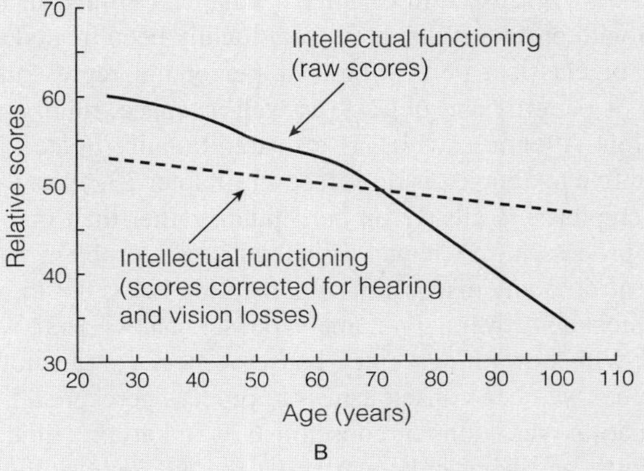

APPLICATION BOX FIGURE (A) Visual acuity and hearing sensitivity decrease with age; (B) the solid curve shows the usually obtained decrease in intellectual functioning obtained, here, as the average of five tests of mental ability. When the effects of vision and hearing declines are removed (in the broken line), however, there is very little evidence of an age-related decline in intellectual functioning (based on Baltes and Lindenberger, 1997).

THE PLAN OF THE BOOK

The orientation of this book is implicit rather than explicit. Although theories are introduced and discussed in the various chapters, no all-encompassing theoretical orientation has been adopted. We have chosen to be "militantly eclectic" in our orientation. Thus, this text is mostly concerned with perceptual and sensory processes. In general, the presentation of the material follows a levels-of-processing approach, in that the first half of the book is concerned with the more basic sensory processes and is organized around specific sensory systems, such as vision or audition, and the second half of the book is concerned with the more clearly perceptual processes that have strong cognitive influences and are often not bound to any single sensory modality. We have tried to make the individual chapters relatively self-contained. We begin by explaining how sensations and perceptions are measured (Chapter 2). We then proceed with the physiological structures and the basic sensory capacities associated with vision. Chapter 3, in addition to introducing the structure of the visual system, also introduces some basic concepts of neural function and a description of some of the modern methods used to study the physical aspects of sensory function. Chapter 4 discusses the basic sensory aspects of vision—namely, brightness and color. The basic structure of the auditory system (Chapter 5) and the sensory aspects of hearing follow (Chapter 6). The other senses—namely taste, smell, touch, and pain—are discussed in Chapter 7. Chapters 8 through 12 deal with problems that have traditionally been treated as part of classical perception, our perceptual representation of patterns and objects, as well as space, time, and motion. Attention, which is also traditionally treated in cognitive textbooks, is discussed in Chapter 13, although the emphasis is clearly on perceptual, rather than memory, processes. In Chapter 14 we address a problem that is central to any discussion of perception but is apt to be the most controversial—namely, consciousness. Here we deal with how things enter consciousness (or do not), whether we need consciousness to process perceptual information, variations of consciousness in certain clinical patients, and what is known about the neurophysiological underpinnings of consciousness. The last two chapters (15 and 16) deal with perceptual diversity, which includes many of the factors that make the perceptual experience of one individual different from that of another. These factors include the changes that occur in the developing individual because of the normal aging process, life history, experience, learning, and personality factors, to name a few.

You will notice that each chapter includes a series of demonstration boxes. These are experimental demonstrations that you can perform for yourself using stimuli provided in the book or materials that are easily found around a house or other living quarters. They illustrate many aspects of the perceptual process. Often they demonstrate concepts that are very difficult to put into words but that, when experienced, are immediately understandable. You are encouraged to try these demonstrations because they are an integral part of the book. In the same way that perception involves interaction with the world, these demonstrations allow you to interact with your senses in a controlled manner and to gain insight into yourself.

In this book we have tried to be as current and up to date as possible; however, in doing so it is possible to lose the history of a subject and to divorce it from the people who actually produced the data we are studying. For this reason each chapter contains approximately three biography boxes. These describe scientists who have contributed significantly to the subject matter under discussion. This is done to give you a feeling not just for the past, but for the broad sweep of interests and passions that have driven researchers to study perception.

We hope that this book will provide you with some understanding of the limits and the abilities of your senses. This knowledge should expand your comprehension of many behavioral phenomena that depend upon perception as a first step. Perception seems to be the final judge of the truth or the falsity of everything we encounter as part of our human experience. How often have you heard the phrase "Seeing is believing" or "I didn't believe it until I saw it with my own two eyes"? Yet, you have already seen in this chapter that such faith in the truthfulness of our conscious percepts is often misplaced. In 500 B.C. Parmenides considered how perception can deceive us, summarizing his feelings in these words: "The eyes and ears are bad witnesses when they are at the service of minds that do not understand their language." In this book we try to teach you their language.

CHAPTER 2

MEASURING PERCEPTION

CHAPTER SUMMARY

Did you hear what I heard? Did you see what I saw? These questions are usually easy to answer when we are in conversation with someone else, but they become tricky to answer when we take them into the perception lab. This is because perception researchers are often interested in finding out very precisely which aspects of an event were experienced by an observer and which aspects were not noticed. The researcher is often also interested in finding out exactly how much time passed before the observer was able to react to the event. To answer these questions, careful procedures must be followed. Sophisticated equipment is even required at times, to enable researchers to present events, time events, and time the responses of observers with precision. The methods that researchers use in coming to a conclusion about what an observer experienced, and when, are the topic of this chapter. If at times some of these procedures seem overly elaborate, it will be good to remind yourself that their primary purpose is to help researchers avoid an experience that is common in everyday conversation: the realization that even though you and your friend were present in the same location, and witnessed the same events, the individual retelling of these events by you and your friend makes it seem as though you were not sharing the same experiences.

The first issue to deal with in the measurement of perception is that our experiences do not have physical features that correspond directly to the events that give rise to them. That is, our perception of the weight of a lifted object is not itself heavy. The object can be put on a scale and weighed in ounces or kilograms. But on what scale do we place our perception of the object's heaviness? In the same way, if we want to know the color of an object, it is possible to analyze the light that is reflected from the object and to describe its composition in terms of the amount of light (intensity) and its color (wavelength). But how do we measure the intensity and color of our perception of that same object? The answer is that we must rely on what people tell us they perceive, and this can lead to problems. To overcome these problems, perception researchers have developed a large and varied set of procedures. Each of these procedures has its strengths and its weaknesses. The goal of this chapter is to introduce you to the most commonly used and thoroughly tested of the procedures. Knowing a little about each of them will help you understand how perception researchers have come to their conclusions about the function of the various perceptual systems that you will read about in the upcoming chapters.

A second issue that complicates the measurement of perception is that only one person has direct access to any particular perceptual experience. This is the person having the experience, the observer. Although we may firmly believe that we are having the same experience as someone else undergoing the same events, or that we can feel what it must be like to "be in someone else's shoes," this is really privileged information. It is privileged in that there is no known way to verify whether two experiences are the same. The technical term for this kind of knowledge is **first person data.** Other terms that mean roughly the same thing are *subjective experience, phenomenology,* and *introspection.*

First person data stand in sharp contrast to the kind of data scientists are more familiar with, which in the field of perception is called **third person data.** These data are objective, in the sense that any other person who follows the same procedures as the experimenter can collect similar results. First person data could never, by definition, pass this test, since there is no way to verify that the details of experience in two persons are identical. But perception researchers, being practical in nature, have not thrown up their hands in despair at being unable to peer directly into the experience of another person. Instead, they have designed measurement procedures that are as fair and as complete as possible, working within the limitations of third person data. If these third person data point to a reliable connection between the presentation of a stimulus and the response of an observer, then they have passed the test required of scientific data in any field and can give us information about what an individual is experiencing.

PSYCHOPHYSICS: A SCIENCE OF EXPERIENCE

Psychophysics is the general name given to the study of the relationship between the physical stimuli in the world and the sensations about them that we experience. The term is credited to Gustav Teodor Fechner, shown in Biography Box 2.1, a physicist and philosopher who set out to turn the thorny mind-body problem of philosophy into a problem that scientists could work on. In order to do this, Fechner believed he had to solve three problems. First, he had to find a way to measure the minimum intensity of a stimulus that we can perceive, which is the problem of **detection.** Second, he had to devise a way to measure how different stimuli must be before they no longer appear to be the same, which is the problem of **discrimination**. Finally, in order to describe the relationship between the intensity of the stimulus and the intensity of our sensation, he had to find a way to measure sensation intensity, and in doing so addressed the problem of **scaling.**

Not only is Fechner's approach to a science of perceptual experience still in use today, but so are many of the specific procedures that he developed. These methods for collecting and analyzing data are used in every aspect of the study of sensation and perception and in many other areas of psychology, including social, personality, environmental, developmental, clinical, and environmental psychology. That is why we begin by following his approach of dividing the general problem of psychophysics into the three more specific and manageable subproblems of detection, discrimination, and scaling. To these three subproblems we add a fourth, that of **identification,** which involves being able to attach a learned label or category name to the stimulus we have encountered. The importance of this aspect of perception has grown in recent years, especially as researchers continue to discover important connections between what we know and what we are able to see.

DETECTION

Our sensory systems are responsive to energy changes in the environment. Energy changes may take the form of electromagnetic (light), mechanical (sound, touch, movement, muscle tension), chemical (tastes, smells), or thermal (heat, cold) stimulation. The problem of detection is the problem of how much of an energy change,

BIOGRAPHY BOX 2.1

FROM ART TO SCIENCE

Gustav Teodor Fechner (1801–1887) was a German philosopher and scientist with a range of interests spanning from religion to biology. He had an early and illustrious career as a professor of physics at the University of Leipzig but was forced to resign because of poor health at the age of 38. Without the day-to-day commitments of being a professor, he turned his attention to a variety of questions, including how to understand beauty in the visual arts. As he told it, it was while awaking from sleep on the morning of October 22, 1850, that he had his great insight concerning how a person's subjective experience could be studied scientifically (Schultz & Schultz, 1996). On one side of the mathematical equation, he placed the subjective experience of the observer (*S*), while on the other side of the equation he placed measurable characterstics of the physical world, expressed in units of just noticeable difference. A term he liked to use for this approach to a science of experience was "bridge psychophysics," because he saw his equation bridging the gap between subjective experience and physical measurement of the material world. These days there is a scientific meeting held each year in honor of Fechner Day on October 22, sponsored by an organization called International Society for Psychophysics (ISP).

starting from zero, is necessary for an individual to see, hear, or otherwise sense it. Fechner defined the **absolute threshold** for a stimulus as one that "lifted the sensation . . . over the threshold of consciousness." The idea is that below some critical intensity level of the stimulus, a person would not be able to detect it. As soon as this threshold intensity is exceeded, however, we would expect the observer to always detect its presence.

This hypothetical relation can be described on a graph called a **psychometric function.** The ordinate (or vertical axis) of the graph is the proportion of stimulus presentations on which an observer says "yes" to the question, "Did you see (or hear, feel, etc.) the stimulus?" The abscissa (or horizontal axis) of the graph is stimulus intensity. Figure 2.1 shows such a graph using arbitrary units for stimulus intensity. Notice that the proportion of "yes" responses takes a sudden step up from 0 to 1.0 when the stimulus reaches a value of 3.5, meaning that the stimulus went from being undetected below this value to being detected all of the time above this value. The absolute threshold indicated by this ideal psychometric function is thus 3.5.

We must also be aware that a stimulus such as a light or a tone never appears in isolation. A constantly present and ever-changing background of sensation always exists. If you place both of your hands over your ears to block out external noises, you will hear what can poetically be called

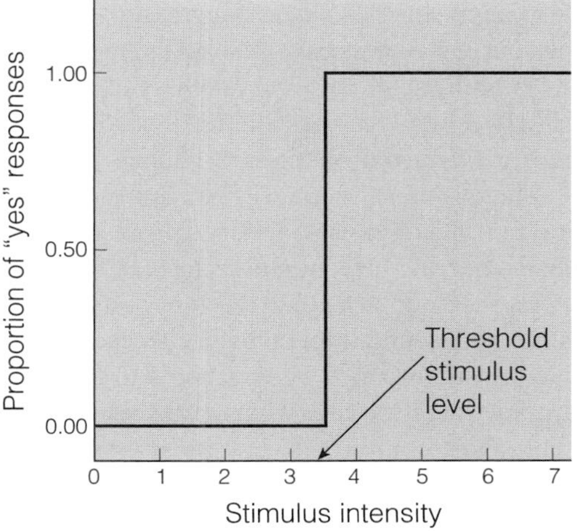

FIGURE 2.1 Absolute threshold.

"the sound of waves from a distant sea" and, somewhat less poetically, "the faint hissing of radio static." Similarly, if you sit in a completely lightproof room in absolute darkness, you will not see complete blackness. Your visual field will instead be filled with a grayish mist, called "cortical gray," and occasionally you will even see tiny "light" flashes here and there. Any stimulus that we ask an observer to detect is superimposed on this background of noise generated from within the observer. This background noise is the result of factors over which we have no control, such as the rushing of blood in our veins and arteries and the spontaneous activity of visually sensitive cells in our eyes. However, this internal noise acts just like stimulation from outside the body and it may help or hinder our ability to detect another stimulus.

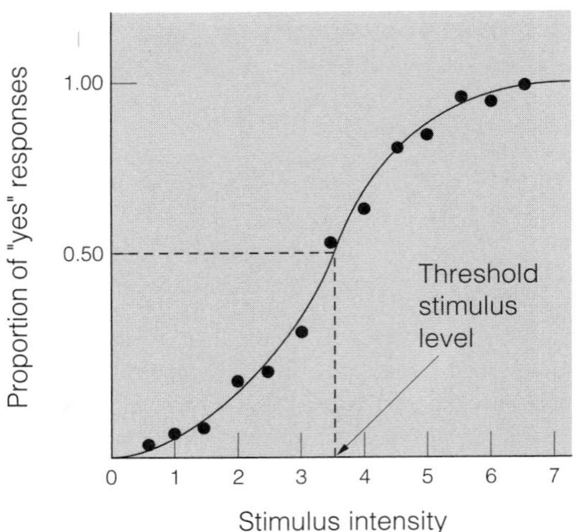

FIGURE 2.2 Typical data from the method of constant stimuli in detection.

Method of Constant Stimuli

How is an absolute threshold measured in practical terms? You can get a feel for this by considering a typical experiment to measure the absolute threshold of hearing. The setting involves a listener wearing headphones in a quiet room. The experimenter selects a set of tones to present. The tones differ in their intensity, some heard very easily and others not heard at all. She presents these tones, one at a time, to the listener. Each is presented many times in an irregular order. The listener is required to respond "yes" when he detects the stimulus and "no" when he does not. This procedure is called the **method of constant stimuli** because a fixed or constant set of stimuli is chosen in advance. Some typical data obtained with this method are presented graphically in Figure 2.2.

We see in Figure 2.2 that as the sound intensity increases, the proportion of "yes" responses, indicating that the person has heard the tone, also increases gradually. This S-shaped curve is commonly obtained using the method of constant stimuli for all sensory systems. But notice the difference between the theoretically ideal absolute threshold in Figure 2.1 and the obtained S-chaped curve in Figure 2.2. There is no sharp transition from "not sensing" to "sensing" in the responses obtained from a person performing the hearing detection task. Instead, the likelihood that a person reports hearing the tone simply increases gradually as the sound level increases. Because there is no dramatic transition point, we are forced to make a somewhat arbitrary decision as to what the absolute threshold is.

A reasonable compromise that most psychophysicists agree on as the absolute threshold is the stimulus intensity that observers detect exactly 50% of the time. This is the point at which the probability of saying "yes" is the same as the probability of saying "no." In Figure 2.2, the dotted line is used to show graphically how the threshold can be determined. First, the data points are fitted with a smooth curve. Then a horizontal line is drawn from the 0.50 value on the ordinate until it intersects the smooth curve. At this point it is extended in a vertical line down to the abscissa. In the example shown in Figure 2.2, the absolute threshold for the listener in the experiment is estimated to be about 3.5 energy units.

Although the method of constant stimuli can produce useful estimates of absolute threshold, its main drawback is that it is time consuming because each stimulus has to be presented a number of times to get a stable estimate of the likelihood that it will be detected. To overcome this limitation, pretesting is sometimes used to make a sensible guess about the rough location of the threshold, so that a more finely graded stimulus set can be centered around it. Although this can reduce the overall number of trials needed for testing, the method is still not really time efficient because many trials will still be used in presenting stimulus intensities that are far away from the actual threshold if an S-shaped function is to be obtained (Simpson, 1988; Watson & Fitzhugh, 1990). In clinical settings, such as a doctor's office where an individual is tested for a possible hearing aid, reducing the time spent determining a threshold can be an important consideration.

Method of Limits

One way to avoid the time-consuming aspects of the method of constant stimuli is to focus only on stimuli near the absolute threshold. The **method of limits** does just that. In this technique, the experimenter begins by presenting an observer with a stimulus (for example, a pure tone) at an intensity high enough to be easily heard and then decreases its intensity in small steps until the observer reports, "I no longer hear it." This is called a *descending series.* On alternate trials the experimenter starts with a tone that cannot be heard and increases the intensity until the observer reports, "I hear it." This is called *an ascending series.* It is assumed that the response changes when the threshold is crossed, and so each series gives an estimate of the absolute threshold as an intensity somewhere between the last two stimuli presented.

When we estimate thresholds from several different series of trials in the method of limits, we find that the "absolute threshold" is not a fixed value as we first thought. For instance, we might find that in one descending series the observer could no longer detect the stimulus when presented with a tone intensity of 50 but in the next descending series a stimulus intensity of only 43 was still detected. Moreover, on average, the descending series yield lower thresholds than the ascending series. It seems that the threshold varies from measurement to measurement, or from moment to moment. We now know that internally-generated noise that we spoke of earlier, plus lapses of attention, slight fatigue, the influence of drugs and other psychological changes can all cause fluctuations of the threshold. It is likely that such threshold fluctuations are responsible for smoothing out the ideal threshold curve into the S-shape we obtain with the method of constant stimuli. Demonstration Box 2.1 shows how you can experience this threshold variability in a simple experiment.

Adaptive Testing

The method of limits is still somewhat inefficient because it is only the stimuli that bracket the threshold (the last two in each testing series) that give any information; the rest tell us nothing. **Adaptive testing** keeps the test stimuli "hovering around" the threshold by adapting the sequence of stimulus presentations to the observer's responses. Consider, for example, the **staircase method** (Bekesy, 1947; Cornsweet, 1962). In this procedure we might start with a descending series of stimuli. Each time the observer says, "Yes, I hear it," we decrease the stimulus intensity by one step. At some point the stimulus becomes too weak to be heard, and the observer will say, "No, I don't hear it." At this point we don't end the series, as we did in the method of limits, but rather we reverse its direction, increasing the stimulus intensity by one step. We continue for as long as required, decreasing the stimulus whenever the observer says "yes" and increasing it whenever the observer says "no." In this way the value of the test stimulus varies around the threshold value as shown in Figure 2.3. This procedure allows the experimenter to "track" the threshold over time, even if sensitivity is changing, such as after administration of some drugs or after adaptation to different background stimuli. When we wish to, after several reversals of direction, we can average the stimulus values at which the reversals occurred to obtain an average threshold value.

The staircase method is the simplest example of the use of adaptive testing to find thresholds. Using the observer's previous responses to determine the stimulus series allows the experimenter to zero in on the threshold quickly and efficiently, with few wasted trials and with a high degree of reliability (Kaernbach, 1991; Meese, 1995). In our example we used the rule "increase intensity by one step if the response to the previous stimulus was 'no' and decrease intensity by one step if the previous response was 'yes.'" Other rules can be used, however, to increase the precision of the method, to avoid judgment biases, or to achieve certain statistical properties in the data (Brown, 1996; Levitt, 1971; Macmillan &

DEMONSTRATION BOX 2.1

THE VARIABILITY OF THE THRESHOLD

For this demonstration you will need a wristwatch (or a clock) that ticks. Place the watch on a table, and move across the room so that you can no longer hear the ticking. If the tick is faint, you may accomplish this merely by moving your head away some distance. Now gradually move toward the watch. Note that you are actually performing a method of limits experiment because the sound level steadily increases as you approach the watch. At some distance from the watch you will begin to hear the source of the sound. This is your momentary threshold. Now hold this position for a few moments, and you will notice that occasionally the sound will fade and that you may have to step forward to reach threshold, whereas at other times it may be noticeably louder, and you may be able to step back and still hear it. These changes are a result of your changing threshold sensitivity.

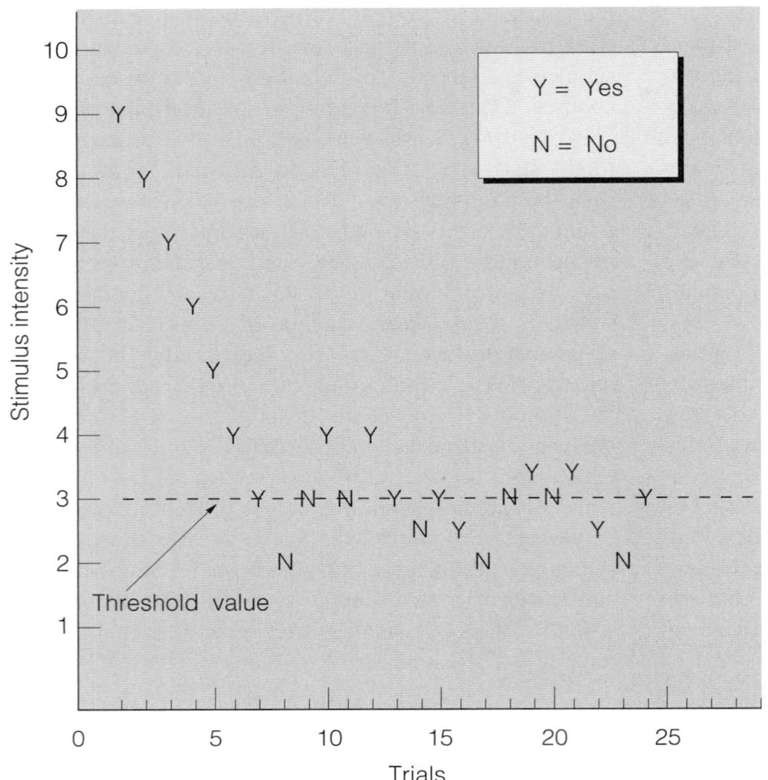

FIGURE 2.3 A portion of a trial-by-trial record (called a *track*) from a run of an adaptive testing technique using a descending staircase procedure where the stimulus intensity was decreased when detected ("yes") and increased when not detected ("no").

Creelman, 1991). The intensity of the step size can also be changed adaptively from trial to trial to achieve even greater efficiency and precision (Kaernbach, 1991). If the series of trials is long enough, there are even some statistical techniques to estimate the entire psychometric function from this trial-by-trial data (Leek, Hanna, & Marshall, 1992). Recently an entire issue of the journal *Perception & Psychophysics* was devoted to papers describing the latest adaptive testing techniques and theory (Macmillan, 2002).

Here are some examples of approximate absolute threshold values as measured by the methods we have just discussed. The human visual system is so sensitive that a candle flame can be seen from a distance of more than 48 km (30 mi) on a dark, clear night. The human auditory system can detect the ticking of a wristwatch in a quiet room at a distance of 6 m (20 ft)—sensitivity beyond this would allow us to hear the sound of air molecules colliding. Furthermore, the average human can taste 1 teaspoon of sugar dissolved in 7 1/2 liters (2 gallons) of water and smell one drop of perfume diffused through the volume of an average three-room apartment.

Signal Detection Theory

All of the techniques we have described so far are based on simply recording the observer's responses of "Yes, I hear it" or "No, I don't hear it." These can be pretty tenuous data on which to base our theories. Suppose an observer felt that this was a "test" of some sort in which it would be good for him to appear to be quite sensitive; he might say "yes" on almost every trial. What would prevent this from happening? Even trustworthy and dedicated people, which includes most observers in psychophysics experiments, might be unsure as to whether or not a very weak stimulus was peeking out from the always-present noise. Under these conditions observers must adopt some decision strategy for responding when they are uncertain. For example, observers could limit the number of "no" responses, feeling that too many "no" responses would make them appear to be hard of hearing.

One way to try to control such response strategies is to insert **catch trials,** on which no stimulus is presented, into the series of trials. An honest and accurate observer should always respond "no" on catch trials because no stimulus was presented. If a "yes" response was recorded on such a trial, it could properly be counted as a guess. In practice, if observers respond "yes" too often on catch trials, they are cautioned against guessing and their estimated threshold is adjusted to take the guesses into account. Over many experiments, however, it has become clear that "yes" responses on catch trials are not always guesses. Sincere, honest observers often report that they really hear something like the tone they are trying to detect, even when it is not there! Are observers in these experiments hallucinating? It seems absurd to believe that, but there is no way to account for such experiences within classical psychophysical theory. Results such as this set the stage for a completely new approach to the problem of detection.

As we have seen, estimates of the absolute threshold can vary not only with changes in an observer's sensitivity, as we would expect, but they can also vary with changes in the way an observer comes to make a decision about what he has just experienced, which is not desirable. **Signal detection theory** attempts to deal with this problem. This is a theory that emerged from the same considerations that are used to analyze scientific experiments and to decide whether an electrical switch is closed or open in a telecommunications device (Green & Swets, 1966/1974; Macmillan & Creelman, 1991). Signal detection theory acknowledges that any stimulus must be detected against a background of ongoing internal noise in our sensory systems as well as ongoing noise in the environment. Thus, on each trial the observer has to decide whether the signal was present in all that noise or whether there was only the usual fluctuating neural noise. For example, a radar operator might be trying to detect on the radar screen the visual signal denoting a radar echo of an approaching airplane against a background of false echoes (of clouds, birds, etc.) and static from the display apparatus. In signal detection theory there is no absolute threshold; there is only a series of observations, each of which must be categorized as either signal present or signal absent. A series of such decisions can be used to deduce how sensitive a person is to a given signal, independent of any motivational or expectation effects that might bias the decisions.

Signal detection theory requires a special type of experiment in order to measure sensitivity and bias. The basic design is shown in Table 2.1. The experiment uses two types of "stimulus" presentations (shown at the left of the table). A *signal absent trial* is like a classical catch trial on which no stimulus is presented and observers see or hear only the noise generated by their sensory system or by the experimenter. On a *signal present trial* the experimenter actually presents the target stimulus. The two possible responses are shown at the top of Table 2.1. Yes indicates that the observer has decided that the signal was present and No indicates that the observer has decided the signal was not present. The combination of the two possible types of trials and the two possible responses leads to four possible outcomes, as indicated by the four cells of Table 2.1. A "yes" on a signal present trial is called a **hit**, whereas a "yes" on a signal absent trial is called a **false alarm**. Similarly, a "no" on a signal absent trial is called a **correct negative**, and a "no" on a signal present trial is called a **miss**.

TABLE 2.1 Outcomes of a Signal Detection Experiment

	Response	
Signal	**Yes**	**No**
Present	Hit	Miss
Absent	False alarm	Correct negative

Consider a typical signal detection experiment designed to measure an observer's ability to detect a tone of a very low intensity in a background of noise that sounds like the static you hear when a radio is tuned between stations. After a ready signal, the observer is required to respond by pushing one button to indicate, "Yes, it was a signal present trial" and a different button to signify, "No, it was not a signal present trial." Table 2.2 shows a typical response pattern for an experiment that has 50% signal present trials and 50% signal absent trials. This **outcome matrix** shows the proportion of trials on which the four possible results occurred. Notice that the proportions in each row must sum to 1.00 because we consider the two types of trials separately.

TABLE 2.2 Outcome Matrix (Proportions) when Stimulus Is Present 50% of the Time

	Response	
Signal	**Yes**	**No**
Present	0.75	0.25
Absent	0.25	0.75

Notice that on 25% of the signal absent trials the observer responded, "Yes, the signal was present." Why should the observer report that a signal was present when it was not? First, the observer is not always sure that whatever was heard was actually the signal. Thus, many nonsensory aspects of the situation might influence the pattern of responding. For example, if the signal is expected to be present on almost every trial, the observer might respond "yes" to even the faintest or most ambiguous of sensations (since she is expecting it to be there most of the time), whereas if the signal is expected to occur only rarely, the observer would be less tempted by ambiguous, faint sensations and might wait until a very strong sensation was experienced before saying "yes." If the signal was expected to occur about half the time, as in Table 2.2, the observer might respond "yes" whenever the sensation was moderately strong.

If this analysis is correct, then we should be able to change the observer's response pattern by changing only his expectations and leaving everything else the same so as not to change his sensitivity. Typical results from additional experiments with the same observer are presented in Table 2.3. In one case there were 90% signal present trials and in the other only 10%. Notice that when the signal occurred frequently, the observer said "yes" often. This resulted in a high proportion of hits, but also in a high proportion of false alarms. The observer said "no" more often when the signal was expected to occur only occasionally, thus reducing the proportion of false alarms but also reducing the proportion of hits.

Because changes in an observer's response strategy change the proportions of hits and false alarms on which we must base estimates of sensitivity, it is important to measure sensitivity independent of those changes. To do this, signal detection theory creates a theoretical picture of how the signal and noise must have appeared to the observer over the course of the experiment so as to generate the obtained outcome matrix. This picture is based on several assumptions. First, as we already mentioned, it is assumed that the amount of internal and external noise an observer must cope with varies from moment to moment. These fluctuations in noise level are caused by physiological, attentional, and other variables in the sensory and perceptual systems of the observer as well as by random fluctuations in the environment, such as the fluctuating light patterns on a radar screen even in the absence of echoes. Signal detection theory represents these variations across time as a **probability distribution** like that shown in Figure 2.4, called the signal absent distribution.

TABLE 2.3 Outcome Matrices (Proportions) for Two Different Conditions

STIMULUS PRESENT 90% OF THE TIME		
	Response	
Signal	Yes	No
Present	0.95	0.05
Absent	0.63	0.37

STIMULUS PRESENT 10% OF THE TIME		
	Response	
Signal	Yes	No
Present	0.35	0.65
Absent	0.04	0.96

In Figure 2.4, the abscissa (horizontal axis) is the sensory activity level during a trial when no signal was presented, and the ordinate (vertical axis) is the relative likelihood of occurrence of any particular sensory activity level over all of the trials in the experiment. On trials when the signal is present, the sensory response produced by the signal adds to whatever activity level was present at that moment, producing the signal present distribution also shown in Figure 2.4. In Figure 2.4 the two distributions have been drawn on different copies of the same axes so that each can be seen clearly. In the theory they always overlap. You can see from Figure 2.4 that many different levels of sensory activity could result with some likelihood greater than zero either from signal present trials or from signal absent trials.

In signal detection theory, the observer is assumed to use a simple rule to make a response on each trial. If the sensation level is above a particular level, called the **criterion** and symbolized with the Greek letter β (beta), the observer says "yes"; if it is below the criterion level, the observer says "no." Following this rule will result in the proportions of hits, false alarms, misses, and correct rejections that we would observe in an outcome matrix. In the theory, the area under the appropriate probability distribution to the right or left of the criterion represents the proportions of the various types of responses given over the course of an experiment, as illustrated in Figure 2.4. For example, the area under the signal present distribution to the right of the criterion (where the observer responds, "Yes, I perceived it") represents the proportion of hits observed in an experiment, whereas the area to the right of the criterion in the signal absent distribution represents the proportion of false alarms.

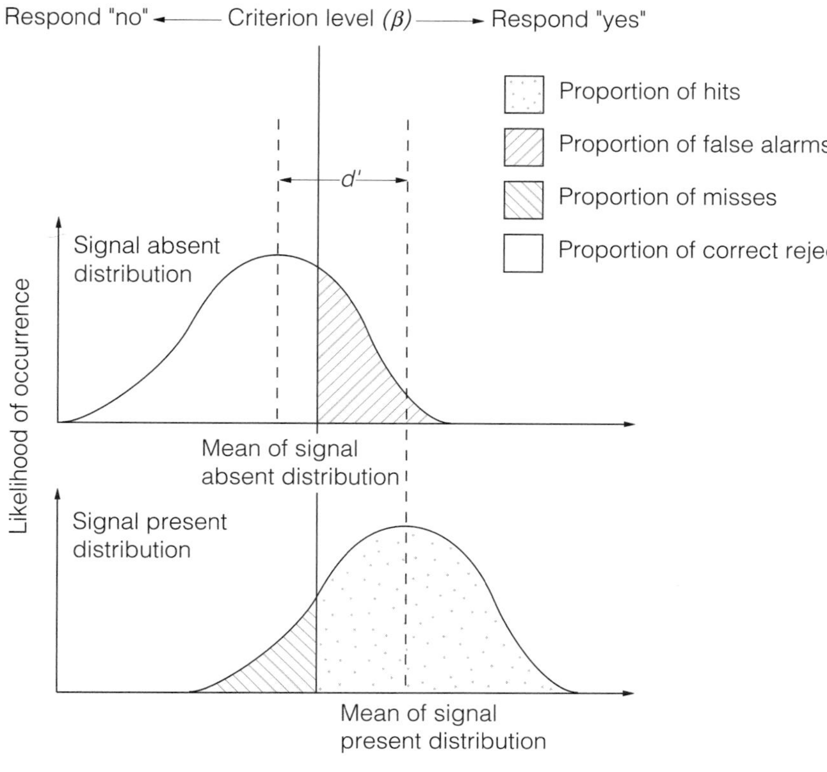

FIGURE 2.4 Illustration of how signal absent and signal present distributions result in hits, misses, false alarms, and correct negatives for a particular criterion setting. Notice that the two curves are actually plotted on the same axes—they are separated for clarity. The curves would overlap if plotted together.

Motivation and expectation will determine where the criterion is placed. For instance, suppose the observer is a radiologist looking for a light spot as evidence of cancer in a set of chest X-rays (Krupinski, Roehrig, Furukawa, 1999; Swensson, 1980). If the radiologist thinks she has found such a spot, she calls the patient back for additional tests. The penalty for a false alarm (additional tests when no cancer is present) involves only some added time and money on the part of the patient. But the penalty for a miss (not catching an instance of real cancer) might be the patient's death. Thus, the radiologist may set a criterion value that is quite low (high relative value of "yes" responses), not wanting to miss any danger signals. This means she will have many hits and few misses, but also many false alarms.

The signal detection theory picture of such a situation, portraying an outcome matrix similar to that at the top of Table 2.3, would look like the one shown in Figure 2.5A. Conversely, if the observer is a witness to a crime who is trying to identify suspects from a set of police photos, he might be more conservative. Here the penalty for a false alarm could be the arrest, trial, and conviction of an innocent person, whereas the penalty for a miss might be only that the prosecution would have less evidence available to prosecute the guilty parties. The witness might set a high criterion (high relative value of "no" responses) in order to avoid false alarms, but at the penalty of reducing the number of hits. The picture for this situation, with an outcome matrix similar to that shown at the bottom of Table 2.3, would resemble that shown in Figure 2.5B.

Although the location of the criterion alters the response pattern, location of the criterion has no effect at all on the **sensitivity** of the observer. In signal detection theory, sensitivity refers to the average amount of sensory activity a given signal adds to the average amount of sensory activity present in the absence of the signal (noise). This is similar to the everyday use of the word *sensitivity*. Thus, a radio receiver that produces a large electrical response, allowing a weak signal to be heard above the background static, is more sensitive than one that produces only a small electrical response

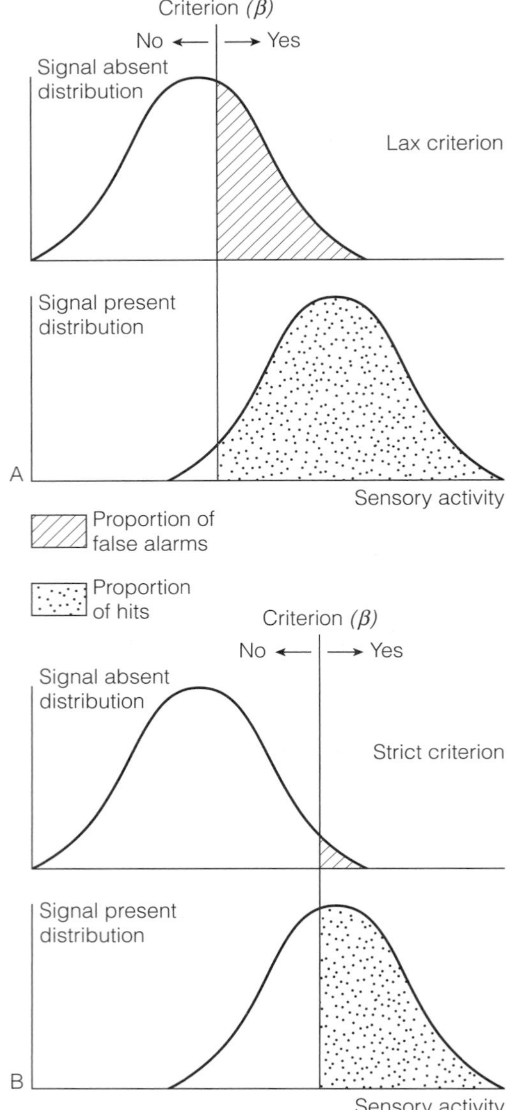

FIGURE 2.5 The effect of motives or expectations on criterion placement and proportion of hits and false alarms.

to that signal, which may then be obscured by static and noise.

In signal detection theory sensitivity is measured by the distance between the centers (averages) of the signal absent and the signal present distributions. This could be interpreted as the difference in average sensation levels as a function of the presence or absence of a signal. We call this distance measure of sensitivity d', which is pronounced "dee prime" (see Figure 2.4). When the two distributions are far apart, and overlap less, as in Figure 2.6B, d' is larger. When they are close together, and overlap more, d' is smaller, as in Figure 2.6A.

The calculation of d' and β can be complex, requiring probability tables or computer programs, and most of you will never have to do this. However, for those of you who would like to try it, or those of you who are doing research in which the signal detection measures that we have discussed might be useful, we have provided Computation Box 2.1, which provides a graphical method for doing this. Using this graphical method to compute d' and β for a few outcome matrices will also greatly aid your understanding of the theory and its use.

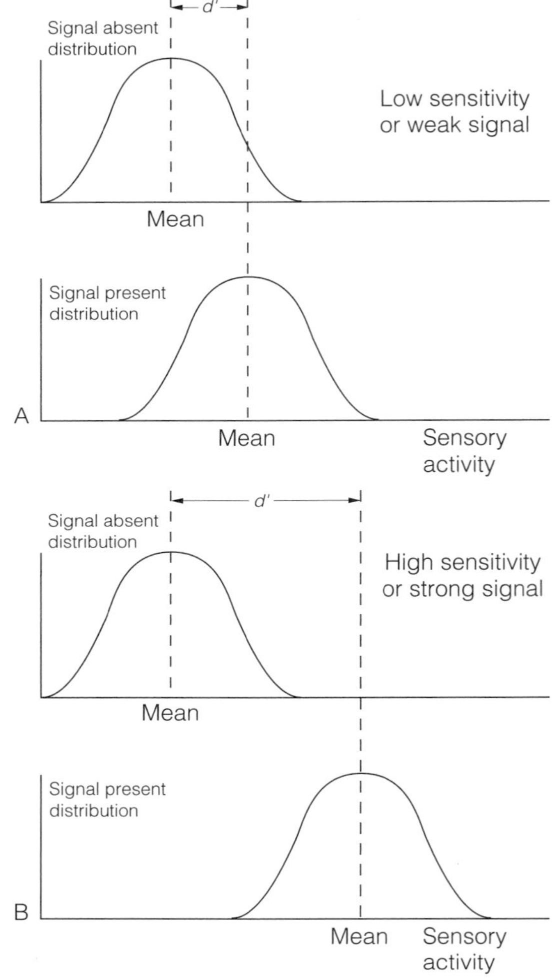

FIGURE 2.6 The effect of sensitivity and signal strength on d'.

COMPUTATION BOX 2.1

CALCULATION OF SIGNAL DETECTION MEASURES D′ *AND* β

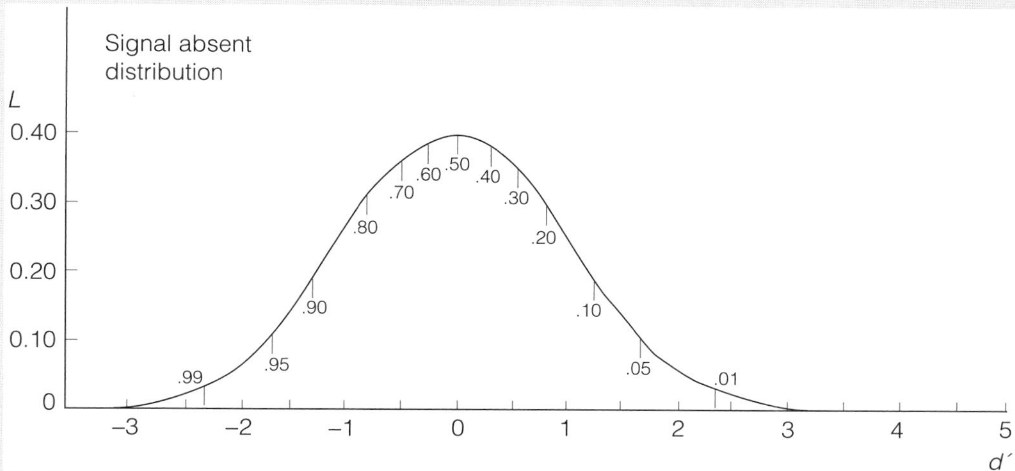

To calculate d' and β using a simple graphic procedure, you will need the sheet of transparent overlay (found inside the front cover) and the diagram of the signal absent distribution. First, tear the overlay along the perforated line to separate the criterion and signal present distribution portions as indicated.

Next, from the outcome of a signal detection experiment, you will need the proportions of hits and false alarms. As an example, we will use the data from Table 2.2.

TO CALCULATE *d′*

1. Put the sheet containing the criterion on top of the diagram of the signal absent distribution. Make sure that the horizontal line of the criterion sheet is superimposed on the horizontal axis of the distribution.
2. Slide the criterion sheet across the sheet below until the criterion (vertical line) is positioned so that it cuts the signal absent distribution curve at the point that represents the proportion of false alarms. From Table 2.2 this is 0.25, so you must estimate the placement between the marked numbers.
3. Holding the criterion sheet stationary, add the signal present distribution sheet to the stack, positioning it so that the horizontal axis is aligned with the other horizontal axes. Adjust it so the criterion meets the signal present distribution curve at the point representing the proportion of hits (in this example it is 0.75).
4. The final stack of two overlay sheets on top of the signal absent distribution should look something like the figure on page 24. Notice that you can see through the overlay sheets to the d'-scale printed on the signal absent distribution diagram. The d'-value can then be read off that scale as the point where the vertical line (which is marked "Read d'" and represents the mean of the signal present distribution) intersects the d'-scale (about 1.35 in the figure on page 24—interpolate carefully).

Now try calculating the values of d' for the two sets of data in Table 2.3. You should find that d is about 1.35, the same as for the data of Table 2.2, in spite of the vast differences in hit and false alarm rates.

TO CALCULATE β

Measuring the criterion requires one small computational step in addition to looking at the graphs.

1. Align a straightedge (ruler or piece of paper) parallel to the superimposed horizontal axes of your pile (without sliding the sheets around), and position it vertically so that you are measuring the height of the curve where the criterion and the signal present curve meet. Read off the value corresponding to the height from the vertical axis (labeled "L" for "Likelihood") where the straightedge crosses it (around 0.34).
2. Next read the height of the curve where the criterion crosses the signal absent curve. (In this example this is the same, with a height of 0.34.)

(continued)

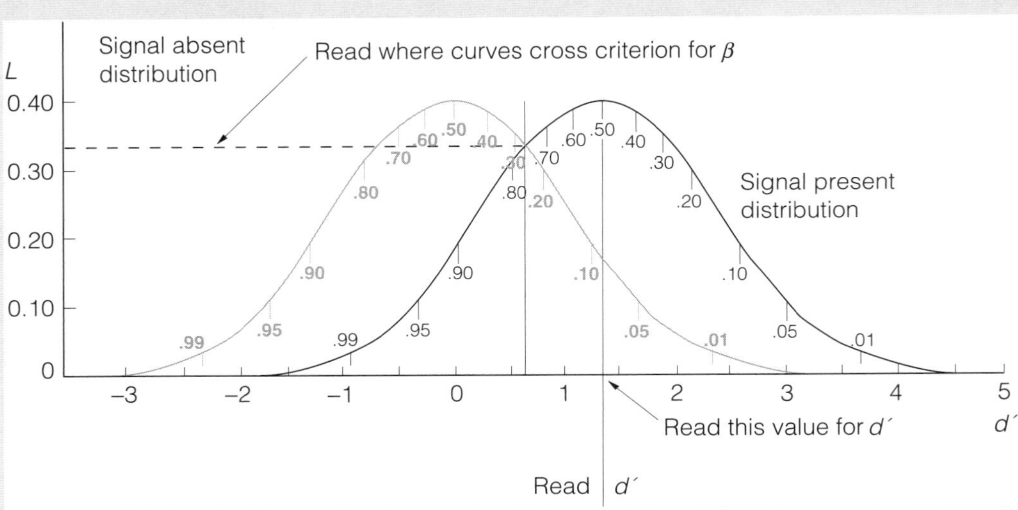

3. To calculate β, divide the height (the *L*-axis value) for the signal present distribution by the height for the signal absent distribution. In the figure, this is $0.34/0.34 = 1.00$, or $\beta = 1.00$. Try calculating β for the two sets of data in Table 2.3. You should find that, because of the very different hit and false alarm rates in the two data sets, the values are also very different. The top data set shows a lax criterion with β less than 1.00 (here around 0.30), whereas the lower data set demonstrates a conservative criterion with β greater than 1.00 (here a bit more than 4.00).

You should save your sheets of transparent overlay with the book so that you can use them for other d' and β calculations. Also note that, although this graphical method is accurate enough for quick estimates of d' and β, psychophysicists use precise numerical tables or complex equations to arrive at these measures with the accuracy needed for research.

Simple Reaction Time

In the methods of stimulus detection we have discussed so far, we have focused on the accuracy of the experience. These methods are designed to determine whether a stimulus had an influence. However, there are many situations in which the speed with which we can detect a stimulus is an equally important, or even more important, aspect of the perceptual situation. Think of the last time you were driving a car or bicycle, and you had to brake hard or swerve to avoid hitting a car that had stopped unexpectedly in your lane. Surely the speed with which you detected that something was now blocking your path was in some sense more important than the accuracy with which you detect the size, color, or specific shape of the vehicle that you needed to avoid. An accurate detection decision that took too long would have placed you at serious risk of injury.

Simple reaction time is defined as the time between the onset of a stimulus and the beginning of an overt response to it. The beginning of the response indicates that the information about the stimulus has passed through the sensory system and has activated the motor systems of your brain. This is clear evidence that your experience has been altered by the stimulus. The concept of simple reaction time was introduced in 1850 by one of the most influential early researchers in perception and physiology, Hermann von Helmholtz, who used it as a crude measure of how quickly nerves can conduct information.

A typical simple reaction time experiment is very much like the task of a swimmer or a track athlete, set to begin a race in the starting position. As soon as the starting gun is sounded, the athlete is permitted to begin moving over the start line. In a perception experiment, a tone or a light would sound, which would be the signal for the observer to press a key as quickly as possible. How much time do you think is needed to initiate a simple movement such as pressing a button in response to a starting signal? Despite the fact that most of us feel that we are actually experiencing events in the world at the same time that they appear, the actual delay before we can respond to a stimulus is surprisingly long. It takes at least 160 milliseconds (a millisecond is one thousandth of a second and is usually abbreviated *ms*) to respond to a tone and at least 180 ms to respond to a light.

Studies of the visual system, of which we will have much more to say in Chapter 3, show that over half of this time, over 120 ms, is taken up in the neural processing of the tone or the light. The time that is required for the visual centers of the brain to activate the centers controlling the muscles is actually the shortest portion of this overall duration. Signals from the visual centers of the brain can be used to activate the muscles of the eye or hand in only 20 to 40 ms.

You might want to think about this the next time you are required to make a rapid decision to bring your vehicle to a stop because a traffic light has turned red. Well over half of the time needed to begin an action will be taken up by your brain's analysis of the change in color of the light. That means over 120 ms will have elapsed and yet you will have barely begun seeing the red light. By the time your foot or hand begins to depress a brake pedal, 200 or more milliseconds will have elapsed. During this time, your vehicle will have continued to travel at its existing speed. This amounts to around one third of a second during which, at a typical highway speed of 100 kilometers an hour (65 miles per hour), your car will have traveled more than its full length and you have not yet accomplished anything that will begin to slow the car. Of course, once the brake has been depressed, the car will have its own time course of coming to a halt. As we often hear in commercials, "individual results will vary."

One of the most important influences on the speed of detection is the intensity of the stimulus. In general, the less intense it is, the slower the reaction time will be. Figure 2.7 shows typical average reaction times to the onset of a tone plotted against the intensity of the tone, collected in a classic experiment by Chocolle (1940). With lower tone intensities, we near the detection threshold, and, although the tone is still always detectable, the reaction times are longer. Similar results have been obtained for visual stimuli (Cattell, 1886; Grice, Nullmeyer, & Schnizlein, 1979).

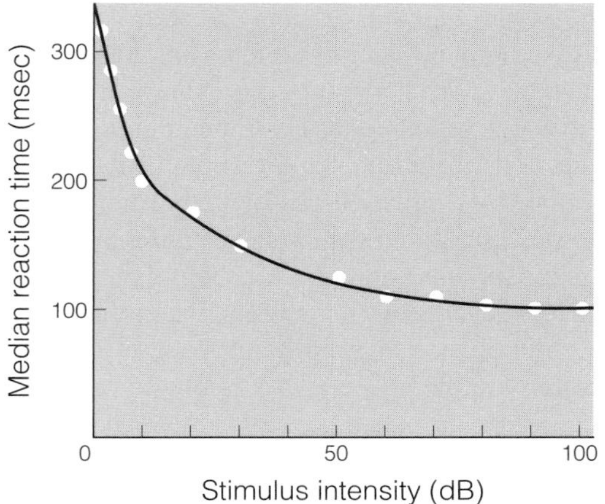

FIGURE 2.7 Effect of stimulus intensity on simple reaction time (based on Chocolle, 1940).

DISCRIMINATION

The recipe called for dividing the gooey dough mixture into two equal portions, one for the top and the other for the bottom of the deep-dish apple pie the cook was preparing. He put about half of the mixture into each of two bowls and then compared them. He decided they were not the same, took about a teaspoonful from one, and put it into the other. "There," he said, "now they are equal. This will be a perfect pie!" This somewhat obsessive cook was engaged in an act of discrimination. He was determining whether two amounts of dough were the same or different. He did not care how much dough was in each bowl; it could have been 200 g or 1000 g. He cared only whether the two bowls had the same amount. Discrimination problems ask, "Is this stimulus different from that one?"

The study of discrimination focuses on the question, "By how much must two stimuli differ in order to be discriminated as not the same?" Suppose we are comparing a computer and a typewriter. Are they the same or different? The answer depends on what aspects are being compared. Both have keyboards and can print words, so they are the same in that way. But computers can compute, and typewriters cannot, so they are different, too. To avoid such confusion, the standard discrimination experiment involves variation of stimuli along only one dimension. Thus, in a study of the discrimination of weights, we might hold the size and shape of our stimuli constant and vary only their weight.

In a typical study, observers are presented with pairs of stimuli and asked to make the responses "heavier" or "lighter" or some similar set of judgments appropriate to the stimulus dimension being judged. Observers are usually not given the option of saying "same" because it has been shown that even when they feel they are just guessing, observers are more often correct than incorrect. Thus, not allowing "same" judgments yields a more accurate measurement of discrimination performance (Brown, 1910). One stimulus intensity, called the **standard,** is the stimulus that the others are compared with. The standard appears on every trial and is compared to a set of similar stimuli differing only along the dimension being studied. These stimuli make up the set of **comparison stimuli.** This experiment is a variant of the method of constant stimuli (which, you may remember, is used to determine the absolute threshold) to which the standard has been added. We are also measuring a threshold here, but this is a threshold for the perception of a difference between the standard and the other stimuli. It is called the **difference threshold.**

Typical results from an experiment in discrimination of lifted weights are displayed in Figure 2.8. In this experiment, the standard (a 100-g weight) was presented with each comparison stimulus (82 to 118 g in 1-g steps) over 700 times. We need plot only the proportion of the presentations on which each comparison stimulus was judged "heavier" than the standard because the proportion of "lighter" judgments can be obtained by subtracting the proportion "heavier" from 1. Notice that as the weight of the comparison stimulus increases, the number of times that the observer judges it "lighter" only gradually shifts to more frequent reports of "heavier." This suggests that, as in the case of the absolute detection threshold, the difference threshold is not sharply delineated at a single value for an individual but may vary over time and conditions. The data result in an S-shaped psychometric function when fitted with a smooth curve, as shown in Figure 2.8.

But what should we take as evidence that a difference has been detected? We cannot use the point on the curve where the comparison stimulus is called "lighter" half of the time and "heavier" half of the time (proportion "heavier" 0.5), since that represents the stimuli that are considered to be exactly the same and therefore neither lighter nor heavier. This is called the **point of subjective equality.** Instead, we are interested in the point at which "heavier" and "lighter" can be distinguished from this point of equality. This can be found half way between the point of subjective equality and perfect discrimination. For example, when the proportion of "heavier" responses equal 0.75 (which is halfway between 0.5 meaning neither heavier or lighter, and 1.0 meaning always heavier), it means that the difference in the "heavier" direction is being noted 50% of the time. Following similar reasoning, when the proportion of "heavier" responses equals 0.25, a difference in the "lighter" direction is being noted 50% of the time. The stimulus region between the 0.25 point and the 0.75 point is called the **interval of uncertainty** since stimuli in that region are perceived as very similar to the standard stimulus. To get the difference threshold, we simply divide this interval by 2, which then gives us an average of the stimulus difference needed to produce either a heavier or a lighter discrimination. Thus the difference threshold for the data in Figure 2.8 is about 4 g. This means that when a pair of stimuli in this experiment were separated by 4 g, the subject was able to detect the difference between them about half the time.

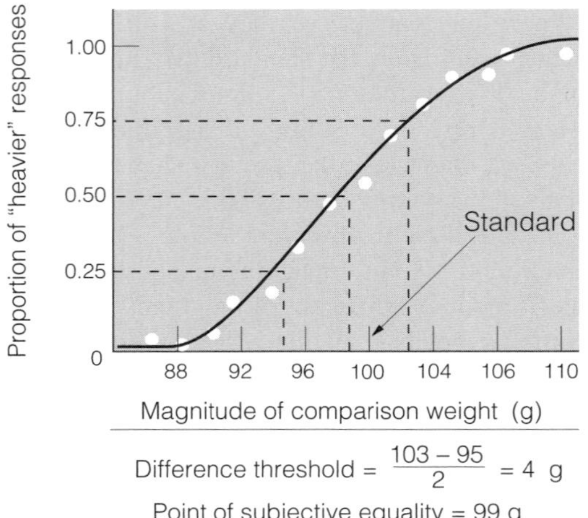

FIGURE 2.8 Typical data from the method of constant stimuli in discrimination with calculations of difference threshold and point of subjective equality.

Notice that the difference threshold is the average of the threshold for "greater than" and the threshold for "less than." It thus represents the threshold for "different" averaged across the direction of the differences. This value is sometimes also referred to as the **just noticeable difference** and often abbreviated as the *jnd.*

If discrimination is good, the difference threshold will be small, meaning that small differences between stimuli will be noticed. In Figure 2.9 the black line shows the psychometric function of an observer with relatively good discrimination ability who has a difference threshold of 0.50 units. The white line shows that of an observer who is less able to discriminate these stimuli and who has a larger difference threshold of 2.00 units. The worse the discrimination ability, the flatter the psychometric function is and the larger the difference threshold. A horizontal line parallel to the abscissa at all points would represent the extreme of no discrimination.

You may have noticed that in the data of Figure 2.8 the point of subjective equality is not equal to the standard. The stimulus that appears to be equal to the standard of 100 g is actually 1 g lighter. This is a typical result in many psychophysical experiments involving the presentation of stimuli that are separated in time. The stimulus presented first (generally the standard) is

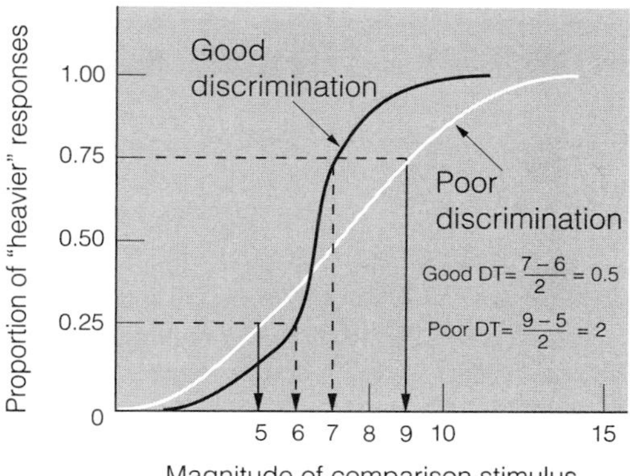

FIGURE 2.9 Difference thresholds (DTs) for observers of different sensitivity.

judged to be less intense than the later stimulus. This effect has been named the **negative time error** (because the standard is judged to be less intense than it should be). It is thought to be an error resulting from the fact that we are judging the currently sensed stimulus against our memory of the previous stimulus and our memories are not as vivid or as sharp as the stimulus currently being perceived (Fechner, 1860/1966; Wolfgang Kohler, 1923).

Weber's Law

A systematic pattern was observed in early studies of discrimination, indicating that the size of the just noticeable difference was related to the size of the standard stimulus (Fechner, 1860/1966; Weber, 1834). A typical example is shown in Figure 2.10, from an experiment in which observers lifted sets of comparison weights in the context of standard weights that were themselves of varying degrees of heaviness. The graph shows that the size of the difference threshold (just noticeable difference) grows in size directly as the weight of the standard stimulus is increased. This means that the difference threshold is not a constant value. It is larger for larger standards by a fixed percentage. For example, if a room contained 10 lit candles and you could just detect the addition of 1 candle, then if the room contained 100 candles it would take an additional 10 candles for you to notice it. This relation between the size of the difference threshold and the magnitude of the standard is called *Weber's law.*

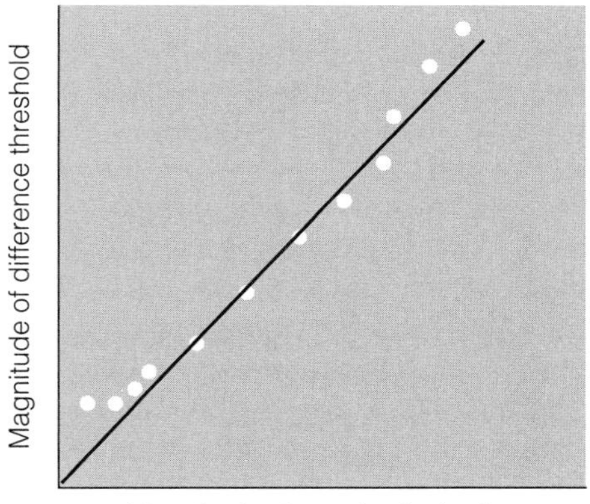

FIGURE 2.10 Effect of intensity of standard on difference threshold.

Weber's law is written as

$$\Delta I = k\, I$$

where ΔI is the difference threshold, I is the intensity (magnitude) of the standard stimulus, and k is a constant. The constant k, called the **Weber fraction,** is equal to $\Delta I/I$. This constant, which is usually less than 1, indicates the proportion by which a standard stimulus must be changed so that the change can be detected 50% of the time. Weber's law states that the Weber fraction is the same for any intensity of standard stimulus. For example, if the Weber fraction for lifted weight is 0.1, it means that for a weight to be discriminated as different than the standard it must differ by 10%. Thus if the standard weight is 10 g, you must add or subtract 1 g to just notice a difference, while if the standard weight is 1000 g, a 100 g difference is needed to be noticed. Thus the larger or more intense the comparison stimulus, the larger the absolute stimulus change must be to be noticed. A simple demonstration of Weber's law is given in Demonstration Box 2.2.

Table 2.4 presents typical Weber fractions (k) for a variety of stimulus types. As you can see, for some stimulus modalities k is relatively large (for example, light and sound intensity), and for some very small (for example, electric shock). Generally speaking, if we have equivalently measured Weber fractions on the same stimulus modality, then larger Weber fractions mean poorer sensitivity to differences along that continuum. For example, the fact that Weber fractions for light intensity are larger in elderly individuals can be interpreted to indicate that such individuals are less sensitive to differences in light intensity than are younger individuals.

Weber's law turns out to be a remarkably good description of our ability to make discriminations. Measurements have been taken in many sense modalities to check the relation. The clearest picture of the results is given by plotting the value of the Weber fraction, $\Delta I/I$,

DEMONSTRATION BOX 2.2

WEBER'S LAW

It is easy to demonstrate Weber's law for the perception of heaviness. You will need three quarters, two envelopes, and your shoes. Take one quarter, and put it into one envelope, and put the remaining two quarters in the other. If you now lift each envelope gently and put it down (use the same hand), it is easy to distinguish the heavier envelope. Now insert one envelope into one of your shoes and the other envelope into your second shoe, and lift them one at a time. The weight difference should be almost imperceptible. In the first instance, the targets differed by the weight of the quarter, and the difference was discriminated easily. In the second instance, although the weight differential was the same (one quarter), the overall stimulus intensity was greater because shoes weigh much more than the envelopes and the quarters alone.

against the standard stimulus intensity. If the Weber fraction is actually constant, we should see a horizontal line, parallel to the horizontal axis. Figure 2.11 shows a composite of data from many sound intensity discrimination experiments. There are small deviations from the expected constancy, which occur at both very low and very high stimulus values. The deviations are probably the result of internal noise at low values and the result of distorted behavior of the sensory systems at extremely high values. You should note that these deviations look especially large only because the graph has been plotted in logarithmic units. The flat part of the curve actually covers nearly 99% of the total range of intensities.

Choice Response Time

We have been discussing situations in which discrimination is very difficult. However, even when stimulus differences are well above the difference threshold, some discriminations are easier to make than others. For example, most people feel that red is more easily differentiated from green than it is from orange, even though we would never actually make an error in discriminating these colors. Because experiments looking for the just noticeable difference depend on observers making errors, they cannot be used to measure detectability or discriminability in situations where all of the stimulus differences are far enough above threshold to be easily perceived. To measure discriminability in such situations, we can measure the response time involved in making the discrimination. **Choice response time** involves making one of several different responses depending on the stimulus presented (for example, press the button on the right for a red light and the button on the left for a green light). Biography Box 2.2 will give you a little background on F. C. Donders, a Dutch scientist who pioneered the use of choice response time for measuring the duration of internal mental processes.

TABLE 2.4 Typical Weber Fractions ($\Delta I/I$) (based on Teghtsoonian, 1971)

Continuum	Weber Fraction
Light intensity	0.079
Sound intensity	0.048
Finger span	0.022
Lifted weight	0.020
Line length	0.029
Taste (salt)	0.083
Electric shock	0.013
Vibration (fingertip)	
60 Hz	0.036
125 Hz	0.046
250 Hz	0.046

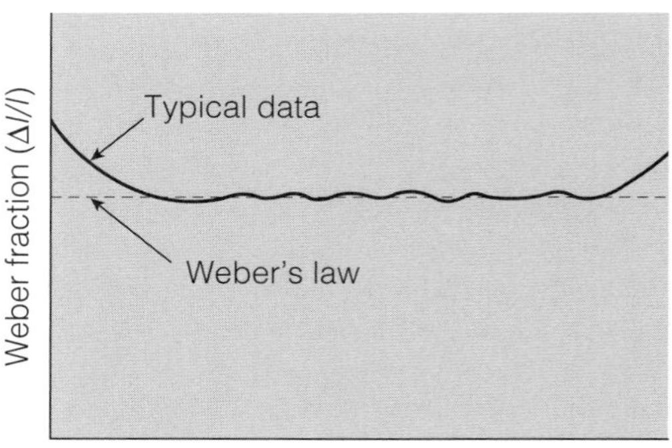

FIGURE 2.11 Typical data for test of Weber's law. The dotted line is predicted by Weber's law: $\Delta I/I = k$.

BIOGRAPHY BOX 2.2

WHAT IS THE SPEED OF THOUGHT?

Even though our sensory experiences and thoughts appear to be instantaneous, seeing and thinking take time. And not a trivial amount of time. It is measureable. Contrary to what you might think at first, the real limit on how quickly we hear something or how rapidly we see an event is not tied to the very rapid speed of light (300,000 kilometers per second or 186,000 miles per second) nor to the much slower speed of sound (0.344 kilometers per second or 0.214 miles per second). Instead the main limit on the speed of our perceptions is the much longer time it takes for neurons to conduct information from one region of the brain to another. Even once a signal has arrived in a brain region, some time must elapse before that region has completed its analysis.

In the mid-1800s, the physicist Hermann von Helmholz began to estimate neural transmission time by stimulating nerves at various distances from a muscle and then measuring the time it took for the muscle to contract. His estimates ranged from 50 to 100 meters per second (165 to 330 feet per second). The Dutch physician ***F. C. Donders (1818–1889),*** extended this idea in 1868 into the realm of purely mental processes by having observers perform two tasks. First, they performed a simple reaction time task to the onset of stimulus, which could be either a tone or a light. Second, they performed a choice response time task with the same stimuli. If a tone occurred, they pressed one key and if a light occurred they pressed another. By subtracting the average simple reaction time from the average choice response time, Donders estimated that the time it took to make a simple decision such as this took between 50 and 100 milliseconds (5 to 10 hundredths of a second). Donder's approach to the measurement of mental processes is still in wide use today. To honor Donder's pioneering achievements in the study of physiology and the mind, the Dutch government commissioned a postage stamp in his honor in 1935.

Another classic study involving choice response time was done by Henmon (1906). In one experiment observers were presented with pairs of lines differing only in length and were told to depress the one of two keys that corresponded to the side on which the line was longer. Henmon found that the smaller the difference between the line lengths, the longer was the response time. He also reported similar results for tones. The more similar two tones were in duration, the longer it took observers to make a response indicating which one was longer. You can experience several other examples of this effect in Demonstration Box 2.3.

The measurement of choice response time is also complicated by the inherent relationship between time and accuracy that we all know well from our experiences taking tests in school. We can usually perform more accurately on a test question if we are given more time. If we are forced to respond quickly, the likelihood of making an error will naturally increase. The general nature of this relationship is illustrated in Figure 2.12. This S-shaped curve relating response accuracy to response time is called a **speed-accuracy trading relationship.**

Response accuracy is limited at the lower end of the curve by the probability of guessing correctly by chance. For instance, if an exam consists of multiple-choice questions with four alternatives, and you know nothing about the material, you would still be expected to guess correctly 25% of the time. On a true-false test, your guessing average should be 50%, even if you know nothing about the material at all. At the upper end of accuracy, performance will be limited by the total amount of information it is possible to have in the situation if no time limit is involved. This may be complete information if the problem is simple, but it may also be less than perfect if the situation is complex.

For choice response time the issue is not the amount of stored information as it is for an exam. At its lower end, the time needed to make a response is limited by the minimum amount of time required for a stimulus to influence a motor neuron, as we discussed earlier. However, the remainder of the relationship between response time and accuracy depends to a large extent on whether speed or accuracy is more important to the observer. If accuracy is of greatest importance, then this can be achieved, but only at the expense of a rather slow response time. If response speed is of utmost importance, then it will be achieved at a cost in response accuracy.

The existence of the speed-accuracy trading relationship means that when discrimination tasks are compared using only response time as the index of performance, there is always uncertainty over whether

DEMONSTRATION BOX 2.3

CHOICE RESPONSE TIME AND STIMULUS DISCRIMINABILITY

A fun-to-do example of the relation between choice response time and discriminability involves card sorting (e.g., Shallice & Vickers, 1964). Take a deck of common playing cards and select out of it 10 of the picture cards (kings, queens, and jacks) and 10 numbered cards from the red suits (hearts and diamonds) to make a new deck of 20 cards. Compose another deck of 20 by using the numbered cards (include the aces) of the black suits (clubs and spades). Shuffle each deck separately and place it in front of you, face down. Next you need a clock or a watch with a sweep second hand. Wait until the second hand reaches the "12," pick up one of the decks, and begin to sort it into two piles. The first deck gets sorted into number and picture cards; the second gets sorted into spades and clubs. Note the time it takes to sort each deck. You may want to repeat the task a couple of times so that you are sorting smoothly. Notice that the sorting time for the spades and clubs (a more difficult task because it involves making small form discrimination on similarly colored cards) is longer than the easier discrimination task of sorting picture and number cards.

the response time differences are the result of a decision to be more accurate in one task, which would naturally prolong the response time, or whether the response time differences reflected real differences in the time for perception at the same level of accuracy. To resolve this uncertainty, researchers usually report measures of response accuracy along with measures of response time in a study of speeded discrimination. If one pair of stimuli is really more difficult to discriminate than another pair, then the more difficult pair will result in both lower average response accuracy and longer average response times. Demonstration Box 2.4 will give you an opportunity to experience the effects of trading response accuracy for speed.

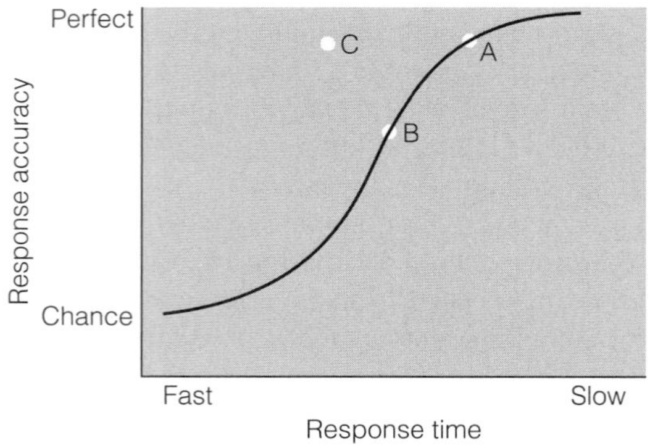

FIGURE 2.12 The relationship between choice response accuracy and choice response time. Performance in discrimination A is actually equal to that of discrimination B. Although discrimination A appears to be the more accurate, this has occurred only because the discrimination was also made in a longer time period. On the other hand, discrimination B appears to be made more rapidly than discrimination A, but only at the cost of a reduced level of accuracy. Only discrimination C can truly be said to be a better performance than either discrimination A or B.

SCALING

The dog trainer glanced at her new St. Bernard pupil and estimated his shoulder height to be 65 cm (26 in.) and his weight to be 70 kg (150 lb). In so doing she was engaged in the process of estimating scale values of her pupil's height and weight. **Scaling** attempts to answer the question, "How much of X is there?" X can be a stimulus intensity in the real world, a sensation magnitude, or the magnitude of other complex psychological variables such as pleasantness or annoyance.

A scale is a mathematical rule by which we assign numbers to objects or events. But not all psychological quantities can be measured in the same way. Some perceptual experiences have an underlying aspect of intensity (for instance, brightness), whereas others do not (such as shape). When we are dealing with an experience in which it makes sense to ask, "How much?" or "How intense?" we have a **prothetic continuum** (Stevens & Galanter, 1957). With prothetic continua, changes in the physical stimulus result in a change in the apparent quantity of the psychological experience. For example, louder sounds seem to have "more" of something than softer sounds do; that something is loudness. This experience can often be connected to the way the sensation is represented in the brain; for example, loudness seems to depend on the total amount of neural activity in auditory areas of the brain, with louder experiences represented

DEMONSTRATION BOX 2.4

THE SPEED-ACCURACY TRADING RELATIONSHIP

Take the two decks of 20 playing cards you created in Demonstration Box 2.3 (number versus picture cards and spades versus clubs) and sort them each again, two times. However, the first time you sort them try to go as quickly as possible, even if that means you make some mistakes. (If you find you are making no mistakes at all, you must speed up and try again.) Then the second time you sort the two decks, make sure you make no mistakes at all. (If you make any this time, you must slow down and try again.) When you are finished, draw a graph such as the one shown in Figure 2.12. Plot your four data points, corresponding to your total sorting time and accuracy level for each of these four speeded sorts. Was the discrimination of number versus picture cards really more difficult than the discrimination of spades versus clubs? If so, then you will find those two data points lying in the lower left side of the graph relative to the two data points for the number versus picture cards. Do the two sorts you made on the same deck of cards seem to fall on an S-shaped curve? They should, because the only difference between these two sorts was your relative emphasis on speed versus accuracy.

by more activity than are softer experiences. Such prothetic continua as loudness can be meaningfully measured on several different types of scales (although some restrictions are necessary; see Geschieder, 1997).

With other perceptions, a change in the physical stimulus results in a change in the apparent quality rather than the apparent quantity of a stimulus. When we have an experience in which the only question it makes sense to ask is "What kind?" we are dealing with a **metathetic continuum.** Thus, a change in the wavelength of a light may cause its appearance to change from red to green. Psychologically, there is no quantitative difference between these two hues; they simply appear to be different. It makes no sense to ask if red is "more" or "less" than green. Occasionally both types of continua will be present in the same sense impressions. For instance, in touch, the amount of pressure applied is a prothetic continuum, but the location of the touch is a metathetic continuum.

Indirect Scaling: Fechner's Law

There are two very different approaches to establishing a scale on which numbers will be assigned to the intensity of sensations. The first is **direct scaling,** in which individuals are asked to assign a number directly to the magnitude of a sensation. This seems easy and straightforward. However, many early psychologists distrusted the accuracy of such direct reports because the concepts of number did not seem as immediate and fundamental to them as sensations and perceptions of tones and lights. For this reason **indirect scaling** methods, based on discrimination ability, formed the basis for the first psychological scales.

When Fechner initially attempted to describe the relation between stimulus intensity and sensation, he first had to invent a way to measure the magnitudes of sensations. He reasoned that because the minimal difference in stimulus intensity that can be sensed between two stimuli is the difference threshold (or just noticeable difference, jnd), one minimal stimulus difference would seem much like any other minimal difference. Technically this means that if we take two dim lights that are separated by one jnd and we take two lights that are much more intense, but again separated by one jnd, we should perceive the two pairs of stimuli as differing by equal sensory steps. Next Fechner assumed that we can count or add jnd's to create a scale that corresponds to the perceived strength of our sensation of a stimulus. A stimulus at absolute threshold intensity was assumed to generate 0 units of sensation magnitude; a stimulus intensity 1 difference threshold above absolute threshold was assumed to generate 1 unit of sensation magnitude (1 jnd of sensation); a stimulus intensity 1 difference threshold above the 1-unit stimulus to generate 2 units of sensation magnitude, and so forth. Thus the number of jnd's of sensation "measured" the sensation intensity. The jnd of sensation was the "unit" of a sensation scale (because all were assumed to represent equal increments of sensation) just as the degree centigrade (or degree Fahrenheit) is the unit of a temperature scale (because all represent equal increments of temperature).

Finally, Fechner assumed that Weber's law (which states that the difference threshold is a fixed proportion of the stimulus magnitude) is correct. As we have seen, this is reasonable for most of the perceptible stimulus range. The relation between the sensation intensity and the intensity of the physical stimulus implied by Fechner's assumptions is shown graphically in Figure 2.13.

This curve is described by the equation

$$S = (1/k)\ln(I/I_0)$$

where S is the magnitude of sensation a stimulus elicits (the number of jnds of sensation above 0 at absolute threshold), I/I_0 is the physical magnitude of the stimulus (intensity [I] relative to the absolute threshold stimulus magnitude [I_0]), $1/k$ is the inverse of the Weber fraction ($1/\Delta I/I = I/\Delta I$), and ln is the natural logarithm (logarithm to the base e). This equation is called **Fechner's law.** The value of $1/k$ will be different for different sensory and psychological continua because it is the inverse of the Weber fraction for the continuum scaled. Basically, this law says that as we increase the magnitude of a physical stimulus, the magnitude of our sensory experience increases rapidly at first, but then more slowly as the stimulus becomes more intense. This has been supported in many studies, which show that sensation intensity, measured with a discrimination measure such as d', is logarithmically related to stimulus intensity.

On a practical level, Fechner's law has proven itself useful; for example, the volume control on your radio varies the physical intensity of the sound logarithmically, although you probably feel that each degree of turning of the knob produces an equal increase in the loudness of the sound. At a theoretical level, Fechner's law is also consistent with physiological data, such as the approximate logarithmic increase in firing rate in sensory neurons with increases in stimulus intensity.

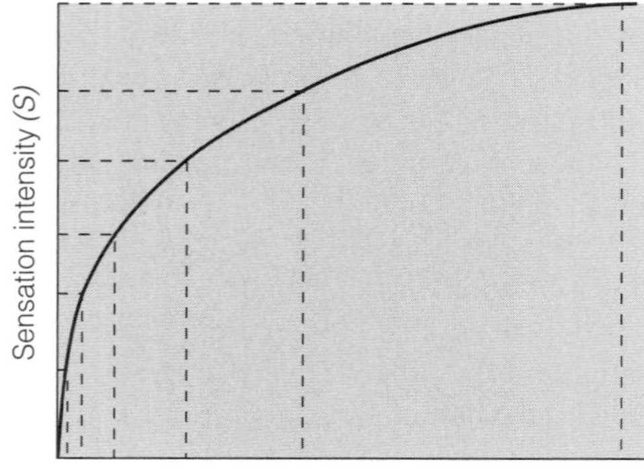

FIGURE 2.13 Fechner's law. It takes larger and larger differences between stimuli (Is) as stimulus intensity increases to give rise to the same size differences between sensations (Ss).

Direct Scaling

Since Fechner's time, many psychophysicists have insisted that indirect scaling is neither necessary nor preferable. Because we are interested in the magnitude of the sensation aroused in an observer by a stimulus, why not simply ask the observer to tell us directly how intense the sensation is? If the observer used numbers in a consistent way to report the sensation magnitude, then those numerical responses could be used directly to establish a scale of measurement.

Category Scaling. In one of the simplest applications of direct scaling, the well-known 1-to-10 category scale is used by observers to place the sensation created by each physical stimulus into 1 of 10 categories, from weakest to strongest. Stimuli are presented one at a time, and observers' average judgment for a particular stimulus intensity is treated as the scale value of sensation magnitude for that intensity. In an early typical study of this sort observers sorted envelopes containing weights into five categories, labeled "1" (for the lightest weights) to "5" (for the heaviest) (Sanford, 1898). When the average category value (y-axis) was plotted against each actual weight (x-axis), the resulting curve was concave downward, very similar to the curve predicted by Fechner's law (Figure 2.13).

Magnitude Estimation: Stevens's Law. Although in category scaling observers are responding directly to their sensation magnitude, there is still some indirectness involved. Most important is that available responses are limited to a few arbitrary category labels. Thus, stimuli that are similar but that give rise to different magnitudes of sensation are often grouped into the same category simply because there aren't enough categories to have one for each stimulus intensity. S. S. Stevens popularized a procedure called magnitude estimation to try and avoid these problems. In this procedure, observers are asked to assign numbers to the magnitudes of the sensations elicited by each of a set of stimuli that vary on some prothetic dimension. Stimuli are usually judged one at a time, and the only restriction on responses is that only numbers larger than zero can be used.

A typical modern magnitude estimation experiment might involve scaling the loudness of a set of pure tones (e.g., Zwislocki & Goodman, 1980). Observers are asked to assign a number to the sensation (loudness) elicited by each tone in such a way that their impression of the magnitude of that number matches the loudness of the tone. Observers are also told that they may use any positive number, including decimals or fractions. They are further told not to pay attention to any stimuli presented earlier or to the responses they might have given to such stimuli but, rather, to concentrate on matching a number to the loudness of the current stimulus.

Stevens originally expected the results of magnitude estimation and other direct scaling experiments to confirm Fechner's law, but many did not. In one such early direct test of Fechner's law, artists were asked to mix a gray that was halfway between a particular black and a white (Plateau, 1872). Fechner's law predicts that this psychological midpoint should correspond to the average of the logarithm of the physical intensity of the black stimulus and that of the white stimulus. Unfortunately, the grays mixed by the artists seemed to fall halfway between the cube roots (1/3 power) of the intensities of the black and the white stimuli. This suggested that the relation between physical and sensory intensity would be better described by a power function such as $S = I^{1/3}$, rather than Fechner's logarithmic function.

Stevens (1956) found that the equation that best described the relation of the average magnitude estimates of loudness to the stimulus intensities was $L = aI^{0.60}$, where L (for "loudness") represents the average magnitude estimates, a is a constant, I is the physical intensity of the sound (sound pressure), and 0.60 is a power to which I is raised. In succeeding years, Stevens and a host of others produced magnitude estimation scales for many other sensory continua. All of these scales seemed to be related to the physical stimulus intensities by the general relation

$$S = aI^m$$

where S is the measure of the sensation intensity and m is a characteristic exponent (power) that differs for different sensory continua. Because this relation states that the magnitude of the sensation is simply the intensity of the physical stimulus raised to some power (m), this relation is often called the **power law** or, after its popularizer, **Stevens's law** (see Biography Box 2.3).

In the power law the magnitude of the sensation elicited by a particular stimulus intensity depends on the size of the exponent. In general, the exponent for any one continuum is quite stable. As long as the experimental situation is kept reasonably standard and the same measures of physical stimulus intensity are used (Myers, 1982), the average exponents produced by different groups of observers for the same continuum are similar. Some of them are small fractions (0.3 for brightness), some are close to 1 (for line length), and others are substantially greater than 1 (up to 3.5 for electric shock). Some typical exponents for several sensory continua are given in Table 2.5.

In Figure 2.14 we show plots of some power functions showing how perceived sensory intensity varies when scaled directly against physical stimulus intensity.

BIOGRAPHY BOX 2.3

PUTTING NUMBERS ON SENSATIONS

Stanley Smith Stevens (1906–1973) was born in Ogden, Utah and raised in a frontier-style Mormon household. In 1933 he received his doctorate in psychology from Harvard University and then immediately was given a teaching position there and remained there on the faculty until his death. In 1962, at his own request, his title was changed and he became the world's first Professor of Psychophysics.

Stevens's early interests were in hearing, and particularly on how our sense of the loudness of a sound was related to the physical stimulus. These interests caused the U.S. Air Force to ask him to set up a lab to study the effects that the intense noise in military aircraft had on their aircrews. Although the lab started humbly in the back of a furnace room, it eventually expanded to some 50 people by the end of the war and became the Laboratory of Psychophysics.

Stevens's popularized a conceptual breakthrough that sounds simple. Since people have no problems assigning numbers to things that indicate their estimates of length in inches or weight in pounds, perhaps people could also assign numbers that indicated the intensity of their sensations, such as the loudness of a sound or the brightness of a light. The very simplicity of this concept brought on much skepticism; however, in Stevens's hands this **method of magnitude estimation** proved to be very useful. In fact, the measures were sufficiently stable to allow Stevens to work out the mathematical relationship between the physical stimulus intensity and our perception of that stimulus. Since his first studies in sound perception, magnitude estimation has been used for virtually all sensory qualities, including common ones such as brightness, pain, warmth, and roughness, and more esoteric ones such as beauty, harmony, and even the heinousness of crimes.

TABLE 2.5 Representative Exponents of the Power Functions Relating Sensation Magnitude to Stimulus Magnitude (based on Stevens, 1961)

Continuum	Exponent	Stimulus Conditions
Loudness	0.60	Both ears
Brightness	0.33	5° target—dark
Brightness	0.50	Point source—dark
Lightness	1.20	Gray papers
Smell	0.55	Coffee odor
Taste	0.80	Saccharine
Taste	1.30	Sucrose
Taste	1.30	Salt
Temperature	1.00	Cold—on arm
Temperature	1.60	Warmth—on arm
Vibration	0.95	60 Hz—on finger
Duration	1.10	White noise stimulus
Finger span	1.30	Thickness of wood blocks
Pressure on palm	1.10	Static force on skin
Heaviness	1.45	Lifted weights
Force of handgrip	1.70	Precision hand dynamometer
Electric shock	3.50	60 Hz—through fingers

Notice that the curves for power functions with different exponents (m) have dramatically different shapes. The curve is concave downward when the exponent is less than 1 (for example, brightness), whereas it is concave upward when the exponent is greater than 1 (for example, electric shock) and a straight line when the exponent equals 1 (for example, apparent length). The immense appeal of the power law is that it allows a vast range of different sensation-magnitude versus stimulus-intensity curves to be captured in the same mathematical function. Moreover, it is relatively easy to estimate what that curve will look like for any set of magnitude estimation judgments. If the power law is a correct description of the relation between magnitude estimations of sensation intensity and stimulus intensity, then logarithms of the magnitude estimates plotted against the logarithms of the stimulus intensities will form a straight line. In Figure 2.15 the curves in Figure 2.14 have been replotted in this way. We can now estimate m from the plotted data by measuring the distances marked Δy and Δx in the figures and computing $m = \Delta y/\Delta x$. The constant a is the point at which the line crosses the ordinate. Demonstration Box 2.5 allows you to perform a magnitude estimation experiment for yourself.

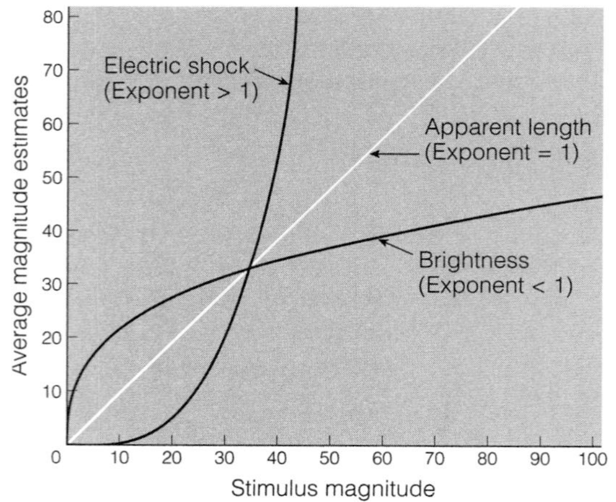

FIGURE 2.14 Power functions for brightness, length, and electric shock. Notice how different exponents give rise to different curves.

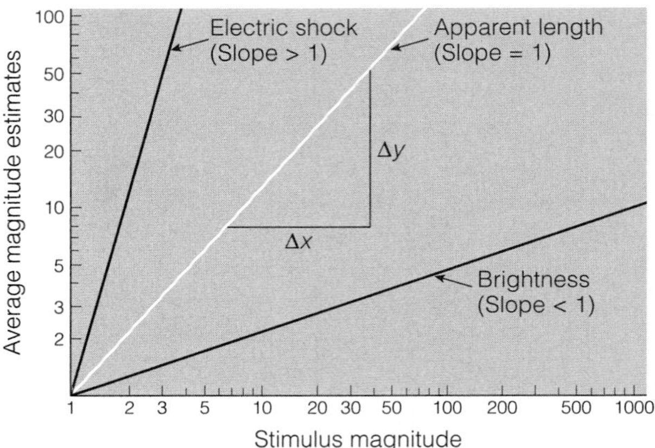

FIGURE 2.15 The same power functions as in Figure 2.14 plotted on logarithmic axes. In such log-log plots, all power functions become straight lines, with the slope of the straight line determined by the exponent (m) of the power function.

You might wonder why category scaling seems to support Fechner's law, whereas magnitude estimates are related to stimulus magnitude by a power law. Actually, Stevens and Galanter (1957) found that category judgments only approximately fit a logarithmic relation. Since then it has been shown that category judgments also fit the power law, but with exponents (m) that are about half the size of those produced by magnitude estimation (Ward, 1974). Torgerson (1961) suggested that these apparently conflicting scaling results reflect different but equally valid ways of judging the same sensory experience. For example, if my 10-kg dog and my 100-kg brother both gain 1 kilogram in weight, we may ask, "Which one gained more?" If we consider the intervals between weights (as is done in category scaling), the answer is "neither" because both have increased by 1 kilo-

DEMONSTRATION BOX 2.5

MAGNITUDE ESTIMATION OF LOUDNESS

To produce a graded set of sound intensities for this demonstration, you will need a long ruler, a coin (we have designed the demonstration for a quarter), an empty tin can or water glass, a soft towel, and a friend. Place the can onto the folded towel and have your friend drop the coin from the designated height so that the coin hits the can on its edge only once and then falls onto the towel (silently, we hope). You should sit with your back to the apparatus.

Ask your friend to drop coins onto the can from heights of 1, 10, 70, 100, and 200 cm in some mixed order. For each sound so produced, call out a number whose magnitude you feel matches the loudness of the sound. You may use any numbers you think appropriate as long as they are greater than 0, including decimals and fractions. Your friend should record the height from which the coin was dropped and the number you gave in each instance. Do this for two or three runs through the stimuli (in different irregular orders), and then average the numbers you called out for each height.

To determine if these judgments follow a power law, plot them on the log-log coordinates provided on the accompanying graph. The vertical axis represents the average magnitude estimates spaced logarithmically, and the horizontal axis represents the sound intensities spaced logarithmically (based on the height of the coin drop). Draw the straight line that best fits (by eye) the data points. Usually the data points fall close to such a line, and any deviations around it are usually fairly random. You can compute the exponent directly (m in the power law $S = aIm$) by computing the slope of the straight line on the graph. To do this, pick two points on the line and measure Δx and Δy with a ruler as done in Figure 2.16. Now divide Δy by Δx, and you should get a value somewhere around 0.30. This is half of the 0.60 value for loudness in Table 2.5 because we have measured sound intensity differently here.

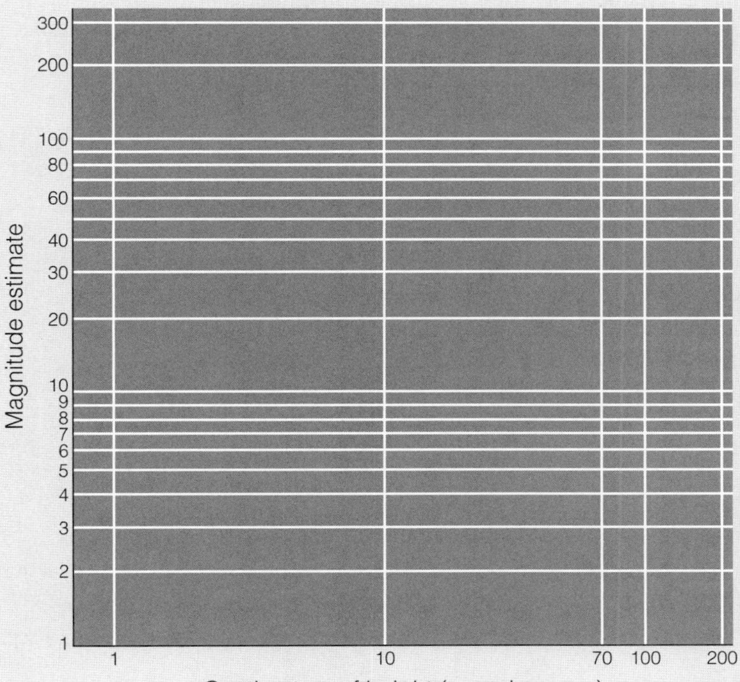

gram. If we consider the ratios between weights (as is implicitly required in magnitude estimation), my dog has increased his body weight by 10% and my brother by only 1%. Thus, my dog exhibited a much greater proportional weight gain. Both types of judgments require estimates of the magnitude of a single event, and both are useful, but the scales (and resultant stimulus-sensation curves) are different (Marks, 1979b; Popper, Parker, & Galanter, 1986).

When scaling techniques are used to measure differences between groups, conditions, or changes in sensory acuity over time, it is often found that the sensitivity of the measures can be improved through training. Observers can learn how to give magnitude estimations according to a power function with a particular exponent, thus providing them with a sort of internal "master" scale of sensory intensity (Berglund, 1991; King & Lockhead, 1981; Ward, 1992). This has been called *constrained scaling* because observers were being constrained to use a particular standard scale (West, Ward, & Khosla, 2000). The advantage of this is that when all sensations are judged against the learned scale, the data are less variable, making comparisons across conditions more reliable. For example, using constrained scaling techniques, Marks, Galanter, and Baird (1995) were able to demonstrate that the loudness of binaural tones (tones presented to both ears) was roughly twice that of monaural tones (tones presented to only one ear). Obviously, in cases such as this, because we have pretrained observers for a given internal scale, we are not interested in the absolute value of their exponents, as we normally are in scaling experiments. Rather, we are seeking sensitive ways to see how conditions change the scaling exponents. These differences provide us with information about the nature of the underlying sensory experiences.

Cross-Modality Matching. Because the size of the power function exponent varies with how response numbers are used, it might seem that these scales tell us more about how humans use numbers than they do about how sensation varies with stimulus intensity (see Baird, 1975). To counter such criticism, S. S. Stevens invented a scaling procedure that does not use numbers at all. In this procedure, an observer adjusts the intensity of a stimulus on one sensory continuum until the magnitude of the sensation it elicits seems to be equal to that elicited by a stimulus from a different sensory

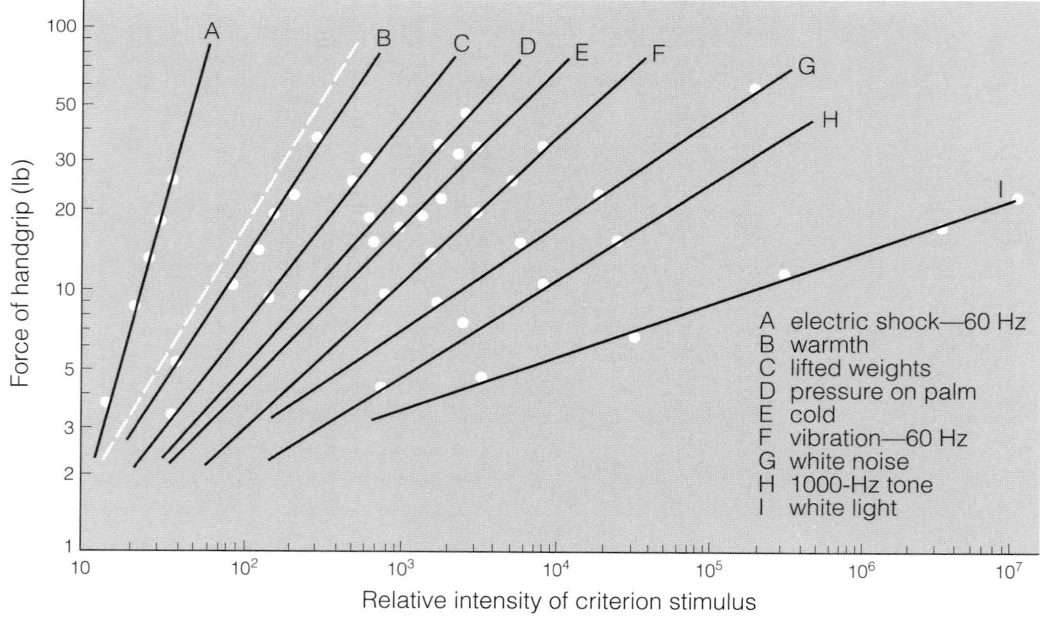

FIGURE 2.16 Cross-modality matching data for nine stimulus continua with force of handgrip as the response continuum. Because the values on both axes are logarithmically spaced, all of the straight lines indicate power function relations between stimulus and response magnitude. The dashed white line has an exponent of 1.0.

(From S. S. Stevens, in W. A. Rosenblith (Ed.), *Sensory Communication.* New York: Wiley, 1961. Copyright 1961 by MIT Press.)

continuum. Thus, you might be asked to squeeze a handgrip until the pressure feels as strong as a particular light is bright. This procedure is called **cross-modality matching** because the observer is asked to match sensation magnitudes across sensory modalities. Actually, the version of magnitude estimation described earlier is also a form of cross-modality matching in which the number continuum is matched to a stimulus continuum (Oyama, 1968; Stevens, 1975). When we plot the data from cross-modality matching experiments on logarithmic axes (as we did for magnitude estimation experiments), we find that the average matches fall onto a straight line. Despite the fact that the observers no longer make numerical estimates, the data still obey the power law for sensation intensities, suggesting that the underlying scale does reflect the relationship between the sensory experience and the physical stimulus, rather than simply the way that people use numbers. Figure 2.16 shows this for a number of modalities matched against handgrip pressure.

IDENTIFICATION

A family doctor listening to the heart sounds of a patient through a stethoscope might be considered to have a discrimination problem to solve. That is, he needs to answer the question, "Are these heart sounds normal or abnormal?" If the doctor makes a decision with respect to how severely abnormal the heart rhythm appears to sound, he might also be considered to have made a scaling decision. A rhythm that is very unusual would be cause for much greater concern and caution than a heart beat with only a slight irregularity. However, both of these psychophysical questions bypass the questions that are probably of greatest concern to the doctor: Exactly what kind of abnormality do the sounds of the stethoscope represent? Is it the kind of irregular heartbeat that many people experience under conditions of stress and anxiety? Or are the sounds best classified as the irregular beat that might be associated with a serious heart condition?

These questions are more complex than the simple discrimination between two alternatives. An answer will clearly involve selecting one option from a large range of possible alternatives. Identifying the heart sounds as consistent with one or another diagnosis will involve linking the current perception to some information that has been experienced in the past and stored in memory. Which category or label in memory best fits the features of the present stimulus? To understand how perception researchers understand this problem of **identification,** we must first introduce you to **information theory.**

Information Theory

The difficulty of an identification task depends in large part on the number of possible stimulus alternatives an observer is asked to distinguish among (see Cutting, 1987). Consider someone who claims he can always identify his favorite brand of beer. Suppose we gave him two unmarked glasses of beer and asked him to sample them and to try to identify his favorite brand. If he did select the correct brand, we would not be very surprised because he would be expected to select his own brand 50% of the time by chance alone, even if he had no prior memory of this beer and was just guessing. On the other hand, if our "expert" successfully selected his own brand of beer out of 25 brands presented to him at random, we would be much more likely to take his claim seriously. This is because now the probability that he could select his brand by chance alone out of 25 alternatives is only 1 in 25.

Psychologists in the 1950s turned to ideas developed by radio and telephone engineers in order to understand the identification problem. Books by Shannon and Weaver (1949) and by Wiener (1961) made it clear that the problems faced by the perception researcher and by the communications engineer were similar. The engineer deals with a message that is transmitted through a communication channel and decoded by someone or something at the receiver's end. The degree to which the final decoded message reflects the original message depends, in part, on the ability of the system to transmit information without distortion. This is what is meant by the *fidelity* of a system. The perception researcher has a similar problem. Stimuli are presented to an observer through a sensory system, and this information is then decoded in the central nervous system. The degree to which the observer's identification of the stimulus corresponds to the actual stimulus will be affected by the ability of the sensory system to handle the stimulus input without distortion. This is what a perception researcher means by *veridical* (meaning accurate) perception.

The system for measuring the performance of a communication channel is known as information theory. It defines the amount of information in a very general way, so that the actual meaning or content of the message is irrelevant. The technical meaning of **information** in this theory is defined as the *reduction of uncertainty,* where uncertainty reflects our need to guess what is there because we don't have enough data to be sure. Thus if someone tells you that this week will contain a Sunday morning, they will have conveyed very little information because we already know that every week contains a Sunday morning. If instead they tell us that on this Sunday morning there will be a parade in honor of Jiffy the Kangaroo, they will have conveyed a great deal more information, because they have specified which one out of a large number of potential alternative events is going to occur.

A useful way to quantify information in this sense is to count how many questions a person must ask to discover which member of a stimulus set has occurred. This is a version of the game of Twenty Questions you may have played as a child. If in a simple version of this game there were only two possible alternatives, A or B, and you wanted to determine which of them was the target, you would only need ask one question, "Is it A?" The answer to this question is sufficient, since "yes" confirms that it was A and "no" tells you that it was B.

Now let's imagine playing the game with four target possibilities, A, B, C, or D. You should be able to find this target with at most two questions. The answer to the first question "Is it A or B?" reduces your number of possible alternatives to two. This is because a "yes" answer confirms that it is a choice between A and B while a "no" answer tells you that it is either C or D. Once we have it down to two alternatives, we already know that only one more question is necessary in order to identify the correct item. Each necessary question, structured to eliminate exactly half of the alternatives, defines a **bit** (from *b*inary dig*it*) of information.

It turns out that the number of questions we need to have answered to find a target in a game of Twenty Questions has a very specific mathematical formula. It is always the logarithm to the base 2 of the total number of possible stimulus alternatives. If you are not familiar with logarithms, it need not concern you here. An easy way to understand how this formula works is to answer the question, "To what power must we raise the number 2, in order to equal the number of stimulus alternatives, where power reflects how many times we have to multiply something by itself?" Trying out a few numbers, we can see that if we have four alternatives we must raise 2 to the second power, since $2 \times 2 = 4$. If we have 16 alternatives we must raise 2 to the fourth power, since $2 \times 2 \times 2 \times 2 = 16$. If we have an uneven multiple of the power of 2, such as the number 29, we can always round our answer to the nearest neighbor, as, for example, $2 \times 2 \times 2 \times 2 \times 2 = 32$. In this case the information content of a game with 29 alternatives would be between 4 and 5 bits.

Channel Capacity

If we follow the lead of perception researchers who have used information theory to understand the problem of identification, we can consider the human observer as a sort of communication channel that is able to transmit information. Our observer may then be represented as in Figure 2.17. A stimulus is presented, and the observer is asked to try to identify it. By "identify" we mean to give a response that is the agreed-on label for the particular stimulus presented. To the extent that the observer's responses match the labels of the stimuli presented, **information transmission** is occurring. That is, if the observer is presented with a stimulus and gives the correct label as a response, information (the correct label) has been transmitted through the channel represented by the observer. If the response matches the stimulus perfectly for all stimuli, then the observer is a perfect information transmitter.

Consider an example in which we are randomly calling out letters from a set of eight: A B C D F G H X. If an observer correctly identifies (response) the letter that we have called out (stimulus), then three bits of information ($\log_2 8 = 3$) have been transmitted to her, since that is how many guesses it would have taken to identify the stimulus if she hadn't heard the number called and was reduced to guessing. But now suppose identification is not perfect; only some of the information available (say one bit) is being transmitted. For instance, if the observer hears a faint "eee" sound, with the first part of the letter cut off, she does not know exactly which letter was called out. However, she can eliminate A, F, H, and X, which have no "eee" sound. Since this reduces the number of stimulus alternatives by half, we would say that she will transmit one bit of information in her response, which will be a guess among the other four alternatives. In general, the greater the probability that the observer will correctly identify the stimulus—that is, the more she "picks up" from the presentations—the more information that has been transmitted to her by the stimulus.

Consider an imaginary experiment in which each of four stimuli was presented 12 times in a random order

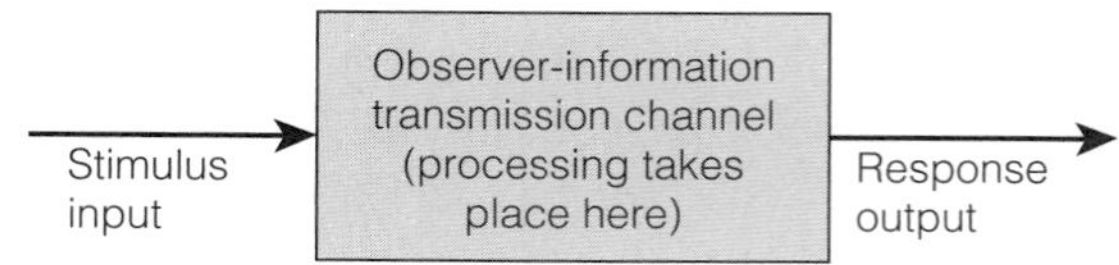

FIGURE 2.17 A human information channel.

and an observer was asked to identify which stimulus was presented on each trial. The data from such an experiment can be summarized in a **confusion matrix,** as shown in Table 2.6 for three different observers. Observer A shows perfect transmission of the two bits of information available ($\log_2 4 = 2$) because the correct response was given to the stimulus on every trial. There are never any errors, or confusions. Observer B shows poorer information transmission. Note that when Stimulus 2 was presented, it was called "2" most of the time but sometimes it was called "1" and sometimes "3." When the response was "2," however, there is a fair likelihood that the stimulus was Stimulus 2. Observer B is much better than Observer C, who seems to have been responding without reference to the stimulus presented. Observer C transmitted none of the available stimulus information.

TABLE 2.6 Stimulus-Response Matrices for Three Observers

OBSERVER A: PERFECT INFORMATION TRANSMISSION

	Response			
Stimulus	**1**	**2**	**3**	**4**
1	12			
2		12		
3			12	
4				12

OBSERVER B: SOME INFORMATION TRANSMISSION

	Response			
Stimulus	**1**	**2**	**3**	**4**
1	8	4		
2	2	8	2	
3		2	8	2
4			4	8

OBSERVER C: NO INFORMATION TRANSMISSION

	Response			
Stimulus	**1**	**2**	**3**	**4**
1	3	3	3	3
2	3	3	3	3
3	3	3	3	3
4	3	3	3	3

How many different stimuli can an observer identify perfectly? If you think of all the people you can name by looking only at their faces, and all the animals you can recognize, and all the places you can identify from pictures, this is truly an enormous number. But think of learning a new group of objects for the first time. Studies looking at this problem have found that there are severe limits on human performance when a group of stimuli vary only along a single physical dimension, such as sound intensity or frequency. The number of stimuli varying along one dimension that an observer can identify perfectly has been found to be surprisingly small. For example, the identification of tones varying only in frequency seems to have a limit of about five different tones (Pollack, 1952), which is equal to 2.3 bits of stimulus information. Information transmission for tones varying only in sound intensity is much the same, around 2.1 bits (Garner, 1953). Studies with different lights varying along a single dimension yielded estimates of 2.34 bits for light intensity, 2.84 bits for size, and 3.08 bits for wavelength (Eriksen and Hake, 1955). Results like this have led researchers to conclude that the human mind is only able to identify about 7 (plus or minus 2) different stimuli that vary along a single physical dimension (Miller, 1956).

This limit is called the observer's **channel capacity.** Figure 2.18 illustrates how channel capacity is measured; each dot represents the information transmission calculated from a separate confusion matrix. Notice that even when the amount of information available in the display is greater than 2.5 bits, the observer can pick up no more information than this limit, meaning that his sensory channel capacity is about 2.5 bits in this situation.

Seven seems to be a very small number of stimuli to be able to identify. We know that musicians, for example, seem able to identify (indeed, sing) hundreds of different songs. Every one of us can certainly identify hundreds of faces and thousands of words. How can this be, in light of our inability to transmit more than about three bits of information per stimulus dimension? The answer clearly lies in the fact that the objects we are typically asked to identify vary along many dimensions simultaneously, not just the one dimension tested in the studies described so far (e.g., Rouder, 2001).

Consider a study that examined the benefits to identification of varying just two rather than one dimension (Pollack, 1953). When observers were asked to identify tones based only on frequency, estimates of information transmission averaged about 1.80 bits. When they were asked to identify tones based only on intensity, information

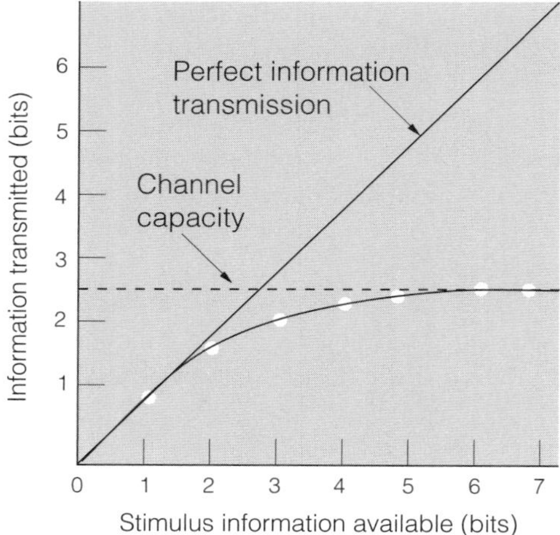

FIGURE 2.18 Channel capacity. The straight diagonal represents perfect information transmission. The curve represents typical performance. The dashed horizontal line is channel capacity.

transmission was about 1.70 bits. However, when both dimensions were varied simultaneously, information transmission was 3.10 bits. This is more than was obtained for either dimension separately. In general, it seems that identification accuracy improves directly as the number of dimensions along which a set of stimuli varies is increased. In some studies, this has permitted information transmission levels to reach as high as 17 bits for a single, briefly flashed stimulus (Anderson & Fitts, 1958). This means that observers could perfectly identify 1 stimulus out of more than 131,000 alternative stimuli.

Identification Time

As with the other psychophysical questions we have considered, performance on identification tasks can be evaluated both with measures of accuracy (e.g., the confusion matrix) and with measures based on response time. Just as choice response times are directly related to the difficulty of a stimulus discrimination, so too is the time required to identify a stimulus, **identification time,** directly related to the difficulty of identification. Many studies have even shown a direct link between identification time and the information contained in a stimulus as indexed by information theory (see Usher & McClelland, 2001).

In a typical experiment of this kind, observers pressed telegraph keys in response to light. When there were a larger number of different possible lights, and therefore a larger number of different possible responses, response times were longer than when the number of stimulus alternatives were small. Data from an early experiment of this kind are shown in Table 2.7 (Merkel, 1885). When the number of stimulus alternatives is expressed in information units or bits, rather than in the original form, there is a straight line function that relates identification time and the number of stimulus alternatives. This relation is now called **Hick's law,** in honor of the researcher who first proposed it (Hick, 1952). It states that identification response time is a linear function of the bits of information in a stimulus. Demonstration Box 2.6 shows how to produce effects like those of Hick's law in a card-sorting task.

Identification time is sensitive to a truly wide range of factors, including some internal ones, such as motivation, attention, and the state of the sensory systems. It is also very sensitive to the observer's past history with that stimulus. For instance, the time required to read a word, which is one of the most frequently studied speeded identification tasks, is influenced by the length of time since that word was last presented (familiarity), by the number of concepts to which that word is associated in the reader's mind (meaning), and even to the vividness of the mental images formed spontaneously when a word is read (concreteness). Because of this exquisite sensitivity to such a wide range of variables, identification time is one of the most popular tools of perception researchers. At the same time, this sensitivity to such a wide range of factors also holds potential pitfalls. The key to the successful use of identification time lies in the ability of the researcher to design an experiment in which all the relevant factors are controlled, except for the factor of critical interest, whether that be the attentional state of the observer, the observer's past history (memory), or the observer's sensory system (see Maddox, 2001).

TABLE 2.7 Reaction Time as a Function of Number of Stimulus Alternatives (based on Merkel, 1885)

Number of Alternatives	Reaction Time (ms)
1	187
2	316
3	364
4	434
5	487
6	534
7	570
8	603
9	619
10	632

DEMONSTRATION BOX 2.6

NUMBER OF STIMULUS ALTERNATIVES AND REACTION TIME

Take a deck of playing cards and separate 16 cards using only the low numbers ace, 2, 3, and 4. Next, make up another deck of 16 cards using 2 each of the 5, 6, 7, 8, 9, 10, jack, and queen. Now shuffle each deck. Measure the time it takes to sort each deck into piles by number (four piles for the first and eight for the second deck) using a watch or clock with a sweep second hand as you did in Demonstration Box 2.3. Notice that the reaction time becomes longer (measured by sorting time) as the number of alternative stimuli that must be recognized and responded to becomes greater. Thus, sorting the four-stimuli deck is more rapid than sorting the eight-stimuli deck.

APPLYING PSYCHOPHYSICS

This summary of psychophysical procedures for answering questions about the detection, discrimination, scaling, and identification of perceptual experiences has only scratched the surface in presenting the procedures and method of analyzing what an individual perceives. There are many other procedures and techniques that you will become familiar with if you continue to study in this area. It is most important, however, to become familiar with the application of these basic methods we *have* discussed to problems and questions you encounter every day. This is much more important than learning more about the wide assortment of methods we have not had the opportunity to cover in this introductory chapter.

A good way to familiarize yourself with the basic issues involved is to get into the habit of thinking about your perceptual experiences in terms of detection, discrimination, scaling, and identification. For example, the next time you are startled suddenly by a loud noise or by a suddenly appearing object in your visual field, take a moment to reflect on it like a psychophysicist might. Do this, of course, after you have settled down from the surprise. What was the first aspect of the experience that you can recall? Was it the *detection* that something unusual was occurring, before you were able to determine what the event was, or perhaps even what modality (vision or hearing) it was occurring in? Or did you have the experience that a particular emotion had been activated prior to the *identification* of what the perceptual event was that actually activated the emotion? Engaging in these exercises will help you become familiar with the different aspects of perceptual experience, from the perspective of psychophysical measurement.

An issue of practical importance that you will soon encounter, once you start examining your world like this, is that many of the experiences that you are interested in, especially the experiences of others, are not very easy to communicate. For instance, you may have, or have had, a pet dog or cat. If so, at some point you probably have found yourself wondering about their perceptual experiences. How are they different from your own experiences? How are they the same? To answer these questions using any of the psychophysical tools we have described, you will first have to figure out a way for your pet to "speak" to you. Before you throw down this book because you think that is impossible, think about the ways in which your pet does communicate to you every day. You may know when it is hungry or expecting food by the way it behaves. You may know when it wants to go outside. You may even know whether it wants to spend time with you or whether it would rather be left alone. What if you were to link some of these naturally occurring behaviors to some perceptual events? Would your dog be able to tell the difference between blue and yellow if you placed her food bowl behind a blue curtain (and not a yellow one) each day, after you had randomly chosen a side for the blue curtain? What about red and green? What about a photograph of you, instead of one of your sister, that would correctly indicate which curtain the food was behind?

This is exactly what perception researchers have done who study the sensory systems of animals. This is also what researchers have done when they study humans who are unable to communicate in the usual ways, including newborn babies, individuals who have never acquired speech because of abnormal development, and patients with cerebral strokes that have left them unable to understand speech.

Finally, you should also bear in mind that the analyses performed by some regions of your brain are more accessible to your own awareness or consciousness than the analyses performed by other regions. To study this aspect of perception, it is important to devise techniques for studying separately the experiences of those parts of our brains that are able to make a verbal report from the experiences of the other parts of our brain that are able to act in some way, though they cannot speak. One example of a nonspeaking perceptual system that we all have is the system that guides where the eyes are aimed in space (Ross, Morrone, Goldberg, & Burr, 2001). This system for guiding the eyes can be fooled by visual illusions that have no influence on the system that governs our perception of where objects are in space. There are other illusions that influence our perception of where things are, even though our eye guidance system is not fooled by them (Deubel, Bridgeman, & Schneider, 1998). We will have more to say about these distinctions in Chapter 14 when we discuss what it means for a perception to be conscious.

The psychophysical measurement techniques that have been introduced in this chapter will appear in many guises throughout the rest of the book. However, it is worth pointing out that the study of sensation and perception goes well beyond these specific measurement techniques. Many perceptual and cognitive psychologists today continue to work on Fechner's original problems. These psychologists are sometimes called fundamental psychophysicists because they are primarily interested in the fundamental concepts of perceptual measurement (such as detection or discrimination) rather than on using psychophysical methods in order to study a sensory system such as vision or audition (e.g., Link, 1993; Norwich, 1993; Ward, 1992). Despite the cumulative progress of more than 130 years of research in measuring perceptual experience, there are still many important basic questions that remain to be answered.

STUDY QUESTIONS

1. What are two features of perceptual experience that make it somewhat more difficult to study scientifically than the subject matter of other sciences?
2. What are the three problems of measurement that Fechner believed had to be solved in order to make psychophysics a true science of experience?
3. Make a list of strengths and weaknesses for the three primary methods of studying detection.
4. Signal detection theory was developed to measure separately two features of a psychophysical judgment. What are they?
5. What mental processes are involved in making a speeded choice response that are not involved in making a speeded simple reaction?
6. What is the basic unit of psychophysical measurement in a discrimination experiment?
7. The speed-accuracy trading relationship is S shaped, meaning that if observers are given more time to make a judgment, they can often also be more accurate. How should the average speed and the average accuracy in two tasks be related to convince you that one task is truly easier than the other?
8. Make a list of strengths and weaknesses for the three primary methods of studying direct scaling.
9. Which psychophysical question has been linked most closely to information theory?
10. What is the basic unit of measurement for the concept of channel capacity?
11. List four factors that influence the speed with which a stimulus can be identified.
12. Describe an experience in which you were startled by an unexpected event. Indicate which aspects of that experience were related to the psychophysical problem of stimulus detection, discrimination, scaling, and identification. In what order did you experience each of these four aspects?

CHAPTER 3

THE VISUAL SYSTEM

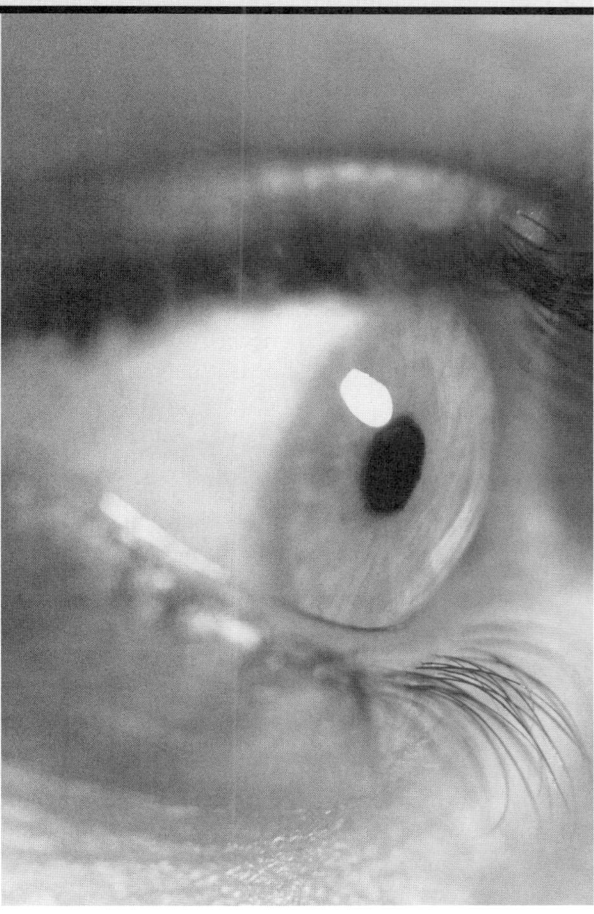

CHAPTER SUMMARY

Every morning you awake to a world filled with sights, sounds, touches, and smells. These are all events that are "out there," in the sense that they are experienced as occurring outside of your own head. You see the alarm clock digits glowing in the dark on the bedside table, you feel the weight of the wrinkled blankets on your skin, and you can even sense that the temperature in the room is warmer than you remembered it to be when you fell asleep. Yet these experiences of the outside world are occurring because of very specific events going on inside your head. You might even say that these experiences are being brought to you courtesy of the human nervous system, which in the adult consists of approximately 100 billion neurons.

In this chapter we will introduce you to some of the basic terms used to describe parts of the nervous system, we will discuss how the nervous system functions, and we will describe how research scientists study the nervous system to see how it works. In all of this, we will focus on vision, which is the system that lets you make contact with the external environment through the physical medium of light. As you will soon see, light does not simply enter your nervous system and deposit a photographic record. That by itself wouldn't result in any vision at all. If it did, then a photo album would be able to see. Instead vision works by a series of transformations. First, light entering your eye is transformed into a signal that the nervous system can understand. This neural signal is then transformed again in a large number of different ways. Some of these transformations make color vision possible; others allow us to see shapes and forms; and still others allow us to reach out and grasp our morning cup of coffee.

You may have heard the old saying, "the eyes are the windows to the world." A very important lesson that we will see repeated many times in our discussion of the visual system is that its design has a great influence on the way we experience the world around us. You already know that the properties of a physical window can greatly affect your appearance of the world outside. If a window is colored, your experience of the world will be tinted; if a window is curved or if it magnifies the view, then so too will be your experience of the world seen through the window. For this reason, it is important for you to understand the physiological makeup of the eye, as well as the way in which the brain transforms the information it receives. These physiological structures and events are ultimately responsible for the way we experience the world.

THE NEURON

The basic building block of the nervous system is the **neuron**. This is a structure consisting of a single cell that can communicate with its neighbors (other single-celled structures) using a combination of electrical and chemical means. Figure 3.1 shows three of the most common types of neurons in the nervous system. A **sensory neuron** conducts information about the outside world to other neurons; an **interneuron** conducts information between neurons; and a **motor neuron** conducts nerve impulses from the central nervous system outward to the muscles. Since each of these neurons is a separate cell, they are each composed of three distinct parts: a **cell body**, an **axon**, and **dendrites**. Many people are surprised to learn that almost all of what we know about the neuron has been discovered within the past 100 years. Biography Box 3.1 will introduce you to two pioneers in this field of research.

The cell body contains the nucleus, which includes the genetic material and a large variety of molecules that govern the functioning of the neuron. The branching structures that receive information from incoming nerve fibers of other neurons are the dendrites. The axons are usually long fibers that conduct nerve impulses toward the many other neurons (or muscle fibers) with which each neuron connects. Axons typically terminate near dendrites of other neurons. Many neurons have axons

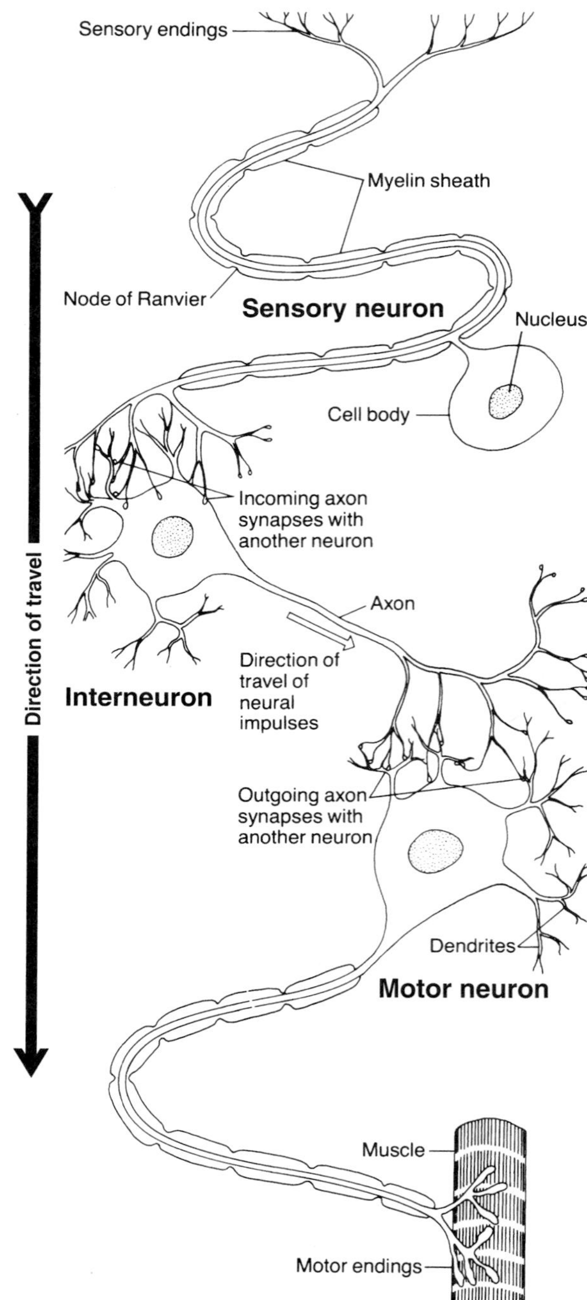

FIGURE 3.1 Neurons of various types and their important parts and connections with each other.

that are covered by protective and nutritive cells called **glial cells**. These form the **myelin sheath** around the axon; the myelin sheath increases the speed at which electrical changes can travel along the axon.

BIOGRAPHY BOX 3.1

TECHNOLOGY AND UNDERSTANDING GO HAND IN HAND

Does the nervous system consist of a tightly interconnected web, in which the activity in some small part is broadcast to the entire network? Or is it best to think of the nervous system as consisting of individual entities, each of which lives by its own rules in communicating with its neighbors? This was a hotly debated question among physiologists at the start of the twentieth century. Microscopic views of the tangled tissue that constitutes the nervous system did little to resolve the debate. Strong arguments were being made on both sides.

On one side of this debate was ***Camillo Golgi (1843–1926),*** an Italian physiologist who had earlier abandoned a career in psychiatry because of financial problems. In the seclusion of a small kitchen converted to a laboratory, in a hospital near Milan, he discovered a technique for staining individual neurons by injecting them with silver nitrate. This process made visible a limited number of neurons at random, which could be observed under the microscope as black structures with well-defined borders. Yet even this discovery did not shake his life-long belief in the inherent connectedness of all nervous tissue.

On the other side of this debate was ***Santiago Ramón y Cajal (1852–1934),*** a Spanish physiologist who was also the main proponent of the "neuron doctrine," the view that the nervous system consisted of anatomically and functionally distinct cells. Although Ramón y Cajal advocated this view long before Golgi staining was in popular use, it was through the use of the staining technique that Ramón y Cajal's views eventually came to dominate popular opinion among physiologists.

For each of their contributions to this discovery, Golgi and Ramón y Cajal were awarded a shared Nobel Prize in Medicine in 1906. Ironically, Camillo Golgi used the opportunity of his acceptance speech to make yet another concerted effort to overturn Ramón y Cajal's neuron doctrine, which his own technological discovery had made possible. Although the neural details of Golgi's views have found little support over the years, his idea of the dynamic interconnectedness of the nervous system is still very strong in the neurosciences, even among those who today believe firmly in the neuron doctrine.

When many axons together form a pathway that carries information from one part of the body to the other, that pathway is called a **nerve**. Sensory information is carried by nerves to the **central nervious system (CNS)**, which consists of the brain and the spinal cord. Within the central nervous system, a pathway is no longer called a nerve but instead is called a **tract**. In addition to the tracts in the central nervous system, which appear as **white matter** because the myelin sheath is white, there are distinct regions containing clusters of many cell bodies that together appear as **gray matter**.

Neuronal Communication

Information is passed from one neuron to another by electrochemical changes. When a neuron is unstimulated or "at rest," the inside is electrically negative with respect to the outside. The typical **resting potential** of a neuron is about −70 millivolts (mV). This is mostly because of the presence of large negatively–charged proteins inside the cell. The most important substances for neural action are sodium and potassium. They are involved in an ongoing biochemical process called the **sodium-potassium pump**, which ejects three sodium molecules from the cell for every two potassium molecules it allows into the cell. The resting state of the neuron therefore represents a chemical equilibrium resulting from the continual flow of these molecules across the cell membrane.

When a neuron is stimulated, either by a physical stimulus such as light (if it is a visual receptor in the eye) or by mechanical pressure (if it is a touch receptor in the skin) or even by another neuron (if it is an interneuron), the electrical potential changes across the cell membrane. A change in the electrical potential from the resting potential toward 0 mV and beyond is called **depolarization**; a change toward an even more negative potential is called **hyperpolarization**.

The most common form of neural response, especially for the interneurons that form the gray matter in the brain, involves a dramatic and rapid change in the electrical state of the neuron, which occurs when depolarization reaches a critical level. An initial brief period of depolarization is suddenly followed by a much larger and more rapid depolarization as sodium flows into the axon through tiny channels. This abrupt change in a cell's state is called an **action potential** or, more simply, a **neural spike**. The entire process of an action potential takes only a few milliseconds (one millisecond = 1 one-thousandth of a second). An example of a slow-motion recording of an action potential is shown in Figure 3.2.

The rapid period of depolarization occurs within about 1 millisecond and is quickly reversed and followed by a period of hyperpolarization that is equally brief. In the 4 to 5 milliseconds that follow this sudden shift in electrical charge, the potential of the neuron again returns to its resting level of −70 mV. The period of hyperpolarization following a spike is called the **refractory period,** and during this time the neuron is much more difficult to excite.

Although it is not the most typical form of neural response observed in the body, for many sensory neurons, the more they are stimulated, the greater is their change in electrical potential. Such quantitative changes in a cell's state are called **graded potentials,** because the electrical state of the cell reflects in a fairly direct way the degree of outside stimulation of the cell at any given moment. Many neurons in the sensory systems, such as in parts of the eye and the inner ear, respond in this way.

For neurons that communicate using action potentials rather than graded potentials, increases in stimulation do not change the *degree* of depolarization in the spike. Rather increases in stimulation change the *number of spikes* that are produced in any given unit of time. Because of this we can summarize the overall activity level of a neuron at any moment in time by referring to its **firing rate.** This leads to a very simple way of understanding neural communication. If you imagine each spike to be a bark from a dog, and the excitement level of the dog is measured by its rate of barking, then a neuron receiving many inputs is like a very yappy dog. A direct line of communication from one region of the brain to another will sound like a version of dog "telephone," where each dog barks to its neighbor in turn, and a region of the brain that is very active will sound like a whole chorus of barking dogs.

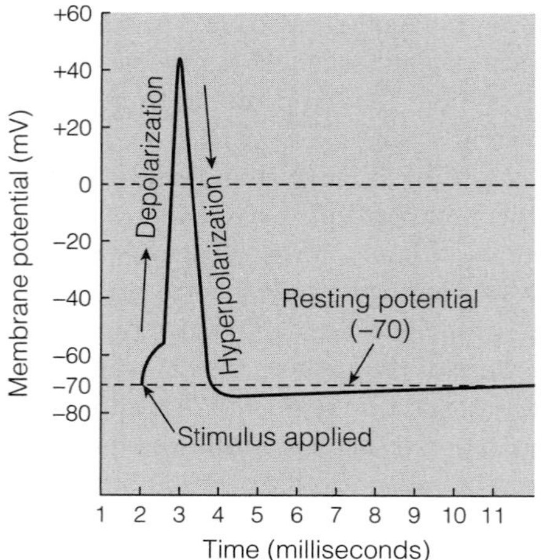

FIGURE 3.2 Voltage changes over time that describe a typical spike or action potential.

In general, spikes are communicated from one neuron to another more quickly when the axons are large. In some of the largest axons ever studied, which were about 500 micrometers in diameter and found in giant squid, spikes were recorded moving along an axon at a rate of 100 feet (35 meters) per second. However, even the thickest axons in humans and other animals require help in communicating at speeds where they are useful for quick sensing of events, followed by fast muscular response to the situation. This help comes from the myelin sheath that surrounds many axons (see Figure 3.1). In myelinated axons, spikes can travel at speeds up to 300 million meters per second, which is near the limit of electrical conduction using the best wire. However, actual communication is much slower than this for several reasons. The most important of these is that every time the axon of one neuron ends and the dendrites of another neuron begin, a complicated chemical process of **synaptic transmission** takes place. Despite this, it is fairly common to record speeds of neural conduction in myelinated axons only 20 micrometers in diameter that reach 120 meters per second.

Ways to Measure Neural Function

The direct study of neural functioning in sensory systems and in the brain tends to be done at one of two different levels. At the microscopic level, the behavior of individual neurons in known sensory pathways or brain regions can be recorded. At the macroscopic level, the functioning of larger brain regions and neural systems is studied. Each of these levels of study depends on its own sophisticated technology and research methods.

Single Neuron Recordings. The spike responses of individual neurons are measured in surgically prepared and anesthetized animals using **microelectrodes.** Usually these consist of tiny glass tubes (the tip might be 0.01 mm in size or smaller) filled with salt water. The electrode is inserted into the cell body or the axon, and the potential difference between the test electrode and a comparison electrode located outside the cell is recorded by a computer. The changes in electrical activity can then be displayed visually on a screen or amplified and converted to sounds that can be heard by the experimenter. Interestingly, when converted to sound, each spike of a neuron does sound a little like the quick "yip" of a dog (or maybe just a pop or a click to the less imaginative listener). Visual renditions of recordings of two series of spikes from a typical neuron are shown in Figure 3.3. The first recording was made from a relatively active neuron that had just recently been stimulated. The second was made from the same neuron when it was at rest, meaning it had not recently been stimulated.

The use of microelectrodes to record the activity of single neurons in the brain has produced some of the most exciting data in the fields of sensory physiology and neuroscience. Generally, the procedure involves the application of a muscle relaxant combined with local anesthetics to eliminate the discomfort from the restraining device used to hold an animal. This must be done in accordance with strict ethical guidelines regarding the treatment of research animals. A **stereotaxic instrument,** together with a standardized map of the brain of the research animal, is used to allow the researcher to place electrodes in very precise locations in the brain or in a nerve.

Figure 3.4 shows a laboratory rat with its head positioned in a stereotaxic instrument. The rat is viewing a screen on which visual patterns can be presented. The microelectrode is attached to the computer, to the visual display, and also to a loudspeaker. The loudspeaker transforms the neural spikes into a series of audible clicks. Researchers can then listen to the neural response, keeping their eyes and hands free to attend to other matters. An increase in the clicking rate means an increase in the firing rate of the cell, and a decrease in clicking rate means a decrease. An increase in firing rate that occurs when a specific stimulus is presented means that the neuron is being excited by that stimulus. A decrease in the firing rate indicates that the stimulus causes an inhibition of the overall activity level of the neuron.

Regional Brain Function. The earliest attempts to study the function of larger areas of the nervous system were based on natural occurrences involving accidents and injury in humans, in which some part of an individual's brain underwent a **lesion** (destruction of neurons and supporting cells) or an **ablation** (removal of neurons and supporting cells). By observing the relation between where a lesion or ablation had occurred and which functions were affected, much information was gained about sensory processing and brain function. This thinking also led to experimental work in the early 1900s that involved the deliberate production of lesions and ablations in animals' brains. Unfortunately, the results of lesion and ablation studies are often difficult to interpret, since the loss of function may be caused by many factors. A crude example is stopping an animal's visual processing by destroying the centers in the brain stem that control breathing, since an animal that cannot breathe dies, and a dead animal can't see. We would not want to conclude from this lesion study that the brainstem is directly involved in processing visual stimuli!

Some of the electrical recording techniques developed for use in monkeys and other nonhuman animals have been applied successfully to patients undergoing surgical treatment for epilepsy (Kreiman, Koch, & Fried, 2000). Part of this treatment involves the temporary placement of electrodes directly into the brain. While the surgery is being undertaken, it is possible to measure the responses of a small number of neurons to pictures of faces, ob-

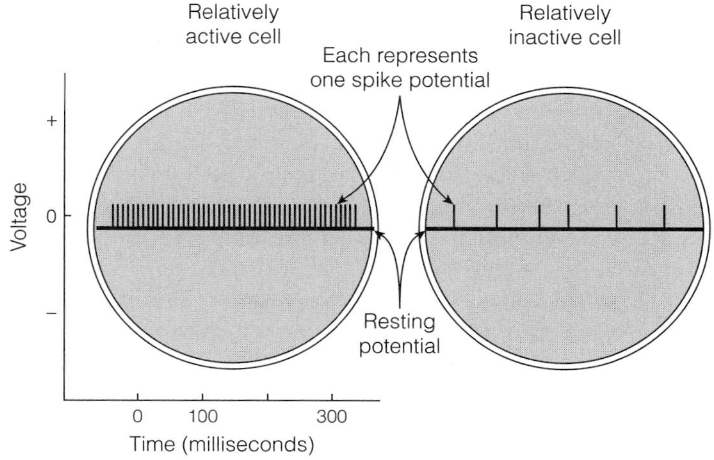

FIGURE 3.3 Two recordings taken from a microelectrode that has been inserted into a neuron that produces action potentials. The pattern of firing is rapid when the neuron is stimulated (A) and infrequent when it is at rest (B).

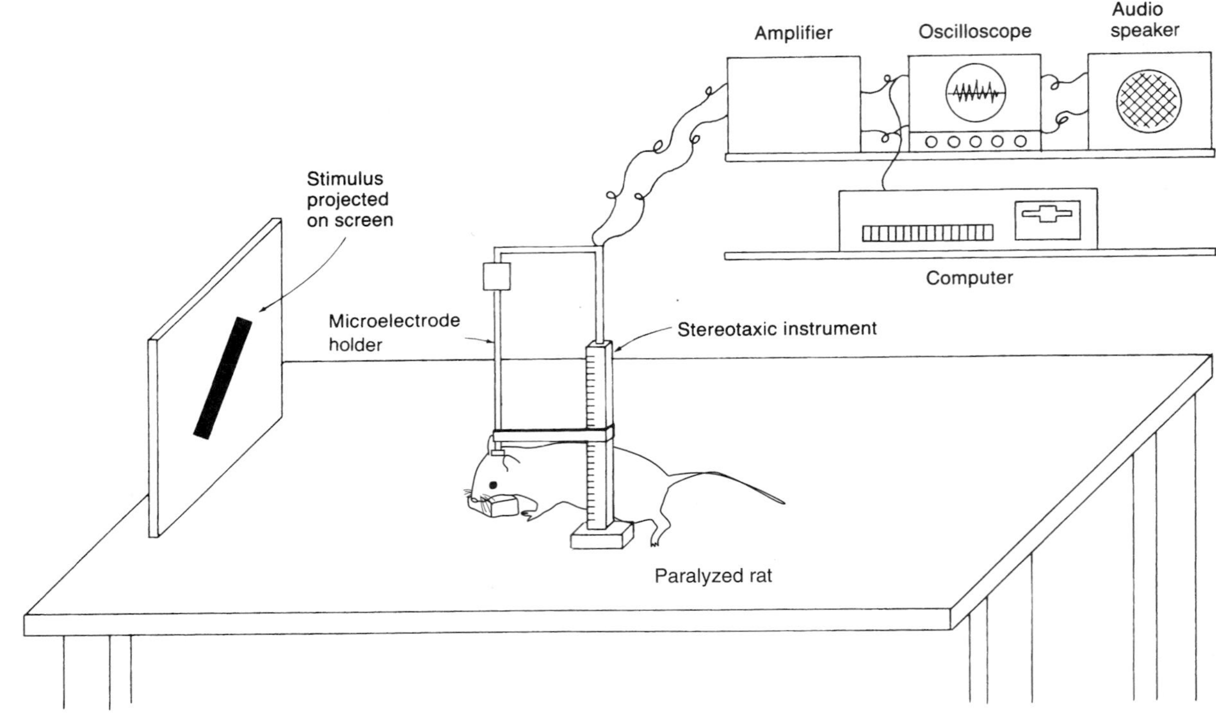

FIGURE 3.4 Setup to record neural activity from the visual cortex of the rat.

jects, and naturalistic scenes. One of the remarkable findings of this research is that neurons that respond selectively to these pictures do so in a very similar way, regardless of whether the pictures are actually presented to the eyes, or only called into the "mind's eye" as a memory.

A more common way to make electrical recordings in humans does not require surgery. All that is required is the placement of small recording electrodes on the scalp. This produces the familiar **electroencephalogram (EEG)**, which reflects the average activity of millions of cells in the outer layers of the brain. Locating a number of electrodes over various regions of the skull allows researchers to infer which areas of the brain are most active during various tasks, and how that activity changes over time (e.g., John, Prichep, Fridman, & Easton, 1988). EEGs that are measured in response to brief sensory stimuli are called **evoked potentials,** and are one of the main tools in the field of cognitive neuroscience.

A slight variation on the electrical recording of human brain activity involves the measurement of magnetic fields also produced by neural electrical activity. This technique is called **magnetoencephalograhy (MEG)**. It can allow more precise localization of the underlying regions of neural activity than EEG does. It also allows measurement of time sequence by allowing researchers to isolate the areas that respond most quickly, those that respond slightly later, and so forth. In this way researchers can trace sensory processing in the brain (see Hari, 1994; Salmelin, Hari, Lounasmaa, & Sams, 1994).

Other techniques for measuring the dynamic functioning of the brain take advantage of the metabolism of neurons. One of the first to be put into regular use was **positron emission tomography (PET)**. PET usually involves the injection of a radioactive form of glucose, which is the major fuel for brain activity. This substance is picked up by the active brain areas that need fuel to sustain their continued activity. However, the particular form of glucose used in PET is difficult to metabolize and accumulates in the active neurons. Thus if the person were viewing a picture, we would expect more glucose to accumulate in the areas of the brain that are responsive to visual events. The radioactive glucose in the brain is detectable by sensitive recorders of radiation. Maps of the active regions of the brain can then be made (e.g., Fox, Mintun, Reiman, & Raichle, 1988). Two such maps (one for visual and another for auditory activities) are shown in Color Plate 1. A PET scan can give a map in which the spatial resolution of active versus inactive regions is only a few millimeters. This is very good compared to EEG and MEG. However, it suffers by comparison in its temporal resolution. It can pick up changes in response over time with a resolution of only about 1 to 2 seconds. As you know, much can change in your perceptual experience over that period of time!

Two other widely used techniques for measuring brain activity also depend upon metabolic changes (Andreasen, 1988). Specifically, they rely on the fact that there is increased blood flow to active brain areas. Since this change in blood flow occurs fairly quickly, it can allow the measurement of rapid changes in the pattern of brain activity. The original method for monitoring these activity changes is called **regional cerebral blood flow (rCBF)**. The technique involves injecting into a person a relatively inert radioactive substance that goes where the blood goes without being absorbed. One of the side affects of neural activity is to briefly dilate the small blood vessels nearby thus increasing blood flow and the amount of radioactivity emitted from these areas (Iadecola, 1993). Detectors placed around the head can detect the increased radioactive emissions from these areas, hence indicating the most active regions in the brain (Berman, Zec, & Weinberger, 1986).

The second method for determining function based upon blood flow is **magnetic resonance imaging** (MRI), which also goes under the name **nuclear magnetic resonance** (NMR). This technique does not involve any added radioactive substances. Rather, it depends on the fact that the atoms of the brain, which are ordinarily oriented in random directions, can be aligned by an outside magnetic field without disturbing their function and then made to spin like tiny gyroscopes by an electromagnetic field in the radio frequency range. When the radio frequency field is turned off, the hydrogen atoms that are a normal component of the brain slow their spinning and release electromagnetic energy. The released energy can be measured, and from it can be deduced the concentration of hydrogen atoms in the region being monitored. This can give very precise pictures of brain structures with no need to expose individuals to radioactive substances.

In the early 1990s, MRI began to be modified to provide information not only about the shapes of structures in the brain, but also about localized brain activity. This modified form of imaging is called **functional magnetic resonance imaging** (fMRI) (Cohen, Noll, & Schneider, 1993). This procedure takes advantage of the fact that the blood protein hemoglobin, which normally binds with oxygen, will show a slight change in its magnetic properties when it releases its oxygen. Because blood flow and amount of oxygen used by neurons increases when neural activity increases, this can pinpoint the most active regions of the brain during perceptual, cognitive, or emotional tasks (e.g., Belliveau, Kennedy, McKinstry, Buchbinder, Weisskoff, Cohen, Vevea, Brady, & Rosen, 1991; Moonen, van Zijl, Frank, Le Bihan, & Becker, 1990). The fMRI technique provides maps of brain activity with a spatial resolution of 1 or 2 millimeters and a temporal resolution of less than a second. As such, it promises to give us a better idea of the regions of the brain that are involved in specific information processing tasks and can also indicate roughly the sequence of brain events that occur during such tasks.

Since 1995, the most recent technological advance in cognitive neuroscience has been a technique called **transcranial magnetic stimulation (TMS)**. It consists of a piece of apparatus that looks a little like a magician's wand with a figure-of-eight at one end. It can be used to mimic a short-lived, reversible, and spatially–focused lesion in a human participant engaged in a wide variety of perceptual and cognitive tasks. The figure-of-eight in this piece of equipment actually delivers a very brief but powerful magnetic discharge. This magnetic burst changes neural functioning in a specific region of the brain for a very brief time. It has been used to induce short-lived blind spots and amnesia in human participants (Corthout, Uttl, Walsh, Hallett, & Cowey, 1999a, 1999b; Hilgetag, Theoret, & Pascual-Leone, 2001). Combined with recording tools such as EEG or MEG, this has given researchers the ability to stimulate the brain noninvasively, at the same time they are recording both the electro-magnetic effects of the jolt and the consequences to perceiving and thinking.

Each of these methods, summarized in Table 3.1, has greatly expanded our knowledge of how the brain processes sensory information. Although researchers are just beginning to tap the potential of these methods, we have already learned enough so that we can begin to form models of how the brain goes about interpreting and responding to sensory events (Posner & Raichle, 1994). The really exciting aspect of these methods is that they allow us to test human beings comfortably, when they are conscious and responding to the stimuli in the world around them, without surgical interventions or pain.

TABLE 3.1 An overview of the main tools used in the past century of research on regional brain function.

Technique	Date of Origin	Main Contribution	Major Weakness
Lesions & ablations	1850–	Localize function	Unclear causation
Single neuron recordings & stimulation	1950–	Receptive field	Almost entirely limited to non-human animals
PET scans	1960–	Localize function	Low temporal resolution
EEG	1970–	High temporal resolution	Low spatial resolution
MEG	1980–	High temporal and spatial resolution	Expensive
fMRI	1990–	Spatial resolution in millimeters	Measures neural activity indirectly
TMS	1995–	Noninvasive lesions during cognition	Uncertain spatial resolution

THE EYE

The eyes of most vertebrate animals, from fish to mammals, have a similar basic structure (Berman, 1991; Dawkins, 1996). They all contain light-sensitive receptors, protected within a dishlike structure, through which light enters by way of a lens. A schematic diagram of the human eye is shown in Figure 3.5. Each eye lies in a bony socket within the skull and is roughly spherical with a diameter of 20 to 25 mm. The outer covering, which is seen as the "white" of the eye, is a strong elastic membrane called the **sclera.** Even though the eye is not made of rigid materials, its shape is maintained by the pressure of interior fluids.

The front of the eye contains a region where the sclera bulges forward to form a clear, domelike window, called the **cornea** (Martin & Holden, 1982). The cornea serves as a simple fixed lens that begins to gather light and concentrate it so that it will eventually form a sharp image on the rear interior surface of the eye. Because the cornea bulges forward, it actually allows for the reception of light from a region slightly behind the observer, as shown in Demonstration Box 3.1.

Between the cornea and the lens is a small chamber filled with a watery fluid called the **aqueous humor.** The larger, main chamber of the eye is filled with a clear, jellylike substance called the **vitreous humor.** Both of these fluids are similar to the cerebrospinal fluid that bathes the inner cavities of the brain. This is not surprising because the neural components of the eye actually develop from the same structures that eventually form the brain.

When we look at the eye of a friend or at our own eye in the mirror, our attention is usually captured by a ring of color. This colored membrane, surrounding a central hole, is the **iris.** When we say that a person has brown eyes, we really are saying that she has brown irises. Iris colors include gray, violet, blue, green, brown, black, and variegated combinations of these. Iris color is genetically determined in the same way as skin color. The function of the iris seems to be to control the amount of light entering the eye. The light enters through the hole in the iris, called the **pupil.** The size of the pupil is controlled by a reflex. When light is bright, the pupil may contract reflexively to as little as 2 mm in diameter, whereas in dim light it may dilate to more than 8 mm. This is about a 16-fold change in the area of the aperture. Demonstration Box 3.2 shows how you may observe the effect of light on pupil size.

The constriction of the pupil in bright light serves an important function, similar to that of reducing the size of the aperture in a camera. Although the overall amount of light entering the eye is reduced, the smaller pupil also leads to the formation of a sharper image at the back of the eye and to a large increase in the range of distances over which objects are simultaneously in focus. In dim light, the ability to discriminate details is less important than the increased sensitivity obtained by increasing the overall amount of light entering the eye, so the pupil increases in size to let in more light. But light levels are not the only reason for changes in pupil size. It also varies with changes in our emotional and attentional levels. When we are really interested in something, the pupils enlarge, as if the eye were trying to gather more light. Smart traders have been known to use this clue to gauge customer interest in an item. Clever customers will sometimes counteract this tactic by wearing dark glasses. The popularity of candlelight dining comes from the fact that the dim light level causes the pupils to dilate and makes lovers appear to be more attentive and interested.

The Crystalline Lens

The **lens** in most vertebrate eyes is located directly behind the pupil. Because the curvature of the lens determines the amount by which light entering it is bent, its

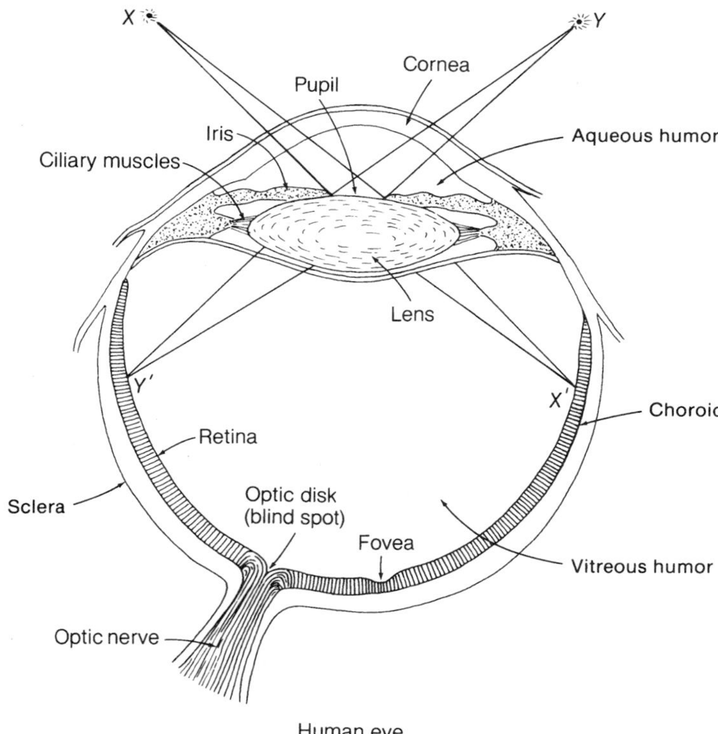

FIGURE 3.5 Structure of the human eye, with a demonstration of the image formation of two targets (*X* and *Y*).

shape is critical in bringing an image into focus at the rear of the eye. The process by which the lens changes its focus is called **accommodation** (Dalziel & Egan, 1982). Back in the mid-1800s Johannes Purkinje demonstrated that the human lens changes focus by changing its shape (see Wade & Brozek, 2001). The natural shape of the human lens tends to be spherical, but when the muscles that control it relax, the pressure of the fluid in the eyeball and the tension of the muscles connecting the lens to the inside wall of the eye cause it to flatten. Under these conditions, distant objects will be in focus. Contraction of the ciliary muscles, from which the lens is suspended, removes some of the tension from the lens, and it takes on a more spherical shape. When it is rounder, near objects are in focus. The effect of lens shape on point of focus is shown in Figure 3.6.

Your age is important in determining how well your lens is able to accommodate for changes in viewing distance. For example, the lens of a newborn infant is in focus only for objects that are approximately 19 cm away, although it is able to accommodate quite well by about 2 months of age (see Chapter 15). After about 40 years of age, the ability of the lens to change focus decreases with age because the inner layers of the lens die, causing the lens to lose some of its elasticity (Weale, 1986). This results in a form of **refractive error** (light-bending or focusing error) called **presbyopia,** which translates to "old sighted." Functionally, this condition increases the near point distance. The **near point** refers to how close an object may be brought to the eye before it can no longer be held in focus and becomes blurry. Thus, older persons without corrective lenses often may be seen holding reading material abnormally far from their faces in order to focus on it adequately.

An eye having normal accommodative (focusing) ability is called **emmetropic.** Sometimes there is too much or too little curvature in the cornea or, alternatively, the eye is too short or too long, so that the accommodative capacity of the lens is not sufficient to bring light from an object into focus. If the eye is too short or if the light rays are not bent sharply enough by the cornea, distant objects are seen clearly, but it is dif-

DEMONSTRATION BOX 3.1

VISION "BEHIND" THE EYE

It is easy to demonstrate that the visual field actually extends to a region somewhat behind the eye. In order to do this, simply choose a point that is some distance in front of your head and stare at it. Now raise your hand to the side of your head as shown in the figure, with your index finger extended upward. Your hand should be out of view when you stare at the distant point. Now, wiggle your finger slightly, and bring your hand slowly forward until the wiggling finger is just barely visible in your peripheral vision. At this point stop and, with your head as still as possible, move your finger directly in toward your head. You will notice that your hand will touch a point on your temple somewhat behind the location of the eye, indicating that you were actually seeing somewhat "behind yourself."

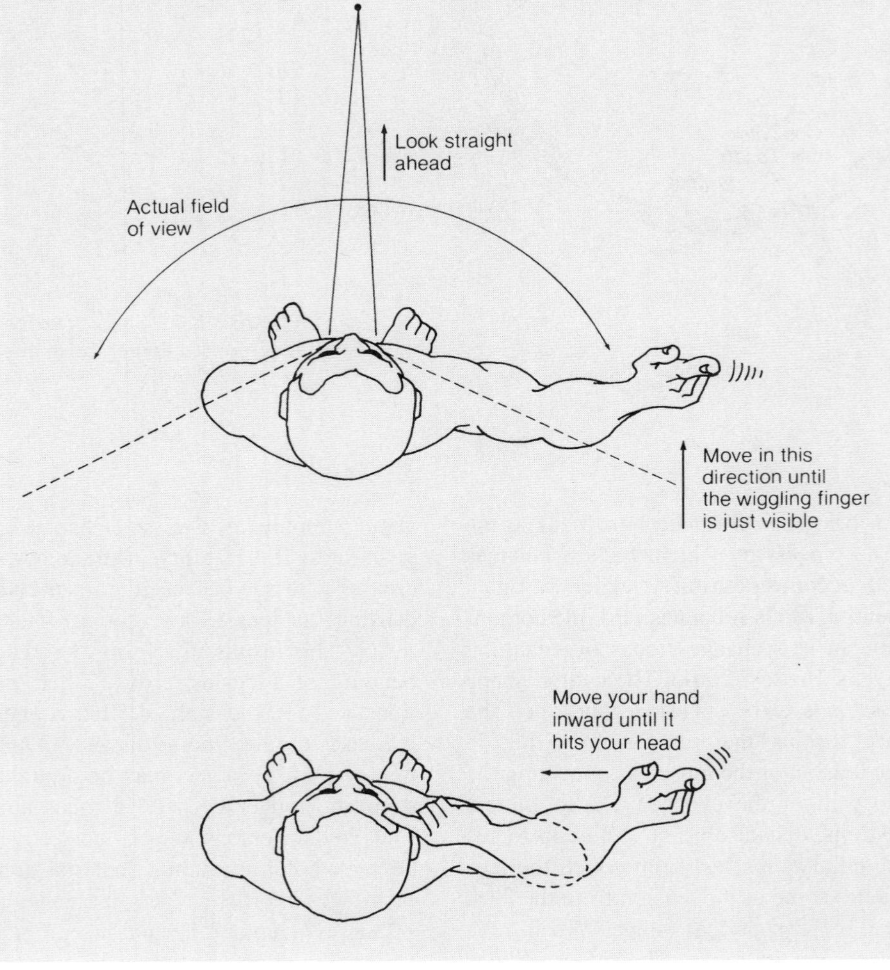

ficult to bring near objects into focus. The common term for this is *farsightedness,* and the technical term is **hypermetropia.** If the eye is too long or if the light rays are bent too sharply by the cornea, near objects are in focus; however, distant objects are blurry. This condition is called *nearsightedness* or **myopia.** The optical situations that result in these difficulties are shown in Figure 3.7.

Another feature of the lens that warrants mention is the fact that it is not perfectly transparent. The lens has a yellowish hue, and the density of this yellow tint increases with age (Coren & Girgus, 1972a). The yellow

DEMONSTRATION BOX 3.2

THE PUPILLARY LIGHT REFLEX

For this demonstration you need a friend. Dim the light in the room, but leave enough light so that you can still see the size of the pupil of your friend's eye. Notice how large your friend's pupil appears to be under these conditions. Now turn on an overhead light or shine the beam of a flashlight into your friend's eye and note how the pupil constricts. Removal of the light will cause the pupil to dilate again. The light reflex of the pupil was the first reflex ever studied by Whytt (1751), who is credited with the discovery of reflex action. It is still sometimes called Whytt's reflex.

pigment screens out some of the ultraviolet light entering the eye. Animals with clear lenses (such as many birds and insects) can see ultraviolet light, as can people who have had their lenses surgically removed (e.g., Hardie & Kirschfeld, 1983). The yellow pigment in the lens also screens out some of the blue light and thus alters our perception of color somewhat. For example, you may have heard individuals arguing over whether a particular color is blue or green. If they are different ages, the source of the argument may lie in the fact that because the lens yellows with age, each is viewing the world through a different yellow filter (see Sasaki & Hockwin, 2002).

Living in bright sunlight contributes in its own way to a yellowing of the lens. Long-term exposure to certain ultraviolet components (UV-B) of sunlight leads to a premature aging effect in which the lens takes on a yellow-brown tint early in adulthood. This is called **phototoxic lens brunescence,** or "browning" of the lens (Javitt & Taylor, 1994). Some researchers have even been able to correlate the presence of specific terms for "blue" in the natural languages spoken in various regions in the world to variations in the levels of this ultraviolet light (Lindsey & Brown, 2002). This suggests that the accelerated aging of the eye that comes about through chronic exposure to ultraviolet light components, rather than cultural reasons, is behind the lack of a distinction for "blue" and "green" in languages that originate in locales with high ultraviolet exposure. In support of this hypothesis, when young North American observers were given a color naming test while wearing strongly tinted yellow sun glasses, they also referred to as "green" colors that ordinarily appeared "blue" (Lindsey & Brown, 2002).

The Retina

The image formed by the cornea and lens of the eye is focused on a screen of neural elements at the back of the eye called the **retina.** The term *retina* derives from the

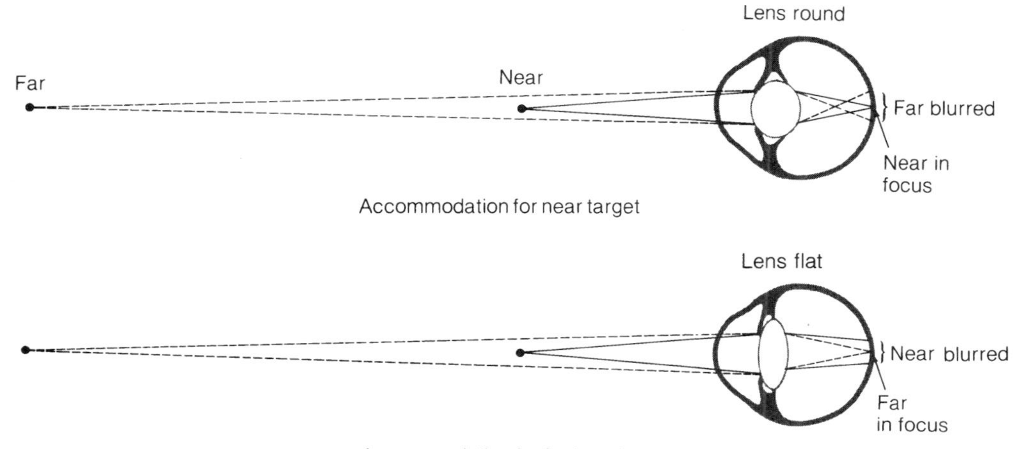

FIGURE 3.6 Accommodation involves the focusing of an image by changing the shape of the crystalline lens.

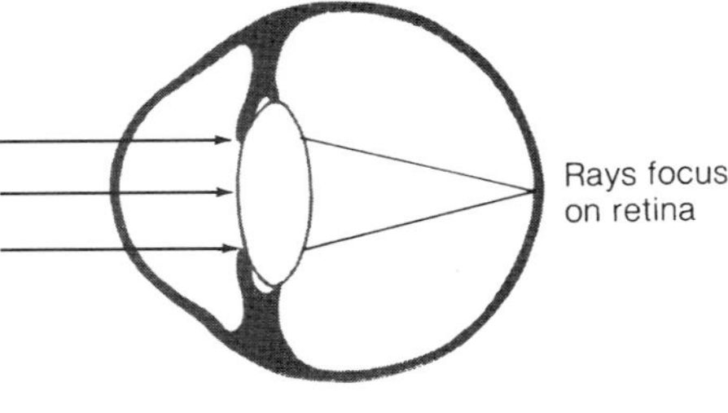

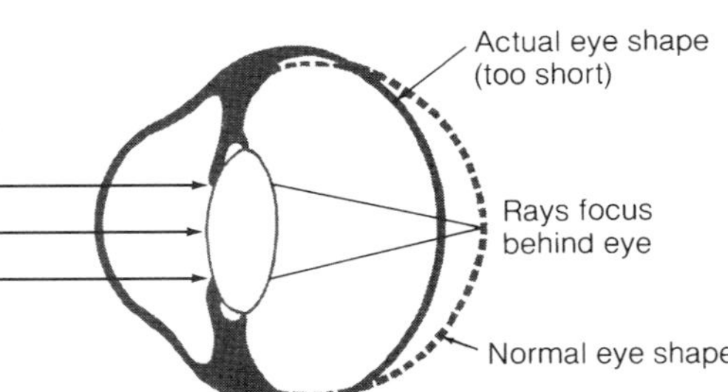

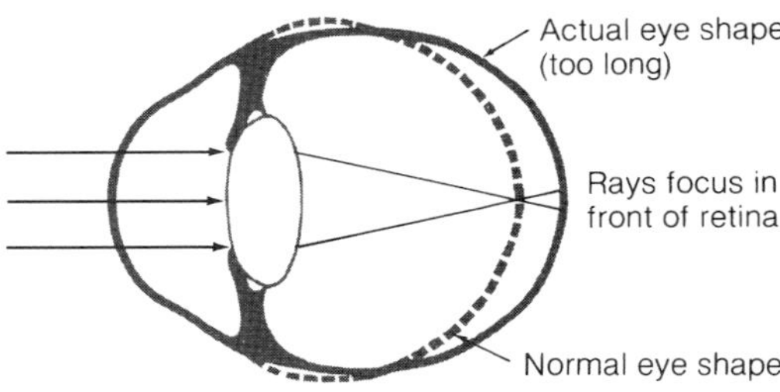

FIGURE 3.7 Three common refractive conditions of the eye.

Latin word meaning "net" because when an eye is opened up surgically (or its interior viewed with an optical device such as an ophthalmoscope) the most salient feature is the network of blood vessels lining the inner cavity of the eye. Demonstration Box 3.3 shows how you can observe these blood vessels in your own eyes.

The sheet of neural elements that makes up the retina extends over most of the interior of the eye. In daylight-active (*diurnal*) animals, a light-absorbing layer called the **pigment epithelium** lies underneath the retina. This dark layer serves the same purpose as the black inner coating in a photographic camera, reducing the amount of reflected and scattered light that could blur or fog the image. In night-active (*nocturnal*) animals, where the detection of light is more important than image clarity, the light that penetrates the retina is reflected back through the retina by a shiny surface known as the **reflecting tapetum.** This permits the light to pass through the retina twice (once as it enters and once as it is reflected out), effectively doubling its intensity. Although this results in a sizeable increase in sensitivity, this increase is obtained at the expense of a considerable fogging and blurring of the image. This is especially true at higher illumination levels. The existence of the reflecting tapetum explains why cats' eyes seem to glow in the dark when a flashlight is pointed toward them.

The retina consists of three major layers of neural tissue and is about the thickness of a sheet of paper (see Figure 3.8). It is here that the light is transformed into a neural response. This initial transformation of a physical entity (light) into a neural signal is called **transduction.** The layer of the retina closest to the scleral wall contains the **photoreceptors.** There are two types of photoreceptors in the human eye, which are distinguishable on the basis of their shapes: long, thin, cylindrical cells called **rods,** and shorter, thicker, and more tapered cells called **cones.** The outer segments of these cells contain pigments that absorb light and start the visual process. The middle layer of the retina consists of **bipolar cells,** which are neurons with two long extended processes. One end makes synapses with the photoreceptors; the other end makes synapses with the large **ganglion cells** in the third layer of the retina.

In addition to the three forward-feeding layers of cells in the retina—photoreceptors, bipolars, and ganglion cells—there are two types of cells that make connections laterally. Closest to the receptor layer are **horizontal cells.** These cells typically have short dendrites and a long horizontal process that extends some distance across the retina. The other lateral connecters are called **amacrine cells,** and are found between the ganglion and bipolar cells. More than 30 types of amacrine cells, differing in size and chemical properties, have been isolated (Rodieck, 2000). Both the horizontal and amacrine cells modify the visual signal and allow adjacent cells in the retina to communicate and interact with one another.

Light reception occurs within the rods and cones. Contrary to what we might expect, the orientation of rods and cones is inverted, with the pigment-bearing end pointing toward the *back* of the eye rather than toward the lens. Thus, the retina may be thought of as a transparent carpet lying upside down on the floor of a room, with the pile of the carpet corresponding to the rods and cones. The incoming light must therefore pass through the carpet (the retina) before reaching the photorecep-

DEMONSTRATION BOX 3.3

MAPPING THE RETINAL BLOOD VESSELS

For this demonstration you will need a pocket penlight and a white paper or light-colored wall. Hold the penlight near the outside canthus (corner) of your eye. Now, shaking the bulb of the penlight up and down, you will see a netlike pattern on the light surface. This pattern is generated by the movements of the shadows of your retinal blood vessels across your retina. By steadily shaking the bulb with one hand and tracing the shadows with the other, you can produce a map of your own retinal blood vessels.

tors. Although this arrangement might appear to be somewhat counterproductive, it actually makes good sense. The photoreceptors use a lot of oxygen, and to meet this need there are many blood vessels in the epithelial layer at the rear of the eye. If the retina were "right-side up," the many blood vessels providing the photoreceptors' blood supply would partially block the light input. Therefore, the "upside-down" organization turns out to be more functional.

The Fovea

Not all parts of the retina are of equal importance in the visual process. The most important section of the human retina is located in the region around the **optic axis,** an imaginary line from the center of the retina that passes through the center of the pupil (see Figure 3.9). If we view a human retina through an ophthalmoscope, we note a yellow patch of pigment located in the region of the origin of the optic axis. This area is called the **macula**, which translates to "yellow spot." Demonstration Box 3.4 describes a procedure in which you can see your own macula. In the center of the macula is a small depression about 0.30 mm in diameter that looks much like the imprint of a pinpoint. This small circular depression is called the **fovea centralis**, which translated is "central pit." The fovea is critical in vision. Whenever you look directly at an object, it means that the eyes are rotated so that the image of the object falls on the fovea. Animals lacking foveas do not need to be able to move their eyes (see Cronly-Dillon & Gregory, 1991).

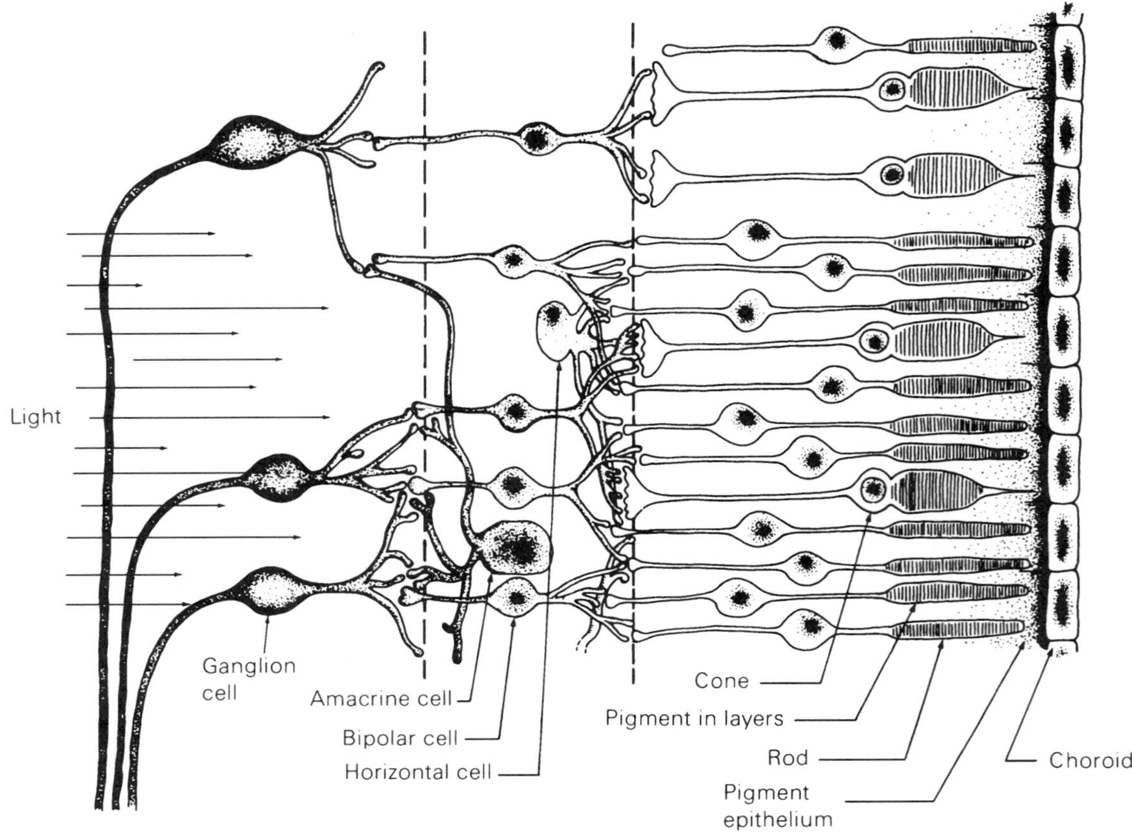

FIGURE 3.8 Schematic diagram of the human retina.

The fovea is shown schematically in Figure 3.10. In the center of the foveal depression, the upper layers of cells are pushed away so that the light passes through a much thinner cellular layer before reaching the photoreceptors. The photoreceptors themselves are very densely packed in this region. This section of the retina contains only cones; there are no rods at all (Osterberg, 1935). Foveal cones also have a different shape than the more peripheral cones depicted in Figure 3.8. They are much longer and thinner (often only 0.001 mm in diameter) and thus somewhat resemble rods. Outside of the fovea the number of cones decreases rapidly. The number of rods, on the other hand, increases rapidly as one leaves the foveal region, reaching a peak concentration at about 20° of visual angle from the fovea and then decreasing again, as shown in Figure 3.9 (Curcio, Sloan, Packer, Hendrickson, & Kalina, 1987).

Rods and Cones

The presence of two types of photoreceptors suggests the existence of two separate visual functions. In the early 1860s the retinal anatomist Max Schultze found that nocturnal animals, such as owls, have retinas that contain only rods. Animals that are diurnal, or active only during the day, such as chipmunks or pigeons, have retinas that consist entirely of cones. Animals that are active in the twilight, or during both day and night, such as rats, monkeys, and humans, have retinas composed of both rods and cones. On the basis of these observations, Schultze offered what has been called the **duplex retina theory** of vision. The rod system, also called **scotopic,** is for vision under dim light conditions, whereas the cone system, also called **photopic,** is for vision under daylight or bright conditions.

Individuals whose retinas contain no rods, or only nonfunctioning rods, seem to have normal vision under daylight conditions. However, as soon as the light dims beyond a certain point (into twilight), they lose all sense of sight and become functionally blind. These individuals suffer from **night blindness** (von Kries, 1895). The implication is that scotopic vision is entirely dependent on rods. The opposite pattern is found for individuals lacking in

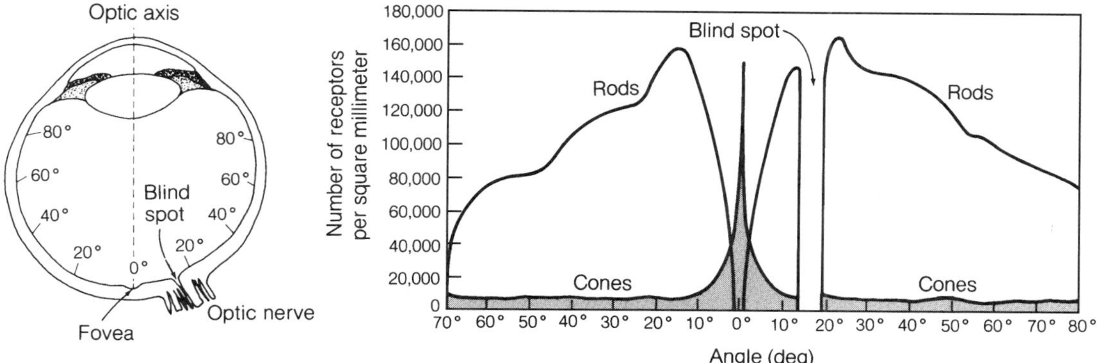

FIGURE 3.9 The distribution of rods and cones in the human retina. The left figure gives the locations on the retina of the "angle" relative to the optic axis on the right figure.

functioning cones. These people find normal levels of daylight painful, totally lack color vision, and have very poor visual acuity. Under dim levels of illumination, however, they function normally (e.g., Sacks, 1997). Such individuals suffer from **day blindness** and provide evidence that a functioning cone system is necessary for both normal photopic vision and for the perception of color.

Before a rod or a cone can signal the presence of light, it must first interact with the light in some way. Such interaction involves absorbing, or capturing, one or more photons. Any substance that absorbs light is called a pigment. A substance that absorbs a lot of light would appear to be darkly pigmented because most of the photons hitting it would be absorbed and very few would be left to bounce back to the eye of the viewer. As we noted earlier, the outer segments of both the rods and the cones contain visual pigments. If you turn back to Figure 3.8, you will see the pigments arranged in layers in the outer segments of the photoreceptors. For rods, the photosensitive pigment is arranged in a stack of around 2000 tiny disks, like coins inside a tube; for cones, the pigment is part of a single large, elaborately folded membrane that forms the layers of photosensitive material (see Wolken, 1995).

Although rods and cones do not contain the same pigments, the biochemical events leading to hyperpolarization in the presence of light are similar for rods and cones (Bridges, 1986; Schnapf & Baylor, 1987). Figure 3.11 shows the process for a schematic rod. The first step is that the pigment bleaches, or loses its apparent coloration, when exposed to light, breaking into two parts. This starts a cascade of photo chemical reactions that results in the closing of the normally open sodium channels in the cell wall, upsetting the balance of sodium and potassium in the cell body of the receptor. This leads to the hyperpolarization we discussed earlier, meaning that the normal negative charge of −40 mV across the receptor cell membrane becomes even more

DEMONSTRATION BOX 3.4

THE MACULAR SPOT

Under appropriate conditions it is possible to see the macular spot in your own eye. In order to do this you will need a dark blue or purple piece of cellophane. Brightly illuminate a piece of white paper with a desk lamp. While looking at the paper with one eye, quickly bring the piece of cellophane between your eye and the paper. Now as you look at the paper you see what appears to be a faint circular shadow in the center of it. The sight of the shadow may last for only a couple of seconds. Sometimes its visibility can be improved by moving the cellophane in front of and away from your eye so that you have a flickering colored field. Some individuals can see the spot when staring at a uniform blue field, such as a clear summer sky. This percept is caused by the fact that the yellow pigment in the macula absorbs the blue light and does not let it pass. This causes a circular shadow, which can be briefly seen. It is often called Maxwell's spot, after James Clerk Maxwell, who noticed its presence during some color-matching experiments.

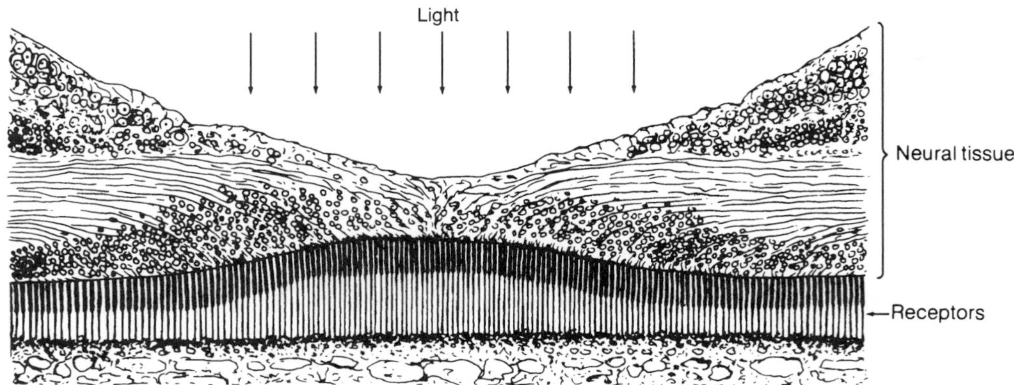

FIGURE 3.10 Sketch of a cross section through the fovea. Light comes from the direction of the top of the page.

negative, perhaps −70 to −80 mV (Schnapf & Baylor, 1987). This hyperpolarization of the receptor cells stimulates the bipolar cells, which in turn stimulate the ganglion cells. At the same time, complex interactions occur between neighboring bipolar and ganglion cells via the lateral connections among horizontal and amacrine cells. The axons of the ganglion cells then carry the resulting neural signals out of the eye toward the brain.

To maintain a sufficient supply of unbleached pigment, chemical reactions in rods and cones continually reassemble the pigments from their constituent parts. The pigment in the rod is called **rhodopsin** (which means "visual red"). Rhodopsin regenerates in the dark

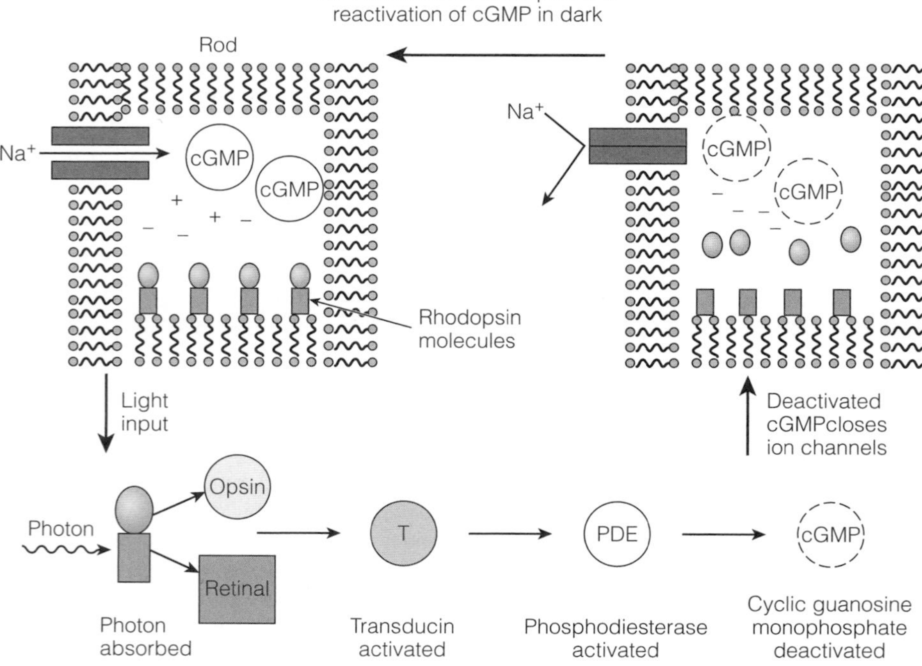

FIGURE 3.11 Cartoon of chain of events in a rod stimulated by light. The Na^+ channel is normally held open by activated cGMP molecules. When photons bleach the rhodopsin molecules, the resulting cascade of photochemical events deactivates the cGMP molecules, closing the Na^+ channel and hyperpolarizing the rod.

BIOGRAPHY BOX 3.2

REMEMBER TO EAT YOUR CARROTS

How many times have you heard an adult remind a child to "Eat all of your vegetables, especially the carrots. You don't want to have poor eyesight." The idea that there is a direct connection between the vitamins contained in some foods and our own physiological function is so widely accepted now that it may be hard to understand that this was a radical idea only 70 years ago.

George Wald (1906–1997) was working as a young scientist in 1933, one who had only recently been awarded his Ph.D., when he was first able to establish a firm link between vitamin A and the visual pigment rhodopsin found in the rod photoreceptors of the eye. At the time even the idea of vitamins was still deeply mysterious. His Ph.D. at Columbia University in New York had been conducted under the supervision of Selig Hecht, a superb vision researcher widely renowned for his precise measurement of visual function and for theories that were consistent with those measurements. But George Wald wanted to find the real substances behind these theoretical ideas. In his own words, "I left Hecht's laboratory with a great desire to lay hands on the molecules for which these were symbols." That desire led him eventually to a physiology lab in Germany, where he was able to isolate vitamin A in the retinae of some frogs, which, as it turns out, were accidentally shipped to the lab in the first place.

George Wald returned to North America in 1934, where he took up a position as lecturer in the Department of Biology at Harvard University. He spent the remainder of his professional career there. He was awarded the Nobel Prize in Medicine in 1967 for his work on the molecular basis of vision, an award he shared with two other pioneers in vision research, Haldan Hartline and Ragnar Granit.

with the help of vitamin A (Boll, 1876). Because vitamin A is vital to this process, the absence of vitamin A in the diet can show up in "epidemics" of night blindness (Wald, 1968). This sometimes happens in isolated communities where fish products or appropriate vegetables containing vitamin A are not available. Folk wisdom tells us that eating carrots will improve our vision and this is correct because carrots are a rich source of vitamin A. The corresponding pigment in the cone is called **iodopsin** (which means "visual purple"). On exposure to light, iodopsin breaks down into several chemical components, some of which are the same as the components of rhodopsin. Biography Box 3.2 will introduce you to a pioneer in the understanding of how rod receptors convert light energy to a neural signal via the pigment rhodopsin.

Neural Responses to Light

The eye transmits visual information to the brain via the long axons of the retinal ganglion cells. This neural pathway, known as the **optic nerve,** exits from the eye by means of a hole through the retina and the scleral wall. At the center of the optic nerve lie the blood vessels that sustain the metabolic needs of the eye. Because this bundle of axons and blood vessels must exit through the retina, there are no photoreceptors in this region. As such, there is also no visual response to light striking this portion of the retina, and so it is appropriately called the **blind spot.** You may demonstrate the absence of vision in this region of your own retina by trying Demonstration Box 3.5.

The nerve impulses transmitted from the eye to the brain via optic nerves are not "raw" sensory data. Rather, they are the result of a large amount of neural processing that has transformed the original optical image in many ways. In order to get a sense of just how much processing has occurred, consider that there are 120 million rods and 5 million cones in each human eye. Yet there are only about 1 million axons making up each optic nerve. Clearly, each receptor cell does not have its own private pipeline to the brain, but rather, the responses of a large number of photoreceptors are represented in the activity of a single optic nerve axon. This transformation comes about because the combined activity of the 125 million rods and cones, plus the output of several million more intervening bipolar, horizontal, and amacrine cells, has converged onto the much smaller number of ganglion cells. We will soon see how the information regarding light is transformed in the eye from the moment it arrives (see Forrester, 2002).

The Receptive Field of a Neuron. As we have noted, information that is carried to the brain by a single ganglion cell axon represents the combined activity of a large number of rods and cones. As such, any single ganglion cell will respond to light that strikes anywhere on a sizeable region of the retina. Such a region of the retina, on which the presence of light alters the firing rate of a cell, is called that cell's **receptive field.** In this way, each ganglion cell responds to light falling on a substantial and often overlapping zone of receptor cells in the retina (see Masland, 2001).

Most contemporary studies of retinal ganglion cells follow in the footsteps of a Nobel Prize–winning scientist, Hartline (1940) and his colleague Kuffler (1953), who first inserted an electrode through the eye of an anesthetized cat and recorded from single ganglion cells in the retina. Generally one finds that when a single small spot of light is displayed on a screen, thereby stimulating the retina of the animal observing it, one of three different types of responses from a ganglion cell might occur. The first type of response is the one typically expected when a neuron is excited: a burst of neural impulses immediately following the onset of the stimulus. This has been dubbed an **on response.** Alternatively, the cell can give a burst of impulses beginning at the termination of a stimulus. Such a response is termed an **off response.** Some responses are hybrids because both the presentation and the removal of the stimulus cause bursts of neural impulses. These are designated **on-off responses.** Typical examples of these responses are shown in Figure 3.12.

When very small lights are used (about 0.2 mm in diameter on the retinal image), the ganglion cell response tends to vary from on, through on-off, to off, depending on the location of the stimulus within the cell's receptive field. A map of the overall shape of the receptive field of a retinal ganglion cell is illustrated in Figure 3.13 for two cells. These receptive fields are roughly circular in shape with two distinct zones: a center and a surrounding re-

DEMONSTRATION BOX 3.5

THE BLIND SPOT

The region of the retina where the optic nerve leaves the eye contains no photoreceptors and thus is blind. You may demonstrate this for yourself by using the figure here. Close your left eye, and with your right eye look at the X in the figure. Keeping your eye on the X, move the page toward you. At some point the little open square will seem to disappear. At this point its image is falling on your blind spot. Notice that when you have the page at the correct distance, not only does the square seem to disappear, but also the line appears to run continuously through the area where the square should be. This indicates that we automatically "fill in" missing information. We fill it in with material that is similar to nearby visible material. This accounts for why you are not normally aware of the blind spot. You are simply supplying the missing information to fill in this "hole" in the visual field.

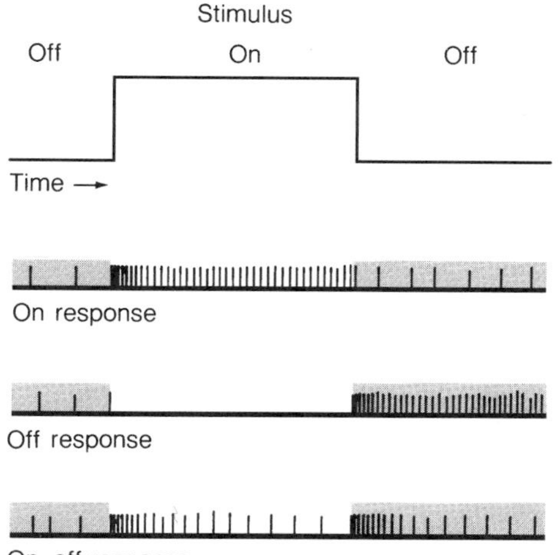

FIGURE 3.12 On, off, and on-off neural responses in the retinal ganglion cells.

gion. For half the ganglion cells the onset of a light falling anywhere within the central zone causes the ganglion cell to respond with a burst of firing. The same light falling anywhere in the surrounding region gives the opposite result. That is, the onset of a light does not produce a response, but its offset does. Between these two regions, roughly at the border between the on and off regions, is a narrow region where the on-off responses occur. The other half of ganglion cells have the opposite arrangement, with the central zone responding to light offsets, the surrounding region to light onsets, and the border region to both on and off responses (see Hicks, Molotchnikoff, & Ono, 1993).

Separate Systems for Light and Dark. The two kinds of ganglion cells that show either the on- or off-center responses are distributed uniformly throughout the retina. Yet they are visibly different under the microscope and they make contact with their respective bipolar and amacrine cells at different levels in the retina. Lateral connections to off-center cells lie closer to the photoreceptors than do the connections for on-center cells (Nelson, Kolb, Robinson, & Mariani, 1981). In addition, these cells maintain their separateness from one another all the way to the visually sensitive regions of the brain (Perry & Silveira, 1988). Some evidence even suggests that specific amacrine cells, with different neurotransmitters, may shape particular receptive field properties in ganglion cells (Dacey, 1988). All of this supports the idea that the processing of relative lightness and darkness may be fundamentally different. The on-center ganglion cells can be thought of as detectors of brightness relative to some average level of intensity, whereas the off-center cells serve as detectors of relative darkness (see also Linberg, Cuenca, Ahnelt, Fisher, & Kolb, 2001).

This possibility was actually speculated about many years before there was any physiological evidence for it, when vision researchers realized that increases in the amount of light shining on a scene had opposite effects

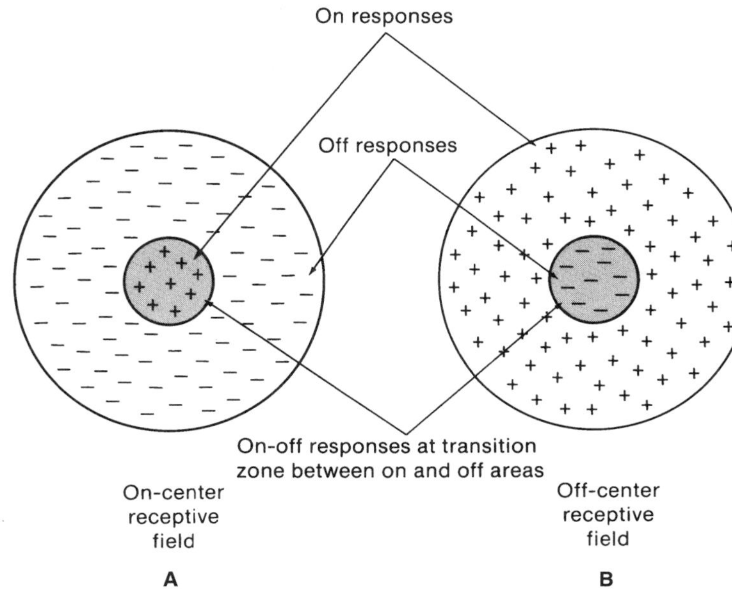

FIGURE 3.13 Circular center-surround retinal receptive fields of (A) an on-center cell and (B) an off-center cell.

on the appearance of surfaces that were relatively light versus those that were relatively dark. Increasing the amount of light causes relatively bright objects to appear even brighter and relatively dark objects to appear even darker (Jameson & Hurvich, 1964). This is a little paradoxical if we think of darkness as being the absence of light. But it begins to make sense if we think of additional light having separate effects on the separate systems for the representation of lightness and darkness. In that case, increasing the overall illumination allows each system to increase its dynamic range (Fiorentini, Baumgartner, Magnussen, Shiller, & Thomas, 1990). This explains why the screen of your television, which appears to be only a dull gray when the television is turned off, is suddenly able to display dark black regions when the screen is turned on.

An important discovery made about 20 years ago has now given direct evidence for the independence of brightness and darkness systems of ganglion cells (Slaughter & Miller, 1981). These researchers applied a chemical called aminophosphonobutyrate (APB) to the retina of the mud puppy (an aquatic salamander). This caused all the on-center ganglion cells to become unresponsive to light, while the off-center cells maintained their normal responses. Since then other researchers have shown that APB blocks the responses of on-center ganglion cells of the cat and the monkey (Shiller, Sandell, & Maunsell, 1986). Animals treated with APB show normal responses to decreases in light but are almost entirely unable to detect increases in light.

Parvo and Magno Ganglion Cells. It has long been known that ganglion cells come in a wide range of sizes (Cajal, 1893), as is illustrated in Figure 3.14. However, only recently have researchers come to general agreement on a system for classifying ganglion cells that takes these size differences into account (Rodieck & Brening, 1983). The cells with the smaller bodies have come to be known as **parvo** cells, whereas those with larger bodies are called **magno** cells (these are Latin terms for small and large, respectively).

It turns out that many anatomical and physiological characteristics are associated with the difference in size (Schiller, 1986; Shapley, 1990). To begin, Figure 3.14 shows that parvo ganglion cells have branches that extend over a much smaller area than do the branches of magno ganglion cells. This means that magno cells have a much broader range when it comes to communicating with neighboring cells. Proportionally, there are many more parvo cells than magno cells, and they differ in terms of their distribution across the retina. Virtually no magno cells have been found in the foveal region, and the number of magno cells increases as we move outward into the peripheral retina.

Associated with these differences in anatomy are several important functional characteristics that have been summarized in Table 3.2 (see also McIlwain, 1996). For instance, magno cells send neural impulses along their axons at speeds of about 40 m per second. This is very fast when compared with parvo cells, which have conduction speeds of only 20 m per second. Although both

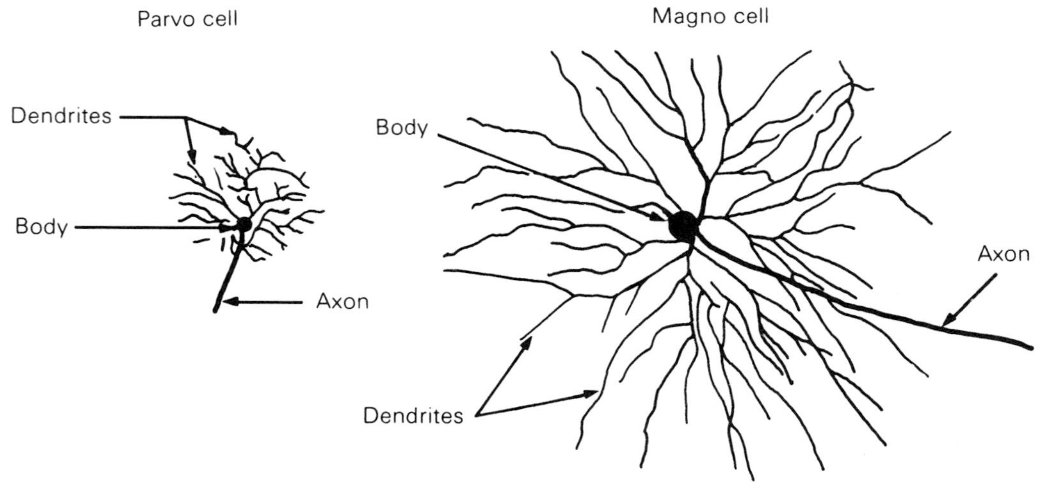

FIGURE 3.14 Examples of parvo and magno cells, taken from a cat retina and laid flat for illustration purposes.

TABLE 3.2 Selected Anatomical and Physiological Differences between Parvo and Magno Ganglion Cells, along with Some Possible Consequences for Behavior

	Parvo	Magno
Anatomical differences	Small cell body Dense branching Short branches Majority of cells	Large cell body Sparse branching Long branches Minority of cells
Physiological differences	Slow conduction rate Sustained response Small receptive field Low-contrast sensitivity Color sensitive	Rapid conduction rate Transient response Large receptive field High-contrast sensitivity Color blind
Possible functional consequences	Detailed form analysis Spatial analysis Color vision	Motion detection Temporal analysis Depth perception

parvo and magno cells have receptive fields with the center-surround, on-off arrangement that we have described, the smaller parvo cells have smaller center-surround receptive fields.

The neural responses of parvo and magno cells also differ over time. When parvo cells are stimulated, they respond in a sustained manner, continuing their neural activity as long as the stimulus remains. Magno cells, on the other hand, have a much more transient response. They tend to give only a brief burst of activity when the stimulus comes on, or when it goes off, and they tend to cease responding quickly thereafter.

Another parvo-magno difference is illustrated in Figure 3.15A, which shows a sketch of the receptive field of a retinal ganglion cell in which half of the field is evenly illuminated with light and the other half is dark. Suppose that we now switched the illumination to the pattern shown as Figure 3.15B or Figure 3.15C. If we were stimulating a parvo cell, it would continue to respond exactly as it had been responding. In other words, as long as the same amount of illumination is present in the center and surround, the parvo cell does not distinguish between the different locations of illumination. However, any switch in the pattern of illumination will provoke a vigorous response in a magno cell. Because small movements of an object cause these kinds of changes in the visual field, magno cells are ideally specialized for movement detection (Kruger, 1981; McIlwain, 1996).

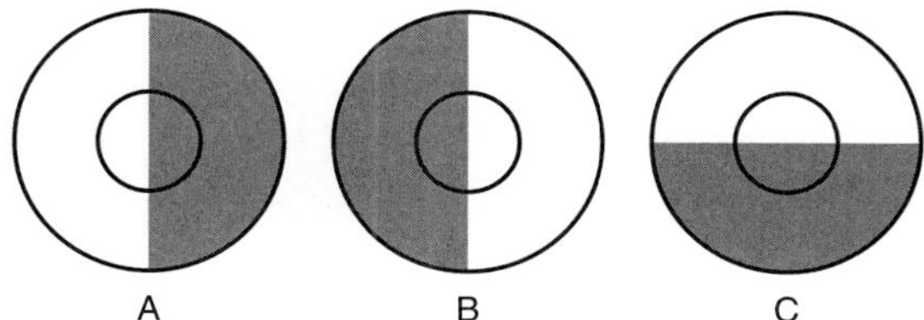

FIGURE 3.15 If the illumination pattern on a center-surround receptive field is half light and half dark, as shown in *A*, and then is shifted to a new orientation (either *B* or *C*), a magno ganglion cell would respond to such a change but a parvo ganglion cell would not.

THE VISUAL BRAIN

The most important concept for our modern understanding of the visual brain is mapping. The concept of a map is very helpful because of our everyday familiarity with roadmaps. A roadmap is an organized representation of information. The lines on the map are not themselves roads and rivers; they refer only to the relationships between these landmarks. In the same way, neural signals in a brain map of the visual field are merely one of many possible ways to represent the original pattern of light. Second, a map preserves certain spatial relations among landmarks but distorts others. For instance, the relative distance between two towns is accurately preserved in a roadmap, as is the relative direction one must travel to move from one town to the other. However, the absolute distance can be determined only by converting the scale units of the map into kilometers or miles; the actual direction can be determined only by referencing the roadmap to true north. The same is true of visual maps in the brain. Relative distances and directions between points of light are preserved, although absolute distances and directions may be greatly distorted. Vision researchers often refer to this kind of representation as being a **topographic map.**

Visual Maps

We can begin our story of how the eye and brain map visual information by examining the relationship between points of light in the visual field of view and specific points on the retina, as shown in Figure 3.16 (see also Swindale, 2001). Imagine the field of view for each eye divided into four quadrants, corresponding to the upper and lower visual field and the nasal and temporal visual field. Then, because of the way in which the cornea and

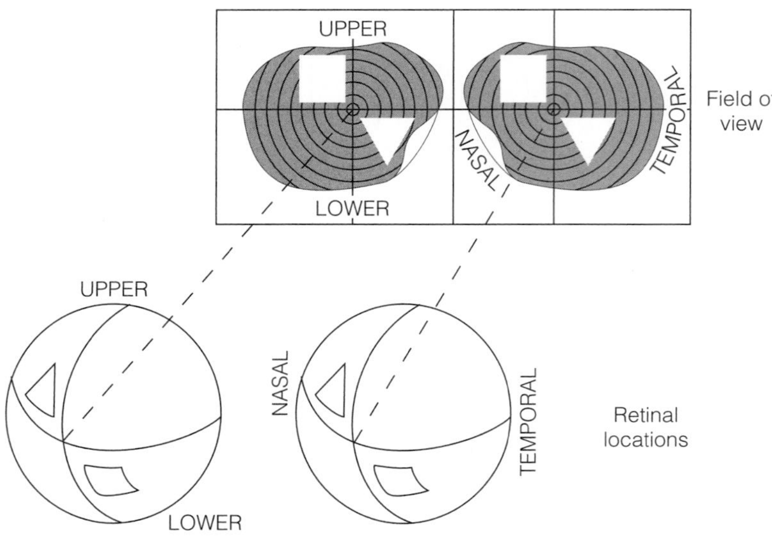

FIGURE 3.16 The relationship between points of light in the visual field and corresponding points on the retina.

the lens diffract light onto the retina, light from the upper visual field is projected onto the lower retinal surface, light from the nasal visual field is projected onto the temporal retinal surface, and so on. In short, the visual image of the world is represented as both upside-down and left-right reversed on the retina. Long ago, some philosophers worried about the problems such mapping transformations might pose for the brain, but this is no longer considered to be a concern, largely because the image on the retina preserves all the important spatial relations in the field of view. Just like a roadmap, no information is lost simply because the roadmap is turned upside down or viewed in a mirror.

The mapping of light into neural signals in the retina is only the first of many maps that are constructed by the visual system. As we noted earlier, the axons of the retinal ganglion cells gather together and exit from the eye at the blind spot. This bundle of axons, which forms the optic nerve, is the beginning of a pathway that eventually ends in the brain. There are two distinct anatomical routes that lead to the common end point, however, and each carries somewhat different information, thereby producing different kinds of maps along the way. We will discuss each of these pathways in the next sections, though you must bear in mind that these separate pathways are always working together because they are in constant communication with each other in the brain (see also Forrester, 2002, and McIlwain, 1996, for more detailed technical descriptions).

Both pathways begin in the same fashion, with the information traveling out of the eyes along the optic nerves. As can be seen in Figure 3.17, the two optic nerves come together at a point that looks like an χ. This point is called the **optic chiasm** (from the Greek letter χ or chi). In primates, which include humans, one half of the optic nerve fibers cross to the opposite side of the brain. These are the fibers that represent the two inside or nasal retinas. Those from the outside or temporal halves of each retina do not cross but continue on the same side. This arrangement means that neural signals from temporal retina of each eye are mapped to the side of the brain on the same side as that eye, whereas signals from the nasal retina of each eye are mapped to the side of the brain that is opposite to that eye. A simpler way to understand this is to remember that all light from the left side of your visual field is mapped onto the right brain and all light from the right side of your visual field of view is mapped onto the left brain (e.g., Jeffery, 2001).

The Tectopulvinar System

The oldest visual pathway, in evolutionary terms, is the **tectopulvinar system.** It is a pathway we share with many other animals, including birds. In humans it is no longer the dominant neural pathway of visual information, but it is still a very important one for the perception

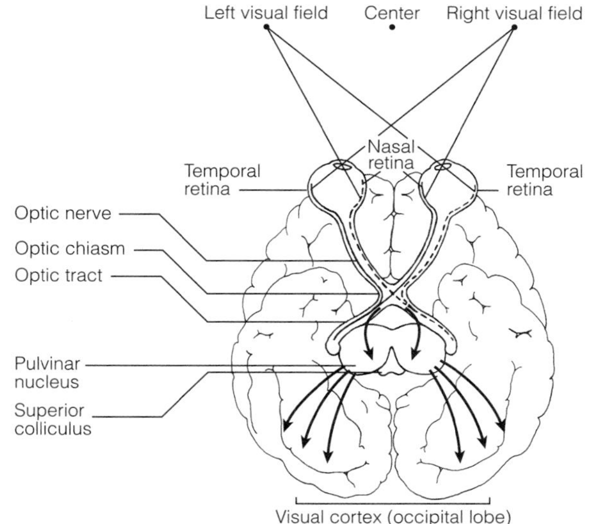

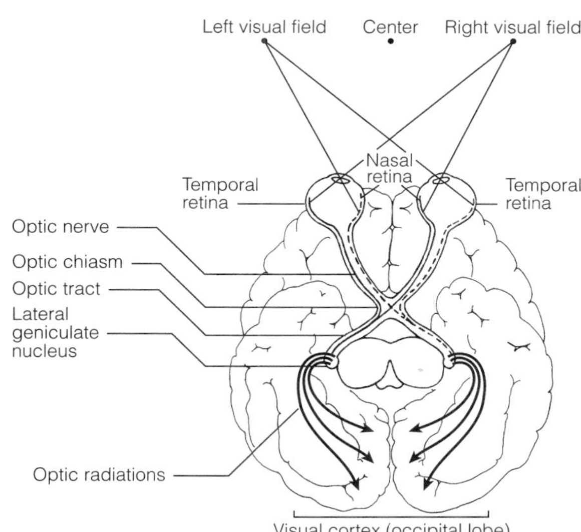

FIGURE 3.17 The two visual pathways from the eye to the visual cortex. (A) The tectopulvinar pathway. (B) The geniculostriate pathway.

of motion and for the control of eye movements (e.g., Casanova, Merabet, Desautels, & Minville, 2001).

The brain structures in the tectopulvinar pathway are indicated in Figure 3.17A. The pathway begins when a number of fibers from the optic tract branch off to the brain stem instead of to the midbrain. The structures that receive these incoming fibers look like four bumps on the roof (dorsal surface) of the brain stem; they are known as the **superior colliculi**. The vast majority of ganglion cells arriving at this location are the magno type in primates, meaning that they have rapid responses and are very sensitive to sudden changes in illumination.

Cells in the upper and intermediate layers of the superior colliculi have receptive fields that are arranged in an orderly topographic manner. The front (or anterior) portion represents the central visual field, whereas the back (posterior) portion represents the visual periphery. The colliculus on the right receives input from ganglion cells that have been stimulated by stimuli in the left visual field; the colliculus on the left responds to stimuli in the right visual field. As we might expect, given the magnocellular input from the retina, these receptive fields are not very sensitive to details of shape, such as orientation, or to color, but they are quite sensitive to motion and location. In the deeper layers the cells begin to exhibit a very interesting property. In addition to being activated by visual input, they can also be driven by auditory and tactile stimuli. This suggests that the superior colliculi are locations where information from the various senses is combined and integrated.

As with other visual centers in the brain, we must keep in mind that the inputs to the superior colliculi do not come only from the retina. This area receives extensive inputs from the primary visual area of the cortex (Area V1) as well as from a cortical visual area thought to be a center for visual motion processing (Area V5). These returning signals are called **back projections** because they represent feedback based on previous information that has already been sent to the brain. Both of these back projections to the superior colliculi are primarily of the magnocellular type, thus contributing to the view that this brain region is important in the analysis of movement and location.

From the superior colliculi the pathway continues on to the **pulvinar** and the **lateral posterior nuclei,** which are located nearby in the thalamus. From here, the fibers project to the cortex. Interestingly, none is destined directly for the primary visual cortex (Area V1), but rather, they connect to cells in the secondary visual areas (Area V2 and beyond).

The tectopulvinar pathway in primates is specialized for the control of eye movements and eye fixations. Even though you are likely not aware of it, you make on average two to four eye movements every moment you are awake. And these are not random events. You are always examining visual locations that are relevant to the visual tasks you are currently undertaking; you are always gauging the length of fixation to the complexity of the information you are inspecting; and you are always on the lookout for new information that may be coming into your field of view. To take all this into account requires a very complex and sophisticated network of brain regions. We now know that the superior colliculi are in constant communication with brain regions in the posterior parietal cortex, the frontal cortex, and other regions of the brain stem and midbrain. Much of the detailed neural circuitry involved is now known because of research over the past 25 years using single-cell recording techniques in awake and behaving monkeys. Some researchers believe it is now the best understood of all sensorimotor systems in primates (Munoz & Wurtz, 1993, 1995; Schall & Thompson, 1999; Wurtz, 1996).

The Geniculostriate System

The dominant pathway for humans and other primates, such as monkeys, is the **geniculostriate system** (Bullier, 2001). The major termination for the optic tract in the primary visual pathway is a structure in the thalamus called the **lateral geniculate nucleus,** shown in Figure 3.17B.

The lateral geniculate is arranged in six distinct layers of cells, as shown in Figure 3.18, each of which contains a topographic map of the visual field. As is the case with the retinal ganglion cells, lateral geniculate cells do not respond to visual stimuli unless the stimulation occurs within their receptive fields. Generally, the receptive fields of the lateral geniculate cells are similar to those of the retinal ganglion cells, in that they have either an on-center and an off-surround, or the reverse arrangement.

Figure 3.18 shows that the layers of cells in the lateral geniculate nucleus alternate between those receiving input from the eye on the same side and those receiving input from the eye on the opposite side. Parvo cells are located in the upper four layers of the lateral geniculate nucleus and receive their input primarily from the parvo ganglion cells in the retina, whereas magno cells are located in the lower two layers and receive input from the magno ganglion cells (Lennie, Trevarthen, Van Essen, & Waessle, 1990; Livingstone & Hubel, 1988). It should not be surprising, then, that the receptive fields of parvo cells have a color-opponent organization, whereas those of many magno cells are equally sensitive to all wavelengths of light. Magno cells are also more sensitive than parvo cells to the magnitude of the change in luminance at an edge (Shapley, 1990). Thus, the division into two parallel streams of processing that began in the retina—a slower-acting one for detailed form and color vision and a faster-acting one for movement perception—continues into the brain (see also Sincich & Horton, 2002).

Just like cells in the superior colliculi of the tectopulvinar pathway, cells in the lateral geniculate nucleus receive neural signals not only from the retina but also from higher visual centers in the cortex. Some estimates of the percentage of lateral geniculate inputs that are back projections of this kind are as high as 80 to 90% (Sherman, 2001). Even at this very early stage of visual processing, then, the signals that continue on to the brain are influenced not only by the incoming pattern of light but are also heavily influenced by the current state of the rest of the brain.

When the axons of the lateral geniculate neurons leave the geniculate, they form a large fan of fibers called the **optic radiations,** as shown in Figure 3.17B. These fibers eventually synapse with cortical neurons in the rear (or posterior) portion of the brain. This general area is known as the **occipital lobe.** Several other labels are now commonly used to refer to different subregions within the occipital lobe. The most popular labeling scheme among vision researchers denotes the different subregions within the occipital lobe as **Visual Area 1** or **V1, Visual Area 2** or **V2,** and so on. In all we now know of more than 36 different regions of the cortex containing neurons that are visually sensitive (e.g., DeYoe & van Essen, 1988; van Essen, 1984). We will restrict our discussion to only the few of these that are reasonably well understood.

Principles of Mapping

There are over 100 million neurons in the visual cortex. Only the smallest fraction of these has been thoroughly studied in attempts to discover their response characteristics. What we do know is based largely on research in which electrical impulses are recorded from single cells, employing the same techniques used in mapping the receptive fields of retinal ganglion and lateral geniculate

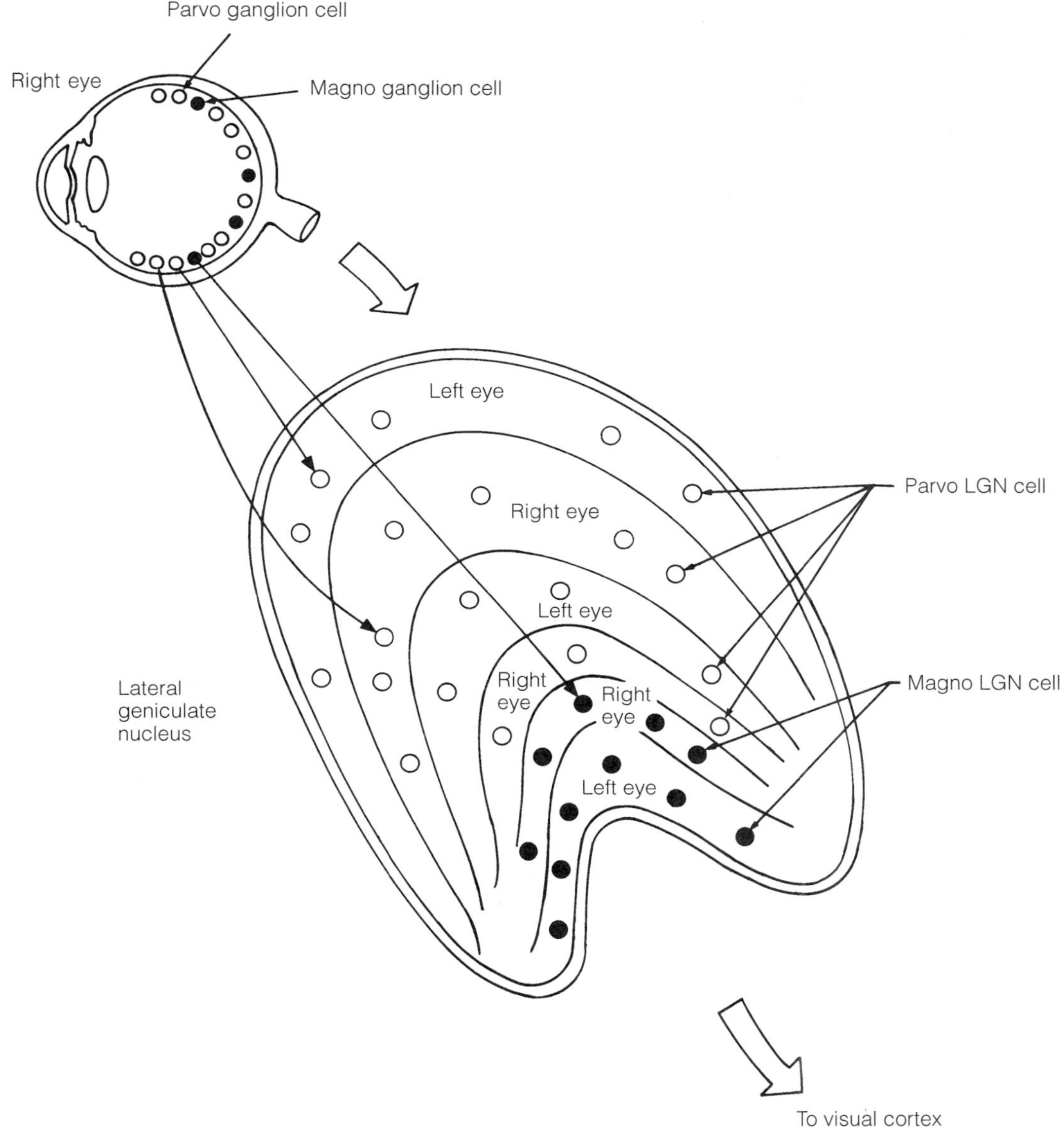

FIGURE 3.18 Layering of cells in the right lateral geniculate nucleus.

cells. Current techniques in this area still owe much to the pioneering work done by David Hubel and Torstein Wiesel, who received the Nobel Prize in 1981. Biography Box 3.3 introduces you to their work.

With the single-cell technique, a researcher can, in principle, probe any one of the millions of neurons in the cortex to see whether that neuron is visually sensitive. However, relying solely on this technique is a little like playing the lottery; you have to be extremely lucky to be presenting a particular neuron's favored stimulus to the relevant portion of the retina at the same time that you are recording its responses with a microelectrode. As you can infer, this is less likely to occur at random than finding the proverbial needle in a haystack.

Researchers use a number of additional techniques to assist them in their search for visually sensitive regions in the cortex. One of the most important of these involves examining the anatomical structure of the cortical cells with

BIOGRAPHY BOX 3.3

FROM SPOTS TO EDGES

When two young neuroscientists, a Canadian by the name of ***David Hubel (1926–)*** and a Swede named ***Torsten Wiesel (1924–)***, stumbled across cortical neurons with receptive fields sensitive to edges, neither was prepared for the finding. The year was 1958 and they were busy beginning their scientific careers. They were hoping that the experiments they were conducting would help them eventually to find secure academic positions as well as to help them find receptive fields in the visual cortex of a cat that were similar to those Hartline and Kuffler had discovered earlier in the lateral geniculate nucleus. Their apparatus for presenting visual stimuli to the cat consisted of 1-by-2 inch glass slides on which they would glue black dots of various diameters. These slides would be inserted into a projection device and moved around the cat's visual field in order to see whether they could evoke any neural activity. Hubel and Wiesel were hoping to find receptive fields that resembled the circular center-surround arrangement with which they were already familiar.

After about 5 hours of frustration, in which the only activity they recorded was the occasional spontaneous burst of firing that a visual neuron makes when at rest, they found an area of the cat's visual field in which they were able to elicit something of a response. However, the stimulus triggering this response did not seem to be the black dot. Instead, it was the faint edge of the glass slide moving across the visual field. When the glass slide was tilted by 20 degrees to one side or the other, the neuron remained silent. Also, when the edge of the slide was moved across the visual field in the opposite direction, the neuron was silent. Only when the edge of the slide was moved through the area in a specific orientation and in a specific direction did the neuron fire vigorously. We now know that Hubel and Wiesel had encountered their first complex cell, a type of neuron that represents 75% of the neurons that have been tested in Area V1. In 1981, these two scientists were honored with the Nobel Prize in Physiology for this and related discoveries.

chemical staining. The effects of these stains can be seen when a slice of cortical tissue is placed under a microscope. What one sees are patches and stripes of cortical tissue that have been affected differently by the stain, suggesting that these regions have common features and may be candidates for distinct brain areas that process specific kinds of information. Single-cell recordings can then be used to determine whether one of the functions served by that region is a visual one.

A second criterion used to identify a cortical region as a visual area is evidence that the region contains a topographic map of the retina. This means that each location that we stimulate on the retinal surface should be directly related to a location where there is activity on the cortical surface. For example, if we have two points, A and B, that we stimulate on the retina, and then we stimulate a point C that is at a location halfway between A and B, we would expect that in the cortex, the neurons responding to C would also lie between the locations of the neurons responding to A and B. However, finding such exact maps on the cortex can sometimes be very tricky because the cortical surface is not flat but, rather, is folded, with convoluted wrinkles, rises, and deep indentations.

A third consideration used to determine the borders of distinct visual regions in the brain is a functional one. Specifically, the receptive field properties of the neurons in a given area should differ from the receptive field properties of those in other visual areas. As we will see later in this chapter, some visual areas contain topographic maps of the retina that are specialized for representing color; others are specialized for orientation of edges; and still others are specialized for the direction of motion.

Despite the many differences that exist between various topographic visual maps, they have a number of interesting features in common. One principle concerns a direct relationship between the amount of cortical tissue devoted to a function and the perceptual importance of that function. In visual topographic maps, it is very common to find large regions devoted to the central retina, with smaller areas of cortical "real estate" devoted to retinal locations farther from the fovea. This allows the average sizes of the receptive fields of neurons to be small in foveal regions, whereas they become increasingly larger as we move away from the center of the retina. Functionally this means that the neurons at the center of the map are able to register much finer details than those in outer reaches of the map. This relationship has been quantified for Area V1, where it has come to be known as **cortical magnification** (Hubel & Wiesel,

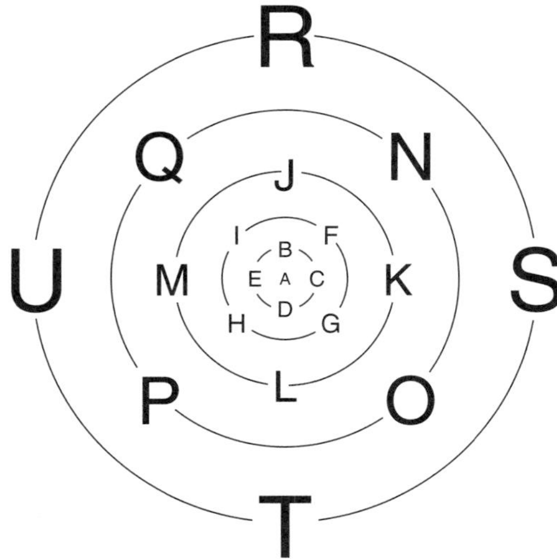

FIGURE 3.19 Letter sizes have been scaled so that when the central *A* is fixated, all other letters are approximately equally easy to read. This illustrates cortical magnification.

1974). A functional illustration of cortical magnification is shown in Figure 3.19, where letters have been scaled in size so that regardless of how far they are from the fovea they are approximately equal in readability.

Primary Visual Cortex

The most important cortical visual region is Area V1 because it is the first stop in the cortex and almost all of the signals received by the other cortical regions pass through it and are returned to it by back projections. For this reason, Area V1 is often referred to as the **primary visual cortex.** Another popular term for the same region is the **striate** ("striped") **cortex,** because when it is chemically stained and vertical slices are examined under the microscope, it has distinct dark stripes running through the middle. These stripes occur because the stain-sensitive variety of cells is more concentrated in middle layers of Area V1 than it is in other neighboring regions of the cortex.

The foveal region of the retina in humans is represented at the extreme rear of the cortex, sometimes referred to as the **occipital pole.** As one moves away from the pole, toward the front of the cortex, more peripheral visual field locations are represented among neurons that are farther away from the pole. The cortical map of the visual field is inverted and left-right reversed like the image on the retina. Locations in the upper half of the visual field are represented below a major convolution at the back of the cortex, known as the **calcarine fissure,** whereas locations in the lower half of the visual field are represented just above the calcarine fissure. The left half of the visual field is represented in the right occipital cortex, whereas the right half of the visual field is represented in the left occipital cortex. Thus, if we divided the V1 cortex into four equal quadrants, damage to the upper-right quadrant would result in blindness for the lower-left quadrant of the visual field.

As so often seems to be the case, the topographical mapping of Area V1 was discovered long before the development of modern staining and microelectrical recordings. The mapping was first discovered through studies of the way visual function was affected by head injuries that occurred in accidents and war. When a piece of visually sensitive primary cortex is damaged, the patient is blind in the corresponding part of the visual field. Such a blind patch in the visual field is called a **scotoma** (meaning "dark spot"). If the blinded region is so large as to encompass an entire quadrant of the visual field, it is called a **quadrantanopia.** If it encompasses an entire half of the visual field, it is referred to as a **hemianopia**. The complete loss of vision as the result of occipital lobe lesions is sometimes called **cortical blindness,** to distinguish it from the blindness caused by damage or malfunction of the eyes and optic tract. The consequences of various kinds of lesions to Area V1 can be seen in Figure 3.20.

It is in the cells of Area V1 that investigators first discovered visual receptive fields that differed in their spatial arrangement from the familiar circular on and off regions of ganglion cells. Instead of being circular, the receptive fields of these cells have an elongated central region that is oriented at a particular angle, along with elongated flanking regions that are opposite in their sign to that of the central region (Hubel & Wiesel, 1979). A schematic diagram of the probable way in which lateral geniculate neurons feed into cells in Area V1 is shown in Figure 3.21A, and the corresponding receptive fields are shown in Figure 3.21B. This particular example illustrates so-called **simple cells.** Simple cells generally have little spontaneous activity and never seem to respond to diffuse illumination covering the whole screen. They may respond weakly to small spots of light. However, the stimulus that really gets them firing vigorously is a dark or light bar that is flashed in the appropriate location and orientation in the receptive field. Because of this preference for edges of a particular angle, simple cells are said to have **orientation specificity** (e.g., Vanduffel, Tootell, Schoups, & Orban, 2002).

A second class of V1 neuron, and one that is actually found more frequently than the simple cell, is the **com-**

VISUAL FIELD LOSS

A. HEMIANOPIA

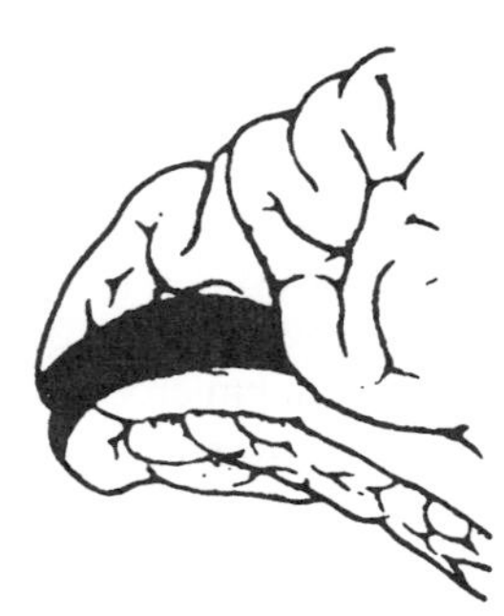

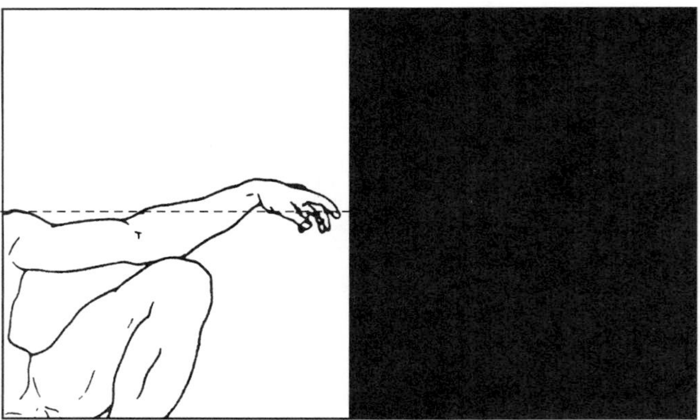

B. SCOTOMA

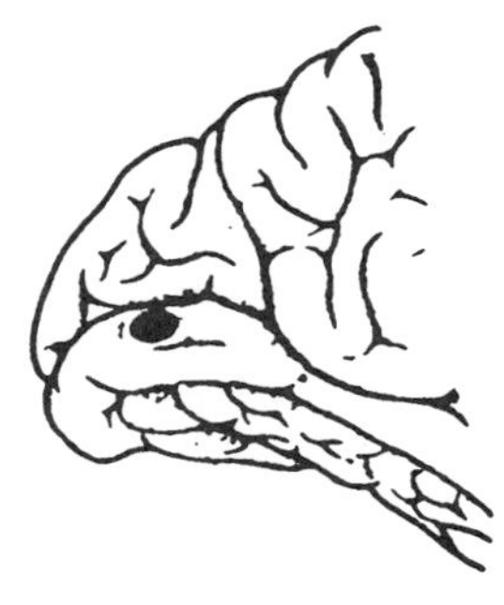

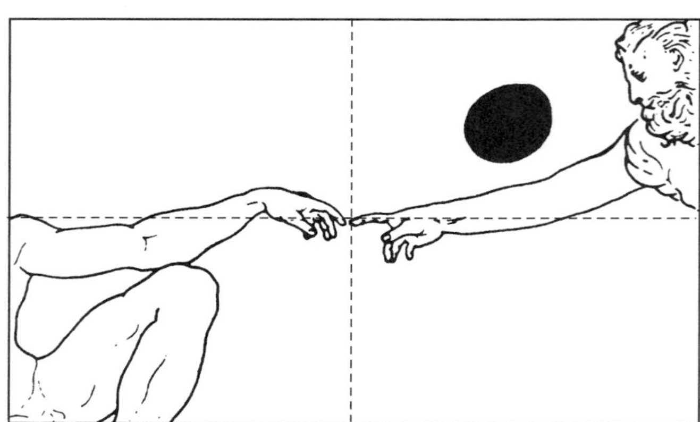

C. QUADRANTANOPIA

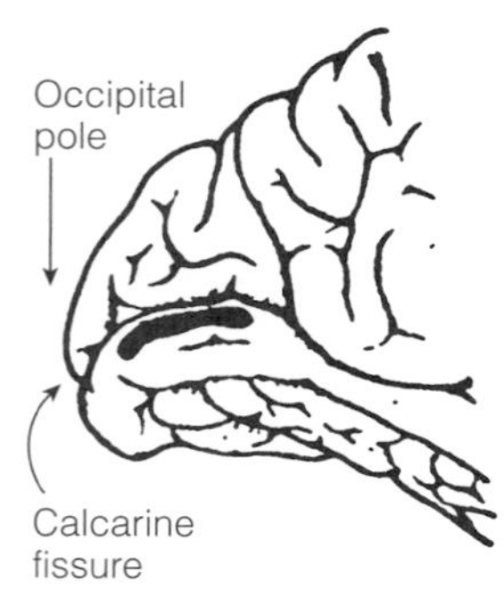

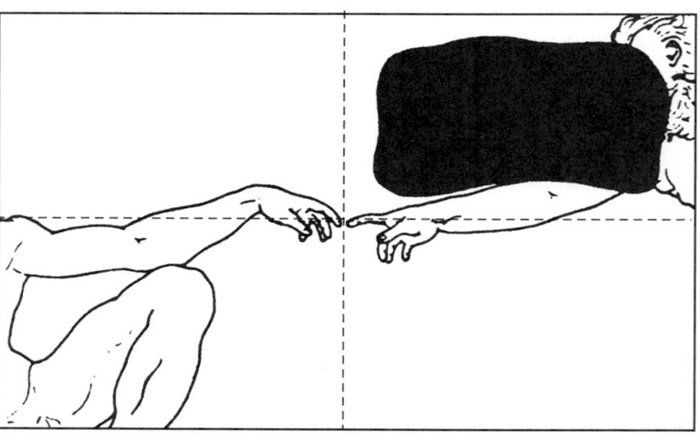

FIGURE 3.20 The consequences of various kinds of lesions to regions of Area V1.

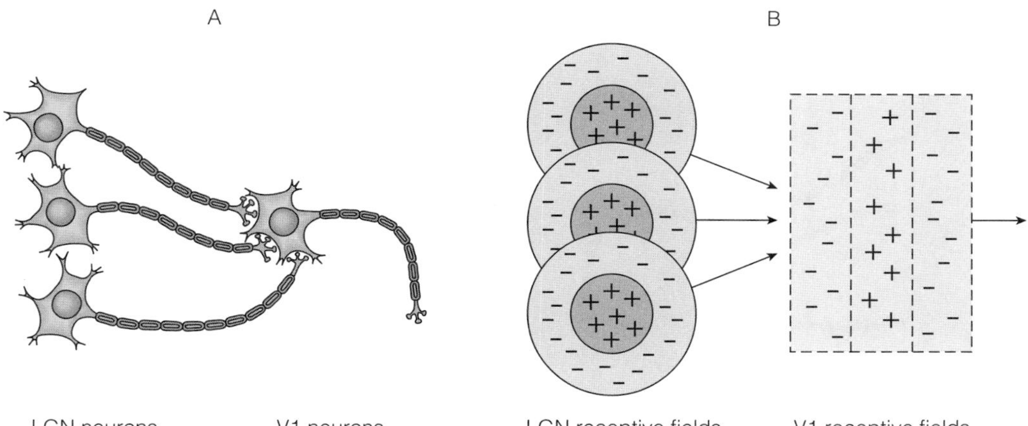

FIGURE 3.21 (A) The circuitry and (B) receptive fields of simple cell in area V1. Circular center-surround receptive fields of lateral geniculate neurons project forward into the elongated orientation-sensitive receptive fields of neurons in Area V1.

plex cell. Its receptive field and probable circuitry is illustrated in Figure 3.22. It is more complex in the sense that it will respond to an edge of particular orientation regardless of where that edge appears within the visual field. As a result, complex cells have larger receptive fields than do simple cells. In addition to responding maximally to oriented edges, complex cells prefer the edge to be moving in a direction that is orthogonal (at 90 degrees) to the orientation of the edge. What they therefore seem to prefer is a bar or edge that is moving in a given direction, anywhere within the receptive field (see Mechler & Ringach, 2002).

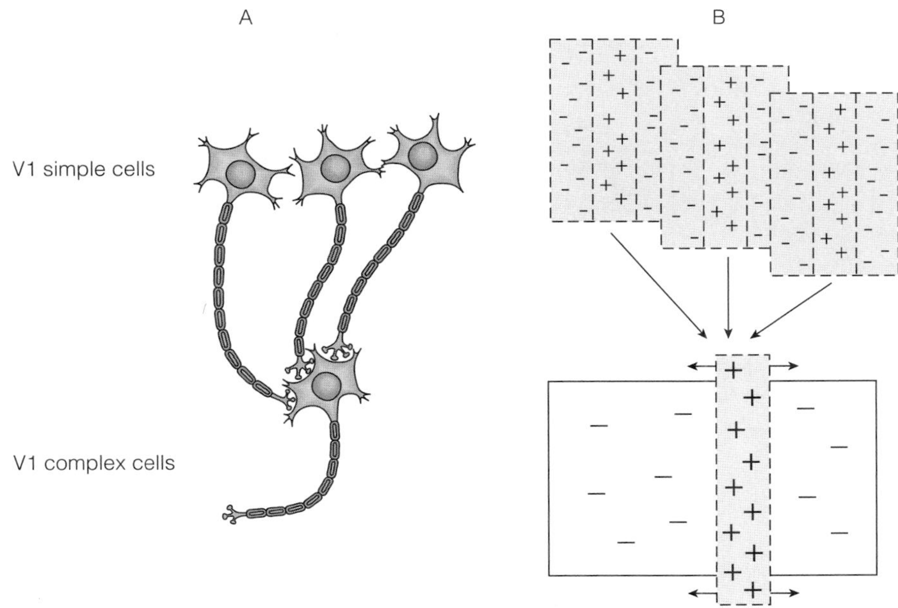

FIGURE 3.22 (A) The circuitry and (B) receptive fields of complex cell in Area V1. These cells are sensitive to the appropriately oriented bar moving orthogonal to their preferred edge, anywhere within their receptive field.

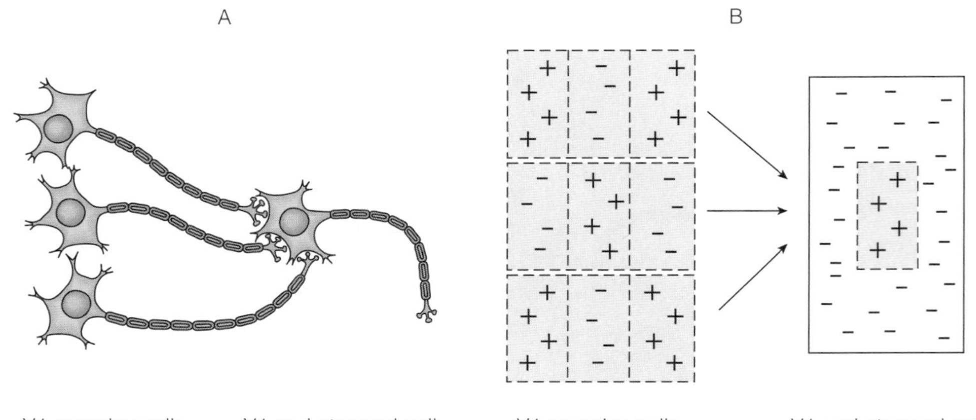

FIGURE 3.23 (A) The circuitry and (B) receptive fields of end-stopped cell in Area V1. These cells are sensitive to a bar that is of a specific length and orientation moving within the receptive field.

The third class of neuron found in Area V1 is the **end-stopped cell.** Its receptive field not only responds to an edge of a particular orientation, moving in a certain direction, but it does so only when the edge is of a specific length. As shown in Figure 3.23, the cell fires most vigorously when a bar of a particular length is moved into its receptive field. Bars that are longer than that actually have an inhibitory effect on the overall response. Also, if the flanking region of the receptive field is stimulated with an edge oriented differently from the edge that triggers the cell in the central region, the cell will continue to respond vigorously. This suggests that the underlying circuitry involves lateral inhibition, in the same way that ganglion cells tend to mutually inhibit their neighbors. What is new here is that the mutual inhibition is based on visual properties such as orientation and direction of motion rather than on simple spatial proximity.

Cells with these receptive field properties are not randomly intermixed in Area V1. The arrangement is intricate. The cells are arranged in six layers, which neuroscientists have numbered layers 1 to 6, beginning at the surface of the cortex. This is depicted in Figure 3.24. Some of these layers have been studied in greater detail, and as a result several sublayers have been given individual names, as can be seen, for example, in Layer 4. Cells in the middle layers, such as Layer 4 in the dia-

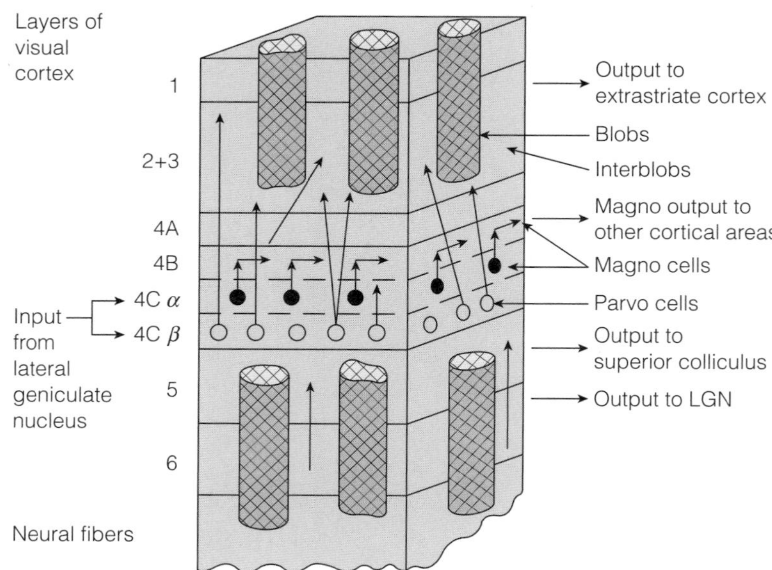

FIGURE 3.24 Location of various visually responsive cells in the layers of the Area V1.

gram, tend to receive input directly from the preceding visual region. In the case of Area V1, this is the lateral geniculate nucleus. Cells in the inner layers tend to send signals back to the lateral geniculate and on to other visual regions of the cortex, whereas cells in the outer and inner layers receive input in the form of back projections from these other visual centers in the brain.

The cell layer in Area V1 receiving inputs directly from the lateral geniculate bodies is Layer 4C. The classification system we saw in the retina and in the lateral geniculate nucleus is also preserved in Layer 4C, with magno cells being found in the top layer labeled 4C-α, and parvo cells being found in the lower layer labeled 4C-β. This is also illustrated in Figure 3.24.

Closer to the cortical surface, specifically in Layers 2, 3, and 4B, we find cells that connect with other visual centers in the cortex. They, too, appear to preserve the parvo-magno distinction, although in a somewhat different form. All of the magno cell inputs from input layer 4C–α go directly into sublayer 4B. This starts the motion-processing pathway because these cells are not sensitive to color but are selective for both orientation and movement.

The parvo cell pathway that departs from Area V1 is a bit more complex because it makes an additional subdivision. A cell-staining technique has shown that there are roughly cylindrical patterns of darkly stained cells in Layers 2 and 3, about 0.2 mm in diameter, that can be seen against a background of lighter cells (Wong-Riley, 1979). These dark regions have been called **blobs** and the light regions **interblobs.** The parvo cells that go into the blobs carry color and contrast information and are likely the origin of a stream of color processing. The cells in the interblob region respond selectively to the orientation of an edge but do not differentiate between edges of different colors (Livingstone & Hubel, 1988; Zeki, 1993).

Layers 5 and 6 of Area V1 also receive back projections from other areas of the visual cortex and contain specialized cells that are reminiscent of the parvo-magno distinction. Receptive fields of cells in Layer 5 are large and sensitive to the direction of stimulus movement, whereas those of cells in Layer 6 are rather long, narrow, and orientation sensitive.

The arrangement of cells across the horizontal surface of the cortex is also highly organized. Cells preferring a

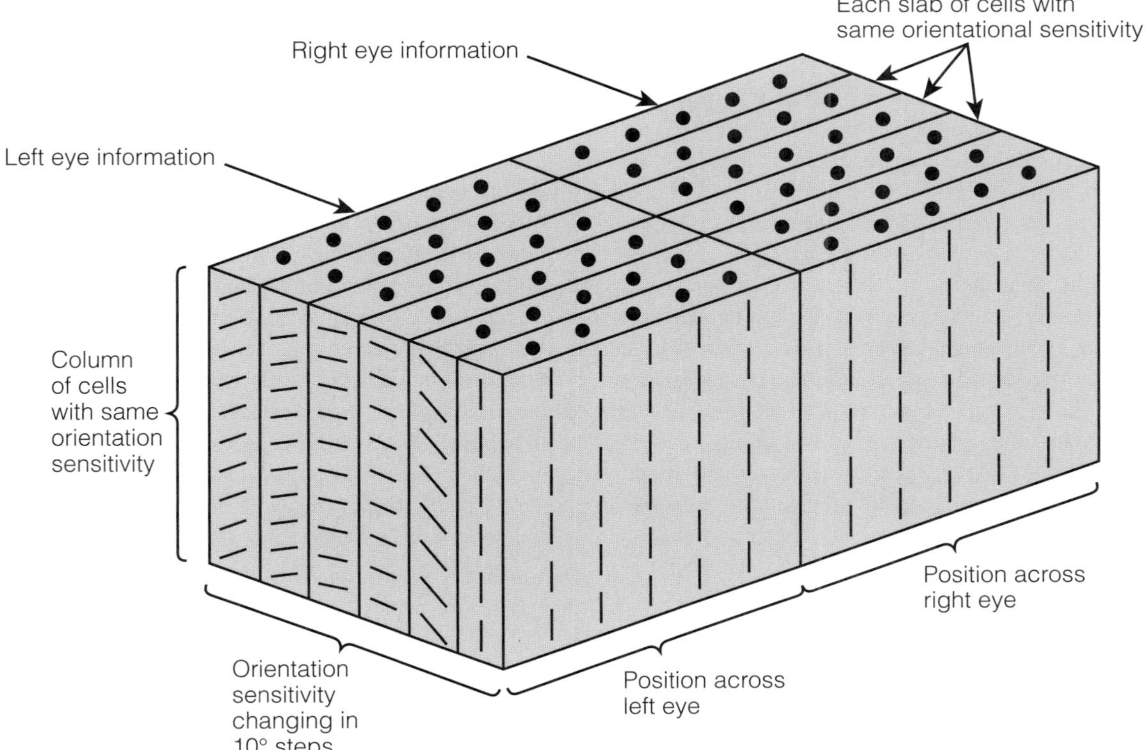

FIGURE 3.25 Diagram of a hypercolumn, which is a small region of visual cortex containing inputs from both eyes and all visual orientations.

particular orientation tend to be grouped into slabs and columns, as shown in Figure 3.25. As we move across the top of the cortex in one direction, the orientation specificity shifts by about 10 degrees per column. Moving in the other direction, we encounter columns of cells that have the same orientation sensitivity but that are more responsive to one particular eye than to the other, hence showing relative **eye dominance** (c.f. Crowley & Katz, 2002). A region of cortex containing all 360 degrees of orientation specificity, and including a region responsive to both the left eye and the right eye, forms a larger unit that neuroscientists call a **hypercolumn.** Such a piece of cortex might be between 0.5 and 1 mm square and 2 mm deep.

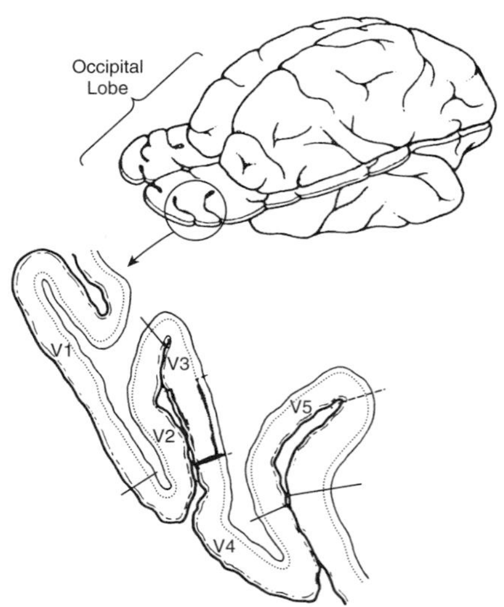

FIGURE 3.26 The locations of Areas V1–V5 in the occipital lobe of the cortex. An imaginary slab has been pulled out from the top drawing and expanded to show more detail.

MULTIPLE PARALLEL PATHWAYS

In addition to all of the functions we have already described for the primary visual cortex, one of its most important functions is to serve as a source for almost all of the other cortical visual maps. From V1, axons send neural messages directly and in parallel to many other visual maps. As a group, these other visual areas in the cortex are sometimes referred to as **prestriate cortex,** because they all lie in front of Area V1, or even as **extrastriate cortex,** where the term *extra* means "beyond" the striate cortex. It is important to note that axons arriving at the other visual areas from Area V1 do not carry the same information to each of these other cortical maps of the visual field. V1 segregates three major types of visual information—form, color, and motion—and routes these outputs to separate cortical regions for processing.

The visual area that is the nearest neighbor to V1 is (not surprisingly) called **Area V2.** It is not readily visible from the cortical surface because much of it is hidden in deep convolutions. Its position in the cortex is shown in Figure 3.26. Area V2 receives some input directly from the geniculate fibers as well as being connected point-to-point with Area V1. One of the most distinctive anatomical features of Area V2 is revealed in response to the same chemical stain that makes the blobs visible in V1. In Area V2 this stain reveals a set of dark stripes running vertically through the cortical tissue, interspersed between lighter stripes. Some of the dark stripes are relatively thick, whereas others are thin. Moreover, in the monkey, thick stripes and thin stripes appear in a repeating pattern separated by the lighter interstripes. Because Areas V1 and V2 represent visual information in similar ways and because both of these visual areas send axons to almost all of the other prestriate visual areas, some researchers now refer to the two areas together as the **V1-V2 complex** (Zeki, 1993).

Area V3: A Map for Form and Local Movement

Area V3 contains a visual map, separate from Areas V1 and V2, that lies largely buried within a fold of the cortex immediately in front of V1. It is shown in Figure 3.26. Some of its input comes directly from V2 and some comes directly from V1, without an intermediate stopover in V2. It is a complete point-to-point correspondence map of the visual field. One of the unique curiosities of V3 is that it has two representations of the foveal region of the retina. This suggests that it is specialized for the detailed kind of visual processing that the fovea is able to support with its high degree of receptor concentration.

Neurons in V3 receive their input both from the magnolike pathway (Layer 4B, thick stripe) and from the parvolike pathway (interblob, interstripe). Their receptive fields tend to be specific for edges of particular orientation; many are sensitive to motion, and most are not sensitive to color (Kaas & Lyon, 2001). Some researchers now see this area as a region specialized for the perception of forms, with additional information about how the forms or figures are moving, rotating, or changing, and there is also evidence that V3 helps in our depth perception by processing stereoscopic cues (Adams & Zeki, 2001).

Area V4: A Map for Color

An important clue to the specialized function of **Area V4,** shown in Figure 3.26, was seen over 100 years ago in a report concerning a 61-year-old woman who had suffered a stroke affecting the occipital lobe of her left hemisphere (Verrey, 1888). What we know now was that the woman's principal lesion lay well outside of Area V1, closer to the area known as V4. The most striking feature of the visual deficits that resulted from the stroke was an inability of the woman to see the world in color in the right half of her field of view. Colors in the left half of her visual field appeared normal, but everything in the right half was seen in shades of gray. Since the time of that report, many other patients have had similar problems stemming from cortical lesions (Zeki, 1990). At times they report a loss of color vision only on one side, and at other times they report a complete loss of color vision. To distinguish this from other forms of color blindness involving abnormal functioning of the retinal cones, this condition is called **cerebral achromatopsia.**

One of the curious features associated with this kind of color blindness is that it is often accompanied by a more general scotoma in the visual periphery. This at first seems paradoxical because color vision is primarily a visual function that is seen in the center of the visual field. However, the related conditions make perfect sense when we consider the locations of Areas V1 and V4 on the cortical surface, as shown in Figure 3.26. It is easy to see that because of their closeness, an injury that could cause a brain lesion in V4 might also cause some damage to the anterior portion of V1, where the peripheral field of view is mapped.

When we looked at the distribution of cones in Figure 3.9, we found that they were most densely concentrated in the central region of the retina in and around the fovea. Because cones carry the color information, it should not be surprising to find that Area V4 is an incomplete map of the visual field, with inputs mostly from the foveal regions of V1 and V2 and including only the central 40 degrees. Perhaps the most interesting property of V4 neurons is that their responses correspond to the perceived color of a surface, rather than to the actual wavelength composition of light that enters the eye (Zeki, 1983). As we will see in Chapter 4, our perception of colors depends not only on the wavelength of the light but also on the viewing conditions, type of illumination, and other stimuli in the environment. For instance, studies of monkeys with damage to V4 show that their basic ability to discriminate different wavelengths of light is still good. What is impaired is their ability to accurately perceive the color of surfaces under changing conditions of illumination (Heywood, Wilson, & Cowey, 1987). Work on humans who have damage to this same area suggests that V4 may be important for perceptually "gluing" the color onto the objects that it belongs to, and thus establishing clear boundaries between regions of the visual field (Gallant, Shoup, & Mazer, 2000).

Area V5: A Map for Global Motion

Area V5, shown in Figure 3.26, is specialized for detecting the speed and direction of motion. The importance of this visual area to everyday perception is made clear in the case of a 43-year-old female patient who had suffered a fairly small localized lesion in Area V5 because of a vascular disorder (Zihl, von Cramon, & Mai, 1983). Along with some lesser problems in performing arithmetic calculations and finding words for common objects, the most striking observation was the patient's inability to see objects in motion. She had difficulty, for example, pouring a cup of coffee because at any moment in time the fluid appeared to be frozen. As a result, she couldn't stop pouring at the right time. Her inability to see movement in a speaker's mouth also made it difficult to follow a conversation. Crossing the street was especially dangerous because she seemed unable to predict the speeds of approaching cars. This condition has been called **cerebral akinetopsia** because it is a form of motion (kinetic) blindness that is entirely cortical in nature.

Neurons in Area V5 receive their input from the thick stripes in V2 and some even directly from neurons in Area V1. Researchers have found that all neurons in V5 are sensitive to motion in one way or another and that over 90% of them are tuned to favor a particular direction. None of the neurons seems concerned with color or form (Zeki, 1974, 1993). There is an important distinction to be made for the way in which the V5 neurons are motion sensitive, relative to those in V3. That is, V5 neurons are sensitive to the overall direction of motion of an entire object, whereas the neurons in V3 seem to be mostly responsive to motion produced along particular edges, such as might occur when an object remains in one place but tilts or rotates (Movshon & Newsome, 1992; Zeki, 1993). To be this sensitive to properties of whole objects, rather than to local attributes of small regions on the retina, V5 neurons have very large receptive fields, indicating that they integrate information over a large retinal area (Zeki & Shipp, 1988). The receptive fields of some neurons in this region are nearly one half of the entire visual field, meaning that they are really concerned with whether or not an object is moving rather than precisely where it is at any moment in time.

The Parietal Lobes: A System for Knowing "Where?"

Up to now we have seen that there are different neural streams for carrying form, motion, and color and specialized cortical maps for the representation of this information (Van Essen & Waessle, 1990; Zeki, 1993). These streams and maps must interact and communicate with one another to produce the many varied aspects of our visual experience. Beyond the occipital lobe, there appear to be at least two distinctly different regions of the brain involved in visual processing, and these are in the parietal and the temporal lobes (Mishkin, Ungerleider, & Macko, 1983). These areas contain additional maps of the visual field, and some very complex visual processing takes place there. A diagram to help you localize these tertiary or "third-order" visual areas is shown in Figure 3.27.

The **parietal lobe** of the cortex seems to be specialized to answer the question "Where is it?" (e.g., Husain & Jackson, 2001). Monkeys with lesions in the parietal cortex have no difficulty learning to identify objects by sight alone; however, they have a great deal of difficulty learning to respond correctly to information about the location of objects (Mishkin & Lewis, 1982). Humans with brain damage to the parietal cortex also appear to be impaired on tasks that require relative location judgments but not on tasks that require simple object identification (Posner, 1988).

Patients who have suffered damage to the posterior parietal portion of the cortex often simply neglect objects in one half of their visual field, especially if the damage is to the right hemisphere (Milner & Goodale, 1995). These patients will sometimes be able to recognize the identity and meaning of an object, at the same time that they have a great deal of difficulty reaching appropriately for the object. This condition is called **optic axatia.** It is important to note that these same patients have no difficulty using other senses to control their reaching. Locating a spot on one arm with the finger of the other is done effortlessly if the spot has been identified by touch. These patients also have no difficulty describing in words the relative locations of objects and their approximate sizes. Their problem is thus neither motoric nor visual in itself. Rather, the problem is restricted to visually controlled action, which appears to be governed by neurons in the parietal lobe.

The Temporal Lobes: A System for Knowing "What?"

The specialty of the **temporal lobe** seems to lie in answering the question "What is it?" The importance of the lower temporal lobe, or **inferotemporal cortex,** in performing this function was discovered by Kluver and Bucy (1937). These researchers were observing monkeys that had undergone surgery to remove most of both tem-

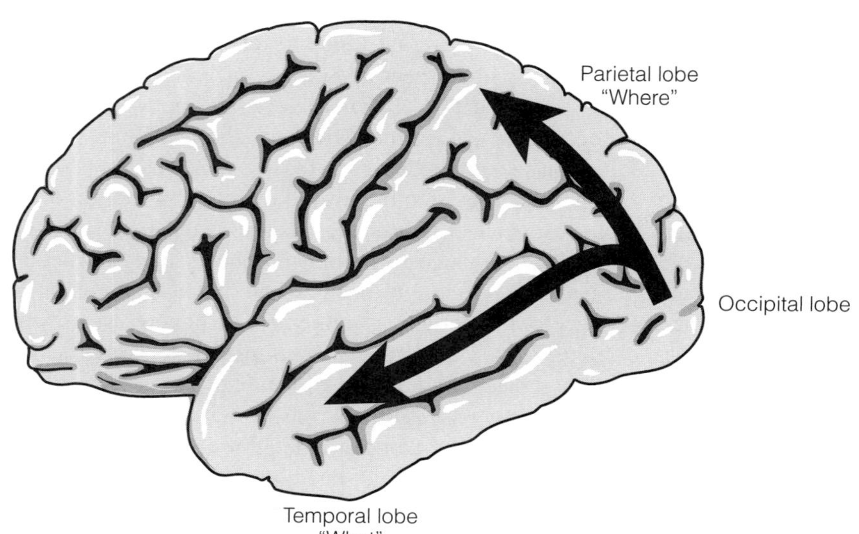

FIGURE 3.27 Two visual pathways that extend beyond the occipital lobe.

poral lobes. The animals could reach for, and accurately pick up, small items, and so they were clearly not blind. However, they appeared to have lost the ability to identify these objects by sight. This syndrome became known as **psychic blindness.** Its clearest manifestation can be seen in animals that are easily able to grasp objects they see but yet are completely unable to learn to discriminate between these objects by sight (Wilson, 1957).

This syndrome in monkeys is similar to a human defect called **visual agnosia** (e.g., Saumier, Arguin, Lefebvre, & Lassonde, 2002). These patients can see all parts of the visual field, but the objects that they see mean nothing to them, as indicated by the title of the popular book, *The Man Who Mistook His Wife for a Hat* (Sacks, 1987).

Investigators recording the responses of single neurons in the inferotemporal cortex of monkeys have made some startling discoveries. They have found neurons that are sensitive to the specific size, shape, color, orientation, and direction of movement of an object (Desimone, Schein, Moran, & Ungerleider, 1985). Gross, Rocha-Miranda, and Bender (1972) reported that one day they accidentally discovered a neuron that, although unresponsive to any particular simple shape, responded vigorously when they waved their hand in front of the screen. They spent the next 12 hours testing various paper cutouts in an attempt to find out what feature triggered this specific unit. When all the stimuli of the set were ranked according to the strength of the response they produced, the experimenters could not find any simple physical dimension that correlated with this rank order. However, the rank order of stimuli, in terms of their ability to drive the neuron, did correlate with their apparent similarity (at least for the experimenters) to the shadow of a monkey's paw. Overall the data suggest that the inferotemporal cortex seems to be specially tuned to recognize objects, perhaps objects that are frequently seen (see Tanaka, 1996).

Even more startling degrees of specificity seem to characterize neurons in the upper region of the temporal lobe, the **superior temporal cortex.** In monkeys, neurons in this region have been found to respond selectively to faces (Bruce, Desimone, & Gross, 1981) and to particular movements of faces, such as back and forth or rotation (Perrett & Mistlin, 1987). The strongest responses are given to the most realistic and most monkey-like of the faces. Distorting the stimulus by removing the eyes, scrambling the features, or presenting a cartoon caricature results in a weaker response. Kendrick and Baldwin (1987) have found similar neurons in sheep that respond preferentially to sheep faces and, interestingly, even to human faces as well. Thus, it is likely that in your temporal cortex there are neurons that respond best to the image of your grandmother, ones that respond to your car, and ones that respond best to each of the other shapes that are familiar to you.

THE PROBLEM OF VISUAL UNITY

By now you must be impressed by the large number of different maps of the visual field that can be found in the cortex. All of these maps are operating at the same time or, as vision researchers say, in parallel, performing specialized tasks that are critical for visual perception, such as identifying and localizing objects and determining their color, shape, and state of motion. We have seen how each of these maps is constructed by careful selection of only some of the information available in the entire field of view. A convenient summary of the pathways leading to these maps, and interactions among them, is shown in Figure 3.28. As you can see from that diagram, the motion map in Area V5 is based largely on the information conveyed by the magnocellular pathway that begins in the ganglion cells of the retina and that is further refined in the cells of Layer 4B in Area V1 and the thick-stripe regions of Area V2 before arriving in Area V5. The color map in Area V4, on the other hand, gets its information from parvo retinal ganglion cells via the blob regions of Area V1 and the thin stripes of Area V2.

This specialized function of so many areas within the cortex leads to the question, "Why are there so many different maps of the visual field?" Wouldn't one map containing all of the information be enough? To help us think about this, we must first remember that the function of the visual system is not to re-create an image of the outside world in the brain. Remember, there is nobody inside your brain who could look at such an image even if it were there. The function of the visual system is to recognize objects, to locate them in space, and to assist individuals to respond appropriately to objects and events in their environment. Many investigators have suggested that the multiple maps in the visual field were created to increase perceptual speed. Processing several lines of information in parallel is very fast and efficient—much like having a series of diagnostic medical tests (e.g., blood, urine analysis, and X-rays) all run at the same time and analyzed in different laboratories, rather than waiting for the first set of test results and then starting the next in some sequential manner (Livingstone & Hubel, 1988; Phillips, Zeki, & Barlow, 1984). Others have pointed out that the computations involved in processing such attributes as motion and color are themselves so different that it is almost a neces-

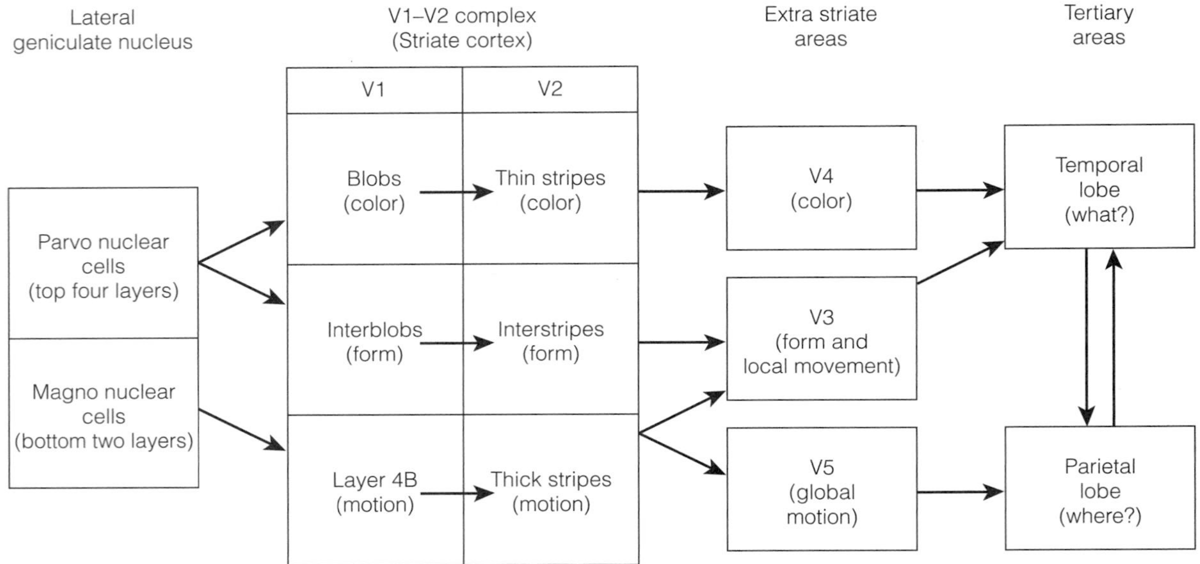

FIGURE 3.28 A highly schematic overview of the geniculostriate visual pathway to the cortex.

sity to keep them isolated from one another (Ballard, Hinton, & Sejnowski, 1983; Zeki, 1993).

Given that there are so many maps, the next question is, "How can our visual experience be that of a single, coherent visual world, given the fact that the processing of the information is fragmented into many separate maps, in many places in the brain, each with separate information processing aims?" We will consider this question in every chapter in this book, but we will look at it again with special interest in Chapter 14, "Consciousness." For now, it is important to remind ourselves that the various neural regions we have described are in constant communication with each other, through both feed-forward and feed-back projections. This means that it is a mistake to think of any of the individual visual processes we have described as occurring in isolation.

Dynamic Receptive Fields

Neuroscientists are beginning to take this more dynamic view of the brain into account in their studies of the behavior of individual cells. They have found, for example, that neurons in Area V1 can be triggered by information that is distant from the classical receptive field as studied originally by Hubel and Wiesel (1962, 1974). When the behavior of neurons is examined more closely for influences of context, it turns out that neurons in Area V1 have receptive fields that are much more dynamic than was originally thought (Albright & Stoner, 2002).

An example is shown in Figure 3.29. In this study by Fiorani, Rosa, Gattass & Rocha-Miranda (1992), the classical receptive field of a neuron was first mapped in the usual way by finding the right combination of visual field location and preferred orientation of an edge. A stationary occluding square that was much larger than the classical receptive field was then placed over the same region. This was to make sure that any activity in the neuron could not be triggered by stimuli in its receptive field as conventionally defined. Several different edges were then swept over regions of visual field that were adjacent to the receptive field, which was itself covered with the occluding square. Remarkably, when an edge was used that extended beyond the receptive field on both sides, the neuron produced a burst of activity that was just as strong as though it had been stimulated directly. This meant that it had been informed about its favorite edge indirectly, by the activity of neighboring neurons. A second important feature of this ability to activate a neuron indirectly is that its firing was delayed slightly relative to the speed with which it responded under direct stimulation. This is probably because its input was arriving via lateral connections and feedback that took slightly longer to develop than did direct stimulation.

Data like these suggest that we may have to change our view of the neurons that process visual information. At this moment we have a presumption that each one is "tuned" for a specific feature or aspect of the visual stim-

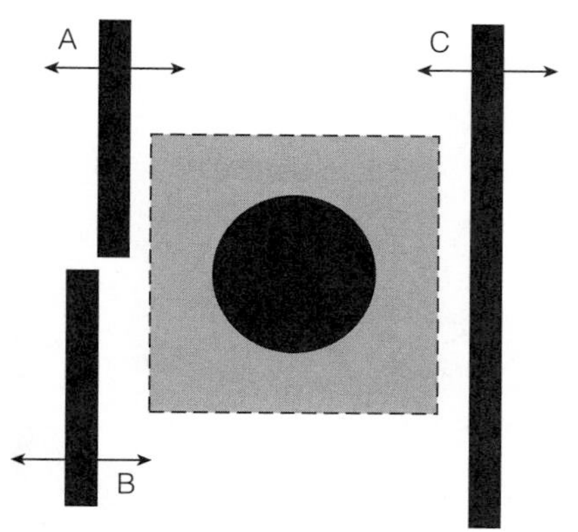

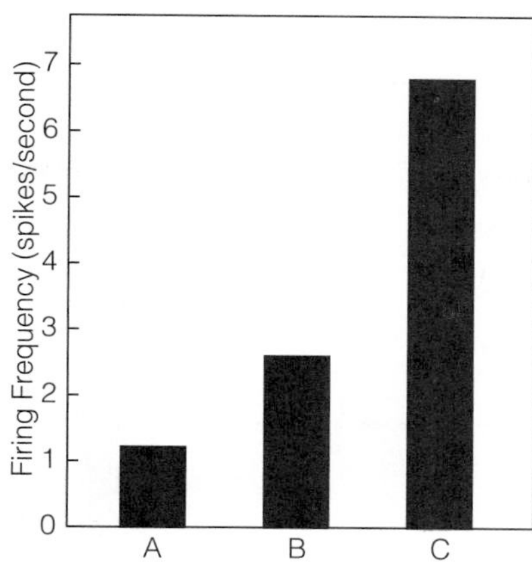

FIGURE 3.29 The black disk illustrates the classical receptive field of a neuron in Area V1. The gray square represents an occluding stimulus that prevents the receptive field from being stimulated directly. The black bars labeled A, B, and C are three different types of moving edge. The graph records the firing rate of the neuron for each of the three types of edge (based on Fiorani et al., 1992).

uli, or perhaps at higher levels, even for specific objects. The more dynamic view suggests that individual visual cortical neurons are part of a network, or a complex circuit. The response of any one unit is not determined solely by one type of information that it receives, but rather reflects everything else going on around it. Thus a given cell may change its "tuning" from one situation to another (c.f. Casagrande, Xu, & Sary, 2002).

STUDY QUESTIONS

1. List the main parts of a neuron and describe the function of each.
2. Describe the way a neuron communicates to other neurons using the sodium-potassium pump.
3. What is the main way in which sensory receptors communicate with other neurons? What about interneurons?
4. List some differences between the microscopic and macroscopic approaches to the study of the nervous system.
5. Draw and label the main structures of the human eye.
6. Draw and label the main layers of neurons within the retina.
7. Ganglion cells come in several different varieties. Describe their differences along two dimensions: on-center versus off-center and parvo versus magno.
8. Show how the visual fields' quadrants are mapped onto the retinal surface. Then show how the visual fields' quadrants are mapped onto Area V1.
9. What are the main differences between the tectopulvinar and the geniculostriate visual pathways?
10. What is a hypercolumn?
11. List three extrastriate visual areas in the cortex and describe the visual impairments that result from damage to each one.
12. How are the temporal and parietal lobes specialized for different aspects of vision?

CHAPTER 4

BRIGHTNESS AND COLOR

CHAPTER SUMMARY

The following scene must have played countless times in horror films and in episodes of *The X-Files:* It is night, and in the darkness two ragged old beachcombers can barely be seen moving along the water's edge. Suddenly, one stops.

"Hey, Charlie, I think there's something out there."

"Wha- What is it?"

"I can't make it out. It's some sort of glow. It looks kinda greenish but it's too dim to make out what it is."

This scene illustrates the most basic property of vision, namely, that it depends on the presence of light. The most primitive visual percepts are simply reactions to the presence of and nature of the incoming energy. These responses are represented in consciousness as a brightness or lightness and the awareness of a color. We often sense the presence of light before sufficient energy exists for us to apprehend shape or form. Thus, the next line of dialogue in the preceding scene usually goes, "It's getting brighter," and then as the energy becomes sufficient for the two characters to apprehend the object itself, "Are those red spots eyes? Oh, my God! It's some sort of creature!" As we shall see, the perception of brightness and color is much more complex and surprising than the script of this particular film.

PHOTOMETRIC UNITS

Electromagnetic energy, or light, can vary along three dimensions: intensity, wavelength, and duration. All dimensions are important in the perception of brightness and color, although brightness varies most directly with intensity whereas color is most dependent on wavelength. Let's start our discussion with brightness, since, at least intuitively, it appears to be a simpler sensory experience, and the measurement of how much light is present seems like it should be an easy matter of physical measurement.

Photometric units are used to describe light, and these units are, by convention, expressed in terms of energy. There are two ways by which light can reach the eye: (a) directly from a radiating source such as a light bulb or a firefly or (b) indirectly by reflection from surfaces that have radiant energy falling on them, such as trees or walls. Different types of measures are used for these different types of light input. All photometric units, however, are ultimately based on the amount of light emitted from a single burning candle. The nature of this standard candle, its photic energy, and the specific measures derived from it have been fixed.

Each different aspect of light is designated by its own name and requires a different measurement unit, and these are summarized in Figure 4.1 for a situation where we have a projector shining light on a screen. Let us begin with the light measures that can be taken with a photometer (a physical light-measuring device). The amount of energy coming from a light source (e.g., the projector bulb) is called its **radiance.** The unit of radiance is the standard candle, which produces an energy of slightly more than 0.001 watt at a wavelength of 555 nm. This quantity of luminous energy is called a **lumen.** The amount of light falling on a surface (e.g., the screen) is another photometric quantity called **illuminance.** The amount of light reflected from a surface is called its **luminance,** and the percentage of light falling on a surface that is reflected is called its **reflectance.** Re-

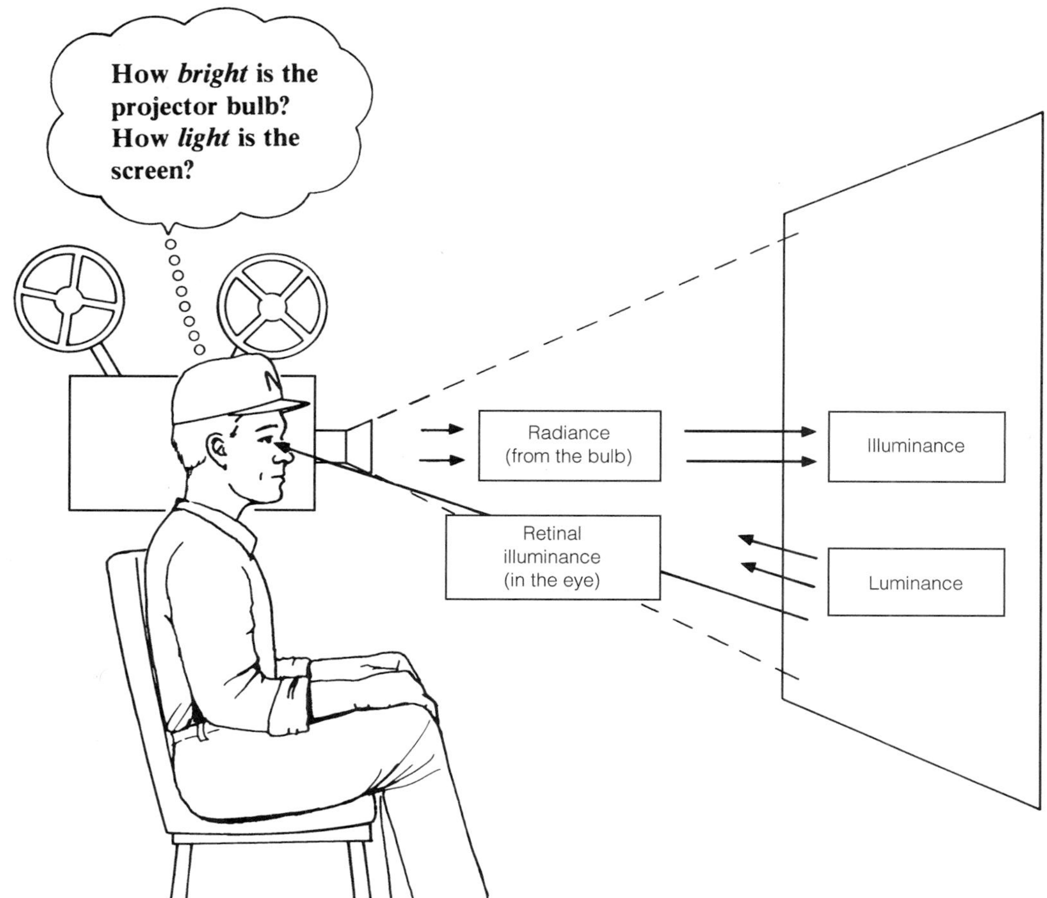

FIGURE 4.1 The relationship between various physical measures of light and psychological judgments of brightness and lightness.

TABLE 4.1 Photometric Units

Photometric Term	What is Measured	Unit	How Measured	Comments
Radiance or luminous flux	Radiant energy from a light source	Lumen	A candela is the light of a 1-lumen source at a distance of 1 m shone on a square meter	Defined in terms of a standard candle (candela)
Illuminance	Light falling on a surface	Lux	1 lumen/m^2	As the source moves farther away illuminance decreases
Luminance	Light reflected from a surface	Candelas per square meter	Luminance = $\frac{\text{Illuminance} \times \text{Reflectance}}{100}$	Independent of distance of eye from surface
Reflectance (albedo)	Proportion of light reflected from surface	Percentage reflectance	Reflectance = $\frac{\text{Luminance}}{\text{Illuminance}} \times 100$	Really ratio of reflected to incident light
Retinal illuminance	Amount of light incident on the retina	Trolands	1 candela/m^2 seen through pupil of 1 mm^2 area	Roughly 0.0036 lumens/m^2 through a 1-mm^2 pupil

flectance is thus 100 times the ratio of luminance to illuminance. The amount of light reaching the retina is called the **retinal illuminance.** Table 4.1 summarizes these photometric quantities, along with how they are measured, the units used, and some of their specific properties.

There are two important measures of our subjective impressions of light intensity in which vision researchers are interested. These are not physical measures but instead are measures of our experience. The first of these is a measure of **brightness,** the phenomenal impression of the amount of light that is being emitted from a source or reflected from a surface. Thus, a subject might be asked to "adjust the amount of light coming from this adjustable patch so that it appears to be the same brightness as that of the test patch." Brightness is the psychological attribute corresponding roughly to the physical measures of illuminance (if the light source is being viewed directly) and luminance (if the light source is being judged indirectly by its effect on a reflecting surface). The second measure is one of **lightness,** the phenomenal impression of the percentage of reflected light relative to the total light falling on a surface. Lightness (sometimes referred to as "whiteness") is the psychological correlate of the physical measure of reflectance. In this case a subject might be asked to "make this adjustable patch appear as if it were cut from the same piece of paper as the test patch." Thus, lightness refers to the observer's impression of whether the pigment of a reflecting surface appears to be white, gray, or black.

Why is it necessary to distinguish between the various physical measurements that we can make and the psychological experience of brightness? It is necessary because the perception of brightness cannot be explained simply by specifying the amount of light reaching the eye. As we noted in Chapter 2, when we plot the magnitude of brightness sensation against the physical stimulus intensity, we get a relationship that is not one to one. Brightness measured by a direct scaling technique (such as magnitude estimation) grows approximately as the cube root of the physical intensity (to be precise, the phenomenal sensation grows at a rate equivalent to the light intensity raised to the 0.33 power). This means that if we had a theater stage illuminated by eight lights and we wished to double the perceived brightness of the area, doubling the number of lights to 16 would not double the perceived brightness but instead would increase it by only one third. If we wanted to double the phenomenal brightness, we would have to increase the number of lights to 64!

Figure 4.2 shows the general shape of this relationship graphically. Notice that the curve in Figure 4.2 resembles the logarithmic curve of Fechner's law (remember Chapter 2 and particularly Figure 2.13). For this reason, various photometric values, such as the brightness scales used in television studios, are frequently presented in logarithmic units, especially when designed for visual purposes. This serves to equalize the sizes of the sensory changes as a function of changes in physical intensity. The unit of brightness in the graph in Figure 4.2 is the **bril,** which was suggested by S. S. Stevens. Each bril represents about 1/10 of a log unit above threshold of detection for a human observer. Some evidence suggests that the magnitude of neural responses in the primary visual cortex is more closely related to our perception of brightness than to the amount of illumination on the retina (Rossi, Rittenhouse, & Paradiso, 1996).

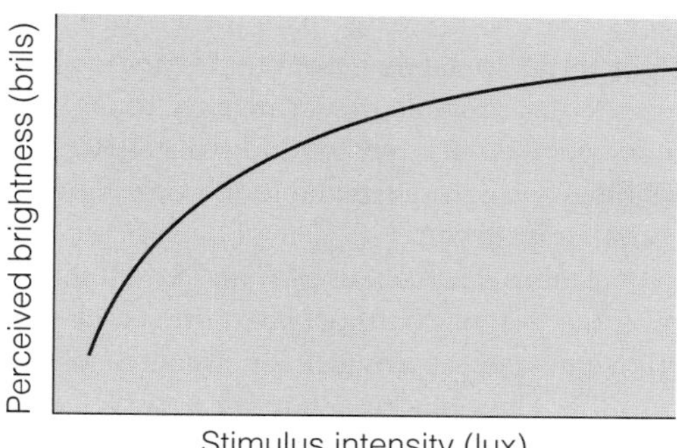

FIGURE 4.2 The nonlinear relationship between stimulus intensity and brightness.

BRIGHTNESS PERCEPTION

Dark and Light Adaptation

The perception of brightness depends on the current state of sensitivity of your eye, in much the same way that the brightness of the final photographic image depends on the sensitivity of the film. An amount of light that may produce a faint image on insensitive film may produce an overly bright image on very sensitive film. You are probably aware that your eyes change in sensitivity when you walk from a darkened room into the bright sunlight. Everything suddenly appears to be so bright and "washed out" that a few moments must pass before objects are clearly visible. The opposite occurs when you walk from a bright outside into a darkened movie theater. Now everything appears to be very dark, and objects are difficult to resolve in the gloom. After a while you can discern objects, although the adaptation to the darkness takes much longer than the adaptation to the brighter environment. We call the process of adaptation to a darker environment **dark adaptation** and that to a brighter environment **light adaptation.** Although we cannot slip off our daylight retina and put on the twilight one in the way that we change film in a camera to accommodate changes in lighting conditions, the sensitivity of our eyes does change through these two adaptation processes.

To monitor the changes in sensitivity associated with dark adaptation, we first adapt an observer to bright light by putting him in a brightly lit room for a few minutes; then we turn off the lights. Now we test to find the observer's absolute threshold for the detection of a light that is shone a bit off center and repeat this measurement at fixed intervals. Such an experiment reveals that the observer at first needs relatively strong stimuli to reach threshold; however, the eye rapidly becomes more sensitive over the first minute or two, at which point it begins to stabilize at a level that is about 100 times more sensitive (2 log units) than when we initially turned off the lights. After about 10 minutes of darkness, the sensitivity begins to increase rapidly again. During this second period, the threshold drops quickly for 5 or 10 minutes, then again stabilizes, reaching a relatively constant level after about a half hour. When we graph the change in threshold for a typical observer, as we have done in Figure 4.3A, we can see a break, or kink, in the sensitivity curve. The kink indicates a change in the rate of dark adaptation.

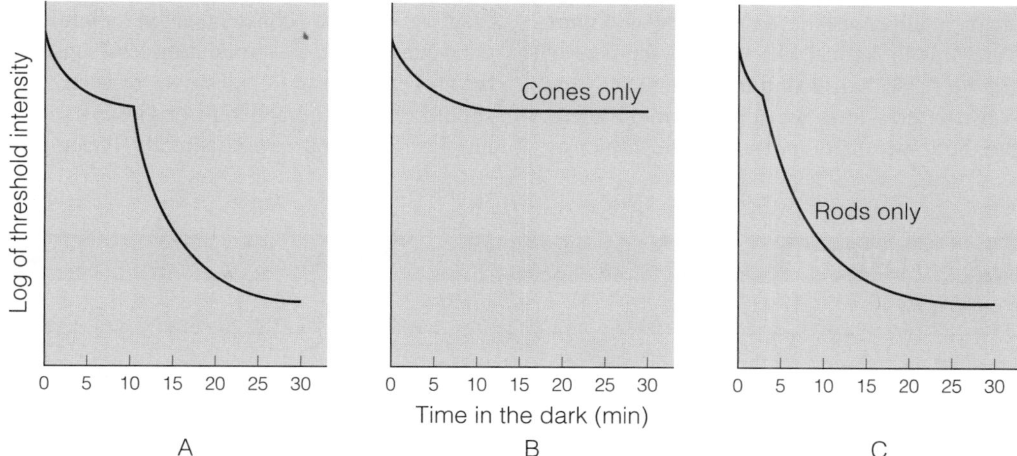

FIGURE 4.3 (A)The normal time course of dark adaptation, (B) dark adaptation in the cones (or central fovea), and (C) dark adaptation in the rods (or periphery).

When a sudden transition or break is found in a curve, it often suggests that a second process has come into operation. This is confirmed here by the fact that there is a marked change that occurs in conscious perception near this sharp break in the curve. For instance, if we used a green-colored light to measure the threshold, the observer would be able to identify the color throughout the first 10 minutes or so of the test session. At about the point at which the threshold suddenly begins to drop again, the light would seem to lose its color and become grayish. This confirms the old proverb, "At night, all cats are gray."

The two distinct portions of the dark adaptation curve are associated with the two types of photoreceptors in the retina, rods and cones. Animals that are active during the twilight hours tend to have mostly rods in their retina while animals that are active during daylight have mostly cones. Cones provide **photopic** or daylight vision (including the perception of color), and rods provide **scotopic** or twilight vision. Humans have both rods and cones, and the two segments of the dark adaptation curve represent separate rod and cone contributions. Cones quickly reach their level of maximal sensitivity while rods take longer to adapt. The rods are more sensitive to light but at the expense of giving up color vision. The point at which the adaptation of the rods catches up to that of the cones is the break in the dark-adaptation curve shown in Figure 4.3A.

We can verify this experimentally. Suppose we return to the experimental situation that we used to track the course of dark adaptation. Now we change the stimulus so that we are focusing a tiny pencil of light only on the central fovea when we take threshold measurements. Because the central fovea contains only cones (Chapter 3), this method allows us to track dark adaptation in cones. Such an experiment gives us the data shown in Figure 4.3B. Notice that this looks just like the first segment of the curve in Figure 4.3A. No second increase in sensitivity occurs, no matter how long we continue in darkness. To demonstrate the lower or rod portion of the curve, we repeat the experiment, except that now we focus our pencil of light about 20 degrees from the center of the fovea, where the retina contains predominantly rods. When we do this, we get the curve shown in Figure 4.3C, in which the first rapid change (attributable to cone action) is almost completely absent.

An even more spectacular way to show the separate rod and cone origin for the two portions of the dark adaptation curve was provided by Hecht and Mandelbaum (1938). They placed a normal observer on a diet deficient in vitamin A for 57 days. Because this vitamin is critical for the synthesis of rhodopsin, the pigment in rods, the diet effectively eliminated the action of these receptors. After 57 days, the observer had a dark adaptation curve similar to that in Figure 4.3B. Not only was the rod portion of the curve almost totally absent, but also the individual was almost completely night blind and unable to see dimly illuminated targets. By the way, the observer completely recovered when he went back to his normal diet. Perhaps similar naturally occurring instances have given carrots (a vegetable high in vitamin A) their reputation for being "good for the eyes."

Overall, these experiments indicate that two separate photoreceptor mechanisms are involved in the perception of brightness: the cone system for brighter illumination and the rod system for dimmer illumination. Demonstration Box 4.1 allows you to see the effects of dark adaptation for yourself.

Retinal Locus

Suppose the perceived brightness of a light depended directly on the sensitivity of the stimulated receptors, as well as on the intensity of the light. If that were the case, then moving a constant light stimulus across the dark-adapted retina, stimulating less-sensitive cones near the fovea and more-sensitive rods in the periphery, should change the apparent brightness of the light. This has been verified experimentally (Drum, 1980; Osaka,

DEMONSTRATION BOX 4.1

DARK ADAPTATION

To show the dramatic increase in sensitivity associated with dark adaptation, you should first carefully blindfold one eye. Use a couple of cotton balls and some tape to do this. After about 30 minutes, darken the room, or step into a reasonably dark closet. Remove the blindfold and compare the sensitivity of your two eyes by alternately opening one eye at a time. The dark-adapted eye should see quite well in the dim illumination, but the other eye will be virtually blind.

1981). Peripheral targets appear brighter than central ones. This finding is also embodied in a bit of folk wisdom. At some time in antiquity people noted that looking directly at a dim object, such as a star, could cause it to disappear from view. For this reason, early astronomers would often look at a point off to the side of a star in order to let its image fall upon the more sensitive peripheral retina (containing mostly rods). This technique allows such a dim target to be perceived more clearly. If you try this yourself, look at a point about 20 degrees from the star that you wish to see. (Twenty degrees of visual angle is about twice the width of your hand held at arm's length.) This allows the star's image to fall on the part of the retina where the density of rods is greatest and gives you maximum sensitivity.

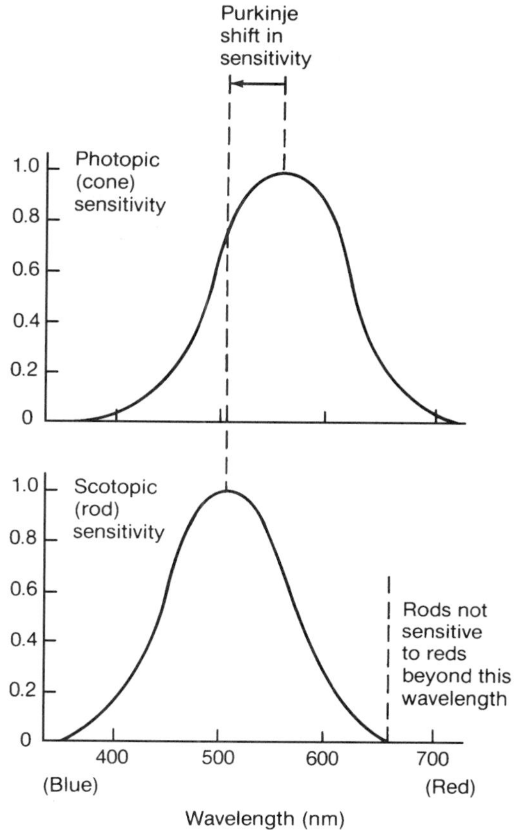

FIGURE 4.4 Differences in relative sensitivity to various wavelengths under photopic and scotopic illumination conditions.

Wavelength

The wavelength of the light will also affect our perception of its brightness. For instance, yellow light (medium wavelengths) almost always appears to be brighter than blue light (short wavelengths). The usual procedure for assessing the relative brightness of lights of different colors is to use a bipartite target. This is simply a circular target that has been divided in half, with one half containing the standard color that is to be matched in brightness and the other half containing the comparison color that is adjustable. Systematically pairing various colors and then matching their brightness provides a set of measures of the relative amounts of energy needed to produce equal sensations of brightness for various wavelengths of light. For convenience, the wavelength requiring the least energy to equal the brightness of the standard is set at a value of 1.0. All other wavelengths, being less effective in producing the brightness sensation, are assigned values less than 1.0, depending on their relative brightnesses.

After this conversion has been made, a curve can be plotted as in Figure 4.4. Such a curve is called a **luminosity curve.** Notice that we actually have two curves in this figure. The first is labeled photopic and represents the results that we would obtain from the matching experiment if the standard were at daylight levels of light intensity. It has a peak sensitivity for wavelengths around 555 nm, and the brightness falls off rapidly for shorter (toward the blue) or longer (toward the red) wavelengths. If we repeat this matching experiment under conditions in which the standard is dim, so that only rod vision is operating, the observer will not be aware of the color of the stimuli, and both halves of the field will appear gray regardless of their wavelength. Nonetheless, some wavelengths will still look brighter than others. Thus, we can map out the luminosity curve that is marked scotopic in Figure 4.4. Under these conditions the curve is somewhat different, with a peak around 505 nm. This curve is shifted toward the short wavelengths, suggesting that we are more sensitive to blue-green light under dim viewing conditions.

The change in the brightness of light of different wavelengths as the intensity is changed was first described by the Czechoslovakian phenomenologist Johannes E. Purkinje, and in his honor this phenomenon is referred to as the **Purkinje shift.** He first noted the change while looking at his garden as twilight was falling. As the light dimmed, the brightnesses of the various colored flowers began to change. Reds that had been bright relative to blues and greens began to look darker, whereas the bluer tones appeared relatively brighter. Because scotopic vision lacks the sensation of color, daylight greens or blues change to moonlight grays, whereas daylight reds change to moonlight blacks. Demonstration Box 4.2 allows you to experience the Purkinje shift in visual sensitivity for yourself.

There is an interesting application of the Purkinje shift. You may remember from watching war movies that the briefing rooms next to airstrips or the control rooms of ships and submarines are often depicted as illuminated by red light. This red is not used solely for dramatic effect in the film but is actually used in such real-world settings. Rods are relatively insensitive to the red end of the spectrum; hence red light is virtually equivalent to no light at all for the rods. However, the cones still function at these longer wavelengths if there is sufficient stimulus intensity, so the cones may be used while the rods are beginning to dark adapt. The dashed line in the bottom part of Figure 4.4 shows a wavelength beyond which the rods no longer function while the cones still do. Thus, pilots about to fly night missions, or sailors about to stand the night watch, can be briefed or can check their instruments under red illumination, then function efficiently in the dark without waiting the many minutes necessary to completely dark adapt.

There is another practical application of this information. In years past fire engines were traditionally painted red since red is such a dramatic color. However, today you are apt to see fire equipment mostly in yellow and yellow-greens (e.g., Color Plate 3). Can you derive why that is the case from the data that we just told you about?

Time and Area

In addition to depending on the intensity, wavelength, and retinal location of the stimulus, our ability to detect a spot of light depends on two other important factors. For instance, a photographer knows that when she is taking a picture under dim illumination she may have to lengthen the exposure time in order to collect enough light to register the image adequately on the film. In bright sunlight a short exposure will usually do. Actually, the same amount of physical energy is necessary to expose the film properly in each case; it just takes longer to collect the requisite amount under dim illumination. In physics this relationship is known as the **Bunsen-Roscoe law.** This law describes the photochemical reaction of any light-sensitive substance, whether it be film or visual pigment. We find that there is a similar tradeoff between stimulus duration and stimulus intensity in vision when we are dealing with the problem of the absolute threshold for brightness perception. There it is known as **Bloch's law.** This means that a weak stimulus must be presented for a long time in order for it to be detected, whereas a more intense stimulus can be presented for a shorter duration and still be detected. This time-versus-

DEMONSTRATION BOX 4.2

THE PURKINJE SHIFT

For this demonstration you will need a dark room and some way of providing a light whose intensity you can vary without altering its color. A good method is to use a television set as a light source. This may be done by tuning the set to an unused channel and turning the contrast control to a minimum. This reduces the visibility of the random dots that normally appear on the screen. Now, if you darken the room so that the television is the only source of illumination, the brightness control on the set will be a means of controlling the room light. An alternate procedure in the absence of a television is to turn on a light in a room and enter a closet, shutting the door after you. The amount of light entering the closet can be controlled by opening the door by differing amounts. Turning your back to the door allows for a diffusion of the light to any target that you wish to be illuminated. Unfortunately, if the outside room is well lit, opening the door by a few centimeters will provide a good deal of light: Hence, control of illumination may be improved by dimming the light in the outside room.

Now, look at Color Plate 2 inside the front cover of this book. Here we have two colored spots, one blue and one red. When viewed in moderate or bright light (the brightness control on the television is set to high, or the closet door is more widely ajar), the blue spot and the red spot appear to be approximately equal in brightness. Now, make the light very dim (close the door almost completely, or turn down the brightness control on the television). In the bright light, you were viewing the spots with cone vision. Now, if you dim the lights sufficiently, only rod vision will be activated. After 5 to 10 minutes, as your eye dark adapts, the blue spot will appear to be significantly brighter than the red spot. In fact, the red spot may actually disappear. The effect may be accentuated by staring at the white spot. This shifts the images away from the fovea to an area of the retina containing a greater number of rods.

intensity tradeoff works only over stimulus durations less than about a tenth of a second and also depends on the wavelength of the stimulus.

The size of a stimulus also affects its detectability. In Chapter 3 we noted that there is a good deal of convergence in the visual system, meaning that a number of rods or cones may synapse with the same bipolar cell and several bipolar cells may converge on the same retinal ganglion cell. Consider a hypothetical example. Suppose that the receipt of four units of neural transmitter per second is sufficient to activate a bipolar cell and that a bipolar cell has four receptors making synapses with it. If we provide a tiny spot of light that is strong enough to elicit only one unit of neurotransmitter per second from the retinal receptor and the light is wide enough to stimulate only two receptors, clearly the bipolar cell will not respond. If we double the size of the stimulus so that all four receptors are illuminated, however, the bipolar cell will receive a total of four units of neurotransmitter per second and will become activated. Thus, as the area of a stimulus increases (even though its intensity does not change), the likelihood increases that we will recruit enough photoreceptors to begin a chain of neural activity that will allow us to detect it. An alternative way of conceptualizing this is in terms of retinal receptive fields, such as those illustrated in Figure 3.13. Increasing the stimulus size might be thought of as simply "filling in" the center of the receptive field with light, thus adding more "on" responses to the overall activity. For relatively small areas, covering visual angles of 10 min of arc or less (about 1 mm viewed at arm's length), there is a tradeoff relationship between area and intensity that is known as **Ricco's law.** Thus, if we increase the area covered by a stimulus, we can decrease its intensity and still be able to detect it and vice versa for a decrease in stimulus size. For stimulus sizes greater than 10 min of visual angle, increasing the area has a reduced effect.

Maximum Sensitivity

After this discussion, you may be wondering just what the ultimate limit of sensitivity might be if the stimulus were adjusted to the optimal wavelength, size, duration, and retinal position and if the observer were fully dark adapted. The classic experiment to answer this question was conducted by Hecht, Schlaer, and Pirenne (1942). They found that the minimum threshold for the perception of a brightness sensation occurred when only 6 quanta of light (photons) were stimulating the retina. Further computations showed that when detection occured, each of the 6 photons was stimulating a different one of six rods. Theoretically we can't get any more sensitive than this! Even at higher levels of illumination, however, it is possible to show that fluctuations of only a few photons may affect our perception of brightness, thus showing the exquisite sensitivity of the eye as a light detector (Krauskopf & Reeves, 1980; Zuidema, Gresnight, Bouman, & Koenderink, 1978).

SPATIAL CONTEXT EFFECTS

Brightness Contrast

Strange as it may seem, our perception of the brightness of targets often depends more on the luminance of adjacent objects than on the luminance of the target itself. Figure 4.5 demonstrates this. Here we have four small squares, each of which is surrounded by a larger square. The central squares all are actually printed in the same gray; thus, the amount of light that reaches your eye from each is the same. Notice, however, that the apparent brightnesses of these small squares are not equal. Their brightnesses vary depending on their background, with the grays printed on dark backgrounds appearing lighter

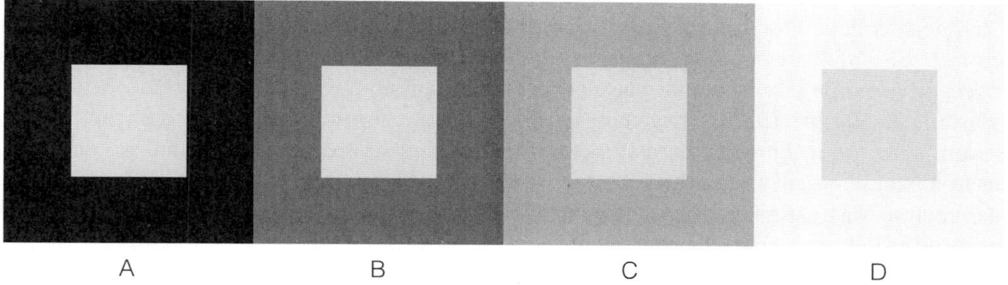

FIGURE 4.5 Simultaneous brightness contrast, showing how the background can alter the perception of the central gray regions.

DEMONSTRATION BOX 4.3

THE INTERACTION OF LUMINANCE AND BACKGROUND

For this experiment you will need your variable light source again (either the closet or the television). Hold up Figure 4.18 and look at the central squares, with your light source providing a low (but not dim) level of illumination. As you increase the level of illumination from its lowest value, the center target in Square A should grow brighter. Now repeat the procedure while looking at the center target in Square D. Notice that as the luminance level increases, this target square actually gets darker. Because all the center squares are identical in reflectance, the differences in their apparent brightness depend solely on their backgrounds. This may seem strange because we tend to associate black with the absence of light. Because you are already in a room or a place that potentially can be darkened, turn off all the light sources and close your eyes (to eliminate any stray illumination). Notice that what you are seeing is not black but, rather, a misty gray (often called cortical gray). Thus, the absence of light is gray, not black. Only in fields that contain some areas of bright illumination can real black be seen.

than the grays printed on light backgrounds. This effect is called **simultaneous brightness contrast.**

Everyday experience tells us that our conscious experience of brightness will increase as the amount of light reaching the eye increases. Unfortunately, our perceptual experiences often defy such "common sense." Despite increases in the amount of light reaching the eye, the brightness of a surface may actually decrease depending on the illumination of the background on which it rests, because simultaneous brightness contrast is greater at higher levels of illumination (Arend, 1993). You can see this effect by following the instructions in Demonstration Box 4.3.

The fact that a light surround depresses the apparent brightness of a target suggests that some form of spatial interaction is present. This interaction must involve some form of inhibition, where an actively stimulated portion of the retina will suppress other nearby retinal activity. Physiological evidence for such inhibitory spatial interaction was first collected using *Limulus* (the horseshoe crab), which has a very large compound eye that makes dissection of individual visual fibers somewhat easier. Nobel Prize winner H. K. Hartline (see Biography Box 4.1) and his frequent collaborator, Floyd Ratliff, were able to demonstrate the inhibitory neural interactions between nearby receptors using a very simple but elegant experiment (Hartline & Ratliff, 1957). They monitored the responses from a neuron in *Limulus* that is functionally equivalent to a ganglion cell. When the receptor attached to this neuron was stimulated with light, of course, the onset of the light increased the activity of the neuron. However, while this neuron was being stimulated, if Hartline and Ratliff illuminated a receptor located a short distance away, it caused a decrease in the response level of the neuron that they were monitoring. This finding demonstrates that visual neurons may be inhibited by the activity of nearby neurons. This process is called **lateral inhibition** because the inhibition acts laterally (sideways) on adjacent neurons. The amount of inhibition that any given neuron applies to its neighbors depends on how strongly it is responding and on how close the neurons are to each other. The more a neuron is stimulated and the closer it is to another neuron, the more intensely it will inhibit the other.

It is now easy to understand why the surface of inner square A is seen to be brighter than the surface of inner square D in Figure 4.5. In the part of the retina exposed to the lightest surround (surround of inner square D), many neurons are active and, as a consequence of this activity, are actively inhibiting their neighbors. This inhibition from the light surround should reduce the response of the receptors exposed to the inner square, making it appear dimmer. The neurons exposed to the inner square on the dark background do not receive as much inhibition from their less strongly stimulated neighbors. Because the amount of stimulation from the inner squares is the same but the neurons exposed to inner square A are undergoing a lesser amount of inhibition, inner square A appears to be brighter. Thus, lateral inhibition provides a basis for explaining brightness contrast effects.

Lateral inhibition can also explain more complex effects observed in other stimulus configurations. In the 1860s, physicist and natural philosopher Ernst Mach studied patterns with an intensity distribution like that shown in Figure 4.6B. In this figure, we have a uniform dark area and a uniform light area, with an intermediate zone that gradually changes from dark to light. However, when we look at the actual stimulus depicted in Figure

BIOGRAPHY BOX 4.1

WHEN TECHNOLOGY IS NOT ENOUGH

Haldan Keffer Hartline (1903–1983) was interested in the responses of individual neurons of the eye when stimulated by light. The problem he faced was that the technology for recording electrical responses of nerves had not been well worked out at the time. Microelectrodes did not yet exist, so the method of measuring electrical responses had to involve isolating a single neural fiber by teasing at the nerve bundle with a needle. Next one would lay a thin string laced with quartz crystals and silver (which could conduct electricity) over the fiber and then stretch that string between strong magnets. When the nerve fiber had an electrical response, it was conducted through the string and caused a slight movement that could be seen (because a mirror arrangement magnified it) and then recorded. Since the whole process involved being able to isolate single nerve fibers and yet keep them alive, Hartline had to find exotic species, whose nerve fibers were easy to tease apart and that did not depend on warm blood to keep them alive. His favorite species thus became the horseshoe crab, *Limulus*, whose retinal fibers were easy to get at, and the frog, whose optic nerve was easily exposed and therefore could be tested while alive—long enough to get a few measures of neural response. Later, when microelectrode technology began, Hartline extended his research to cats. His work, conducted at the University of Pennsylvania, Johns Hopkins University, and Rockefeller University, mapped out the regular relationships between neural response and the intensity of light reaching the eye. More important, he was the first to demonstrate that increasing light exposure to certain retinal receptors could actually inhibit or decrease the response of other nearby receptors. This was the breakthrough that allowed us to begin to understand how information is coded in the visual system, and it earned him the Nobel Prize in 1967.

4.6A, we do not see a gradual change in brightness flanked by two uniform areas. Instead, two bands or blurry lines are visible at the points marked by the arrows in the figure. One is darker than any other part of the figure, and the other is brighter. They are called **Mach bands,** in honor of their discoverer. Their presence can be explained by lateral inhibition.

We have indicated the location of some retinal ganglion cells illuminated by the Mach band–producing pattern in Figure 4.6C. Cell *b* is stimulated by bright incoming light, but it is also strongly inhibited by the activity of the adjacent cells *a* and *c*. Cell *d* is stimulated to the same extent as cell *b*. But on one side it is strongly inhibited by *c*, whereas on the other side it is somewhat more weakly inhibited by *e*, which is not receiving as much light. The important thing to understand here is that cells *b* and *d* have the same degree of stimulation, but *d* is less strongly inhibited. In this case, we might expect that *d*'s response will be more vigorous than that in cells like *b*. This should cause the region around *d* to appear relatively brighter. Next consider cell *i*. It is not stimulated very much, but neither are the nearby cells *h* and *j*. This means that *i* is not being strongly inhibited by surrounding units. Cell *g* is receiving the same small amount of stimulation as *i*. However, whereas *g* is weakly inhibited on one side by *h*, it is more strongly in-

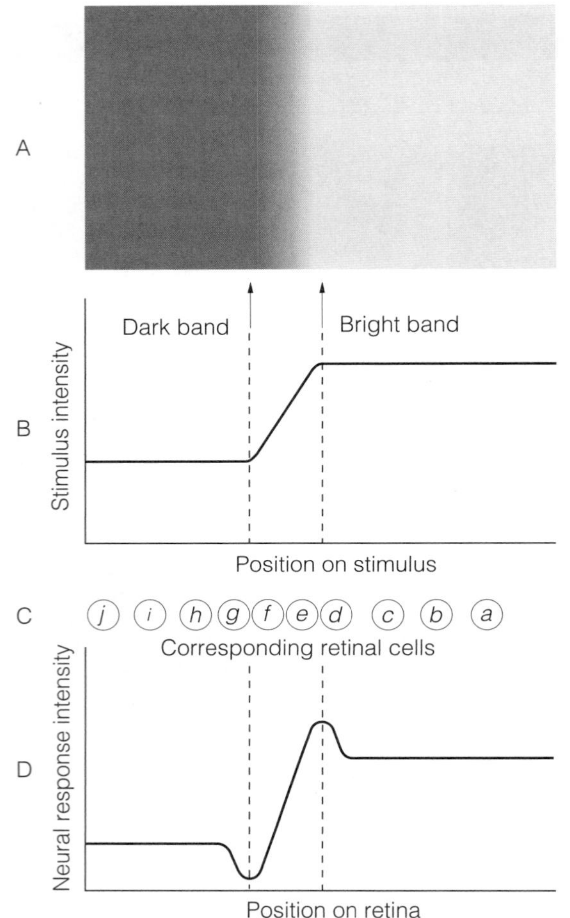

FIGURE 4.6 (A) A Mach band pattern, (B) the actual distribution of stimulus intensity, (C) corresponding retinal cells (see the text), and (D) neural response intensity distribution (A and B based on Cornsweet, 1970).

hibited on the other side by *f*, which is responding more vigorously because of the higher intensity of light falling on it. Thus, although *g* and *i* receive the same amount of stimulation, *g* is more strongly inhibited than *i*. This means that its response will be lower, causing an apparently darker region to appear there. The relationship between the input and the neural (and perceptual) response is diagrammed in Figure 4.6D. It is easy to produce a Mach band pattern for yourself, as shown in Demonstration Box 4.4.

It seems likely that a wide array of brightness perception phenomena can be explained by theories that assume particular patterns of inhibitory and excitatory interactions between sensory neurons; however, such interactions may be occurring not only on the retina, but also higher up in the brain (e.g., Dresp & Grossberg, 1999; Kelly & Grossberg, 1999). The physiology of the retina implies that such inhibitory effects should take place over a limited distance and that targets that are relatively far away from one another should not be affected. Many recent studies have used what are called Mondrian patterns to show that this is not the case. Mondrian patterns are named after abstract artist Piet Mondrian, whose works often consisted of a complex arrangement of squares of different hues and lightnesses. If we have a pattern of squares of varying degrees of lightness, it has been observed that introducing a very light one decreases the apparent brightness of all of the others, even if they are a long distance away. To explain such "global" effects, some more cognitive and computational mechanisms have been suggested.

Perhaps the most researched global mechanism is based on **brightness anchoring.** This principle suggests that the highest luminance in a pattern tends to appear white and serves as a standard by which all of the other luminances are perceived. When that highest luminance increases, the standard against which the others are judged is raised, and all other surfaces in the scene appear to be darker, not because they have changed, but rather because they are now darker relative to the highest one. Several studies suggest that some sort of cognitive or computational process much like this is taking place (e.g., Gilchrist, Kossyfidis, Bonato, Agostini, Cataliotti, Li, Spehar, Annan, & Economou, 1999).

Brightness Assimilation

Given that brightness effects such as simultaneous brightness contrast need more than lateral inhibitory interactions to explain them fully, it should not surprise us to find that high-level cognitive processing and computational mechanisms may play a role in other brightness phenomena. For example, in many instances predictions made from either lateral inhibitory or excitatory considerations can be wrong. One example of such an effect can be seen in Figure 4.7. The two rings shown in this figure are composed of the same color of gray and lie atop the same sharp background edge of black and white. The only difference between the two rings is that thin black lines have been drawn through the ring in Figure 4.7B to connect the background edge from top to bottom. Despite the fact that lateral inhibition would lead us to expect that the half of the ring on the white background will be seen as darker than the half on the black background, the gray ring in A appears to be uniform in brightness. Compare this with the ring in B, which does

DEMONSTRATION BOX 4.4

MACH BANDS

Mach band patterns do not reproduce well in print. This is probably because the range of luminances possible from ink on paper is not very large. It is easy to produce your own Mach band pattern using a distribution of light. All you need is a card or a book that is opaque and has a straight edge, and a large light source. If you are in a room that has fluorescent or large frosted light fixtures in the ceiling, these produce a fine uniform source of illumination.

When you hold the card near a surface, you cast a shadow. As shown in the accompanying diagram, a full shadow appears under the surface and full light on the other side. In between is a graded shadow, the penumbra, which gradually moves from light to dark. Hold the card still and look at the brightness pattern—you will easily see the dark and light Mach bands. You may increase the visibility of the bands by moving the card closer to the surface. This reduces the size of the penumbra and makes the area of gradual change in intensity steeper, as shown in the diagram. Because this puts the bright and dim areas nearer one another, it enhances the effect of the inhibitory process.

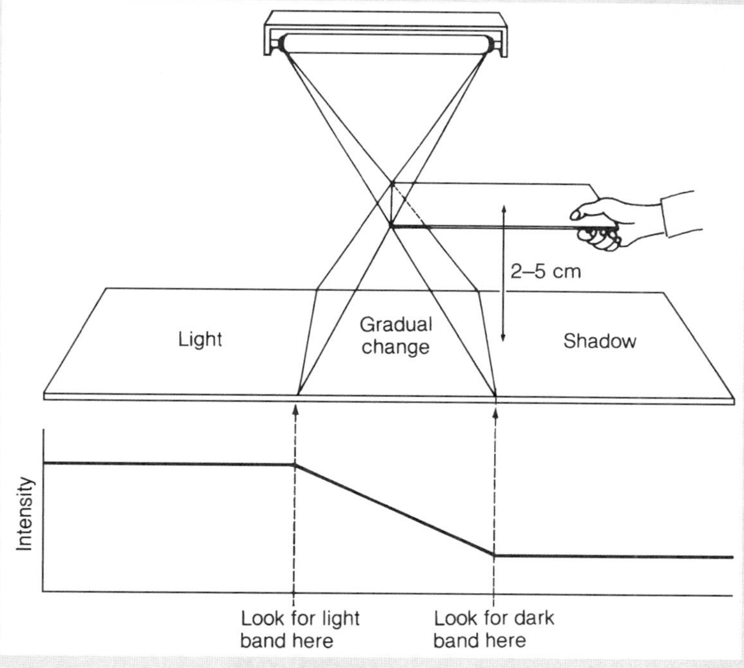

show the expected simultaneous brightness contrast. It appears that the thin lines are enough to bias the interpretation of the display so that it is seen as two half rings of different brightness laid side by side. The absence of the lines in A biases the perception of the ring toward a single-colored object on top of the background, and thus no contrast effects are seen, and both sides of the ring appear to be an "average" gray (Koffka, 1935).

Another example where cognitive effects may alter or override the effects of lateral inhibition on brightness is seen in Figure 4.8. The gray under the white stripes is identical to that under the black stripes. Notice, however, that the gray under the white stripes appears to be lighter than the gray under the black stripes. This is the opposite of the prediction we would make based on lateral inhibition. The white stripes should darken the gray rather than lighten it. The phenomenal impression, then, is the reverse of brightness contrast, and it is called **brightness assimilation** (Shapley & Reid, 1985).

Peripheral physiological contributions to brightness assimilation are suggested by the fact that it seems to occur only when the test stripes of white or black fall within the spatial summation zones of ganglion receptive fields. If the stimuli are increased in size to the point

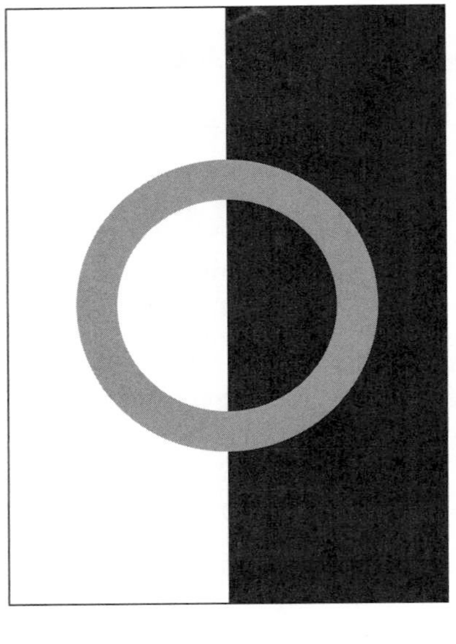

A

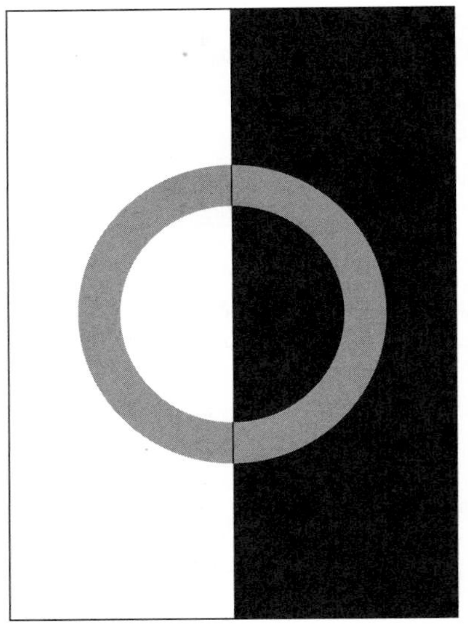

B

FIGURE 4.7 Brightness contrast is influenced by the cognitive interpretation given to a form. The gray rings in A and B are identical, except for the thin black lines in B.

where the gray and white (or black) stripes taken together fall into the off or inhibitory region of the receptive field, then brightness contrast is once again observed (Anstis, 1975). However, higher-level processes may play a role in this effect, too. Some of these higher-level processes involve computation of an average illumination level across the scene. As this average goes up or down, our perceptions of the brightnesses of individual regions are "dragged" in the direction of the average as long as they are not too extreme (Heinemann & Chase, 1995). This is much like the social inference that we might make when we infer that a person is wealthy because that person lives in the same neighborhood where many wealthy people live.

A

B

FIGURE 4.8 Brightness assimilation, where the gray under the white stripes appears lighter than the gray under the black.

There is some evidence that how we distribute our attention over a pattern influences whether brightness contrast or brightness assimilation occurs. In general, the part of the visual field to which we are attending—or at least the part that is viewed as the figure or object, rather than the background—shows greater brightness contrast (Brussell & Festinger, 1973; Coren, 1969). The background regions that are not directly attended to then show brightness assimilation (Festinger, Coren, & Rivers, 1970). You can demonstrate this for yourself by focusing your concentration on the gray in Figure 4.8 for a few moments. Soon the grays will appear to differ in a contrast direction rather than show brightness assimilation.

COLOR

For many animal species, the perception of light and dark is not enough. For them the additional ability of color vision is a matter of life and death. For instance, if bees lacked color vision, their task of locating the nectar-bearing flowers hidden among shrubs, grasses, or leaves would be almost impossible. The very survival of bees depends on the ability to spot a glint of color that indicates the presence of blossoms. Some evolutionary psychologists speculate that human ancestors developed the particular kind of color vision system we now have in response to a specific environment (e.g., Regan, Julliot, Simmen, Vienot, Charles-Dominique, & Mollon, 2001). This was one of tropical trees bearing fruit that were too

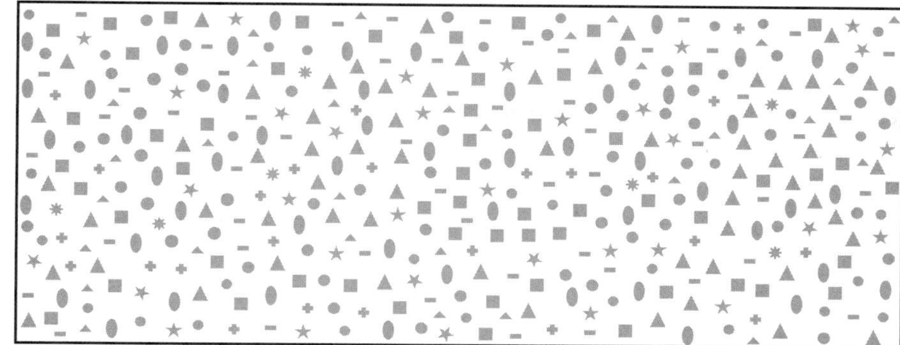

FIGURE 4.9 Can you find the hidden word? If not, turn to Color Plate 3.

large to be taken by birds and that were yellow or orange in color when ripe. One example is the tree family Sapotaceae. These trees offer a color signal of their nutritious fruit only to animals such as monkeys and humans, whose visual systems contain at least three different types of "color-tuned" light receptors. For an example of the advantage conveyed by color, look at Figure 4.9.

THE COLOR STIMULUS

The human eye registers as visible light wavelengths between 360 and 760 nm. Sir Isaac Newton was able to show that stimuli of different wavelengths within this range produce different color sensations. Newton's experiment was simple. He took a glass prism and allowed some sunlight to pass through it from a slit in a window shade. When he held a sheet of white paper on the other side of the prism, the light no longer appeared to be white; rather, it took the form of a colored spectrum, looking much like the arrangement of lights in a rainbow (see Figure 4.10A). Newton knew that light bends when passing through a prism and that the amount of bending (technically called refraction) depends on wavelength. There is less refraction of the longer wavelengths (600–760 nm) and more of the shorter (360–500 nm). Thus, a prism takes various wavelengths of light, which make up sunlight, and separates them according to wavelength. The fact that we see this spread of light as varying in hue seems to show that color perception depends on the wavelength of the light. Table 4.2 shows some typical color names associated with some selected wavelengths of light.

Newton also inserted another prism (in the opposite orientation) so that the light was now refracted in the direction opposite to the effect of the original prism. This, of course, recombined all of these wavelengths into a single beam. Now when he placed a piece of paper into this beam it again appeared to be white, with no hint of the original colors that went into the combination. This indicates that the sensation of white results from a mixture of many different wavelengths (see Figure 4.10B).

An important technical distinction should be made here. Figure 4.10 does not describe how white light is broken up into "colored light." Colored light does not exist; rather, what does exist is visible radiation of different wavelengths. If there were no observer there would be no color. When we talk about the color stimulus, we

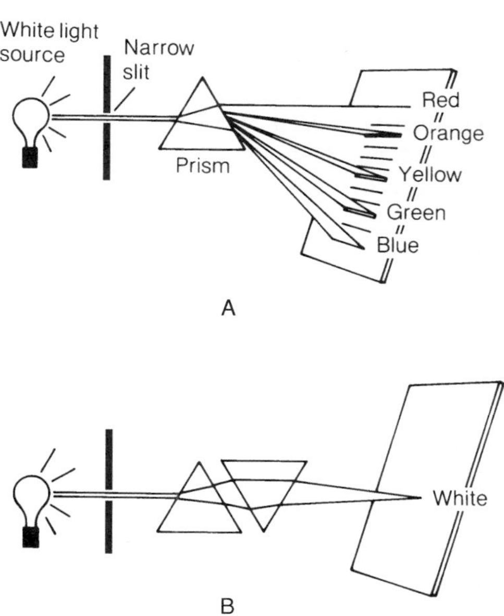

FIGURE 4.10 Newton's experiments: (A) separation of white light into its various wavelengths gives the color spectrum; (B) recombination of spectral lights gives white light.

TABLE 4.2 Wavelengths of Light and Associated Color Sensations

Color Name	Wavelength (nm)
Violet	450
Blue	470
Cyan	495
Green	510
Yellow-Green	560
Yellow	575
Orange	600
Red	660
Purple	Not a spectral color but a mixture of "red" and "blue"

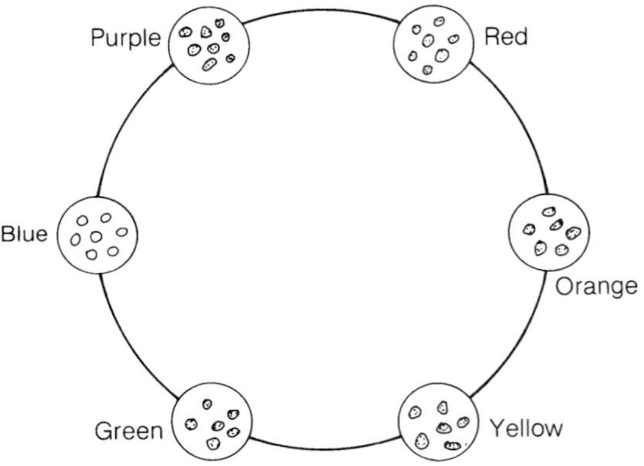

FIGURE 4.11 A primitive color circle for encoding the colors of pebbles.

should actually speak of radiation of different wavelengths because the sensations of red, green, blue, or any other color reside in the observer. Having made this technical distinction, we must admit that it is extremely convenient to talk about red light or green light, and for the sake of brevity we will not hesitate to do so in some of our later descriptions. Remember, however, that when we refer to "blue light," we are referring to those wavelengths of light that elicit the sensation of blue, namely, the shorter wavelengths in the visible spectrum.

Objects appear to be the color they are because they reflect to our eyes only selected wavelengths of light. Thus an apple viewed in white light appears to be red because all of the wavelengths except the longer (red-appearing) ones have been absorbed by the surface of the apple. Colored objects or surfaces contain pigments that selectively absorb some wavelengths of light, whereas the rest are reflected and thus reach your eye. It is this selective "subtraction" of some wavelengths from the incoming light that gives an object its color. If a surface does not selectively absorb any of the visible wavelengths reaching it but reflects them all uniformly, it appears white or gray, rather than colored. Color filters work in much the same way, that is, by absorbing some wavelengths of light. For instance, if a white light is projected through a green filter, the resulting beam is green because the filter has absorbed most of the long and short wavelengths, allowing only the medium-range, or green-appearing, wavelengths to reach the eye.

Color Appearance Systems

Suppose you were marooned on a desert island that had a beach covered with many colored pebbles. Lacking anything else to do, you set about the task of classifying the colors of all of the pebbles in some meaningful way. The first classification scheme that might come to mind would involve grouping stones together on the basis of their hues. Thus, you would end up with a pile of red stones and another of green stones and so forth. After you have your piles of stones, you would next have to look for some meaningful arrangement for the piles. You see that orange seems to fall, in terms of appearance, somewhere between red and yellow. The yellow-greens, of course, seem to fall between yellow and green. After you reach the blue end of your line of stones, however, you might find yourself running into a bit of a problem. The purple stones seem to fall somewhere between the blues and the reds, which means that a straight-line arrangement is not adequate. Instead, you might arrange the pebbles as shown in Figure 4.11.

This crude color arrangement scheme is circular in form. You have probably seen it before in books on art, decorating, or design, where it is usually called the **color circle** or **color wheel.** In this arrangement, you have separated the colors according to **hue,** which is the psychological dimension that most clearly corresponds to variations in wavelength. Often when we use the word *color,* in everyday life and in this chapter, we are actually referring to hue. Let us consider the effect of wavelength on sensation by looking at the effects produced by pure or **monochromatic** stimuli. Monochromatic (from the Greek *mono* meaning "one" and *chroma* meaning "color") stimuli contain only one wavelength. These stimuli are similar to those found in the spectrum generated by Newton's prismatic separation of light and therefore are often called **spectral colors.** Such monochromatic stimuli do not include all the hues found in the color wheel. For instance, we find that there is no single wavelength that produces the sensation of purple. This sensation requires a mixture of blue and red wavelengths.

Meanwhile, back on the beach, it has become clear that our color wheel classification scheme based only on the psychological attribute of hue seems incomplete. A close look at the piles of pebbles reveals marked color differences. For instance, among the red pebbles you might find that some are a deep red color and others are pink; another group may be almost pure white with only a hint of red coloration. This observation corresponds to the physical dimension of **purity.** Clearly the purest color you could get would correspond to a monochromatic or spectral hue, and as you add other wavelengths, or white light, the color would appear to become "washed out." This psychological attribute of color appearance is called **saturation.** It is easy to integrate saturation into the color circle by simply placing white in the center. Now imagine that the various degrees of saturation correspond to positions along the spokes or radii emanating from the center of the wheel. The center represents white (or gray), and the perimeter represents the purest or most saturated color possible. Figure 4.12 shows the color wheel now modified to include saturation. Notice that the point corresponding to pink (a moderately desaturated red) is plotted near the center along the line connecting red and white, whereas crimson is plotted farther away from the center along the same line.

To the average observer, hue and saturation do not completely describe all of the visible nuances of color. It is possible to have two colors match in both of these attributes but still appear to be different. For instance, a blue spot of light projected onto a screen would not appear to be the same as another spot identical in all regards except that it has been dimmed by putting a light-reducing filter in front of it. Thus, the sensory quality of **brightness** (which we discussed earlier in this chapter) must be worked into our system of describing colors. Because we have already used the two dimensions capable of being reproduced on a flat piece of paper, it is clear that the addition of a third color dimension (brightness) forces us to use a solid instead of a flat representation.

The shape of the three-dimensional color "space" can be derived from common observation if we recognize that at high brightness levels colors appear to be "washed out," whereas at low brightness levels colors appear to be "weak" or "muddy," meaning that they are of low saturation. Thus, the hue circle must shrink at these extremes because there saturation seems to vary over a confined range, and very high degrees of saturation are never observed at very high or low levels of brightness.

If we combine the three psychological attributes of hue, saturation, and brightness, we get something that looks like Figure 4.13, which appears to be a pair of cones placed base to base. This is called the **color spindle** or the **color solid.** The central core as we move up or down represents brightness and is composed of all the

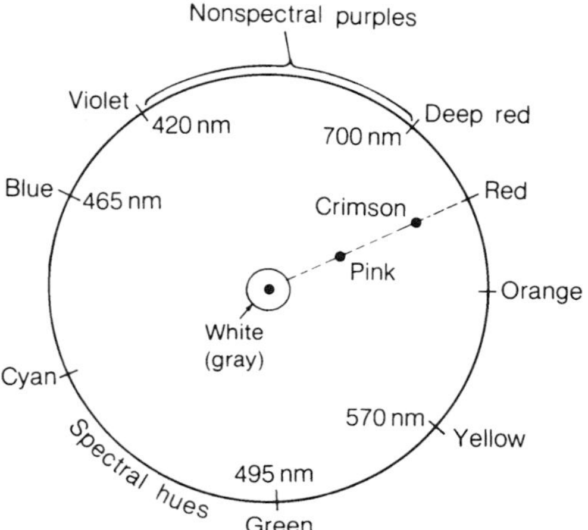

FIGURE 4.12 The color circle modified to allow the encoding of both hue and saturation. Spectral colors are on the outer rim; white is in the center.

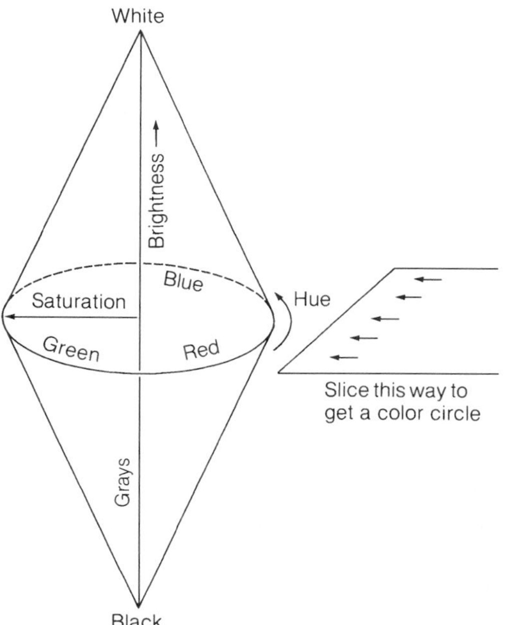

FIGURE 4.13 The color solid.

BIOGRAPHY BOX 4.2

A TRULY COLORFUL RESEARCHER

Hermann von Helmholtz (1821–1894) was a towering intellect who is claimed by many disciplines. Most of his best-known work was done when he was a professor at Bonn, Heidelberg, and finally Berlin. Among his many accomplishments in physics and mathematics are his study of, and quantification of, the law of conservation of energy and his studies of thermodynamics and vortex motions in fluids. His research in physiology included the first measurement of the speed of neural transmission, which also involved the invention of the reaction time methodology used today in all aspects of psychology. He also worked extensively on hearing, developing resonance theory, which opened the door to our understanding of how the ear analyzes tones. In addition, he provided an analysis of musical harmony that has proven to be useful to musicians as well as psychologists. In perception he is best known for his work on the trichromatic theory of color vision, which included his studies of color mixing and research on color blindness. However, he did not stop there. Helmholtz studied many other visual phenomena and is credited with our first understanding of how the eye focuses by changing the shape of the crystalline lens, and also with the invention of the ophthalmoscope. Helmholtz was an exciting and popular lecturer who believed that the public should be educated about science. He even carried this forward by participating in a number of well-received scientific presentations at the World's Fair in Paris in 1899, the same world's fair for which the Eiffel Tower was built.

grays running from white (at the top) to black (at the bottom). We can imagine that at each brightness level, if we sliced through the color solid in the direction shown in the diagram, we would get a color circle in which the hue would be represented along the perimeter. Totally desaturated colors (the grays) are at the central core, as we've already noted; hence saturation is represented by moving from the center outward. This is the basic representation used in many color appearance systems. Probably the most popular in use among psychologists is the one developed by Munsell (1915) and modified by Newhall, Nickerson, and Judd (1943) to agree with the way typical observers arrange color stimuli. To catalog the various colors we use a **color atlas,** in which each page represents a horizontal or a vertical slice through the color solid. Color samples that illustrate colors found in varying locations in the color solid are given in such atlases, allowing the observer to identify and label any given test color.

Mixing Colors

One of the most important facts about color vision was discovered in the 1850s by the German physicist and physiologist, Hermann von Helmholtz (see Biography Box 4.2), and the Scottish physicist, James Clerk Maxwell. These researchers found that human observers were sometimes completely unable to tell the difference between two colored stimuli, even though one stimulus was composed of a monochromatic light and the other was composed of three monochromatic lights in various amounts. (Any two colors that appear to be the same, even though they are really made up of different wavelengths of light, are called **metameric colors.**) They also found that by combining an appropriate set of three different-colored monochromatic light sources in appropriate amounts, they could create a color that perfectly matched another monochromatic color. Three monochromatic wavelengths that allow such matches are generally called **primaries.** Actually, the choice of the wavelengths for the primaries turned out to be rather arbitrary. Primary colors need be only reasonably far apart from one another, with the additional requirement that the mixture of any two of them alone will not match the third one.

The fact that any given color can be matched by a mixture of three appropriately selected primary colors suggests an alternate way of specifying the hue of a stimulus, namely, in terms of the proportion of the three primaries needed to reach this match. Geometrically this suggests a triangular space with a primary color at each corner. Color mixtures may then be represented in the same way as they are on the color circle. Thus, yellow—which is a mixture of red and green—is represented by a point on the line between red and green. If we add more red the point moves toward the red primary, and if we add more green it moves toward the green. As in the color circle, white is represented by a point in the middle and is composed of an equal proportion of the three primaries. Also, as in the color circle, a red of lower saturation (the whitish red or pink) would be represented by a point moved inward toward the center. Such a diagram is shown in Figure 4.14.

Additive Mixing of Lights. The process of combining different wavelengths of light in order to produce new colors is called **additive color mixing.** The consequences of mixing lights from the three primary wavelengths red, green, and blue are shown in Figure 4.15A. Let's begin by imagining that we projected a red disk of light onto a screen, perhaps by placing a red filter in front of a spotlight. If we now projected a deep blue (almost violet) disk onto the screen (using a blue filter and a second spotlight) so that it partially overlapped the red disk, the light reaching our eyes from the overlapping region would contain both red and blue light. Finally, if we repeated the procedure with a third spotlight and a green filter, arranging things so that a green disk of light was partly overlapping both the red disk and the blue disk, we would create a region in the center containing red, blue, and green light. Each time we created a new overlap of color disks, we would be adding to the mixture of

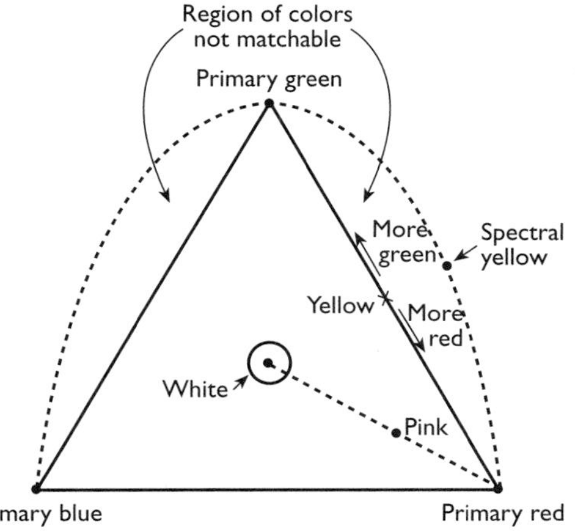

FIGURE 4.14 Specifying colors using a color triangle.

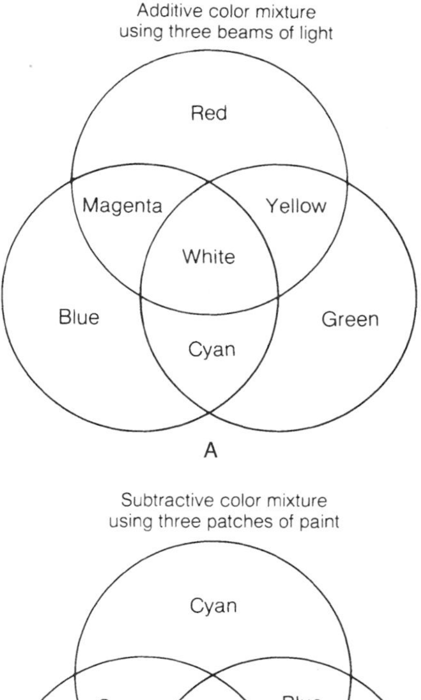

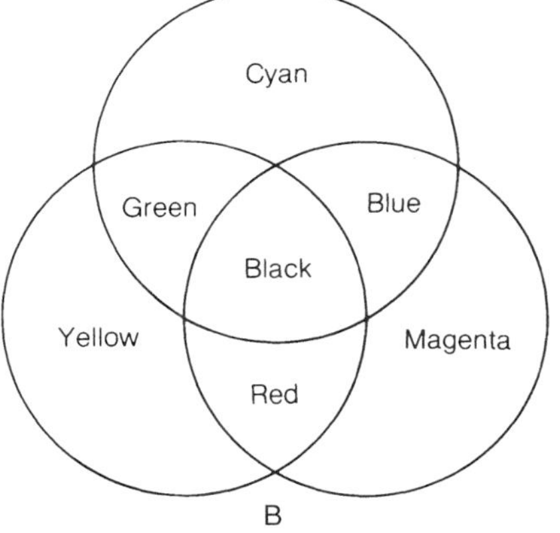

FIGURE 4.15 Color-mixture systems: (A) additive, (B) subtractive.

DEMONSTRATION BOX 4.5

ADDITIVE COLOR MIXTURE

For this you will need a television and a magnifying glass. If you hold the magnifying glass up to the screen, you will see that each region is made up of a series of tiny dots or rectangles. When you sit at normal viewing distance, you can no longer resolve the individual dots. They have combined within the eye to give you an additive color mixture. Now find a region of the screen that appears to be yellow. If the magnifying glass is strong enough to resolve the individual elements, you will see only dots consisting of reds and greens. Now find a place on the screen that appears to be white. The same magnification now shows that it is really equally illuminated red, green, and blue dots. A similar technique was used by the French painter Georges Seurat, who replaced the traditional irregular brush stroke used in painting with meticulously placed dots of color. Thus, instead of mixing paints on his palette, he allowed the mixture to be accomplished optically within the eye of the onlooker viewing the painting from an appropriate distance.

wavelengths reaching the eye. At the place where red and blue overlap, we see a lighter hue that is reddish-purple, often called magenta. Where the blue and the green overlap, we see a lighter hue that is greenish-blue, usually called cyan. Where the red and green overlap, many people are surprised to find that we now see yellow. Finally, where all three beams overlap, we see only white. Another form of additive color mixture can be seen using Demonstration Box 4.5

Subtractive Mixing of Pigments. A form of color mixing that most students are more familiar with, and that is perfectly predictable from the physics of light, is the mixing of paints or pigments. Mixing paints in order to produce new colors is called **subtractive color mixing** because each addition of pigment to the mix results in more wavelengths being absorbed by the pigments and thus in less light being reflected toward the eye of the observer. As every student learns in grade school, if you mix all the paints in your palette together, you will certainly not produce white. Instead, you will get a dark shade of gray or even black.

As an example, consider an object with a red surface, such as a tomato. Its red appearance means that the surface pigment absorbs most of the short and medium wavelengths, reflecting to your eyes only the long (red) wavelengths. A pigment that looks similar to grass green might absorb most of the long wavelengths and the short wavelengths, reflecting to your eye mainly middle wavelengths. Thus, when you mix red and green paints together, you end up with a mixture in which only the middle wavelengths are reflected by the green; yet these are absorbed by the red pigment. Hence, you are essentially subtracting all of the wavelengths, leaving only a muddy gray appearance.

Some consequences of mixing paints are illustrated in Figure 4.15B. Note that in order to produce the full range of colors from only three primary pigments, you have to begin with primaries that are not pure in wavelength. Indeed, you will get the best results if you begin with pigments that reflect a rather broad range of wavelengths. This is because mixing pigments can only decrease the range of wavelengths that are being reflected. That is, each addition of pigment to the mix will prevent some additional wavelengths from being reflected to the eye. Therefore, the brightest colors will be found at the periphery of the subtractive color mixing diagram in Figure 4.15B, with the darkest possible color, black, appearing in the center.

In the diagram you can see the consequences of mixing cyan (reflecting the short and middle wavelengths), magenta (reflecting the long and short wavelengths), and yellow (reflecting the middle and long wavelengths). Because the cyan pigment absorbs all the long wavelengths and the magenta absorbs all the middle wavelengths, their mixture absorbs both the long and the middle wavelengths, leaving us only with the short or blue-appearing portion of the spectrum. Similarly, a mixture of magenta and yellow absorbs both the short and middle wavelengths, leaving us with long-wavelength or red-appearing pigment. Finally, when we combine yellow with cyan, we find that the yellow subtracts the short wavelengths and the cyan subtracts the long wavelengths; hence only the middle or green-appearing wavelengths remain.

In the everyday world pigment mixtures are actually much harder to predict than this because the wavelength-absorbing property of pigments is very complex. For example, Figure 4.16 shows the wavelengths reflected by some typical pigments. Notice how irregularly

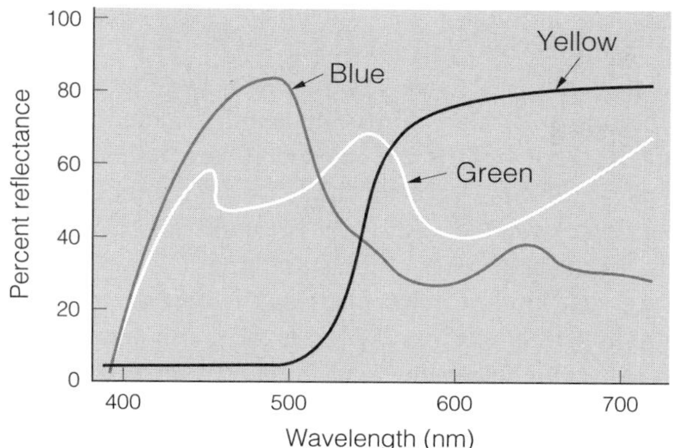

FIGURE 4.16 The relative wavelength composition of a blue, a yellow, and a green pigment.

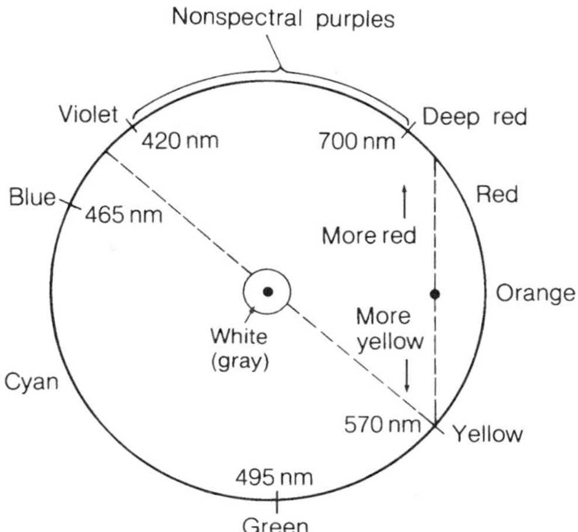

FIGURE 4.17 Using the color circle to predict color mixtures.

they reflect the light, and imagine the problems in predicting what the resultant mixes might reflect and absorb.

Color Spaces

The color circle, which we have already discussed, provides a convenient means of predicting the appearance of additive color mixtures. Note that the spacing of colors around its circumference corresponds to the way the various hues appear to an average observer—which is not identical to a regular spacing according to wavelength. To use the color circle to predict a color mixture is actually simple. Suppose we mix a spectral red (about 650 nm) with a spectral yellow (about 570 nm). We can depict this as in Figure 4.17, where the resultant mixture is represented by the line connecting these two colors. If we combine the yellow and the red in equal proportions, we will get a color that corresponds to the dot in the center of the line. We can determine what this color will look like by simply drawing a line from the center of the color circle through the dot to the perimeter. When this is done, we find that we get an orange corresponding to about a 600-nm spectral stimulus. Increasing the amount of yellow shifts the point along the line in the direction closer to the yellow hue. Adding more red shifts the point along the line in the other direction. You will notice that we started out with two spectral, or pure, hues (marked on the perimeter); however, the resultant mixed color is no longer on the perimeter but is closer to the center of the color circle. The purest colors possible (the spectral colors) are placed on the perimeter of the color circle; more desaturated colors are found closer to the center of the circle (nearer white or gray). From this we can conclude that any color mixture is less saturated than either of the two component colors that went into it. No mixture of colors can ever be quite as saturated as a monochromatic or spectral color.

An interesting effect occurs when we mix two colors that are exactly opposite to each other on the color circle. For instance, mixing a violet with a yellow along the line shown in Figure 4.17 results in a colorless gray. This is because, when the proportions are correct, this mixture lies in the center of the circle. Colors whose mixture produces such an achromatic gray are known as **complementary colors.**

In 1931 the Commission Internationale de l'Eclairage (CIE) standardized the procedure for specifying the color of a stimulus. The members of this group decided to use a color space created by the mixing of three primary colors. Unfortunately, if we select any three normal spectral colors as primaries, a number of perceptual and mathematical problems result. The major perceptual problem is the fact that there are other spectral colors that cannot be represented within the triangle. For instance, a pure spectral yellow cannot be represented (unless it is one of the primaries, which creates other problems) because any color mixture can never be as saturated as the pure spectral color itself. To solve this perceptual problem, the CIE members selected three hypothetical primary colors. They arranged the primaries at the corners of the triangle shown in Figure 4.18. These imaginary primary colors are more saturated than any real colors can be. (Remember that this is done so that all perceptually visible colors can be represented within the space.) Notice that we have labeled the hori-

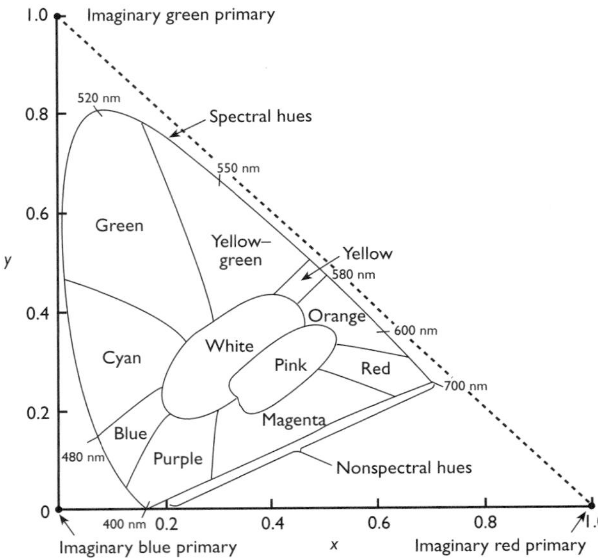

FIGURE 4.18 The CIE chromaticity space, which is a variant of the color triangle system using three imaginary "super" primaries.

zontal and vertical axes of the triangle with the labels x and y.

We can now represent any color as a point in the color space. The reason we can plot a mixture of three colors by using a point that has only two spatial coordinates is because the **CIE chromaticity space** has been arranged so that y represents the proportion of green in the mixture and x represents the proportion of red in the mixture. Clearly the proportions of red and green and blue in any mixture must sum to a proportion of 1.0 (you can think of these as representing percentages where all the items must sum to 100% of the light). If we know the proportions of green and red in the mixture, we need only subtract the sum of these from 1.0 to find the proportion of blue. The actual colors that can be perceived do not fill the full triangle (remember that the primaries we are using are imaginary "supersaturated" colors). Instead, they fill a horseshoe-shaped area with the spectral colors forming the outside boundary. We have labeled this area on the figure so that you can see the regions filled by various colors. Thus, if we had a color specified as $0.2x$ and $0.6y$, we would know that it is composed of 20% red, 60% green, and (subtracting 80% from a total of 100%) 20% blue. Looking at the figure, you can find the point described by these x- and y-coordinates and see that this color would look green.

Notice that brightness is not represented anywhere on this diagram. As in the color space we discussed earlier, brightness requires a third dimension. The color space in the figure can be pictured as a single slice through a three-dimensional color space, just as we demonstrated in Figure 4.13. This third dimension is called z. Using the CIE color system, we can specify any color stimulus by its **tristimulus values,** which are simply the x- and y-coordinates for the hue of the stimulus and a z-coordinate for the brightness of the stimulus.

Another kind of color space that is becoming increasingly important in everyday life is the color space used in modern color televisions and computer screens. For the purposes of producing a color image, a screen of this kind is divided into many distinct columns and rows. At the intersection of each column and row is a tiny rectangle called a pixel, which is short for "picture element." Each pixel on the screen is illuminated by light from three different electron guns, a red or long-wavelength-emitting gun, a green or middle-wavelength-emitting gun, and a blue or short-wavelength-emitting gun. By varying the relative contribution of each of these three guns, a very large number of colors can be shown at each pixel location. For example, if all three guns are turned off, the pixel will appear to be black; if all three guns are turned on to their maximum amount, the pixel will appear to be white; if only one of the guns is turned on to its maximum, the pixel will appear to be a highly saturated red, green, or blue, respectively. The color space underlying this form of color imaging is called **red-green-blue** (or simply **RGB**) **space** and is shown in Figure 4.19. It is a three-dimensional space, just as the color solid and the CIE color space; however, it is a cube in which each axis represents the amount of red, green, or blue in the color stimulus, while the line that runs from the corner representing black (all colors off) diagonally up to the corner representing white (all colors on) contains all of the grays. Moving away from this gray line toward any corner increases the saturation of the color.

The most important practical difference between the color solid and RGB space is that the color solid is intended to represent all of the colors that a human observer can possibly see. The RGB space, on the other hand, describes only those colors that can be produced by a particular television or monitor screen. You can explore such a color space using Demonstration Box 4.6.

THE PHYSIOLOGY OF COLOR VISION

To this point, we have dealt with the physical stimulus, some aspects of combining various wavelengths of light, and some methods of specifying the appearance of a color. None of the foregoing descriptions specifies how a

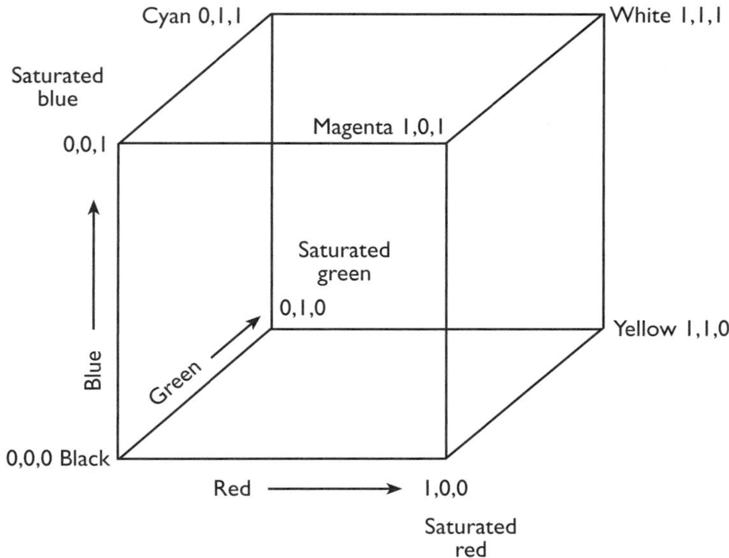

FIGURE 4.19 The RGB color space.

particular color sensation arises. In order to understand this, we must deal with both physiological and psychological factors. Let us consider these in light of the two major theoretical positions that have emerged during the past 150 years.

Trichromatic Color Theory

Much research has gone into the search for the physiological basis of color vision. Earlier in this chapter you learned about scotopic (that is, dim) levels of illumination, when only the rods are active and no color vision is found. On the basis of these observations, we can deduce cones are the retinal receptors that provide the first stage of the color response, but how do they do it? A first guess might be that there is a different cone for each perceptible color, or, alternatively, each cone could have a different neural response, a sort of Morse code, that it could signal for each color. However, most normal people can discriminate the differences among around 2 mil-

DEMONSTRATION BOX 4.6

COLOR MIXTURES IN RGB SPACE

This demonstration requires a computer with a color monitor and any application, such as Microsoft Word, Microsoft Powerpoint, Adobe Illustrator, or Adobe Photoshop Corel Draw, that will allow you to choose some custom colors for rendering fonts, shapes, or backgrounds. Consult the Help command for the software you have if you don't already know where to select the custom color option. Once you have selected custom colors, you will find that there are several options regarding something called a color picker. These include such names as HLS Picker, CMYK Picker, and RGB Picker. For this demonstration, select the RGB Picker, which refers to a color selection scheme based on the three primary colors red (R), green (G), and blue (B). Each of these colors has a sliding scale associated with it that can range from 0 to 100%. The colors that result from any combination of values on these three scales will be shown to you in a box called "New," "Test," or "Sample."

Begin by sliding all three scales down to 0%; your newly mixed color should be black since you have called for no light from any of the three primary colors. Next slide each of the scales to 100%, one at a time, to confirm that the R scale really gives you red colors, the G scale gives you green, and the B scale gives you blue. Slide all three scales to 100% to confirm that equal amounts of all three colors creates the color white. Next try mixing red and green to get a banana-like yellow. You can move the slides around to explore the color space and perhaps to match some sample colors from colored papers, paints, or parts of pictures that you have around.

lion colors under usual conditions and around 8 million colors under best conditions (McCamy, 1998; Pointer, 1998) making either the concept of separate cones or separate codes for each color completely unrealistic.

The first good solution to how we discriminate colors was suggested almost two centuries ago by Thomas Young (1773–1829). Young concluded that we need only a few different retinal receptors, each with a different wavelength sensitivity, to allow us to perceive the number of colors we do. He speculated that perhaps as few as three different kinds of receptors would do. When Helmholtz and Maxwell were able to show that normal observers needed a mixture of only three primaries to match any color stimulus, this was taken as evidence for the presence of three different types of cones in the retina, long before it was possible to make a direct observation of the anatomy of a cone. Because the usual color-matching primaries consisted of a red, a green, and a blue, it was presumed that there are three types of receptors, one responsive to long wavelengths (usually called the L cone), one to medium wavelengths (M cone), and one to short wavelengths of light (S cone). This **trichromatic theory** (from the Greek *tri* meaning "three" and *chroma* meaning "color") finds some very convincing support from studies of people with defective color vision.

Color Vision Defects. Virtually all individuals differ from what is usually called "normal" or "average" color vision in some way or another (Neitz & Jacobs, 1986). However, some people show drastic deficiencies in their ability to discriminate colored stimuli and, in popular language, are said to suffer from **color blindness.** This term is much too strong because only a very small percentage of individuals are totally incapable of discriminating hues. According to the trichromatic theory of color vision, we can predict five different varieties of color abnormality. The first, and most drastic, would be found in those who have no functioning cones. Because all of their seeing would be done only with the rod system, they would be expected to have no color discrimination ability. In addition, they should have relatively poor visual acuity (20/200 or less) and find photopic, or daylight, levels of illumination to be uncomfortable. Their night vision, on the other hand, should be normal. It is estimated that only 1 in 300,000 individuals has no functioning cones at all (Sharpe & Nordby, 1989).

A slightly less drastic malady is one in which only one variety of cone is functioning in addition to the rods. With this problem, vision should be possible under both photopic and scotopic conditions, but there would still be a lack of any color discrimination ability. The individual with no functioning cones, or the one with only one functioning cone type, responds to light in much the way that a sheet of black and white film does. All colors are recorded simply as gradations in intensity of the response. Such individuals are called **monochromats** (from the Greek *mono* meaning "one" and *chroma* meaning "color").

It is much more common for individuals to have a malfunction in only one of the three varieties of cones. Given two functioning cone systems, these people should have some color perception, though it would differ from that of a normal observer. In effect, they should be able to match all other colors with a mixture of only two primaries. Such individuals are usually called **dichromats** (the Greek *di* means "two"). The existence of such individuals has been known since the 1700s. The English chemist John Dalton (1766–1844) was a dichromat, a fact he learned rather late in his life. Supposedly, it first came to his attention when he wore a scarlet robe to receive his Ph.D. degree. Because he was a Quaker, a sect that shuns bright colors, this caused quite a stir, until it became clear that yarn dyed scarlet, gray, or dark blue-green all appeared to be the same to him.

There are three predictable forms of dichromacy, depending on whether it is the red-, green-, or blue-responding cones that are inoperative. The specific confusions are predictable from the color-matching curves of normal observers. Dalton's type of color defect is usually referred to as **protanopia** (the Greek prefix *prota* means "first," and red light is generally designated as the first primary). A protanope would be insensitive to long wavelengths normally perceived as red light because his L cones are not functioning properly. If a red light were made much brighter than a green light, a protanope could easily confuse them, whereas a color-normal observer would perceive both that the red light was brighter than the green and also that they differed in hue.

The most common form of dichromacy is called **deuteranopia** (the Greek prefix *deutera* means "second," and green light is by convention the second primary). Individuals with deuteranopia have a malfunction in the M cone system. They are still able to respond to green light; however, they cannot distinguish green from certain combinations of red and blue.

Trichromatic theory also predicts that there is a third form of dichromacy that is caused by the absence or malfunction of the S cone system. Although a name existed for this phenomenon, **tritanopia** (from the Greek *tritan,* for the "third" primary, blue), there was no confirmed report of this difficulty until about 1950, when a magazine article containing a special color-vision test plate appeared as part of an intensive search throughout England and discovered 17 individuals with this rare problem. Instead of seeing the spectrum as composed of blue and of yellow as do other dichromats, tritanopes see the long wavelengths as red and the shorter ones as bluish-green. The discovery of this last class of individuals provides strong support for a trichromatic theory of color vision.

Color defects are fairly common. Some instances of it are relatively mild and result in what is called **anomalous trichromatism.** Color matches made by individuals with this problem require more red **(protoanomaly)** or more green **(deuteranomaly)** than do color matches of normal observers. If we count all individuals with any form of color deficiency, we find that just over 8% of males show color weaknesses, whereas slightly less than 0.05% of females show similar weaknesses. Color defects are genetically transmitted on the X chromosome, accounting for their uneven transmission in males and females, and studies have conclusively mapped the pattern of this transmission (Botstein, 1986; Nathans, 1987; Nathans, Piantanida, Eddy, Shows, & Hogness, 1986).

Which colors does a dichromat actually see? It is difficult to know how the colors seen by a dichromat compare with those seen by a color-normal observer. However, a glimpse into the visual world of the color defective has been provided by a rare person who was deuteranopic in her left eye but color normal in her right eye. Graham and Hsia (1958) had this observer adjust the color seen by her normal eye so that it appeared to be the same hue as the color seen by her defective eye. The results of her matches are shown in Figure 4.20. As can be seen from this figure, the colors over the entire range of red to green (from about 700 to 502 nm) all appeared to have the same yellow hue (about 570 nm), and all of the colors from green to violet appeared to be blue (matching a 470-nm stimulus). The region that appears to be blue-green to the normal observer (around 502 nm) was perceived as being a neutral gray in the defective eye. Researchers have confirmed these results by comparing the color-matching and color-naming performance of dichromats with color-normal observers (Paramei, 1996). Knowledge of the nature of the color confusions among dichromats allowed Coren and Hakstian (1988, 1995) to develop a simple questionnaire that assesses whether individuals are likely to be color blind. You can test yourself with this questionnaire using Demonstration Box 4.7.

Given the fact that in the United States alone, some 11,000,000 men and 900,000 women have some form of inherited color blindness, it is not surprising to find that

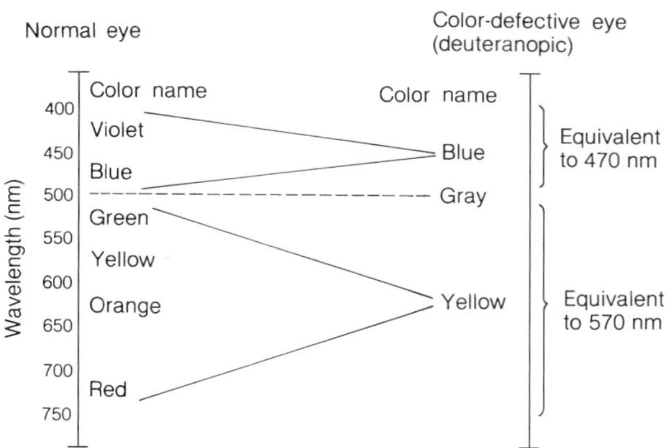

FIGURE 4.20 Color matches of a normal eye to a "color-blind" eye (deuteranopic) in the same observer (based on Graham & Hsia, 1958).

attempts have been made to create prosthetics that could allow color-blind individuals to make normal color distinctions. The most common technique involves placing a red filter over one eye (in the form of a contact lens or eyeglasses). This darkens the blues and greens. The perceptual effect of this is typically to make reds look fluorescent and greens take on a sort of a luster. People wearing such lenses can also alternately wink each eye to help determine the color of a traffic light. While such viewing devices may help color discrimination in some circumstances, there is some evidence that there is a tradeoff resulting in some reduction of visual acuity and depth perception (Sharpe & Jägle, 2001).

Physiological Basis of Trichromatic Theory. Although the data from color mixing and color defects seem to support a trichromatic theory of color vision, direct physiological evidence for the three cone pigments did not appear until the 1960s. The measurement procedure involved is conceptually simple but technically difficult (Bowmaker & Dartnall, 1980; Brown & Wald, 1964; Marks, Dobelle, & MacNichol, 1964). It involves a device called a **microspectrophotometer.** With this device a narrow beam of monochromatic light is focused on the pigment-bearing outer segment of a cone. As tiny amounts of light of various wavelengths are passed through the cone, the amount of light absorbed at each wavelength is measured. The more light of a given wavelength is absorbed by the cone pigment, the more sensitive is the cone to light of that particular wavelength. The data showed that most mammals, with the exception of some primates, are dichromats with an S cone and a cone that responds best

DEMONSTRATION BOX 4.7

COLOR VISION SCREENING INVENTORY

To see if you may have a color-vision deficit, simply take this test, which is the Color Vision Screening Inventory* developed by Coren and Hakstian (1987, 1988). For each question you should select the response that best describes you and your behaviors. You can select from among the following response alternatives: Never (or almost never), Seldom, Occasionally, Frequently, Always (or almost always). Simply circle the letter corresponding to the first letter of your choice.

1. Do you have difficulty discriminating between yellow and orange? N S O F A
2. Do you have difficulty discriminating between yellow and green? N S O F A
3. Do you have difficulty discriminating between gray and blue-green? N S O F A
4. Do you have difficulty discriminating between red and brown? N S O F A
5. Do you have difficulty discriminating between green and brown? N S O F A
6. Do you have difficulty discriminating between pale green and pale red? N S O F A
7. Do you have difficulty discriminating between blue and purple? N S O F A
8. Do the color names that you use disagree with those that other people use? N S O F A
9. Are the colors of traffic lights difficult to distinguish? N S O F A
10. Do you tend to confuse colors? N S O F A

Scoring Instructions

Responses are scored 1 for Never, 2 for Seldom, 3 for Occasionally, 4 for Frequently, and 5 for Always. Simply add together your scores for the 10 questions. If your score is 17 or higher, you have an 81% likelihood of failing a standard screening test for color vision. If your score is in this range, you might want to get your color vision tested by your doctor or in a perception laboratory.

to a wavelength between the usual L and M cones, which we can call an LM cone (Jacobs, 1993).

Although researchers are still refining the detailed description of the cone pigments, the general pattern of the results is clear. In normal humans there are three major groups of cones. A typical set of measurements, taken from a human eye that had to be surgically removed (Bowmaker & Dartnall, 1980), shows maximum absorptions in the ranges of 420 nm, 534 nm, and 564 nm, respectively. Figure 4.21 shows the relative absorption of these three pigments (where 1.0 is the maximum amount absorbed by the pigment). Clearly, on the basis of their sensitivity peaks, these are not really tuned to the blue, green, and red primaries that we use in color mixing experiments but rather the S cones are tuned to violet, the M cones to yellow-green, and the L cones to orange. Also shown in the figure is the relative sensitivity function for the rods in this same eye. These receptors have a maximum absorption of 498 nm when measured with the same technique. There is now some psychophysical evidence that under **mezopic** illumination (intermediate light levels when both rods and cones are active to some degree) rods do seem to contribute a color and their activity is interpreted as blue (Buck, 2001).

Because the cones are differentially distributed across the retina, our color response is different over different portions of the eye (Roorda & Williams, 1999). There are virtually no S cones in the central foveal region, which suggests that all observers are dichromats, specifically tritanopes, for small targets seen in central vision. This conclusion has been verified using psychophysical techniques (Tuck & Long, 1990; Williams, MacLeod, & Hayhoe, 1981). The S cones are also relatively rare in comparison with L and M cones, comprising only about 10% of all cones. The relative rarity of S cones probably also explains why blue contributes less than red or green to many aspects of the visual process (e.g., Kaiser & Boynton, 1985).

Sensitivity to blue light first increases and then decreases with increasing distance from the fovea. Sensitivity to green light diminishes with increasing distance from the fovea and disappears at about 40 degrees from the fovea. A similar pattern holds for sensitivity to red and yellow light, with color responses disappearing in the order green, red, yellow, and blue as distance from the

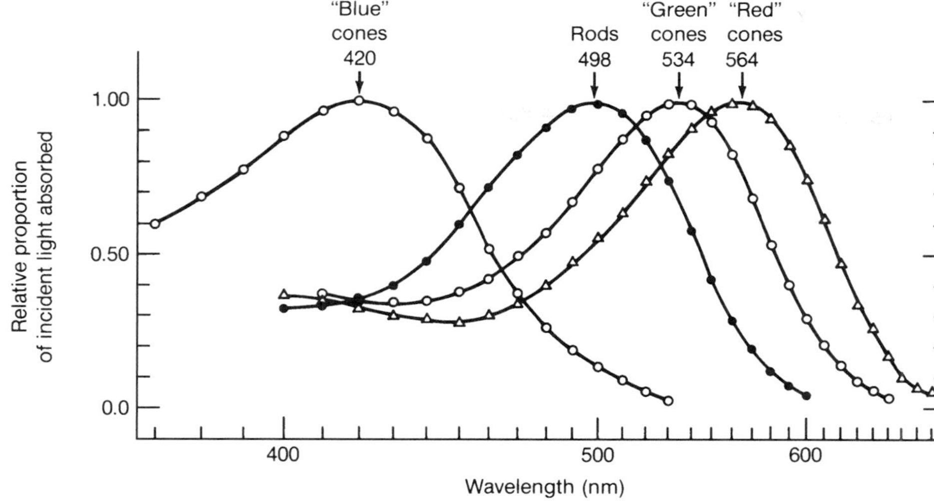

FIGURE 4.21 The relative absorption of various wavelengths of light by the three different cone types and the rods of a human (based on Bowmaker & Dartnall, 1980).

fovea increases. In the far periphery of the retina, we are totally color blind. The exact distance, however, depends on the size of the stimulus. We can discriminate the colors of larger stimuli farther out on the peripheral retina (Johnson, 1986). To see how your own color discrimination varies across the retina, try Demonstration Box 4.8.

Color responses are also sufficiently different between observers, even among those with normal color vision, to suggest that there may be systematic individual differences in cone photopigments (Neitz & Jacobs, 1986; Webster, Miyahara, Malkoc, & Raker, 2000). Over the past 20 years it has become clear that some women are capable of making finer color discriminations than most men. While some people thought that this had to do with culture or sex roles, it has now become clear that some women have a retina that is genetically structured in a different way. This comes about because the genes for the L and M cones are both on the X chromosome and are close enough to form an unstable arrangement. In some cases, instead of making two color-sensitive cone types they actually make one cone type with an intermediate LM sensitivity. If a woman has this defective chromosome and it is passed on to a male, he becomes color blind (a dichromat) since he only has one X chromosome, paired with the shorter Y chromosome; hence there is nothing to correct the defect. However, since women have two X chromosomes, they can have one that produces the normal long and middle wavelength cone types plus one that produces the defective intermediate cone. Such a woman appears to be color normal but actually has four cone types. This would make her a **tetrachromat** (from the Greek *tetra* for four and *chroma* for color). Tetrachromat women would be more color sensitive than the normal person with only three cone types and would actually

DEMONSTRATION BOX 4.8

COLOR-SENSITIVE ZONES ON THE RETINA

Color perception is best in the central region of the retina (excluding the small central region of the fovea, which is blue blind). You can observe the changes in color discrimination for different parts of the retina by taking a small orange piece of paper and placing it on a gray surface. Keeping your head fixed, look off to the side of the orange target. If you keep moving your eyes outward (away from the target), you stimulate more peripheral parts of the retina. Eventually you will reach a point where the orange will look yellowish, meaning that you have now imaged it beyond the red-sensitive zone. If you continue moving your eyes outward, you may even hit a point where the orange no longer looks colored at all but merely appears gray. Your eye will have to move farther to get these changes in color appearance if the orange patch is larger (see Johnson, 1986).

need four primary colors to match all of the colors that they see. To see what this means perceptually, we can have people look at a spectrum (such as that created by Newton's prism) and ask them how many distinct bands of color they see in it. A normal trichromatic person will see between 7 and 8, a color defective dichromat will see between 5 and 6, while these tetrachromatic women will see 10 discrete bands of color (Jameson, Highnote, & Wasserman, 2001). Sex differences are also seen in some monkeys, such as marmosets and squirrel monkeys, where the males are dichromats and the females are trichromats (Jacobs, 1993).

Opponent-Process Theory

The German physiologist Ewald Hering (see Biography Box 4.3) was not completely satisfied with the trichromatic theory of color vision, not because of physiological considerations but rather because of subjective experiences associated with color. For instance, when languages are examined to determine the labels we use to denote different color categories, most have 11 basic terms, which in English correspond to the desaturated colors white, gray, and black, and then the common colors red, green, blue, yellow, orange, purple, brown, and pink. However, when observers are presented with a large number of color samples and asked to pick out those that appear to be pure (defined as not showing any trace of being a mixture of colors), they tend to pick out four, rather than three, colors. These unique colors almost always include a red, a green, and a blue, as trichromatic theory predicts; however, they also include a yellow (e.g., Schirillo, 2001).

With these four primary colors people seem able to describe the color of their world. Researchers have shown that if you ask observers to adjust the percentage red, percentage yellow, percentage green, and percentage blue in any test color (adding up to 100%), they can comfortably describe the entire range of visible hues (Gordon, Abramov, & Chan, 1994). The percentages of each of the four perceptual primaries that observers give to match any spectral color is shown in Figure 4.22. These results cannot be attributed simply to learning or language use. For example, Bornstein, Kessen, and Weiskopf (1976) showed that 4-month-old infants tend to see the spectrum as if it were divided into four hue categories. They did this by repeatedly presenting a given wavelength of a light until the infants became visually bored and stopped looking at the light (a process called habituation). They next monitored how much time an infant spent looking at a second wavelength of light. They found that when the second wavelength was selected from another hue name category (based on the adult data), the infants spent more time looking at it than they did at a wavelength selected from the same hue category. The infants acted as if stimuli in the same hue category were more similar than those from different categories; hence it seems they were categorizing hues into the same four groups that the adults do.

Hering looked at another aspect of the subjective experience of hue. He noted that certain color combinations are never reported by observers, for instance, a yellowish blue or a greenish red. This led Hering to suggest hypothetical neural processes in which the four pri-

BIOGRAPHY BOX 4.3

THE COLORFUL RESEARCHER'S OPPONENT

Trained as a physiologist, ***Ewald Hering (1834–1918)*** made contributions to our understanding of liver function and how the vagus nerve helps to control breathing. His perceptual research at the University of Leipzig, where he was a professor, included studies of brightness and also studies of our temperature sense and adaptation to hot and cold. He is best known, however, for his work on the opponent process theory of color vision. He viewed himself as being in a sort of intellectual combat with Helmholtz over which view of color vision would prevail. He also opposed Helmholtz on other fronts, including his theory of hearing and harmony. A particular point of conflict was Helmholtz's general philosophy of perception, which allowed for cognitive and learning processes to assist people in trying to understand what they are sensing. Hering preferred a nativist approach in which our ability to judge space, depth, and form is inherited and automatic. This idea was later adopted by Gestalt psychologists. Few people know about the competitive hostility that existed between Hering and Helmholtz; however, most researchers accept the fact that both were correct (at different levels in the visual system) in their theories of color vision.

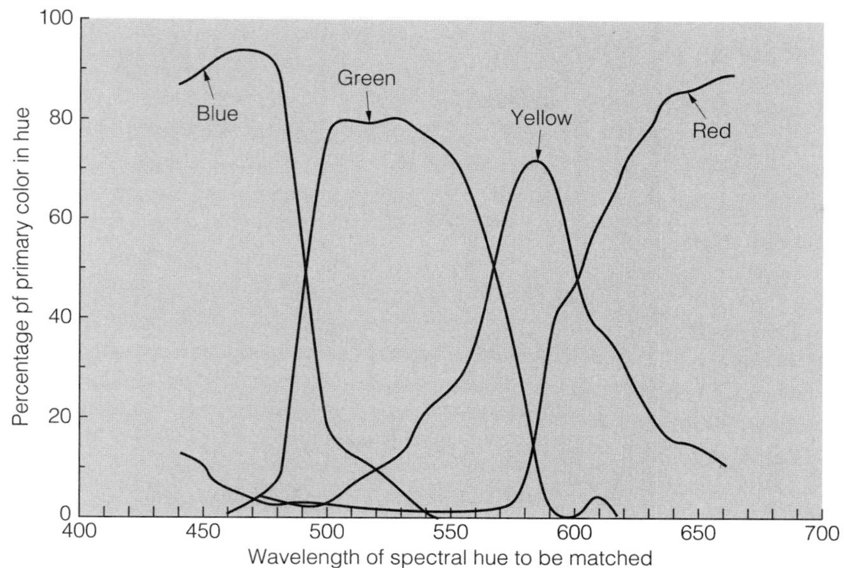

FIGURE 4.22 When subjects are asked "What percentage of the four primary colors (red, yellow, green and blue) would you need to mix in order to match the color you are looking at?" they can comfortably respond to every spectral hue. This figure gives the relative percentages from a typical group of subjects (based on data from Gordon, Abramov, & Chan, 1994).

maries are arranged in opposing pairs. One **opponent process** would signal the presence of red or green, and a separate process would signal blue or yellow. An example of such a process would be a single neuron whose activity rate increased with the presence of one color (red) and decreased in the presence of its opponent color (green). Because the neuron's activity cannot increase and decrease simultaneously, one could never have a reddish green. A different opponent-process cell might respond similarly to blue and yellow. A third unit was suggested to account for brightness perception. This was called a black-white opponent process, after the fact that black and white are treated psychologically as if they are "pure colors" (see Quinn, Wooten, & Ludman, 1985). But we need not limit the discussion to speculation based on color appearances alone because physiological evidence bears directly on the issue of opponent-process coding of color information.

Physiological Basis of Opponent-Process Theory. When Hering first suggested an opponent-process mechanism for the neural encoding of hue information, there was no physiological evidence to support such a speculation. Perhaps the single most important finding of twentieth-century sensory physiology was that neural responses are subject to both excitatory and inhibitory influences caused by interaction between neighboring units. We introduced several such systems in Chapter 3. In fact, earlier in this chapter we saw that certain brightness phenomena, such as brightness contrast and Mach bands, can be explained by the presence of a spatially opponent mechanism on the retina, where excitation in one region might cause inhibition in another. If we could also find *spectrally* opponent organization, where stimulation by one wavelength of light causes excitation in a neuron and stimulation by a wavelength in another region of the spectrum causes inhibition of that cell's neural response, then we would have a physiological unit that corresponds to the mechanism postulated by Hering.

We already know that there are three cone types as predicted by trichromatic theory. However, by the time we reach the level of the retinal ganglion cells, there is clearly an opponent-process coding just as Hering predicted. In addition, there is a spatial distribution to these responses that is similar to the center-surround organization of receptive fields we discussed in Chapter 3. Suppose we shine a tiny red spot (which stimulates L cones) on the eye while recording from a retinal ganglion cell. In some cases, as the size of the spot increases, the vigorousness of the neural response increases up to some point. After that, further increases in the size of the red spot have no further influence on the cell's response. Notice that this is very different from the type of response seen when white light is used (as in Chapter 3), where increasing the size of the spot starts to produce a reduction of response rate as it begins to enter the inhibitory region of the receptive field. If we repeat the experiment with a green spot (stimulating M cones), we find that the cell appears unresponsive when the green spot is in the center of the receptive field. However, as the spot becomes larger or as it is moved into the surround field, the resting level of activity is reduced. Thus, we have a cell that has the property of being excited by red and inhibited by green if the stimulus is the appropriate size and in the appropriate location on the retina. We also find an equal number of cells with the opposite organization (green excitatory center, red inhibitory surround). These can be called L-M color opponent or color antagonistic ganglion cells after the principal cone inputs producing the red versus green antagonistic cells that Hering suggested.

There is a second class of opponent process ganglion cells where the input colors are blue (from S cones) and yellow (L plus M cones), which then produce S-LM color antagonistic cells (see Gordon & Abramov, 2001). There is a difference, however, in the spatial organization of these. Consistent with the relative scarcity of S cones in the eye, the receptive fields of these ganglion cells are not very selective spatially. That is, there is not the usual center versus annulus arrangement, and these cells respond to blue and yellow light over their entire receptive field in much the same way. You can see the receptive field arrangement of these cells in Figure 4.23.

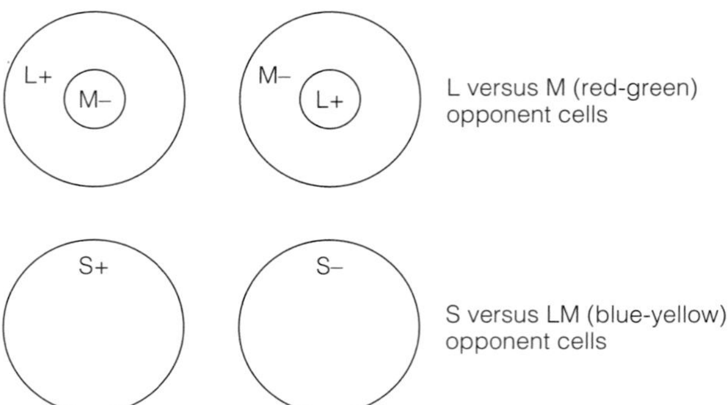

FIGURE 4.23 Pattern of color opponent responses found in retinal ganglion cells. Note that there is no spatial specificity for the S versus LM (blue-yellow) cells, but there is the center-surround spatial separation for the L versus M (red-green) cells. Note + means activity increases when appropriately stimulated and – means decreases.

Notice that we only had to proceed two layers of cells into the retinal processing hierarchy to reach the level of ganglion cells, and here already color seems to be arranged according to four primary colors (blue, yellow, red, and green), with these four colors being further organized into two pairs of oppositional colors (blue versus yellow, and red versus green). Of the two pathways leaving the retina, the tectopulvinar, which passes information on through the superior colliculus, does not seem to carry much if any color information. The color information goes through the geniculostriate pathways, and the first stop is at the lateral geniculate. DeValois and DeValois (1980) found that neurons in the lateral geniculate of monkeys are also color coded, similar to the color-coded retinal ganglion cells; however, when the eye was stimulated by large spots of light, the response pattern of some neurons changed. Some neurons responded more vigorously when the eye was stimulated with short wavelengths of light and decreased their response rate below their spontaneous (dark) activity level for long wavelengths of light. Other neurons acted in exactly an opposite manner. Each class of cells had different patterns of response as a function of wavelength, similar to what is needed for a red-green neuron and a blue-yellow neuron. Because the lateral geniculate receives its input directly from the retinal ganglion cells, this is exactly the pattern of results we would expect. Thus, returning to our example, if we have a red excitatory center in a receptive field, we should get increased response for a large-area red light, whereas the green inhibitory surround would completely ignore its presence. Conversely, a large green spot would cause an inhibitory response and be ignored by the red excitatory center, and so forth. Typical responses from lateral geniculate neurons to large spots of light can be seen in Figure 4.24. There are three neuron types. One responds differentially to short and moderately long wavelengths (blue-yellow), one responds differentially to moderately short and long wavelengths (red-green), and one does not show different opponent processing but, rather, responds simply to the amount of luminance reaching the eye. The spectrally tuned neurons code both chromatic and spatial information in the responses. This means that whether a given wavelength will produce an increase or a decrease in neural response may also vary as the spatial position of the stimulus spot is varied within the receptive field of the neuron.

How can a four-primary, opponent-process (or "push-pull") system exist when we already have provided physiological and psychophysical evidence indicating that the retina operates with a three-color pigment system? An example of how neurons might be wired to result in antagonistic activity based on the wavelength of the stimulus is shown in Figure 4.25. It requires only that certain cones excite neurons farther along in the system and that other cones inhibit the response rates of those neurons. Engineers hit on a similar system when they designed color television transmission. The color in the original scene is first analyzed into its red, green, and blue components by the camera and then transformed

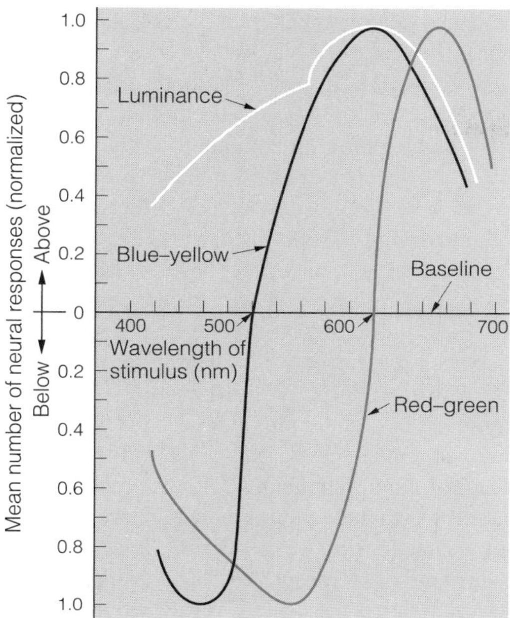

FIGURE 4.24 The neural response rate for cells in the lateral geniculate relative to their resting response rate, for stimulation by lights of different wavelengths (based on DeValois & DeValois, 1975).

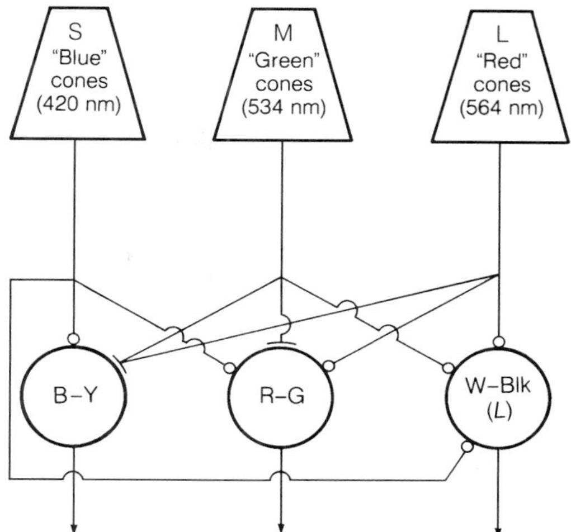

FIGURE 4.25 Schematic diagram indicating how a three-pigment system might be connected to produce opponent-process neural responses. The lines represent the connections. The round and the flat connections differ in that one is excitatory and the other is inhibitory (which is which is arbitrary). Numbers indicate the wavelength of maximum sensitivity.

into two color-difference (or opponent-process) signals (plus an intensity signal). After reception at their distant location, the signals are reconverted into red, green, and blue signals by the television set. This technique was selected because it requires considerably less information to be transmitted through each channel, thus providing good fidelity and increased economy. Perhaps similar considerations underlie the organization of our visual systems.

Color Channels and Cortical Coding

There has been a recent explosion of knowledge about how color information is encoded in the nervous system. Let us begin with the lateral geniculate, where the opponent-process color neurons are found. As we indicated in Chapter 3, the lateral geniculate is composed of six well-defined layers (three receiving input from each eye). These layers can be subdivided on the basis of the size of neurons in each. The upper four tiers are small cells and hence are called the **parvocellular** layers (from the Latin *parvo* meaning "small"). They account for around 70% of the geniculate neurons. The bottom two tiers are called the **magnocellular** layers (from the Latin *magno* meaning "large"), and account for 10% of the neurons. Separate streams of information flow through these layers. In addition, some neurons are interleaved between the parvocellular layers, account for the other 10% of the geniculate neurons, and seem to be associated with yet another stream of information (see Frishman, 2001). These are called the **koniocellular** layers (from the Greek *konio* for dust, since they appear visually as a thin grainy layer of dark dust between the parvocellular layers). The opponent color neurons, which make up about 90% of the neurons in the geniculostriate system, seem to be concentrated in the four parvocellular layers and the koniocellular layers, while the magnocellular channel seems to be specialized to carry brightness information. L-M (red-green) opponent neurons are most commonly found in the parvocellular layers, while S-LM (blue-yellow) are most frequently found in the koniocellular layers (Hendry & Reid, 2000). Thus there actually may be different pathways for the red-green and the blue-yellow information, with different types of color-tuned ganglion cells sending their information to different layers of the lateral geniculate (Dacey, 2000).

As we saw in Chapter 3, the separation of color and brightness channels continues on up through the cortex. New physiological techniques have allowed us to study the organization of color processing in the brain. For example, one staining technique has shown that the distribution of color-sensitive neurons in the primary visual cortex (V1) is not uniform; rather, there are patches of such neurons, which show up when stained as dark, slightly irregular oval regions, each about 0.2 mm in diameter. These regions, given the unsophisticated name of **blobs** by researchers, are shown in Figure 4.26. Many of the color-coded neurons from the parvocellular and koniocellular channels have connections in the blobs of V1, whereas the regions between the blobs **(interblobs)** receive some parvocellular inputs plus the magnocellular inputs that are concerned with brightness, form, motion, and other information that is not color related (Shostak, Ding, Mavity-Hudson, & Casagrande, 2002; Zrenner, Abramov, Akita, Cowey, Livingstone, & Valberg, 1990).

If we use an electrode to record from the neurons in a cortical blob, we find the usual opponent process that involves an increase in response when the eye is stimulated with some colors and a decrease in response when stimulated with others. Once again, there is a spatial factor in this response. For example, stimulating the center of the neuron's receptive field with L (red) light would cause the neuron to increase its activity, whereas stimulating the surrounding with M (green) light would cause the neuron to decrease its activity. Neurons in the blob regions have generally circular receptive fields and thus are not very sensitive to differences in edge orientation. They are also not very sensitive to motion signals (Shapley, 1990).

In Layer 4 of V1 in the cortex and in Area V4 of the extrastriate cortex, there are neurons that have a double opponent organization. Such a neuron might increase its activity when the center of its receptive field is stimulated with L (red) light but actually decrease its firing when the surround is stimulated with L light. The opposite organization is seen for responses to M (green) light in the same cell, with an M spot on the center of the receptive field producing a decrease in response and a green spot on the surround producing an increase in firing (De Valois, Cottaris, Elfar, Mahon, & Wilson, 2000). A diagram of both a simple opponent-process cell and a double opponent-process cell is given in Figure 4.27.

The most important feature of the double opponent arrangement is that the neuron is responsive to the difference in wavelength between light in the center and light in the surround of its receptive field. This means that such a cell would signal the same level of activity, for example, regardless of whether the center was stimulated by red and the surround by gray or the center was stimulated by gray and the surround by green, provided that the red-green difference was equivalent in the two cases. Such a neuron is ideally suited to being sensitive to the color differences between surfaces, even though the surfaces are both illuminated by light of yet another wave-

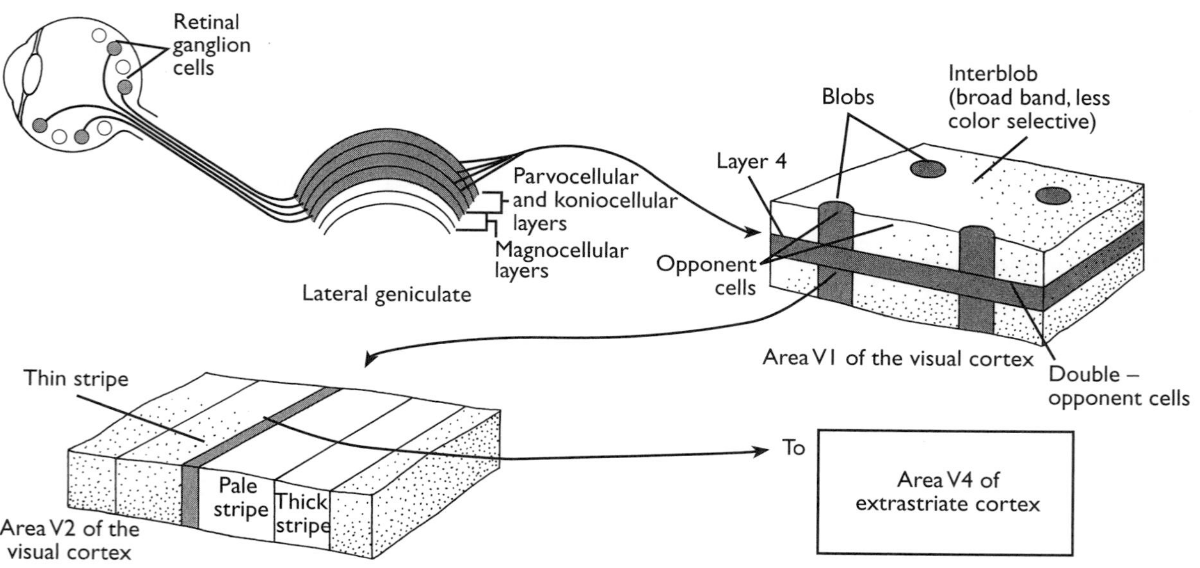

FIGURE 4.26 The major color channel in the visual system contains information from the parvocellular and koniocellular channels and is shown here, beginning with the eye, passing through the lateral geniculate and then through cortical regions V1 and V2.

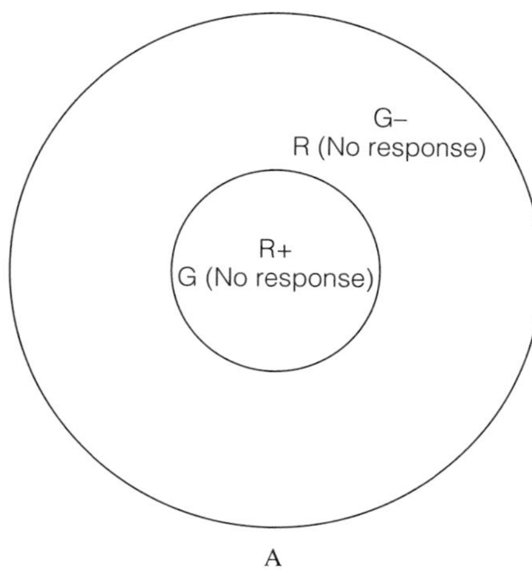

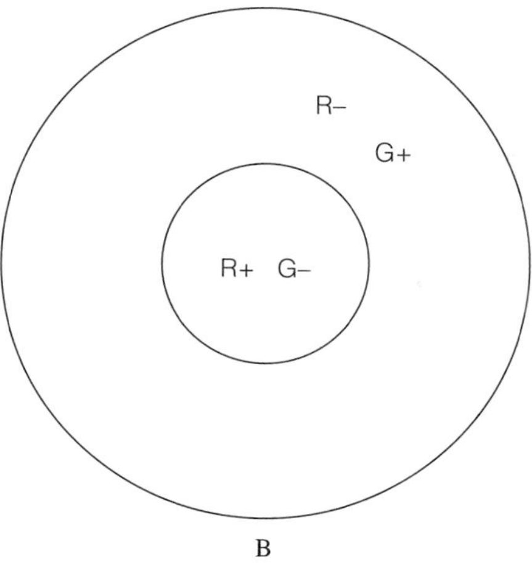

FIGURE 4.27 Receptive fields of typical color-opponent (A) and double-opponent (B) cells, recorded in the cortex.

length. This is exactly what is required for us to be able to see colors as the same under different illumination conditions, such as those introduced by shadowing, colored filters such as sunglasses, and unusual lighting. We will take up this topic of color constancy again in Chapter 10.

The separation of color processing from other visual attributes in the visual cortex continues up through higher levels, with the color-weak magnocellular channel ending up in a different place than does the color-strong parvocellular channel. In Area V2, the organization shifts to "stripes" (this term is again based on the way in which regions accept various stains). The color-coded neurons concentrate into what appears as dark thin stripes; the color-weak magnocellular inputs go into dark thick stripes; whereas mixed inputs form wide pale stripes (see Figure 4.26).

Beyond the V1-V2 complex, there is growing evidence for a specialized color processing center in Area V4, as we described in Chapter 3. Much of this evidence now comes from brain imaging studies that use positron emission tomography (PET), which measures blood flow from increased metabolic activity in the cerebral cortex, or functional magnetic resonance imaging (fMRI), which measures changes in blood oxygen level that occur as groups of neurons become active. The advantage of these techniques is that they are noninvasive and

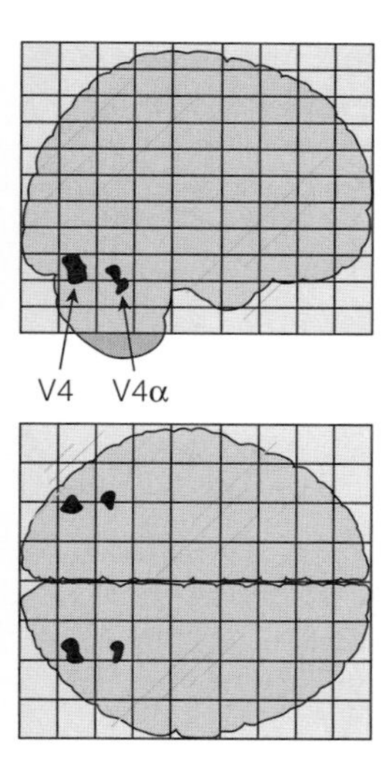

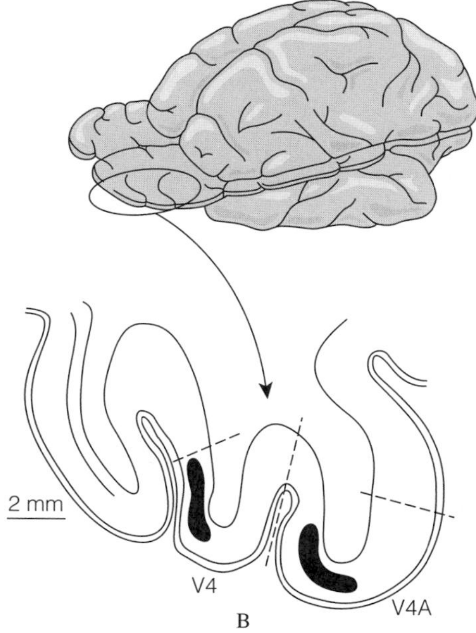

FIGURE 4.28 Locations of color-processing areas in V4 and V4α in the human brain as revealed by PET and fMRI. (A) Dark blobs show active areas for colored vs black-and-white visual stimuli. (B) Precise locations of V4 and V4α in extra striate cortex.

the subjects can be normal human observers viewing colored images. In humans, cortical color centers can be found in posterior V4, which is similar to that found in monkeys, and in a more anterior center V4α, which is not found in the monkey brain. The location of these centers can be seen in Figure 4.28. Note that in Figures 4.28A and 4.28B we are looking at a "glass brain," which means that the centers are not actually on the surface but deeper in the brain. Figure 4.28C shows the same centers as if a slice were taken through the brain and pulled out like a dresser drawer. The suggestion is that these two centers process color differently, since V4 is mapped directly to positions on the retina and can assign a color to a location in space, while V4α responds to combinations of colors, even mixing them across the two eyes (Bartels & Zeki, 2000). However, we still have much to learn about the way in which these brain centers process color.

Although our knowledge about the neural coding of colors is increasing, there are still some obvious puzzles left to be solved. One deals with the appearance of **subjective colors.** These are perceived colors, in the absence of the appropriate wavelengths of light, that can be made to appear in certain flickering black-and-white displays. Some theories suggested that this could indicate that color information was being coded via some sort of neural Morse code rather than the spatial opponent-process system that current data suggest (e.g., Festinger, Allyn, & White, 1971; Young, 1977). More recent theories suggest that these colors may arise because of the interaction between the magnocellular system, which carries brightness information, and the parvocellular system which carries color information (Le Rohellec & Viénot, 2001). The color could come about because the parvocellular system is slower and is still responding even after the magnocellular system has indicated that a flash of colorless light has come and gone, thus leaving us with the impression of color. However, there are still many puzzling aspects of subjective color that remain unexplained. A procedure for creating subjective colors for yourself is shown in Demonstration Box 4.9. You

DEMONSTRATION BOX 4.9

SUBJECTIVE COLORS

You have already encountered subjective colors in Demonstration Box 1.3, where colors appeared in a stationary stimulus. A more powerful set of subjective colors, produced by flickering black-and-white patterns, began as a toy invented by C. E. Benham in 1894. It was painted on a top and meant to be spun; hence the pattern is often referred to as **Benham's top.** The pattern is shown in the figure. Cut out this pattern (or carefully reproduce it), and mount it on a piece of thin cardboard. Punch a hole in the marked center region, and insert a nail or a round pencil. Now spin the pattern as shown. Colors should appear when the pattern is spun at a moderate speed. If you are spinning it clockwise, the inner bands should be slightly red, the next yellow, then green, and the last blue or violet. The order of the colors should reverse if you spin the pattern counterclockwise. The color effects arise because of the specific patterns of flickering white and black set up by each band. These patterns mimic the flashing on-and-off light patterns used to study subjective colors in a laboratory setting. If you alter the adaptive state of your eye by staring at a white surface for a minute, you will notice that the perceived colors on each line will be different (Karvellas, Pokorny, Smith, & Tanczos, 1979).

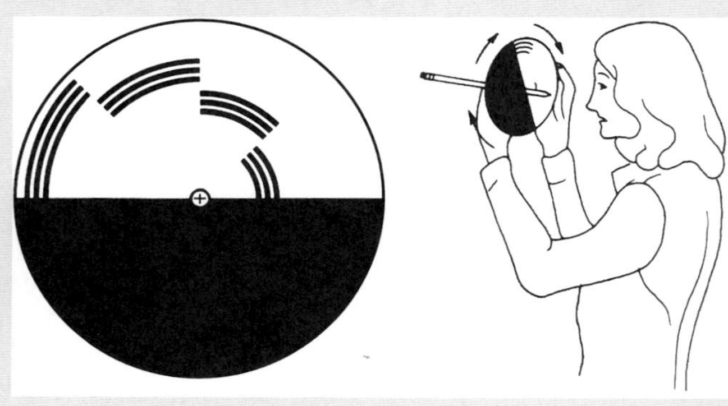

might also want to look back at Demonstration Box 1.3, which shows how subjective colors can come about in stationary patterns (which is yet another colorful puzzle).

COLOR PERCEPTION

Although subjective colors baffle us at the moment, they do demonstrate that the wavelengths of light that are present are not the only factors that determine our perception of hue. Here we describe a number of other factors can alter the perceived color.

Intensity and Duration

Both physiological and psychophysical evidence suggest that color information and brightness information are carried by different visual channels, yet it is also clear that the perception of hue may be affected by the intensity of the stimulus (e.g., Emmerson & Ross, 1986). If intensity levels are low, only rods will be active and no color will be seen. But even beyond the cone threshold the perceived hue of a stimulus will change depending on the stimulus intensity. Specifically, if we increase the intensity of red or yellow-green stimuli, they not only appear brighter but also begin to take on a more yellow hue. Similarly, blue-greens and violets begin to appear bluer when the intensity is increased. This phenomenon is called the **Bezold-Brucke effect,** in honor of its two discoverers. It is easy to demonstrate, as is shown in Demonstration Box 4.10. Some researchers believe that the Bezold-Brucke effect comes about because the red-green opponent-process cells are slightly more sensitive than the blue-yellow cells (Coren & Keith, 1970; Nagy, 1980). Thus, we can discriminate between red and green at lower intensity levels. Because the blue-yellow units become active only at higher intensity levels, hues may tend to be dominated by these colors when stimuli are bright.

Prolonged exposure to colored stimuli also produces a shift in the perception of hue. For instance, if you viewed the world through a deep red filter for a sufficient period of time, you would find that when the filter was removed the world would take on a blue-green tint. This fatiguing of a specific color response is called **chromatic adaptation.** It is believed that these adaptation effects are due either to selective bleaching of one particular photopigment or to fatigue of one aspect of the neural response of an opponent-process system (e.g., Shevell, 2001; Vimal, Pokorny, & Smith, 1987). Imagine looking through a red filter for a long period of time. The red-catching pigment becomes bleached, or the red response in the red-green opponent-process cells becomes fatigued. Now, when you view a white surface, the absence of red pigment (or the weakness of the red response) causes the blue and green systems to account for a greater proportion of the total activity. This gives the white a cyan (blue-green) tint. When such fatigue effects due to prolonged stimulation are localized to only one region of the retina, they are called **afterimages.** Demonstration Box 4.11 provides a stimulus for the production of color afterimages. You will notice when performing this demonstration that the hue of the afterimage tends to be the complementary hue of the stimulus producing the afterimage.

DEMONSTRATION BOX 4.10

THE BEZOLD-BRUCKE EFFECT

For this demonstration you will need three pieces of colored cellophane, glass, or celluloid to serve as color filters. One should be red, the other green, and the last yellow. Take a white sheet of paper that is brightly illuminated with room lighting, and cast a shadow over one half of the paper. Looking through the red filter, you will notice that the hue of the red seen on the bright half of the paper is noticeably yellower than the hue seen on the shadowed portion. When you peer through the green filter, you should experience the same effect. However, looking through a yellow filter should not cause an apparent change in hue. Thus, the brighter you make a red or a green, the more yellow it will appear. This is a demonstration of the hue shift, associated with increasing stimulus intensity, called the Bezold-Brucke effect.

Another way to see this effect is to look at an incandescent lightbulb (60–100 W) through the red or green filter. You will notice that the lightbulb appears to be yellow, despite the presence of the filter. Because the red filter allows only the long (red) wavelengths of light to pass and the green allows only the middle (green) wavelengths through, no yellow is reaching your eye. The yellow appearance of the bulb is caused by the Bezold-Brucke hue shift that occurs when the intensity of the stimulus is high.

DEMONSTRATION BOX 4.11

COLOR AFTERIMAGES

You can easily demonstrate negative or complementary color afterimages using Color Plate 5. Here you see four square patches of color: red, green, blue, and yellow. Notice the black X in the middle of this pattern. Stare at the black X for about 2 minutes while keeping the plate under reasonably bright illumination. At the end of this period, transfer your gaze to the black X to the right of the figure. You should see a pattern of colored squares that is the exact complement of the pattern originally viewed. Where the red patch was, you will see green; where the green patch was, you will see red; where the blue patch was, you will see yellow; and where the yellow patch was, you will see blue. These are the complementary color afterimages caused by the fatiguing of the various color responses during the time you were staring at the color patches.

Spatial Interactions

Earlier in this chapter you learned that the brightness of a stimulus can be affected by the intensity of adjacent stimuli. The general nature of the interaction is inhibitory, so a bright surround makes a central area appear dim. Inhibitory interactions between adjacent color systems can also occur, and they result in hue shifts. The phenomenon is called **simultaneous color contrast.** Consider Color Plate 6. Notice that this figure has four brightly colored patches, each of which surrounds a small central square. The square on the red patch appears to be slightly green, and that on the green appears to be slightly red. The square on the blue patch appears to be slightly yellow, and that on the yellow patch appears to be slightly blue. However, each square is exactly the same gray. You might be able to increase the strength of this effect by viewing Color Plate 6 through a sheet of tracing paper or thin tissue.

There is a lot of similarity between color interactions and brightness interactions. In color contrast, for instance, there is evidence for inhibitory or opponent process interactions both at the retinal level and higher up in the cortex, which together influence the colors that an observer sees when there are adjacent fields of different colored stimuli (e.g., Brenner & Cornelissen, 2002; Shevell & Wei, 2000). In addition to color contrast there is a **color assimilation effect,** very similar to the brightness assimilation effect we observed in Figure 4.8, where gratings of thin colored lines result in a spreading of the color to adjacent gray rather than causing contrast, as in Figure 4.5 (Smith, Jin, & Pokorny, 2001).

Cognitive Factors in Color Perception

There is evidence from certain clinical cases that color is a special sensory quality that is independent of other aspects of our ability to interpret the world. For example, there are some patients who, through brain injury, lose their ability to recognize objects but keep their ability to recognize colors, while others lose their ability to perceive colors while keeping their ability to recognize objects (e.g., Miceli, Fouch, Capasso, Shelton, Tomaiuolo, & Caramazza, 2001). However, there are also subtle interactions between color perception and other cognitive processes.

The remembered color of familiar objects often differs from the objects' actual color. When observers are shown color samples and later asked to match them from an array of colored chips, systematic errors are made. Observers tend to pick chips of greater brightness when asked to remember bright colors and of greater darkness when asked to remember dark colors. When asked to remember and match colors of familiar objects with characteristic hues, we remember apples or tomatoes as being more red than the actual objects, bananas are more yellow in memory than in the bunch, and grass is greener than it is on the lawn (Newhall, Burnham, & Clark, 1957; Yendrikhovskij, Blommaert, & de-Ridder, 1999). Because of this memory effect, many film manufacturers have chosen to modify the spectral reproduction ability of color film so that the reproduced colors are richer than they are in nature.

Memory and color perception can also interact in another way. If we are asked to remember scenes that are presented in black and white or in color, we will remember the colored scenes more accurately (Wichmann, Sharpe, & Gegenfurtner, 2002). However, this is only the case if the scene is colored in normal hues. Strangely colored skies, oddly colored objects, and so forth are not remembered accurately. With such interactions between color and cognition it should not be surprising to find that diseases that impair our cognitive abilities, such as Alzheimer's disease, also impair our abilities to discriminate and match colors to figures (Sala, Kinnear, Spinnler, & Stangalino, 2000).

Color does more than provide us with additional information about stimuli; it has emotional consequences, affecting our mood and perception of the world in subtle ways. Color can even produce sensory impressions that are characteristic of other senses. It is almost universal to call the short-wavelength (blue) colors "cool," whereas the longer wavelengths (yellow) tend to be called "warm. In an era when the conservation of energy is important, it is interesting to note that people will actually turn a heat control to a higher setting in a blue room than they will in a yellow room. It is as if they are trying to compensate thermally for the coolness that has been visually induced (Boynton, 1971). There is even some suggestion that the color of a substance can affect how it appears to smell to us (Gilbert & Martin, 1996; Zellner & Kautz, 1990).

Our moods can also vary along with our perception of color and brightness. Patients suffering from depression are more likely to agree that the lights in their surroundings seem dimmer than usual (Friberg & Borrero, 2000). The probability that they see the world as less bright is correlated with the depth of their depression. Two thirds of the patients categorized as severely depressed responded that their environment appeared dimmer than usual compared to only 21% of moderately and 14% of mildly depressed patients. Depressed patients are also much more likely to agree with the statement , "I notice that everything seems gray/cloudy/drab/lacking color," suggesting a reduced color sensitivity when they are suffering from this mood extreme (Barrick, Taylor, & Correa, 2002). All of these findings emphasize that color is a psychological achievement, not simply a direct effect of the physical variation of wavelengths of light. If you still doubt this statement, it will be instructive to turn back to Demonstration Box 1.3 or Demonstration Box 4.9 in this chapter to see colors develop in your mind where no physical variations in wavelength exist.

STUDY QUESTIONS

1. What is the difference between luminance and illuminance, and which photometric units would you use for each?
2. Give four examples of instances where the perceived brightness of a stimulus or target is not just dependent on the amount of light reaching the eye.
3. Which brightness and color phenomena depend on inhibitory interactions?
4. What evidence can you provide to disprove the statement that "the perception of color depends solely on the wavelength of the light reaching the eye"?
5. There are three psychological dimensions or aspects of color appearance. What are they, and which physical qualities of the stimulus do they most closely correspond to?
6. Do the data on color blindness support the trichromatic or opponent process theory? Why?
7. Which perceptual observations led to the suggestion of an opponent process theory of color vision?
8. Which visual channels of information transmission are associated with color vision, and how do they handle the color information?
9. What is the Bezold-Brucke effect? Why does it occur?
10. What is the evidence that color perception is affected by, or interacts with, more cognitive processes?

CHAPTER 5

THE AUDITORY SYSTEM

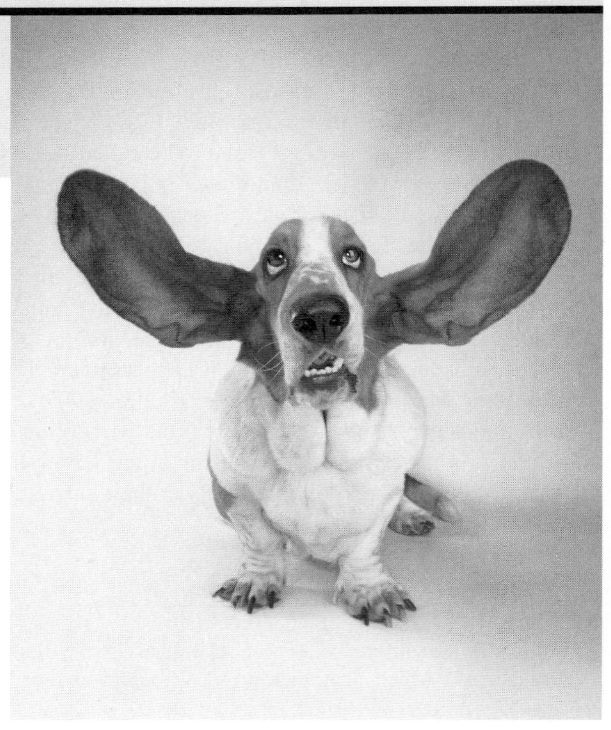

CHAPTER SUMMARY

It is one of those strange twists of history that while studying the physiology of the ear in order to help the deaf, Alexander Graham Bell developed an early version of that indispensable modern communication device: the telephone. Modern scientists are still studying auditory physiology, and others are realizing Bell's dream by developing devices that can be permanently implanted into the ear to allow the deaf to hear again. In this chapter we will take a fascinating journey down the ear canal and into the brain to explore the mechanical and neural structures that underlie our perception of sound. During this journey we will encounter a mechanical marvel, the cochlea, which fills a space of only 2 cubic centimeters but has over 1 million moving parts (Hudspeth, 1985), and the subtle and complicated neural mechanism that underlies our understanding of speech and our appreciation of music.

SOUND

Sound, to a physicist, is a series of changes in mechanical pressure in an elastic medium, such as air or water. When sound is very intense, such as at a rock concert, you can actually feel the mechanical pulsations being transmitted through the air, especially those from the bass instruments, which may cause the floor, your seat, and even your body to vibrate in resonance with them. To see how such waves come about, think about what happens when a guitarist plucks a guitar string to make a sound. The string vibrates, moving rapidly back and forth in space. This movement causes the strand of steel to collide with the air molecules around it. These molecules in turn collide with others, causing air compression as the string moves forward and rarefaction as it moves

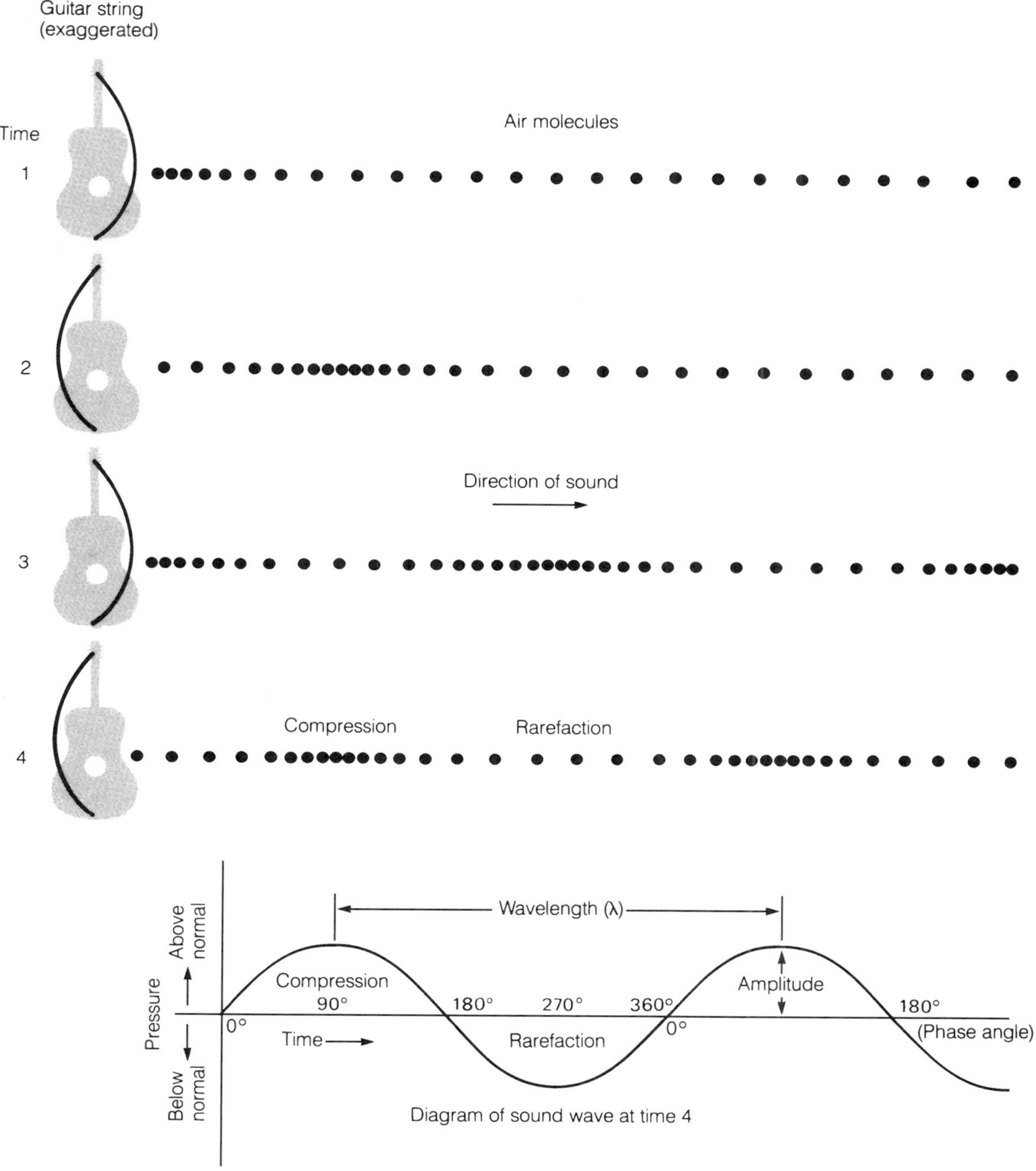

FIGURE 5.1 The nature and description of a simple sound wave in air.

back. The result is a **wave** of mechanical energy, as shown in Figure 5.1. This wave can then be picked up by a microphone, amplified electrically, and then sent to speakers that change the variations in electrical voltage to vibrations of the speaker cone, which compress the air in front of them causing the much more intense pressure waves you hear.

Sound waves can be transmitted for great distances, even though the individual molecules of the medium vibrate only over very small distances. This is done when air molecules collide with those next to them, thus moving the pressure wave through space. Each of these collisions loses a bit of energy, so the pressure variations are less intense as the sound wave moves away from the source. This means

BIOGRAPHY BOX 5.1

RESEARCH AT THE SPEED OF SOUND

Ernst Mach (1838–1916) was an Austrian physicist and philosopher who is probably best known for the fact that his name is attached to the speed of sound (which is about 340 m/second, or 1224 km/hour, in air at ground level). He discovered that the speed of sound varies depending on the medium that it moves through. Today we use a speed measuring scale (using Mach numbers) that takes the medium into account. Thus a speed of Mach 2 is twice the speed of sound in the medium being measured. Working mostly at the University of Prague and later at the University of Vienna, Mach established important principles of optics, mechanics, and wave dynamics. However, throughout his long academic career Mach was interested in the psychology and physiology of sensation. He made many fascinating discoveries in this field, including another phenomenon that bears his name, Mach bands, the tendency of the human eye to see bright or dark bands near the boundaries between areas of sharply differing illumination (see Chapter 4).

One of his most famous works, *Analysis of the Sensations* (1886), was a brilliant blend of physics, physiology, psychology, and philosophy. In this book, Mach argued that the sole content of knowledge is sensation and that material objects can be understood only in terms of the sensations they cause. Mach didn't think there was any such thing as absolute time or absolute space, but only those derived from relationships between objects and between object and perceiver. These ideas had a great influence on Albert Einstein, who incorporated them into his *general theory of relativity.*

that its ability to move or vibrate other objects, such as our eardrums, grows weaker the farther we are from a sound source. Because sound involves the vibration of parts of the medium through which it travels, it cannot pass through a vacuum. The necessity of a medium for the existence and propagation of sound waves was demonstrated by Robert Boyle in 1660. He suspended his watch by a thread in a jar and observed that its ticking sound gradually faded away as he pumped the air out of the jar. Many of the important properties of sound were worked out by Ernst Mach, who is described in Biography Box 5.1.

A Simple Sound Wave

The simplest sound wave is a sine wave, often called a **pure tone.** The lower part of Figure 5.1 shows a plot of air pressure as it varies over time for a pure tone in air. The **wavelength** (represented by the Greek letter λ, pronounced *lamda*) is the distance from one peak of the wave to the next, which also represents a single **cycle** from one maximum pressure through a pressure minimum and back to the maximum again**.** The **frequency** (f) of the wave is the number of cycles completed during one second. Frequency is expressed in **Hertz** (Hz), named after the German physicist Heinrich R. Hertz. One Hertz is equivalent to one **cycle per second.** Sound frequency is the most important (but not the only) factor determining the pitch of a sound that we hear. Just as in music, *pitch* refers to whether we are experiencing a high or a low note or tone. The range of frequencies that seem to have pitch for people with normal hearing is from about 20 to 20,000 Hz. Pure tones below 20 Hz are experienced as vibration, whereas those above 20,000 Hz are not heard at all except by young children (although your dog can still hear these tones).

The **pressure amplitude** is the change in pressure produced by the sound wave. This is a relative measure that compares the maximum pressure change in the sound (measured as force per unit area in dyne/cm^2) to normal atmospheric pressure (about 1,000,000 dyne/cm^2 at sea level). The maximum pressure difference the human ear can tolerate is about 280 dyne/cm^2 above or below atmospheric pressure, whereas the minimum pressure difference detectable is about 0.0002 dyne/cm^2. For a sound wave with pressure amplitude equal to 0.0002 dyne/cm^2, the air molecules are displaced by about 0.0000000001 cm, which is about one tenth the diameter of a hydrogen molecule. This means that the ear is an extremely sensitive organ with a broad response range.

A much more convenient way to talk about such a wide range of sound pressure changes involves a logarithmic scale (based upon the powers of 10), again comparing the current pressure to a reference level. The unit used is called the **Bel** in honor of Alexander Graham Bell. Because the Bel is rather large relative to normal hearing levels, we typically express **sound pressure levels** in **decibels** (dB); a decibel is one tenth of a Bel. The formula for sound pressure level (in dB) is

$$\text{dB} = 20 \log\left(\frac{p}{p_0}\right)$$

where p is the sound pressure amplitude and p_0 (usually 0.0002 dyne/cm^2) is the reference pressure. This reference pressure was not completely arbitrary. It represents the average threshold for hearing of healthy young individuals. Table 5.1 gives typical values of sound pressure levels for some representative sounds and illustrates how loudness increases as the sound pressure level increases. Sound pressure amplitude is the most important (but not the only) determinant of loudness.

TABLE 5.1 Sound Pressure Levels of Various Sound Sources (P_0 = 0.0002 dyne/cm^2)

Source	Sound Level (dB)
Manned spacecraft launch (from 45 m)	180
Loudest rock band on record	160
Pain threshold (approximate)	140
Large jet motor (at 22 m)	120
Loudest human shout on record	111
Heavy auto traffic	100
Conversation (at about 1 m)	60
Quiet office	40
Soft whisper	20
Threshold of hearing	0

A final important aspect of sound waves is the **phase angle.** Phase angle refers to the particular part of the compression-rarefaction cycle a wave has reached at any designated instant of time. A single cycle of a sine wave is assigned 360° (as in circular motion). A pure tone begins with 0° of phase angle at the point of zero pressure difference, followed by the compression peak at 90°, another zero-pressure-difference point at 180°, and the rarefaction (pressure minimum, sometimes called a *valley*) at 270° as shown in Figure 5.1. Thus, any point in a cycle can be specified by number of degrees from 0° to 360°. If two pure tones are at exactly the same place in their respective cycles (so that their peaks and valleys coincide), they are said to be **in phase.** If their peaks and valleys do not coincide, the two tones are **out of phase.** How much they are out of phase is expressed in terms of **relative phase,** the difference between their respective phase angles. If one tone is at 90° (its peak) when another is at 180° (crossing the zero-pressure-difference line), then the two are 90° out of phase.

Because sound waves consist of variations of mechanical pressure over time, different pure tones that occur at the same time can interact with each, effectively adding or subtracting pressure from the total sound signal. If two pure tones of the same frequency are perfectly in phase (0° out of phase), their pressure changes coincide and the amplitude of the resulting tone is the sum of those of the two tones. If the two tones are 180° out of phase, one reaches its minimum when the other is reaching its maximum and the pressure amplitude of the resulting tone is the difference of those of the two tones. If these out of phase tones also had the same pressure amplitude, they would actually cancel each other completely. This principle is used in **active noise suppression** to eliminate unwanted sounds. In a typical system a computer analyzes inputs from a microphone and then generates through a speaker sounds that are 180° out of phase with the unwanted sounds. The broadcast sounds cancel the noise, and it is not heard. Active noise suppression systems are currently being designed for cars, airplanes, and other noisy environments where the characteristics of the noise do not change too rapidly. You already can buy a pair of headphones that use active noise suppression to lessen noise in an airplane.

Everyday sounds are more complex than pure tones. Only a few sound sources, such as tuning forks or electronic instruments, produce pure tones. Sounds produced by musical instruments, the human voice, automobiles, waterfalls, and so on have much more complex patterns of compression and rarefaction. These complexities result from the interaction of many different sound waves

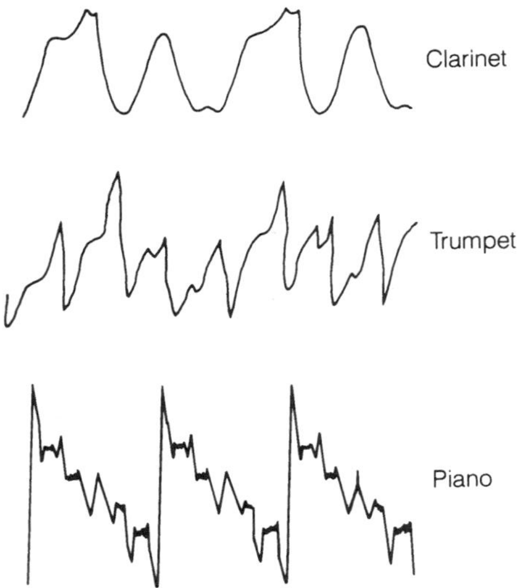

FIGURE 5.2 Complex sound waves produced by three musical instruments.

of different frequencies and phases that add and subtract from each other to create a new sound. Complex sounds are referred to as having an additional psychological property called **timbre.** We can tell the difference when the same note is played on a trumpet, a clarinet, a piano, and a violin quite easily. This is because they have different timbres, meaning that they produce different wave forms even when they are playing the same musical note as shown in Figure 5.2. Demonstration Box 5.1 shows you how to experience our extraordinary ability to identify complex sounds through their timbre.

Complex sounds, such as those in Figure 5.2, can be described by analyzing them into the sets of simpler waves, which added together produce the more complicated wave forms in the first place. This method was invented by the French scientist J. B. J. Fourier. Mathematically what Fourier proved was that any continuous, periodic waveform can be represented as the

DEMONSTRATION BOX 5.1

PERCEPTION OF TIMBRE

Perhaps the most primitive musical instrument is the human hand, used (usually in pairs) to clap rhythms. As in any musical instrument, the shape and orientation of the surrounding parts will alter the complex components of the resultant sound, hence the timbre that we hear. There seem to be only a few basic ways of clapping, and people have the remarkable ability to distinguish which is occurring from the sound alone (Repp, 1987). Try holding your hands in the configuration shown in Configuration A of the figure so that your hands are aligned and flat. Clap a few times, listening closely to the sound. Now hold your hands in Configuration B, with your hands oblique and slightly cupped. Clap a few times, again listening closely to the sound. Configuration B generates more low-frequency sounds in the mixture than Configuration A. You should be able to distinguish the different claps quite clearly. You can also hear differences if the palms are crossed while clapping, if you clap with your fingers around your palm, and so forth. It might be fun to have someone else now clap while you are not looking and see if you can approximate what his or her hand positions are. If you can, you are responding to the timbre of the sounds and performing some form of analysis of the complex sounds actually present into their constituent components, which then allows you to recognize their source. Similar spectral analyses allow us to recognize voices, musical instruments, and a wide variety of natural sounds.

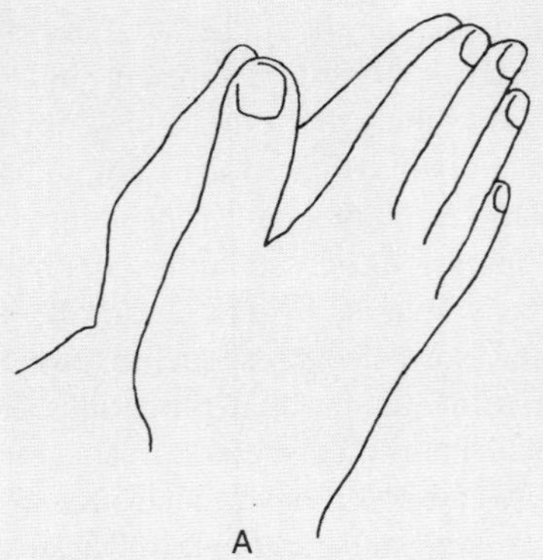

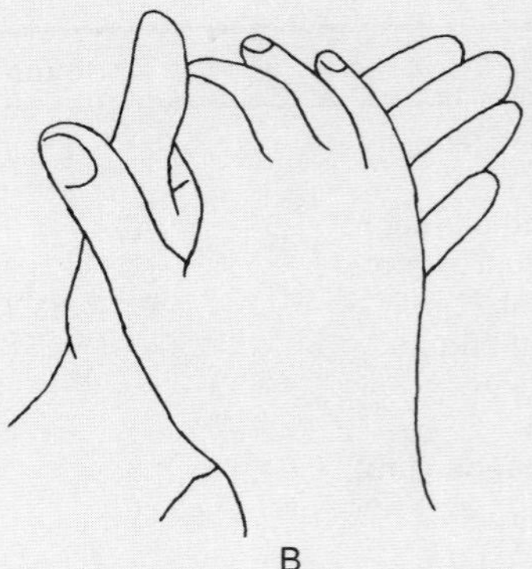

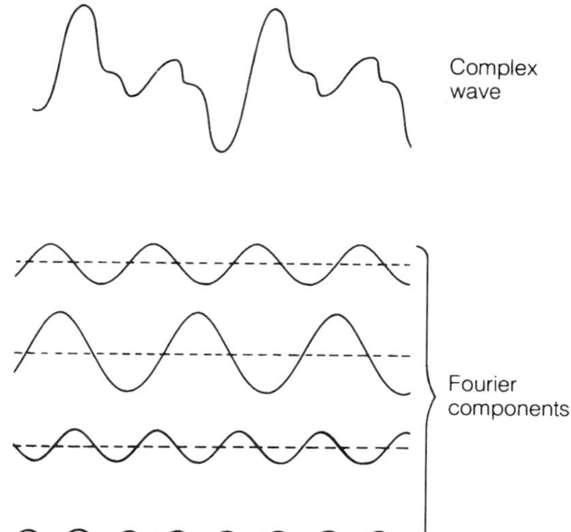

FIGURE 5.3 Fourier components (sine waves) of a complex sound wave.

sum of a set of simple sine waves with appropriate wavelengths, phases, and amplitudes. Figure 5.3 shows an example of the decomposition of a complex waveform into such a set of sine waves (which are sometimes called **Fourier components**). Speech sounds also may be analyzed into their Fourier components, with results that are very useful for the understanding of speech perception (see Chapter 6). In fact, the ear performs a mechanical Fourier analysis on complex sounds, allowing you to hear the various simple sounds that went into the complex sound. This fact is known as **Ohm's acoustical law** after the physicist George Ohm. You may demonstrate this effect for yourself using Demonstration Box 5.2.

THE STRUCTURE OF THE EAR

Evolution and the Anatomy of the Ear

The human ear is an extremely complex biological system, yet biologists have traced its origins to simple organs in primitive animals (Stebbins, 1980; van Bergeijk, 1967). All vertebrate ears seem to have evolved from the sense of touch. Whether primitive or advanced, they seem to be specializations of groups of cells with protruding hairs that, like the hairs on the skin of your arm, are designed to respond to mechanical stimulation. In fact, the skin is sometimes used to demonstrate certain phenomena associated with human hearing.

One of the first developments in the evolution of the mammalian ear was the lateral line. The lateral line is a row of nerve endings in the skin of fish and some amphibians that gets its name because it shows up as a visible line of contrasting color on the skin. These nerve endings are wrapped around sensory hairs that are embedded in jellylike masses that are exposed to the surrounding water. As the water vibrates from the motions of prey, predators, or other events, the waterlike jelly vibrates as well, causing the sensory hairs to bend, thus stimulating the nerve endings and signaling the vibration to the animal's brain. Detection of vibrations is useful to such animals, especially when vision or other sensory systems cannot function well. For example, the lateral line system in one Antarctic fish is tuned very precisely to the vibrations made by the plankton it feeds on, helping the fish find prey during the 6 months of darkness the region experiences (Montgomery & MacDonald, 1987).

In addition to the lateral line system, some types of fish have primitive internal ears that work on much the same principles as do human ears. These internal ears probably evolved from a specialized, deeply sunken part

DEMONSTRATION BOX 5.2

OHM'S ACOUSTICAL LAW

This demonstration is done with a piano or a guitar, but if neither is available, use three glasses filled with water to different heights so that they produce a fairly high note, a middle note, and a low note when tapped with a butter knife. Now have some friends strike the high, middle, and low notes simultaneously a few times. Without their telling you, have them drop out one note, sounding only two a few times, then put it back in. Notice that it is easy to determine which of the three notes was added or subtracted, despite the fact that the chord formed by these notes is a complex sound pattern. The individual sounds do not lose their identities and can be discriminated from the others in the complex sound. With enough practice a person can learn to separate as many as six or seven different components of a complex chord or "clang." The separation of sound components by the auditory system is known as Ohm's acoustical law.

of the lateral line system. This part of the lateral line developed into an internal structure called a **labyrinth** because it has looping passages. The labyrinth is fluid filled, and there are tiny hairs that protrude into the fluid and bend when it moves in response to sound stimulation from the water outside. The hairs are attached to sensory nerves that signal the fish's brain when they are bent. Some of the elements in this simple ear are similar to those found in humans, including the composition of the fluid in the labyrinth, which is the same as that in the human inner ear.

Mammals, birds, and the crocodilian reptiles, lizards and snakes, and turtles all have a more complex labyrinth that contains a membrane covered with sensory cells from which (of course) tiny hairs protrude. This evolved about 200 to 250 million years ago when the ancestors of these classes of animals moved from the water to the land. In mammals, birds, and the crocodilian reptiles the labyrinth became a structure that we call the **cochlea.** Its name, which means "shell," is derived from its coiled snail-shell appearance in mammals. The cochlea contains two different types of hair cells with specialized functions that evolved about 150 to 200 million years ago (Manley & Köpp, 1998). These hair cells are rather a late evolutionary development and first appear in snakes and lizards. Figure 5.4 summarizes the evolution of the ear. Once you have finished this chapter and know more about the specific components of the auditory system, you might find it interesting to glance back at this figure again to see the sequence of how these evolved.

All mammalian ears have the same basic parts, although they differ somewhat in proportions (with the elephant, of course, having one of the largest). They also differ in sensitivity. Bats, whales, and dogs have extraordinarily keen hearing over a very wide range of frequencies. The ears of mammals differ from those of birds, reptiles, and fish in that mammalian ears typically have three small bones to transmit vibrations to the labyrinth, rather than a single bone, as found in these other species. Bekesy (1960), in a classic series of detailed studies, established that all of these various types of ears function in a similar manner. He was able to link many of the performance differences with differences in the physical properties of the ears such as the size of the ear canal and the length of the cochlea. Thus, the human ear, with which we will be concerned in this chapter, is a part of a large family of roughly equivalent organs. This makes it possible to extend the results of studies of other animals' ears to the human auditory system.

Physiology of the Human Ear

Now let us consider the structures of the human ear as they react to the reception of a sound. Figure 5.5 is a schematic representation of the human ear. Let us begin

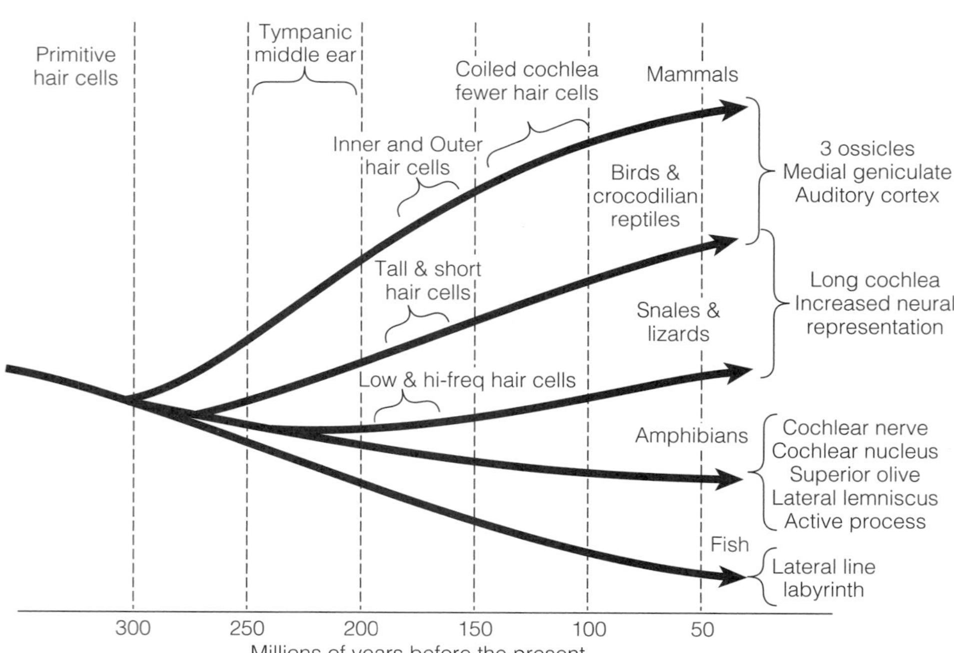

FIGURE 5.4 Major developments in the evolution of the ear.

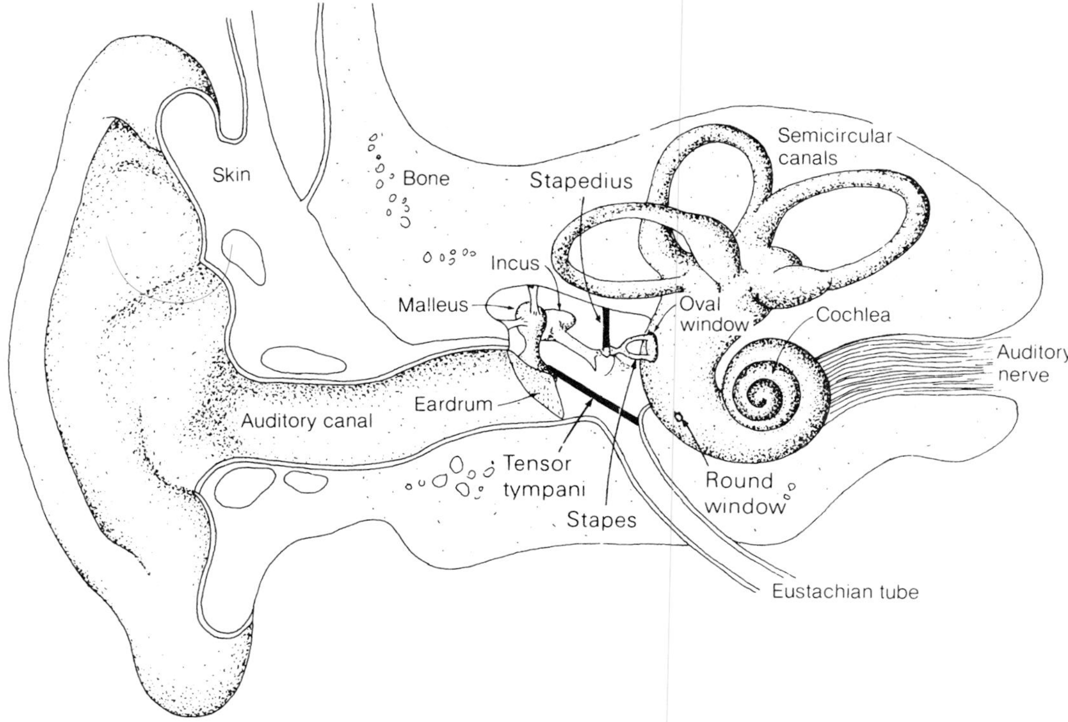

FIGURE 5.5 The human ear (based on Lindsay & Norman, 1977).

by looking at the **outer ear.** The **pinna** is the "ear" that poets and lovers talk about, namely the fleshy part of the visible from the outside. Only mammals have pinnae, which channel sound waves into the **ear canal,** which is technically called the **external auditory meatus.** Pinnae also affect sound localization, as you will see in Chapter 6. Some mammals, such as bats and dogs, can move their pinnae which gives them some ability to select the direction from which sounds are received.

Sound waves that reach the ear move along the ear canal until they encounter the **eardrum** (or **tympanum**). The ear canal acts as a passive amplifier increasing the amplitude of certain sound frequencies through resonance. In humans, sounds with frequencies between 2000 and 7000 Hz (which carry some speech information) benefit from such amplification. The eardrum vibrates in phase with the incoming sound waves, moving faster for high-frequency sounds and more slowly for low-frequency sounds. As we mentioned earlier, these vibratory movements are small. The detailed structures of the ear canal, the eardrum, and the air chambers beyond the eardrum all are important in shaping the way the ear responds to sounds (Rabbitt, 1990; Stinson & Khanna, 1989).

The vibrations of the eardrum are transmitted to the transducer mechanism in the cochlea by three tiny bones (**ossicles**) in the **middle ear:** the **malleus** ("hammer"), the **incus** ("anvil"), and the **stapes** ("stirrup") (see Figure 5.6). The stapes connects to the cochlea via a small membrane-covered opening called the **oval window.** In some common clinical conditions the ossicles cannot conduct sound vibrations, often because they are fused together or because there is a break in the chain connections. This results in a hearing loss called **conduction deafness.** Surgery can sometimes restore the ability to carry vibrations from the eardrum to the oval window, partially relieving this condition.

In addition to conducting vibrations to the oval window, the middle ear also amplifies them. Amplification is necessary because the eardrum, to which the malleus is attached, is a large, easy-to-move flap of skin, whereas the part of the inner ear that must be moved by the stapes, the oval window, is small and difficult to move because it is at the bottom of a long tube filled with fluid. The middle ear increases the pressure applied to the oval window in three ways (Pickles, 1988). First, and most important, the area of the oval window is only about one fifteenth that of the vibrating area of the eardrum. From physics

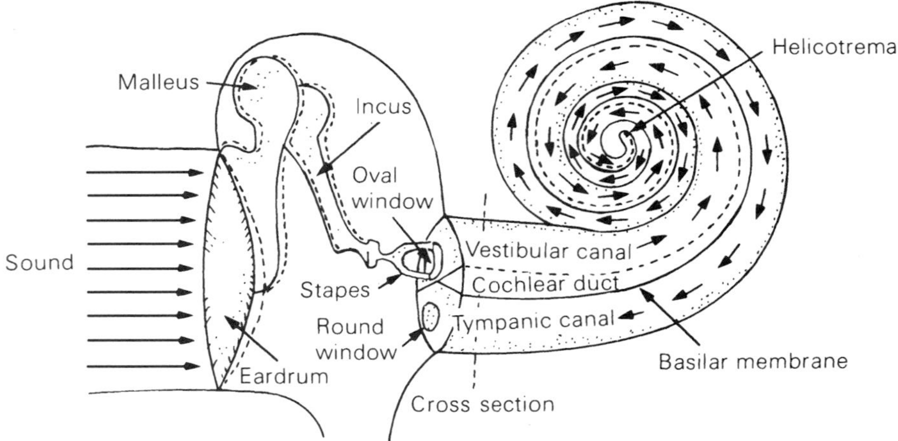

FIGURE 5.6 Movements of the eardrum in response to sound are transmitted by the ossicles to the fluid in the canals of the coiled cochlea.

we know that when the same force is applied uniformly to two surfaces of different areas, the smaller surface will receive the greater force per unit area. Hence, the difference in vibrating area between the eardrum and oval window causes the pressure exerted by the stapes on the oval window to be about 15 times greater than that of the sound wave on the eardrum. The other pressure-increasing mechanisms are more subtle. They depend on the lever action of the malleus and incus and on the way the eardrum buckles as it moves. These two processes increase the force applied by the stapes to the oval window by decreasing its velocity of movement relative to that of the eardrum. In total, the force applied at the stapes is amplified by a factor of about 30 over that of the sound wave on the eardrum by these properties of the middle ear. This mechanical amplification means that much fainter sounds can now reach the threshold of hearing.

Somewhat paradoxically, the middle ear can also *decrease* the pressure at the oval window relative to that at the eardrum. This is a protective mechanism designed to reduce damage to the ear caused by high sound pressure levels. Low to moderate sound pressures cause the stapes to push directly on the oval window. For high sound pressures, however, the stapes moves at an angle that greatly reduces the force it applies to the oval window. In addition, high-level sounds of low frequency cause muscles attached to the malleus and the stapes to contract reflexively, thus decreasing the movements of the ossicles and decreasing the force applied at the oval window (see Figure 5.5 for the locations of these muscles). These mechanisms reduce the pressure of what otherwise might be damaging sounds.

The ossicles of the middle ear are surrounded by air. The pressure of this air in the middle ear is kept approximately equal to that of the surrounding atmosphere by means of the **eustachian tube,** which opens into the back of the throat. This is important because a pressure differential would cause the eardrum to bulge and stiffen, resulting in less responsiveness to the sound striking it (Rabbitt, 1990). If the eustachian tube were not present, the pressure in the middle ear would gradually drop because of absorption of the air by the surrounding tissue. However, the two eustachian tubes open briefly every time we swallow, allowing air to flow into the two middle ear cavities from the mouth and lungs. This equalizes the air pressure on both sides of the eardrum. Sometimes, for example, when we have a head cold, the eustachian tubes become blocked, and the pressure in our middle ears cannot be equalized to that of the outside air, which may be painful and even cause temporary hearing loss. Similar problems can arise when we are climbing or descending in an airplane; the cabin pressure may become considerably lower or higher than the pressure within our middle ears unless we equalize the pressure by swallowing or by pressing our nostrils together and blowing gently. The eustachian tubes can also be a route by which bacteria can travel to the middle ear and cause infections that can also result in temporary hearing loss. This problem, called **otitis media,** often happens when infants or young children get colds because their eustachian tubes are short. In otitis media, fluid builds up in the middle ear, causing the eardrum to bulge painfully and sometimes to burst in cases of severe infection.

Vibrations of the stapes are transmitted to the **inner ear** via the oval window, which is the boundary between the middle and inner ears. The oval window is at the base of the **vestibular canal,** one of three tubes that form the cochlea (Figures 5.6 and 5.7). The far end of the vestibular canal (called the *apex*) is connected to another tube, the **tympanic canal.** This connection is a sort of short

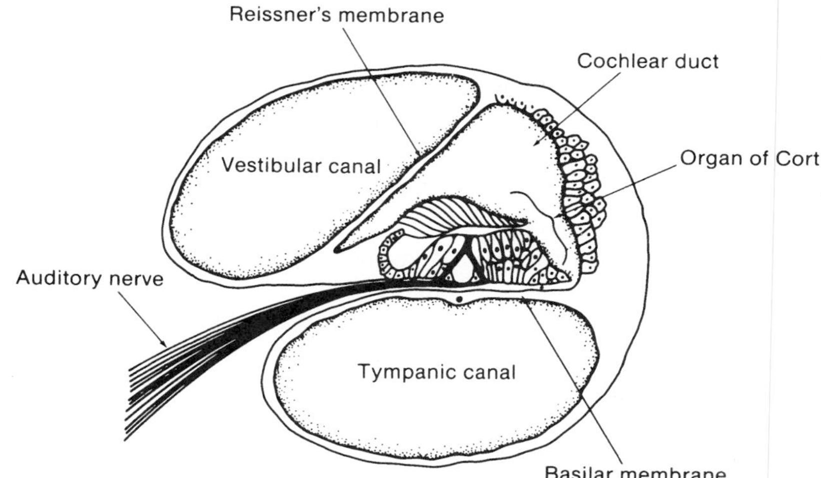

FIGURE 5.7 Cross-section of the cochlea reveals its three canals and the organ of Corti, the auditory receptor.

section of bent corridor called the **helicotrema.** The tympanic canal has its own membrane-covered opening at its base, which separates it from the airspace in the middle ear. This is called the **round window.** These canals are filled with **perilymph**, a fluid resembling salt water. Because perilymph is not compressible, movements of the stapes can cause the round window to bulge out or flex in from the applied pressure.

The third canal of the cochlea, the **cochlear duct** (or *scala media*), is relatively self-contained. It neither contacts the middle ear nor joins the vestibular or tympanic canals. It is formed by two membranes, **Reissner's membrane** and the **basilar membrane.** Together they form a crude triangle with the wall of the cochlea (Figure 5.7). The cochlear duct is filled with **endolymph,** a fluid that is more viscous than perilymph. Reissner's membrane is only two cells thick and has no function other than to form one wall of the cochlear duct. The basilar membrane, however, supports the structures that convert the movements of the cochlear fluid into neural signals.

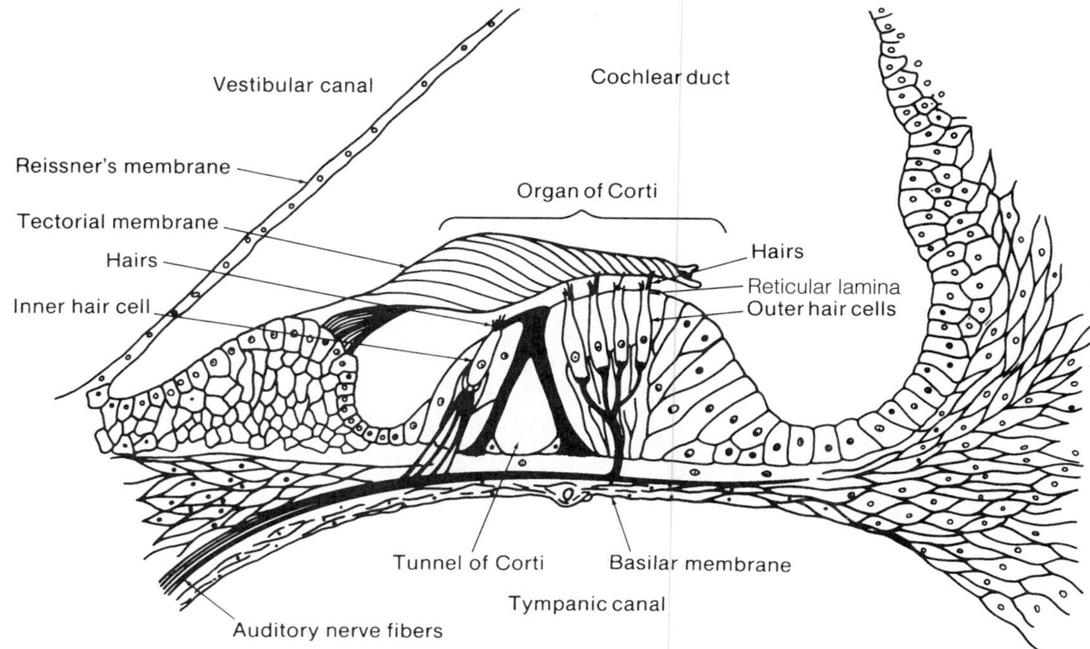

FIGURE 5.8 The detailed structure of the organ of Corti (based on Gulick, 1971).

In humans the basilar membrane is about 30 mm long. It is narrower (0.08 mm) near the base and wider (0.5 mm) at the apex. It is also about 100 times stiffer at the base than at the apex. This tapering of the basilar membrane is necessary to maintain the efficient transfer of energy between middle and inner ears at low frequencies (Shera & Zweig, 1991).

A third membrane within the cochlear duct is also important. The **tectorial membrane** extends into the cochlear duct from Reissner's membrane, and hairs from some of the cells of the **organ of Corti** are embedded in it (Figure 5.8). The organ of Corti contains the hair cells that convert mechanical action in the cochlea into neural signals that are sent to the brain.

The organ of Corti rests on the basilar membrane along its entire length. It contains about 15,000 cells that resemble the cells of the skin in that hairs protrude from them. The hairs are formed from a core made of a protein called *actin* and a covering of another protein called *myosin*. A single row of about 3000 **inner hair cells** is found on the inner side (inner relative to the outside wall of the cochlea—the left side in Figure 5.8), and then there is a space and next to it are three to five rows of **outer hair cells.** *Inner hair* cells have about 40 to 60 hairs each. These hairs extend into the endolymph that fills the cochlear duct but do not actually touch the tectorial membrane (Lim, 1980). *Outer hair* cells have more hairs, as many as 100 to 120 very tiny hairs protruding from each one. The tallest of these outer hairs are firmly embedded in the tectorial membrane; the shorter hairs apparently do not touch the membrane. The hairs on outer hair cells are arranged in V- or W-shaped rows, whereas those on the inner hair cells form straight rows (Photo 5.1).

For both inner and outer hair cells, the sets of hairs of different sizes protruding from a single cell are arranged in order of size and form a **hair bundle.** Each hair in a bundle is connected to nearby hairs in the same bundle by linking filaments. In addition, for all but the tallest hairs, each hair is connected at its tip to the side of its taller neighbor by a thin filament called a **tip link** (see Photo 5.2). This tip link appears to have a core of actin, similar to the hairs themselves (Osborne, Comis, & Pickles, 1988; Pickles et al., 1989). Because of these links, all of the hairs in a hair bundle tend to move together. When they bend toward the longer hairs, the tip links will pull on the cell membrane at the tips of the shorter hairs and on the sides of the taller hairs. This arrangement of hairs and filaments is important for the transduction of sound in the organ of Corti, as you will see in a while.

It has recently been shown that mutations in the genes that regulate the structure of actin and myosin can cause

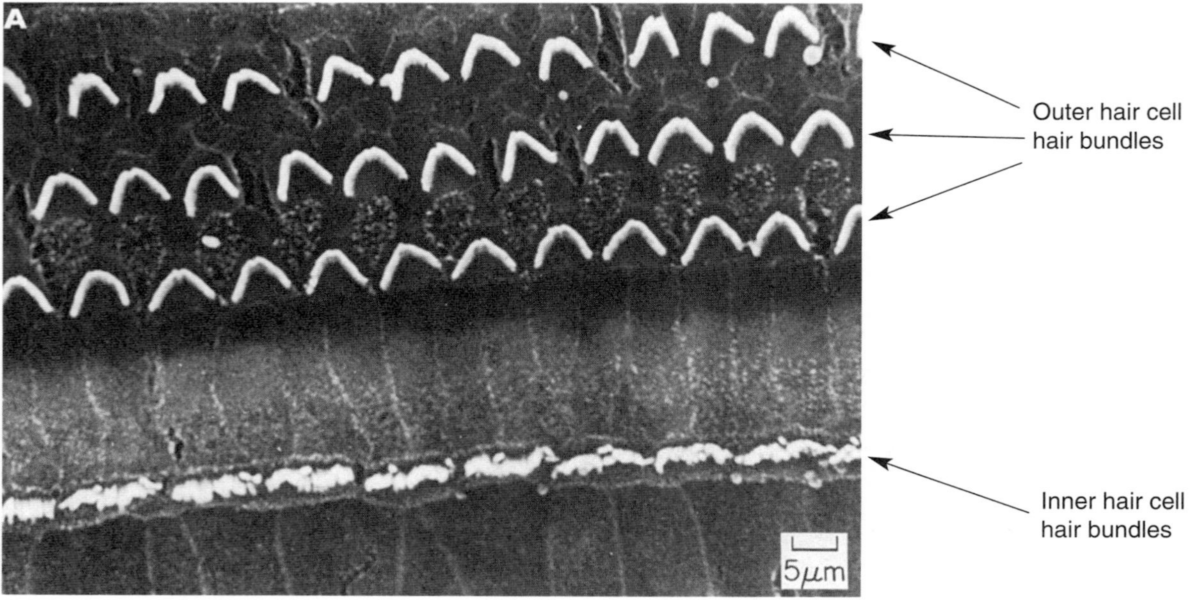

PHOTO 5.1 Scanning electron micrograph of the organ of Corti from the top with the tectorial membrane removed to expose the hair bundles of the outer and inner hair cells (from Pickles, 1988).

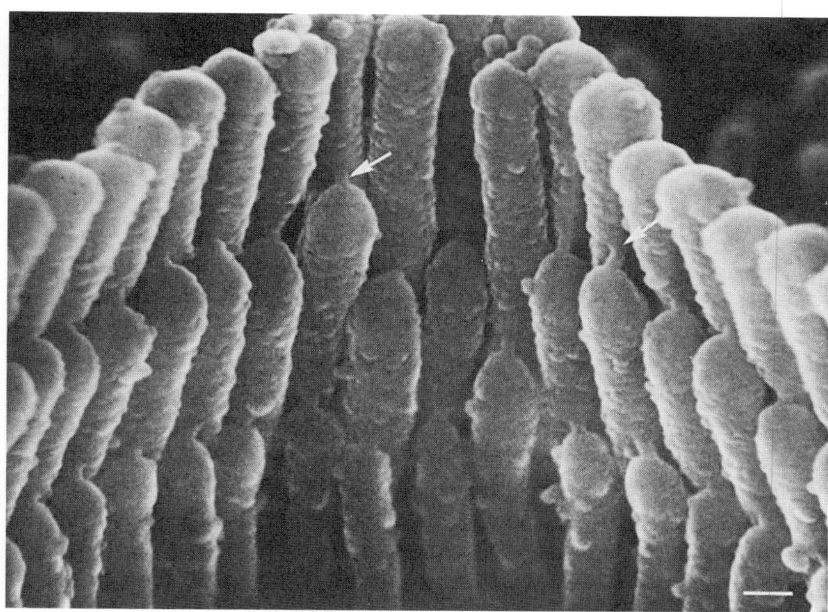

PHOTO 5.2 Scanning electron micrograph of an outer-hair-cell hair bundle, showing the graded sizes of the hairs and the tip links connecting the tips of the shorter hairs to the sides of the taller ones (from Pickles, 1988).

deafness, presumably by causing structural defects in the hairs and their bundles that interfere with their function in transduction (e.g., Lynch et al., 1997). Hair cells can also be damaged, usually in the form of hair breakage, by stimulation from high-pressure-level sounds. It was long believed that such damage, causing sensorineural deafness, was irreversible in mammals. However, there is mounting evidence that hair cells can be stimulated to regenerate, even in humans (Staecker & Van De Water, 1998; Warchol et al., 1993).

About 30,000 nerve fibers make connections with the base of the hair cells in the cochlea and also go to neurons located in the **spiral ganglion.** For about 95% of these (the so-called **type 1** fibers) each makes a connection with an *inner* hair cell. How many connections are made with each hair cell depends upon where you are in the cochlea. About 15 type 1 fibers connect to each inner hair cell in the middle of the cochlea, while only 3 or 4 fibers connect to each inner hair cell at the base and apex (Spoendlin & Schrott, 1989). Each of the remaining 5% of the fibers (called **type 2 fibers)** connects to *outer* hair cells. These involve many more connections and each type 2 fiber may make contact with around 10 outer hair cells (Spoendlin, 1978). Figure 5.9 shows how projections of the spiral ganglion neurons innervate the cochlea.

Type 1 fibers have large diameter axons and are covered with a myelin sheath that allows them to conduct neural impulses considerably faster than do the small-diameter, unmyelinated type 2 fibers. In addition, the two types of fibers originate from differently-shaped spiral ganglion cells (Kiang, Rho, Northrop, Liberman, & Ryugo, 1982). The fact that there are so many differences between these two types of fibers suggests that each might carry different types of auditory information. It is likely that actual information about sounds is carried by the fibers that innervate the inner hair cells. The fibers

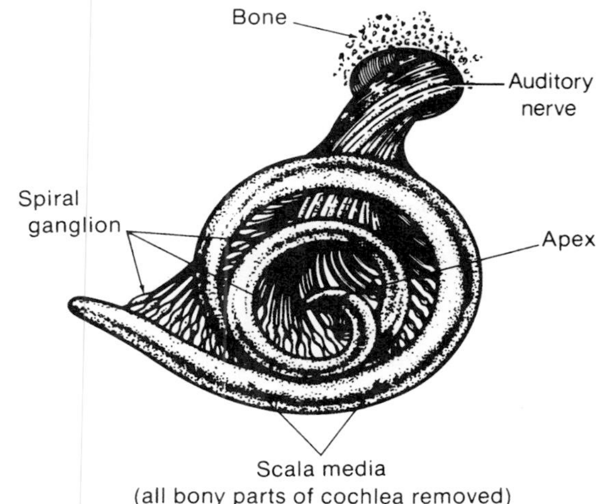

FIGURE 5.9 A view of the cochlea with the bone and other covering removed, leaving only the soft membrane and neural tissue.

that innervate the outer hair cells seem to be involved in some sort of feedback loop that modifies the respon-sive'ness of the inner hair cells to sounds of particular frequencies and play a role in what we will come to call an *active process* (see Zwislocki, 2002).

The axons of the spiral ganglion cells make up the auditory nerve—the neural pathway to the higher auditory centers in the brain (Figure 5.9). Complex feedback loops and inputs from the higher brain centers sent to the cochlea seem to be fairly common in the auditory system. Thus the hair cells not only send sensory (*afferent*) information to the central nervous system via the spiral ganglion but also receive out-going (*efferent*) signals from nuclei in the **superior olive**, which is part of the brain stem (see Figure 5.18; Sahley, Nodar, & Musiek, 1997). Hair cells in every species receive this kind of feedback information (e.g., Manley & Köpp, 1998).

Why should we have signals from higher centers coming into the ear? It seems most likely that these inputs control processes that are designed to protect the ear from damage by intense sounds. Inputs from the superior olive on the opposite, or *contralateral*, side of the head is referred to as the *crossed pathway*. These control the protective processes for high-level *binaural* sounds (sounds reaching both ears) but are relatively unaffected by background noise (Puel, Bobbin, & Fallon, 1988). Input from the superior olive on the same, or *ipsilateral*, side of the head is referred to as the *uncrossed pathway*. This pathway is activated only by high-level monaural sounds (affecting one ear preferentially) in a noisy background (Ramesh, 2000). When maximum protection of the auditory system is needed, such as intense sounds with noise-filled backgrounds (like rock concerts?), both systems are activated. The crossed pathway to the outer hair cells is also involved in changing the responsiveness of the basilar membrane to certain frequencies (modifying the so-called tuning curves, which we discuss in the next section) and thus they also may be associated with the focusing of attention on certain aspects of the auditory stimulation (Pickles, 1988; Xiao & Suga, 2002; and Chapter 12).

Mechanical Tuning on the Basilar Membrane

When the stapes vibrates against the oval window, it causes the fluid to move down the vestibular canal. This vibration eventually reaches the helicotrema and then moves around the bend to cause fluid motion in the tectorial canal. Together these movements cause a sort of shearing action that produces pressure waves across the cochlear duct (e.g., Olson, 1999). These pressure waves, in turn, cause mechanical waves to travel down the basilar membrane from the stiffer, narrower base (near the oval window) to the looser, broader apex (Kitzes, Gibson, Rose, & Hind, 1978). The traveling wave that is produced is a sort of a kink, or local bending, that moves down the length of the membrane, much like what happens when a whip is cracked. Figure 5.10 is a schematic drawing of such a wave. You can explore the properties of traveling waves for yourself by fixing a piece of cloth, such as a scarf, at one end with a pile of heavy books and moving the other end up and down (as uniformly as possible) at various frequencies. The speed and distance of travel will vary with the frequency with which you move the free end. The existence of traveling waves on the basilar membrane was demonstrated by Georg von Bekesy (e.g., 1960), who received the Nobel Prize for his work on the mechanics of the ear and is discussed in Biography Box 5.2.

Variations in elasticity and width of the basilar membrane are responsible for the direction and the speed of the traveling wave. These mechanical properties then make up a *passive process* that causes differences in the amplitude of the traveling wave based on the frequency of the sound input. Bekesy demonstrated that traveling waves caused by low-frequency sounds grow steadily in size as they travel down the basilar toward the apex. Traveling waves associated with low frequencies do not reach their maximum until they reach a place near the apex. Those caused by higher frequency sounds, however, don't travel as far down the basilar membrane. The maximum wave amplitude for a high-frequency tone is much nearer to the base of the membrane where the stapes is attached to the cochlea, and the energy of such a wave then quickly dissipates. This is shown in Figure 5.11, which displays traveling wave amplitude at different places along the basilar membrane for pure tones of different frequencies (see also Greenwood, 1990). This mechanical analysis of sound by the basilar membrane is the basis for Ohm's acoustical law. Demonstration Box 5.3 shows you how to experience the difference in the ability of low- and high-frequency waves to travel down a membrane.

Measurements have demonstrated that the response of the basilar membrane is very sharply tuned to the frequency of the stimulating sound; that is, the curves shown in Figure 5.11 are sharply peaked. Variations in the stiffness and thickness of the basilar membrane along its length are not sufficient to explain these very sharp mechanical tuning curves. The additional tuning arises from mechanical amplification by an **active process** that

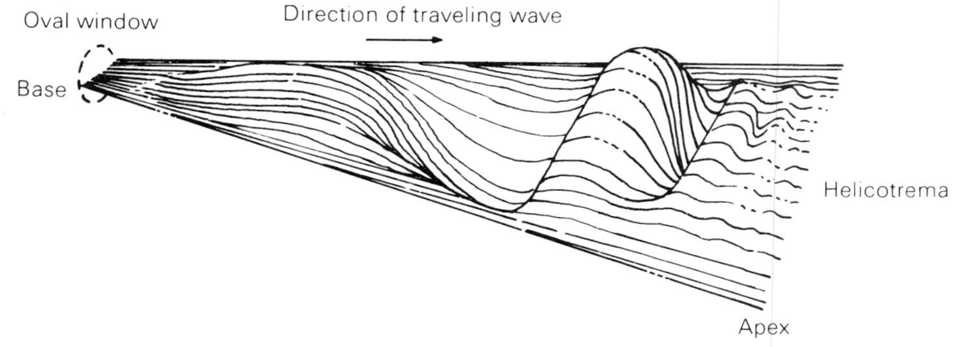

FIGURE 5.10 A traveling wave on the basilar membrane.

BIOGRAPHY BOX 5.2

TRAVELING WAVES ON THE COCHLEA

Georg von Békésy (1899–1972) is another physicist who did important work in audition. He is most famous for his discovery of traveling mechanical waves on the basilar membrane. This discovery arose out of his early work at the Hungarian Telephone and Post Office Laboratory in Budapest. At that time he was working on problems of telecommunications. While trying to create the best design for a telephone earphone, he began to feel a need to know exactly what was going on in the inner ear. To accomplish this he developed an anatomical technique that allowed rapid, nondestructive dissection of the cochlea. The story is told that he became a nuisance in both the autopsy rooms of the Budapest hospitals (where he searched for recently deceased bodies that he could plunder for their cochleas), and also the mechanical workshops of the Post Office Laboratory (where he used the drill press to grind away the bone surrounding the cochleas, leaving the press full of human-bone dust for the returning workers to find in the morning).

Békésy observed the shape of the traveling waves by tracking the motion of particles of silver sprinkled on the nearly transparent basilar membrane in a strobe light whose rate he adjusted to equal that of the vibration. He was awarded the Nobel Prize in Physiology and Medicine in 1961 for his discovery. Békésy went on to make many other contributions to both hearing and other sensory sciences. In particular, he was one of the first to study lateral inhibition in the skin, an idea that arose from his mechanical model of the cochlea applied to the forearm. After World War II he moved to Harvard University, and after retirement at age 65, he continued his research at the University of Hawaii, where he remained until his death. When he died in 1972 he left a large collection of paintings, statues, and artifacts that is now owned by the Nobel Foundation.

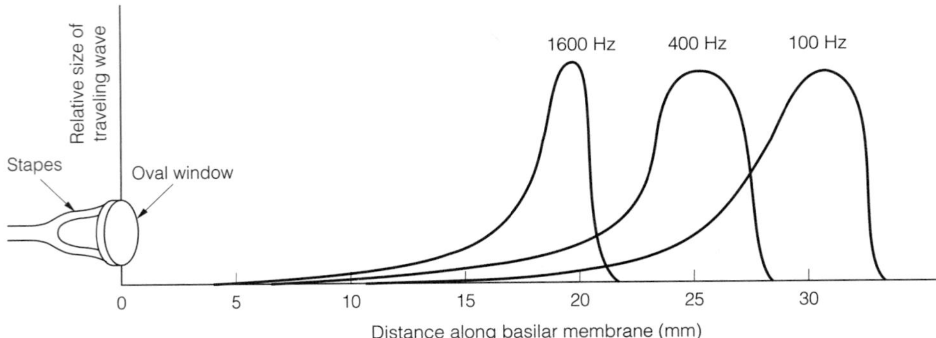

FIGURE 5.11 A graph of the relative sizes of traveling waves along the basilar membrane for three different frequencies of tone. Notice that as the frequency increases, the waves reach their maxima nearer the oval window and stapes (base).

modifies the mechanical vibrations before they reach the inner hair cells, thus sharpening the mechanical tuning of the basilar membrane (see Moore, 2001). Figure 5.12 illustrates how this process might work by adding energy to the traveling wave just before it peaks, thereby raising the peak and making the drop-off after the peak even sharper.

The most recent evidence indicates that there may be more than one active mechanism at work, possibly one for reptiles such as frogs and turtles and an additional one for mammals, birds, and the crocodilian reptiles (Manley & Köpp, 1998). The mechanism in the bull frog's sacculus (which has hair bundles similar to those of outer hair cells) relies on spontaneous movements of the hair bundle that are produced by a molecular "motor" inside the hairs. When stimulated by a sine wave at the frequency of the spontaneous movements, the resulting motions of the hair bundle are greater than they are when the motor is disabled (Martin, Hudspeth, & Jülicher, 2001). Thus, the hairs themselves add the required energy to their own motion when stimulated with a motion to which they are tuned. Some researchers believe that this mechanism is also present in mammals because various chemicals, such as the salicylates found in aspirin, abolish mechanical amplification in both reptiles and mammals (Stewart & Hudspeth, 2000).

The active process mechanism of the bullfrog, however, does not seem to be the whole story in mammalian hearing, where movements of the outer hair cells are the source of the mechanical amplification. The outer hair cells contract in response to changes in voltage across their cell membrane (e.g., Brownell, Bader, Bertrand, & De Ribaupierre, 1985). The voltage changes that stimulate these movements typically arise via efferent inputs such as those from the superior olive via the crossed olivo-cochlear bundle, or from the bending of the hairs caused by the traveling wave itself (see the next section). The protein prestin, found in the cell membrane of the outer hair cells, has been shown to be the "motor" that is driven by these voltage

DEMONSTRATION BOX 5.3

THE SKIN AS A MODEL FOR THE BASILAR MEMBRANE

The basilar membrane is set into vibration by incoming sound stimuli. How the membrane vibrates, however, depends on the frequency of the sound input. Low frequencies tend to cause vibrations of significant magnitude along the entire length of the membrane; high frequencies cause vibrations that are significant only near the base. You can easily demonstrate the frequency-specific nature of the vibration by using your finger as a model of the basilar membrane because skin has about the same resiliency and elasticity. Place your finger in your mouth, resting your fingertip firmly against the front of your teeth. Now make a loud, low sound (try to imitate the low sound of a foghorn), and notice that your entire finger seems to vibrate, perhaps all the way down to the knuckle at its base. Next make a high-pitched sound (try to imitate the whistling of a teakettle or the test tone on a TV station that has ended the day's broadcasting). Notice that the feeling of vibration covers only a tiny region, perhaps your fingertip or down to the first joint. In a similar fashion, low sound frequencies induce waves that extend over the length of the basilar membrane, whereas higher frequency waves are restricted spatially in their effects.

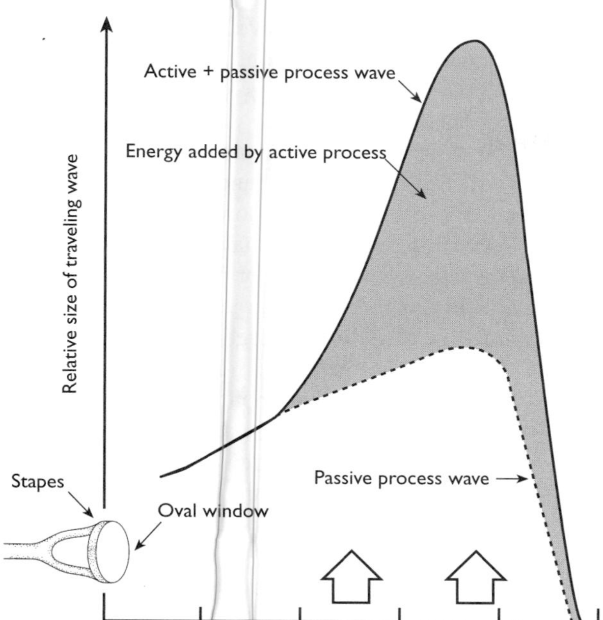

FIGURE 5.12 Illustration of how the active process in the organ of Corti might sharpen mechanical tuning curves by amplifying traveling waves just before their peaks (based on Pickles, 1988).

changes, causing the hair cell to become shorter (e.g., Liberman et al., 2001). When the outer hair cell gets shorter, it pulls the tectorial membrane toward the basilar membrane, altering the phase of the traveling wave in the two membranes by 90°. This turns out to be just the amount required to make them resonate in a manner that addes energy to the traveling wave on the basilar membrane (Nilsen & Russell, 1999). This mechanism operates near the peak of the traveling wave, as shown in Figure 5.12. Additional amplification is provided by electro-mechanical interactions of the outer hair cells arising from the fact that they are all embedded in the reticular lamina, so that when one cell moves its neighbors are subjected to mechanical and electrical forces (Zhao & Santos-Sacchi, 1999). These interactions resemble lateral inhibition in that they sharpen the tuning of the basilar membrane by suppressing the traveling wave everywhere but near its peak. Since abolishing the prestin-driven mechanism seems to eliminate most if not all of the amplification observed in the mammalian ear, it is possible that this mechanism is the only one operating in mammals (Nilsen & Russell, 1999), and a different mechanism operates in the bull frog and other similar reptiles.

An interesting consequence of mechanical activity in the cochlea is that sounds are actually *emitted* by the ear (Kemp, 1978). Some of these **otoacoustic emissions** occur spontaneously, whereas others are evoked by a sound input. Otoacoustic emissions can be fairly intense (over 20 dB), and they differ depending on how they are stimulated (Lonsbury-Martin et al., 1990). Stimulation of one ear by sound can alter spontaneous otoacoustic emissions from the other ear (e.g., Harrison & Burns, 1993). Evoked otoacoustic emissions can be used to estimate cochlear tuning in humans, and these estimates agree with the latest behavioral measurements, showing that frequency tuning curves in the human auditory system are much sharper than was previously believed (Shera, Guinan, & Oxenham, 2002).

Spontaneous otoacoustic emissions arise from the operation of the active process that amplifies the traveling waves. Evidence for this comes from examination of the effects of some common drugs, such as aspirin and quinine sulfate, which can cause both hearing loss and tinnitus (ringing in the ears). Both of these drugs also reduce the ability of the outer hair cells to move. Administration of aspirin eliminates spontaneous otoacoustic emissions in monkeys (Martin, Lonsbury-Martin, Probst, & Coats, 1988), geckos (Stewart & Hudspeth, 2000), and humans (Wier, Pasanen, & McFadden, 1988), although it does not alter otoacoustic emissions that are evoked by external sound stimuli. Administration of quinine sulfate eliminates or reduces both spontaneous and evoked otoacoustic emissions in humans (McFadden & Pasanen, 1994). Thus, drugs that reduce the ability of the outer hair cells to move also reduce otoacoustic emissions, suggesting that these internally generated sounds may arise from the activity of these hair cells.

Mechanism of Transduction

Mechanical vibrations in the ear are changed into electrochemical fluctuations, which are the code of the central nervous system, through a process known as **transduction.** This happens in the organ of Corti, which rests on the basilar membrane. Traveling waves that move down the basilar membrane also cause it to move sideways with respect to the tectorial membrane. Both inner and outer hair cells are attached at their base to structures connected to the basilar membrane. Because the longest hairs of the outer hair cells are embedded in the tectorial membrane, the shearing force between the two membranes results in a mechanical pressure that causes these hairs to bend. The inner hair cell hairs, which are not attached to the tectorial membrane, are bent when they are swept through the viscous fluid (endolymph) in the cochlear duct by the movement of the basilar membrane (Raftenberg, 1990). Although this seems to be a less efficient way of producing bending, there appear to be no differences in the absolute sensitivities of the inner and outer hair cells (Dallos, Santos-Sacchi, & Flock, 1982).

The bending of hairs is transduced into electrical changes in the hair cells by a mechanism that involves the tip links that go from the shorter hairs to their longer neighbors (Hudspeth, 1985; Pickles, Comis, & Osborne, 1984). Figure 5.13 illustrates one way in which this mechanism could work. As shown in the figure, each end of each shorter hair seems to have a pore that functions like a little "trapdoor" (Hudspeth, 1985; Strassmaier & Gillespie, 2002). When the hair is standing straight or is bent away from or perpendicular to the direction of the tallest hairs, the trapdoor "rattles around" a bit (because of impacts with the surrounding molecules) but is open only about 1% of the time (shown closed in Figure 5.13A). Potassium ions, which have a positive charge, flow into the hair whenever one or more pores are open. The inward flow of positive charge is just balanced by the outward flow of positive charge caused by other ion "pumps" elsewhere in the cell, maintaining the cell's resting membrane potential at about –60 mV (see Chapter 3). When the hair is bent in the direction of the tallest hairs, however, the tip link attached to the trapdoor pulls on it and keeps it open more of the time, allowing more positively charged potassium ions to flow into the cell (Figure 5.13B). This causes a depolarization (making the inside of the cell more positive relative to the outside) that may go up to 20 mV. This electrical event triggers the release of neurotransmitter substances from the bottom of the hair cell. These neurotransmitters stimulate the dendrites of the spiral ganglion cells, which then generate the action potentials that go up the auditory nerve to higher brain centers. Although the molecular nature of the pore through which the potassium ions flow is not known at this time, it is likely to be similar to other mechanical transduction channels, such as those in mechanoreceptors in the fly (Strassmaier & Gillespie, 2002). Many of the recent findings on the transudation mechanism of hair cells and the active process involved in amplifying the auditory response have come from the research of Albert James Hudspeth, who is discussed in Biography Box 5.3.

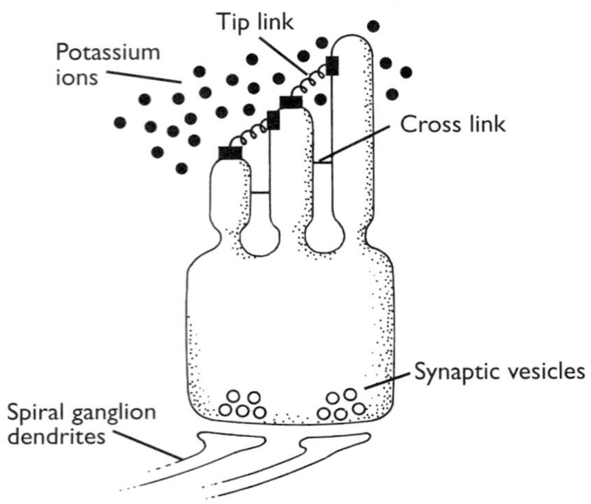

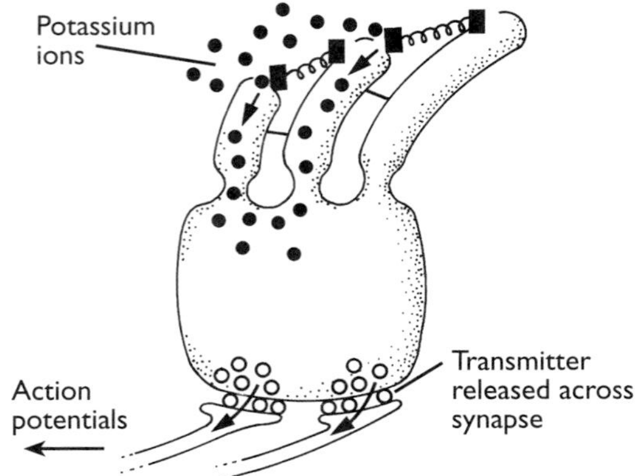

FIGURE 5.13 Model of transduction in hair cells. (A) No sound, hairs not bent, trapdoor closed, potassium ions excluded, no transmitter released, no action potentials; (B) sound present, hairs bent, trapdoor open, potassium ions enter, transmitter released, action potentials in auditory nerve.

ELECTRICAL ACTIVITY OF THE AUDITORY NERVE

After transduction in the cochlea, the information in a sound is encoded into patterns of electrical activity in the auditory nerve. To study the neural processing of auditory information, we use the same techniques of electrophysiological recording that are used to investigate the visual system. The most common technique involves inserting tiny electrodes into neurons in the auditory pathways of nonhuman animals and recording their electrical activity in response to various sound stimuli. More recently, brain-imaging techniques such as PET, fMRI, MEG, and EEG are revealing exciting information about where and how the human brain processes auditory in-

BIOGRAPHY BOX 5.3

TRAP DOORS IN THE INNER EAR

Albert James Hudspeth (1945–) who is both an M.D. and a Ph.D., is an Investigator at the Howard Hughes Medical Institute and F. M. Kirby Professor and Head of the Laboratory of Sensory Neuroscience at Rockefeller University. After receiving his A.B. in biochemistry at Harvard in 1967, he continued on there to earn his graduate degrees. After a year at the famous Karolinska Hospital in Stockholm, he joined the faculty of California Institute of Technology in 1975 and then moved through several universities before finally settling at Rockefeller in 1995. During those years he worked ceaselessly on the biophysical and molecular bases of hearing and equilibrium, in particular on the function, degeneration, and potential for replacement of the hair cells of the inner ear. He and James Pickles, independently, headed research groups that identified and characterized the tip links on the hair cells. He noticed the tiny pores at the end of these tip links, which he called "trap doors." He helped to establish that the opening and closing of these trap doors these are part of the final steps that convert the mechanical energy of the vibrating fluid in the cochlea into electrochemical energy that can trigger neural responses in the auditory pathways.

More recently he has been working on the active mechanism of mechanical amplification in vertebrates that do not possess outer hair cells. His discovery that each hair bundle contains an energy source capable of performing mechanical work also helps us understand the role of "molecular motors" in biological systems.

In addition to studying the process of mechanical transduction, Hudspeth also works to discover the genetic basis of human deafness and tries to devise ways to stimulate replacement of damaged or congenitally malformed or absent hair cells. This work might ultimately help hearing-disabled adults and might also help in alleviating disorders such as tinnitus (ringing in the ears) that are usually associated with malfunction of the cochlea.

formation. If you are unfamiliar with these procedures, now would be a good time to glance back at Chapter 3 (pages 48–49), where they are described in some detail.

The axons from spiral ganglion neurons make up the auditory nerve. Recording spike potentials from these reveals several types of responses to sounds. Figure 5.14 shows the minimum sound pressure levels of pure tones

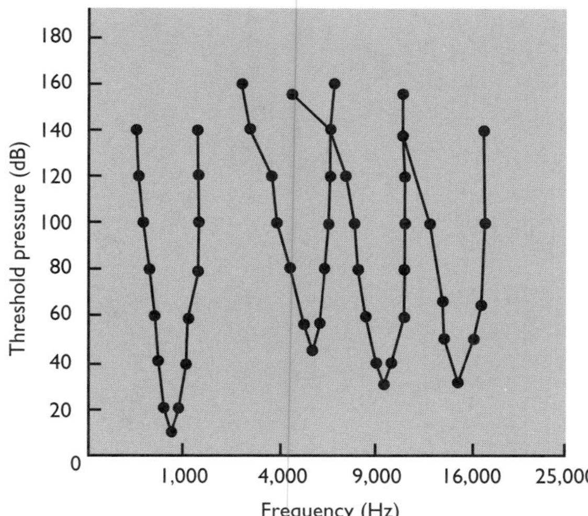

FIGURE 5.14 Threshold response curves for auditory nerve fibers in the cat (based on Whitfield, 1968).

needed to trigger a response that is above the resting rate in these auditory nerve neurons. These are the neural equivalent of absolute thresholds (see Chapter 2). Notice that the sensitivity varies with the frequency of the sound. The resulting curves are called **threshold response curves,** and, as can be seen from the figure, each neuron has a **characteristic frequency** for which its neural absolute threshold is lowest. Neurons that respond to pure tones in this way are called **tuned neurons** (tuned in the same sense that we tune a radio to accurately receive one particular station's broadcast frequency). The sensitivity of such neurons decreases (the threshold is higher) as we move away from the characteristic frequency in either direction. Another way of describing auditory neuron tuning is to display a **tuning curve** showing how its firing rate in response to a tone of constant intensity varies as we change the frequency of the tone. An example is shown in Figure 5.15. The spiral ganglion contains neurons tuned to frequencies spanning the entire range of hearing.

This auditory nerve fiber tuning arises from the mechanical properties of the basilar membrane and the active process we discussed earlier. Most of the tuned auditory nerve fibers that have been studied are connected to inner hair cells (Liberman, 1982). Remember that the basilar membrane's vibratory response to a pure tone is a finely tuned function of the tone's frequency,

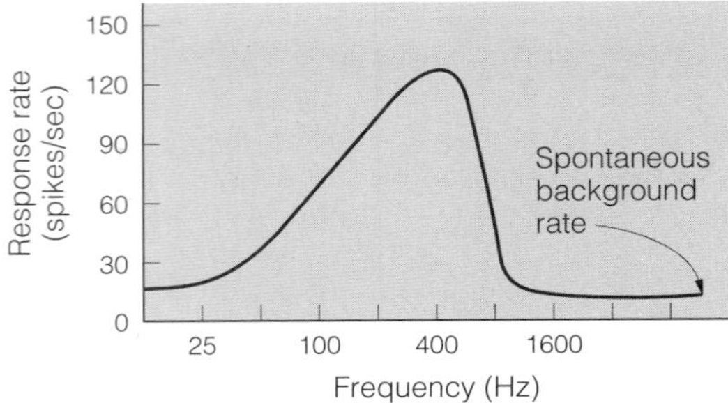

FIGURE 5.15 Tuning curve of a typical auditory nerve fiber (based on Lindsay & Norman, 1977).

and it is this vibration that causes the inner hair cells' hair bundle to bend and in turn to initiate the neural response. A particular inner hair cell is sensitive to traveling waves on the basilar membrane that peak near the location of that cell. The frequency of the tone causing that peak vibration is the frequency to which neurons that are attached with that hair cell are tuned. Other frequencies of the same intensity will cause less vigorous movement of the basilar membrane at that location, which in turn results in less vigorous bending of the hair bundle of the hair cell and less vigorous responding of the neurons connected to it. The outer hair cells also show frequency tuning. As we discussed earlier, their responses contribute through the active process to the precise mechanical tuning of the living basilar membrane and thus affect the responses of inner hair cells indirectly.

The effect that outer hair cell responses have on the responses of the inner hair cells is demonstrated in a phenomenon called **two-tone suppression** (Rose, Galambos, & Hughs, 1959; Sachs & Kiang, 1968). Suppose that we are recording the activity of an auditory nerve fiber and it is responding vigorously to a pure tone at its characteristic frequency. If a second tone of a different frequency (but moderately close to the tuned frequency) is briefly presented, the response rate in the tuned neuron drops. This two-tone suppression disappears when outer hair cells have been selectively damaged by a drug (Schmiedt, Zwislocki, & Hamernik, 1980). One can also produce similar suppression with only one tone and direct stimulation of the outer hair cells (Geisler, Yates, Patuzzi, & Johnstone, 1990). Moreover, two-tone suppression also occurs with otoacoustic emissions, which reflect the active process mediated by the outer hair cells (Brass & Kemp, 1993). Thus, two-tone suppression probably arises from mechanical actions of outer hair cells stimulated by the second tone that act much like lateral-inhibition in vision. These reduce the response of the basilar membrane nearby and thus diminish the response intensity that the inner hair cells would normally produce for the first tone (Zhao & Santos-Sacchi, 1999).

Auditory nerve neurons, similar to other sensory neurons, also display **neural adaptation.** When first stimulated by a moderately intense pure tone at its characteristic frequency, an auditory nerve neuron responds vigorously. However, if the stimulation continues unchanged, the firing rate drops over time, eventually reaching a much lower rate near the background rate. Different auditory nerve neurons display different time courses for adaptation and these occur in stages. Some show very rapid rate of adaptation and one or more slower stages later. Some show only the later, slower adaptation rates. The adaptation curve of a neuron displaying an early very rapid adaptation stage, and a somewhat later slower stage is shown in Figure 5.16.

In this typical spiral ganglion neuron from a guinea pig, the firing rate fell to about one third of the initial rate by about 25 ms after stimulus onset and then decreased more gradually over the next several hundred milliseconds (Yates, Robertson, & Johnstone, 1985). Some auditory nerve neurons continue to adapt for several seconds (long-term adaptation) or even several minutes (very long-term adaptation; Javel, 1996). It is thought that the various phases of adaptation correspond to various stages in the depletion of available neurotransmitters at synapses with the inner hair cells (Javel, 1996). The long-term adaptation effects are thought to be the neural basis for

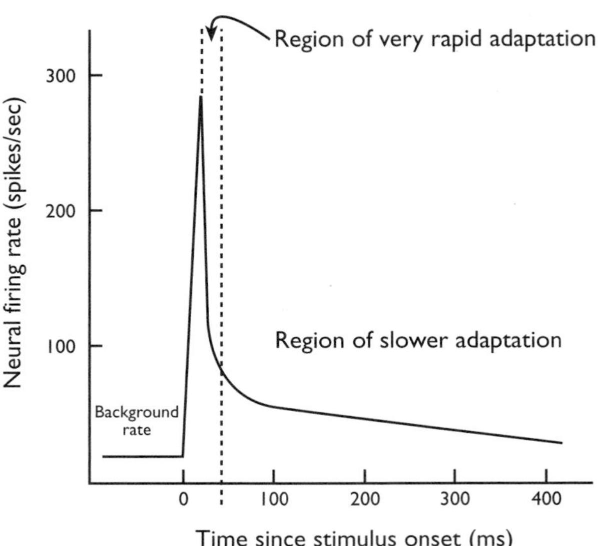

FIGURE 5.16 Neural adaptation in a typical auditory nerve fiber.

auditory perceptual adaptation, which is the decrease in the perceived loudness of a low-level pure tone that is listened to for a long period of time.

Auditory nerve responses to pure tones can help us to understand how information about intensity and frequency of sound is represented in the auditory system. For example, we have already seen that there are tuned neurons that respond best to a limited range of frequencies. In addition, it can be shown that the frequency of low-frequency sounds can be encoded directly in the rate of firing in the auditory nerve—sort of counting the pressure peaks with neural responses (Johnson, 1980; Rose, Brugge, Anderson, & Hind, 1967). Consider a 100-Hz pure tone. If it is highly likely that some neurons fire at each compression peak in the sound wave, but unlikely that any fire at any other times, the overall firing rate in the auditory nerve will be around 100 Hz. Notice that no individual neuron has to fire at 100 Hz for the overall firing rate to occur at that frequency. It is necessary only that each neuron have the greatest probability of firing at the compression peak. Thus, each neuron would tend to fire in phase with the sound wave, although one may fire only about every second peak, whereas another fires only about every fifth peak. This is called **phase locking.** For many neurons firing on different cycles of the sound wave but phase locked to its compression peak, there will tend to be at least several spikes occurring at every peak of the wave, and thus the auditory nerve will display volleys of spikes at a rate equal to the frequency of the stimulating sound. Also, even if each individual neuron is adapting to the sound and firing ever more slowly, the overall firing in the auditory nerve will still occur at the stimulating frequency as long as at least a few neurons fire at each peak. The ability of the whole auditory nerve to fire at the frequency of the stimulating sound wave up to a limit of about 4000 Hz, and thus to send information about sound frequency to higher auditory centers, is a central component in the *volley theory* of pitch perception, which we will discuss more fully in Chapter 6.

Intensity information is coded differently by the tuned auditory neurons. Although there may be many spiral ganglion neurons tuned to the same frequency, the response thresholds for neurons with the same characteristic frequency can differ over a range of 20 dB (Evans, 1975). Moreover, although tuned neurons do fire more rapidly as the sound pressure level increases, they only do this up to about 30 to 50 dB above their threshold. At this point the neuron is firing as fast as it can (technically it is **saturated**). With this ceiling, the firing rate of a tuned neuron can encode only a limited range of low to moderate sound pressures. On the other hand, the greater a sound's pressure amplitude, the more individual neurons will fire in response to it. A particular pure tone of high enough pressure will recruit responses from neurons that are not tuned to its frequency but, rather, are tuned to nearby frequencies and thus have higher thresholds for this tone. Both the 20-dB range of response thresholds and the recruitment of off-frequency neurons allow a much wider range of sound pressures to be encoded by *how many* neurons are firing.

The resulting state of affairs is that for any given pure tone input there is a population of auditory nerve neurons all firing at different response rates. This situation is represented in Figure 5.17A for two levels of pressure.

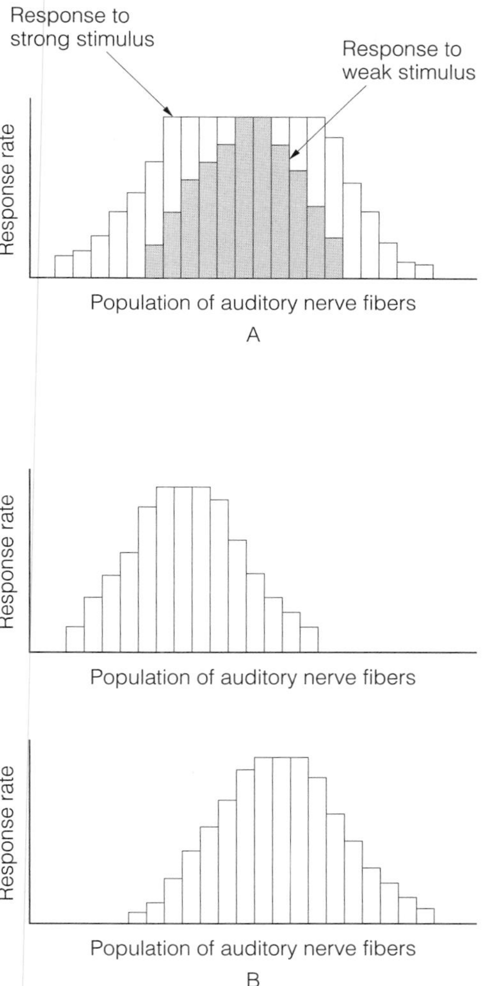

FIGURE 5.17 Hypothetical distributions of response rates for the population of auditory nerve fibers firing in response to (A) weak versus strong stimuli of the same frequency and (B) stimuli of the same strength but of different frequencies.

Stimuli of different frequencies tend to cause different populations of neurons to fire above their background rates, as is shown in Figure 5.17B. The entire pattern of auditory nerve activity is different for different stimuli. Frequency seems to be encoded by *which* tuned neurons are firing and low-frequency sounds by *how fast* the auditory nerve as a whole is firing, whereas sound intensity seems to be encoded by *how many* tuned neurons are firing (Whitfield, 1978) and very low-pressure sounds by how fast specific tuned neurons are firing (Viemeister, 1988).

Our increasing understanding of how the auditory nerve encodes frequency and pressure of pure tones has allowed people with certain kinds of hearing disabilities to recover some auditory function. As mentioned earlier, if the hair cells do not function normally, either because they were damaged or congenitally malformed, a person has a sensorineural hearing loss. This results in raised thresholds, distorted tuning curves, and sometimes in ringing in the ears (tinnitus) caused by hair cell or neural activity in the absence of sound. Although it is so far difficult to do anything about too much neural activity, other than to mask it, it is possible to help people who have too little neural response to sounds. This is accomplished by inserting **cochlear implants** into the ear (Schindler & Merzenich, 1985). People who have been deafened later in life seem to benefit more from cochlear implants than do those who have been deaf from an early age. It seems that the development of sign language in the early deaf, in which somatosensory processing invades the auditory cortex, prevents the later-installed cochlear implants from utilizing auditory cortical processing (Lee et al., 2001).

A cochlear implant consists of a microphone to pick up the sounds, a computer to analyze them into their frequency components, and a series of electrodes that have been implanted at different points along the basilar membrane where the traveling waves corresponding to different sound frequencies peak. The computer sends tiny electrical signals to the electrodes to stimulate the auditory nerve to fire similarly to the way it is made to fire by the hair cells in normal-hearing people. Deaf patients with such devices can discriminate the frequencies of different sounds and can even recognize speech sounds quite well, especially when a speech preprocessor is attached to the cochlear implant to isolate certain speech-relevant frequency changes. For example, there is a recent finding suggesting that adding white noise to speech signals might improve speech perception in implant recipients, although the mechanism for this is not yet clear (Morse & Evans, 1996). Placing more emphasis on temporal coding of frequency by stimulating the auditory nerve at the frequencies in the sound input also seems to improve speech perception in those with implants (Moller, 1999). Even music can now be appreciated through implants, especially by people who receive some musical training after receiving their implants (Gfeller, Witt, Kim, Adamek, & Coffman, 2000). Clearly we are coming ever closer to the dream of providing a full range of hearing experience for people with this form of deafness. There is now hope even for people who lack a functioning auditory nerve because more central implants, farther along the pathway to the brain, are being developed (Shannon & Otto, 1990).

THE AUDITORY PATHWAYS

Figure 5.18 diagrams the principal brain centers and pathways in which the information carried by the auditory nerve is processed. To keep this relatively simple, most of the arrows represent the **feedforward sweep** of auditory processing (see Chapter 3 for a more general discussion of feedforward and feedback sweeps). This means that for most arrows from one area to another there is another projecting back from the receiving area to the originating area, the **feedback sweep.** Although many of these loops have yet to be studied in the auditory system, loops among cortical areas and between the medial geniculate nucleus and the auditory cortex are quite likely implicated in our conscious awareness of sounds (Chapter 14).

Remember that it is the axons from the spiral ganglion neurons that make up the auditory nerve projects to the **cochlear nucleus,** located in the lower rear part of the brain. As shown in the figure, the auditory nerve axons enter the **ventral** (front) **cochlear nucleus,** where each divides into at least two branches. One branch connects to neurons in the ventral cochlear nucleus, and the other proceeds to the **dorsal** (back) **cochlear nucleus.** The neurons of the ventral cochlear nucleus send about half of their axons to the superior olive located on the *same* side of the brain and about half to the superior olive on the *opposite* side of the brain. The axons from the dorsal cochlear nucleus all cross over to the opposite side of the brain and eventually terminate in the **inferior colliculus.** Thus, it appears that much of the auditory information from the right ear is initially sent to the left side of the brain and vice versa.

The two superior olives send most of their afferent (sensory input) fibers to the inferior colliculi (which are located just below the superior colliculi, which are so

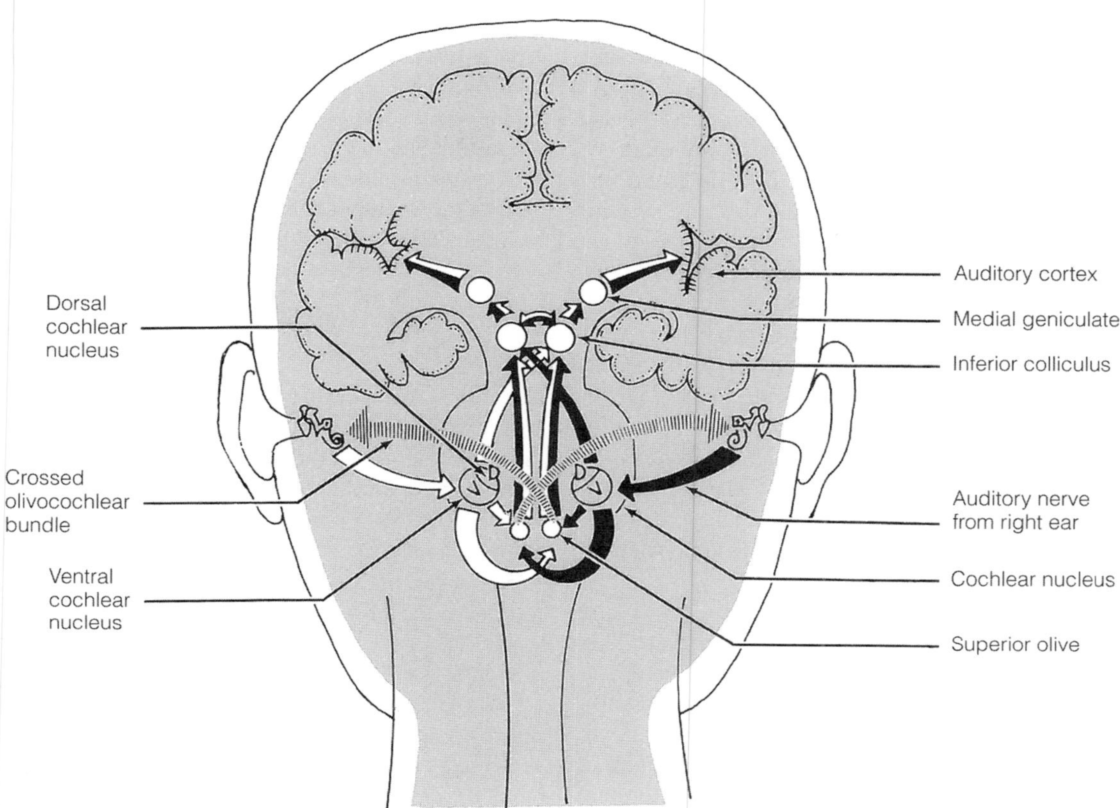

FIGURE 5.18 The major auditory pathways in the brain.

important for vision, as discussed in Chapter 3). We mentioned in an earlier section that as part of the protective process for the ears, special neurons in the superior olives also send efferent fibers back to the cochlear nuclei and to the hair cells in the cochlea to modify their response to incoming sounds (Sahley, Nodar, & Musiek, 1997). One group of neurons sends efferent fibers to synapse on the afferent fibers innervating the inner hair cells, mostly on the same side of the brain. Another group sends efferent fibers to synapse directly on the outer hair cells, mostly on the other side of the brain, via the crossed olivocochlear bundle. This means that at the level of the inferior colliculus, considerable fiber crossing takes place from one side of the brain to the other so that each inferior colliculus has information from both ears.

Some neurons in the inferior colliculi send axons to the **medial geniculate** nuclei, and some send axons to the deep layers of the superior colliculi. The deep layers of the superior colliculi contain multimodal neurons that respond to the locations of lights, sounds, and touches (Stein & Meredith, 1993). One function of the superior colliculus appears to be the integration of visual and even tactile information about the location of the source of the sound relative to the listener. This can then be used to control eye, head, and body movements, and it may possibly play a role in how we direct our attention to objects in the world (Chapter 12).

From the medial geniculate nuclei, fibers project to a part of the superior temporal cortex called the **primary auditory projection area,** or A1. The secondary auditory cortex, A2, which lies in a belt around A1, also receives axons directly from the medial geniculate, although fewer of them. Most of its input is from neurons in A1. The general locations of these brain regions are pictured in Figure 5.19. Unfortunately, as can be seen in Figure 5.18, much of the auditory cortex is not on the surface but, rather, is tucked into a fold called Heschl's gyrus. That means that a simple side of the brain does not show much of the auditory cortex. Several other areas also process auditory stimuli, including areas adjacent to A1 and A2, some of the somatosensory cortex, and Wernicke's area, which processes speech stimuli, and the posterior parietal cortex, which appears to contain spatial maps for auditory, visual and somatosensory stimuli. Like the primary visual cortex (V1), the primary auditory cortex (A1) is arranged in layers (six of them).

Figure 5.19 also indicates that just like we found for vision, there is a general division of the auditory system into **what** and **where** (or possibly, **how**) subsystems (e.g., Rauschecker & Tian, 2000). The parts of the auditory system that process speech and identify voices, musical melodies, and the sound signatures of environmental events are located mostly in the superior temporal lobe and seem to converge with the object and motion identification parts of the visual system in the inferior temporal lobe. The locations of environmental events creating sounds, on the other hand, seem to be processed mostly in the parietal lobe, possibly converging with visual and tactile (if in touch range) information about those events.

Although this division of the auditory system in what and where pathways is still being developed, there is a great deal of evidence that it makes sense. First, detailed single-unit studies of the monkey auditory system support the suggestion that source identification (what) and location information (where) are processed in different places in the brain. The front part of the auditory cortex is more selective for type of sound (especially monkey calls) and the back part more selective for spatial location (e.g., Tian, Reser, Durham, Kustov & Rauschecker, 2001). There also seem to be separate pathways into the prefrontal cortex for these two functions (Romanski et al., 1999). In humans, this part of the cortex is involved in discriminating the locations of overlapping complex sounds (Zatorre, Bouffard, Ahad, & Belin, 2002). In addition, lesions in the inferior parietal lobe and the top of the auditory cortex among others, disturb sound localization ability, whereas lesions in the front and bottom of the auditory cortex disturb recognition of sounds (Clarke et al., 2002). Finally, several studies of humans using brain imaging have converged on the right inferior parietal cortex as the most active area during sound localization (e.g., Alain et al., 2001; Weeks et al., 1999; Zatorre, et al., 2002).

Electrical Activity of the Lower Auditory Centers

Remember that the majority of auditory nerve neurons are tuned to a characteristic frequency, although some may respond only to clicks or other stimuli that are not pure tones. Similar tuned neurons are found in the cochlear nucleus, superior olive, inferior colliculus, and medial geniculate. Also, as described earlier for the auditory nerve, there is a region of nearby frequencies that produces an inhibition of response (as in two-tone suppression) in these same cells, possibly also mediated by the outer hair cells.

In addition to the frequency tuning of neurons, several more complex response patterns appear in the more central nuclei of the auditory pathway, and these seem designed to register specific aspects of the sound stimulus. For instance, neurons in the cochlear nucleus of adult cats can be categorized into several types on the basis of their response to a simple tone (Pfeiffer, 1966). **Onset neurons** give a burst of responses immediately after the onset of a tone and then cease responding, no matter how long the tone persists. **Pauser neurons** exhibit a similar burst of firing at the onset of a tone, but this is followed by a pause and then a weaker sustained response until the tone is turned off. **Chopper neurons** give repeated

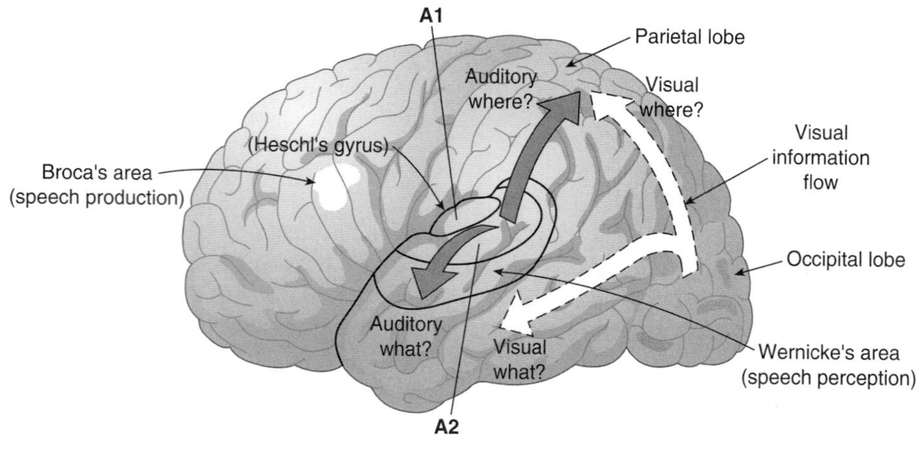

FIGURE 5.19 The principal regions of the cortex responsive to sound (much not visible because they go into the fissures), with alternate labeling systems. Dotted pathways represent the visual what-where system.

bursts of firing followed by short pauses, with the vigor of successive bursts decreasing. **Primary-like neurons** give an initial vigorous burst of firing when the tone is turned on; then the firing rate decays to a lower level that is sustained for the duration of the tone. These cochlear nucleus neurons have been shown to be capable of encoding some crucial aspects of speech sounds (Palmer, Winter, & Darwin, 1986), especially using phase locking to encode regular variations in sound amplitude (Rhode & Greenberg, 1994). These are somewhat reminiscent of the cells in the visual pathways that were tuned to specific pattern features.

Several other types of neurons can be found in one or more of these auditory nuclei. For example, **offset neurons** reduce their response rate below their spontaneous activity level at the onset of the tone and then give a burst of activity at its offset. An interesting variation of this is a tuned neuron that increases its activity at the onset of a tone at a characteristic frequency but reduces its activity at the onset of a tone having a slightly different frequency. At a conceptual level this kind of responding might remind you of the on-center/off-surround neurons observed in the visual system (Chapter 3). Rather than having a receptive field that consists of a region in space, these neurons have receptive fields consisting of a band of frequencies. The response pattern for such a neuron in the medial geniculate is the roughly W-shaped pattern in Figure 5.20 (Webster & Atkin, 1975).

Because different points along the basilar membrane vibrate most strongly for different frequencies of sounds, we say that the response of the basilar membrane is **tonotopic** (from the Greek *tono* for "tone" and *topus* for "place"). This spatial encoding of frequency is preserved in the auditory nerve and appears throughout all of the subcortical auditory areas: cochlear nucleus (Rose, Galambos, & Hughes, 1960), superior olive (Pickles, 1988), inferior colliculus (Martin, Webster, & Service, 1988), and medial geniculate (Rouiller, Rodrigues-Dagaeff, Simm, De Ribaupierre, Villa, & De Ribaupierre, 1989). The tonotopic organization of the basilar membrane can be seen even at the level of the primary auditory cortex (Phillips, 1993). It produces a frequency "map" where progression across the cortex is associated with a systematic rise or fall in frequency responsiveness.

The finding that sound frequencies are spatially mapped into regions of the cortex has been confirmed in humans using brain-imaging techniques. The maximum brain activity observed in both the primary auditory cortex (Romani, Williamson, & Kaufman, 1982) and secondary areas of the auditory cortex (Cansino, Williamson, & Karron, 1994) varies in depth as the frequency of the stimulating tone varies. Because the response is at a greater depth the higher the frequency, the neurons responding to higher frequencies must be located on the cortical surface within Heschl's gyrus. For example, recent fMRI studies of humans show an orderly arrangement of frequency tunings of neurons along Heschl's gyrus where each millimeter of anatomical distance corresponded to a change in frequency tuning of about one acoustical octave (Engelien, Yang, Engelien et al., 2002).

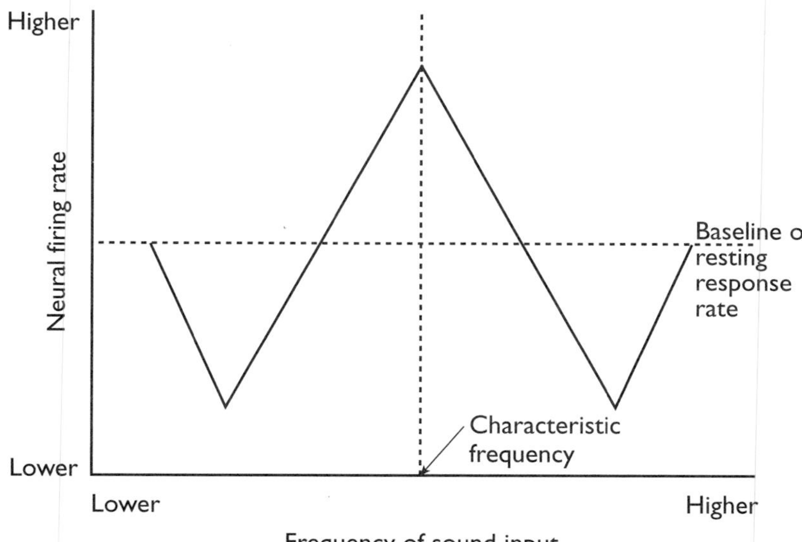

FIGURE 5.20 Schematic representation of a frequency-specific receptive field in the medial geniculate with an excitatory center for the characteristic frequency and inhibitory flanks for near frequencies.

As in the case of vision, there may be several different maps in different parts of the cortex and there may be differences between the right and left sides of the brain. Recent recordings of auditory evoked potentials from within the cortex were made on humans who had intractable epilepsy (Liegois-Chauvel et al., 2001). The tonotopic maps in these patients were much clearer in the right temporal lobe than in the left. In addition, imaging studies of human pitch processing confirm that the right auditory cortex is specialized for processing slowly changing narrow-band sounds, like melodies, whereas the left auditory cortex is specialized for processing more rapidly changing, broad-band sounds, like speech (Zatorre, Belin, & Penhune, 2002).

THE AUDITORY CORTEX

It probably seems to you that the auditory processing centers seem to contain a remarkable number of different cells tuned for a variety of different features. As we go further up the auditory processing stream, this conclusion becomes inescapable. Neurons in the auditory cortex exhibit a variety of complex responses to sound stimuli. Among the approximately 60% of the neurons that respond to pure tones, there those that respond to the onset of a particular sound (on responses), those that respond to the offset of a sound (off responses), and those that respond to both (on-off responses). These responses are either excitatory (increases over the resting neural response level) or inhibitory (decreases relative to the resting level) (see Figure 5.21). These responses closely resemble the response patterns of visual system neurons (Chapter 3). The other 40% of auditory cortical neurons seem to have "special tuning" in that they respond selectively to more complex sounds, including noise bursts, clangs, or clicks. There appear to be more ordinary tuned neurons in A1 and more specially tuned neurons that respond to more complex sounds in other auditory cortical areas (Alho et al., 1996). The responses of neurons in A1 are usually transient, such as on, off, and on-off responses, whereas responses in the belt areas are usually of the more sustained excitatory or inhibitory types (Seifritz et al., 2002).

Temporal coding also seems to play some role in coding auditory signals. For slowly varying sounds we often find synchronized activity involving many neurons, much like the phase-locked responses of auditory nerve neurons used to signal lower frequencies. In contrast, nonsynchronized rate coding is used to represent rapidly-varying sounds (Lu, Liang & Wang, 2001). These differences in responding may be related to the

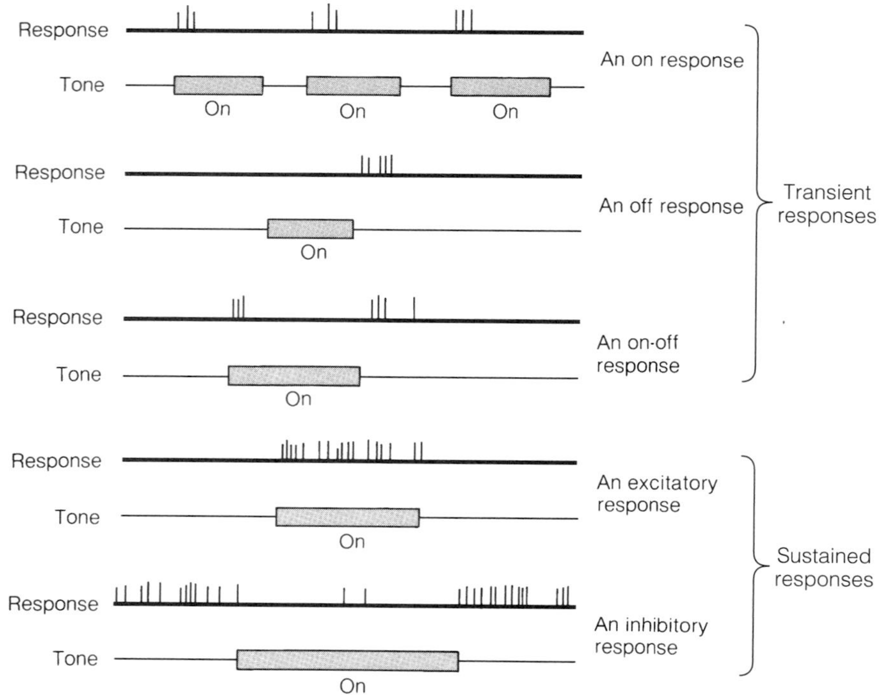

FIGURE 5.21 Different types of response to pure tones recorded from neurons in the auditory cortex of the cat (based on Whitfield, 1967).

two different types of neural synapes (one associated with sustained and the other with transient auditory inputs) recently discovered in the primary auditory cortex of mice (Atzori et al., 2001).

Among the tuned neurons in A1, about 30% also seem to have some kind of additional amplitude tuning and respond only to a limited range of sound amplitudes within their preferred frequency ranges (Phillips, 1993). To consider another form of special tuning, there is recent evidence suggesting that there are neurons in the dorsal region of the cat's auditory cortex that are tuned for the duration, rather than the frequency or amplitude, of sounds (He, Hashikawa, Ojima, & Kinouchi, 1997). Finally, some neurons in the right posterior auditory cortex respond best to moving sound sources, providing a basis for tracking important, sound-emitting environmental events (Baumgart, Gaschler-Markefski, Woldorff, Heinze, & Scheich, 1999).

An interesting group of specially tuned neurons found in the auditory cortex of the cat is the **frequency sweep detectors** (Whitfield & Evans, 1965). These neurons respond only to sounds that change frequency in a specific direction and range. Some frequency sweep detectors respond to increases but not to decreases in frequency within the same frequency range, whereas others respond to decreases in frequency but not to increases. A third type responds only to increases in frequency for low-frequency tones. Such neurons would help the cat discriminate between various types of cat meows, yowls, and screeches. Because these types of stimuli are also often encountered in human speech and music, such detectors, if present in people, could have an important role in our ability to understand spoken language and musical sequences.

Frequency sweep detectors respond selectively to sound patterns in much the same way that visual cortical neurons respond selectively to light patterns. There are even auditory analogs to the face and paw "detectors" observed in the visual parts of the temporal cortex (see Chapter 3). For instance, there are neurons in the cat auditory cortex that respond with a unique pattern of activity to recordings of certain cat vocalizations (Watanabe & Katsuki, 1974). What is more, these cortical neurons do not respond with the same pattern of activity to any of the individual components of the cat vocalization—only to the full sound sequence. This indicates that the neurons are integrating the outputs of neurons from lower levels of the auditory pathway that do respond to simpler components of the sound pattern. It seems that the lower level neurons are detecting the various features of the vocalization, and the cortical neuron is responding only to the combination of all of the features (Whitfield, 1980). Similar research has been done in primates. Cells in the auditory cortex of the squirrel monkey seem to be sensitive to the vocalizations of other squirrel monkeys (Swarbrick & Whitfield, 1972). As in the cat, some of these cells are unresponsive to the presentation of simple tones, although they respond vigorously to the presentation of extremely complex vocalizations (Funkenstein, Nelson, Winter, Wolberg, & Newman, 1971).

Sometimes, instead of special tuning of a neuron, there is a special form of coding across the auditory cortex. For instance, the "twitter" call of the common marmoset is faithfully, although abstractly, represented in the synchronized firing of primary auditory cortical neurons dispersed across Area A1 (Wang, Merzenich, Beitel, & Schreiner, 1995).

Particular regions in the brain may be designated for decoding special complex signals. As you will learn later in Chapter 6, in humans there are particular areas, mostly in the left hemisphere of the brain, that are important for analyzing speech sounds. In macaque monkeys, destruction of Areas A1 and A2 on the left side of the brain abolishes their ability to discriminate such complex vocalizations (Heffner & Heffner, 1984). This implies that monkeys may have a primitive analog to the speech perception areas of humans. This would be consistent with the fact that temporal response patterns of neurons in the monkey auditory cortex can encode certain important features of human speech, such as voice-onset time, which we will also talk about in the next chapter (Steinschneider, Schroeder, Arezzo, & Vaughan, 1995). This may be a fairly specialized ability in higher species, such as primates, because an investigation of the auditory cortex of cats failed to reveal an ability to encode this information (Eggermont, 1995).

The human auditory cortex has specialized mechanisms to analyze speech and musical sounds (e.g., Zatorre, et al., 2002). The left auditory cortex and nearby areas are extensively involved in the processing of speech sounds. It has been suggested that these mechanisms may be language specific rather than sound specific because the auditory cortex in the left hemisphere is active even during lip reading in the absence of auditory stimuli (Calvert et al., 1997). There is even a part of the secondary auditory cortex that is specialized to process voices, perhaps to connect information about who is speaking with information about what they are saying (Belin, Zatorre, Lafaille, Ahad, & Pike, 2000). This area of auditory cortex is analogous to the specialized visual face processing area located in the right inferior temporal cortex (Figure 5.19), although voice sensitivity appears in both hemispheres. On the other hand, some aspects of music perception seem to be processed mostly by the auditory cortex on the right side of human brains, probably because the right auditory cortex is specialized for processing spectral information about sounds.

One of the more interesting recent findings is that the organization of the auditory cortex, like that of visual and somatosensory cortex, is not static but rather changes with experience. Not only is it "invaded" by visual and touch processing in the early deaf (e.g., Lee et al., 2001), but it also changes over relatively short periods of time with conditioning and learning. For example, simply training people to better discriminate nearby frequencies of pure tones changed the way the auditory cortex responded to the trained frequencies (e.g., Menning, Roberts, & Pantev, 2000). In other animals, such training enlarges the cortical representation of the trained frequencies, although this alone does not seem sufficient to explain the performance change (Talwar & Gerstein, 2001). In Chapter 6 we mention also several studies of changes in musicians' brains as a result of their musical training.

It should be clear that there are some very important similarities between auditory and visual systems, as well as some differences in function related to the unique stimuli to which the two respond. It has recently been suggested that any differences are more apparent than real and that a common set of functional principles underlies all primary sensory areas (Shamma, 2001). Some of these commonalities obviously include tuning of cells for special features, as well as for such basic qualities as stimulus intensity. Nonetheless, hearing is not vision and there are some unique aspects of the auditory process that show up when we consider the perceptual questions that directly address what it is that people actually hear, rather than merely how that sound is registered in the nervous system.

STUDY QUESTIONS

1. Describe how the ear analyzes a complex sound into its different frequency components.
2. How does the middle ear protect the inner ear from overstimulation caused by high-level sounds?
3. Describe the inner, middle, and outer ears and indicate the function of each one.
4. How does the cochlea transduce mechanical energy into electrochemical energy?
5. Why are neural tuning curves so sharp when passive basilar membrane tuning curves are not?
6. Describe the feedforward sweep of auditory processing centers in the brain.
7. Describe the function of at least one feedback loop in the auditory system.
8. How does the analysis of sound in the auditory system resemble the analysis of light in the visual system?
9. In what way is the auditory cortex asymmetric?
10. Where is speech processed in the auditory system? Is this the same or different from where music is processed? Why?

CHAPTER 6

HEARING

CHAPTER SUMMARY

Sound is the medium for spoken language, which is arguably what makes humans different from other animals. It is also the medium for screams of pain and sighs of love. A jet airliner passing overhead can make us wince, the sound of a gurgling brook can help us relax, a great symphony performance can move us to tears, a rock band can excite us. Sound has powerful effects on human behavior. The "soundscape" is rich with meaning for humans, and this richness is reflected in the psychological experience of sound. In this chapter we will describe what we hear and something of how we hear it, dealing first with the basic sensations associated with sound and then considering music and speech perception.

DETECTION OF SOUNDS

The simplest auditory experience is detecting that a sound is present. In a classic study at Bell Telephone Laboratories, Sivian and White (1933) measured absolute thresholds for pure-tone stimuli under carefully controlled conditions for several different sound frequencies. Figure 6.1 summarizes their results. Absolute threshold varies with sound frequency. The ear is most sensitive to sounds with frequencies between 1000 and 5,000 Hz, being about 100 times less sensitive to a sound at 100 Hz than to a sound at 3000 Hz. Notice that the **minimum audible fields** (sounds presented in an open space, or free field) are considerably lower than the **min-**

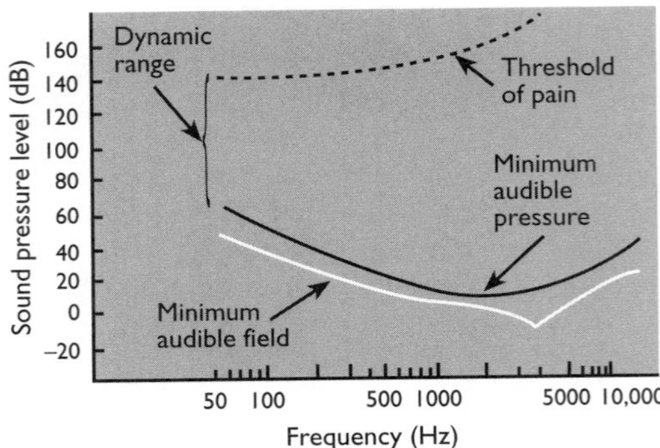

FIGURE 6.1 The dynamic range of hearing from minimum audible sound pressure levels to the threshold of pain (based on Sivian & White, 1933).

imum audible pressures (sounds presented through earphones). More recent measurements suggest that the values may be around 5 dB lower in the region of 2000 to 4000 Hz (Betke, 1991).

Thresholds are lower in a free field mostly because of the existence of resonances and amplifications due to the sound collecting nature of the pinna and the shape of ear canal. These effectively increase the sound pressure at the eardrum. We are most sensitive to sounds of 3000 to 4000 Hz in free-field presentation, which is also the natural resonance frequency range of the external ear canal. Interestingly, screams of agony or terror, especially those of females, sometimes have peaks in the 3000-Hz range (Milne & Milne, 1967), and many speech sounds have important components in this region. Demonstration Box 6.1 shows how to create a situation in which you can experience how your ability to detect sounds varies with their frequency.

If our ears were any more sensitive that they are, we would actually hear the sound of blood rushing through the tiny vessels in the middle and inner ears and the random noise generated by the motion of the air molecules banging against the eardrum (Hudspeth, 1985). When sounds are very intense, however, we experience pain. The difference between the absolute threshold for hearing and the pain threshold defines the **dynamic range** of the ear for any given frequency of sound (see Figure 6.1). The dynamic range can be up to 150 dB for frequencies between about 1000 and 5000 Hz, equivalent to a 7.5-millionfold difference in sound pressure. Few stereo systems can match that! Young adults can hear sounds with frequencies between about 20 and 20,000 Hz, and some young children can hear sounds with frequencies up to 27,000 Hz. Unfortunately, as we age we progressively lose sensitivity, particularly for higher frequencies. Demonstration Box 6.2 describes a simple test for the upper frequency limit of your own hearing.

Several factors other than frequency and pressure determine our ability to detect sounds. One is the duration of the sound. The auditory system sums sound energy across time, acting as if a fixed total amount of sound en-

DEMONSTRATION BOX 6.1

SOUND FREQUENCY AND THRESHOLD

Many people are aware of the problems associated with replaying recorded music so that it sounds as it did when it was recorded. Recording techniques reproduce the sound frequencies produced by musical instruments, but the replay is often at a lower intensity. Many sounds of musical instruments lie in low or high-frequency ranges where the absolute threshold is substantially higher than in the midrange of frequencies. Thus, unless you listen to recordings of an orchestra at reasonable intensity levels, you will not hear sounds at many of the frequencies produced by the instruments. Many high-quality audio amplifiers have been modified to include circuits that compensate for such psychological mechanisms by boosting the level of very low and very high frequency sounds.

For this demonstration you will need a radio or another sound source that produces orchestral music. A cheaper unit, such as a portable radio or your car radio, both of which lack automatic loudness compensation circuits, would be perfect (or you might be able to disable the ones on a more expensive unit). Find a station (or a CD, MP3, etc.) where a full orchestra is playing. Turn down the sound, and listen to the instruments you can hear. Now, gradually turn up the sound. As you do this, you will find that you become more aware of the bass violin and cello; the larger brass pieces, such as the tuba; some of the lower notes of the harp or bassoon; and some of the higher tones from the violins, flutes, and piccolos. When the volume has been considerably increased so that you can hear the entire orchestra and many of the pieces (placing your ear close to the speaker helps), gradually turn down the volume again. Now many of the lower and higher frequency instruments seem to disappear as certain frequencies they produce drop below threshold. The middle frequencies of the orchestra, however, are still quite audible.

DEMONSTRATION BOX 6.2

HIGH-FREQUENCY HEARING LIMITS

You can make a simple test of your own high-frequency hearing using your television set. Turn it on, and then lower the sound completely. Now lean over the back of your set and listen for a soft, high-pitched whine. If you can hear it, this means that you can detect frequencies on the order of 16,000 Hz. Now, try this test on someone who is considerably older than you are and then with someone who is much younger. You should find that the older individual cannot hear this sound, whereas the younger one can. You might also try moving away from the set (if possible) until you can just hear the sound. This is your threshold distance. Now have your other observers do the same, and determine their threshold distances. The greater your threshold distance, the more sensitive your ear is to these high-frequency sounds.

ergy is necessary to stimulate the ear sufficiently so that we hear a sound. The required amount of energy required for hearing can arrive as a high pressure over a short time interval or as a lower pressure over a longer time interval. This relationship is called **Hughes's law** and applies to sounds from 1 ms to about 200 ms duration. The auditory system also sums sound energy across frequency. Suppose we present an observer with two tones of different frequencies; however, each one has only about half the pressure needed to reach threshold. Surprisingly, the observer often reports hearing a sound. The tones cannot differ in frequency by too much, however, or else summation will not occur. Just as there is a critical duration beyond which temporal summation does not occur, there is a **critical band** of frequencies beyond which adding tones does not facilitate detection (Scharf, 1975). The critical band is much narrower for low frequencies than for high frequencies. Figure 6.2 demonstrates how the critical bandwidth varies with frequency.

Another type of summation in the auditory system is across ears. Sound presentations to one ear are called **monaural** (from the roots mon for "one" and aural for "ear"), whereas those to two ears are called **binaural** (from the root bi for "two"). The threshold for binaural presentation is about one half that for monaural presentation (Chocolle, 1962). Binaural thresholds can be lower than monaural thresholds even if the sounds are not presented simultaneously to the two ears. For example, if two subthreshold tones are presented to the ears one at a time, within a total duration of less than 200 ms, the combined sound will be detected 50% of the time even if each individual tone is only one half the monaural threshold level (Schenkel, 1967). In this case, temporal summation has combined with summation across the two ears. Biography Box 6.1 features a modern researcher of acoustical psychophysics.

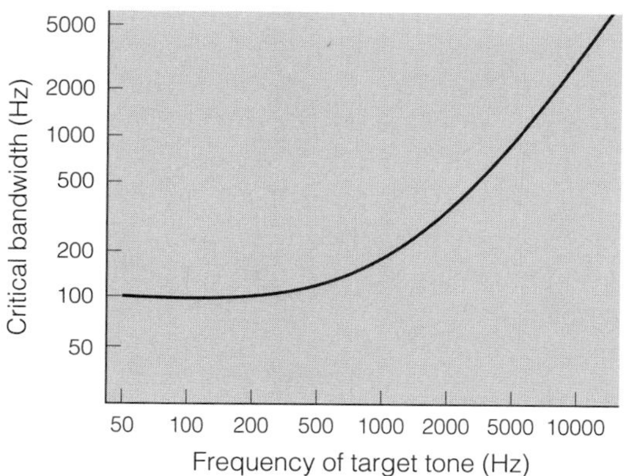

FIGURE 6.2 The relation between critical bandwidth, within which added tones will facilitate detection, and frequency of target tone.

Auditory Masking

In our modern, noisy, world it is common to experience **auditory masking.** This happens when sound we want to hear is obscured by sound we don't want to hear (labeled *noise*), such as in a crowded nightclub or near a busy highway. Sounds can combine physically and the results of sound inputs can interact when they have their effect on the basilar membrane, and even later on in the auditory pathway. If we present an observer with a sound that is audible by itself, adding another sound may result in the observer's losing the ability to hear the first one. We usually say that the second sound is *masking* the first (the *target*); hence we will call this added sound a *masker*. When target and masker are presented at the same time, we have **simultaneous masking.**

A masking sound does not necessarily make *all* other sounds more difficult to hear. Zwicker (1958) showed this by measuring absolute thresholds for target tones of various frequencies presented both alone and simultaneously with a narrow band of noise with a middle frequency of 1200 Hz. As you can see from Figure 6.3, the higher the

BIOGRAPHY BOX 6.1

PROFILE OF A PSYCHOACOUSTICIAN

Although he is probably best known for his leadership role in the application of signal detection theory to psychophysics (see Chapter 2), ***David M. Green*** has made numerous important contributions to our understanding of hearing. His textbook on hearing (Green, 1976) is a fascinating blend of explanations of fundamental concepts and arguments and analyses unique to his rigorous scientific perspective. He has published hundreds of articles and chapters ranging from studies of the foundations of hearing, signal detection and decision analyses, to applied theory and technique in communication, methods for measurement of auditory attention, and mathematical analyses of psychological data. He has demonstrated his broad expertise by serving on panels analyzing such issues as whether the recordings from police radios at the JFK assassination indicated a second gunman, whether and how supersonic flyovers and sonic booms can be controlled, and the effect on whales of deep sea explosions used to study the ocean's currents. Just before he retired from active academic life he produced a series of studies and a summary book on *Profile Analysis* (Green, 1987). Profile analysis shows how people can detect even very small differences between the "spectral profiles" of complex sounds. Profile analysis is one of the main approaches to the analysis of the relation between global and local processing of auditory events.

level of the masking noise, the higher the level of the target tone had to be for it to be audible. The most striking aspect of Figure 6.3, however, is the asymmetry of the masking effect. The greatest masking (resulting in the highest target thresholds) is found for tones with frequencies similar to that of the masker (in this example 1200 Hz). While there is also substantial masking of tones higher in frequency than the masking sound, tones of a lower frequency are relatively unaffected by the masker. For people with sensorineural hearing loss (caused by damage to hair cells or auditory nerve cells), this **upward spread of masking** effect is even more pronounced (Gagne, 1988). You can experience some of these masking effects by performing Demonstration Box 6.3.

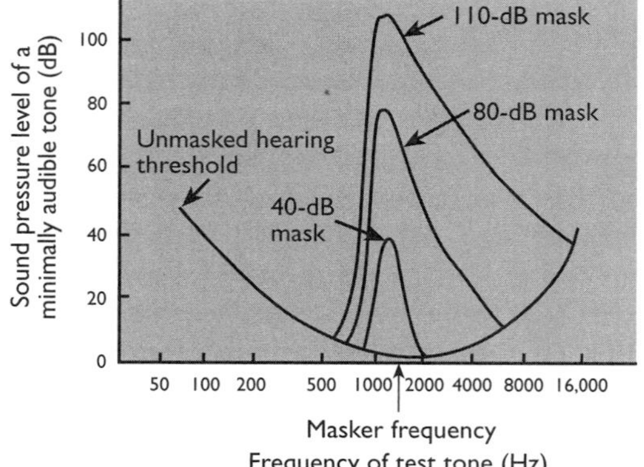

FIGURE 6.3 Thresholds for a pure-tone target in the presence of a narrow band of masking noise centered at 1200 Hz. The higher the curve, the higher the threshold, hence the more effective the masking (based on Zwicker, 1958).

Why does simultaneous masking spread upward in frequency? Turn back to Figure 5.11, which shows how the vibration pattern of the basilar membrane varies with the frequency of a pure tone. Notice that tones of low frequencies produce a very broad vibration pattern, extending over much of the membrane, whereas tones of higher frequencies produce vibration patterns nearer to the oval window (where the stapes is transmitting the vibrations) don't extend as far along the membrane. Now look at Figure 6.4, which shows the effects of two tones on the vibration of the basilar membrane. In the top row (left column) you see that when the target tone is weak and the target tone is of a lower frequency than the masking noise, the target tone's vibration pattern extends beyond the flank of the vibration pattern produced by the masker, allowing the target to be detected. However, when the target tone is of a higher frequency than the masking noise (top row, right column), the target tone's vibration pattern is completely covered by that of the masker, and the target is not detectable as a separate tone. The sound pressure of the higher frequency test tone in the presence of lower frequency noise must be increased substantially (bottom row, right column) before its vibration pattern at last extends beyond that of the masker and it can be detected as a separate tone.

Masking sounds can decrease audibility of a target sound even when they are not presented at the same time. **Forward masking** occurs when the masker is presented *before* the target and **backward masking** occurs when the masker is presented *after* the target. Forward

DEMONSTRATION BOX 6.3

AUDITORY MASKING

To experience several different masking phenomena, you need two major sources of sound—one for a masking sound and one for the target sound that will be masked. Good sources are the noise of a car engine for a masking sound and the car radio for a source of target sounds. If you have a car with a radio, get into it and turn on the radio without starting the engine. Find some music with a good range of frequencies. Classical music is best, but any music will do. Modern music with a lot of steel guitar (country) or electrically amplified guitar (rock) is also good. Take particular note of sounds at the high and the low frequencies. Turn the volume knob on the radio to a level where you can just barely hear these frequencies. Now start the car motor. Press on the accelerator (with the car out of gear!) to make the engine turn over at high revolutions per minute (open the windows if your car interior is well-insulated). This creates a source of intense broad-band masking noise. Now listen for the high and the low frequencies that were clearly audible in the music before you started the car engine. Turn up the volume until the high and low frequencies (which should now be masked) are just barely audible again, and take notice of the difference between the volume settings before and after the noise was introduced. You could map out a masking curve for particular frequencies in a piece of music by varying the revolutions per minute of the motor to vary the level of the noise and by varying the frequency of the sounds whose audibility you are using as a criterion for radio volume adjustment. Note that even with high-level masking noise, you can still hear the middle frequencies, where most of the singing is, whereas the higher and lower frequencies are masked. This is a reflection of the superior sensitivity of the ear to these frequencies. You can also experience speech masking in your car. When the masking noise is of sufficient level (be careful not to damage your engine), even the middle frequencies (where most speech sounds occur) are masked, and you cannot understand the singer or the radio announcer.

masking increases with the level of the masking sounds and is smaller when the time interval between the mask and the target is larger. If sounds are separated by more than about 300 ms, there is no measurable masking (see Zwislocki, 1978). Forward masking also shows the upward spread of masking, but we can't explain it just from interaction of excitation patterns on the basilar membrane. This is because the masker is no longer present when the target is presented at a later time. That means that more central neural processes must be involved. It is likely that the masker is lowering the sensitivity of the hair cells, or their synapses with auditory nerve fibers, thus raising the threshold for the target. It is also possible that more intense maskers cause the basilar membrane to "ring," or continue to vibrate, for up to 10 ms after they are turned off (Carlyon, 1988). Backward masking is a more elusive phenomenon but it does occur. For instance, the ability to hear a click is reduced if a more intense click follows it by up to 25 ms. A masking noise may increase the threshold for a tone that is turned on up to 40 ms earlier (Wright, 1964). Unfortunately, at this time the mechanism causing backward masking is not well understood.

Central masking occurs when target and mask are presented simultaneously to different ears, although the masker must be about 50 dB more intense than in simultaneous masking. Here there can be no interaction of vibration patterns on a single basilar membrane, and the masking is therefore assumed to arise from interactions in more central brain areas. Because of the absence of basilar membrane interaction, there is much less upward spread of central masking (Zwislocki, Damianopoulos, Buining, & Glantz, 1967), but it still does occur for very low-frequency masking sounds (Billings & Stokinger, 1977).

Sound Discrimination

Riesz (1928), working at the Bell Telephone Laboratories, did the classic study of sound pressure discrimination. He measured the Weber fraction for sound pressure (the proportion by which the pressure of a sound must be different from that of a standard in order for the difference to be detected 50% of the time—see Chapter 2) using of different sound frequencies. Figure 6.5 shows Riesz's results for four different frequencies. As you can see, the Weber fraction is smallest (discrimination is best) for stimuli in the middle range of frequencies (1000 Hz and 4000 Hz). Our ability to discriminate sound pressure differences is somewhat worse at higher or lower frequencies, although the difference is not always as large as Riesz found it to be (e.g., Florentine, Buus, &

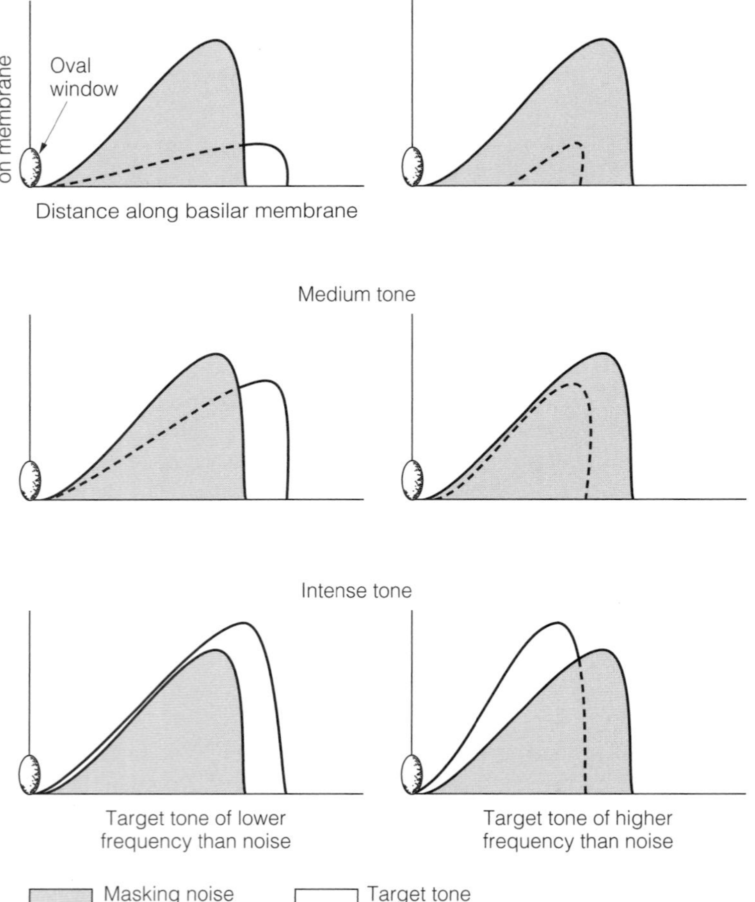

FIGURE 6.4 The interactions of patterns of vibration of the basilar membrane resulting from a target and a noise stimulus (based on Scharf, 1964).

Mason, 1987). For middle sound levels and frequencies, however, the Weber fraction is relatively constant. In this range the auditory system can detect differences of about 10 to 20% in sound pressure (as low as 5% under optimal conditions) across the broad span of frequencies and pressures that include the kind of sounds we most often hear in everyday life.

In general, modern studies have found that Riesz's description of changes in discrimination with sound pressure and frequency replicates well (Ward & Davidson, 1993). Also, just as in sound detection, sound pressure-difference thresholds are about 33% smaller for sounds presented simultaneously to both ears than for those presented only to a single ear (Jesteadt & Weir, 1977). This is because the binaural presentation gives the observer two chances to hear the difference, rather than just the single chance available when monaural presentation is used. Similarly, the pressure-difference threshold is smaller the longer a sound lasts, over a range of 2 ms to 2 sec (Florentine, 1986). The longer stimulus durations give more information about the pressure difference and thus more opportunity to detect it.

The classic study of frequency discrimination also was done at the Bell Telephone Laboratories—this time by Shower and Biddulph (1931). Figure 6.6 shows Shower and Biddulph's measurements of the Weber fraction for frequency for several different sound pressure levels over a broad range of frequencies. Here the Weber fraction is $\Delta f/f$, where f is the frequency of a continuous standard tone and Δf is the brief change in frequency of the standard that can just be detected. Notice that the Weber fraction is fairly constant and quite small (around 0.005) for moderate-level tones above 1000 Hz. This means that if a continuous 1000-Hz standard tone was

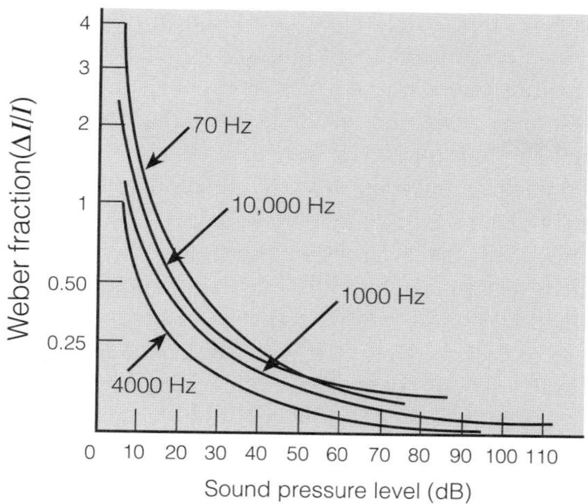

FIGURE 6.5 Sound pressure discrimination measured in terms of the Weber fraction for various sound pressure levels and frequencies of standard stimuli. Note that the Weber fractions are given in intensity (I) units, which are equivalent to pressure squared (based on Riesz, 1928).

changed by only 5 Hz (to 1005 Hz), this small modulation would be detected half the time. At lower levels our discrimination of frequency differences is not quite this good. Here too, modern studies confirm the work of Shower & Biddulph (Wier, Jesteadt, & Green, 1977). Finally, as was the case for pressure discrimination, binaural frequency difference thresholds are about 33% smaller than are monaural ones (Jesteadt & Wier, 1977).

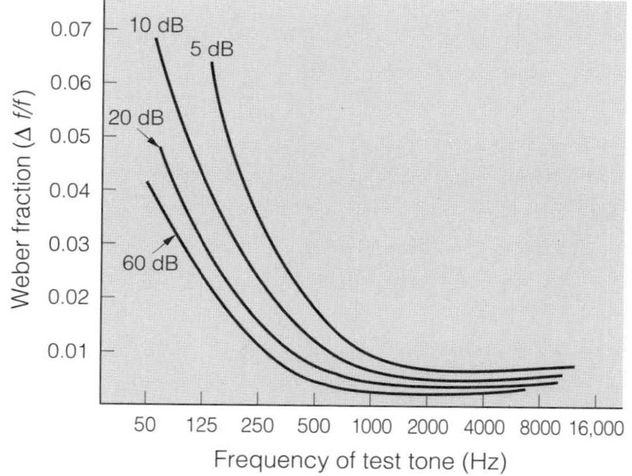

FIGURE 6.6 Frequency discrimination measured in terms of the Weber fraction for various sound pressure levels and frequencies of standard stimuli (based on Shower & Biddulph, 1931).

Sound Localization

Every sound seems to come from some location in space: from the right or left, in front or behind, above or below our bodies. Some sounds appear to come from close by, others from a distance. Our auditory systems construct a sort of auditory space, with our bodies at the center, within which sounds can be localized and their sources approached ("Hey, Jan, nice to see you!") or avoided ("Grrrrooowwwlll").

Interear Difference Cues. Several distinct cues indicate the **azimuth,** or angular difference from the straight-ahead direction, of a sound source. Figure 6.7 shows a typical situation where a sound is coming from a source at 45° left azimuth. Notice that one ear receives the sound on a direct path from the source whereas the other ear is in the **sound shadow.** The shadowed ear receives only those sounds that are bent around the head or diffracted by the edge of the head. This means that the sound pressure at the shadowed ear is lower than that at the ear receiving the sound directly. This **sound level difference** between the ears is larger the farther the sound source is from 0° azimuth (Middlebrooks, Mak-

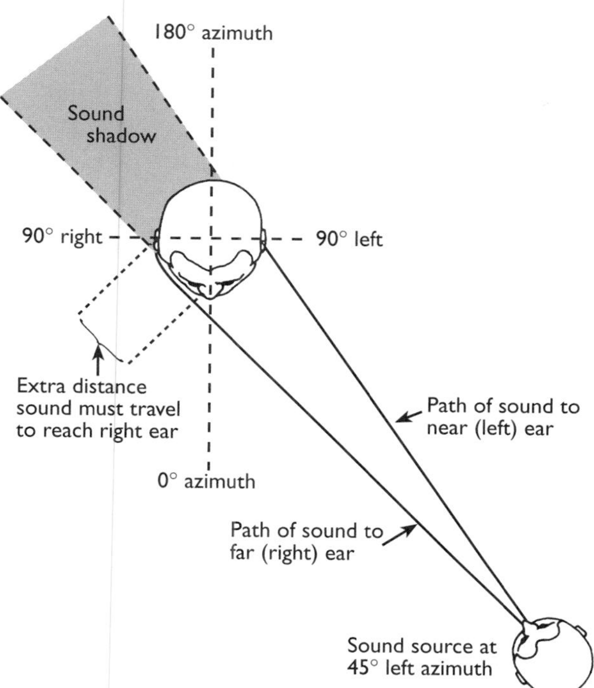

FIGURE 6.7 The path of sound to the two ears for a sound source at 45 left azimuth (based on Lindsay & Norman, 1977).

ous, & Green, 1989). Also, although sound waves with frequency lower than 3000 Hz bend around the head, higher frequency sound waves tend to rush right past the shadowed ear. This exaggerates the intensity differences caused by the presence of a sound shadow for higher frequency sounds. The increase in sound level difference with increasing azimuth serves as a cue to the direction the sound came from. A large sound level difference between the two ears indicates that the sound source is off to one side, at a large azimuth. The greatest intensity difference occurs when the sound source is at 90° azimuth. The ear receiving the louder input is closest to the sound source and is perceived to be so.

Unless a sound source is at 0° or 180° azimuth, sound must travel different distances to reach the two ears. Because sound takes time to travel through space, there is a **time difference** in the arrival of the sound at the two ears. For example, for a sound at 90° azimuth in either direction, the ear closer to the sound is stimulated approximately 0.8 ms earlier than is the farther ear. Of course, the time difference is 0 for sounds at 0° (straight ahead) or 180° (directly behind the head) azimuths. Intermediate azimuths result in intermediate values for this time difference. Time difference is a cue to the location of a sound source and results in the experience of an apparent azimuth for it. You may demonstrate the effects of the time difference on azimuth perception for yourself by using Demonstration Box 6.4.

Interear intensity and time differences occur in a correlated fashion for naturally occurring complex sounds, as illustrated in Figure 6.8. That is, if a complex sound occurs at 45 left azimuth, it will both be louder at the left ear and arrive there earlier. Sounds for which the two cues are in conflict (for example, louder at the left ear but arriving at the right ear earlier) are perceived differently from those for which the two cues are consistent (Gaik, 1993). In particular, artificial sounds giving conflicting cues are often perceived to be somehow "unnatural" and to emanate from more than one location at once.

Back in 1907 Lord Raleigh proposed a two-process theory of sound localization. He suggested that we local-

DEMONSTRATION BOX 6.4

TIME DIFFERENCES AND AUDITORY DIRECTION

For this demonstration you will need a length of rubber hose or flexible plastic tube. Hold one end up to each ear, as shown in the figure. Now, have a friend tap the tube using a pencil. At the point where she taps, a sound wave starts moving in both directions down the tube. If she taps so that there is a longer section of tube on one side, the sound must travel farther before reaching one of your ears. This delay is perceived as a shift in direction of the sound. Notice how the sound seems to change direction as different parts of the tube are tapped, causing different patterns of sound delays.

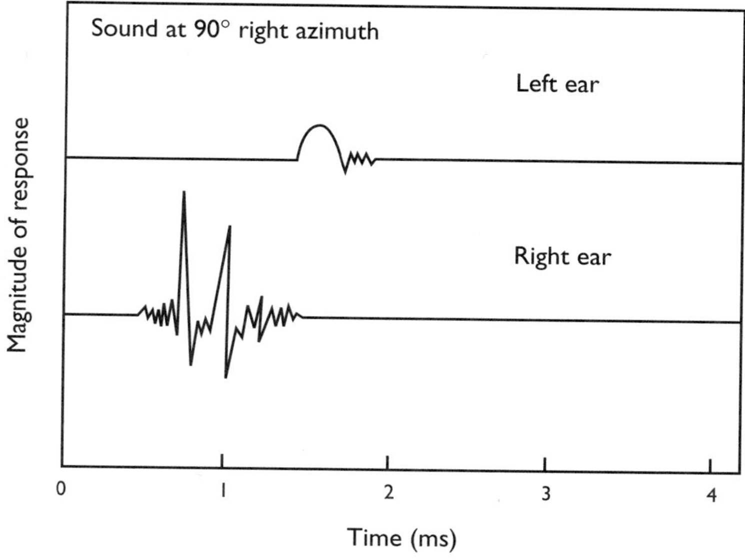

FIGURE 6.8 Responses of the two ears to a brief sound at 90 right azimuth, showing both the sound pressure level and time difference between the responses (based on Gaik, 1993, Fig. 1, p. 99).

ize *low-frequency sounds by using time differences* at the two ears caused by differences in distance from the source, while we localize *high-frequency sounds by using the sound intensity differences* at the two ears caused by the sound shadow. This theory can be tested by asking listeners with eyes closed to point to the location of various sound sources and recording their errors. Figure 6.9 shows the results of one such experiment (Stevens & Newman, 1934); here errors are averaged over all locations at a particular frequency. As you can see, most errors occurred in the region of 1500 to 3000 Hz. There were fewer errors above and below this frequency range. This indicates the efficient use of at least one cue in the low- and high-frequency ranges. Performance is worst at middle frequencies, however, where neither cue to localization is particularly useful. This interpretation has been confirmed by work on the **minimum audible angle,** which is the smallest amount of spatial separation of two sequentially presented acoustic events that can just be detected (Mills, 1958). The minimum audible angle varies with the frequency and location of the sound sources. We are most sensitive to horizontal position changes when a sound source is centered in front of our nose (near 0 azimuth) but most sensitive to vertical position changes when the sound is located at 90 azimuth, which is directly to the side (Makous & Middlebrooks, 1990; Perrott & Saberi, 1990).

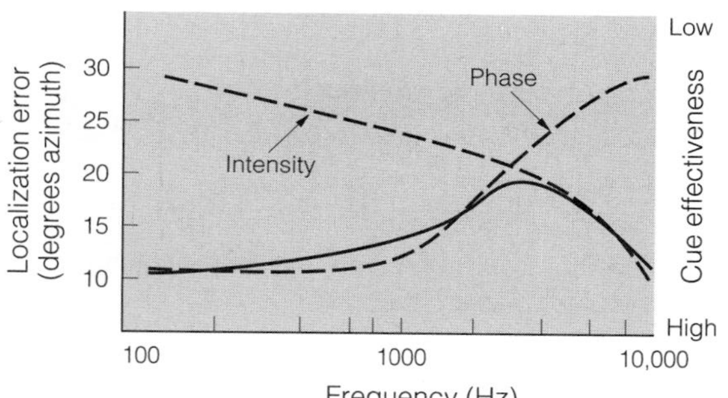

FIGURE 6.9 Relative cue effectiveness in arbitrary units for interaural intensity and phase differences (dashed lines) as a function of frequency. The solid line shows mean localization errors as a function of frequency. (From Gulick, 1971. Copyright 1971 by Oxford University Press, Inc. Reprinted by permission. Data from Stevens & Newman, 1934.)

Reverberation and Other Cues. When we are in an ordinary room, the sound from any source goes bouncing around the room, reflecting from the walls, ceiling, and floor many times. This means that the same sound stimulus can be received at the ear a number of times with various delays. Figure 6.10 illustrates this phenomenon. Why don't we experience an overwhelming auditory confusion as these sounds ricochet around us? Typically, only the earliest arriving of the many echoes of a particular sound is heard as a separate acoustic event. The echoes that arrive several milliseconds later are treated as part of that original event, not as new events. We do not experience echoes as separate events until the reflecting surface is far enough away so that the echoes take a substantial time to reach us (more than 35 ms or so).

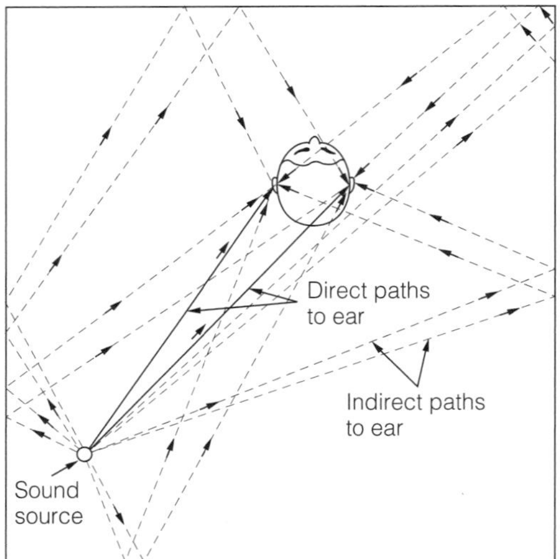

FIGURE 6.10 Some of the echoes produced by sound reflecting from the walls of a room (from Lindsay & Norman, 1977).

When sounds are separated by less than 35 ms, the fused sound tends to appear to be located at the source of the earliest-arriving sound. Thus if two sounds are separated by 2 ms, the one that arrives first is 6 to 10 times more important effective in determining the perceived direction of the sound source (Wallach, Newman, & Rosenzweig, 1949). This is also true when the first sound low-frequency and the later is a high-frequency, but not if it is the high-frequency sound that arrives first (Shinn-Cunningham, Zurek, Durlach, & Clifton, 1995). This fusion of sounds and their early echoes into one auditory event, and the localization of that fused sound at the source of the earliest-arriving sound, is called the **precedence effect.** It occurs in all mammals and even in insects (Wyttenbach & Hoy, 1993). It is an important factor in our ability to listen selectively to one sound source even though it may be surrounded by a large group of competing sounds (see the discussion of the cocktail party problem in Chapter 13). You can experience the precedence effect by trying Demonstration Box 6.5.

Sometimes echoes can affect the apparent location of sound sources. Blind individuals use echoes to help them locate and avoid obstacles (Worchel & Dallenbach, 1947). Echoes also provide cues to the distance of sound sources. As a sound source moves away from a listener, the amount of sound that directly reaches the ears decreases more rapidly than the amount reaching the ears after reverberation. Thus, the relative amount of "**reverberation sound,**" which has a distinct quality, like an echo, is a cue to the distance of a sound source from an observer (Mershon, Ballenger, Little, McMurtry, & Buchanan, 1989).

Another cue to distance is the frequency makeup, or spectrum, of a complex sound. Sounds composed mostly of high frequencies seem to come from quite nearby, and the more the sound is dominated by low-frequency components, the farther away its source appears to be. Through experience with a variety of sounds, we learn that more distant sounds typically are more dominated by low-frequency components, perhaps because the high-frequency components are more easily blocked by intervening obstructions (Butler, Levy, & Neff, 1980).

Learning is also involved in the perception that louder sounds are nearer than softer sounds. In fact, everything else being equal, nearer sounds do have a higher intensity than sounds from the same source at a greater dis-

DEMONSTRATION BOX 6.5

PRECEDENCE AND THE ONE-SPEAKER STEREO ILLUSION

For this demonstration you will need a radio, phonograph, or tape recorder that has stereo speakers located about 2 m apart. Turn on some music, and stand about midway between the two speakers, facing a point between them. You will notice that the sound seems to envelop you. It comes from both sides, and you can clearly identify sounds coming from one speaker or the other. Take a few steps (you need not go very far) toward one side where a speaker is located. After only a step or two you will suddenly find that all the sound seems to be coming from the speaker nearest you. You no longer get any sensation of sound coming from the more distant speaker (although it still affects sound quality, as you can demonstrate by turning it off). A few steps to the other side will reverse this effect, making it appear as though all of the sound is coming from the other speaker. As you move toward a speaker, you alter the time it takes for the sound to reach your ears. The precedence process then takes the sound arriving first and emphasizes it, giving you the impression that all the sound emanates from that source.

tance. Differences in sound distance are thus reliably coded by differences in sound pressure (Ashmead, LeRoy, & Odom, 1990). Through experience we build up memories of, for example, how much farther shouts carry than do whispers. In later encounters we can use this knowledge to judge how far away a sound source may be (Philbeck & Mershon, 2002).

A final important cue to the distance of a sound source is the presence of a compelling visual object that could be the source. The ventriloquist's dummy seems to be talking because its mouth moves and the ventriloquist's does not (if the ventriloquist is any good). Echoes and reverberation play no role in this effect (Mershon, Desaulniers, & Amerson, 1980). In addition, the illusion that a sound is coming from a likely visual object can be so compelling that it can affect the perceived loudness of the sound. If the sound seems to emanate from a visual object that is far away, we will have the illusion that it is louder than a similar that seems to come from a place that is close by (Mershon, Desaulniers, Kiefer, & Amerson, 1981). Observers seem to correct for the fact that actual sound pressure diminishes rapidly as the distance from the sound source increases, a phenomenon termed **loudness constancy** (see Chapter 10).

Virtual Auditory Space. The pinnae, head, neck, shoulders, and other nearby body parts affect different frequencies of sound differently. Interactions between body parts and sound can delay (Batteau, 1967) or amplify (Butler, 1987) sounds of different frequencies by different amounts, providing cues as to the location of complex sound sources, especially their elevation (e.g., Asano, Suzuki, & Sone, 1990; Perrett & Noble, 1995). Actually, the two ears both contribute (different) spectral cues as to elevation, at least until the ear that is farther from the source is deep in the sound shadow, at which point only the cues from the nearer ear matter (Morimoto, 2001). All of these effects can be summarized by the **head-related transfer function,** or **HRTF.** The HRTF is a mathematical description of exactly how each frequency in a sound is amplified or damped by the body parts near the ears, depending on its direction. The HRTF describes all of the information available at the two ears regarding the location of a sound source. It is possible to alter sound presented through headphones or speakers in the ways it would have been altered in the free field, and thus to simulate what a listener would receive in the free field. When this is done the listener has a compelling impression that the sound source is located "out there" in the three-dimensional world rather than is emanating from headphones or speakers (Wightman & Kistler, 1989).

Such "virtual" sound sources can be localized almost as well as real ones, provided that "virtual" head movements are allowed and sufficient exposure obtained (e.g., Bronkhorst, 1995). The HRTFs of different people are, of course, not the same, simply because body parts differ in size and shape between individuals. However, humans are sufficiently similar so that a "generic" HRTF from a representative listener does create virtual auditory space with headphone-presented sounds for other listeners and permits nearly as good localization performance as do individualized HRTFs (Wenzel, Arruda, Kistler, & Wightman, 1993). This result promises that a new type of human-machine interface technology, a virtual acoustic display, might be constructed using a standard HRTF that would work for most people. This is already available in many home computers, and it allows some convincing experiences of sounds differing in location in many video games (c.f. Macpherson & Middlebrooks, 2002). Someday, airplane cockpits and air traffic control displays, computers, and advanced communications systems might include virtual acoustic displays that will significantly enhance both the usefulness of the machines and the richness of our experience of them (see ASVA 97, 1997).

Physiological Mechanisms. The auditory system contains neural units that respond to both time differences and sound pressure differences between the two ears and that may, in turn, signal the location of a sound source. Some neurons in the superior olives (e.g., Tollin & Yin, 2002a, 2002b), inferior colliculi (e.g., Semple & Kitzes, 1987), and auditory cortex (e.g., Recanzone, Guard, & Phan, 2000) of various birds and mammals respond best to binaural stimuli that reach the two ears at slightly different times or pressures. Different neurons have different "best" interaural time differences or different "best" interaural pressure differences. This means that different neurons are "tuned" to particular time or intensity differences. Some neurons are also tuned to spectral differences that indicate elevation of the sound source (Aitkin & Martin, 1990). We could say that these tuned neurons encode sound location much as neurons tuned to sounds of different frequencies encode sound frequency. It is possible that such neurons constitute a kind of map of auditory space, with each neuron having a region of auditory space to which it responds best, a sort of "auditory receptive field" much like the visual receptive fields discussed in Chapter 3.

One problem with this idea, however, is that the receptive fields of these neurons are too large to account for the degree of accuracy that people show when actually localizing sounds. It is possible that interaction of time difference and pressure difference detectors might give rise to higher-level neurons that have more restricted receptive fields that might allow a fairly accurate mapping of auditory space. One way this could happen is that *change* in time difference and/or pressure difference cues could be coded more precisely than the absolute values of these cues. The localization mechanism adapts very quickly to sounds that don't change, but an adapted localization mechanism responds vigorously again as soon as a stimulus change occurs (Hafter & Buell, 1990). In cats, gerbils, and rats, inferior colliculus neurons respond more accurately to changes in time difference than to the time difference itself (Spitzer & Semple, 1991).

Another possibility is that the map of auditory space could be based on, or at least calibrated by, the more precise map of visual space. Visual maps of space clearly calibrate auditory maps in the barn owl (Knudsen & Knudsen, 1989), especially in the superior colliculus (Knudsen & Brainerd, 1991). The deep layers of the superior colliculi of mammals also contain coordinated visual, auditory, and tactile maps of space (Stein & Meredith, 1993), making such a hypothesis more likely to be true. The finding that humans who became blind at an early age are also less accurate in localizing sounds in the vertical plane seems to confirm this speculation (Zwiers, Van Opstal, & Cruysberg, 2001). The same study, however, found no differences between the blind and normal-sighted observers in azimuth localization accuracy, indicating that the time and intensity difference cues used for the horizontal plane may be adequately calibrated without vision.

A final possibility is that neurons in auditory cortex (or at least A1) are not precisely tuned to sound location, perhaps because they do not participate directly in computing sound location but instead pass on the relevant information to higher cortical centers that do so (Schnupp, Mrsic-Flogel, & King, 2001). Subcortical time difference and pressure difference detectors, however, could contribute to location-specific *patterns* of cortical firing, similar to the across-fiber patterns that are thought to encode different smell stimuli (see Chapter 7; Middlebrooks, Clock, Xu, & Green, 1994). In this case, a specific place would then be coded by a specific pattern of response. This approach is supported by the fact that such across-fiber patterns in the auditory cortex of cats seem to vary more precisely with the location of stimulating sounds than do the rates of firing of individual neurons (Middlebrooks et al., 1994), and also that both firing rates and timing are necessary to accurately account for how the auditory cortex encodes sound locations (Xu, Furukawa, & Middlebrooks, 2000). Such patterns of firing could form two broadly tuned channels, one for each hemisphere of the brain, which then corresponds with each side of the world. Here the apparent azimuth corresponding to a sound's location is represented as the relationship between the firing rates in the two channels. Firing patterns of neurons in the inferior colliculi of guinea pigs are consistent with this theory (McAlpine, Jiang, & Palmer, 2001).

SUBJECTIVE DIMENSIONS OF SOUNDS

For a long time people believed that there is a direct and relatively simple correspondence between subjective experiences of sounds and physical properties of sounds. In particular, the subjective dimension of **loudness** was thought to be a direct reflection of sound pressure, and that of **pitch** was thought to reflect sound frequency. However, the subjective qualities of loudness and pitch were found to be complex perceptions that depend on the interaction of several physical characteristics of the stimulus, as well as on the physical and psychological state of the listener. And that's not all. In addition to loudness and pitch, we can differentiate many other qualitatively different experiences associated with sound stimuli. These include the **perceived location** of a sound (where it seems to come from), its **perceived duration** (how extended in time it appears to be), its **timbre** (that complex quality that allows us to distinguish a note played on a clarinet from the same note played on a violin), its **volume** (the sense in which it fills space and seems large or small), and its **density** (a complex feeling of the compactness or hardness of the sound), as well as **consonance** or **dissonance** (how two sounds seem to "go together" or to "clash"). Of these dimensions of sound experience, pitch and loudness are indeed "privileged" because people can classify sounds faster on the basis of pitch and loudness than on the basis of volume or other subjective qualities (Grau & Nelson, 1988). Pitch and loudness do interact with one another in such tasks, however, and either can interfere with perception of timbre (e.g., Melara & Marks, 1990).

Loudness

Of course, everything else being equal, loudness does vary directly and dramatically with sound pressure. The experience of loudness, however, is not identical with sound pressure. Many other factors influence our experience of the loudness of a sound. Thus, decibels of sound pressure are *not* measures of loudness. Instead, to measure loudness we use psychophysical scaling procedures such as those discussed in Chapter 2. For example, average magnitude estimations of loudness (L) are a power function of sound pressure (P): $L = aP^{0.6}$, where a is a constant (Stevens, 1956). The exponent of 0.6 indicates that the power function rises steeply for low sound pressures and then levels off for higher sound pressures (see Chapter 2). The value of the power function exponent for loudness depends on the specific stimuli used and the test conditions employed (Marks, 1974). For example, the exponent varies with stimulus frequency; it is substantially larger than 0.6 for frequencies lower than 400 Hz (Hellman & Zwislocki, 1968; Ward, 1990).

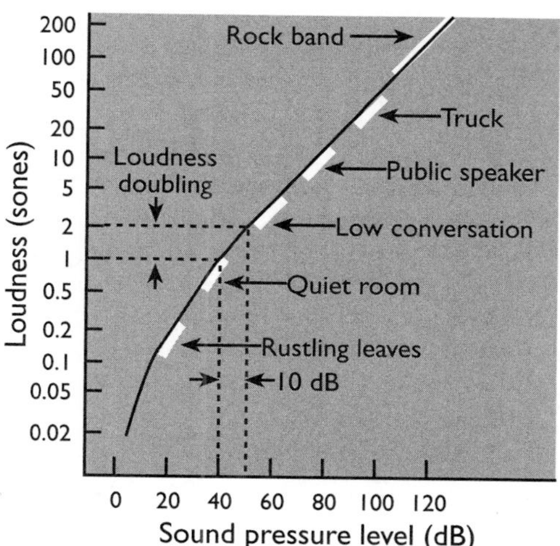

FIGURE 6.11 The relationship between loudness (measured in sones) and sound pressure level (measured in decibels).

Based on his own and others' work, Stevens suggested a new unit by which to measure loudness. Any sound whose loudness matches that of the standard sound, a 1000-Hz stimulus at a level of 40 dB, is said to have a loudness of 1 **sone.** For most of the range of audible sound pressures there is a linear relationship between the logarithm of loudness in sones and sound pressure in dB. To double the loudness (for instance, from 1 to 2 sones) we have to increase the level of the sound by about 10 dB. For very weak sounds (below 30 dB), however, doubling the loudness requires much smaller increases in level (e.g., Canévet, Hellman, & Scharf, 1986). This relationship is shown in Figure 6.11, which also shows the loudness in sones of some typical sounds. Table 6.1 summarizes essential aspects of sones and other audiometric units discussed in this chapter.

The loudness of a tone is affected by several other properties of sound, such as frequency, duration and complexity. The effect of frequency can be summarized in an **equal loudness contour,** which shows the sound pressure levels at which tones of different frequencies appear to be equally loud as a standard tone. Figure 6.12 shows equal loudness contours for several different sound pressure levels of the 1000-Hz standard tone. If tones of different frequencies sounded equally loud when they were the same level, all of the contours would be horizontal straight lines. Notice that these contours rise and fall with frequency, however, much as the contour for absolute threshold at the bottom of the graph does. This means that tones of equal level but of different frequencies differ in loudness. Tones in the 1000 to 5000 Hz range of frequencies sound considerably louder than tones of equal level outside this range.

TABLE 6.1 Audiometric Units

Audiometric Term	Unit	What is Measured	How Measured
Pressure amplitude	Dyne/cm^2	Variation of sound pressure from atmospheric	Measure peak compressive force per 1 cm^2 area
Sound pressure level	Decibel (dB)	Ratio of pressure amplitudes of two sounds	20 log (P/P_0)
Frequency	Hertz (Hz)	Number of cycles of compression/rarefaction	Count cycles per second
Loudness	Sone	Subjective impression of sound intensity	1 sone = loudness of 1000-Hz tone at 40 dB
Pitch	Mel	Subjective impression of sound frequency	Pitch of 1000-Hz tone at 40 dB is 1,000 mels

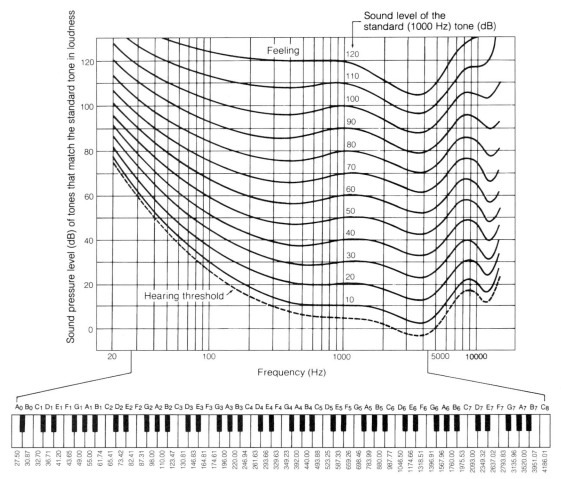

FIGURE 6.12 Equal loudness contours. (From Lindsay & Norman, 1977. Data from Robinson & Dadson, 1956.)

For tones briefer than about 200 ms, we must increase sound pressure level of a shorter tone to match the loudness of a longer tone. This effect of duration on loudness can also be summarized by an equal loudness contour, such as the one in Figure 6.13. According to this curve, a 2-ms burst of sound must have a level of about 16 dB in order to sound as loud as a 10-ms, 10-dB burst. This effect of duration on loudness is similar to Hughes's law for absolute thresholds and is consistent with the idea that the auditory system sums the energy of sounds arriving over a 200-ms time window (Gulick, 1971). The auditory system also sums loudness across critical frequency bands. This is called **spectral loudness summation.** Interestingly, temporal and spectral loudness summation interact, with less spectral summation the longer the duration of the tones being added (Verhey & Kollmeir, 2002).

The auditory system also sums energy across the two ears for loudness as it does for absolute thresholds, so that a binaural presentation sounds about twice as loud

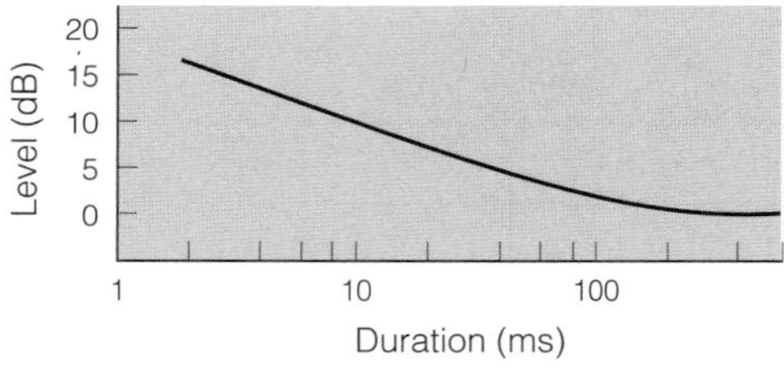

FIGURE 6.13 Equal loudness contour showing the changes in level needed to maintain a constant loudness as the duration of the standard is varied. (From Gulick, 1971. Copyright 1971 by Oxford University Press, Inc. Reprinted by permission.)

as a monaural presentation of the same tone (Levelt, Riemersma, & Bunt, 1972; Schneider & Cohen, 1997). You can demonstrate this for yourself using a radio, stereo, or television. First, experience the loudness of the sound of the TV when you listen with both ears. Then cover one ear, and notice how the loudness diminishes. The mechanism that sums loudnesses from the two ears is separate from the one that sums loudnesses over time (Algom, Rubin, & Cohen-Raz, 1989).

The sound from rock concerts, conversation, and waterfalls is complex, it is composed of many different frequencies. For example, consider a complex sound that includes all the frequencies in some range (its **bandwidth**) around a particular frequency. We can create a different kind of equal loudness contour by asking listeners to adjust the level of a 1000-Hz pure tone until its loudness matches that of this complex sound for a range of different bandwidths. We keep the overall level of the sound the same by decreasing the level of each frequency component as bandwidth increases. Figure 6.14 displays an equal loudness contour for this complex sound. Increasing the bandwidth does not affect the loudness of the sound for bandwidths below about 160 Hz. Above this bandwidth, however, loudness begins to increase as we include a greater number of frequencies, although the total level of the sound remains unchanged (Scharf, 1978).

Acoustical Pitch

The pitch of a sound can be quite different depending on context. **Musical pitch,** which characterizes sounds in a musical context, is discussed in the section on music. **Acoustical pitch,** which we discuss here, refers to the pitch of isolated sounds, or at least sounds in a nonmusical context. The most important physical determinant of acoustical pitch is the frequency of the sound stimulus. Robert Hooke demonstrated this relationship in 1681. He placed a card against a rotating, notched wheel. The resulting vibrations of the card created a sound wave—a sort of rough buzzing musical note. When the rotation rate was increased, the frequency of vibration of the card increased, and so did the pitch of the note. For centuries thereafter, the terms pitch and frequency were used interchangeably on the assumption that pitch rises and falls in exact step with frequency. However, this assumption is incorrect.

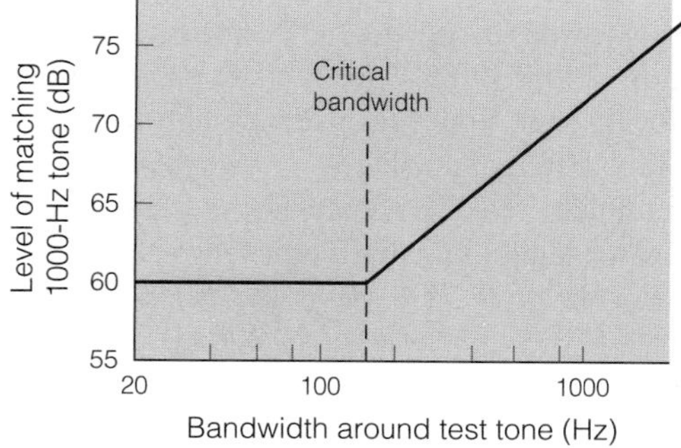

FIGURE 6.14 The effect on loudness of increasing the bandwidth of frequencies in a complex tone (based on Gulick, 1971).

The most useful scale for acoustical pitch is the **mel** scale proposed by Stevens, Volkman, and Newman (1937). It was constructed by asking listeners to produce equal pitch intervals by adjusting the frequencies of a set of isolated pure tones. To specify pitch on the mel scale we use the same standard sound as that used for sones: a 1000-Hz, 40-dB pure tone. The pitch of this tone is said to be 1000 mels. Although its major determinant is frequency, acoustical pitch measured in mels is not exactly proportional to either frequency or to log frequency. The nonlinear relationship of the mel scale to log frequency is shown in Figure 6.15A.

Factors other than frequency affect the pitch of a sound, the major one being its pressure. We can produce **equal pitch contours** by asking a listener either to adjust the pressure level of one of two tones that differ in frequency until the two tones match in pitch (Stevens, 1935) or to adjust the frequency of one of two tones that differ in level until the tones match in pitch (Gulick, 1971). Figure 6.16 shows some equal pitch contours measured by Stevens (1935). The graph shows the percentage change in the frequency necessary to keep the pitch constant as level is changed. The ordinate was chosen so that lines curving upward mean that the pitch is increasing and lines curving downward mean that the pitch is decreasing. As the figure shows, varying the pressure level of a tone alters its pitch. For high frequency tones pitch tends to rise as level increases, whereas for lower frequency tones an increase in level tends to lower pitch.

Theories of Pitch Perception

Consider a complex sound composed of several different pure tones. The auditory system conducts a crude Fourier analysis of this complex sound (Ohm's law), and a listener can discern the presence of the various components. For instance, if two tones are played simultaneously, we hear a musical chord containing two distinct components that differ in pitch—we do not hear a single

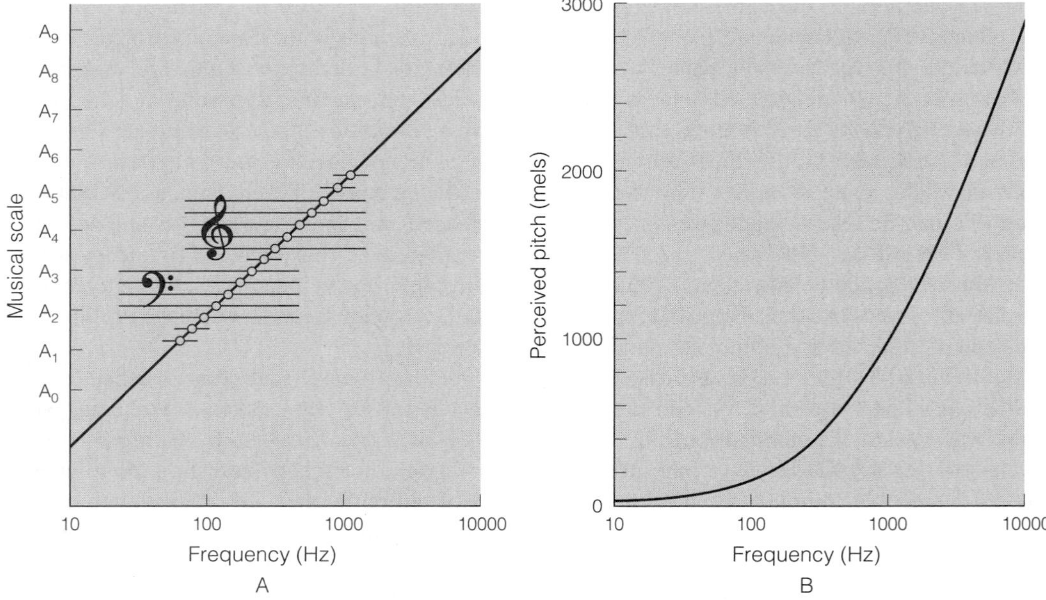

FIGURE 6.15 (A) The relationship between the log frequency and musical scale and (B) the relationship between mels and log frequency (from Lindsay & Norman, 1977).

unitary sound (as you discovered in Demonstration Box 5.2).

We call the lowest-frequency, and usually most intense, pure tone in such a complex sound the **fundamental.** Musical instruments tend to produce complex sounds containing both a fundamental and **harmonics,** frequencies higher than the fundamental. Harmonics, or, musically, overtones, are whole number multiples of the fundamental frequency. For example, when a musical instrument plays the musical note A_3, the complex wave form produced will contain the fundamental, at 220 Hz, and also some sound energy at 440 Hz, 880 Hz, 1320 Hz, and so forth. The timbre of an instrument depends on the specific harmonics, or overtones, it produces. Different instruments emphasize different overtones. It is the number and relative strength of the overtones that allow us to distinguish a piano's A_3 from a guitar's A_3. The pitch of a complex sound is largely determined by the frequency of the fundamental, whereas its timbre is determined by the harmonics, and by other, more complex features (McAdams, Winsberg, Donnadieu, De Soete, & Krimphoff, 1995). Table 6.2, created by Helmholtz in the mid-1800s, shows how various combinations of harmonics produce different subjective impressions.

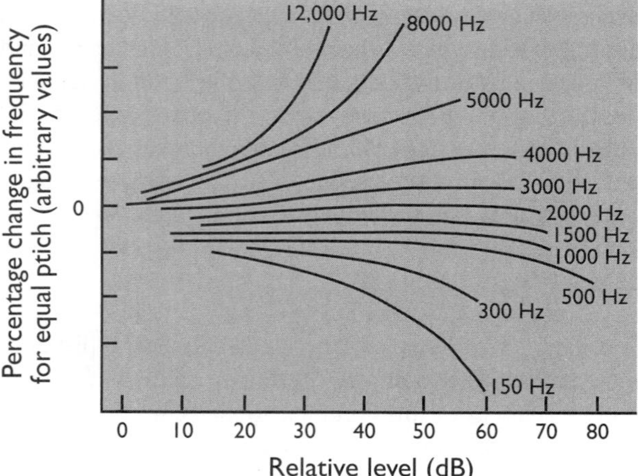

FIGURE 6.16 The relationship between apparent pitch and sound level for one listener (based on Stevens, 1935).

The fundamental frequency is the greatest common denominator of all of the harmonics present in a complex sound. For example, 300 Hz is the fundamental of the harmonics 600 Hz, 900 Hz, and 1200 Hz. An interesting illusion results when we listen to a complex sound made up of just the harmonics without the fundamental (e.g., the harmonics above without 300 Hz): The pitch of the sound with the **missing fundamental** sounds the same as the pitch of a sound that contains both fundamental

TABLE 6.2 Sound Composition and Timbre (based on Helmholtz, 1863/1930)

Makeup of Complex Tone	Subjective Impression
Fundamental alone	Soft
Fundamental plus first harmonic	Mellow
Fundamental plus several harmonics	Broad or full
Fundamental plus high harmonics	Sharp
Fundamental intense, harmonics less intense	Full
Harmonics intense, fundamental less intense	Hollow
Odd harmonics (for example, 1, 3, 5) dominating	Nasal
Frequency ratios of 16 : 15, 9 : 8, 15 : 8, 7 : 5, or 7 : 6	Rough or screeching

and harmonics. Animals, such as cats, birds, and monkeys, are also subject to this illusion (Tomlinson & Schwarz, 1988). Furthermore, MEG recordings (see Appendix) from the primary auditory cortex (A1) of humans show the same response when a missing fundamental sound is presented as when the complex sound contains the fundamental (Pantev, Hoke, Lutkenhoner, & Lehnertz, 1989).

Although the missing fundamental illusion may seem of only passing interest, it actually plays an important role in testing the two major theories of pitch. The first is based on the **place principle,** and the second is based on the **frequency principle.** The place principle asserts that different pitches are encoded as different places of maximum vibration along the basilar membrane, whereas the frequency principle asserts that pitch is encoded in terms of the overall frequency of firing in the auditory nerve.

The place principle was proposed more than 100 years ago by Helmholtz. Intrigued by Ohm's law (see Chapter 5), he suggested that some parts of the basilar membrane resonate to (that is, vibrate in sympathy with) low-frequency tones, whereas other parts resonate to tones of higher frequency. The place principle was confirmed and modified by Bekesy in a series of precise experiments for which he won the Nobel prize (see Bekesy, 1960). Bekesy discovered that high-frequency tones maximally stimulate the narrower, tighter base of the basilar membrane near the oval window, and tones of lower frequencies cause their largest effects farther toward its wider, looser apex. Basilar membrane action is not as simple as Helmholtz's resonance notion, however, because waves of activation travel down the membrane. Moreover, as we discussed in Chapter 5, complex interactions between outer hair cells and the basilar membrane sharpen the its tuning (the active process).

Although it was the dominant theory of pitch perception for many years, the place principle always had difficulty explaining the missing fundamental illusion. Both Helmholtz and Bekesy suggested that the illusion arose because of distortion introduced by the mechanism of the ear. Bekesy (1960) argued that the basilar membrane responds "as if" the fundamental is also physically present. This means that it can be masked by a sound that activates the same place on the basilar membrane. Unfortunately, this doesn't happen. Consider, for example, a pair of tones, such as 2000 and 2400 Hz, which produce a missing fundamental of 400 Hz. A sufficiently high level band of noise, centered around 400 Hz and played at the same time as the missing fundamental sound, should mask the (missing) fundamental. Nevertheless, despite the presence of this noise, the pitch of the complex sound is still perceived to be that of the fundamental (Patterson, 1969). This rules out the suggested place theory distortion mechanism for the missing-fundamental phenomenon.

The frequency principle can explain the missing-fundamental "illusion," and why the missing fundamental is not abolished by masking at the fundamental frequency. The frequency principle also has a long history, having been championed by August Seeback in the 1840s (Green, 1976) and then revived by Wever (1970) and Goldstein (1973). According to the frequency principle, pitch is determined by the overall pattern of spike potentials traveling up the auditory nerve, the number of which rises and falls depending on the number of spiral ganglion neurons firing at any moment. These neurons tend to fire around the moments of peak compression in the stimulating sound wave (phase locking), so that for tones of up to about 4000 Hz the overall frequency of firing in the auditory nerve tracks the frequency of the tone (see Chapter 5). For example, a tone of 500 Hz produces about 500 bursts of spike potentials per second in the auditory nerve. In the frequency principle, pitch is determined by the frequency of these bursts. Modern research indicates this temporal coding of frequency information is very important in both music and speech perception (e.g., Kral, 2000), with the more global aspects more important for speech and the more local ones for melody perception (Smith, Delgutte, & Oxenham, 2002).

According to the frequency principle, the missing fundamental is signaled by the neurons that respond to harmonics below 4000 Hz. Adding or masking the fun-

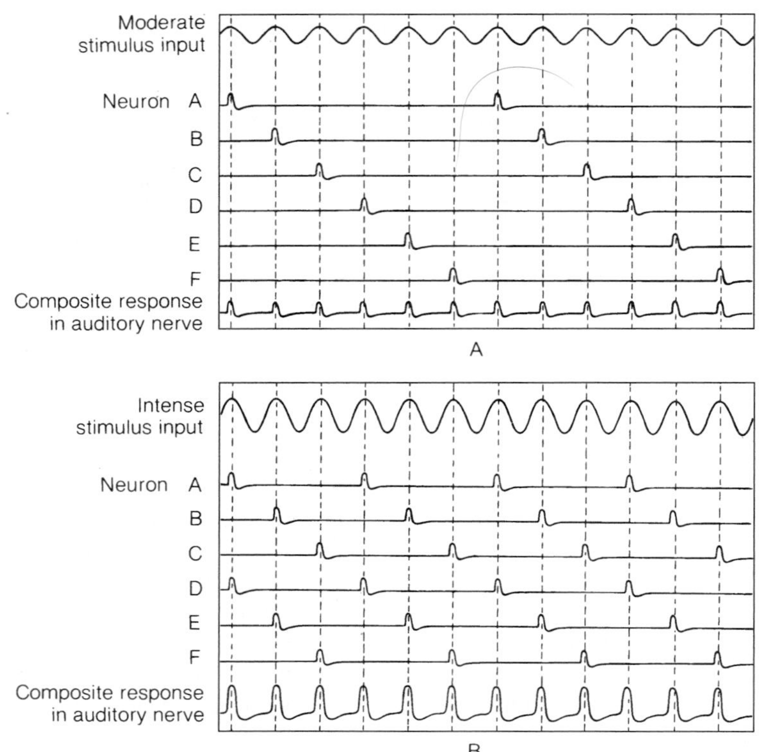

FIGURE 6.17 The volley principle. Note that the composite neural response follows the frequency of the stimulus. However, for the weaker stimulus (A) fewer neurons fire in each volley than fire for the stronger stimulus (B).

damental frequency would not alter this pattern of firing, since bursts of firing at, say, 2000 and 2400 Hz produce even bigger bursts at 400 Hz. This is because every fifth burst of the 2000-Hz series coincides with every sixth burst of the 2400-Hz series. Thus, whether the neurons responsive to 400 Hz are firing or not makes little difference to the pattern of bursts produced by the harmonics in the auditory nerve. On the other hand, if we mask the response to the harmonics by presenting a high-frequency band of noise, centered at 2200 Hz and extending for several hundred hertz on either side of it, the missing fundamental is no longer heard (Patterson, 1969). Clearly the response to the harmonics, which determines the auditory nerve firing pattern, is necessary for the missing fundamental to be perceived.

How can the auditory nerve carry bursts of spike potentials up to about 4000 Hz when individual neurons fire at no more than about 500 Hz? This is explained in terms of a **volley principle** that describes how neurons fire in groups or squads (Wever, 1970). While one neuron is "reloading" (actually resting between spike potentials), its neighbor might be firing. The overall effect in the auditory nerve is a burst of activity for each pressure peak in the sound input, although different neurons are firing at different times. An example of how this might work is shown in Figure 6.17.

Figure 6.17 also shows how pressure and frequency coding in the auditory nerve can be distinguished. An increase in the pressure of a sound, although not changing the volley frequency, would increase the number of neurons firing at each pressure peak, both by stimulating additional neurons that had not previously been firing and by increasing the firing rate in those neurons that were not yet saturated. Thus, frequency could be represented by the frequency of volleys and pressure by the number of responses per volley. Auditory cortical processing could then render these into the experiences of pitch and loudness, respectively.

Because both the place principle and the frequency principle are well supported by research, a definitive explanation of pitch probably will have to include aspects of both theories. Wever (1970) proposed that in humans pitch is mediated by the frequency principle for frequencies lower than about 4000 Hz (the theoretical upper limit for volleying). For frequencies from 500 to 20,000 Hz, the place principle can explain pitch perception. Below 500 Hz, however, the vibration pattern on the basilar membrane is too broad to explain our excellent pitch discrimination by the place theory, so frequency theory is needed to explain performance in this frequency range. Notice that for frequencies between 500 and 4000 Hz, both principles apply. This could help explain the superior performance of the ear for sounds in this range. For frequencies outside this range, we must rely on only one mechanism; thus performance is poorer.

AUDITORY SCENE ANALYSIS

Everyday sounds are not simple, isolated, and meaningless pure tones or noise bursts. We are surrounded most of the time by a multitude of complex hisses, squeaks, booms, chirps, and roars, as well as a constant stream of words and music that pours out of our social gatherings. Such sounds contain diagnostic information about important events (Ballas, 1993; Lakatos, McAdams, & Caussé, 1997). How do our auditory systems and the rest of our brains deal with this enormous flow of sound to produce the rich auditory world, filled with sounding objects, events, and locations, that we experience?

Analogously to vision, we can consider our auditory surroundings as an **auditory scene** (Bregman, 1990; Yost, 2001). An auditory scene may consist of any number of sound-producing events. Each sound source or event varies in spectrum (the amplitude of sound at each frequency), duration, location, time, and so forth. The sound from these various events combines to produce the pattern of acoustic energy received by the ear. We must build separate mental representations of the events from the sound mixture we receive. To do this, we must infer backward from the mixture of sounds we receive to the events that generated them. This process is called **auditory scene analysis** and it is implemented by a complex network of brain areas including auditory cortices and other parts of the temporal lobe as well as the posterior association cortices (Alain, Arnott, & Picton, 2001). Then, in order to build a coherent picture of the world, we must integrate the mental representation of the auditory scene with the representation of the accompanying visual scene, involving most of the visual system of the brain as well. Figure 6.18 illustrates the problem.

Auditory scene analysis involves at least two mechanisms. The first is a fast, involuntary, probably innate process of **auditory grouping.** The second involves imposition of **auditory schemas,** which are higher-level hypotheses or expectations based on knowledge of familiar sounds (Bregman, 1990). The auditory grouping mechanism uses several sources of information. First, the continuous flow of sound received by the ear is analyzed into separate time chunks and grouped according to shared frequency ranges. Each time/frequency segment is represented in terms of level, temporal change, frequency change, location, and other variables. Sounds that have similar patterns over time or that have similar frequency spectra are grouped into separate **auditory streams:** groups of sounds that "belong together" because they appear to emanate from the same source.

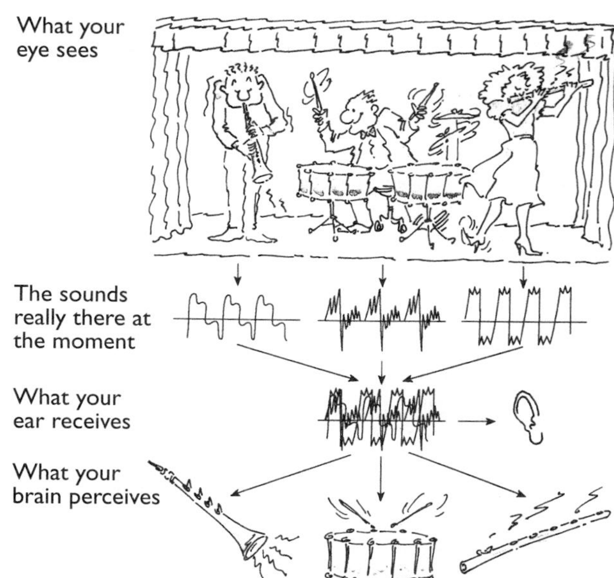

FIGURE 6.18 The problem of auditory scene analysis.

Auditory grouping processes have been studied extensively in the laboratory (see Bregman, 1990), and we know a lot about what affects their operation. For example, the faster a series of sounds is presented, the easier it is to separate out the different streams. Similarly, the more different the locations from which two sounds come, the easier it is to hear them as separate streams. Try Demonstration Box 6.6 to experience this for yourself. More examples can be found on Bregman and Ahad's CD (1996). Auditory streams in music are facilitated by differences in timbre of the instruments and in the timing of musical notes (Iverson, 1995). Biography Box 6.2 will introduce you to a pioneer in research on auditory scene analysis.

Auditory grouping can create some interesting illusions. For example, when a longer pure tone is repeatedly alternated with a short noise burst, the pure tone is heard as continuing through the train of noise bursts, although it is really turned off while each noise burst is on (Warren, 1984). Similarly, continuous frequency changes

DEMONSTRATION BOX 6.6

AUDITORY STREAMING

One of the most powerful factors in allowing us to create auditory or visual groupings of stimuli involves differences in spatial location. For instance, in the figure accompanying this box you will see an example of a problem involving visual scene analysis. The line of print in the top part of the figure contains a mixture of two messages. They are very difficult to separate. However, when they are separated slightly in location, the two messages are easily understood.

An analogous process operates in interpreting separate but similar sound sources. You can experience this by using two portable tape players or radios with earphones. First tune each so you can hear only static. Now change the tone control so that one of the sounds is a high-pitched static and the other is low pitched, and turn the volume up on each. Place one earphone from each radio set next to each other (you might use a rubber band to hold them close), and hold the pair of sounding earphones near and slightly in front of one ear. Notice how difficult it is to separate the mixture of sounds into two high- and low-pitched streams. Next, remove the rubber band, and hold one earphone near, but slightly in front of, one ear and the other earphone in the same relative position near your other ear. Notice how much easier it is to separate out the two streams. The intensity differences of the two sounds at the two ears allow them easily to be assigned to different locations, and thus to different streams, and you hear a higher pitched and a lower pitched noise separately, each emanating from a different sound source.

BIOGRAPHY BOX 6.2

MAKING THE SCENE IN AUDITION

Albert S. Bregman, the "father of auditory scene analysis" earned a B.A. in philosophy and an M.A. in social psychology from the University of Toronto and a Ph.D. in human memory from Yale University. He had not one stitch of training in auditory psychophysics when he arrived at McGill University to teach cognitive psychology in 1965, after a stint at The Center for Cognitive Studies at Harvard University. However, in about 1969, he "happened to employ a rapid sequence of unrelated sounds in an experiment on auditory learning. It became apparent that the perceived sequence was not the actual sequence of sounds, and this observation launched me into the study of auditory perception, a pursuit that has lasted since then" (from Bregman's Web site). He actually considered his lack of training in audition to be an advantage, and it certainly proved to be no disadvantage, as Bregman proceeded to develop those first informal observations into a powerful paradigm called "auditory scene analysis." Although we described this paradigm in this chapter, and indicated its relevance to both music and speech perception, we didn't have space to describe its vast range of other implications. Neuroscience, music theory, audiology, engineering, and computer science have all been fertile fields for applications of Bregman's ideas. Indeed, he was awarded the Jacques-Rousseau medal for interdisciplinary contributions because of this far-reaching influence. In particular, auditory scene analysis has influenced acoustic technology in computer speech recognition and led to improvements in hearing tests, hearing aids and audio systems. The paradigm of auditory scene analysis meshes nicely with modern approaches to visual scene analysis. This close relationship promises an even more far-reaching paradigm with its roots in the powerful auditory concepts developed from a serendipitous observation by a cognitive psychologist who, although untrained in audition, possessed an even more important tool: a ready mind.

are perceived to be continuous even when interrupted by noise bursts (Kluender & Jenison, 1992). Apparently the auditory system is interpreting this auditory scene as if a continuous pure tone, representing a single event, were repeatedly being masked by short noise bursts representing others, much as we hear a sustained trumpet note from a radio as continuous, even though parts of it are masked by the clanking of pots or plates in the kitchen as we fix dinner.

Learned schemas also help us interpret the auditory scene. These schemas contain detailed knowledge about regular patterns of sounds that have particular meanings. For example, a skilled auto mechanic can listen to an ailing engine and separate out the squeaking noise made by a degenerating water pump from the many roars, hisses, clanks, and buzzes made by the other components of the engine. A schema could induce "inattentional deafness" (see Chapter 13), because while listening to the water pump the mechanic might not be aware of the flapping sound that indicates that the engine's fan belt is loose. The schema-based process allows a sound that is selected by attention to be processed better, but it can actually impair processing of the unattended sounds (Bregman, 1990; Mack & Rock, 1998).

Schema-based scene analysis processes take longer to operate than the grouping processes do; however, they are also capable of integrating sounds over longer periods of time. Schemas appear to be activated by detecting all or part of a known pattern in the sound input. The schema selects out the sounds appearing in "its" pattern for use in constructing "its" event, and this construction then contributes to the interpretation of the auditory scene. Each person's schemas are different because they depend on each person's unique learning history. However, auditory grouping and auditory schemas work with other perceptual and cognitive processes (such as those of vision) to create our world of perceptual objects from the booming, buzzing confusion confronted by our sensory systems. Next, we will discuss some of the most sophisticated examples of auditory scene analysis as we consider music and speech perception.

MUSIC

We would probably all agree that the random pounding of a typical three-year-old on the keys of a piano, although perhaps music to a parent's ears, does not qualify as music for the rest of us. If we hear a concert pianist playing a piece by Chopin, however, even if our tastes do not include classical music, nearly all of us would at least agree that we are listening to music. Both "performers" are using the same 88 piano keys; both are producing a series of sounds that vary in loudness, pitch, timbre, and duration; and yet one produces noise and the other music. We perceive as music only those series of sounds that possess certain structural relationships. A child's random pounding of the keys on the piano or a series of isolated pure tones in a pitch judgment experiment lack those relationships. After we perceive a sequence of sounds as music, however, an entirely new set of phenomena emerges, and even the perception of individual sounds is different (Krumhansl, 1990; Jordain, 2000). Moreover, music can affect peoples' emotional state, and the distribution of the neurotransmitter serotonin that is associated with feeling "up" or "down" (Evers & Suhr, 2000).

Musical Pitch

One of the most striking examples of the perceptual phenomena that differentiate musical perception from other forms of auditory perception is the difference between musical pitch and acoustical pitch. We already described the mel scale for acoustical pitch. For both the mel scale and the musical scale, sounds vary along the dimension of **tone height,** which is simply whether a sound appears to be of higher or lower pitch. In music, however, there are additional relationships among **musical notes,** sounds that are identified as forming music, that influence musical pitch.

One important relationship for musical pitch involves the concept of the **octave.** In the common scale—*do, re, mi, fa, so, la, ti, do*—the second *do* is one octave higher than the first *do.* For any two sounds separated by an octave, the fundamental frequency of the higher is exactly twice the frequency of the lower. Thus, middle C (or C_4) on a piano has a fundamental frequency of 261.6 Hz, and the C one octave higher, C_5, has a fundamental frequency of 523.2 Hz. On the **equal temperament scale,** octaves are all considered to be equal pitch differences, so that the pitch difference between C_3 and C_4 is the same as that between C_4 and C_5. This means that musical pitch on the equal temperament scale is proportional to the logarithm of frequency, as depicted in Figure 6.15B. The figure shows the large discrepancies between the mel scale and the musical scale. For instance, the one-octave difference between C_3 and C_4 corresponds to 167 mels, whereas the one-octave difference between C_6 and C_7 corresponds to 508 mels. Such measurements confirm the feeling, often expressed by musicians, that the higher musical octaves sound "larger" than the lower ones. It is as if there is more "psychological distance" between the keys at the high end of the piano than between those at the low end.

Musical notes that have the same relative position in an octave (such as two *do*s, or C notes, separated by one or more octaves) seem more similar to each other than do notes that have different relative positions in the octave (such as C and G, or *do* and *so*). The surprising aspect of this is that it means that notes that are fairly close in frequency, such as C_4 (262.6 Hz) and F_4 (349.3 Hz), sound less similar than notes that are farther away in frequency, such as C_4 and C_5 (523.2 Hz). This tendency for musical notes with similar positions within an octave to sound similar means that the single dimension of tone height (with low notes at the bottom and high notes at the top) will not suffice to describe our perception of musical pitch. This is reminiscent of the situation for color perception discussed in Chapter 4. Remember that we needed a three-dimensional arrangement to describe our perception of color, with hues arranged in a circle and brightness on a dimension perpendicular to the plane of the circle. The required additional aspect of musical pitch is called **tone chroma** to emphasize its similarity to hue. All musical notes with the same name (e.g., C or G) share the same chroma. Like hue, chroma is represented by a circle. To represent both height (one dimensional) and chroma (two dimensional) together graphically, we must use a three-dimensional scheme, much as we did for color. Such a scheme was first proposed in 1846 by Drobisch, who recommended using a helical representation, an idea that has persisted until the present (Krumhansl, 1990; Shepard, 1982). Figure 6.19 shows the musical pitch helix. One complete turn of the helix (a 360 rotation in the horizontal plane) describes a single octave. All notes with the same name fall on a vertical line connecting the helix to the same point on the chroma circle at the bottom, and all sound similar.

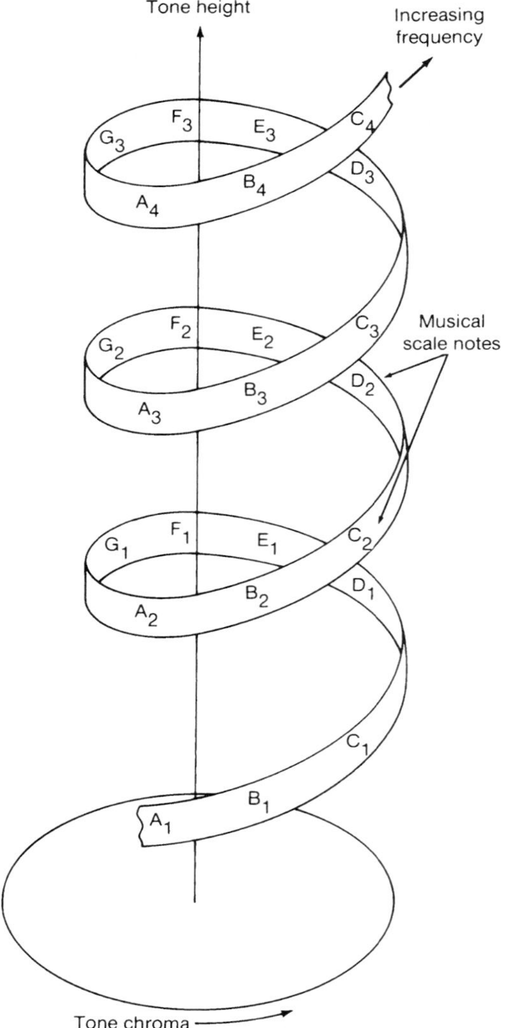

FIGURE 6.19 A regular helix represents the two aspects of musical pitch: height and chroma.

How well can people identify musical notes? In musical contexts, we frequently hear of individuals who have **perfect (or absolute) pitch** (see W. D. Ward, 1999, for a review). Such people are able to identify a musical note that is played on an instrument even when the note is presented in complete isolation from other notes (although they do occasionally misidentify the octave where it is located because of the perceptual similarity we have already discussed). The ability is generally limited to some musicians who began musical training before the age of six, although individuals with Williams syndrome (a genetic disease that limits cognitive abilities) also have amazing pitch identification ability (Lenhoff, Perales, & Hickok, 2001), and the capacity to develop it seems to be inheritable (Drayna, Manichaikul, de Lange, Sneider, & Spector, 2001). When musicians with perfect pitch are presented with pure sine-wave tones, however, they can identify the notes correctly only about half the time (Lockhead & Byrd, 1981). This is still a lot better than those without perfect pitch, who tend to be correct on only about 8% of the trials, but it is nowhere near "perfect." Moreover, even nonmusicians can have good memory for pitch and tempo in some situations. For example, mothers can sing the same song to their infants in virtually the identical pitch and tempo on instances 1 week apart (Bergeson & Trehub, 2002). Similarly, nonmusicians can identify departures from the pitch of familiar TV themes better than would be expected based on their ability to identify isolated musical notes (Schellenberg & Trehub, 2003).

Remember that the acoustical pitch of a complex sound is mostly determined by the fundamental frequency. A pure tone contains only one frequency, which is by definition the fundamental. When a note is played on a musical instrument, however, different harmonics give timbre, or complexity, to the sound. Because people with perfect pitch for musical notes do relatively poorly when identifying pure tones, they must be using the harmonics to aid in identification. From self-reports we know that people with perfect musical pitch judge chroma by comparing the test note with an internally-generated standard, whereas people without perfect pitch seem simply to guess at chroma. When those with perfect pitch are asked to identify **musical intervals** (the spacing between musical notes) relative to an *externally presented* standard, however, they are able to do well with a piano-like C note, a common internal standard, but only poorly when the reference note is F#, out-of-tune C, or out-of-tune E. Those without perfect pitch can judge musical intervals equally well for any external standard (Miyazaki, 1995). It seems that those with perfect pitch rely on it even in relative-pitch tasks, to their detriment when identifying pitch intervals relative to an unfamiliar standard. Perfect pitch does seem to arise from a specialization of the brain: The left-hemisphere auditory association cortex of musicians with perfect pitch is relatively larger than that of musicians without perfect pitch and that of nonmusicians (Schlaug & Jancke, 1995). Consistent with this structural difference, evoked brain responses to auditory stimuli of musicians with perfect pitch are quite different from those of nonmusicians (e.g., Hirata, Kuriki, & Pantev, 1999). Among musicians, however, the difference is marginal between those who have absolute pitch and those who rely on relative pitch (Hantz & Kreilick, 1995). Musical training seems to give rise to effective pitch judgment strategies and similar brain activity regardless of the presence of absolute pitch-related specializations.

Chords represent some of the special relationships that define music and create musical notes out of isolated complex sounds (e.g., Krumhansl, Bharucha, & Kessler, 1982). A **chord** is created by playing three or more musical notes at the same time. Each chord is defined in terms of the ratios of the fundamental frequencies of the notes that make it up. Chords whose respective components have the same ratios are given the same name, no matter what octave they are from. For example, an E major chord is composed of the notes E, G#, and B no matter whether the notes are three octaves up from the lowest on the piano (E_4, $G\#_4$, and B_4) or six octaves up (E_7, $G\#_7$, and B_7). This aspect of musical pitch also is consistent with the helix shown in Figure 6.19, where spacing between adjacent notes is equal on a logarithmic scale, because the musical intervals between the notes of a chord remain the same regardless of tone height or absolute frequency of those notes.

Musical Forms

In addition to the local aspects such as individual notes, musical intervals, and chords, music also exhibits global properties. One of the most important is **melody,** which refers to the sequence of pitch changes in a series of notes. Melody is a global property because it depends on the perception of musical notes in relationship to one another rather than in terms of their individual features (Cuddy, Cohen, & Mewhort, 1981; Deutsch, 1978). The various intervals and proportions that make up melody define the **contour** of a piece of music. Musical contour closely resembles visual contour in that the rises and drops in frequency of the musical notes resemble the variations in luminance that create edges in the visual field. The musical contours in Figure 6.20 are the same even though they are in different positions on the musical scale. Musical contour is so compelling that even trained musicians can miss a distortion in a piece of music, provided the contour remains intact (Krumhansl, 1990). Musicians, on the other hand, are extremely sensitive to changes in contour. In fact, melodies can be recognized on the basis of contour alone, although performance is better when the local cues are also available (Dowling, Kwak, & Andrews, 1995).

We also organize the sequence of different notes and chords that make up a piece of music in a hierarchical fashion (e.g., Bharucha, 1996; Serafine & Glassman, 1989). Combinations of notes form **motifs** (sometimes written as **motive** but still pronounced "**mo-teef**"), combinations of motifs form **phrases,** and so on (Deutsch, 1978). These combinations arise from the processes that perform auditory scene analysis. The grouping processes group the notes into different "streams," and the learned schemas organize the notes into motifs and phrases. The schemas are based on musical conventions acquired either through formal training or through exposure to recorded and live music performances (e.g., Crawley, Acker-Mills, Pastore, & Weil, 2002; Deliege & Melen, 1996). Schemas can be so powerful that they can affect preferences for the way musical instruments are tuned (Loosen, 1995), detection of changes in melodic struc-

FIGURE 6.20 When a melodic sequence is transposed to different positions on the musical scale (A) it still retains the same contour (B).

ture (Trainor & Trehub, 1994), and perception of musical tension (Bigand, Parncutt, & Lerdahl, 1996).

At least some of the Gestalt laws of grouping that we discussed in Chapter 8 also apply to the grouping of musical notes (Deutsch, 1978). One is the law of **proximity** (see Figure 8.27B), by which notes that are close in musical pitch are grouped together, whereas notes that are far apart are grouped into different musical forms. A striking example occurs when two familiar melodies are played to a listener, one to each ear, using a similar range of musical notes and thus a similar pitch range for each (Bregman, 1990). The notes for each melody are alternated in sequence to the two ears (e.g., Note 1 of Melody 1 to the right ear followed by Note 2 of Melody 1 to the left ear, then back to the right ear for Note 3, etc., while Note 1 of Melody 2 was played to the left ear first, followed by Note 2 of Melody 2 to the right ear, and so forth). As you might expect, the listener hears only an unorganized batch of musical notes and is unable to identify the two tunes. However, as the two melodies are separated gradually in pitch range—one becoming progressively higher, the other progressively lower—the listener becomes able to identify the two familiar melodies even though they are "split" across the two ears.

Different types of musical instruments play the same notes with different timbres, which gives them their characteristic sounds and allows us to identify which instrument is playing any given note. When several instruments play simultaneously, the listener tends to group those of similar timbre into the same stream, an auditory example of the Gestalt law of **similarity** (Figure 8.27D). In symphonic music, this principle is used to separate phrases that have a similar fundamental frequency range but a different musical message. Also, timbre provides an additional principle of grouping to that of pitch range when different instruments play different parts of a piece (as in the lead and rhythm guitar parts of a piece of modern rock music).

The Gestalt law of **good continuation** (Figure 8.27F) applies when sequences of pitch changes in the same direction (for example, *do, re, mi, fa, sol, la, ti*) tend to be perceived as part of the same sequence, whereas changes in direction of change (for example, *do, re, mi, fa, mi, re, do*) tend to act as boundaries between segments (Deutsch & Feroe, 1981).

If you would like to hear effects based on these principles, you might try to obtain Dowling and Harwood's (1986) book, Perry's (1999) book, Deutsch's (1995) CD, or Bregman & Ahad's (1996) CD; all contain examples

FIGURE 6.21 Three musical phrases in which the melodic contour is the same and the notes differ only in duration.

of the many musical illusions and paradoxes that arise from these grouping processes.

In addition to height and chroma, musical notes vary in duration. Note duration dramatically affects our perception of melody. For example, Figure 6.21 presents three musical excerpts that all have the same contour. They differ only in the duration for which the notes are held, but this causes a tremendous difference in the melody we perceive. The first excerpt is the beginning of the familiar American folk song "Red River Valley," the second is the opening of Mozart's Serenade in D, and the third is the beginning of the second movement of Beethoven's Symphony No. 5. If you play a musical instrument or sing you may want to try performing these phrases for yourself, just to hear how different they sound. Or you could obtain the three passages on recorded media and compare them on your stereo.

Rhythm and **tempo** arise from the durations of musical notes (e.g., Krumhansl, 2000). Tempo is the perceived speed associated with the presentation of the sounds, and rhythm is the perceived organization in time. Listeners spontaneously organize even a simple sequence of identical sounds into subsequences consisting of an accented sound followed by at least one, and sometimes several, unaccented sounds (Bolton, 1894). Thus, a clock goes "**tick,** tock, **tick,** tock," even though every ticking sound is identical. This spontaneous organization happens when the sounds occur at rates between 10 per second and 1 every 2 seconds, and is strongest at rates of 2 to 3 sounds per second. In the perception of music, these induced rhythms are superimposed on the deliberately manipulated rhythmical structure of the music. The overall rhythmic organization of the music interacts with the organization induced by the variations in pitch of the musical notes, affecting the perceived melodic structure of the music (e.g., Bigand, 1997; Handel & Oshinsky, 1981). The overall rhythmical structure can be so compelling that people can, from hearing a recording of a popular song many times, sing it from memory—long after their last hearing of it—at just about the tempo at which it was performed on the recording (Levitin & Cook, 1996). Demonstration Box 6.7 shows how sounds may be rhythmically grouped together by variations in timing and also by differences in the timbre of the notes.

As we mentioned previously, learned schemas also play a role in music perception. Music listeners rely on such schemas to "fill in" aspects of the melody and to impose structure on the various music streams (e.g., DeWitt & Samuel, 1990). Even ratings of the subjective "goodness" of individual notes within a larger melodic sequence are strongly affected by the types of music to which both musicians and non-musicians have been most exposed (Krumhansl, 1985). Studies of brain responses to musical stimuli indicate that such effects arise from the high-level interpretive response to the music rather than the lower-level perceptual aspects (Besson & Faita, 1995). Moreover, differences in learned schemas between musicians and nonmusicians are correlated with differences in brain structure, including a larger anterior corpus callosum in musicians (Schlaug & Jäncke, 1995). When asked to make difficult judgments about music, musicians tend to rely on processing in the left hemisphere of the brain (also the language hemisphere for most people), whereas nonmusicians tend to rely on the right hemisphere (e.g., Evers, Dannert, Roedding, Roetter & Ringlestein, 1999).

Infants seem to be born with an equal ability to perceive music from all cultures, but the development of learned schemas for the music of our native culture restricts our ability to interpret music from other cultures. For example, six-month-old North American infants are equally able to detect "mistakes" in a traditional Western major scale and a Javanese **pelog** scale that was not part of their birth culture, whereas North American adults are

DEMONSTRATION BOX 6.7

RHYTHMIC GROUPING

In this demonstration you will produce a series of tapping sounds as stimuli. In order to indicate how your taps should be distributed in time, let us establish a sort of rhythmic notation. Whenever we present a **V** it indicates a tap, whereas a hyphen indicates a brief pause. First, tap this simple sequence: **VV-V.** Listen carefully, and notice that the first two taps seem to "go together" or form a unit, but the last seems to stand alone. Now, repeat this sequence of taps several times and try to mentally change this organization so you have two groups, with the first tap **(V)** forming one and the last two taps **(V-V)** forming the other. Notice that no effort of will allows you to do this. The two taps that are close together in time seem to go together and the other does not. This is analogous to the Gestalt principle of grouping by proximity that we discuss in Chapter 10.

Next, try the sequence VVV-V-V-VVV-V-V-VVV, and so on. Notice that this is a repetition of three quick taps, followed by two slow taps. Notice that now the three taps from one group, and the two slow taps form another, perceptually. It is virtually impossible to hear this any other way. This is analogous to the Gestalt principle of similarity (the visual analogue is shown in Figure 11.11).

While you are tapping, you can see that perceptual groups or clusters can be formed by frequency or timbre differences despite the absence of rhythmic differences. Begin by steadily tapping a surface with your pencil. Make sure the tapping rhythm is steady and unchanging. Now take a piece of paper and slip it between the surface and your pencil and notice that the sound quality changes. Without changing your rhythm, slip the paper in and out so that you are tapping **table, table, paper, paper, table, table,** and so on. Notice that the sounds seem to take on a grouping, with the table taps together and the paper taps together, and it seems, despite the fact that you are tapping quite steadily and monotonously, that the sounds have a rhythm that goes **table, table,** pause, **paper, paper,** pause, **table, table,** and so forth. Here, grouping by perceived similarity has imposed an apparent rhythm on the sound sequence.

much better at detecting "mistakes" in their native Western scale (Lynch & Eilers, 1990). Also, infants' ability to detect changes to melodies is unaffected by whether such changes are predictable from Western musical conventions, whereas adults raised in North America do much better with changes that wouldn't occur in Western music (Trainor & Trehub, 1992). This "tuning" of the auditory perceptual system by experience occurs for language learning, as we will see later in this chapter.

Music is important in every culture, and the field of music perception and cognition is far broader and deeper than those few aspects we have discussed. Many books (e.g., Bregman, 1990; Deutsch, 1999; Jourdain, 1997; Krumhansl, 1990) and journals (e.g., *Music Perception* and *Psychomusicology*) reveal these other aspects in detail. In the future, comparisons between the music of different cultures promise insight into which aspects of music depend on learning the musical vocabulary of a particular culture and which depend on mechanisms that characterize all human beings (e.g., Deutsch, 1999; Perlman & Krumhansl, 1996; Serafini, 1995). Similarly, comparisons between species that produce music (e.g., among varieties of songbirds, between songbirds and humans) may reveal the neural mechanisms that are critical to various aspects of music perception (e.g., Brenowitz, 1991; Hulse & Page, 1988). Finally, we are just beginning to understand the biological foundations of music (Zatorre & Peretz, 2001).

SPEECH

Anyone who has studied a second language has probably shared the frustrating experience of listening to what seems a stream of nearly continuous speech in the "second" language without understanding a word of it. In our "first" language we can understand speech at rates of up to about 50 discrete sound units per second, although speech usually proceeds at only about 12 units per second (Foulke & Sticht, 1969). In contrast, the order of nonspeech sounds, such as tones, buzzes, and hisses, can only be determined if they occur at a much slower rate of about two-thirds of a unit per second (Warren, Obusek, Farmer, & Warren, 1969). You might have noticed the very rapid speech used by radio and TV advertisers. Listeners must somehow "normalize" such rapid speech, because it distorts important temporal cues (e.g., Pind, 1995).

In our native language we can compensate for a wide variety of large distortions of the speech signal, for example, when people speak with different accents, with a mouthful of food, or while holding their nose (Remez, Rubin, Pisoni, & Carrell, 1981). And although the distortions introduced by telephones and radios don't affect the intelligibility of speech in our native language, it can have embarrassing effects on our understanding of a "second" or later language (e.g., Warren, Reiner, Bashford, & Brubaker, 1995). We easily understand conversations despite a background of noise, even when the noise level is only 6 dB less than the speech intensity. In fact, even if the speech and noise are the same intensity, we can identify about 50% of single words, and we can understand speech on a familiar topic even if the speech level is lower than that of the noise.

In some ways speech perception is a kind of auditory form perception and follows principles similar to those of music perception and auditory scene analysis. In other ways, however, speech is special, not only because of the important role it plays in human affairs, but also because there are special mechanisms for producing and perceiving speech.

The Speech Stimulus

As Liberman and Mattingly (1985) put it, "the objects of speech perception are the intended phonetic gestures of the speaker" (p. 2). Thus, the goal of the speech perception process is to develop in the listener's consciousness a meaningful representation of what a speaker **intended to say,** producing auditory perceptual objects similar to the visual ones we discussed in Chapter 10.

Linguists describe the auditory speech stimulus in terms of how each speech sound is produced **(phonetics)** and how specific sounds distinguish words in a language **(phonemics)**. These follow the same rules in every human language, although the specific sounds and the rules for combining them can be quite different (e.g., Clark & Clark, 1977; Ladefoged, 1975). Although our discussion is limited to spoken American English, a similar analysis can be done for any language, including nonspoken languages like American Sign Language.

In American English speech, the vocal apparatus produces two basic types of speech sounds: **vowels** and **consonants.** They are produced by alternating sequences of opening and closing the **vocal tract** (the air passages in our throats, mouths, and nasal areas) while air from the lungs flows through it. Typically, closing movements of the **articulators** (the parts of the vocal tract used to shape speech sounds, such as teeth, tongue, lips, and palates) produce consonants, and opening movements produce vowels.

Consonants are classified according to **voicing, manner,** and **place. Voiced** consonants, such as the **b** in "bat," are produced when the airflow constriction is followed in less than about 30 msec by vibration of the vocal cords, whereas **unvoiced** consonants, such as the **p** in "pat," are produced when the vocal cords don't begin vibrating until more than about 40 ms after the constriction. **Stops,** such as the **p** in "stop," are formed by completely stopping the flow of air and then suddenly releasing it. **Fricatives,** such as the **f** in "fricative," are formed by stopping the flow through the nose, but leaving a small opening for air to flow from the mouth. **Nasals,** such as the **n** in "nasal," are produced by closing the mouth so that air from the lungs flows through the nose. Finally, the lips or the lips against the teeth control the flow of air from the lungs in **labial** consonants such the **b** in "bat," whereas positioning the tongue at various places inside the mouth produces **alveolar** (at the ridge behind the teeth, **t** in "tin"), **palatal** (against the hard palate, **n** in "gnat"), or **velar** (against the velum, the soft palate at the top of the throat, **c** in "cot") consonants.

Vowels are produced by vibrating the vocal cords as air moves out of the lungs through the open mouth. Which vowel is produced depends on the position and height of the tongue, which form the shape of the resonating chamber in your mouth. For example, the **ee** in "beet" is produced with the tongue at the front and quite high up in the mouth, whereas the **o** in "pot" is produced with the tongue at the back and low in the mouth. Rounding of the lips also affects vowel production. The **o** in "who" is **rounded** because the lips are rounded to produce it, whereas the **e** in "he" is **unrounded** because the lips are flat when it is produced.

Linguists have created a system of speech sounds that is sufficient to describe any utterance in any language. In this system a speech sound that is used in a language to distinguish one word from another is called a **phoneme.** Every language has its own set of phonemes. Some have only a few (Hawaiian has 11), whereas others require 60 (some African dialects) or more. Table 6.3 lists the 40 major phonemes of American English and the symbols used by the International Phonetic Association (IPA) to refer to them. When we refer to a phoneme in this text we will print it in bold type and give an example word in quotes (e.g., the **p** in "pod"). Try saying the various example words in Table 6.3, paying attention to how the sounds of the phonemes correspond to the way the sounds are produced (their phonetic, or articulatory, features).

Because every phoneme has a unique description in terms of its articulatory features (e.g., the **b** in "bat" is voiced, bilabial, stop), there is a one-to-one correspondence between the phonetic and phonemic descriptions of words. Unfortunately, it is often impossible to isolate the acoustic properties of the speech signal that correspond to a particular speech sound in a particular utterance. This is because in normal speech, movements of our articulators often produce sounds relevant to three phonemes simultaneously (the end of one, the middle of another, and the beginning of a third—this is called **coarticulation**).

It is useful to have a means of displaying the speech sound signal so that we can describe relationships be-

TABLE 6.3 The Major Phonemes of North American English

Consonants				Vowels			
p	pea	θ	thigh	i	beet	o	go
b	beet	ð	thy	i	bit	ɔ	ought
m	man	s	see	e	ate	a	dot
t	toy	ʒ	measure	ɛ	bet	ə	sofa
d	dog	tʃ	chip	æ	bat	ɜ	urn
n	neat	dʒ	jet	u	boot	ai	bite
k	kill	l	lap	U	put	aU	out
g	good	r	rope	ʌ	but	ɔi	toy
f	foot	y	year	ʋ	odd	ou	own
ç	huge	w	wet				
h	hot	ŋ	sing				
v	vote	z	zip				
ʍ	when	ʃ	show				

Note: The phonetic symbol is to the left of each column, and its sound corresponds to the part of the word represented in bold type. Some vowel and consonant combinations are also shown.

tween phonetic or acoustic features and the perceived speech units. In the **speech spectrogram** illustrated in Figure 6.22, the horizontal axis shows time from the onset of a speech sound, and the vertical axis shows the frequencies of the sine wave components that make it up (see Chapter 5). The moment-to-moment variations in amplitudes of the different components are represented by the varying darknesses of the smudges: The darker the smudge, the greater the amplitude of the component. Figure 6.22 displays large-amplitude components at frequencies from about 300 to 700 Hz in all of the syllables. These components last about 200 ms for the "bab" syllable and about 300 ms for the "gag" syllable.

The bands of dark smudges in Figure 6.22 are called **formants.** Formants arise because the sound waves created by the passage of air from the lungs across the vocal cords and out through the articulators are affected by the positions of the various parts of the vocal tract. At least four formants can be distinguished for each of the syllables in Figure 6.22. The one at the lowest frequency (around 500 Hz in the figure) is called the **first formant** and is produced by the shape of the pharynx (wall of the throat). The **second formant,** at about 1400 to 1500 Hz in the different parts of Figure 6.22, is produced by the shape of the oral cavity. Higher formants are produced by complex resonances of the vocal tract, including the nasal passages.

In general, vowels and consonants can be distinguished in speech spectrograms. The relative positions of the various formants roughly correspond to the different vowel sounds. Using artificial speech stimuli, it has been shown that only the first two formants are needed to create sounds that listeners readily identify as vowels; hence from here on we will refer to only the first two formants. Figure 6.23 shows those formants for a set of vowel sounds spoken by an adult male. Because people have different-sized mouths, noses, and throat passages, they have different ranges of possible shape changes. This means that the first and second formants will appear at a range of different frequencies across different speakers. Figure 6.23 also shows, for comparison, one vowel spo-

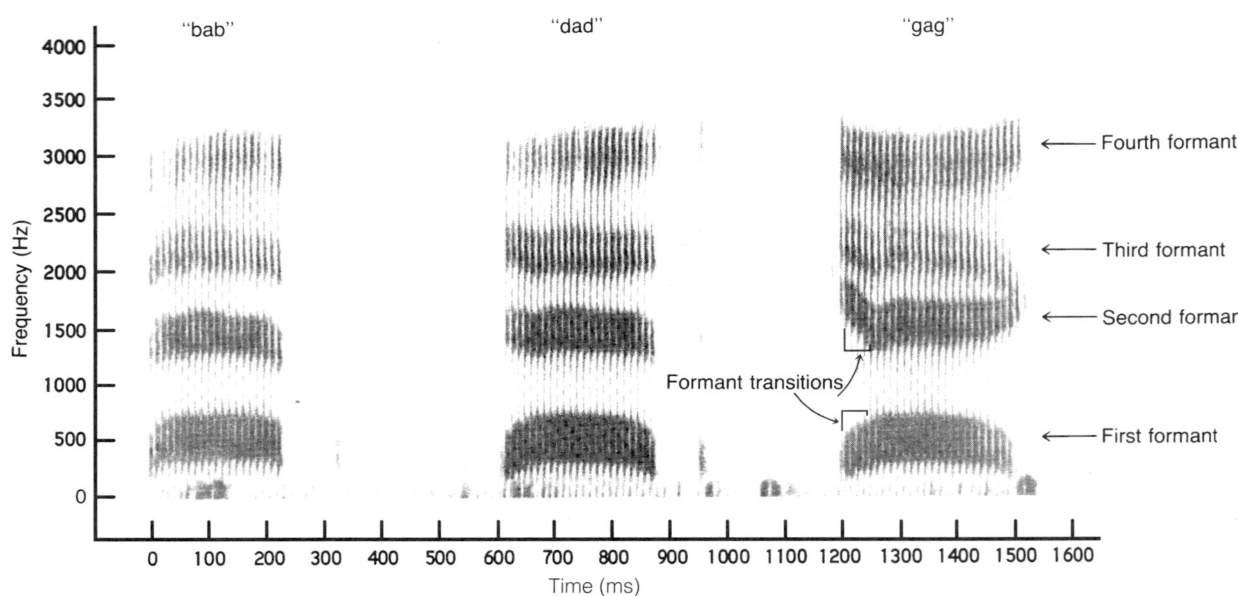

FIGURE 6.22 Speech spectrogram of the words "bab," "dad," and "gag," spoken with a British accent (based on Ladefoged, 1975).

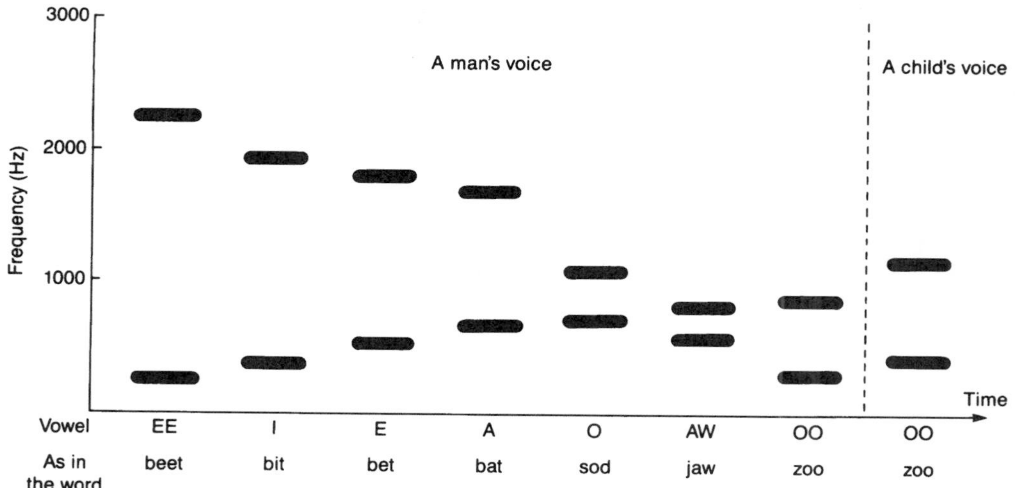

FIGURE 6.23 The first two formants for a series of vowel sounds made by an adult male voice. For comparison, the last vowel sound is shown also as it would be made by a child's voice.

ken by a child. Notice that for the same vowel sound corresponding formants are located at higher frequencies for the child than for the adult.

Consonants are generally indicated by **formant transitions,** which are changes of formants over an interval of less than 100 m. Typical formant transitions are identified in Figure 6.22 and drawn schematically in Figure 6.24. Notice in Figure 6.24 that as the second formant transition changes, the consonant changes from **b** to **d** to **g,** although the vowel sound (represented by the two formants after the transitions) remains the **o** in "sod."

Simple speech sounds of the sort just described do produce predictable perceptual responses, yet in natural speech the signal is not so regular. The theoretically expected components are often missing or distorted. Because of coarticulation there is seldom a precise correspondence between the acoustic properties of the stimulus and the perception of the speech signal. Although it is possible to obtain a precise acoustic description of any utterance in terms of a speech spectrogram, it is not always possible to say exactly which aspects of that spectrogram are meaningfully related to speech perception. For example, look at the

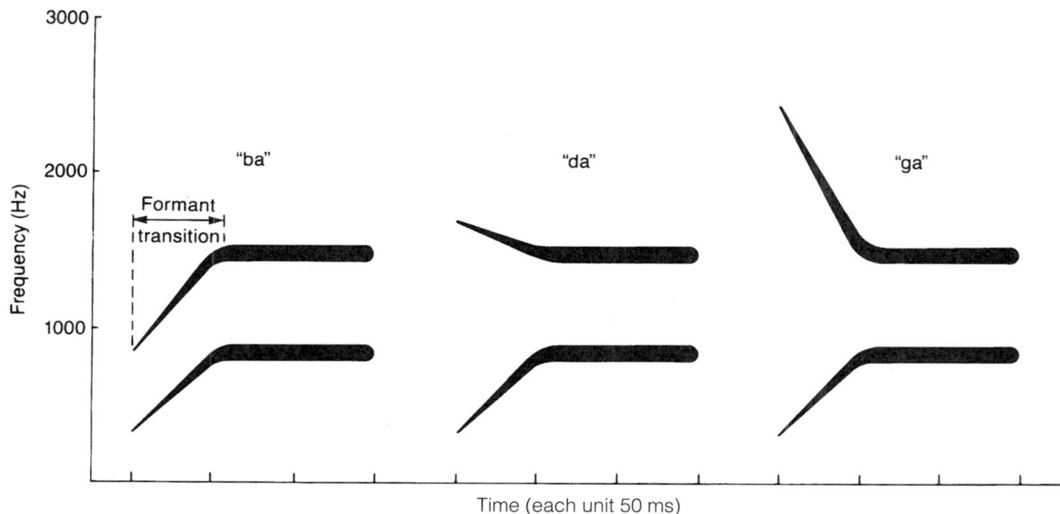

FIGURE 6.24 Changes in the formant transition cause a systematic change in the consonant sound heard for the same vowel. The vowel sound is the o in "sod."

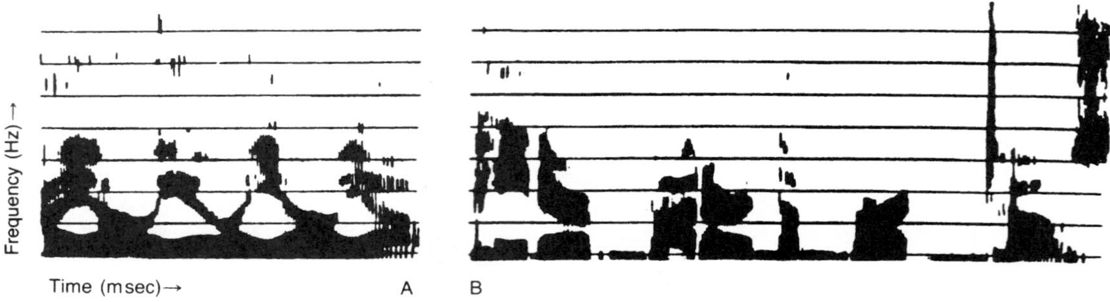

FIGURE 6.25 Speech spectrograms of natural utterances (adapted from Pisoni & Luce, 1986).

two speech spectrograms in Figure 6.25. Spectrogram A represents an utterance of "I owe you a yoyo" and spectrogram B is of the utterance "Peter buttered the burnt toast." Can you find distinct parts of the spectrogram that represent the various vowels and consonants in the utterances?

Perhaps we should look for higher-level regularities or patterns of relationships rather than acoustic properties of individual speech units to explain our perceptions. In music we recognize a melody played on a piano as the same melody when it is played on the clarinet even though no two corresponding sounds are ever the same. The melody is carried in the relationships among the notes rather than in the absolute properties of the individual sounds. A global analysis based on relationships instead of individual acoustic components seems to be required in speech perception as well, considering that we are able to comprehend the same message from such a wide variety of speakers.

Ambiguity and Invariance

Our perception of the speech signal differs from its acoustic properties in several ways. For instance, we hear speech in segments that we interpret as phonemes, words, or phrases separated by pauses. Natural speech, however, usually occurs in a continuous stream, without any obvious breaks or other "markers" corresponding to the perceived pauses (e.g., Chomsky & Miller, 1963). The speech signal also lacks **linearity,** the idea that for each phoneme in an utterance we should be able to find a corresponding segment of the physical speech signal. Linearity also requires that the order of acoustic segments must correspond to the order of phonemes. One example of linearity failure is the children's ditty "mares eat oats and does eat oats and little lambs eat ivy." If you hear someone read it for the first time it will probably sound like "marsee doats and dosee doats . . .". After you know what it means, you begin to hear "breaks" in the acoustic stream where none physically exist.

Another problem is with **acoustic-phonetic invariance,** the notion that there must be some **constant set** of acoustic features associated with each perceived phoneme. For example, the formant transition representing a particular consonant must be present every time this consonant is perceived. Unfortunately, such invariance does not characterize natural speech. In some cases very different acoustic signals can be perceived as the same phoneme. For example, when we hear the consonant **d** in combination with the vowel **ee,** to form the **dee** in "deep," the second formant transition is a rise in frequency; when we hear **d** in combination with **o,** to form the **do** in "dope," the second formant transition is a drop in frequency; and when we hear the **d** in combination with **e,** forming the **de** in "deck," there is no second formant transition at all! This situation violates linearity because the information about **d** does not correspond to a specific segment of the acoustic signal (for example, the second formant transition). It also violates invariance because the acoustic cue for **d** depends on the context (here the vowel it is paired with) rather than a specific set of invariant acoustic features. This lack of correspondence between phonemes and acoustic features makes it difficult to determine exactly what will be perceived given only the acoustic input. This was also illustrated earlier in Figure 6.25.

Is Speech Special?

In some respects, speech is special and different from other perceptual stimuli. Speech is produced by humans to communicate linguistic information, something only humans do naturally. Speech **sounds** special to the listener; there is a distinct difference between our perception of speech and of other sounds. By special, however, speech researchers usually mean the proposal that the perception of speech is accomplished by a specialized set of neural mechanisms in humans (e.g., Liberman, 1982, 1996). It is generally agreed that such special neural mechanisms exist. First, there are two special areas in the brain identified with speech processing: Wernicke's area, in the superior part of the left temporal lobe of the cortex, for speech perception; and Broca's area, in the rear part of the left frontal lobe of the cortex, for speech production. In most humans the left hemisphere of the brain seems to be specialized for speech and language (see Coren, 1992). Damage to the left side of the brain is more likely to produce disruption in speech comprehension or production, presumably because the areas damaged are specialized to perform those functions (e.g., Kolb & Whishaw, 1990). The exclusive role of particular parts of the left hemisphere in speech processing (and not in processing of other auditory stimuli) has been identified by the most recently developed brain imaging techniques, including positron emission tomography (PET—Fiez & Raichle, 1995; Söderfeldt et al., 1997; Zatorre, Meyer, Gjedde, & Evans, 1996) and functional magnetic resonance imaging (fMRI—Binder et al., 1994, 1996). (See Chapter 3 for a description of PET and fMRI.) In fact, the auditory cortex of the left hemisphere contains language-specific memory traces of recently encountered phonemes that are absent for equally complex nonspeech acoustic stimuli (Näätänen et al., 1997). It is reasonable to expect people's perceptions to reflect this specialized neural processing of speech.

Categorical perception is one phenomenon that suggests a special speech mode of auditory processing (Liberman, Harris, Hoffman, & Griffith, 1957). A prominent example involves the voicing of stop consonants. The time at which the onset of voicing occurs can be viewed as a stimulus continuum, ranging from about 0 to 70 ms or so after the stop. From auditory psychophysics we would expect that as we varied the voice onset time we would get a gradual change of the perception of voicing, leading to a gradual change of the identified consonant from, say, the **b** in "bad" to the **p** in "pad," with perhaps some region around 30 to 40 ms in which the phoneme was ambiguous. Surprisingly, this does not typically occur. Rather, as shown in Figure 6.26A, for all voice onset times less than about 35 ms listeners hear a voiced consonant—say, **b**—and for all voice onset times greater than that they hear an unvoiced consonant, say, **p.** The value of voice onset time that divides the **b** (voiced) region from the **p** (unvoiced) region is called the **phonemic boundary.** Moreover, if listeners are presented with pairs of sounds with voice onset times on the same side of the phonemic boundary (say, 10 ms versus 20 ms before voice onset), they have a very hard time discriminating them at all, whereas if stimuli with the same voice-onset-time difference come from opposite sides of the boundary (say, 30 and 40 ms), discrimination is very good. Consonants show this categorical perception, but vowels do not.

Early demonstrations of categorical consonant perception led many researchers to conclude that some special kind of mechanism must exist to process and categorize acoustic cues defining the various consonants. Later data, however, have muddied the picture (see Pisoni & Luce, 1986, for a review). Similar categorization effects can occur for nonspeech stimuli such as "plucked" versus "bowed" sounds of violins (Cutting, 1976), "chirps" versus "bleats" (Pastore & Li, 1990), and simple temporal rhythms (Schulze, 1989). Moreover, phoneme boundaries are perceived in a categorical way in nonhuman species such as macaque monkeys (May & Moody, 1989; Morse & Molfese, 1987), Japanese quail (Kluender, Diehl, & Killeen, 1987; Kuhl & Padden, 1983), and border collies (Adams & Molfese, 1987), none of which should be expected to have a special mechanism for human speech processing. The monkey auditory cortex (A1) responds to voicing onset only for a stimulus on the unvoiced side of the phonemic boundary, thus reflecting the perceptual boundary (Steinschneider, Schroeder, Arezzo, & Vaughan, 1995). Even crickets dis-

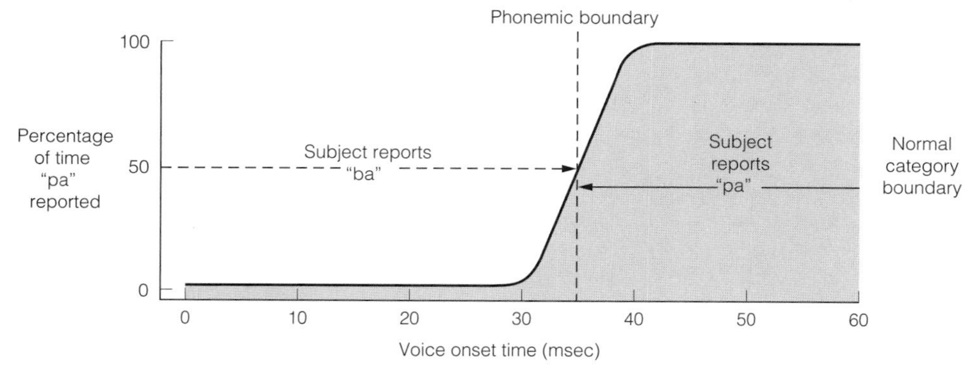

FIGURE 6.26 Typical results of an experiment on categorical perception of phonemes.

play categorical perception of pure tones that attract (frequency lower than 16,000 Hz) and repel (frequency higher than 16,000 Hz) them (Wyttenbach, May, & Hoy, 1996). These and other data, although still controversial, indicate that at the very least, both speech processing and nonspeech processing are based on a rich, abstract auditory code generated from the input sound (Sawusch & Gagnon, 1995).

Another perceptual phenomenon that seems to imply that speech is special is the **McGurk effect** (McGurk & MacDonald, 1976). This involves a form of **cross-modal integration** in which what we see affects what we hear. In the McGurk effect, the listener is exposed to a series of speech sounds—for example, "da"—and at the same time to a movie or video of a face articulating speech sounds in synchrony with the speech sounds. When the visually presented articulator movements are congruent with the speech sounds, speech perception is normal. However, when the visual and auditory inputs are incongruent—for example, the sound is "ba," but the face is making the articulatory movements associated with "ga"—the percept is often a compromise phonetic percept, in this case "da." You can experience a similar effect caused by the cross-modal integration of speech cues by trying Demonstration Box 6.8. This suggests that visual information and auditory information about speech are being integrated before the phoneme is categorized (see Massaro, 1987). The McGurk effect seems to be stronger for syllables and weaker for complete words (Easton & Basala, 1982). This implies that visual speech information is not powerful enough to overcome a combination of auditory and semantic information. Only when the visual information and auditory information are about equally strong does the conflict produce the "in-between" percept.

Of course, in normal speech the visual and auditory information are usually consistent, and both help to communicate the intended phonetic gestures of the speaker. Speech perception probably involves such a mechanism because most linguistic communication takes place, and is learned by the child, in a face-to-face mode where both types of cues are available. However, we don't **need** visual cues to understand speech. For example, we understand speech on the radio, even at higher than normal presentation rates, as in commercials. Moreover, category boundaries between consonants are affected by exposure to the presented sound in a McGurk paradigm ("da" in the example) and not by the perceived sound (e.g., "da"; Roberts & Summerfield, 1981). In this case auditory processing seems to take precedence over speech processing. Finally, other theories can account for the auditory-visual cue integration of the McGurk effect (e.g., Massaro, 1987). Thus, it is likely that there is a rich interaction between "ordinary" auditory processing, which is really not so ordinary, and the "special" processing of speech sounds.

Context

Because the function of speech is to convey meaning, and because the same sound may signify different meanings, there must be some way to disambiguate speech sounds. The **context** in which the speech occurs can serve this

DEMONSTRATION BOX 6.8

CROSS-MODAL INTEGRATION OF CUES

For this demonstration you need access to a television set and a radio. Bring the radio into the same room as the television set and turn them both on. Tune the radio to a point between channels so a hissing or roaring sound comes from the speaker. Tune the television set to a newscast or other show where a person is talking steadily, looking directly into the camera. Set the volume of the television set to a medium setting so that you can comfortably understand what is being said but low enough so that when the radio noise is turned to a high level you can't hear the television. Now, close your eyes and turn up the radio noise until you can't understand what the speaker on the television is saying, then lower the radio noise until you can just barely understand the speaker, and finally raise it a bit so you can't again. Now, open your eyes. In the presence of the visual cues as to what is being said, you will find that you now can understand the television speaker when you see his or her face. The effect will be similar to turning down the noise slightly, except that all you did was add the visual cues. When you close your eyes again, you should find it again impossible to understand the television speaker's speech. The additional information you are obtaining visually by watching the speaker talk is clearly having an effect on the intelligibility of the speech. These visual cues are particularly important anywhere the intelligibility of speech is reduced by the presence of noise, such as at a noisy party or on a noisy downtown street, or if your hearing is not very acute. Thus, many hearing-impaired people find it easier to understand speech when they are looking at a speaker's face.

DEMONSTRATION BOX 6.9

CONTEXT AND SPEECH PERCEPTION

In the absence of an appropriate context, even common words are often difficult to identify. To see how context interacts with speech perception, read the following phrase in a smooth, rapid conversational style to a friend: "In mud eels are, in clay none are." Ask your friend to write down the phrase exactly as he or she heard it. Now you should provide a context by telling your listener that you are going to read a sentence from a book that describes where various types of amphibians can be found. Then read the preceding sentence again at the same speed you did before. After your listener writes down what was heard this time, you can compare the sentences (or nonsentences) that were heard with and without the context. Without the context you might find responses such as "In middies, sar, in clay nanar" or "In may deals are, en clainanar"(Reddy, 1976). Here the words in the sentence are difficult to identify when presented rapidly, and a strange and largely meaningless set of segments is generated. When the proper context is supplied, however, the same speech sounds are correctly segmented into words and are interpreted as meaningful elements.

function, as it often does for vision (see Chapter 10). This occurs regularly in the case of **homophones,** which are words that sound alike when spoken but convey different meanings—such as **be** and **bee, rain** and **reign,** and **no** and **know.** Interestingly, other words that sound quite different to us, such as **married** and **buried,** are produced by speakers using nearly identical movements of the mouth and lips. These **homophenes** are difficult for lip-readers to discriminate out of context. Demonstration Box 6.9 presents an example of how context affects our ability to extract the meaning of speech stimuli.

There are a great many context effects in speech perception (see Liberman & Mattingly, 1985; Sawusch, 1986). In demonstrating another, Day (1968, 1970) presented sound sequences to both ears of listeners at roughly the same times. For example, if the left ear received **b-a-n-k-e-t** the right ear received **l-a-n-k-e-t.** Many of the listeners fused the two sequences into the word **blanket,** even when **lanket** preceded **banket** by several milliseconds; other listeners heard only the separate sound sequences. But no one heard **lbanket,** which is a sequence of phonemes that does not occur in English. The possible meaningful words that **can** occur in speech provided a context that influenced what was perceived in this ambiguous speech stimulus.

Yet another indication of the importance of context is that even trained listeners are unable to accurately transcribe spoken passages phonetically in an unknown language, simply because of their lack of understanding of the meaning of what they are transcribing (Shockey & Reddy, 1974). Even in a known language, listeners can identify less than 50% of a set of words extracted from a stream of recorded speech and presented in isolation (Pollack & Pickett, 1964). If those same words are presented surrounded by some of the words in the original recorded utterance, identification is much better. The more acoustic, syntactic, or semantic context is provided, the better listeners are at identifying the words.

Context can actually induce a listener to fill in a gap in continuous speech. Warren (1970) presented listeners with a taped sentence: "The state governors met with their respective legislatures convening in the capital city." The sound of the first **s** in "legislatures" was deleted and replaced by the sound of a cough. Nineteen of 20 listeners reported nothing unusual about the sentence. They restored the missing phoneme; hence the effect was named the **phonemic restoration effect.** The effect is powerful: restored phonemes can cause shifts of phonemic categorical boundaries (Samuel, 1997).

The likelihood that a phoneme will be restored depends on both meaning and acoustic cues (Bashford, Warren, & Brown, 1996; Samuel, 1996). Phonemic restoration is more likely the more cues available (Trout & Poser, 1990), the more ways a missing sound can make a meaningful (Samuel, 1987), and the more predictable the context makes a missing part (Bronkhorst, Bosman, & Smoorenburg, 1993). In effect, we hear the speech units that the immediate context suggests should be in the phrase, even if they are not physically present.

Theories of Speech Perception

Many theories have been proposed to explain the phenomena of speech perception. No one theory has achieved a consensus, although **trace theory** and **cohort theory** seem to be leading the race (Miller & Eimas, 1995). Theories of speech perception can be grouped by **level of analysis,** whether they deal with the identification of phonemes or of words, and by whether they utilize **active** or **passive processing** (Nusbaum & Schwab,

1986). Passive processing, like the data-driven processing we discussed in Chapter 10, involves a sequence of events that is relatively fixed and works at a sensory level. After the message is sensed and filtered, it is then mapped fairly directly onto the acoustic or articulatory features of the language. Active processing involves a much more extensive interaction between low-level sensing of acoustic features and higher level processes involving analysis of context and knowledge of speech production and articulation. Both active and passive models may rely on general acoustic processing rules or may invoke "special" speech analysis processes.

Many passive theories incorporate the notions of **feature detectors** or **template matching.** Feature detectors for speech are usually conceptualized as neurons specialized for the detection of specific aspects of the speech signal, much the way specific neurons in the visual cortex selectively respond to aspects of the visual stimulus such as line orientation (see Chapter 3). An auditory template may be viewed as a stored abstract representation of certain aspects of speech that develops as a function of experience and serves the same function as a feature detector. Both the feature detectors and any rules to integrate them into percepts can be "special" to speech perception (e.g., Eimas & Corbit, 1973).

Some passive theories stress that ordinary auditory processes are sufficient to explain speech perception at the level of phonemes (e.g., Fant, 1967; Massaro, 1987; Samuel & Kat, 1996). These **auditory theories** usually postulate several stages of processing. The first consists of "ordinary" auditory processing, including analysis of a complex sound into its simple sine wave components, auditory feature analysis, and auditory pattern processing. The next stage then applies more specialized (but not necessarily "special") rules to the output(s) of the first stage(s), integrating them to produce perception of phonemes. A good example of this approach that uses words, rather than phonemes, as the unit is Klatt's (1980) Lexical Access From Spectra (LAFS) model. In this model the listener does a spectral analysis of the input signal, matching the results to a set of templates of features stored in memory. Words are then identified from the set of features detected in the input. In this model there is no need to describe segments or phonemes or other linguistic entities; the speech input is directly matched to words in memory by a fixed process. Figure 6.27A gives a schematic representation of a generalized passive model.

Active models of speech perception usually involve analysis of the context in which the speech is occurring, the expectations of the listener, the distribution of attentional resources, and memory. One prominent active model of word identification is called **cohort theory** (Marslen-Wilson, 1980, 1989). In this model passive analysis initially identifies the phoneme(s) of a word. These then activate a "cohort" of words in memory that have similar phonemes (e.g., all words beginning with **st,** such as "stop," "stall," "stride") in proportion to how similar they are to the identified phoneme(s). Finally, other acoustic or phonetic information, and the goodness of fit between cohort members and the ever-developing meaning of the discourse, eliminate all words in the cohort except the most appropriate one.

Another prominent active theory, which has been implemented as a computer model, is McClelland and Elman's (1986) **trace theory.** This theory implements passive feature detection at three interacting levels: (1) acoustic feature detectors whose output is the input to (2) phoneme detectors whose output is the input to (3) word detectors. The various detectors and other processors, referred to in the computer model as **nodes,** are highly interconnected. Activating one node tends to activate all the nodes to which it is connected, both at the same level and at other higher or lower levels. This is actually a complex model in which various levels may interact with one another in a looping fashion, with higher levels "tuning" or altering the weighting given to specific features at lower levels.

All active theories have in common high-level decisional processes superimposed on the initial feature-extraction results. Thus, the speech we "hear" may be determined by factors other than the actual acoustic signal. A diagram of a generalized active speech-processing theory is shown in Figure 6.27B.

The **motor theory** first proposed by Liberman, Cooper, Shankweiler, and Studdert-Kennedy (1967) and more recently revised by Liberman and Mattingly (1985, 1989; Liberman, 1996) has both active and passive elements. It considers the identification of phonemes considered as the intended phonetic **gestures** of a speaker. In this theory, perception of speech sounds is accomplished by a "special" processing mode that is both innate and part of the more general specialization for language that humans possess. The theory assumes that the same evolutionary adaptations of the mammalian motor system that made speech possible for humans also gave rise to a system for perceiving the resulting speech sounds based on the way they were produced. In this theory, intended speech gestures are inferred from an acoustic/visual speech signal based on an abstract representation of the articulatory movements the listener would use to produce that speech signal.

As an example of how this system might work, remember that the **d** in **dee** as in "deep" is perceived as the same **d** as that in **do** as in "dope," although they are quite

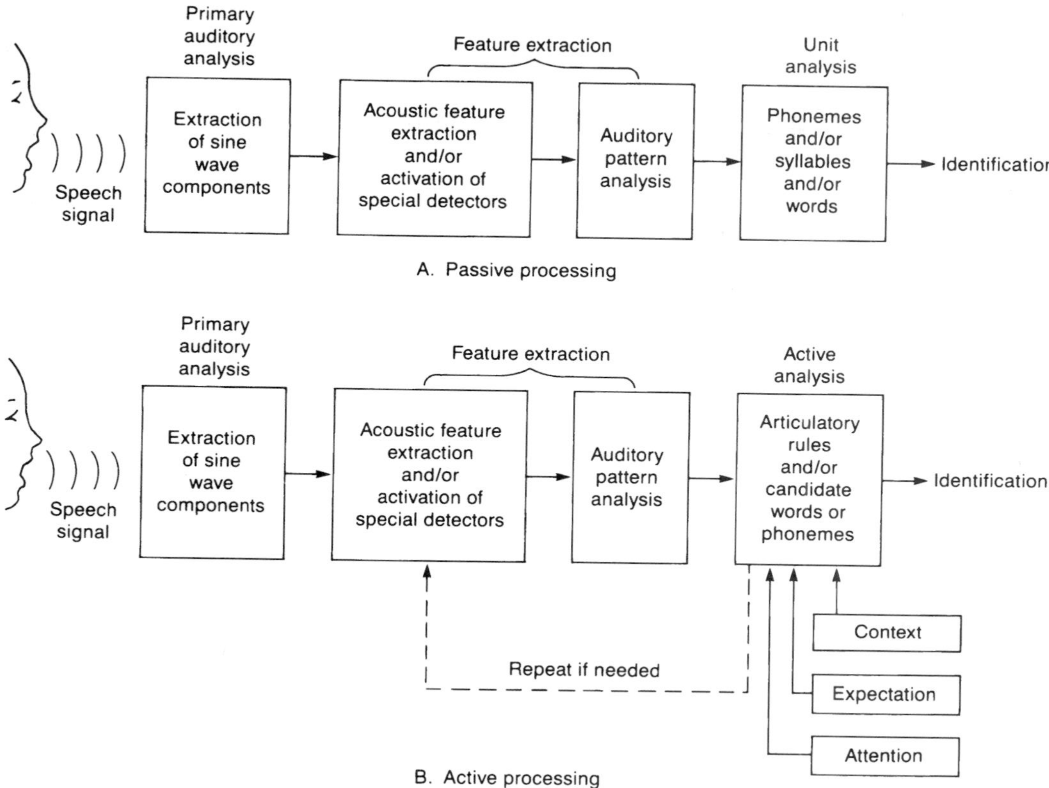

FIGURE 6.27 Diagrammatic representation of the differences between generalized passive (A) and active (B) models of speech processing.

different acoustically. According to motor theory, both are heard as **d** because the listener would use equivalent articulatory movements to produce the **d** phoneme for both utterances. The fact that the actual sounds of the two **d**s are not the same is irrelevant, just as pitch of voice, speed of speech, and other sound-distorting factors are irrelevant. Biography Box 6.3 introduces you to the leading theorist of motor theory.

The motor theory of speech perception remains controversial. For example, perceived pitch of vowels is much more sensitive to temporal displacements of acoustic components than are non-speech complex sounds (Hukin & Darwin, 1995); vowel quality (analogous to timbre) of static vowel sounds can be identified at much shorter durations than can the pitch (octave or note) of the sounds (Robinson & Patterson, 1996); and humans perceive the similarities among vowels differently than do monkeys (Sinnott, Brown, Malik, & Kressley, 1997). All of these findings point to some kind of special processing of speech sounds by humans. Nonetheless, other data continue to indicate that at least some of these special properties of speech sounds are *not* specific to humans (Kluender & Lotto, 1994), and debates continue to rage about whether we hear sounds or "tongues" (Fowler, 1996; Lindblom, 1996; Ohala, 1996; O'Shaughnessy, 1996; Remez, 1996; Stevens, 1996).

No one theory or level of analysis has come to dominate speech perception. In fact, there appears to be a gradual blurring of some of the distinctions. For instance, we have seen that active models begin with a passive-processing, feature-extraction component, whereas some of the passive-processing models may allow active processing when the signal is degraded or conditions are difficult (Fant, 1967; Massaro, 1987). The motor theory also has both active and passive aspects. In addition some investigators have proposed that both general auditory processes and special speech processes are necessary to account for all the data (e.g., Pisoni, 1973; Werker & Logan, 1985). Certainly there can be no argument as to whether an auditory mode of processing exists. The problem speech theorists still must contend with is just how "special" speech perception is and how much of what is heard is in the signal and how much is constructed in the mind of the listener.

BIOGRAPHY BOX 6.3

A "SPECIALIST" IN SPEECH

For over 30 years ***Alvin M. Liberman (1917–2000)*** championed the motor theory of speech perception, trading volleys with a variety of foes, and always insisting that "speech is special." He arrived at this conclusion after dozens of experiments stimulated by one of his few failures. After World War II he had been asked to develop a reading machine for the blind. The idea was to have the machine scan printed text and produce a distinctive sound for each letter of the alphabet. Unfortunately, years of work by Liberman and his colleagues at Haskins Laboratories (now one of the preeminent centers for speech and language research and technology) failed to produce a machine that worked any better than a simple translation into Morse code. This was not satisfactory, since Morse code can only be followed at about 1/10 the normal speaking rate, unbearably slow when reading a novel or a textbook before an exam. So why was speech such a good carrier of linguistic information? Liberman realized that speech evolved along with language as its acoustic carrier. Moreover, speech sounds overlap, producing a very fast, but also very complex, acoustic encoding of language. Liberman also argued that humans' ability to perceive that rapid, complex signal and decode the intended phonemes co-evolved along with the ability to produce speech, producing a unique send-receive linguistic system that would be very difficult to improve upon. Interestingly, modern synthetic speech-producing systems rely on the acoustic cues to the vowels and consonants discovered by Liberman and his colleagues in the course of developing this theory. In his later years he often collaborated with his wife and others to champion the "alphabetic principle" approach to reading, based on the discovery that the ability to break a word down into its component vowels and consonants, called "phoneme awareness," is critical for learning to read alphabetic print.

STUDY QUESTIONS

1. Describe the three most important influences on our ability to detect and to discriminate sounds.
2. Why are low frequency sounds better maskers than are high frequency sounds?
3. What are the two major mechanisms of sound localization and how do they work?
4. Describe the two kinds of equal loudness contours.
5. What is the missing fundamental and why is it important in pitch perception?
6. How does the volley principle rescue the frequency theory of pitch?
7. What is auditory scene analysis and why is it important?
8. How is musical pitch different from acoustical pitch?
9. How do the Gestalt principles affect how we hear music?
10. What is special about speech perception?
11. Describe at least one passive model and one active model of speech perception.
12. What aspects of auditory scene analysis do music and speech have in common?

CHAPTER 7

TASTE, SMELL, TOUCH, AND PAIN

CHAPTER SUMMARY

Helen Keller was born both blind and deaf. She lived in a perceptual world restricted to smells, tastes, touches, and feelings of warmth and cold and pain (the so-called *minor senses*). Such a world is difficult to imagine for those who can see and hear, but these "minor senses" provided Helen Keller with a rich and varied perceptual life. Even linguistic communication is possible, as her teacher demonstrated when she taught her to communicate by tapping of her finger on her teacher's palm and receiving taps back as an answer. Moreover, many species of animals rely almost exclusively on taste, smell, touch, and pain for survival-related information about the world. In this chapter we briefly survey these *anything-but-minor* sensory systems.

TASTE

As well as providing some of the spice of life, the pleasure and disgust provided by our sense of taste serve a survival function. A reasonable rule of thumb, at least for natural substances, is that bad tastes signal harmful, indigestible, or poisonous substances, whereas good tastes signal useful, digestible substances. Taste can help us avoid too much of a good thing because the pleasantness and intensity of sweet and salty tastes are reduced when we are full (e.g., Scott, 1990). Protective taste can lead to paradoxes, however, such as when foods like hot peppers containing capsaicin cause a "burning" sensation when chewed. Although nearly everyone initially (and sometimes tearfully) rejects such "hot" foods, most people can learn to appreciate them because a moderate amount of such irritation is not harmful (Zellner, 1991). Another example is the "delicious" or umami taste given to Chinese food by monosodium glutamate (MSG), which in large amounts can cause "Chinese-restaurant syndrome," an uncomfortable, nauseated, dry-mouthed sleeplessness.

Our gustatory *(taste)* sense evolved from direct interactions of the first living things with the giant bowl of chemical soup in which they were immersed. Substances suspended or dissolved in water were important to their survival. Some provided food, some gave warning, and some caused destruction. The most primitive one-celled organisms did not possess sensory systems like vision that require large numbers of specialized cells. They relied on direct chemical or mechanical interactions with their environment through their cell membrane. In contrast, multicelled animals use a "division of labor" with specialized receptors to pick up chemical information from the surroundings. For example, fish have pits lined with receptors responsive to a variety of chemical and mechanical stimuli. Insects and other invertebrates have such receptors located on their antennae.

Although two anatomically separate systems eventually developed, in the primordial sea there was little differentiation between taste and smell. When life moved onto land, however, the two chemical receptor systems became differentiated. The taste system became a "close-up" sense, which provided the last check on the acceptability of food. Smell turned out to be useful as a distance sense, although it also retained an important function in dealing with food.

Taste Stimuli and Receptors

The physical stimuli for the taste system are water-soluble substances. The concentration of a chemical substance is related to the intensity of the taste we experience. Which aspects of the stimulus give rise to the different taste qualities is now becoming known through sophisticated biochemical and molecular biological studies of isolated receptor cells.

It is useful to distinguish six primary taste qualities. The first four, **sweet, salty, sour,** and **bitter,** have been known since antiquity (e.g., Henning, 1916). The other two, **umami** (commonly described as a kind of "meaty" or "savory" taste) and **fat,** have been suggested only recently. The umami receptor has now actually been isolated (Nelson et al., 2002) while the fat receptor is predicted by other findings and some theoretical considerations (Gilbertson, 1998).

Each taste quality is associated with different molecules, called **tastants.** Sweet taste generally arises from organic molecules, which are made up mostly of carbon, hydrogen, and oxygen in different combinations. These molecules are commonly called sugars, alcohols, and so forth. Other sweet substances, like aspartame and cyclamates, are also organic chemicals, but they are quite different from "natural" sweeteners, such as sugars, in their molecular structure. Bitter taste is related to sweet taste. Many substances that taste sweet in small amounts taste bitter in large amounts (e.g., saccharin). Also, several substances containing nitrogen, such as strychnine, caffeine, quinine, and nicotine, taste bitter.

Salty taste is elicited by molecules that, when dissolved in water, break into two electrically charged parts called **ions.** For example, each molecule of table salt is composed of two atoms: one sodium (Na) and one chlorine (Cl). When dissolved in water, the atoms break apart. The sodium atom is now a positively charged ion (written Na^+), and the chlorine atom is a negatively charged ion (written Cl^-). Some salts taste bitter in high concentrations, and in very low concentrations most salts taste sweet.

Sour substances also break up into two parts when in solution, but they are usually acids (such as hydrochloric, sulfuric, acetic, and nitric) rather than salts. In all of these substances, hydrogen is the positively charged ion (H^+). The presence of the hydrogen ion is directly related to the sour taste of such acids. Umami taste is elicited by amino acids such as L-glutamine (which is actually part of the seasoning MSG); some amino acids, however, taste sweet. Fat taste arises from free fatty acids that are transported though the saliva by special proteins secreted in the mouth.

The receptors that respond to taste stimuli are groups of cells called **taste buds** that are found in three types of little bumps on the tongue called **papillae** (Figure 7.1). **Fungiform papillae** are shaped like little mushrooms (fungi) and are found at the tip and the sides of the tongue. **Foliate papillae** make up a series of folds (folia) along the sides of the rear portion of the tongue. **Circumvallate papillae** are shaped like flattened hills, with a circular trench or valley surrounding them, and are located at the back of the tongue. The arrowhead-shaped **filiform papillae** contain no taste buds; they help to abrade food into small, easy-to-dissolve bits. Some taste receptors are also scattered over parts of the mouth other than the tongue, such as on the **soft palate** (the back portion of the roof of your mouth). Figure 7.2A shows how the taste buds are distributed within a circumvallate papilla. Each taste bud consists of several receptor cells

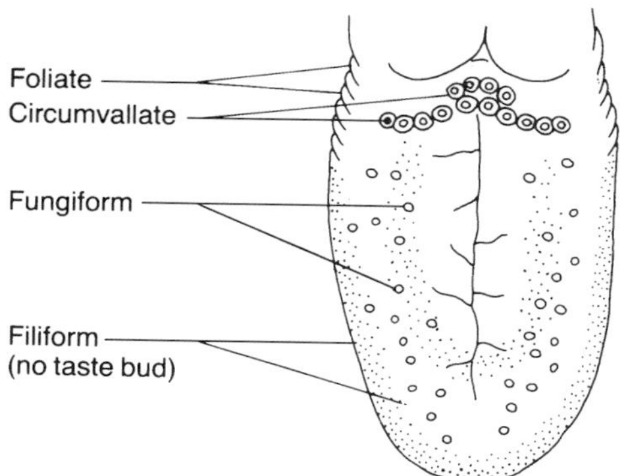

FIGURE 7.1 A diagram of the human tongue showing the locations of the different types of papillae.

(perhaps up to 30) of different types as well as undeveloped basal cells (Figure 7.2B). There are about 10,000 taste buds in your mouth when you are young, but their number decreases with age.

Within each taste bud the individual cells are continually developing. Each taste receptor cell has a life span of only a few days; thus the composition of the taste bud is always changing, with some immature cells (around the outside), some mature cells (near the inside), and some dying cells always present (Beidler & Smallman, 1965). The taste receptor cells are a specialized variation of skin cells. This explains their short life span, because all skin cells are periodically replaced. Slender projections (called **microvilli**) from the top end of each cell lie near an opening onto the surface of the tongue called a **taste pore.**

Tastants interact with receptors and ion channels on the microvilli. There are several different transduction mechanisms to turn chemical stimulation into a neural response (Figure 7.3; Gilbertson, Damak, & Margolskee, 2000), and each of the microvilli can have more than one of these. For instance, the transduction of salty-tasting NaCl (table salt) and KCl is accomplished by the flow of sodium or potassium ions directly through passive channels in the cell membrane. In sour-taste transduction, hydrogen ions flow through the same channels and also block the usual flow of potassium ions through other channels in the cell membrane. All of these mechanisms directly depolarize the taste bud. Sweet- and bitter-tasting molecules are transduced by complicated mechanisms involving specific receptors in the microvilli cell membrane (Figure 7.3; Montmayeur & Matsunami, 2002). When appropriate molecules latch onto the receptors, either positive ions flow across the cell membrane, again directly depolarizing the cell, or the concentrations of various other molecules inside the cell change in a cascading fashion. Similar mechanisms are at work in the newly discovered amino-acid receptor, which mediates the taste of umami (Nelson et al., 2002). There also seem to be mechanisms to transduce "fat" taste; one is by fatty acid molecules blocking the flow of potassium ions out of the cell (Gilbertson, 1998). All of these mechanisms lead to a rise in the amount of Ca^{2+} inside the cell, and this, in turn, causes the release of neurotransmitter molecules across the synapses of the taste buds with the taste nerves, causing spike potentials to travel up the taste nerves.

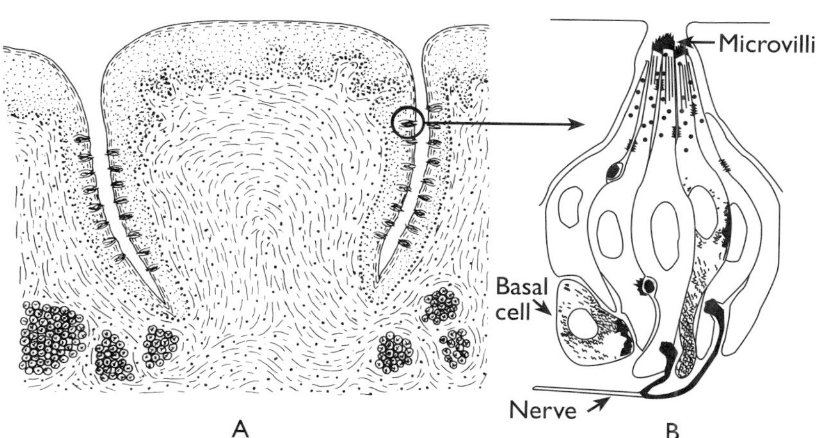

FIGURE 7.2 (A) A typical papilla with taste buds; one is circled (from Wyburn et al., 1964); (B) drawing of a single taste bud (from Smith, 1997).

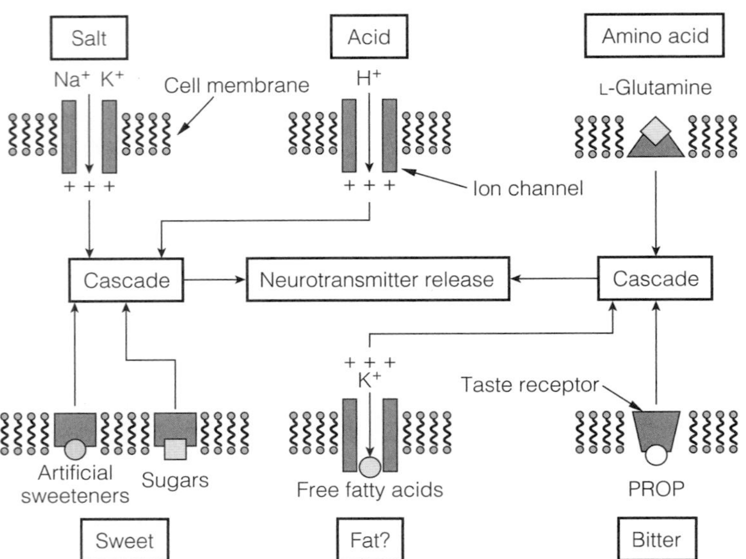

FIGURE 7.3 Some of the most important taste transduction mechanisms. Regions at the top and bottom are outside the cell membrane; the cascade boxes represent a variety of different intracellular mechanisms, from complex second messenger systems to simple depolarization, all resulting in an increase in intracellular Ca^{2+} and thus release of neurotransmitter across the synapses with taste nerves.

Neural Pathways and Responses

Three large nerves (the **chorda tympani, vagus,** and **glossopharyngeal**) carry fibers from the taste buds. They run from the tongue to the several nuclei in the **solitary tract** (which is located in the medulla—the place where the spinal cord widens to form the brain stem). In addition, there is the **common chemical sense,** which is sensitive to a wide variety of different stimuli, including certain tastes such as those associated with hot peppers and ginger. This system is separate from the taste system and in humans consists mostly of the **trigeminal nerve** of the head and its free nerve endings in the mouth and nasal cavity.

From the nuclei in the solitary tract, taste information is carried via a set of pathways called the **medial lemniscus** to the taste center of the **thalamus,** which is situated at the top of the rear-central portion of the thalamus (**ventral posterior nuclei**). The thalamic taste area projects to three areas in the cortex and also to the limbic system, including to the amygdala. Two cortical projections terminate at the base of the primary somatosensory cortex (near where touch on the face is projected), and the third at the **anterior-insular cortex,** which is a part of the frontal cortex under the front end of the temporal cortex. An interesting finding is that neurons in the somatosensory cortex respond to both touch and taste, and taste and touch neurons are also mixed together there. There may also be connections between neurons processing thermal sensations and those coding for tastes, since purely thermal stimulation of the tongue can cause taste sensations (Cruz & Green, 2000).

Studies of nonhuman animals have shown that taste fibers encode the intensity (concentration of molecules) of a tastant in their overall rate of firing. One of the few human studies capitalized on the fact that taste pathways from the front of the tongue must be cut during a certain kind of ear operation (Diamant, Funakoshi, Strom, & Zotterman, 1963). Before the taste pathway was cut, its electrical activity in response to various concentrations of table salt applied to the tongue was recorded. In all of the patients the amount of neural response was roughly proportional to the logarithm of the concentration of the salt solution.

How is taste **quality** or identity (including its pleasantness) encoded? Most receptor cells seem to respond to most or all of the types of tastants although with apparently different degrees of response for particular groups of tastants (Kimura & Beidler, 1961; Smith & St. John, 1999). This broad responsiveness is consistent with the fact that each contains several different transducer mechanisms. Most of the taste cells in the thalamus also respond to all tastants (Doetsch, Ganchrow, Nelson, & Erickson, 1969). In addition, there are some neurons in the cortex that are tuned to the apparently pleasantness of tastes. Some of these respond to tastants that are pleasant but not to unpleasant tasting ones, while other neurons do the reverse. Thus these neurons actually encoding the hedonic value of taste molecules (Smith & St. John, 1999).

The fact that most fibers respond to all tastes is not a problem because each has a different pattern of sensitivities, so that taste quality can be encoded through an

across-fiber pattern of neural activity (Pfaffman, 1955; Biography Box 7.1). Figure 7.4 shows how this might work for four of the basic tastes. Notice that although all of the fibers respond to all taste inputs to some extent, the pattern of firing across the four diagrammed fibers is different for each quality. Thus, for a sugar stimulus (S) we find Fiber A responding vigorously, Fiber B moderately, and Fibers C and D only weakly. For salt (NaCl) Fibers A and D respond weakly, whereas Fiber B responds strongly and Fiber C nearly as vigorously. Erickson (1963) was able to show such distinct across-fiber pattern differences, which become somewhat less distinct in the thalamus (Doetsch et al., 1969).

Another way to interpret the firing patterns displayed in Figure 7.4 is the **labeled-line theory** (Pfaffman, 1974). The basic idea is that each taste fiber is labeled as if it had one taste quality and that is the one that it is most sensitive to. Thus, when Fiber A in Figure 7.4 responds, because its "best" stimuli are sugars its activity simply signals a sweet taste, whereas Fiber B would signal a salty taste, and so forth. This is consistent with the fact that different sugars are indiscriminable from each other when their taste intensities are equated (Breslin, Beauchamp, & Pugh, 1996). It also means that a simple stimulus, such as table salt (NaCl), could have a complex taste if it activated several types of fibers. This does appear to happen because at different concentrations table salt can trigger both salt and sweet or salt and sour sensations (Bartoshuk, 1978). Moreover, although maltose is indistinguishable from other sugars at low concentrations, it can be discriminated from them at high concentrations, presumably because it activates an additional labeled line (Breslin et al., 1996). Considered in this way, the labeled-line theory is compatible with the across-fiber pattern approach, except that its code for taste quality is a profile across a few fiber types rather than a pattern across many thousands of unique fibers.

Most of the modern research indicates that some kind of across-fiber pattern must be operating at cortical levels because the meaning of the response in each neuron depends on responses of other neurons. Each cell codes many properties including intensity, several taste qualities, and also possibly hedonic value. Moreover, again we find interactions between taste and somatosensory regions, which provides the possibility of complex feedback loops and neural interplay (Katz, Nicolelis & Simon, 2002). When the taste stimulus first encounters the mouth, there is a somatosensory response for the first 200 ms, followed by a gustatory response. After 1 sec a new somatosensory response follows based on palatability-specific movements of the face and mouth as the tastant's hedonic content is now coded (Ugh! Spit! Mmmmm . . . chew, swallow). This is very reminiscent of the *facial feedback theory of emotions*, which main-

BIOGRAPHY BOX 7.1

A MAN OF MANY SENSES

Carl Pfaffman (1913–1999) pioneered the study of the electrophysiology of taste and smell. Pfaffman was interested in virtually all of the senses *except* the major senses of vision and hearing and made breakthroughs in all of them. After completing a bachelor's degree at Brown University, he earned a second one while on a Rhodes Scholarship at Oxford University and then worked with Lord Adrian, who received the Nobel Prize for his work on the electrophysiology of the nervous system, while earning his Ph.D. at Cambridge University. His Ph.D. work was the beginning of over 40 years of discoveries about how taste nerves respond to taste stimuli. In that work he discovered that, in general, taste nerves respond to a wide variety of taste stimuli, so that a given taste stimulus would elicit responding, at different rates, in many taste fibers. Apparently, a pattern of firing across many taste fibers represented the taste of any particular stimulus, an *across-fiber pattern*. It now seems that both labeled-line and across-fiber pattern coding of both taste and smell stimuli can be found in many if not all mammals. Pfaffman also pioneered in the study of mammalian pheromones, and work that he began on the effects of pheromones on primary sensory input is still being done. All of this pioneering work had great influence on the way that psychology developed after World War II, in particular helping to generate interest in the new field of behavioral neuroscience. Pfaffman spent much of the latter part of his career at Rockefeller University and taught many students whose names appear in this chapter as having made other fundamental contributions to the science of taste and smell. However, he also had time to do work on the sense of touch and is also credited with the first evidence of directionally sensitive touch receptors. Throughout his long career, Pfaffman seemed to be able to "sniff out" the topics that were ripe for progress, and then go on to make fundamental contributions to them.

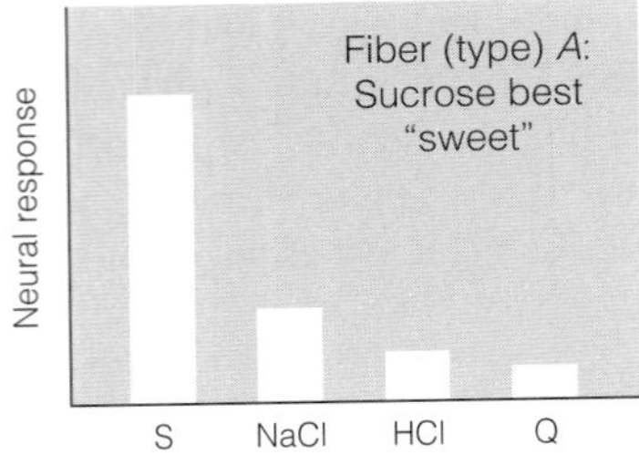

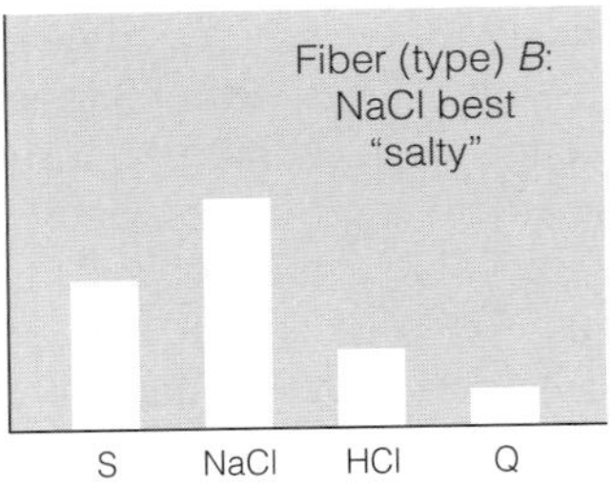

Stimulus

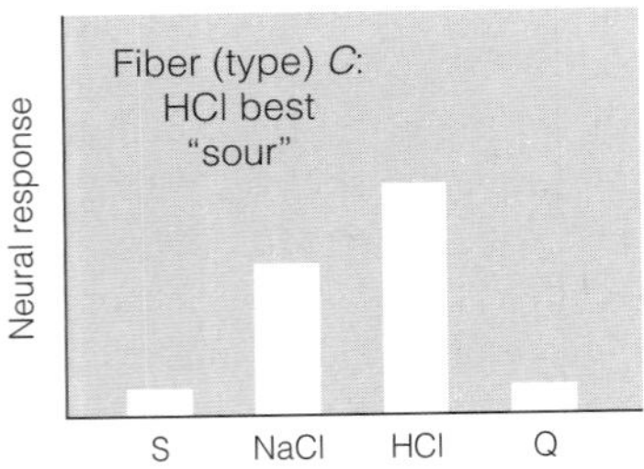

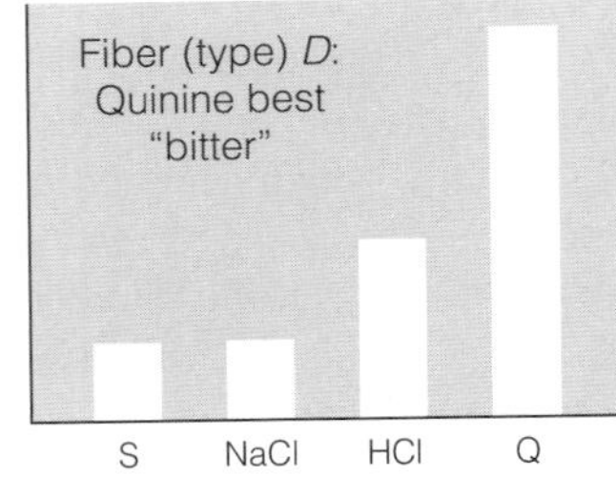

Stimulus

FIGURE 7.4 Using the across-fiber pattern theory, consider each graph to represent the response of a unique taste fiber to the various stimuli. Using the labeled-line theory, consider each graph to represent the average response of a group of more or less equivalent taste fibers.

tains that the actual facial expressions provide somatosensory feedback, which then modifies the emotions we are feeling (e.g., Neumann & Strack, 2000); only here the facial feedback is modifying our emotional or hedonic response to a taste.

Taste Thresholds and Adaptation

Absolute taste thresholds vary with the particular taste stimulus, how it is measured, viscosity and temperature, the current or previous presence of other taste stimuli, and the part of the tongue or mouth stimulated. Thus several factors must be specified when we describe taste sensitivity.

The **molar concentration** is the most useful measure of stimulus intensity (Pfaffman, Bartoshuk, & McBurney, 1971). A solution has a concentration of 1 **mole** if the molecular weight of a particular substance (in grams) is dissolved in enough water to make 1 liter of solution. Different solutions with the same molar concentrations have the same number of stimulus molecules in a given volume of liquid.

Figure 7.5 shows how absolute thresholds for various stimuli measured in this way vary across four different parts of the tongue and the soft palate, presumably because receptor densities vary in the same way. The front of the tongue is very sensitive to bitter taste, but the soft palate is even more sensitive. The tip and back of the tongue are most sensitive to sweet, whereas the front and sides are most sensitive to salt. Sensitivity to "hot" tastes, such as those associated with chili peppers, also differs from place to place in the mouth. Demonstration Box 7.1 helps you explore these differences.

Individuals also differ dramatically in absolute sensitivity to certain tastes. Blakeslee and Salmon (1935) measured the absolute thresholds of 47 people for 17 different substances. Many, such as table salt or saccharin, had a narrow range of thresholds. For some, however, such as vanillin or phenylthiocarbamide (PTC), large individual differences in sensitivity were found. In fact, some people are apparently "taste blind," or **ageusic,** to them; at ordinary concentrations they cannot taste them at all. If the concentration is high enough, however, even the ageusic can taste PTC's bitterness. Ageusia for PTC is similar to color blindness (discussed in Chapter 4) in that both appear to have a genetic component and tend to run in families.

People who are ageusic for PTC also tend to be insensitive to the bitter taste of caffeine in coffee (Hall, Bartoshuk, Cain, & Stevens, 1975). Conversely, PTC tasters also find that potassium chloride (KCl) tastes bitter and that the taste of a preservative found in many foods, sodium benzoate, is readily noticeable (Bartoshuk, Rifkin, Marks, & Hooper, 1988). Further studies with a chemical relative of PTC, called PROP, revealed that some cheeses taste more bitter and some sweeteners

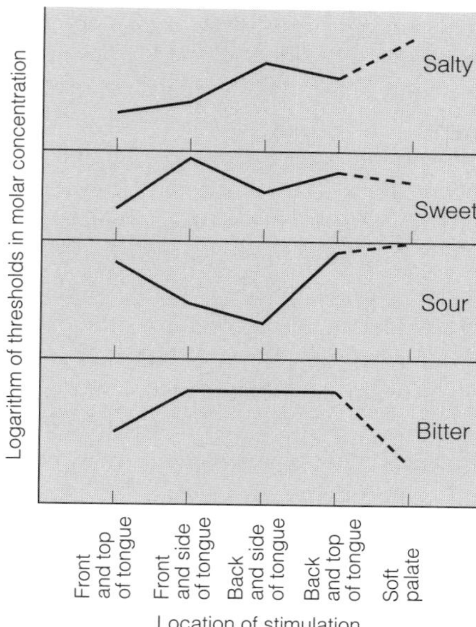

FIGURE 7.5 Average absolute thresholds for four different taste stimuli at four locations on the tongue and at a location on the soft palate (based on Collings, 1974).

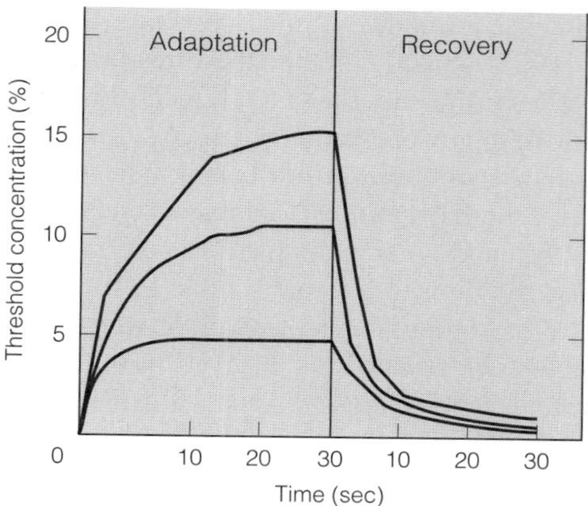

FIGURE 7.6 Adaptation and recovery from adaptation to continued stimulation of the tongue with table salt (NaCl). The three curves represent three different adapting concentrations. The time axis represents the amount of exposure to the adapting concentration, or recovery time, before determination of absolute threshold. Note the resemblance to dark adaptation curves (see Chapter 4; based on Hahn, 1934).

taste sweeter to PROP tasters. In general, those who are most sensitive to PROP (called "*supertasters*") find many taste stimuli to be more bitter, and "hot" stimuli to be hotter, than those who are less sensitive (Bartoshuk, 1993), probably because PROP supertasters have more taste buds (and thus receptors) on their tongues. All of these results will probably eventually be explained by genetic variation in the number and efficiency of the bitter and sweet transduction mechanisms in different individuals.

The taste system adapts very readily to continued stimulation by the same tastant, temporarily raising the absolute threshold for that tastant. Figure 7.6 shows an example of the effects of previous stimulation with table salt (NaCl) on absolute threshold for table salt. As you can see from the figure, absolute threshold varies both with exposure duration and with concentration (see also Szabo, Bujas, Adjukovic, Mayer, & Vodanovic, 1997). Similar effects can be demonstrated for the effects of adaptation on sensory intensity (Gent, 1979). This sort of adaptation helps explain why at dinner some people resalt their food again and again. As they eat, they adapt to the salty taste and come to need more salt to experience the taste at the same level. You can avoid resalting your food if you eat something that is not salty between bites of salty food. As Figure 7.6 shows, recovery from threshold adaptation is virtually complete in about 10 sec, no matter how much salt was tasted previously. Taste intensity, however, takes longer to recover than does absolute threshold, up to 2 minutes after adaptation to a moder-

DEMONSTRATION BOX 7.1

VARIATIONS IN TASTE SENSITIVITY

Although you all have probably experienced spicy "hot" foods on numerous occasions, you may not know that sensitivity to hot spices varies over the mouth. For example, the tip of the tongue is most sensitive to red and black peppers, and the anterior (hard) palate and cheek are least sensitive (Lawless & Stevens, 1988). You could demonstrate this for yourself by placing several drops of Tabasco sauce or other hot sauce (which contain hot red peppers) on the tip of a cotton swab or a bit of paper napkin twirled around a pencil or toothpick. Touch this "taste stimulator" to different parts of your mouth and tongue, and notice how the sensations differ in strength for different locations.

ately intense stimulus (Bujas, Szabo, Adjukovic, & Mayer, 1991). Taken together these results suggest that to experience the full flavor of a meal, one should eat slowly, with many pauses between bites of food.

Through **cross-adaptation** tasting one substance can also affect the threshold for (and the subsequent taste of) other substances. For example, adaptation to one salt will raise the threshold to other salts. In some cases, exposure to one stimulus may actually **lower** the threshold to another taste stimulus or make its taste more intense. This special type of cross-adaptation is called **potentiation.** Thus, adaptation to an acid, although reducing the sourness of another acid, may increase the sweetness of a sugar. Adaptation to urea (the bitter substance contained in human urine) will increase the intensity of salty sensations (McBurney, 1969). You can experience dramatic examples of potentiation and cross-adaptation by trying Demonstration Box 7.2.

Taste Intensity

Our ability to discriminate taste intensity differences is really quite poor for all taste stimuli. The Weber fraction (the proportion by which the more intense of two stimuli must be larger than the other for them to be discriminated; see Chapter 2) ranges from a relatively poor 0.10 to an awful 1.0, making taste the least sensitive of the senses by this criterion (Pfaffman et al., 1971). Moreover, the Weber fraction for the bitter taste increases as we age, especially for high concentrations of the taste stimulus. For example, for high concentrations of caffeine, the Weber fraction is about 0.4 for young people and around 2.3 for the elderly (Gilmore & Murphy, 1989). However, the Weber fraction for sucrose (common table sugar) is about 0.15 regardless of age.

As for other sensory experiences, magnitude estimations of taste intensity are a power function of stimulus intensity, $S = aI^m$, where S is the magnitude estimation of how intense the taste is, I is the molar concentration, a is a constant, and m is an exponent that describes the rate of change of the perceived intensity of the taste (see Chapter 2). Under standard conditions the exponent m is usually around 1.0 (i.e., for table salt it is about 0.9, for quinine hydrochloride it is about 0.9, for hydrochloric acid it is 1.0, and for sucrose it is 1.0; e.g., Norwich, 1984). However, the exponent does vary with state of adaptation (Meiselman, Bose, & Nykvist, 1972) and with age, being somewhat smaller for sour and bitter substances for the elderly (Bartoshuk, 1988).

Several studies have compared neurophysiological recordings from taste nerves with psychophysical data collected at the same time. They have shown that both neural and psychophysical responses vary with stimulus intensity in a similar fashion (e.g., Borg, Diamant, Oakley, Strom, & Zotterman, 1967). It seems likely that our taste intensity is related to the overall amount of neural activity evoked by the stimulus, which in turn depends on the molar concentration of the stimulus. However, more than just stimulus concentration is involved in our sensation of the intensity of a single taste because our perception may be affected by the presence of other taste stimuli in mixtures (which is how most tastes are experienced). For example, when half of a 10% fructose solution is replaced by less-sweet-tasting sucrose, the

DEMONSTRATION BOX 7.2

POTENTIATION AND CROSS-ADAPTATION

Have you ever drunk some orange juice right after brushing your teeth in the morning and noticed that it tasted terrible? If so, you were experiencing the effects of sodium laurel sulphate, the detergent in toothpaste, on your taste system's response to citric acid. Citric acid, which is what makes orange juice and lemon juice taste sour, tastes only slightly bitter at very high concentrations. However, stimulation of the taste cells with sodium laurel sulphate causes this bitter taste to increase greatly in intensity, making it noticeable at lower concentrations, such as those found in orange or lemon juice (Bartoshuk, 1988). If you have never experienced this, try the following. Wash your mouth out by swishing with pure water. Then taste some orange (or lemon) juice. Notice that the bitter taste is very faint if it is there at all. Now brush your teeth, and rinse thoroughly to get rid of the other toothpaste tastes, such as mint, which tastes sweet. Again taste the orange or lemon juice. Notice how the bitter taste has increased in intensity, but the sourness has not changed much at all. Sodium laurel sulphate also decreases the intensity of sweet, salty, and bitter tastes somewhat. You can try to experience these effects by repeating the orange juice experiment just described with sugar water, salt water, and cold coffee. It would be best to do these other experiments on different days so that adaptation effects do not confound your taste sensations.

DEMONSTRATION BOX 7.3

PUTTING OUT THE FIRE

You may have had the experience of putting too much pepper or other hot spice in your mouth and finding the burning too much to bear. Or you may have been prevented from eating some tasty dish because it was "too hot." These are circumstances in which you want to reduce the intensity of sensations arising from stimulation of your common chemical sense. Surprisingly, the effectiveness of swishing various liquids in your mouth to put out the fire depends to some extent on how they taste (Stevens & Lawless, 1986). The most effective liquid has a sweet (for example, soda pop) or sour (for example, lemon or other citrus juice) taste and is at a cool temperature. Bitter-tasting substances (for example, quinine or possibly beer) do not seem to help any more than simply waiting for the burning to cease, and salty substances are intermediate in effect. The cool temperature explains some but not all of the cooling effect because different tastants at the same temperature have different effects. If you are daring, you might try swishing some *diluted* Tabasco sauce around in your mouth until it begins to burn and then experimenting with different quenching substances to see whether you can confirm these results. Remember to leave plenty of time between trials for the burning sensation to fade completely.

mixture actually tastes **sweeter** (sometimes called **synergism**—McBride, 1993). Similarly, taste intensity from application of a stimulus to one site can be decreased by application of the same taste stimulus elsewhere on the tongue or in the mouth, probably because taste nerves mutually inhibit one another (Bartoshuk, 1988). Mixtures of different taste stimuli display even more complex interactions. For example, adding sucrose to a sour-tasting citric acid solution can decrease its perceived sourness; yet, at the same time it makes the citrus taste more intense—which is a highly profitable state of affairs for soft drink companies making lemon-flavored drinks (McBride, 1993). Demonstration Box 7.3 provides one way in which you can explore a complex interaction between taste intensities.

SMELL

A properly trained search and rescue or police dog can follow the track of a single individual even when it has been entangled with the tracks of many others. The dog is smelling the fatty acids that seep through the shoes of the suspect, even though these are present in incredibly small amounts. For example, each human footprint contains only about 0.00000000004 grams of valeric acid, a typical fatty acid secreted by glands in the sole of the foot. No wonder criminals fear such dogs and often confess voluntarily when tracked and caught through this astounding "nose work."

Because we seldom see a human sniffing the ground to find out who has been there recently or exploring a new room by sniffing the furniture, we tend to think that smell is unimportant. Although much of our perceptual processing of odors seems to be done at a relatively unconscious level, our sense of smell plays a role that is far from minor. For example, for humans as well as other animals, foul odors often signify danger in the sense of putrefied or spoiled substances that are no longer safely edible. Perhaps even more important, although it is very difficult to recall or to name smells, the experience of a particular smell at a particular moment can stimulate a flood of memories of episodes in which that smell was present (e.g., Proust, 1912; Herz & Engen, 1996). These "memories of times past" are often rich in emotional tones. Thus, the scent of cinnamon might evoke feelings of joy associated with your mother baking apple pies. Such smell-evoked memories may be necessary for normal biological functioning. For example, if a recently mated female mouse smells a strange male's urine before her fertilized egg implants in her uterus, implantation will likely fail. This will also happen if she "forgets" what her mate smells like, either because she was separated from him for 50 days or because a part of the olfactory system responsible for these memories was interfered with (Brennan, Kaba, & Keverne, 1990).

In many common situations, smell works together with taste. If we have experienced nausea after eating a distinctive food, we can acquire a **conditioned taste aversion** to that food, based especially on how it smells, which will make us avoid that food in the future (e.g., Bartoshuk, 1990). When we have a bad head cold, food seems flavorless; yet our nasal passages are most affected by the cold, not our mouths, where the taste receptors are located.

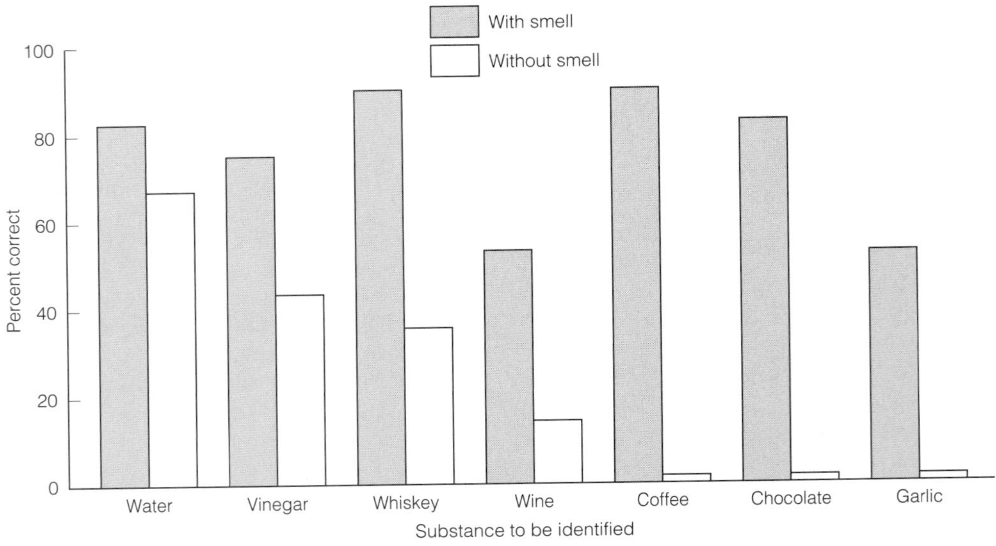

FIGURE 7.7 Identification of some common foods with and without smell (based on Mozel, Smith, Smith, Sullivan, & Swender, 1969).

When our nasal passages are swollen or clogged with extra mucus, smell stimuli cannot reach our olfactory receptors. This affects both our ability to smell and to experience flavor because much of the richness and subtlety of our experiences of the flavors of food and drink come from their odors (e.g., Brillat-Savarin, 1825/1971; Murphy & Cain, 1980). When we cannot smell, our ability to identify foods by taste alone is significantly inferior, unfortunately for some of our most preferred foods, as Figure 7.7 shows. Demonstration Box 7.4 allows you to experience this for yourself without waiting for a head cold.

Smell acts as if it has two separate modes of action that may result in different perceptual experiences and different forms of information extraction (e.g., Bartoshuk & Beauchamp, 1994). The first is associated with our experience of the flavors of food. It is triggered when **odorants** (molecules that can be smelled) are pumped from the mouth into the nasal cavity while we are chew-

DEMONSTRATION BOX 7.4

FLAVOR WITHOUT SMELL

The simplest way to experience flavor without smell is to pinch your nostrils closed before coming near the substance to be tasted, and then put some of that substance into your mouth and swish it around while paying attention to its flavor. Then release your nostrils, open your mouth slightly, and breathe in gently through both mouth and nose. You should experience a significant change in the flavor when you do this. Try it for the various substances listed in Figure 7.6 and any others you can think of. Your experiences with nose pinched approximate those of elderly people who have experienced large deficits in their sense of smell.

It is rather easy to show that food identification is impaired when the sense of smell is absent. You simply need to get a friend to help you. First prepare several different substances to be identified—the ones listed in Figure 7.6 will do. They should be in a liquid state (mash up the garlic and mix it with water). Then seat your friend at some distance from the solutions, and blindfold him or her. For each substance, first ask him to pinch his nose, and, when he has done that, put some of the solution in his mouth and ask for its name. After he has tried that, tell him to release his nostrils and again attempt to name the substance. Repeat this for each substance, and several friends if you can, and see how closely the results match those of Figure 7.6.

ing and swallowing food. The second is a distance sense that occurs when molecules emitted by external objects or organisms are sniffed through the nostrils into the nasal cavity. It is interesting to note that there are times when "distant smell" and "food smell" give different impressions. For instance, Limburger cheese has a distant smell that is quite strong and, most people think, offensive, but it has a food smell when in the mouth that contributes in a positive way to the flavor of the cheese, which many people find quite pleasing.

Smell Stimuli and Receptors

Ordinary odorants must come from volatile substances, those having a gaseous state at ordinary temperatures—in other words, something that can evaporate, because air currents carry the molecules to the smell receptors in the nose. However, the most volatile substances do not necessarily smell the strongest. Pure water, which is very volatile, has no smell at all. In fact, the extent to which an odorant separates itself chemically from water **(hydrophobicity)** is highly correlated with the intensity of its smell (Greenberg, 1981). Conversely, musk (a secretion obtained from some deer and beavers) has low volatility; yet, it is a very powerful odorant and is used in making some of our most expensive perfumes.

The receptive cells of the olfactory system, called **primary olfactory neurons,** are located in a relatively small area in the upper nasal passages (Figure 7.8) called the **olfactory epithelium,** which literally translates as "*smell skin*." Humans have about 6 million olfactory neurons (Doty, 2001), each of which expresses just one receptor type, most probably chosen at random (Ebrahimi & Chess, 1998). Each primary olfactory neuron sends a long extension (called the **olfactory rod**) to the surface of the olfactory epithelium and also sends its axons toward the brain. Remarkably, the olfactory epithelium is the site of continuous production of new olfactory neurons from the basal cells (Figure 7.8). Although some olfactory neurons live for a long time, others live for only a few weeks, so that continuing neurogenesis is necessary to maintain a full complement of receptor types (Doty, 2001).

A number of **olfactory cilia** protrude from a knob at the end of the olfactory rod. There are around 6 to 8 cilia per olfactory rod in humans but around 100 to 150 in dogs (T. S. Brown, 1975). The olfactory cilia contain the receptor molecules to which odorant molecules become bound. There are around 1000 different types of receptors, all members of a family called G-coupled protein

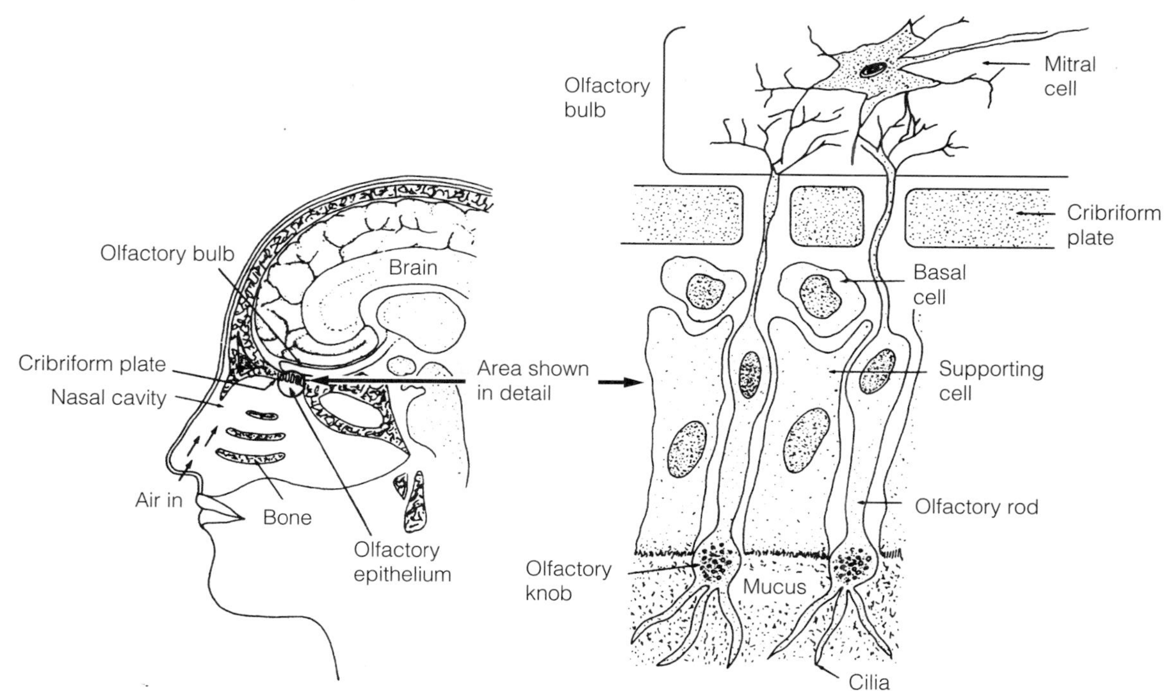

FIGURE 7.8 Anatomy of the olfactory system and a detail of the structure of the olfactory epithelium and olfactory bulb.

receptors, which happens to be the largest family of genes in mammals (Edrahimi & Chess 1998). The cilia are hairlike structures embedded in a special type of watery mucus secreted by Bowman's glands. This mucus contains many substances, some of which protect the receptors and the brain from infections, and many molecules of a special protein called **olfactory binding protein** (or **OBP** for short) that can attach to normally hydrophobic odorant molecules that would ordinarily be repelled from the watery mucus. It is likely that each odorant molecule bound to an OBP molecule is transported to and detached from each of several receptor molecules by the continually moving stream of mucus sweeping across the cilia (Nickell, 1997).

Cloning and molecular biology have revealed the mechanism by which the brief interaction of an odorant molecule with a receptor molecule causes an electrical response in the primary olfactory neuron. The process was originally suggested by Amoore's (1970) **lock-and-key theory,** in which specific proteins in the cell walls of the cilia form reversible chemical bonds with specific parts of particular odorant molecules. Recent research has confirmed this experimentally (e.g., Nickell, 1997). The momentary bonding of stimulus and receptor molecules initiates a cascade of other biochemical processes that results in action potentials in the axon. The chain of events is outlined in Figure 7.9. It begins when an odorant molecule bonds with a receptor, activating a specific protein, called G_{olf} (Jones & Reed, 1989). This event, with the help of another molecule (guanosine triphosphate), activates an enzyme called adenylate cyclase, which in turn causes cAMP (cyclic adenosine monophosphate) to be produced (Bakalyar & Reed, 1990; Brand et al., 1989). The cAMP acts as a sort of a key and opens ion channels in the cell membrane, allowing sodium ions to enter, depolarizing the cell and causing spike potentials to travel up its axon (see also Firestein & Werblin, 1989). In addition to opening sodium channels, cAMP also opens Ca^{2+} channels. The increase in Ca^{2+} in turn activates channels by which Cl^- flows out of the cell, providing considerable amplification of the response to a particular odorant, and thus generating enough neural activity for the detection of even faint odorants (Menini, 1999).

Neural Pathways and Responses

The primary olfactory neurons send their axons in about 30 to 40 bundles (Doty, 2001) through tiny holes in a bone at the top of the nasal cavity (the cribriform plate) to form the **olfactory nerve.** The nerve goes straight to the bottom layer of the many-layered **olfactory bulb.** This bulb is located in front of and below the main mass of the brain (see Figure 7.8). The passage of the olfactory nerve through the cribriform plate makes it vulnerable to being severed when the head suddenly starts or stops moving in a particular direction. Many people who have had head injuries—for example, in automobile accidents—have lost their sense of smell for this reason.

The axons of the receptors and the dendrites of neurons from the olfactory bulb form complex clusters of

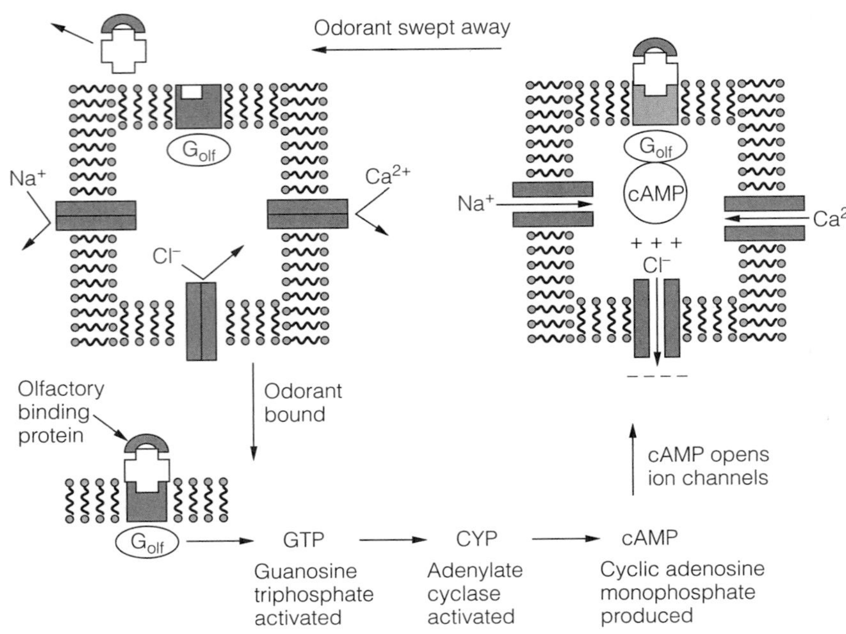

FIGURE 7.9 The standard olfactory transduction process. Note that there are about 1000 different types of receptor molecules (the notched boxes), but only one type per receptor neuron.

connections, called **glomeruli,** in the bulb. Each type of receptor neuron sends axons to a particular pair of targeted glomeruli (e.g., Belluscio, Lodovichi, Feinstein, Mombaerts, & Katz, 2002). Thus receptors and glomeruli are organized so that a pattern of neural activity across the glomeruli indicates stimulation by specific odorants. In effect there is a sort of an "odorant map" (Korsching, 2002) similar to the stimulus maps found in visual and auditory systems. This pattern of glomerulus activation is modified by interneurons that surround the glomeruli and produce a pattern of both excitation and inhibition (Smith & Jahr, 2002). These look much like the lateral inhibitory processes that we find in brightness and edge processing in vision (see Chapters 4 and 8). Such neural interactions sharpen the "receptive field" of glomeruli tuned to a particular odorant by suppressing activity of glomeruli tuned to other odorants and also synchronize the firing of the neurons projecting to more central areas (Korsching, 2002).

Different olfactory neurons have different destinations. One type of olfactory bulb neuron sends axons directly along the **lateral olfactory tract** to the primary sensory cortex for smell, called the **piriform cortex,** in the temporal lobe. Another type of neuron sends axons both to the smell cortex and to several lower brain centers, especially the limbic system including especially the amygdala, which is involved in our experience of emotion and memory (remember how easily smells can evoke memories and feelings). There are about 1000 times more axons in the olfactory nerve than leave the olfactory bulb, indicating that many receptor cells contribute to the activity of each of the cells in the olfactory bulb and later centers (Allison, 1953). From the primary smell cortex the neural pathways become extremely complex, including projections to the thalamus and several other cortical areas. Imaging experiments with humans also find activation of cerebellum (see Doty, 2001). Apparently the cerebellum monitors the incoming air stream and controls sniffing to maximize the strength of odorant sensations. Other imaging studies have discovered that different sniffing or smelling tasks engage different sets of brain areas (Savic, 2002). Moreover, such experiments have also revealed that unpleasant odors activate left amygdala and left piriform cortex more than do pleasant or neutral odors, and smelling familiar odorants activates semantic association areas as well. Thus, neural responses to odorants often involve the limbic system and cortical association areas in the earliest processing of olfactory stimulation, unlike vision and hearing in which considerable cortical processing is accomplished before limbic activation begins.

As is typical for sensory systems, several studies have found that the intensity of the neural response varies directly with the intensity of the stimulus. However, most contemporary investigators have focused on the more difficult problem of how different smell qualities are encoded. They have tried to find evidence of specific types of receptors for different types of stimuli. In an early study, Gesteland, Lettvin, Pitts, and Rojas (1963) recorded both the slow potential change and the spike potentials generated in the axons of single receptors in the olfactory epithelium in response to the same stimuli. These two types of electrical responses are shown one on top of the other in Figure 7.10. As you can see, this particular receptor responded vigorously to musk, less to nitrobenzene, hardly at all to benzonitrite, and not at all to pyridine. Gesteland and colleagues thought that these responses indicated the existence of the sought-after receptor types, although they were cautious in making this interpretation. Such caution was well founded because later recordings from single cells in the epithelium, olfactory bulb, and cortical and lower brain centers that receive olfactory information have found that each neuron responds to a broad range of stimuli, although not all odorants, much as the taste microvilli do (e.g., Kauer, 1987). Across-fiber patterns similar to those found in taste seem to be present in the olfactory system, and the "code" for smell qualities probably will be found in these patterns (Erickson & Schiffman, 1975; Kauer, 1987).

Smell Thresholds and Adaptation

De Vries and Stuiver (1961) calculated that it takes at most eight odorant molecules arriving at the olfactory epithelium to activate a single receptor cell in the human. Considering all aspects of the manner in which mole-

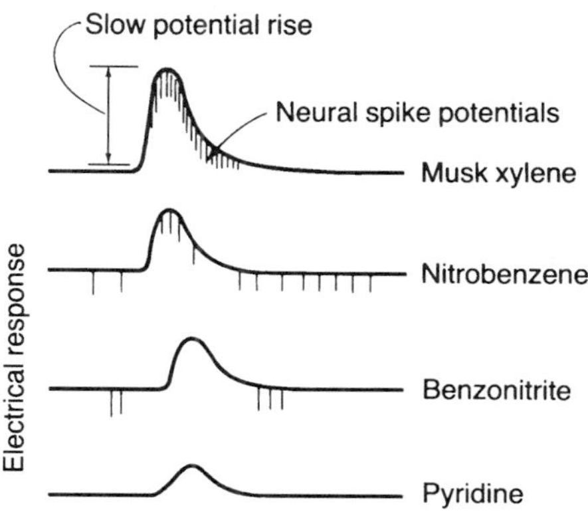

FIGURE 7.10 Slow potential and spike potential responses of olfactory receptor cells to four different smell stimuli (based on Gesteland et al., 1963).

cules of odorants are distributed in the nose, they further argued that a single primary olfactory neuron can generate action potentials in response to contact by one odorant molecule; this can occur because of the amplifier in the transduction mechanism discussed earlier. This is the greatest sensitivity that any single receptor could have. Thus, considering only the functional properties of primary olfactory neurons, a dog (or any other animal) can't be more sensitive than a human. The actual difference in olfactory ability then comes from the fact that dogs have about 200 times more cilia than humans have; the surface area of the cilia in German Shepard dogs is roughly 3000 times (70,000 cm^2 versus 22 cm^2) that of humans. Thus, the likelihood that a very weak odorant will actually stimulate a primary olfactory neuron and produce a noticeable sensation is far greater for the dog (see Marshall & Moulton, 1981).

Measurements of humans' absolute thresholds for various odors give values that vary across psychophysical methods (e.g., Berglund, Hogman, & Johansson, 1988). They depend on the purity of the odorant, the way it is delivered to the olfactory epithelium, and how the stimulus intensity is measured. Moreover, individuals' thresholds for the same substance vary dramatically from moment to moment (Stevens, Cain, & Burke, 1988). Different substances also have different average thresholds.

Smell sensitivity differs reliably across individuals (e.g., Stevens et al., 1988). It is possible to have an "odor blindness," or **anosmia,** to certain substances. Amoore and colleagues (e.g., Amoore, Pelosi, & Forrester, 1977) have reported 76 different anosmias ranging from the gentle smell of vanilla to the pungent smell of skunk. Some of these anosmias are quite common (for instance, one out of three people cannot smell the camphorous odor of 1,8 cineole), whereas others are quite rare (e.g., only 1 of 1000 people cannot smell the putrid odor of *n*-butyl mercaptan; see Pelosi & Pisanelli, 1981). Such specific anosmias are consistent with the fact that there are a very large number of receptor types, and that each odorant stimulates only one or a few types of receptors. When a specific receptor protein is missing, perhaps because of a missing or malfunctioning gene, then the person with the missing receptor protein has a specific anosmia. Disease can also give rise to olfactory dysfunction, and modern standardized tests of olfactory function, such as the UPSIT (Doty, 2001; see Biography Box 7.2), have identified many such diseases.

Prolonged exposure to an odorant causes adaptation that affects thresholds, perceived intensity (Cain & Engen, 1969), and even pleasantness of odors (Cain & Johnson, 1978). One of the great disappointments of wine tasting is that the aroma of even a great wine seems to be experienced strongly only for the first few sniffs. Adaptation rapidly weakens our experience of pleasant smells and flavors unless frequent breaks of about 15 sec are taken. Luckily, continuous sniffing also weakens the less-pleasant odors of sweaty bodies, paint fumes, and air pollution.

In a classic set of experiments, Moncrieff (1956) studied the effects of previous exposure to an odorant on the threshold for that same odorant **(self-adaptation)** and on that of different odorants **(cross-adaptation).** The largest sensitivity decrease was found for self-adaptation. Cross-adaptation varied with the similarity of the smells of the two stimuli. Odorants with similar smells gave larger cross-adaptation effects than did those that differed in smell. Surprisingly, all of the adapting odors used by Moncrieff had some effect on observers' sensitivity for the others. Sometimes even odorants that are perceptually and chemically different can show cross-adaptation (Pierce & Wysocki, 1996). The several odorants that can interact with any one receptor, and the number of different receptors that can bind a given odorant, prevent any simple scheme from reliably predicting cross-adaptation effects. You can experience self- and cross-adaptation for yourself by trying Demonstration Box 7.5.

The unadapted olfactory system seems to be about as sensitive as the visual or auditory system in discriminating changes in intensity, with Weber fractions as low as 0.05, meaning that a change in intensity of only 5% can be detected about half of the time (Cain, 1977). Interestingly, smell intensities can be discriminated better if the odorants enter the right nostril than if they enter the left nostril (Zatorre & Jones-Gotman, 1990). Because the olfactory pathways stay on the same side of the brain as where they begin, this, along with other evidence, may indicate that the right hemisphere of the brain is more specialized for certain types of olfactory processing, although it is also true that unpleasant smells tend to selectively activate the left amygdala and the left smell cortex.

Pheromones

Some smells have been said to have a special biological significance for all animals, including humans. Ellis (1905) pointed out that both men and women often emit strong odors during sexual excitement, and some authors have speculated that human behavior may be strongly influenced by such olfactory stimuli (e.g., Comfort, 1971; Kohl & Francoeur, 1995). Chemicals secreted by ani-

BIOGRAPHY BOX 7.2

SCRATCH N' SNIFF PSYCHOPHYSICS

Richard Doty (1944–) has a passion for understanding the chemical senses, both the basic mechanisms of how they function and the many ways in which that function can go wrong. One of his most enduring contributions will surely be the development of the UPSIT (the University of Pennsylvania Smell Identification Test), which allows standardized psychophysical tests of olfactory function. Utilizing the microencapsulated odorants developed by the perfume industry, this highly reliable scratch n' sniff test has norms based on nearly 4000 persons and has been administered to over 180,000 persons in controlled tests. A survey of 11 million subscribers was conducted by *The National Geographic* using this test, resulting in some interesting profiles of smell abilities across different populations. Much of what we know about differences in smell abilities between men and women, and changes in smell ability with aging, smoking, and work place exposure to chemicals has been learned using this test or one of its variants or competitors. Perhaps most dramatically, using such tests Doty and his colleagues have discovered over 30 diseases that result in smell loss, ranging from obvious ones like nasopharyngeal carcinoma (cancer of the nasal passages) to schizophrenia, psychopathy, and attention deficit disorder. There is promise of using such smell loss as an advance warning of diseases like Alzheimer's and Parkinson's, where new methods of early treatment might be preventative. Doty is the Director of the Smell and Taste Center at the University of Pennsylvania, where he is also a Professor in the School of Medicine. He received his Ph.D. in 1971 from Michigan State University.

In addition to fundamental work in taste and smell, he investigates the mechanisms of pathological smell loss and helps those with such loss to understand and deal with their dysfunction. He is much sought after for this clinical expertise and is often the first to be asked for an opinion when a new taste or smell disorder is discovered.

DEMONSTRATION BOX 7.5

SMELL ADAPTATION

You experience self-adaptation of odorants every day. The next time you notice a strong odor, take several deep sniffs, and then take a more usual sniff and pay close attention to the intensity of the odor as compared to what you at first experienced. You should notice a significant decrease in sensation intensity. Alternately, prepare yourself a cup of coffee or aromatic tea, keeping your nostrils pinched while you do. When the steaming cup is in front of you, release your nostrils and take a gentle sniff, noting the intensity of the odor. Then take several deep sniffs followed by another gentle sniff, and compare the odor intensity during the final gentle sniff to that during the first gentle sniff.

It is a bit more difficult to demonstrate cross-adaptation because the effects are weaker and not systematic. You should use your own judgment and explore a range of odorants using the general method described here. When two odorants you wish to test have been obtained, first step into another room, where you cannot smell them, and take several deep sniffs. Then approach the odorants with pinched nose. Release your nostrils near the first (test) odorant, and take a gentle sniff, noting the intensity of the odor. Then take several deep sniffs of the other (adapting) odorant, and return to the test odorant and take another gentle sniff. Compare the odor intensity on this sniff to the first one. If it is less intense, you have experienced cross-adaptation; if it is more intense, you have experienced facilitation, as sometimes happens with biologically significant odors (see Engen, 1982).

mals that transmit information to other animals (usually of the same species) are called **pheromones.** Although it is clear that pheromones strongly influence behavior in many animal species, the possibility that pheromones strongly affect human behavior is controversial. As you might expect, manufacturers of colognes and perfumes, ever searching for ways to enhance the sales of their products, have responded to this suggestion by marketing products that contain suspected human pheromones.

Pheromones were discovered and first studied in insects such as ants, bees, and termites, where they are the dominant form of social communication (Wilson, 1971). There are two major types of pheromones: **releasers,** which "release," or automatically trigger, a specific behavioral response, and **primers,** which trigger glandular and other physiological activities. Insects attract their mates, recruit others for food gathering or fighting, and recognize each other and their own species via releasers. Queen ants, bees, and termites control swarming, new queen production, and the proportion of types of workers using primers. An insect pheromone is usually a **specific chemical** produced by a **specific gland** and detected by a **specific receptor.** Insect behavior often seems programmed to respond directly to the controlling influence of pheromones.

Mammals, of course, are much more complex animals than insects, and the effects of pheromones on their behavior are more subtle. Nonetheless, many pheromone-related effects, both primer- and releaser-like, have been found in several species, including rodents, dogs, and monkeys (e.g., Dulac, 2000). An example of a releaser-like effect is the odor of a female dog in heat attracting male dogs (Goodwin, Gooding, & Regnier, 1979). In monkeys, female vaginal secretions called **copulins** have a more subtle effect on male sexual behavior in monkeys (e.g., Goldfoot, 1981; Michael, Keverne, & Bonsall, 1971). In most amphibians, reptiles and mammals, pheromones are secreted by specific glands and detected and processed by the **accessory olfactory system,** which consists of the **vomeronasal organs,** a special set of smell receptors for detecting heavy pheromone molecules—the accessory olfactory bulb, and projections to areas of the brain involved in reproductive behavior (Wysocki & Meredith, 1987). Altering the response of the accessory olfactory system to pheromones—for example, by knocking out the genes that control expression of a pheromone receptor—results in altered reproductive behavior (e.g., Del Punta et al., 2002).

The behavioral effects of pheromones on humans are likely to be indirect because social and learning factors influence our behavior more than they do that of other mammals. Moreover, although humans do have vomeronasal organs at the base of the nasal chamber, there appear to be few if any nerves leading away from the area, and we have no accessory olfactory bulb at all (e.g., Doty, 2001). Although it appears that humans do not possess a functional accessory olfactory system, nonetheless, pheromone-like odorants still do activate the hypothalamus, where sexual preference may be determined—with men's activated by the female-related odorant and women's activated by the male-related odorant (Savic, Berglund, Gulyas, & Roland, 2001). This activation, is likely mediated by the connections of the primary olfactory system to the hypothalamus, since a follow-up study with male anosmics whose vomeronasal organ was normal found no such activation.

Smells do seem to play an important, although probably subordinate, role in some aspects of human social behavior. First, people can reliably detect their own body odor from among a set of similar stimuli contributed by other people (e.g., McBurney, Levine, & Cavanaugh, 1977). People also can identify the sex of an odor donor, using both quality ("musky" male versus "sweet" female—Russell, 1976) and intensity (strong and unpleasant male versus weaker and more pleasant female—Doty, 1985), based on hand odor (Wallace, 1977) or breath odor (Doty, Green, Ram, & Yankell, 1982), as well as body odor. Females are better at this (e.g., Doty et al., 1982) and at all aspects of odor identification (Doty, Applebaum, Zusho, & Settle, 1985).

Even very young babies can identify the scent of their mothers' breast (e.g., MacFarlane, 1975) and their mothers' armpit odor (Cernoch & Porter, 1985). Female newborns can even develop a preference for an artificial odorant from mere exposure to it (Balogh & Porter, 1986). However, accurate odor identification in adults requires sufficient experience with the odor and its source (e.g., Schab, 1991). Because the relationship between parents and children promotes such experience, we might expect parents to recognize the odors of their own offspring and expect siblings to recognize each others' odors, and they do (e.g., Porter, Balogh, Cernoch, & Franchi, 1986).

Because humans are sensitive to biological odors, even without a functioning accessory olfactory system, perhaps they are also sensitive to pheromones. Alpha androstenol is a sex-attractant pheromone for pigs that is also present in human apocrine (a gland in the underarm region) sweat. Does it play a role in human sexual attraction? In spite of several intriguing results, such as small effects of alpha androstenol on ratings of job candidates

BIOGRAPHY BOX 7.3

PHEROMONES RAGE IN WOMEN'S DORMS

Martha K. McClintock (1948–) made her first contribution to science in her honor's thesis at Wellesley College in 1969. This proved to be a landmark study based on her informal observation that the menstrual cycles of her friends and acquaintances in her dorm at Wellesley seemed to be more synchronized than would be expected by chance. Her more systematic study was published in *Nature* in 1971 and constituted the first evidence ever published of the influence of pheromones in humans. The paper launched her on a continuing study of pheromones, sexual behavior, and the social regulation of disease. One of her most recent publications was a paper in *Nature* describing an elegant experiment that reaffirms the influence of female underarm pheromones on the reproductive cycle of women, in particular the timing of their menstrual periods, capping 35 years of study of this difficult topic. A Professor in the Psychology Department and Director of the Institute of Mind and Biology at the University of Chicago, Dr. McClintock (Ph.D., University of Pennsylvania, 1974), is much sought after for her expertise on the human female reproductive system, as well as her work on human regulatory, or priming, pheromones.

(Cowley, Johnson, & Brooksbank, 1977), sexual attractiveness (Kirk-Smith, Booth, Carroll, & Davies, 1978), and seat choice in a dentist's waiting room (Kirk-Smith & Booth, 1980), there is no unequivocal evidence that human behavior could be **controlled,** to the extent seen in lower mammals and insects, by such pheromones (Rogel, 1978).

It is possible that there are less dramatic effects of pheromones on human reproductive functioning. For example, male underarm secretions influence the regularity of the female menstrual cycle (Cutler, Preti, Krieger, Huggins, Garcia, & Lawley, 1986), whereas female underarm secretions influence the synchrony of females' cycles (McClintock, 1971, 1998; Preti, Cutler, Garcia, Huggins, & Lawley, 1986; see Biography Box 7.3). These are primerlike effects because they involve physiological changes and not specific behaviors. They can be important moderators of activity and preference, but they do not have direct and powerful immediate influences on human behavior that is found in other mammals.

TOUCH

Pressure on any part of the skin that covers the surface of our body can evoke the sensation of touch, and the major components of most sexual experiences are touch sensations. The very act of touching another person, in Western society, is considered to be an act of considerable intimacy, whether it is the gentle touch of a friend or lover or the violent punch of an aggressor. Touches from parents and siblings are crucial for normal social development, as Harlow's well known studies of monkeys with surrogate mothers showed (Harlow, 1959). The senses of touch, pain, warmth and cold all arise from receptors embedded in the skin and their associated neural pathways, which we will describe before discussing touch and pain in more detail.

Skin Stimuli and Receptors

The skin responds to a variety of physical stimuli. When an object deforms the skin surface we experience touch or pressure. When an object bends any hair on our body we also experience touch. The temperature of the object with which we touch the skin causes a sensation of warmth or cold depending on the temperatures of the object relative to that of the skin. Finally, mild electrical stimulation causes a type of touch sensation, and sometimes warmth or cold, whereas intense electrical stimulation, strong pressure, and extreme temperatures usually result in pain.

Figure 7.11 shows the most important structures in **hairy skin,** which covers most of the human body. A different kind of skin, **glabrous skin,** has no hairs and is found on the palms of the hands, soles of the feet, parts of fingers and toes, lips, and genitals. All skin consists of two basic layers. The outermost, the **epidermis,** consists of several layers of tough dead cells covering a single layer of living cells. The living layer, called the **dermis,** divides constantly to generate the dead protective layers above. Most of the nerve endings in hairy skin are found in the dermis. However, some glabrous skin has a thick outer layer of dead cells that contains many free nerve endings, which makes it effective protection but also extremely sensitive to stimulation. Under the two layers of skin cells is usually a layer of fat cells. In addition to

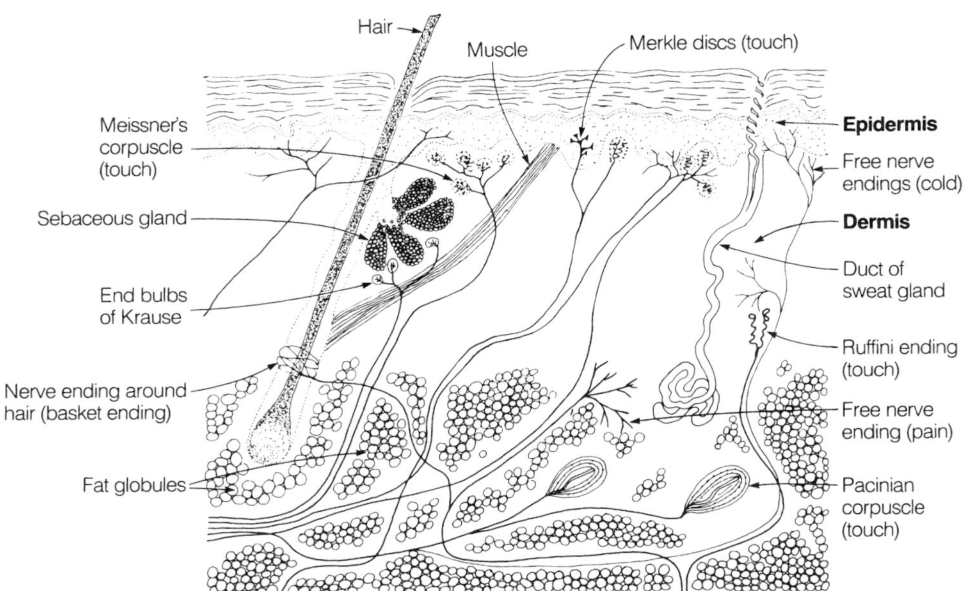

FIGURE 7.11 A piece of hairy skin in cross-section (based on Woolard, Weddell, & Harpman, 1940).

these, the skin contains a variety of hairs, muscles, glands, arteries, veins, and capillaries.

Figure 7.11 also shows some of the most common nerve endings in the skin. Nerve endings with small bodies or swellings on the dendrites, including the **Pacinian corpuscles, Meissner corpuscles, Merkel disks,** and **Ruffini endings,** are called "corpuscular" and are associated with nerve fibers that are particularly responsive to touch stimuli. We will discuss in a later section how the type of corpuscular ending and its location within the skin together determine the touch function subserved by the neuron (Johnson, 2001). "Noncorpuscular" or **free nerve endings** in subcutaneous fat are associated with pain fibers (Vierck, 1978). Free nerve endings projecting into the epidermis may be associated with cold fibers, which increase their firing rate when skin temperature drops, or with warm fibers, which increase their firing rate when skin temperature rises (Hensel, 1981). They may also be the endings of pain fibers (Perl, 1984).

As an example of how a skin receptor responds to stimulation, consider the very common **Pacinian corpuscle** (Figure 7.11). Loewenstein and his colleagues peeled away the surrounding layers of the cell (much as we would peel an onion) to allow them to touch the axon itself (Loewenstein, 1960). They showed that a mechanical stimulus operates directly on the axon of the nerve by deforming its membrane. This deformation causes numerous tiny holes in the membrane to open, allowing positive ions to flow into the cell and depolarize it. The depolarization generates an action potential in the myelinated axon and carries the message of stimulation to the brain. Temperature probably acts by controlling chemical reactions that affect the flow of ions across the cell's membrane, whereas electrical stimuli probably trigger spike potentials directly.

Neural Pathways and Responses

The organization of receptors and neural pathways for the skin senses depends on both the **type of nerve fiber** and **the place of termination** of the pathway in the cortex. The type of nerve fiber is important because different types of nerve fibers carry different kinds of information. Fibers can be classified in at least three ways: (1) according to the class of stimulus that most easily excites them (mechanical, temperature, or noxious), (2) according to the way they respond to those stimuli (slow- or fast-adapting), and (3) according to whether they have large, ill-defined receptive fields or small, well-defined ones. By **receptive field** here we mean much the same thing we did for vision (Chapter 3), except that here we refer to that region of the *skin* that, when stimulated, causes responses in a particular neural fiber. The receptive fields in the skin possess the same sort of excitatory-center, inhibitory-surround organization found in the visual system (e.g., Bekesy, 1967). Demonstration Box 7.6 shows how you can demonstrate this organization for yourself with touch stimuli.

Under the criteria described earlier, humans have been shown to have four different types of fibers that respond to mechanical deformation of glabrous skin: fibers

DEMONSTRATION BOX 7.6

INHIBITORY INTERACTIONS ON THE SKIN

In this demonstration you will see how skin sensations interact. You will need two fairly sharp pointed objects, such as two toothpicks or two bristles from a hairbrush. The demonstration will work better if you ask a friend to control the stimuli. Do not use anything like a knife because you will be pushing the point quite strongly against your skin. First, try pressing one point against the skin of your palm. Notice the spread of sensation around the stimulated point. Now put the two points as close together as you possibly can. Push them together on the same place on your palm. Notice that you feel only one point, although two are present. Now move the two stimulating points slightly apart. You should *still* feel only one point. Repeat this procedure several times, moving the points apart by a little more each time and paying careful attention to whether the sensation feels like two points or one on your skin. If you are pushing hard enough and paying close attention to your sensations, at just about the separation where the two points begin to feel like two distinct points on the skin, you should have a surprising experience. The magnitude of the sensation from the two points should diminish greatly, perhaps vanish altogether for a short time. The sensation should be very faint, even though two toothpicks (or brush bristles) are pushing with some force against the skin. As you then move the points even farther apart, you will perceive two distinct, full-strength sensations, appropriately separate on the skin. This phenomenon is explained by the overlapping of regions of excitation and inhibition in adjacent receptive fields of the skin, as shown in the accompanying figure.

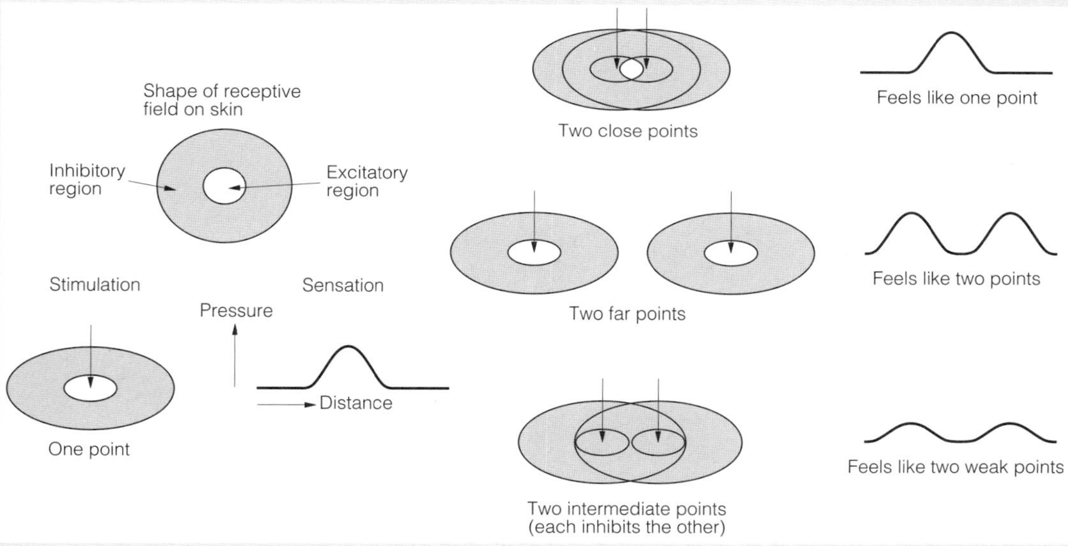

with small, well-defined receptive fields that adapt either rapidly or slowly and fibers with large, ill-defined receptive fields that adapt either rapidly or slowly (Greenspan & Bolanowski, 1996; Vallbo, 1981). Such fiber types are reminiscent of the parvo and magno pathways associated with the nerve fibers that leave the retina of the eye (Chapter 3).

The place on the skin where a particular nerve ending is found determines the location in the brain to which the information is sent, regardless of the type of fiber it represents. All of the sensory information from the skin is sent to the spinal cord through 31 pairs of nerves (one member of each pair for each side of the body). There are also four cranial nerves that collect cutaneous information from the head region. These inputs are gathered into two main pathways to the brain, each of which seems to carry different types of information (Figure 7.12).

The first pathway, the **dorsal column,** is composed of large, fast-conducting fibers and mostly receives input from the large, myelinated, fast-conducting (40 m/sec) Aβ fibers that terminate in corpuscular endings in the skin. This pathway ascends the spinal cord on the same

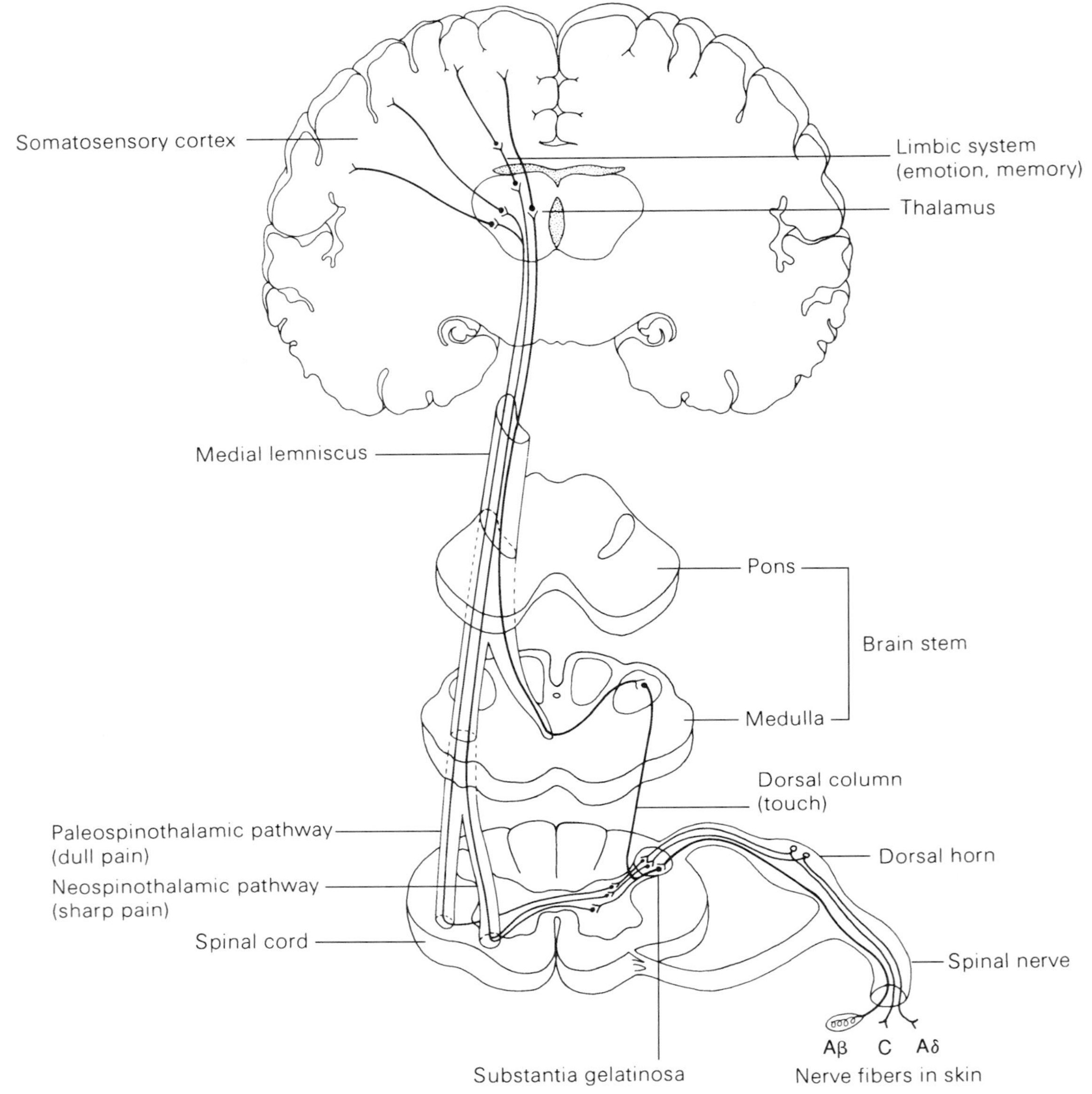

FIGURE 7.12 Schematic drawing of some of the important neural pathways from the skin to the brain. The sections of the spinal cord and brain stem are horizontal; that of the brain is vertical.

side of the body until it reaches the brain stem, where most of the nerve fibers cross over to the other side. It then continues to the **thalamus** and finally to the **somatosensory cortex** located in the **parietal** region of the brain (Figure 7.13). Thus, touch information is sent to the somatosensory cortex on the opposite side of the body from where it started. This is mostly a touch pathway, although temperature fibers have also been found (Hensel, 1981).

The second pathway, the **spinothalamic pathway,** is made up of many short axons instead of a few long ones. Its two branches, the **paleospinothalamic** (**paleo** means "old") and the **neospinothalamic** (**neo** means "new"), join with the dorsal column at the brain stem to form the **medial lemniscus.** The paleospinothalamic pathway is older in an evolutionary sense and signals dull or burning pain—it receives most of its input from the small, unmyelinated, slow-conducting (< 2.5 m/sec) C fibers that

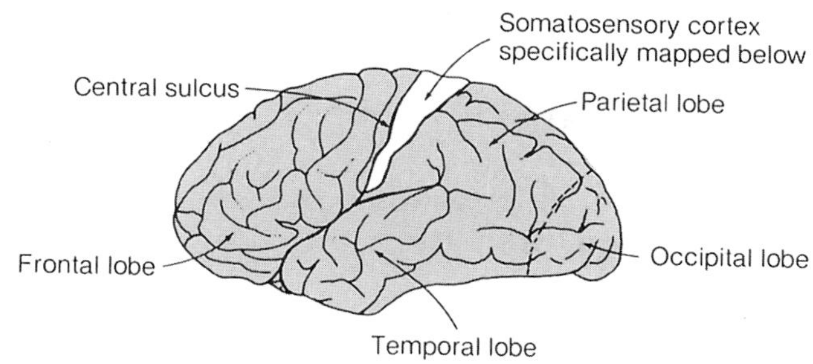

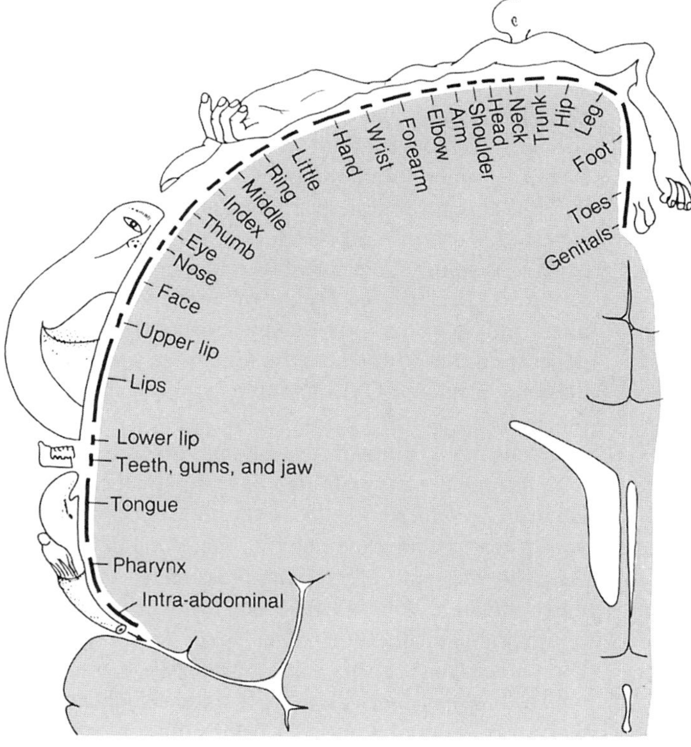

FIGURE 7.13 Penfield and Rasmussen's (1950) topographic map of projections of "touch" nerve fibers on the somatosensory cortex. The length of the line next to the drawing of each body part is proportional to the area of somatosensory cortex subserving that body part. (From *The Cerebral Cortex of Man,* by W. Penfield and T. Rasmussen. Copyright 1950 by Macmillan Publishing Co., renewed 1978 by Theodore Rasmussen.)

terminate in the skin. The neospinothalamic pathway signals sharp or pricking pain and probably receives most of its input from the small, myelinated, but slower-conducting (5 to 20 m/sec) Aδ fibers that terminate in the skin. It also receives some input from the large, fast-conducting Aβ fibers. The two spinothalamic pathways ascend on the opposite side of the spinal cord from where their input fibers terminate in the skin and then project to several areas of the brain, the most important being the thalamus and the **limbic system** (responsible for emotion and memory). Fibers from these areas then go to the somatosensory cortex. These pathways seem to carry some information about temperature and touch but signal mostly noxious stimulation. Interestingly, the unmyelinated C fibers also appear to mediate sensual touch, that is, the skin-to-skin gentle touch of hairy skin that seems to be necessary for normal social behavior and a healthy emotional life (Olausson et al., 2002). Stimulation of the skin in this manner elicits activity in limbic areas in humans but not in somatosensory cortex.

There are two major parts of the somatosensory cortex, **S1** and **S2,** and many subsidiary areas (Burton & Sinclair, 1996). S1 has several identifiable layers (Kaas, 1983). Thalamic neurons project mainly to one or more layers in S1, depending on where they come from. S1 neurons then project to S2 (Pons, Garraghty, Friedman, & Mishkin, 1987). Neurons in the many areas of somatosensory cortex connect with each other in very complex ways, following hierarchical rules very similar to those that characterize connections in the visual cortex, including back projections between areas (e.g., Iwamura, 1998; see also Chapter 3).

Touch at each location on the body is represented by a corresponding location of activity in the somatosensory cortex (e.g., Burton & Sinclair, 1996). In effect, the body is mapped onto the cortex. In their now classic research, Penfield and Rasmussen (1950) worked out the actual pattern of the relationship in humans by electrically stimulating the somatosensory cortex of patients who were having brain operations. As each place on the cortex was stimulated, the patients reported the sensation felt, such as a tingling of the left leg, an itch of the right hand, and so forth. The resulting map of the body is shown in Figure 7.13. Notice that the spatial location of stimulation on the skin is preserved in the spatial location of activity in the cortex. You can experience one of the consequences of a cortical map that encodes the stimulation of adjacent regions of the skin into adjacent regions of cortical activity by trying Demonstration Box 7.7.

The somatosensory map of the skin is not fixed, however, and may change if sensory input is permanently lost from some region of the skin, even in adulthood. For example, in monkeys deprived of innervation from an arm, over the period of a year or more, the region of S1 that previously encoded touch and pain information from that arm modifies itself to encode information from adjacent regions of the skin (Pons, Garraghty, Ommaya, Kaas, Taub, & Mishkin, 1991). Even short-term experience can change the map. For example, practice at discriminating the frequency of vibrations applied to the fingers in different ways, either three adjacent fingers together or the first and last of the three excluding the middle one, can modify the somatosensory representation of the middle finger so that it either joins the others (fusion) or separates from them (segregation), respectively (Liu, Gaetz, Bosnyak, & Roberts, 2000). These and other forms of neural plasticity in somatosensory cortex probably result from modification of the synapses between neurons coding the relevant locations based on exactly *when* the synapses are active, whether nearly simultaneously (< 10 ms) or only at longer intervals (e.g., Fox, Glazewski, & Schulze, 2000). That the timing of neural activity should play a role in modifying the somatosensory map is to be expected since the cortical representation of touch location is accomplished in S1 by the precise timing of the first spike from several fibers that all innervate the same location (Petersen, Panzeri, & Diamond, 2002).

Touch Thresholds, Adaptation, and Intensity

One of the most striking aspects of our sense of touch is how our sensitivity varies from one region of the body to another. Figure 7.14A shows representative absolute touch thresholds for several different regions of the body. Such thresholds are obtained by applying a small rod or hair to the surface of the skin with differing amounts of force per unit area, which changes the tension of the skin. The abrupt change in skin tension, or **strain,** is the stimulus for touch (Frey & Kiesow, 1899; Biography Box 7.4), much as an abrupt change in light intensity is the stimulus for vision (see Chapter 4). When the same rigid rod is used for all skin loci, these thresholds can be expressed simply in terms of the amount of force applied to the rod because the area over which the force is applied (the tip of the rod) remains constant. This has been done in Figure 7.14, where the higher the bar, the greater the force needed for absolute threshold and the lower the sensitivity.

Even more dramatic variations of threshold exist within a relatively small area of skin, say the surface of the arm. To experience this, explore a 2 × 2-cm area on your forearm with a toothpick or hairbrush bristle, pressing with the same very light pressure every time you touch the skin. You will find that you can feel the touch of the bristle distinctly on some spots, whereas on others you will feel only a very faint touch or none at all.

A vibrating touch stimulus is easier to detect than is the single touch of a bristle. The absolute threshold for a vibrating stimulus depends on the vibration frequency, much as the threshold of hearing depends on the frequency of a sound wave. Also, similar to the ear, the skin is sensitive only to a limited range of vibration frequencies, from about 40 Hz to about 2500 Hz. The absolute threshold for a vibrating stimulus is somewhat lower when the skin is warmer. This effect is restricted to vibration frequencies over 100 Hz for glabrous skin, but it occurs at all frequencies for hairy skin (Verrillo & Bolanowski, 1986). Cooling increases the touch threshold on the tongue, at least for intermediate vibration frequencies (Green, 1987).

There seems to be a minimum absolute threshold measurable for touch, similar to vision and smell. Vallbo (1983) placed a subcutaneous electrode in a rapidly adapting nerve fiber in the hand of an awake human vol-

DEMONSTRATION BOX 7.7

ARISTOTLE'S ILLUSION

The famous Greek philosopher-scientist Aristotle noticed an interesting illusion of touch that is quite easy to demonstrate. Hold your fingers as shown in Figure A, and touch the point between them with a pencil, as shown. Notice that you feel one item touching you and the sensation of one single touch. Now cross your fingers as shown in Figure B, touching yourself again with a pencil in the place indicated between the fingers. Notice that you feel two distinct touches. The effect may be stronger if you close your eyes during the touches. The simplest and most plausible explanation of the illusion is that when the pencil is stimulating the inside of the two fingers (Figure A), the touch information is being sent to overlapping or adjacent areas of the touch cortex, resulting in the sensation of one touch. When the pencil is stimulating the outsides of the two fingers because of your finger contortions, the information is being sent to two separate areas of the touch cortex, allowing you to experience two distinct touches. Such a cortical mapping is quite reasonable because commonly a single object between two fingers would be expected to stimulate adjacent skin surfaces and hence should be encoded as a single touch source. It is normally not possible, however, for a single object to stimulate the outsides of two different fingers, and so two different touches should be experienced in these circumstances. The cortical mapping reflects these common situations. It seems that whether the fingers are actually crossed or not, all processing makes the assumption that they are uncrossed (Benedetti, 1985).

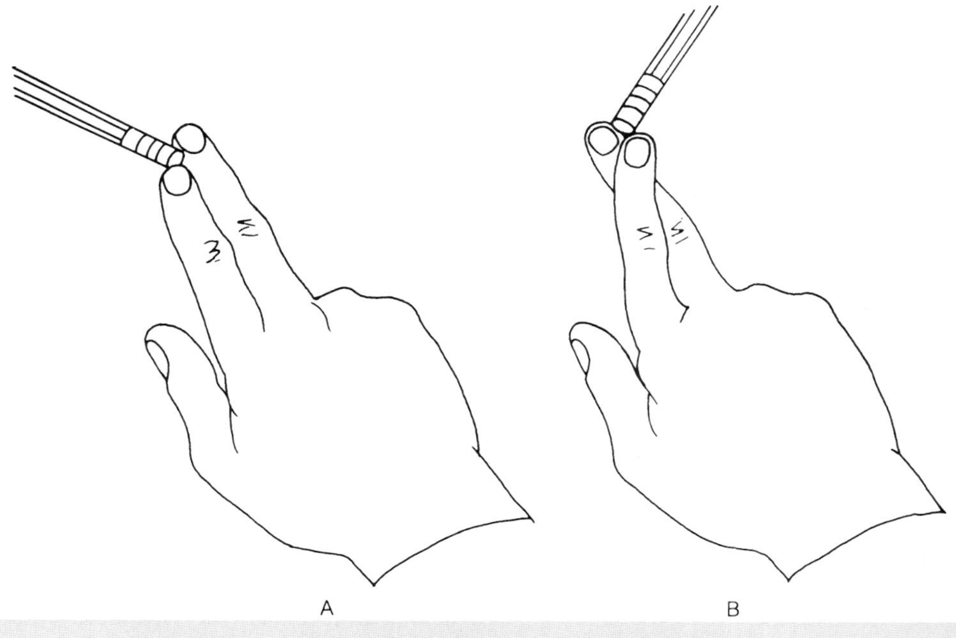

unteer. He found that a single spike potential in the fiber, stimulated by a 10-μm (millionth of a meter) movement of a tiny probe placed on the skin, produced a detectable sensation. Obviously, at the neural level, we can't get any more sensitive than the ability to experience a single spike potential as a conscious touch sensation.

One aspect of all tactile experience is that each touch sensation is localized at a particular place on the skin. Our ability to localize a touch sensation accurately is directly related to the amount of neural representation the touched place has in somatosensory cortex. In general, the greater the area of the cortex representing a particular region of the body, the smaller the errors of localization for that region (the relative cortical representation of areas of the body was shown in Figure 7.13). One way of expressing localization accuracy is the **two-point threshold.** This threshold arises from the discovery by Weber in the 1830s that two-touch stimuli (such as the

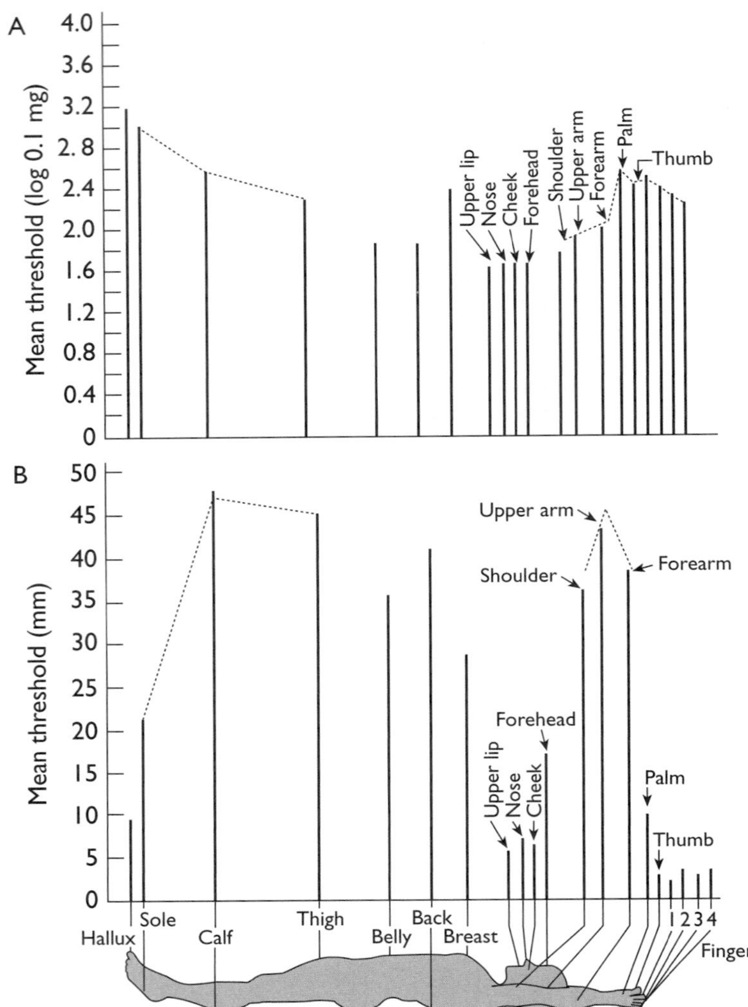

FIGURE 7.14 (A) Representative absolute thresholds for different regions of the skin. (B) Representative two-point thresholds for different regions of the skin (based on S. Weinstein in D. R. Kenshalo (Ed.), *The Skin Senses,* 1968, Charles C. Thomas, Publisher, Springfield, Illinois).

points of a drawing compass) will be felt as a single touch if they stimulate points that are very close together on the skin. The two-point threshold is a measure of how far apart the two touch stimuli must be on the skin before they are felt as two—rather than one—touches. A comprehensive determination of two-point threshold was provided by Weinstein (1968), and a summary of some of his results is shown in Figure 7.14B, where higher bars mean that the points must be farther apart to be discriminated. Notice the remarkable sensitivity of the lower face, the hands, and the feet. Presumably this reflects the use of these areas in manipulation of objects and in locomotion and also the larger areas of cortex associated with each.

As in the case of all other sensations, touch is subject to adaptation. Applying a stimulus to the skin and observing the gradual disappearance of the sensation can show this. For example, when you first get dressed in the morning you may be (uncomfortably) aware of your belt or waistband, but after a while the sensation from it fades from consciousness. Zigler (1932) measured touch adaptation for several different areas of the body. He found that the heavier the stimulus, the longer it took for the sensation to disappear, but that the larger the area covered by the stimulus, the less time it took for the sensation to disappear. You can explore touch adaptation by trying Demonstration Box 7.8.

Adaptation can also be measured by asking an observer to adjust the intensity of a briefly presented stimulus until the sensation associated with it matches that associated with another stimulus to which adaptation has been taking place over some time period. The difference

BIOGRAPHY BOX 7.4

HORSE(HAIR)ING AROUND WITH TOUCH

Maxmilian Ruppert Franz von Frey (1852–1932) made a methodological breakthrough in the 1890s when he discovered that, when pressed against the skin until they bent, horse hairs tend to apply a single downward force that was not proportional to how much they were bent in doing the pressing. In contrast, for a common spring the downward force on the surface where the tip is resting is directly proportional to how much it is bent; the more bending the more force is applied at the tip. These horse hairs, however, always exerted the same force when they were bent, and this force depended on the stiffness, length, and diameter of the hair. This observation looks like merely an odd finding of interest to physicists; however, it was a vital finding for the study of the sense of touch. This fact allowed reproducible tests of touch sensitivity by different people and on different occasions without the need to measure precisely how much force was being applied by the experimenter. All that the experimenter had to do was to press a calibrated hair against the skin until it bent to provide a constant known touch stimulus. Seizing on this opportunity, von Frey used these hairs to explore tactile sensation. In particular, he discovered pain spots and measured touch thresholds for a variety of different skin areas. Now most aesthesiometers (devices for exploring the sense of touch) are called von Frey aethesiometers in honor of his pioneering work, although most are now made with true monofilaments (for example, nylon). These aesthesiometers are used for clinical purposes too, since a variety of diseases either increase or decrease sensitivity of the skin to such touches. In particular, various pathologies of the skin nerves can be diagnosed in this way, as well as some degenerative diseases such as multiple sclerosis. Max von Frey began his career with a medical degree from the University of Leipzig in 1877 and assumed various research and teaching posts until he became, in 1899, Professor of Physiology at the University of Würzburg, where he remained for the duration of his career. He published many articles and books during his distinguished career, and his von Frey hairs are now used worldwide in clinical medicine and in research.

between the intensities of the two stimuli is a measure of the amount of adaptation that has taken place. Using this technique, Frey and Goldman (1915) determined that adaptation to touch stimuli is similar to that for other modalities; it is very rapid for the first second or so and then gradually slows down. After 3 sec, the sensation level has decreased to about one quarter of the beginning value.

Bekesy (1959) used this same technique to measure the time course of adaptation for vibratory stimuli, which generally takes longer than that for static stimuli. Again, different parts of the body respond differently. On the lip, adaptation is complete after about 20 sec. On the forearm, however, loss of sensation is more gradual, and adaptation is not complete even after 60 sec. These longer adaptation times are consistent with the more effective vibratory stimulus.

Vibrating stimuli are also used to study the perceived intensity of touch sensations. Magnitude estimates of the intensity of a 60-Hz vibratory stimulus on the fingertip follow a power function of stimulus intensity with an exponent of about 0.95—nearly a linear relationship (Collins & Cholewiak, 1994). Magnitude estimates of single mechanical pulses applied to the skin of the hand are also a power function of stimulus intensity, but with a somewhat lower exponent for glabrous skin (about 0.70)

DEMONSTRATION BOX 7.8

TOUCH ADAPTATION

For this demonstration, you will need a watch with a sweep second hand, two pieces of cardboard (cut into small circles with diameters of about 1 cm and about 4 cm), and a friend. Lay one piece of cardboard on the skin of your friend's back, and record the amount of time before the sensation of touch disappears. Repeat this with the other piece of cardboard. Try the experiment again, only this time press gently on each cardboard. Notice that the lighter touches and the larger surface-area stimulations disappear faster from consciousness. Thus, they show faster adaptation.

than for hairy skin (about 1.05) (Hamalainen & Jarvilehto, 1981).

We mentioned earlier that similar to sound sensitivity in the ear, the skin's sensitivity for vibration is different for different stimulus frequencies (e.g., Marks, 1979a). Correspondingly, for a given physical pressure, some vibration frequencies give a more intense touch sensation than others. Figure 7.15 shows a set of equal sensation curves, for a vibrating stimulus on the skin, that looks somewhat similar to the equal loudness contours presented in Figure 6.12. Every point on a given line represents the same perceived touch intensity. Maximum touch sensitivity occurs in the region of 200 to 400 Hz. Notice that stimulus intensity in Figure 7.15 is measured in decibels (compared to a displacement of the vibrator surface by 1 μm, which represents 0 dB). This is similar to decibels of sound pressure (Chapter 6).

Other similarities between responses of the skin to vibrations and the ear to sound arise both because of the similarity of the vibratory stimuli to the pressure variations in sound and because the basilar membrane (where sound is registered in the cochlea) actually evolved from hairy skin. Thus discrimination of the intensities of vibrating stimuli follows Weber's law as closely as that of sound intensities does (Gescheider, Bolanowski, Verrillo, Arpajian, & Ryan, 1990). Psychophysical channel capacity is similar for touch and sound intensity at about 2 bits maximum (Rabinowitz, Houtsma, Durlach, & Delhorne, 1987). Just as in sound, forward, backward, and simultaneous masking occurs. On the skin masking happens when a vibrating stimulus is applied in the presence of another vibrating stimulus. The magnitude of masking decreases as the time interval between target and mask increases (Gescheider, Bolanowski, & Verrillo, 1989).

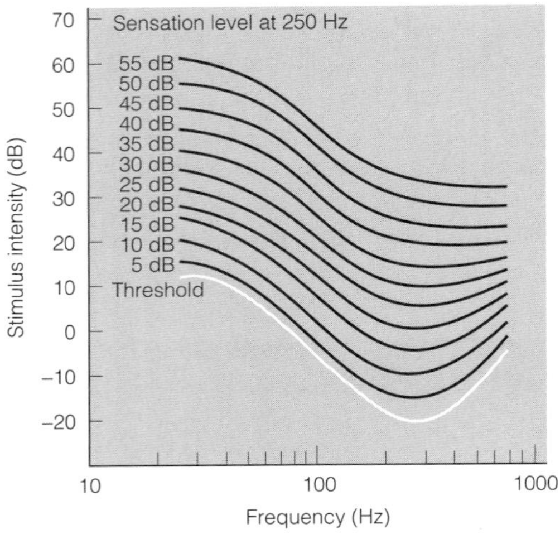

FIGURE 7.15 Equal sensation contours for a vibrating stimulus. These contours are similar to equal loudness contours over the same range of frequencies (see Figure 7.12) (from Verrillo, Fraioli, & Smith, 1969).

The skin is different from the ear in that there are four distinct receptor and afferent nerve systems, or **channels,** for touch rather than the single system in the ear. Each of the four systems has distinct psychophysical properties, some of which are summarized in Table 7.1. The Pacinian system (composed of Pacinian corpuscles and their nerves) seems to be most sensitive to high-frequency vibrations, in the region around 250 Hz (Verrillo, 1968), whereas each of the three non-Pacinian systems (RA, SA1, and SA2) has a different, generally lower, operating range of frequencies (e.g., Greenspan & Bolanowski, 1996). The psychophysical properties of each channel depend on both the mechanical properties of the skin and on those of the specific receptor stimulated (e.g., Van Doren, 1989). Each channel is specialized for a particular perceptual task (Table 1; Johnson, 2001). Although stimulation of only one channel is required for a sensation to be perceived, our touch sensations usually result from a blend of activity in all four channels, as each responds to a different aspect of a particular touch stimulus (Greenspan & Bolanowski, 1996).

In addition to passively perceiving vibrating stimuli, we perceive "roughness," which is actually based on changes in pressure associated with textured surfaces moving over our skin surface. Our sensitivity for roughness varies over the body, with greatest sensitivity on the lips, fingers, and forearms and least sensitivity on the heels, back, and thighs (J. C. Stevens, 1990). These relative sensitivities are similar to those for absolute sensitivity to the pressure of a single point (Figure 7.14A). Roughness is perceived similarly whether the surface or the body part moves to produce the stimulus (Heller, 1989). Actually vision and touch perform similarly in discriminating relatively rough textures; however, touch is superior to vision for discriminating smoother textures (Heller, 1989).

Tactile and Haptic Pattern Perception

The sense of touch can discriminate and recognize complex objects (Klatzky, Lederman, & Metzger, 1985), although it tends to respond best to different aspects of objects than the visual system does (Klatzky, Lederman, & Reed, 1987). Louis Braille exploited this ability when he created his tactile pattern alphabet, which enables blind people to read. In this alphabet, patterns of raised

TABLE 7.1 The Four-Channel Model of Touch Sensation for Glabrous Skin[a]

Characteristic of Channel	Channels			
	Pacinian	RA	SA2	SA1
Adaptational property	Rapid	Rapid	Slow	Slow
Receptive field size	Large	Small	Large	Small
Receptor ending	Pacinian	Meissner	Ruffini	Merkel
Stimulus	Vibration	Fast indent	Stretch	Indentation
Sensation	Vibration	Flutter	Buzz-like	Pressure
Frequency range	40–500 Hz	2–40 Hz	100–500 Hz	0.4–2.0 Hz
Temporal summation	Yes	No	No	Indeterminate
Spatial summation	Yes	No	?	No
Perceptual function	Hand-held object motion	Grip slip	Hand shape	Form, texture

[a]Based on Greenspan & Bolanowski, 1996, Johnson, 2001.

dots on paper play the role of the patterns of ink on paper that constitute written language for sighted people. The high speed with which an experienced blind person can read a Braille-rendered text reflects not only long hours of practice (as does any form of reading) but also the remarkable sensitivity of the touch system.

A way of conveying information that more directly substitutes tactile patterns for visual patterns is the **vision substitution system** (White, Saunders, Scadden, Bach-y-Rita, & Collins, 1970). Here, a television camera scans a visual pattern, and the output of the camera is converted into a pattern of vibrating points on the skin of the back of a blind (or blindfolded) observer. The observer can move the camera to view different parts of the visual scene. When visual stimuli are converted to tactile patterns in this way, observers can recognize up to 25 different stimulus patterns. Even the relative distances of various objects in a scene can be perceived from the tactile pattern, and illusions are experienced as well. These findings raise questions similar to those raised by visual and auditory pattern perception. For example, we might ask if there are feature detectors for touch. These and other findings (e.g., Horner, 1991) also remind us of the importance of high-level cognitive processes in even the simplest types of perceptual experiences.

Reading in Braille requires that the reading material be translated into raised bump patterns on heavy paper. This is expensive, and takes time, which means that blind people could be deprived of access to newspapers and magazines, which are published in large numbers and must be available quickly to be of most value. There are electromechanical devices which turn print into touch patterns. One of the first of these was the **Optacon** (Bliss, Katcher, Rogers, & Shepard, 1970), which scans each printed letter and turns it into a raised pattern which also vibrates. After 50 hours of training, blind users of the Optacon can read untreated material at 20 words per minute. Experienced users attain rates as high as 60 words per minute. Interestingly, sighted users can also achieve excellent performance, although they exhibit large individual differences (Cholewiak & Collins, 1997).

The tactile perceptual system can also aid the hearing impaired. Several devices have been developed in which an array of electrodes or vibrators is used to transmit speech information to the skin of hearing-impaired people. In these devices, the prominent frequency components in speech are translated into vibration at different places on the skin, and people can learn to recognize the vibratory patterns as words. Devices such as the *Tickle Talker* (Cowan, Alcantara, Blamey, & Clark, 1988), the *Queens vocoder* (Brooks & Frost, 1983), and the *Tacticon* (Weisenberger, Broadstone, & Saunders, 1989) all have been shown to be useful, especially in conjunction with lip-reading.

The Optacon and similar devices also have been used for research into the mechanisms of tactile pattern perception. As we mentioned earlier, presentation of one pattern on the skin can **mask** another, making it more difficult to recognize (J. C. Craig, 1978). Some of this masking may be due to competing responses to internal representations of the two tactile patterns (J. C. Craig, 1995; Horner, 1997). For example, if a letter pattern is presented on the Optacon and then followed immediately by a rectangular pattern, observers have a harder time identifying the letter than if no masking pattern was presented. This is called **backward masking** because the masking pattern seems to act backward in time to interfere with the perception of the earlier target. **Forward masking** also occurs with tactile patterns; here, the masking pattern is presented first, followed by the target. As in audition and vision, masking studies often reveal basic mechanisms of tactile perception. For example, there is usually more backward masking when the time interval between target and mask is short and more forward masking when the time interval is long (J. C. Craig, 1983). This is consistent with the idea that perceptual representations of tactile features persist for about 1200 ms (e.g., Craig & Evans, 1987) and reveals something about how those representations are integrated over time (Evans, 1987). Masking effects are similar for all body locations, although pattern discrimination and recognition in the absence of masking varies with location on the body (Cholewiak & Craig, 1984). The ability to localize tactile stimuli is similarly subject to backward, forward, and simultaneous masking and depends on the time interval between mask and target (J. C. Craig, 1989). Masking of identification is usually most effective when the mask and target occur at the same location (but see Horner, 1997), whereas masking of localizability is most effective when mask and target occur at different locations (J. C. Craig, 1989).

We have been talking about receptors that respond to mechanically encoded information from the world around us when contact is made with our skin. There is also a vast amount of touchlike information available from within our own bodies. Thus, we can determine by feel alone whether our bodies are moving or stationary (Chapter 12), and we can also determine the position and movement of our body parts. The neural processing of this information and the sensations we feel, called collectively **kinesthesis,** bear striking resemblances to touch.

In the most complex organisms, several specialized receptor systems inform the brain about the position of the limbs or the orientation of the body. Our bodies are literally enmeshed in a web of sensory receptors that accurately monitor the positions of various body parts so that appropriate action can be initiated and controlled. In many cases the signals of these sensory systems are not consciously perceived but, rather, are used in controlling reflex actions that maintain an upright posture. When these signals are perceived, they give rise to the sensations of force or weight, which are often used to help guide our voluntary movements, as in sports or other skilled motor performance, and also our identification of objects that can be touched but not seen.

When we move our limbs about actively through the world, we perceive objects through a combination of tactile and kinesthetic sensations caused by our mechanical interaction with them. Such experiences play an important role in perceptual development as vision and touch calibrate each other (Chapter 15), and they can also be important under conditions in which visual and auditory information about the world is missing or impoverished, such as when stumbling about in a dark bedroom. Our experience of the world based on a combination of tactile and kinesthetic sensation is called **haptic perception** (Gibson, 1966).

People are very good at identifying ordinary objects presented haptically (Klatzky, Lederman, & Metzger, 1985). One important type of haptic information about objects is their size (extension in space). Our ability to discriminate lengths using only haptic perception is quite good. For example, the difference threshold for length for objects between 10 mm and 20 mm is about 1 mm, indicating a Weber fraction of 0.05 to 0.10 (Durlach et al., 1989). Haptic length discrimination does not follow Weber's law very well, however, because the Weber fraction tends to decrease for larger objects. Nonetheless, channel capacity is about 2 bits for haptic length, similar to visually-perceived length (Durlach et al., 1989).

Several other haptic attributes of objects can be reliably discriminated and are often used in haptic object identification. One is surface texture (Lederman, Browse, & Klatzky, 1988), which is often integrated with the perception of hardness (Klatzky, Lederman, & Reed, 1989), and also with perception of any curvature of the object surface (Pont, Kappers, & Koenderink, 1997). Moreover, even a brief "haptic glance" at an object can sometimes suffice to identify it through detection of one or more of these characteristic properties, although free haptic exploration (which means freely feeling around the object) is necessary to achieve the highest levels of accuracy (Klatzky & Lederman, 1995).

Sometimes the cues to haptic shape perception are quite subtle. Figure 7.16 illustrates an intriguing experimental setup that shows that the shape of solid objects can often be identified when they are merely wielded by a handle and their edges and contours are not seen or touched. This appears to occur because observers can sense haptically the moments of inertia and resistance to rotation around various axes of the objects. It also indicates that the distribution of mass of an object can play a role in the perception of its shape (Burton, Turvey, & Solomon, 1990), orientation (Turvey et al., 1992), and where it is grasped (Pagano, Kinsella-Shaw, Cassidy, & Turvey, 1994). Furthermore, such wielding of a rod can yield information about objects struck with it, such as size (Barac-Cikoja & Turvey, 1993) and distance

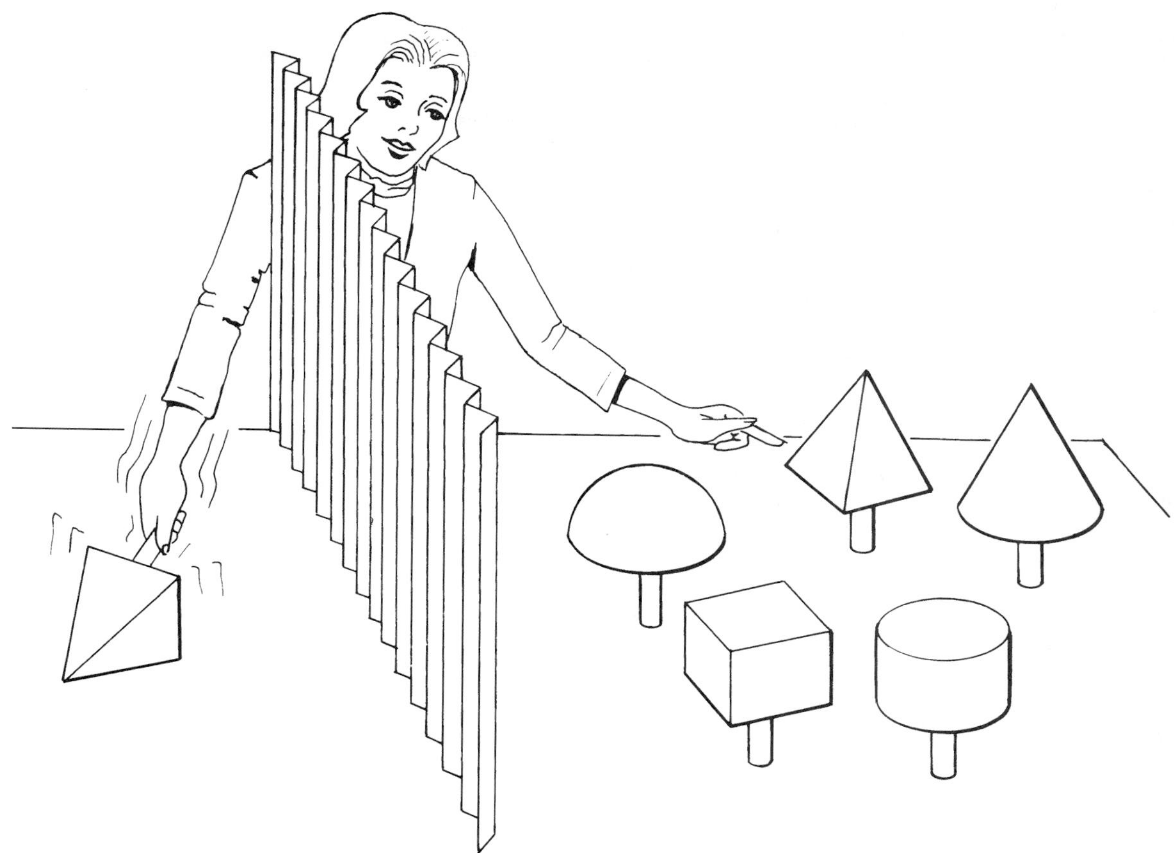

FIGURE 7.16 Experimental setup for recognition of objects based on haptic information, especially the distribution of mass in the object (based on Burton, Turvey, & Solomon, 1990).

(Barac-Cikoja & Turvey, 1995). This is the same process by which the information received by tapping a cane aids blind people by providing cues as to both sizes and distances of objects in the world. This same process seems to assist normally sighted individuals in maintaining body orientation and posture in the dark or when their eyes are closed (Jeka, Easton, Bentzen, & Lackner, 1996).

Haptic perception is closely related to vision in some ways, in that we can often recognize an object that we explored only by touch when we later see it, or vice versa, suggesting that there is at least partial equivalence between visual and haptic representations of objects (Gibson, 1966). Another example of the close visual-haptic relationship is that some visual patterns that cause illusions, such as one line being perceived as longer than another although they are the same length, also occur when three-dimensional models of the patterns are explored by touch alone (e.g., Heller, Calcaterra, Burson, & Green, 1997). Finally, haptic exploration is often used to assist visual recognition when making difficult discriminations (Klatzky, Lederman, & Matula, 1993). In fact, when vision and touch disagree on a difficult-to-judge object property, such as size, touch can dominate vision if responses are rendered haptically as well (Hershberger & Misceo, 1996).

An application of haptic perception is found in the **Tadoma** method of assisting speech perception by people who are both blind and hearing impaired, as Helen Keller was. In Tadoma, an observer touches the speech articulators (the parts of the face and neck that produce speech sounds, e.g., lips, jaw, etc.). From the motions of the articulators perceived by the "haptic listener," the words said by the speaker can be recognized with a good deal of accuracy (Norton et al., 1977). You can experience Tadoma in Demonstration Box 7.9.

DEMONSTRATION BOX 7.9

TADOMA WITH YOUR FRIENDS

When perceiving speech using Tadoma, the perceiver places his or her hand on the face and neck of the speaker, with the thumb across the middle of the lips and the fingers fanned out across the face and neck as in the figure in this box. To try this for yourself, get a friend to whisper the words listed below while you monitor the person's articulators as shown in the figure. Pay attention to the in-and-out movements of the lips, the up-and-down movements of the jaw, and the flow of air from the mouth (the cure of larynx vibration is abolished by the need to whisper if you have normal hearing). You should have your eyes closed and put earplugs or cotton in your ears so visual information and auditory information are absent. Your friend should read the words very slowly, in an irregular order, and (because you are new at this method of perceiving speech) with exaggerated movements. There should be a pause after each word for you to guess what the word was. For an even more difficult test, your friend should choose words you have not seen and use normal movements of the articulators, although he or she should still speak slowly. Some words that are relatively easy to discriminate are *you, me, yes, why, but, candy, tree,* and *push.* Reverse roles so your friend can try it, too.

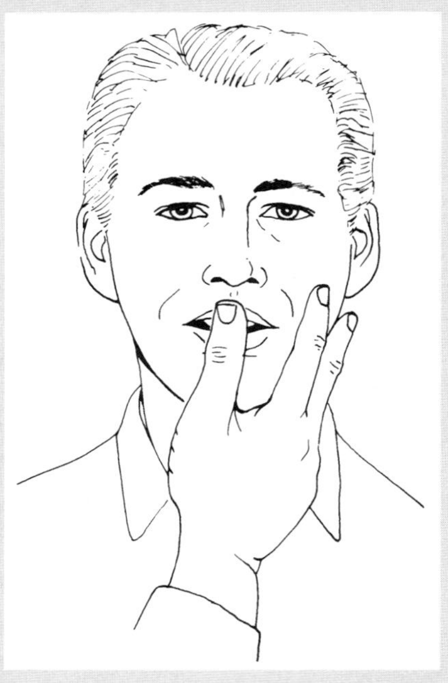

PAIN

Pain is an imperative and complex experience. It is usually associated with damage to the body of an animal, and its experience is accompanied by myriad emotions and thoughts. Many sensory psychologists consider pain to be a sensation; other psychologists argue that pain is not a sensation at all but, rather, an emotion or a bodily state akin to hunger or thirst (e.g., Wall, 1979). Perhaps the best view is a compromise. There are certainly identifiable sensory characteristics of the experience of pain. Pain has absolute and differential thresholds, it adapts, and it has definable and separate physiological pathways and projection areas in the brain. Furthermore, its intensity dimension is separable from the intensity dimension of nonpainful stimuli in the same modality (Janal, Clark, & Carroll, 1991). In these ways pain acts like a sensory system, and we will treat it here as a unique sensory modality.

Pain Stimuli and Receptors

Pain evolved to assist the survival of animals in two ways. First, animals must be able to avoid, or at least quickly terminate, environmental situations that could harm them. Light, sound, touch, and temperature, when they occur at very high intensities or for prolonged durations, can destroy body tissues and sensory receptors. If potentially harmful intensities are not recognized fast enough the organism may perish. Second, pain provides information to individuals so that they may cope appropriately with an injury if it does happen, such as inducing individuals to be still in order that healing may occur or to seek treatment for the injury. Sometimes individuals may receive serious injuries and not feel pain until sometime later (Melzack, Wall, & Ty, 1982). Under certain circumstances this is adaptive because when the injury first occurs, actions such as escaping or fighting for one's life are more adaptive, and pain would only interfere. A delay in the perception of pain until it is safe to engage in healing-promoting behaviors may save an individual's life (see Wall, 1979). During the healing phase, the stimulus for pain is the injury itself, and the function of the pain is not to warn but to promote recovery by reducing activity that may make the injury worse. This function is accomplished because the inflammation that accompanies injury or disease stimulates changes in the pain receptors, and increases in the substances they respond to such as **endovanilloids,** which are internally generated substances related to *capsaicinm* (the same chemical that gives hot peppers, such as jalapeños their bite) which, in turn, enhances the pain response (e.g., Di Marzo, Blumberg, & Szallasi, 2002). Without this pain sense to warn and immobilize, we would have a hard time living long enough to reproduce, which is often the unfortunate fate of those humans who are born without a well-functioning pain sense (see Sternbach, 1963). For example, Melzack and Wall (1988) reported a case of a woman who died at 29 years of age of massive infections caused by damage to her skin and bones from abrasions and unhealed injuries, especially to her joints, that she simply had not detected because she lacked adequate pain sensitivity.

The pain receptors are the free nerve endings with which the skin and the rest of the body are well supplied. As we mentioned earlier in this chapter, free nerve endings in the subcutaneous fat under the dermis of the skin have been found to be connected to nerve fibers associated with pain (see Vierck, 1978). The position of these endings in the subcutaneous fat makes them respond only to high-intensity stimuli, whether mechanical or temperature. Other pain fibers terminate in the epidermis; these endings are wrapped in a Schwann cell sheath, which allows them to retain a high stimulation threshold even in this more exposed location (Perl, 1984). Many such nerve fibers contain vanilloid receptors that are sensitive to heat, acid, and capsaicin (a vanilloid). These receptors mediate burning pain, especially that caused by endovanilloids generated by inflammation that we mentioned above (Di Marzo et al., 2002). Pain can also arise in the absence of activity of receptors because central pain-signalling neurons become more excitable as a result of changes caused by injury or disease, and fire even when only normally innocuous inputs are stimulating them (Scholz & Woolf, 2002).

Pain receptors occur on two types of nerve fibers, small myelinated Aδ fibers and even smaller unmyelinated C fibers. These fibers have relatively high thresholds and respond only to noxious stimuli, such as pinches, pin pricks, or extreme temperatures (e.g., Lynn & Perl, 1996). The Aδ fibers are especially sensitive to noxious mechanical stimuli, whereas the C fibers respond to all kinds of noxious stimuli (they are often called **polymodal nociceptors**—from the Latin *nocere,* "to hurt" + [re]ceptor). Remember we remarked in the "Touch" section that mild stimulation of the C fibers also can give rise to a pleasurable sensation, sensual touch. C fibers typically terminate in free nerve endings in the subcuta-

DEMONSTRATION BOX 7.10

THE PRODUCTION OF DOUBLE PAIN

This demonstration uses the method of Sinclair and Stokes (1964) to generate two pains for the price of one. Double pain is experienced only under certain conditions. When these conditions are met, people report a first sharp, stinging sensation, followed about 1 sec later by a more-intense burning pain that may spread to a wider area and fades more gradually. Although most people, under the appropriate conditions, experience this sequence without being told what to expect, we are telling you now so that you will have a good chance to experience it. For this demonstration you will need to find a source of hot water, something to measure its temperature, and two medium-sized bowls to hold it in. You need to produce two water baths: one at 35°C (95°F) and one at 57°C (135°F). If you have access to a thermometer (a meat thermometer is fine for this demonstration), this would obviously be the best way to measure the temperatures of the baths. If you do not have a thermometer, simply mix 3½ cups of very hot tap water with 3½ cups of cold tap water for the 35°C bath. To keep it at about this temperature, add a little hot water every minute or so. To create the 57°C bath, combine 6⅔ cups of hot tap water with ⅓ cup of cold tap water.

Immerse your entire hand in the 35°C bath for about 10 min. When this time has elapsed, mix the 57°C bath, and carefully insert your finger into it until the water comes up past the second joint of the finger. Count "one-thousand-one" to yourself, and then withdraw your finger. Pay careful attention to the sensations you experience. Notice that first you feel a sharp stinging and then about a second later a burning feeling. You may try the experiment again and again without fear of any damage if you immerse your hand in the 35°C bath between trials, and always limit your immersion in the 57°C bath to 1 sec. If you wish, you can try varying the temperatures of the two baths to find the limits of the conditions under which the phenomenon will occur. Also, in calculating the formulas for the two baths, we assumed that the cold tap water in your area has a temperature of about 10°C (50°F), and the hot tap water a temperature of about 60°C (140°F). If your water temperatures vary significantly from these, you will have to adjust the proportions of each to make up the baths.

neous fat of the skin or deep in muscles and joints, whereas the Aδ fiber ends are wrapped in Schwann cells and terminate in the epidermis. Aδ and C fibers connect mainly with the spinothalamic pathway and are now generally acknowledged to be "the" pain fibers. Apparently the fast Aβ fibers and the dorsal column pathway are specialized for highly discriminative processing of tactile information, whereas the slower Aδ and C fibers and spinothalamic pathway carry information such as pain, temperature, and only rudimentary touch. This relationship was first suggested in 1920 by Henry Head.

The particular organization of the pain pathways leads to some interesting phenomena. For example, **double pain** is the experience of two distinct peaks of pain, differing in quality and separated in time, arising from a single pain stimulus. It is now generally accepted that the first, sharp or pricking, pain arises from the response of the somewhat faster-conducting Aδ fibers to the noxious stimulus, whereas the second, dull or burning pain, arises from the slower-conducting C fibers (e.g., Willis, 1985). You can experience this by trying Demonstration Box 7.10.

Neural Responses to Pain Stimuli

The electrophysiology of pain has been studied by applying noxious stimuli, such as electric shock, pinching, or pricking, to animals and recording the responses of neurons at various levels of the nervous system. In this way it has been discovered that certain neurons fire only when their receptive fields are stimulated by stimuli that we perceive as being painful. For example, such neurons have been found in the thalamus of monkeys (Bushnell and Duncan, 1989), in the primary somatosensory area (S1) of rats (Lamour, Willer, & Guilbaud, 1983) and monkeys (Kenshalo & Isensee, 1983) and may also occur in the secondary somatosensory area, S2 (see Willis, 1985). Studies using PET scans have identified three different areas in the human cerebral cortex that respond when painful heat or vibration is applied to the skin: the anterior cingulate gyrus, S1, and S2 (e.g., Coghill et al., 1994). It is clear that both the thalamus and the cortex play roles in pain perception. Probably several brain areas contribute to the pain experience.

Perhaps the most interesting electrophysiological fact about pain is that the nerve fibers involved in pain and those involved in tactile and kinesthetic sensations interact, sometimes in opposition to each other. Melzack and Wall (1988; Biography Box 7.5) devised an ingenious conceptual model of pain, called the **gate-control theory,** based on the interaction of two of these fiber types (Figure 7.17). This theory provides the foundation for most modern accounts of pain phenomena and has re-

BIOGRAPHY BOX 7.5

THE GATES OF PAIN

Ronald Melzack (1929–) was born in Montreal, Canada and worked with the great Canadian neurophysiologist D.O. Hebb while obtaining a Ph.D. from McGill University in 1954. Some time later, when he was studying patients who had phantom limb pain after amputations, he realized that pain sometimes seems to lose its survival value, often continuing for a long time after damaged tissue has healed. In contrast, sometimes great damage can be sustained without any pain at all, as when horribly wounded soldiers refuse pain medication because they feel no pain to warrant it. These realizations, along with discoveries in the anatomy and physiology of the pain pathways (in particular, the inhibitory role of the substantia gelatinosa in the spinal cord) led Melzack and his colleague Patrick Wall to propose the gate-control theory of pain that we discuss in this chapter. Published in *Science* in 1965, the theory provided a theoretical framework for three decades of work on the functional anatomy of pain, as well as explaining many mysteries. Although displaced from its central role in research by the discovery of endogenous opiates, the theory still has its adherents and still influences modern pain research. In addition to contributions to understanding the physiology of pain, Melzack is also famous for the McGill Pain Questionnaire to measure the subjective experience of pain. Based on Melzack's collection and categorization of hundreds of words used to describe pain, such "burning," "searing," "throbbing," and so forth, the questionnaire allows patients to describe precisely the pain they are feeling, allowing both accurate diagnosis of diseases and more effective pain control by drugs and other procedures. This questionnaire is now used in pain clinics and cancer hospices everywhere in the world. Although Melzack is now retired from his position as Professor of Psychology at McGill University and Research Director of the Pain Clinic at Montreal General Hospital, he still edits the very influential and widely-used *Textbook of Pain*, a 1500-page tome that is indispensable for those who study and treat pain.

ceived both anatomical and experimental support (e.g., Humphries, Johnson, & Long, 1996).

The action of the gate-control theory of pain is described in Figure 7.17. Notice that both low-threshold, *fast* (Aβ) sensory fibers and high-threshold, *slow* (Aδ and C) sensory fibers have connections with the **substantia gelatinosa** (a group of neurons in the spinal cord; see also Figure 7.12) and with the **transmission cells (T cells).** The T cells are some of the *slow-conducting* fibers that make up the spinothalamic pathway and send pain information up the spinal cord to the brain, whereas the substantia gelatinosa serves as the gate that may or may not allow the T cells to send their pain signals. Basically, the fast Aβ fibers close this gate, whereas the slow fibers open it. Notice in Figure 7.17 that the connections of both the fast and the slow fibers to the T cells are marked with a plus sign, meaning that they increase neural activity in those cells. The actions of these fibers on the substantia gelatinosa cells are different,

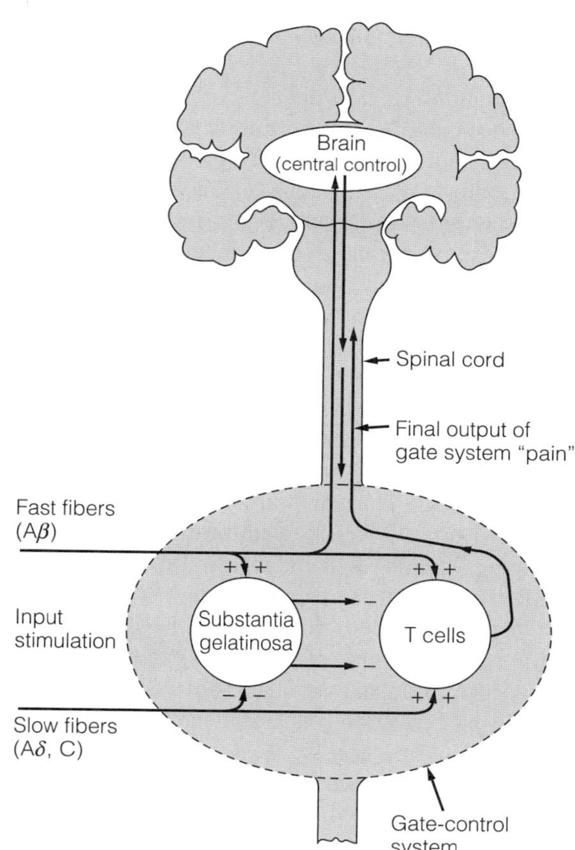

FIGURE 7.17 An illustration of the gate-control theory of pain.

however. The fast fibers excite the neurons in the substantia gelatinosa (+), whereas the slow Aδ and C fibers inhibit their action (−). When the T cells are sufficiently active, we experience pain. A light touch would mostly stimulate the fast fibers, which have lower thresholds. This would excite the substantia gelatinosa neurons, causing them to inhibit the T cells, thus canceling the excitation of the T cells by the fast fibers and keeping them below the activity level sensed as pain. A noxious stimulus, however, would stimulate the higher threshold slow fibers as well as the fast fibers. Because the slow fibers inhibit the substantia gelatinosa cells, canceling their excitation by the fast fibers, the substantia gelatinosa neurons no longer inhibit the T cells, which can fire more vigorously in response to input from both fast and slow fibers, and pain is experienced.

Generally speaking, chemical analgesics act to inhibit the slow fibers but do not affect the fast fibers. This allows the substantia gelatinosa to inhibit the T cells and keep the pain gate closed. Another way to close the pain gate (at least somewhat) is to rub or vibrate the skin around an area where you have hurt yourself, thus stimulating the fast fibers in the surrounding skin, which will stimulate the substantia gelatinosa and close the gate. However, higher-level processes can also participate because fast fibers transmit information directly through the dorsal column to the brain, which can in turn send information back down the spinal cord to modify the gate-control system, which may explain how some people can mentally reduce their feelings of pain. Melzack and Casey (1968) suggested that this central pathway to the gate may respond to cognitive and emotional events signaled by the brain, which may be capable of changing the nature of a potentially painful experience. There is experimental evidence that the descending pathways can inhibit responses of spinal cord neurons to noxious stimuli (e.g., Light, 1992).

Pain Thresholds, Intensity, and Adaptation

To treat pain as a sensation, it is useful to define a pain threshold. This is taken to be the intensity of a stimulus that will just barely produce a sensation of pain. As in touch, there are specific tiny points on the skin that respond selectively to pain. These "pain points," also discovered by Frey (Biography Box 7.4), give the sensation of pain for stimuli that do not produce painful sensations when applied to other places on the skin. Pain points correspond to the receptive fields of the pain fibers (e.g., Lynn & Perl, 1996). The distribution of such pain points over the body seems quite variable, as can be seen from

TABLE 7.2 Distribution of Pain Sensitivity[a]

Skin Region	Pain Points (cm^2)
Back of knee	232
Neck region	228
Bend of elbow	224
Shoulder blade	212
Inside of forearm	203
Back of hand	188
Forehead	184
Buttocks	180
Eyelid	172
Scalp	144
Ball of thumb	60
Sole of foot	48
Tip of nose	44

[a]Based on Geldard, 1972.

Table 7.2. Pain thresholds vary in the oral-facial regions as well, with the tongue and inside of the lip being less sensitive than other parts to heat-induced pain (Green, 1985).

A major advance in measuring pain thresholds was made by Hardy, Wolff, and Goodell (1943). They used a device that focused an intense beam of light on the ink-blackened forehead of a subject in order to produce a controllable, precisely measurable pain stimulus. They called this device a **dolorimeter,** from the Latin *dolor* meaning "pain" and *meter* meaning "to measure." The exact thresholds measured in this way are of little importance because the units of any pain threshold stimulus vary with the pain-producing device or stimulus modality. More important, Hardy and colleagues (1943) were able to show that pain thresholds act like the thresholds for other sensations. Pain thresholds are relatively stable as long as the conditions are stable, but they vary systematically with changes in the neurological, pharmacological (drugs), or psychological state of the individual. These results have been replicated many times. One odd fact is that even social situations have been shown to affect pain thresholds (Craig, 1978).

Whether two pains are the same or different in intensity can be discriminated, indicating that there is also a meaningful difference threshold for pain. The first good measurement of the difference threshold was done by Hardy, Wolff, and Goodell (1947) using a modification of the dolorimeter. To accomplish this the authors subjected themselves to both a large amount of pain and considerable tissue damage. They even moved the site of the painful stimulation from the forehead to the forearm because the latter was more easily cared for when blistered by the pain stimuli. These rather extreme measures resulted in some very important results. Hardy and colleagues (1947) found that the difference threshold is reproducible under constant conditions. Moreover, they also found that the Weber fraction remains remarkably constant (as Weber's law would assert) at about 0.04 (a mere 4% stimulus change) over quite a large range of pain intensities. This indicates that we are quite sensitive to variations in pain intensity. Weber fractions increase dramatically at only the highest stimulus intensities. At the extremes, however, the data were not very reliable because the skin damage being sustained made it difficult for the author/observers to concentrate on the pain intensities. More recently, signal detection theory has been successfully applied to the study of pain discrimination, although great care must be taken in doing this (e.g., Irwin et al., 1994).

Hardy and colleagues (1947) also created the first scale of pain intensity. Because they had established the validity of Weber's law for pain, they merely added up **jnds,** as Fechner had done (Chapter 2), to create the **dol scale** based on the discriminability of painful stimuli. Later scales of pain intensity have been created by more direct methods (see Gracely & Naliboff, 1996). Magnitude estimations of the intensity of pain produced by electric shocks follow a power function with an exponent between 2 and 3.5, making this the sensory modality with the largest power function exponent for any sensory modality (Algom & Lubel, 1994, Rollman & Harris, 1987). The exponent varies as a function of the nature of the pain stimulus and again we find that the social context in which the pain is measured makes a difference (e.g., Craig, Best, & Ward, 1975).

An interesting aspect of pain perception is that pain experience from different sources can add together to produce a higher intensity of experienced pain than either one alone. This is true both within modalities and across modalities. Thus, noxious stimulation of two teeth at the same time lowers the pain threshold compared to stimulating a single tooth and turns mild discomfort into pain (Brown, Beeler, Kloka, & Fields, 1985). Also, pain from shock and loud noise experienced together is roughly the linear sum of the pains experienced separately (Algom, Raphaeli, & Cohen-Raz, 1986).

Does pain adapt? In 1939, Dallenbach demonstrated that pain caused by needles, heat, and cold does indeed adapt. Heat-induced pain has been studied by having observers judge the degree of experienced pain as they sat with their hands in hot water over a period of time (Hardy, Stolwijk, & Hoffman, 1968). As can be seen from Figure 7.18, adaptation was complete for the lower

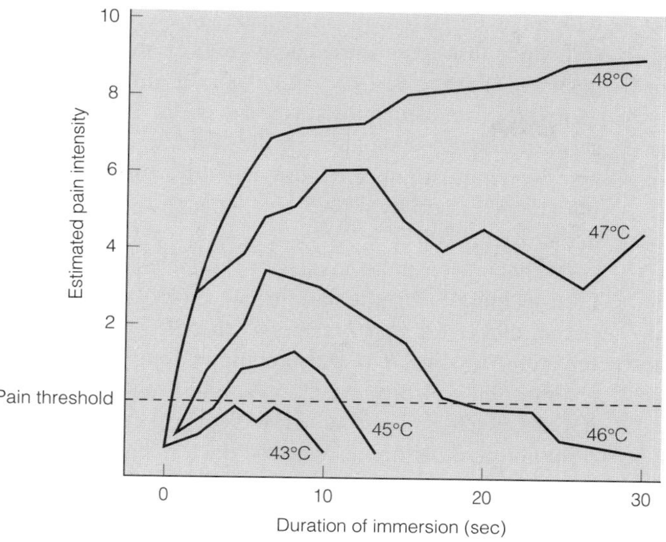

FIGURE 7.18 Average estimations of pain intensity from hot water immersions of different temperatures at different durations.

temperature pain stimuli, which were only mildly painful, and less complete for the more painful stimuli. Adaptation may not take place at all for extremely painful stimuli, although it has been shown that even dental pain adapts (Ernst, Lee, Dworkin, & Zaretsky, 1986). Demonstration Box 7.11 allows you to experience pain adaptation, but be careful—that water is hot!

Analgesia and Endogenous Opiates

Because pain is unpleasant, we seek to minimize it. Yet, pain often persists or may occur for the first time well after a damaging stimulus is gone. As we already mentioned, pain sensations are designed to induce individuals to remain relatively immobile, which aids healing. However, modern humans are not content to accept this immobilizing pain, nor do they desire to experience the pain from surgery or illness. Thus, we have assembled an impressive array of **analgesics** (which reduce pain but not the detection of touch, cold, and warmth) and **anesthetics** (which eliminate all sensations and may even result in unconsciousness) to rid ourselves of pain. The major focus of much pain research is to discover new ways to get rid of pain (e.g., Scholz & Woolf, 2002). The most potent and reliable method of pain relief is to ingest (for example, aspirin) or inject (for example, novocaine) chemicals into our bodies. We also apply sprays or salves to cut or burned skin to achieve local anesthesia. For more severe pain we resort to narcotic drugs (such as morphine, an opium derivative) or opt for unconsciousness (as with ether or chloroform).

DEMONSTRATION BOX 7.11

PAIN ADAPTATION

All you need for this demonstration is a fairly hot water bath, hot enough to cause mild pain but not hot enough to burn your skin. A pan or bowl of water at about 46°C would be ideal. You can make such a bath by mixing hot and cold tap water. Assuming your average cold tap water is about 10°C and the average hot is about 60°C, it would take about 1 cup of cold water and 3 cups of hot water. Alternatively, you could measure with a meat thermometer, or simply add cold water to the hot until you get a mildly painful sensation when you immerse your finger in the bath.

When you have your bath of water, immediately immerse a finger in it and pay attention to the intensity of the painful sensation. It should begin to diminish after about 5 to 10 seconds and may vanish entirely after about 20 seconds. Now place a finger from your other hand into the bath. The sensation of pain you experience on that finger is evidence that adaptation to the pain has taken place, rather than a disappearance of pain because the water cooled down.

It was while studying how opium-based drugs like morphine produce analgesia that researchers discovered **endogenous opiates** (opium-like chemicals that generated from within). These chemicals, interact with specific receptors in the brain to produce analgesic effects (Kosterlitz & McKnight, 1981). At least two major classes of internally generated chemicals, the **enkephalins** and the **endorphins,** have significant analgesic effects and seem to react with the same sites that opium based drugs do (e.g., Yaksh, 1984). When administered via injection, the endorphins have more potent and longer lasting effects. The opium-like action of these endogenous substances is further demonstrated by the fact that their analgesic effect can be blocked by the administration of **naloxone,** a chemical that blocks the action of opiates such as morphine and heroin and is often administered to those who have taken overdoses. Administration of naloxone by itself makes people who are under stress more sensitive to pain, presumably because it blocks the effectiveness of endogenous opiates released naturally under these circumstances (Schull, Kaplan, & O'Brien, 1981).

Our conscious experience of pain intensity is affected not only by the magnitude of the pain stimulus but also by concentrations of these "chemical regulators," which are generated internally and act directly on specific areas of the central nervous system. Study of endogenous opiate systems may also provide clues to the mechanisms involved in nonchemical methods for the reduction of pain. For example, Willer, Dehen, and Cambier (1981) found that the psychological stress caused by the anticipation of a painful shock resulted in analgesic effects. Presumably the stress triggered the endogenous opiate system to protect the individual from the expected pain (see also Lewis, Terman, Shavit, Nelson, & Liebeskind, 1984). Similarly, women during the last 2 weeks of pregnancy experience significant increases in pain thresholds, which reduces their discomfort (Cogan & Spinnato, 1986). This is not confined to humans. Pregnant rats also experience the same threshold increases, and this effect is reduced by injection of opiate antagonist chemicals (Gintzler, 1980).

The endogenous opiate system may also be involved in some of the more "mysterious" reports of reduced pain sensitivity. Take the case of placebo effects, such as the pain reduction people experience when they take a pill that they think is an analgesic but is really an inert substance. These effects are sometimes reversible by naloxone, suggesting that an endogenous opiate system is involved. Recently, it was shown that naloxone blocks the "open injection" effect in which visible injections with a needle give more analgesia than hidden injections (infusions through a intravenous line) of an opioid analgesic (Petrovic, Kalso, Petersson, & Ingvar, 2002). Moreover, neuroimaging evidence from a PET study showed that the same areas of the brain, in particular the anterior cingulate nucleus, are activated both by an opioid analgesic and by a placebo (Amanzio, Pollo, Maggi, & Benedetti, 2001).

Perhaps even more mysterious is the traditional Chinese technique for alleviating pain called **acupuncture** (from the Latin *acus* meaning "needle" and *pungere* meaning "to sting"). In this technique, long, thin needles are inserted at various sites on the body. These needles may be twirled, heated, or have electrical current passed through them. Although Western doctors have been cautious about accepting acupuncture as a valid means of reducing pain, many studies support its effectiveness (Mamtani & Cimino, 2002). Many studies have now established that pain reduction achieved through acupuncture is mediated by release of endogenous opiates (e.g., He, 1987).

The brain-chemical interaction we have been discussing provides only an incomplete picture of the factors influencing our perception of pain. For instance, many forms of pain reduction, such as that achieved via hypnosis, do *not* appear to be mediated by endogenous opiates (e.g., Kosterlitz & McKnight, 1981). It seems that humans have at least two pain control systems, and only one of them involves endogenous opiates (e.g., Akil & Watson, 1980).

Some of the most interesting analgesic procedures involve cognitive processes. These include such techniques as suggestion, attitude, concentration of attention, and social modeling (e.g., Wolff & Goodell, 1943). The efficacy and interpretation of these techniques vary, but there is no doubt that they result in dramatic changes in pain thresholds. For instance, social modeling, where observers see another person's reactions to painful stimuli before judging the painfulness of the same stimuli for themselves, has been reported to affect both d' (Craig & Coren, 1975) and physiological reactivity to painful electric shocks (Craig & Prkachin, 1978). Similarly, when people are attending to a stimulus modality that is different from the one in which a painful stimulus is presented, they experience significantly less pain and can less accurately and quickly discriminate levels of the painful stimulus (Miron, Duncan, & Bushnell, 1989).

The perception of pain involves several different mechanisms. These mechanisms may be integrated within the gate-control theory of pain that we discussed earlier. According to this theory, pain is experienced when the T cells are firing at a high enough rate. The theory describes a spinal gate controlled not only by fast- and slow-conducting sensory fibers but also, as we noted earlier, by inputs from higher levels of the nervous system. Thus, cognitive factors, motivational states, attentional factors, or other stimulation, such as high-intensity hissing noises, electricity, or music, could all be responsible for controlling the gate via the pathway **descending** from the brain to the spinal cord gate (e.g., Light, 1992). These descending pathways seem to be strongly implicated in analgesia caused by release of endogenous opiates. Perhaps activation of the descending pathways causes release of endogenous opiates into the spinal cord, thus decreasing firing of the T cells (Watkins & Mayer, 1982). However, the mechanism involving the substantia gelatinosa does **not** seem to use endogenous opiates to produce its effects.

STUDY QUESTIONS

1. What are the six major types of tastes and how is each transduced?
2. What kind of code does the brain use to represent different tastes?
3. What effects can tasting one tastant have on the taste of another?
4. Describe how odorants cause activity in the olfactory nerve.
5. Why is some animals' sense of smell so much more acute than others'?
6. Describe the role that pheromones play in human behavior.
7. Describe the four types of touch receptors both anatomically and in terms of what each is specialized to respond to.
8. What are the differences and similarities between neural fibers that signal touch and those that signal pain?
9. Describe the gate control theory of pain modulation.
10. What role do endorphins play in pain regulation?

CHAPTER 8

PATTERNS AND EDGES

CHAPTER SUMMARY

If I analyzed the stimuli reaching me this moment in my office, a photometer might tell me that there are about 241 distinct light intensity levels, and a colorimeter might register the presence of 672 different wavelengths of light, which combine in different ways to make up 8184 different discriminable colors. These different intensities and hues are arranged in over a million different regions in space in front of me, and these regions each have some sort of boundaries with their neighbors, thus causing tens of millions of abrupt, visible stimulus changes. But when I look at my office, do I see hundreds of brightness levels, thousands of colors, or millions of unique stimulus changes distributed over space? No, I see a simple scene, containing my computer, with a page of text on monitor's screen, a few books scattered across the desk, with more on the shelves above it, and to my right I see my youngest puppy curled up asleep.

At the simplest level one could say that my perception is organized into meaningful patterns rather than consisting of a clutter of undifferentiated individual stimuli. What is truly astonishing is the way in which this organization comes about. It is effortless, automatic, and fails to astonish the person actually doing the perceiving. To understand this all a bit better, look at Figure 8.1. You probably have no difficulty recognizing the fact that although the drawing is incomplete, it depicts a scene with two dogs looking at a seated cat. Most of you can probably even make a guess as to the likely breeds of the dogs. However there are no dogs or cats present in this stimu-

FIGURE 8.1 The perceptual system automatically, and without any sense of effort, organizes and integrates these 33 black blobs into 3 meaningful figures.

lus. There are simply 33 black blotches on a white background. What you see as the German-Shepherd-type dog on the left is actually just a group of 11 black blotches, the Poodle on the right is just 11 different blotches, and the cat in the middle is made up of the remaining 11 black blotches.

The more closely you consider this pattern, the more amazing your perception of it appears to be. Why do you see three shapes not 33? Why are they organized the way they are? Look at the bottom of what appears to be the German Shepherd's mouth and note its distance from the cat's ear. The lower part of the mouth and the ear are seen as parts of two different figures. Yet that gap is actually a bit smaller than the gap between the upper and lower part of the cat's chest, which are seen as belonging to one figure. Similarly, the bottom of the Poodle's front feet is closer to the cat's tail than is the lower segment of that tail, yet in perception both pieces of the tail are part of the same figure and different from the figure we see as the Poodle. How we organize our world into figures and patterns is the question we will deal with in this chapter. Later on, after we have learned about how we interpret depth and distance into our perception (Chapter 9), we can turn to the issue of how we see objects and scenes (Chapter 10).

CONTOUR PERCEPTION

The fundamental building block for any visual pattern is the contour. Four fundamental characteristics of light are important to vision: intensity, wavelength, and the distribution of light over space and over time. **Contours** or "edges" could be defined technically as sudden changes in light intensity across space. A visual system that is sensitive to spatial changes in intensity has the basic equipment necessary to perceive spatial structure and hence contours.

At the most basic level, the visual system seems to divide the visual field into regions of relatively uniform brightness (Palmer & Rock, 1994), which are commonly referred to as **shapes.** Shapes are separated from the background, or from other shapes, by contours. A **first-order contour** is a region in the retinal image where the light intensity (or wavelength composition) changes abruptly. The central rectangle in Figure 8.2A is an example of a luminance contour, defined by light intensity differences (but it could have been a color difference). Examples of first-order contours in the everyday world can be found at the edge of a blackboard, the outline of the moon against the night sky, and the silhouette of a person. Note that a black line on a sheet of white paper,

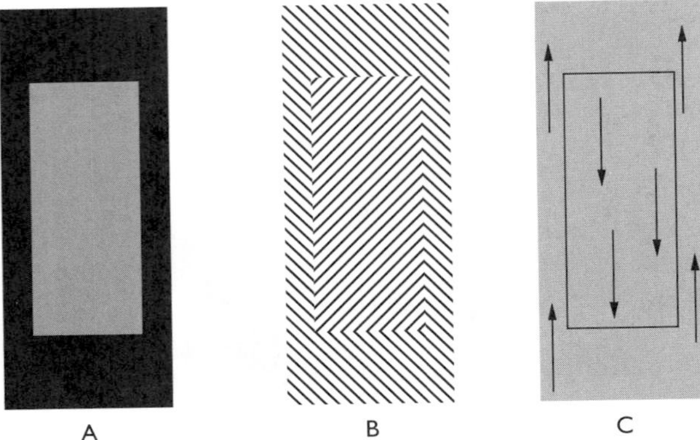

FIGURE 8.2 A is an example of a first-order contour based on luminance. B is a second-order contour based on line orientation, while C illustrates another second-order contour that would emerge if the central rectangle of texture pattern was moving down and the outside moving up.

strictly speaking, consists of two contours: one where the white paper changes to black line and another where the black line changes back to white paper. The artistic convention of using a line on a flat surface to represent an edge in the real world seems to be based on a very primitive perceptual tendency to interpret lines as contours.

There are other classes of contours, however, and these are dependent on the way in which we perceptually organize the visual field. Figure 8.2B shows a central rectangle, which does not depend on luminance or wavelength characteristics but occurs simply because of the texture differences (here in line orientations) in different parts of the field. It appears to be bounded by contours that define it, but these contours are not physically there, they are **emergent** or **second-order contours** that are constructed by the perceptual system from the first-order contours that *are* present. For this reason they are often referred to as **subjective contours.** Subjective contours can come about in many ways, such as in Figure 8.2C, which attempts to illustrate the fact that if different regions of the visual field were moving in different directions or at different speeds, such as a rectangular section of the field with the texture elements moving downward while the rest of the field has the elements moving upward, you would see a subjectively contoured rectangle in the region where we have drawn in the lines here. Second-order contours can also come about because of depth cue that add the third dimension to our world, as you will see in the next chapter.

As we saw in Chapter 3, the visual cortex is really tuned for detecting first order contours, since the orientation specific cells in V1 are activated by luminance or color differences. These "edge detection" or "line detection" cells signal the presence of a contour, and the variously oriented contours are then pieced together in higher regions of the cortex to form the shapes and patterns that this chapter is concerned with.

Contours are the basic building blocks of visual perception; in their absence we actually lose our ability to see. We can demonstrate this by looking into a **Ganzfeld** (German for "whole field"). A Ganzfeld is a visual field that contains no abrupt luminance changes and thus no contours. When observers look into a Ganzfeld, they usually report seeing "a shapeless fog that goes on forever." Any hint of color soon fades to gray, even if the entire field is illuminated with, say, green or blue or red light (Cohen, 1958). Many observers even experience perceptual **blank out,** a feeling that they *can't see,* after prolonged viewing, but this is not attributable to any loss in the ability of the individuals to detect changes in luminance if they do occur (e.g., Knau, 2000). This subjective feeling of blindness disappears, and the sense of seeing returns, the instant any kind of luminance change, flicker or local brightness difference is introduced into the visual field (Avant, 1965).

Blank out can occur in natural environments as well. For instance, **snow blindness** is a kind of natural blank out, caused by the lack of contour in the retinal image when the visual field contains a lot of snow and ice, and it affects around 3% of climbers on snow-covered mountains (Basnyat & Litch, 1997). The snow and ice scatter much of the light in all directions and together are often very uniform in texture, which creates a kind of natural Ganzfeld. You can experience some of these sensations for yourself by trying Demonstration Box 8.1.

VISUAL ACUITY

Contours define the shapes we see and details that distinguish one shape from another. Obviously, if the details are very small or the stimulus changes that define the contour are not very large, they will be difficult to see. **Visual acuity** refers to the ability of the eye to resolve details. There are different types of visual acuity, each dependent on the specific task or specific detail to be resolved. The type of visual acuity most commonly measured is **recognition acuity,** which was introduced by Herman Snellen (1862). He created the familiar eye chart found in most ophthalmologists' or optometrists' offices, consisting of rows of letters of progressively smaller size. The observer is asked simply to identify the

DEMONSTRATION BOX 8.1

THE GANZFELD

Although Ganzfeld situations have been produced with elaborate laboratory equipment, there are several simple ways to produce a Ganzfeld that will allow you to experience this contourless field for yourself. You can take a table tennis ball and cut it in half, placing one half over each eye, or you can use two white plastic spoons (like those probably available in any campus cafeteria) to produce a Ganzfeld by placing the bowl of a spoon over each eye as shown in the accompanying figure. Direct your gaze toward a light source (a fluorescent lamp, say) prior to placing the objects before your eyes so that your field of view will be flooded with diffuse, contourless light. Stay in this position for a few minutes and monitor any changes or alterations in your conscious perceptual experience. If the light originally had a tint, you will soon notice that the color will fade into a gray. After a while you will suddenly feel that you cannot see. This feeling of blindness is called **blank out.** It seems that in the absence of contours in the field, vision ceases. If a friend now casts a shadow over part of the field (say, with a pencil across the spoons), vision will immediately return with the introduction of this contour.

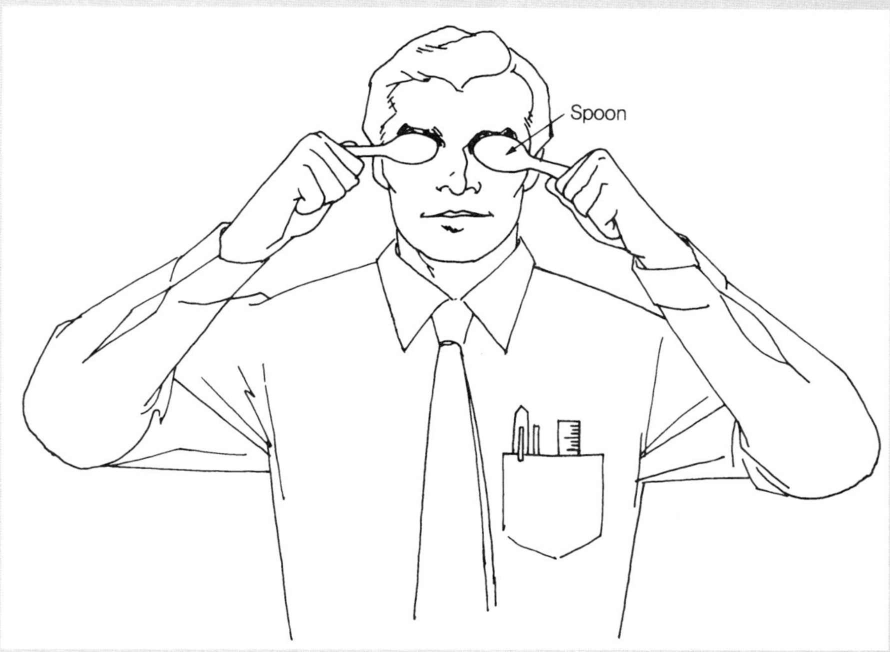

letters on the chart, and the size of the smallest letters identified determines acuity. Acuity is usually measured relative to the performance of a normal observer. The usual means of reporting it is a fraction where the numerator indicates the test distance and the denominator indicates the distance at which a normal observer can correctly identify the test item. Thus, an acuity of 6/6 indicates that an observer is able to identify letters from a distance of 6 meters that a normal observer can also read from 6 meters, which means that his acuity is normal. You may be more familiar with the designation 20/20—6 m is equivalent to 20 ft. An acuity of 6/9 (or 20/30) would mean that an observer is able to read letters from 6 m that are large enough for a normal observer to read from a distance of 9 m. Here, the visual acuity is somewhat less than normal. The big E at the top of the standard acuity chart represents 6/60 or 20/200.

A more general means of specifying the limits of acuity is to use the minimum **visual angle** of a detail that can be resolved. The visual angle is a measure of the size of the retinal image. Figure 8.3 shows what is meant by visual angle and demonstrates a simple computation

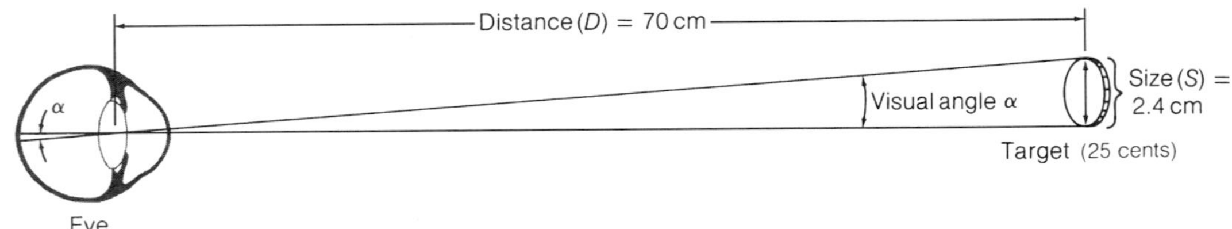

FIGURE 8.3 Computation of the visual angle of the image of a quarter viewed a distance of 70 cm (approximately arm's length), where the observer's line of sight is perpendicular to the lower edge of the coin. Tangent of visual angle α = size/distance; therefore, tan $\alpha = S/D = 2.4/70 = 0.034$. Thus, α is approximately 2°.

based on the size and the distance of the object. Generally speaking, a normal observer can reliably resolve details of 1 min of arc (1/60 of a degree; about the size of a quarter seen at a distance of 81 m, which is nearly the length of a football field), although different tasks often produce different limits of acuity (Beck & Schwartz, 1979).

The identification of letters on a Snellen chart is not the best way to measure acuity because letters differ in their degree of identifiability. For instance, O and Q and P and F are letter pairs that are easily confused, whereas L and W and O and I are easy to discriminate. Because these differences might affect acuity measurements, E. Landolt (1889) introduced a different recognition task that used circles with a gap in them as targets (see Figure 8.4). The gap can be oriented either up, down, to the right, or to the left, and the observer's task is to indicate the position of the gap. The circles differ in size, and the smallest detectable gap is the measure of acuity.

Several other tasks are used to measure visual acuity (see Zadnik, 1997). The most primitive measure of acuity is the specification of the smallest target of any type that can be detected. The relationship between brightness perception and the acuity task is most apparent for this task where the target is a light line or spot against a dark background or a dark line or spot against a light background. **Vernier** or **directional acuity** requires an observer to distinguish a broken line from an unbroken line. **Resolution** or **grating acuity** is measured by an observer's ability to detect a gap between two bars or the orientation of a grid of lines. This particular form of acuity task has certain theoretical implications, which we will discuss in the next section. Figure 8.4 shows examples of the previously mentioned acuity targets with arrows pointing to the crucial detail. Notice that each detail is merely a region of the visual field where there is a change in luminance.

It is even possible to estimate people's visual acuity without using any visual targets by simply asking them about their everyday experiences in viewing the world. Because we normally use both eyes and our ability to see a detail will depend on the eye with the better acuity, such an estimate will really be of our "best eye" acuity. Coren and Hakstian (1989) developed a self-report acuity screening inventory that correlates 0.83 with laboratory measures of best-eye visual acuity. You can test yourself with it, using Demonstration Box 8.2.

It is reasonable to expect that the minimum resolvable detail would be determined by the size of the retinal receptors or the size of the retinal receptive fields. Thus, in order to distinguish whether one or two spots of light are present, it might be expected that it would be necessary to have at least one unstimulated retinal receptor (or receptive field) between two light-stimulated retinal receptors (or receptive fields). Surprisingly, for tasks such as vernier acuity, people can resolve much finer details than

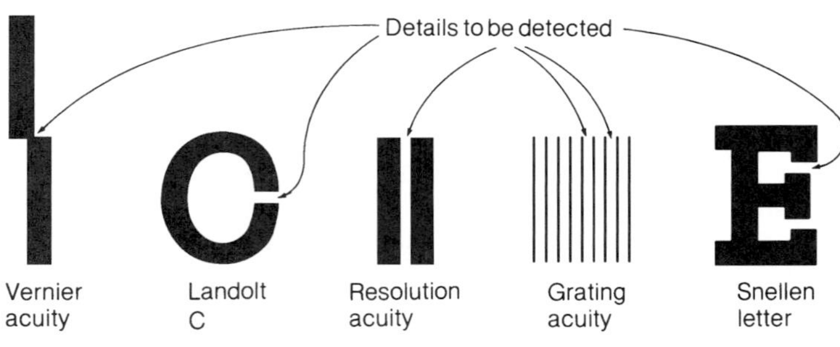

FIGURE 8.4 Some typical acuity targets and the details to be discriminated.

DEMONSTRATION BOX 8.2

ACUITY SCREENING INVENTORY

To get an estimate of your own best-eye visual acuity, simply take this test, which is the Acuity Screening Inventory* developed by Coren and Hakstian (1989). The questionnaire deals with a number of common visual situations. For each question you should select the response that best describes you and your behaviors. You can select from among the following response alternatives: Never (or almost never), Seldom, Occasionally, Frequently, Always (or almost always). Simply circle the letter that corresponds to the first letter of your choice.

1. Do you find most book print too small to read easily without glasses or contact lenses? N S O F A
2. Can you recognize people if you see them at a distance when you are not wearing any corrective lenses? N S O F A
3. Do you notice that far objects appear fuzzy when you are not wearing glasses or contact lenses? N S O F A
4. Do you notice that near objects appear fuzzy when you are not wearing glasses or contact lenses? N S O F A
5. Do you wear glasses or contact lenses? N S O F A
6. Can you read easily in dim light without any corrective lenses? N S O F A
7. Do you think that you may need glasses? N S O F A
8. Would you say that your vision is as good as most people's? N S O F A

Answer the following two questions using Good, Average, Slightly below average, Poor, Very poor (circle the first letter corresponding to your choice).

9. Without glasses or contact lenses, the clearness or sharpness of vision in my right eye is G A S P V
10. Without glasses or contact lenses, the clearness or sharpness of vision in my left eye is G A S P V

Scoring instructions:

For Questions 1, 3, 4, 5, and 7, responses are scored from 1 for "Never," 2 for "Seldom," 3 for "Occasionally," 4 for "Frequently," and 5 for "Always." For Questions 2, 6, and 8, reverse the scoring so that responses are scored from 1 for "Always" up to 5 for "Never." For Questions 9 and 10, scoring goes from 1 for "Good" to 5 for "Very Poor." Your acuity score is just the sum of these 10 items. Now just check the following table for your predicted Snellen acuity score (this prediction should be plus or minus one line on the eye chart).

ASI SCALE TOTAL	PREDICTED BEST-EYE SNELLEN ACUITY
10 to 18	20/20 (or better)
19 to 25	20/30
26 to 32	20/40
33 to 38	20/60
39 to 50	20/100 (or worse)

*The Acuity Screening Inventory is copyrighted to SC Psychological Enterprises and is reprinted with permission.

might be expected on the basis of these considerations. Under optimal conditions, acuities of 5 sec (one second of arc is 1/3600 of a degree) or less are possible, despite the fact that the smallest receptive fields are around 25 times larger than this (Klein & Levi, 1985). In fact, this is about one sixth the diameter of the smallest retinal cones. Resolution of details less than about 10 sec is often referred to as **hyperacuity** (Westheimer, 1979) because visual performance seems to have gone beyond the resolution imposed by the physical size of the receptors. Some theorists explain this paradox by proposing models of complex neural circuitry and statistical pooling of neural responses (Skottun, 2000; Wilson, 1986). Others believe that the responses of single cells can account for hyperacuity but that these cells are higher up in the chain of processing than ganglion cells are. For instance, there is electrophysiological evidence that a vernier stimulus (like the broken line in Figure 8.4) excites a different orientation-tuned simple cell in the primary visual cortex (see Chapter 3) than does a line without the break (Swindale & Cynader, 1986). This would suggest that hyperacuity might exist because high-level cells are specifically tuned to particular "acuity details," like gaps, breaks, or offsets. Because vernier acuity is so sensitive, it has been suggested that the patterns of "range lights" or "leading lights" that are used to assist the navigation of ships would be more effective if the lights appeared as line segments, rather than as points of light on the navigational towers (Coren, Whitehead, Baca, & Patten, 1995).

Factors Affecting Visual Acuity

Because acuity tasks are closely related to brightness discrimination, it is not surprising to find that acuity varies as a function of the many factors shown to be important in the perception of brightness including color and intensity of the targets (Ruttiger & Lee, 2000). Another example of this relationship is illustrated by the fact that the adaptive state of the eye determines the minimum details that can be discriminated under particular viewing conditions (Howard, Tregear, & Werner, 2000; Lie, 1980). Thus, if you step out of the bright sunlight into a dim room, you may find it impossible to read even the large type of the headlines of a newspaper for a few moments. As your eyes adapt to the dim surroundings, however, you can soon easily read even fine print. Even a brief flash of light, bright enough to alter an observer's state of adaptation, markedly reduces an observer's ability to detect and recognize acuity targets.

The detection of details in acuity targets also shows an interaction between time and stimulus intensity, very much like that described by Bloch's law for brightness detection. This means that we can increase the likelihood that a detail will be detected either by increasing the difference between the intensity of the target and that of its background or by increasing the amount of time that the observer views the stimulus (e.g., Ridder, McCulloch, & Herbert, 1998). Although Bloch's law holds only for times less than 100 milliseconds (ms) for brightness detection, the tradeoff between time and intensity holds for up to 300 ms in acuity tasks in which observers are trying to detect pattern details (Kahneman, Norman, & Kubovy, 1967).

Retinal position is also as important for acuity as it is for brightness perception (Levi, McGraw, & Klein, 2000). The figure in Demonstration Box 8.3 allows you to experience the drastic reductions in visual acuity for targets that are imaged some distance from the fovea. When we measure relative acuity for various locations on the retina, we find that it varies as shown in Figure 8.5. Notice that acuity is best in the central fovea and drops off rapidly as we move into the periphery. This curve looks remarkably like the distribution of cones across the retina diagrammed in Figure 3.9. It also looks much like the distribution of parvo ganglion cells in the retina (Wandell, 1995). Direct physiological measurement of the responsiveness of parvo and magno cells shows that parvo cells have smaller receptive fields and sustain their responses to stationary stimuli. This has led several researchers to suggest that the limits of visual acuity are set by the prevalence of parvo cells, or cells with characteristics similar to parvo cells, which are best designed for detection and analysis of small details in stationary visual arrays (e.g., Palmer, 1999).

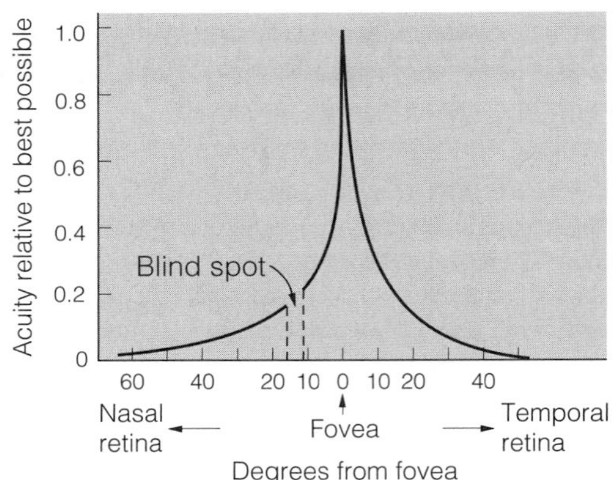

FIGURE 8.5 The distribution of visual acuity across the retina.

The part of the retina that is highest in visual acuity contains mostly cones, which send their signals to parvo ganglion cells. Because cones operate only at high levels

DEMONSTRATION BOX 8.3

VISUAL ACUITY AS A FUNCTION OF RETINAL LOCATION

Visual acuity is best in the fovea. The range of clear vision extends less than 10° away from the foveal center. Lay this book flat on the table and view the accompanying diagram from a distance of approximately 12 cm. Cover your left eye with your left hand and look directly at the point marked "0." Without moving your right eye, you will note that the letter over the 0 mark is relatively clear and that the letter at 5° is also legible. However, the letters at 10° and beyond begin to appear fuzzy, and the letters at 40° and 50° are virtually unreadable.

K	B	X	M	P	A	S
+	+	+	+	+	+	+
50°	40°	30°	20°	10°	5°	0°

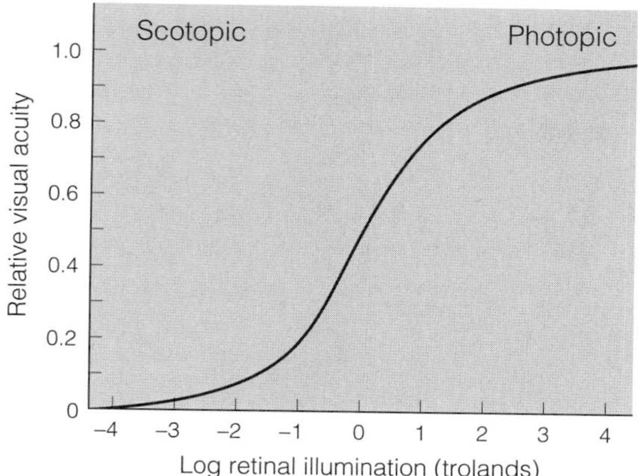

FIGURE 8.6 The effect of illumination on visual acuity.

of illumination, we could then predict that there would be better acuity at high illumination levels. When we measure the relationship between acuity and illumination directly, we obtain the curve shown in Figure 8.6. Notice that when the illumination is low, in the scotopic (rod) range, acuity is poor, and it improves only slightly as the light intensity is increased. However, as we begin to shift into the photopic (cone) range, acuity improves rapidly. Of course, at too high a light level the acuity is reduced again because of the effects of glare (not shown).

One aspect of the relationship between acuity and illumination has important implications for some common situations. In 1789 Lord Maskelyne, director of the Royal Greenwich Observatory, noticed that he became noticeably nearsighted at night. This tendency to accommodate the eye inappropriately near, even when the object of interest is far away, is called **night myopia** (Leibowitz, Post, Brandt, & Dichgans, 1982). One of the contributing factors is the fact that the pupil is usually quite dilated under dim lighting conditions, contributing to the amount of light scatter in the eye. This degrades the sharpness of the retinal image, interfering with our ability to see details under twilight and nighttime observation conditions. Such an additional reduction of acuity under dim illumination may be an important component in nighttime driving accidents.

SPATIAL FREQUENCY ANALYSIS

A complete description of the relationship between brightness perception and acuity must take into account a great deal of information. Imagine any test pattern of light. Next realize that when this pattern stimulates the eye, there are 125 million or more retinal receptors per eye, each receiving an amount of light ranging from 0 up to many millions of units. Pity the poor perceptual researcher who must now find a method of describing all of this activity (not to mention the poor brain that must interpret the visual pattern that caused it). If we had to analyze every point of light and its intensity before we could see patterns or make statements about brightness perception and acuity, we would have little time left over for other behaviors. Many researchers realized this and began to look for some reasonably small set of relationships among the variables that affect brightness perception that could be used to describe visual arrays, hoping that such a simplified description might yield deeper insight into the way in which visual stimuli are analyzed by the brain.

In some ways, the most successful attempt to summarize brightness and acuity data to date has involved the use of a mathematical technique based on **Fourier's theorem.** In the present context this theorem implies that it is possible to analyze any pattern of stimuli into a series of simpler sine wave patterns. In Chapter 6 we applied the theorem to complex sound waves, in which sound pressure level at some point in space varies over time in an irregular but repeated pattern. For our current problem we are concerned with how light intensity varies across space, namely across the retinal image. According to Fourier's theorem, we can analyze any pattern of light intensity across space into a series of simpler sine wave patterns, each of which would be seen as a regularly varying pattern of light and dark if seen alone.

You might recall from your study of trigonometry that a sine wave is simply a regular, smooth, periodically repeating function that can be precisely specified mathematically. Figure 8.7A shows a graph of a sine wave and beside it a distribution of light that varies in the same way, growing more intense (brighter) where the function rises and less intense where it falls. Such a light distribution is called a **sine wave grating** because the intensity of reflected light from the page varies sinusoidally as we move horizontally across the figure, and the whole pattern forms a sort of blurry grating or grid. When applied to light distributions, Fourier's theorem states that by adding together (scientists call this synthesizing) a number of such gratings we can produce any specified light distribution. Moreover, although individual sine wave patterns have only gradual changes in intensity, by adding many of them together we can produce even light distributions that contain sharp corners, such as that shown in Figure 8.7B. Figure 8.7B is called a **square wave grating** because the light changes are sharp and give a boxlike intensity pattern. Successive addition of the appropriate frequencies of sine waves (or, more accu-

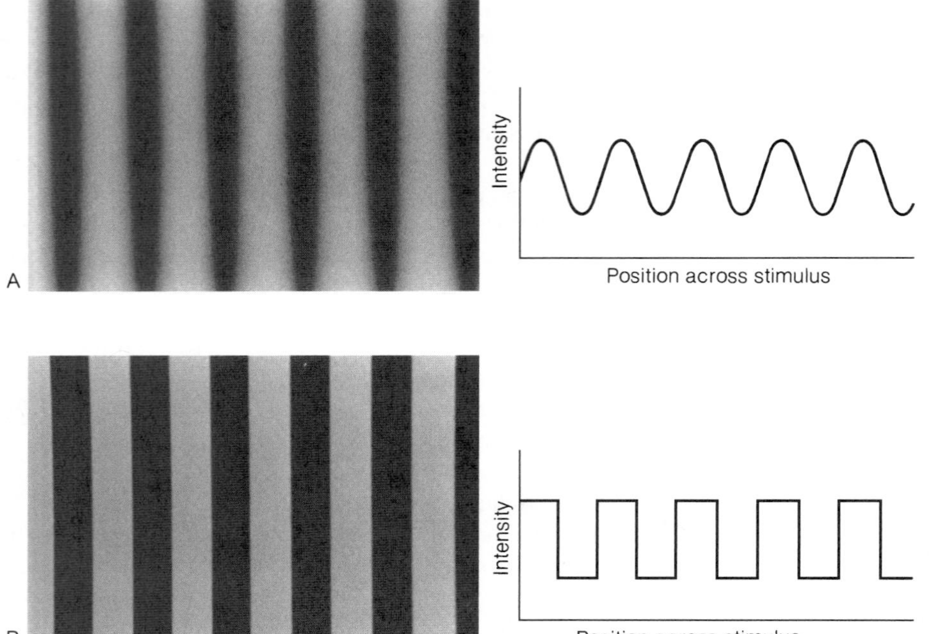

FIGURE 8.7 (A) A sine wave spatial distribution of light and (B) a square wave spatial distribution of light.

rately, the sine wave variations in light intensity that they represent) gradually gives a better and better approximation of the sharp corners of the square wave grating, as can be seen in Figure 8.8.

You might think that adding sine waves can give you only repeating patterns or gratings, such as in Figure 8.7. This is not true. According to the rules of Fourier synthesis any pattern, whether repeating or not, can be created by combining appropriate sine waves. Thus, Figure 8.9 shows a single bright bar on a dark background. Below it are the first few sine wave variations in intensity that would be added to produce the bar. Notice that after only the fourth wave pattern has been added, we have already started to create a single bright feature. Addition of other sine waves will ultimately make the bar sharper.

If we take this approach to describing the patterns of light that act as stimuli to our visual systems, we no longer have to catalog the intensity of every point in the pattern. Now we can describe a light pattern precisely with a relatively compact mathematical expression indi-

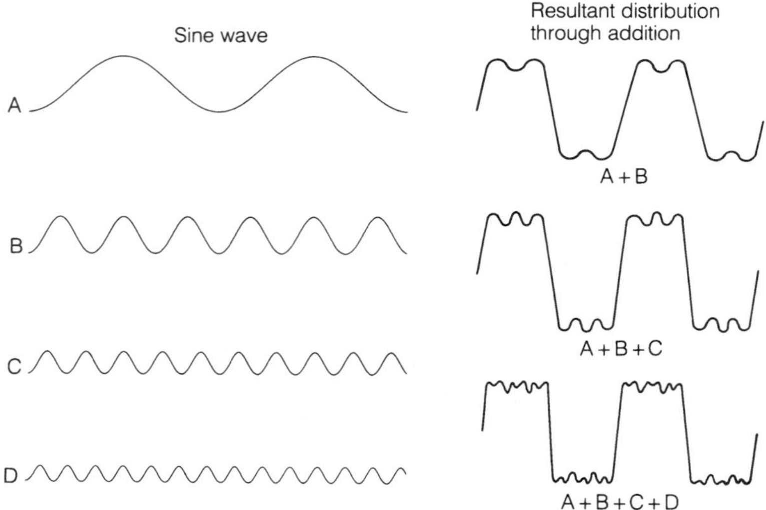

FIGURE 8.8 Gradually adding higher frequency sine waves of lower amplitude to the distribution leads to better approximations of a square wave through the process of Fourier synthesis.

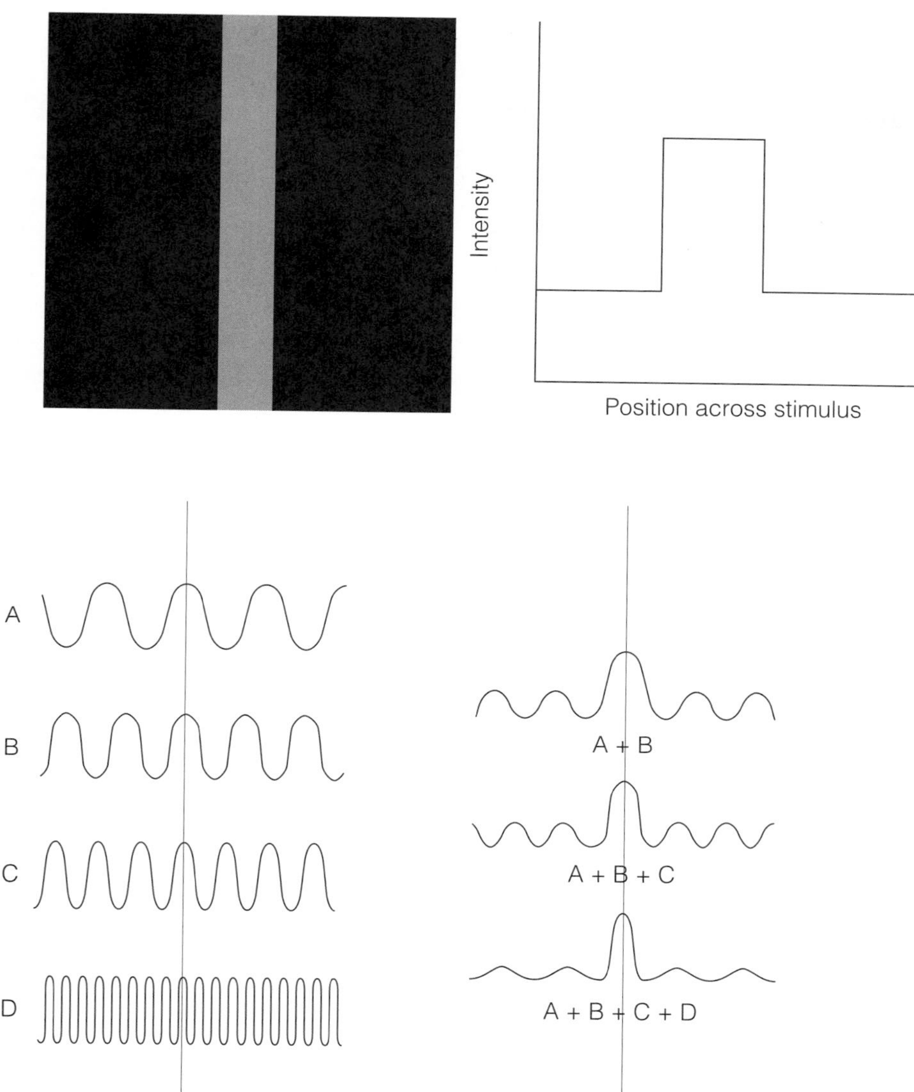

FIGURE 8.9 Gradually adding higher frequency sine waves of the same amplitude to the distribution leads to an approximation of a single bright bar of light.

cating the particular set of sine wave gratings to be added together to reproduce it. Even if the mathematics sometimes becomes complex, the resulting description is still far simpler than a catalog of the light hitting 125 million or more individual retinal receptors. (See Graham, 1989, for a more complete introduction to Fourier analysis of visual patterns.)

Modulation Transfer Function

Fourier analysis (breaking up a pattern into its component sine waves) and Fourier synthesis (adding together a set of sine wave variations to create a more complex pattern) provide more than a simple shorthand for the description of light patterns. They serve as powerful tools that may be used to analyze how the visual system responds to stimuli. Consider for a moment how an optical engineer tests the fidelity of a photographic system (that is, how well the final photo reproduces the actual light variations in the real world). He would start with a simple easily defined set of patterns, such as the gratings shown in Figure 8.10. Some of the gratings will have very broad bars and spaces. In such gratings the light intensity rises and falls slowly as we move across the extent of the pattern; hence they are said to have *low spatial frequencies*. Here frequency simply refers to the

A

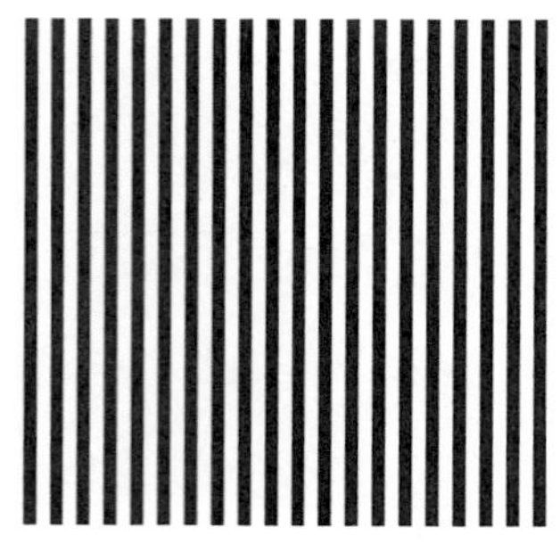
B

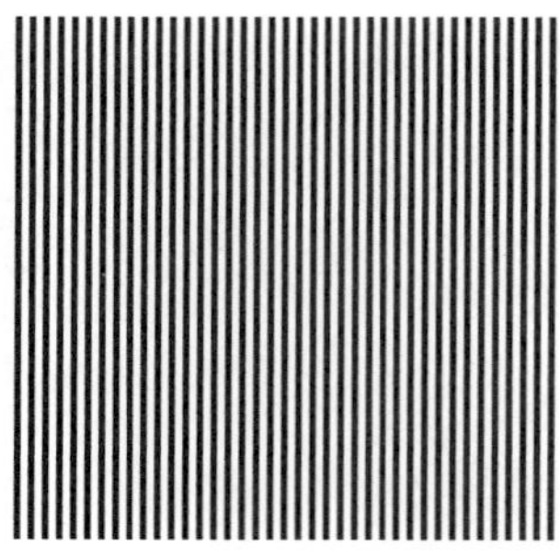
C

FIGURE 8.10 The effect of physical contrast and spatial frequency on the apparent contrast of patterns. A has a smaller physical contrast than B or C. Notice that the higher-frequency pattern (C) has less apparent contrast than the lower frequency pattern (B).

number of times that the light level goes from dark to light and back measured over one degree of visual angle. Other gratings will have narrow bars and spaces. In these gratings the light intensity changes many times as we move across space; hence they are said to have *high spatial frequencies*. The next step is to photograph each grating using the system we are testing and check to see how well each one is reproduced. At some point, when the bars and spaces become quite narrow, the system will reach its resolution limit. At this point the photographic lens can no longer faithfully reproduce the pattern and all of the bars and spaces will merge into a gray blur. We can modify this procedure to measure visual acuity of human observers.

The optical engineer will report his analysis of the fidelity of a system in terms of the maximum number of lines per inch that can be resolved. Typically, very finely spaced arrays of lines cannot be resolved. The final image is therefore blurred, and we would say that the high frequencies are cut off or attenuated. A graphic or mathematical description of the way in which certain spatial frequencies are accurately reproduced while others are lost because the system cannot resolve them is called the **spatial modulation transfer function.** This label indicates that we are looking at how well the luminance changes (technically "modulations") that occur over a fixed measure of space are accurately reproduced or decoded when they are "transferred" or sent through the optical system.

When visual scientists began to adapt this kind of analysis to measure the resolution ability of the eye, they found that one important factor was the **contrast,** which is a measure of the difference between the highest and the lowest luminance levels in the pattern. Actually the most convenient measure is a **contrast ratio,** which is just the difference between maximum and minimum luminance levels divided by some average or pooled estimate of the overall amount of light. The convenient thing about the contrast ratio is that it doesn't change if you uniformly increase or decrease the amount of light falling on an image or a grating (see Walraven, Enroth-Cugell, Hood, McLeod, & Schnapf, 1990, for a more complete discussion of contrast ratios).

Several procedures have been used to assess the visual system's ability to resolve changes in light intensity over space. One procedure, called **contrast matching,** can be used to measure the modulation transfer function in humans. Consider Gratings A and B in Figure 8.10. Although both are square wave gratings, they differ in terms of their physical contrast ratio—Grating A has a smaller contrast ratio than Grating B because the maximum difference in A is between black and midgray, whereas in B it is between the same black and a higher intensity, white region. Now consider the difference between Gratings B and C. Both are square wave gratings, but B has a lower spatial frequency (wider bars) than C. Although the physical contrast is the same for B and C (both are the same black ink with the same white interspaces) they don't look the same. Typically C appears to have less contrast, meaning that black stripes appear a bit lighter and the white stripes a bit darker in C than in B. You can increase this difference by propping the book up and stepping back a foot or two. The reduced contrast in C suggests that the visual system is not doing as good a job in transferring the image from the real world to your consciousness. In a contrast matching task, observers are asked to adjust the intensity of the light and dark regions of such targets (or more usually, sine wave gratings) until they appear to have the same contrast. In this way, we map the differences in visibility of various spatial frequencies.

An alternative method of measuring sensitivity to various spatial frequencies involves measuring the **contrast threshold.** This is the amount of contrast needed for you to detect that there is a grating present in the pattern, rather than a uniform gray. Either of these techniques will give us a representation of how sensitivity changes as we change the spatial frequency of the stimuli. In these ways we can map out the modulation transfer function where the stimulus modulations (or intensity changes in the environment) are being transferred to (detected in) the observer's conscious experience of the pattern.

When we measure a typical modulation transfer function for a human observer, it looks like the solid line shown in Figure 8.11. Notice that the threshold contrast ratio is plotted backward (e.g., with higher contrast thresholds lower on the vertical axis). This is done so that when we look at the figure the height of the curve will represent the observer's sensitivity. Clearly, the curve is highest at around 6 cycles per degree (6 cycles of the sine wave over each degree of visual angle). This means that human observers are most sensitive in this region and we can detect stimuli of around 6 cycles per degree even if the contrast ratio is quite low. Sensitivity decreases rapidly for the higher spatial frequencies, meaning that we need more contrast to see these stimuli. This loss at higher frequencies is probably a result of the fact that the eye is an optical system, containing a lens, and any such system has a high-frequency cutoff. Notice also that there is some loss of resolution in the lower spatial frequencies (less than 6 cycles per degree). This loss results from the fact that as the bars and spaces become wider, lateral inhibition (the same process that produces Mach bands and simultaneous brightness contrast—see Chapter 4) is less effective. Lateral inhibition normally helps to sharpen the neural response to contours. Thus it appears that we are most sensitive to luminance changes when they occur at intermediate spatial frequencies.

The modulation transfer function provides a convenient basis for predicting the apparent brightness of many types of stimulus configurations. Furthermore, as a summary of the spatial frequencies that we can detect at any given contrast level, it serves as a measure of our visual acuity. For instance, if you draw a horizontal line across Figure 8.11 at any contrast level, only the frequencies for which the transfer function curve is above the line will be visible.

Because the modulation transfer function serves as a sort of a summary of our visual acuity and responsiveness to light, we can use it to compare the visual resolution ability of various groups of individuals. For instance, we know that there are changes in the modulation transfer function as we grow older, with a general reduction in sensitivity to higher spatial frequencies. These changes accurately predict not only reductions in visual acuity with age but also changes in certain aspects of our depth perception (stereopsis) measured by other techniques (Greene & Madden, 1987). Figure 8.12

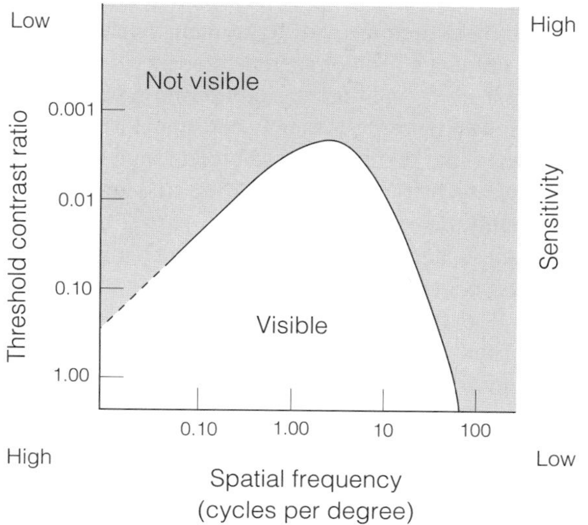

FIGURE 8.11 The modulation transfer function, which shows the relative visibility of targets of various spatial frequencies.

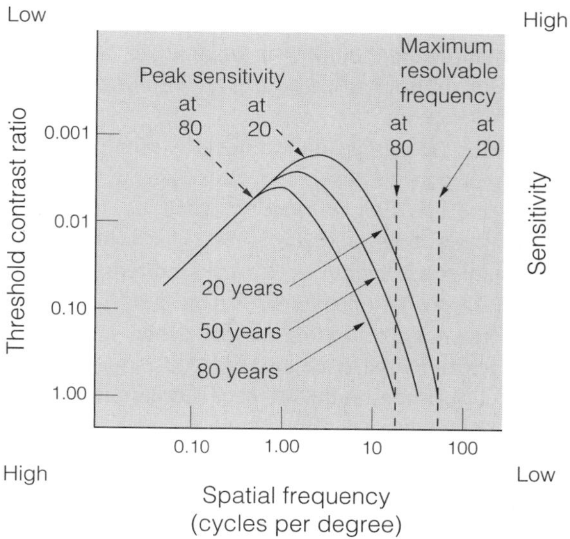

FIGURE 8.12 Changes in the modulation transfer function with age, showing the loss of sensitivity for high spatial frequencies and a general reduction in sensitivity (based on Owsley, Sekuler, & Siemensen, 1983).

shows the modulation transfer functions from groups of 20-, 50-, and 80-year-olds (Owsley, Sekuler, & Siemensen, 1983). Notice that the highest frequency visible steadily drops with age (meaning that smaller details or narrower stripes can't be seen). This might be expected if the optical or focusing ability of the lens was diminishing (see Chapter 15). Notice that the peak sensitivity (the highest point on the curve) is lower with age, indicating that visual responsiveness is lower (needs more contrast to reach threshold). Finally, the peak sensitivity, representing the spatial frequency that would appear to have the greatest contrast, is also shifted toward lower frequencies, suggesting that wider stripes or gratings are relatively more effective stimuli when we are older. All of this acuity and brightness response information, and more, can be derived from comparing modulation transfer functions, which explains the popularity of this method of data presentation.

Neural Spatial Frequency Channels

Imagine an extremely self-assured scientist sitting at his home computer, complete with all of the programs necessary to do Fourier analyses of any light patterns that might happen to be of importance or interest, muttering to himself, "If I find Fourier analysis so useful in analyzing patterns of light, maybe the visual system does, too. Perhaps the visual system is set up to conduct some sort of spatial frequency analysis for any given pattern of light. Certainly, if it did, it would benefit from the same sort of concise description of the incoming light pattern that I obtain and could thus also avoid the separate analysis of millions of responses of millions of individual photoreceptors."

Actually, this suggestion is not as strange as it might seem. At a general level, the first stage of spatial frequency analysis can be accomplished by mechanisms that we know exist and have already discussed. These mechanisms are the circularly organized retinal receptive fields described in Chapter 3. Recall that each of these has an excitatory, or on, region that, when stimulated by light, gives an increase in neural response rate, and an inhibitory, or off, region that gives a decrease in the neural response rate when stimulated by light (and a burst of responses upon the light's termination). Before we discuss how such an arrangement can do a spatial frequency analysis, we must introduce a bit of terminology. Every cycle of a sine wave grating has both a dark and a light phase, as we saw in Figure 8.7. This means that the dark stripe (or the light stripe) would be one half of the sine wave cycle. Now we suggest to you that every circular receptive field is, in effect, "tuned" to a sine wave frequency whose half cycle is equal to the size of its central excitatory or inhibitory region. To visualize this type of structure, consider Figure 8.13.

Suppose that we have an on-center receptive field of the size illustrated in the figure. If the spatial frequency is too low—that is to say, the stripes are too wide—the fields of illumination will fall on both the center and the surround. Even though the central "on" region (+) of the field is stimulated, there is an equal degree of stimulation of the inhibitory surrounding "off" regions (−) of the receptive field so the two types of responses tend to cancel each other out. Thus, the total response of the ganglion cell with this receptive field is low. Now consider the other extreme, where the spatial frequency is very high, and there are many stripes falling across the field. The on and off regions of the field would each be stimulated by about equal proportions of light and dark, again producing little or no net response. Finally, consider a spatial frequency in which the half cycle width is approximately the same as the central region of the receptive field. If the bright stripe now covers the central region of the on-center cell, there will be a vigorous on response. There will be little inhibition from the surrounding off region, which lies mostly in darkness from the dark half of the cycle. Thus, the net response to this grating would be relatively stronger than to any other grating. Notice that the same sort of analysis of spatial frequency can occur in the off-center cell, except that here the optimal response is obtained when the dark half of the cycle is over the central region of the receptive field. Each receptive field is maximally responsive to a specific spatial frequency of light intensity changes.

This crude analysis of spatial frequencies could serve as the first step of a Fourier decomposition of the incoming stimulus pattern if a few additional requirements were met. First, there must be a broad range of receptive field sizes so that "tuning" would be fine enough to approximately determine sufficiently many of the spatial frequencies that make up the pattern. This requirement seems to be easily fulfilled because, as we noted in Chapter 3, parvo and magno cells differ quite a bit in the speed of and nature of their responses. They also differ in their ranges of receptive field size, with parvo cells tuned for higher spatial frequencies than are magno cells (Ellemberg, Hammarrenger, Lepore, Roy, & Guillemot, 2002). Thus, there may be a number of different channels in the visual system, each tuned to a different range of spatial frequencies. There is some evidence that the magnolike low spatial frequency channels interact with, and can inhibit, the parvolike higher spatial frequency

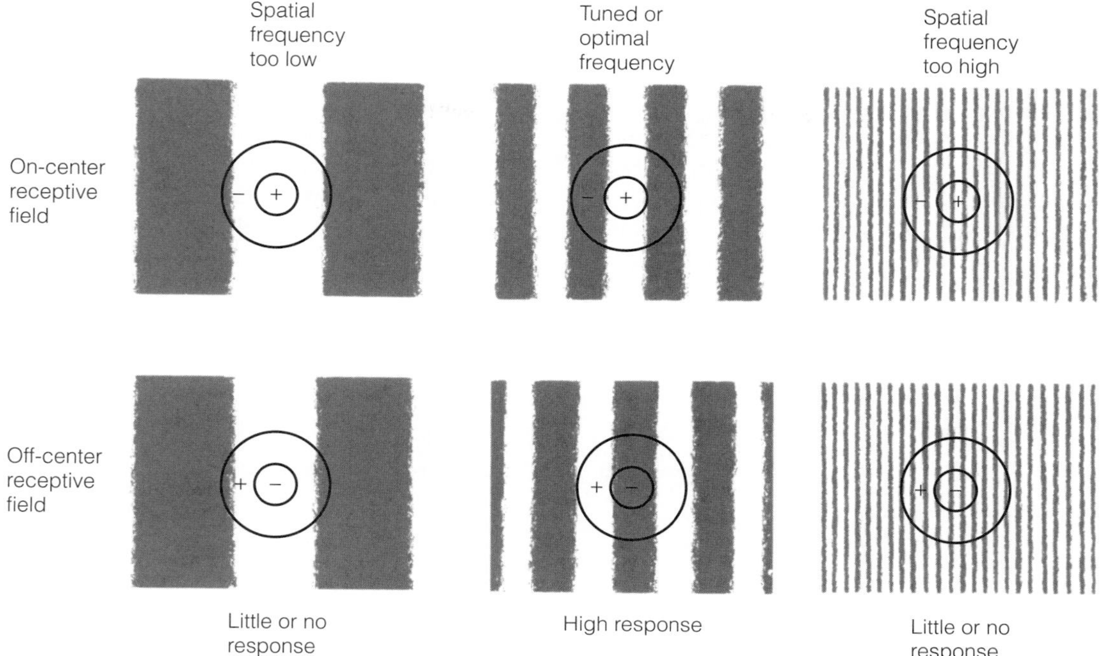

FIGURE 8.13 A demonstration of how a circular receptive field organization of a particular size can perform a crude spatial frequency analysis.

channels (Hughes, 1986; Olzak, 1986). Moreover, a model assuming as few as six such channels (or receptive field sizes) can explain some of the remarkable feats of acuity that people are capable of, namely the hyperacuity we discussed earlier in which resolution ability is better than would be predicted on the basis of the physical size of the retinal receptors (e.g., Skottun, 2000).

Of course, for such Fourier analysis to be of value perceptually, there must be high-level neurons, perhaps in the visual cortex, that preserve the spatial frequency information extracted by the tuned receptive fields of the retinal ganglion cells. There is evidence that such neurons exist in the cortex. These neurons have not only preferred edge orientations to which they respond maximally but also preferred ranges of spatial frequency (DeValois & DeValois, 1987). Although the existence of such neurons does not prove that Fourier analysis occurs in the visual system, it at least suggests that the equipment to perform such an analysis does exist.

Neurons as Spatial Filters

The neural mechanisms that are capable of performing a crude Fourier analysis of the visual image are often referred to as **neural filters.** The term *filter* is used here because these cells are thought to respond by firing most rapidly when a specific visual pattern excites them and to fire much less rapidly to any other patterns. In effect, they are filtering out all but a select set of stimuli and passing on information about only those to which they are "tuned," much like a radio tuner passes on to the amplifier only information carried on a specific radio frequency. The neurons we are considering respond by firing more or less, depending on the extent to which the spatial frequencies in the image match the filter characteristics.

It has been suggested that the center-surround cells we described in Figure 8.13 are themselves the results of the actions of other neural filters occurring earlier in the visual system, some of which are still hypothetical and have not yet been physically isolated. They probably result from particular neural networks of connections in the retina. These earlier filters are really quite simple. If we look at their response pattern over a single slice of space, most of them increase their responsiveness toward the center of the field and then tail off again, giving us a familiar bell-shaped distribution, as is shown in the leftmost part of Figure 8.14A. These distributions were mathematically described by Carl Fredrich Gauss in the early 1800s, and hence are called Gaussian distributions.

Filters with such distributions of response can have either wide or narrow spreads and low or high peaks (compare the leftmost distributions in Figures 8.14A and 8.14B). Another important feature is that these filters can be either excitatory (meaning that neural responses increase toward the center of the filter's field) or inhibitory (meaning that neural responses actually decrease the likelihood that other nearby neurons will react). Combining an excitatory and an inhibitory distribution has the same arithmetic effect as subtracting the value representing the inhibitory distribution of responses from those representing the excitatory. Hence, the spatial filter that results from the combination of these is referred to as the **difference of Gaussian filters,** or, more affectionately, **DOG** filters. Note that the net effect of combining two bell-shaped spatial filters, where the wider one is effectively subtracted from the narrower, is to create a filter with all the essential characteristics of an on-center receptive field, as shown in Figure 8.14A. An off-center receptive field can be modeled by simply subtracting the narrower of the two bell-shaped curves from the wider one, as shown in Figure 8.14B. Both of these arrangements are certainly plausible for ganglion cells because these cells have inputs from other cells with receptive

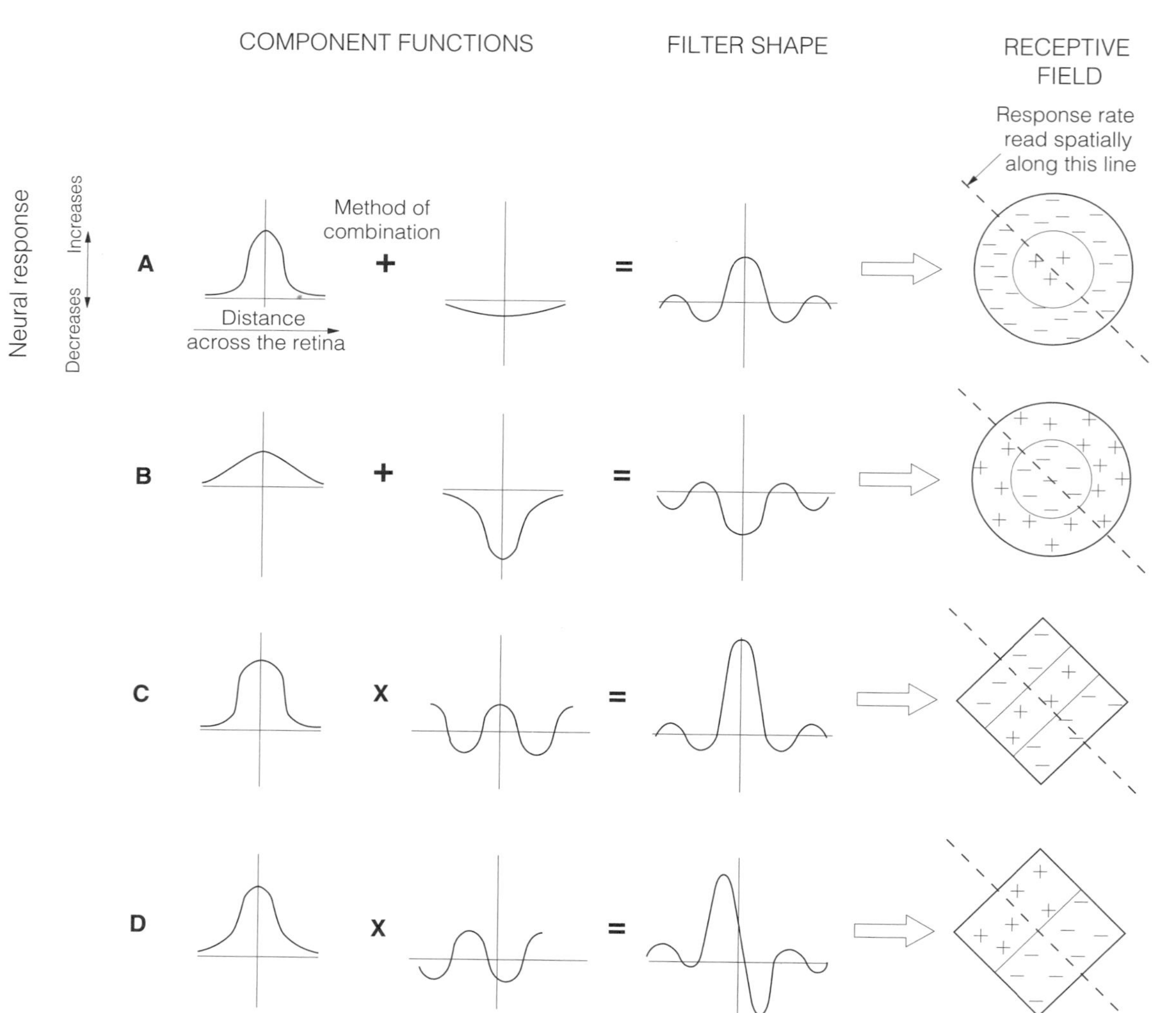

FIGURE 8.14 Subtracting one bell-shaped curve from another of a different width yields a *difference of Gaussian* function that performs spatial filtering like a center-surround ganglion cell (as in A and B). Multiplying a bell-shaped curve with a sine function produces a *Gabor* function that performs like an orientation-specific line detection (C) or edge detection (D) neuron in the visual cortex.

fields in a variety of sizes. This has led computational vision scientists to build models of the retina with DOG filters (e.g., Fiorentini, Baumgartner, Magnussen, Shiller, & Thomas, 1990).

Mathematically speaking, Fourier analysis is a "simple" analysis procedure since it only looks at one dimension at a time. More recently it has been suggested that more complex mechanisms may actually be used by the visual system (e.g., Sutter & Hwang, 1999; Tijsseling & Gluck, 2002). The most useful of these seems to be the **Gabor filter,** which is named after Dennis Gabor, the Nobel Prize–winning physicist who analyzed such filters and used them to develop the theory on which holograms are based. It is not appropriate to work out the mathematics of such filters here; however, you can think of a Gabor filter as a combination of a bell-shaped Gaussian distribution with a sine wave, and the important result of this is that it results in a new kind of filter that has an orientation in two dimensions and can produce responses that look like the orientation specific neurons in the visual cortex that respond best to bars or edges with a specific tilt (c.f. Adini & Sagi, 2001). Gabor filters are shown in Figures 8.14C and 8.14D. As with the DOG filter, Gabor filters are used by many computational vision scientists because they are thought to be plausible models of the way in which the primary visual cortex processes a visual image (see Manahilov & Simpson, 2001). Thus, in the same way that we found many different "maps" of sensory qualities and information dimensions in the cortex, some visual physiologists regard the processing of information in the visual system as the application of a complex series of many different filters to the incoming information (e.g., Van Essen, Anderson, & Felleman, 1992). Others argue that even if we cannot find specific physiological mechanisms that correspond to Gaussian and sine wave filters, the use of these mathematical concepts to describe differences among various visual feature detectors may help to simplify our understanding of them. At the very least, it allows computational vision scientists to represent feature-specific cells in mathematical terms for later use and manipulation in their theories.

Although spatial frequency analysis and visual filtering seem to provide useful or promising approaches to the problems of brightness and acuity, they do not provide us with the complete answer (Meese, Hess, & Williams, 2001). Our final perception of a particular brightness, size, or detail resolution often requires the operation of all levels of the perceptual system, including higher cognitive processes.

CONTOUR INTERACTIONS

There is a conceptual trap that a person's thinking might fall into when talking about neural filters. That is the idea that our perception of a contour is a fairly passive event that simply involves the filter that matches the incoming stimulus passing the stimulus information on. The fact is, as we hinted in our discussion of Mach bands in Chapter 4, the neural circuitry associated with center surround and orientation specific cells in the visual system exaggerates any edges that are encountered. This exaggeration is accomplished through the interaction of excitatory and inhibitory responses in a region of the visual field. The importance of these kinds of neural interactions was studied by Floyd Ratliff, who is described in Biography Box 8.1. The consequences of interactions of this sort can be easily seen in Figure 8.15A.

Figure 8.15A is nothing more than a regular arrangement of black squares with white interspaces that is called the **Hermann grid.** The interesting aspect of this figure is the presence of gray smudges at the intersections between the black squares. One of the disconcerting aspects of this perception is that when you try to look directly at one of these gray spots, it disappears—only those intersections that are not currently being fixated appear to have the gray smudges.

The diagram in Figure 8.15B illustrates what is going on at the ganglion cell level. A receptive field that is center-excitatory and aligned with an intersection will have a larger net amount of inhibition in its surround than will a same-size receptive field centered in the space between two squares. This means that, relatively speaking, the intersections will be registered by ganglion cells as containing less light than the vertical and horizontal regions between squares. But why doesn't this illusion occur at the intersection that is being fixated directly? This is because the receptive fields are smallest for neurons in the foveal region of the retina, and they increase in size with distance from the fovea. Therefore, the receptive field size that is ideal for producing the illusion in the visual periphery will, by definition, be larger than the receptive fields that are active when the pattern is examined at the center of gaze. Viewing the pattern up very close will increase the retinal size of the spaces in the pattern stimulating the periphery and, as you would predict, will also reduce the strength of the illusion as the contour distances no longer "match" the receptive field sizes.

Another way that contour interactions have been studied is by looking at how detection thresholds for a contour change as a function of the presence of other contours in the vicinity. The most tyical effect of nearby

BIOGRAPHY BOX 8.1

A CRAB'S-EYE VIEW OF CONTOURS

Floyd Ratliff (1919–1999) got his undergraduate degree at Colorado College and then went to Brown University to train under Lorrin Riggs. He then went to Johns Hopkins University to work with the first of two Nobel Prize laureates with whom he would do research, H. K. Hartline. His second Nobel Prize–winning collaborator was G. von Bekesy, with whom he worked at Harvard University. He then rejoined Hartline at Rockefeller University, where he continued to work for the rest of his career.

Ratliff wanted to study the first stages of neural processing in the eye; however, this was extremely difficult in the mid-1950s, since visual cells are small, axons are difficult to tease apart mechanically, and any interruption of blood flow causes them to die quickly. He solved his problem by choosing the horseshoe crab (*limulus*) as his subject. This unusual creature has some wonderful characteristics as far as visual scientists are concerned. It has large compound eyes (like a fly's but larger), and the neurons from each little eyelet are widely spaced and easy to access and identify. Furthermore, the eye can be kept alive and functioning for hours, even when completely removed from the crab. Ratliff's work on contour-resolving mechanisms and lateral inhibition in this strange eye continued with Hartline and provided the first quantitative description of information processing in a portion of the visual system. It also represented the first use of computerized data collection in neurophysiology. Our first understanding of the importance of inhibitory interactions in the perception of contours comes from this research. His contribution to science was recognized when he was elected to the National Academy of Sciences.

Ratliff was not only interested in vision at the neural level, but also in the psychophysics of what people actually see. For this reason he studied contour perception by using visibility and brightness "illusions" that are apparent in phenomena like Mach bands (see Chapter 4). However, his interests extended well beyond edges and brightness. Ratliff was extremely interested in the relationship between art and science and was fascinated by the extent to which the intuitions of great artists seemed to anticipate many of the conceptual advances in the neuroscience and psychology of vision. Eight years after he officially retired from university life, he published a book that specifically addressed this topic. It was entitled *"Paul Signac and Color in Neo-Impressionism,"* and it demonstrated that artistic aesthetics and visual science have much in common.

contours is to reduce our visual acuity for any one of the group of contours, a phenomenon that is known as **crowding** (e.g., Liu & Arditi, 2001). One explanation for this phenomenon is that the same excitatory and inhibitory neural interactions that *enhance* the visibility of contours make it more difficult to perceive contours under certain conditions. This is most likely to occur when the spacing is such that the neural response to one contour interferes with that of others nearby. An interesting aspect of this is that actually seeing the interfering contour is not necessary, since a stimulus that is subthreshold for conscious perception may still be strong enough to excite a neural response. (This has been demonstrated by Fiorentini et al., 1990). Furthermore, it should also be the case that certain spacings between the contours (e.g., when the inhibitory field of one contour overlaps the excitatory response of another) should result in increased contour detection thresholds, but at other, much nearer, spacings (when the excitation fields overlap) we should find facilitation, and hence lower thresholds. This is what is usually found, as shown in Figure 8.16. One potentially useful additional finding is that crowding effects are much greater in certain clinical conditions. This is particularly the case in **amblyopia exanopsia,** which is associated with diminished visual acuity, often in one eye, but usually without any obvious visual pathology (e.g., Levi, Hariharan, & Klein, 2002). This visual problem might result from a failure of the neural contour detection and enhancement mechanisms at the level of the organization of simple receptive fields.

Masking and Metacontrast

Interactions such as crowding do not occur only for the perception of simple contours and cannot be fully explained by the way ganglion cells communicate with one another. Indeed it appears that the concepts of **spatial summation** for closely neighboring stimuli and **lateral inhibition** among slightly more distant stimuli are general design principles of the brain. For example, the perception of many forms, including letters, shapes, and pictures, is influenced negatively by the presence of other forms in the near vicinity (e.g., Hess, Cristyn, &

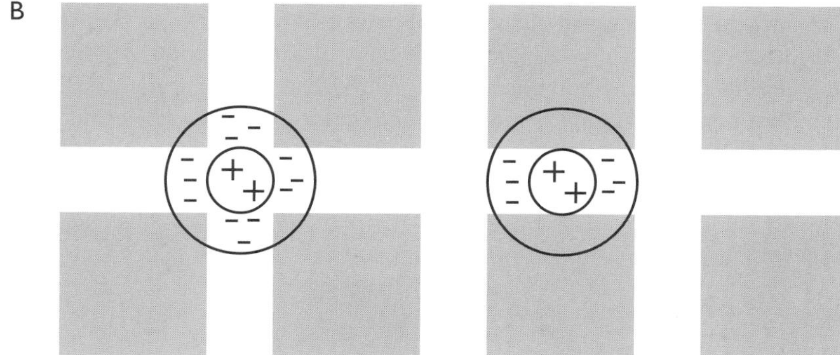

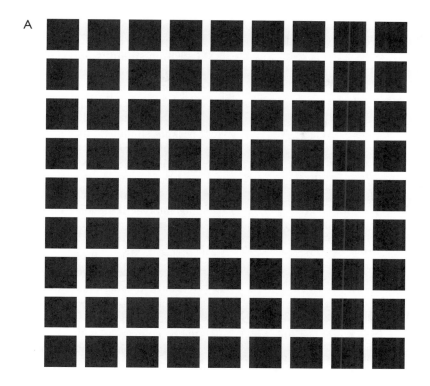

FIGURE 8.15 (A) The Hermann grid. (B) A sketch of the response of two ganglion cell receptive fields, one centered on an intersection of the grid, the other centered on a space between two square elements.

Chaudhry, 2001). However, there is one aspect of contour interaction that has been extensively studied and that depends on the timing of stimuli as well as on their spatial relationships. This is called **visual masking.**

At the most general level, visual masking refers to a reduction in the visibility of a contour or target that is caused by the presentation of a second stimulus that is close to the target in space and/or time. Thus the crowding phenomenon discussed previously is often referred to as **simultaneous masking** (He, Cavanagh, & Intriligator, 1996; LaBerge & Brown, 1989) because the target stimuli and those that flank it are presented at the same time (see Figure 8.17A). There are several ways to separate the target stimulus in time from the one that is supposed to interact with it. First we can present the target stimulus for a brief period of time and then immediately follow or replace it with a masking stimulus that consists of some array of contours that overlap the same position in

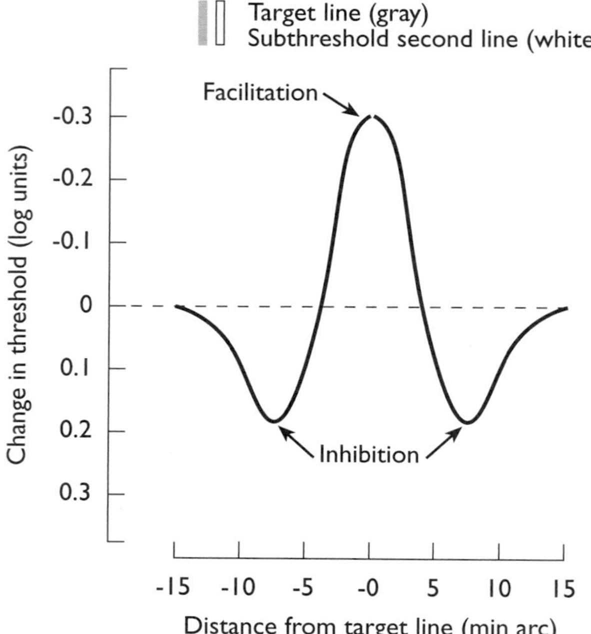

FIGURE 8.16 The change in the threshold of detection for a small target bar (gray) as a function of the distance between the target bar and a second subthreshold bar of similar size (white).

space. This is known as **pattern masking** and is shown in Figure 8.17B. An alternative is to show the target stimulus and then follow it with a masking stimulus that contains closely adjacent, but non-overlapping contours. This is sometimes referred to as **metacontrast** and is shown in Figure 8.17C.

What you actually see when the target and the mask are separated in time depends on the **interstimulus interval or stimulus onset asynchrony,** which is simply the time between the presentation of the target and the presentation of the mask. For example, a target that is highly visible when presented briefly by itself can be made completely invisible by the later presentation of a masking stimulus. Since this involves affecting the visibility of a target that was presented earlier and is now gone, it is called **backward masking.** In effect, it works backward in time, affecting an event that has already ended. The amount of masking depends on the interstimulus interval. If the mask occurs too early, or too late, the amount of masking is reduced. Generally speaking, backward masking is strongest when a brief interval of about 50 to 100 milliseconds intervenes between the presentation of the target and the mask.

For both pattern masking and metacontrast, it appears that masking is the result of the neural units that are specialized for the analysis of specific visual attributes actively competing with other units in their region by sending inhibitory signals to neighboring units that are proportional to their current level of activation (Wilkinson, Wilson, & Ellemberg, 1997). Most typically, researchers think that the occurrence of the masking stimulus interrupts the processing of the target stimulus before it is completed, and thus much information about it is lost before it can be consciously registered. One class of such theories postulates the existence of two neural channels. The first is fast acting but short lived, while the second is slower but longer lasting. The faster channel signals the stimulus onset while the slower channel contains information about the shape and color

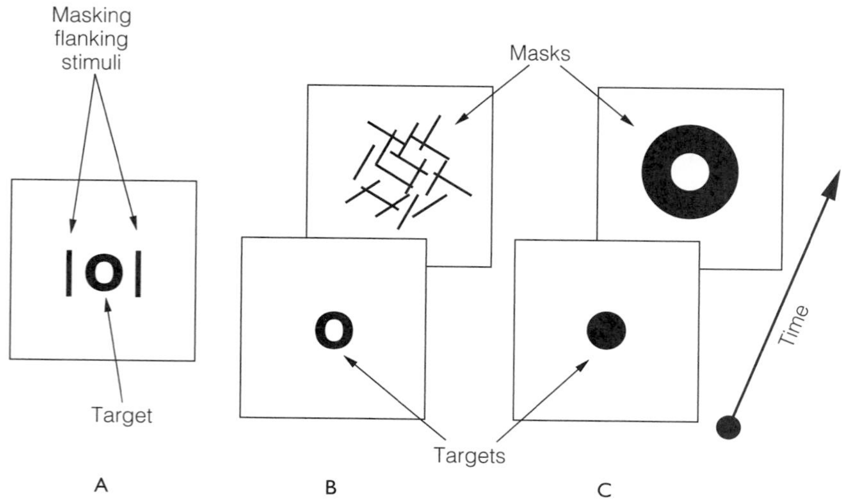

FIGURE 8.17 Various configurations used to produce masking. (A) Simultaneous masking. (B) Pattern masking. (C) Metacontrast.

of the target. The appearance of the fast signal from the mask overtakes the processing of the slower signal from the target and thus reduces our ability to perceive the target accurately (see Breitmeyer & Ogmen, 2000, for a review). It certainly is the case that even in the primary visual cortex, V1, the presence of a masking stimulus can interfere with normal processing of contours and patterns (Lamme, Zipser, & Spekreijse, 2002). There is also evidence that higher-level cognitive processing and attentional factors may be involved in the masking process (e.g., Kawahara, Di Lollo, & Enns, 2001). Two clear facts emerge from all of this research: First, contours are not perceived instantaneously but require substantial time for processing, and second, the processing of one contour can interfere or interact with the processing of others.

Contour Detection

Our considerations so far suggest that detection of a contour involves more than just a luminance or a wavelength difference in the world and an edge-detecting neuron in our brain or visual system. This becomes even clearer when we recognize that in the natural world the perception of contours can be very complex. If you look around you right now, you will notice that some contours defining objects are partly occluded from view by objects that lie nearer to you than those contours. Other contours are not associated with very much contrast because the color and luminance on either side of the edge are very similar. Still other contours do not define the edge of an object at all but are instead the result of shadows cast by other objects standing between a light source and the surface on which the shadows have been cast. Therefore, in order to analyze an image appropriately, your visual system must be able to group contours that truly belong together; it must be able to boost the signal of parts of contours that are very faint in the image; and it must be able to assign some contours to the status of "surface edge" and other contours to the status of "shadow edge."

Vision scientists who study the computational aspects of contour detection have discovered a number of ingenious mathematical tools to help them detect contours in an image (e.g., Rolls & Deco, 2002). Most of these tools involve examining the gradient of image intensity in a local region of the image in order to find the precise location in which the intensity is changing most rapidly. All of these locations are then represented in a **contour map,** which is a representation of the original image in which only the edges have been preserved and coded as points (e.g., van Tonder & Ejima, 2000). Figure 8.18B shows a typical contour map for the photograph shown in Figure 8.18A, generated by using a simple contour-finding algorithm. Note that because of imperfect lighting in the original photograph and because of noise in the edge-finding process, some portions of the real contours have been omitted and other markings that do not represent real contours have been added. The next task for both an artificial vision machine and for a human visual system is to determine which edges belong together, which should be discarded, and which edges need to be added because they are missing from the map.

One way in which contour grouping has been studied in human vision is to ask observers to indicate the shapes hidden in pictures such as those shown in Figure 8.19 (Beck & Rosenfeld, 1989; Field & Hayes, 1993). These textures are generated by randomly sprinkling small elements such as short bars all over an image. Among the randomly oriented elements, however, is a continuous

A

B

FIGURE 8.18 (A) A black and white photograph of a scene. (B) The same photograph in which all edges have been replaced by contours.

A

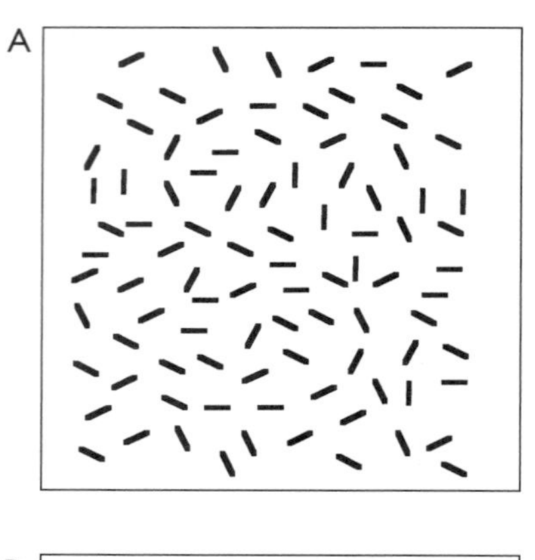

C

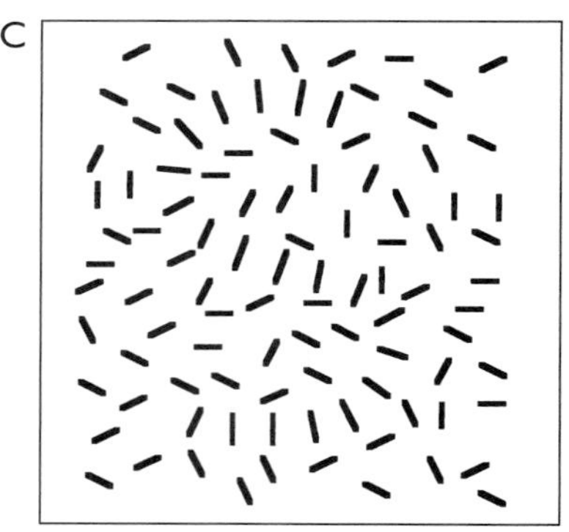

B

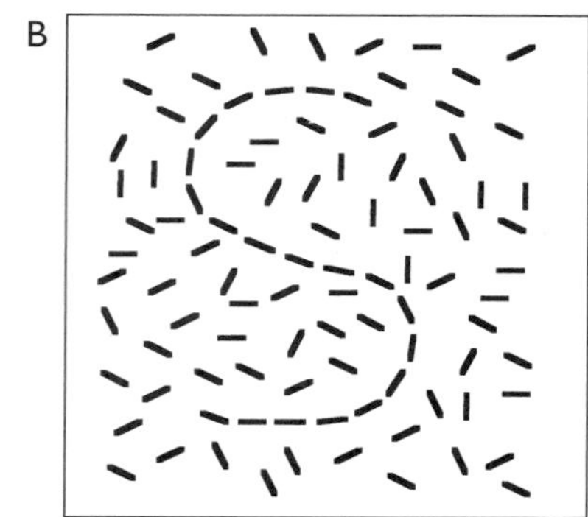

D

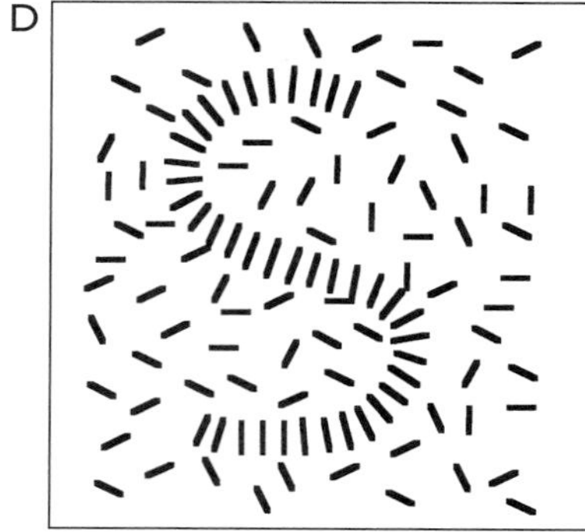

FIGURE 8.19 There is an S-shape configuration in each of these randomly textured patterns. (A) Large spacing between the bars in the S shape. (B) Small spacing between the bars in the S shape. (C) Small spacing between the bars, but the bars are all rotated by 90°. (D) Bars are rotated by 90°, but their spacing has been reduced by one half.

curved line of elements. Which S shapes are easiest to see? You will probably not be surprised to see that bars that are farther apart, as in Figure 8.19A, are more difficult to group into a continuous line than are bars that are closer together, as in Figure 8.19B. However, note that the relative orientation of the bars is also very important. Figure 8.19C contains the same number of bars as does Figure 8.17B, but instead of being aligned on their long axis each of the bars has been oriented at 90 degrees to its original orientation. As you can see, it is extremely difficult to group the bars on this basis. Only when the density of the bars is increased twofold, as in Figure 8.19D, is the S shape once again easily visible. Findings such as these indicate that there is a cooperative grouping process in human vision that seeks to extend edges as well as a competitive grouping process that seeks to inhibit the grouping of edges that do not have the same orientation. If the visual system were focusing its efforts on extracting contour maps, then line drawings (which are the equivalent of good contour maps) should be processed more quickly and easily then real-world patterns with shading and texture. This is not the case, however, and such drawings actually require more time to process than the richer scene they were derived from (Attwood, Harris, & Sullivan, 2001).

Finally, it is important to keep in mind that for contour perception to occur, there must be not only spatial variation in the intensity of light but also variation over time in the pattern of illumination on the retina. In Chapter 11 you will see that several temporal factors are important in the perception of contours.

FEATURE EXTRACTION

The shapes that emerge into our consciousness from the retinal image can be said to possess **features** that differentiate them from other shapes. For example, if you have ever picked raspberries or blackberries, you will recall that the image of a ripe berry consists of a curved and roughly oval shape. Sometimes these shapes overlap the leaves of the plant, and sometimes they are themselves overlapped by leaves or other berries. A ripe berry will tend to be larger than the others, will have a texture of bumps that is coarser than the others, and will reflect a darker "reddish" or "purplish" color. The so-called **relevant features** of the ripe berry are those that help you differentiate it from the others. In this case these features are size, texture, and color.

Perception researchers use several different experimental methods to help them determine what the basic features are for the human visual system. One of these is the **visual search** task, in which an observer looks for the presence of a single target item and the experimenter varies the total number of search items in the display from trial to trial. An example of two of these displays is shown in Figures 8.20A and 8.20B. If the time it takes for the subject to find the target stays approximately the same as the number of items is increased, the target is said to "pop out," and the feature that differentiates the target item from the distracting items is thought to be a basic visual feature (e.g., Krummenacher, Hermann, & Heller, 2002).

In a related task, subjects are asked to identify the presence or the location of an "odd" region in a briefly flashed display consisting of tiny figural elements. Two examples of displays from such a **texture segregation** task are shown in Figures 8.18C and Figure 18.D. If subjects are able to find the "odd" region in a display shown for less than 100 ms, the region is again said to pop out, and the feature that differentiates the elements in the "odd" region from background elements is believed to be a basic visual feature.

These two tasks, and others, tend to agree in their identification of a number of basic visual features of shape, including color, brightness, orientation, length, and curvature (Ramachandran & Anstis, 1986; Treisman, Cavanaugh, Fischer, Ramachandran, & vonder Heydt, 1990). In addition, these simple features can sometimes be combined in a hierarchical fashion to create **emergent features.** These are **Gestalts** or larger configurations that cannot be explained by simply examining the component parts, as shown in Figure 8.21. These emergent features sometimes behave just like simpler features in visual search and other feature detection tasks (Enns, 1990b; Enns & Prinzmetal, 1984). Some of the important emergent features identified to date include spatial relations among contours, such as line crossings, line endings, and line closure (e.g., Elder & Zucker, 1993, 1994). Still other emergent features can be traced to the three-dimensional orientation of surfaces (Aks & Enns, 1996; Enns & Rensink, 1991), the direction of scene lighting (Enns & Rensink, 1990; Ramachandran, 1988), and surfaces defined by common motion (Prophet, Hoffman, & Cicerone, 2001), stereo-depth perception (Heider, Spillmann, & Peterhans, 2002), and pictorial depth cues (Enns, 1992). In these latter cases the "features" can no longer be defined with respect to the contours and shapes in the image but instead must be defined with respect to the three-dimensional visual world that has been interpreted from the image.

An alternative way to characterize visual features is to trace them to a physiological base, as, for example, the neurons in the visual system that are tuned for specific types of contours, edges, angles, and so on. These detectors serve as **templates** and feature identification involves matching the retinal image to these physiological templates. New templates can be built through learning and experience so that higher-level features can be extracted and ultimately compared to memories of perceptual objects at a third stage to determine the identity of the stimulus (e.g., Hurlbert, 2000).

The classical theory based on this kind of reasoning was originally called **Pandemonium** because each stage

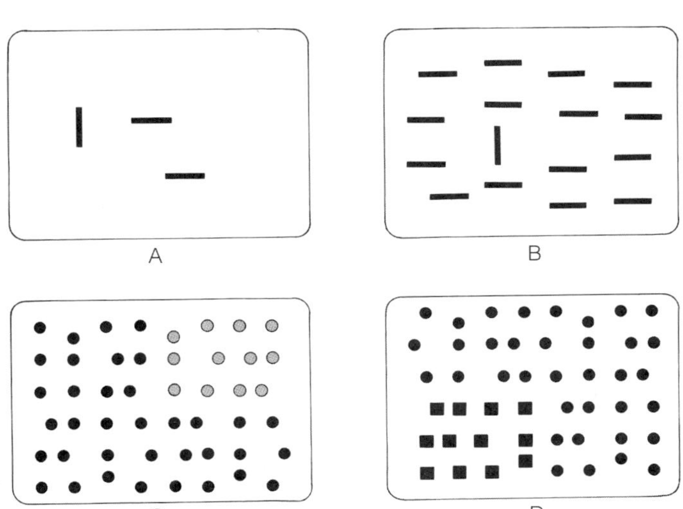

FIGURE 8.20 (A and B) Displays from a typical visual search experiment in which the target is a vertical bar. This target is easy to find, regardless of the number of horizontal bars present. (C and D) Displays from a typical texture segregation experiment in which the elements in the "odd" region differ in brightness or in shape from the elements in the "background" region.

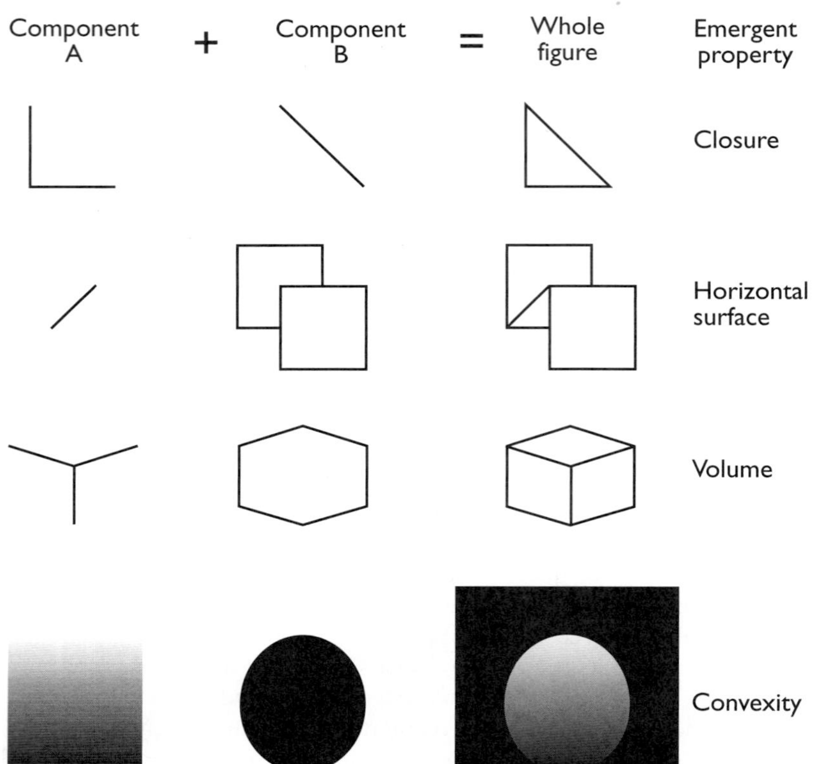

FIGURE 8.21 When component figures are added together, emergent features are sometimes created that cannot be explained by examining the component parts (based on Enns, 1990b; Pomerantz, 1986; Ramachandran, 1986).

in the analysis of an input pattern was originally conceived of as a group of hypothetical **demons** (in reality the output of template matching units) shouting out the results of their analyses (Selfridge, 1959). Figure 8.22 shows how the theory works. In the first stage, an **image demon** passes on the contents of the retinal image to each of a set of **feature demons** (feature-specific cortical units). These feature demons shout when they detect "their" feature in the input pattern. These shouts are listened to by the **cognitive demons,** each of which is listening for a particular combination of shouts from feature demons (these are higher-level learned templates). As the information is analyzed by the feature demons, the cognitive demons start "shouting" when they find a feature appropriate to their own pattern, and the more features they find, the louder they shout. A **decision demon** listens to the "pandemonium" caused by the shouting of the various cognitive demons. It chooses the cognitive demon (or pattern) that is making the most noise as the one that is most likely to be the pattern presented to the sensory system.

Template-based models of feature extraction, such as Pandemonium, do predict certain aspects of pattern recognition, such as the specific pattern of mistakes people make when trying to identify alphabetic characters (see Ashby & Perrin, 1988), as well as accounting for between-letter confusions that depend on minute details of the letters, such as size, type font, and the like (Sanocki, 1987). Machines that read letters and addresses often use feature templates as the first stage of recognizing the writing that they are looking at, and template-based models have been used successfully to explain how we recognize degraded patterns or those presented in a "perceptually noisy" environment (e.g., Manjeshwar & Wilson, 2001).

Finally, one of the original hopes of the Fourier analysis approach described earlier, was that after the extraction of the spatial frequency components that make up a shape, these sine wave variations in brightness (Fourier components) would be found to be the features used to identify perceptual objects. It has now been shown that this approach cannot work if the Fourier analysis is applied over the entire visual field, but it still appears to be useful if the analysis is done over smaller regions, around the size of cortical receptive fields (see Mallot, 2000).

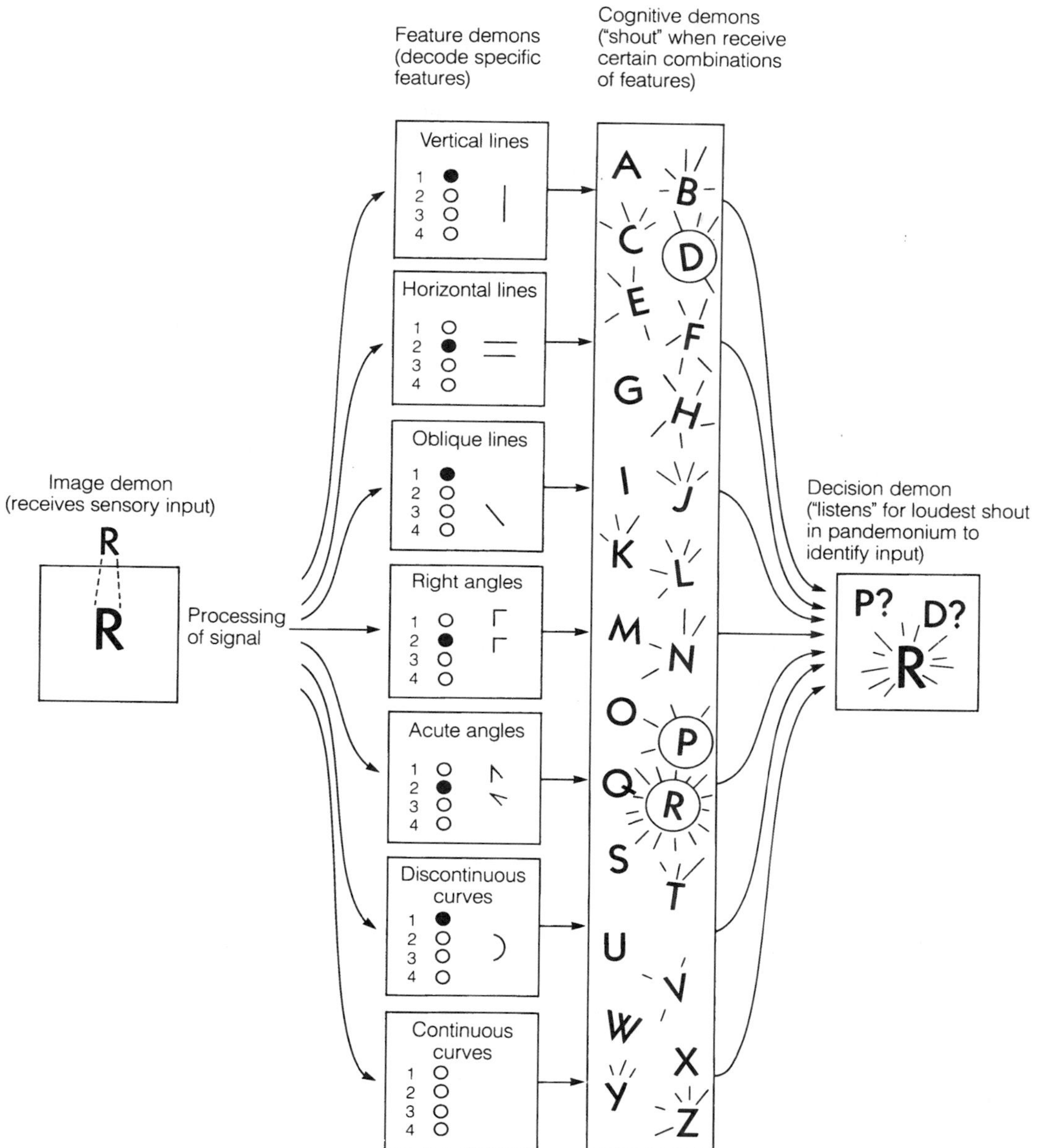

FIGURE 8.22 The Pandemonium model in action. The number of times each type of feature is registered by the feature demons is indicated by which circle is blackened in each box.

Unfortunately, the spatial frequency approach is really different from other forms of feature analysis in more ways than its mathematical description. First, the spatial frequency components are not apparent to consciousness and thus are not useful in describing what we see. Second, they are not always closely related to what is actually perceived. For example, regions of the visual array that are clearly different in their Fourier components sometimes do not appear to be perceptibly different (Caelli, 1988). This approach does have the advantage, however, that the set of possible Fourier components is not as arbitrary as the feature list seems to be and does not change with the set of shapes. Some researchers therefore feel that it may still prove to be useful for the description of our perception of forms (see Rolls & Deco, 2002, for a review).

PERCEPTUAL ORGANIZATION

At the beginning of this chapter we noted that one of the most striking aspects of perception is that it is organized. That is, under normal viewing conditions our visual systems operate to produce perceptible figures, objects, and meaningful patterns, as we saw in Figure 8.1. These figures and coherent patterns that we experience in consciousness exist only in our minds, and they are the result of several levels of active processing and interpretation applied to the retinal image. You can experience the way in which this organization process works when you look at Figure 8.23. It is simply a field filled with triangles, but pay attention to the direction that they are pointing. Notice that sometimes they all point to the right, sometimes up and to the left, sometimes down and to the left. Not only does the organization and interpretation of the figure change, but it changes in a systematic and regular manner. *All* of the triangles switch direction together. It is not a few scattered triangles pointed right, some down-left, and so forth to create a random array. Rather the perception is not only organized but it renders our interpretation of the stimulus into something that is regular and systematic. Thus perception seems to be trying to make the world simpler and more interpretable. But what rules and methods does it use to achieve this?

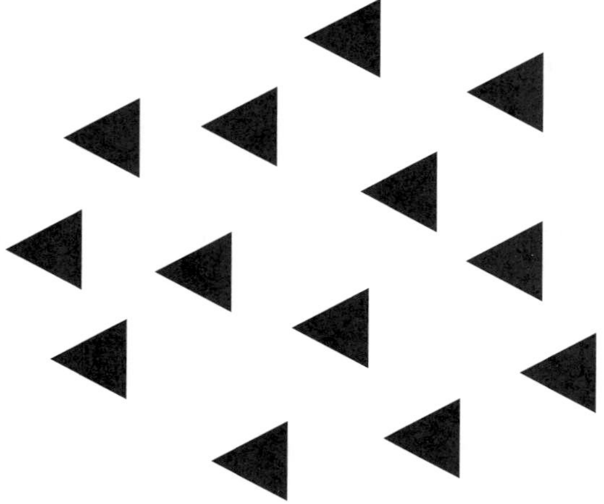

FIGURE 8.23 Notice that the direction that these triangles seem to be pointing changes over time, but these changes affect *all* of the triangles simultaneously.

FIGURE AND GROUND

The Gestalt psychologists Max Wertheimer, Kurt Koffka, and Wolfgang Kohler were the first to systematically research the general question of how all perception comes to be organized into patterns, shapes, and forms (see Biography Box 8.2). **Gestalt** is a German word that can be translated as "form," "whole," or even "whole form." The Gestaltists were interested in processes that cause certain visual elements to seem to be part of the same figure or grouping and certain others to seem to belong to other figures or groups. They formulated several laws of perceptual organization that govern the emergence of a visual figure (Wertheimer, 1923). Their basic observation was that elements or features within a visual pattern do not seem to operate independently. At the phenomenal level, there appear to be attractive "forces" among the various elements that cause them to form meaningful and coherent figures, much as gravity organizes the planets, sun, and moons of our solar system. The Gestaltists described how certain regular properties of relations among elements within a pattern bring about the emergence of stable figures.

Perhaps the most primitive example of perceptual organization is when we see a two-dimensional **figure** (say, a black spot) on background (e.g., the expanse of white paper on which the spot is drawn). A figure is simply a group of contours that has some kind of objectlike properties in our consciousness. A shape can be a figure, but shapes can also form part of the background (or **ground**) from which the figure emerges. Thus, a ball resting on a field of grass is a figure (here, a round shape) resting on a ground consisting of many elongated shapes (the blades of grass). How can we tell the difference between a figure and its ground? For example, how can you differentiate the book you are reading from the table on which it rests or the printed words from the page? On your retina the blobs of contours that make up figures and grounds are all run together, intersecting and overlapping, but somehow the visual system separates the book from the table and the words from the page.

To begin with, this separation is a psychological achievement and not simply a description of the physical stimulus. This can be seen in Figure 8.24A. Pay attention to what you see inside the gray frame. Is it a set of black arrows pointing upward on a white background or a set of white arrows pointing downward on a black background? As you look at this figure for a few moments, the two pattern organizations will alternate in consciousness, demonstrating that the organization into figure and

BIOGRAPHY BOX 8.2

THE WHOLE IS DIFFERENT THAN THE SUM OF ITS PARTS

Max Wertheimer (1880–1943) was born in Prague and educated at the universities of Prague, Berlin, and Würzburg before assuming a post at Frankfurt. He recalled that it was in 1910, while traveling by train, that he thought of the general notion that was to become the basis of Gestalt psychology, namely that perception was organized and that simple knowledge of the parts of a stimulus could not always predict what the perception of the whole might be. At the next major stop he got off of the train and bought a toy stroboscope (a device allowing successive still pictures to be exposed at a constant rate of speed so that movement can be perceived). Working in his hotel room, he verified the basic principles of an apparent movement illusion (the Phi phenomenon), which would serve as an example of the general principle. The vacation was forgotten, as he rushed to the university and borrowed a tachistoscope to test his ideas. His first two experimental subjects were Wolfgang Kohler and Kurt Koffka, the two men who were destined to be second only to Wertheimer in their contributions to Gestalt psychology in the years to come. Together these three worked out the general principles of figural organization that we know of as the Gestalt laws.

Gestalt psychology was viewed as a revolution against the idea that knowledge of the sensory elements was all that was needed, and these elements were somehow simply bundled up by association processes to become the conscious percept. It was a widespread revolution, since the same organizational principles that group elements in visual patterns were believed to be in operation in other sensory realms, such as hearing. In addition, Gestalt organization was supposed to affect other mental operations, such as thinking, learning, and even social processes. Thus the Gestalt psychologists extended their research well beyond pattern perception.

In 1933 Wertheimer left Germany to escape the rising tide of Nazism and anti-Semitism and assumed a position at the Graduate Faculty of the New School for Social Research in New York City. Koffka and Kohler also ended up in the United States. There were some beneficial outcomes as a result of their exile from Germany, namely, that Gestalt psychological concepts, which were relatively unknown in America, now became a popular subject of active research and eventually achieved broad acceptance. Another unforeseen benefit was that Wertheimer got to meet Albert Einstein. Wertheimer spent many hours with Einstein, getting him to trace each step of the thinking that had led him to derive the *theory of relativity*. Insights from these conversations, combined with his knowledge of Gestalt principles of organization, led to his last book, *Productive Thinking*. It was an attack on the educational methods of the time, which were based on memorization, repetition, and routine practice. Instead he offered methods of taking advantage of the general organizational principles of the mind to form meaningful cognitive units. This idea is still being pursued by educational theorists.

ground is in your mind, not in the stimulus. Notice also that the white and black arrows are not perceived at the same time. You "know" that both are possible, but you can't "see" both at the same time. It is impossible for a given part of a visual pattern to be simultaneously interpreted as both figure and ground.

A number of factors can influence whether something is seen as figure or ground (see Palmer, 2002). Generally

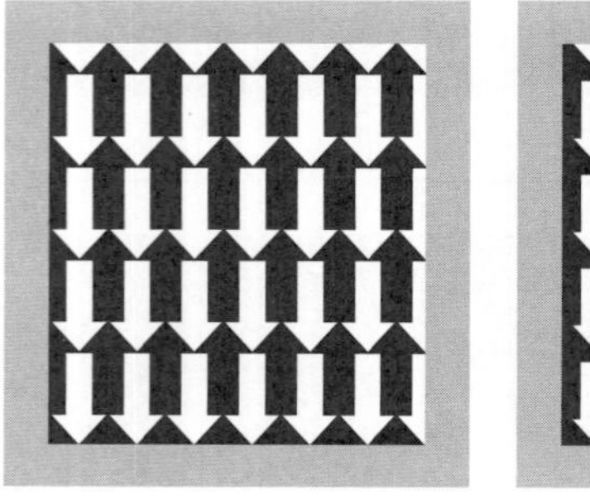

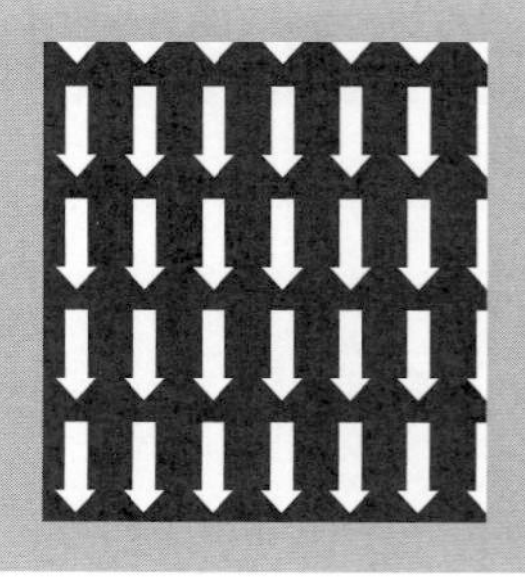

A B

FIGURE 8.24 (A) A reversible figure-ground stimulus in which sometimes you see black arrows pointing upward and sometimes see white arrows pointing down. (B) Smaller stimuli are more likely to be seen as figures; thus it is much easier to see the white arrows pointing down and there is much less alternation between the black and white arrows in this array.

speaking, the smaller an area or a shape is, the more likely it is to be seen as a figure. This is demonstrated in Figure 8.24B, where it is easier to see the white arrows as figures because they are smaller than the upward-pointing black arrows. Also, there is a bias toward seeing the lower region of a pattern as the figure (Vecera, Vogel, & Woodman, 2002). This can be seen in Figure 8.25, where one sees black, wavelike curlicues in A but white ones in B, even though B is just A inverted so that the white is now in the lower region. Flip the book to see the figure ground relationship reverse for these figures.

After a particular interpretation has been arrived at—for example, the white arrows in Figure 8.24A—figure and ground take on distinct properties. When the white area is seen as the figure, it appears to be in front of the black area seen as the ground, and the contours in the pattern seem to belong to the white arrows. However, when the interpretation changes, the contours are now seen to belong to the black arrows, and the black figures appear to be closer and in front of the white background. Furthermore, figures appear to be more "thing-like" and appear to have a shape, whereas the ground appears formless (e.g., Baylis & Cale, 2001). Figures are seen as "richer" and more meaningful and are remembered more easily. Figures also contrast more than the ground, appearing brighter or darker than equivalent patches of light that form part of the background (Coren, 1969). Finally, the stimuli seen as figures are processed or registered in greater detail than stimuli seen as ground (Weisstein & Wong, 1986).

Figural Grouping

Most forms or shapes we see are composed of a number of elements. We have already observed that the organization of elements into perceptual objects involves an active constructive process. We can see the action of this "urge to organize" elements into shapes in Figure 8.26, where the many possible organizations of the elements into circles of various sizes, ovals, rectangles, and some less regular shapes, seem to alternate in a rapid, unstable manner.

The Gestalt researchers studied the way in which elements in visual patterns tend to become organized into formlike or objectlike perceptions. They listed the various principles they discovered in the form of what are now called the **Gestalt laws of perceptual organization.** These "laws" help to explain the way in which we organize sounds as well as visual forms or events over time (e.g., Palmer, 2002). To illustrate these principles of organization, we can start with the 12 dots shown in Figure 8.27A. These appear as a fairly random and meaningless collection of elements. In Figure 8.27B, however, we see four columns of dots. This is an example of the

FIGURE 8.25 There is a bias toward seeing stimuli in the lower part of an array as figures. Thus, in A you see a black wave and in B a white one, even though A and B are the same figure, merely inverted.

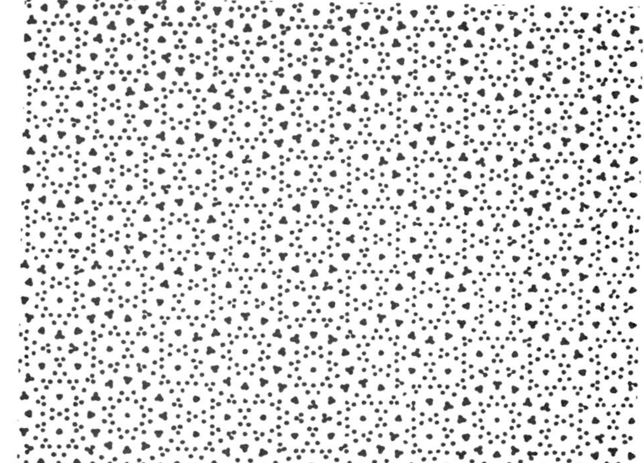

FIGURE 8.26 A stimulus revealing the "urge to organize." There are many possible organizations of the various small elements, and the visual pattern you see is continually changing as you shift from one organization to another.

law of proximity, which states that elements close to one another tend to be perceived as a unit or figure. In Figure 8.27C we have altered the spacing so that now we see three rows. The rows or columns are basically lines of figural elements that we experience via this perceptual organizing mechanism.

If we change the brightness, color, or shape of some of the elements, we can see in operation the **law of similarity,** which maintains that similar objects tend to be grouped together. For example, in Figure 8.27D the elements are all equally spaced; however, we again see three rows because black circles are grouped with other black circles and gray circles with other gray circles. In Figure 8.27E the spacing is the same as Figure 8.27D; however, we now see four columns because similar shaped elements are grouped together.

Observers who are asked to describe Figure 8.27F usually say they see two intersecting straight lines of dots rather than a > and a < shaped collection of dots meeting at the center. This is an example of the **law of good continuation,** which states that elements that appear to follow in the same direction (as in a straight line or simple curve) tend to be grouped together. When elements are in motion, elements that move together are said to have **common fate,** which is a sort of variant of good continuation that states that elements that move together tend to be grouped together. This is sometimes referred to as the **law of common motion.**

Figure 8.28A is an example of the **law of closure,** which states that we tend to ignore gaps between elements in order to form a closed figure. Here we perceive a square despite the fact that it is made up of 12 discrete dots with large spaces between them. Closure is a powerful organizer of perception, and it often works in conjunction with other mechanisms. Thus Figure 8.28B appears as an unpatterned jumble of dots; however, by making some of the dots distinctive, hereby changing their brightness and texture as in Figure 8.28C, we get a grouping by similarity, which immediately is organized by closure into a square, even though the positions of the dots in Figure 8.28B and Figure 8.28C are identical.

Most of the basic Gestalt laws of perceptual organization had been described by the mid-1930s; however, we are still refining our knowledge about them and even discovering some that the original Gestaltists did not explore (e.g., Gillam, 2002; Kellman, 2000). There is an overriding principle in all of them, however, and that is

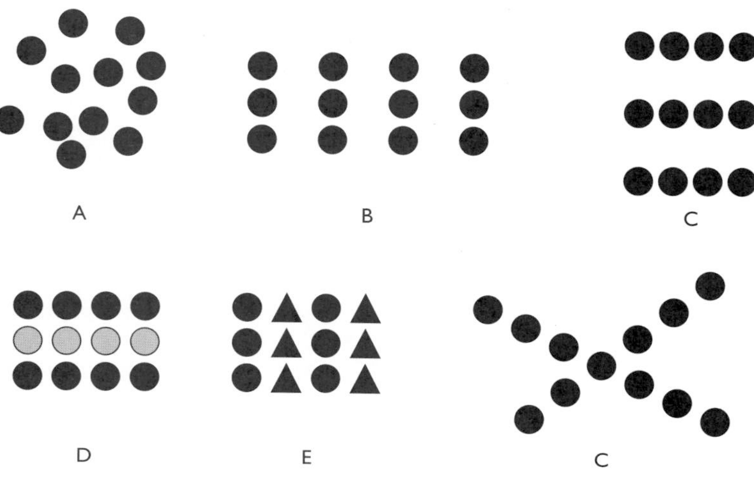

FIGURE 8.27 Gestalt principles of perceptual organization. (A) a group of 12 dots seen as a cluster with no internal organization. Change in *proximity* causes the 12 dots to be seen as 4 columns (B) or 3 rows (C). *Similarity* of color causes the perception of 3 rows (D) and similarity of shape causes the perception of 4 columns (E). *Good continuation* causes (F) to be seen as two intersecting lines of dots rather than > and < shaped arrays of dots meeting at their apex.

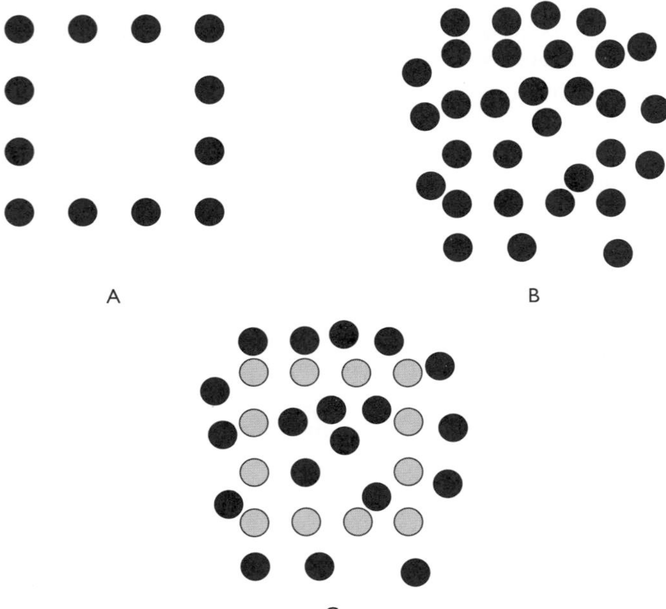

FIGURE 8.28 *Closure* causes these 12 dots immediately to be seen as a square (A). In (B) this same square is perceptually lost in a jumble of other dots, while (C) shows how grouping by similarity (of brightness and texture) can combine with the law of closure to allow the square to be easily seen again.

an attempt to create perceptually the most stable, consistent, and simplest forms and patterns possible within a given visual array. The Gestalt psychologists treated this process as if it were yet another rule of perceptual organization, calling the process the **law of Pragnanz.** It states that the organization of the visual array into perceptual objects will always be as "good" as the prevailing conditions allow. Here the meaning of **good** encompasses concepts such as **regularity, simplicity,** and **symmetry.** Thus in one study observers were asked either to judge or to produce triangles and quadrilaterals that were "most typical" of each class of figures. There was a pronounced bias toward selecting figures that had equal corner angles and equal side lengths, in other words, figures that were the most regular and symmetrical (Feldman, 2000).

DEMONSTRATION BOX 8.4

PRAGNANZ

Look at the accompanying figures for a moment and (without looking back again) draw them on a separate piece of paper. When you have finished, return to this box.

Now carefully compare the figures you drew to the actual figures. Did you pick up the fact that the "circle" is actually a tilted ellipse? That the "square" contains no right angles? That the "triangle" has two rounded corners and an open one? That the "X" is actually made up of curved lines? Look back at your reproductions. If you drew (or remembered) just a good circle, square, triangle, and X, your percepts have been "cleaned up" by the action of Pragnanz.

The law of Pragnanz is also a way of saying that the perceptual systems work to produce a perceptual world that conveys the "essence" of the real world, that is, to assure that the information about the real world is correctly interpreted. In fact, the German word **Pragnanz** means approximately "conveying the essence of something." Because prevailing conditions are sometimes not ideal, as in line drawings or on a foggy night, the essence can be "better" than the reality. Seeing complex patterns of contours as perceptual objects makes further processing of the vast array of information in the retinal image simpler and faster (Oyama, 1986; Yantis, 1992). Demonstration Box 8.4 allows you to explore the concept of Pragnanz further.

Pragnanz allows us perceptually to "heal" broken patterns, which are actually more common than complete patterns in the visual field. This is because we are so often confronted with scenes in which our view of one figure is partly blocked by other figures that are interposed in front of them, effectively breaking up the contour's shape. Thus in Figure 8.29 we effortlessly recognize each shape, even though none of the ones that we are asked are identify are seen in their entirety. Each one appears to be partially occluded by another and all are, therefore, incomplete.

Whether Pragnanz can trigger closure and accurate object identification depends on the nature of the contours we are presented with. Look at Figure 8.30A. Despite the large amount of black interposed in front of the gray figures, our visual system is able effortlessly to group together the correct portions of the image. In this figure, several copies of a familiar letter of the alphabet (B) can be seen lying in various orientations underneath some spilled ink. Familiarity with the occluded objects is clearly *not* a sufficient condition for this to occur, as shown in Figure 8.30B. This figure contains the same letter fragments, but the occluding spots of black ink have been removed—observers find these letters almost

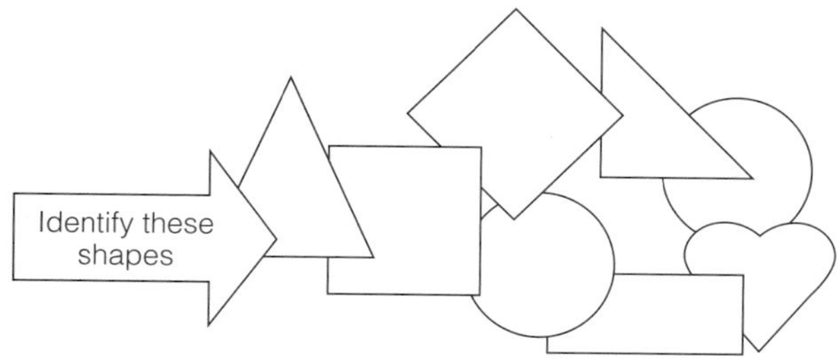

FIGURE 8.29 *Pragnanz* allows you to easily recognize the 8 shapes to the right of the arrow, even though not one of them is visible in its entirety.

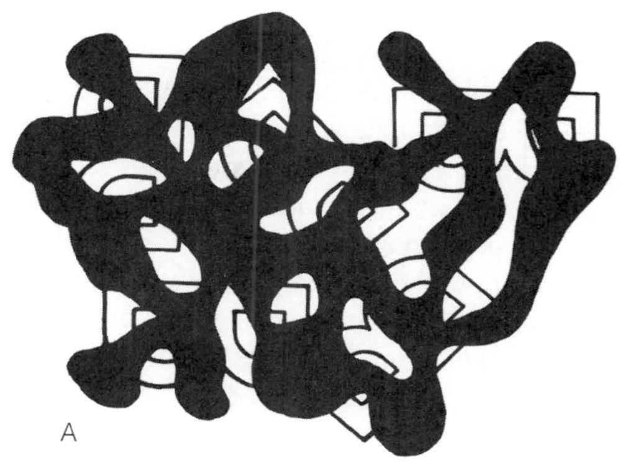

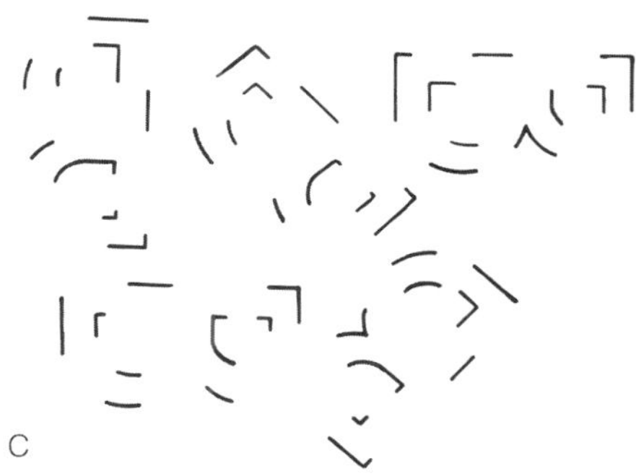

FIGURE 8.30 (A) Several copies of the letter B are lying beneath some spilled ink, but they are easy to read. (B) The same letter fragments, without the ink as an occluding object, are very difficult to read. (C) When only the intrinsic contours of the letters are shown, the letters are easy to read, despite the absence of any ink to act as an occluding object (based on Brown & Koch, 1991).

impossible to decipher even when they know which letters to look for (Bregman, 1981; Kanisza, 1979). Thus, the grouping that is occurring in Figure 8.30A must be following some rules that work regardless of the meaning of the objects.

One suggestion is that shape contours are "labeled" very early in the grouping process as either **intrinsic contours** (meaning they belong to the figure) or **extrinsic contours** (meaning they are simply a consequence of one object interposed in front of another; another). The intrinsic contours of the ink spilled in Figure 8.30A can be traced to form continuous shapes. Extrinsic contours (where the ink crosses the underlying letters) serve as a signal that allows the intrinsic contours of the letter B to be "filled in" underneath the occluding black ink. In Figure 8.30B the shape fragments that have been drawn are a combination of intrinsic contours of the letter B and extrinsic contours caused by the ink spill. In this case the visual system has no way of knowing which is which because the interposing figure is not visible; hence the "filling in process" is not invoked. Now examine Figure 8.30C. Here only the intrinsic contours of the letter B have been retained, and so the letters are once again quite readable (Brown & Koch, 1991). It appears that correct contour labeling can be achieved in a number of ways, including the assignment of contours to different depth planes—such as the ink being seen in front of the Bs (see Nakayama, Shimojo, & Silverman, 1989). Sometimes the characteristics of the contours determine the labels. For instance, at approximately T-shaped intersections between contours the stem of the T intersection is labeled intrinsic and is seen as part of the more distant figure, whereas the crossbar is labeled extrinsic and is part of the nearer, interposing figure (Enns & Rensink, 1991; Kellman & Shipley, 1990).

Pragnanz, combined with other organization processes can actually create the perception of contours even when there are no luminance or color changes physically present. These are called **subjective contours** or **illusory contours** (Petry & Meyer, 1987; Purghé & Coren, 1992). Thus the white square in the center of Figure 8.31A exists only perceptually, not physically. Seeing the square, however, does simplify the pattern as the law of Pragnanz predicts, thus giving us five simple, regular and symmetrical figures (four black circles and a white square) instead of four irregular shapes (circles with chunks removed in different locations). Figure 8.31B shows an even greater simplification. Here you see an irregular white shape (like a distorted hourglass or dumbbell) in resting on seven black circles. This is much simpler and more regular than what is physically present, which is eight difficult-to-describe, irregular, and asymmetrical black blobs. Both of these subjective contour figures illustrate how a figure can emerge from a two-dimensional array without the contribution of any intrinsic contours. The only contours used to define them are extrinsic contours that occur when these figures occlude the shapes underneath them. Many of the most convinc-

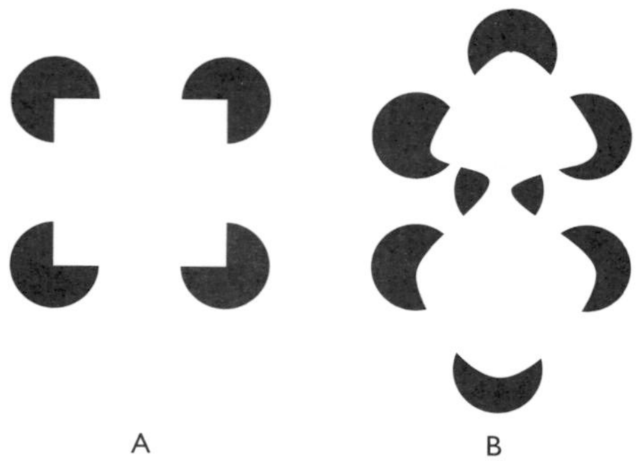

FIGURE 8.31 The white square in (A) and the distorted hourglass or dumbbell shape in (B) do not exist in the stimulus array but rather are outlined in subjective contours that come about through the operation of Pragnanz.

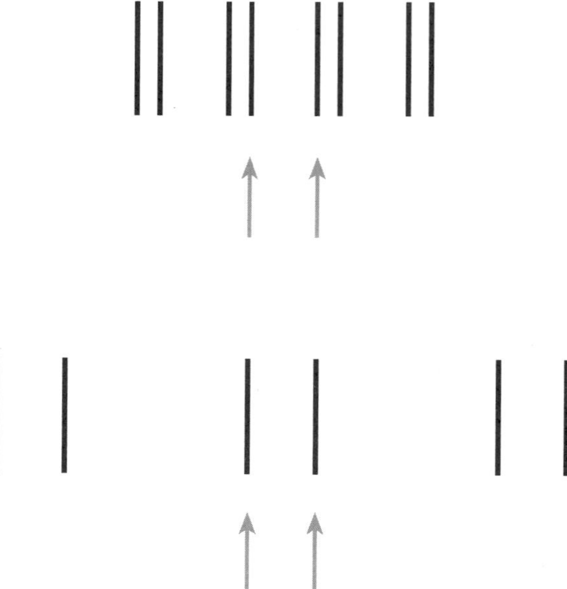

FIGURE 8.32 The space between the elements in the same unit grouped by proximity (lower portion of the figure) appears to be smaller than that same space where the proximity cue groups them into different units (upper figure).

BIOGRAPHY BOX 8.3

SEEING WHAT IS NOT THERE

Gaetano Kanizsa (1913–1993), who has been called one of the founders of Italian experimental psychology, was virtually unknown in North America until the 1970s. Although he was born in Trieste, his parents were from Hungary and Slovenia. Kanizsa got his doctorate at Padua where he worked under Vittorio Benussi. Benussi had trained in Germany and had been influenced by Gestalt thinking there. Kanizsa absorbed this influence and soon came to think of himself as being very close to the kind of thinking and research associated with Wertheimer, Koffka, and Kohler. Kanizsa then returned to Trieste to take a university position and remained there until the end of his career.

Most of the Gestaltists, and the majority of Italian psychologists at the time, were very theoretically oriented. Kanizsa was not particularly theoretical (although many of his studies and demonstrations make important theoretical points). He was a fine artist and liked to draw and manipulate figures. He would often say that he considered himself, not a psychologist, but rather a "thing-ologist." It was while manipulating some figures that he noticed that they contained some contours that were visible in consciousness but were not actually drawn. These were *subjective contours.* He began to explore these phantom contours in a series of papers and soon had not only developed configurations that had strong illusory lines and shapes but also some configurations where transparent figures could be seen where none existed. He felt that these figures illustrated some of the deeper mechanisms of perceptual organization.

Since Kanizsa published only in Italian, his work went unnoticed among English-speaking psychologists. However, Stanley Coren, then at the Graduate Faculty of the New School For Social Research (where Wertheimer had been), stumbled across some of the figures that Kanizsa had drawn. He was so impressed by the strength of the contours that he set about trying to discover what mechanisms caused them and published his results in the *Psychological Review* in 1972. A broad range of perceptual psychologists thus came into contact with Kanizsa's figures and were just as impressed by them as Coren had been. As a result, hundreds of articles came out exploring them or modifying these patterns to produce novel effects. Kanizsa's name thus became as well known in North America as in Italy.

Subjective contours have now been found to be an extremely common occurrence and are found not only in stationary line drawings but also in motion displays, stereoscopic depth configurations, and even in three-dimensional constructions. An interesting fate has overtaken them, however. They are now more often used as tools to explore many other psychological problems. These cover a broad range of issues, including perceptual development, neurophysiolgical processing in the brain, contour formation, learning, the nature of consciousness and even clinical conditions, such as schizophrenia. They have the advantage over many other possible stimuli that they must be constructed in the mind by organizing certain elements that are presented. Thus one gets to study perceptions that are in the mind but never were part of what was processed by the retina. They are now seen so often that one must be reminded that they really began as merely a particularly powerful demonstration of perceptual organization.

---

ing subjective contour configurations were first discovered by Gaetano Kanizsa, who is discussed in Biography Box 8.3.

It is important to note that subjective contours seem to be due to the overall configuration and relationships among the visual elements in the display that triggers this form of perceptual organization rather than due to any easily discovered neural image processing mechanism (e.g., Gillam & Nakayama, 2002). However, in many ways subjective contours seem to share many common processing mechanisms with real contours (see Kellman, Guttman, & Wickens, 2001) and even can be seen by very young infants (e.g., Arterbery, 2001).

The Gestalt principles not only produce the perception of figures that are not there, they are so powerful that they are responsible for distorting our perception of relationships between contours that *are* physically present. For example, the internal distances between parts of a pattern that are organized into the same group, or figure, are underestimated relative to the same distances when the same parts represent the space between different perceptual groups (Coren & Girgus, 1980; Enns & Girgus, 1985). Figure 8.32 illustrates these effects. The figure shows two different groupings formed by operation of the law of proximity. The distance between the two lines pointed to by the arrows in each part is identical, yet that distance seems larger in the upper part, where the lines are parts of two different groups. Such distortions support and enhance the operation of the Gestalt laws to form perceptual objects from discrete parts of the visual array.

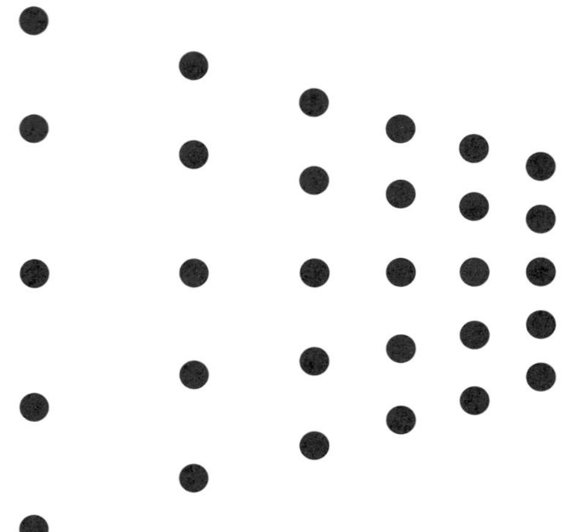

FIGURE 8.33 Grouping into rows or columns depends on the perception of surface depth. If the surface is seen as receding in depth, then the apparent proximity rather than the retinal proximity between dots determines grouping.

The Gestalt principles also interact in important ways with other aspects of form and space perception. For instance, by studying the perception of arrays of dots such as that in Figure 8.33, some researchers have found that both retinal proximity and perceived proximity are important determinants of the way in which the dots are perceptually grouped (Rock & Brosgole, 1964). If observers see the dots in Figure 8.33 as being attached to a flat surface such as the page, then grouping is influenced primarily by the proximity between dots as measured in the retinal image. On the other hand, if observers perceive the dots as being attached to a surface that is inclined to the right and thus the right edge is receding away from the observers, then the apparent proximity between the dots on the perceived surface determines whether row or column organization is seen. Related experiments examining the law of proximity and the perceptual completion of partially occluding objects (Palmer, Neff, & Beck, 1996) and the law of similarity and perceived lightness (Rock, Nijhawan, Palmer, & Tudor, 1992) have shown that figural grouping often depends on the *apparent* or *perceived* proximity, similarity, and continuation. This suggests that the principles of grouping interact with other perceptual mechanisms, such as depth perception (Chapter 9) or object and scene perception (Chapter 10).

Texture Segregation

Subjective contours demonstrate that shapes and figures can be formed by changes in the stimulus pattern other than those of intensity or wavelength. One common way of defining figure boundaries involves separating regions of the visual image based on differences in **visual texture.** Visual textures are collections of tiny contour elements or shapes that do not differ in average brightness or color. For example, in Figure 8.34 you will see three regions defined by different textures—one a texture of L's, the second a texture of T's, and the third a texture of tilted T's. Notice that there is apparently a boundary, or contour, on either side of the central region populated by upright T's. These contours are a form of subjective contour because they are not actually present in the stimulation and are generally referred to as **textural contours.**

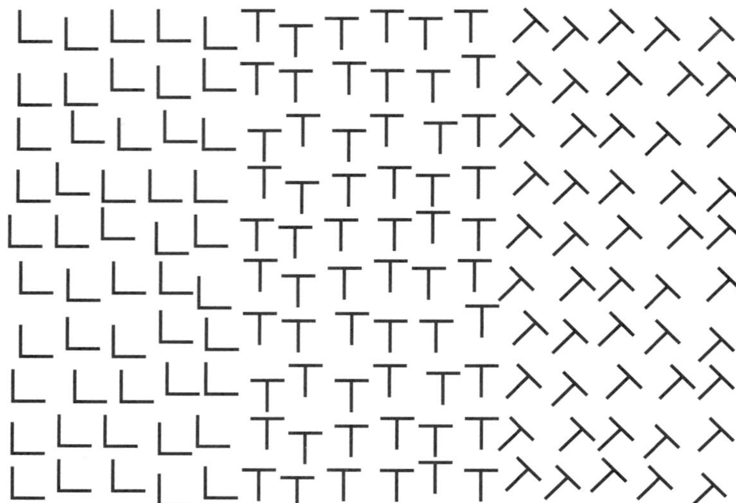

FIGURE 8.34 Examples of weak and strong texture boundaries.

The ease with which you can make out shapes defined only by textural contours depends on the nature of the textural elements. It has often been suggested that the segregation of parts of the field on the basis of textural elements is really an example of grouping by similarity, which we discussed earlier. From this perspective, the element properties that permit effortless texture segregation can be taken to be those properties that are analyzed automatically by the visual system. Good examples of both weak and strong texture properties are shown in Figure 8.34. Although people judge a T shape in isolation to be less similar to (and therefore more distinctive from) an L shape than to a tilted T shape, these judgments do not predict what happens when entire regions of a texture are made up of these shapes (Beck, 1982). The texture boundary between the L's and the upright T's is much less apparent in Figure 8.34 than the texture boundary between the upright T's and the tilted T's. Apparently, the orientation of element contours is a much more important aspect of their contribution to texture regions and edges than is the local spatial relations between the contours of each L or T.

Texture segregation is usually easy and automatic when there are differences in the number, density, or type of a few classes of local features that are generically called **textons** (Julesz & Bergen, 1983). Textons include elongated **blobs** of a particular color, length, width, or orientation; line ends, called **terminators;** and places where blobs cross each other, called **intersections.** The spaces between textons are also important and are sometimes referred to as **anti-textons** (see van Tonder & Ejima, 2000). For example, if you look carefully you can see a square shape in the upper right central region of Figure 8.35A. It is defined by a boundary between elements that have no terminators and elements that have three terminators. Notice that all of the elements are made up of exactly the same parts or blobs: a slanted line in two different orientations and a "corner" in four different orientations. This region of texture is difficult to perceptually segregate because the local texture elements differ only in how these parts are put together, and there are no differences in the spacing between elements to help you. The pattern becomes easier to see, however, after you have looked at the figure several times.

The square shape in the central region of Figure 8.35B is even more difficult to see. You will probably be able to find its boundaries only if you find two different elements somewhere and then systematically follow neighboring pairs of elements in order to find where the boundary is. The central region in this texture is composed of elements that resemble the number 10 in one of four orientations. The outer region is composed of elements that resemble the letter S, either regular or mirror imaged and upright or lying down. Because the S element and the 10 element are both composed of the identical blob parts and there are no other textons (e.g., number of terminators or intersections) to distinguish them, this texture-defined square is very difficult to detect even after many viewings of the pattern.

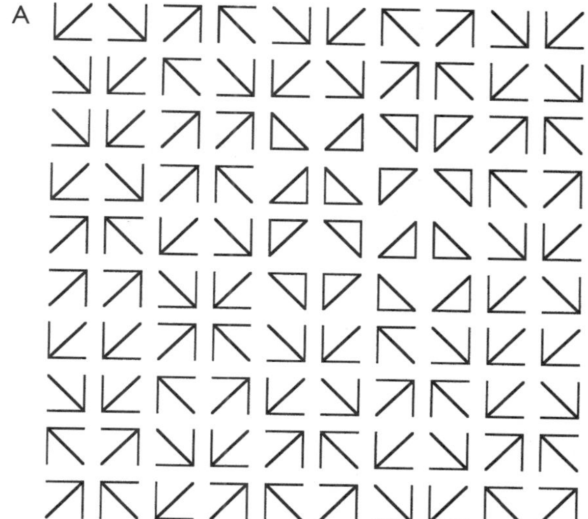

FIGURE 8.35 Texture boundaries defined by (A) a difference in the number of element terminators and closure and (B) a difference only in the presence of closure.

Although analysis of textons may help, it has become clear that certain aspects of the textural elements themselves make it easier or more difficult for us perceptually to separate the field into shapes and contours based on texture (e.g., Sturzel & Spillmann, 2001). Thus color, brightness, and relative contrast can sometimes overpower shape differences in our perception of textural regions (e.g., Callaghan, 1989). Different stimulus dimensions can become important for texture segregation depending on the type of judgment that the observer is asked to make (Heaps & Handel, 1999), with uniqueness relative to other nearby texture elements being a more important factor than the specific dimensions of the physical stimulus (e.g., Enns, 1986).

Spatial Frequency Analysis and Texture Boundaries

Several investigators have been successful in developing computational models of texture segregation that hypothesize that there are contour-detecting receptive fields, such as are found in the striate visual cortex, that do a spatial frequency analysis on regions of the visual field (e.g., see Gurnsey & Fleet, 2001; Wilkinson, Wilson, & Ellemberg, 1997). These receptive fields are usually described mathematically as **Fourier** and **Gabor** filters, which we discussed earlier in this chapter. The main idea is that all regions of an image are analyzed simultaneously to determine which spatial frequencies are present. When the filters that best fit one region of an image are substantially different from the filters that best fit another region, we see the regions as distinct and segregate them perceptually, treating the different regions as forms with contours. The differences between best-fitting filters can be based either on spatial frequency (e.g., if the grain or coarseness of the texture changes from region to region), on orientation (e.g., if the predominant element orientation changes between regions), or on both spatial frequency and orientation.

One of the important discoveries made in comparing the performance of computational models with that of human observers attempting to detect texture boundaries is that human texture segregation is sensitive to the polarity of the luminance relations between elements and the background (Sutter, Beck, & Graham, 1989). **Positive polarity** refers to an element's being brighter than the background; **negative polarity** refers to an element's being darker than the background. As shown in Figure 8.36A, if a texture pattern is composed of alternating bands of dark and light elements, then a change in the orientation of the bands from vertical to diagonal is readily detected, and we see two regions defined by their patterns. The orientation of receptive fields suitable for de-

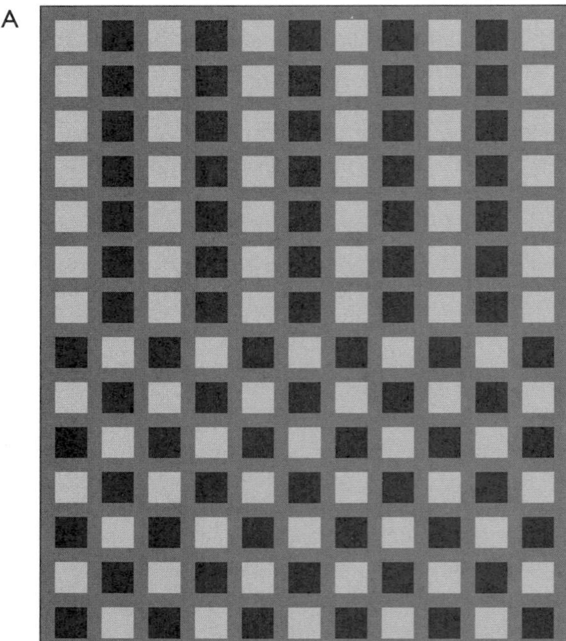

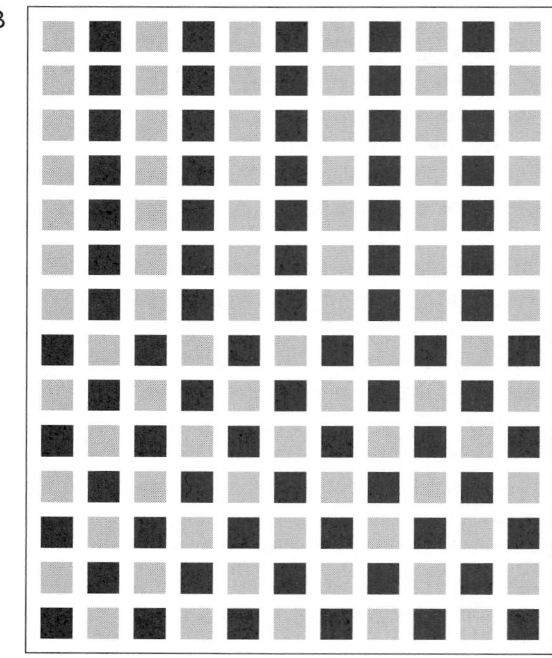

FIGURE 8.36 (A) Dark and light texture elements shown against a background of intermediate gray. (B) The same texture elements shown against a background that is lighter than both elements.

tecting the bands in the vertical region of the texture would be different from the orientation of receptive fields suitable for detecting the bands in the diagonal region.

However, a comparison of Figure 8.36A with Figure 8.36B shows that this is true only if the dark and light elements also differ in contrast polarity. In Figure 8.36A the background level of gray lies **between** the level used to draw the dark and the light elements so that the dark elements are darker than the background (negative polarity), while the light elements are lighter than the background (positive polarity). In Figure 8.33B the same values of gray have been used for the dark and light elements, but the background level has been changed so that both the dark and light texture elements have the same polarity in that both are darker than the background. Now the segregation of the two regions of the pattern based on textural differences is much more ambiguous. This sensitivity to the polarity of the contrast between elements and backgrounds indicates that automatic texture segregation is based on some very crude comparisons (e.g., whether the contrast polarity is the same or different) and does not take full advantage of the quantitative information available in the computational models. In the real world texture elements are not always uniform but may have internal variations in brightness. In that case the polarity at the corners or where there are changes in direction of the contour seem to be weighted more by the perceptual system (Branka, 2002).

In an earlier study of figure and ground, Julesz (1978) argued that texture segregation by these kinds of mechanisms is an "early warning" system that draws attention to regions requiring finer analysis. The texture boundary detection is accomplished by background processes, whereas the finer, more detailed analysis of important shapes is accomplished by figural processes. This argument has been interpreted in two ways. The first is that it suggests that regions defined by **higher spatial frequencies** (e.g., smaller details or sharper contours) are more likely to be seen as being figures.

A demonstration of this relationship between spatial frequency analyses and the perception of figures comes from Klymenko and Weisstein (1986). They found that when regions of a visual field were defined by different spatial frequency gratings, the regions containing the higher spatial frequency grating were more likely to be seen as a figure. Regions containing the lower frequency gratings were more likely to be seen as ground. Look at Figure 8.37A, and notice that it has an unstable figure-ground organization much like Figure 8.24A. Here you can see either a Maltese-type cross as the figure or a sort of a fat X. These perceptual organizations alternate in consciousness and are roughly equal in their strength. In Figure 8.37B, however, your first impression will probably be of a striped Maltese cross on a black background, and, although there is still some alternation between this figural organization and a black X, the cross will tend to dominate in consciousness because the stripes provide more high spatial frequencies in the areas associated with them. You can see that it is not just a function of brightness differences, since in Figure 8.37C the higher frequencies are now on the darker X component, which is more easily seen than the now white Maltese cross.

There is an important implication of these results linking spatial frequency to figure perception. Higher-frequency analyses are more likely to be accomplished by the parvocellular system (see Chapter 3), which also has higher visual acuity for fine details. Thus figure perception may be more intimately associated with the parvocellular than with the low-spatial-resolution magnocellular system.

While we are thinking about the underlying physical mechanisms associated with perceptual organization, we should consider a second implication of Julesz's argument. If texture segregation is an early alerting mechanism that draws attention to likely figures, it also should occur relatively early in the visual processing stream. Consistent with this is the observation that patterns that evoke texture segregation produce distinct response patterns as early as the primary visual cortex, V1 (Nothdurft, Gallant, & Van Essen, 2000). However, texture segregation not only guides attentional and information processing strategies but is affected by them. Hence it is

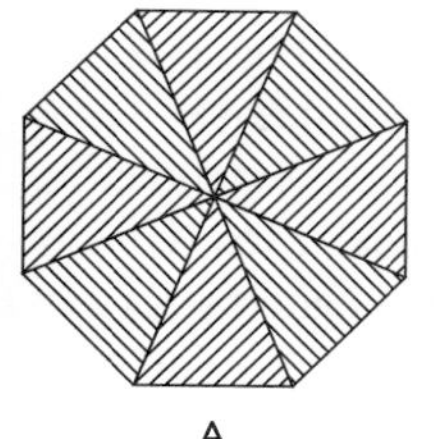

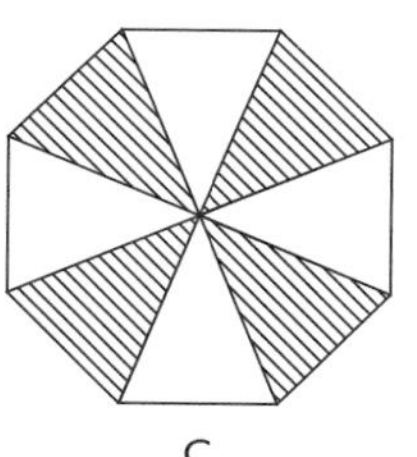

FIGURE 8.37 (A) has an unstable figure-ground relationship where a striped Maltese cross will alternate in consciousness with a striped "fat" X. In (B) the Maltese cross dominates in consciousness because it has more high-frequency components than the uniform black X. (C) demonstrates that it is always the figure with the higher spatial frequencies and not a matter of relative brightness, since now the striped X dominates over the white Maltese cross.

not surprising that later complex processing portions of the cortex, V3 and V4, also seem to be involved in this aspect of perceptual organization (e.g., Kastner, de Weerd, & Ungerleider, 2000).

INFORMATION, SYMMETRY, AND GOOD FIGURES

When we spoke about the law of Pragnanz, we introduced the notion of "figural goodness." Although we referred to "good" figures as being regular and symmetrical, this definition is too imprecise and limited for many situations and stimuli. For example, can we determine whether the letter F differs from the letter R in terms of figural goodness given that neither demonstrates regularity or symmetry? Several solutions to this problem have been suggested, but there still seems to be no consensus. One reasonable scheme involves defining figural goodness in terms of the amount and complexity of information needed to describe a particular stimulus or perceptual organization (e.g., Leeuwenburg, 1988). One of the earliest attempts to do this was that of Hochberg and Brooks (1960), who used a formula to compute figural complexity based on the number of angles, the number of different-sized angles, and the number of separate line segments in the image of the figure. This computation was supposed to represent the amount of information needed to identify the figure when perceived in a particular way.

To help illustrate this approach, Figure 8.38 shows figures varying in image complexity from A (most complex) to D (least complex). Figures with the lowest complexity are apt to be seen as two dimensional; thus Figure 8.38D is usually seen to be a flat puzzle made up of interlocking triangles. When figures are seen as three dimensional, greater image complexity is usually involved. Thus, although it is possible in principle to see Figure 8.38D as a three-dimensional cube (sort of a variation of Figure 8.38A, but tilted a bit), to do so would involve considering 24 angles (4 on each cube face) instead of the 18 angles (3 from each triangle) that are needed to describe the figure as flat. Generally it is the organization with the lowest figural complexity that is most likely to be seen, as if the visual system was biased toward doing the least amount of processing possible when viewing any stimulus.

Closely related to the Hochberg and Brooks computations is an alternative method of looking at the amount of information in a figure and its consequences for perception. This method was suggested by Attneave (1955), who

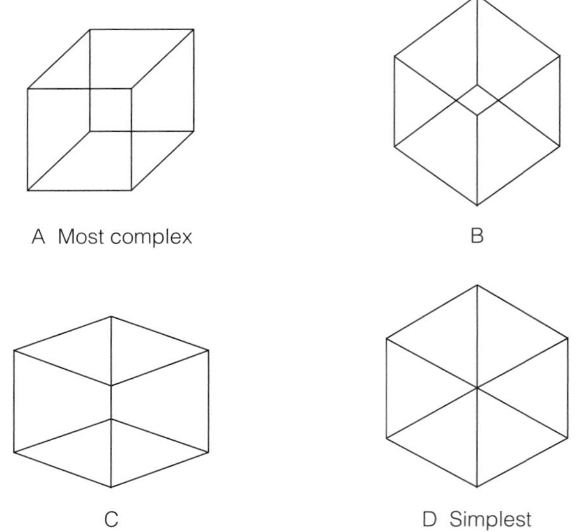

FIGURE 8.38 Various projections of a cube. The figures are more likely to be seen as two dimensional as the viewer moves from the most complex (A) to the least complex (D).

tried to quantify the figural goodness of patterns using **information theory** (which we discussed in Chapter 2). To see how information theory applies to patterns, consider Figure 8.39, where we have broken up the parts of larger images into separate smaller **cells** (you can think of these as pixels). We will call the whole stimulus array a **matrix.** Notice that we can construct a variety of patterns by simply filling in cells. Suppose we asked you to guess the figure present, without actually seeing it, by simply guessing whether each cell was black or white. Because each guess deals with two alternatives, the answer to each contains one **bit** of information, as we pointed out in Chapter 2. If we filled in the pattern randomly, in order to guess the complete pattern you would need 64 guesses (one for each cell) or 64 bits of information (one for each guess needed). If we told you that the left side was the mirror image of the right side, called a **vertically symmetrical** pattern because mirror images are symmetrical around a vertical line, you would need to guess only 32 cells either on the right or on the left in order to guess the pattern, thus reducing the amount of information to 32 bits. Therefore, a vertically symmetrical figure, such as Figure 8.39B, contains less information than an asymmetrical figure, such as Figure 8.39A. Figure 8.39C, which is symmetrical around vertical, horizontal, and diagonal axes, contains even less information than the other two patterns (16 bits) because only one corner (16 cells) must be known before the entire pattern can be derived.

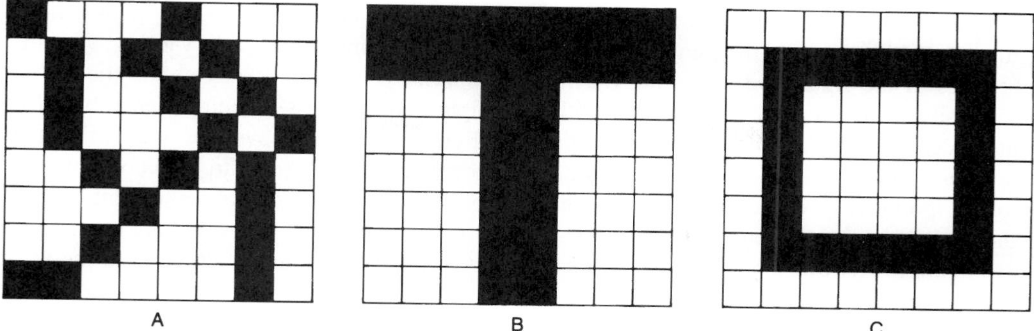

FIGURE 8.39 Examples of symmetry in patterns: (A) no symmetry, (B) symmetry around a vertical axis, (C) symmetry around both horizontal and vertical axes.

Because good figures are generally symmetrical and regular, we can now see that they also contain less information. This means that they should thus be easier to remember and easier to recognize or to pick out. Studies do show that closed "good" figures, or symmetrical low-information patterns, are much easier to recognize than those composed of the same features in a different arrangement (see Tyler, 2002). However, all kinds of symmetry are not equal. Look at Figure 8.40A. It is symmetrical around a vertical axis (the dotted line), meaning that the right and left halves of the figure are identical mirror images of each other. It is very easy to see that Figure 8.40A is symmetrical while 8.40B is not. Now look at Figure 8.40C, which is symmetrical around a horizontal axis (meaning the top and bottom halves of the figure are mirror images). It takes people longer to recognize horizontal symmetry and also longer to detect deviations from horizontal symmetry as in Figure 8.40D. One reason for this is probably evolutionary in nature, since most biological organisms, especially animals, such as humans, are symmetrical around a vertical axis, when viewed from the front. It would certainly be of adaptive value to be able to detect quickly figures that might be people, predators, or prey, staring directly in your direction (see Wilson & Wilkinson, 2002).

It is easy to recognize that Figure 8.41A is symmetrical; however, our perception of Figure 8.41B is that it is

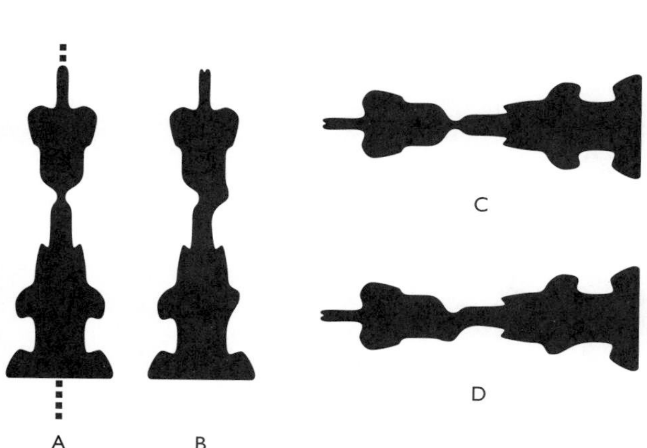

FIGURE 8.40 (A) is easily seen as being symmetrical around a vertical axis (dotted line) and the deviations from vertical symmetry are easily seen in (B). It takes longer to detect the horizontal axis symmetry in (C) and even longer to detect the differences between top and bottom that make (D) asymmetrical.

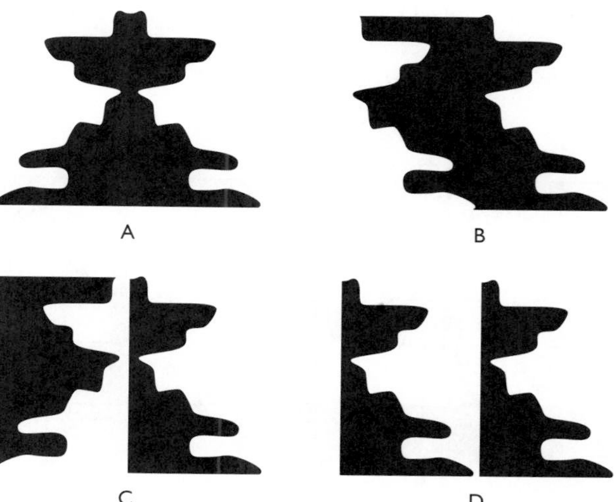

FIGURE 8.41 The symmetry in (A) is easily seen; however, the repetition of the right and left side contours in (B) is not, since each convexity on the right is a concavity on the left and visa versa. By changing the color of the leftmost contours, the repetition in (D) is now easier to see (because the convexities and concavities now match) while it is now the symmetry in (C) that becomes more difficult to discern.

not, and that it is an irregular shape. Actually, Figure 8.41B is regular since the contours that make up the left and the right sides of the figure are identical. The fact that we do not easily see the regularity associated with a repeated contour demonstrates another aspect of the perception of patterns, namely, that we encode figures as a pattern of convex portions (protuberances or parts that stick out) and concave portions (indentations or parts that go in). In Figure 8.41A every part that is convex on the right side is also convex on the left side, while in Figure 8.41B every part that is convex on the right side is concave on the left side. In Figure 8.41C and D, we have reversed the colors on the left and now it is easy to see that Figure 8.41D is regular since convexities and concavities are identical, while it is much harder to see the regularity in Figure 8.41C, which now has the problem of reversed convexities and concavities (see Baylis & Driver, 2001). One reason why patterns of protrusions and indentations are important is that they allow us perceptually to divide a figure into parts, which then allows us to examine and compare relationships and differences between figures more easily (e.g., Singh & Hoffman, 2001). We will come back to this issue of convexity and concavity when we talk about object perception in Chapter 10.

Our judgments of symmetry can be affected by a number of other factors, such as whether there are a lot of different aspects of the pattern that are varying (e.g., color or brightness) in addition to spatial and contour elements. It is easier to pick out symmetries if only a few stimulus dimensions are varying (Huang & Pashler, 2002). Symmetry not only guides the way we attend to a figure and process its components, but also the way we divide our attention over the figure affects our perception of symmetry. We seem to focus our attention on one aspect of the stimulus pattern and filter out the others when we make our symmetry judgments, as can be seen in Figure 8.42. If you pay attention to the white squares, it is obvious that the pattern is symmetrical around the vertical axis; however, paying attention to the black squares produces the perception of a pattern that is symmetrical around a horizontal axis.

Finally, symmetry and regularity not only simplify our perception of the world, but they appeal to us at an aesthetic level. Generally speaking, people find symmetrical patterns to be artistically pleasing, with mirror image symmetries being the most pleasing of all (e.g., Washburn & Humphrey, 2001). In addition, our idea of the physical beauty of a person, particularly of their face, is strongly biased toward regular and symmetrical features (e.g., Zebrowitz & Rhodes, 2002). Furthermore, this bias does not seem to be culturally determined (e.g., Rhodes, Yoshikawa, Clark, Lee, McKay, & Akamatsu, 2001). Since Pragnanz biases us to see all stimulus patterns as more regular and symmetrical, it must then be helping us not only to encode visual patterns more rapidly and efficiently but also to view our friends and lovers as more attractive!

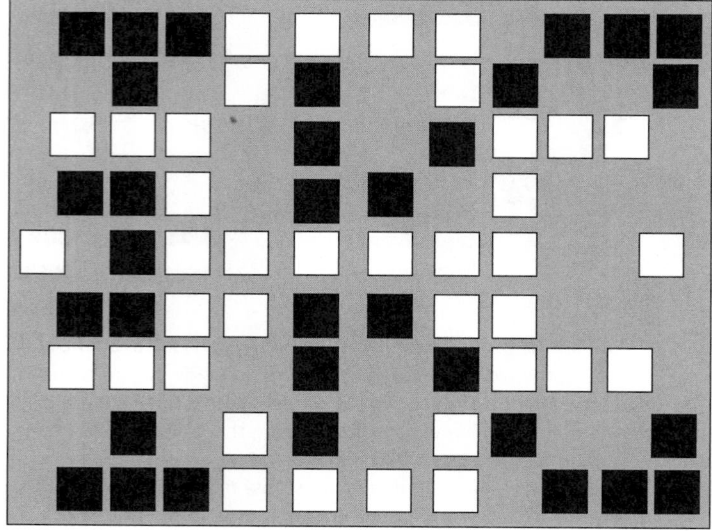

FIGURE 8.42 At first glance this appears to be a random, unsymmetrical, pattern of squares; however, focusing your attention on the white squares produces the perception of vertical symmetry while focusing your attention on the dark squares produces the perception of symmetry around a horizontal axis.

STUDY QUESTIONS

1. Describe the various types and classes of contours. Does there always need to be a luminance or color difference for the perception of a contour? If not, then how else does the perception of an edge come about?
2. Describe the various tests or measures of visual acuity. How is acuity measured and reported? Is it possible to have an acuity of 20/10? Explain your answer.
3. A variety of factors influence visual acuity. List these and describe how variation in each would affect visual acuity.
4. What is spatial frequency analysis and why is it an attractive set of procedures for many visual scientists?
5. Some researchers now report visual performance by describing the modulation transfer function of an individual or a group. What are the advantages of this over normal acuity measures?
6. Describe how neural systems might be able to perform a spatial frequency analysis. Also describe a perceptual experience that seems to be predicted by such a neural analysis system.
7. What is meant by masking? Describe the types of paradigms that have been used to produce it as well as the neural mechanisms that might cause it.
8. Why is texture segregation considered to be a form of contour perception? What factors influence texture segregation, and how?
9. How has the analysis of feature extraction contributed to our perception of patterns and edges? What mechanisms underlie these?
10. List the Gestalt principles of behavioral organization and draw or describe an example of each.
11. What are subjective contours, and what do they tell us about the perception of patterns and edges?
12. What is Pragnanz, and what relationship does it have to information theory? What is the relationship between symmetry and Pragnanz, and are there different types of symmetry?

CHAPTER 9

SPACE

CHAPTER SUMMARY

In 1621 Robert Burton noted that "All places are distant from heaven alike." Perhaps for a clergyman-philosopher such a description of spatial relations was sufficient. Yet, for you, a simple mortal trying to pick up a cup of coffee from the tabletop, much more precision is needed. You must be able to judge how far the cup is from your hand with a good deal of accuracy, lest you end up with a messy puddle of hot fluid. Your very life may depend on your precision in judging depth and distance, as when you sense that you are standing near the edge of a cliff or are driving your car along a mountain road. You cannot get cut by a knife edge pictured in a flat photograph, but the real blade extending toward you in space can produce painful contact. Thus, accomplishing our daily tasks safely depends on the accuracy of our spatial perception.

TYPES OF DEPTH PERCEPTION

Our perception of depth has at least two different aspects. The first involves the perception of the actual distance of an object, such as how far away a pencil is on a desk. This is an estimate of **absolute distance,** which involves a process called **egocentric localization.** Most of us are familiar with the word egocentric in its everyday use—you are egocentric if you are concerned only about your own activities and their effect on yourself. In the context of space perception, egocentric means where our bodies are positioned relative to other objects in the external environment. The second aspect of space perception involves the perception of relative distance, such as whether the pencil is lying nearer to the book or to the coffee cup, which are also on the desk. The judgment of relative distance requires the observer to make **object-relative localizations,** which are estimates of the distances between objects in the environment. The judgment of relative distance is also involved in the perception of whether an object is flat (as in a two-dimensional picture) or solid (three-dimensional), in that this requires estimation of the spatial relationships between parts of an object.

The accomplishment involved in seeing objects in depth is quite amazing considering that the basic information available to the nervous system is just a flat image on our retinas. The question of how we convert this two-dimensional image into our three-dimensional conscious impression of the world has stimulated a number of different theoretical approaches. Before discussing the research on this problem, we will briefly summarize these approaches. (Recall that we introduced three different theoretical approaches in Chapter 1.)

One approach is called **direct perception** (Michaels & Carello, 1981) and is characterized by the work of J. J. Gibson (e.g., 1979). Three assumptions are central to direct perception. The first is that all the information we need to see three dimensionally is present in the retinal image or in relationships among parts of the retinal image. The second is that the visual scene is analyzed by the brain in terms of whole objects and surfaces rather than in terms of elementary stimulus attributes such as edges, colors, and specific locations that together make up objects. Finally, direct perception assumes that the impression of depth or distance arises immediately in the observer on viewing the stimulus and needs no further computation or any additional information based on inferences or experience (see Sedgwick, 2001).

An alternative approach is used by scientists who view visual processing as being similar to information processing done by a computer. These scientists have been influenced by developments in **artificial intelligence,** which is a part of computer science that attempts to design machines that behave "intelligently," such as machines that can interpret visual information. There are actually two different types of these scientists. The first is interested in designing robots that can perform tasks for humans based on visual input. The second is interested in designing computer programs that will duplicate the processing steps actually used by a human observer when viewing visual stimuli such as pictures. For this second group the computer program actually serves the same function as a theory, in that it can be used to predict what a person might see in particular circumstances. Because of this, the computer programs, or the description of the processes used to create the programs, are often referred to as **computational theories** of vision. One of the best known of these computational theorists was David Marr (1982). He began with one of the assumptions made in direct perception, namely, that all the information we need to derive three dimensionality is present in the visual inputs. However, he departed from the direct perception view, in the manner of all computational theorists, when he suggested that the accurate interpretation of three dimensionality requires a number of complex computations and several stages of analysis (see also Edelman & Intrator, 2002).

A variation on the computational theories involves the idea of the **modularity of perception.** This approach was first offered by Jerry Fodor (1983), and it viewed the mind as a distinct set of units or modules, each of which is complete in itself and has a specific function with dedicated neural hardware that can do a specific bit of processing or computation. This allows the perceptual analysis to be quick yet does not require any conscious intervention. Perception can then take the output of many modules and pass it on to higher centers where cognitive processes can come into play (see Nakayama, 2001).

There is yet another important version of perceptual theory that is based on the assumption that our perceptual representation of the world is much richer and more accurate than might be expected on the basis of the information contained in the visual image alone. This approach, which might be called **intelligent perception,** originated with Helmholtz in 1867 and has carried on in many labs through to the present (see Fahle & Poggio, 2002). It suggests that perception is like other mental processes in that, in addition to the information available at the moment, we can use information based on our previous experience, our expectations, and so forth. In other words, our visual perception of space may involve "going beyond" the information given in the visual image. Some of this information may be nonvisual in nature, such as material derived from our past history, and the selection of this information may be affected by our cognitive processing strategies. Because this approach emphasizes the combining of several sources of information to "build" or "assemble" our conscious experience of what is "out there," such theories have also been called **constructive theories** of perception.

Although it is likely that each of these approaches is valid for some aspects of the perceptual process (cf. Coren & Girgus, 1978; Uttal, 1981), theorists who favor particular approaches tend to try to isolate different factors when they consider the perception of depth or distance. For instance, a theorist interested in direct perception might concentrate on looking at aspects of the stimulus and relationships between stimuli in the retinal image, whereas a theorist who believes in constructive perception may focus on the cognitive interpretive processes called into play when we attempt to comprehend the three-dimensional nature of the world. All of these approaches, however, usually begin by attempting to isolate the **cues** for depth. These are signals in the stimulus that we are often not consciously aware of but that function to shape our perceptual responses.

PICTORIAL DEPTH CUES

When you look at a realistic painting or a photograph, you find it easy to perceive the spatial relationships among the various items portrayed. Your impression of the relative distances in such scenes is based on a set of cues, appropriately called **pictorial depth cues.** These cues are also called **monocular cues** because they not only appear in pictures but also are available when only one eye is used to view a scene. Remember that the image on the retina is essentially two-dimensional (we will have more to say about this in Chapter 10). To understand these depth cues we must first recognize that visual experience usually depends on the transfer of light reflected from an object in the external world to the eye of the observer. A number of depth cues depend on characteristic ways in which light travels to the eye and on ways in which it is affected by the medium (usually air) through which it passes. Other depth cues depend on how light interacts with objects and also on the geometry of images.

Interposition or Occlusion

The vast majority of objects in the world are not transparent. Because light reflected from distant objects cannot pass through opaque objects that stand between them and the observer, a nearer object tends to block the view of a more distant one. This depth cue is called **interposition** or **occlusion.** It is easy to see that the cat in Figure 9.1 is nearer than the woman's leg because the view of the leg is partially covered by the image of the cat. Notice that interposition is a cue for relative depth only. It indicates that the cat is nearer than the woman's leg but not how far away the cat or the man is.

Although the cues for occlusion can be global, such as the fact that part of our view of an object that we know (or assume) is singular and complete may be blocked, there are also subtle local cues for occlusion.

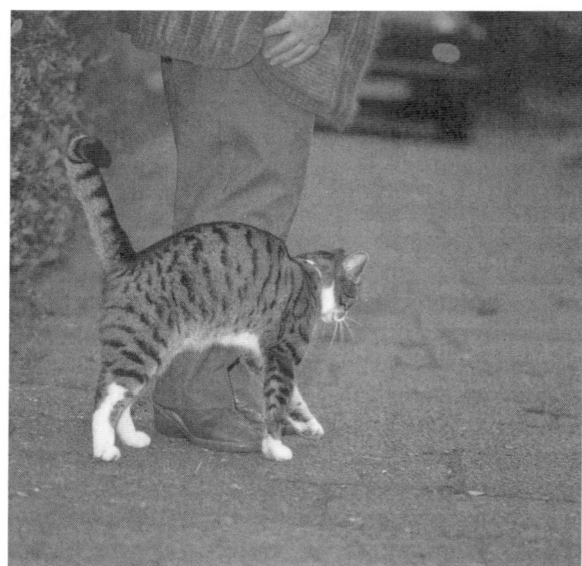

FIGURE 9.1 Interposition as a depth cue is illustrated by the fact that the cat is seen as closer than the woman's leg because it partially blocks the view of the leg.

One of the most pervasive of these is the so-called T-junction (see Rubin, 2002). The defining characteristic is a smooth, continuous contour (one that would fit the characteristics of *good continuation* as defined in the Gestalt principles we discussed in the previous chapter) against which another contour abruptly ends. The classic form of the T-junction is shown in Figure 9.2A. Notice that the object with the continuous contour (here the "roof" of the T) is seen as in front of and occluding the other figure. It is still a T-junction when it is turned on its side as in Figure 9.2B, and the continuous contour is still seen as in front. Don't get too literal about the "T" nomenclature, since it often looks more like a Y as in Figures 9.2C, D, and E; however, the continuous contour is always seen as part of the figure in front. There is also another common variation of a local a local cue for occlusion, which is an L shaped junction, where the object with the L contour is seen as being nearer to the observer, as in Figure 9.2F.

One of the most interesting findings with regard to interposition is that the absence of stimulation from the occluded part of an object, for example the part of the man's leg that is behind the cat in Figure 9.1, is only rarely brought into our consciousness. Instead, the visual system usually "fills in" the occluded portion of an object very rapidly and automatically, and we act as if the whole object were present and visible (Gerbino & Salmaso, 1987; Sekuler & Palmer, 1992). For example,

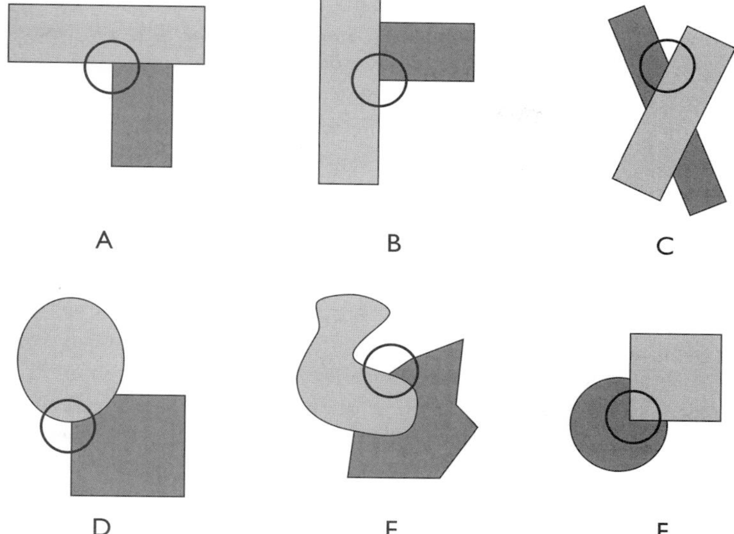

FIGURE 9.2 Intersections that indicate occlusion (enclosed by black circles): (A) is the classic form of the T-junction with the object with the long continuous contour seen as nearer; (B) is a T-Junction rotated 90 degrees; (C, D, & E) variants that look more like Y's than T's; however, the object with the long continuous contour is seen as closer; (F) is an L-junction where the object with the L contours is seen as nearer.

several studies have shown that subjects are able to make a speeded "same-different" response to pairs of shapes just as rapidly when one member of the pair is partly occluded as when both members of the pair are completely visible (Shore & Enns, 1997). Careful investigation of the amount of time needed for the "filling in" to be complete suggests that it occurs within the first 100 to 200 ms of processing (Sekuler & Palmer, 1992). Increasing the number and quality of other depth cues in the scene can reduce this time to less than 100 ms (Bruno & Bertamini, 1997).

The perceptual completion of the occluded figure is often referred to as an **amodal completion,** meaning that the missing parts of the figure are perceptually present even though there are no physical stimuli to support that conclusion (see Sekuler & Murray, 2001). Thus in Figure 9.3A we amodally "see" a circle that is partially blocked by a square, so that both figures are in our consciousness as in Figure 9.3B, which shows the figures as if the square were transparent. However, there is no reason that the physical actual situation might not be something like Figure 9.3C, where the figure is actually the stylized symbol for a male rather than a regular circle, or even Figure 9.3D, where there is not even any overlap but merely an irregular figure abutted to a square. Generally speaking, there is a preference to amodally complete the occluded figure in a manner that produces the simplest, and most regular object, much like the operation of the law of Pragnanz that we discussed in Chapter 8 (see Van Lier, 2001).

Shading and Shadows

The fact that light cannot pass through most objects gives rise to the interposition cue. The fact that light usually travels in straight lines gives us another cue for relative depth. This means that surfaces facing the light source will be relatively bright, whereas surfaces away

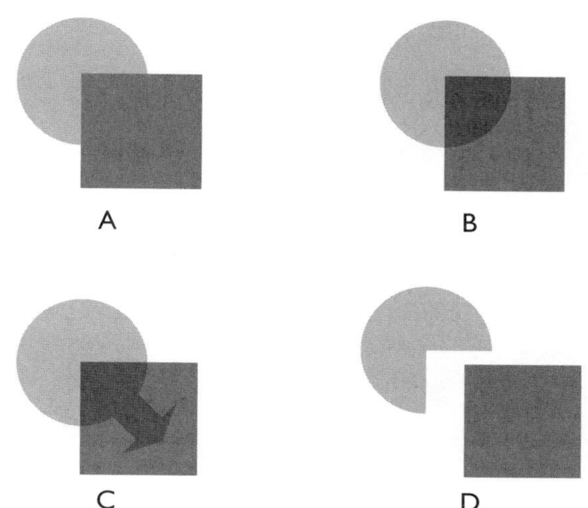

FIGURE 9.3 (A) is a typical occlusion array in which we amodally complete the occluded figure as if the two figures were as in (B). However, the hidden figure could look like what is seen in (C) or it might not even be hidden at all but shaped like what is seen in (D) and merely abutted against the square.

from the light source will be in shadow. Particular patterns of shadow can provide information about the relative shape of solid objects. Thus, if light comes from above, the lower part of an ingoing dent or "dimple" will catch more of the light, whereas the upper part will be in relative shadow. For an outgoing protrusion or "pimple" the top part will be bright and the lower part in shadow. This is illustrated in the picture of "pimples and dimples" shown in Figure 9.4. As it stands you see a square made up of "dents" or "dimples" surrounded by a field of "bumps" or "pimples." If you turn this book upside down, the light and shadow patterns in the figure reverse, and now the square is made up of protruding bumps, whereas the background is a field of ingoing dents (cf. Berbaum, Bever, & Chung, 1984; Ramachandran, 1988).

Clearly, for the shading cue to work consistently in Figure 9.4, we must be assuming that the light is coming from above (which it does in most everyday situations). If the light were coming from another direction, the shading pattern would be different. If you hold the figure so that it is at 90 degrees (e.g., the shadows are either to the left or right), the perception becomes unstable and will flip back and forth between the depth organizations. This perceptual shift will occur simultaneously for all of the figures of both types, almost as though the visual system can't represent more than one light source at a time (see Conner, 2001). Observers do seem to use their knowledge or presumptions about the location of the light source to help them accurately perceive the three-dimensional nature of objects using the shading cue (Berbaum, Bever, & Chung, 1983; Enns & Rensink,

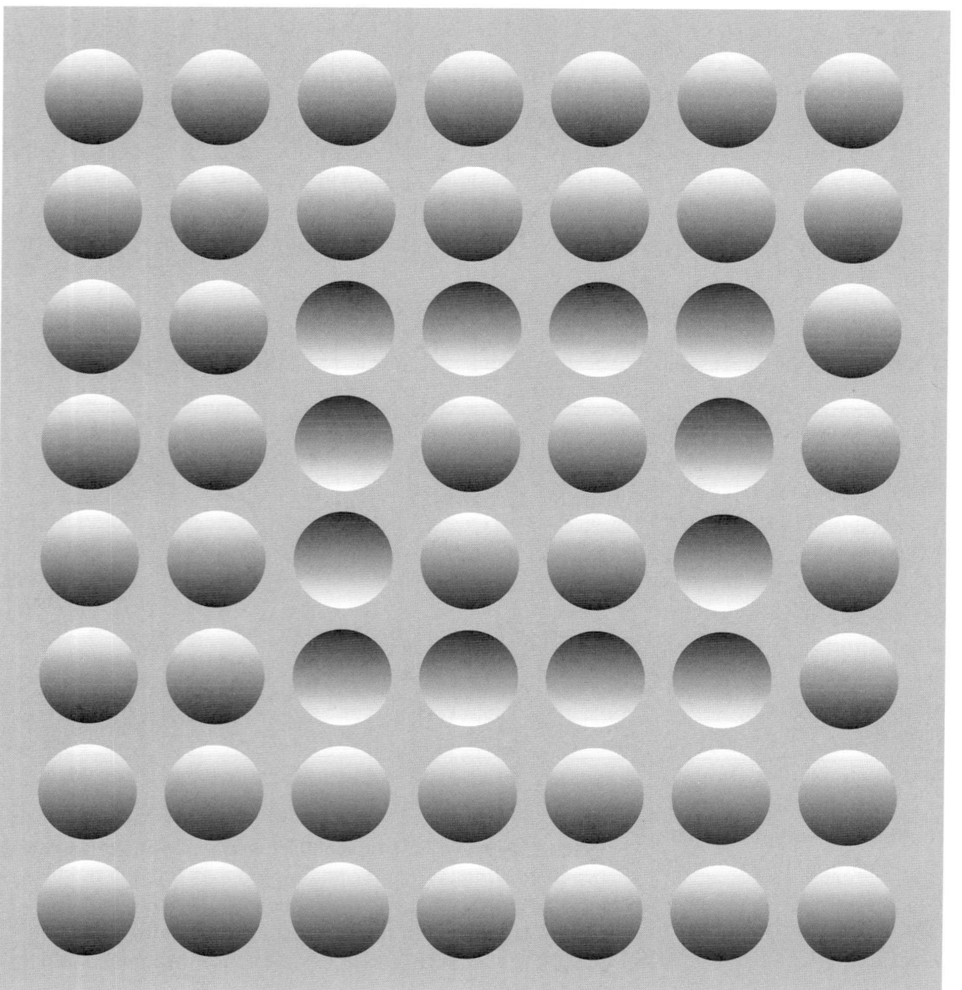

FIGURE 9.4 Shading makes it clear that we are looking at a central square made up of "dimples" or "dents" with a background of "pimples" or "bumps." Turning the figure upside down reverses the shadow pattern and also reverses the perceived depth relationships so that we see a square made up of pimples and a background of dimples.

1990). However, these effects are tied to retinal or head-centered coordinates rather than to gravitational coordinates. You can verify this by lying on your side and keeping the figure in the same orientation as your head. In this case the three-dimensional shape effects remain the same (Howard, Bergstrom, & Ohmi, 1990). This is surprising since light sources (with few exceptions, such as miner's helmets) are stable with relationship to gravity but not in relationship to our head position. Since visual information originates in retinal locations and the neural transformation into gravitational coordinates would be time-consuming and difficult, the visual system seems to have adopted the simpler, usually correct assumption of a light source above the head rather than the more accurate assumption of a light source above the ground. However, the linking of the depth interpretation to retinal coordinates seems to suggest an underlying neural bias. Recent recordings from Area V4 of the cortex is consistent with this, since specific neurons were found that appear to be selectively tuned for brightness patterns with the shadows on the top versus the shadows on the bottom (Hanazawa & Komatsu, 2001).

The shading pattern on an object or surface is actually only one of the cues associated with shadows. The shading that defines the shape of an object can be called an **attached shadow** because the pattern of light that serves as a cue to its three-dimensional shape is actually distributed over the object itself (see Figure 9.5). Another factor that can affect the shading pattern, however, is the presence of a second object or surface lying in the path of the light source. Such an object will give rise to a **cast shadow,** such as can be seen in Figure 9.5.

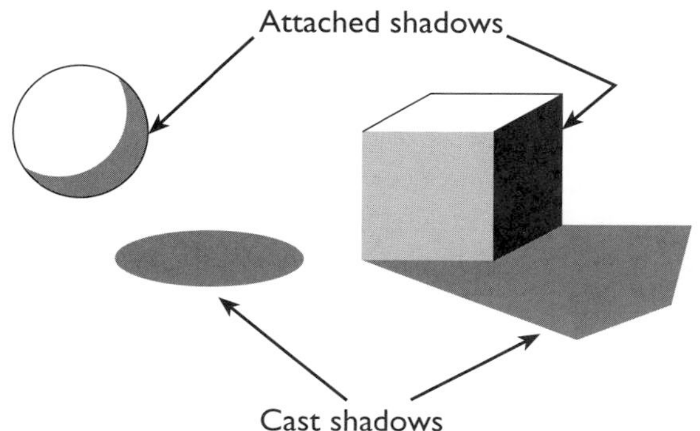

FIGURE 9.5 Two types of shadows that give us different information about depth. **Attached shadows** help to indicate the intrinsic shape of an object, and **cast shadows** indicate the relative distance of an object from another object or surface.

Attached and cast shadows share a number of attributes in the way they signal information about the visual world. For example, the direction from which light in a scene is being cast is given in a similar way by attached and cast shadows: Both shadows fall away from the source of light. The relation between the brightness of a shadow and the surrounding surface is also similar for both kinds of shadows: Shadows are invariably darker than the surfaces on which they are projected. Research shows that the human visual system has a broad tolerance for the interpretation of shapes as shadows, provided that they follow these rough guidelines (Cavanagh & Leclerc, 1989), while inconsistent shadows can impair perceptual identification (Castiello, 2001).

Research on the perception of shadows, however, also indicates that the visual system uses different information from cast shadows than from attached shadows in analyzing the visual world. Consider the shape of an object. Whereas attached shadows (shading) provide considerable information about surface shape via pattern of light and dark regions, cast shadows signal shape only through a distorted silhouette of the objects casting the shadows. When it comes to the determination of relative depth and distance, the two types of shadow again differ in their information content. Whereas the attached shadow can provide only information about object shape, observers are able to use the distance between objects and cast shadows to determine the relative depth of objects (Madison, Thompson, Kersten, Shirley, & Smits, 2001). Specifically, the more separated the object is from its cast shadow, the greater will be the perceived distance between the object and the shadowed surface (Allen, 2001). A compelling illusion of motion based on this principle occurs where a stationary target shape seen against a checkerboard pattern can be made to appear to move toward and away from the viewer simply by moving a cast shadow toward and away from the target shape (Kersten & Knill, 1996). Figure 9.6 shows successive shadow positions, and as the cast shadow seems to move farther away from the figure, the figure seems to loom at a higher distance above the checkered surface.

Aerial Perspective

The partial and complete blockage of light by objects gave us our first two pictorial cues for relative depth. Another cue for depth emerges from the fact that the air is filled with light-absorbing and light-scattering particles even on the clearest of days. As light passes through the air, some of it is absorbed, and other light is scattered by the minute particles of dust and moisture. Large particles

Time 1

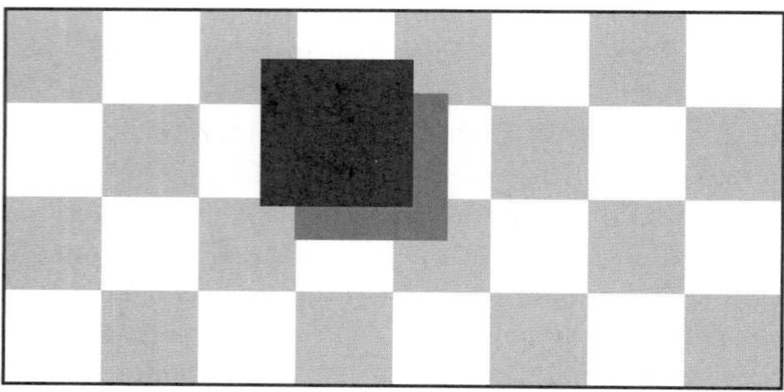

Time 2

Time 3

FIGURE 9.6 The stationary black square can be made to appear to move toward and away from the viewer simply by moving the gray cast shadow toward and away from the black square (drawn based on description by Kersten & Knill, 1996).

(such as dust) scatter the light uniformly, causing a uniform distribution of light or a blurring of the image. For particles that are small in comparison to the various wavelengths of light (such as minute bits of water vapor), the degree of scatter depends on the specific wavelength. In general, shorter wavelengths (blue) are scattered more than longer wavelengths (Uttal, 1981). The combined effect of these phenomena produces the cue called **aerial perspective,** in which the image of a very distant object, such as a distant mountain, will be slightly bluer in hue and hazier or less distinct in appearance than the images of nearer objects that are physically the same color.

Such changes in appearance can provide information about the absolute distances of relatively faraway objects (see Howard, 2002). In some geographic regions (such as the prairies of the United States and Canada), this can lead to considerable errors in distance judgments because the clear, dry air reduces aerial perspective. Thus, a plateau that appears to be only 1 or 2 miles away on a clear day, when looking across a dry sector of Wyoming, may actually be 20 or 30 miles from the observer. Conversely, this explains why objects seen in the morning fog or a mist appear to be farther away than when seen in bright midday sun (Ross, 1975).

An interesting variant of the aerial perspective cue is usually referred to as **relative brightness** or **relative contrast.** The light from more distant objects must travel through the atmosphere for a greater distance and may be subject to increased absorption or scattering of the light by the particles in the air. Thus, a more distant object may appear to be less bright. The scattering of the light may also cause an overall reduction in relative contrast. In the absence of any other cues, you will tend to see the brighter of two identical objects as closer, and even when other cues are present, reduced contrast is associated with seeing objects as more distant (Rohaly & Wilson, 1999). An example of aerial perspective and relative contrast can be seen in Color Plate 7.

Retinal and Familiar Size

As an object moves farther away, its **retinal image size** begins to diminish. One country song captured this effect in a lyric that went, "If you see me getting smaller I'm leaving." The geometry of this situation is shown in Figure 9.7, where the more distant person is casting a smaller retinal image. We tend to use these relative differences in retinal image size as a cue for relative distance, as in Figure 9.8, where we see a row of puppies that seems to recede into the distance because of their decreasing image size. Thus, the comparison of the sizes of objects in the visual field, relative to each other, is an important part of the process of perceiving relative distance.

Retinal image size is a cue used both by direct perception and by computational theories of perception. There is, however, another size cue that is important in

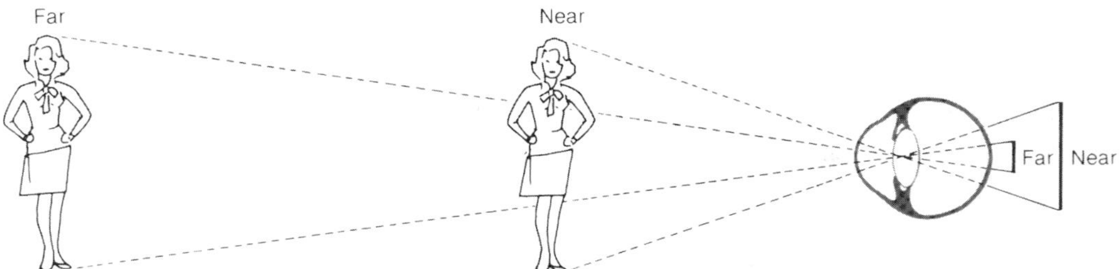

FIGURE 9.7 Objects of the same physical size produce smaller retinal angle sizes with increasing distance from the observer. Thus, relatively speaking, smaller images are perceived to be more distant.

constructive theories. This has nothing to do with image size but, rather, with your previous experience with the usual or **familiar size** of the object. For example, playing cards all tend to be around the same size. In a classic experiment Ittelson (1951) presented to observers three playing cards, under **reduction conditions.** This was usually a darkened room with all other depth cues removed. One of the playing cards was normal in size, a second was twice normal size, and a third was one half of normal size. He found that observers tended to judge the double-sized playing cards as being much closer to them and the half-sized cards as being much more distant than the normal-sized card. This is the same process that causes you to see the dogs in Figure 9.8 as receding into the distance. You assume that all of these images are about the same "dog size" and use this familiar size information in conjunction with the changing retinal size to gain the impression of changes in relative distance.

As long as the objects are well-known and the distances not too extreme, familiar size can give you absolute depth information, not merely relative depth information (Fitzpatrick, Pasnak, & Tyer, 1982; Marotta & Goodale, 2001). Thus, if we see a very tiny elephant, we can use our knowledge that elephants are relatively large creatures to deduce that the elephant has not shrunk in size but, rather, is far away from us. You may demonstrate the effect of familiar size for yourself by following the instructions in Demonstration Box 9.1.

Linear Perspective

There is a well-known pictorial depth cue that may be seen as an extension of the retinal-image-size cue to distance. This cue is **linear perspective.** For example, look at Figure 9.9, which is adapted from a book published in 1604 by Jan Vredman de Vries on how to depict perspective in drawings. In this schematic scene we notice that physically parallel lines, such as those defining the paving blocks making up the floor, seem to converge as objects become more distant. So do the hypothetical lines that connect all the tops and all the bottoms of the pillars, all of which are supposed to be physically the same size. This illustrates the fact that parallel lines in the real world, such as railroad tracks, appear to con-

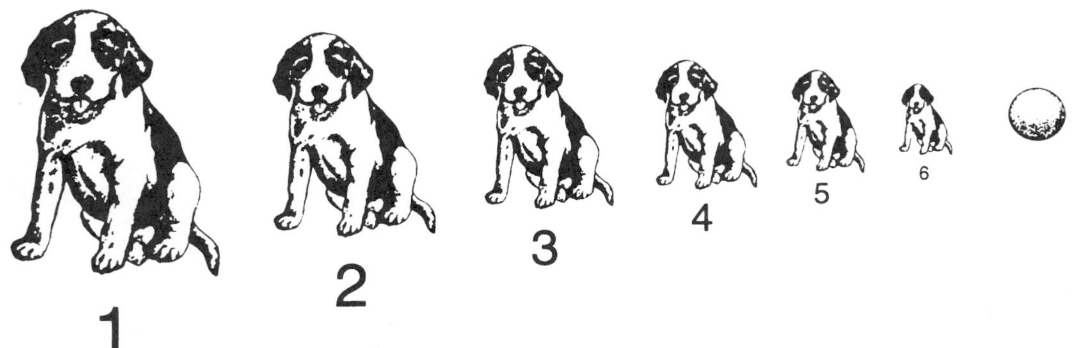

FIGURE 9.8 Relative size differences are interpreted as cues for relative distance. Thus, we see a row of puppies that seems to recede into the distance because of their decreasing image size.

DEMONSTRATION BOX 9.1

FAMILIAR SIZE AND DISTANCE

Look at Figure 9.8. Notice that the row of puppies seems to recede into the distance. Off to the right is a ball. If we told you that it is a tennis ball or a baseball, you would have no difficulty in deciding which dog is at the same distance away from you as the ball. After you decide this, return to this box.

Now, suppose we told you that the ball is really a volleyball or a basketball. Which dog is the same distance as the basketball? Notice that the ball apparently "moved backward" in depth when you assumed it was a larger object. This shows how knowledge of the size of an object can affect our judgment of the distance of the object, giving us the **familiar size** cue to distance.

verge, and objects appear to get smaller and smaller in a systematic fashion as their distance increases. Eventually they reach a **vanishing point,** where all the perspective lines converge, and objects diminish to invisibility. This point is usually on the horizon, as shown in the figure. This is a simple geometric effect that occurs in the real world and when we project a three-dimensional scene onto a two-dimensional surface. It provides a powerful relative depth cue (e.g., Braunstein & Liter, 1993). Hence, it is easy to determine that Pillar B is farther away than Pillar A by utilizing the perspective cue.

Texture Gradients

James J. Gibson (1966, 1979) suggested an interesting way of combining both linear perspective and relative

FIGURE 9.9 An example of linear perspective, in which physically parallel lines seem to converge as they grow more distant. Notice that the lines have been extrapolated to show a vanishing point on the horizon.

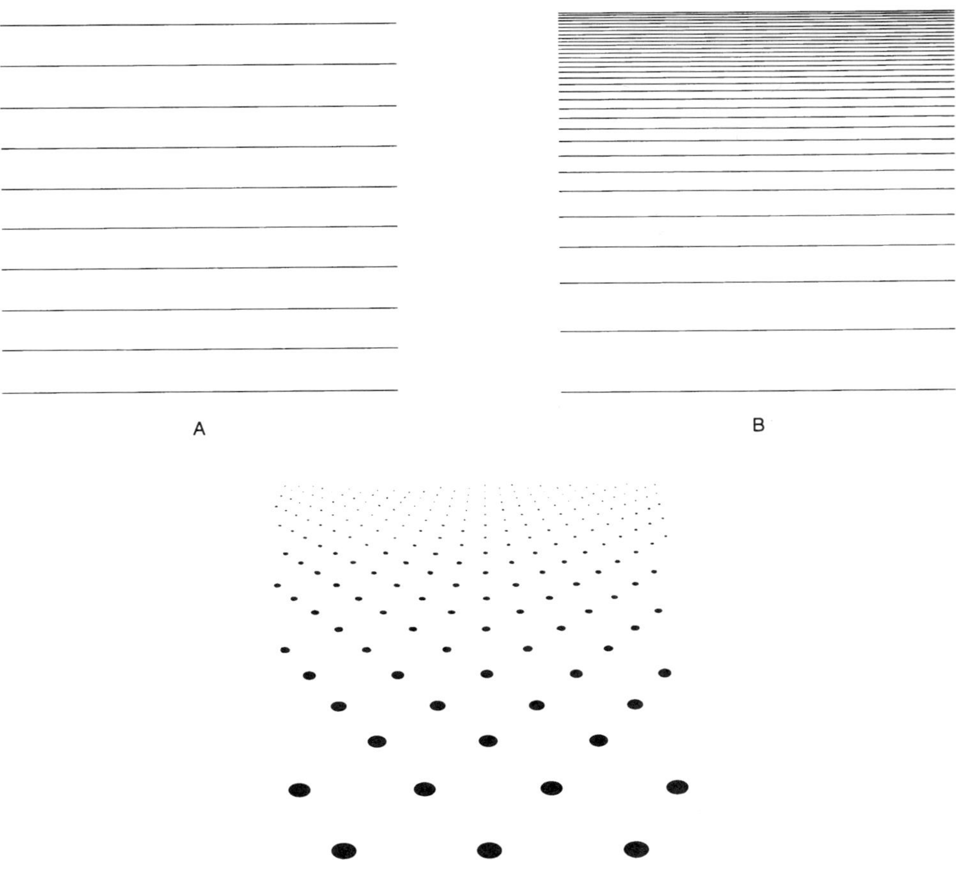

FIGURE 9.10 Examples of texture gradients are shown in B and C, which appear as surfaces receding in depth. In A there are no decreases in element size or spacing, and thus the perception is of a flat surface.

size information into one cue, which he referred to as **texture gradient.** A visual texture is loosely defined as any collection of objects in the visual image (Caelli, 1982), and the gradient (continuous change) is the change in the relative size and compactness of these object elements. The more distant parts of a texture have smaller elements that are more densely packed together. The depth impression associated with texture gradients is sometimes called **detail perspective.** Figure 9.10A shows a texture of lines. Because the texture is uniform, it shows little depth and looks much like a flat wall or garage door. If we introduce a gradient, however, as is done in Figure 9.10B, with the lines becoming more compact as we move toward the top, we now get an impression of depth. An even stronger impression of depth appears if we allow the gradient to appear in the horizontal placing of elements as well as the vertical, as can be seen in the texture of dots in Figure 9.10C.

One important type of information contained in texture gradients emerges from the fact that sudden changes in texture usually signal a change in the direction or distance of a surface. Thus, Figure 9.11A shows how the gradient changes from floor to wall, and Figure 9.10B shows how the gradient changes at a cliff or step-down. The perception of depth obtained from texture gradients can be quite striking. Texture helps us to define the shapes of solid objects (Li & Zaidi, 2000), as well as delicate variations in distance, as shown in the undulating surface depicted by texture cues alone in Figure 9.12 (cf. Todd & Akerstrom, 1987). Texture gradients rely on a more global analysis of stimulus relationships, and that level of analysis dominated the life of

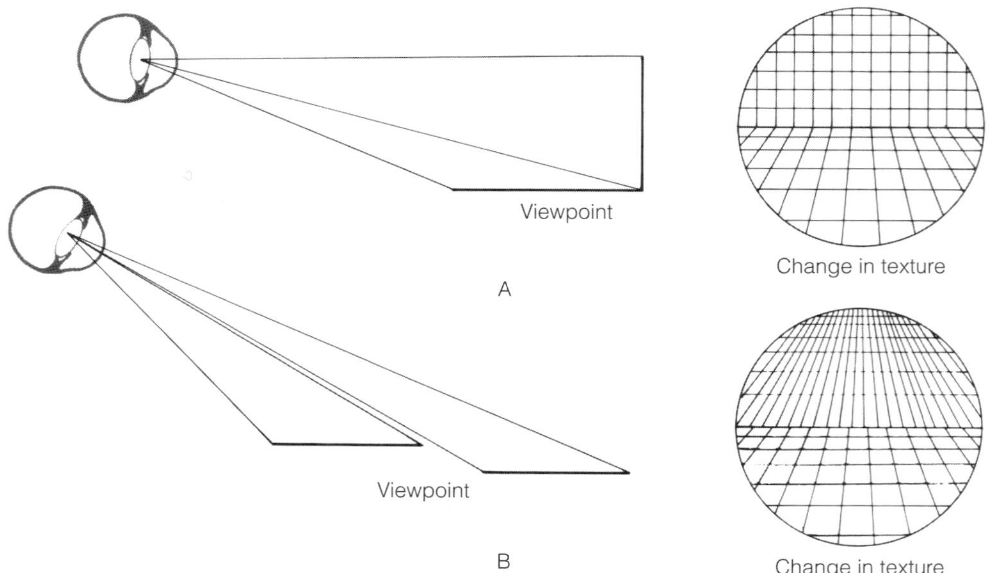

FIGURE 9.11 How texture changes at a corner (A) and an edge next to a sharp drop in depth (B).

their discover, James J. Gibson, who is described in Biography Box 9.1.

Height in the Plane

Another cue to distance depends on the relationships between objects as their images are projected onto our retinas. This cue is **height in the plane,** or **relative height,** and refers to where an object is relative to the horizon line. In Figure 9.13, Post B seems farther away than Post A because the base of Post B is closer to the horizon line. Hence, it is said to be "higher in the plane," or "higher in the picture plane," if we consider this as a two-dimensional projection. The reverse holds for targets above the horizon. Bird C seems farther away than Bird D because Bird C is "lower in the picture plane." In other words, proximity to the horizon line signals the greater distance.

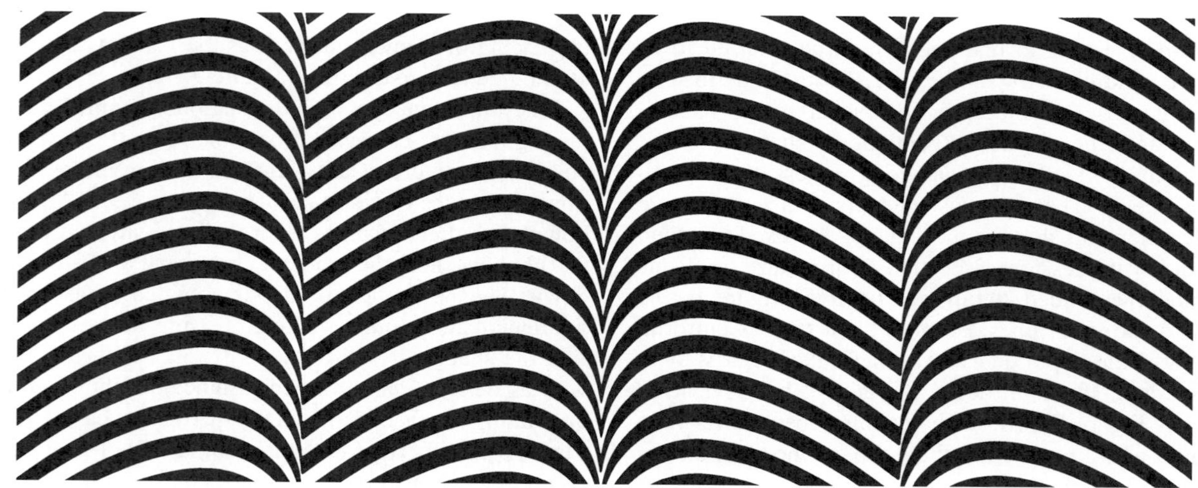

FIGURE 9.12 This rippling or undulating surface is defined completely on the basis of variations in texture density.

BIOGRAPHY BOX 9.1

THE MANY TEXTURES OF PERCEPTION

James J. Gibson (1904–1979) is one of the most appreciated psychologists in the field of depth perception and motion perception, yet his theoretical views can still arouse passionate debate, both pro and con, nearly a half a century after he began to introduce them. Gibson studied at Northwestern University and then went on to Princeton for his Ph.D. His first teaching position was at Smith College, where he met Kurt Koffka, one of the founders of Gestalt Psychology (see Chapter 8), and although he was never converted to Gestalt theory, the idea that one must look at the relationships described by the whole pattern of stimuli and not at individual elements stuck with him and became a foundation of his own thinking.

It was while serving in the U.S. Air Force during World War II that Gibson began to think seriously about depth perception. This was an important problem, since the ability to judge depth, distance, and speed of motion are crucial to a pilot, especially if he was trying to land on the relatively tiny platform of the aircraft carriers of that era. After the war Gibson published his research and speculations in one of the most influential books ever written about depth perception, *The Perception of the Visual World* (Gibson, 1950). The book was important not only because it described a new emergent cue for depth (namely, the texture gradient) but because it redefined how researchers were to look at the visual world. Gibson suggested that we look not only at individual stimuli but rather at surfaces, textures, and edges. This book also described the way in which stimuli change and flow as an individual moves, which would become the foundation for much research on motion perception.

Gibson moved on to Cornell, where he stayed for the rest of his career. It was there that he met his wife, the developmental psychologist Eleanor Jack Gibson (Chapter 16), and they collaborated on several important papers on perceptual learning.

At the theoretical level, Gibson became the leader of a new movement in perception. It was originally called direct perception since he felt that information was directly extracted from the environment, without any inferential steps, intervening variables or mechanisms, or learned associations. The task of the psychologist was to find those aspects of the stimulus array that gave the best information and were relied on most heavily by the perceiver. The last phase of his theorizing has led to what is often referred to as ecological psychology. This shifted the analysis to look for those aspects of the stimulus that provide a behaving organism with information about opportunities for interaction with the environment (which he called *affordances*). He believed that an active organism receives a continuous flow of information, and some of these channels of information provide invariant and stable information about the world. Later computational theorists would accept that as one of the basic postulates for their own approach to perception.

FIGURE 9.13 Height in the plane and proximity to the horizon will determine which elements in the diagram are perceived as more distant. In this case, B and C are seen as being farther away because they are closer to the horizon.

PHYSIOLOGICAL CUES FOR DEPTH

Until now we have considered only cues for depth that can be found in the retinal image itself. There are other cues for distance that come about because of the way the visual system responds to or interacts with the visual stimulus. These may be called **structural** or **physiological cues** because they arise from muscular responses and adjustments of the eye.

Accommodation

When we discussed the physiology of the eye in Chapter 3, we described how the crystalline lens responds to targets at different distances from us. We noted that the shape of the lens must change (actually its amount of curvature changes) in order to keep the retinal image in clear focus (Dalziel & Egan, 1982). This process is called **accommodation.** Only one particular curvature will clearly focus the retinal image of an object viewed at a particular distance from the eye. Relaxed accommodation, where the lens is relatively flattened, is necessary if distant objects are to be clearly focused on the retina, whereas a strongly curved lens is needed to image closer objects on the retinal surface. As we change the tension on the ciliary muscles, which control the lens shape, feedback from these muscular changes can provide us with some additional nonvisual information about the distance of the object we are looking at.

In addition to feedback from the act of accommodation, the presence or absence of blur due to an object being out of focus can serve as a cue for relative distance. It has been shown that in the absence of all other depth information, observers can judge that two spots of light presented in complete darkness are at different distances. This is probably because accommodation cannot be correct for two stimuli at different distances at the same time; hence, one of the lights will be slightly blurred and out of focus, suggesting that the targets are not equidistant (Kaufman, 1974).

There is some controversy over the utility of accommodation as a cue to depth in everyday situations. Accommodation is rather slow in its effects and is also limited in the range of observer-to-object distances over which it is useful. For example, for objects at a distance of around 3 m, the lens has fully relaxed accommodation and doesn't flatten out any farther, regardless of how far away an object is. There is a similar limit for close objects. If a target is within 20 cm of your face, your lens has reached its point of maximum curvature. It is within the range of 20 to 300 cm that accommodation seems likely to provide a useful auxiliary cue for distance, where it seems to work in combination with other cues for depth (e.g., Mather & Smith, 2000). It seems most useful when glimpses of targets occur at different times, however, since the change in accommodation from one view to the next is easily sensed as a change in the object's distance (Mon-Williams & Tresilian, 2000).

Convergence and Divergence

Another potential distance cue comes from the fact that we have two eyes. Two-eyed perception is referred to as **binocular,** from *bi* meaning "two" and *ocula* meaning "eye." Because (as we learned in Chapter 3) the best visual acuity is obtained when the image of an object is focused on the two foveas, eye movements are executed to bring the image to this region of each eye. If the eyes move in different directions, this is called **vergence movement.** If an object is close to you, you must rotate your eyes inward (toward the nose) in order to focus its image on the fovea. Such a movement is called **convergence** (the root *con* means "toward"). When a target is farther away, the eyes must move away from each other in an outward rotation (toward the temples); hence, this movement is called **divergence** (from the root *di* meaning "apart"). Different degrees of convergence and divergence are shown in Figure 9.14.

Each target distance, up to about 6 m, is associated with a unique angle between the eyes called the **convergence angle,** as indicated in Figure 9.14. To achieve each eye position, a unique pattern of muscular contractions must occur. Feedback from such vergence movements could be useful in determining the distances of objects, although there has been some controversy about how useful and reliable such information is as a depth cue (Rivest & Ono, 1989). It seems that information from convergence is given greater weight when the depth information it signals is consistent with that from other available cues (Tresilian & Mon-Williams, 2000). Thus convergence and accommodation acting together may provide accurate absolute depth information, especially when the only visible stimulus is a single point of light whose distance observers are asked to judge (Morrison & Whiteside, 1984).

Perhaps one reason why convergence and accommodation are somewhat weaker cues for depth is the fact that the eye will use other depth cues preferentially to adjust the eye. Thus there is some evidence that the eyes will attempt to converge and accommodate as if they were looking at objects at various distances in response to the available depth cues from other sources (e.g., Takeda, Hashimoto, Hiruma, & Fukui, 1999) even when

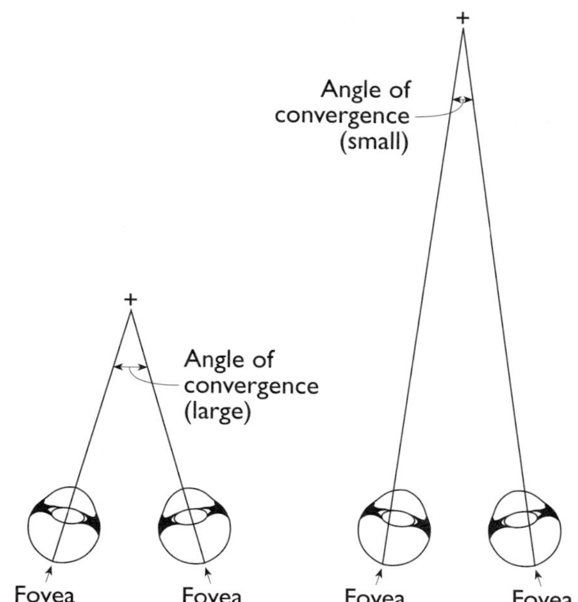

FIGURE 9.14 Convergence angle changes as a function of fixation distance. This may provide some information about target distance.

these cues are in paintings and line drawings (Enright, 1987a, 1987b).

MOTION AND MOTION PARALLAX

Except for the physiological cues, all of the cues to depth we have discussed so far can be defined with respect to a single static or unchanging image, such as a photograph or a painting. However, most of our perception of depth occurs in an environment in which the observer is in motion (because of body, head, or eye movements) and very often one in which objects are in motion as well. This gives the visual system the opportunity to compare multiple images over time, each slightly different depending on the speed of movement. Therefore, it should not be surprising that when we add motion to the incoming visual pattern, some additional depth cues appear.

One of these movement cues concerns the pattern of motion of an object as you travel past it. Suppose you are traveling in a car or bus and looking at the scene in Figure 9.15. Suppose also that your direction of movement is from right to left and that you are gazing at the spot marked "fixation point." Under these conditions, all of the objects closer to you than the fixation point will appear to move in a direction opposite to your movement, whereas objects that are farther away will appear to move in the same direction you are moving. Not only the

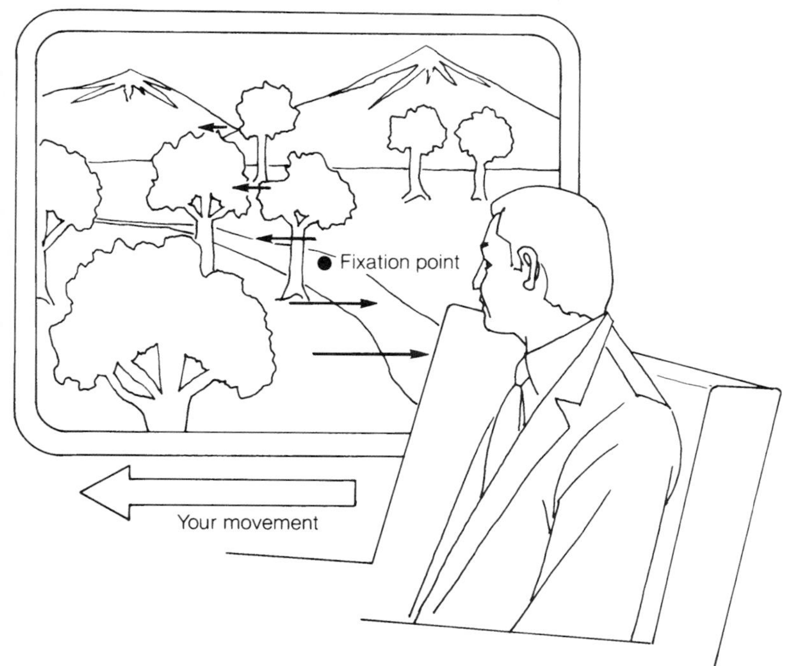

FIGURE 9.15 Motion parallax. When an observer moves, objects at varying distances from the observer will move in different directions at differing speeds. These differences can serve as cues for the relative distances of the objects.

direction but also the speed of movement vary with the objects' proximity to you and to your point of fixation—the nearer the object is to the retina, the faster will be its motion across the retina relative to other objects. This cue to distance is called **motion parallax.** Motion parallax is a good cue for relative distance (to tell you which of several objects is nearer or farther from you) but is not very good at giving you absolute distance, such as how many meters away from you an object is located (Bradshaw, Parton, & Glennerster, 2000).

Your whole body does not have to be moving to generate motion parallax. This cue can also be generated simply by swinging your head back and forth while your body is stationary, giving you very good information about the depth of objects if they are not too distant from you (Ono & Rogers, 1988). The accuracy of depth perception depends on the speed with which the head is moving (Ujike & Ono, 2001). Motion parallax based on body movements is treated differently than is optical motion from environmental events (Wexler, Panerai, Lamouret, & Droulez, 2001). An obvious reason for this is that we must somehow enter the actual body movements into our calculations when computing depth estimates based on the relative motion of images across our retinas. Thus it is not surprising to find that there are specialized areas in the brain that respond to this kind of optical motion (Nishiike, Nakagawa, Tonoike, Takeda, & Kubo, 2001). These areas are located in the temporal lobes of the brain very near the areas that monitor the vestibular system. The vestibular system responds to body and head movements and will be discussed further in Chapter 12.

A special form of motion parallax occurs when an object moves or rotates. The relative pattern of movement of parts of the object can give us information about its three-dimensional shape (e.g., Carpenter & Dugan, 1983; Doner, Lappin, & Perfetto, 1984). The fact that motion cues can give us information about the relative

DEMONSTRATION BOX 9.2

THE KINETIC DEPTH EFFECT

To see how subtle motion parallax effects can create the impression of a three-dimensional form in a two-dimensional pattern, you will need a candle and a piece of stiff wire (a coat hanger or a long pipe cleaner will do). Bend the wire into a random three-dimensional shape. Now light the candle and darken the room. Place the bent wire so it casts a shadow on a blank wall, as shown in the figure. Notice that when the shape is absolutely motionless, the shadow is seen as a flat pattern of lines. Now if you rotate the shape with your hand, the shadow suddenly changes perceptually, becoming a three-dimensional object that cannot be seen as flat, despite the fact that you are viewing a two-dimensional shadow. This phenomenon is also sometimes referred to as **depth from motion.**

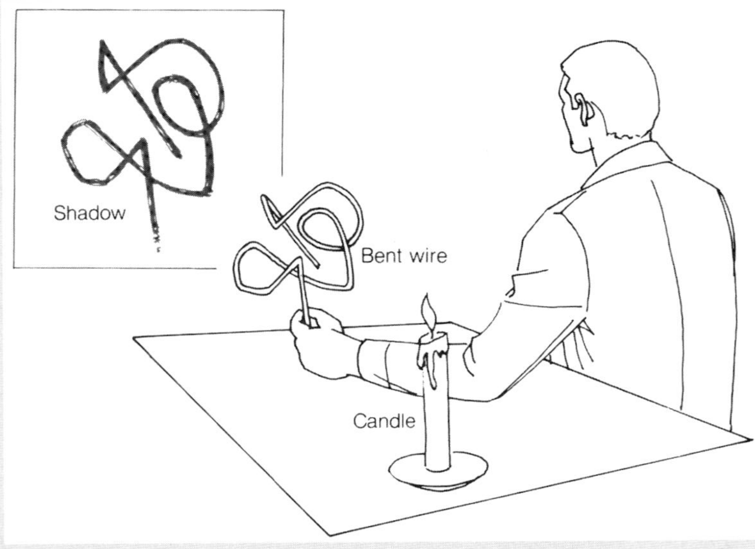

depth of parts of an object has been called the **kinetic depth effect** or **structure-from-motion** (Hogervorst & Eagle, 2000). Demonstration Box 9.2 allows you to see this phenomenon for yourself. In Chapter 12 ("Motion") you will also learn how motion parallax can give you information about the direction of your movements through space.

BINOCULAR DEPTH PERCEPTION

Just as motion provides the visual system with multiple images to compare, thereby giving it additional cues to depth, the fact that we have two eyes confers a great advantage in trying to estimate relative depth. For example, in many common tasks involving judgments of relative depth, such as threading a needle, inserting items into slots, or even placing cards behind alphabetic dividers in a box, many people perform up to 30% faster and more accurately when using both eyes than they do with one eye alone (Sheedy, Bailey, Buri, & Bass, 1986). For this reason, many occupations or tasks that require good distance-judging proficiency also require screening for **stereopsis,** which is the ability to extract depth information from the binocular views. Poor stereopsis can prevent a person from becoming an airplane pilot or even from driving a car.

Cues for Stereopsis

The specific cue for binocular depth perception (stereopsis) depends on the fact that, in humans and many other animals, the two eyes are horizontally separated but overlap in their view of the world. In humans, the dis-

DEMONSTRATION BOX 9.3

BINOCULAR DISPARITY

You can see the difference between the views of your eyes by holding a pencil up near your nose, as shown. The tip of the pencil should be toward you and angled slightly downward. Now alternately close each eye. The pencil seems to swing back and forth. With your right eye open, it appears angled toward the left; with the left eye open, it appears angled toward the right. With both eyes open, the fused view is of a pencil straight ahead of your nose.

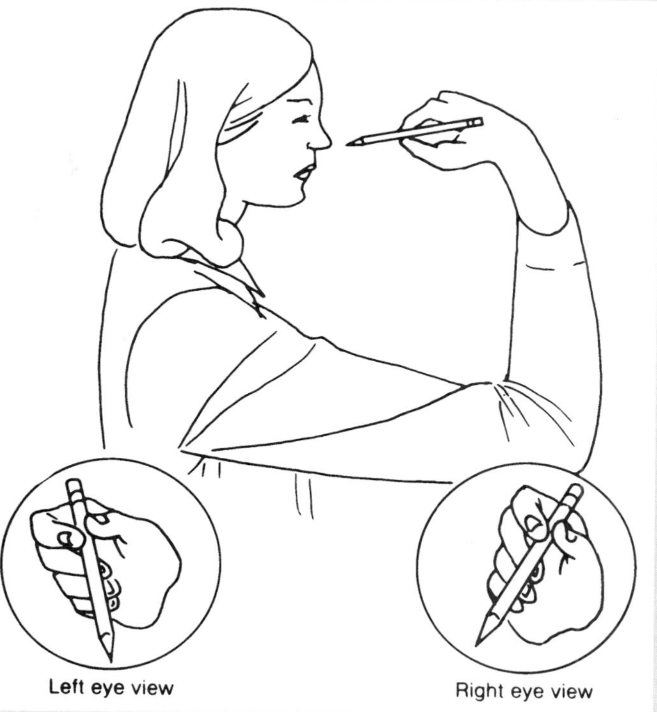

tance between the two pupils can be up to 6.5 cm. Because of this separation, each eye has a different view of the objects seen by both eyes and hence a different image of the world. We call the differences between the two eyes' images **binocular disparity.** You can see how different the images may be by following the instructions in Demonstration Box 9.3.

The process by which we merge these disparate images into a single unified percept is called **fusion.** As a process, however, fusion is fairly limited in its range of operation, and many parts of the total visual image do not fuse. This failure of the two eyes' views to merge completely gives rise to double vision or **diplopia.** Under normal viewing conditions you are not usually consciously aware of this diplopia; however, you can readily learn to see the double images in the unfused portion of the visual field. Demonstration Box 9.4 shows how this is done.

In Demonstration Box 9.4 you should have noticed that the pattern of double images is different depending on whether the unfused image is in front of or in back of the target you fixated. In the demonstration we defined these patterns as **crossed** versus **uncrossed disparity.** Objects more distant than the point of fixation are seen in uncrossed disparity, whereas closer objects are seen with crossed disparity. Hence, we can use the type of double image as a cue to relative distance. Only objects at about the same distance as the target we are fixating will be fused and seen singly. When we map out all of the points where targets are at about the same convergence or fixation distance in visual space, we trace out an imaginary curved plane called the **horopter.** A narrow region on either side of this hypothetical plane includes all points in visual space that are fused into single images. It is called **Panum's area.** Figure 9.16 contains a diagram of the horopter and Panum's area. The size and shape of Panum's area actually change a bit with varying fixation distances. However, for every fixation distance there is a zone in the visual field where the disparate images are seen as fused into a single object.

The process of fusion has also been studied in terms of **corresponding retinal points.** These are areas on the retina that represent a common direction or location according to the map of the visual field represented in the

DEMONSTRATION BOX 9.4

DOUBLE IMAGES AND DISPARITY

Find a piece of transparent colored material, such as cellophane (any hue will work). Place it before your right eye. If you wear glasses, you can affix it to the frame over the lens in front of your right eye; if not, use a piece of tape to hold it to your forehead. Now align two index fingers directly in front of your nose with the closer finger about 10 to 20 cm from your nose and the farther finger about 8 cm behind the closer one.

Now that you have arranged the appropriate situation, fixate your nearer finger. However, simultaneously try to pay attention to what the far finger looks like. This is a pretty difficult feat to accomplish at first, but with practice you should be able to fixate one target while simultaneously paying attention to what is going on beyond the fixated area. When you fixate the near target, you will notice that two images of the far target will be seen. The fact that one eye is viewing the image through a colored filter should help make the presence of double images beyond the fixation point more apparent. If you switch your fixation to the farther object, the closer of the two targets will appear as a double image. Targets that lie away from the area surrounding the point of fixation are not fused into a single image. They produce disparate retinal images. Disparate (unfused) images are always present in the visual field; however, we are usually not aware of them unless forced to attend to them, as in this demonstration.

After you have become comfortable with this procedure, fixate the near target and then close your right eye. You should notice that the image of the far target (the uncolored image) appears to lie to the left of the nearer, fixated object. Now close the left eye and open the right, and you will notice the opposite. The image of the far target (the colored image) now appears to lie to the right of the nearer, fixated target. The fact that the right eye is seeing the right disparate image and the left eye is seeing the left disparate image means that when both eyes are open, the far target is seen in uncrossed disparity. The opposite will happen if you change your fixation to the far target. Now the closer object appears as diplopic (double). If you once again alternately close each eye, you will notice that the right eye is now seeing the image that lies to the left of the fixated target (the colored image), while the left eye is viewing the image that lies to the right. In the case of double images that lie closer to us than the point of fixation, we have a situation of crossed disparity. As the text explains, these differences in disparity may be a cue to distance.

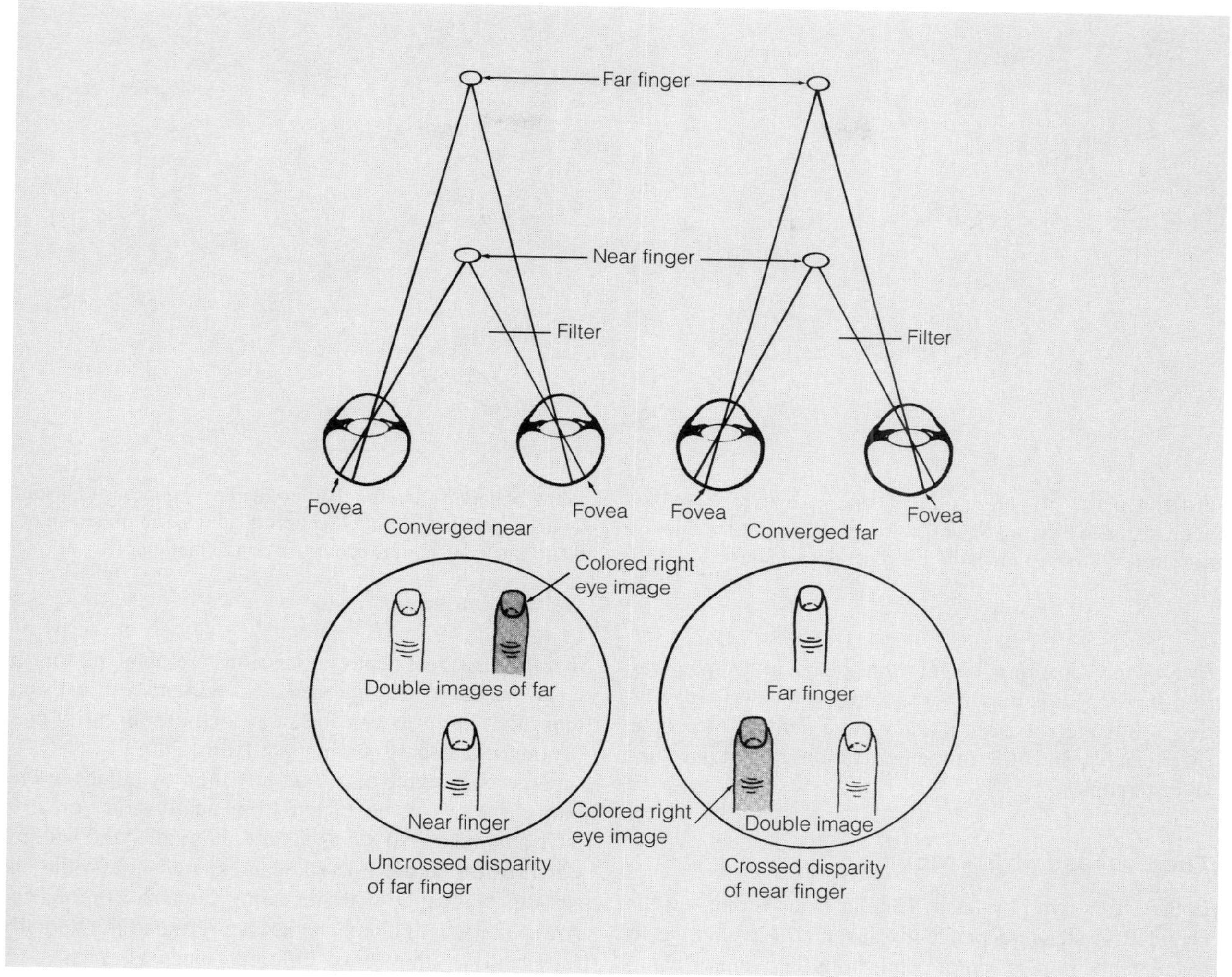

visual areas of the brain. The foveas of the two eyes are corresponding retinal points, and, according to this conceptualization, the horopter represents the zone in visual space that stimulates corresponding retinal points for one fixation distance.

There are large individual differences in stereoscopic depth perception. **Percent stereopsis** is a measure of an individual's sensitivity, and it is similar to Snellen acuity or decibels of hearing loss in that it is based on a comparison to a fixed value for "normal" or average stereopsis. In this case **100% stereopsis** refers to an ability to accurately interpret a depth difference based on a binocular disparity difference of 20 sec of visual angle. In most states in the United States an individual must have a minimum of 65% stereopsis (the ability to resolve depth given by disparity of 59 sec of visual angle) to get an unrestricted automobile driver's license. Persons with less than this degree of stereopsis may still be able to ascertain depth differences based on binocular disparity alone if the differences are large enough. People with only 25% stereopsis would require a binocular disparity of 286 sec of visual angle (almost 5 degrees) to detect any depth differences. Such disparity levels will seldom be encountered under normal circumstances; hence, such people will have no functionally usable stereopsis to assist in the accurate manipulation of objects within arm's length, and they will not benefit from binocular disparity when trying to catch a ball or when engaging in activities where precise relative depth judgments are important. It is possible for you to estimate your stereopsis ability without the use of laboratory instruments, using the inventory developed by Coren and Hakstian (1996). This

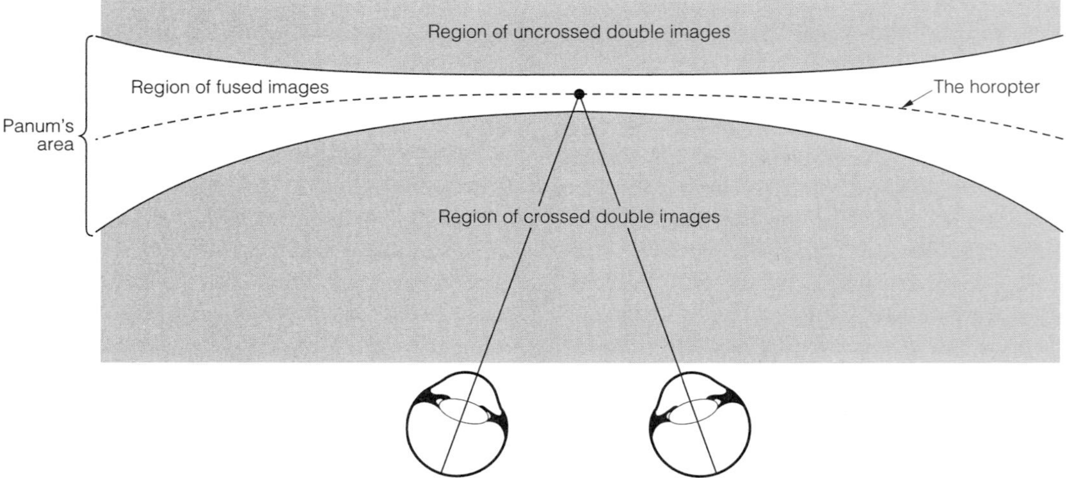

FIGURE 9.16 The horopter and Panum's area for one fixation distance. The regions of fusion and disparate images are shown. Crossed disparity is present at distances closer to the observer than the fixation distance; uncrossed disparity is present beyond the fixation distance. The presence of disparate images may provide a cue to distance.

Stereopsis Screening Inventory appears in Demonstration Box 9.5. It is important to know your own capabilities in this area because a fairly large number of people (between 5% and 10% of the population) do not have usable stereopsis.

The Process of Stereopsis

In the 1830s two physicists, Charles Wheatstone and Sir David Brewster, independently invented a technique to re-create the impression of depth from flat pictures using only the binocular disparity cue (see Wade, 1984). Their technique involves recreating the disparate views each eye would see and representing them to the eyes in the form of drawings or photographs. Thus, in Figure 9.17A, we have two rods at different distances from the observer. If we drew the image each eye sees, we would get something like Figure 9.17B. Notice that the images are disparate because the rods are more widely separated in the right eye's image than in the left eye's image. Now the resulting images are viewed in an optical instrument known as a **stereoscope,** which places different stimuli into the two eyes simultaneously, as shown in Figure 9.17C. When this is done, the disparate images fuse, and the objects are seen as if they were an actual three-dimensional scene. For a period of time every Victorian living room had a stereoscope and a set of travel pictures of famous places that had been taken using a camera with two lenses and shutters. This produced the "visual magic" of depth from flat images. Recent research shows that the strongest depth impressions are obtained for objects that have well-defined textures and vertical contours that seem to provide more definite disparity cues (Thomas, Goldberg, Cannon, & Hillis, 2002).

A certain degree of insight into the way binocular disparity works can be gotten from an illusion you may have stumbled across by accident. It is called the **wallpaper illusion** because people can experience it while observing wallpaper with repeating elements or objects. Any pattern with elements that are repeated horizontally (especially if they have different spacings, such as in Figure 9.18) can produce the illusion of depth. There are two ways to see this depth. However, before starting to view these patterns, remember that you must have adequate stereopsis ability (see Demonstration Box 9.5) or you are just wasting your time. Second, even among people who have normal stereopsis, some achieve the fusion into depth much more slowly than others (Tam & Stelmach, 1998), so don't panic, just keep at it.

The first viewing method will give you crossed disparity. Place your finger close to the middle of Figure 9.18 and focus on it. Now draw your finger back closer to you while you try to keep the finger in focus (and in fused vision). Try, at the same time, to attend to the pattern behind your finger. It will start to blur, but at some point you will notice that the three lines appear to be at different depths, with the "smiley faces" closest and the blue dots most distant. For many people the fused depth will "lock in" and you can remove your finger and look at this "illusory" depth that stereopsis has provided you.

DEMONSTRATION BOX 9.5

STEREOPSIS SCREENING INVENTORY

To get an estimate of your own stereopsis, simply take this test. It is the Stereopsis Screening Inventory* developed by Coren and Hakstian (1996). Scores on this test correlate (r = 0.80) with laboratory measures of stereoscopic depth sensitivity. The questionnaire deals with a number of common visual situations. For each question you should select the response that best describes you and your behaviors. You can select from among the following response alternatives: Never (or almost never), Seldom, Occasionally, Frequently, Always (or almost always). Simply circle the letter that corresponds to the first letter of your choice.

1. Do you find most book print too small to be read easily without glasses or contact lenses? N S O F A
2. When you were a child, did your parents or teachers tell you that you were holding the book too close to your eyes? N S O F A
3. Are you troubled by temporary losses of vision in one or both eyes? N S O F A
4. Do your eyes feel "tired," especially at the end of the workday? N S O F A
5. Do you wear glasses or contact lenses? N S O F A
6. Do you think that you may need glasses? N S O F A
7. Would you say that your vision is as good as most people's? N S O F A

Answer these last two questions using Good, Average, Slightly Below Average, Poor, or Very Poor (circle the first letter corresponding to your choice).

8. Without glasses or contact lenses, the clearness or sharpness of vision in my right eye is G A S P V
9. Without glasses or contact lenses, the clearness or sharpness of vision in my left eye is G A S P V

Scoring Instructions

Responses to Questions 1 to 6 are scored as 1 for "Never," 2 for "Seldom," 3 for "Occasionally," 4 for "Frequently," and 5 for "Always." Question 7 is reverse scored ("Never" 5 to "Always" 1). For Questions 8 and 9, scoring goes from 1 for "Good" to 5 for "Very Poor." You next need to compute a tenth score, which is simply the absolute (unsigned) difference between Questions 8 and 9 (e.g., if the response to Question 8 was "Good" and to Question 9 was "Slightly Below Average," the tenth entry in the total would be the absolute difference of 1 minus 3, which is 2). Now add these 10 scores (your nine answers plus the computed tenth value) to get your total score.

If your total score is 17 or less, you have better than 65% stereopsis, and for most everyday situations your binocular depth perception is normal. If your total score is 18 to 30, you have an 84% chance of having a moderate to strong stereopsis deficit (65% to 25% stereopsis). Although you may be able to use binocular depth information if the disparities are large, you have enough of a depth loss that you have a high probability of failing the depth perception test used for most automobile driver's licenses. With scores of 31 or higher there is an 81% chance that you are among the 5% to 10% of the population who have no functional stereopsis (stereopsis less than 25%).

*Copyright SC Psychological Enterprises reprinted with permission.

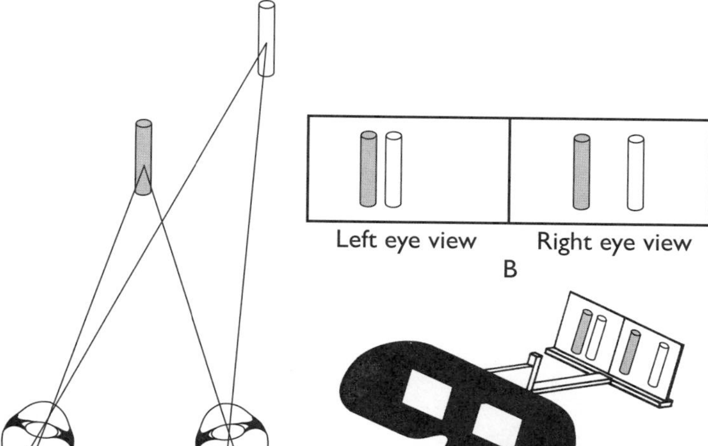

FIGURE 9.17 Disparate retinal images. (A) The two retinal images of a scene are different because the two eyes view the world from slightly different directions. (B) A stereogram is a flat representation that mimics the differences between the two retinal images. (C) A stereogram is viewed in a stereoscope that allows for the separate but simultaneous stimulation of the two eyes. The perceptual phenomenon is called **stereopsis.**

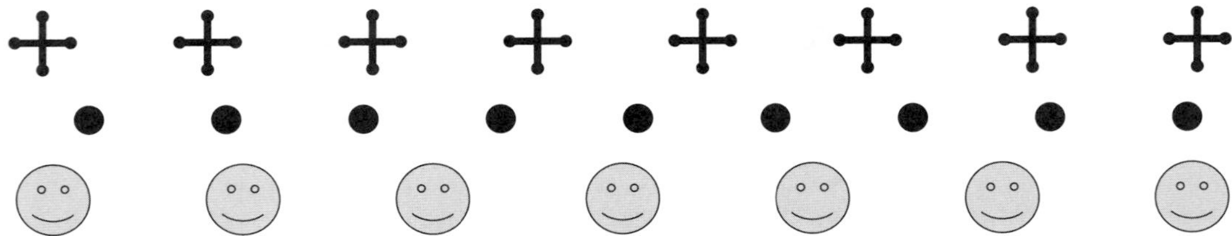

FIGURE 9.18 Stimulus pattern for the wallpaper illusion—these three lines of figures will be seen as floating at different distances depending on whether crossed or uncrossed disparity is used. The text provides instructions for viewing this figure.

In this view the smiley faces appear to be closer to you (and the dots appear to be most distant). Figure 9.19A gives you a bird's eye view as to what is happening.

To see the depth change with uncrossed disparity, you should move your head so close to the book that the tip of your nose nearly touches it. Stare straight ahead into the distance as though you could see right through the page. Next pull your head slowly back away from the page. Don't change the focus of your eyes just keep looking into the distance. As soon as you see the differences in the depth start to emerge, it is probably best to stay where you are. For some people the depth relationship will lock in, and then you can move your head and even try to position your finger so that it is at the same distance as the illusory elements that appear to be floating in space in front of you. In this view the smiley faces appear to be more distant than the dots, and Figure 9.19B shows this relationship geometrically.

With the information you gained from the wallpaper illusion, you can now understand the basis of the "magic eye" posters that became so popular in the 1990s. Most were pictures that appeared to be colorful two-dimensional patterns. These were based on the same principles as the wallpaper illusion. Since they sprang into three-dimensional depth when viewed with the eyes converged in front of (crossed disparity) or behind (uncrossed disparity), they are often called **autostereograms**, and we will encounter one of these in Demonstration Box 9.6.

Understanding how stereopsis is achieved is more difficult than setting up the conditions that allow us to see binocular depth. There have been several computational approaches to this problem, most of which involve selecting a particular location in space and then comparing and computing the relative positions of parts of the images. From such computations it was hoped that the relative depth of the objects being viewed could be derived

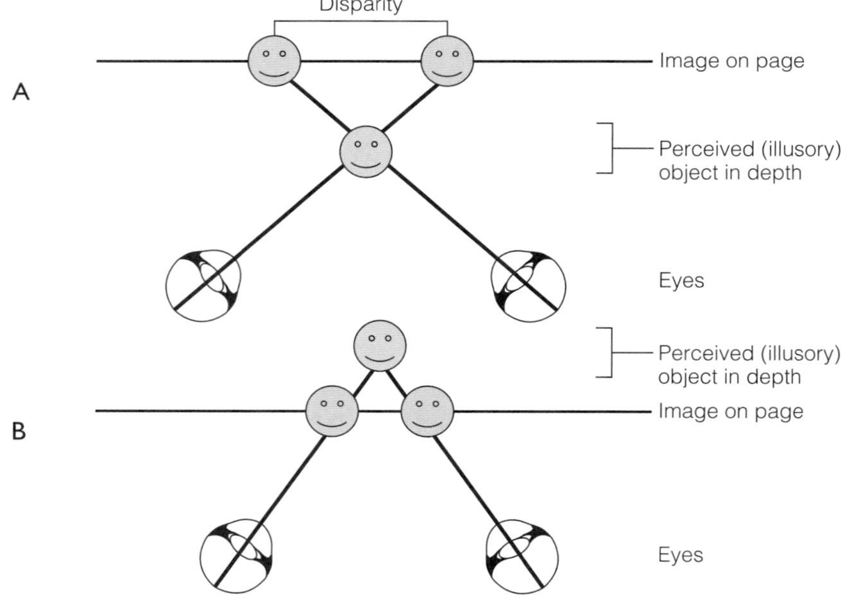

FIGURE 9.19 An overhead view of the wallpaper illusion. (A) When the eyes are converged on a point that is nearer than the image plane, corresponding images in the two eyes appear to be nearer to the eyes than the page. (B) When the eyes converge on a farther point, corresponding images in the eyes are seen as farther away.

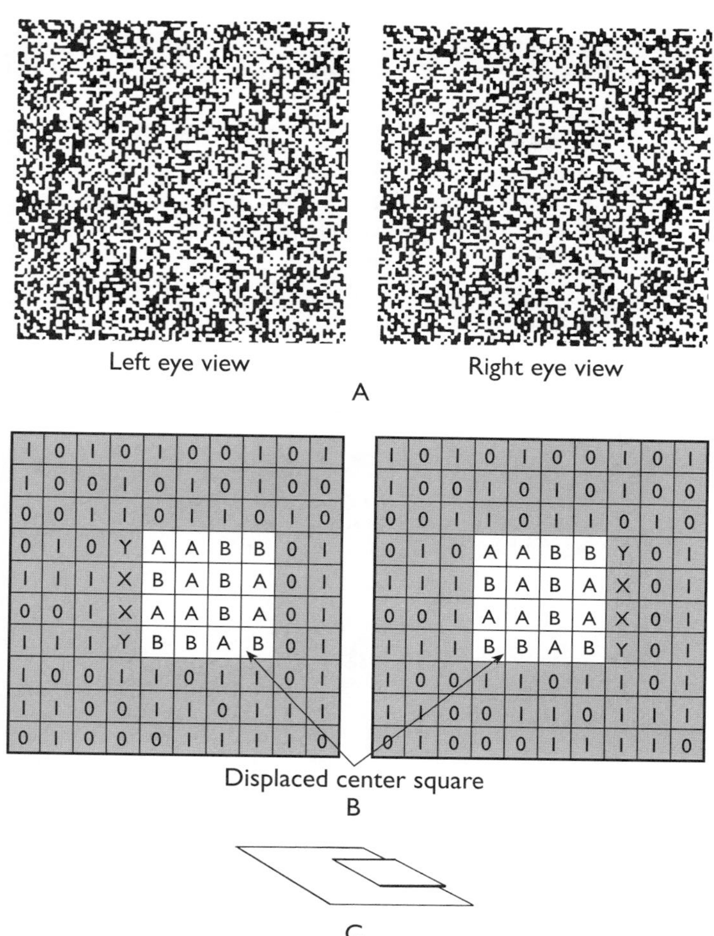

FIGURE 9.20 (A) is a random-dot stereogram. (B) shows how (A) is constructed, and (C) illustrates that a central square is seen floating above the background when the two views are combined in a stereoscope. (From B. Julesz, *Foundations of Cyclopean Perception.* Copyright 1971 by the University of Chicago Press.)

(e.g., Marr & Poggio, 1979; Mayhew & Frisby, 1980). Although interesting, these approaches have not yet provided a "breakthrough" conceptualization, although, as will be seen later, they do provide some descriptively useful suggestions.

The most provocative findings about stereopsis have actually come from direct physiological measurement. The first important results date from the late 1960s, when investigators began to find disparity-tuned detectors in the visual cortex of the cat (e.g., Bishop & Pettigrew, 1986). These detectors are neurons that are finely tuned to small differences in the relative horizontal placement of images in the two eyes (Bishop, 1981). For example, suppose there is no disparity in the images of the two eyes and a particular neuron responds maximally to this condition. This particular neuron would represent a spatial position that lies on the horopter, or the zone of fused images in external space. In a like manner, other neurons may be tuned to particular disparities that represent locations in space that lie in front of or behind the horopter. This means that rather large populations of cortical neurons would be needed to represent all of the possible disparity values in the visual scene.

It is now clear that the mere existence of disparity-tuned detectors is not enough to explain stereoscopic depth perception. The problem is illustrated in Figure 9.20, which contains a random-dot stereoscopic display. These displays can be used to demonstrate the notion of **global stereopsis,** or the perception of depth in the absence of monocular shape or form (Julesz, 1971). This aspect of depth perception comes about because of disparity cues built into the dot patterns. Figure 9.20 shows how this disparity, which consists of a horizontal shift in a group of these random dots, is created. An example of an autostereogram made up of random dots is shown in Demonstration Box 9.6. The evolution and importance of the random dot stereogram can be traced in Biography

DEMONSTRATION BOX 9.6

RANDOM-DOT AUTOSTEREOGRAMS AND GLOBAL STEREOPSIS

You may demonstrate how depth cues can bring about the perception of binocular form by using the accompanying figure. This figure is made up of relatively random dots and short streaks, so it provides no local information for depth. Try to view this first using the technique we used to get uncrossed disparity in the wallpaper illusion (this was the method that started with your nose close to the image and you "looking through" page). Once stereoscopic fusion is achieved, it is easy to determine what object is defined via global stereopsis. For those of you who need a hint, there are two dinosaurs in here (one a triceratops and one a stegasaurous).

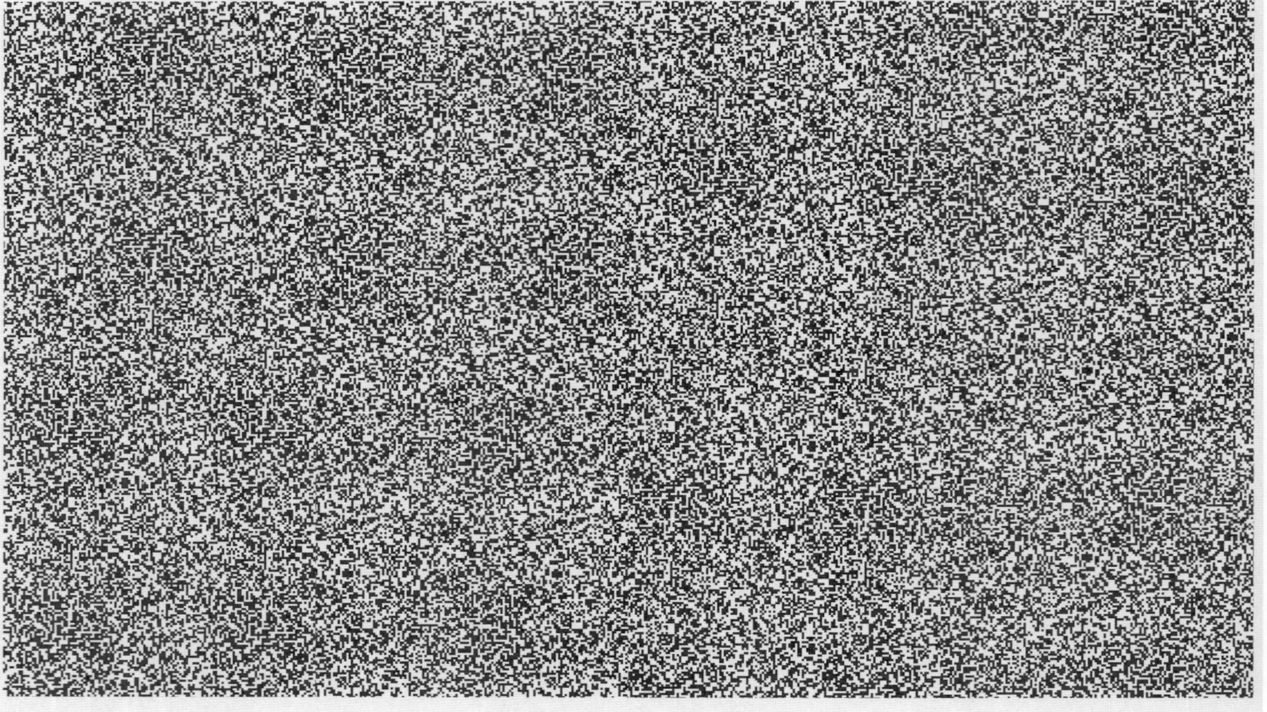

Box 9.2, which describes the career of their inventor, Bela Julesz.

You might suppose that because there is disparity built into the random-dot stimulus, neurons tuned for such information should be capable of detecting depth from these arrays. However, it is not quite that simple, mainly because the stimulus is composed of identical dot elements rather than discrete and identifiable contours. If stereopsis is based on the action of disparity-tuned detectors, each of which responds to one disparity value in the array, any dot potentially could be combined with any other dot. Each of the many possible combinations would produce a different depth perception. The task for the visual system is to find the dots in one eye that correspond to the same dots in the other eye—this is called solving the **correspondence problem** by computational researchers. To solve this problem there must be a method of eliminating or avoiding false combinations and selecting only correct disparity pairs.

Computational theorists have proposed very sophisticated computer programs to do exactly this. Many of these are based on the idea that disparity detectors tuned to the same disparity mutually facilitate one another, whereas those of different disparities inhibit one another (Burt & Julesz, 1980; Marr, 1982; Mayhew & Frisby, 1980). Mathematically it can be shown that with a population of detectors working together in this fashion, only one depth solution would be common to this

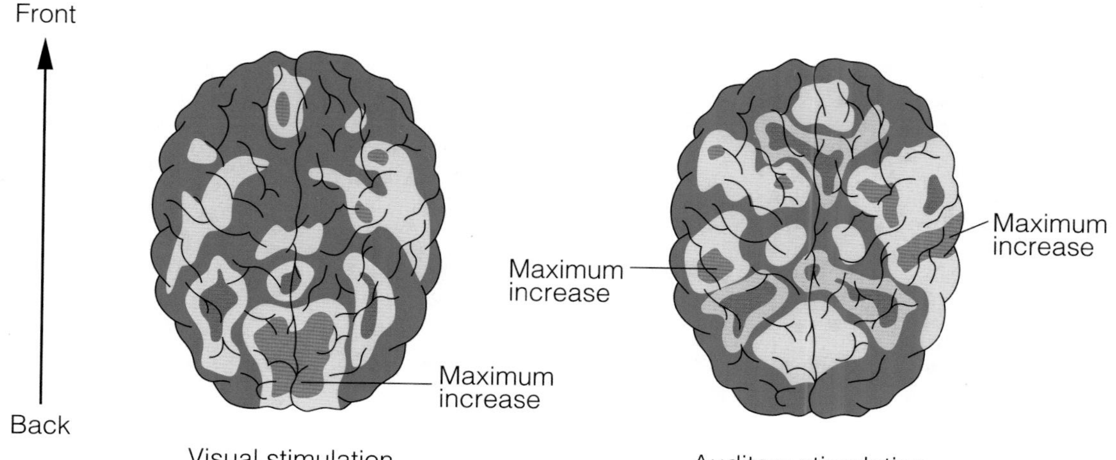

COLOR PLATE 1 A typical colorized map of the brain resulting from measurements of neural activity via a PET scan. Areas of highest activity are indicated by the reds and yellows; areas of lowest activity are indicated by the blues. Arrows point to the region of highest specific activity when an individual is stimulated visually (looking at a change pattern of colors) or auditorially (hearing a complex sequence of tones).

COLOR PLATE 2

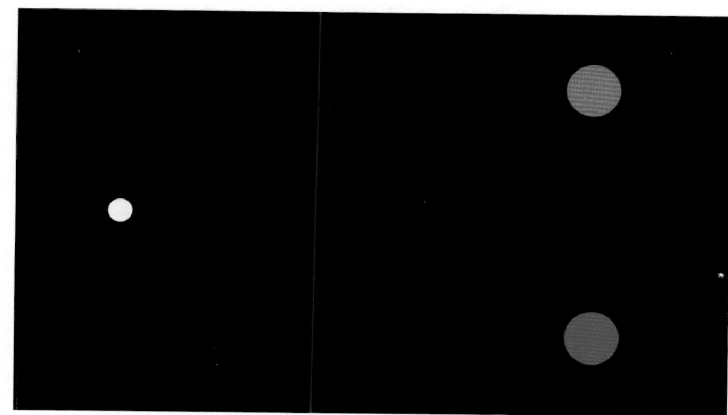

COLOR PLATE 3

COLOR PLATE 4

COLOR PLATE 5

COLOR PLATE 6

COLOR PLATE 7

COLOR PLATE 8

A Read through this list of color names as quickly as possible.
Read from right to left across each line.

RED	YELLOW	BLUE	GREEN
RED	GREEN	YELLOW	BLUE
YELLOW	GREEN	BLUE	RED
BLUE	RED	GREEN	YELLOW
RED	GREEN	BLUE	YELLOW

B Name each of these color patches as quickly as possible.
Name from left to right across each line.

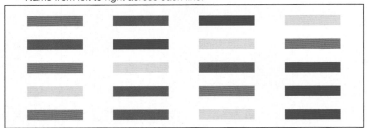

C Name the color of ink in which each word is printed as quickly as possible.
Name from left to right across each line.

RED	BLUE	GREEN	YELLOW
YELLOW	BLUE	RED	GREEN
BLUE	YELLOW	GREEN	RED
GREEN	BLUE	YELLOW	RED
BLUE	YELLOW	RED	GREEN

COLOR PLATE 9

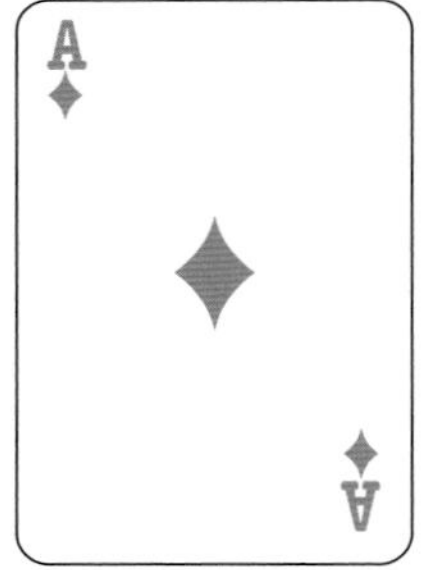

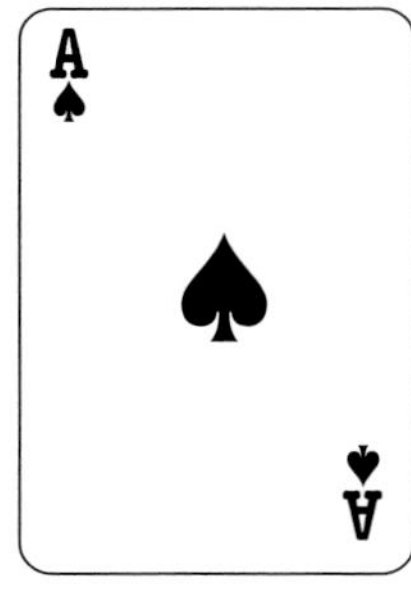
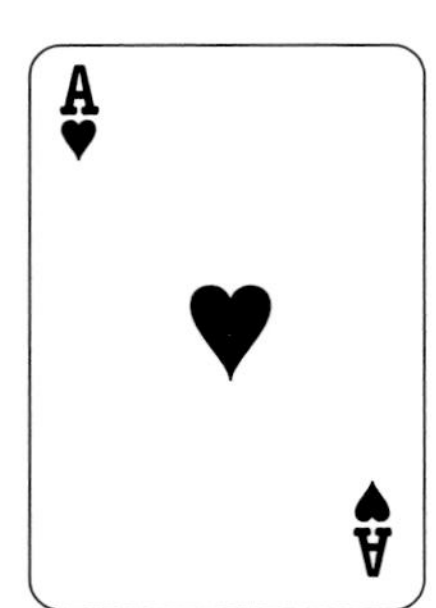
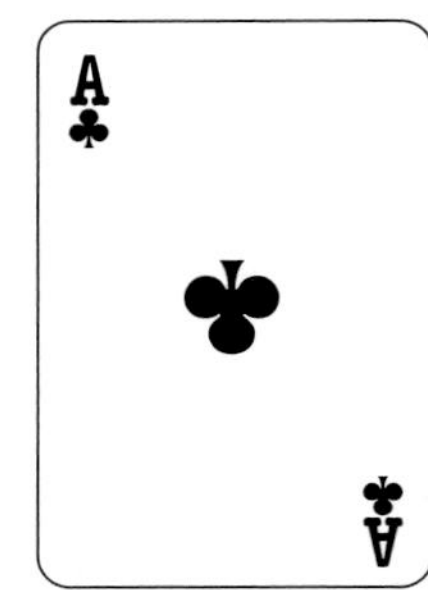

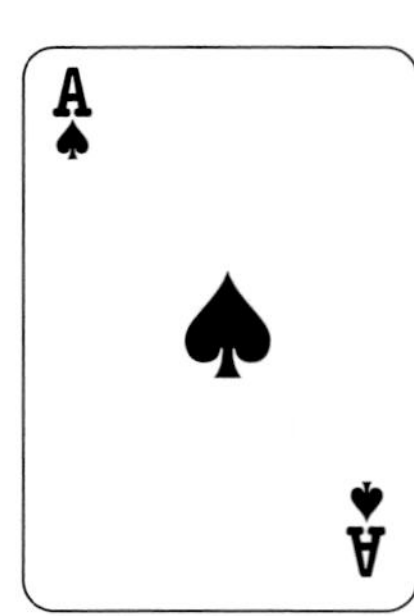

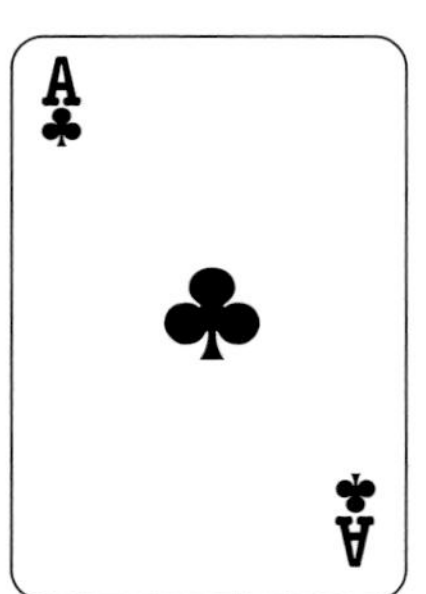

BIOGRAPHY BOX 9.2

DOTS IN DEPTH AND SPECKLES IN SPACE

Probably the most important methodological tool for studying stereoscopic depth perception was invented by a man who started out as an electrical engineer. ***Bela Julesz*** obtained his diploma in electrical engineering in 1950 at the Technical University, in Budapest, Hungary, and then went on to earn a Ph.D. in engineering at the Hungarian Academy of Sciences in 1956. AT&T's Bell Laboratories hired him because of his research on communications systems. Television was in its infancy at that time, and Julesz was working on some technical aspects of TV, when his interests turned to concerns about the perceptual apparatus of the individual viewing it. From then on his research concerned itself with vision, particularly depth perception and pattern recognition.

The random-dot stereogram came about in the late 1950s as a means of testing stereopsis without large visible contours. Some of the first of these simply involved taking a piece of coarse sandpaper and placing a figure cut out of a another similar sheet of sandpaper on it. The cutout could then be moved from side to side to provide retinal disparity in photographs taken of the these displays. These photos were then viewed in a stereoscope, where the cutout now appeared to hover in depth. Today elaborate computer programs quickly generate random-dot stereograms and random-dot autostereograms of virtually any image that can be scanned into them.

A recent survey of the literature showed that more than 80% of all studies involving stereopsis within the last 5 years have used random-dot stereograms as the stimuli. The reason is obvious: There is no way to "fake" or to "guess" the nature of the figure. Unless you have binocular depth perception, the individual views simply make no sense.

Julesz left Bell Laboratories and went on to become the Director of the Laboratory of Vision Research at Rutgers University in New Jersey. He has received many awards for his research, including election to the U.S. National Academy of Sciences and to the Society of Experimental Psychologists for his work on visual processing. He was also honored by the country of his birth by being named as a member of the Hungarian Academy of Sciences.

facilitatory-inhibitory process, and only one global stereoscopic view would be seen (Julesz & Schumer, 1981). Together, these programs have come to be called **cooperative algorithms** for achieving stereopsis in the absence of familiar shapes and forms.

In this instance, computational theorists do seem to have reached a solution similar to that suggested by physiological investigators. Both attempt to explain the random-dot stereo problem by assuming that neurons tuned to the same disparity cooperate, whereas those tuned to different disparities inhibit each other. For many years this idea was only a theoretical possibility, based on Hubel and Weisel's (1962) observation that the receptive fields of most cells in the striate cortex (V1) could be stimulated through either eye (Mustillo, 1985). Since the 1970s, however, this idea has received increasing support from electrophysiological recordings made on alert, behaving monkeys. Gian Poggio and his colleagues (e.g., Poggio & Poggio, 1984; Poggio & Talbot, 1981) have been able to identify two classes of disparity-sensitive neurons in the striate cortex. One type of neuron is sensitive to disparities tuned over a narrow range around the fixation point; the other type is sensitive to crossed (signaling "near") and uncrossed (signaling "far") disparities. Within each of these classes, cells can be further subdivided into those with excitatory responses and those with inhibitory responses. For instance, a cell with an excitatory response to crossed disparity will give an inhibitory response to uncrossed disparities and vice versa. Thus, all of the components for a cooperative algorithm for stereo depth appear to be present already in the first cortical region of visual processing (Aslin & Dumais, 1980; DeValois & DeValois, 1980).

Our understanding of stereoscopic depth processing is still evolving, however, and simple computational analyses may not suffice. For example, it has now become clear that although disparity is processed in area V1, stereoscopic depth is not (e.g., Cummings & Parker, 2000). Once disparity is detected higher visual centers get involved, with much of the actual depth processing going in V3 (Backus, Fleet, Parker, & Heeger, 2001). From V3 information is passed on to the parietal lobes (e.g., Adams & Zeki, 2001), where, as we shall see later in our discussion of consciousness (Chapter 14), various properties that make up our perception of an object are "glued together." This makes sense because differences in color as well as differences in contour can be processed as disparity and used to create stereoscopic depth (e.g., Domini, Blaser, & Cicerone, 2000). Thus under certain circumstances stereoscopic depth may not be fully processed until there is some sense of a coherent object in view (e.g., Yin, Kellman, & Shipley, 2000). With so many higher cortical centers involved in processing depth it should not be surprising to find that even modest amounts of alcohol intake can cause significant loss of the ability to judge depth based on stereopsis (e.g., Wegner & Fahle, 1999), a fact that may contribute to many alcohol-related traffic accidents.

INTERACTION OF DEPTH CUES

Although each of the cues for depth we have discussed is sufficient, by itself, to give the conscious impression of a three-dimensional arrangement in space, the accuracy of our perception of depth often depends on the interaction of several cues. Under normal conditions, if a cue such as interposition suggests that your friend Fred is standing closer to you than your friend Maria is, other cues, such as relative size, height in the plane, and binocular disparity, will tend to confirm this relationship. Chaotic and conflicting cues, such as those shown in William Hogarth's 1754 engraving False Perspective (Figure 9.21), virtually never occur in "real-world" settings.

How do cues for depth combine? A first guess is that an observer's sensitivity to a difference in distance when several cues are available is approximately the arithmetic sum of the sensitivities obtained with each cue alone, although this proves to be too simple given the actual data (e.g., Jacobs, 2002). In general, addition of depth cues does increase the accuracy of depth estimates (cf. Massaro, 1988). For example, when relative size, height in the plane, occlusion, and motion parallax (Bruno & Cutting, 1988) are all consistent, they add to one another. Similar effects have been found for motion parallax and binocular disparity (Rogers & Collett, 1989). In fact, there is some suggestion that individuals who have the best abilities to combine depth cues actually produce the best depth estimates (Westerman & Cribbin, 1998).

Sometimes the addition of depth cues creates a new "emergent" depth cue. Thus it is possible to argue that texture gradients are really just an emergent property of the combination of relative size, height in the plane, and perspective. Another case involves perception of depth when motion is involved. For example, consider what happens to the image on your retina as you watch an automobile on a highway pass by a house that lies between you and the highway. One cue to the relative depths of these objects is, of course, occlusion—the more distant automobile will be only partially visible for some period of time and perhaps entirely occluded for a brief period. Another cue is given by motion—the car will be moving at a faster speed on your retina than the house as you move your head. However, the combination of these two cues produces an important emergent property with regard to the visible contours of the automobile and the house. Portions of the surface of the auto will disappear as it moves behind the house (deletion), and then portions of the surface will again become visible when it emerges (accretion). **Surface deletion** and **surface accretion** can be powerful cues to depth, even when defined only with random-dot displays. The stimuli that are deleted or accreted over time are perceived to lie in a plane behind the dots that may move but remain visible (Craton & Yonas, 1990).

Another depth cue that emerges from a combination of simpler cues is that of **stereomotion,** or a difference in the relative rates of motion with the images in the two eyes (Regan et al., 1990). If an object such as a baseball is hurtling toward you on a direct collision course with your head, the edge of the ball that projects onto your left eye will be moving across the retina at exactly the same rate, albeit in the opposite direction, as the edge of the ball that projects to your right eye. On the other hand, if the ball is coming toward you at an angle, such as might happen if it were to narrowly miss your head, then the rate of motion in one eye will be faster than in the other. Thus, this cue involves a comparison between image motion in the two eyes. In fact, investigators have found neurons in the striate cortex of cats and monkeys that are sensitive to leftward motion in one eye at the same time that they are sensitive to rightward motion in the other eye (Cynader & Regan, 1978; Poggio & Talbot, 1981). Some of these neurons are tuned sharply enough to be able to detect objects on a "near miss" collision course, whereas others are tuned to detect "a hit in the head" (Regan et al., 1990).

The process of combining cues, however, is not a straightforward matter of addition. In some cases one depth cue is favored over others if there is any conflict, for example, stereopsis dominates image blur (Mather & Smith, 2000), and texture cues can dominate relative motion cues (O'Brien & Johnston, 2000). In some cases the conclusion reached by processing determines which cue dominates. Thus when you are catching a ball, its visual size is changing as it approaches and its disparity is changing as well. Both cues are being processed; however, the arrival time of the ball is judged on the basis of whichever of the two cues says it will arrive soonest (Rushton & Wann, 1999). In many cases, the relative influence of cues will depend on learning and experience (see Jacobs, 2002). Generally speaking, the cue that

FIGURE 9.21 Ambiguity of depth cues gives a confusing, difficult interpretation to a scene, as shown in Hogarth's 1754 engraving *False Perspective.* The more you study this figure, the more contradictory depth cues you find.

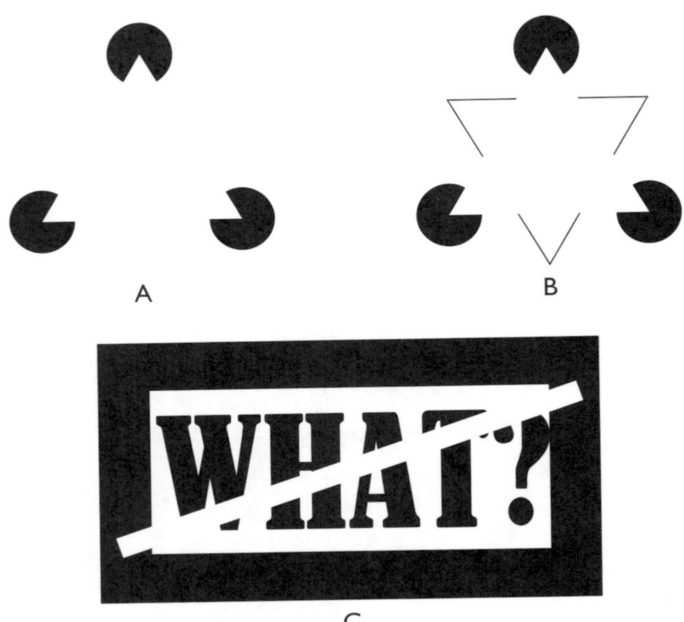

FIGURE 9.22 A white triangle, defined by subjective contours that are not physically present, appears in A, created by occlusion cues against the black disks. In B, adding another occluded figure (inverted triangle) makes the subjective contour stronger. C demonstrates a more explicit use of the occlusion cue to define a subjectively seen thin white bar.

proves to be the most reliable in a situation is weighted most heavily (Jacobs & Fine, 1999).

When depth cues are in conflict they can actually result in a *reduction* in the perception of depth. The most common example of this occurs in viewing pictures. In pictures there are perceptual cues that suggest that the picture is flat (e.g., stereopsis, motion parallax, and surface texture of the paper), which compete with the monocular cues for depth in the picture (e.g., height in the plane, relative size, linear perspective, texture gradients). The stronger the cues for flatness, the lower the weight given to the depth cues in the picture, meaning that the scene depicted in the picture looks less three dimensional (see Miller, 1999).

Depth cues interact not only with each other, but also with other aspects of perception such as the formation of contours and edges and the perception of brightness. Consider Figure 9.22A. What most people will see is a white triangle with its corners resting on three black disks. The triangle is brighter than the background and the edges that define it, although visible, are somewhat indistinct. This is because the triangle is not physically there. As we noted in Chapter 8 in our discussion of perceptual organization (e.g., figure versus ground), contours that are not physically present on the retina but are perceptually visible are called **subjective contours** or **illusory contours** (Petry & Meyer, 1987; Purghé & Coren, 1992). The importance of subjective contours in the present context is that, although many factors can contribute to the formation of subjective contours (e.g., Coren, 1991; Halpern, 1981; Ware, 1981), the presence of depth cues seems to provide a powerful impetus to organize parts of the field into simple figures and to create the perception of contours. Thus in Figure 9.22A we interpret the pie slice shaped "bites" in the black disks as a cue for occlusion and mentally create the contours of the figure that must be occluding them. If we add an additional occlusion cue, as in Figure 9.22B, where the pattern is consistent with a triangle not only occluding the disks but also occluding an inverted triangle drawn with black lines, then the subjective contour becomes stronger. In fact, any form of occlusion cue, if it is strong enough, can produce a subjective contour, as in Figure 9.22C, where the thin white bar partially blocking the word "What?" is bounded only by subjective contours and is not physically present.

Coren (1972) suggested that occlusion is not special in its ability to produce subjective contours, and that any depth cue would suffice. Obviously, the contours you saw in Demonstration Box 9.6 were subjective in nature and they were created by the disparity cue for depth. In Figure 9.23, we have the word "Shadows," which seems to be cut out of white cardboard and hovers over a white background. However, the contours defining the letters are not physically present but are subjectively produced by the presence of shadow cues for letters above a surface. In Figure 9.24A another potential depth cue (difference in texture density) defines a subjectively seen edge

SHADOWS

FIGURE 9.23 These subjectively contour defined letters are triggered by shadows that would be a cue for depth had the letters been physically present.

as if there was a clifflike drop-off. In Figure 9.24B, we add some additional depth cues, such as the suggestion of perspective, a bit of aerial perspective by making the elements that are supposed to be nearer darker and more distinct, and also a bit of relative size by making these lines somewhat thicker. This addition of other depth cues makes the subjective contour defining the cliff much stronger. Even infants as young as 8 months of age see subjective contours and treat figures defined by them as if they were real objects in depth (e.g., Csibra, 2001).

There is good evidence that these subjective contours are not simply a result of local retinal effects but rather depend on our ability to organize the world into surfaces seen at varying distances (e.g., Gillam & Nakayama, 2002). Furthermore, these contours produced by depth cues act, in many ways like real (physically present) contours (e.g., Coren & Harland, 1994), interact with real contours (e.g., Poom, 2001), and may even be processed in the same regions of the brain that process physical contours (e.g., Heider, Spillmann, & Peterhans, 2002).

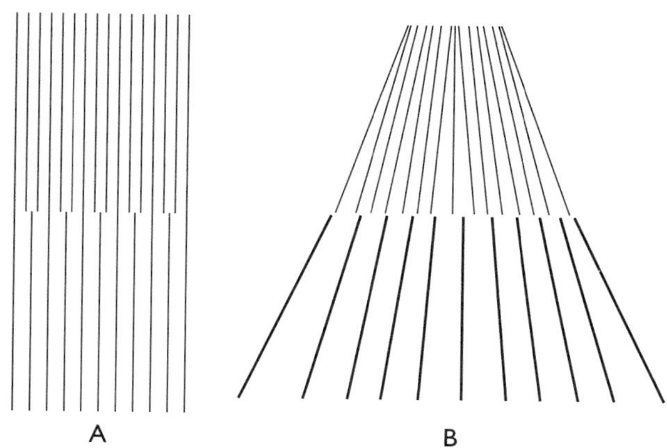

FIGURE 9.24 In A a subjective contour edge is defined by differences in texture density. In B the addition of depth cues, linear perspective, aerial perspective (nearer lines are darker), and relative size (nearer lines are wider) makes the subjective contour stronger and the edge look more like the drop-off at a cliff.

PERCEPTION OF DIRECTION

Three-dimensional depth is only one aspect of our perception of space. The perception of the location of an object will also include its **egocentric direction,** which is its direction relative to our bodies (e.g., how far to the right or left the football is relative to my body). This is contrasted with the **allocentric** direction, which is the object or stimulus relative direction (e.g., how far to the right or left of the elephant is the mouse). There are actually two types of egocentric directional judgments that we integrate in a complex fashion to give us our sense of up, down, right, and left (Howard, 1982). The first one is called **bodycentric** direction. It uses as a reference location the midline of the body, an imaginary vertical line parallel to the spine passing through the navel. The second is called **headcentric** direction, where the midline of the head is used as another reference location for right and left. The midline of the head is an imaginary vertical line centered on the nose. Of course, bodycentric and headcentric directions are potentially different because it is possible to rotate the head independently of the body. The distinction between these two aspects of direction is shown in Figure 9.25. This distinction is particularly relevant for pilots involved in air and space flight, where the body is strapped into a vehicle that is not necessarily moving in a bodycentric direction. Studies in which the body orientation has been fixed in a misaligned position relative to its motion through space have shown that the perception of heading is accurate provided that the head and eyes are free to move. If the head is also fixed in a misaligned position, then there is a systematic distortion in the perceived heading in the direction of the misalignment (Telford & Howard, 1996).

Most of the research on direction has concentrated on one aspect of headcentric perception we can refer to as the **visual straight ahead**. We usually define our notion of "straight ahead" as a direction in front of us, oriented around the midline of the head (Cutting & Vishton, 1997), although this can be biased by the position of our eyes in our head as well (e.g., Becker & Saglam, 2001). The visual **egocenter** is the position in the head that serves as our reference point for the deter-

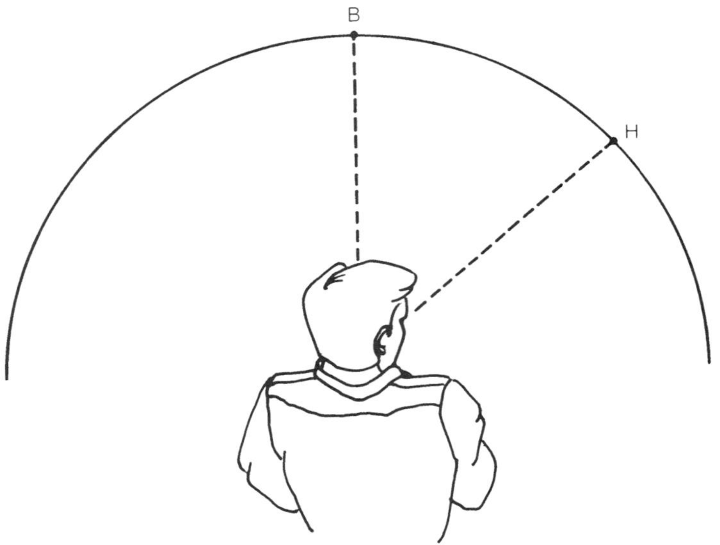

FIGURE 9.25 The distinction between bodycentric and headcentric directions. Point B is straight ahead of the body midline, whereas Point H is straight ahead of the midline of the head. Notice, however, that these two straight-ahead directions can be two different points in visual space.

mination of headcentric straight ahead. In general, however, it appears that we compute a straight ahead that is apparently located in front of the middle of the head. Researchers often refer to this as the location pointed to by a hypothetical **Cyclopean eye,** a name derived from the mythical Greek giant Cyclops, who had a single eye in the middle of his forehead. Demonstration Box 9.7 shows how you can experience for yourself the referring of the visual direction of the two eyes to this common egocenter.

DEMONSTRATION BOX 9.7

THE COMMON VISUAL DIRECTION OF THE TWO EYES

You can experience how the visual directions of the two eyes are referred to one common direction in the center of the head. First, take a sheet of stiff cardboard (20 by 27 cm will do), and place it in front of the eyes, as shown in the figure. Put a dot in the middle of the far end of the cardboard, and stare at it while a friend marks the exact center position of each of your pupils on the end of the cardboard closest to your face. Next, draw lines from these marked points until they form an angle, or V (as pictured). Finally, reposition the cardboard in front of your face at a point slightly below your eyes. Now, stare at the far point where the two drawn lines intersect, and you should see, in addition to the two lines you have drawn, a somewhat more shadowy line running between them. This "new" line is the fusion of the views of the two eyes and should appear to point directly at a spot close to the midline of the head. This demonstrates that although the direction of each eye's view is different (as shown by the spatial separation between the two drawn lines converging on the far point on which you are fixating), the visual direction of the combined binocular view is referred to a common point between the eyes. This point is called the egocenter, or the Cyclopean eye.

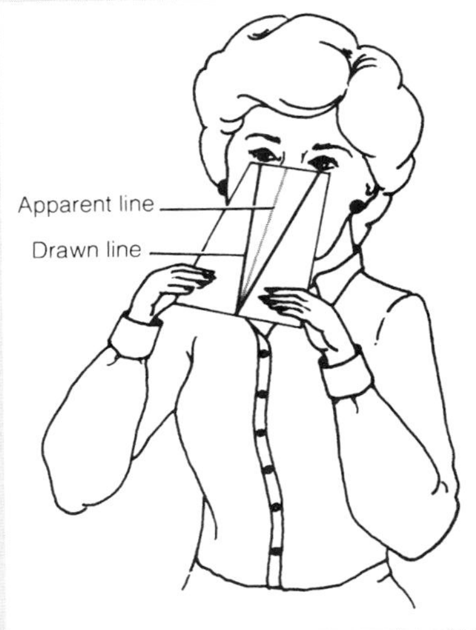

BIOGRAPHY BOX 9.3

WHEN UP AND DOWN ARE NOT DIRECTIONS

***Ian P. Howard* (1927–)** was born in England and received his education at the University of Manchester and the University of Durham. He was always interested in visual perception and the perception of depth or distance, but his major contributions are the advancement of our understanding of direction perception and how people manage to orient themselves in their environment. It is curious that a year before he got his doctoral degree (1965) he was already writing about what would turn out to be his mid- and late-life passion, namely the perceptual problems that people might encounter when traveling in outer space. The problem for astronauts is that they have no gravitational influences to assist them in orienting themselves. In other words, the directions associated with up and down now longer can be guided by gravity but must depend completely on vision.

Howard taught at New York University and the University of Toronto and then went on to become the Chairman of the Psychology Department at York University in Canada. His research skills combined with his organizational skills allowed him to become a director at the Human Performance in Space Laboratory at the Centre for Research in Earth and Space Technology in 1988, and then in 1993 he assumed the post as Senior Scientist at the Centre for Research in Earth and Space Technology. Now, with the help of NASA, he finally had the chance to separate gravitational from visual influences on our sense of direction and orientation.

The equipment and experimental settings for such research can be difficult and exotic. Some studies were conducted under parabolic flight conditions (where an airplane enters into a high-speed controlled dive to give a few moments of weightlessness). Others were conducted while suspended in a large sphere that looks like a furnished room or the Space Lab interior. The subject and the room can be independently rotated so that gravitational and visual cues can be in active conflict. These studies have been augmented by other studies (again sometimes with a suspended subject) by using a helmet that provides a computer-created, stereoscopic, virtual environment. Finally, Howard's studies were moved to the space shuttle and Space Lab for testing with real working astronauts over extended periods of up to 16 days. The results suggest that vision dominates over all other senses in determining our sense of direction and orientation. Howard's work shows how theoretical and "pure" laboratory science can interact with real-world problems. You can be sure that experimental subjects sitting in a darkened room, pointing at dots of light, had no inkling that their data would one day help fly humans safely into outer space, to the moon, and perhaps beyond.

Eye Movements and Direction

Several variables affect our sense of the direction of objects. Stimulus factors are, of course, important; the more stimuli available, the more stable our directional judgments, which accounts for the fact that our ability to judge direction is much less stable in the dark. Also, visual configurations influence the judgment of direction. For example, if you are looking at a square or rectangle that is not exactly centered in your visual field, there will be a tendency for you to judge the straight-ahead direction in terms of the center of this displaced square or rectangle. It is as if the perceptual system confuses what is straight ahead of the observer with what is centered with respect to the other contents in the visual field (Roelofs, 1935; Royden & Hildreth, 1996). However, nonvisual factors also play a role in directional localization.

In a previous section we saw how eye movements, in the form of convergence and divergence, convey information about the distances of objects. It would also seem reasonable that feedback from eye movements could help in determining the visual direction of an object. At least two sources of eye movement information could be used to compute the direction of an object in space. The first arises from the movement commands sent to the eye muscles (the **efference copy**); the second (the **afference copy**) arises from feedback from the eye movement itself. One study examined the influence of the efference copy by having subjects judge the straight ahead while pressing a finger lightly against the side of their eyeball—hence moving the eye without efference from the eye muscles (Bridgeman & Graziano, 1989). Observers showed very little influence of this manipulation when judging straight ahead in a normal visual environment, but their judgments were considerably biased in the direction of the finger press when they were made while viewing a blank field with no landmarks. Although there is controversy about whether efference or afference information is more important (see Donaldson, 2000), it seems clear that eye movement information does play a role in localizing targets in space (Banks & Ehrlich, 1996).

There are many examples demonstrating how eye movements affect our localization of objects. The information about object localization seems to be associated with where the eyes are pointing at any given moment. Imagine that the fovea of the eye serves as a reference point. In the absence of other information, we localize an object as being in the direction that the fovea is pointing when we try to look at it. This means that if we accurately image the object on the fovea, we will accurately perceive its direction. If, on the contrary, we inaccurately point our eyes, such as when the eyes lag behind a moving object that we are trying to track (see Chapter 12 on motion), we should inaccurately localize it. There is evidence that this is exactly what happens, and this can cause striking perceptual distortions (e.g., Coren, Bradley, Hoenig, & Girgus, 1975), despite mechanisms that attempt to compensate for such problems (Van Beers, Wolpert, & Haggard, 2001). In addition, the role of eye movements in object localization can be subtle. For example, there is a suggestion that the eye movement does not actually have to be made; the eye movement we compute in order to move the eye at some later time may bias our perception of direction (e.g., Coren, 1986; Hershberger, 1987).

There is mounting evidence that the perceptions of egocentric and allocentric direction are processed independently (e.g., Eggert, Ditterich, & Straube, 2001). This makes some sense since egocentric direction is needed if we are actually going to interact physically with objects in the environment by performing some action, while allocentric localization provides us with an accurate perceptual "map" of objects in the world, which we can then enter into memory (cf. Goodale, 2001). The current evidence is that both are ultimately processed in the parietal lobe; however, they use different specific cortical centers. This has been determined by looking at the effects of various cortical lesions (Landis, 2000) as well as by functional magnetic resonance imaging in humans (Galati, Lobel, Vallar, Berthoz, Pizzamiglio, & Le Bihan, 2000). In these computations eye movements are used differently. They seem to be an important source of information for egocentric direction computations but much less important for processing allocentric localizations (Brenner & Cornelissen, 2000).

Eye Dominance and Perceived Direction

We have considered eye movements of either eye to be interchangeable, but some evidence suggests that the two eyes are not used equivalently in the computation of visual direction. Before we consider this evidence, it is important to understand that there are some tasks we habitually do with one eye. In sighting tasks where only one eye can be used at a time (such as in looking through a telescope), 65% of all observers consistently use their right eye, whereas the remainder consistently use their left (Coren, Porac, & Duncan, 1981). The preferred eye for such tasks is usually called the **sighting-dominant eye** (Porac & Coren, 1981; Ruggieri, Cei, Ceridono, & Bergerone, 1980). Demonstration Box 9.8 shows how you can determine which eye is your sighting-dominant eye.

For the purposes of our discussion of the perception of direction, sighting dominance is important because the visual direction associated with straight ahead is more strongly influenced by the dominant eye (Porac & Coren, 1976, 1981). This certainly does not mean that only one eye is used to determine visual direction (Ono & Weber, 1981). Rather, it means that the location of the egocenter, or Cyclopean eye, is biased toward the side of the sighting-dominant eye (Barbeito, 1981). For instance, Porac and Coren (1986) tested observers in a totally darkened room and had them set a point of light so that it appeared to be visually straight ahead. Whether observers used only one or both eyes, they tended to set the point so that it was closer to the side of the dominant eye rather than midway between the two eyes.

DEMONSTRATION BOX 9.8

SIGHTING DOMINANCE AND THE STRAIGHT-AHEAD DIRECTION

The visual straight ahead may depend on a single eye (Porac & Coren, 1976, 1981; Walls, 1951). Try the following demonstration to see how this works. Stand in front of a wall at a distance of about 3 m. Pick a point on the wall that is directly in front of you (a small crack or bump will do). Now, with both eyes open, quickly stretch out your arm and align your fingertip with the point on the distant wall. When the alignment has been completed, alternately close each eye. You will find that the point on the distant wall will shift out of alignment for one of the eyes. However, the other eye will seem to be aligned with the point on the wall whether one or both eyes are opened. The eye that maintains the alignment is called the sighting-dominant eye. You will notice that regardless of which hand you use to perform the alignment, you will tend to line up a near (your fingertip) and a distant (the point on the wall) target in terms of the same eye. The presence of a sighting-dominant eye, and our tendency to make a straight-ahead alignment in terms of this eye, indicates that the locus of the egocentric straight-ahead direction may be shifted toward the side of the sighting-dominant eye.

Another interesting consequence of eye dominance and sighting concerns head posture. Many people display a noticeable head tilt in their everyday posture—a head tilt that becomes more pronounced when they are asked to judge the alignment of objects in depth. Research has shown that individuals with right-eye dominance tilt their heads to the left, whereas those with left-eye dominance tilt their heads to the right. Both types of individuals appear to tilt their heads in order to help maintain a line of sight that is consistent with a body-centered coordinate system (Previc, 1994). In addition, when the head is turned to the side, the dominant eye may briefly yield to the other eye, perhaps because the usually nondominant eye is now in an orientation that gives it a better or more comfortable view (Khan & Crawford, 2001).

DEVELOPMENT OF SPACE PERCEPTION

We will deal with the development of many aspects of space perception later in Chapter 15; however, it is worth while to consider briefly some developmental issues to help clarify a theoretical question. One of the most common ways to assess whether there is a constructive aspect to space perception is to observe the behavior of young organisms when they are placed in situations that call on their abilities to perceive distance or direction (see Rader, 1997). Because infants and young animals have limited experience with the world, their abilities to deal with such situations should shed some light on the role of inborn versus learned components in the perception of visual space.

Species Differences

The evidence is clear that in certain simpler animals the perception of direction and distance is inborn. For example, in salamanders it is possible to rotate the eye 180 degrees, thus inverting the retina. When this is done, animals consistently swim and snap in the opposite direction when presented with a food lure (Sperry, 1943). Because the same results occur when similar operations are performed during the animals' embryonic stage, it is clear that visual direction is related innately to the location of retinal stimulation in this species (Stone, 1960). Similarly, immediately after birth chicks peck at small objects with reasonable accuracy. When experimenters optically displaced the images of the targets to one side (using special lenses attached to hoods), the chicks proceeded to peck systematically to one side. This pattern of inaccuracy showed little improvement over time, suggesting that this response to the apparent direction of stimuli was not changeable by experience (Hess, 1950). In higher animals, such as mammals, experience may play a larger role.

Other research shows that several species of young animals, in addition to human infants, show evidence of visual "filling in" of the occluded portion of an object (Johnson, Bremner, Slater, & Mason, 2000). These animals, which include mice (Kanizsa, Renzi, Conte, Compostela, & Guerani, 1993) and newborn chicks (Regolin & Vallortigara, 1995), behave toward partly occluded objects in the same way that they behave toward the objects that are completely visible. Whether or not these animals use the interposition cues of occlusion to interpret the relative depth of the objects is still not known. It is somewhat surprising to find that there are some animals, such as pigeons, that, although tested using the same procedures, do not show this capability (Sekuler & Lee, 1996).

To determine which factors may be influenced by experience in a species, investigators frequently use controlled-rearing procedures, such as rearing an animal in total darkness from birth until testing. Such dark rearing eliminates all externally generated visual experience. If experience with various visual depth cues is necessary for the development of normal depth perception, these dark-reared animals should have measurable deficits when required to respond to distance cues. If depth perception simply matures as the animal ages, then restricting the animal's visual experience should not affect its behavior, and the only important variable should be its chronological age.

A simple and popular procedure for measuring depth perception in young animals uses an apparatus called the **visual cliff** (Walk & Gibson, 1961). A diagram of a typical visual cliff arrangement is shown in Figure 9.26. Basically it consists of two sections, divided by a "start platform." Each section provides a different depth impression. The "shallow" side is a piece of glass that lies directly over a patterned surface. The "deep" side has the same type of patterned surface but looks like a sharp drop because the surface is placed at some distance below the glass. For testing, a young animal is placed on the central starting platform that separates the apparently shallow and deep surfaces. It is assumed that from this position the subject can see that the shallow side is safe, whereas the deep side, with its simulated clifflike drop-off, would be perceived as being dangerous. Investigators make the presumption that if the animal consistently chooses the shallow over the deep side, then it can perceive the difference in apparent depth and is attempting to avoid a fall.

Several different types of animals have been tested on the visual cliff, including rats, chickens, turtles, goats, sheep, pigs, cats, dogs, monkeys, and humans (Green & Davies, 1993; Walk & Gibson, 1961). In all cases, even when testing very young animals, there was a preference for the shallow over the deep side of the cliff. There were some interesting species differences, however, which seemed to be related to the habitat features of the natural environment for the various species (Sloane, Shea, Proctor, & Dewsbury, 1978). For instance, aquatic animals, such as certain turtles, did not show the marked preference for the shallow side that the other, more landbound species displayed. Perhaps the survival value of cliff avoidance may not be as pronounced in animals that spend much of their lives swimming because changes in depth of water are not as perilous as sudden sharp drops on land.

Experience and Depth Perception

Although the cross-species differences observed in depth perception are of interest, the visual cliff apparatus has

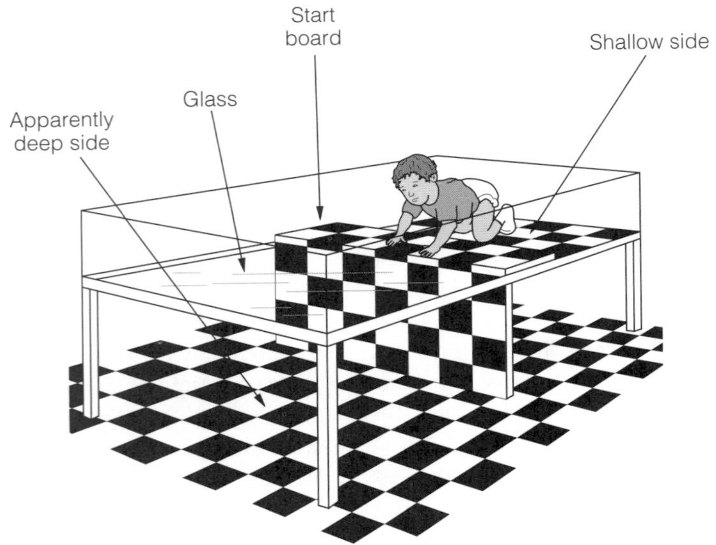

FIGURE 9.26 The visual cliff.

been used primarily to generate data concerning the development of depth perception (e.g., Rader, 1997). A combination of controlled rearing followed by observations of behavior on the visual cliff has been the experimental technique most commonly used in animal studies. In general, the findings have suggested that experience and innate factors interact to produce an animal's ability to perceive depth. For example, when cats or rats are reared in the dark, they show little depth discrimination on the visual cliff when first tested. However, as they receive more and more experience in a lighted world, their depth discrimination rapidly improves until they are indistinguishable from normally reared animals (Tees & Midgley, 1978).

When the visual experience takes place also is important. There seem to be **sensitive periods** in an animal's development, referring to the fact that there are particular ages and particular durations of time when depriving an animal of a particular type of visual experience may produce the largest perceptual deficits (Timney, 1985). For instance, a study by Tees (1974) showed how deprivation of visual experience during a sensitive period can affect later depth perception. Dark reared rats were compared to light-reared rats on their preference for the deep versus the shallow side of the visual cliff. The amount of time that the animals were dark reared was varied, and, in addition, the strength of the depth information was varied by varying the distance to the bottom of the deep side of the visual cliff. In this study, the age of the animal, the amount of distance information, and the amount of visual experience all interacted. It was only among the animals that had been dark reared for a comparatively long time (60 to 90 days) that the effects of rearing conditions revealed themselves. For these animals, although depth could be discriminated when the drop-off was large, there was an insensitivity to weaker distance cues. These data indicate that there may be inborn components in the ability of rats to discriminate depth on the visual cliff. These are probably sharpened through experience with depth cues in the environment, a finding supported by other research as well (e.g., Kaye, Mitchell, & Cynader, 1982).

The developmental time course and the effects of experience seem to be different for the various depth cues (see also Atkinson, 2000). We know that binocular depth perception develops quite early because evidence for the use of binocular disparity for a depth cue may be found in young infants (Birch, Shimojo, & Held, 1985) even using random dot stereograms such as in Figure 9.20 (Fox, Aslin, Shea, & Dumais, 1980). When viewing sterograms with special glasses, these infants can see a figure floating in front of a background only if they can combine the disparate information from the two eyes' views. Such patterns (as in Figure 9.20 or even in Demonstration Box 9.6) are meaningless unless you can make use of the disparity cues hidden in each monocular view. Infants will spend a longer time looking at a visible figure than at a random pattern of dots. This can tell us if they are seeing the three-dimensional image. Calloway, Lloyd, and Henson (2001) used such random dot stereograms and found that prior to 8 weeks of age none of the infants made any differential viewing responses, even with very large disparities. By 9 to 16 weeks, however, 50% of them showed evidence of binocular depth perception. After 17 weeks more than 90% of the infants showed a clear ability to use stereopsis. This is consistent with earlier animal work, which suggested that the use of monocular cues for depth is much more dependent on specific experience than is binocular depth perception (Eichengreen, Coren, & Nachmias, 1966).

The ability to use kinetic depth information seems to develop at about the same time that the ability to use binocular depth information appears, at roughly 3 to 5 months of age (Owsley, 1983; Yonas & Granrud, 1985b). One biologically important aspect of depth perception, namely sensitivity to information about object motion toward the body (which may indicate an impending collision), seems to be present at an even earlier age. It has been measured at ages as young as 2 to 3 weeks (Yonas, 1981). Even at this young age, infants will blink their eyes when presented with an object that seems to be moving closer and seems to be growing close enough to hit them in the head.

Studies of sensitivity to monocular pictorial depth cues have revealed a slower developmental process. For example, it takes until 6 to 7 months of age for infants to reliably respond to linear perspective information (e.g., Arterberry & Yonas, 1989), familiar size (Granrud, Haake, & Yonas, 1985), texture gradients (Arterberry & Yonas, 1989; Yonas & Granrud, 1986), and concavity-convexity specified by shading (Granrud & Yonas, 1985). Use of more complex cues, such as the perception of relative depth in a picture based on the direction of shadows cast in the pictorial representation, may not appear until the age of 3 years (Yonas, Goldsmith, & Hallstrom, 1978).

Perhaps the earliest use of a monocular cue is that of occlusion. By the age of only 3 months, infants are already sensitive to the presence of T-junctions, which indicate that one object is blocking or occluding another (Bhatt & Bertin, 2001). By 4 months of age an infant not only can tell that an object that is partially blocked is farther away but also can make adultlike presumptions as to what the shape of the partially occluded item is (Johnson, Bremner, Slater, & Mason, 2000).

Developmental studies indicate that the perception of depth and distance cannot be understood fully unless we assume that some components are explained by inborn factors, whereas others may require active experience to emerge (cf. Atkinson, 2000; Gwiazda & Birch, 2001). These studies suggest that adhering strictly either to a direct perception viewpoint or to a constructive perception viewpoint might be too limiting. Innate components of perception must mature, and certain types of experience can help or hinder the achievement of a high level of perceptual functioning. Some aspects of depth perception seem to be given directly, and others require memory and experience to allow them to function properly.

STUDY QUESTIONS

1. Occlusion is a cue for relative depth or distance. What does it refer to, and what are the local stimulus elements that serve as clues that occlusion is taking place?
2. There are two types of shadows. What are they, and what depth information does each of them convey?
3. Relative size is not sufficient to determine the distanced of a viewed object. What other aspect of size perception is needed, and how does it influence our perception of depth?
4. What is a "vanishing point"? Where is it usually found? Which depth cue makes use of it?
5. What is a texture gradient? Which theorist is it associated with, and which theoretical approach did it eventually lead to?
6. There is an exception to the rule that items higher in the picture plane are seen as more distant. What is that exception? Can you reformulate the rule to account for the usual case and the exception?
7. What is the difference between crossed and uncrossed disparity? Can you demonstrate this difference simply?
8. Why are random dot stereograms important as methodological tools? Why are random dot stereograms important theoretically?
9. What is the difference between egocentric and allocentric direction? Are they processed the same way? Do they have different behavioral functions?
10. There is some evidence that certain aspects of depth perception are inborn while others take longer to develop. Which cues fall into each category? Which cue processing abilities take the longest to develop?

CHAPTER **10**

OBJECT AND SCENE PERCEPTION

CHAPTER SUMMARY

When we look around the world, we see individual entities called **objects,** (such as this book, a pencil, a desk) as well as objects and surfaces in relation to one another, called **scenes** (such as the pencil resting on the desk). Each object appears to have a relatively enduring set of properties, such as its size, its shape, its color, and the texture of its surfaces. Scenes, too, have their own intrinsic properties, such as the spatial relations that exist among the various objects, the lighting conditions that illuminate the scene, and the overall dimensions of the environment in which the scene occurs. Now consider a very simple problem. Suppose that you are presented with several rectangles made of cardboard and you are asked to say which one is the largest. If the difference in their physical size is not too small, you would probably have little trouble giving the correct answer. But how did you reach your conclusion? Many people would probably give an answer like this: "The largest rectangle is the one that produces the largest image in my eye." However, this answer would be wrong, as can be seen from Figure 10.1. There we have three different rectangles; the image of each is the same size on your retina, and yet each is a representation of a different-sized cardboard rectangle "out there" in the "real world." The smallest of these pictured objects would be only a few centimeters on each side "out there," whereas the largest would be over a meter in width and length.

FIGURE 10.1 Three rectangles whose retinal images are all the same size, although each appears to be different in size than the others.

Seeing the cards in Figure 10.1 as being three very differently sized objects sums up in a nutshell one of the most important problems in vision. The problem is that we see objects and scenes, which are physical entities in a three-dimensional environment, and yet their perception comes about solely through the analysis of images, which are two-dimensional projections of light onto the surfaces of our retinas. How does our visual brain make the leap from image to scene? In this chapter we will consider this problem from a number of perspectives. But first we will begin by considering the general problem of the information that is available to the brain in coming to the conclusion that the three cards shown in Figure 10.1 are not all the same size.

THE PROBLEM OF VISUAL SCENE PERCEPTION

The world we see is composed of objects such as trees, buildings and coffee cups, among other things. The only information we receive about these objects through vision lies in the pattern of light that is reflected from these objects. This pattern of light, called the **image,** can be thought of as a two-dimensional array. Each point in the array can itself be further specified in terms of its total intensity of light (brightness) and its wavelength (hue). These two factors, the intensity and wavelength of each point of light in the image, are determined by four general aspects of the environment, as shown in Figure 10.2.

The first of these aspects is the **light-source** and refers to the direction and intensity of the light-producing regions in the environment. For example, in a natural outdoor scene, there is only one important primary source, the sun. Most light reflected from the various objects in the environment originates from this source, although reflections of light from one surface to another may provide secondary sources of illumination. The light reflected to earth on a moonlit night is an example of such secondary light. In an indoor scene, there may, of course, be more than one primary light source (e.g., windows admitting sunlight, several light bulbs) and many secondary sources (e.g., reflecting walls).

A second factor that determines the nature of the image is the **surface reflectance** of the various objects that come in contact with the light. As discussed in Chapter 4, some surfaces absorb light from one region of the wavelength spectrum more than from other regions, leading to the perception of differently colored surfaces. Thus, if one surface absorbs the short and middle wavelengths and reflects only the longer wavelengths, the portion of the retinal image that corresponds to the image of this surface will contain only long wavelengths or red-appearing light. In addition to these wavelength reflectance characteristics, surfaces differ in the total amount of light they absorb. Some surfaces are highly reflecting and thus look glossy or mirror like; others absorb much of the incident light and thus are matte or dull.

A third aspect is the **surface orientation** of each of the visible surfaces in the scene. Surface orientation is determined with reference to an imaginary line perpendicular to the surface, which is called the *surface normal*. For instance, a surface oriented for optimal light reflection would be one in which the angle between the direction of the light source and the surface was exactly the same as the angle between the direction of the viewer

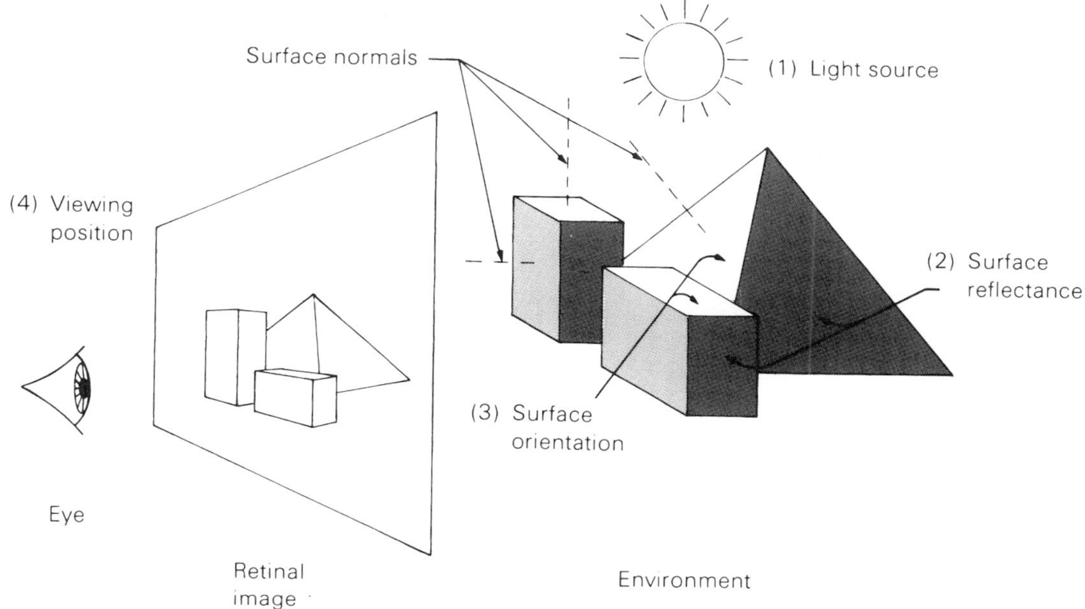

FIGURE 10.2 Four properties of the visual environment that together determine the intensity and wavelength of each point in an image: (1) light source, (2) reflectances, (3) surface orientations, and (4) viewing position. The surface normals (dotted lines) are also noted for some surfaces.

and the surface normal. As these two angles become more unequal, less and less light will be reflected from the objects onto the image. For example, the surface of the pyramid that is facing the eye in Figure 10.2 is reflecting more light to it than are the block surfaces that are facing the same way. This is because the angle between this surface and the light source is approximately equal to the angle between the surface and the eye.

The fourth aspect is the **viewing position,** specifically the relationship between the viewer's eye and the scene. If a viewer moves around in the environment with respect to a scene, the image projected from the scene will change accordingly. This change will occur despite the fact that the light sources, surface reflectance, and surface orientations have not changed at all relative to one another.

These four aspects of the viewing situation, then, determine the distribution of light in the image that is available to a viewer. This simple fact has fooled many people into thinking that the problem of form perception is fairly straightforward. The faulty argument goes something like this: If the two-dimensional retinal image is completely determined by these four aspects of the three-dimensional world (namely, light source, reflectances, surface orientation, and viewing position), then it should be possible to examine an image and decompose it in a way that will give us a precise description of that world and the objects in it. What this reasoning fails to take into account is that any given retinal image could have been produced by a potentially infinite number of scenes.

The ambiguity of the scene information in any resulting image is shown in Figure 10.3. Suppose that a viewer is looking at a trapezoidal shape that is lying on the ground oriented so that its shorter edge is close and its longer edge is farther away (Figure 10.3A). The image that it would cast on the eye would be a rectangle. However, an object that was truly rectangular, if it was being viewed straight on, as shown in Figure 10.3B would cast the same image. In fact an irregular rhombus shape viewed from a particular angle, such as Figure 10.3C would also cast a rectangular image on the eye. It is clear that on the basis of the information given in the image shape itself, one would be unable to say which of these three shapes were being viewed in the scene. Unless the viewer knows something about the orientation of the shape with respect to himself, the image does not contain enough information to differentiate between many alternatives. This illustrates how our perception of an object's shape is intertwined with our assumption of our viewing position relative to that object.

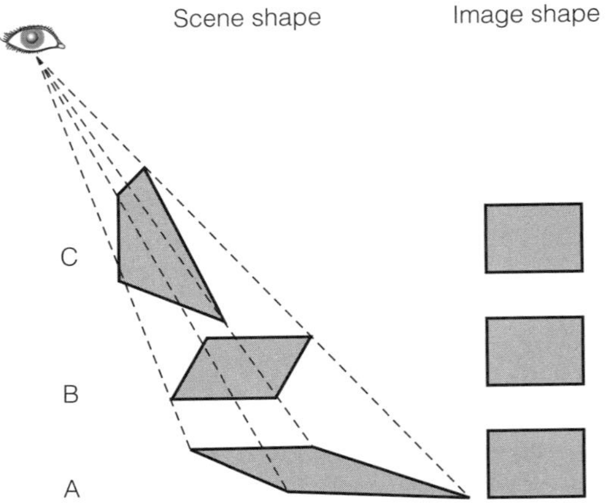

FIGURE 10.3 The inherent ambiguity of a two-dimensional image is illustrated here, showing a variety of three-dimensional shapes that would all generate the same two-dimensional outline in the image formed at the eye, which lies at the tip of the pyramid of imaginary dotted lines extending from the obliquely viewed square (A). B is a true rectangle viewed straight on, while C is a rhombus that still projects a square image to the eye.

What makes the problem of object perception so fascinating is that it is being solved by our visual systems every moment that our eyes are open, without even a hint of effort on our part. It is only when attempts have been made to understand the visual system with mathematical equations (Gosselin & Schyns, 2001; Grossberg, 1987) or to build a functioning visual system by machine (Clark, Troscianko, Campbell, & Thomas, 2000; Riesenhuber & Poggio, 2000) that the enormous complexity of this problem becomes apparent. This is therefore an area in which there is still a large gap between what we know our visual system is able to do and our very limited understanding of how it is accomplished. Biography Box 10.1 will introduce you to an individual who probably did more than any other scientist in the past century to bridge this gap.

In this chapter, we will show you how this problem has been approached from a number of different perspectives by perception researchers. Because a general solution to this problem has not yet been discovered, it is a very exciting and rapidly changing area of research. Rest assured that when a general solution is discovered, you will know about it almost immediately, since it will mean that a wide range of machines of convenience will become available on the consumer market. These will likely range from machines that are able to play tennis with you, to machines that will act as butlers in your house, and even to machines that will be able to perform surgery on you with a minimal amount of tissue damage, because the tools are so much smaller than a

BIOGRAPHY BOX 10.1

WILL MACHINES EVER BE ABLE TO SEE LIKE WE DO?

A young mathematician and psychologist, ***David Marr (1945–1980),*** did more than any other scientist in the twentieth century to make this dream a reality. His genius seemed to lie in being able to think and write in such a way that scientists from three distinctly different disciplines (visual psychophysics, animal biology, and artificial intelligence) were able to speak to one another about visual perception. The new scientific field that emerged in the 1970s partly as a result of his research became known as **computational vision.** This research field is very active today and is noted for the equal emphasis it gives to research findings in human vision, neuroscience and computer simulations.

The way that David Marr envisioned that these three areas of research would work together is summarized in the three levels of understanding that he believed were necessary for any complete theory of vision. These levels are arranged hierarchically from most abstract to most concrete. Most important, none of these levels can be reduced to another; each is essential for a complete understanding. The **computational** level attempts to state exactly what the visual problem is that needs to be solved. The **algorithm** level specifies various ways that the problem could be solved in principle. The **implementation** level describes the actual equipment, be it neurons or silicon chips, that are used to compute the algorithm and accomplish the task.

This computational approach was summarized in one of the most widely cited scientific books of all time, *Vision*, a book that David Marr authored shortly before he died of leukemia at the age of 35 (Marr, 1982). Today the many accomplishments of his short life are recognized by the prestigious Marr Prize that is awarded every two years to the best paper given at the International Conference of Computer Vision, a conference attended by psychologists, neuroscientists, and computer scientists.

surgeon's hands. In each case, the reason these machines are not available right now is because scientists are lacking a general purpose solution to the problem of recovering the three-dimensional structure of a scene from the two-dimensional images that can be recorded by a camera viewing that same scene (e.g., Neumann, Pessoa, & Hansen, 2001).

RECOVERING THE THIRD DIMENSION

The four general factors of a scene that determine what an image will look like to a viewer form a tightly interconnected web. This means that if any three of these aspects are known (or can be measured), then the fourth aspect can be determined by following the laws of geometry. The problem posed for human vision (and for all biological visual systems more generally) is that most of the time not even three of these factors can be known with certainty. This leaves the visual system with some guesses to make if it has any hope at all of coming to a firm conclusion about the shape and position of the objects being viewed. The more "intelligent" these guesses are, meaning the more they are based on clues that are generally reliable, the more accurate vision will be. In this section we will consider some of the clues used by the human visual system to make rapid guesses about the scene properties it is viewing. These clues have often been discovered through the study of **visual illusions.** Illusions often occur in situations in which the guess made by the visual system about one of the scene factors is inappropriate. By studying these situations carefully, the general rules used by the visual system can be discovered.

Let's consider some of the working assumptions that the visual system makes when it is trying to interpret a scene.

Scenes are Lit from Above

A smooth variation in the luminance of an image is called **shading.** On its own, without considering the larger context, a local region of shading can arise for a large number of reasons. A surface of an object could be curved so that some parts of it reflect greater amounts of light to the eye than others, as we observed when we looked at the various cues for the perception of depth (Chapter 9). On the other hand, the pigment on the surface may in fact be graded, so that some regions of the surface are really darker than others and there may be no variation in depth at all. To introduce even more ambiguity, it is possible that the shading came about because we are viewing the penumbra of a shadow cast by another object onto a surface.

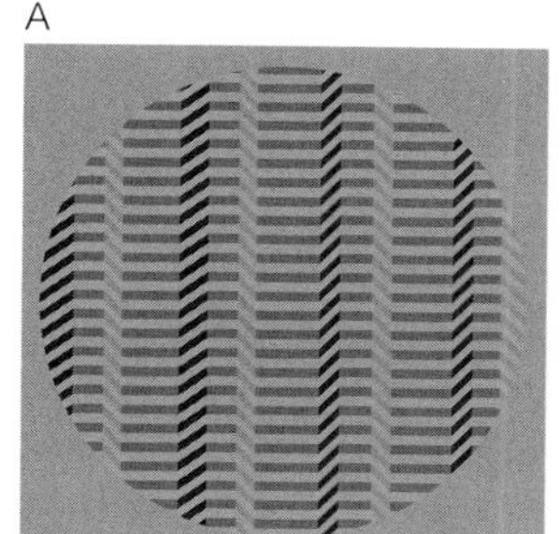

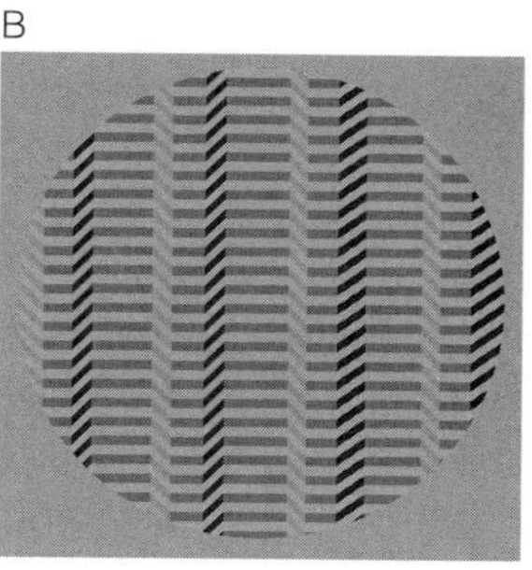

FIGURE 10.4 Displays such as these tend to be seen as depicting (A) thin corrugated ridges among wide spaces and (B) wide corrugated ridges among thin spaces. Turning the book upside down to view the same display will reverse the interpretations. What the human viewer brings to the situation is the assumption that light shines from above. (From Mamassian, P., & Landy, M.S. (2001). Interaction of visual prior constraints. *Vision Research,* 41, 2653–2668.)

As shown in Figure 10.4, the visual system tends to interpret shading with the assumption that light shines from above the scene (e.g., Mamassian & Landy, 2001; Sun & Perona, 1998). This resolves one of the inherent ambiguities of scene perception, which is whether to interpret the shaded region as bending away or toward the viewer. If a scene is lit from above, then the gradient of luminance that runs from light to dark must represent a surface curvature that is also bulging toward the viewer (a convexity). The opposite pattern of shading would correspond to a bulging away from the viewer (a concavity).

Surfaces are Generally Convex

Pictures of surfaces with minimal cues for three-dimensional shape are generally interpreted as being convex (meaning that they are seen as bumps coming out at you rather than concave dents or hollows). As shown in Figure 10.5, this bias can be seen when images of common objects, such as potatoes and faces, are formed from hollow casts of the original objects. Even though the original object may be a hollow cast (generally concave), an image of it will usually appear to look solid (generally convex). This bias can even override the previous one, that light generally shines from above. A picture of a face that is actually a hollow mask lit from above will appear as a convex face lit from below (Ramachandran,

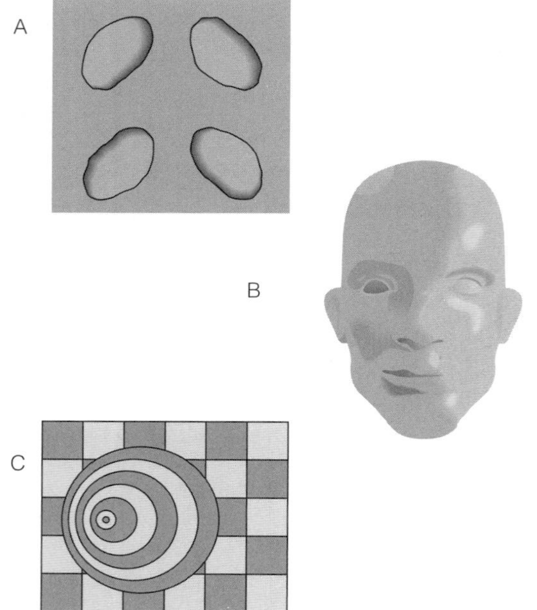

FIGURE 10.5 (A) potatoes lit from all directions, (B) a face lit from the side, and (C) a texture gradient with no shading. All of these surfaces appear to be generally convex, even though the geometry of the situation could just as accurately specify pictures of hollow masks of these objects and surfaces.

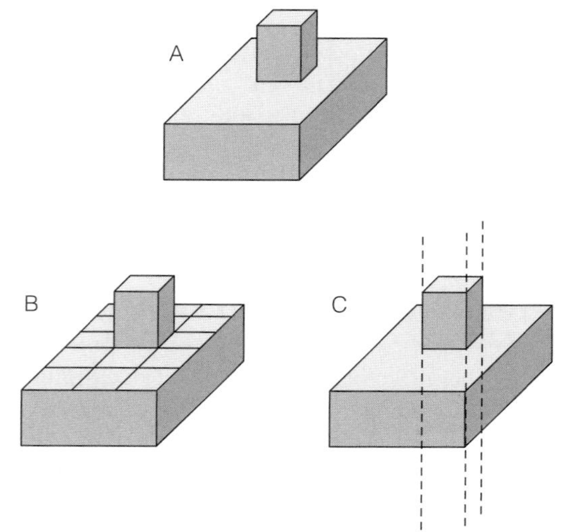

FIGURE 10.6 Objects are generally seen as resting on surfaces even when those surfaces are not explicitly shown. The picture shown in A could be the situation shown in B or C. Human observers overwhelmingly tend to see the smaller cube as though it were resting on the larger block beneath it, as depicted in B, and not as though it were floating above it, as in C.

1988). This bias even extends to arbitrary texture gradients depicting surfaces where no shading is involved. The texture shown in Figure 10.5C appears to bulge out toward the viewer rather than to recede into the page.

Objects are Attached to Surfaces

The visual system tends to presume that objects rest on surfaces, even when those surfaces are not really visible. For example, in Figure 10.6A, the smaller cube appears to rest on the surface of the larger block beneath it as in Figure 10.6B, even though it could just as easily be floating a short distance above the larger cube, with its front right edges vertically aligned, as shown in Figure 10.6C (Albert & Tse, 2000).

Objects are Generally Viewed from Above

The visual system has a strong bias toward interpreting objects as though they are being viewed from above rather than from below. This bias is evident in the Schroeder stairs illusion, as shown in Figure 10.7. The most frequent interpretation of this picture is that of a set of stairs in which the wall labeled A is the surface nearest to the viewer, which means that the triangle is on the first riser of the set of stairs and the disk is on the first tread. But another interpretation is possible. The wall labeled B can instead be seen as the surface nearest to the viewer, in which case the stairs are being viewed from below and the triangle is now on the first tread and the disk on the first riser. If you find it difficult to see this interpretation, because of the natural bias to view surfaces from above, simply rotate your head (or the book) so that the letter B is upright on your retina. Now slowly rotate your head (or the book) back to the original viewing po-

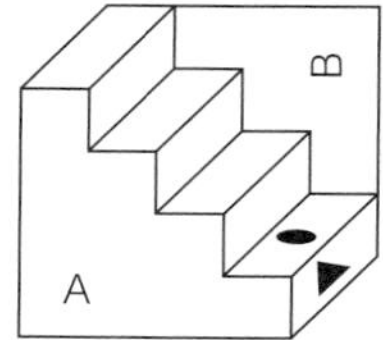

FIGURE 10.7 The Schroeder stairs illusion is an ambiguous set of stairs that can be viewed as though from above (making surface A to be the wall nearest the viewer) or from below (making surface B the wall nearest the viewer). The first interpretation is more frequent, reflecting the bias in human vision to view objects and surfaces from above.

sition and see if you can maintain that interpretation. Most people find it difficult to do so because of the bias to view surfaces from above.

A Generic Viewpoint

One of the most general biases of human vision is to interpret a relation between two or more edges as though it will hold for a variety of possible viewpoints. For example, consider the three lines that meet at the junction in Figure 10.8. This pattern could have been the result of viewing three lines floating in the air or suspended from a ceiling at different distances from you. In such a case it could be pure coincidence that from the vantage point from which you happen to view them, the three innermost line ends happen to meet at the same place in the image. If that were the case, then a simple movement of your head in one direction or the other would reveal that the three line ends do not meet at the same place in the scene. Human vision tends to ignore these low-probability coincidences and focuses instead on interpretations that assume the edge relations shown in the image are generally true and would hold when the object was viewed from a variety of different angles and positions. This is the **generic viewpoint** interpretation.

This combination of five assumptions regarding scene perception, namely that light shines from above, that surfaces are generally convex, that objects tend to rest on surfaces, that scenes are generally viewed from above, and that images are generally generic for a scene, can readily be extended to the interpretation of whole scenes. Consider the picture in Figure 10.9A. It clearly depicts a scene containing three-dimensional objects of specific shapes and in a particular spatial arrangement even though the shapes are all silhouettes containing no interior detail. None of the shapes even occludes another, though the two large shapes partially occlude the horizon. Under the surface convexity assumption, the depicted shapes are blobs and not holes. Under the surface attachment assumption, the blobs are resting on a surface that helps to determine the shape of their lower edge. Under the generic viewpoint assumption, the remaining round edges of these blobs would continue to be round if the viewpoint on the scene was shifted.

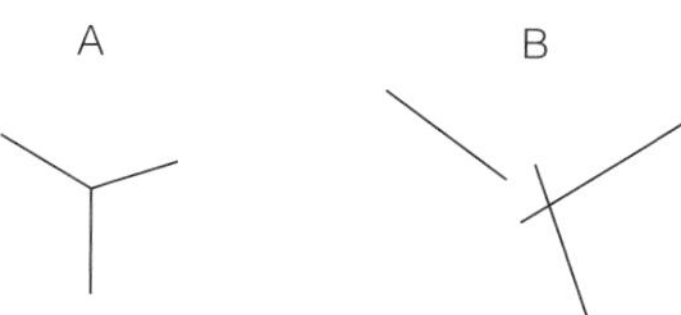

FIGURE 10.8 Generic viewpoint of edges. (A) The three lines are assumed to correspond to three edges that meet at a single point in the scene. (B) If movement of the head or the scene were to reveal the line relations shown here, we would be genuinely surprised.

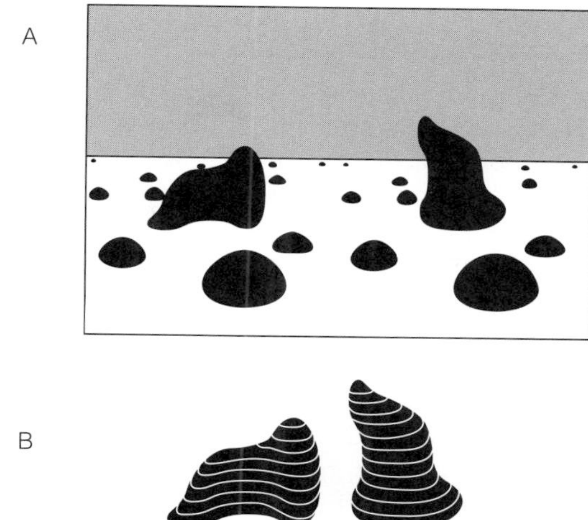

FIGURE 10.9 (A) An image of solid blobs that nonetheless appears to depict a three-dimensional scene. (B) Iso-elevation contours show how different these two blobs are in a three-dimensional interpretation even though they have the same image dimensions. Rotate the page by 90 degrees to see their similar outline shapes. (From Albert, 2001).

The largest two black blobs in Figure 10.9A are especially interesting because they seem to have particular indentations and rounded surfaces that are nowhere specified by shading, texture, or occlusion. From what does their three-dimensional shape derive? Figure 10.9B illustrates the equal elevation contours of these shapes under the assumption that they are resting on the same surface. Clearly these are very different three-dimensional shapes under this assumption. However, now imagine that the shape on the right side is rotated 90 degrees in the counterclockwise direction (or do it by physically rotating the book). When this is done it becomes clear that both silhouettes are identical in shape. This difference in their three-dimensional appearance, despite the identical nature of their two-dimensional outline, illustrates the power of interpretation that has been added by simply putting the principles of surface attachment and generic viewpoint into play. The fascinating part of all of this is that it takes no apparent mental effort on our part. These assumptions are simply there and always ready to be put to work in perceiving a scene.

PERCEPTUAL CONSTANCY

If the only information we had about a scene came through the momentary images in our eyes, our world would be more chaotic than anything that Alice experienced in Wonderland. Friends would appear to get larger as they came closer to us and then shrink as they went away. A piece of white paper would appear black when viewed in the moonlight because the amount of light in the image is no greater under these conditions than in the image of a piece of coal viewed in daylight. This same piece of paper would appear to change shape continually as its shape on the retina changed from rectangle to trapezoid when viewed from different positions. The color of the paper would be blue under fluorescent lighting and yellow under incandescent lighting.

Fortunately, our perception of objects and scenes is much more constant than the ever-changing image of the same scene on our retinas. Most of the time our friends appear to remain the same size, even though they may be viewed from various distances. The piece of paper remains a white rectangle, although you might sense the fact that the color or intensity of the light falling on it, or its angle of tilt relative to you, has changed. This is what is meant by **perceptual constancy,** namely that our perceptions of objects and scenes do not vary nearly as much as the fluctuations in the images of those same objects and scenes. In this section we will consider four different visual constancies.

Size Constancy

To understand size constancy, you must first understand what happens to the retinal images of objects as our distance from them varies. As the distance between the eye and the object grows larger, the size of the retinal image grows smaller. This relationship is shown in Figure 10.10. Retinal image size is usually expressed and measured in terms of visual angle. The visual angle for S_1 (Stimulus 1) is α_1 and for S_2 is α_2. Like other angles, these are expressed in degrees, minutes, and seconds of arc. As an example, the image size of a quarter (a 25-cent coin) held at arm's length is about 2 degrees, whereas at a distance of about 80 m the quarter would have a visual angle of only 1 min of arc. At a distance of 5 km (around 3 miles) it would have the tiny retinal image size of only 1 sec of arc. Thus, as its distance from an observer increases, its retinal image size gets smaller.

The ability to see an object as being the same size (always the size of a 25-cent coin in our previous example), despite changes in objective distance and retinal image size, is called **size constancy.** To accomplish this feat we therefore have to take into account the distance of an object in determining its size. In Figure 10.11A, we see three men standing in a courtyard. All three appear to be about the same size, even though the retinal image size of the apparently most distant individual is only about one third that of the apparently nearest one. In other words, we estimate distance and size together and adjust our perception of size in accordance with our distance judgment. This has the effect of perceptually enlarging more distant objects. You can see how this constancy scaling works by looking at Figure 10.11B, where all the images of the men are exactly the same size. Here the constancy scaling correction becomes more obvious because it makes the apparently farthest man appear much larger than we would expect a man to be at that distance

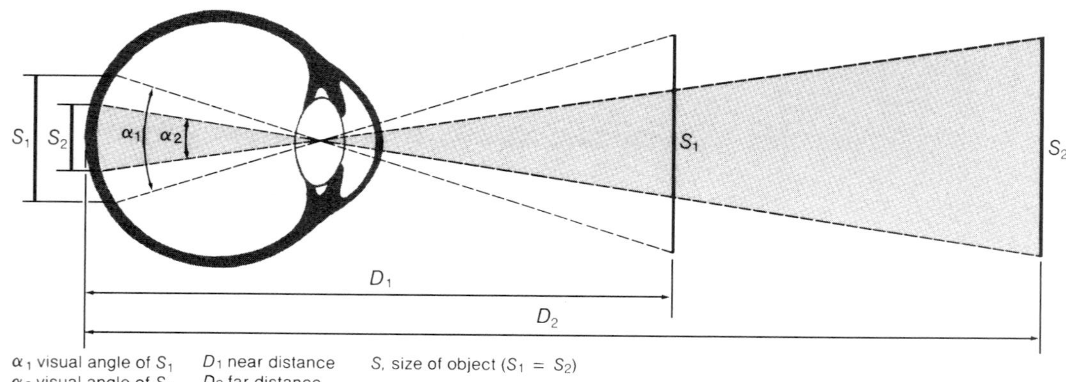

FIGURE 10.10 The visual angle of an object. Although the physical size (S) of two different objects is the same, changes in distance (D) will result in changes in the size of the visual angle (α). Here (α_1) of object S_1, which is closer to the eye, is larger than (α_2) of object S_2, which is farther from the eye.

FIGURE 10.11 (A) Three men whose retinal image grows smaller as they appear to be more distant. Our visual system believes the smaller images are actually farther away and is therefore able to assume a constant actual size of all three men. (B) When the images of the men all remain the same size, even though some of them appear to be more distant, the more distant men are seen as larger in size. This is an illusion that is based on the same assumptions that normally would lead us to the perception of size constancy.

from us. This demonstrates that changes in apparent distance alter our perception of apparent size. By the way, this is not simply a learned predisposition that we have picked up from viewing pictures, since animals, such as baboons, who, presumably have not spent much time viewing pictures and photographs, also show this same illusion (Barbet & Fagot, 2002). A very direct experience of size constancy you can try for yourself is described in Demonstration Box 10.1.

To study the close link in perception between the apparent size of an object and its apparent distance from the viewer, many experiments have varied the number and type of cues to distance that a viewer has available. In general, the greater the number of cues to distance, meaning the stronger will be the sense that an object is farther away, the stronger is the size constancy effect (Collett & Parker, 1998). Even when the cues to distance do not come from the image, but are only physiological cues, such as vergence of the eyes and accommodation (Chapter 9), size constancy is stronger when more information about distance is available to the observer (Mehan, 1993; Roscoe, 1989).

A clear demonstration of this relationship was provided by Leibowitz and Moore (1966). These authors varied the degree of accommodation and convergence in observers by inserting prisms and lenses between the eyes and the stimuli, which were presented against an otherwise blank background. This forced observers to adjust their convergence and accommodation to either apparently closer or farther distances if the stimuli were to be seen in focus and the binocular image was to be fused. Even though the retinal sizes of the stimuli remained constant, these depth cues influenced the perceived sizes of the stimuli, such that stimuli that appeared to be more distant were also judged to be larger. The effects of binocular disparity, another powerful cue to apparent distance, on size constancy can be experienced by following instructions in Demonstration Box 10.2.

Size Constancy in Picture Perception. Visual illusions based on size constancy occur very commonly in pictures, where there is often ambiguity about the apparent distance from the viewer and size of objects (Ross & Plug, 1998). Much of this ambiguity arises from the dual nature of pictures, which we discussed in Chapter 9. This refers to the fact that when we are viewing pictures, certain depth cues indicate to us that the surface of the picture is flat. At the same time, other depth cues in the picture itself are indicating to us that some of the depicted objects are farther away from us than other objects. Thus, at one level we are treating pictures as if they were three dimensional, while at the same time we are

DEMONSTRATION BOX 10.1

SIZE CONSTANCY AND APPARENT DISTANCE

An easy way to demonstrate how apparent distance affects apparent size requires that you carefully fixate the point marked X in the accompanying white square while holding the book under a strong light. After a minute or so, you will form an afterimage of the square. To see the afterimage, simply transfer your gaze to a blank piece of paper. On this paper you will see a ghostly dark square that is the afterimage. Now shift your gaze so that you are looking at a more distant, light-colored wall. Again you will see the dark square afterimage projected against the wall, but now it will appear to be much larger in size. The afterimage is not changing its retinal size and therefore its visual angle, because it has been 'painted' onto your retina. However, when you project it against surfaces at varying distances from you, its apparent size changes. It appears to be larger when projected on a more distant surface and smaller on a nearer surface. This is an example of how size perception and distance perception interact to achieve size constancy. This relationship between apparent size and distance is often called **Emmert's law.**

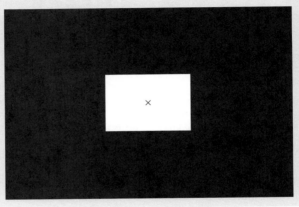

representing the picture in consciousness as a flat two-dimensional array.

One of the most common examples of a pictorial illusion that arises because of a size constancy interpretation is shown in Figure 10.12C, where two horizontal lines of equal length are drawn between two converging vertical lines. Notice that the upper line appears to be slightly longer. This is called the **Ponzo illusion.** It is actually an illusion only in the sense that there seems to be no need for depth or distance to be seen in this figure. Yet the illusion is caused by the fact that the two converging lines are automatically and unconsciously interpreted as cues

DEMONSTRATION BOX 10.2

ADDITIONAL DEPTH CUES STRENGTHEN SIZE CONSTANCY

Hold out both of your hands with their backs toward you. One hand should be relatively near you (about 20 cm or 8 in. should do), and the other should be out at arm's length. At first glance, both hands should appear to be about the same size. Now, remove the binocular disparity depth cue by closing one eye. Keeping your hands at these different distances and your head very steady (to prevent motion parallax as a further depth cue), move your distant hand to the side until its image appears to be just next to the near one. Now when you compare the size of the two hands, it should be clear to you that the more distant one appears smaller than the near one, showing a clear weakening of size constancy. You can restore the size constancy by adding additional depth cues. You can do this by opening both eyes and by swinging your head from side to side. This will make your hands once again appear to be the same size even when held at different distances from you.

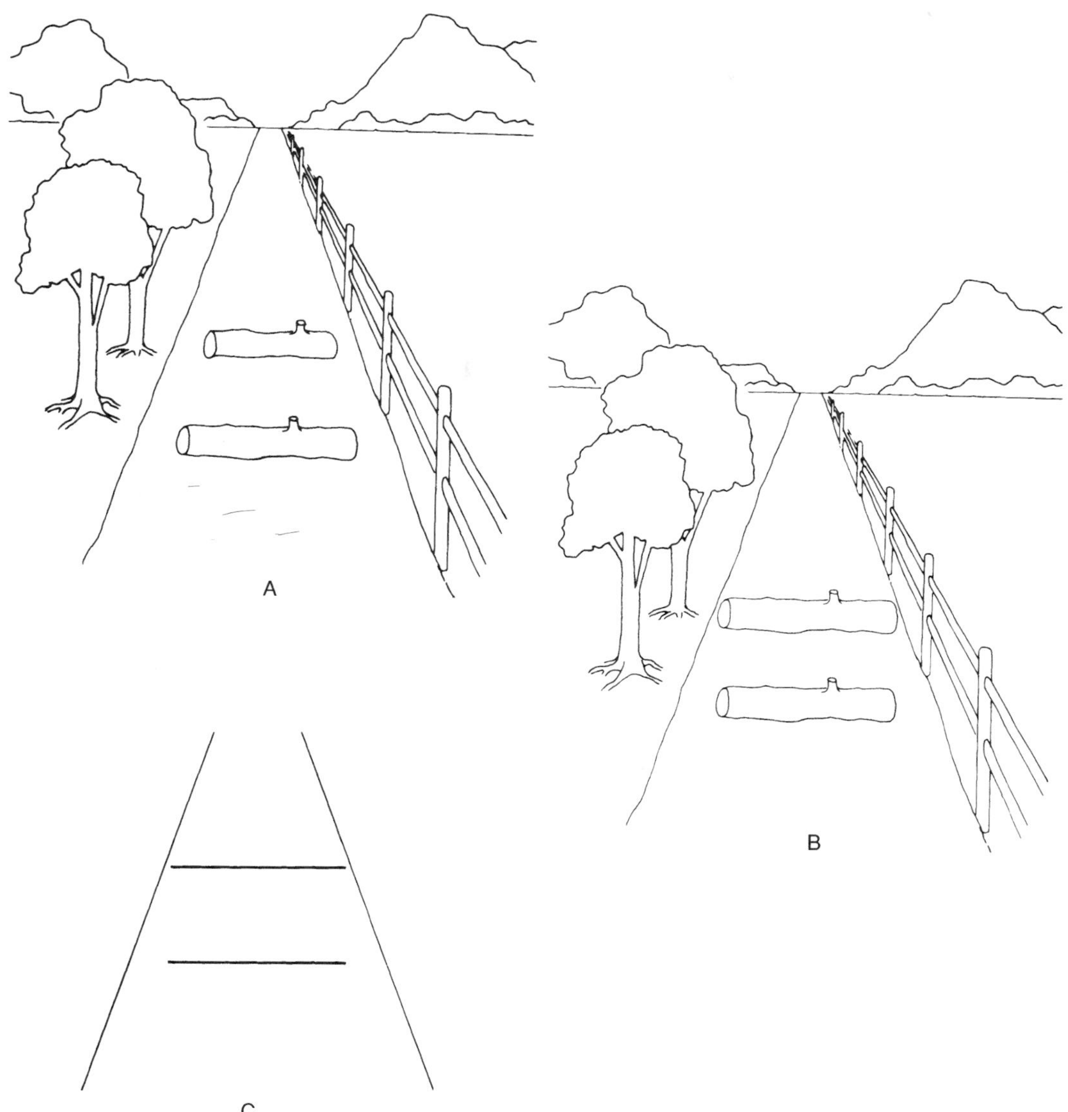

FIGURE 10.12 (A) Two logs that appear to be the same size but at different distances from the viewer. This interpretation is consistent with both the position of the two logs in the picture (the upper one seems farther away) and with their relative size (the upper one is smaller). (B) Two logs that are identical in their pictorial size. Because the upper log appears to be farther away, it now also appears to be larger than the lower log, following the appearance of the Ponzo illusion in C, where the upper horizontal line appears to be longer than the lower one.

to distance by human observers (Coren & Girgus, 1977; Gillam, 1980).

Once we make the context for distance less ambiguous and give a clear meaning to the horizontal stimuli, as shown in Figure 10.12 for the pictures marked A and B, the reason for the illusion is easier to understand. For picture A the two logs in the road have been drawn as different sizes on the paper and the distance cues in the picture (perspective, texture, and height in the plane) indicate that the upper log is more distant. Because of size constancy we see it as being the same size as the closer log. In picture B we have two logs that appear to be different in size, with the more distant one seemingly longer than the closer one, although they have been drawn to be exactly the same physical size on the page. This too represents the operation of size constancy. To the extent that the picture mimics conditions in the real world, the upper log appears to be more distant. In the real world, it could cause the same-sized retinal image as the lower log only under conditions in which it was physically longer. Because in the picture the logs have been drawn the same size, the constancy scaling mechanism has correctly adjusted our perception.

A more subtle version of a size constancy illusion is shown in Figure 10.13. Here the vertical line marked A appears to be shorter than the vertical line marked B, although they are equal actually in length. This is called the **Mueller-Lyer illusion.** It involves several different visual mechanisms (Coren, 1997; Coren, Porac, Aks, & Morikawa, 1988; McClellan & Bernstein, 1984), but one of the most important is size constancy (Coren, 1999; Coren & Girgus, 1978). To see how this comes about, note that when the arrow heads are pointing away from the vertical line, the configuration of lines mimic the perspective cues of the outside of a building, as shown in picture C. When the arrow heads point toward the vertical line they mimic an interior corner of a room, as shown in D. It is easy to see in these more elaborated pictures that the arrow heads imply increases or decreases in distance away from the plane of the picture. The operation of size constancy therefore enlarges the apparent length of B relative to A, because it is judged to be at a relatively farther distance. It is important to note again that the Mueller-Lyer display is an illusion of size only in the sense that no depth or distance is intended in the picture. This makes the application of size constancy inappropriate in this situation.

If we deliberately emphasize the depth cues to the basic Mueller-Lyer lines, we can get a particularly powerful illusion effect. This is shown in Figure 10.14, where the depth effects shown in Figure 10.13 have been accentuated. Here the two heavy vertical lines are the same physical length but they appear to be very different in length because of the action of size constancy. Studies have also shown that if the depth cues at each end of the line contradict one another, then the size of the illusion is greatly reduced (Nijhawan, 1991).

Size Constancy and the Moon. The most spectacular illusion involving size constancy in everyday life is undoubtedly the **moon illusion.** This occurs when the moon on the horizon appears to be larger than the moon when it is high in the sky, despite the fact that it is exactly the same-sized disk on our retina at all points throughout the night. In fact, it is almost exactly one half of a degree of visual angle, which is about one quarter of the width of your thumb, held out at arm's length (Hershenson, 1989; Kaufman & Rock, 1989). The reason its size appears to differ depending on where in the sky it appears is an inappropriate application of size constancy. This leads to much the same perceptual result as the pictorial illusions shown in Figures 10.11 and 10.12.

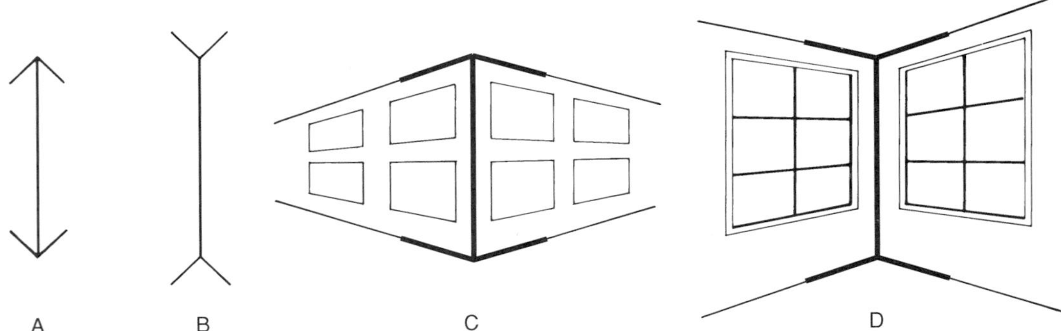

FIGURE 10.13 (A) The underestimated segment of the Mueller-Lyer illusion. (B) The overestimated segment. (C and D) The corresponding perspective configurations.

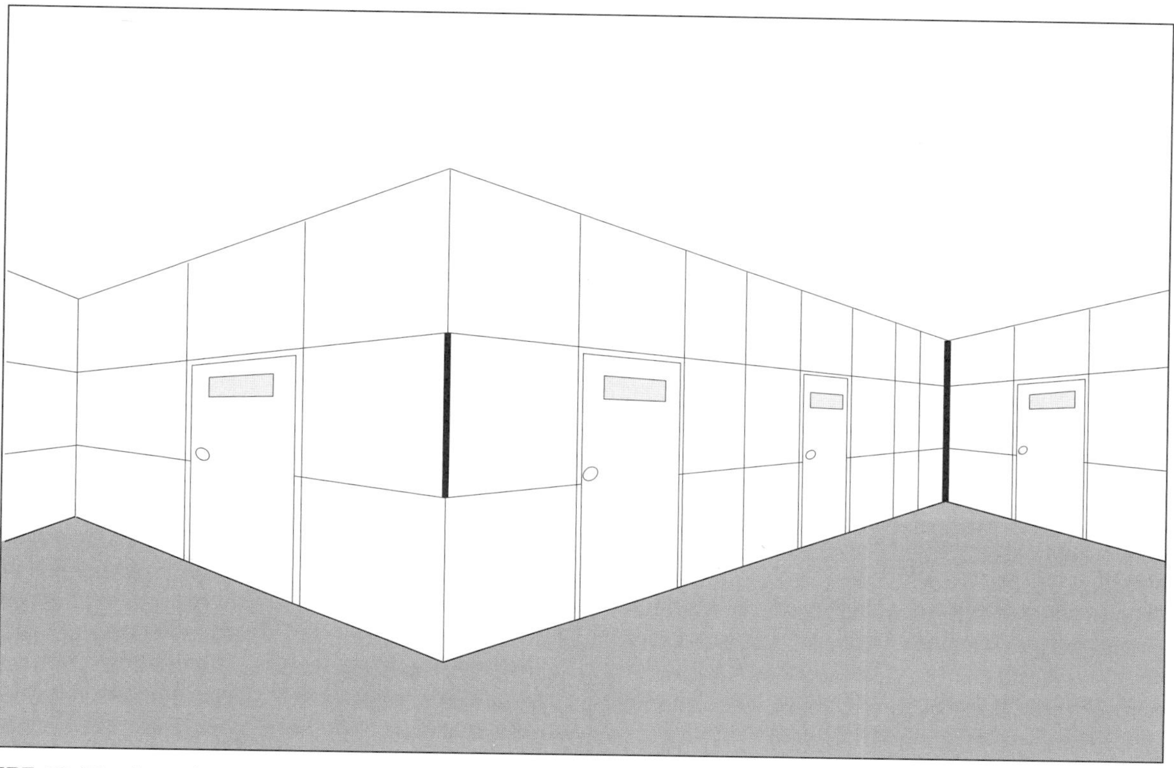

FIGURE 10.14 A version of the Mueller-Lyer illusion in which the depth relationships are accentuated. The two heavy vertical lines are identical in their length on the page.

Our visual system behaves as though the moon is being seen on the "surface" of the sky. All our modern knowledge about where the moon really is and how large it really is has no influence on the much more basic tendency of our brain to "see" the moon and the stars as though they were painted on a large dome. To make matters worse, this dome, as far as the brain is concerned, is like the interior of a large, upside down, flattened bowl, as shown in Figure 10.15. This places the moon on the horizon at a much greater distance from us than the moon at its zenith.

But you are probably wondering why the brain would unconsciously arrive at the conclusion that the sky is a flattened dome. This seems to be because when you look toward the horizon, you have a large number of depth cues for distance, such as texture gradients, familiar objects, and perspective cues, indicating that the moon is farther away than even the most distant point you can see on earth. On the other hand, when you look up, there is only black sky and perhaps a few clouds and stars. There are no visual cues at all indicating how large or how far away these objects are in the night sky. Our brains seem to assume, in the absence of any contradictory knowledge, that the distance from us to these objects must not be very great. This means that the moon is assumed to be farther away when on the horizon than when at zenith. Size constancy gets applied to these assumptions and the moon's apparent size gets adjusted accordingly.

This interpretation of the moon illusion has been supported by many studies (e.g., Kaufman & Kaufman, 2000; Ross & Plug, 2002). Most have taken the approach of varying the number and type of depth cues present in the situation, to see whether judgments of the moon's size are influenced by these factors governing perceived distance. For example, even when the moon is only drawn in pictures, judgments of the perceived size of a two-dimensional disk in the picture, representing the moon, are directly related to the number and strength of depth cues in the picture (Coren & Aks, 1990). In the three-dimensional world, you can easily verify for yourself that a reduction in the perceived distance of the moon will weaken the illusion. That is, if you are athletic enough to perform this demonstration. Pick an evening when the moon is on the horizon and looks quite large.

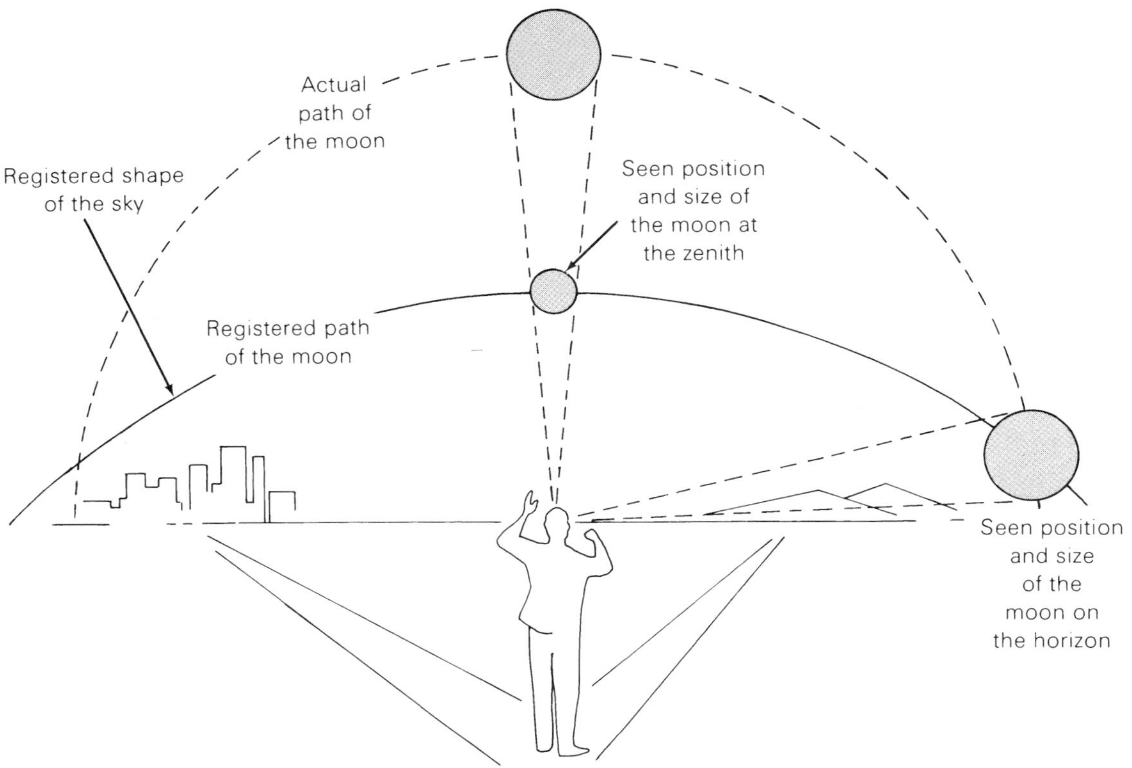

FIGURE 10.15 The fact that the moon appears to be more distant from us when it is at the horizon than when it is overhead is the main factor resulting in the moon illusion.

Now, turn your back to the moon and bend over and view it through your legs. With your head and the scene upside down, the depth cues that you will see will no longer look normal, and you will find that the moon appears to be much smaller in size than when viewed in the usual way. Coren (1992) performed a version of this experiment using a slightly more decorous technique to accomplish the same thing. He simply turned a picture containing the moon upside down and found that the moon illusion in pictures was also decreased. Again this happens because the depth cues are weakened by viewing them in an unusual orientation.

Shape Constancy

Each perceptual constancy involves an analysis of the variable and fluctuating properties of the visual image in order to come to a conclusion about what the actual dimensions and qualities of an object might be. For size constancy, this means seeing an object as a certain size despite wide variations in the size of its image on our retinas. **Shape constancy** refers, in a similar way, to the perception of the enduring shape of an object, despite wide variations in the shape that is projected from that object to our eyes.

To see why shape constancy is necessary, consider what happens when you view a rectangular card from different angles, as in Figure 10.16. As we increase the tilt of the card, the retinal image becomes more like a trapezoid, with the formerly vertical sides tapering outward. Yet, a card held at these angles will still look rectangular. The same happens when we swing a door outward. The large changes in the shape of the retinal image must be dealt with if the door is still to appear to be rectangular. This requires information from other sources than the shape of the door itself, because the shape of the retinal image will not resolve the ambiguity concerning the actual shape of the door. Following the instructions in Demonstration Box 10.3 will help you to experience the operation of shape constancy through a strong visual illusion.

There is a very close relationship between size constancy and shape constancy because both depend on distance perception for their operation. For size constancy,

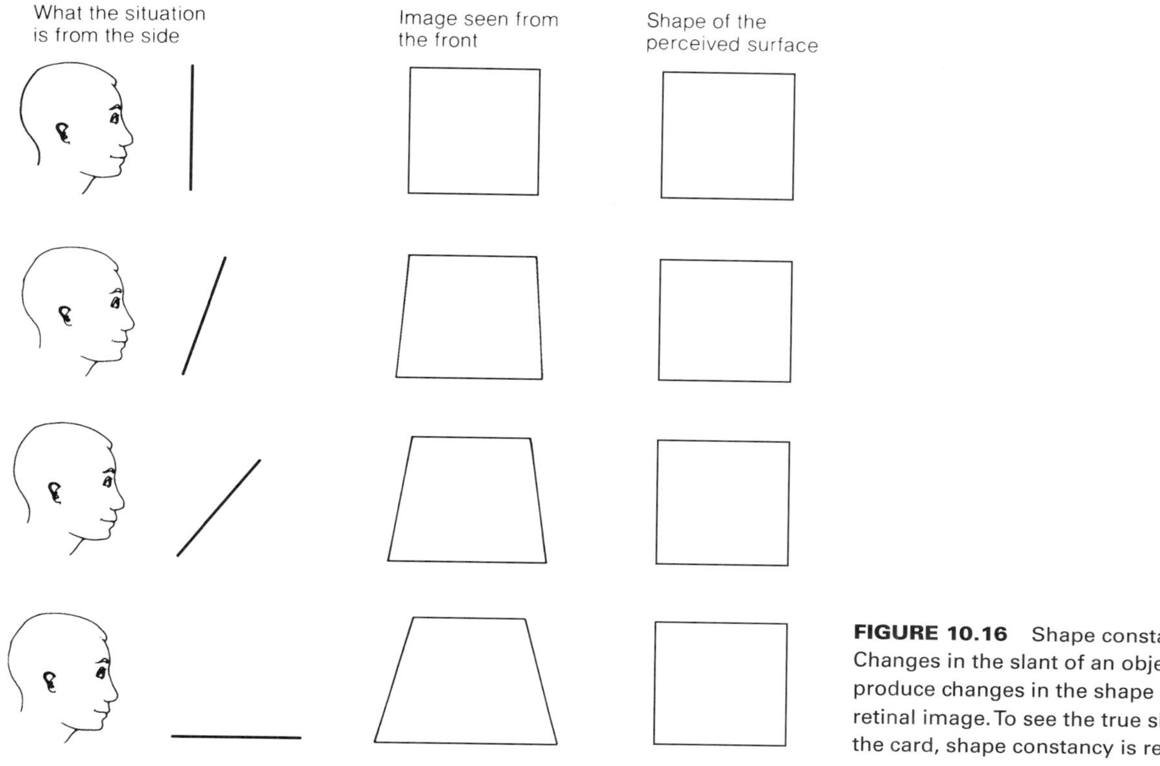

FIGURE 10.16 Shape constancy. Changes in the slant of an object will produce changes in the shape of the retinal image. To see the true shape of the card, shape constancy is required.

DEMONSTRATION BOX 10.3

SHAPE CONSTANCY

Look closely at the two gray box tops in the figure. Are they the same shape? Now take a small piece of paper and trace the gray top of one box. Cut out this shape so that you can superimpose it on each of the two box tops (note that to place the cutout on the second shape you will have to rotate it by 90 degrees). What you will find is that the gray box tops are exactly the same shape for each box. The reason they do not look to be the same shape in the picture is that you automatically and unconsciously have interpreted the box tops as being rectangular shapes that are receding in depth. In that interpretation, one shape is much longer than the other, whereas the other shape is much wider.

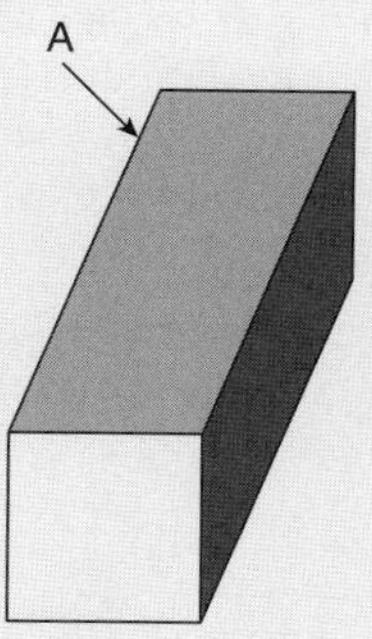

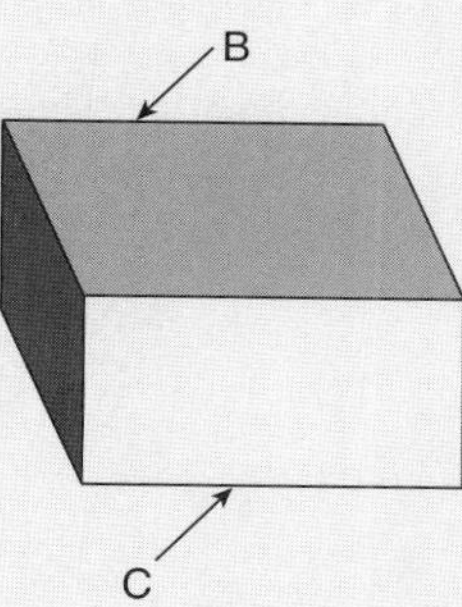

perceived distance is used to gauge the actual size of an object relative to other objects. For shape constancy the perceived distance is used to gauge the relative distance of different parts of the same object from the observer, such as the nearer and farther point of an object's surface from the observer. When we are talking about different distances to parts of the same object, we are referring to an object's orientation in space or *slant*. You can experience the relationship between size constancy and shape constancy by following the instructions in Demonstration Box 10.4.

In three-dimensional environments that are seen with no limitations on viewing time, observers tend to perceive the shape and slant of objects with remarkable accuracy. Just as we saw in the case of size constancy, if we reduce the number of available depth cues or prevent observers from using other contextual information that would indicate the degree of slant, the operation of shape constancy becomes less effective and our perception begins to resemble the situation on the retinal image rather than the situation in the scene (Doorschot, Kappers, & Koenderink, 2001; Niall, 1990).

Observers use several strategies to assist in the judgment of slant. For example, in Figure 10.17A, we have the shape of the familiar letter E. This shape has a typical or a normative orientation based on our experience with it. We tend to use such normative information to infer whether the shape we are currently viewing is upright, rotated, or tilted (e.g., Braine, Plastow, & Greene, 1987). Even in the absence of such prior experience with a shape, we make certain assumptions about shape orientation. For example, we tend to assume that the longest dimension (sometimes called the principal axis) represents the upright dimension of an object (Sekuler, 1996). Thus, we are apt to consider the rectangle shown in Figure 10.17B as being less tilted than that shown in Figure 10.17C (Humphreys, 1984).

The apparent slant of objects is also affected by their perceived relationship to one another in a scene. Consider a very simple scene consisting of only the pair of boxes shown in Figure 10.18A. Notice that the boxes are drawn so as to be seen in three dimensions and that their perceived orientation in space is different; one box is slanted upward toward the front while the other is slanted upward toward the back. Shift your attention to edges of the sides of each box that are nearest to one another; these are the inside edges that we have indicated with arrows in Part B of the figure. Now consider the relative orientation of these edges, and you will notice that they do not appear to be parallel to one another. Instead, the extensions of these edges appear to diverge as they move toward the top of the drawings. This is called the **box alignment illusion,** because in fact these edges are physically parallel in the picture. To help convince you that this is in fact an illusion, simply turn the page upside down. If the edges were diverging toward the top of the page before, then they now ought to appear to converge as your eye moves up. Yet, these particular edges of the two boxes still appear to diverge toward the top of the page.

DEMONSTRATION BOX 10.4

SIZE CONSTANCY AND SHAPE CONSTANCY INTERACT

Look at the box in the accompanying figure. Most people believe that a dime will fit inside the top of this box. Try placing a dime (flat on one face) into the box. Does it fit? The reason that the top surface of this box appeared to be large enough to accommodate the dime is that you made a shape constancy and a size constancy correction. The shape constancy correction changed the appearance of the top of the box into a square receding in depth. The size constancy correction made the sides of the box appear to be equal in length. Look back at the box and notice that its real physical shape is a parallelogram, not a square.

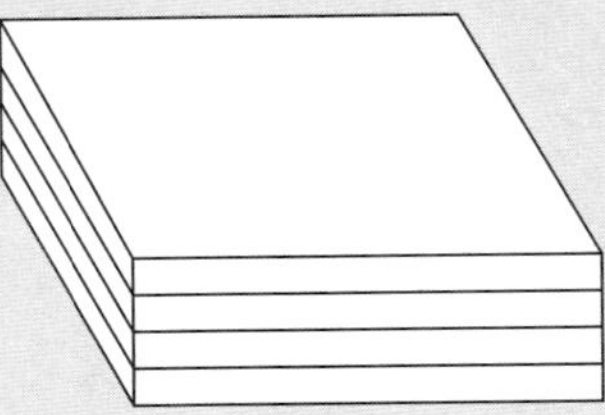

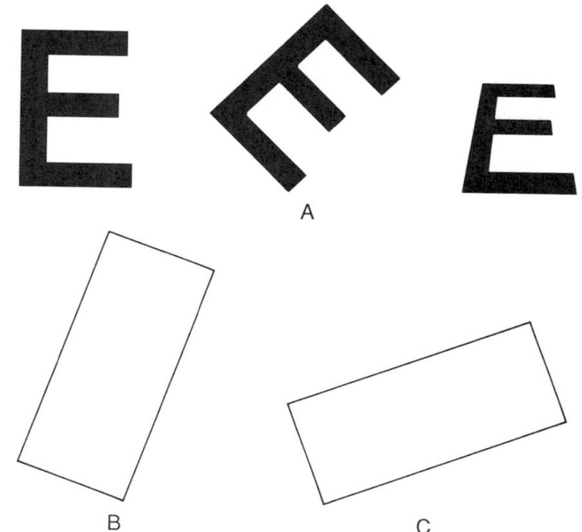

FIGURE 10.17 (A) We can tell how some shapes are tilted in space because of our familiarity with them. For less common shapes, we assume that the longest axis indicates "upright." For this reason, we tend to see B as being less tilted than C, even though both are tilted exactly the same amount from the horizontal.

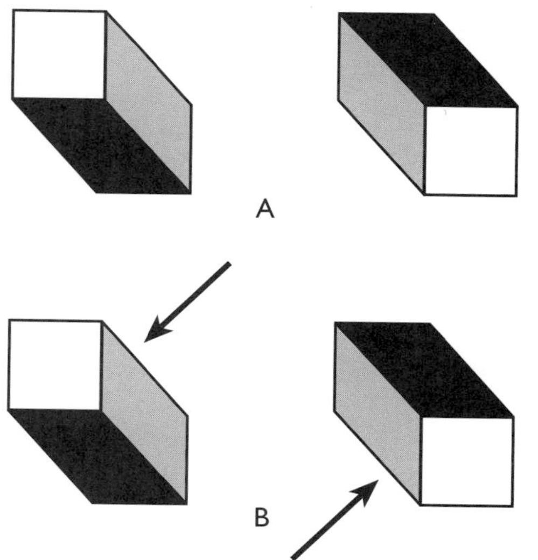

FIGURE 10.18 The box alignment illusion. Look at the long inside edges of the boxes in A (the edges to look at are pointed to by arrows in B). Notice that these two edges in A do not appear to be parallel but, rather, seem to diverge toward the top of the figure. Now turn the page upside down and notice that these edges still appear to diverge toward the top of the figure. Of course, both of these perceptions cannot be correct, and indeed they are not. The two edges are physically parallel on the page.

Research with the box alignment illusion has shown that it depends on the assumptions observers make about linear perspective in this scene (Enns & Coren, 1995). As we discussed in Chapter 9, the vanishing point of a picture is the place where all of the perspective lines converge. Even though no vanishing point has been drawn in this picture, observers seem to insist on using the implied perspective information in the boxes to infer its location, and this affects their perception of the shape and tilt of the objects. This has been confirmed by superimposing pictures of these boxes on pictures of scenes that have a visible vanishing point. This strongly influences the box alignment illusion, much like the manipulation of depth cues affects other aspects of size constancy and shape constancy that we have discussed.

Lightness Constancy

How light (as opposed to dark) an object appears to be is also affected by a perceptual constancy. It is in our interest to know what proportion of light is reflected from an object's surface, independent of the amount of light that is shining onto the surface. This is what is meant by **lightness constancy** (sometimes referred to as *brightness constancy*). To help you understand what is involved in being able to see the lightness of an object, you need to remind yourself that the total amount of light we receive from any point in a retinal image is determined by two factors. The first is the amount of light from all light sources in the scene that falls on the object. This is called **external illuminance.** The second is the **surface reflectance** (sometimes called the *albedo*), which is the proportion of light falling on the object that is reflected to the eye of the observer. For example, a white surface will reflect most (perhaps 80 to 90%) of the light that falls on it. In contrast, a black surface will absorb a great deal of light, and the proportion reflected will be small (often less than 4 to 5%). This means that when viewed under the same light the white appears lighter than the black. However, suppose that the two surfaces were viewed under different illuminations. To achieve lightness constancy we must have some way of subtracting away the contribution of external illuminance to the image.

Under everyday viewing conditions we are good at being able to judge the lightness (or surface reflectance) of an object. That is, a piece of white paper will tend to look very light in appearance when viewed in bright sunlight, when viewed through colored sunglasses, when viewed in a room with dim lighting, and even when viewed by light from a single flickering candle. Similarly, a piece of coal viewed in bright sunlight will still appear black even though it may be reflecting a greater amount of light to the eye than would a piece of white paper viewed in ordinary room light. For example, a piece of coal reflecting only 5% of the 1000 units of sunlight falling onto it would be providing you with a greater overall intensity of light than a piece of white paper that reflected 90% of the 50 units of light falling onto it from a candle. Because of lightness constancy, the coal reflecting 50 units would still appear to be blacker than the paper reflecting only 45 units. Somehow we are able to judge these differences in lightness without becoming confused by the total amount of light.

Two types of explanation have been given for lightness constancy. The first involves a computation that could be based directly on the patterns of light intensity in the image. A computation that works well for many situations is called the **ratio principle** and is illustrated in Figure 10.19. Suppose you are looking at a white tabletop with a reflectance of 80% on which is resting a gray piece of paper with a reflectance of 40%. They are illuminated by a light source of 100 units of intensity. The amount of light reaching your eye would then be 80 units from the table and 40 units from the paper. Suppose that an identical piece of paper is seen in shadow so that the intensity of the light in the shadow is only half the original 100 units (i.e., 50 units). Now the amount of light reaching your eye from the table and the paper is 40 and 20 units, respectively. On the basis of the amount of light reaching your eye, we might now predict that the shadowed white tabletop would appear to be gray and similar in lightness to the gray paper viewed under the intense illumination. This, however, is not the case—the white still appears white and the gray appears gray. It is not the total retinal illumination that matters but, rather, the ratio of the intensities of the two patches of light on the retina (Wallach, 1972). In this situation, the light from the white surface is twice as intense as that from the gray surface, regardless of the intensity of the external illumination. What has remained constant is the ratio of 2 to 1 (Jacobsen & Gilchrist, 1988).

Several refinements of this ratio principle allow it to explain a somewhat larger range of situations than the simple one illustrated in Figure 10.19. For example, one version of it is called the retinex theory (Land, 1986),

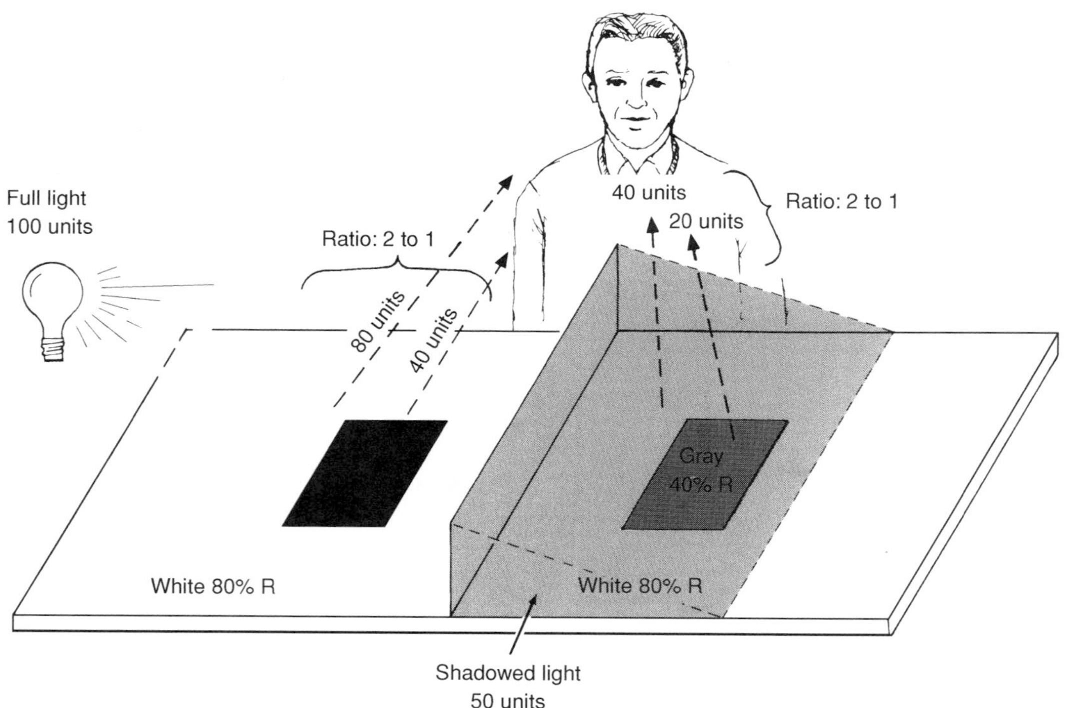

FIGURE 10.19 The ratio principle in lightness constancy. Notice that the ratio of the amount of light reaching the eye of the observer from the background and the target remains constant regardless of the amount of light falling on the two surfaces.

which specifies that gradual changes in illuminance are ignored and ratios are computed only over neighboring edges that are sharp. Surfaces that are separated by a wide distance in the image can be compared by computing the illuminance ratios at all of the boundaries between them. This theory has been very successful in allowing the ratio principle to be extended to situations that more closely resemble naturalistic scenes, where there are many gradual and complex changes in the illumination falling on a number of regions with different reflectance levels.

At a physiological level in the eye, the ratio principle of lightness constancy might operate through the mechanism of lateral inhibition (which we discussed in Chapter 3) (Cornsweet, 1985; Gilchrist, 1988; Shapley, 1986). For this to work, we must assume that the amount of lateral inhibition from one ganglion cell to the next becomes greater as the intensity of the retinal illumination is increased. The idea is that greater levels of light intensity not only produce a larger neural response in the excited areas, but they also produce more inhibition of adjacent areas. Because the larger amount of inhibition would subtract from the greater excitation, it could offset the larger response of the eye to more intense illumination. This would leave the overall neural response of the eye relatively the same regardless of the average intensity of the light input. If the inhibition and excitation are balanced in this way, any changes in the overall illumination should leave the ratio of the neural responses to dark and light surfaces relatively unchanged. One way to fool the system, however, would be to alter the intensity of the background alone because this affects the nature of the neural response even though the illumination of the target area has remained the same. This means that a change in the object's relationship to its background could affect how well lightness constancy works, and this has been shown to be the case (Schirillo & Arend, 1995). There is no need for these interactions to be confined to the retina since similar inhibitory mechanisms have been found in the primary visual cortex (VI) which could also contribute to lightness constancy (MacEvoy & Paradiso, 2001).

A second explanation for lightness constancy begins with the ratio principle but then adds a number of factors. One of the most important of these involves an initial evaluation of the sources of illumination in the scene. The need for such an evaluation is shown in a classic experiment involving a concealed light source (Gelb, 1929), illustrated in Figure 10.20. A black disk was placed against a gray background. Out of sight from the observer a strong light source was used to illuminate the black disk so that the borders of the disk and the region

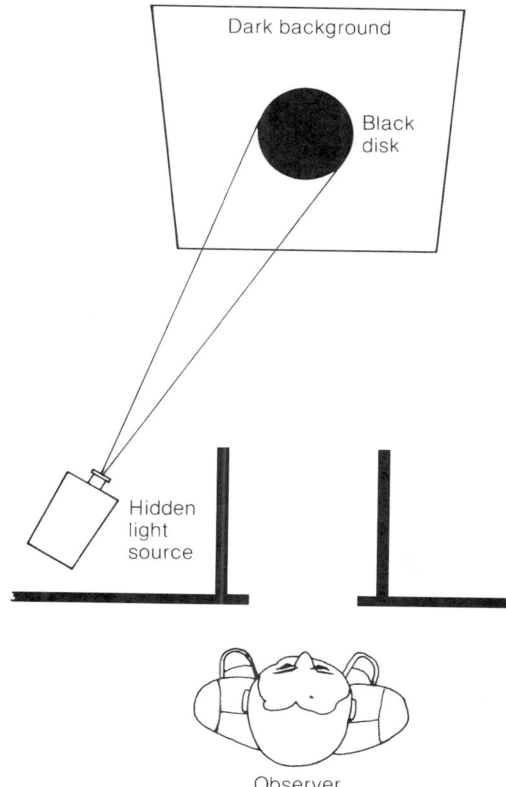

FIGURE 10.20 Experimental situation used by Gelb (1929) to test for lightness constancy when a light source was hidden from view.

lit by the spotlight were coincident. Although the disk was black, observers reported seeing a white disk in dim light rather than a very brightly lit black disk. Of course, this represents a complete failure of lightness constancy. If constancy were operating, the observers would see the black disk as black even though it was very brightly lit.

Lightness constancy was restored in this situation by a very simple manipulation. When the experimenter placed a piece of white paper partly in front of the brightly lit black disk, the disk immediately looked black. In other words, with the addition of the reference white paper to indicate the source of the light, constancy returned. As soon as the piece of white paper was removed, however, the black disk returned to its former white appearance. These results show that successful lightness constancy depends on observers making the correct attribution with regard to the lighting conditions in the scene. Demonstration Box 10.5 shows how our assumptions about the illumination falling on a surface can affect its perceived lightness.

DEMONSTRATION BOX 10.5

LIGHTNESS CONSTANCY

To a certain extent, lightness constancy depends on assumptions that the observer makes about the nature of the world. Consider the gray tube shown here. Notice that the gray of the interior of the tube appears to be lighter than the gray of the exterior. In fact, they are the same gray. Coren and Komoda (1973) suggested that this apparent lightness difference involves a cognitive adjustment based on presumptions we make about the environment. If the tube were real, its interior would be likely to receive less light than its exterior. In the tube pictured here, however, the same amount of light reaches the eye from both the apparent interior and the apparent exterior surfaces. This could happen only if the interior surface reflects a greater proportion of the light than reaches it; in other words, the internal surface must have a greater reflectance. This demonstration shows one way lightness constancy operates. The visual system makes presumptions about the amount of light reaching surfaces and adjusts the perceptual experience so that the apparent lightness corresponds to the assumed relative reflectances, rather than to the actual distribution of light reaching the eye.

Also notice one other interesting aspect of the tube shown here, namely that either the right- or the left-hand portion can be viewed as the interior or the exterior surface. A figure that can assume several different orientations depending on one's point of view is called a *reversible figure.* Notice how the apparent lightness difference between the two sides changes, depending on whether you see the right or the left side as the interior surface. The apparent inner surface, regardless of whether it is the right or the left, appears to be the lighter one.

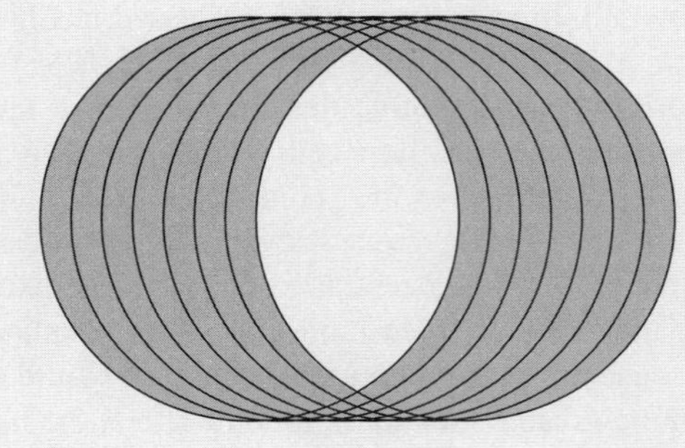

Another important factor is **anchoring,** which means that one stimulus is chosen as a reference or an anchor and the lightnesses of all other stimuli are judged against that anchor. A variety of principles seem to be adopted by the perceptual system to select the brightness anchor. Commonly the anchor is simply the brightest or the largest stimulus in the field, although this choice may be modified by other factors (Gilchrist et al., 1999). As in the case of the other constancies we have looked at, the more available cues the better the constancy. In the case of lightness constancy this means that the more articulated the field is (meaning the more different lightness levels that are visible), the better the lightness constancy (Gilchrist & Annan, 2002). Biography Box 10.2 will introduce you to a researcher who has done much to demonstrate the important role of visual scene analysis in the achievement of lightness constancy.

Color Constancy

We have seen how the perceived size, shape, and lightness of objects remain relatively constant in our consciousness regardless of changes in the retinal image. The perceived color or hue of an object has a similar enduring quality in the face of different lighting conditions. This is called **color constancy.** This means that within limits, we will see a red apple as red whether it is viewed under the white light of the sun, fluorescent light that has a dominant blue hue, or incandescent light that is basically yellow. Color constancy is our ability to detect the surface color of an object despite variations in the color of the external illumination falling onto it.

Just as in lightness constancy, our perception of color is not based completely on an object's image on the retina but, rather, also depends on its relationship to surrounding stimuli (e.g., Jenness & Shevell, 1995; Land, 1986). Color constancy is significantly better when there are many objects around to serve as comparison stimuli. You can prove this for yourself by using Demonstration Box 10.6.

There is a much similarity in the theories used to explain lightness constancy and color constancy. For instance, the ratio principle has been elaborated into several more complex models that make comparisons at boundaries along three different dimensions: red-green, blue-yellow, and black-white (Brainard, Wandell, &

BIOGRAPHY BOX 10.2

WHAT SHADE OF GRAY IS IT? IT'S NOT AS BLACK AND WHITE AS YOU THINK

When a young perception researcher, ***Alan Gilchrist (1944–),*** started his research on lightness constancy about 30 years ago, the prevailing view was that the ratio principle was behind our ability to see how light (or dark) an object surface was. Moreover, the ratio principle was believed to be implemented in the ganglion neurons of the retina through the mechanism of lateral inhibition. A paper in the journal *Science* by Alan Gilchrist in 1977 and a follow-up paper in *Scientific American* in 1979 are generally credited with changing this view almost overnight. The experiment was elegantly simple. The stimulus was a standard display for simultaneous brightness contrast, in which a gray patch changes its appearance, depending on whether it is surrounded by a lighter or a darker patch (Chapter 4). The new finding was that this illusion was greater when the two surrounding regions were believed by the observer to be illuminated by different levels of light. Since Alan Gilchrist had kept the physical luminance levels constant in all conditions, this difference in illusion could not be attributed to the operation of the ratio principle. How the observer was interpreting the scene as a whole was making all the difference.

Since that time, improvements in computer graphics have been exploited by many researchers to produce a wide variety of compelling demonstrations of this kind. The perception of surface orientation, shadows, transparency, surface shading, and occlusion have all been used to alter the interpretation of how light a surface appears. The main question in lightness constancy has now shifted from how the ratio principle is implemented to a search for the precise rules that are used to determine which surfaces should be included in its computation. This has led Gilchrist to propose the idea that what is needed is just a single anchoring stimulus against which all other stimuli in the environment will be judged. The problem of how this anchor stimulus is selected is complex and has several answers; however, the final solution may well tell us about how certain aspects of attention and object or scene perception work, as well as help to explain our perception of lightness.

Alan Gilchrist is currently a very active member of the Department of Psychology at Rutgers University in New Jersey and a member of the Organizing Committee of the annual meetings of the Vision Sciences Society, held in Sarasota, Florida.

Chichilnisky, 1993; Dannemiller, 1989). There are also theories of color constancy that draw on additional sources of information. For instance, cues about the nature of illumination falling on a surface would allow us to correct for color shifts. Our prior knowledge about the identity of the object being viewed can also be used to maintain constancy. Thus, a banana may appear yellow in red light, in part simply because we know that it is a banana (Jameson & Hurvich, 1989; Jin & Shevell, 1996).

In the case of color constancy, however, there seem to be physiological mechanisms going well beyond lateral interactions in the eye that also play a role. For instance, tissue damage to visual Area V4 of the cortex of monkeys does not affect color discrimination, but it does produce noticeably poor performance on tasks that require color constancy (Kulikowski, Walsh, McKeefry, Butler, & Carden 1994). Human stroke victims who are unfortunate enough to suffer brain damage in a closely related brain site, near the fusiform gyrus in the temporal lobe (Chapter 3), also seem to lose the ability to make color constant comparisons, though all of their color sensitivity is not lost (Zeki, Aglioti, McKeefry, & Berlucchi,

DEMONSTRATION BOX 10.6

CONTEXT AND COLOR CONSTANCY

The greater the number of other colors in a scene, the better your color constancy tends to be. To demonstrate this you will need a magazine photo with a rich arrangement of vibrant colors, a piece of black stiff paper with a small hole (around a quarter of an inch or 7 mm) punched or cut into it, a desk lamp, and a piece of colored acetate or cellophane that can serve as a color filter. Any number of colors will work well; we will simply assume it is blue for this discussion. Turn off all of the room lights except for the desk lamp. Now place the black paper with the hole over the color photo so that only a small patch of white is visible through the hole. The hole should be filled with a color that is obviously white in appearance. Now slide the color filter under the black piece of paper so that the hole reveals the original white spot as seen through the color filter. The color patch will now definitely appear to be a shade of blue, since the hole will be filled with a combination of the original white color combined with the color of the blue filter.

In this limited viewing condition, where only a small patch of color can be seen, color constancy is clearly not working. You are unable to separate the color of the photo from the color of the filter. But now remove the black piece of paper so that the whole scene is exposed, but still viewed through the blue filter. In a few seconds you will begin to make out all of the original colors of the photo, and even the small white patch you were viewing through the hole in the black paper will look white again, despite the fact that this same color looked blue when it was the only color visible. Thus, color constancy has been restored in the presence of a varied number of different-colored surfaces in the scene.

1999). At the same time, some very primitive animals, such as goldfish and other lower vertebrates, can demonstrate sophisticated color constancy in their behavior (Dorr & Neumeyer, 1996; Neumeyer, 1998).

The major physiological mechanisms involved in color constancy are those associated with adaptation processes (Webster & Mollon, 1995). Note that any changes in the color of the illumination will tend to change the wavelength composition of the retinal image over a large region. If, for instance, we shine reddish light on an object, the image will become much more red overall. Without any adaptation process, the surface should then also appear redder because of the increased activity of the red-responsive cones. However, this increased activity in any given color channel leads to faster chromatic adaptation (see Chapter 4), which is the process by which a cone's response to a particular colored stimulus is weakened with continuous exposure. The greater red response will lead initially to more vigorous activity, which in turn leads to faster adaptation in the red cones, which then makes the object seem less red than it otherwise would, thus canceling out the effect of the colored illumination (Werner & Walraven, 1982). In effect, the added red of the illuminant is effectively subtracted by the adaptation process. Obviously, the more that you are exposed to a colored illuminant, both in terms of the time and the area filled by the light, the more adaptation there will be and the more color constancy there will be (e.g., Uchikawa, Uchikawa, & Boynton, 1989). It may take up to 15 min of exposure to the colored illuminant before full color constancy is achieved and for objects to appear to be the same hues that they would be if they were seen in white light (Kuriki & Uchikawa, 1996).

Position Constancy

In this last section on visual constancies, we will cover another rather important one known as **position constancy.** This refers to the fact that even though objects are often in motion across our retina, we do not experience them as moving. Instead we interpret this movement as properly belonging to the eye, head, and body movements we are making almost all of the time. Position constancy is controlled by feedback mechanisms from our eye and head movements. These signals are combined with the actual movements of the visual image across the retina to effectively "cancel them out," leaving us with the perception of a stationary world.

A closer examination of what is involved in position constancy reveals that there are actually two different aspects of object position that must be distinguished from one another. The first concerns the position of objects relative to one another. As I move around an otherwise stationary scene, these relations remain the same despite my ongoing change in viewpoint on the scene. We can call this **object position constancy.** A related, but different, aspect of position constancy is the relative position of objects with respect to me, called **egocentric direction constancy.** My spatial relationships with the objects in the environment are changing dynamically as I move about in it, but what is it that counts as "me" for calculating these spatial relations? Another way to ask the same question is, With respect to what aspect of my body is egocentric direction determined? To gain an understanding of how this question is different from object position constancy, think about the three different ways in which the visual "straight ahead" can be defined, which we discussed in Chapter 9. There is the "ahead" with respect to the center of my gaze, there is the "ahead" that is defined relative to where my nose is pointing, and there is an "ahead" that is aligned with the trunk of my body. As you can easily demonstrate for yourself, changes in eye position do not change the perceived position of objects with respect to you, at least not in the way that changes in head and body position do. To experience this, look at an object that is straight ahead of your body. Now shift your head to one side. The object will no longer seem to be lying directly straight ahead. This indicates that we tend to use the head as the reference for egocentric direction (see Chapter 12 on motion). However, just because the object is now perceived to lie in a different direction with respect to me, its position in the scene has not changed at all with the head movement you made. Object position constancy and egocentric direction constancy are therefore separate aspects of the larger concept of position constancy (Shebilske, 1977). All probably work via some form of neural feedback loop that monitors eye and body movements and then "subtracts" these from any seen visual motion (e.g., Kleiser & Skrandies, 2000).

Varieties of Constancy

There are many other perceptual constancies, some well known, some less known. For example, there is an auditory version of size constancy called loudness constancy. In this situation, the loudness of a sound source remains constant, even when the sound level at the ear diminishes because of movement away from the source (Zahorik & Wightman, 2001). There is even a kind of odor constancy. When you are sniffing an object, a deep sniff will tend to pull more of the odorous molecules into your nose. We know that if we artificially give a large puff of some vapors to you, it will smell more intense than a smaller puff (e.g., Rehn, 1978). Yet when you actually sniff something, its "smelliness" remains constant despite the strength of your sniff, hence demonstrating odor constancy (Teghtsoonian, Teghtsoonian, Berglund, & Berglund, 1978).

As we discussed these perceptual constancies, you may have noticed a pattern beginning to emerge. The purpose of perception is to gain information about the nature of the external environment and the objects in it. The viewing conditions, our relationship to objects, and our own exploratory behaviors will frequently change the pattern of light falling onto our eyes. The visual constancies can be thought of as "corrections" that take into account the ongoing conditions. This allows us to extract a stable set of object properties from the continuous flow of sensory inputs at our receptors. Were it not for the constancies we have discussed, objects would have no permanent properties in consciousness at all. Consciousness and sanity would be difficult to sustain in a world of such unpredictable changes.

WHAT IS A VISUAL OBJECT?

In our discussion so far we have been proceeding as though it was perfectly clear what an object is. Objects are people, chairs, and coffee mugs. But this begs the question of how our visual system, as well as any of our other sensory systems, is able to determine the boundaries of one of these objects, or even which parts of an image belong to one object and which parts belong to another. Giving a satisfactory definition of *object* in this sense turns out to be a very difficult thing to do.

One of the main reasons for this difficulty has to do with the distinction we made between images and scenes at the beginning of this chapter. Physical objects exist in a three-dimensional world of more or less solid bodies that are more or less connected. If some part of an object moves, other parts of the same object move as well. Therefore, if we restricted ourselves to a definition of *object* in the three-dimensional world of the scene, it might be possible to define objects as something like "molecules that adhere together and that move together." The problem is that this definition is not as helpful when it comes to the world of reflected light in the image. Here *object* must be given a definition based solely on the properties of an object that can be conveyed by light. This is more than a philosophical point. It means that our definition of a visual object will be unable to distinguish between real objects that give rise to a particular image, and virtual objects as seen in pictures and movies, provided they give rise to the same image. At the same time, this does not mean that we can reduce our discussion of visual objects to the level of two-dimensional images. As we have seen many times already, vision is fundamentally about the conscious experience of, and action upon, objects that are "out there." Image processing is an important aspect of vision, because that is the raw material that the visual system has to work with, but it is only useful to the extent that it allows us to see objects in the external world. This is the sense in which the visual system sees objects and not merely images.

But having distinguished between real objects and objects in images, it turns out that visual objects are still notoriously difficult to define. There is certainly no definition of *object* at this time that will satisfy all vision scientists. In this section we will consider several ways of thinking about what a visual object is. There seems to be enough truth in each of these approaches to suggest that when a coherent definition of a visual object is finally available, it will include some aspects of all of these ideas.

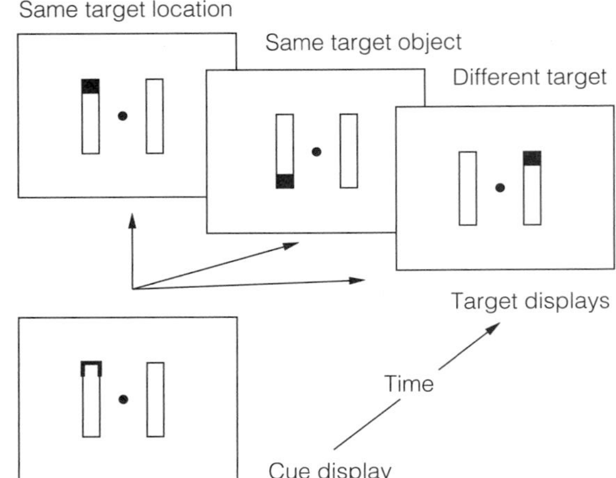

FIGURE 10.21 The display sequence for testing covert orienting to one of four display locations. The upside-down U at one end of the left-side rectangle in the cue display speeds the perception of not only a square target that appears in the same location, but it also speeds the perception of the square when it appears elsewhere within the same object.

The Object as the Focus of Attention

When we view a typical scene under conditions of normal viewing, we make a series of eye movements to acquire details from its various regions. This is necessary because only a small region of the retina near the fovea is able to register visual information with a high degree of clarity, as we discussed in Chapter 3. Yet, even when we are prevented from making physical changes in eye position over time, either because we are instructed to maintain fixation in the center of the picture or because the picture is flashed on and then turned off before our eyes have a chance to move, there is still a sense in which we can choose to view one object and not another. This mental selection process is called **covert spatial orienting,** in order to distinguish it from the **overt spatial orienting** that is involved in making eye movements. It is the mental process we use when we surreptitiously want to inspect someone or something in our visual field without letting others know where we are looking. Athletes in many team sports are experts in this skill, which allows them to pass to teammates without looking directly at them and to avoid opponents who are approaching without losing sight of the ball or the puck.

Many studies have shown that covert spatial orienting results in visual benefits for the attended objects. This means, of course, that objects that are not the focus of covert orienting are seen less well. In the early studies on this topic, researchers tended to think of the mental process of covert orienting as similar to a spotlight that could shine on a region of the visual field and increase the visible detail of the objects located there. However, careful studies conducted on this question make it clear that the enhancement of vision that occurs for attended regions of the visual field often applies to something that resembles focusing on a thing rather than on a region of space.

For example, in one study of covert orienting the visual sequence consisted of the displays shown in Figure 10.21 (Egly, Driver, & Rafal, 1994). The displays contained a pair of rectangles that could be oriented either vertically or horizontally. At the beginning of each sequence there was a cue display, consisting of a brief brightening of one end of a rectangle. This was followed after a brief interval by the presentation of a dark square in one of the four ends of the rectangles. The viewer's task was simply to respond as rapidly as possible to the onset of the dark square by pressing a computer key.

Targets that appeared in the same location as the briefly presented cue were responded to more rapidly than were targets in one of the three other noncued locations. This is the standard visibility benefit that accompanies successful covert orienting. However, the important result for our present question about the role of objects in perception was that there was also a benefit for targets that appeared at the other end of the same rectangle as the cue. If covert orienting was strictly a spatial mechanism, like the beam of a flashlight, then targets that appeared at the other end of the cued rectangle and targets that appeared in an adjacent location to the cued rectangle should have been responded to equally slowly. This object-based benefit of covert orienting suggests that, at a minimum, the definition of an object for vision must include a collection of visual features (such as edges in this case) that are connected.

Other studies have gone on to demonstrate that the connection among edges need not be image based for these benefits of covert orienting to occur. For example, if a nearer object partially occludes the rectangles in Figure 10.21, so that the rectangles appear to extend behind the nearer object, then the benefits of same-object cueing are still obtained (Moore, Yantis, & Vaughan, 1998; Yantis, 1995). Studies that have segmented the visual display into different depth planes using stereo viewing or motion parallax have also found that the benefits of attention extend to collections of edges that appear to belong to the same object (He & Nakayama, 1992). Thus, a visual object appears to be the perceptual unit around which the concept of attention is based. "Aspects of the world that can be attended together" is therefore a good starting point for a definition of object. Biography Box 10.3 introduces you to a perception researcher who has been very influential in pointing out the role of the observer in defining the "visual object."

BIOGRAPHY BOX 10.3

WHAT CAN LINE DRAWINGS TELL US ABOUT OBJECT PERCEPTION?

Julian Hochberg (1923–) has been asking what defines a visual object for over 50 years. In the late 1950s, in collaboration with his wife, Virginia Brooks, he performed a daring experiment with one of their own children. They raised their son for the first two years of his life with no exposure to pictures of any kind in order to see whether he would be able to identify objects using only line drawings. To be sure that he could identify the same objects in the real world, they waited until his vocabulary included the names of objects they wished to test. The experiment was heroic because it meant that television, magazines, books, and product wrappers were not in his environment. On occasional rides in the car, his older sister was assigned the task of shielding his eyes from road signs. At the age of 2 years, the child passed the test of naming line-drawn objects with flying colors. The conclusion was that no special learning was required to recognize objects based only on a pictorial representation of their edges.

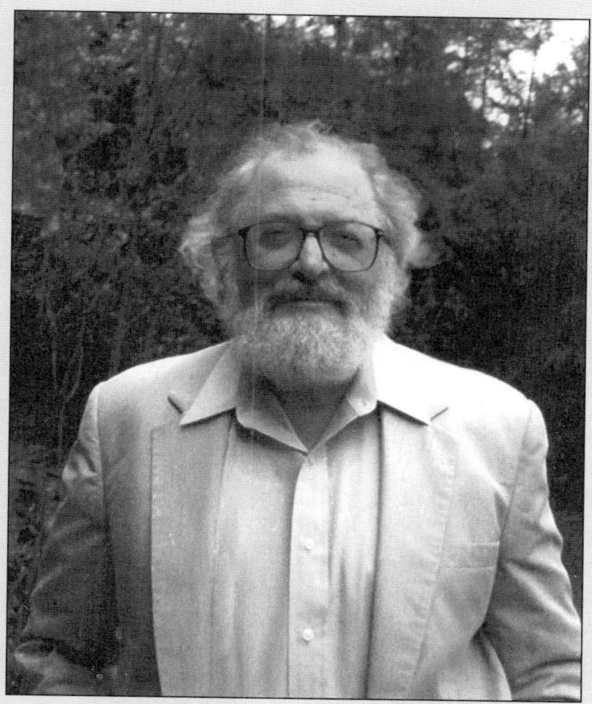

In research during the 1970s, Julian Hochberg exploited drawings of "impossible objects," which are simplified versions of the famous Dutch artist M. C. Escher. His experiments demonstrated that an entire physical object is very rarely seen in a single glance, but rather that a single glance permits the perception of details in only a very small region of the visual field. He speculated that the reason we don't experience this severe tunnel vision in everyday life is that we form abstract schematic representations of those portions of the visual field that are not currently at the focus of our attention. He also proposed that **mental schemata** are what allow us to comprehend movie sequences, even when the sequence consists of cuts and changes in viewpoint. These ideas have been rediscovered in the late 1990s by researchers who study **change blindness.** This is the finding that large changes made to a scene will go unnoticed by a human observer unless focused visual attention is devoted to the object undergoing the change.

Julian Hochberg was a professor in the Department of Psychology of Columbia University in New York city for many years. He is now retired and enjoys the status of Professor Emeritus in that department.

The Object as Figure

Back in Chapter 8, when we spoke of the Gestalt organizing principles in perception, we introduced the concept of **figure** and **ground.** These concepts play an important role in our understanding of objects, so let us renew our acquaintance with them here. A quick glance at any image leaves us with the impression that some of the regions have a definite shape to them and other regions are much less well defined. Figure 10.22 is a highly simplified image of this kind. The white region resembles a vase and the black regions resemble the faces of two people in profile. When the vase is being seen, the black region seems to extend indefinitely behind the white central figure. Clearly, the white-black edge is not perceptually neutral with respect to the shapes on each side of the edge. If it has been assigned by the visual system to the white region, then it does not belong in the same sense to the black region. **Figure** is the term used by vision scientists to describe the shape that has "ownership" of the edge at an image boundary; **ground** is the term they use to describe the shape whose visible boundaries are defined by the "accident" of one object occluding another.

The biases of figure-ground organization in human vision have been the focus of research for more than 100 years. These biases can be described and illustrated in simple terms with respect to two shapes in the image that share a luminance edge. Of these two shapes, the one that will more likely be seen as the figure, all other factors being equal, is the shape that is more enclosed, is smaller in size, has a greater contrast with the background, is more convex, has more parallel edges, has greater symmetry, is more three dimensional in appearance, has a straight-edged base, and is of greater familiarity to the viewer (Peterson, 2000).

FIGURE 10.22 An image that can be seen either as a pair of black figures (faces) against a white ground or a single white figure (vase) against a continuous black ground.

Many of these factors usually work in concert to define regions of an image that correspond to objects in the scene. This means that these factors help to determine which side of an edge will take ownership in the interpretation of the image as having figure and ground regions. In addition to these benefits of edge ownership, which reduces the inherent ambiguity at an edge, there are also very helpful and automatic benefits of figure-ground organization. For instance, spatial attention is automatically directed to figure regions of an image rather than to ground regions (Peterson, 2000; Peterson, de Gelder, Rapcsak, Gerhardstein, & Bachoud-Lévi, 2000). There is also better memory for figure than for ground shapes (Baylis & Driver, 1995). From this perspective then, the objects of vision correspond to those regions of the image that have been given the assignment of figure rather than ground.

The Object Defined by Convexity

Compare the shape labeled A in Figure 10.23 with the shapes labeled B and C. Which of these two shapes appears to be more similar to A? Most viewers choose C as the more similar one (Attneave, 1974; Hoffman & Richards, 1984). Let's see why by examining these shapes in a little more detail. A careful inspection will show that only B shares the same rough edge as A. In fact, these two shapes are exact complements of one another. This means that they would fit together like interlocking puzzle pieces. The edges of shape C, on the other hand, are not the same as those of shape A. Although at first glance C may appear to be merely the mirror image of A, a closer look reveals that two of its lower bulging regions have been swapped. What is it that makes these two shapes with different edges appear to be more similar than the complementary shapes with the identical edges?

Some vision researchers think that this illustrates a tendency for the visual system to organize scenes into regions of maximum convexity (Hoffman, 1998). Each region of maximum convexity can be considered an object **part,** with the region of deepest concavity between parts representing the place where parts have been joined. This would mean that a shape such as that in Figure 10.23A actually consists of five parts (bulges) whereas the shape labeled B consists of a total of four parts (bulges). In contrast, shape C shares the same number

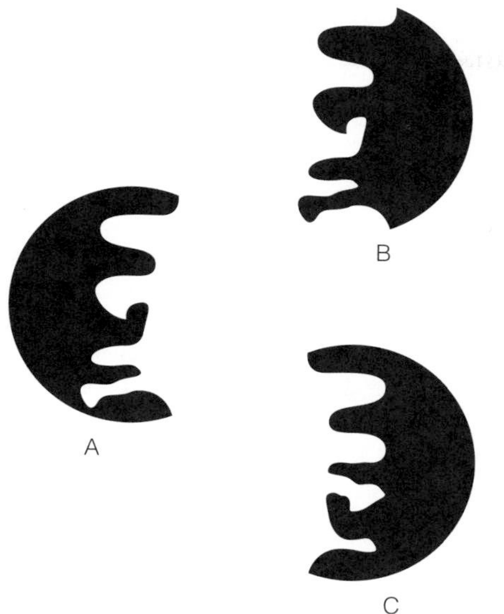

FIGURE 10.23 Is the shape labeled A most similar to B or C? Even though the edges of B are most similar to A, since they fit together like a jigsaw puzzle, people tend to chose C as the most similar to A. They do this even though the details in the two figures are quite different (compare the third and fourth protuberance in each figure). What is similar is the structure of A and C as defined by regions of convexity.

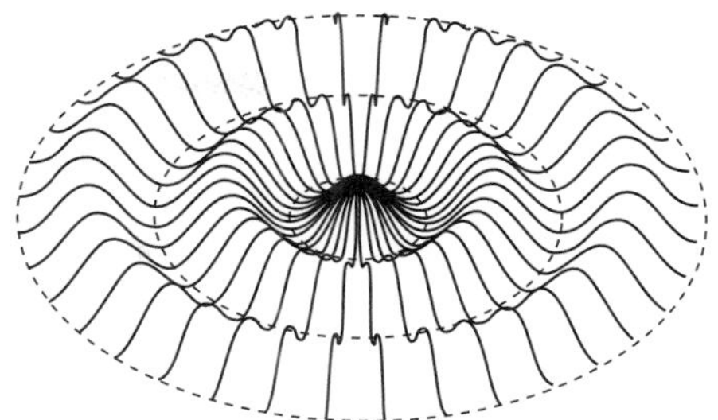

FIGURE 10.24 Are the dashed lines lying on the border between parts or in the center of the parts in this three-dimensional object? Now turn the book upside down and answer the same question.

and rough location of the parts in A and so it has greater overall similarity. According to this view, a visual object is a collection of interconnected parts of this kind. Presumably the factors that unify any given collection of parts would be similar to the factors that might unify a collection of edges. These would likely include contiguity (touching) and similarity in properties of luminance, hue, texture, and motion, as discussed in Chapter 8. The important difference in this view of objects, however, would be that the units over which "object belongingness" would be calculated would be regions of maximum convexity, which is a property of shape, rather than similarity among the more locally defined properties of an edge.

A nice feature of the definition of visual objects based on convex parts is that it can be readily extended into the third dimension. Look at the display in Figure 10.24, first in the orientation in which it appears on the page and then by turning the book upside down. In the upright orientation the corrugated surface seems to consist of a center bump and two concentric ridges—three convex parts in total. The dotted lines lie in the valleys between the parts. When the book is held upside down, the same display consists of a central donut-shaped ring and one and a half concentric ridges—a half of a part has gone missing. Consistent with this interpretation, the dotted lines now lie on the tops of the ridges and the outermost ridge can be seen to be incomplete.

Problems of Scale

A rather glaring problem with all of the definitions of a visual object so far is that they fail to consider that the visual world is structured at more than one level. As you know from much past experience, it is not difficult to interact with the world at a number of different levels. For example, most visual scenes can be examined using the rather broad characteristics found in the lower spatial frequencies of an image (Chapter 8), which correspond roughly to the coarse shapes seen if one blurs the image entering the eye. Or the same scene can be examined for the detail found only in the high spatial frequencies, the kinds of detail that are only visible with properly corrected visual acuity at the center of your gaze. Visual objects defined at one level of structure in the scene may or may not correspond to visual objects defined at another level.

Researchers have addressed this problem by examining the perception of stimuli that have been carefully constructed to contain different kinds of information at each of several levels. These are called **hierarchical stimuli,** because the objects defined at one level of structure can be artificially manipulated independent of the objects defined at the other level of structure. For example, look at the displays in Figure 10.25 and try to determine as quickly as you can, how many letter H's have been drawn. Did you find all 37? Or did you miss some H's? Did some H's take longer to find than others? If you look again you will see that the target letter H appears at two different levels in A and C and at only one level in B and D.

DEMONSTRATION BOX 10.7

THE ROLE OF LOCAL FEATURES IN OBJECT PERCEPTION

Harmon (1973) and Harmon and Julesz (1973) have presented an interesting set of demonstrations that illustrate how local features can interfere with a more global percept. One of their demonstrations is presented in the figure shown in this box. It is a computer processed block representation of a photograph. The brightness information from this scan has been locally averaged, so the brightness value in each of the squares is an average of a number of brightness samples taken in that area of the picture. This technique can be used to see if such local brightness information can elicit the percept of the original photograph. To try this, look at the figure at normal reading distance. Do you recognize the person? Try again, viewing from 2 m this time. (It will also help if you squint your eyes.) If you follow these instructions, you should be able to identify this block portrait as a very famous historical person. If not, the name of the individual is printed upside down in the bottom right-hand corner of this page. (From Harmon & Julesz, 1973. Copyright 1973 by the American Association for the Advancement of Science. Used by permission.)

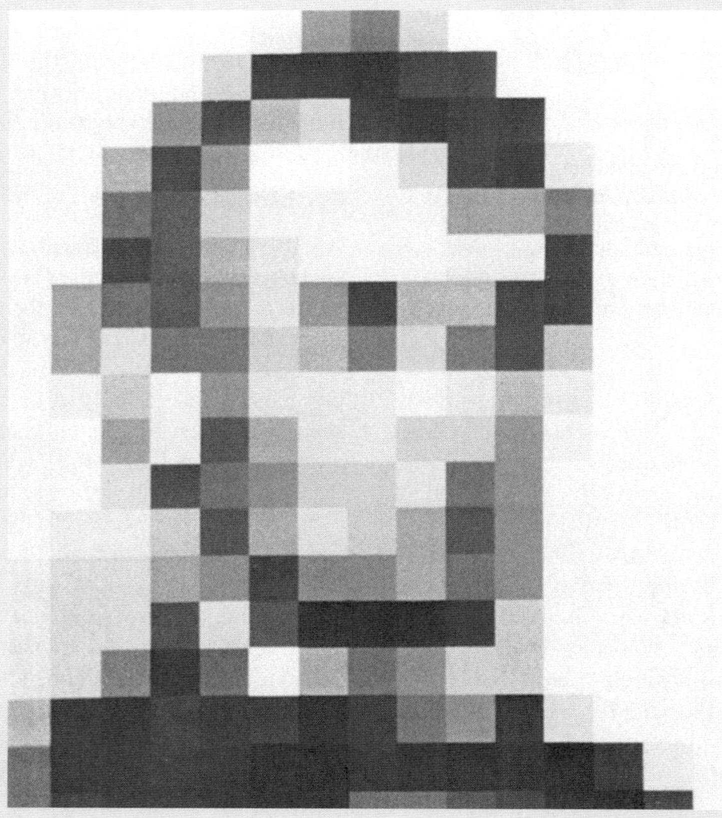

Abraham Lincoln

Each stimulus in Figure 10.25 consists of two levels of letters, a larger or **global** letter H in each case and many smaller or **local** letters. These local letters are also H in stimuli A and C and are S in stimuli B and D. Each small letter is made up in turn of even more local features such as individual line segments, and each of these segments could be subdivided into even smaller local features such as microdots of ink, if we had a large enough magnifying glass. Thus, the terms *local* and *global* are relative; we must specify what level of detail we are referring to when we use them. You can see for yourself the importance of local features in object identification by trying Demonstration Box 10.7.

```
H         H        S         S
H         H        S         S
H         H        S         S
H         H        S         S
H H H H H H        S S S S S S
H         H        S         S
H         H        S         S
H         H        S         S
H         H        S         S

     A                  B

H         H        S         S

H         H        S         S

H    H    H        S    S    S

H         H        S         S

H         H        S         S

     C                  D
```

FIGURE 10.25 Examples of hierarchical letter stimuli that have two distinct levels of detail.

Research with hierarchical stimuli has shown that within certain limits of scale, viewers are faster to find target objects when they are at the more global level of structure than when they are at the more local level of structure (Navon, 1977). This corresponds literally to being able to see the "forest" before the "trees." In Figure 10.25, it means that you were likely able to find the target letter H more quickly when it formed the larger pattern than when it was contained at the level of the small letters. This is true even though the local level of structure contained multiple copies of the same information (there are 22 small H's in A!). One reason the global structure can be seen more quickly is that low spatial frequency information is transmitted through the visual system more rapidly than high spatial frequency information. This means it can be carried on the rapid magnocellular or M-stream of processing (Chapter 3).

Other factors come into play as well. If the patterns are very large, so that the smallest details at the local level are themselves large enough to activate the M-stream system and global level of structure falls outside of the normal bounds of these receptive fields, then targets at the local level of structure will be seen first (Kinchla & Wolfe, 1979). Also, the relative density of the local elements plays an important role in determining which level of targets is seen first (Martin, 1979). More distant spacing of the smaller letters will make the global level more difficult to see and closer spacing of these letters will make the global level easier to see. You may have experienced something of this effect when searching for the large H in the more sparsely populated patterns of C and D. All of the preceding factors are affected by how observers distribute attention to the figure. Observers are able to voluntarily direct their attention either to global or local aspects of the figure and thus give priority to that level of structure (Robertson, Egly, Lamb, & Kerth, 1993), although this takes measurable time and mental effort (Ward, 1985).

A complete definition of visual object has to take into account the hierarchical nature of most scenes and the dynamic interaction between a scene and the observer's goals. This can be seen in the question of whether the whole human body, the face, or some specific facial feature corresponds to the visual object. The answer is clearly, "it depends." For some tasks such as lip-reading, the appropriate level of structure that corresponds to the visual object is undoubtedly the mouth. For other tasks, such as reading someone's emotional expression or determining someone's identity, the appropriate level of analysis for the visual object is the whole face. Recognizing someone by their gait from a distance is an example in which the whole body is the object of analysis.

OBJECT IDENTIFICATION

Look at Figure 10.26 and study it for a minute or so. You have never seen it before because it was especially constructed to make a point. It is clearly an object, but what is it? Now look at it again. You will recognize it because

FIGURE 10.26 An object that you have never seen before.

you have seen it before (just a few seconds or so ago), although you still are not able to identify it (it is not even a real object). You experience familiarity, but the object makes no sense. Now study it a little longer. Eventually you may begin to think it resembles some objects you have seen before; perhaps it is a distorted version of a streetside hot dog vendor's cart or perhaps a child's toy. The longer you look at it, the more associations it generates, although it still doesn't have a name. If we told you that it is a "horned wheeler," the name might suggest that it is an apparatus for conveying or transporting things, although how or why still might be a puzzle.

Every day, practically every moment, we identify perceptual objects like the one in Figure 10.26, although they are seldom as novel. Actually, the ability to see a stimulus as an object is often not sufficient. Our very survival may depend on our *recognizing* an object as something we have seen before and on our *categorizing* that object so that we can retrieve information about its likely behavior or the behavior we should perform in its presence. How do we go about identifying objects?

Data Driven versus Conceptually Driven Processing

All modern theories of visual object identification distinguish between two qualitative types of psychological processes. One type is referred to as **data driven,** because it begins with the arrival of sensory information at the receptors. This type of processing is characterized by a fixed set of rules or procedures that is applied to all incoming data. In a sense, the data themselves are said to "drive" the process because the visual patterns that are encountered will automatically trigger certain operations. In vision, these processes would include the registration of distinctive features in the image, such as luminance differences, contours, and other attributes that distinguish one pattern from another. To some extent, the perceptual grouping processes discussed in Chapter 8 can be considered data driven, since they lead to such reliable effects as subjective contours, the good continuation of a broken line, and filling in when a nearer object occludes our view of a more distant object. Our perception of Figure 10.26 could also be considered data driven, since we were able to determine its shape and the relations between its various parts without having a previously stored representation with which to compare it.

The second type of process is called **conceptually driven,** and its importance is illustrated in Demonstration Box 10.8. In this type of processing, higher-level processes such as memories of past experiences, general organizational strategies, and expectations based on knowledge of the world and previous events or the surrounding context guide an active search for certain patterns in the stimulus input.

An example of conceptually driven vision can be seen in the initial perception of a dark thing flashing through the air on a playground. If we were in a playground in which people were playing ball, we might initially treat the stimulus as a ball someone had thrown and quickly check to make sure it wasn't heading in our direction. If instead we were in a quiet garden park, our first tendency might be to treat the stimulus as a bird flying by. If it were dusk, we might even suspect a bat. These different initial perceptions would certainly lead to a different outcome for our behavior because we might not check the flight path of the stimulus with the same diligence in the garden park as we would in a playground. As this example shows, both data driven and conceptually driven processes must occur for perception to be complete. If only data driven processing occurred, we would not be able to take full advantage of our tremendous amount of experience with the visual world to enhance our perceptual functioning and to make it more efficient. This is especially important in poor visual environments and in situations where time to act is of the essence. If only conceptually driven processing occurred, we would see only what we expected to see and would likely make too many mistakes to survive.

Object Parts versus Views

Once the data driven processes have analyzed the image, and the conceptually driven processes have been activated in order to assist in the object identification process, a very large problem still remains. On what basis are the features of the image to be linked to the concepts in memory? This is an area of vision research that is fraught with real difficulty and many controversies. At one extreme, some researchers have proposed that the visual brain contains a "library" of three-dimensional models (Brooks, 1981; Lowe, 1987). Each model is an entry in the library and corresponds to a different object. However, this approach soon runs into problems of logical plausibility. Rough calculations of the number of different objects a typical human will recognize over a lifetime leaves one with the realization that the vast number of neurons in the brain devoted to object recognition is still no match for the vast array of different objects you have already seen and could recognize. There is also the problem of how to add new models to the library each time a new object is encountered.

DEMONSTRATION BOX 10.8

CONCEPTUALLY DRIVEN PROCESSING

The figure in this box is a drawing of an animal you have seen many times before. Do you know what it is? If not, turn the page and look at the hint given in the figure there. In the figure on the next page, the cow's head is outlined. Now look back at the figure here. Having once identified the cow, you may wonder how you missed it in your first glance at this picture.

The difference between your experience during the first look at the figure and your experience during the second look (after you knew what it was a picture of) illustrates the distinction between data driven and conceptually driven visual processes. In the first viewing, the data driven processes extracted shapes of various sizes and with various features. You then tried to match this collection of features with objects in your long-term memory. Perhaps you thought it was an aerial photograph of the Great Lakes or some other familiar scene. In the second viewing, your memory representations of a cow influenced the way you grouped the shapes in the picture. From now on, your memory will contain a record of this picture, and you will probably be unable to look at the figure (even weeks from now) without seeing the cow immediately.

A more realistic proposal is that the visual object "library" consists of a much smaller set of three dimensional model *parts* or *components*, such that any object, including new ones, can be modeled quickly by assembling the necessary parts into the correct spatial arrangement. Now the problem becomes, which parts? Selecting too few parts or the wrong parts will leave many objects unrecognizable. Selecting too many parts may lead to the same problem encountered when each object was represented by its own model.

A set of parts that has met with some success, in both efforts to achieve vision by computer (Hummel & Biederman, 1992; Pentland, 1986) and in efforts to account for human performance in object recognition tasks (Leeuwenburg, 1988), is shown in Figure 10.27. These parts are called **geons** (short for geometric ions). They are all variations of a generalized cylinder (Biederman, 1987). They are simple convex solids that consist of a main **axis of elongation** and a **cross section.** Both of these aspects of a simple solid can be varied along a few well-chosen dimensions, so that from the combination of two basic types of axes (straight or curved), two types of cross section (straight or curved), three types of cross-section symmetry (asymmetrical, reflection symmetry, or rotational symmetry), and three types of cross-section change across the axis (constant, expanding, or contracting), a total of 36 different simple solids can be generated as the basis set of the three-dimensional library. For obvious reasons, this approach to object identification is called **identification by parts.**

Solution to Demonstration Box 10.8

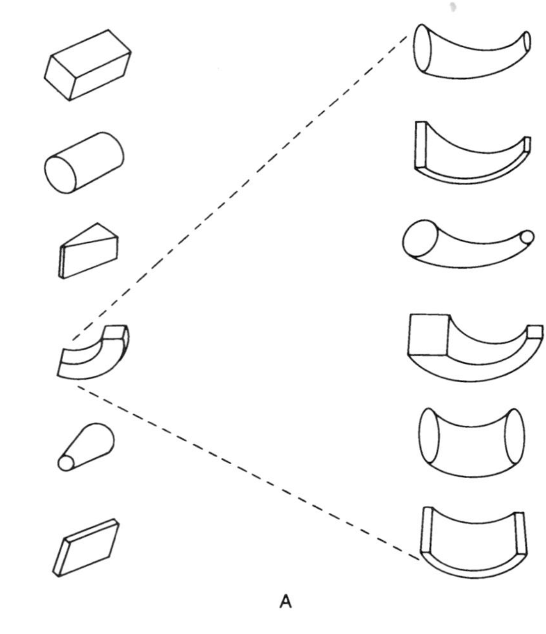

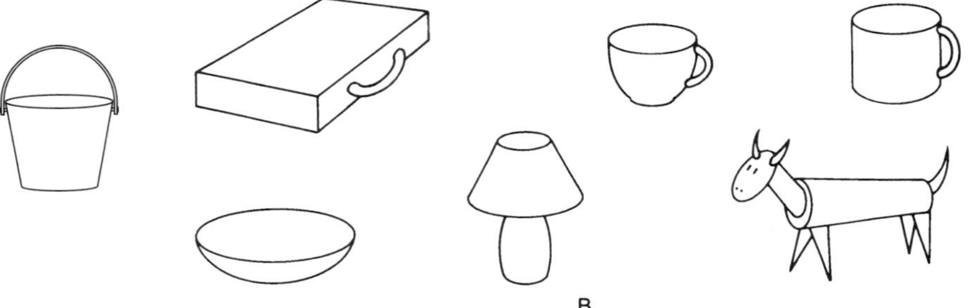

FIGURE 10.27 (A) On the left is a partial set of geons, from any one of which many variants can be created (as on the right for one of them) by varying the basic parameters. (B) Some of the objects that can be created from geons (based on Biederman, 1987).

Once an object in an image has been analyzed in terms of its geons, it is possible to link this description to known objects in long term memory. In this approach, memory consists of a "library" in which familiar objects have been described in terms of geons. Take something as simple as a pail, for example, and illustrated in Figure 10.27. Past experience with pails has taught you that this class of objects consists of a wide cylinder in vertical orientation, topped by a long thin cylinder with a curved axis of elongation. This object may have the same components as another object such as the coffee mug also shown in Figure 10.27, but it is critically different in the spatial relations that exist among these two parts. This sort of scheme can readily model lamps, suitcases, and drawers, among other objects.

A clear strength of this approach is the way it strikes a nice balance between being well defined and open ended. It is well defined in the sense that the proposed parts have clear definitions and they are of a manageable number. At the same time it is open ended, meaning that the possibility always exists for new objects to be added to the memory store of known objects without having to increase the basis set of model parts. Thus geons are, in some respect, similar to a spatial alphabet, and the stored information about the specific parts involved in an object and their particular spatial relations to one another are similar to a dictionary.

Another strength of identification by parts is that it accounts in a very natural way for the problem of object constancy. The constant or invariant aspects of objects that are captured by this approach are their descriptions in terms of these simple parts. Provided that there are sufficient clues in the image to the presence of the appropriate parts, object recognition can proceed, regardless of the particular lighting conditions, object orientation, viewing angle, and viewing distance that might pertain to the image.

But there is at least one glaring weakness in this approach. It is that some objects can be modeled much more readily by geons than other objects. Crumpled newspapers, clothes, human faces, and trees spring readily to mind as examples of objects that do not have simple geon descriptions. Advocates of the geon approach respond to this criticism by pointing out that complications of scale and detail can be worked out with a little extra effort. For example, from a distance, it may be perfectly appropriate to model a crumpled newspaper as a lumpy but generally spherical solid object. If greater detail is desired, each roughly planar surface in the crumple can be modeled as a separate solid. But as this example shows, modeling the right level of detail is only half the problem. How is a library entry in long-term memory supposed to know that a newspaper can be modeled as either of these two possibilities? The spatial relation among parts is no longer a simple solution.

In response to problems such as these, yet another approach to the problem of object identification has been growing in popularity. This approach begins by building on a known strength of the human brain, which is the capacity to store and retrieve large numbers of different patterns. What if objects were stored in long-term memory by a collection of views that had been acquired over time? These views would not have to be photographic in quality. Rather they could be abstract, structural descriptions of an object, or mental schemas. The important difference from identification by parts is that these descriptions would represent views of an object from a particular vantage point and distance. Together, the various views of a known object would be stored in something like a photo album, and these albums could be linked in a giant web of connections, so that relations among objects could be represented by their links in the web. This is called **identification by views** (Tarr & Bülthoff, 1998).

It is clear that a single view of each object would be insufficient to achieve object constancy. Multiple views would have to be included if an object was to be correctly matched to its proper photo album. But it is also clear that not all possible views would be needed. Novel views of an object could still permit recognition of the object if there was a mechanism for rapidly calculating the similarity between views. Pattern comparisons involving a large set is also something at which the human brain seems to be particularly adept.

One obvious weakness of identification by views approach is that it does not easily account for the fact that human vision is very adept in its handling of objects in three-dimensional space. Especially when it comes to action toward objects, vision is capable of computing very precise three-dimensional relations. It is not at all clear how this can be accomplished by using a large number of discrete views. A second weakness is that there is no obvious way in which the part structure of objects can be captured in a multiple view theory of object recognition.

At this point in the ongoing debate it is still too early to decide whether identification by components or by views is the better approach. These two approaches may even turn out to be specialized for different kinds of object recognition. In particular, recognition by parts seems ready made for distinguishing general classes of objects such as pails and coffee mugs. It is much more difficult to imagine it being used to discriminate my coffee cup from yours, which probably differ not in their parts but in their surface markings. On the other hand, recognition by views seems more naturally suited to the problem of distinguishing individuals such as "Fred" from "George." At the same time, it does not appear to have a ready made way to distinguish among general classes of objects, such as faces of women versus faces of men.

SCENE PERCEPTION

In the final section of this chapter it is time to return to the larger question of scene perception, which refers to perception of the relations among objects and the larger context in which individual objects are seen. We will focus on two important kinds of information about a scene that are critical for perceptual understanding. The first is the **gist** or meaning of a scene. Gist is provided by the objects that are associated with one another in the environment and by the meaning of the scene in terms of our perceptual and behavioral goals. The second is the spatial arrangement of the objects, which we will call **layout.**

Gist

Object identification rarely occurs in isolation. Look at Figure 10.28. Most people see two lines of characters, the top line being A, B, C, D, E, F and the bottom line being 10, 11, 12, 13, 14. Now look closely at the forms you saw as B and 13. They are identical in the image. Yet the same form was interpreted as a letter B in the context of other letters and as a number 13 in the context of other numbers. Your identification of these perceptual objects has therefore been affected by conceptually driven processes reflecting the other stimuli that formed the context.

Another example of the effect of context on identification comes from a study in which observers were asked to identify objects presented after they had seen either an appropriate or an inappropriate context for those objects (Palmer, 1975a). For example, in Figure 10.29 the loaf of bread (A) would be appropriate in the context of the kitchen counter displayed there, but the mailbox (B) would be inappropriate. Objects presented after appropriate scenes were more readily identified than were the same objects presented after inappropriate scenes. It seems that what you see immediately before the presentation of a stimulus evokes a series of expectations about objects likely to be present. When the next object seen matches these expectations, identification is easier.

A, B, C, D, E, F
10, 11, 12, 13, 14

FIGURE 10.28 The effect of context on pattern recognition. The B and the 13 are identical figures.

Face perception seems to work the same way (Palmer, 1975b). Look at Figure 10.30. Notice that when seen as part of a face, any bump or line will suffice to depict a feature. When we take these features out of context, they do not really portray the objects very well. We actually require more of a detailed presentation (such as those in Figure 10.30C) to identify facial features unambiguously when presented in isolation. Thus, in this situation the conceptually driven expectations compensate for lack of detail in the data driven feature extraction process.

The incredible speed with which the general meaning of a scene can be determined was revealed in a very elegant way by studies conducted on the perception of rapid-fire sequences of images (Chun & Potter, 1995; Potter, 1993; 1999). These researchers presented viewers with brief glimpses of 15 or more images in a row, under two different viewing instructions. In one condition, the category detection task, viewers were given a verbal category such as 'a picnic' or 'a classroom' before seeing the sequence of images. Their task at the end of the sequence of views was to indicate whether any picture matched that description. In a second condition, the new-old recognition task, viewers were first shown the same sequence and then shown either one of the original images in the sequence (called an *old* picture) or an image that had not been presented (called a *new* picture). They were again given a twofold choice: Was this picture old or new? Think about these two tasks for a moment. Which do you think would be easier—preparing yourself to see an unpredictable picture and sort it into a known general category, or simply identifying whether a picture was one you had seen a short time ago?

The interesting answer is that the new-old recognition task is actually much more difficult than the category detection task when the images are shown at high speeds. When the images were flashed at a rate of 10 per second (100 milliseconds per image), accuracy in category detection was over 80% correct, which is reasonably good performance given these high speeds. However, new-old recognition accuracy was only a little more than 50% correct, which is near the chance level of performance. This means that we are able to use vision to comprehend

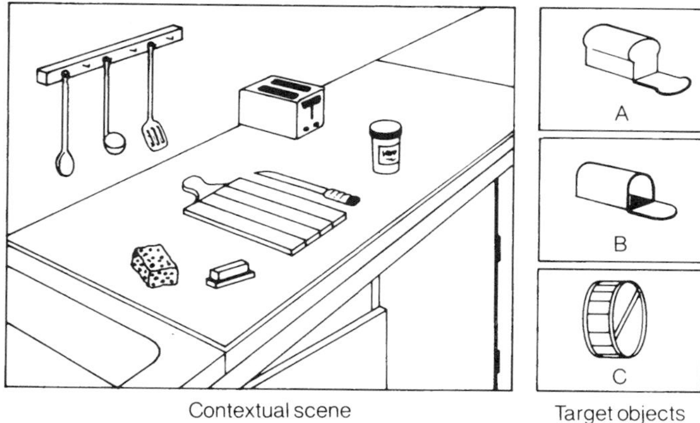

FIGURE 10.29 Context and target stimuli used by Palmer (1975a).

the meaning of pictures shown at this rate—in this case to assign it correctly to a rather abstract verbal category—but we are unable at the same time to form a short-lived memory of the picture that can survive the second or two that intervenes between the presentation of the original picture and the test picture. You may have had a similar experience when you viewed a rapid-fire sequence of television images in a music video or a commercial. Each of the images appears to be seen vividly and clearly, though a second later you may be unable to recall the specific content of more than one of the images.

What is preventing the visual system from forming longer lasting memories of these rapid fire images? An important clue is revealed when recognition accuracy is examined separately for each picture in the series. New-old recognition accuracy is at chance levels for each picture except the last one. The last picture can be matched very accurately to the test picture even though it is shown for exactly the same 100 milliseconds as the preceding pictures. This means that the short time each picture is displayed is not the critical factor in the poor memory. Rather, the problem is that before the contents of each picture can formed into some kind of a lasting representation, visual details from a new picture have written over the sensory information from the old picture. Apparently, it takes longer than one tenth of a second to form lasting memories of unpredictable pictures. At the same time, a glimpse that is shorter than one tenth of a second is enough to permit a pre-existing idea, such as a verbal picture category, to be matched against the information in the glimpse.

One effective way to study how the visual system represents the gist of a scene is to measure how sensitive viewers are to various kinds of changes made to a scene following an interruption in viewing, such as when an eye movement is made, a change in viewpoint occurs, or the scene is briefly blanked and redisplayed. To help you think about this, try the card trick in Demonstration Box 10.9 before reading any further.

This trick fools many people and may have fooled you for two simple reasons. Both of these reasons are key to a general understanding of scene perception. First, human observers generally assume that the world is stable. Objects do not mysteriously appear and disappear. Second, human observers generally do not detect

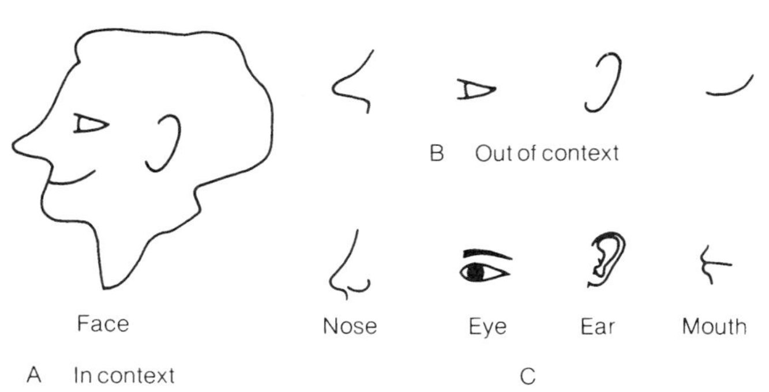

FIGURE 10.30 Facial components are easily recognized in context (A), but out of context they are much less identifiable (B) unless they are made more detailed (C; Palmer, 1975b). (From Norman, Rumelhart, & the LNR Research Group, 1975. Copyright 1975 by W. H. Freeman and Co. Used by permission.)

DEMONSTRATION BOX 10.9

SCENE PERCEPTION

Look at the pictures of the six playing cards. Select only one of these cards to remember. Make sure you don't tell anyone which card you have chosen. Now turn the page to the set of cards on the next page. The secret card you selected has disappeared! How does this trick work? The text explains.

changes to objects that they have not attended. The cards that were viewed but not selected for memory were only registered at the crude categorical level of "face card." The specific combinations of face (jack, queen, etc.) and suit (hearts, spades, etc.) were not individually coded and in fact cannot be coded rapidly for six different objects that are so similar.

But now imagine what would have happened in the card trick if we had replaced the original six cards with five completely different objects such as snapshots of people or coffee holders. Needless to say, the card trick would be a complete flop, since the audience would know instantly that all of the original cards had been removed. The reason you may not have noticed this the first time is that you preserved the *gist* of the scene between views. Both the original six cards and the replaced five cards were of the category "face cards." By carefully manipulating the kinds of changes that can be made between views without alerting the viewers to these changes, researchers are coming to understand how the gist of a scene is represented.

In one study (Henderson & Hollingworth, 2002), viewers were shown typical indoor scenes (e.g., offices, kitchens) under the instruction that these pictures would be shown again later in a memory test and that some of the objects in the picture might change unexpectedly. Any such change that was noticed should be reported immediately. Certain objects in the scenes were designated as "target objects" by the experimenters and were changed during the execution of an eye movement in the normal course of inspecting the scene. For example, suppose that the target object consisted of a book lying on a desk. At some point during the viewing the book might be completely deleted (replaced by the background of the desk), replaced with an object of another type (a coffee mug), replaced with an object of the same type (a book of different dimensions and color), or replaced with the same object rotated by 90 degrees. The result was that object deletions were detected most frequently, followed by replacements by an object of another type. Both of these changes affected the meaning of the scene. Replacements by objects of the same type, and by the same object rotated, did not change the gist of the scene and were detected much less frequently, just as you might expect from thinking about the card trick.

Not only does the semantic analysis of a scene occur very rapidly, helping to guide the more detailed attention processes to specific objects, it also leads to the formation of very stable long-term memories for scenes. However, it is important to remember that these memories are rather removed from the specific details in the scenes. The apparent price of this long-term and very stable memory for scenes is a level of abstraction that is not sensitive to the particulars of most of the objects in the scene. This level of abstraction is called **schematic memory** by many researchers because it is rich in meaning, but at the same time impoverished in its retention of specific details incidental to this meaning.

The amazing memory we all have for scene gist was first documented in the 1960s when researchers began to show participants hundreds of typical summer vacation photographs, each for only a few seconds, and then tested

participants' memory using the new-old recognition task (Haber, 1970; Standing, 1973). This was done by dividing any particular set of photos in half, showing one half of the photos as pictures to be remembered, and then testing on the full set of photos. A chance level of accuracy in such a test would therefore be 50%. Most of these studies found recognition accuracy to be well over 90% when memory was tested the same day. Some studies found accuracy to be over 70% several days and even weeks later. Visual scenes can therefore be retained for long periods of time as measured by recognition accuracy.

The abstract nature of the memory involved is revealed by other studies that examine sensitivity to more subtle differences in the picture than merely whether it belonged to an original and somewhat haphazard set of vacation slides. In one especially revealing study (Potter, O'Connor, & Oliva, 2002) participants viewed sets of slides that were taken in a panoramic series at a city intersection, an intersection they had never seen before, in order to learn where the camera had been placed in the intersection. When they were later tested with a new set of pictures that were each displaced laterally by 30 degrees from the original views, they had no trouble correctly indicating where the camera had been placed to take these views. In other words, they were now familiar with the scene and had specific metric information about it. Yet, in a new-old recognition test they were unable to discriminate these new slides from the old slides at a better than chance level. What they had apparently learned from the original set of slides was a fairly detailed mental map of the city intersection. The original slides had served as the medium for this learning. The specific images in the slides, however, had not been committed to a form of memory that permitted them detection of which slides from among all the views had been presented during the learning phase.

This process of abstraction is not something that only happens over time, similar to the fading of a photo left too long in the sun. Rather it can be shown to occur as soon as the picture is presented. Demonstration Box 10.10 will allow you to experience this process of abstraction for yourself. Try this exercise on yourself before reading further, in order to benefit from the full impact of the experience.

The tendency to fill in a drawing with more detail about the background is called **scene boundary extension** (Intraub, 1997). It occurs not only in drawings but also can be seen in new-old recognition tasks conducted immediately after a picture is presented. In this case participants select as "old" pictures that contain more of the background than was actually shown. The illusion is an example of the viewer's vision literally going beyond what was seen in the picture. In this case it is an appropriate and entirely beneficial illusion.

Layout

The **layout** of a scene refers to the relative locations of the objects and surfaces in the scene. Along with some details of the attended objects, and the general gist of the scene, a single glance at a scene leaves the visual system with quite rich information about the relative locations of objects. Often these locations can be remembered as having been occupied or filled by an object, even though the identity or other features of the object at a given location cannot be remembered.

One of the main reasons the spatial layout of a scene can be seen and responded to rather independently of the particular objects that make up the scene, and even their meaning, is that there are specialized brain regions devoted to the representation of the positions of objects in space. This can be seen in the expression of many neuropsychological conditions. For instance, patients who have had a stroke that has damaged tissue in the temporal lobes (Chapter 2) may be unable to recognize objects even though there is no doubt about where these

DEMONSTRATION BOX 10.10

IMMEDIATE MEMORY FOR SCENE DETAILS

Examine the picture for only a few seconds in order to form as detailed a memory of it as you can. Now cover the picture and try to draw it from memory as best you can.

Once you have completed the drawing, score it for the following details. How many trash cans were drawn? How many pickets were shown in the drawing of the picket fence? Now check your drawing with the original. The typical finding from studies involving this task is that participants are quite accurate in their drawings of the central objects. However, they often draw more background items than were actually shown, in this case they overestimate the number of pickets shown in the fence (Intraub, 1997).

objects are positioned in space. One of these cases was described very vividly by Oliver Sacks in his best-selling book, *The Man Who Mistook His Wife for a Hat*. This patient was leaving the doctor's office one day when he casually reached over to his wife's head, rather than to the coat rack, in an effort to grasp his hat. More formal testing revealed that the patient had the spared visual ability to see where objects were located in space. His reach and grasp were also appropriate to the distance and shape of these objects. What he had lost was the ability to identify the meaning of the objects he could locate. Patients with damage to the parietal lobes sometimes lose the ability to locate objects in space even though they have no trouble correctly identifying these objects.

Spatial layout is a property of scenes about which we seem to acquire a great deal of information, even when we are not consciously aware of it. One series of studies making this point in a very convincing way involves a standard visual search task of moderate difficulty (Chun & Jiang, 1998). This task involves the presentation of a target shape (e.g., a T in one of four orientations) among a large number of distracter shapes (e.g., L's in any one of four orientations) in a random configuration or layout. The experimental manipulation is whether these layouts, which are initially determined completely at random, are repeated during the course of the experiment or not. The finding is that when as many as 12 different random layouts are repeated, search for the target is much faster and more accurate than when the layouts are newly generated on each trial. In the same experiment, a new-old recognition test of the repeated layouts, administered after the search task, showed that participants were only at chance levels in trying to guess which layouts had been repeated and which had never been presented in the search task.

This discussion of object and scene perception has covered a wide range of research, but it has also probably left you with many remaining questions. Researchers still have a long way to go to put object perception on the same kind of solid foundation that we seem to have in our understanding of color vision and edge perception. Many investigators are working both to refine the theories that may be useful and to construct artificial means of performing the necessary computations (e.g., Horn, 1986; Pentland, 1986; Ullman, 1996). Ultimately, however, the usefulness to psychology of such approaches will depend on whether they provide us with any insights as to how the brain actually processes the visual information in a biological system, such as in humans. It is truly humbling to realize that understanding the simple act of identifying a pencil that may be lying on the desk in front of you remains a problem about which there are many theories but still no firm answers.

STUDY QUESTIONS

1. What are the major differences between a visual scene and a visual image? Why is it important to keep them distinct in the study of vision?
2. What are the four major characteristics of a scene that, taken together, determine the visual image?
3. List five assumptions about an image that the human visual system tends to hold and that generally help to interpret the contents of an image.
4. Try to draw a simple picture such that two objects in the picture appear to be the same size even though they are quite different in their actual size on the page. Now add a third object that is physically the same size as one of the first two but that appears to be larger.
5. Which two factors together determine the total amount of light that is reflected to the eye from a surface in a scene?
6. Describe three different ways to approach the question of what defines a visual object.
7. Compare and contrast data driven versus conceptually driven visual processes.
8. List one strength and one weakness of the theory that objects are identified by their parts. Do the same for the theory that objects are identified using multiple views.
9. What is meant by the gist of a visual scene? How does it influence object perception?
10. Was the man who mistook his wife for a hat impaired in his ability to locate objects in space or in his ability to identify objects? Where was his brain damage?

CHAPTER 11

TIME

CHAPTER SUMMARY

Albert Einstein, the Nobel Prize–winning physicist, often thought about the meaning of time and ultimately concluded that "the distinction between past, present and future is only an illusion, however persistent" (Einstein & Besso, 1972). He came to this conclusion when he realized that these concepts had no meaning aside from their relationship to a particular observer. While this conclusion may make it difficult for a physicist to analyze time objectively, for the psychologist it means that the concept is not so different from many other concepts of perception, such as space, shape, color, and motion. Each of these are first of all modes by which we perceive and think about our world. While each of these modes clearly has links to the physical conditions under which we live (e.g., color begins with variations in wavelength, shape begins with edges), at the level of perception each of these modes involves a reality that is unique to the observer. As we will see in this chapter, the time dimension is every bit as important to our perception of the world around us as is color, shape, and space.

THE IMPORTANCE OF TIME TO PERCEPTION

If you were to end your study of perception with the previous chapters on patterns (Chapter 8), space (Chapter 9), or objects and scenes (Chapter 10), you might be forgiven for thinking that the spatial arrangement of stimuli is the most important aspect of visual perception. The perception of three-dimensional depth, visual direction, and the size and locations of objects is all based on our brain's ability to process information about the spatial layout of the environment. You might even think that all of the information needed to create these percepts comes directly from the retinal images or the relationship between the retinal images of the two eyes. What we will learn in this chapter on time perception and in the next chapter on motion perception, however, is that much of this processing is strongly dependent on the perception of the temporal relationships between spatial patterns and objects.

Events Are the Units of Perception

Do still photographs or videotape records give you a more realistic record of the important moments in your life? Most people will say confidently that videotape places an observer "inside the action" to a greater extent than does a series of still photographs. What is it that is recorded on videotape that is lost when recorded in a series of slides? Is it that videotape merely contains more information, by virtue of the large number of still photographs contained within a video sequence? Research shows that it is more than that. Indeed, it is something more centrally related to the way in which the brain processes information.

Our brain responds to change and the basic unit of our perceptual experience is the **event.** Events consist of relations among objects and actions. Although object perception is a necessary ingredient for the perception of an event, as is the perception of an action, of greatest importance to the perceiver are the answers to the questions "Who is doing what to whom?" and "What is happening to me or around me?" The answers to these questions permit observers to plan future actions of their own.

In many ways, events are similar to sentences or phrases in natural language. Although language consists of single units like nouns and verbs, its meaning is not in these components themselves, but rather it is the sequence or timing of those units that conveys the meaning. For instance, there is a great difference between a "man-eating shark" and a "shark-eating man." Although both of these phrases contain the same elements, it is the sequence or timing of the arrival of these stimuli at the eye or ear that determines the actual meaning that we perceive. In the same way, the term *event* refers to a series of stimuli that unfold over time (c.f., Ward, 2002). Our ability to understand actions or the relations that exist between objects depends on this unfolding. Therefore, our perception is limited when most of the time dimension is lost, as it is when we are viewing still photographs.

Actually, moment-to-moment changes in stimulation are necessary even for us to be able to perceive a still picture or a drawing. Even if you try to stare at a picture and not move your eyes at all, your retinal image is continually in motion. This comes about because of eye movements over which we have little control. Some of these are small involuntary drifting movements. In addition, the eye is jiggling or shivering in its socket because of tiny **microsaccades.** These microsaccades occur many times a second and cause the retinal image to shimmy from place to place on the retina no matter how hard we try to hold our eyes completely still. The end result of all this eye movement is that contours in the retinal image are continually moving over a number of different retinal receptors. This means that the output from any given receptor in the eye will actually vary over time with a series of on and off signals as the image bounces around on the retinal surface.

To see how important these momentary changes are to perception, we can eliminate the effects of microsaccades using a now classic technique involving **stabilized retinal images.** This requires an observer to wear a special contact lens that moves with the eye and has a mirror or a tiny projector mounted on it (e.g., Pritchard, Heron, & Hebb, 1960; Riggs, Ratliff, Cornsweet, & Cornsweet, 1953; Yarbus, 1967). In effect, this "glues the image in place." The image stays on the same retinal receptors no matter how the eye moves. What do you see when the temporal variations in the retinal image are removed? Nothing. When a person views a stabilized image, he or she finds that over a period of only a few seconds, the entire visual field fades from consciousness (e.g., Tulunay & Olson, 1996). The contours disappear in chunks, and the color also fades away. If we now flicker the image on and off, the pattern will reappear in consciousness and, if the flicker rate is high enough, it will stay in view (Cornsweet, 1956). Flickering the image has simply reintroduced some of the temporal changes in the retinal image that we removed through the stabilizing technique. The disappearance of the perception of pattern when the retinal image is stabilized, and its reappearance when the retinal image is flickered, supports the idea that change over time is the critical property for stimulating the individual receptors. Without change, receptors soon cease to respond differently from neighboring receptors, and thus we lose the ability detect the presence of a contour (Norwich, 1983). Therefore, for pattern vision to occur, there must not only be spatial variation in the intensity of light, as in patterns of edges, but there also must be variation in the pattern of illumination over time.

We have already provided you with a demonstration of the disappearance and the reappearance of a stabilized image with flickering stimulation back in Demonstration Box 3.3 (see Chapter 3), which you might want to look at again. In that demonstration you mapped the pattern of blood vessels that lie above your retina. Ordinarily you don't see these blood vessels because they create a stabilized image on your retina as light passes through them. They are always in the same place, so they create no temporal changes in stimulation of the receptors. By moving a flashlight placed at the corner of the eye, however, you cause their shadows to move across the retina. With these momentary temporal variations you have effectively destabilized these images, which is why they become visible. You will note that as soon as you stop moving the flashlight, in effect stopping the temporal change, the blood vessels disappear, since their image is now stabilized again.

Another demonstration you can try for yourself involves taking advantage of the fact that in your visual periphery you are sensitive to movement but not to shape. Have someone wave an object or their finger around at the side of your visual field. You will find that the movement is seen but it is impossible to identify the shape of the object. Even more important, when the movement stops, the object will become invisible. You may be surprised to learn that only the most complex mammals, which includes humans, have visual systems that can signal the brain in the absence of movement in the stimuli. More primitive animals cannot see stationary objects at all—remember the velociraptors in Jurassic Park. That means that the jiggling effect caused by the microsaccades is not a flaw in our visual system, but rather a mechanism that evolved to provide continuous temporal variation by moving the retinal image, which, in turn, allows us to see aspects of the stationary environment that are often invisible to lower animals.

Percepts Emerge over Time

One fact about perception that would be of great interest to mystical philosophers is that our perception of an event does not occur in "real time," but rather we live in the past. Despite what you may believe, our perception of such ongoing ordinary events as an approaching car or of a thrown baseball is not instantaneous. We see the world in what a video technician would refer to as "taped delay," with our consciousness always lagging behind the reality. The puzzle then is, if we only perceive events that are already past, how is it even possible for us to interact accurately with objects in the world? Why don't more of us walk blithely in front of moving cars or fail to duck in time to avoid being hit by projectiles? Before we try to answer these important questions, let us provide some important background information about the known temporal relationships between physical events and their perception.

We begin with the timing between an extremely simple visual stimulus and its associated percept. This relationship is illustrated in Figure 11.1. The stimulus is a

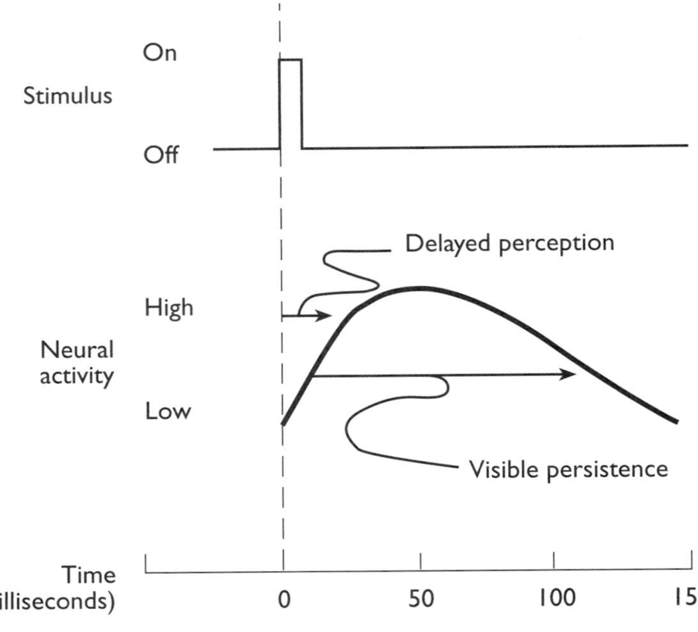

FIGURE 11.1 The temporal relationship between a brief flash of light and associated activity in visually sensitive neurons.

1-millisecond (ms) flash of light over a small region of the retina, say one tenth of a degree. The neural activity associated with this flash of light begins with a small delay following the onset of the light, but once started, the neural activity will continue for a duration that is much longer than the duration of the original brief flash. Our conscious experience of the flash depends on the duration of the neural activity, not the physical duration of the flash. This means that the perceived duration of the light will be a sort of illusion in that it will appear longer than it actually is. Technically we refer to this overestimation of the length of a stimulus as **visible persistence.** The duration of this visual persistence depends on the adaptive state of the eye. Thus our conscious experience of a one ms flash will last approximately 100 ms under light-adapted conditions (predominantly cone vision) and as long as 400 ms under dark-adapted conditions (rod vision) (Coltheart, 1980; Di Lollo, 1980, 1984; Di Lollo & Bishof, 1995).

Some of you are probably relieved by Figure 11.1 since it indicates that the delay between the eye receiving the stimulus and the onset of our neural response (our "taped delay") is really quite small and might not have much impact in our everyday life. However, we must remind ourselves that the relationship shown in Figure 11.1 refers only to the first layers of neurons that respond in the visual system. It takes between 10 and 50 ms for visual signals to reach the lateral geniculate nucleus of the brain, and it takes another 20 to 50 ms for information to reach the primary visual cortex. From the visual cortex it takes yet another 50 to 100 ms for information to reach centers in the frontal parts of the brain responsible for our action and planning and perhaps even consciousness (DeValois & DeValois, 1991). Therefore, the time that elapses between a visual stimulus hitting our retina and our ability to act can be quite large, potentially posing us with significant problems in being able to respond effectively to threats and opportunities in our visual environments.

To put the "taped delay" of perception in perspective, consider that under the most ideal set of circumstances, it will take an automobile driver over 200 ms to perceive a red light at an intersection and make and implement the decision to apply the brakes. Well over half of this time is taken up in the visual analysis of the light itself. For example, it will take around 40 ms for the red light to reach the lateral geniculate nucleus, another 20 ms for it to reach area V1, another 20 ms for it to reach the color area V4, and then another 40 ms for this information to reach centers in the frontal parts of the brain responsible for action, planning, and perhaps even consciousness. So at this point 120 ms have elapsed and the red light has only been "seen." Once the red light is perceived and interpreted, the initiation of muscle responses, is by comparison, quite fast, taking only 10 to 15 ms (Woodworth, 1938). If we put all this together it means that if you are traveling at a speed of 65 miles per hour (around 100 kph), by the time you have become conscious of the stimulus that will require you to stop, your car has already travelled an additional 20 feet (6 meters) and you still haven't even made the slightest movement toward the brake pedal. That process may take another 60 ms, leaving only 20 ms for the activation of the appropriate muscles themselves. Remember that this is an analysis of perception under ideal conditions. As we often hear, individual results will vary, depending on the current conditions of the observer and the environment.

Some recent experiments have helped to shed light on the ways in which the brain compensates for the handicap of registering visual information in "taped delay." In short, the brain appears to have built-in mechanisms to anticipate where stimuli will be in advance. In one study (Nihjawan, 1994), observers viewed a thin bar smoothly rotating about its center on a viewing screen, as shown in Figure 11.2. At unpredictable intervals an extension of the bar was briefly flashed on and off. If perception was instantaneous with the stimulus, or even if there was a constant delay between the presentation of a stimulus

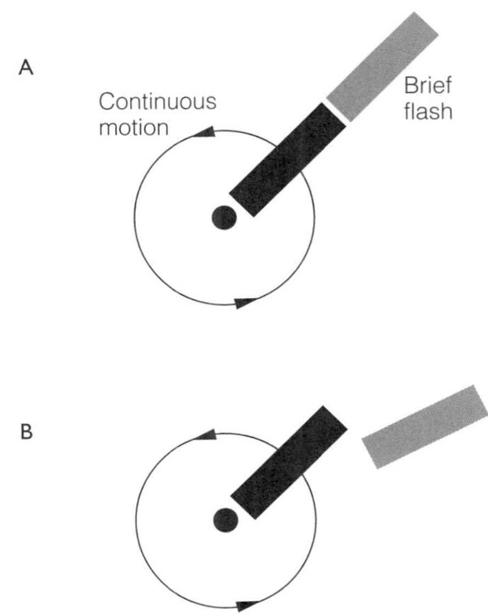

FIGURE 11.2 (A) The sequence of visual displays used to study the flash-lag effect. (B) What observers see when shown this sequence of displays.

and its associated percept, then observers should have seen the brief flash as an outward extension of the rotating bar. However, what they saw in response to the brief flash was a second bar appearing briefly in a location trailing well behind the location of where a true extension would be. For this reason, this effect has come to be called the **flash-lag illusion.** It is as though perception of the smoothly rotating bar is made possible by mechanisms of anticipation, whereas the perception of the briefly flashed extension to the bar is seen as a different stimulus because its unpredictable nature does not fit into the anticipated pattern. Similar flash-lag results have been reported for stationary stimuli involving color changes (Sheth, Nijhawan, & Shimojo, 2000), showing that the perception of events is delayed for other features besides spatial position.

In a related physiological study (Sillito, Jones, Gerstein, & West, 1994), researchers were able to record activity from cells in the lateral geniculate nucleus of cat, both when these cells were influenced only by incoming visual information concerning motion and when these cells were also connected to neurons descending from the primary visual cortex. The descending neurons were shown to **prime** the cells in the lateral geniculate nucleus, so that these cells needed less activity than usual to respond in favor of the direction of motion signaled by the cortex. The authors suggested that the function of the cortical feedback was to test for the presence of certain patterns in the input and to lock onto them very quickly when they were found. This research therefore reveals neural circuits that can help the observer overcome the inherent "taped-delay" aspect of perception. However, in order for it to work, higher visual centers must be given enough information to develop an anticipatory hypothesis that can be used to "tune" the lower visual centers for some expected types of stimuli. Such anticipation could be based on recently acquired information, as in the case of viewing a smoothly rotating bar (Nihjawan, 1994), or they could be based on longer-term memories of what to expect in a given circumstance (Stelmach & Herdman, 1991).

As soon as we introduce the possibility of more than one event occurring in succession, very complex relationships begin to emerge between the timing of physical events and their perception. Remember that we started our discussion with a simple 1-ms flash of light. Now let's consider that flash, followed shortly thereafter by another 1-ms flash of light. Two very different percepts will occur, depending on whether or not the second flash occupies the same spatial location as the first flash.

If we have two brief flashes being shown in succession in separate spatial locations, as shown in Figure 11.3, the perceptual result is **temporal integration,** meaning that the two flashes appear to form a single unified stimulus. Temporal integration has been studied very effectively by using a pattern of dots, as is also

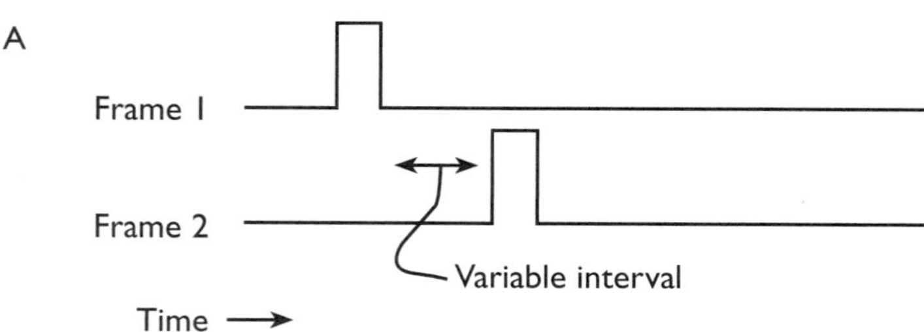

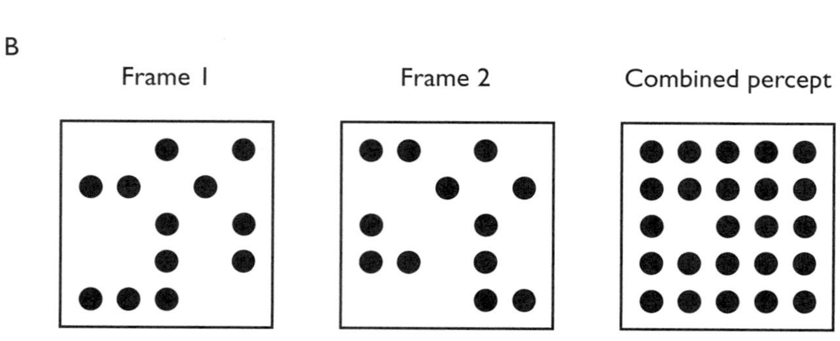

FIGURE 11.3 A method for studying temporal integration. Two display frames are each presented for 1 ms and at varying intervals from one another. Twelve dots are displayed in each frame, such that when the frames are superimposed, one dot in the 5×5 matrix is missing. Observers are asked to report the location of the missing dot. Accuracy in this task declines steadily over intervals from 0 to 100 ms (based on Di Lollo, 1980, 1984).

shown in Figure 11.3 (Di Lollo, 1980, 1984). We start out with a square pattern matrix that can contain 25 dots arranged in 5 rows and 5 columns. In the first 1-ms flash, we present 12 of these dots in randomly selected positions, while in the second one msec flash, 12 different dots are shown. This means that one dot is missing. The observers' task is to locate the position of the missing dot. The only way observers can do this is by integrating information about dot locations across the two flashes. The large number of dots (12 in each frame) and the randomness of the missing location make it impossible to do this task by any conventional use of short-term memory, which usually holds only seven or so elements. If the two flashes are shown with an interval of 0 to 50 ms separating the two events, then accuracy in identifying the missing dot is quite high because the visible persistence bridges the time gap and integrates the two views. In fact, subjects are often unaware that there were two flashes, and appear to see all 24 dots as if they had been flashed on at the same time. However, by the time 100 ms has elapsed in light-adapted viewing conditions, accuracy in the task is approaching chance levels (1 in 25, or 4%) and subjects report seeing two successive groups of dots that they simply can't integrate in any way.

If we have two brief flashes being shown in succession, but in the same spatial location as illustrated in Figure 11.4, the perceptual result is different. Here we may find that the second of the two flashes will be perceived more accurately than the first (Breitmeyer, 1984; Michaels & Turvey, 1979). This is often referred to as **backward masking,** because it is believed that the stimulus that occurred later in time interferes with the processing of the earlier stimulus. This phenomenon was studied in an elegant experiment by Bachman and Allik (1976). These researchers presented two simple shapes in rapid succession in the same spatial location. Each shape was chosen randomly from the set shown in Figure 11.4, flashed for 10 ms, and observers were asked to identify both shapes. When the two shapes were shown simultaneously, accuracy was equally poor for both shapes, showing the difficulty of identifying each shape in the composite display. However, as the interval between the two flashes increased, the patterns of accuracy for the first and second shapes began to deviate substantially from one another. Whereas accuracy for the second shape improved steadily with an increased delay between flashes, accuracy for the first shape plunged even lower before beginning to improve with increased delay. The **J-shaped masking** pattern of accuracy shown for the first shape is evidence that there is a perceptual competition when two objects are flashed in quick succession. The fact that this pattern is only seen for the first object indicates that it is the temporally later shape that wins the competition.

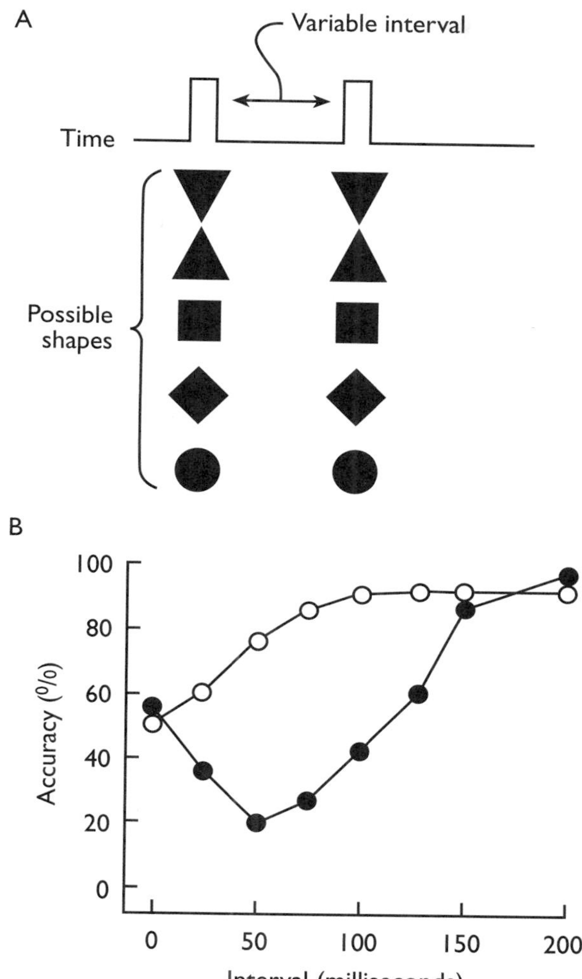

FIGURE 11.4 A method for studying visual masking. Two shapes are presented in rapid succession in the same spatial location. Observers are asked to report the identity of both shapes. When the shapes are shown simultaneously, accuracy is equally poor for both shapes because each shape is camouflaged by the other. However, with an increasing interval between shapes, accuracy for the first shape (black circles) is impaired more than accuracy for the second shape (open circles) (based on Bachman and Allik, 1976).

Spatial Analyses Require Time

The last point we want to make in order to convince you that time is equally important to space in perception is to consider the analysis of spatial layout itself. Examine the picture shown at the top in Figure 11.5, which is a reproduction of a famous print by the Dutch artist M. C. Escher. What is involved in understanding the spatial layout depicted in this print? Sometime after we begin viewing this picture we realize that there are some glaring inconsistencies in the three-dimensional structure of the building. Some of the apparently straight posts connecting the lower and upper floors begin on a portion of the building nearest to us and end on a portion of the building that is farthest away. What does it take for us to detect these inconsistencies? Why aren't they detected immediately upon being shown the picture?

It turns out that the inconsistencies can only be detected by comparing the depicted spatial structure over regions of the picture that are somewhat removed from each other. What the artist has cleverly done is to draw a building with depth relationships that are locally consistent everywhere. This means that each of the connections shown between two or more contours does not violate any principles of perspective drawing. This is shown for each of the two regions highlighted in Figure 11.5B. However, M. C. Escher has fooled the eye through violations of global consistency, changing the depth assignment of a given edge somewhere between these two locally consistent regions.

Why can't the eye detect these global inconsistencies immediately? The main reason is that the fovea has only a very limited spatial range over which it has acuity for fine spatial detail. The depicted structure in two regions can therefore only be compared after an eye movement has been made; the two regions of structure cannot be seen simultaneously. The same process of integrating successive bits of information over time goes on in the perception of more common objects and scenes. Thus you may feel that you see a face all at one time, yet di-

A

B

FIGURE 11.5 (A) Belvedere by the Dutch artist M. C. Escher. (B) The same picture, highlighting two regions that are each locally consistent in their depiction of depth and surface relations but that are globally inconsistent with one another.

rect measures show that you look at the eyes, the mouth, the nose, and the frame made by the hair over a period of a second and more, and then integrate the information over the viewing time to make one coherent percept.

You might think that viewing scenes at a distance, or after a proportional size reduction could eliminate some of the need for temporal integration. Viewing the same image but reduced in size would allow more of the scene to stimulate the fovea of the eye, and fewer time-consuming eye movements would be needed. Unfortunately, this is not the case, because information processing time is not only affected by the size of the area being scanned but also by the amount of information in that area. Thus reducing the size of the stimulus increases the amount of detail that is packed into increasingly smaller portions of the retina. Apparently, the spotlight of attention, or the **mind's eye,** is limited in the amount of detail it can register at once, and so the detection of inconsistency still takes a comparable amount of time, despite no physical eye movements being necessary to acquire all the information (Enns & King, 1990). This demonstration therefore illustrates the need for even apparently simple spatial analyses to require processing over time. Only by comparing information acquired at different points in time can the correct spatial analysis of a scene be completed.

TEMPORAL PROPERTIES OF THE VISUAL SYSTEM

Temporal Resolution

How sensitive are the eye and brain to changes in illumination over time? As with most of the other questions of this sort we have seen, the answer is not simple, since different parts of the visual system have different sensitivities. Physiological studies have shown that the activity of retinal receptors in the eye can resolve a flickering light at rates of up to several hundred cycles per second, although the sensitivity of neurons in the primary visual cortex to change over time is much less. Our conscious awareness of changes in light over time is even more crude. For example, when observers are asked to discriminate a light that is rapidly flickering on and off from one that is steadily on, the measured **critical fusion frequency,** or **CFF,** can fall anywhere between 10 and 60 cycles per second. This is a very broad range, since a stimulus flicking at 10 cycles per second corresponds to a light turned on and off repeatedly for 50 ms durations while at 60 cycles per second on and off periods are only 8.3 ms in length.

Our temporal resolution as measured by the CFF varies over this wide range because it is sensitive to a number of variables, including the current level of light or dark adaptation, the intensity of the light, the distance of the light from the fovea, and the wavelength composition of the light. Table 11.1 provides a summary of these effects. Note that the CFF showing the greatest temporal resolution (highest frequency) would be obtained with the combination of a light adapted eye, a stimulus of high intensity, viewed in the visual periphery, and, in this bright light situation, the color of the stimulus doesn't matter. A CFF showing the least resolution (lowest flicker rate) would be obtained in an observer that was dark adapted, with a light of low intensity, viewed in the fovea, and of long wavelength composition (i.e., red).

An important factor in our discussion of sensitivity to temporal changes in illumination is the distinction between the parvocellular and magnocellular pathways of the visual system. As we saw in Chapter 3 (Visual Pathways), these pathways diverge as early as the retinal ganglion cells, where it is observed that magnocellular neurons respond primarily to the onset or offset of light in their receptive fields, whereas parvocellular neurons respond in a more sustained fashion to the

TABLE 11.1 Factors that Influence Critical Fusion Frequency, the Ability to Discriminate a Flickering from a Steady Light

	CRITICAL FUSION FREQUENCY (CYCLES PER SECOND)					
Variables	10	20	30	40	50	60
adaptation	dark adapted ←	→	→	→	→ light adapted	
luminance	very dim ←	→	→	→	→ very bright	
retinal location				fovea ←	→ periphery	
stimulus size				under 0.5° ←	→ over 10.0°	
wavelength						
dim light	red – green – blue					
bright light				←	all hues	→

steady stream of light. This division of labor is maintained into the higher visual centers of the cortex, where the dorsal pathway receives a larger degree of input from the magnocellular system and the ventral pathway receives a larger degree of input from the parvocellular system. Psychophysicists refer in a functional way to this distinction by using the terms **transient** versus **sustained** channels of the visual system. Demonstration Box 11.1 will help to remind you that your experience of *where* something is, which depends on the rapid transient (magnocellular-dorsal) system, often occurs before your experience of *what* the object is, which depends on the slower sustained (parvocellular-ventral) system.

Recent research has made it clear that it is the magnocellular pathway (transient channel) that is largely responsible for the time keeping operations of vision. This was demonstrated very convincingly in a recent study (Leonards & Singer, 1997). Observers were asked to determine whether there were one or two flashes of light presented on any trial. The actual stimuli were either a single 50-ms flash of light or a pair of 50-ms flashes separated by a 50-ms interval. Since these are the only stimuli visible, this task is extremely easy. Observers typically discriminated these two events with an accuracy of over 95%. However, introducing an irrelevant flash of light, anywhere else in the visual field, and within approximately 250 ms from the test flash greatly impaired the observers' accuracy in discriminating the single flash from the double flash.

Leonards and Singer (1997) subsequently examined the important characteristics of this distracting flash in relation to the test flashes. Low-contrast flashes were chosen to activate the magno pathway selectively; equiluminant chromatic flashes were used to activate the parvo pathway selectively; and high-contrast flashes were used to activate both pathways simultaneously. The researchers found that a low-contrast distracter flash could disrupt accuracy for all kinds of test flashes. On the other hand, accuracy for low-contrast test flashes was not disrupted by high-contrast and colored distracter flashes. This indicates that the specialized magno pathway conveys information about the precise timing of flashes. It can therefore be disrupted by other magno signals that are irrelevant to the task, and it can influence the perceived temporal structure of information conveyed primarily by the parvo system.

Both because the magno pathway is the most important time keeper for vision, and because we are far less consciously aware of its activities than we are of those of the parvo pathway, some aspects of the temporal organization of perception do not fall within the awareness of our conscious experiences. For instance, cycling patterns of visual events that recur over very short periods of time can be used effectively to organize a display into figure and ground even when the basis for these perceptions is not obvious to us (Usher & Donnelly, 1998). In one study, observers were shown displays containing many small bars, in many different orientations, with each bar moving independently in a different direction (Alais,

DEMONSTRATION BOX 11.1

SEEING "WHERE" BEFORE "WHAT"

There are many situations in the everyday world that allow us to see some visual attributes of an object before other attributes. Think of this the next time you try to identify an approaching vehicle from a distance on an open road, try to identify a bird from a distance, or try to find your friend in a busy airport. In each of these circumstances you will know where something is with considerable precision, long before you are able to identify what it is. For example, from a distance, the approaching vehicle may be a truck or a car. You will likely know in which lane it is traveling well in advance of seeing its specific make. It is a general principle of vision that an object's location in space can be determined well ahead of its color and shape. This is because the motion characteristics of an object involve changes in spatial position over time, which are signals that are carried by the faster magnocellular-dorsal visual pathway. Expert bird watchers are well aware of this and often use the movement pattern of the bird as a more reliable indicator of its species than either its color or shape, which may be uncertain from a distance. The same principles hold true for finding your friend at an airport. You will be able to determine where individual people are well in advance of knowing who they are. From a distance, the movements your friend makes in walking and gesturing, which are carried by the magnocellular-dorsal visual pathway, will probably be a more rapid clue to their identity than your friend's facial features, which are carried by the parvocellular-ventral visual pathway.

Blake, & Lee, 1998). At completely unpredictable intervals, any single bar could suddenly reverse its direction of motion. These displays look very much like the random snowstorm seen on your TV when it is not tuned to a specific channel. There is no order to be seen in the spatial pattern of luminance, edge orientation, or motion direction.

Yet it was easy to create visible order in these displays by adding a pattern that consisted entirely of changes over time. If the randomly moving bars in one region, such as a central square, changed their direction at the same time, then those bars formed a square figure that could be seen against the ground of the other bars that were switching their direction of motion at random intervals. This effect occurred even though the many different directions of motion in the central square were completely unrelated to one another and the changes in direction were determined completely at random. These "in concert" or synchronized changes resulted in a visible shape even when the rate of change was as high as 50 times per second. That corresponds to a reversal in the direction of motion on average every 20 ms. Despite the short-lived and unpredictable nature of each of the events involved, observers could see the geometric form defined by these correlated changes in time easily and accurately. Yet they were unable to say what made the form different from the background. Biography Box 11.1 introduces an individual who is often credited with discovering the important role that temporal synchrony plays in neural communication.

Visible Persistence

Is the phenomenon of visible persistence we discussed earlier of general benefit to the visual system, or it is a nuisance? Does visible persistence give us the ability to perform some tasks that would be impossible without it, or does it simply reflect the inherent sluggishness of a

BIOGRAPHY BOX 11.1

NEURONS COMMUNICATE BY FIRING IN SYNCHRONY

Wolf Singer (1943–), a neuroscientist at the Max-Planck-Institute for Brain Research in Frankfurt, Germany, is generally credited with one of the most important discoveries in the past 25 years, concerning the ways in which neurons communicate with one another. His discovery was that active neurons have a tendency to cause other neurons with which they are connected to fire with precisely the same temporal pattern on a millisecond scale. This is called **neuronal synchrony.** Since his initial discoveries, Dr. Singer has pursued the possibility that neural synchrony acts as important neural signal in a wide variety of ways. One of the most exciting of these ideas, one that has not yet been proven directly, is that neural synchrony forms the basis of consciousness, with the contents of our consciousness corresponding to the activity of those neurons that at any moment are closely synchronized. Synchrony is also very likely the basis for our perception of the **perceptual now.**

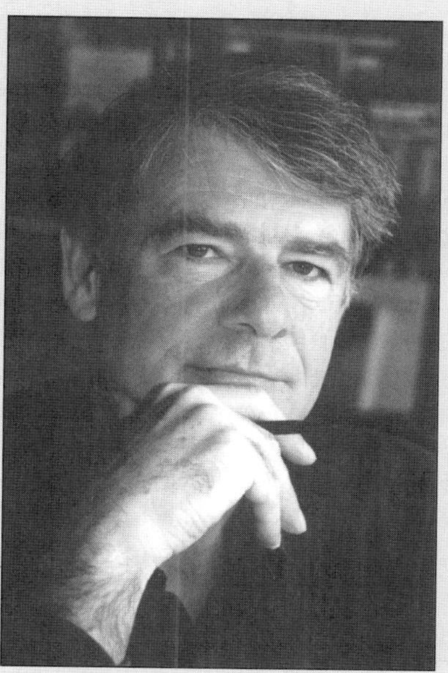

An interesting feature of neural synchrony is that the firing coincidences seem to increase and decrease in cycles, creating waves of activation that repeat themselves between 20 and 60 times a second. These waves of coincidence are called **oscillations** and many neuroscientists are now interpreting them as a sign that two brain regions are in communication with each other concerning the same visual object. Researchers studying human vision can measure these oscillations noninvasively, while an experimental participant is performing a visual task, by recording small changes in brain voltages from a cap of electrodes worn by the participant. These techniques, known as recordings of event-related potentials, or ERPs (Chapter 3), are at present the most direct way of studying the temporal microstructure of brain activity in humans.

visual system that is built from relatively slow-acting neurons? Actually, visible persistence can sometimes be a help or a hindrance, depending on the task we are asked to perform.

One place where our technological society has come to rely on visible persistence is in the realm of video display devices. A modern television or computer screen consists of many rows and columns of picture elements, affectionately called **pixels** by engineers. Each pixel can be triggered to give an assigned light of a certain intensity and wavelength composition, by turning on an electron gun at that location. However, the electron gun only turns on any given pixel at some specified place on the screen for an extremely brief period of time. In fact, each pixel on the screen is turned on and off in succession, starting from the upper left-hand pixel and moving to the lower right-hand pixel. Each pixel is illuminated once every 15 to 16 ms, so that all the pixels are lit, or, technically, **refreshed,** 60 to 75 times a second. The chemical phosphor used at each pixel location on the screen does permit light to persist for some time longer than when the electron gun is actually on, but for the vast majority of the cycle, each pixel is turned off.

If our visual systems did not have visible persistence and were sensitive to the actual time-related changes going on across the television screen, we would see a single dot of light changing color while it traveled rapidly from left to right and from the top to the bottom of the screen. This would be repeated more than 60 times a second. If we add just a little visible persistence, then the screen would appear as a snowy flickering pattern with alternating regions of light and dark and we would not see very realistic images. However, because our visual system has much lower temporal resolution than the television, we see a stable picture in which all the pixels appear to be illuminated simultaneously. Some mammals such as dogs have better temporal resolution ability than do humans, so that they do see an unstable flickering image. That is one reason why your TV does not usually capture your dog's attention, even if it is showing a picture of Lassie romping across the screen.

Despite the marvelous invention that is modern television, we suspect that humans did not evolve a visible persistence function primarily to facilitate our television viewing pleasure. Are there places in the *natural* world where visible persistence would be of benefit? The answer is "yes," and the reason is best understood when we compare some of the functions of the human visual system to that of a camera. In the design of any optical device, whether biological or artificial, some decision must be made with regard to the physical tradeoff that exists between the duration of light exposure and the intensity of exposure. If there is plenty of illumination, then the stimulus only has to be exposed for the brief time needed to register the pattern of light. This corresponds to a fast shutter speed on a camera and little persistence of neural activity in the lower visual levels of humans. If illumination levels are low, however, then a longer time window of persistence, or a slower shutter speed, is needed to register the same pattern of light. Generally speaking, the dimmer the stimulus, the more time it must be exposed in order for the optical image to affect photographic film or retinal receptors.

In the course of human evolution, numerous compromises have been made to achieve a degree of visible persistence that is sufficient to activate neurons at higher levels but that is not so great that the temporal resolution necessary for our survival is lost. Furthermore, we have seen that nature has arranged it so that the duration of persistence is changed dynamically, such that when we are dark adapted or when we are looking at dimmer stimuli, visible persistence is longer giving us a greater opportunity to detect the presence of a pattern.

There are cases, however, where the degree of visible persistence that exists in human vision is clearly detrimental to optimal visual functioning. But, here again, we see that some attempt is made by higher brain processes to compensate for the task-specific deficiencies of lower visual processes. A good example is **motion smear,** which refers to the trail of visible persistence that is left by an object in motion. You have probably seen this before in the dark, where quickly moving a light, such as a small flashlight, a lit cigarette, or a burning ember from a campfire, allows you to see a visible streak. The persistence of the streak is long enough to allow you to make visible circles and forms. Motion smear, however, does not require either dark conditions or very bright stimuli to be present. Demonstration Box 11.2 shows how to experience this phenomenon.

In general, motion smear contributes to difficulty in seeing the precise shape of an object in motion, although it may assist in determining its trajectory. Research has shown that there is substantial **suppression of motion smear** when an object in motion follows a predictable path (Breitmeyer, 1989). In one study, (Hogben & Di Lollo, 1985), observers were asked to indicate the number of dots that could be seen simultaneously on an imaginary circle. In reality, a single dot was being plotted on the screen at any point in time, but its location changed from moment to moment. Visible persistence was the basis for observers seeing simultaneous dots. When the dot was plotted randomly on the circle, observers could see 6 to 7 dots because of visible persistence. However, when the dot followed a predictable

DEMONSTRATION BOX 11.2

MOTION SMEAR

Motion smear is the result of visible persistence when an object moves quickly across your visual field. You can easily experience this smear in daylight by holding one finger in front of your face and wagging it back and forth quickly as is shown in the figure. What you will see is an image with two fingers, one at each end of the swing, plus an additional blurred shape corresponding to your moving finger in the midportion of the movement path. The multiple fingers and the blur are evidence of the visible persistence. This same persistence can decrease your ability to resolve more complex moving targets. To see this, now hold up two, three, or four spread fingers. Wag your hand back and forth as you did before. Again you see something at the end of each swing and a blur between, but the images of the various fingers are all superimposed on the still persistent images of the others, making it virtually impossible to clearly make out how many separate fingers are moving back and forth in front of your face. In the dark, motion smear is even greater, permitting you to spell out letters of your name in the air with a burning ember from a campfire or a lit cigarette.

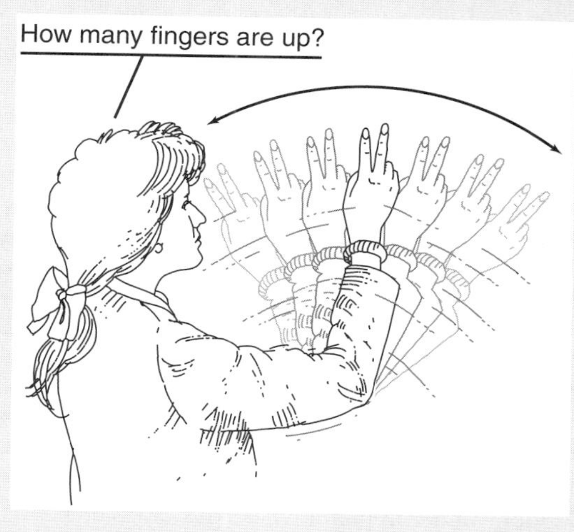

circular path on the screen, observers could only see 2 to 3 dots, meaning that the visible persistence was reduced. The same thing happens for continuously moving targets. If you know where the target is going, some of the smear is suppressed. Studies of patients with selectively compromised magno visual pathways do not show as strong a pattern of suppression, suggesting that the suppression of motion smear is conveyed by the magno pathway inhibiting the parvo stream (Tassinari, Campara, Laercia, Chilosi, Martignoni, & Marzi, 1994).

Visual Masking

The likelihood that you can see a target is greatly reduced if the stimulus is presented when there is another target nearby in both location and time. This is referred to as **visual masking.** In principle, there can be **forward masking,** meaning that when two stimuli are presented, the first stimulus interferes with the perception of the second; there can be **simultaneous masking,** meaning that perception is impaired by the presence of an extraneous stimulus presented at the same time; and there can be **backward masking,** meaning that the presence of the second stimulus interferes with the perception of the first one as we discussed earlier. Forward masking is actually the weakest of the three types. It only occurs if the first stimulus is very close in time (100 ms or less) to the second, and gets stronger as the interval between stimuli approaches zero. Thus, although in a strict sense, this can be called forward masking, as far as the visual system is concerned it is likely that it is really the same thing as simultaneous masking. Because of factors such as visible persistence, the visual system is simply responding too slowly to recognize that the two stimuli did not appear at the same time. The finding supports an interpretation of forward and simultaneous masking suggesting that adding more contours or "noise" to the masking stimulus increases both forms of masking. This means that target identification is being made difficult in the same way that adding camouflage to an object in a scene makes object identification more difficult (Enns & Di Lollo, 2000).

Backward masking is different, in that the strongest effects do not always occur when the target and mask are presented close together in time. This can be observed clearly when we compare **monoptic masking,** in which the target and mask are presented to only one eye, with **dichoptic masking,** where the target is presented to one eye and the masking stimulus to the other (Breitmeyer, 1984). Monoptic masking usually produces the strongest effects when the target and mask are presented simultaneously, with the strength of masking declining as the mask is delayed following the presentation of the target. This strong masking with simultaneous presentation can be attributed to the problems of camouflage we discussed earlier. However, what many studies have found for dichoptic masking can be seen in Figure 11.6. In this figure, target identification accuracy is plotted as a function of the time between target and mask. The resulting curve is U shaped, meaning that the target is still visible when the mask is presented simultaneously but that masking increases (target visibility decreases) as the interval between the target and the mask approaches 50 to 100 ms. If we make the time between the stimuli even greater, approaching 200 ms or more, then the masking effect diminishes and the target becomes visible again.

When masking occurs under dichoptic conditions, we can be confident that low-level or early mechanisms involving interactions in the retina or optic nerve cannot be responsible for the interference. This is because the information from the two eyes only combines to form a single view higher up in the visual system. The U-shaped masking function that occurs for dichoptic masking therefore indicates that some factor other than camouflage is responsible.

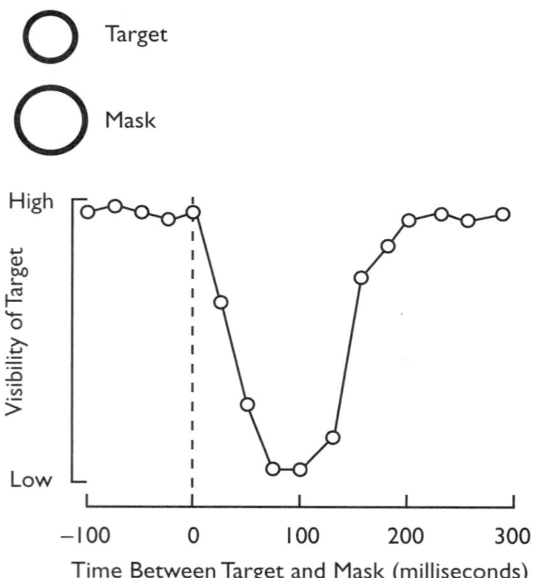

FIGURE 11.6 A typical masking function where the visibility of the target is most strongly interfered with when the masking stimulus follows the target stimulus by around 100 ms.

Varying the number of potential target stimuli gives us additional information about the mechanisms responsible for backward masking (Breitmeyer, & Ogmen, 2000). When only one potential target is presented in a display, followed by a mask, accuracy impairments occur only when the mask arrives within 100 ms or so. However, when there are 12 potential items, backward masking extends to almost half a second (500 ms). Masking results with multiple targets are different in other ways as well. For instance, the degree of masking with a single item is strongly influenced by the intensity of the mask, with brighter masks producing more masking. When there are many possible targets, however, varying the brightness of the mask seems to have little effect.

Findings such as these have led some to theorize that there are two important aspects of backward masking: masking by **temporal integration** and masking by **object substitution** (Breitmeyer, & Ogmen, 2000; Enns & Di Lollo, 1997, 2000). Masking by integration essentially applies to forward and simultaneous masking, as well as that portion of backward masking that occurs within a 100-ms window. The problem for the visual system is that the target and mask patterns are essentially fused or integrated into a single pattern, making the resolution of the two separate stimuli difficult. Backward masking by **object substitution** involves a very different kind of perceptual problem. It is based on the presumption that it takes a certain amount of time for a target to be processed well enough so that we can recognize it. Masking then comes about when processing of a first pattern (the target) is not completed before a second pattern (the mask) appears in the same spatial location and requires use of the same visual analyzing units. This conflict does not involve the early stages of visual processing where contours are defined, but instead involves a competition for the higher-level mechanisms involved in object recognition (Enns, 2002; Enns & Di Lollo, 1997, 2000). Biography Box 11.2 introduces a vision researcher who has proposed a comprehensive theoretical framework for understanding visual masking in terms of interactions between the transient and sustained visual pathways.

Although we have been concerned only with backward masking effects for visual perception, it is important to note that similar effects occur for hearing (e.g., Hartley, Wright, Hogan & Moore, 2000). Such auditory masking is important when we are trying to hear specific sounds and words in a noisy environment. In the auditory realm we do not piece together visual objects or patterns, but most usually words and sentences; hence such masking has an important influence on our understand-

BIOGRAPHY BOX 11.2

UNDERSTANDING VISION BY LOOKING AT INVISIBLE OBJECTS.

Bruno Breitmeyer (1946–   ) has done more than any other modern vision researcher to advance our understanding of visual masking. His book *Visual Masking: An Integrative Approach* (1984) has been treated as the "bible" of visual masking for almost 20 years by many vision researchers.

The theoretical approach proposed by Dr. Breitmeyer is that visual perception involves dynamic interactions between the transient (magnocellular-dorsal) and sustained (parvocellular-ventral) pathways. From this perspective, an important aspect of backward visual masking is the effect that the transient signal of the later arriving mask has on the sustained signal of the target display presented earlier in time. Because the visual system must remain tuned to see new events, it appears to be wired so that transient signals generated by the sudden appearance of an object act to inhibit or suppress sustained signals from objects that have already been viewed. These suppressive effects can therefore render an object invisible or 'masked' that would otherwise be completely visible, if it had not been followed in time by a new object in the same location.

Dr. Breitmeyer is currently a Professor in the Department of Psychology at the University of Houston. He is actively involved in many research projects in which the dynamic interactions between transient and sustained visual signals are important. These include the study of visual attention, motion perception, reading disabilities, and schizophrenia.

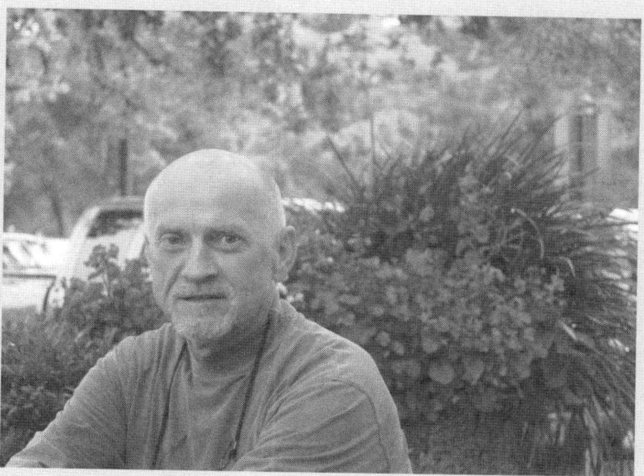

ing of language in our everyday environment (e.g., Perry & Ziegler, 2002). Most important, it demonstrates that the influence that time has on perception is not limited to vision alone, despite the fact that we have been concentrating mainly on visual examples in this chapter.

PERCEPTUAL ORGANIZATION OVER TIME

Time becomes a problem when we try to figure out which parts of the flow of information belong together because they are part of a stream of stimuli that simply take a while to unfold, as compared to those stimuli that should be seen as separate, because that they are really from different events but just happen to be occurring very close together in time. These are fundamental problems confronted by every perceptual system. Some researchers have referred to these problems as the temporal stability versus plasticity dilemma (Grossberg, 1995), because they seem to highlight a tension between two necessary but opposing forces. One is the force toward perceptual stability, necessary in a world where the information from even a rigid and stationary object is constantly undergoing change over time, simply because the stimulus changes as we move and change our angle of view, or other stimuli enter the visual field, perhaps partly blocking our view. The second force is toward perceptual plasticity, which is the process by which we attempt to segregate the parts of the sensory array because more than one object or event has been presented coincidentally in time.

Perceptual Stability

The force toward perceptual stability has been studied using several important auditory illusions. One of the simplest is called the **auditory continuity illusion** (Grossberg, 1995; Warren, 1984). Suppose you hear a steady tone that shuts off for a moment and then turns on again. Obviously you will hear a silent gap in the tone. Suppose, however, that instead of silence, we fill that gap with a broad-band noise (sort of a burst of static) that turns on just as the tone shuts off and turns off when the tone starts again as shown in Figure 11.7. Under certain conditions you will hear the tone as though it had been continuously on, even during the noise. The perception that the tone continues through the noise (even though it is not physically present) is the auditory continuity illusion. The illusion disappears, so that now you don't have the illusion that the tone continued during the noise, if the tone does not turn on again after the noise burst turns off. In the illusion situation it should be obvious that your brain does not know whether the tone will start again until after the noise has been shut off. Therefore, what you experience is a construction by your brain that has been assembled after all the parts of the pattern of signals have been presented. This construction helps to provide continuity for the perception of a single event, across breaks or interruptions in the signal that occur because of extraneous stimuli in the environment. You might think of this the next time you hear the continuous note of a saxophone on the radio in your kitchen, despite it being interrupted by clanks from the pots or dishes you are working with.

We encountered a related illusion in the section on speech and music perception in Chapter 6. When speech is involved the effect is called the **phonemic restoration effect** (Samuel, 1997). In this case, the auditory system of the listener supplies missing parts of speech when the stream of speech is interrupted by other sounds. The missing information is determined from the meaningful content of the sentence in which the speech sequence is perceived. In effect, listeners hear the speech units that the immediate context suggests should be in the phrase, even if they are not physically present.

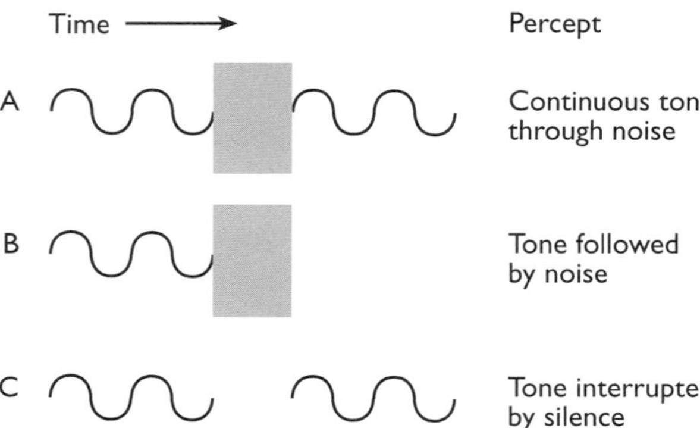

FIGURE 11.7 The auditory continuity illusion. (A) If a stimulus consists of a tone (wavy line), followed by a brief period of noise (rectangle), and then the tone again, you will hear the tone continuing through the noise. (B) If the tone does not turn on again, you will not hear the tone during the noise. (C) If the period of interruption is not filled by noise, the tone will be heard with an interruption (based on Grossberg, 1995).

Again, showing the pervasive involvement of time and the sequence of events in perception, we also find that the visual system can be shown to behave in similar ways. When we see a target (say a black disk) that apparently moves behind another target (say a white square) so that what is really stimulating our retina is a disk with a notch or a bite taken out of it, we still "see" the disk as a complete circle, just partially obscured from view (Murray, Sekuler, & Bennett, 2001; Shore & Enns, 1997). What is happening here is that the perceptual system is "filling in" to effectively "heal" stimuli and make them perceptually whole in order to correct for briefly-occurring distortions or gaps. This, by the way, is one reason why you don't see gaps caused by your blind spot in visual stimuli. The filling-in process completes the stimuli as our eyes move over the field. Only by effectively limiting the changes over time and focusing our attention on the unchanging stimulus do we become aware of our blind spot, as we showed you in Demonstration Box 3.5 (Chapter 3). Perhaps even more striking than the filling-in phenomenon is the way in which the visual system provides the illusion of continuity and completeness in object perception, even though, at any given moment, only a small portion of an object may be actually visible. You can demonstrate this for yourself using Demonstration Box 11.3.

Perceptual Plasticity

The force toward perceptual plasticity can be seen in our everyday ability to segment the continuous stream of acoustic information associated with spoken speech into individual words. To remind yourself of the complexity of this problem, think back to the last time you heard a conversation between two people in a language you did not understand. How well would you do if you were asked to indicate the beginnings and endings of words in that stream of speech? This turns out to be a very difficult task because the pauses in the stream of sounds rarely coincides with the boundaries between words. The raw acoustical information gives us very little reliable information on its own. However, if we are familiar with a language, the problem once again seems very easy. The difference is that we are familiar with the words that can possibly be spoken and so we use that knowledge to segment sounds that have no real physical breaks.

Even within the experience of hearing a familiar language, the role of context can be shown to be critically important in the segmentation process. Imagine hearing the sounds associated with "I'd like anicetea" in one of two contexts: first, at an outdoor cafe near the beach on a summer day, and then in one of those cozy French

DEMONSTRATION BOX 11.3

FIGURAL INTEGRATION

It is rare that we see an object in its entirety. Either we or the object are moving about, resulting in glimpses that are partially occluded by other objects (for example, a dog running through some trees). Yet we have no difficulty identifying the object. Parks (1965) studied this phenomenon by moving a shape behind a narrow window, or slit. His surprising result was that a wide variety of shapes could be easily recognized, even though the shape was never seen except as a series of fragments. Because of one of the shapes Parks used, the phenomenon of easy identification of shapes presented by moving them behind a slit has come to be called **Park's camel.**

In order to experience Park's camel for yourself, have a friend pass various objects (including himself or herself) behind a narrow slit created by a door that is slightly ajar (Shimojo & Richards, 1986). Try varying the size of the slit and the speed with which the object passes across it. You will find that over a surprisingly wide range of size and speed conditions the object will be identifiable. Also, pay attention to the strength of the feeling you will have that the **entire** object is present, even though at any moment you are only receiving a fragmentary view of it. When the conditions are optimal, that impression is very strong. This demonstrates the importance of the integration over time required to create the perceptual object out of a chaotic and constantly changing retinal image.

pastry shops in midwinter. The person serving you would undoubtedly hear two very different messages, despite the acoustical streams being identical in the two settings.

The role of context in perceiving visual motion is equally important. Consider two displays created by Ramachandran and Anstis (1986). The first consists of simply alternating the views shown as frames 1 and 2 in Figure 11.8A. What an observer reports seeing here is a single small dot that is flashing on and off beside a stationary larger square. In Figure 11.8B, three additional dots have been added. Alternating frames 1 and 2 makes those three dots appear to move first right then left in a repetitive manner. You might think that the dot beside the square will flash on and off as before. However, observers see something completely different. The original dot now seems to be moving behind the square and then reemerging in a repetitive manner. In the context of other dots that appear to move, the brain acts as if it is now most plausible that the original small dot is doing the same thing and so a motion signal is attributed to that dot, even though there is no local evidence that the dot is moving. We will learn more about apparent motion in the next chapter.

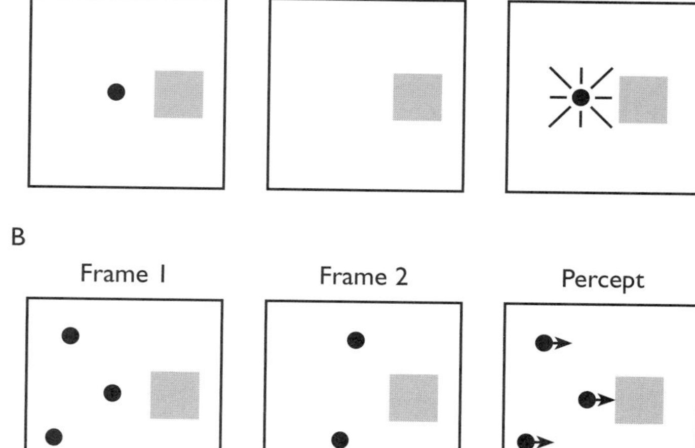

FIGURE 11.8 Visual displays consisting of two frames that are flashed repeatedly. (A) A single small dot is seen flickering on and off beside a stationary larger square. (B) The same small dot is now seen moving behind the square and back again. The only thing different in this display from the previous one is that there are other dots which appear to be moving back and forth as a group (based on Ramachandran & Anstis, 1986).

THE PERCEPTION OF THE PASSAGE OF TIME

Your sense of the passage of time is a perceptual experience. Up to now we have been considering the relationship between physical stimuli and our perceptual experiences. However, in the case of perceiving the passing of time, the situation is less clear. There certainly is no readily visible "time organ" for such stimuli to impinge on. Our notion of time may be associated with some form of internal clock that we consult like a wristwatch to determine the span of an event, but it also seems tied to our experience of change (see Aschersleben, Bachmann, & Muesseler, 1999). It is through the concept of change that time and motion become intertwined. Changes that occur in a sequence are often associated with a perception of time passing, whereas, as you will learn in Chapter 12, changes in location over time may, under the proper conditions, be perceived as motion.

The concept of time is fundamental to the way in which human beings perceive, think, and act. For example, every natural language in the world has separate verb tenses for past, present, and future, plus innumerable modifiers to specify time more precisely, such as yesterday, today, recently, in an hour, while, during, after, and hundreds more (Bentham, 1985). Despite this centrality of time to our experience, the study of time perception is complex, since time is not *a thing* that, like an apple, may be perceived directly in isolation of the events around it. In fact, time involves two qualities of our perception that seem to be added to our consciousness but yet cannot be linked directly to simple physical dimensions (see Roeckelein, 2000). These qualities are an awareness of a present moment and the impression that time passes. Let us call these the concepts of now and flow, respectively (Michon, 1985).

The concept of **now** is always with us, and has been described by William James (1890) as the "saddle-back of time with a certain length of its own, on which we sit perched, and from which we look in two directions into time." Sometimes called the **subjective now,** it is the few seconds of our current experience of ongoing consciousness; all else is either past or future. However, it is important to remember that even this subjective present is actually in the "near past," if we take into account the "taped-delay" nature of our conscious experience that we discussed at the beginning of this chapter. For this reason, many philosophers refer to our immediate experiences as occurring in the **specious now.** With this phrase they are referring to the fact that our subjective now seems forever doomed to be about the immediate past rather than the actual present.

Most psychologists are not as concerned about the philosophical implications of this problem as they are concerned about the practical problems of being forced to live in the "near past" (although see Roeckelein, 2000). They are interested in why it is that humans don't walk into dangerous, fast-moving traffic more often than they already do. What visual signals are humans using when they are able to duck unconsciously and automatically in order to avoid being hit in the head by a flying object? For this reason, we usually measure the performance of observers in real time rather than the conscious reports of observers about their experience of the same events. Yet, almost without fail, when the performance and experience aspects of perception are compared directly, the conscious experience of events usually lags behind the performance aspects by several hundred ms or even up to half a second (Libet, 1999, 2002; Libet, Gleason, Wright, & Pearl, 1983; Libet, Wright, Feinstein, & Pearl, 1992). We will have more to say about this relationship in our discussion of consciousness in Chapter 14.

Although **flow** is an equally fundamental perceptual attribute of time to now, it actually can be broken down into a number of different measurable aspects of experience (Brown, 1990). Each of these additional facets of time perception may be different from the others and may involve unique physiological or information processing mechanisms. One of the most common judgments that we make about time flow is **duration estimation.** This is simply our perception of how much time has elapsed between two events, such as the time that lapses between when you turn on the stove and when a pot of water boils. We usually use units such as seconds or minutes to describe duration. Next, we have the perception of **order** or **sequence,** which involves the determination of which event came first, second, and so forth. Without this you could never remember telephone numbers that someone has just read to you correctly. The minimal case of the perception of sequence involves determining the time interval that must separate two events before they are perceived as occurring one after the other, rather than at the same moment. This judgment involves the discrimination between the experience of **simultaneity** and that of **successiveness.** The last aspect of flow is somewhat less perceptual but still requires time estimation. It is the anticipation or **planning of an ordered sequence** of events before they actually occur. This is especially important in playing musical instruments, or in actions such as speech production where we

BIOGRAPHY BOX 11.3

MAKING TIME FOR TIME

Paul Fraisse (1911–1996) may well be credited for bringing the study of the perception of time into the laboratory. Fraisse was initially educated in philosophy and theology with the notion that he would ultimately become a priest. While he was studying at the Catholic University at Louvain, however, he met the psychologist Albert Michotte who was studying the perception of visual events and became entranced with both science and issues involving time. Following World War II (during which he was captured by the Germans, escaped, then recaptured, only to escape again using false papers), he began his studies in time perception. Unfortunately, the dominant orientation of postwar psychology was behaviorism, which could not deal very well with the idea of time perception since, after all, time is not a "stimulus" and hence one should not talk of perceiving it. Fraisse, however, was able to demonstrate systematic relationships between time intervals and perception. He divided temporal events into three levels depending on their apparent duration. Events lasting less than 100 ms appear instantaneous and duration is meaningless. Between 100 ms and 5 seconds, there is a feeling of duration of an event that is still occurring in the psychological present. For stimuli or intervals greater than 5 seconds there is the sense that they have slipped out of the present and they have some kind of a past that must be addressed by memory. Fraisse lived long enough to see the advent of cognitive psychological approaches, when the notion of time as a stimulus as well as the legitimacy of time perception were no longer issues of controversy. In addition to his scientific work at what is now Université René Descartes, Fraisse is also credited with shaping French psychology and psychological education. This was done as the Director of the Institute of Psychology (which unified psychological research and study in several major institutions in the Paris region). He received many awards and served as the President of the French Society of Psychology as well.

automatically plan and execute an ordered sequence of sounds to produce meaningful utterances. It was the French psychologist Paul Fraisse who first gained scientific acceptance for the study of these issues of time perception, and he is discussed in Biography Box 11.3.

When we look for the mechanisms by which we perceive time, we find that two general processes have been suggested. We may call these "clock" theories, since each gives a mechanism that determines how we monitor the passage of time. The first involves a **biological clock** and assumes that there is some physiological mechanism that we can use as timer for our perception of time. Thus, just as the eye is an organ that monitors light, our biological clock monitors time. The second involves the notion of a **cognitive clock,** where time is derived via some cognitive process that is based on things like how much sensory information is processed, how many events occur within a given interval, or how much attention is paid to ongoing cognitive events. In this latter viewpoint time is constructed rather than simply monitored. Both types of clocks may exist, and each may be used for different types of time perception.

Biological Clocks

Many physical phenomena have their own rhythms or timing. There are day-night cycles, cycles of the moon, cycles of the seasons, and many others. Living organisms often display similar rhythmic activities. Many flowers open and close at particular times of the day. In animals there are physiological and behavioral processes that cycle regularly. One proposal about the way time is perceived is based on the idea that the flow of subjective time is related to some body mechanism that acts in a periodic manner, with each period serving as one "tick" of the biological timer. Anything that alters the speed of our physiological processes would then be expected to alter our perception of the speed at which time passes.

Circadian Rhythms. One of the most obvious examples of an apparently timed behavior is the sleep-wakefulness cycle that runs through a regular daily rhythm or the hunting and feeding patterns of animals that repeat every 24 hours (Groos & Daan, 1985; Rijnsdorp Daan, & Dijkstra, 1981). There are also more subtle physiological processes that have their own periodic changes. For example, the pulse, blood pressure, and temperature of the body show day-night variations in humans as well as in many other animals. There is a more than 1°C difference in body temperature between the coolest point, which occurs during the night, and the warmest point, which occurs during the afternoon (Coren, 1997). These are all examples of a **circadian rhythm,** which comes from the Latin *circa,* meaning "approximately," and *dies,* meaning "day." Thus, a circadian rhythm is one that varies with a cycle of roughly 24 hours.

So much rhythmic activity in behavior suggests control by some internal biological clock. Alternatively, it may be that these repetitive 24-hour changes are simply a function of the regular changes in light and temperature that occur in the day-night cycle. Thus, an animal might become active in the presence of daylight when it can see more clearly and the temperature is a bit higher, and it is this activity that then alters the physiological function. The "built-in" approximately 24-hour cycle, however, can be demonstrated experimentally in the absence of light or temperature changes. For example, suppose that we find ourselves in a constant-light environment, where there are no changing cues that show the passage of time. Under these conditions our biological clock will "run free," gaining or losing time like a not-too-accurate clock. Although different people will have different cycle lengths, most of us will begin to live a "day" that is approximately 25 hours long (e.g., Aschoff, 1981).

If the internal biological clock is set for about 25 hours, why do our internal and behavioral rhythms continue on a 24-hour cycle? Why doesn't our daily activity cycle drift out of phase with local time? This is because there is a mechanism that synchronizes the internal timer with local time. From the behavioral point of view, the most salient aspect of local time is the alternation of light and dark cycles. To be an accurate reference against local time, a biological clock must be synchronized with the local day-night cycle, and it must have a stable period that is relatively free of unpredictable environmental fluctuation. This process of synchronization is called **entrainment.** If there were no such mechanism, traveling across the continent, where the sun might rise 3 hours earlier relative to the current setting of your biological clock, would leave you 3 hours "out of step" with your new environment. There is, of course, some disruption of your time sense from such trips in the form of jet lag, which accounts for the sight of newly arrived Europeans wandering through the lobbies of New York hotels at 4 or 5 A.M., looking for an open restaurant to have breakfast in. Because of their great speed of travel, their circadian rhythms are still set to Paris, Moscow, or some other European time. Body time does eventually adapt to the new time zone at a rate of 1/2 to 1 hour per day. This adaptation comes about through entrainment of the biological clock to the local environmental sunlight-to-darkness cycle (e.g., Coren, 1997).

To use the traditional term, we would say that light is the primary **zeitgeber** (German for "time giver"). There is much evidence, based on several species of animals including humans, that shows the internal clock is synchronized to light (e.g., Johnson & Hastings, 1986). A brief flash of light will reset the biological clocks of animals reared in constant darkness, either advancing it or retarding it, depending on when the flash occurs (Aschoff, 1979). If there is no regular light cycle, however, other environmental stimuli, such as daily fluctuations in temperature, may serve as zeitgebers to set the internal timer.

Is there a single physiological structure that might serve as the biological clock? Researchers have isolated several regions in the hypothalamus that seem to be important to maintaining the circadian rhythm (Gerkema & Groos, 1990). The most important of these is called the **suprachiasmic nucleus** (which we will abbreviate as the SCN), and it is located very near the optic chiasm, as can be seen in Figure 11.9. The SCN is really a very tiny organ of the body, containing only a few thousand cells; however, it has a large effect on our behavior. The timing function of this brain structure is easily demonstrated. For example, rats are nocturnal animals, sleeping during the day and foraging at night. Destroying the SCN abolishes this pattern. The animal still sleeps the same amount of time, but the circadian pattern is gone and it sleeps in random periods throughout the day and night (Stephan and Nunez, 1977). Tumours in this region have the same effect in humans (Fulton & Bailey, 1929). Furthermore, electrical stimulation of the SCN in animals will reset the biological clock, in much the same way that brief flashes of light do for dark-reared animals (Rusak & Groos, 1982). Because light is the primary zeitgeber for the circadian clock, we would expect that the SCN would receive inputs from the visual system, and it does (e.g., Groos & Meijer, 1985). It also may be affected by a hormone secreted by the pineal gland (which is also light sensitive). This hormone, called **melatonin,** is normally secreted at night (or after a period of light exposure) and appears to reset the circadian clock in the SCN (Cassone, 1990; Wever, 1990).

If light is needed to keep our internal clocks synchronized to local time, this raises an interesting question. What happens to blind people who can't see light? Can they reset their biological clock? About 76% of blind people report that they have difficulty falling asleep at their usual bedtime and these difficulties are cyclical in nature, which is exactly what you would expect if blind people had a free-running internal clock that was an hour or so longer than 24 hours. Coren (1997) reviewed several studies that have looked at individual blind people over a longer term and confirmed that their internal cir-

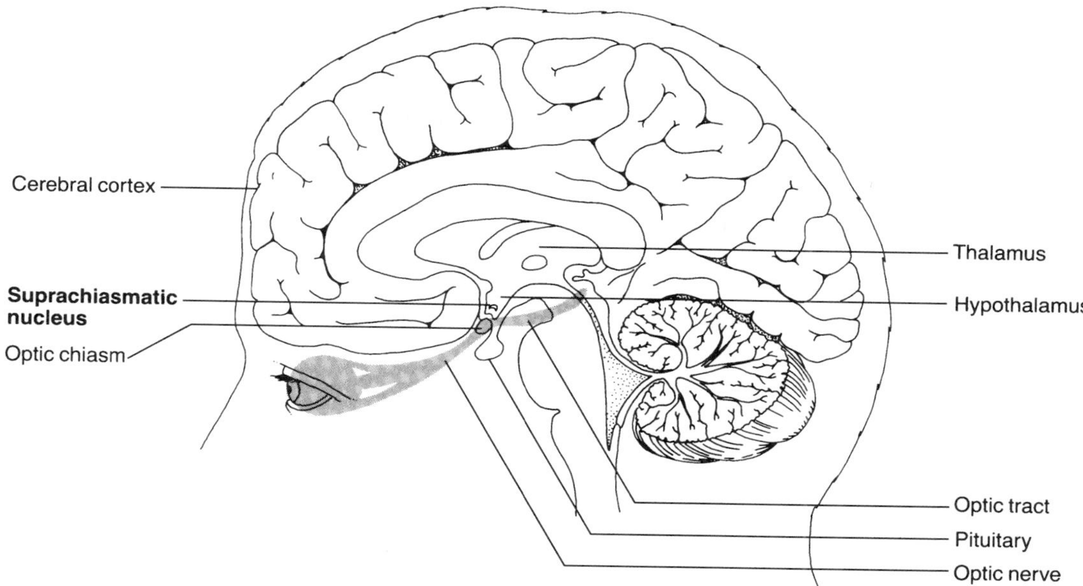

FIGURE 11.9 The location of the suprachiasmatic nucleus of the hypothalamus, which is thought to be the basis of the biological clock that maintains circadian rhythms.

cadian timer is not resetting normally. For example, one study of a completely blind man monitored an 80-day period. His periods of sleep gradually drifted so that for a week he was sleeping during the night but by two weeks later his maximum periods of sleepiness were during the day. This pattern of behavior was consistent with an individual whose internal clock was set at a day length of 24.9 hours. Thus the absence of a normal light sense in the blind seems to hamper more than their ability to process visual information. It also puts them in a situation where their body time drifts, leaving their normal sleep and waking cycles out of step with those who have normal sight.

Short-Term Timers. Although our circadian rhythms are maintained by an internal biological clock, we often make estimates of times that are considerably shorter than 24 hours. We can accurately determine which of two time intervals was longer, when each was less than a second in duration. A "slow" circadian clock would be useless for this task, which suggests that there are probably several biological clocks in animals. For example, destroying the SCN does not affect the cyclic change in body temperature (Fuller et al., 1981), nor does it seem to affect some shorter-cycling biological rhythms. In much the same way that we might use a stopwatch to measure short intervals, our wristwatch to measure longer ones, and a calender to measure even longer periods of time, there seem to be different biological clocks for different aspects of behavior (c.f. Lewis & Walsh, 2002).

Heartbeats, electrical activity in the brain, breathing, hormonal and metabolic activities, and even walking steps have at one time or another been suggested as candidates for an internal biological timing mechanism. More recently, however, focus has shifted to a variety of brain centers, with the idea that there is no single biological clock, but rather a neural "clock shop," with different timers for short and long times and for times that are associated with attentional shifts (see Meck & Benson, 2002). More attention is now being focused on the prefrontal and frontostriatal cortex, since damage to these areas seems to affect time-related judgments.

Rather than looking at long time intervals, some researchers have gone to the other extreme and asked what is the shortest time interval we can sense. Experimentally, they asked the question, What is the minimum time separation needed for two events to be perceived as occurring at different times (successively) rather than at the same time (simultaneously)? The answers to this question seem to cluster around two different time units, one very short, around 30-ms, and the other a bit longer at around 100-ms.

The 30-ms unit seems to be the smallest time difference that can be discriminated reliably when human observers are asked to make judgments of temporal order, such as answering the question "Which of two objects appeared first?" (Enns, Brehaut, & Shore, 1999; Poppel, 1997). The 30-ms unit also appears often in studies measuring response time. For example, studies in which observers are asked to react as quickly as possible to a display have indicated that short-term memory can be scanned at about the rate of 25 to 30 ms per item (e.g., Sternberg, 1975). The detection of different vowel sounds in speech seems to require only 20 to 30 ms (Hermes, 1990). The timing of well-trained motor tasks, such as typing or piano playing, also seems to support a 30-ms internal timing organization (Shaffer, 1985).

Other researchers have come to a similar conclusion by looking at **micropatterns,** which are variations in a stimulus that occur so quickly that there is no corresponding change in the perception. The classic studies are those of Efron (Efron, 1967, 1973; Yund, Morgan, & Efron, 1983), who found that a 20-ms stimulus composed of 10 ms of red light followed by 10 ms of green light was not perceptibly different from one in which the green was presented before the red. Both appeared yellow, provided that the visible persistence of the second patch of color was eliminated. Eriksen and Collins (1968) used a set of patterns that, if seen by themselves, seemed random. If, however, two patterns were superimposed, either physically or psychologically, they contained a word. Eriksen and Collins found that when observers were shown patterns sequentially, recognition for the word was highest when the interval between the patterns was about 25 ms. This implies that the perception of simultaneity is maintained over only a 25-ms interval.

The unit of 30 ms also shows up in analyses of the distribution of eye movements and motor actions made in response to visual events. For example, when distributions of simple motor responses are examined, either of hand responses made to signal the onset of a light or of eye movements made in response to a moving target in the visual field, the distributions typically contain a wide range of response times, as shown in Figure 11.10. Some movements are initiated as early as 100 ms while others take as long as 400 ms, but the vast bulk of the responses occur in the window of time stretching from 150 to 250 ms. What a number of researchers have noted is that there appear to be a number of smaller peaks superimposed on these larger response time distributions. These smaller peaks seem to recur every 30 ms or so. It seems likely then that the 30-ms unit corresponds to the minimum time that must elapse between peaks in the waves of neural activity that are used to communicate between

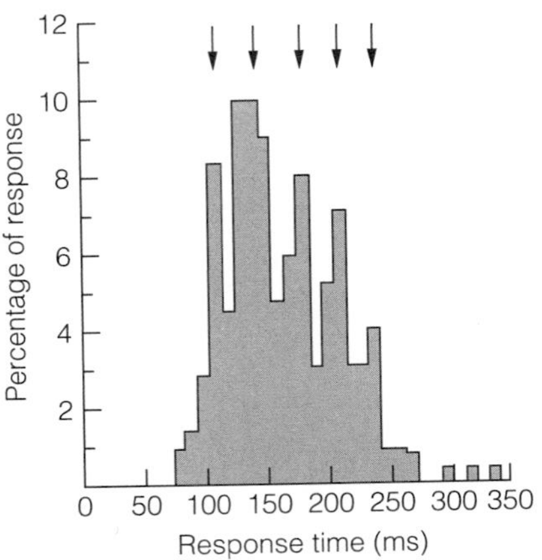

FIGURE 11.10 A typical distribution of response times in a manual simple reaction time task or in an eye movement latency task. The larger distribution of responses is overlaid with peaks every 30 ms or so, as indicated by the arrows (based on Poppel, 1997).

brain regions. In this way 30 ms may form the smallest perceptual unit because it is the most irreducible unit of neural communication (Poppel, 1997).

One hundred msecs seems to be the smallest irreducible unit of time when researchers attempt to measure the time required to consciously perceive an object. We have already come across this time interval in our discussions of **temporal integration** and **backward masking.** In the case of temporal integration, two discrete flashes can be fused into a single perception provided that they occur within 100 ms of each other. When it comes to object identification, the time interval between the onset of the target display and the onset of the mask needs to be around 100 ms in order for the target object to avoid being influenced by backward masking. This same unit of time has been called the **perceptual moment** by researchers interested in quantifying the basic time unit of perceptual experience (Stroud, 1955). Based on several research findings, Stroud estimated that each moment of experience is about 100 ms in duration, which would be the shortest perceived duration a stimulus can have. In addition, stimuli presented within the same moment either would be perceived as occurring simultaneously, or, depending on the nature of the stimulus, would not be distinguishable from each other. Stimuli presented in different moments would be perceived as being successive.

White (1963) attempted to measure the perceptual moment by having observers estimate the number of clicks they heard. He presented the clicks at different rates up to 25 per second. Observers were fairly accurate at rates of up to 5 per second; at the highest click rates, however, observers still estimated a presentation rate of about 6 to 7 clicks per second. This corresponds to a perceived rate of 1 stimulus every 150 ms. Thus, information could not be processed in "chunks" smaller than 150 ms, which would be the resolution limit of the internal timer.

In another study, Efron (1967) presented two brief pulses of light and asked observers to say which one was longer. One of the flashes was always 1 ms in duration; the other was of a variable duration. Both flashes were always seen as being of the same length until the exposure time of the variable flash exceeded a value of 60 or 70 ms. At this duration, the variable flash was seen as being longer than the 1-ms flash. Efron concluded that the minimum duration of a stimulus in consciousness (which should be one perceptual moment) was around 60 or 70 ms.

An interesting "reverse" demonstration of the perceptual moment comes from Intraub (1985), who presented a series of pictures to subjects at a rate of one every 111 ms. One of these pictures always had a frame around it, and observers were simply asked to indicate which picture had the frame. On 54% of the trials, subjects reported that the frame was around the picture that appeared before or after the correct one, probably because the two pictures fell within the same perceptual moment.

Perhaps the source of difficulty in nailing down the perceptual moment and our ability to perceive stimuli as successive rather than simultaneous comes from the fact that different tasks, situations, and physiological factors can all influence our perceptual speed (e.g., Kolers & Brewster, 1985; Ulrich, 1987). Recent work shows that the minimal resolvable time varies with age (Feeney, Howard, & Howard, 2002), the presence of various drugs such as alcohol (e.g., Jones, Chronister, & Kennedy, 1998) and even as a function of the way in which attention is distributed (Carver & Brown, 1997). Thus the best that we can say at this time is that, depending on the specific task, the minimum perceptual duration (or the time between ticks of the fastest biological clock) is probably between 25 and 150 ms.

A final brief unit of time to consider is the duration over which a perceptual event can be reproduced in motor actions by a human observer. Several studies have shown that the duration of a simple visual event can be reproduced fairly accurately over the period of about one half second to 3 seconds, as shown in Figure 11.11 (see Poppel, 1997). The function relating the duration of the reproduced response to the duration of the event is fairly faithful in a 1-to-1 fashion for up to 3 seconds. After that it begins to fall off sharply. Another place the 3-second unit is important is in the duration of perceptual states associated with bistable images such as the ambiguous Necker cube shown in Figure 11.12. Although every observer switches from one percept to the other at different times, the duration of stable states has an average of near

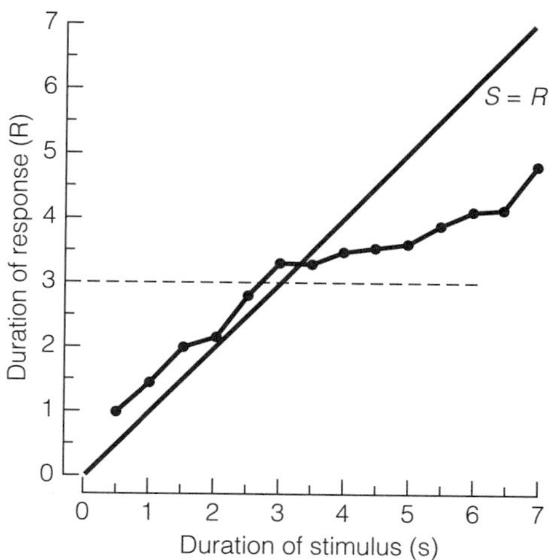

FIGURE 11.11 Visual events lasting between one half second and three seconds can be reproduced faithfully in human motor actions. After that there is still a lawful relationship in the reproduction of visual durations, but it is no longer a direct one. The small constant error of 300 to 500 ms seen for the shorter durations is thought to reflect the delay between the intention to end the motor response and its actual termination (based on Poppel, 1997).

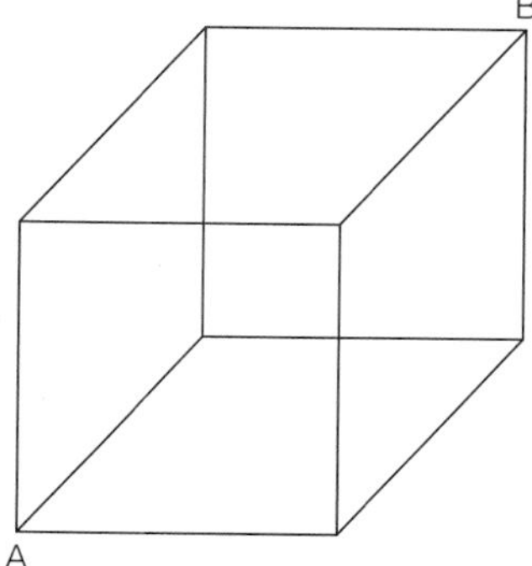

FIGURE 11.12 The Necker cube, in which the face with corner A sometimes appears to be nearer than the face with corner B, but then the figure reverses so that the face with corner B appears nearer. Reversals occur at around 3-second intervals.

3 seconds. It is likely that the **subjective now** of our conscious experience is also linked to this time unit. It is as though every 3 seconds, the brain shakes itself off and says, "What's new?" This probably provides us with the adaptive benefits of staying flexibly attuned to our changing world.

Biological Pacemaker. To the extent that there is a biological timer that serves as a sort of **pacemaker**, ticking away internal time, it would be reasonable to expect that it would speed up or slow down along with other physiological processes in the body. Hoagland (1933) verified this when his wife became ill with a high fever. He asked her to estimate the duration of 1 minute by counting to 60 at a rate of one number per second. When her body temperature was approximately 39°C (103°F), her perceived minute was only 37.5 seconds by objective clock time. This suggests that at higher body temperatures the speed of physiological activities increases, and this causes the pacemaker to tick more rapidly than usual. Thus, when asked to reproduce a given physical time interval, a person with a high body temperature produces an interval that is too short. An alternative way of looking at this is to note how our perception of physical (clock) time will seem to change when psychological time is running quickly. A given physical duration will appear to be too long if the psychological clock is ticking faster than the physical clock, therefore giving more ticks per unit time than normally occurs (see Figure 11.13).

If an increase in body temperature increases apparent duration, then lowering body temperature should have the opposite effect. This was found by Baddeley (1966), who tested scuba divers diving in cold water off the coast of Wales. Like Hoagland, he asked his subjects to count to 60 at a rate of one number per second. After the dive, when their body temperature was approximately 1°C lower than it had been before entering the water, his subjects required approximately 70 s to count to 60. This indicates that their pacemakers were ticking at a slower rate than the external clock. Counting time using the slower ticking rate of their internal timer led them to underestimate the passage of clock time. In other words, when your internal clock is too slow, physical time seems to whiz by (see Figure 11.13). Similar variations in time estimates have been obtained using natural daily variations in body temperature (Campbell, Murphy, & Boothroyd, 2001; Shurtleff, Raslear, & Simmons, 1990). You may demonstrate the effects of temperature on your own time sense by trying Demonstration Box 11.4.

If we have an internal biological clock, then anything that affects the rate of physiological function might also affect our estimates of time. For instance, fatigue usually slows physiological functioning. Thus, the longer you are awake (or the greater the pressure for sleep), the slower your biological clock, and the more likely that when asked to estimate the passage of an hour your estimate will be longer than a physical clock hour because of shortened time experience (Aschoff, 1984; Daan, Beersma, & Borbely, 1984). Similarly, generally anaesthetics lead to a shortening of time experience (Adam, Rosner, Hosick, & Clark, 1971). Conversely, many investigations have found that drugs like amphetamines and caffeine (both of which are stimulants) lead to a lengthening of time experience (Frankenhauser, 1959). Drugs such as marijuana, mescaline, psilocybin, and LSD also seem to produce a lengthening of perceived time relative to a nondrug state (Weil, Zinberg, & Nelson, 1968). It has been argued that all these changes in time perception are caused by acceleration or decelera-

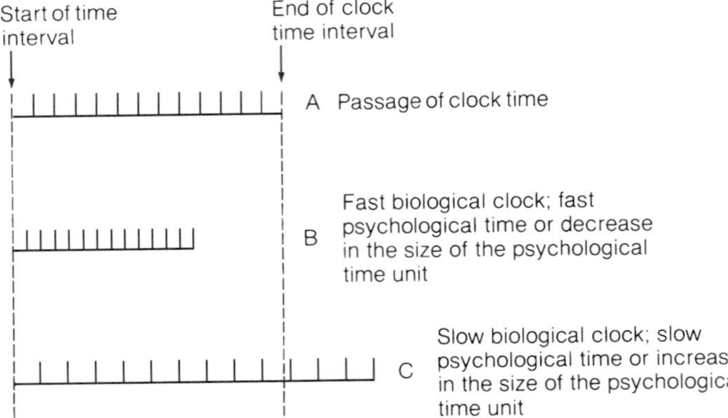

FIGURE 11.13 Each tick mark on these lines represents a unit of time. Those in A are clock time; those in B and C are ticks of the biological clock. Notice that in B the internal clock is faster, so that the same amount of clock time seems psychologically longer (more ticks) and time "drags by." For C, the internal clock is slower and so the same amount of clock time seems subjectively much shorter (fewer ticks).

DEMONSTRATION BOX 11.4

BODY TEMPERATURE AND TIME PERCEPTION

This demonstration is based on an experiment performed by Pfaff (1968). We know that our body temperature can fluctuate as much as 1°C during the course of a day. It is at its lowest point early in the day and tends to rise throughout the afternoon. Given this, try the following observations. On rising in the morning, try counting to 60 at the rate of what you perceive to be one number per second. You will probably need a friend to keep track of clock time for you so that you can relate your perceived minute to a clock minute. Then take your temperature. (Do not take your temperature before you count; otherwise it may bias your counting rate.) Do this several times throughout the day, and keep a record of your results. If the theory is supported, you should find that your counting time will shorten (relative to a clock minute) as your body temperature increases. Thus, as the body clock speeds up, the passage of time tends to be overestimated, and "clock" time seems to pass more slowly.

tion of the pacemaker that serves as our internal timer. An interesting recent confirmation of this line of reasoning has come from the study of hyperactive children with attention deficit disorders. Their hyperactivity is associated with an acceleration of many of their neural processes, which should include their internal biological clock. As predicted by this line of reasoning, physical time seems to pass more slowly and duration estimates become longer in these hyperactive children (Barkley, Murphy, & Bush, 2001).

Cognitive Clocks

When you say that two minutes sitting on a hot stove feels like two hours but two hours sitting with your loved one seems like two minutes, you are expressing the central tenet of most cognitive clock theories of time perception. These theories are based on the presumption that the perception of the passage of time is based not on physical time but rather on the mental processes that occur during an interval. In effect, time is not directly perceived, but rather "constructed" or inferred unconsciously from the cognitive processes that are involved (Fraisse, 1963). This predicts that the kind of tasks a person is doing will change that person's perception of time. Among the factors that increase the subjective perception of duration are an increase in the number of events occurring during the interval (e.g., Poynter & Holma, 1985), an increase in the complexity of the events that occur (e.g., Block, 1978), an increase in the difficulty of the cognitive processes that are required (e.g., Hicks, Miller, & Kinsbourne, 1976), and an increase in the degree of attention given to the passage of time (e.g., Brown, 1985; Enns, Brehaut, & Shore, 1999). All of these factors lengthen the perception of how much time has passed, and all are consistent with the idea that the rate at which the cognitive clock ticks is affected by how internal mental events are processed.

Change. One idea is that the ticking rate of the cognitive clock is dependent on the **mental monitoring** of change. The greater the number of events, or the more changes that occur, during an interval, the faster your cognitive clock ticks and thus the longer is your estimate of the amount of time that has passed. Several studies seem to support this idea. A duration filled with stimulus events is perceived as longer than an identical time period empty of any external events, a phenomenon known as the **filled duration illusion.** What the events are, whether tones, light flashes, words, or drawings, seems less important than the number of changes (e.g., Avant, Lyman, & Antes, 1975; Hicks, Miller, Gaes, & Bierman, 1977; Poynter & Holma, 1985). For example, simply causing a target to flicker will increase estimates of the length of time it was visible (Droit-Volet & Wearden, 2001). Conversely, observers placed in conditions of **restricted environmental stimulation,** where they remain for periods of 24 hours or longer reclining in a soundproof, darkened chamber, tend to underestimate drastically the amount of time they have spent in the chamber (Suedfeld, 1981). This underestimation occurs, presumably, because so few stimulus events have transpired during the interval.

Processing Effort. How difficult stimuli are to process, the amount of attention and memory storage they require, and the amount of mental workload have also been shown to affect our perception of the duration of a time interval (Brown & Boltz, 2002). For example, we tend to judge the brief presentation of a word to be longer in duration than a blank interval of the same length (Thomas & Weaver, 1975). Furthermore, the presentation interval of familiar words is judged to be shorter than the presentation interval of meaningless verbal stimuli (Avant & Lyman, 1975) and presentations of nonfamiliar words appear to take longer than familiar words (Warm & McCray, 1969). In both instances, an increase in the amount of information processing required during the interval (a word versus a blank and a meaningless group of letters versus a word) leads to an increase in the estimated duration of the interval. This is consistent with a **processing effort model** of time perception. Similarly, the more items you store in memory, during an interval of time, the longer you judge the time to be (Mulligan & Schiffman, 1979), a notion sometimes called the **storage size model** of time perception. Both are based on the presumption that the ticking rate of the cognitive clock is dependent on the amount of cognitive activity actually engaged in.

Temporal versus Nontemporal Attention. Both the number of events processed and the degree of effort involved in processing those events affect our cognitive clock time, but the results are complicated by the way the observer is attending to the task. A simple example of this is given by the old homily "a watched pot never boils," which suggests that the more attention you pay to the passage of time, the longer the time interval appears to be (e.g., Block, George, & Reed, 1980; Cahoon & Edmonds, 1980). This may be called the **temporal processing model** of time perception.

One of the best examples of the temporal processing model is the fact that, when we are told in advance that we will have to judge the time that a task takes, we tend to judge the duration as longer than if we are unexpectedly asked to judge the time after the task is completed (e.g., Brown, 1985; McClain, 1983). Simply telling observers that they will later have to estimate the time that has passed causes them to pay attention to, and perhaps to order, internal events and external physical events in a way that increases the perceived duration of the task.

Conversely, anything that draws our attention away from actually monitoring the passage of time should shorten our sense of time passing. For instance, making the task we are working on more difficult makes it harder to attend to time directly. For this reason, we find that estimates of the duration of difficult tasks are usually shorter than estimates of the duration of easy tasks (e.g., Arlin, 1986; McClain, 1983). Sometimes, directing attention toward or away from the passage of time may even reverse the filled duration illusion, which we discussed earlier, since it is more difficult to process many events in an interval while at the same time attending to the flow of time itself (e.g., Zakay, Nitzan, & Glicksohn, 1983). Demonstration Box 11.5 shows how attention to time and task difficulty interact to affect our perception of the passage of time.

It should be clear from the preceding discussion that in the same way that there are a number of biological clocks that can interact in complex ways to give us a sense of the passage of time, there are also a number of cognitive clocks, or at least a number of ways to set the speed of a single cognitive clock (c.f. Grondin, 2001). One interesting aspect of this is the effect of an observer's age on the perceived passage of time (e.g., Lustig & Meck, 2001). We all remember how, as children, the time between birthdays seemed endless. There is now a good deal of evidence that as people age, the passage of larger units of time (such as days, months, or even years)

DEMONSTRATION BOX 11.5

TIME PERCEPTION AND ATTENTIONAL FACTORS

For this demonstration you will need a stopwatch or a watch with a sweep second hand. Do each step **before** you read the instructions for the next one.

1. Sitting quietly, note the time and then, with your eyes closed and with no counting, estimate the passage of 30 s. Then open your eyes.
2. Next, note the time, look away from the watch, and start to count backward from 571 by threes (e.g., 571, 568, 565, etc.). Be sure to count out loud. When you feel that 30 s has passed, stop counting and note the amount of time that has elapsed.
3. Compare the two time estimates. The first one should be shorter than the second one because your cognitive clock was moving slower when you were attending only to the passage of time and faster when you were dividing your attention between the counting task and the monitoring of time (see Figure 11.9).

seems to be much faster (Joubert, 1990). One possible explanation for is this is that the total amount of time that you have experienced serves as a reference level, and the perceived duration of any time interval is compared to this baseline. Thus when you are 5 years old, the passage of a year represents the passage of an interval equivalent to 20% of your life span so it seems to drag by. When you are 50, however, a year represents only 2% of your elapsed time experience and therefore it seems to zip past more quickly.

STUDY QUESTIONS

1. What happens to visual perception when there is no variation in the image over time? Why?
2. What important lesson about vision is illustrated by the flash-lag illusion?
3. What determines whether two images presented in rapid succession will result in temporal integration of the two images or visual masking of one image by the other?
4. List three factors that influence critical fusion frequency.
5. How does visible persistence contribute to your enjoyment of moving pictures?
6. What is the difference between monoptic and dichoptic visual masking?
7. In what way does the auditory continuity illusion show that the brain goes "beyond the information given"?
8. What is the relationship between the objective passage of time and the perceived passage of time?
9. Make a list of several different units of time that seem to recur in studies of time perception. What do these different "clocks" tell us about how time perception is governed in the brain?
10. How is perceived time influenced by body temperature? What does this tell us about how our brain keeps time?

CHAPTER 12

MOTION

CHAPTER SUMMARY

Perception is not static, but changes continually over time. Many of these changes are like successive "snapshots," such as glancing from one page to another or shifting your gaze from one building to another as you stand in the street, but many other changes are more continuous in nature, such as the sight of a car moving in the street beside you or a bird flying through the air. These perceptual experiences have the added quality of perceived motion.

Your initial feeling might be that the perception of motion is really a simple thing. You might even think that all you need for motion to be perceived is the image of a visual stimulus moving across your retina. But this is far from the truth. You will learn in this chapter that motion perception involves some very complex interactions among several different sensory and motor systems, including vision, proprioception, eye movement control, and locomotion. For example, we only rarely experience the world under conditions in which we are not also in motion. On a daily basis we walk from place to place, ride in our cars and on trains, and even move our head while talking to other people and reading. From this perspective, motion across the retinal surface is a relatively minor factor in the interplay between systems (Sekuler, Ball, Tynan, & Machmer, 1982).

To give you a sense of some of the complexity involved, consider some examples of everyday situations in which the perception of motion is critical to your understanding and appropriate action. For instance, in many cases you can perceive movement when the image of the stimulus is stationary on your retina. This happens when we follow a moving person with our eyes. If we are tracking the person carefully, her image will be relatively fixed on the same retinal location, and yet we will still see her as moving. There are other times when there is motion in the retinal image we receive and yet we do not see any movement. This occurs when our eyes move from one person to another in a conversation in which we are sitting among our friends. Despite the fact that the images of the people slide across our retinal receptors, we see them as remaining perfectly stationary in their seats. Finally, there are times when both our eyes and a visual stimulus are stationary, but we still see movement! This can occur when we view a solitary light like a candle glowing in the dark, or when we view a stationary object against a moving background. In both of these cases an object that is actually stationary appears to move around against an apparently stationary background (Duncker, 1929).

The perception of motion in objects that are perfectly stationary can even occur in full daylight, as illustrated in Figure 12.1. Look at the center of the rings while you slowly move your head toward and then away from the page. You will see the rings appear to rotate, with the inner ring rotating in an opposite direction to the outer ring. This is an illusion of motion in a stationary picture (Pinna & Brelstaff, 2000). It depends on an analysis in which the retinal signals for expansion and contraction (this is what the rings are actually doing on your retina as you move closer and farther) are incorrectly interpreted as signals for rotation around the ring (Gurnsey, Sally, Potechin, & Mancini, 2002).

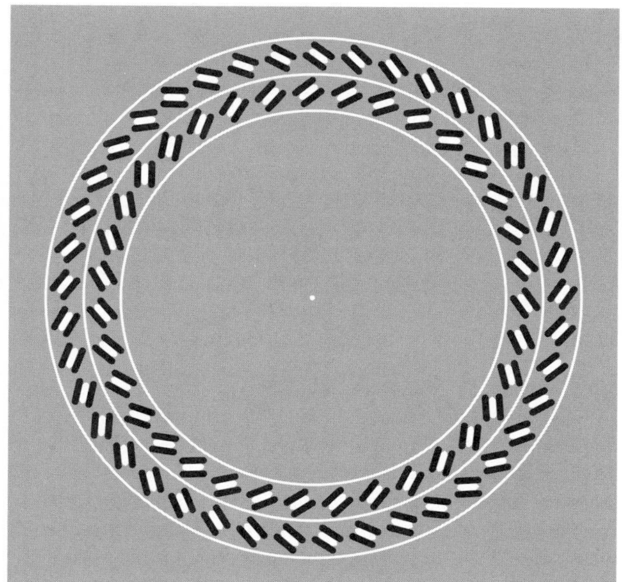

FIGURE 12.1 The rotating wheel illusion (based on Pinna & Brelstaff, 2000). Watch what happens to the appearance of the rings as you look at the center dot and move your head slowly forward and backward.

As you can see from these examples, the perception of motion is much more complex than it first appears. We will approach our understanding of it in this chapter by first considering the way our nervous system processes different aspects of motion. We will then consider several features of the visual stimulus that are unique to an analysis of motion. With this background, we will be prepared to consider the wide variety of human functions that receive benefits from our ability to perceive motion. In all of this, we will have to be constantly reminded of the important nonvisual factors that contribute to our experience of motion and stability. To aid our understanding of these factors, we will end the chapter with a section on our finely tuned sense of balance.

PHYSIOLOGICAL BASIS FOR MOTION PERCEPTION

Is the perception of motion a primary aspect of vision, like color and form perception, or is it an experience that is derived from some other more primitive aspects of vision, such as the perception of space and of time? Many years ago this was a hotly debated question, since an answer was not obvious from an examination of the physical relations involved. The science of physics revealed only that the motion of an object was directly related to its spatial location at different points in time. If we use M to symbolize motion velocity, S to denote spatial location, and T to denote time, then this relationship could be written in any one of three ways. For instance, $M = S/T$ suggests that motion is computed from the elements of time and space. But $S = M \times T$ is an equally valid description of the same relationship and it implies that motion and time are the primary experiences. Finally, the relationship could even be written as $T = S/M$, which would imply that space and motion are the primary visual experiences from which a perception of time is derived.

Most researchers who study motion perception now regard this last expression as the one that is closest to the way visual perception actually works. This is because neurons have been found in the visual systems of primates and other animals that code directly for the properties of both space and motion. As we saw in Chapter 3, most of the visually sensitive regions in the brain are organized on the basis of spatial location. We also mentioned that there are single neurons that are sensitive to the presence of motion in a particular direction and at a particular velocity in their receptive fields, and this will become important here. However, in Chapter 11 we noted that no neurons had been found to date that seemed to be specifically sensitive to the passage of time. In this sense, then, motion perception is every bit as basic to the design of the visual system as is the visual property of the color or the orientation of an edge.

But to be fair to earlier researchers, we also have to mention that the primacy of motion was suspected long before there was any single-neuron evidence in favor of this position. Biography Box 12.1 will introduce you to the first researcher to make this suggestion. For instance, one of the oldest visual illusions known to vision researchers is the **waterfall illusion.** If you stare, for a minute or two, at an image that is moving continuously in one direction (such as a waterfall) and then shift your gaze to a stationary image (such as the bank beside the waterfall), you will see an image moving in the opposite direction for a short period of time. This suggests that there are neurons that have become fatigued, in the same way that staring at a large color patch seems to fatigue color-sensitive neurons, thereby influencing subsequent color perception in the direction of the complementary color. In this case, the fatigue seems to bias the system in favor of seeing motion in a direction *opposite* to that of the original stimulus. PET scans have even localized the area of the brain where these cells are located, as being in V5, the medial temporal part of the brain where many motion specific cells are found (Hautzel, et al., 2001).

The psychophysical technique used to study the waterfall illusion in the laboratory is called **selective adaptation** (Sekuler, 1975). It involves exposing the eye to a moving pattern such as a field of stripes. Prolonged viewing of such a stimulus temporarily reduces an observer's ability to detect motion in the same direction as the stripes (Hunzelmann & Spillmann, 1984). However, this drop in sensitivity does not carry over to faster or slower movements, nor does it generalize to movements in the opposite direction (Dawson & Di Lollo, 1990; Wright & Johnston, 1985). Thus, the selective adaptation procedure gives results consistent with the idea that our brains contain movement-sensitive cells that are tuned to a particular direction and speed. To experience another interesting illusion that researchers believe is caused by the fatigue of motion-sensitive cells, try the demonstration in Demonstration Box 12.1.

Another demonstration of the primary status of motion can be seen in the separate nature of the perceptual experiences associated with an object's motion and shape. In many instances, motion can be perceived quite independently of the shape and color involved. An example of this can be seen in **apparent motion** displays, which involve two stationary displays being rapidly interchanged. If one display consists, say, of a white square on the right side of the field and the other consists of a white square on the left side, alternating these views at the correct speed will give the impression of a white square moving left and right in an oscillating manner. But this motion depends very little on whether the two objects are identical, similar, or extremely different in color and shape, provided that there is only one object in

BIOGRAPHY BOX 12.1

AN ARGUMENT FOR MOTION PRIMACY

Sigmund Exner (1846–1926) was a nineteenth-century Austrian scientist and a colleague of Hermann von Helmholtz. He is credited with being the first to hypothesize the existence of specialized neural mechanisms for motion perception, particularly in the periphery of the eye.

Exner's reasoning began from the simple observation that the appearance of motion could be achieved by the successive presentation of two stationary images. Today we call this **apparent motion,** and it is widely used in television and movies. The only technology Exner had available for the presentation of two successive images was sparks of electricity. The existence of such a powerful illusion from such a simple stimulus, Exner argued, meant that neurons specialized for the detection of real motion were being fooled.

However, his careful experimentation revealed an even stronger argument than the mere existence of apparent motion. Exner noted that the perception of movement could be obtained even from two sparks that were so close together that they could not be distinguished when presented simultaneously. This made it impossible to argue that observers were inferring (either consciously or unconsciously) the presence of motion from more primary knowledge of spatial position and time. Instead, it followed that motion perception must be a primary sensation in its own right.

DEMONSTRATION BOX 12.1

MOTION AFTEREFFECT

The **motion aftereffect** demonstrated here is called the *spiral aftereffect* because the stimulus used to produce it is a rotating spiral. Photocopy or trace the picture below onto a stiff piece of cardboard cut into a circle. Puncture the center of the cardboard and place it onto an old record turntable or spin it on the end of a pencil. Stare at the rotating spiral pattern for about a minute before stopping the rotation completely. While the disk was spinning the spiral pattern seemed to expand. Now it should appear to be shrinking, even though it is casting a stationary image on your retina. The shrinking appearance is caused by a selective adaptation or fatiguing of motion detectors tuned to the particular movements involved during the period the disk was spinning. The 60 seconds of viewing will result in an aftereffect that lasts for only about 10 to 15 seconds (Hershenson & Bader, 1990). If you want to examine the selective nature of the adaptation process, repeat the demonstration but this time increase or decrease the speed of the spinning. This should have predictable consequences on the rate at which the pattern seems to shrink during the aftereffect.

each frame. A white square and a red circle will still generate the feeling of motion, now accompanied by some sort of apparently "magical" distortion in color and shape.

During the 1960s and 1970s, the hypothesis that motion was a primary sensation was confirmed in physiological studies. These studies revealed that the visual systems of many animals contained individual neurons that are sensitive to movement. Neurons sensitive to a visual target moving in a particular direction were first described in frogs (Maturana, Lettvin, McCulloch, & Pitts, 1960), but soon after in many other avian and mammalian species (see Hausen, 1982). It was found that motion perception occurs at a very early level of processing in simpler organisms. In many nonhuman animals, such as rabbits, the earliest (most peripheral) neurons that are able to discriminate the direction of motion are found in the retina, specifically, in the ganglion layer of neurons. In other animals, such as the cat, less than 1% of the retinal ganglion neurons are direction selective, meaning that motion is processed at higher levels. By the time we get to monkeys, no motion sensitive ganglion neurons can be found (Rodieck, 1979). It is widely believed that the first neurons to show selectivity for motion in primates, including humans, are located in the superior colliculus and the primary visual cortex.

Neurons that are sensitive to the direction and to the speed of movement are believed by most researchers to arise from a specific arrangement of neurons such as is shown in Figure 12.2 (Marr & Ullman, 1981; Reichardt, 1961; van Santen & Sperling, 1985). The generic name given to this arrangement of neurons is the **Reichardt detector,** named after the researcher who first proposed it. This model requires at least three different neuronal units to make it work. The two cells at the top of the diagram (A and B) behave like the simple cortical cells we discussed in Chapter 3; their receptive fields (shown in the figure) are each tuned to edges of a particular orientation. The neural signals from these two cells are compared with one another by the third cell (C) shown in the lower part of the diagram, but only after the signal from cell A has been delayed by some small amount of time. The purpose of the delay is to compensate for the movement of the stimulus, which will cause successive neural receptive fields to be stimulated. If the two signals (A and B) arrive at about the same time, then the comparator cell (C) will fire vigorously, signaling a moving stimulus. Each Reichardt detector is tuned for a particular direction and speed of movement. The system drawn in Figure 12.2 will signal the presence of a rightward motion, since movement from B to A (leftward) will produce signals that do not arrive at the same time. It is also tuned for a particular speed, and this tuning depends on the length of time that the signal from cell A is delayed. Shorter delays are needed to synchronize the signals corresponding to a faster-moving stimulus.

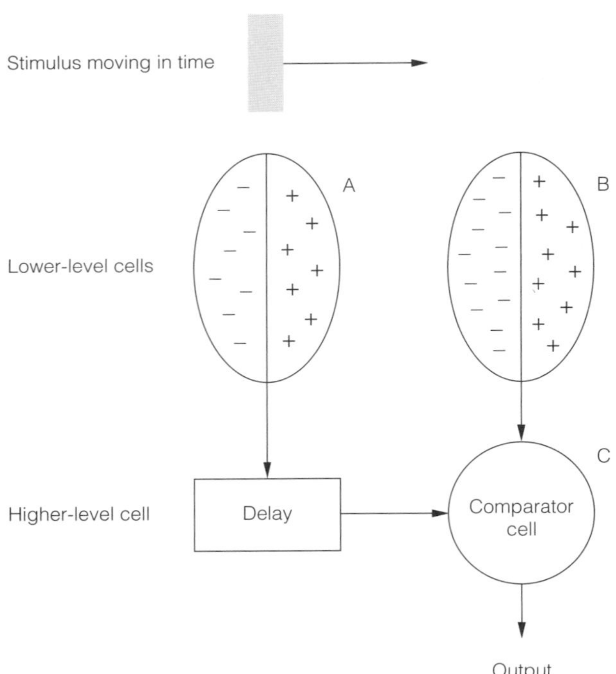

FIGURE 12.2 A computational model of motion detection that is consistent with physiological evidence (based on Reichardt, 1961).

In Chapter 3, we considered evidence from anatomical, physiological and clinical neuropsychology that suggested that there are different pathways in the visual system for different kinds of information (e.g., Livingstone & Hubel, 1988). If we consider first the two most general visual pathways in primates, we find that it is the older tectopulvinar pathway (evolutionarily speaking) that is more involved in motion perception than the newer geniculostriate pathway. There are some suggestions that the tectopulvinar pathway may be entirely specialized for the perception of movement, along with the control of responses that involve moving stimuli, such as some kinds of eye movements (Flandrin & Jeannerod, 1981; Guitton, Crommelink, & Roucoux, 1980).

Within the geniculostriate system, there is an important subdivision that is also relevant. Specifically, the magnocellular system is more responsive to moving stimuli, while the parvocellular system is more involved in form and color perception (DeYoe & van Essen, 1988; Zeki, 1993). When we first encountered the magnocellular pathway in Chapter 3 we noted that it was better suited than the parvocellular pathway to the perception of rapid rates of movement since cells in this pathway respond to any change in stimulation. Sustained response cells are more oriented toward the detection of details and hence are better suited for the perception of form, or very slow movement (McKeefry, 2001).

Magno ganglion cells are also not distributed equally across the retina. Rather they are more abundant in the peripheral retina than at the fovea. This helps to explain why the apparent speed of a moving target depends on where it is in the visual field, with motion in the periphery appearing to be of a higher velocity (Campbell & Maffei, 1981). The flipside of this is that our ability to detect very slow target movements (up to about 1.5 degree per second) decreases with distance from the fovea (Choudhurt & Crossey, 1981). For higher target velocities, however, our ability to detect target movement increases with distance from the fovea. At moderate to fast velocities, the peripheral retina seems better able to detect movement (because of the increased proportion of transient response cells) even though the decrease in acuity may be so great that the observer may not be able to recognize the shape of what is moving (Bhatia, 1975; Brown, 1972). This is why you sometimes see a TV screen flickering when you catch a glimpse of it far in the periphery of your visual field. Out there, the transient cells are sensitive enough to make out the actual movements of the raster that paints each line on the TV screen.

The importance of the magnocellular system in motion perception can be shown using a technique involving **isoluminant patterns.** These are patterns of lines or forms that are distinguished from their backgrounds only on the basis of the hue dimension of color. All luminance differences have been eliminated (hence the terms **iso-,** meaning the same, and **luminant,** referring to light intensity). The usefulness of these patterns is based on the fact that the magnocellular system responds much better to luminance differences than it does to hue differences. It is the parvocellular system that can detect patterns that are based only on hue differences. This explains why, when we use moving isoluminant stimuli, we may be able to see the pattern quite well; however, the speed and even the direction of movement is often difficult to determine (Cavanagh, Tyler, & Fareau, 1984; Lindsey & Teller, 1990; Troscianko & Fahle, 1988). These findings indicate that the color-blind, but luminance–sensitive, magnocellular system is more involved in motion perception than the color-sensitive parvocellular system (cf. Burr & Corsale, 2001).

In monkeys and humans there are two main regions of the cerebral cortex that contain many neurons with the characteristics of Reichardt detectors: the primary visual cortex and the temporal lobe (Newsome & Pare, 1988). The specific portions of the temporal lobe that contain these neurons are called the **medial temporal** area and the **medial superior temporal** areas, and these are sometimes referred to as cortical area V5 in monkeys (see Figure 12.3). While it is the case that there are neurons in the primary visual cortex (V1) that respond to direction of motion (e.g., Maunsell & Van Essen, 1983), it appears that V5 is the part of the brain that is most highly specialized for motion perception. It is here that we process coherent movement of objects and arrays as well as motion related "events" such as the onset of movement (e.g., Kable, Lease-Spellmeyer, & Chatterjee, 2002). In addition, V5 contains neurons that are not only specialized to detect and respond to motion, but also are specifically tuned to the speeds of moving stimuli (e.g., Perrone & Thiele, 2002).

Laboratory studies combining behavior and physiology in monkeys have helped to illustrate the different roles played by the primary visual cortex and the temporal lobe in the perception of motion (Movshon & Newsome, 1992; Newsome, Britten, & Movshon, 1989). In monkeys, the motion-sensitive region of the temporal lobe corresponds to the human region (V5). Recording from single neurons in this region has shown that almost all of them are strongly direction selective. This means that they give a strong response to stimuli moving in their preferred direction and actually show an inhibited response (below the resting rate of activity) to stimuli moving in other directions. An important way in which

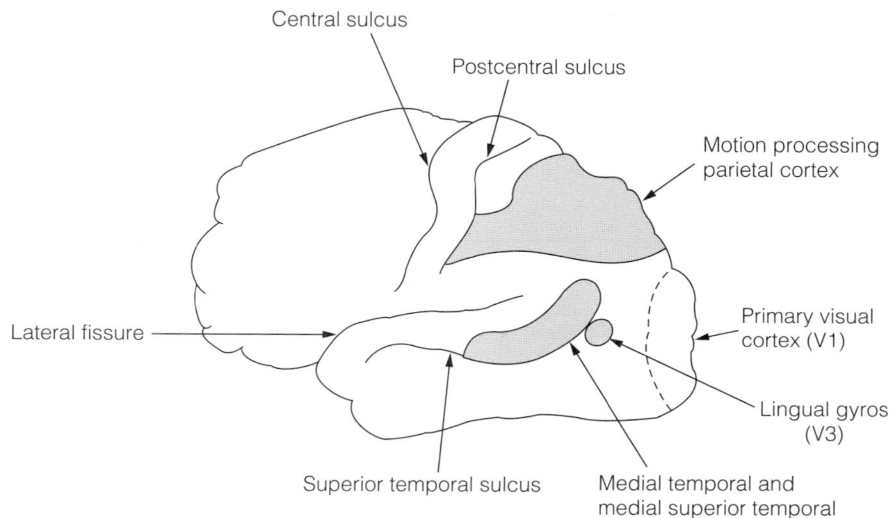

FIGURE 12.3 The **medial temporal** and **medial superior temporal** regions of the cortex most involved in motion perception.

these neurons differ from motion-sensitive neurons in the primary visual cortex (Area V1) is that they have large receptive fields. In contrast to the receptive field of a neuron in V1, which may be only a few minutes of arc in size, the receptive fields of neurons in V5 may extend up to 1/4 of the entire visual field. This has been interpreted as meaning that these neurons are actually integrating the activity of many motion-sensitive neurons in V1.

The unique roles played by neurons in areas V1 and V5 can be seen by using specifically designed motion stimuli. One of these looks very much like the "snow" on an untuned TV channel. It is actually a rapid series of video frames containing dots in randomly chosen locations. This is illustrated in Figure 12.4. The correlation between the movements of dots in successive frames is called **motion coherence.** If the dots in each frame are placed randomly, without any regard to previous or successive frames, then the motion coherence is said to be zero. However, if 50% of the dots in successive frames move in the same direction, with a consistent trajectory, then the motion coherence of the display increases to 50%. Finally, if all of the dots are matched, so that the entire screen of dots is translated in the same direction and by the same amount from frame to frame, then the motion coherence is 100%.

Human observers are highly sensitive to small correlations in these displays, sometimes being able to detect motion coherence that involves as few as 5% of the dots. The most optimal conditions seem to occur when the correlated dots are moving together at about 2 degrees per second, which involves a dot displacement of 0.1 degree every 50 ms. Sensitivity also increases with the size of the visual field that is taken up by the display. Unlike many other psychophysical tasks, which do not improve when the display grows larger than about 1 degree, sensitivity to motion coherence continues to improve until the displays are about 20 degrees in diameter.

Studies of monkeys have shown that only the neurons in Area V5 are sensitive to the global direction of motion in displays such as these (Movshon & Newsome, 1992). Neurons in Area V1, because of their small receptive field size, are only sensitive to the direction of motion for a single dot in a small region of the display. As a result, these neurons are unable to distinguish a dot that is moving coherently with other dots from a dot that is moving completely independently. In sharp contrast to this, a neuron in Area V5 will fire selectively to a random dot display when the motion coherence is as low as 5%.

One of the most exciting aspects of this research is that the thresholds determined for individual neurons match almost exactly with those determined from the behavior of a monkey who has been trained to indicate the perceived direction of motion in a random dot display. That is, the degree of coherence required to activate an individual neuron is the same degree of coherence required for the accurate discrimination of motion as indicated by the monkey's responses. To further confirm this relationship, studies of small lesions in Area V5 in one hemisphere of the brain have been shown to decrease the behavioral sensitivity of the monkey to coherent motion displays in the opposite visual field. For the visual field corresponding to the unlesioned hemisphere, however, the threshold for motion coherence is unimpaired (Movshon & Newsome, 1992).

The importance of the temporal lobe (including V5) in motion perception has been made vividly apparent in clinical cases where patients with temporal lobe damage can still see stationary shapes and colors but can no longer perceive motion. One of the most famous cases of a cortical form of motion blindness occurred in a woman who suffered bilateral brain damage, including damage to the temporal lobes. She reported that she had no trouble recognizing a car when she saw one, but she was no longer able to judge its speed. The simple act of pouring a cup of coffee also became virtually impossible, since

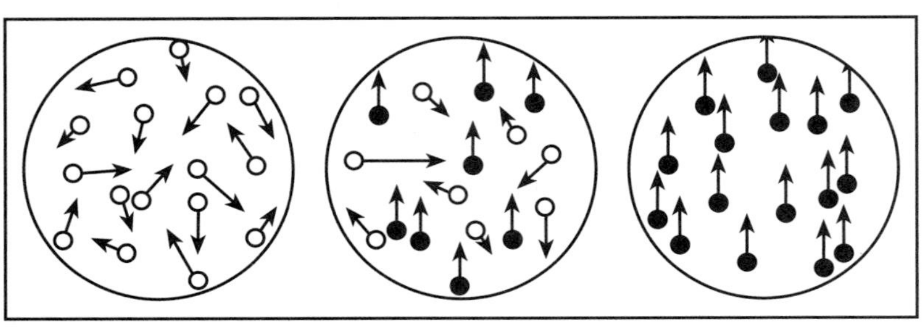

FIGURE 12.4 Schematic illustrations of three random dot kinematograms with different degrees of motion coherence. (A) Motion is said to have 0% coherence because there is no relationship between the locations of dots in successive frames. (B) Motion is partially coherent motion because half (50%) of the dots have the same trajectory in successive frames. (C) Motion is completely coherent (100%) because all dots move in the same direction and at the same speed.

the woman could no longer see the dynamic flow of the fluid nor the steady rise of the liquid level (Hess, Baker & Zihl, 1989; Zihl, von Cramon, & Mai, 1983).

STIMULUS FACTORS IN MOTION PERCEPTION

Generally speaking, there are two principal ways by which we perceive motion. The first involves detecting shifts in the relative positions of parts of the visual image; the second involves using our eyes to follow a moving target. Many researchers believe these involve different perceptual systems, so we will call the system that responds to image changes the **image-retina system** and the one that interprets motion from our eye and head movements the **eye-head system** (Gregory, 1978). Since the image-retina system involves only optical image changes, we will consider it first, postponing our discussion of the eye-head system until we consider the important role played by visual motion in tracking objects with our eyes.

Motion Thresholds

We begin with the question of how much movement is needed in the image before we can perceive motion. To answer this question, we usually measure a movement threshold for a single dot or edge, just as we measured thresholds for the minimum amount of light or sound needed for sensation (see Chapter 2). Our sensitivity to the movement of an external target depends on several variables. In experimental settings, absolute movement thresholds have usually been studied using a small point of light that moves against some sort of stationary background, as in one of the earliest studies by Hermann Aubert (1886). He found that observers could detect the movement of a luminous dot in the dark, 50 cm from the eye, when it was moving at about 2.5 mm per second (which is about one fifth of a degree of visual angle per second).

Target movement alone, however, is not enough to allow us to describe motion thresholds. Motion perception often involves the recognition that relationships are changing between visual stimuli, which means that we are also dealing with relative movement thresholds. Some interactions among visual targets, such as occur when part of a moving surface systematically blocks our view of another surface, or exposes our view to a new surface, can assist the perception of motion (Kaiser & Calderone, 1991). Perhaps the best situation for detecting target movement is when there is some motionless reference point, such as a stationary feature nearby or on the background, which forms the **visual context.** An example might be a stationary square frame surrounding the target. Under these circumstances we find that observers are much more sensitive (e.g., Palmer, 1986). The minimum movement that can be detected in the presence of a stationary visual context is about 0.25 mm per second or 0.03 degree of visual angle per second (as compared to 0.2 deg/sec for a single target with no stationary context). This is an incredible degree of movement sensitivity. If a snail were to crawl across a desk 1.5 m wide at this rate, it would take it 1 hour and 40 minutes to go from end to end. Such motion sensitivity does not require movement across the field, but it can also be found when detecting small oscillations or "vibrations" in visual targets (e.g., Lappin, Donnelly, & Kojima, 2001).

Our ability to judge the difference between two velocities is similarly facilitated by the presence of other stimuli that are stationary (Bonnet, 1984). Some researchers contend that the image-retina system really involves two different sources of motion information. The first is **subject-relative change,** where the only information is the movement of the target relative to the observer's position in space. The second is called **object-relative change,** which is the movement of target relative to other objects. This kind of motion creates a change in the overall configuration of the visible pattern and therefore may involve processes similar to form perception (e.g., Mack, Heuer, Fendrich, Vilardi, & Chambers, 1985; Wallach, Becklen, & Nitzberg, 1985). Of these two types of change, measurements of detection and discrimination show that humans are much more sensitive to object-relative change. This advantage for object-relative change is also in evidence very early in life, with human infants being able to demonstrate their awareness of this kinds of change as early as 8 weeks of age (Dannemiller & Freeland, 1991).

The Motion Correspondence Problem

As soon as we consider the possibility of seeing the motion of more than a single dot or edge in an image several new problems arise. One of these is the **motion correspondence problem.** Consider the stimulus situation shown in Figure 12.5. At the start (Time 1) three spots of light appear at one side of a screen. A fraction of a second later they are replaced by three identical spots of light on the other side of the screen (Time 2). What the observer sees is motion, as though each of the three spots had moved across the screen toward the right. However, this is not the only logically possible motion. Since all of the spots are identical, there are a large number of different patterns of movement that might have been seen, and two examples (which observers never actually see) are shown at the bottom of Figure 12.5.

The reason that some paths of motion are seen and others are not has to do with the fact that the perception of motion seems to follow certain rules (e.g., Dawson, 1991). These rules include a preference for proximity in space—the shortest possible movement between two images will tend to be seen (Burt & Sperling, 1981)—and also a preference for proximity in time—the motion that requires the slowest speed will tend to be seen (Dawson & Pylyshyn, 1988). Thus the correspondence problem is most often solved perceptually by following the shortest distance between two neighboring stimuli in the longest period of time.

The Aperture Problem

A second problem that occurs with multiple stimuli in motion has to do with the inherent ambiguity of the signal registered by each individual Reichardt-type motion sensor. Recall that each such sensor can be specifically tuned for motion in a given direction and of a specific velocity. The problem arises when one considers the large number of different stimuli that can activate any single detector. Consider the Reichardt detector shown in Figure 12.2. It would be activated by a vertically oriented edge moving horizontally (from left to right) across the retina at a given speed. However, it would also be activated by an obliquely oriented edge that passed over it more quickly. In fact, a very large number of combinations involving orientation and speed of a moving contour would activate the same unit. In principle, then, the output of a single Reichardt detector does not specify the motion of an edge with very much precision. It can only indicate that motion has been detected in a very general direction (e.g., rightward) and of a very general speed (e.g., moderate).

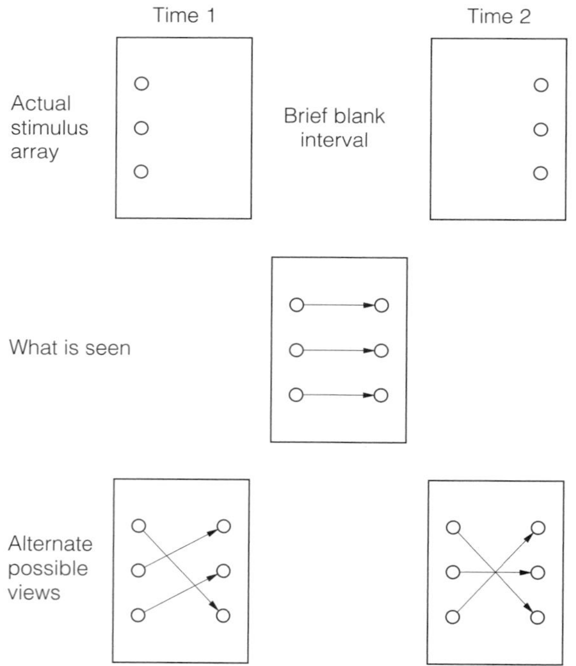

FIGURE 12.5 The correspondence problem. A stimulus involving three spots of light flashed on one side of a screen and then the other a moment later is seen as the simple apparent movement of the three spots of light as shown in the central frame. Logically, however, there are many other forms of motion that could be seen, including those shown in the bottom frames.

This is called the **aperture problem,** because if we were viewing figures moving behind a stationary aperture we might get erroneous movement information. The nature of this problem is illustrated in Figure 12.6, where the different local motion signals correspond to different regions of a simple shape such as a diamond. Depending on where each aperture is, the movement of a local edge of the diamond shape is consistent with different motion signals. In order to see the motion of the shape as a whole, information from these various apertures must be integrated. Studies of the responses of single neurons in the monkey to stimuli such as these indicate that while the neurons in cortical area V1 are sensitive to the local or aperture motion signal (e.g., orthogonal to the local edge orientation), neurons in cortical area V5 are sensitive to the direction of motion of the shape as a whole (Movshon, Adelson, Gizzi, & Newsome, 1985).

An understanding of the aperture problem gives us insight into the illusion we introduced in Figure 12.1. Look at it once again. When your head moves toward the image, the interior rings of elements appear to move in a counterclockwise direction while the outside ring of elements appear to move in a clockwise direction. Let us consider in detail for a moment only the interior ring of elements, which is illustrated in schematic form in Figure 12.7. From your understanding of the discussion so far, you will be confident that when your head moves toward the image, the retinal image of the ring will be growing in size. This is illustrated by the four bold arrows that surround the ring in Figure 12.7. Now imagine that Reichardt-type motion detectors are analyzing the dominant direction of motion at each element location in the ring. Because these elements consist of edges that are all oriented at 45 degrees with respect to the circle, the

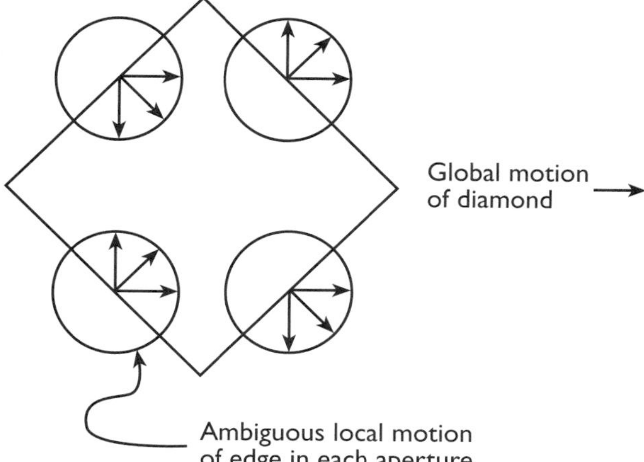

FIGURE 12.6 The aperture problem. An object in motion, such as the diamond shape, has both a motion that corresponds to the object as a whole (global motion) and a number of motion signals that differ from one another (local motions). Because individual motion sensors consider only a small region of any given image, information from the local signals must be integrated by the visual system in order to determine the global direction of an object in motion.

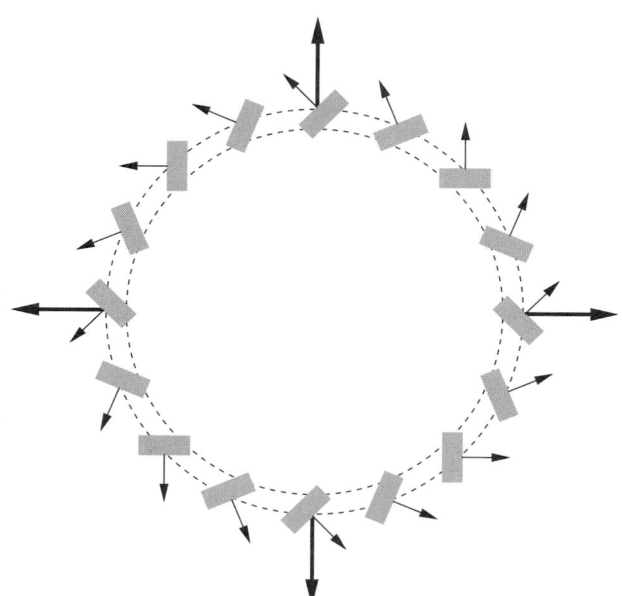

FIGURE 12.7 A schematic illustration of the global (bold arrows) and local (light arrows) directions of motion for the interior ring in Figure 12.1, when your head is moving toward the center of the ring.

local motion at each element location will be at an oblique angle with respect to the circle. This is illustrated by the light oblique arrows that surround the ring. Your visual system is thus faced with putting together two different pieces of information with respect to the motions on your retina from the inner ring. First, as your head moves forward the ring grows in its overall size, which is readily attributed to the fact that your head is getting closer to the page on which the image is resting. Second, the local motion is generally in a counterclockwise direction. On the basis of these two pieces of information, is not unreasonable for your visual system to come to the conclusion that although the ring remains the same size when your head moves forward and backward, it is undergoing rotational motion in a direction orthogonal to the local element edges.

Induced Motion

Another problem associated with the perception of motion in complex arrays involves determining which objects are moving and which are stationary. A well-known example of a misattribution of motion was first described by Duncker (1929), who studied the perception of a bright dot displayed in an otherwise featureless dark room. When the dot was moved very slowly, observers were not certain whether or not it was moving. However, when a stationary dot was placed near the moving dot (in effect becoming the visual context), it became clear that one of the dots was in motion (due to the object-relative changes). Curiously though, observers could not identify which of the two dots was moving. Duncker next changed the context stimulus by making it a rectangular luminous frame that was stationary and surrounded the dot. Under these circumstances there was no ambiguity and observers were able to tell that the dot rather than the frame was in motion.

Duncker next varied the conditions so that the dot was stationary and the surrounding rectangular frame was moving. Under these circumstances an illusion appeared, in that observers reported that the stationary dot was moving rather than the frame. Duncker called this **induced motion,** since the perceived movement of the dot was brought about by the real movement of the surrounding context. This is similar to the perception that the moon is moving behind the clouds, when actually the clouds are moving quickly while the moon's motion is actually negligible in comparison. The clouds provide a surrounding context that is in motion and, consistent with the principle that Duncker discovered in the laboratory, they induce an apparent motion of the not-detectably moving moon. Under appropriate circumstances this can produce massive mislocalizations when you try to reach for a target that is apparently moving but physically is not (e.g., Soechting, Engel, & Flanders, 2001).

Induced movement effects are most dramatic when the context is moving slowly rather than quickly (Wallach & Becklen, 1983). Square frame shapes are more effective than circular frames and large surrounds are more effective than small ones (Michael & Sherrick, 1986), although it appears that it is the part of the visual context that is closest to the target that is most responsible for the illusion (Schulman, 1979). Furthermore, in order to induce motion, the target and the background must be at the same distance from the observer. If the frame that supplies the context is too far in front of or behind the target, no motion will be induced (Gogel and Koslow, 1972). You can produce induced motion yourself by following the instructions in Demonstration Box 12.2.

Real versus Apparent Motion

In addition to induced motion, there are many other circumstances where the perception of motion does not require a stimulus that is actually moving in the world. All that is required for a vivid impression of motion is that a stimulus be appropriately displaced in space and time. This observation has been used to great advantage by advertisers and lighted sign manufacturers in every major city of the world. The signs that appear to have moving messages in them, such as bouncing arrows or borders in motion, actually consist of a series of stationary light bulbs that flash on and off in succession.

One of the early psychological researchers who studied this phenomenon was Max Wertheimer (1912). Beginning with two lines separated in space, which could be flashed on and off sequentially, he varied the time interval between the offset of the first line and the onset of the second (we call this variable period the **interstimulus interval**). When the interstimulus interval was very brief, observers saw two lines appear simultaneously, because of the phenomenon of visible persistence that we discussed in Chapter 11. If the interval was long, the observers saw a line appear and disappear, followed by a second line appearing in a different location. However, for some intermediate interstimulus intervals Wertheimer's observers reported that they saw a line appear and then move from the first position in space to the second. Although initially called *phi movement,* we now refer to this experience of movement between successively presented stationary stimuli as **apparent motion,** to distinguish it from **real motion,** where the stimulus actually occupies each location in space between its initial point and its ending point. You can demonstrate this type of apparent movement for yourself by following the instructions in Demonstration Box 12.3.

The fact that the eye and brain can be fooled into seeing motion from a rapidly presented sequence of still stimulus frames might seem to be an interesting but not very useful curiosity. Yet every time you go to the cinema, you are paying to see two hours of an apparent motion illusion. Each frame in the film you watch is actually stationary, being exchanged for a new frame about 24 times a second. Television and computer screens work in much the same way, with static frames changing about 30 times a second in television and 60 times a second on your personal computer.

If the perception of movement that occurs when viewing apparent motion differs little, if at all, from the perception of movement derived from objects that are really moving in the three-dimensional world, you might be tempted to ask why it is important that researchers even make the distinction between real and apparent move-

DEMONSTRATION BOX 12.2

INDUCED MOVEMENT

To induce movement in a stationary target, all you need is a sheet of clear cellophane or glass and a sheet of white paper. In the middle of the white paper draw a small dot. On the clear cellophane draw a large rectangle, about 10 cm by 16 cm (4 in by 6 in), using a felt-tip marker or a grease pencil. Now lay the clear sheet over the paper so that the dot is enclosed by the rectangle and is near one of its sides. Look steadily at the dot and *slowly* move the cellophane across the paper. You will notice that the dot appears to move in the direction opposite the motion of the rectangle. The effect is strongest when the dot is near the sides of the rectangle, where object-relative change plays a role. Increasing the speed of movement should reduce the amount of induced motion you percieve. Why?

DEMONSTRATION BOX 12.3

APPARENT MOVEMENT

To see apparent movement similar to that described by Wertheimer, simply hold your index finger vertically a short distance in front of your nose. Look at any distant target (such as a mark on the far wall of the room). Relax your eyes and alternately wink each eye. You should see your finger in a different place with each eye. Now, begin to rhythmically open and close each eye in turn (remembering to keep your eyes relaxed). At slow rates you should see your finger "jump" from side to side; however, at some moderate rate of winking you should see the finger appear to actually "move" from one position to the other.

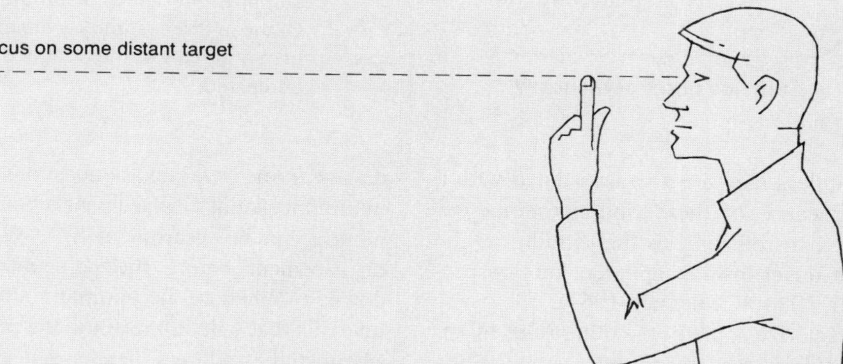

ment. The answer, as is so often the case, depends on the perspective we take. From the point of view of the neural motion signals produced in the brain, the two types of stimuli are indistinguishable. Both will stimulate Reichardt-type motion sensors in exactly the same way, provided that the spatial and temporal displacements are comparable (Burr, Ross, & Morrone, 1986). In fact, apparent motion can cause motion adaptation effects similar to those that cause the waterfall illusion (cf. Piehler & Pantle, 2001). However, from the perspective of the person designing a moving visual display there is a great deal of difference. In a display with objects that actually move over time, the observer's perception of motion will be limited only by the temporal and spatial limits of the visual system. In a display consisting of apparent motion, the perception of motion will also depend on the rules used by the visual system to fill in the physically absent motion information. This is not to say that apparent motion and real motion are processed identically at all levels of the visual system. Recent fMRI studies on humans suggests that the functional equivalence of apparent motion and real motion occurs at the primary visual cortex (V1). At the higher levels of visual processing, namely V5, the response are different, suggesting that the medial temporal cortex is actively involved in "constructing" the apparent motion out of the nonmoving input displays (Muckli, et al., 2002).

Our impression of apparent motion is dependent on both the distance between the stimuli at successive points in time and the time that elapses between the successive presentations. Generally speaking, when the stimuli are separated by larger distances, longer time intervals between the stimuli are needed for apparent motion to be perceived (Farrell, 1983). However, careful analysis of the temporal aspects of apparent motion displays reveals that there are really three different variables involved. These are illustrated in Figure 12.8. In addition to the **interstimulus interval,** which we have already discussed, there is the duration of the stimulus in each frame (**frame duration**), as well as the time that elapses between the onset of one frame and the onset of the next frame. This variable is often referred to as **stimulus onset asynchrony,** or simply **SOA.** Systematic comparisons of the effects of each of these variables, alone and in combination, have revealed that the primary determinant of the perception of motion is the stimulus onset asynchrony. Manipulations of frame duration and interstimulus interval do not have much influence on the per-

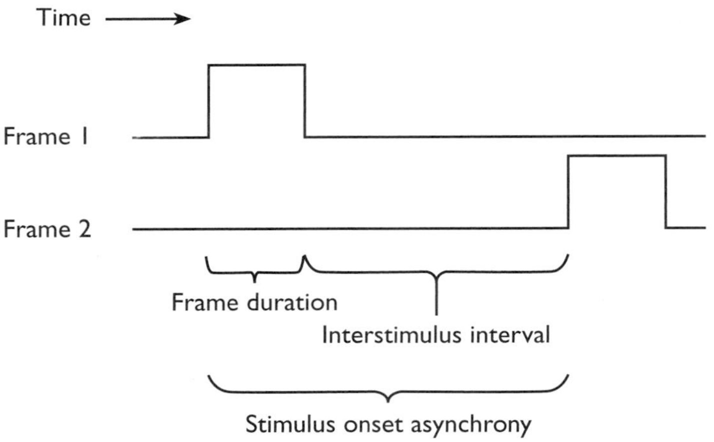

FIGURE 12.8 The three temporal variables of apparent motion displays: frame duration, interstimulus interval, and stimulus onset asynchrony. Of these three, stimulus onset asynchrony is the best predictor of the quality of motion that will be perceived.

ception of motion unless they are also associated with a change in SOA. Because of these findings, some researchers have taken to referring to this finding as the **SOA law** (or **onset-onset law**) of apparent motion perception (Breitmeyer, 1984; Kahneman, 1967).

In trying to characterize some of the other rules of apparent motion perception, researchers have come to the conclusion that there is an important and fundamental difference between two kinds of apparent motion displays. One kind of display corresponds to the motion sequences shown on television and in movies, where each successive frame lasts only a few milliseconds and the spatial displacements of an object from frame to frame are only a few minutes of arc. These are called **short-range motion** displays. The other kind of display is like those studied by the early Gestalt psychologists (e.g., Wertheimer, 1912) and as seen in some neon advertising signs, which involve apparent motion of only one or two objects over much larger spatial displacements with longer temporal intervals. These are called **long-range motion** displays.

Short-Range Motion Perception. The short-range motion displays that are usually studied in the laboratory consist of randomly located dots in each frame of the sequence. We have already discussed one version of these, the random-dot displays resembling an untuned TV channel that used to study motion coherence. A more general name that is often used to refer to random-dot displays used to create motion sequences is **random-dot kinematogram,** often abbreviated as **RDK.**

If we begin with a single frame of randomly located dots and create an RDK by displacing all of the dots, either horizontally or vertically, by the same amount in successive frames, we can ask questions such as, "What is the minimum spatial displacement over which the direction of motion can be discriminated?" "What is the maximum displacement before the perception of motion breaks down?" "What are the minimum and maximum temporal intervals that will still result in the perception of motion?" Many studies addressing such questions have shown that reliable motion perception only occurs when the spatial displacements are small (around 5 to 15 minutes of arc) and the temporal intervals are short (around 20 to 80 milliseconds). With apparent motion generated in this way, as long as the dots in successive frames are of the same luminance, we can even produce motion aftereffects, similar to those described in Demonstration Box 12.1 (e.g., Anstis, 1978; Braddick, 1974; Nakayama, 1985).

Long-Range Motion Perception. Most of the long-range motion displays that have been studied consist of only a small number of stimuli. In these displays, motion is seen over distances much greater than the optimal 15 minutes of visual angle for short-range motion. Distances may actually include separations of many degrees across the visual field. The time between successive frames that produces the perception of motion can also be much longer; sometimes even longer than 200 ms. The perceptual processes for long-range motion are determined less by the stimulus factors and seem to be based on more complex inferential procedures. For instance, it often seems as though the brain is unwilling to conclude that the disappearance of one stimulus should be followed shortly thereafter by the sudden and independent appearance of an identical stimulus nearby. Therefore, an inference is made that the original stimulus must have moved to this new location. Described this way, the process seems to involve a form of "logic" or simplifying principle, which derives apparent motion as a reasonable interpretation of the stimulus changes observed (e.g., Rock, 1983).

Long-range apparent motion also demonstrates a good deal of "tolerance" in its interpretation of the way the correspondence problem should be solved. For example, suppose we present a display of alternately flashing and spatially separated stimuli at a rate we know produces the sensation of motion. Now suppose that the target on the right is red and the one on the left is green. Will we still see motion? The answer is that we will see a target both moving and changing color as it moves. We can get apparent motion not only between targets of different colors but between targets with different shapes, sizes, brightnesses, and orientations, and in most of these situations the target seems to be transformed while it is moving (e.g., Anstis & Mather, 1985; Kolers & von Grunau, 1976).

The stimulus inputs to the long-range motion process can also be considerably more abstract than stimuli for the short-range process (Cavanagh & Mather, 1989). Figure 12.9 illustrates this point in two ways. When Figure 12.9A is alternated with Figure 12.9B every 200 ms or so, observers see a dot-covered square jumping back and forth with its corners resting on the quartets of large black disks (Ramachandran & Anstis, 1986). To appreciate how much interpretation is involved in this perception, note that the "jumping square" is defined by illusory or subjective edges and not any physical edges. The dots covering the subjective square do not move nor are they displaced physically at all (this means that the retinal images of the dots are fixed in the same place regardless of whether the square is seen at the right or left). Yet in our perception there is apparent movement of the dots. It appears as though the square not only jumps back and forth, but that it takes the dots covering it with them. Thus all of the dots are also seen jumping right and left, despite the fact that nothing is actually moving across the retina.

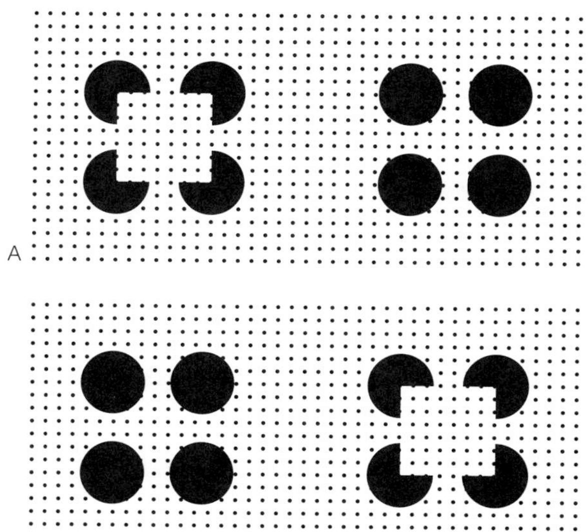

FIGURE 12.9 Two stimulus displays (A and B) that are alternated to produce the apparent motion of subjective squares.

Long-range apparent motion adapts flexibly to other conditions in the visual field. If you place an object in the pathway of the apparent movement, the perceived path of motion will seem to deflect around the object (Berbaum & Lenel, 1983). If a particular pathway is suggested, by, for instance, briefly flashing a curved path between the two flickering stimuli, the apparent motion will seem to follow that pathway (Shepard & Zare, 1983). If the stimulus looks like a solid object, the path the apparent motion follows can be complex and even involve motions that appear to be three dimensional (rather than simply side to side) (e.g., Hecht & Proffitt, 1991). It is as if the observer was trying to "figure out" how the object could have gotten from the position and orientation that it had at Time 1 to the position and orientation that it has at Time 2, while still remaining a solid and real object. All these factors suggest that higher-level cognitive processing mechanisms play a role in the perception of apparent motion in long-range displays (Rock, 1983).

Some researchers have considered the empirical differences between the perception of motion in short-range and long-range displays and have theorized that perception in each is determined by two fundamentally different systems. One system may be governed by primitive and preattentive short-range processes and the other by cognitively influenced and attention-limited long-range processes (Braddick, 1980; Petersik, 1989). Others have reasoned that the distinction is really one of different types of motion sensors, the short range displays activating Reichardt-type sensors, with small time and space parameters, that take only luminance changes as input. The long-range displays in turn are said to activate sensors with much larger spatio-temporal windows that are stimulated by luminance, color, texture, and even motion (Burr, Ross, & Morrone, 1986; Cavanagh & Mather, 1989).

THE MANY PURPOSES OF MOTION PERCEPTION

Just as the perception of color has a wide variety of different uses, ranging from its assistance in depth perception, to object identification, to the determination of whether a fruit is ripe enough to eat, so too does motion perception play many different roles. It is a mistake to think that just because a process such as motion perception is very basic to the visual system as a whole, it therefore will only be used in very stereotyped ways. In this section we will examine the role played by an analysis of motion in functions ranging from the breaking of camouflage, to the perception of "blame" in an interaction between two objects, and to our ability to recognize someone based solely on the way they move.

Figure-Ground Relations

One of the most basic functions of motion perception is that of segmenting figure from ground. In many simple animals, such as sea crabs and frogs, the visual system is relatively inactive unless a moving stimulus is present. It is as though these simple visual systems are interested only in "seeing" what is changing in their environment. Things that change correspond to "figure" or objects of possible interest, whether they be possible enemies, mates, or food.

In human vision, the way that motion assists in determining figure-ground relationships is described by the Gestalt principle of **common fate** (Wertheimer, 1923). Simply stated, this principle states that portions of an image that move together tend to be part of the same object or surface. The perceptual power of this law can be observed by following the instructions in Demonstration Box 12.4. Because of common fate, the perception of motion helps us identify objects, aside from any precise estimates of speed or direction. Those portions of the image that move together (or don't move when the background is moving) will tend to stand out perceptually and are thus excellent candidates for closer attention by the visual system.

Another example of how motion perception helps us divide the world into coherent figures, objects, and surfaces is seen in the random dot kinematogram illustrated in Figure 12.10. This type of display has been used to study the rules of perceptual grouping when relative motion differences are the only cues to shape and surface boundaries. The construction of these displays is very similar to the random dot stereograms discussed in Chapter 9, except that the two frames are now shown successively in time rather than stereoscopically. In both displays there is a region of dots in one frame that has been displaced horizontally relative to the same region of dots in the other frame. When the two frames are shown in alternating fashion, the displaced region appears to oscillate horizontally over time. Not only does this figural region segregate perceptually from the background as a distinct shape, but it also appears to be closer to the observer than the background.

The appearance of the oscillating figure as nearer than the background is consistent with what is happening to the individual dots at the edge of the figure. Over time, dots in the background are being successively deleted and redrawn as the oscillating edge moves back and forth over the background (Shipley & Kellman, 1994; Yonas & Craton, 1987, 1990). These are therefore the local cues in the random dot kinematogram to the depth cue identified as **motion parallax** in Chapter 9.

DEMONSTRATION BOX 12.4

COMMON FATE

For this demonstration you will need two sheets of transparent plastic, a pen that will write on the sheets, and a white piece of paper. The sheets and pens used for making displays visible by overhead projectors will serve the purpose very well. On one of the sheets draw 30 to 40 same-size dots at random so that they look like they have been sprinkled on the sheet. On the other, use dots to draw a simple shape such as a triangle or a letter of the alphabet, using only 4 to 6 dots. Be careful to make these dots the same size and shape as the random dots on the first sheet. Now place the two sheets of transparency on top of one another, preferably on a white sheet of paper. You should no longer be able to see the shape outlined by the few dots on the second sheet. Now keep one of the sheets stationary and move the other. Suddenly the shape will spring to life, either as a moving figure over a stationary field of dots or as a stationary figure in a moving field of dots. This illustrates the Gestalt law of common fate. Note how quickly your ability to identify the dots belonging to the shape disappears once the motion stops. This is also a very simple example of a **structure from motion** display, which we will discuss later in the chapter.

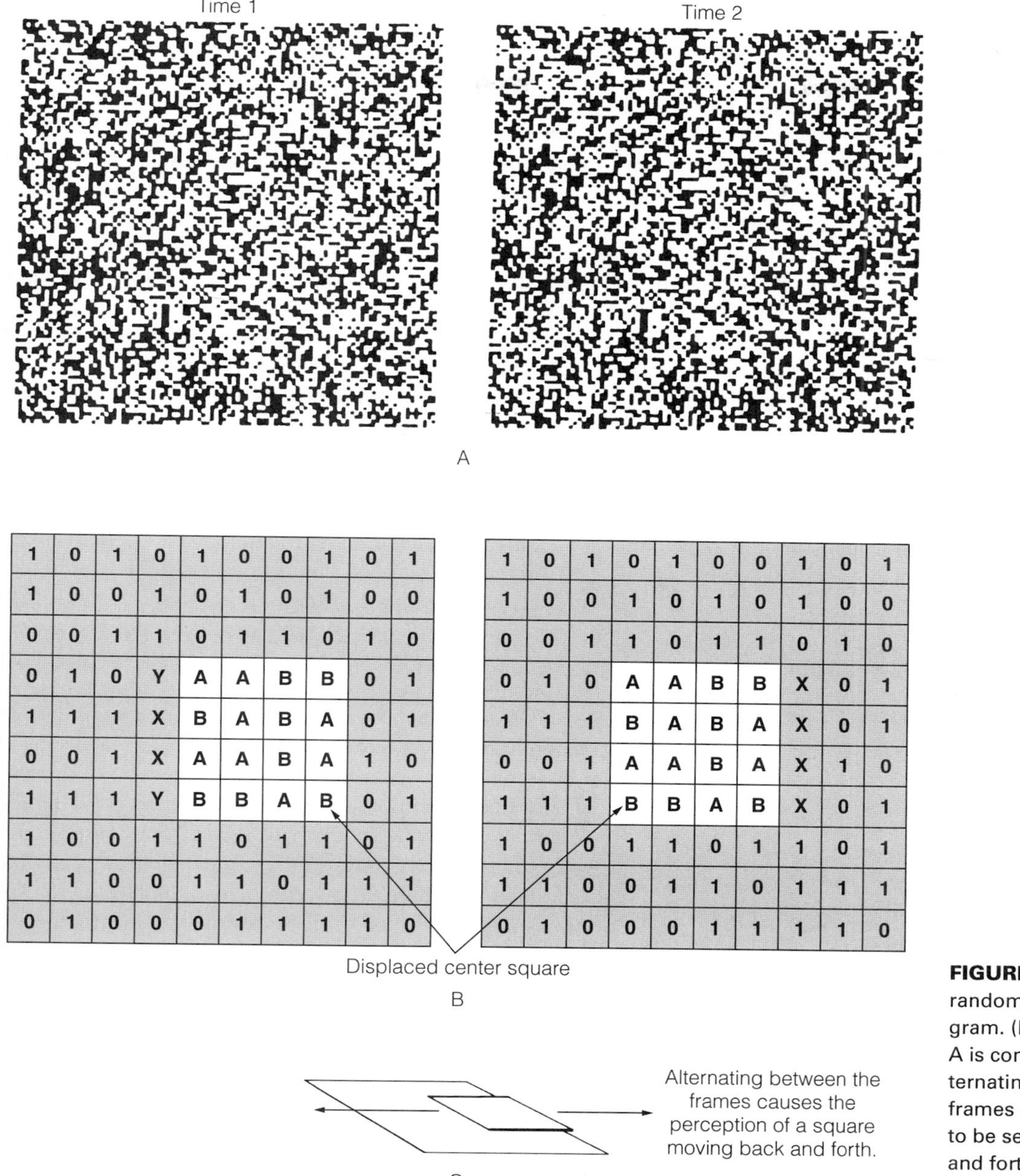

FIGURE 12.10 (A) A random-dot kinematogram. (B) Details of how A is constructed. (C) Alternating between the frames causes a square to be seen moving back and forth in front of the background.

Object Shape and Depth

A function of motion perception that is closely related to figure-ground assignment, but that is even more sophisticated, is the perception of object shape and three-dimensional surface structure. Consider those portions of a three-dimensional object that are visible from a single snapshot. Now compare the information gained from watching the same object move through space, or by moving around the object when it is stationary. In both cases, the visual system is given multiple views or vantage points of the same object. Just as the two views given by each of the two eyes can help to resolve the three-dimensional structure of an image, so too can the multiple images acquired through motion be used to determine its three-dimensional structure.

Some subtle modifications to a random dot kinematogram can make it useful for studying the role of motion in the perception of three-dimensional shapes and surfaces. Consider the display illustrated in Figure 12.11. It starts once again as a random collection of dots in the first frame but in successive frames each dot is displaced along the trajectory that would correspond to the location of a randomly chosen dot on the surface of a transparent cylinder. Observers viewing this display see a vivid image of a transparent cylinder rotating in depth. The dots corresponding to the surface that are depicted further away from the observer are seen as moving in a different direction and at a different depth plane from the dots corresponding to the apparently nearer surface.

Demonstrations such as the one illustrated in Figure 12.11 show that relative motion information alone is sufficient to enable the processes responsible for shape perception to operate. The process is sometimes called **structure from motion** by researchers who are interested in the computational aspects of three-dimensional vision. Detailed analyses of the geometry of the displays that produce these percepts have revealed that the three-dimensional structure of a rigid object can be determined mathematically from a minimum of four dots viewed over a minimum of three different frames in the sequence (Ullman, 1979). However, the perceptual system seems to ignore these mathematical limits and stable perception of structure from motion can be obtained by as few as three dots (Caudek, Domini, & Di Luca, 2002). It does so by integrating the motions across time and thus obtaining additional information to form a stable percept.

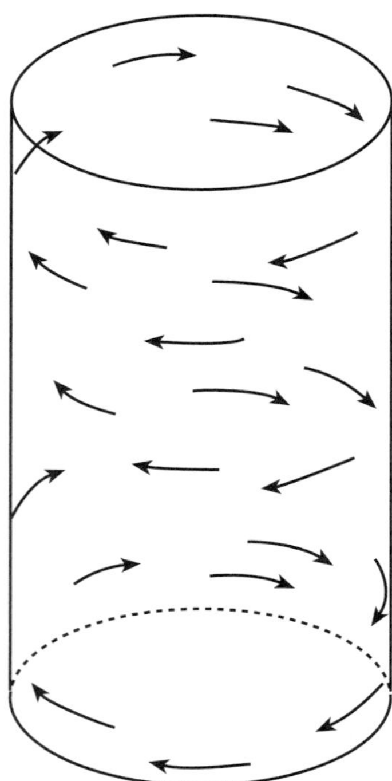

FIGURE 12.11 A random-dot kinematogram, which appears to the viewer as a cylinder rotating about its vertical axis in three dimensions. Because observers see the dots as transparent moving surfaces, even though there is no shading or edge information in the image, these displays are used to study the perception of three-dimensional structure from motion.

It is also worth reminding the reader that the structure from motion problem is closely related to the **kinetic depth effect** described in Chapter 9. There we saw that the three-dimensional shape of an object could be determined quite easily from only its silhouette, provided that the object was undergoing rotation about one of its axes. With the random-dot kinematogram shown in Figure 12.11, we see that the three-dimensional shape of an object can be recovered successfully by the visual system even when the silhouette of the object is no longer explicitly present.

Although the physiological basis of structure from motion is not yet clear, it is again Area V5 that seems to be implicated, specifically the dorsal section of the medial superior temporal cortex. Here about 18% of the neurons respond selectively to motion cues corresponding to tilted surfaces and 24% to those indicating slanted surfaces (Sugihara, Murakami, Shenoy, Andersen, & Komatsu, 2002). Thus V5 is involved in "constructing" a percept using a motion component—here an object and surfaces out of motion cues.

Object Identification

The motion characteristics of an object are often themselves powerful cues to the identity of that object. In fact, under certain circumstances, some objects can only be identified by their unique pattern of motion. Take, for example, the problem of identifying a bird in flight. From a sufficient distance, the shape, size, and color cues of the bird have been rendered essentially useless; only a moving dark blob can be discerned. However, the motion cues still tell a powerful story. The larger the bird, the slower will be the beat of its wings. By this technique alone, a large raptor such as an eagle can be distinguished from a finch or a starling. Expert bird watchers are in fact able to use motion cues alone to discriminate birds of the same size and color, such as bald eagles versus turkey vultures and golden eagles versus hawks.

One of the more finely tuned skills that humans possess in this regard is the ability to identify other humans and their activities solely from the patterns of motion made by their trunk and limbs. Studies examining this ability refer to it as **biological motion** perception (e.g., Johansson, 1976a). In a series of studies now considered to be classics in the area of motion perception, Gunnar Johansson (Biography Box 12.2) began by asking "Will an observer be able to identify the motions associated with the act of walking even in the absence of any other information, such as sight of the person?" To answer this question Johansson developed a clever technique. He attached small lights to the major joints of an individual (shoulders, elbows, wrists, hips, knees, and ankles), as shown in Figure 12.12A. He then made a motion picture film of the person as he moved around in a darkened room. When observers later watched the film, they only saw a pattern of lights moving about in total darkness. Nonetheless, they were able to identify the pattern as a person walking or running, even when they only got to see the motion for as short an exposure as 200 ms (Johansson, von Hofsten, & Jansson, 1980). Observers were also easily able to detect abnormalities, such as the simulation of a small limp.

In another experiment, two people with similar arrays of lights were filmed while performing a spirited folk dance. Figure 12.12B shows a series of positions from the folk dance in which the black dots mark the positions of the lights. Once again, even with only a moving pattern of lights, observers had no difficulty identifying the motion as a dancing couple (Johansson, 1976b). Infants as young as 4 months of age seem to notice that biological motion is different from other forms of motion and prefer to watch patterns of the sort we have been dis-

BIOGRAPHY BOX 12.2

I CAN TELL BY THE WAY YOU MOVE . . .

Gunnar Johansson (1911–) was a young Swedish vision researcher in the 1950s, working on his doctoral dissertation, when he discovered that the motion of human beings in action held a great deal of information regarding their identity and their intentions. To get at this motion information in a pure a form as possible, he attached small flashlight bulbs to the main joints of human actors and filmed them moving about in complete darkness. Observers who viewed the films, but did not know how they were created, had no trouble seeing vivid impressions of human figures. Using only these movies containing a few isolated points of light in motion, they could identify whether the actors were male or female, and they could identify the activities the actors were engaged in such as dancing, walking, or participating in gymnastics. Observers were even able to specifically identify their friends by observing these moving points of light alone.

This pioneering research has had an enormous influence on the field of vision research, since it helped to isolate the critical information used by humans in their analysis of visual motion. At the same time, it has had an equally large influence on the study of human movement and kinematics and on the analysis of motion by artificial seeing machines. The American Psychological Association honored him with a Distinguished Scientific Career Award in 1986.

Gunnar Johansson began as a professor in the Department of Psychology at Uppsala University, Sweden, in 1956. At the age of 80, when he was still active in research, his department honored him with a symposium that was attended by many of the researchers he had influenced with his research. These papers have been collected in a book edited by Jansson, Bergstrom, and Epstein (1994), appropriately titled *Perceiving Events and Objects.*

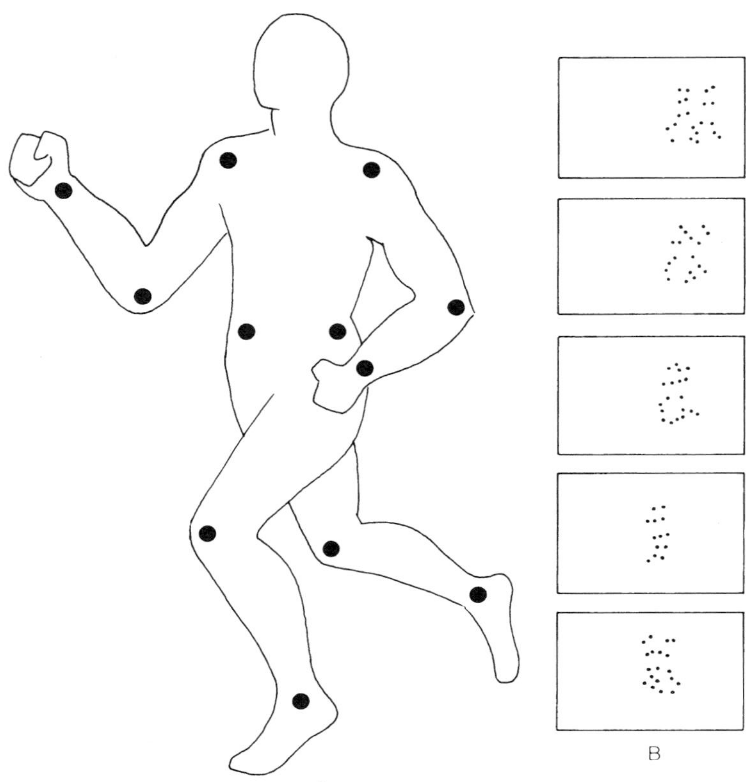

FIGURE 12.12 An example of the type of displays used by investigators to study patterns of humans in motion. A indicates the positions of lights affixed to individuals and B shows a sequence of movement positions made by a dancing couple.

cussing, rather than random patterns of lights moving (Fox & McDaniel, 1982).

Our precision in recognizing individuals based only on their biological motion patterns is really striking. For example, in one study researchers photographed a group of people who were acquainted with one another. These people were photographed with only lighted portions of several joints visible. Several months later these same individuals were invited to watch the films and attempt to identify themselves and their friends in the motion picture. People were able to identify themselves and others correctly on many trials, although their performance was not perfect. The investigators also asked their observers how they went about making their identifications of various individuals in the film. People tended to mention a variety of motion components such as the speed, bounciness, and rhythm of the walker, the amount of arm swing, or the length of steps as features that allowed them to make their identification. In other studies, these same investigators found that observers could tell, even under these conditions, whether a person was a male or a female, despite seeing only a moving pattern of dots. In fact, it was not necessary for all the body joints to be represented in the light display for people to make correct identifications. Even when only the ankles were represented, observers could detect the sex of the walker. They could also make these gender identifications within about 5 seconds of viewing (e.g., Cutting & Kozlowski, 1977; Cutting & Proffitt, 1981). Thus, different motion patterns characterize each sex and each individual.

Much work is being done to determine the nature of the information used to identify individuals, and from this some fairly sophisticated computer programs have been developed to create simulated biological motion patterns. For instance, Cutting, Proffitt, and Kozlowski (1978) proposed that the torso of the body acts like a flat spring with the limbs in symmetrical motion around it. This, along with certain individual differences in bodily dimensions (such as the relative widths of the shoulders and hips), provides a center of movement that is not necessarily associated with any body part; however, it organizes the coherent motion of the body parts in an individual fashion making identification possible. Perhaps it is patterns of biological motion such as this that enable us to identify people in light too dim to allow us to see their faces. It also probably explains how you can identify people walking down the street, even though they may be too far away for you to make out their features or may have their backs to you.

Recent work suggests that biological motion may be of sufficient importance to our survival as to warrant its own specialized region of cortical processing (e.g., Pavlova, et al., 2003). Recent fMRI brain imaging studies suggest that the lingual gyrus, which is between the temporal cortex (containing V5) and the occipital cortex (see Figure 12.3) and probably corresponds to Area V3 in monkeys, is especially important in recognizing biological motion (Servos, Osu, Santi, & Kawato, 2002). Human movement images activate this area, and there is little overlap with the areas associated with object recognition or linear motion perception.

Event Perception

Motion perception is critical to our perception of larger event sequences that involve multiple objects and actors. In fact, it allows us to come to a conclusion about "what happened" and "whose fault it is" long before we have had the opportunity to consider the same events with conscious deliberation. While we might like to think that we don't necessarily "jump to conclusions" in our reasoning about the causes and effects of what we see, researchers have provided us with powerful demonstrations illustrating that this is, in fact, exactly what we do. Our visual systems seem to be designed at the simplest and earliest levels of analysis to draw conclusions about "cause." As with most illusions, this one probably works to our advantage most of the time, because we live in a world in which effects do have causes. But once we are disconnected from this world, through the use of artificial displays such as computer screens and animated movies, the processes leading to this illusion can be studied. Biography Box 12.3 introduces you to the pioneering researcher in this area, Albert Michotte.

Figure 12.13 illustrates a short movie sequence consisting of two identical looking disks, beginning with one on the left and one in the center. After a short time, the disk on the left moves right, toward the center disk. When it reaches the center disk it stops and the center disk moves at the same rate toward the right. This is a sequence of images in which there is an objective correlation between the movements of the two disks. The disk in the center moves in the same way as the disk on the left, but only after the disk on the left has moved to make contact with the center disk. Given such a correlation between the two disks, we should reasonably be able to see the events as corresponding to several different scenarios. We might see the two disks as each being moved by an outside force (a third unseen agent), we might see the two disks as each moving on their own (merely a coincidence or correlation), or we might see the first disk as causing the second disk to move (a causal connection).

Observers shown this movie invariably see the left disk as "hitting" the other one and thus causing it to move (e.g., Scholl & Tremoulet, 2000). This perception of causation is compelling and irresistible, even when you know that they are just two disks, programmed by another human, to move on the screen. You know full well that

BIOGRAPHY BOX 12.3

THE CARTOON SCREEN COMES TO LIFE

Albert Michotte (1881–1965), a professor at Louvain University in Belgium, opened up a new line of psychological research in 1946 when he published a book whose English title would eventually be, *The Perception of Causality.* To conduct this research, he constructed some elaborate mechanical contraptions that permitted him to manipulate the appearance of two objects on a projection screen. Each of the objects could move left and right at various speeds and with various delays. His approach was to show these displays to people and simply ask them to describe what they saw.

Among his most striking findings was that small variation in the movements of the objects produced large variation in the way observers described what they saw. Their verbal description included words attributing motivations, emotions, age, gender, and relationships between the two objects. They would say, for example, "The little ball is trying to play with the big ball, but the big ball doesn't want to play so he chases the little ball away. But the little ball is stubborn and keeps bothering the big ball. Finally, the big ball gets mad and leaves."

Today, animators take for granted the principles discovered by Michotte for the perception of causation and animacy. Ironically, over the same period vision scientists have been much slower to accept these principles as an integral aspect of their understanding of motion perception. For many of them it is simply too difficult to imagine that such emotionally laden concepts could be directly linked to the lowest levels of motion perception.

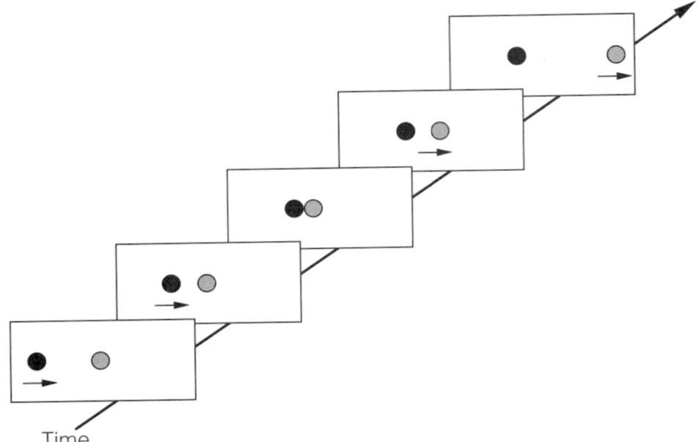

FIGURE 12.13 A short movie sequence that is seen by all human observers as involving a ball on the left bumping the ball on the right and then causing the ball on the right to move.

these are not billiard balls or bowling balls. Yet you can't help seeing the left disk making an impact that moves the other one, according to an everyday and unspoken understanding of the laws of physics. Your visual system simply leaps to this unfounded conclusion, as does the visual system of adult participants from non-Western cultures (Hashimoto, 1966; Morris & Peng, 1994) and infants as young as six months (Leslie, 1986; Schlottmann, 1999).

Other, equally unwarranted and yet equally irresistible conclusions are drawn by the visual system for even more complex causal connections. Several of these are illustrated in Figure 12.14 (White & Milne, 1997, 1998). In fact, it takes very little to create a movie in which observers see the geometric shapes as "being alive" and of having "goals" that they attempt to achieve through a variety of self-selected strategies. For instance, if a small disk moves around the screen in concert with a larger triangle (that is, the disk tends to move first and the triangle tends to lag behind in both space and time), then observers are sure that the triangle is "pursuing" the disk (Heider & Simmel, 1944). This conclusion becomes even more unavoidable if the small disk moves around some larger stationary shapes in such a way that it is no longer "in the triangle's line of sight." Of course, the triangle has no "sight" at all, but that doesn't prevent us from interpreting its behavior as though it did. If the triangle ceases its "pursuit" every time the disk is behind a larger object, we irresistibly see the "hiding" strategy of the disk as being successful and the "seeking" strategy of the triangle as being thwarted by this tactic.

It is these aspects of visual motion processing that cartoon animators exploit in order to create convincing artificial characters and storylines. The way they design their displays is critical to the success of an animated movie because the visual system "makes up its mind" very quickly about the causal relations among objects in motion, much more quickly than the moviegoer is able to reason about these same events.

Object Speed and Direction

One of the most obvious functions served by motion perception—an evaluation of the velocity (speed and direction) of objects relative to other objects and to us—has turned out to be one of the most difficult to understand. This is somewhat paradoxical, because even animals

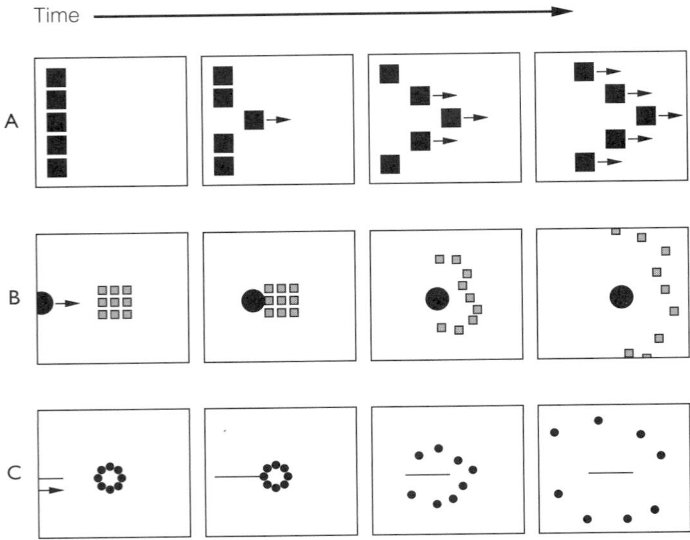

FIGURE 12.14 Simple movie sequences that are interpreted as (A) the center square pulling the remaining squares, (B) the moving disk scattering the small squares, and (C) the line puncturing and bursting the circle of dots.

with the simplest of visual systems are equipped with precise collision detection and avoidance mechanisms. House flies, for instance, are exquisitely prepared to adjust the landing configuration of their limbs and body in correspondence to the slant of an approaching surface. They have turned out to be a model experimental animal for the investigation of this function of motion perception (Reichardt & Poggio, 1979).

But despite the importance of this function of motion perception and its presence in the lowliest of creatures, the truth is that vision researchers do not have a clear sense of the mechanisms involved in being able to catch a baseball or of being able to predict that one runner is going to beat another runner to a base. There is a growing consensus that one reason this problem has been so difficult to solve is that, first, there are actually a number of different problems and, second, each problem likely can be solved in several different ways by the adaptive human brain. Thus, any single-minded approach is almost guaranteed to fail to account for all of the experimental data (Regan & Gray, 2000; Tresilian, 1999).

One very important source of information about what motion researchers refer to as **time to collision,** referring to judgments about whether and when two objects will collide, was actually suggested by the science fiction author Sir Fred Hoyle in his novel *The Black Cloud* (1959). People in this novel are faced with the impending doom of an interstellar cloud that is on a collision course with the earth. "How long have we got?" is on everyone's mind. Hoyle provided an ingeniously simple method for answering this question, without the need for any measurements of the object's actual distance nor the velocity of the observer. In short, he showed that an object's time to collision can be obtained from the ratio of the object's size on the retina to the rate of change in its retinal size over time. This results in the equation shown in Figure 12.15, which has come to be known as **tau** (Lee, 1976).

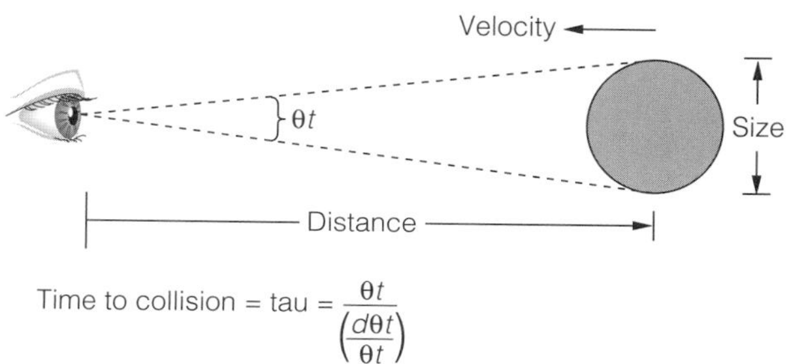

FIGURE 12.15 **Time to collision** refers to the time that will elapse before the observer collides with an object that is moving at a constant velocity. It can be calculated by this equation, which is known as **tau** (Lee, 1976).

But **tau** is not the only source of information available for judging time to collision, nor is it even available under all circumstances in which collision estimates are required. For example, it is only useful when object velocity is held constant and when the impending collision is with the observer. Consider the four typical laboratory tasks that are used to measure the perception of time to collision in Figure 12.16, where the length of each arrow represents the speed of the object. In Figure 12.16A two moving objects are approaching a central goal at different relative speeds. At some point the two objects disappear from the screen and the observer is asked to indicate which object will arrive first. Figure 12.16B illustrates a similar task with the exception that both objects are approaching from the same direction. At some point the faster one will overtake the slower one, but will it be before or after they reach the goal? The task in Figure 12.16C is similar with the exception that objects are approaching the goal from orthogonal directions. In Figure 12.16D the task is to decide whether the looming disk on the left or the right will reach the observer first.

In these situations observers are able to use any information that they think will help them make accurate judgments. When observers are not given any feedback on their ongoing performance, what they tend to do is to base their judgments on simple rules such as "the one that was closer when the items disappeared." This rule works for many displays, but it fails when the speed of the item farther behind is actually fast enough to overcome the gap in the remaining time. Interestingly, when ongoing accuracy feedback is provided, the rules that are used begin to take more of the variables into account and the performance of the observer becomes sensitive to the relevant variables (e.g., Bootsma & Oudejans, 1993).

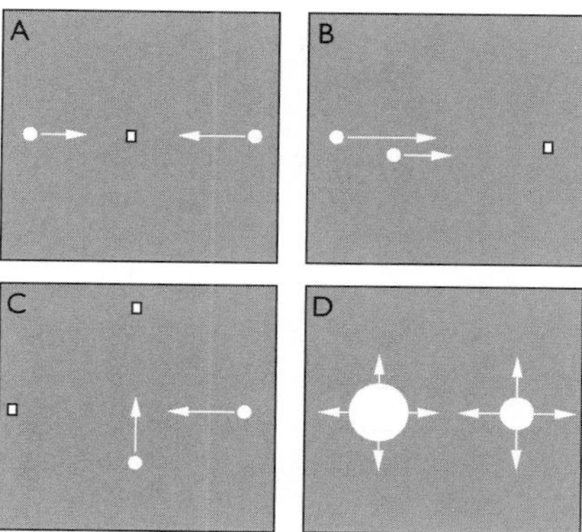

FIGURE 12.16 Four typical laboratory tasks used to study the perception of time to collision. The length of the arrow indicates the relative speed of the objects.

One common situation in which tau is not available as a source of information concerns the task of intercepting an object that is not currently on a collision course with the line of sight. This is the task faced every day, for example, by baseball athletes that have to run in order to catch a ball hit into the field (Tresilian, 1993, 1994; Von Hofsten, 1983). Recent analyses of what baseball players actually do when confronted with this task indicates that they select a running path toward a hit baseball that maintains a **linear optical trajectory** of the moving ball on their retinas (McBeath, Shaffer, & Kaiser, 1995; Shaffer & McBeath, 2002). This means that fielders run so as to maintain the path of the ball on their retina in as straight a line as possible.

This is illustrated in Figure 12.17. A ball hit from home plate into the field will follow a parabolic trajectory. Fielders that are successful in catching the ball tend to run in such a way that the path that the ball takes across their retina maintains a straight line. This means that they will speed up and slow down appropriately if the optical trajectory of the ball deviates from this straight line. It also means that they will tend to run along a curved path to intercept the ball, since the geometry of the situation dictates that doing so is the only way to maintain a linear trajectory. Finally, this analysis helps to explain why it is easier to intercept accurately a ball that is hit to one side than a ball that is approaching head on. This is because trying to maintain a linear trajectory for a ball hit to the side will incidentally place the fielder in the correct location for the catch. In contrast, a ball hit from straight on is already on a linear optical trajectory and so its ultimate contact point with the field cannot be determined from the effort that is needed in order to establish this trajectory in the first place.

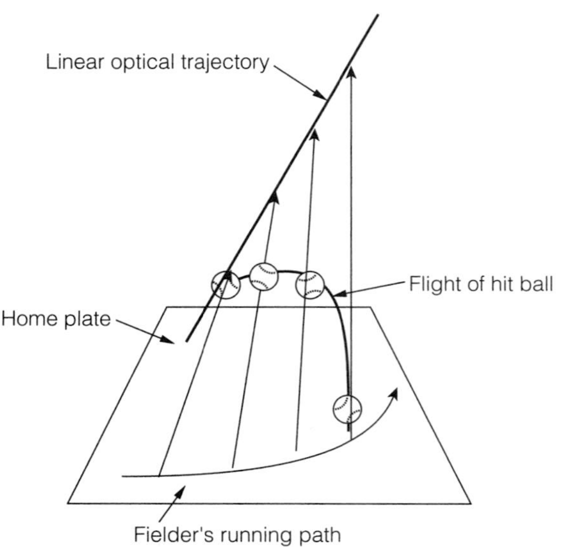

FIGURE 12.17 A fielder trying to catch a baseball tends to run so as to maintain a straight-line path of the ball on the retina. This is called the **linear optical trajectory.**

Tracking Motion with the Eyes

One very important function of motion perception is to enable the eye movement system to track an object that is in motion. As we have seen, our retinas are designed with only a very small region around the fovea that is capable of registering fine spatial detail. If our goal is to identify the fine detail of moving objects, it becomes essential that the image on our retina be fixed. This can only be accomplished by making eye movements that coincide with the movement of the object.

In our discussion so far we have focused on the visual stimulus factors that contribute to our perception of motion, such as movement of the image across the retina. To that extent we have been concerned with the image-retina movement system, as shown in Figure 12.18A. We now turn our attention to the **eye-head motion** system, shown in Figure 12.18B.

This system enables us to detect the movement of external objects even when the image remains in a fixed position on the retina. This most commonly occurs when we move our eyes to follow the path of a physically moving object, as when we track an automobile moving down the highway. This kind of eye movement is called **smooth pursuit movement.** It is designed to keep the image of the target on the fovea, which is the part of the retina that can register the greatest detail. Of course, these eye movements themselves depend on the accurate detection of motion by some part of the visual system that can direct the eyes' movements correctly.

Perhaps the most intriguing aspect of the **eye-head motion** system is that it operates largely without our awareness, meaning that we are not conscious of the commands sent to the eyes to maintain fixation on an object. The neural basis for smooth pursuit eye tracking seems to include the older tectopulvinar visual system we discussed earlier, in conjunction with the **vestibular system** (Parker, 1980), which we will discuss later in this chapter.

Once you start paying attention to the smooth pursuit eye movements you make on a daily basis, you will find that there are actually two different kinds. The one we have been talking about, which allows us to keep a moving object at the center of our gaze, is called **voluntary pursuit movement.** The second type is **reflex pursuit**

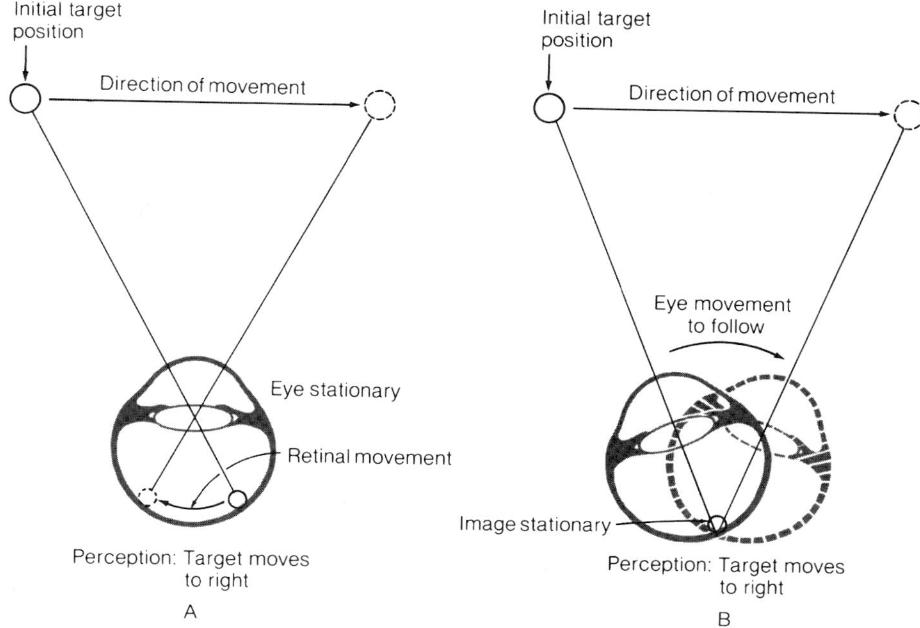

FIGURE 12.18 (A) The image-retina movement system. The image of the moving object stimulates the retina when the eyes are held stationary. This gives information about object motion, possibly as a result of the involvement of movement detecting cells. (B) One of the functions of the eye-head movement system. When the eye pursues a moving target, the image remains stationary on the fovea of the eye, but we still perceive the movement of the object.

movement, which keeps images of objects relatively fixed in one place on your retina despite the fact that your head may be moving. An example of this is shown in Figure 12.19, where the individual is steadily looking at the lens of the camera. Notice that the eyes seem to remain stationary while the head seems to rotate around them. Actually the eyes are tracking in the direction opposite to the head movement in order to keep the target on the fovea. Perhaps not surprisingly, reflex pursuit eye movements are found only in animals that have foveas (Post & Leibowitz, 1985; Raymond, Shapiro, & Rose, 1984).

One of the real puzzles of motion perception is how we are able to perceive the motion of a target that remains motionless on the retina, as happens during smooth pursuit eye movements. One important source of information is the **object-relative change** that can be detected between the stationary target image on the fovea and the retinal motion of the background caused by the eye tracking the target (Pola & Wyatt, 1988). However, suppose that the image of the target remains on the fovea but that there is no patterned background to provide object-relative information to suggest movement. The only way the observer can know the path or the speed of an object is to monitor the path and speed of the tracking eye movements (Epstein & Hanson, 1977; Rock & Halper, 1969). Actually the eye movements do not have to be executed

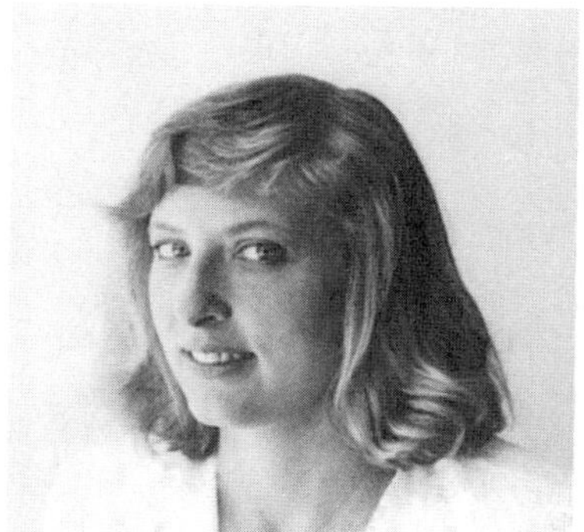

FIGURE 12.19 Reflex pursuit eye movements are used to keep the image of an object fixed on your retina even though you move your head. Here the individual is looking at the camera while rotating her head. Notice how these vestibularly controlled movements keep the eyes fixed while the head seems to rotate around them.

to affect perception, simply their calculation and the preparation for movement influences many aspects of our perception of the moving stimuli (Coren, 1986).

If our perception of the motion of an object depends on information from the eye movements used to track the object, then this implies that anything that alters the direction or speed of motion of the eye should also alter our perception of the movement of the object. Such alterations or misperceptions occur regularly. For instance, the eye does not pursue moving targets with perfect accuracy, but rather tends to follow some distance behind the target. The degree to which the eye lags behind is dependent on the speed of the target (Fender, 1971; Puckett & Steinman, 1969), and under some circumstances the eye never really catches up to the stimulus (Young, 1971). This can cause distortions in the size or the shape of the path the eye follows (Coren, Bradley, Hoenig, & Girgus, 1975).

A good example of this is the **Aubert-Fleischl effect** (e.g., Freeman, 2002). If we estimate the speed of a target when we are tracking it as it moves in front of a stationary background, it appears to move more slowly than it would if we were holding our eyes still by fixating on a point on the stationary background. Because our pursuit eye movements tend to lag behind targets, an observer will not only underestimate the velocity of a target that is tracked with the eyes but also will tend to underestimate the distance the target has moved (Mack & Herman, 1972). It is also possible that there is some form of active inhibition that occurs at the cortical level to reduce perceptual sensitivity to the full field motion of the background stimuli in the direction opposite to the eye movements (Lindner, Schwarz, & Ilg, 2001). Demonstration Box 12.5 allows you to see the Aubert-Fleischl effect for yourself.

There are some circumstances where our own eye or head movements produce movements of the visual image across the retina very similar to those that might occur if the scene were actually in motion. One important function of the eye-head system is to compensate for such movements, so that we continue to see the world as being stationary even though we are moving (e.g., Joseph & Crane, 2001). This process of compensating for eye movements is called **position constancy,** and the fact that objects seem to maintain a fixed position relative to us, despite rotations of both our head and eyes, is called **direction constancy.** Careful measurements show that we are very good at distinguishing image movements caused by target movements from those caused by our own movements (Wallach, 1987).

Although we do not know exactly how this movement compensation system works, it must include a system that monitors the changing position of the eye relative to the position of the head, either when we are tracking a moving target or when we are making eye movements to scan a stationary scene (Howard, 1982). Two classes of theory have been proposed to explain how the eye-head movement system accomplishes this.

DEMONSTRATION BOX 12.5

THE AUBERT-FLEISCHL EFFECT

To experience the underestimation of both speed and distance moved when you track a target, begin by practicing a movement that will serve as your tracking target. With your eyes closed, swing your hand back and forth in front of you at a moderate speed and in a rhythmic fashion as shown in the figure. When you are moving with a nice regular tempo, open your eyes, look straight ahead, and judge the speed and distance your hand is moving. Now look directly at your finger and track it. Notice that your hand seems to be moving more slowly, and the size of the back-and-forth movement (the path length) appears to be shorter. The apparent path length seems shorter probably because when you are tracking the target, information about the extent of the motion comes from the eye-head system, and your tracking movements lag behind the physical target, resulting in a slower overall velocity and a shorter eye-movement path length.

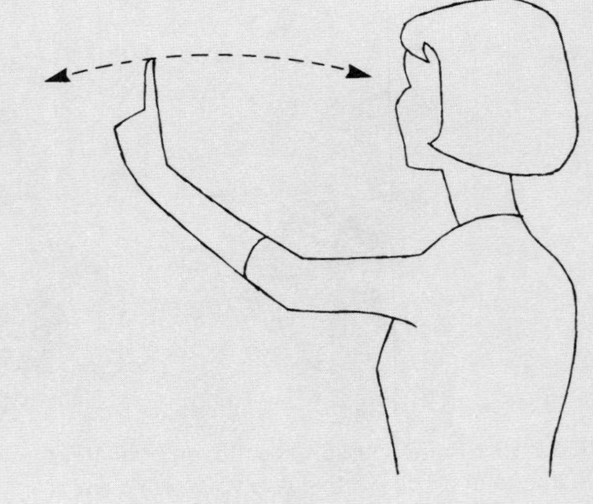

DEMONSTRATION BOX 12.6

OUTFLOW THEORY OF POSITION CONSTANCY

Place your hand over one eye and try tapping or pushing (through the eyelid) the side of your other (uncovered) eye very gently with your fingertip. This rotates the eye in a movement similar to one that could be initiated by the brain. However, in this case the brain has not sent a signal to the extraocular muscles to move the eye. When the eye is rotated in this passive fashion, the visual field will be seen to jog in the direction opposite to the movement of the eye, and to the same extent that the eye actually moved (e.g., Miller, Moore, & Wooten, 1984). Thus, the stability of the visual field holds only for eye movements initiated by signals from the brain. Passive eye movements result in an apparent movement of the visual field. It seems as though the action of the eye-head system requires that the signals to and/or from the eye muscles be compared to signals arriving from the retina indicating changes in retinal image position (Matin, 1982).

Sir Charles Sherrington (1906) suggested that motion is detected via feedback information from the six extraocular muscles that control the eye movements. This feedback information, called **proprioceptive** or **eye position information,** enables the visual system to monitor eye position. The proprioceptive information tells the brain that the eyes have moved, and in turn this information allows the brain to interpret movement across the retina as being observer generated rather than object generated. In support of this theory, there is evidence that some neurons in the superior colliculus and visual cortex of the cat monitor eye position (Berkley, 1982; Kurtz & Butter, 1980). These neurons fire at different rates depending on the extent and direction of eye movement (Donaldson & Long, 1980). Sherrington's theory is often called an **inflow theory** because it is the information "flowing in" from the eye muscles to the brain that is the crucial message for the interpretation of movement.

A different theory about how the eye-head system compensates for self-generated movements of the visual image was offered by Hermann von Helmholtz (1909/1962). He suggested that when the brain initiates an eye movement, efferent signals (motor commands) are sent out telling the eyes to move. Copies of these signals, sent to central regions of the visual system, can be used to indicate that movement information coming from the retina is caused by the eyes moving rather than by movement of stimuli in the world. Since the interpretation of the origin of movement is based on information from the message sent out from the brain that initiates an eye movement, this is called an **outflow theory.** As in the case of inflow information, there are neurons in the cerebellum and in the cortex of monkeys that contain information about eye position. Since these neurons respond before the actual movement takes place, they could represent the source of outflow information registering the intention to move rather than the movements themselves (Miles & Fuller, 1975). To see how outflow information might compensate for eye movements, try the exercise suggested by Helmholtz in Demonstration Box 12.6.

Many vision researchers now think it is likely that both inflow and outflow are needed to provide a full explanation of the eye-head movement system (e.g., O'Regan & Noe, 2001). There are probably times when the inflow information about eye position from the motor system is more reliable than outflow information from the cortical commands sent to the motor system. Table 12.1 gives a summary of the relationship between the image-retina and eye-head movement systems. Demonstration Box 12.7 gives another interesting illustration of the relationships between eye movements and the perception of motion.

Motion of the Self

In the nineteenth century there was a fairground ride called the Haunted Swing. In this ride, people entered a boat-shaped enclosure and artificial scenery was slowly swung backward and forward outside the windows. This resulted in an incredibly strong illusion that the chamber was rocking, and people felt all of the bodily sensations of real motion, including a feeling of loss of their postural stability that made them sway, and even vertigo (Howard, 1982; Wood, 1985). There are also everyday examples of this effect. You have probably had the experience of sitting in a bus or a train parked next to another vehicle. All at once the adjacent vehicle starts to move. However, instead of correctly attributing the movement to the vehicle beside you, you have a powerful sensation of yourself in motion. This is a case of induced move-

TABLE 12.1 The Effect of Retinal Image Change and Eye Movements on the Perception of Motion

Target Motion	Motor-Eye Signal	Retinal Motion	Appearance
	Image-Retina System		
No	None	None	Stationary target
Yes	None	Yes	Target motion
	Eye-Head System		
No	Saccade	Yes	Stationary target
Yes	Pursuit	No	Target motion
No	Passive push with finger	Yes	Target motion in opposite direction

ment, such as we discussed earlier, but it has the added features that it is an induced movement of the self. This is called **vection** (Dichgans & Brandt, 1978) and it is important because it reveals the interplay between the visual and vestibular systems in the perception of body motion. Vection is responsible for the very powerful sense that we are moving that is produced in many virtual environments where the individual is surrounded by flowing visual stimuli (e.g., Hettinger, 2002).

Our perception of **self-motion** depends on an analysis of the continually changing aspects of the retinal image as we move. Consider our most typical motion, which is forward in depth. Although a number of sources of information are important in this situation (see Larish & Flach, 1990), some particular features of the visual array seem to be particularly useful. As we move forward, the visual array in front of us is a radially expanding pattern in the center of our visual field and a laterally translating pattern in our periphery.

For example, consider the pattern shown in Figure 12.20A. Here the arrows represent the flow of the visual array as if you were moving toward the door marked A. Images of objects around door A (that is, those stimuli to its sides or above or below it) expand radially outward and into the periphery as you move forward. This flow of stimuli has been called **streaming perspective** (Gibson,

DEMONSTRATION BOX 12.7

AFTERIMAGES AND APPARENT MOVEMENT

You can readily experience one of the ways the eye-head movement system differentiates external from observer movement. The first thing needed is to generate a *stabilized retinal image*. Ordinarily, the retinal image is in constant motion and stimulates varying groups of receptors at a rapid rate. However, by quickly satiating or fatiguing a single group of retinal receptors, we can generate an image that maintains its position regardless of eye movements. Many of you are probably familiar with the technique used to give rise to such an image if you have ever had your picture taken with a flashbulb attached to the camera. If you looked at the light while it flashed, you may have noticed a purple dot that tended to linger in your field of view for some time after the picture was taken. This purple dot is called an *afterimage*. It is one example of a stabilized retinal image. The afterimage does not shift position on the retina. It stays in a constant position regardless of how we move our eyes. We can use the afterimage to demonstrate the operation of the head-eye movement system.

Perhaps the easiest way to generate an afterimage is to look at a rather bright but small source of light for a brief period of time. Make a 1-cm hole in an index card and hold it up in front of a lightbulb. Look at the hole for a few moments, and this should provide a clearly visible afterimage when you look away from the light. Now notice that each time you move your eyes the afterimage seems to jump in the same direction. This apparent movement is due to the action of the eye-head system.

Commands have been issued to the eye to move, yet the image remains on the same place on the retina. This could occur only if the image had moved as much as the eye (see Table 12.1). You may also notice that the image sometimes seems to drift smoothly from place to place. Again, the image never moves; the movement is signaled from the movements of your eyes. This is one example of how the action of the eye-head movement system can lead to illusions of motion.

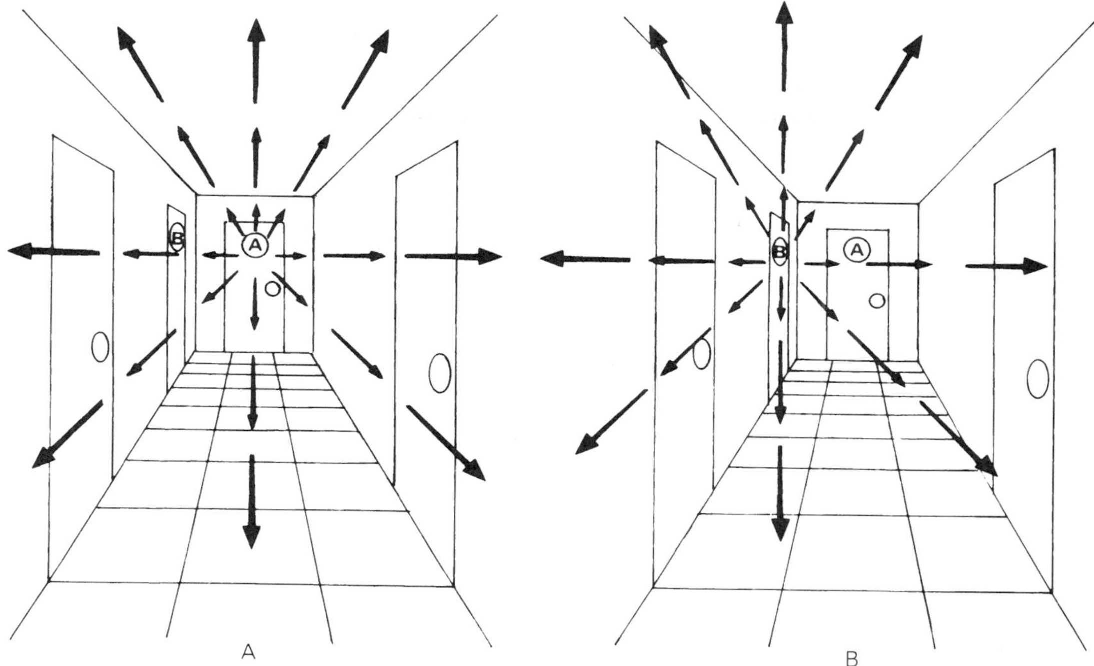

FIGURE 12.20 Streaming perspective. Figure A shows the pattern of flow or expansion of stimuli as it would appear if you were moving toward door A. The length of the arrows indicates the rate of change or speed of expansion, with longer arrows meaning faster change. B shows how the pattern of stimulus flow changes if you were now moving toward door B, rather than straight down the hallway.

1979). If your path were angled so you were going toward the door marked B, the optical transformation pattern would be similar to that in Figure 12.20B. In both cases, the center of this outward flow, which is called the **focus of expansion,** indicates the direction of your movement. Although the specific patterns shown by the streaming perspective of targets in the field will vary as you move your eyes (e.g., Regan & Beverly, 1982), it is still easy to direct your movements by keeping the door you wish to reach in the center of the outward flow of stimuli (Warren & Hannon, 1988).

If we present you with a steadily moving pattern that is the equivalent of a natural streaming-perspective pattern, you will feel as though you are moving (Hettinger, 2002). If the pattern is expanding radially, as in Figure 12.20, you will feel as though your body is moving forward. If the pattern is moved steadily to the side, you will feel that you are moving (or starting to lean or tilt) sideways, or even rotating if the pattern surrounds you. Adding stereoscopic information to the optical flow will also increase the sense of self-motion (Palmisano, 2002).

There is a consensus that the central visual field is more specialized for object motion, whereas stimulation of the peripheral visual field is necessary to induce the feeling of self-motion. Thus, patterns that extend into the periphery tend to produce strong feelings of vection (Delorme & Martin, 1986). If the speed of flow is not too fast, and the pattern is correct, visually induced self-motion can be experienced even for smaller central patterns (Andersen & Braunstein, 1985; Stoffregen, 1985).

The relatively greater contribution of the peripheral retina to vection may explain why the feelings of self-motion can be so strong when you view motion pictures with an oversized or wraparound screen. Many viewers of such large visual displays feel all the bodily effects normally associated with the equivalent self-motion. This suggests that the visual and vestibular inputs must have some common neural pathways and centers. This would be a sensible arrangement since the vestibular system only responds to accelerations or decelerations of body motions. As we will see in the next section, after any prolonged period of constant velocity the vestibular system ceases to respond and only visual input is used to indicate movement of the self.

To the extent that vestibular and visual information can each produce similar feelings of self-motion, it should not be surprising to find that there are neurons in the vestibular nuclei whose rates of firing are influenced by signals suggesting bodily motion, whether such signals come directly from the vestibular organs or from visual centers (Waespe & Henn, 1977). There seems to be a complex interaction between the visual and the nonvisual inputs to give us this feeling of self-motion (DiZio & Lackner, 1986; Henn, Cohen, & Young, 1980). This is confirmed by recent brain scanning studies that have found that the temporal cortex areas associated with motion perception (V5) as well as the parietal areas associated with vestibular function are activated during self-motion (Nishiike, Nakagawa, Tonoike, Takeda, & Kubo, 2001). Some other brain scanning studies have further suggested that the two halves of the brain are not equally involved in self-motion, and it may be that the right hemisphere is more important for this aspect of perception (Peuskens, Sunaert, Dupont, Van Hecke, & Orban, 2001).

The situation is really very complicated, however. Sometimes when the illusion of self-motion is produced, the mismatch between visual and vestibular signals can produce unpleasant feelings. In some individuals there are even symptoms of motion sickness (complete with nausea and vomiting) caused by the lack of agreement between visual and vestibular signals (Stern, Koch, Leibowitz, Lindblad, Shupert, & Stewart, 1985). With continued exposure, individuals become used to this situation and the symptoms usually disappear (Hu, Grant, Stern, & Koch, 1991).

A SENSE OF BALANCE

The **vestibular system** informs us about the position of our body in space using evolutionarily old mechanical mechanisms. Signals from this system interact with signals from the visual motion centers to provide an integrated picture with regard to self-motion and the motion of other objects in our immediate environment. Working together, the vestibular and the visual systems are coordinated for the maintenance of an upright posture and in the control of eye position as we move our heads and bodies (see Goebel & Highstein, 2002). For the most part, these operations take place outside of consciousness. But before we consider the interplay between these two systems, let us first consider the basic structure and physiology of the vestibular system.

Some of the most primitive animals have organs that are sensitive to changes in motion of the body. In primitive invertebrates such as the crayfish these are called **statocysts.** Each consists of a fluid-filled cavity that is lined with hair cells. In the cavity is a tiny stone, called a **statolith** or "still stone," that rests on the hairs. When the animal accelerates, the stone tends to lag behind because of its inertia, thus bending the hairs on which it rests. This action generates an electrical response to the movement. If the animal is tilted, the stone rolls along over a number of different hairs, bending them and generating a different response indicating tilt. The function of such organs is to signal the animal's orientation with respect to gravity. More advanced invertebrates, such as the squid or octopus, have multichambered statocysts that approach vertebrate vestibular organs in complexity, with the ability to detect acceleration in several planes (Stephens & Young, 1982).

Primitive vertebrates have organs that have a similar function; they are called **otocysts** and the bones they contain are called **otoliths.** Notice that these terms each contain the root **oto** meaning "ear." These organs are usually closely associated with the ears, since both the auditory receptors and the vestibular organs probably evolved from hairy skin. In mammals, these organs are protected by the bones of the skull from possibly damaging outside forces. In humans, the **bony labyrinth** in the head contains the cochlea (which is the auditory organ), and the **semicircular canals,** the **utricle,** and the **saccule,** which comprise the vestibular organs (see Figure 12.21).

Vestibular Stimuli and Receptors

The effective physical stimulus for any vestibular organ is change in the rate of motion, or **acceleration.** This occurs whenever we move through space, whether we jump up and down, take off in a jet plane, or simply stand up and walk. The semicircular canals and their associated receptor organs seem particularly well suited for monitoring rotary acceleration (as when turning around or falling down). The other two organs, the utricle and the saccule, seem mainly to respond to linear acceleration (as when taking off in a plane). The movement-receptive portion of the semicircular canals is called the **crista,** which is found in a swelling (called an **ampulla**) at the base of each semicircular canal (see Figure 12.22). The crista consists of an array of sensory cells from which tiny hairs protrude, as shown in Figure 12.22A. These hairs are embedded in a jellylike material called the **cupola.** When your head accelerates, the inertia of the fluid in the canals causes the cupola to move in the opposite direction. This in turn causes the hairs to bend, generating neural responses, just as the hair cells do in

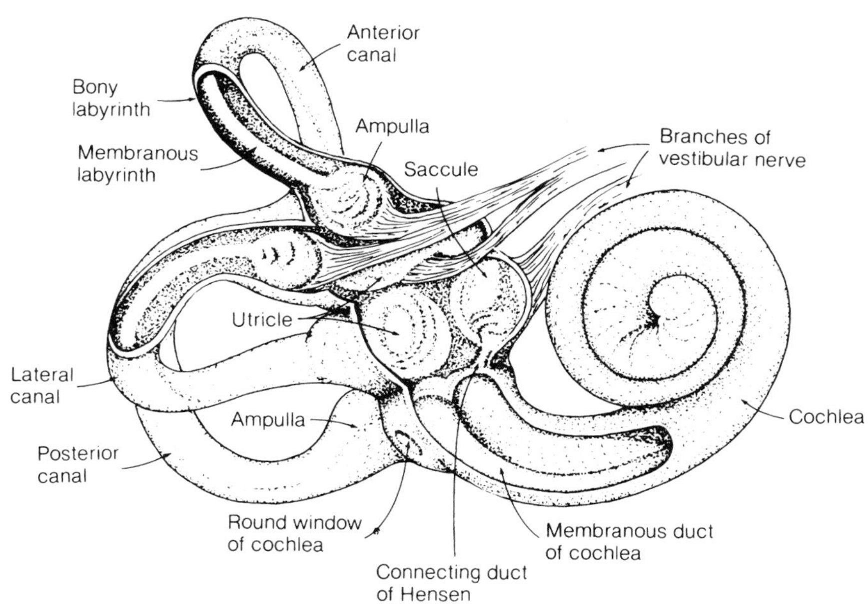

FIGURE 12.21 A diagram of the right inner ear showing the cochlea (which houses the auditory receptor), the semicircular canals, the utricle, and the saccule (from Geldard, 1972).

the ear. As your head continues to move at a particular rate of speed, the cupola gradually comes back to its resting position, no longer bending the hairs, and no longer causing a response in the sensory cells. This is why the effective stimulus is acceleration rather than steady movement.

The receptor organ found in the utricle and the saccule is called the **macula**, shown in Figure 12.22B. It functions much like the statocyst we discussed before. As in the crista, tiny hairs protrude from the sensory cells in the macula. These hairs are embedded in a jelly-like substance covered by a membrane containing otoliths, which lags behind when the head is accelerated, bending the hair cells and generating an electrical response. When the jelly and hairs catch up to the rest of the head, which would happen if the acceleration ceased and motion became steady, the hairs are no longer bent. This means no response would be generated, even though the head could be traveling at thousands of kilometers per hour relative to the earth.

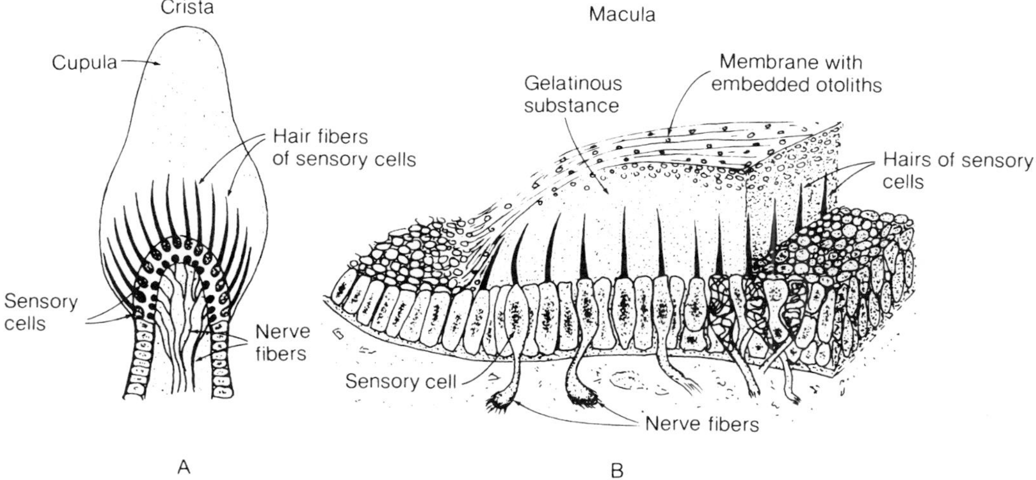

FIGURE 12.22 (A) Diagram of the crista, the receptor found in the ampulla of each semicircular canal. (B) Diagram of the macula, the receptor found in the utricle and the saccule (from Geldard, 1972).

Neural Responses in the Vestibular Sense

The hair cells from both the crista and the macula send their information to the brainstem via the eighth cranial nerve. From there most of the nerve fibers go to the **vestibular nuclei,** which are in the brainstem. After this the sensory pathways become complicated and somewhat obscure. There are projections to the cerebellum and to the cortex, but they are different in different animals (Correia & Guedry, 1978). It is important to note that most of the fibers leaving the vestibular nuclei are motor or **efferent fibers.** One major group of these fibers forms a pathway to the muscles that move the eyes. Szentagothai (1950) discovered that each pair of eye muscles receives fibers from a different semicircular canal. The arrangement indicates that muscles that move the eye in a particular plane are controlled by nerve fibers that originate in one of the semicircular canals that responds to acceleration in that plane. Acceleration in a particular direction causes compensatory eye movements in the opposite direction. This allows the eyes to remain fixed on an object even though the head is turning in various directions. The relationship between eye movements and vestibular stimulation is shown in Demonstration Box 12.8.

Lowenstein and Sand (1940) performed a classic study that illustrates the electrophysiology of the vestibular system. They recorded the electrical activity of single nerve fibers from the crista of a ray (a kind of fish) while the entire labyrinth was rotated on a turntable. They found that as long as the head was accelerating, the fibers responded. The fibres increased their firing rate above the resting rate for acceleration in one direction, and decreased it below the resting rate when the acceleration was in the opposite direction. Thus, as in other sensory systems, both excitatory and inhibitory responses to physical stimuli occur. Lowenstein and Sand also showed that the magnitude of the response (impulses per second in single fibers) varies directly with the magnitude of the stimulating acceleration. So stimulus intensity seems to be encoded in a manner similar to that in other sensory systems. There are at least two other types of nerve fibers: One always responds to acceleration (regardless of direction) with an increase in firing rate, and the other only responds with a decrease in firing rate.

The fibers connected to the hair cells of the macula respond to their stimuli somewhat more simply. Two types of responses have been described. The first is an increase in the rate of neural firing when the head is tilted; the second is a rate increase when the head is returned to its original position (Wyburn, Pickford, & Hurst, 1964). Although there have been some studies of cortical responses to acceleration of the head, little is known in detail about these responses. One fact that has emerged is that inputs from vestibular, kinesthetic, and visual systems converge in the cortex, so that our sensations of "turning" and the like depend in a complex way on all of these inputs (Mergner, Anastasopoulos, Becker, & Deecke, 1981; Parker, 1980). One striking example of this complex interaction is the phenomenon of motion sickness, which is often caused by a mismatch between visual and vestibular or kinesthetic inputs. A great deal of effort is being put into studying this aspect of human reaction, especially because of its importance in space travel, which involves zero-gravity conditions, meaning that the proprioceptive cues normally associated with that feature of the environment are no longer available.

Taken all together, it is now easy to see how the perception of motion is a good example of **sensory convergence,** a process by which several inputs combine to produce a single coherent perception. Of course, we are often not conscious of all, or even most, of the compo-

DEMONSTRATION BOX 12.8

VESTIBULAR STIMULATION AND EYE MOVEMENTS

For this demonstration you will need a friend and a little space. Have your friend hold her arms out and spin around (like a whirling ice skater) until she becomes dizzy. This continuous rotation sets up currents in the semicircular canals that trigger the compensatory eye-movement system. Now stop your friend from turning and look into her eyes. You will notice that her eyes drift steadily in one direction and then snap back and start to drift again. This type of repetitive eye movement is called nystagmus. It is a reflex movement evoked automatically by the vestibular stimulation caused by fluid currents in the semicircular canals.

nents that have gone into the computation. In the case of motion perception, we have seen that the apparently visual experience of motion may contain proprioceptive inputs from eye movements and the vestibular sense, or copies of efferent commands issued to the eye muscles, even though our conscious impression remains strictly visual. As seems to be so often the case in perception, the percept we experience in our consciousness is an amalgam of many sources even though to us it may seem to be a simple experience.

STUDY QUESTIONS

1. What are the main arguments in favor of the position that motion is a primary aspect of visual perception?
2. What is the waterfall illusion, and how can it be used to illustrate selective adaptation?
3. What visual pathways in the brain are specialized for motion perception?
4. What is the aperture problem in motion perception?
5. Describe two everyday situations in which you might be expected to experience vection.
6. What are three critical ingredients for the perception of smooth apparent motion?
7. Describe how the perception of structure from motion is similar to stereovision.
8. How does the maintenance of a linear optical trajectory help a fielder catch a baseball?
9. What is the most important function accomplished by smooth pursuit eye movements?
10. Describe how streaming perspective is a key to the perception of one's own motion.
11. What mechanical events initiate processing in the vestibular sensory system?
12. What is meant by sensory convergence?

CHAPTER 13

ATTENTION

CHAPTER SUMMARY

My experience is what I agree to attend to. Only those items which I notice, shape my mind—without selective interest, experience is an utter chaos.

(William James, 1890, p. 402)

Our open eyes, our ears, skin, noses, and tongues are nearly continuously receptive to the changes in light, sound, touch, smells, and tastes their receptors were evolved to encode. Our ability to process this enormous river of information, however, is limited. Most of the time only one of the many streams of sensory input seems to fill our minds, and the others fade to the periphery of awareness (James, 1890). The various ways by which we select among all that is there to be looked at, listened to, felt, smelled, or tasted are often grouped together under the general label of **attention.**

VARIETIES OF ATTENTION

Imagine the following: You are reading this book, and various extraneous events distract you in spite of the riveting text! You get a cramp in your foot and stretch it; a fire engine whoops by outside, and you listen until the siren stops somewhere down the block; a flicker of movement in the periphery of your visual field causes you to look toward the door to the room as your roommate enters bringing you a midnight snack (you wish!). In this fantasy of college life, each of several important events demands an **orienting** response. That is, your attention is drawn, or pulled, to a source of sudden change in your sensory world. You might give only brief attention to some events, as when you stretch your foot. You might listen to (the fire siren) or look at (your roommate)

BIOGRAPHY BOX 13.1

FILTERING OUT THE NOISE

Donald Broadbent (1926–1993) is responsible for bringing the topic of attention back into the realm of psychological research. By the 1950s, behaviorism dominated North American psychological research. Concepts such as attention, set, and awareness were ignored in the rush to publish new cumulative records of responses and graphs of errors and correct discriminations. Even "superstitious" behaviors were reduced to sequences of bar presses and key pecks in animals. Into this hostile environment rode Donald Broadbent of Cambridge University in Britain. He had just spent the trying years of World War II focused on the vigilance of radar operators and on pilot fatigue. This had taught him two research "tricks": (a) Seek applied problems to generate research ideas, and (2) test abstract theories of mental processes in applied settings. These turned out to be very practical tricks, since government funding of pure research was still a largely unrealized fantasy at that time. His careful experimental work, often in factories or other work places, and his insightful theoretical ideas, particularly espousing the information processing approach culminated in his 1958 book on *Perception and Communication.* This book and the ideas it contained formed much of the impetus for the so-called "cognitive revolution" that brought the scientific study of mental life out of psychology's behaviorist closet and into the beginnings of the intense scrutiny it receives today.

Broadbent is perhaps best known today for his filter theory of attention, in which one of the many streams of sensory input is selected for high-level analysis on the basis of mostly physical features, such as location in space, characteristic features such as frequency range (for sounds such as voices) or color (for visual stimuli), presaging the guided search and top-down control of attention theories we review in this chapter. This theory generated numerous alternatives and competing theories and influenced several generations of experimental psychologists. During his illustrious career Broadbent wrote several other books, including 1961's *Behavior* , 1971's *Decision and Stress,* and 1973's *In Defense of Empirical Psychology,* as well as many journal articles reporting his research. He continued to give inspiring talks at various universities until near his death. A hallmark of his thought was simple elegance, and he treated every topic he addressed in this way, proposing elegantly simple frameworks in which to understand important results in attention, decision making, memory, and the effects of stress, fatigue, and noise on work performance. He was Professor of Psychology, and from 1958 to 1974 the Director of the Medical Research Council Applied Psychology Unit, at Cambridge University.

other events for longer periods of time. Although you attend to some stimuli, you exclude many others. Hence, while listening to the siren you are probably unaware of the goldfish swimming in its bowl or the refrigerator humming in the next room. We say you are **filtering** out the extraneous events, attending to only one of the several available distinct and separable sources of information about the world, which we refer to as **information channels** (Broadbent, 1958; Biography Box 13.1).

Continuing the fantasy, perhaps your attention wanders for a moment from the page, and you think of the exam scheduled for tomorrow in calculus. You wonder where your notes are and look up, scanning your room for the green binder you will be poring over in a few minutes. You are **searching** for a relevant stimulus in the environment, scanning your sensory world for particular features or combinations of features. Finally, just as you are about to start studying your math notes, you pause, realizing that it is at about this time every night that the wolves in the zoo next door begin to howl at the moon. You listen for a few moments. Yes, there they are, right on time. You were expecting something to happen and in **preparing** for that event you momentarily attended to "empty space" until it did.

As implied by our fantasy, it is tempting to say that attention determines what reaches conscious awareness (e.g., Taylor, 2002). Unfortunately, this is too simple. For example, Lamme (2003) argued that it makes more sense to consider attention as selecting from among already conscious visual experiences those that we will be able to report about and to which we will give special processing. This implies that we are aware of information, at least in vision, that we are not attending to, and that there is additional visual information about which we are unaware. The exact relationship between these two ill-defined terms will probably not be decided until considerably more research has been done on each.

In what follows, we describe in more detail some of what is known about how attention operates in orienting, filtering, searching, and preparing. We discuss mostly vi-

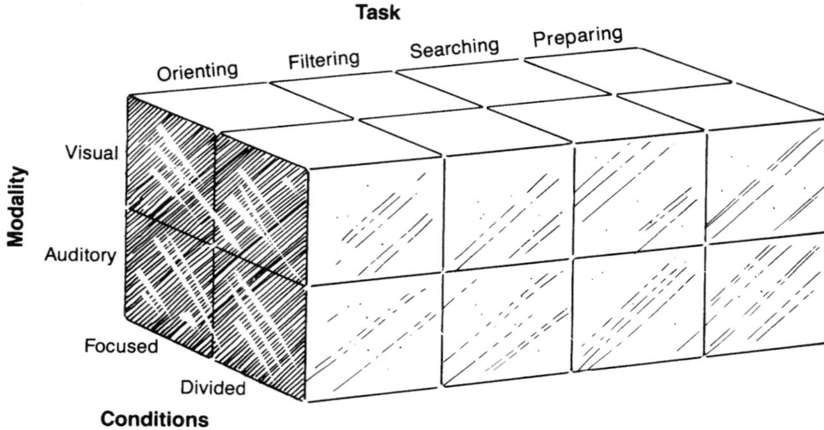

FIGURE 13.1 A representation of various perceptual attention situations dealt with in this chapter.

sion and audition because most work has been done on these, but our conclusions apply to the other modalities as well. By way of definition, we also point out that each of the tasks we described can involve paying attention to a single target or event **(focused attention)** or dividing it among several of them **(divided attention).** Figure 13.1 summarizes the framework for describing attention we will use in this chapter.

In recent years several particular issues or problems of attention within this very general framework have generated much research. For example, there have been many studies of the interaction between the goal-directed aspects of our attention and the tendency for salient features of the environment to "capture" our attention and to distract us from these goals (Egeth & Yantis, 1997). Another group of studies have focused on how extensive practice with a task changes the amount of attention that is required (Pashler, Johnston, & Ruthruff, 2001). One of the most exciting new areas of study has focused on how insensitive we are to changes in our visual world when these changes occur to objects that are not the at the center of our attention (Rensink, 2002). All of these issues and more will arise as we discuss the major tasks of attention outlined in Figure 13.1.

ORIENTING

The simplest way to select among several stimulus inputs is to **orient** our sensory receptors toward one set of stimuli and away from another. We might say that we do not passively see or hear but, rather, that we actively **look** or **listen** in order to see and hear. In other words, we must pay attention in order to explicitly perceive events in our world (e.g., Mack & Rock, 1998).

Orienting Reflex

We have all seen a dog or a cat prick up its ears and turn its head toward a sudden sound. The animal is performing the most primitive form of **orienting response,** which involves adjusting the sense organs, by turning eyes, head, and/or body, so they can optimally pick up information about the event. Responses such as flicking the eye in the direction of a sound or peripheral movement occur automatically and are collectively referred to as the **orienting reflex.** The orienting reflex is so reliable that eye and head turns toward sounds have been used to test the hearing of newborn infants (e.g., Muir & Field, 1979). The most effective orienting stimuli are loud sounds, suddenly appearing bright lights, changes in contours, or movements in the peripheral visual field that are not regular, predictable occurrences. Interestingly, the sudden offset of a light or sound that has been present for a while can also elicit the orienting reflex.

Several behaviors other than eye, head, or body turning follow the onset of a sudden event. These include postural adjustments, skin conductance changes, pupil dilation, decrease in heart rate, a pause in breathing, and constriction of the peripheral blood vessels (e.g., Rohrbaugh, 1984). It is as though we had an internal "model" of the immediate world of stimuli around us. When we notice a departure of stimulus input from that model, we reflexively orient to that stimulus in order to update that model as quickly as possible (Sokolov, 1975). If the same stimulus occurs repeatedly, it becomes an expected part of our model of the world, and our orienting reflex toward it becomes weaker, even if the stimulus is strong. With a change in the nature of the stimulus, however, the reflex recovers to full strength.

Covert Orienting

The **overt orienting** response to sudden changes in the environment is usually accompanied by another, unseen orienting response, the fixing of attention on the event or object that elicited the reflex. This unseen attentional orienting is called **covert orienting.** The combination of overt and covert orienting to an event usually results in enhanced perception of that event, including faster identification and awareness of its significance. Although this hidden orienting of attention usually occurs in association with overt orienting, whether reflexive or voluntary, several researchers have pointed out that it is possible to covertly attend to an event or stimulus without making any overt sign that we are doing so. For example, Helmholtz (1909/1962) observed that he could direct his visual attention around the visual field without making an eye movement or changing accommodation or convergence. Thus, we can consider covert attention orienting separately from overt orienting behaviors, although the two are surely closely related.

A common example of covert orienting is when we become aware of somebody in the room mentioning our name at a party while having a conversation with the person in front of us. Most modern attention research takes for granted that overt orienting can be dissociated from paying attention. Typically in attention experiments eye, head and body movements are strictly controlled, or made irrelevant by using headphones or very short stimulus presentations. Such controlled presentations allow researchers to separate the effects of overt orienting from covert shifts of attention. Thus, in the following discussion we will use the words **covert orienting** to refer only to situations in which attention is focused on a particular object or event, but an overt orienting response is absent or irrelevant.

There are many ways our attention can be drawn to objects or events in the environment. A dramatic example capitalizes on the fact that visual stimuli seem to be more capable of drawing our attention to particular locations in space than do auditory stimuli. This is the phenomenon ventriloquists depend on, called **visual capture,** in which a sound is mislocated at its apparent visual source. Although the ventriloquism effect itself does not involve the capture of attention (e.g., Vroomen, Bertelson, & deGelder, 2001), the drawing of attention to the apparent visual source of a sound can actually enhance the processing of speech sounds in the presence of other distracting speech sounds (Driver, 1996). Demonstration Box 13.1 allows you to experience visual capture for yourself.

An important demonstration of how attention can be captured by a visual event was made by Yantis and Jonides (1984; Jonides & Yantis, 1988). They showed that under some conditions the abrupt appearance of a stimulus in the visual field captures visual attention and facilitates responding to that stimulus. In their experiment they asked observers to say whether a particular target letter was present or not in a field of other distracting letters. On a typical trial, one letter appeared abruptly in the visual field while three others appeared gradually by the fading of selected lines in figures that had been displayed previously (Figure 13.2). Sometimes the target letter was the abruptly appearing letter; sometimes it was one of the gradually appearing letters. When the target appeared abruptly, observers detected it significantly more quickly than when it faded on. It seems that attention was drawn first to the abruptly appearing letter, and if it was the target, a positive response could immediately be made. If the abrupt-onset letter wasn't the target, then attention had to be directed toward the other letters before a response could be made, slowing the response.

Other studies have confirmed the ability of an abrupt-onset stimulus to attract attention. They found that when such a stimulus preceded the occurrence of a target by about 100 ms the target information was processed optimally. It seems that attention is automatically attracted to the spatial location of an abrupt-onset stimulus within about 100 ms of its appearance, without the need to voluntarily orient (e.g., Müller & Humphreys, 1991). It is not inevitable that attention is pulled toward such abrupt stimuli, however, because you can keep attention from being captured by voluntarily focusing your attention elsewhere (Yantis & Jonides, 1990). Moreover, if the observer's task does not require attending to abrupt-onset stimuli, for example, if the target is defined by a color difference, then abrupt-onset stimuli also may not capture attention, whereas color-difference stimuli will (e.g., Folk, Remington, & Johnston, 1992; see Pashler, Johnston, & Ruthruff, 2001, for a review).

In Yantis and Jonides's experiments and in most others, the abrupt-onset stimuli are also new perceptual objects in the visual field. Is attention drawn to any abrupt luminance change in the visual field, or is it drawn only to those that represent new perceptual objects? Actually, attention seems to be tuned to notice the appearance of objects because it is drawn to the abrupt appearance of a new perceptual object even if its appearance is not accompanied by a luminance change—conversely, a salient

DEMONSTRATION BOX 13.1

VISUAL CAPTURE

Visual capture is a phenomenon in which attention is caught by a visual stimulus in a way that results in an illusion of auditory localization. Whenever you are listening to a sound, such as a voice talking, there is a tendency to try to identify visual events, or objects, that could be causing the sound. When the ventriloquist's dummy is moving its mouth and limbs and the ventriloquist is talking without moving **his** mouth, then the location of the voice is "captured" by the dummy's movements, and you **hear** the ventriloquist's voice coming from its mouth, even though it is really the ventriloquist speaking.

You can demonstrate this effect for yourself by obtaining two television sets (or going to a store that sells them and asking to use two of theirs for a "scientific demonstration"). Place them side by side, about 500 cm apart, and tune both sets to the same newscast, talk show, or other show in which the sound is highly correlated with the picture. (You could also use a radio and a television set, tuning in to a simulcast show such as some concerts.) Now turn off the sound on one of the sets and turn off the picture on the other. Move back a short distance and look at a place between the two sets while paying attention to the picture-displaying set. The sound seems to come from that set, even though its sound is turned off. It actually doesn't matter where you look; the sound will seem to come from the set with the picture. You could also try moving the sets apart to see how powerful the phenomenon is. You will be surprised at how far apart these sets can be before the actual sound source dominates. By the way, this also explains why when you are watching a film the sound seems to come from the actors' mouths, even though the speakers may be located at the side of the film screen, or even in the back of the room.

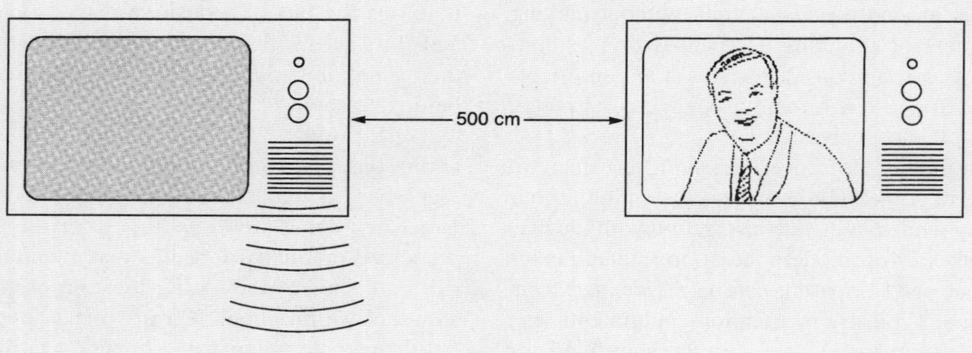

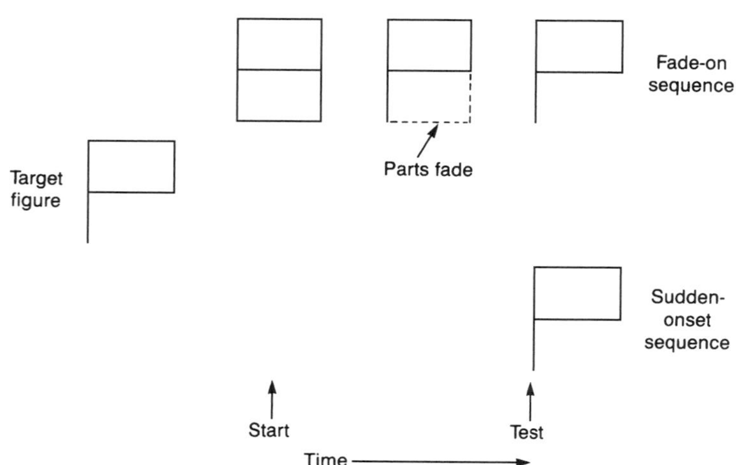

FIGURE 13.2 The upper sequence shows a gradual-onset stimulus, whereas the lower sequence shows a sudden-onset stimulus in the Yantis and Jonides (1984) study. Sudden-onset stimuli were more easily detected.

luminance change that is not associated with the appearance of a new object does not capture attention (Enns, Austen, Di Lollo, Rauschenberger, & Yantis, 2001; Yantis & Hillstrom, 1994). If attention is captured, it is possible to ask whether it is now oriented to the object itself or just toward the location of the object (see Duncan, 1984). Many studies have shown attention is associated with perceptual objects regardless of their location (or even if they move to new locations); however, some resources may also be allocated toward processing spatial location. Thus, attention is drawn both to a new perceptual object and to its location, and which dominates at any one moment depends on the perceptual task (see Egeth & Yantis, 1997, for a review).

Attention capture also happens in hearing. For example, in the early experiments on divided attention, subjects were given a different message in each of their two ears by means of headphones. They were asked to pay attention to and repeat the message they were hearing in one ear **(shadowing)** while another message was delivered to the other ear. When an abrupt or distinctive sound or an unexpected change, such as a switch from a male to a female voice, occurred in the unshadowed ear, subjects tended to "stumble" or lose the continuity of their shadowing (e.g., Kahneman, 1973). Apparently, their attention was drawn to the unshadowed message, causing them to fail to hear the attended message and thus interrupting the smooth flow of shadowing. More recent experiments have confirmed the ability of an abrupt-onset sound to trigger involuntary orienting of auditory attention, both to the frequency of the abrupt-onset sound (e.g., Scharf, 1989; Ward, 1997) and to its location (e.g., Spence & Driver, 1994). Moreover, as in visual orienting, whether an abrupt-onset sound orients attention to its location depends on the task. If the task is spatial, then attention is oriented to the location of abrupt-onset sounds, whereas if it is nonspatial, for example, a frequency discrimination task, then attention is not oriented to the location of previously occurring abrupt-onset sounds (McDonald & Ward, 1999).

Finally, abrupt-onset stimuli in one modality can capture attention in another modality. For example, a glint of sunlight off a motorcycle will capture our auditory attention (e.g., Ward, 1994), as will a pistol shot capture our visual attention (e.g., Spence & Driver 1997). When attention is captured cross-modally in this way, processing of stimuli that occur at the attended location is enhanced (e.g., McDonald, Teder-Sälejärvi, & Hillyard, 2000). Such cross-modal attention capture happens for all combinations of modalities that have been tested so far (e.g., Spence & McDonald, 2003).

In the situations discussed earlier, attention was drawn to some conspicuous stimulus somewhere in the visual or auditory field. In many modern studies of orienting, a special abrupt-onset stimulus, which we will call a **direct cue,** is presented in advance of a target to be responded to for just this purpose. Responses to targets that appear near the cued location are facilitated, relative to those to targets that appear elsewhere, for about 100 to 200 ms after cue onset if the cue doesn't predict the target's location and for up to 1 second if it does (see Wright & Ward, 1998, for a review). Orienting, filtering, and searching all depend on the presence of one or more direct cues toward which attention is either automatically drawn (orienting) or voluntarily directed (filtering or searching). When we receive information in advance about where or when something is likely to happen (we call this a **symbolic cue**), attentional phenomena appear to be somewhat different. This suggests that our expectations interact with how we direct our attention, a matter discussed later under **preparing.**

The Attentional Gaze

A useful way of conceptualizing some of the findings in covert visual orienting and visual searching is a metaphor that we will call the **attentional gaze.** Other terms have been suggested for this concept (e.g., a **zoom lens** by Eriksen & Hoffman, 1972; a **spotlight** by Hernandez-Peon, 1964; the **mind's eye** by Jonides, 1980), but attentional gaze is the most general. In this metaphor, we imagine that your attention can "gaze" about independently of where your eyes are looking. In orienting, attention can be drawn to a direct cue anywhere in the visual field where there is adequate acuity and sensitivity to register it, either by an abrupt onset, as earlier, or by other conspicuous differences in movement, shape, or color.

Covert shifts in the attentional gaze seem to behave in a way similar to physical movements of the eye, in that attention seems to jump from Point A to Point B like a saccade, although it seems to take no longer to move a large distance than a small one (Tsal, 1983). Also, like physical eye movements, attention usually cannot be drawn to more than one location in the visual field at any instant in time (e.g., Yantis & Jonides, 1984). Auditory attention also can be drawn to particular spatial locations in a way similar to that of visual attention (e.g., McDonald & Ward, 1999).

The fact that the attentional gaze can be shifted without accompanying eye (or head) movements raises the question of how these two systems are coordinated.

Under normal circumstances a direct cue will attract both a shift in attentional gaze and an eye movement to the location of the stimulus. However, as you may have noted in listening to a boring conversation, an eye movement to a location of greater interest can be suppressed voluntarily (Klein, 1980), although it is rare for attention not to be attracted by a conspicuous event, at least momentarily. Experimental studies of the attentional gaze show that it can shift much faster than the eye—it reaches a stimulus location before the eye does and seems to help to guide the eye to the proper location (e.g., Remington, 1980). These experiments suggest that the attentional gaze and the gaze of the eyes are related, much like the gaze of the eyes and movement of the hand are related in the everyday act of reaching. Under normal circumstances the eyes will first move to the object of interest and then help guide the hand to the correct location. An eye movement can occur without a hand movement necessarily following, however, and hand movements can be made even with one's eyes closed.

Three aspects of the attentional gaze are important in the processing of sensory information. At any one moment attention may be described as having a **locus,** an **extent,** and a **detail set.** As noted earlier, the attentional gaze shifts around much as your eyes move to take in visual information. After attention is located at a particular place, or **locus,** in the visual field, processing of stimuli occurring at or near that locus is improved. The **extent** of the area over which attention is spread can be controlled by making the direct cue larger or smaller; processing efficiency is less the greater the extent over which attention is spread (e.g., LaBerge & Brown, 1989). Processing is also less efficient for stimuli that are farther away from the center of an attended region of any size (Eriksen & St. James, 1986).

Finally, there is some evidence that the attentional gaze is set or calibrated for a particular level of detail at any one time. In the visual modality, for example, this **detail set** tends to direct the focus of attention to elements of a particular relative size. Several studies have shown that observers can focus selectively on either the more global (relatively larger) aspects or the more local (relatively smaller) aspects in a visual form. Thus, if we have a large figure made up of smaller distinct components (as in Figure 10-25), attention can be set either for the large figure or for its smaller elements. When attention is set for one level of detail, processing of features at the other level is poorer (Hoffman, 1980). This effect may be mediated by separate brain mechanisms that are invoked for the different levels of detail (e.g., Lamb & Yund, 1996). Experiments in which observers searched for global or local forms of varying structures indicate that the global-level processing mechanism may be an attention-demanding grouping operation (Enns & Kingstone, 1995). An example of the effects of detail set is given in Demonstration Box 13.2.

The Neurophysiology of Orienting

Over the past 20 years researchers studying the physiology of the brain have begun to examine some of the neural mechanisms of orienting. Several areas of the monkey brain contain single neurons that fire more vigorously (firing **enhancement**) when the monkey is attending to visual stimuli in their receptive fields than they do when the same target is not attended to (e.g., Mountcastle, Motter, Steinmetz, & Sestokas, 1987). (Recall from Chapter 3 that the **receptive field** of a sensory neuron is that region of the stimulus field in which the occurrence of a stimulus can produce a response from that neuron.) Some of the cortical areas involved in orienting attention can be seen in Figure 13.3A. Deeper in

DEMONSTRATION BOX 13.2

LEVEL OF DETAIL AND ATTENTION

How many times in your life have you looked at a penny? Probably thousands. Take a piece of paper and, from memory, draw both sides of a penny. There is no need to be artistic; just try to represent all the figures, words, numbers, and dates on a penny, each in its proper place. Next, compare your drawings to an actual penny. It is likely that you will find at least one error, and probably several, in the material you include and your placement of it. The reason for this is that it is possible to recognize a penny based on a fairly global set of characteristics, namely its size, shape, and color. So your **detail set** when attending to pennies has probably seldom been small enough to pick out the local characteristics, regardless of the thousands of times you have looked at one. This could be considered to be an example of inattentional blindness, for when you pay attention to a particular detail, such as where the date is placed, it is easy to see and to remember (for a while, anyway).

A

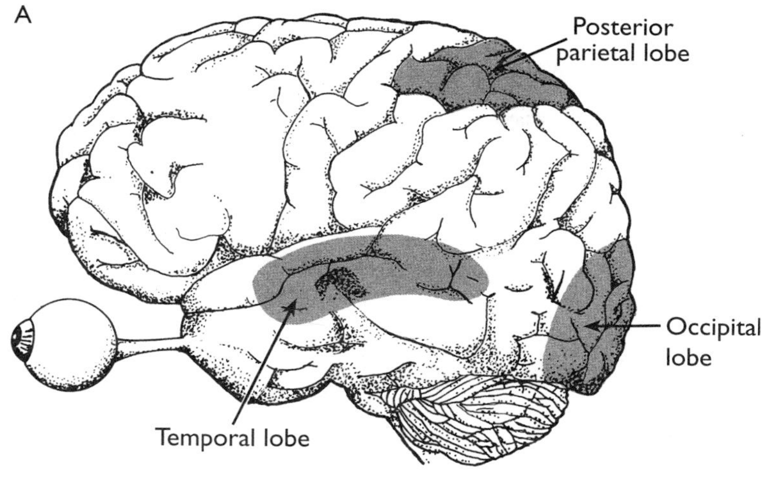

B

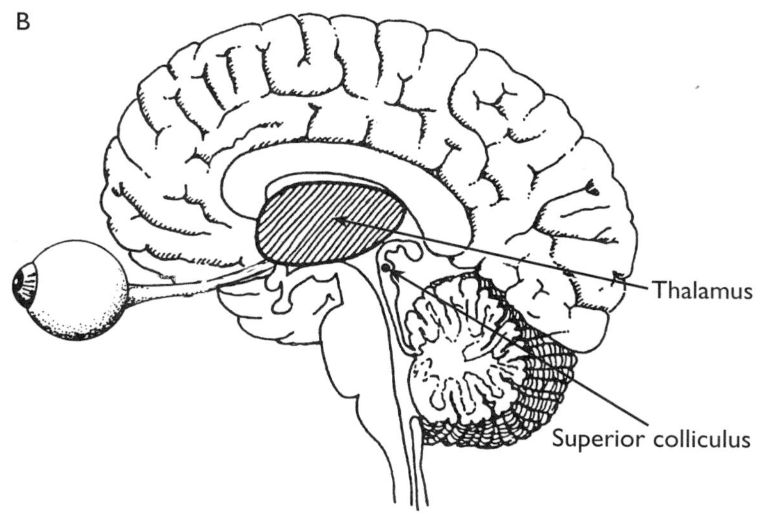

FIGURE 13.3 Areas of the brain involved in attention to visual stimuli. (A) The posterior parietal lobe (covert orienting and filtering) and the temporal and occipital lobes (sites of enhanced activity for attended representations) are located on the cortical surface. (B) The superior colliculus (overt eye movements and covert orienting) and the thalamus (filtering) are located in the brain stem and midbrain, respectively, and are seen here in a sagittal section (slice vertically through the middle of the brain).

the brain, the **thalamus** and the **superior colliculus** are involved in orienting visual attention. The superior colliculi (plural) are the upper pair of hill-like bumps on the top of the brain stem, and they can be seen in Figure 13.3B, which is a view of a brain that has been split down the middle to show the deeper structures. The superficial layers of the superior colliculi contain many neurons that fire when a stimulus appears at a specific location in the visual field. They fire even more vigorously (enhancement) when the monkey makes an overt eye movement toward the stimulus at that location (Wurtz, Goldberg, & Robinson, 1980). These neurons are not simply recording or initiating eye movements, however, because they do not respond at all when eye movements are made in complete darkness. Rather, they show enhanced firing only for eye movements accompanied by a shift in attention toward a visual target, with the increased firing rate of the neurons beginning 50 ms after the target is flashed onto the screen, while the eye movement that follows begins around 200 ms later.

To differentiate overt from covert orienting, we can use an experimental situation like the one shown in Figure 13.4. This involves a screen on which a visual stimulus can be projected and a lever that a monkey can press or release to indicate that it has seen a particular stimulus. In Figure 13.4A the monkey is looking at a point in the center of the screen and neither overtly nor covertly orienting to the target. In Figure 13.4B the monkey has shifted its eyes to the stimulus, demonstrating overt orienting. In Figure 13.4C the monkey has responded to the stimulus with a lever press, indicating covert orienting, but has not moved its eyes, so there is no overt orienting. Recordings of neural activity from the superior colliculus while monkeys performed the

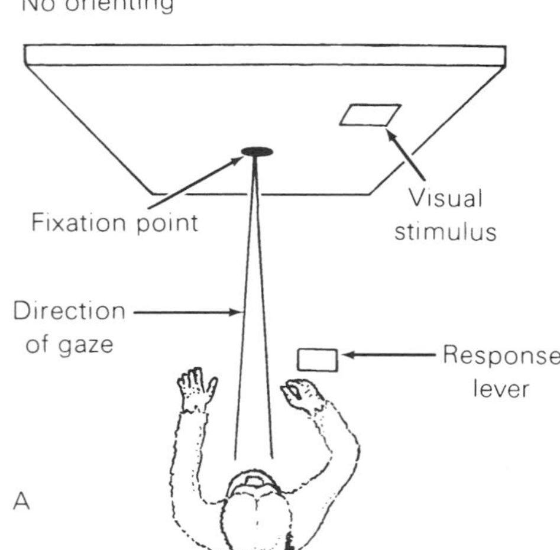

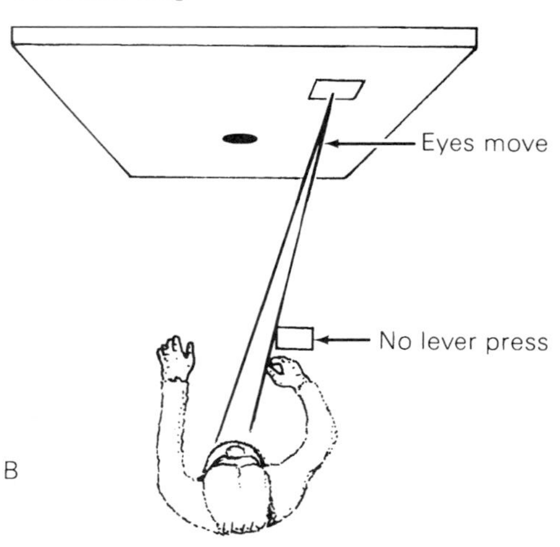

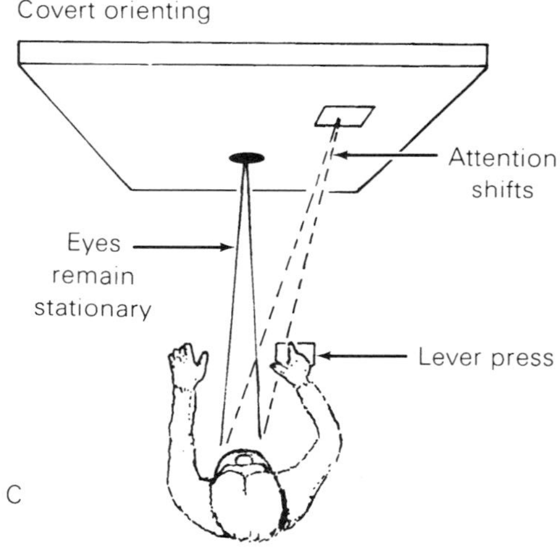

FIGURE 13.4 Conditions used to test for various attention functions in the brains of monkeys. (A) No eye movement or response (no orienting). (B) Eye movement only (overt orienting). (C) Lever press with no eye movement (covert orienting).

tasks in Figures 13.4B and 13.4C indicate that firing enhancement occurred only for the overt orienting displayed in Figure 13.4B and not for the covert orienting displayed in Figure 13.4C.

A similar experiment was done in which a direct cue was presented before the target appeared but no eye movement was made (as in Figure 13.4C), and a recording was made of a superior colliculus superficial-layer neuron's response to the target in its receptive field (Robinson & Kertzman, 1995). The monkey pressed the response key faster when the target appeared close to the cued location than when it appeared far away (such as in the opposite hemifield), regardless of whether or not the cue was in the neuron's receptive field. The response of the neuron to the target, however, was enhanced only if the cue previously appeared in its receptive field. These and other results (e.g., LaBerge, 1995) indicate that the role of some superior colliculus neurons might be to act as triggers for shifts of attention, which then may be followed with overt orienting via eye movements directed at the abrupt-onset stimuli.

The **posterior parietal lobe,** a part of the cortex that lies toward the back of the brain and above the occipital lobes, has also been implicated in attention orienting. The response of neurons in this area are enhanced both when a monkey makes an eye movement toward a target and when the monkey keeps its eyes fixed but responds to the target stimulus with a button press, as in Figure 13.4C (e.g., Mountcastle et al., 1987). Posterior parietal lobe neurons have also been studied in a cue-target paradigm in the absence of eye movements, as discussed for the superior colliculus earlier (e.g., Robinson, Bowman, & Kertzman, 1995). Again, manual responding was faster when a target appeared near a cued location. However, in this case, firing of neurons was always affected when a target followed a cue in roughly the same location even if the cue was not in the neuron's receptive field.

These results suggest that the parietal lobe is an important brain area for directing the **covert** attentional gaze, although it is also involved in overt orienting. Because each hemisphere of the brain receives direct inputs from only one side of the visual field, this may explain why damage to the posterior parietal lobe can result in **hemifield neglect,** which is the inability to pay attention to and to notice stimuli from one half of the visual field (De Renzi, 1982—see also Chapter 14). It also can explain why covert visual orienting is disrupted by lesions of the parietal lobe caused by strokes (Posner, Walker, Friedrich, & Rafal, 1984). Evidence from people with such lesions indicates that the two hemispheres may operate differently in covert orienting, with the left posterior parietal cortex relatively more specialized for shifting attention between objects, in particular for disengaging attention from attended objects in order to shift to a new object (Egly, Driver, & Rafal, 1994). Injuries to either the left or right parietal cortex impair the ability to shift attention away from a currently attended location.

An **electroencephalogram (EEG)** can be used to observe the electrical activity of the brain in humans while they are attending to a stimulus. The EEG displays the voltage of electrical fields created by the brain and recorded from electrodes attached to various locations on the scalp with a small amount of conducting paste (Chapter 3). This allows the measurement of **event-related potentials,** which are tiny changes in the brain's electrical activity caused by a stimulus such as those we have been discussing. Recording is synchronized to start with the stimulus event, and many trials are averaged to produce an indication of the time course of the brain activity (graph in Figure 13.5A). Traditionally in EEGs the positive voltages are plotted in a downward direction

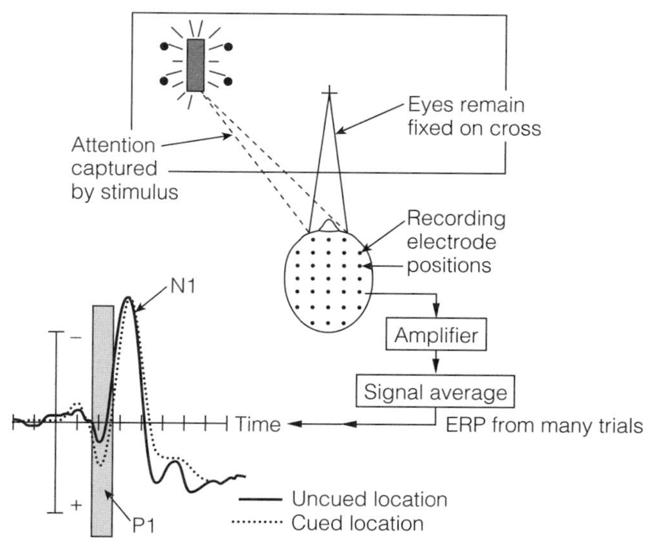

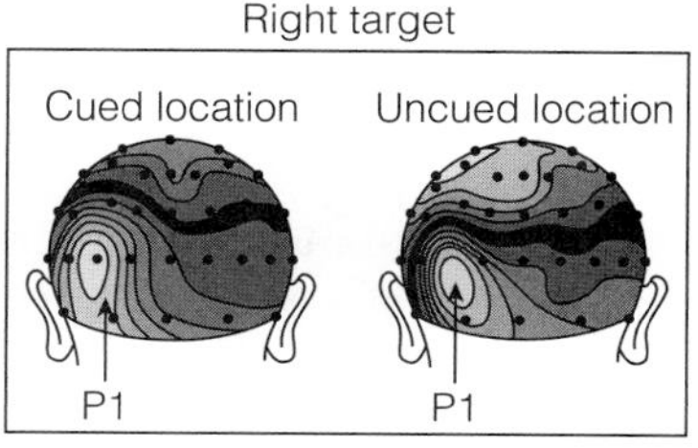

FIGURE 13.5 (A) Visual display, electroencephalograph recording, and event-related potentials for visual attention capture paradigm. (B) Topographic maps of voltages recorded at the peak of the P1 component showing a maximum (lightest color) in the occipital cortex (data from Hopfinger & Mangun, 1998).

(and negative voltages upward) in the display of event-related potentials, just the opposite of the way graphs are usually plotted. Particular changes in voltage over time are called components, and these are labeled in terms of how and when they occur. Figure 13.5A shows both the P1 (first positive-going component) and N1 (first negative-going component) elicited by the onset of the vertical bar in the display in the top part of the figure.

Figure 13.5A actually displays two event-related potentials, that (dotted line) elicited by the visual target after attention was captured by a direct cue (four dots) occurring at the same location about 100 ms before the target, and that (solid line) elicited by a target that was preceded by a direct cue on the other side of the display (Hopfinger & Mangun, 1998). It is clear that the P1 elicited by the cued target is larger (more positive) than that elicited by the uncued target, indicating that the capture of attention by the direct cue facilitated processing of the subsequent visual target at its location.

When event-related potentials are recorded from many sites on the scalp, topographic maps of the voltages can be constructed that represent how the voltage changes across the scalp. Figure 13.5B shows maps indicating that the P1 component is largest in the lateral occipital cortex, in areas where visual stimuli are processed, and thus that processing in the occipital cortex was enhanced by the previous capture of attention by the cue. Similar results have been obtained for cross-modal capture of attention by both auditory (e.g., McDonald & Ward, 2000) and visual (McDonald, Teder-Sälejärvi, Heraldez, & Hillyard, 2001) stimuli, although the effects tend to begin somewhat later for cross-modal capture. A recent fMRI study indicates that the effects of attentional capture across modalities may be mediated by reentrant feedback from the modality processing the capturing cue to that processing the target (Macaluso, Frith, & Driver, 2000), although care must be taken to differentiate between ventriloquism-like cross-modal sensory integration and true crossmodal attentional capture (McDonald, Teder-Sälejärvi, & Ward, 2001).

FILTERING

Having oriented, either covertly or overtly, to an environmental event, we may continue to attend to (look at, listen to) that event to the exclusion of other events. When we do this we are **filtering** out all information except that from the spatial location or perceptual object to which we are attending, a single information channel. How well can we do this? What affects how efficiently we can select one information source and filter out others? What happens to the information to which we don't attend? Everyday experience suggests that attended stimuli seem sharp and clear and are easy to recall, whereas unattended stimuli are less distinct and more difficult to remember. Careful experimental research confirms these informal impressions.

The Cocktail Party Phenomenon

A noisy party is a good example of a situation that requires attentional filtering. Imagine a typical party with loud music and lots of people talking, including someone talking to you. You hear a significant or familiar voice, and you covertly orient toward a conversation off to one side, even while you occasionally nod and say "uh-huh" in response to the person standing in front of you, who thinks you are paying attention to him. Suddenly you are startled to see the person with whom you had been "talking" give a sniff and walk away rapidly, obviously angry at you. You are puzzled because you can't remember a thing that person has said in the last 5 minutes. However, you remember perfectly what your former sweetheart said in the other conversation to which you **were** listening covertly. Apparently you very effectively filtered out everything else, including whatever it was you nodded at that caused your conversational partner to walk away.

Colin Cherry (1953), in a classic article, investigated some of the problems exemplified in the behavior we just described. He introduced the experimental technique called **shadowing** in order to control how his observers oriented their auditory attention. In this technique, an observer is presented with two messages through two different information channels. For example, the two channels could be the two ears (one message to each ear, a technique called **dichotic listening**), or one message could be presented visually and the other auditorially, or the two messages could be presented at different locations in space. The observer must repeat aloud (that is, follow along with, or "shadow") one of the messages as it is presented. Cherry demonstrated that observers could orient to one message and filter out the other.

The difficulty of shadowing depends on the nature of the message: Shadowing prose, such as a selection from a story, is relatively easy; shadowing random lists of words is more difficult; and shadowing nonsense syllables (e.g., **orp, vak, bij**) is the most difficult of all. Clearly, meaning and grammatical structure help us to attend to one message and filter out others. Shadowing is also easier if the messages come from two different places in space, are different in pitch (e.g., one male voice and one female voice), or are presented at different speeds. For an example of how this works, try Demonstration Box 13.3.

What happens to inputs we don't attend to, in other words, those we have "filtered out"? Cherry (1953) found that listeners could remember very little of the rejected message in the shadowing task. In difficult shadowing tasks, even though they knew that they would later be asked about it, listeners were unable to remember words that had been repeatedly presented in the unshadowed message (Moray, 1959). Did the listeners simply not hear the unshadowed message, or did the shadowed message somehow interfere with their memory of the unshadowed message? Both Cherry and Moray had waited for some time after the shadowing task was completed to ask about the unshadowed message. Perhaps the unshadowed message was heard, maybe the words were actually recognized, but they were forgotten quickly because they weren't entered into a long-lasting memory. Perhaps we must pay attention to an input in order to remember it for longer than a few seconds. This idea was tested by interrupting listeners' shadowing and

DEMONSTRATION BOX 13.3

SELECTIVE ATTENTION AND THE PRECEDENCE EFFECT

You may remember our discussion of the precedence effect from Chapter 6, where we listed some variables that affect our ability to localize the position of sound sources in space. When sounds are emitted in enclosed spaces, they tend to cause echoes as they bounce from walls, ceilings, and floors. However, we can still make a correct localization of the sound source because the sound emanating directly from this source will reach our ears before its echoes. The auditory system is sensitive to these time differences and can use this information in the localization of sound-producing sources. The direction of the sound emanating directly from the sound source takes precedence over other sounds in localization, hence the name **precedence effect.**

The precedence effect can also be helpful in selective attention, when we are attempting to process one of many simultaneously occurring stimulus events. A good example of this is found in cocktail party situations, where you may try to follow one of many competing conversations. This aspect of selective attention is helped by the spatial and temporal separations of the auditory inputs. You can demonstrate this for yourself with the aid of two friends (preferably of the same sex) and a doorway. First have your friends stand as shown in Figure A, while each reads passages from a book or newspaper simultaneously. Notice that even with your eyes closed you can easily separate and locate the two messages. Now stand out of the direct line of sight (and sound) of each friend, as shown in Figure B. In this situation the messages must travel indirectly out through the open door. This means that they will tend to reach you at the same time and come from the same direction. Now, again with your eyes closed, notice how difficult it is to locate the voices and to separate their messages.

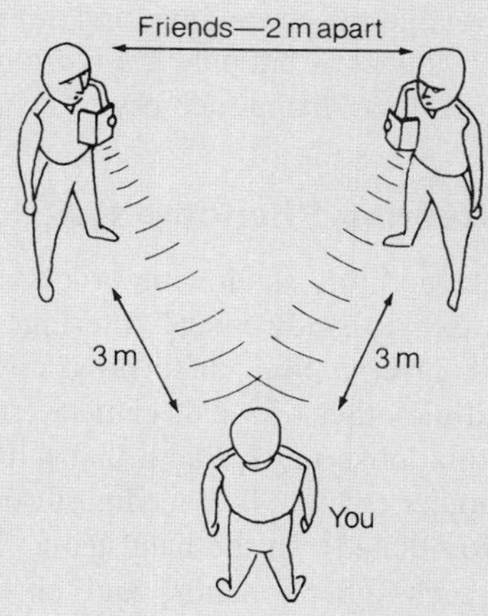

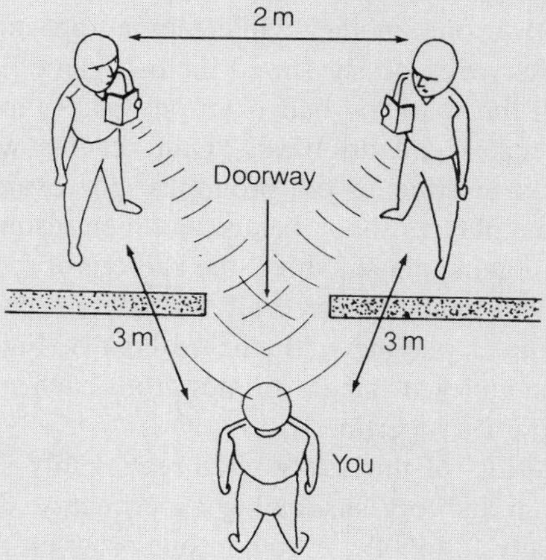

asking them to report what had just been presented to the unshadowed ear (Norman, 1969). Listeners recalled about the last five to seven words, numbers, or whatever units were being shadowed, indicating that information in the unshadowed channel did reach short-term memory.

More recent tests added a method to detect momentary shifts of attention to the unshadowed ear and found that people could remember material from the unshadowed channel only if they had shifted attention to that channel during the presentation of that material (Wood & Cowan, 1995a). Even a powerful stimulus such as their own name in the unshadowed ear was detected by only about 34% of listeners (Wood & Cowan, 1995b). The only people who recalled hearing their own name made attentional shifts to the unshadowed channel immediately after their name occurred, and in addition they recalled an average of two words following the occurrence of their name. It seems that material in the unshadowed ear is available for processing, and attention, for a short while after it occurs, but unless it is attended to it is not entered into a long-lasting memory.

The Video Overlap Phenomenon

An analog of the auditory shadowing task described earlier has been used to study visual filtering (Neisser & Becklin, 1975). Overlapping video programs, one of a hand game and the other of a ball game were presented to observers (this looks much like a badly tuned television, where another channel is "bleeding through" to the channel that you dialed). In the hand game, the players tried to slap each other's hands, and observers who "shadowed" this game had to report each attacking stroke (but not feints). In the ball game, players threw a basketball to one another while moving around irregularly. Observers who shadowed the ball game had to report each throw of the ball from one player to another (but not fakes and dribbles). "Odd" events were also sometimes inserted in the programs (for example, the hand game players shook hands, and then resumed play, or the ball game players threw the ball out of the picture, played with an imaginary ball for a few seconds, and then resumed playing with the real ball). Figure 13.6 shows examples of single frames from each game and the two frames superimposed.

The results of this study were remarkably similar to those from auditory shadowing experiments. Observers could easily follow the events in one program presented alone, as would be expected. They also had little difficulty following the events of one program when the other one was superimposed on it, although they did make a few more errors in this condition. Moreover, the odd events in the shadowed programs were almost always noticed, whereas the odd events in the unshadowed programs were almost never noticed. For example, only 1 of 24 subjects noticed the handshake in the hand game while shadowing the ball game; no subjects noticed the ball disappear in the ball game while they were watching the hand game. The reports that did occur were vague and uncertain and usually not correct. When asked, a few subjects felt that there might be something unusual about the unshadowed program, but they didn't know what it was. Most subjects noticed nothing unusual at all. This indicates that, like auditory filtering, visual filtering allows little of the filtered-out information to make a lasting impression, a result that has been verified in many different situations (e.g., Rock & Guttman, 1981). You can experience a similar type of visual shadowing, and its effect on memory for the unshadowed message, by trying Demonstration Box 13.4. It is also possible to re-create Neisser and Becklin's display and to try their task by feeding the outputs of two video players through a cable splitter (reversed) into a single TV set cable input. You will have the most success with this latter approach if you use two prerecorded video programs that are set in stable scenes with very different content, for example, a basketball game and a hockey game. Don't forget to turn off the sound!

Modern replications of the video overlap phenomenon have gone even further in demonstrating the importance of attention to noticing events in a visual scene. For example, Simons and Chabris (1999) created a film of two different teams playing basketball and introduced as unexpected events either a woman with an umbrella walking across the floor or a person in a gorilla suit walking across the floor. Even when these objects were fully opaque, and even when the gorilla stopped and thumped its chest, many viewers failed to notice their presence. Even dramatic stimuli in simple displays can pass by unnoticed if attention is directed elsewhere. This was called **inattentional blindness** by Mack and Rock (1998).

A related phenomenon is **change blindness** (e.g., Rensink, 2002). In the typical change blindness demonstration a scene is presented for a brief period, followed by a blank and then the same scene with a single change, for example, a picture of a 747 aircraft and another of the same aircraft with one engine missing. This sequence is repeated until a viewer points out the change, which can take many seconds. Unless attention finally alights on the engine that is missing in one view, the change is not

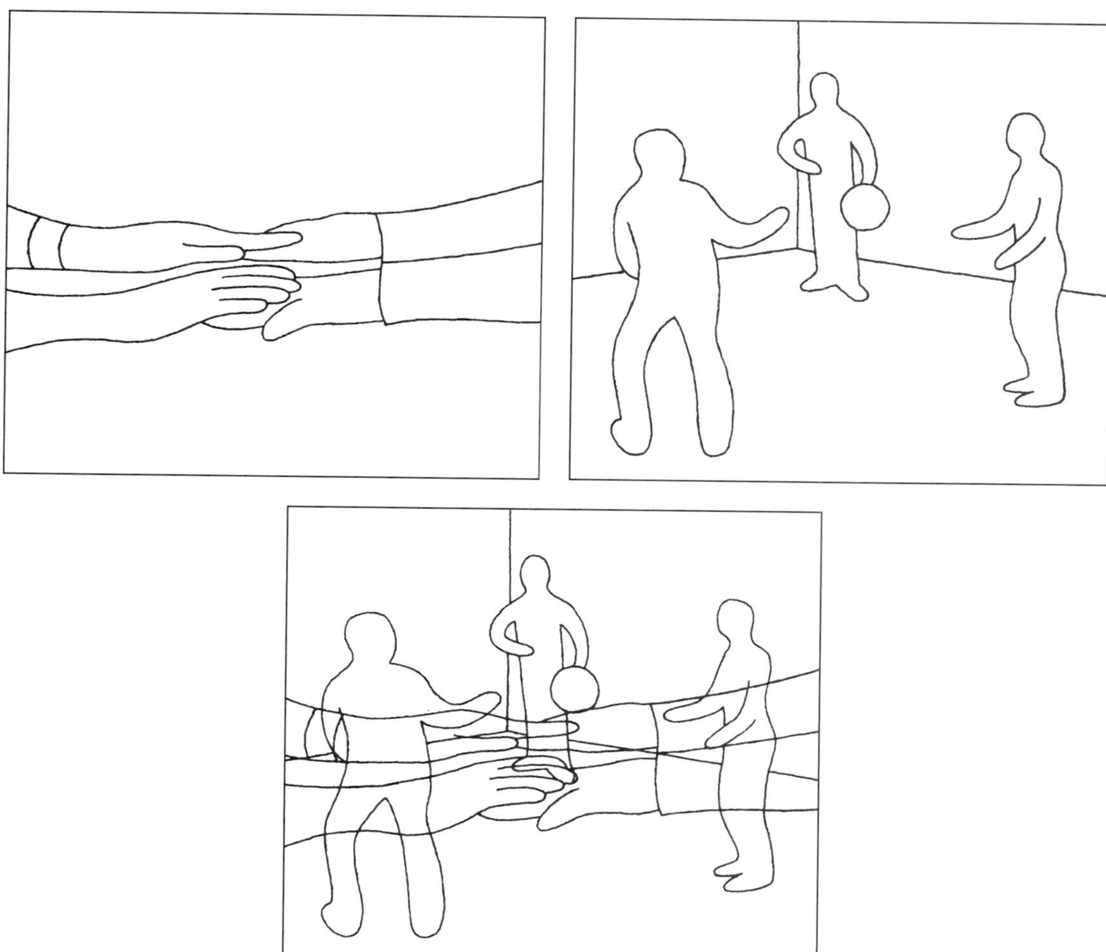

FIGURE 13.6 Outline tracings of isolated frames from the video overlap experiment. (A) Hand game only. (B) Ball game only. (C) Hand game and ball game superimposed (from Neisser & Becklin, 1975).

apparent (Rensink, O'Regan, & Clark, 1997). This and similar results have led some researchers to argue that much of our visual experience is not as solid and complete as it seems. Rather, attention acts to solidify only part of a rather volatile and dynamic representation of the world and only as long as that part is attended (see Rensink, 2002). In this view attention is not filtering out the unattended material, it is rather giving life to the attended material.

The Neurophysiology of Filtering

Where in the brain might filtering of this sort occur? We have described how the **superior colliculus** and the **posterior parietal lobe** of the brain are involved in shifting our attention to various locations or objects in the visual field. However, filtering involves more than simply attending to one object or location and ignoring others. We can choose to attend to one of several stimuli that appear in the same general location. We can also choose to focus on the color rather than the shape of an object or on its texture rather than on its size.

One important brain area in which the behavior of single neurons is affected by attention is the **temporal lobe** of the cortex (e.g., Moran & Desimone, 1985). The temporal lobe is pointed out in Figure 13.3A. You may recall from Chapter 3 that the lower part of the temporal lobe seems to be specialized to answer the question "What is it?"—that is, to identify objects. To study how attention affects the activity of neurons in this area, re-

DEMONSTRATION BOX 13.4

VISUAL SHADOWING AND MEMORY

In the accompanying passage, the relevant message is shaded, and the irrelevant message is printed in the normal fashion. You are to read the shaded passage aloud as rapidly as possible, ignoring the irrelevant (unshaded) message. Now without cheating and looking back, write down all the words you remember from the irrelevant message. Go back and read the shaded passage again, but this time stop after each line to write down the words you recall from the irrelevant message (without looking back at it). You should find that the list of remembered words is longer when your reading is interrupted and you are not asked to recall all of the irrelevant message at once (from Lindsay & Norman, 1977).

In performing an experiment like this one on man attention car it house is boy critically hat important shoe that candy the old material horse that tree is pen being phone read cow by book the hot subject tape for pin the stand relevant view task sky be read cohesive man and car grammatically house complete boy but hat without shoe either candy being horse so tree easy pen that phone full cow attention book is hot not tape required pin in stand order view to sky read red it not too difficult

searchers trained monkeys to attend to one of two stimuli. For example, a monkey might be rewarded with food for pressing a button every time a red rectangle appeared on the screen. This was called the "attended" stimulus. Responses to other stimuli, such as a green rectangle, were not rewarded, and soon the monkey learned to ignore them. They were called the "unattended" stimuli. The researchers then recorded from a single neuron in the temporal lobe that responded best to one of the stimuli, for example, a neuron that normally responded to a red rectangle shown anywhere in its fairly large receptive field. If the monkey was paying attention to the red rectangle, the neuron responded vigorously. Moreover, the neuron seemed to become less sensitive to other stimuli simultaneously present in its receptive field, as if the receptive field had shrunk to fit the boundaries of the attended stimulus. When the red rectangle was present but was not being attended to, because it was no longer being reinforced, the neuron's rate of firing was dramatically lower. Somehow attention had relatively enhanced the response of the temporal lobe neuron to the red rectangle.

This enhancement may be accomplished in part by the activity of the **thalamus,** in particular the pulvinar nucleus, the largest nucleus in the thalamus (LaBerge, 1995). Figure 13.3B shows the general location of the thalamus, which lies in the midbrain, underneath the cortex. The anatomy of several thalamic nuclei is ideally suited for involvement in attentional modulation of responses in sensory and motor areas (Guillery, Feig, & Lozsádi, 1998). These nuclei both send projections to and receive them from many cortical areas, including the temporal cortex, the posterior parietal cortex, and the prefrontal cortex (where voluntary actions are believed to originate). Several studies have indicated that the pulvinar nucleus in particular shows elevated activity when attention must be used to filter out distracting stimuli. For example, Liotta, Fox, and LaBerge (1994) monitored the activity of the pulvinar nucleus of human subjects by PET while the subjects performed either a task that required filtering as well as covert orienting (pressing a button when an O appeared at the center of the letter group to the left of the fixation dot in Figure 13.7A) or a task that required only covert orienting (pressing a button whenever an O appeared to the right of the fixation dot in Figure 13.7B). The activity of the pulvinar nucleus was significantly elevated when the task required filtering compared to when it did not. Similarly, another PET study found that the thalamus was active when a person was required to respond to only a particular attribute of a visual object, for instance, its color or size, and to ignore other attributes (Corbetta, Miezin, Dobmeyer, Shulman, & Petersen, 1991). LaBerge (1995) has argued that this and other evidence imply that the pulvinar nucleus of the thalamus assists in attentional filtering (when instructed to do so by other parts of the brain) by selectively enhancing activity in sensory cortical areas such as the temporal lobe.

Event-related potential experiments have also uncovered effects of attentional filtering on brain activity. An early study Hillyard, Hink, Schwent, and Picton (1973) found that the N1 component of the event-related potential (see Figure 13.5) to an attended sound was larger than that to the same sound when it was unattended.

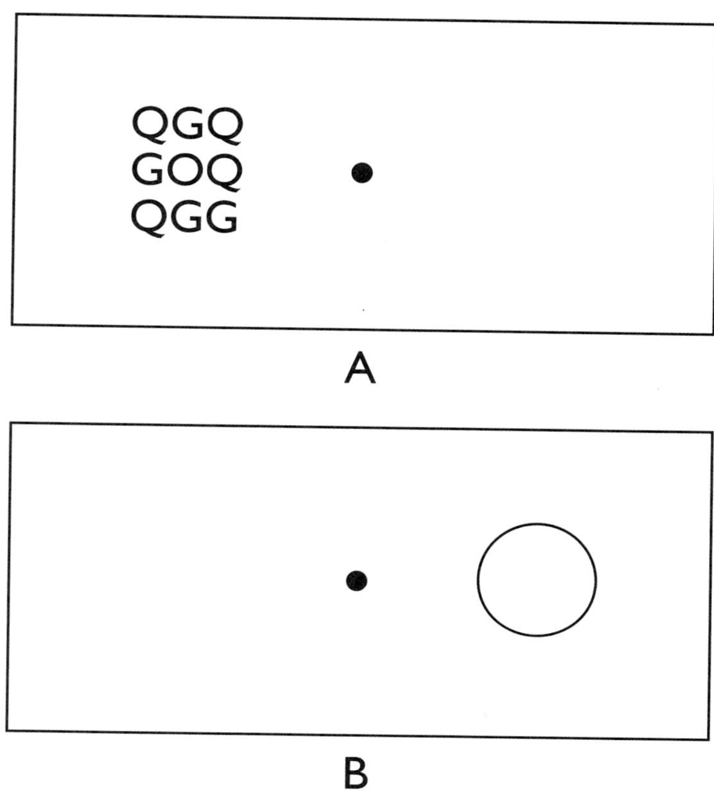

FIGURE 13.7 Stimuli used to ascertain which areas of the brain are involved in filtering. (A) Attending to the center O, and filtering out the other letters, causes much activity in the pulvinar nucleus of the thalamus. (B) Because attending to the large O does not involve filtering, activity in the thalamus is much lower than for the stimulus in (A).

They used a task much like the shadowing task invented by Cherry. More recent studies have shown that in addition, attending to a particular stream of sounds results in a processing negativity that can extend until 300 ms or more after the sound onset (e.g., Näätanän, 1992). Attending produces special processing of the attended information channel that can begin as early as 50 ms after a stimulus occurs.

Divided Attention

An important question relevant to perception is whether it is possible to pay attention to more than one source of information at the same time and, if so, whether performance suffers compared to when only one channel is attended. In the visual filtering experiment (the hand game and the ball game) discussed earlier, observers were also asked to try to **divide** their attention and to shadow both programs simultaneously. That is, they had to report both attacks in the hand game and throws in the ball game. When they tried to do this, performance deteriorated dramatically. Observers missed many more events and typically said the task was "demanding" or even "impossible." Moreover, presenting the two programs to different eyes **(dichoptic presentation)** made the divided attention task no easier. Thus, dividing visual attention between two (or more) sources is very difficult; usually we can look at only one thing at a time. This effect is most dramatic when the competing channels are spatially separated. Under some conditions, attention can be paid to two aspects of a single object at once without depressing performance, whereas when the two aspects characterize two objects separated in space, performance is worse when attention must be divided between them (Bonnel & Prinzmetal, 1998).

Dividing attention between two auditory information channels is similarly difficult. Of course, it is impossible to verbally shadow two messages at once because we cannot say two things at once. However, people have been asked to listen to messages (in this case, word lists) in both ears and later to distinguish words they had heard from distracters (Levy, 1971, cited in Kahneman, 1973). Recognition performance was far poorer when people were trying to pay attention to both ears than when listening to only one ear and filtering out the other. You may have had similar experiences at a party when trying to listen to two interesting conversations at once. It is possible to switch back and forth between them, but if they are at all demanding, a great deal of the information of each one will be lost.

Divided attention is easier if the information channels are in different modalities, such as vision and audition, although performance still suffers in comparison to attention focused on only one channel, whenever the dual task is at all difficult, such as identifying words, lights, or sounds (Bonnel & Hafter, 1998; Treisman & Davies, 1972). Usually, the only time when there is no decline in performance under divided attention is when the task is very easy, such as responding to a simple signal as soon as it occurs in either of two modalities (e.g., Miller, 1982). However, in the vast majority of cases, divided-attention performance is considerably worse than focused-attention performance.

Finally, it is worth mentioning that dividing attention between two demanding tasks does become easier with extensive practice. We all have experienced doing two, or more, things at once, such as driving a car and carrying on a conversation, or reading a book, chewing on a sandwich, and scratching our head. A skilled typist can type at a high rate and shadow a message at the same time with almost no loss of efficiency at either task (Shaffer, 1975). Extensive practice in typing has made that skill "automatic" for the typist. **Automatic processing** requires less attention than does **controlled processing,** allowing more attention to be allocated to the less-automatic skill (shadowing, in this case). We discuss **automaticity** more fully in the next section.

SEARCHING

Imagine you are waiting in an airport for a loved one to arrive home from a trip abroad. The plane arrives, and a flood of people surges through the arrival door. Your eyes flick back and forth across the confusion, searching for that beloved face. You don't bother looking at the people's clothes because you know she is wearing a new outfit, and you don't know what it looks like. You are looking for the peculiar combination of longish coal-black hair, large nose, and wide-set eyes that you remember so well. Someone near you suddenly shouts to a large man in a bright orange suit, who waves in reply. The shouter confides to you that she has an easy time finding her husband at the airport because he always wears that silly suit and "sticks out like a sore thumb." We have been describing a typical circumstance where we know what we are looking (or listening) for and must search a field of "distracters" to find it. This task is one of the most popular for studying attention, partly because it is easy to implement in the laboratory and partly because it has important implications for everyday life.

Eye Movements and Visual Searching

It is much easier to study "looking for" than "listening for" because there is an obvious external indicator of visual searching—overt eye movements. Our eyes are constantly exploring the visual field with high-speed ballistic movements called **saccades.** Demonstration Box 13.5 will show you an easy way to observe saccades in someone who is reading.

The path taken by our eyes as they move (or, more correctly, jerk—*saccader* is French for "to jerk") over the visual field is determined by our intentions, by our previous experience, and by the way the eye movement system works. We will consider each of these influences in turn.

Meaning and expectation help to direct where we look in a visual scene. For example, Yarbus (1967) recorded eye movement patterns while observers looked at pictures with different intentions in mind. Figure 13.8 shows observers' eye movement patterns for a typical picture (A) when asked to estimate either the ages of the individuals in the picture (B) or their wealth (C). Clearly,

DEMONSTRATION BOX 13.5

SACCADIC EYE MOVEMENTS

For this demonstration you will need a volunteer to help you. The materials you will need are a stiff piece of paper with a small hole punched in it and a piece of reading material for your partner. Sit facing your partner at a distance of 2 to 3 ft. Ask your partner to read the passage silently and to move his or her eyes as smoothly as possible. While your partner is reading, look at one of the eyes through the peephole in the stiff piece of paper. Adjust the viewing distance so that only your partner's eye is in view. You should now be able to see each small jerking movement (saccade) as the eye moves across the page. Note that you can identify the end of a line in the passage by the long saccade that is made every so often. You may also be able to tell when your partner goes back to reread some words that were not understood on the first scan.

FIGURE 13.8 Eye-movement patterns made when viewing the picture (A) varied depending on whether the viewer was asked the ages of the individuals in the picture (Scan Pattern B) or their wealth (Scan Pattern C). (From Yarbus, 1967. Copyright Plenum Publishing Company. Reprinted by permission.)

people looked at different places in order to find information relevant to the different questions.

People rapidly learn to inspect spatial locations in a systematic order to detect targets that may be present. Although this is a fairly efficient process for adults, it does not appear to be fully developed until children are about 6 or 7 years of age (e.g., Cohen, 1981) and unfortunately becomes more difficult again for the elderly (Rabbitt, 1984). People also use their knowledge of the world to guide visual inspection. If a scene has been jumbled by randomly interchanging different areas, as has been done in Figure 13.9, people have a harder time locating a target object, such as a store sign (Biederman, Glass, & Stacey, 1973). We also look at unusual objects in a visual scene longer when we find them (A. Friedman, 1979). Perhaps because of this, unexpected objects tend to be remembered and recognized more easily, and exchanges of one unusual object for another (a cow for a car in a living room) are noticed far more often than are exchanges of one usual object for another (a chair for a table in a living room; A. Friedman, 1979). Unfortunately, all of this efficient inspecting doesn't mean that we see everything in a scene. As we discussed earlier, the phenomenon of change blindness indicates that we must pay attention to a particular part of a natural scene in order to notice changes occurring in that part even if they are quite obvious once we are attending to them.

There is also evidence of an important process that could contribute to the constant search for novelty in our looking patterns. This process has been called **inhibition of return** because it refers to a decreased likelihood that people will move their eyes and their attentional gaze back to a location they have recently looked at (e.g., Posner & Cohen, 1984). Inhibition of return has been studied in several different experimental paradigms. In one of them, subjects are asked repeatedly to detect visual targets. Some targets occur in locations previously occupied by targets presented earlier, whereas others occur in previously empty locations. Even after relatively long intervals between targets, from about 1/2 second to 2 seconds, responses to targets appearing where targets had appeared earlier are slower than to targets appearing in new locations (Maylor & Hockey, 1985). Responding to objects that have moved location is also slowed when a target appears in the new location (Tipper, Driver, & Weaver, 1991) or in the old location (Tipper, Weaver, Jerreat, & Burak, 1994). Inhibition of return has been observed even in infants as young as 6 months of age (Rothbart, Posner, & Boylan, 1990). Also, several studies have now confirmed that inhibition of return does occur for target locations previously searched in a visual search task and that search is thereby made more efficient (e.g., Klein, 1988).

The study of inhibition of return is very active (see Klein, 2000 for a review), and several proposals as to the mechanisms that cause it are currently being investigated. It has been proposed that inhibition of return arises from a bias against returning attention to a previously attended

FIGURE 13.9 It is easier to find a target object in a coherent, natural scene (above) than in the same scene randomly jumbled (opposite page; from Biederman et al., 1973).

site or object because the information has already been extracted from it (Posner & Cohen, 1984), arises from a sensory refractoriness at the previously stimulated site (Posner & Cohen, 1984), or arises from various motor inhibitions, including those involved in suppressing an eye movement or other motor response relative to the site of an abrupt-onset stimulus (Posner, Rafal, Choate, & Vaughan, 1985). Inhibition of return has also been found in the auditory modality (Ward, 1994) and across modalities (Spence & Driver, 1998), suggesting that whatever the mechanism, it is general. The neurophysiological evidence also suggests this. The enhancements of processing that are indicated by larger components or processing negativities for attended stimuli are reversed (e.g., McDonald, Ward, & Kiehl, 1999, for visual targets) or absent (Prime, Tata, & Ward, 2003, for auditory targets) when inhibition of return is present. So far none of this evidence has been sufficient to rule out any of the aforementioned mechanisms, although it does indicate that perceptual processing might be affected by at least one of them, probably the attentional one.

Feature versus Conjunction Searching

A common laboratory task used to study visual search involves asking an observer to scan a display of letters (or other forms) in order to find a specified target letter (or form). In one early study, observers searched for particular targets in a list of letters arranged in 50 six-letter lines (Neisser, 1967). With practice they came to perform a top-to-bottom search at great speed (as fast as 60 letters/second). Several factors, however, affected their search speed. For instance, when the target was an angular letter (W, Z, X) and the other letters (distracters) were roundish (O, Q, C), observers searched much more quickly than when the target was more similar to the distracters (e.g., G). When a search target differs from all distracters by possessing a feature they don't have, for example, an angled line, the search is called a **feature search.** When the only way to detect the target is to detect a conjunction (or particular combination) of features (such as the particular angles and their orientations that distinguish between a W and an M), it is called a **conjunction search.** In general, feature searches are much

FIGURE 13.9 (*Continued*)

easier than conjunction searches, which has led them to be called "easy" and "difficult" searches respectively. Neisser's subjects typically reported that when they were searching the list, particularly when the target was very different from the distracters, the nontarget letters were just a blur, and they did not "see" individual letters. In fact, the target often just "popped out" of the array. This is a characteristic phenomenon of feature search, which is also sometimes called "pop-out" search.

Neisser (1967) argued that there is a "preattentive" level of processing that segregates a visual scene into figure and ground, a distinction we discussed in Chapter 8. When there are clear feature differences between the target and the distracting items, the target becomes readily visible because the distracters are lumped together as ground, and the target stands out as a figure by the action of this preattentive process alone. The notion is that similar elements are grouped together automatically, and the ones that don't fit seem to leap into consciousness, perhaps by capturing attention. This isn't possible when the target and background items closely resemble each other (Duncan & Humphreys, 1989). Here, closer attention and scrutiny are needed to detect specific elements (e.g., Julesz, 1980).

The differences between feature and conjunction search have been extensively explored (e.g., Treisman, 1986a). The really striking result is that when feature search is possible, the number of distracting items doesn't seem to affect searching speed. The target simply pops out of the display, and the search is said to be accomplished in **parallel** (meaning that all of the items are effectively processed at the same time). However, when conjunction search is required, the number of distracters does affect search speed. This can be seen clearly in some prototypical data illustrated in Figure 13.10. In a conjunction search we seem to be comparing each of the distracters, one at a time, with the image of the target and responding only when they match. Such an orderly and sequential set of comparisons is often referred to as a **serial search.**

To explain this kind of data, Treisman and colleagues offered a **feature integration theory** (see Chapter 10;

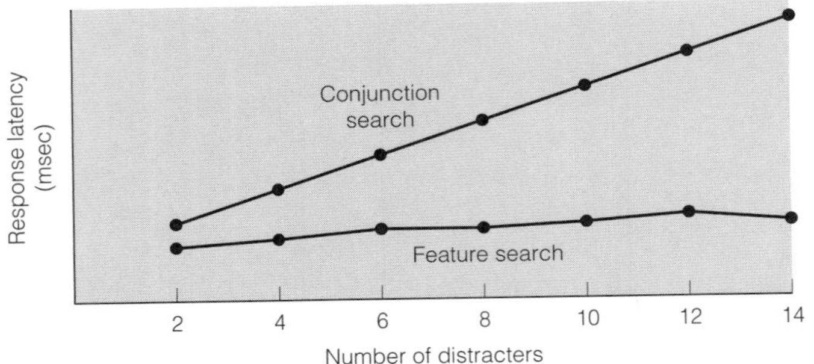

FIGURE 13.10 The relation between response latency to report the presence of a target and the number of distracting items that must be checked. The function is almost flat for feature search and much steeper for conjunction search (based on Treisman, 1982).

Biography Box 13.2). It suggests that each feature of a stimulus (such as color, size, or shape) is registered separately. When an object must be identified from a combination of features, a correct analysis can be achieved only if attention is focused on one location at a time. Recalling our discussion of the attentional gaze, we might say that features occurring in a single attentional "glance" are combined to form an object. This process of combination and comparison takes time and effort. If attention is diverted or overloaded or if presentation is brief, errors in localization of features may occur (Prinzmetal, Henderson, & Ivry, 1995), and we may attribute the wrong features to a particular item and either miss the target or select a wrong target (e.g., Prinzmetal, 1981). Demonstration Box 13.6 gives you an opportunity to try feature and conjunction searches for yourself.

Sometimes conjunctions of simple features also result in a very rapid search—even in "pop-out." Several examples of such displays are shown in Figure 13.11. Demonstrations such as these have been used to argue that the

BIOGRAPHY BOX 13.2

IN SEARCH OF A THEORY OF ATTENTION

Anne Treisman (1935–) was one of many psychologists who was greatly influenced by Donald Broadbent's 1958 book. She had just finished her second undergraduate degree at Cambridge in psychology in 1957 (the first was in 1956 in modern and medieval languages) and entered graduate school at Oxford University, where she received her Ph.D. in 1962 for a thesis entitled *Selective Attention and Speech Perception.* In this thesis and subsequent publications she modified Broadbent's notion of an attention filter, preferring a metaphor of each information channel possessing in attenuator, like the volume control on a stereo, that could be turned up or down to emphasize some sensory input at the expense of others. She built this theory on data showing that the attention filter is not absolute—some information, especially that with semantic importance such as one's name—gets through even when attention is closely engaged elsewhere. Treisman continued to work on attention, and in the early 1980s, while at the University of British Columbia, she and her students published a number of papers that proposed and developed, again based on solid empirical evidence, the influential feature-integration theory of object perception that we discuss in this chapter. One of the trademarks of her empirical research is the clever use of visual search tasks to determine which features of visual objects are easily noticed ("pop-out") of a visual search display. Treisman has received numerous awards for her research in attention and object perception, among them election to Fellowship in the Royal Society of London, election to the U.S. National Academy of Sciences and the American Academy of Arts and Sciences, and has received the American Psychological Association's 1990 Distinguished Scientific Contribution Award. Now a professor at Princeton University, Treisman continues to pursue her research into visual attention, object perception, and memory.

elementary features of forms with respect to attention are not **situation properties** but, rather, **object properties** (e.g., Ramachandran, 1988). We saw in Chapter 10 that situation properties are the relatively variable features of a scene, such as the shapes and colors that change with viewpoint and lighting. In contrast, object properties, such as the relative orientation of an object and surface curvature, tend to remain constant over changes in the observer's viewpoint and scene lighting.

Feature integration theory asserts that attention must be moved sequentially from place to place in a conjunction search or in any other difficult search, but that this is not necessary in a feature search, where the relevant feature pops out from the display. However, there is evidence that in some circumstances attention is used serially even in easy feature searches and that it tends to be allocated to features of the target in conjunction searches (Kim & Cave, 1995). Thus, the same mechanisms may underlie feature search and conjunction search. Moreover, it has also been argued that if the experimental data are carefully scrutinized, the differences described earlier between feature search and conjunction search are more apparent than real (Wolfe, 1998).

Automatic versus Controlled Searching

Practicing and adopting helpful strategies can improve search performance. For example, a conjunction search may be treated as two simple feature searches under some circumstances (e.g., Egeth, Virzi, & Garbart, 1984; Kaptein, Theeuwes, & van der Heijden, 1995). This has been called **guided search** (e.g., Wolfe, Cave, & Franzel, 1989) It means that in Demonstration Box 13.6 you might be able to look only at the white letters in Array C, ignoring the black letters, while searching for the white O. By treating the white objects as figures and the black objects as ground, you can rule out preattentively a large number of distracters on the basis of a simple feature difference from the target, leaving you with only a second simple feature search to complete. There is some evidence from experiments with patients who have had their corpus callosum cut (horseshoe-shaped white area in Figure 13.3B), thus restricting communication between the two cerebral hemispheres, that guided search is apparently mediated by the left hemisphere of the brain, similar to language and other high-level cognitive processes (Kingstone, Enns, Mangun, & Gazzaniga, 1995).

Another strategy that sometimes speeds search is to group items together into smaller sets of stimuli. If stimulus sets are small enough (say, two to eight items), attention operates as if all items are checked at the same time **(parallel search),** rather than sequentially as in serial search. Using such a grouping strategy, a person can search the smaller arrays in parallel for both features and conjunctions (Pashler, 1987).

When observers have been able to practice for a very long time on a task that always demands the same response under the same conditions, the nature of the search process seems to change—search time gradually becomes independent of the number of distracters present. In a typical study of this kind, some observers searched for a fixed set of targets (say, the letters H, S,

DEMONSTRATION BOX 13.6

FEATURE AND CONJUNCTION SEARCH

In each of these arrays of visual forms there are targets to find. The target is a white O. Scan each array quickly, only once, and write down how many targets you see. Notice in each array how difficult or easy it is to find the targets. Do this before reading further.

Now you can know that Arrays A and B required a feature search (in A the feature was brightness; in B it was shape), whereas Array C required a conjunction search (for both brightness and shape). There were three targets in each array. Did you get them all? Most people find the conjunction search to be the most difficult of these tasks, and if they are apt to miss any targets it will be in Array C.

A
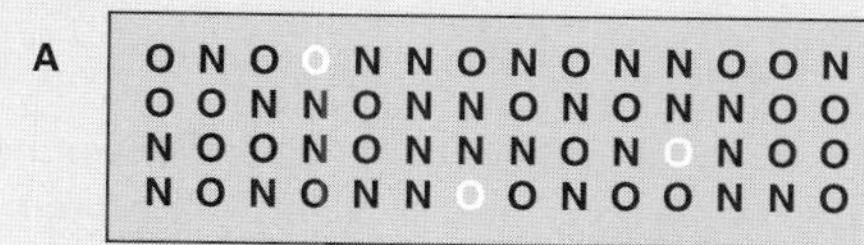

B
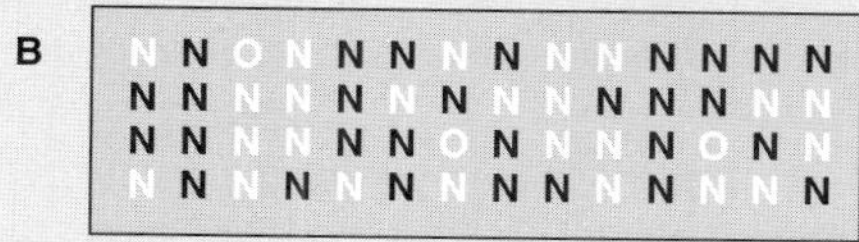

C
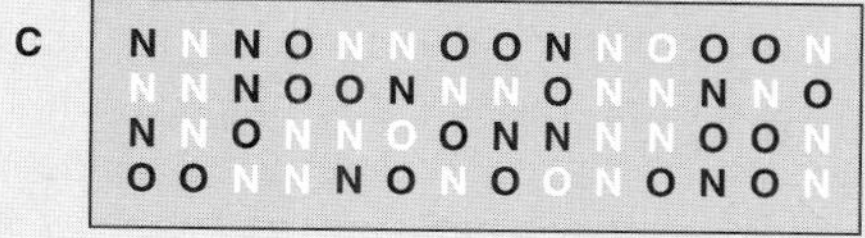

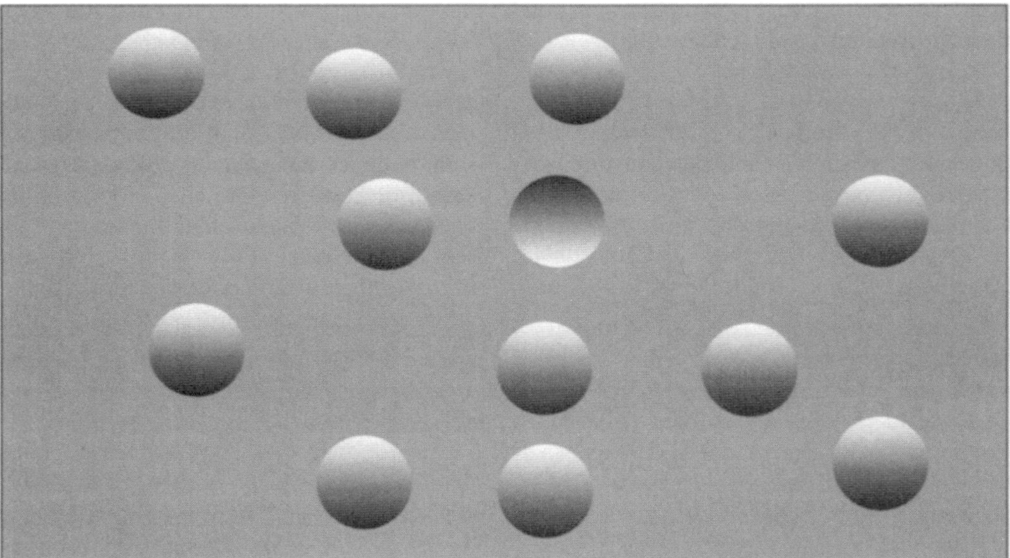

FIGURE 13.11 Examples of conjunctions of simple features that pop out in a visual search. In (A) each item consists of shapes defined by three diamonds—only the spatial relations of the diamonds distinguish the target item from the distracting items (based on Enns & Rensink, 1990). In (B) each item consists of a shaded circle—only the direction of the shading distinguishes the target item from the distracting items (based on Ramachandran, 1988).

and T) among a fixed set of distracters (say, the digits 1 to 9). At first, the more distracters in the display, the longer it took to find the target. However, after 14 days of practice (over 4000 searches) on the same task, the number of distracters in the display ceased to matter. It took the same amount of time to find the target regardless of the number of distracters (Schneider & Shiffrin, 1977; Shiffrin & Schneider, 1977). Figure 13.12 shows this result graphically. It seems that before much practice the search is typical of conjunction searches and is serial in nature (this is often called **controlled processing**). After a lot of practice in a consistent environment the

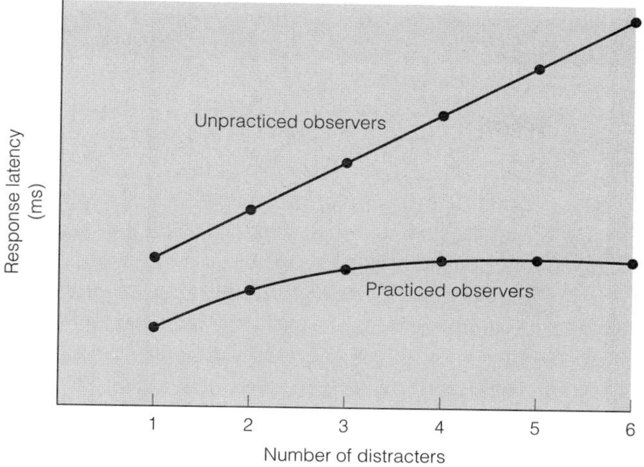

FIGURE 13.12 The relation between response latency to report the presence of a target and the number of distracters to be checked. This function is steeper for unpracticed than for practiced observers (based on Glass & Holyoak, 1986).

search is said to be **automatic,** rather like a simple feature search. A similar result has been obtained for an auditory detection task (Poltrock, Lansman, & Hunt, 1982), which indicates that automatic and controlled processing are not limited to vision, but occur in other modalities as well.

The shift from controlled to automatic processing that occurs with practice is accompanied by several other changes (Schneider, Dumais, & Shiffrin, 1984). On the negative side, for example, it becomes more difficult to prevent responding to targets for which search has become automatic, even if we wish to ignore them. We also don't remember as well the things found and responded to under automatic control. On the positive side, however, it is possible to do other tasks at the same time as engaging in an automatic search, and the added tasks won't interfere with the search. Actually, many lapses of attention in everyday life can be traced to such seemingly automatic processes and their inevitable effects (see Reason, 1984). You can experience for yourself the powerfully automatic nature of reading words, and how this can interfere with other tasks, by trying the demonstration of the **Stroop effect** in Demonstration Box 13.7.

Is it possible that when a process is truly automatic it requires no attentional resources at all? A "yes" answer to this question is given by a clear but rather extreme position called **strong automaticity** (Schneider et al., 1984). However, several results are incompatible with this position. For example, reading in the Stroop effect demonstrated in Demonstration Box 13.7 is supposed to be automatic. However, the Stroop effect is much weaker when the colored ink and the incompatible color name are spatially separated than when they occur in the same place (Kahneman & Treisman, 1984). Strong automaticity would require that as long as the word could be read automatically it wouldn't matter where it was; yet it seems that it is possible to filter out the incompatible color word if it isn't part of the same perceptual object. This and other similar results favor a weaker notion of automatic processing (e.g., Cooke, Breen, & Schvaneveldt, 1987).

More recent results from dual-task (or divided attention) experiments confirm that practice can dramatically improve performance in such situations, but usually only by reducing how much time each processing act requires and not by eliminating the need for attention altogether (see Pashler et al., 2001). Thus the more recent results also favor a weaker position on automaticity.

A somewhat different approach to explaining the effect of practice on search speed emphasizes the acquisition of knowledge (Logan, 1988) or the development of **skill** in accomplishing various perceptual tasks (Neisser, 1976). Here the suggestion is that the effects of practice do not simply involve a switch from controlled to automatic processing but, rather, that a different **strategy** is being used to accomplish the same task (Cheng, 1985). A nonperceptual example would be adding a group of identical numbers, such as 22222. This could be accomplished by adding each of the numbers to a running sum, by learning the multiplication rule and calculating 5×2, or by simply committing to memory the answer to the question, "What is 5 times 2?" In this view, extensive practice allows a new strategy to be learned or new knowledge to be used, rather than causing a transition from controlled to automatic processing. The more recent work on this approach confirms the basic idea but has still not defined exactly what is going on during and after the acquisition of skill (Pashler et al., 2001).

DEMONSTRATION BOX 13.7

THE STROOP EFFECT

The **Stroop effect** is an interesting example of how well-learned material can interfere with our ability to attend to the demands of a task. In 1935 Stroop found that observers had difficulty screening out meaningful information even when it was irrelevant to the task. He devised three situations. In the first he recorded how long it took individuals to read a list of color names, such as *red* and *green*, printed in black ink. He then took an equal number of color patches and recorded how long it took observers to name each one of the series. Then he took a color name and printed it in a color of ink that did not coincide with the linguistic information (for example, the word *blue* printed in red ink). When he had observers name the ink color in this last series, he found that they often erroneously read the printed color name rather than the ink color name; therefore, it took them much longer to read through this last series. The Stroop effect demonstrates that meaningful linguistic information is difficult to ignore, and the automatic expectations that have come to be associated with the presence of words often take over, resulting in difficulties in focusing attention.

Color Plate 8?? is an example of the Stroop Color Word Test, so you can try this for yourself. Have a friend time you either with the second hand of a watch or with a stopwatch as you read each group. Start timing with the command "Go" and read across the lines in exactly the same fashion for each group. When the last response is made in each group, stop timing and note your response time. You should find that reading the color names will take the least amount of time, whereas naming the colors of the ink when the printed word names a different color will take you the most time. Naming the color patches will fall between these two.

The Neurophysiology of Searching

In recent years the search for the neural correlates of visual search has been fruitful. For example, as mentioned earlier, guided search seems to be controlled by the left hemisphere of the brain. One of the more definitive results has been the demonstration that attention does indeed move through a visual display as a difficult conjunction search is undertaken. This has been demonstrated by developing an event-related potential measure of where attention is focused in a visual display, called the **N2Pc.** It is indicated by a more negative voltage over the occipital cortex on the side of the brain opposite to the locus of attention about 200 to 300 ms after the target appears, as indicated in by the arrow in Figure 13.13B (Luck & Hillyard, 1994). In order to show that attention moves to each item that is searched in a difficult conjunction search, it was necessary to use a search display like that in Figure 13.13A (Woodman & Luck, 1999). Targets in this display were always colored and distractors were black, and subjects had to say whether a square with a gap on the left side was present in the array. Do you see it in the figure? Targets were present on half of the trials. However, on 75% of the target-present trials the target was presented in one particular color called C_{75}, and on the other 25% in a different color called C_{25}, biasing the order in which subjects searched the display. For example, if C_{75} was blue and C_{25} was green, subjects would search the blue square first and then the green one, ignoring the other two colored squares and the distractors. C_{75} and C_{25} could occur either on the same side (hemifield) or on different sides of the display. The left side of Figure 13.13B shows the N2Pc when they occurred on the same side, indicating that attention was being paid to that side of the display. The right side of Figure 13.13B shows what happened when C_{75} and C_{25} occurred on opposite sides of the display: The N2Pc first indicated that attention was being paid to C_{75} and then indicated that attention had switched to C_{25} in the other hemifield. Thus, as they searched the display for the target with the gap on the left, they first attended to the most likely object, C_{75}, and then switched their attention to the least likely, C_{25}, doing a serial search of the display.

Vigilance and Arousal

Sometimes we are asked to search for targets that appear very rarely. Therefore, we must sustain a high level of readiness (see the Preparing section on page 414) for an indefinite, sometimes long, time. Examples include a radar technician who is watching for the signal of a particular type of aircraft that flies by only occasionally, and a quality control inspector on an assembly line where damaged or substandard items seldom appear. These observers are performing **vigilance** tasks. Research into vigilance began after it was noticed during World War II that the likelihood of radar operators detecting echoes of

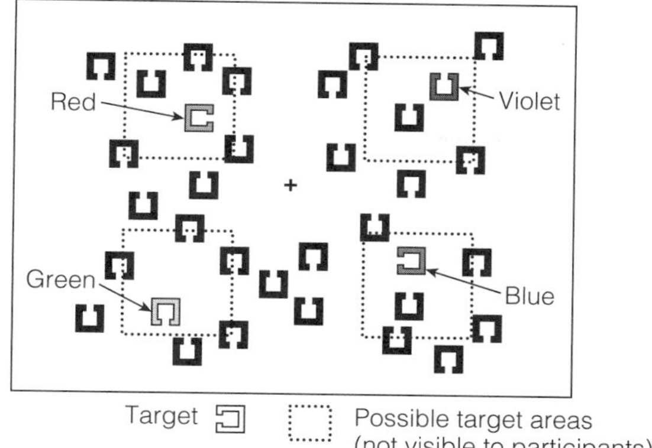

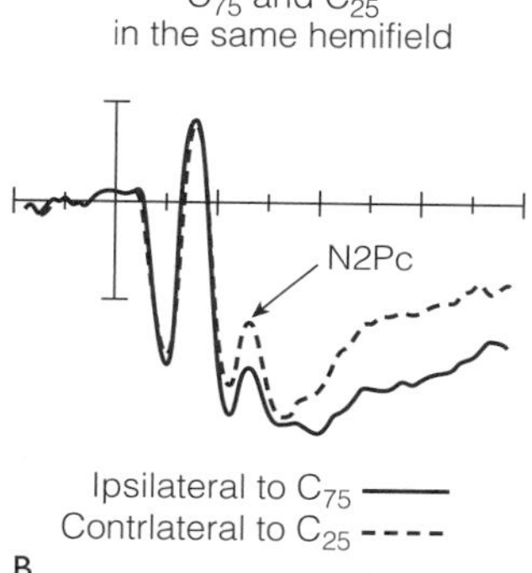

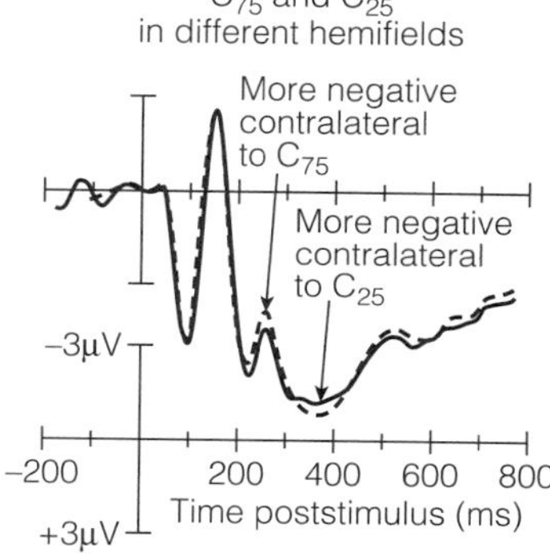

FIGURE 13.13 (A) Visual search display used by Woodman and Luck (1999). (B) N2Pc components when C_{75} and C_{25} were in the same visual hemifield (left) and in different hemifields (right), the latter showing the shift indicating that attention is shifting from item to item in the visual field (after Woodman & Luck, 1999).

enemy planes tended to decrease the longer they had been on duty. After the war, experiments began to explore how attention sustains itself, particularly in boring search tasks with infrequent target stimuli.

In the original experiments on vigilance observers watched a display similar to a clock face around which a clock hand moved in steps. They pressed a key each time they saw the hand take a double step. After only 1/2 hour of watching, observers began to report fewer and fewer double steps, missing almost 25% of them (Mackworth, 1948). Physical fatigue didn't seem to be a reasonable explanation of the drop in performance because the workload was very light. Perhaps the visual system itself was becoming less sensitive, or perhaps the observer was just as sensitive to the double steps but simply failed to respond on some occasions.

The scene was set for the application of signal detection theory (Chapter 2). A decrease in sensitivity of the visual system would be reflected in a decrease in the sensitivity measure, d'. A change in the observer's motivation would be reflected in a change in the criterion, β, which measures response bias. Signal detection theory analysis of this experiment showed that d' did not change over time, but β did. The longer observers had to maintain vigilance, the less "willing" they became to report that the rare event they searched for had actually occurred (e.g., Broadbent & Gregory, 1963). Subsequent research indicated that extensive training can decrease or eliminate such vigilance decrements (e.g., Fisk & Schneider, 1981). Apparently, setting the criterion for responding in such tasks is a function of alertness, or the way available attention is allocated to the task at hand (Parasuraman, 1984).

Does sensitivity (d') ever change in a vigilance task? Yes, it does, and usually for the worse. A meta-analysis of many studies of the sensitivity decrement indicated that four major factors affect the size of the decrement (see Howe, Warm, & Dember, 1995). When the task is a sensory discrimination, as in detecting the presence of a particular visual stimulus, and individual stimuli are presented successively, the decrement increases dramatically with the number of events (mostly nontarget) per unit time (**event rate**). However, if sensory stimuli are presented simultaneously for discrimination, as in saying which of two lines is longer, sensitivity actually increases as event rate increases. On the other hand, for cognitive discrimination tasks, as in classifying a letter, the trends are exactly the opposite: a modest increase in sensitivity with event rate for successive tasks and a dramatic decrease for simultaneous tasks. Moreover, for simultaneous presentation, the decrement is much larger for sensory tasks than for cognitive tasks, except at high event rates, whereas for successive presentation, the decrement is greater for cognitive tasks, again except for high event rates, where they are similar. Finally, the vigilance decrement also depends on overall sensitivity, with greater declines for tasks that have high initial sensitivity.

A major part of maintaining attention seems to be a certain degree of physiological arousal. We adopt certain body positions, tense specific muscle groups, and have the feeling of "concentrating" whenever we are vigilant. Apparently most of us already believe that if we are highly aroused physiologically we will perform better in tasks that require concentration, because we often attempt to raise our arousal level with stimulants such as the caffeine in coffee, for example, before important exams. Is this belief justified? The relation between arousal and performance in general is perhaps most elegantly expressed in the well-known **Yerkes-Dodson law** (Yerkes & Dodson, 1908). Figure 13.14 shows this relation graphically. Contrary to what we may believe, performance doesn't always get better the more highly aroused we are. In fact, overall performance of any task peaks at an intermediate level of arousal. This intermediate level is lower for difficult tasks than for easy tasks, suggesting that very difficult tasks are best performed under low levels of arousal (e.g., Easterbrook, 1959), so perhaps you shouldn't be drinking coffee before a very difficult exam (unless you didn't get enough sleep).

The level of arousal also influences the way in which attention is allocated. This has been studied by artificially inducing arousal through the administration of mild electrical shocks to the subject's fingers (e.g., Shapiro & Johnson, 1987) or by playing anxiety-inducing music (Shapiro & Lim, 1989). Subjects who were moderately aroused in this way were more likely to detect brief tones than they were to detect brief flashes of light, even though these signals were equally detectable when the subjects were not aroused (Shapiro & Egerman, 1984). Moderately aroused subjects were also more likely to detect brief visual flashes in the visual periphery than in the center of the visual field (Shapiro & Lim, 1989). These findings suggest that arousal associated with negative outcomes assists our "early warning" mechanisms. When confronted with danger, humans are probably better off to be more vigilant to sounds than to sights (alerting them to dangers they cannot see) and to visual events in the periphery rather than those at fixation (alerting them to new dangers entering the visual field). Some recent work using brain imaging techniques has begun to uncover the complex relationship among arousal, attention, and vigilance. In one experiment, increasing reaction time to auditory targets over the vigilance period was associated with decreasing activity in the left medial thalamus, an area thought to mediate attentional preparation to respond (Paus et al., 1997).

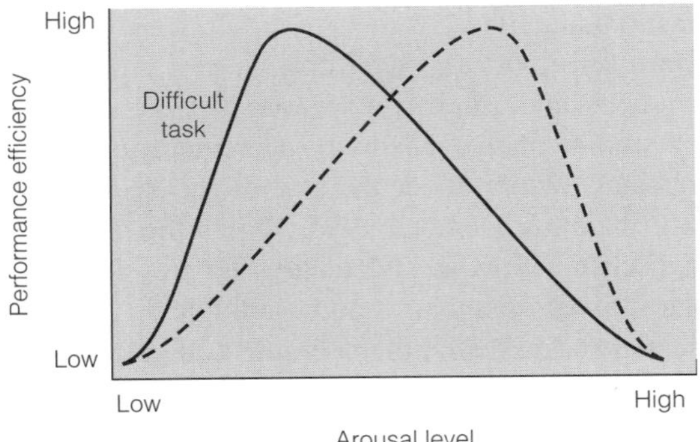

FIGURE 13.14 Yerkes-Dodson law. Performance is best at intermediate levels of arousal, and performance peaks at lower levels of arousal for difficult tasks than for easy tasks.

PREPARING

Knowing exactly when or where an important signal will occur is often difficult. For this reason we have orienting mechanisms that draw our attention to conspicuous stimuli. We also have search strategies that allow us to investigate likely locations where important stimuli might be. However, sometimes our past experience predicts where or when an important event will happen, or we get an advance cue (called a **symbolic cue**) about where or when the event will happen. The information creates in us an **expectancy** about the event, and we may **prepare** for its occurrence by aligning attention with the location and time of the expected event (LaBerge, 1995). For example, imagine you are back in the airport, this time trying to monitor two doors at once through only one of which your beloved will arrive. Suddenly the loudspeaker announces that most of the passengers disembarking from her flight will arrive through Gate 21 (the left one of the two doors). Although you know that still doesn't guarantee it will be *the* door, you find yourself more often shifting your attention to the left door. You are actively preparing for something to happen there by changing your attentional state.

BIOGRAPHY BOX 13.3

AN ENGAGING BUT SHIFTY MODEL OF ATTENTION

Michael Posner (1936–) received his B.S. in 1957 from the University of Washington and his Ph.D. in 1962 from the University of Michigan. During the 1960s and 1970s at the University of Oregon, he worked on applications of information processing theory to memory and skilled performance that culminated in his 1978 book *Chronometric Explorations of Mind*, which became very influential, especially for its exploitation of response time for making inferences about cognitive processes. In the late 1970s he and his students developed a paradigm for studying the covert orienting of attention, a topic that had languished since Helmholtz described it in his informal observations in the middle 1800s. Posner's work, published in several papers in the late 1970s and early 1980s, generated literally hundreds of studies of attention orienting, some of which we describe in this chapter. His metaphorical model of attention switching, involving the operations of disengaging attention from a location, shifting it to a new one, and reengaging it there, mediated by the posterior parietal cortex, the superior colliculus, and the thalamus, respectively, still dominates the orienting literature. Moreover, Posner's discovery in 1984, with Cohen, of the phenomenon of inhibition of return, generated one of the largest-ever bodies of experimental and theoretical work dedicated to a single phenomenon. Work on inhibition of return is still vigorously pursued, with new ramifications discovered every month.

Finally, Posner is famous for being one the main instigators of the field of cognitive neuroscience. When he went to the University of Washington in the 1980s to work with, among others, Steven Peterson and Marcus Raichle on the brain mechanisms responsible for attention orienting, using the latest brain imaging technology, he was starting yet another subcareer. Out of this work emerged a popular and revealing 1994 book with Raichle, *Images of Mind*, which constitutes a manifesto for the cognitive neurosciences. Posner has had a lifelong interest in the development of attention and other cognitive processes and this interest culminated in the founding of the Sackler Institute for Developmental Psychobiology at Weill Medical College of Cornell University, where he is now a psychology professor in the medical college's Psychiatry Department. A member of the U.S. National Academy of Sciences and recipient of the American Psychological Association's Distinguished Scientific Contribution award, Posner is one of the most influential cognitive scientists alive today.

Costs and Benefits of Symbolic Cues

A clear demonstration of the effects of symbolic cues on performance resulted from experiments conducted by Posner and his colleagues (e.g., Posner, 1980, Biography Box 13.3). They asked observers to press a key when they detected a flash of light either to the right or to the left of a fixation point. On half of the trials (the **neutral** trials), the observers fixated a plus sign in the middle of the visual field, and the flash occurred randomly on one side or the other. On the other half of the trials, observers received in advance of the flash a symbolic cue: an arrow pointing either right or left and located where the plus was located on the neutral trials. These were the **cued** trials. On 80% of the cued trials the flash occurred on the side to which the arrow pointed (**valid-cue** trials), and on the other 20% it occurred on the opposite side (**invalid-cue** trials). The observers were not allowed to move their eyes away from either the plus or the arrow; they could only covertly orient their attention. Figure 13.15A shows a summary of these conditions.

Figure 13.15B shows typical results. The average reaction time on neutral trials, about 245 ms, is a baseline that indicates what performance level we would expect without any location-specific attentional preparation stimulated by the symbolic cue. From Figure 13.15B you can see that it took about 30 ms less than that baseline to respond to the flash on the valid-cue trials (the **benefit** of a valid symbolic cue), but it took over 50 ms more than

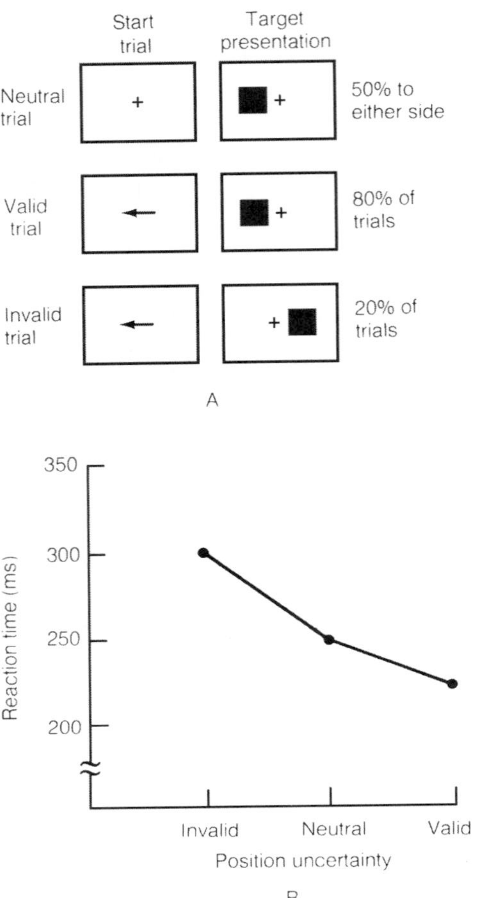

FIGURE 13.15 (A) Stimulus presentations used to study the effects of preparation on detection. (B) Results of reaction-time study of preparation showing the costs (invalid-cue reaction time minus neutral-cue reaction time) and benefits (neutral-cue reaction time minus valid-cue reaction time) of advance knowledge of stimulus location (based on Posner, 1980).

the baseline to respond to the flash on invalid-cue trials (the **cost** of an invalid symbolic cue). The costs and benefits of symbolic cues have been interpreted by Posner (1980), and others, as indicating that an informative symbolic cue can stimulate the covert orienting of attention in preparation for an event, even in the absence of a stimulus at that location in the visual field on which to focus the attentional gaze.

The effects of preparing for an event by orienting attention directed by symbolic cues depend on a number of factors. A somewhat different experimental situation involves a visual field that contains several small empty boxes to which attention can be covertly oriented in response to a symbolic cue. Under these conditions it has been found that the maximum costs and benefits of symbolic cues do not occur immediately but, rather, take at least 300 to 500 ms after the appearance of the cue to produce their full effect (Shepard & Müller, 1989). Thus, preparatory attentional alignments in response to a symbolic cue take much longer than does covert orienting in response to an abruptly appearing direct cue, which occurs in about 100 ms. Part of this extra time must be the time necessary to decode the meaning of the symbolic cue and to initiate the indicated covert shift of attention voluntarily. The voluntary nature of such attention shifts is supported by the fact that symbolic cues can be ignored easily, especially if the subject discovers that, in a particular situation, the available symbolic cues are often wrong (Jonides, 1981). The slower, voluntary alignment of attention in response to a symbolic cue is not automatic. Orienting of attention in response to a symbolic cue can be interrupted by the occurrence of another, attention-grabbing, stimulus (Müller & Rabbitt, 1989), although highly informative symbolic cues can direct attention to a location where it can be sustained even in the face of the occurrence of abrupt-onset stimuli at other locations (Yantis & Jonides, 1990). The costs and benefits associated with symbolic cues affect a broad range of tasks, including detection, identification, and discrimination (Downing, 1988).

Moreover, more natural, ecologically relevant stimuli, such as a pair of eyes gazing in a particular direction, appear to cause people to prepare for a stimulus at the indicated location, accompanied by faster response to stimuli occurring there (e.g., Friesen & Kingstone, 1998). This phenomenon is certainly related to the fact that gaze following, that is looking where someone else is looking, is an attentional strategy exhibited by even very young children and by other primates.

Attention preparation is not limited to visual cues and events. Auditory events (such as the howling of the wolves in the introduction) can be expected and prepared for as well. For instance, imagine you are expecting your mother to come home any minute now. You are expecting to hear her cheery "Hello" in her usual rather high-pitched voice. At this moment your father shouts to you to come help him in the basement. You don't hear him calling, and a minute later he storms into the room, demanding to know why you weren't responding to him. You explain that you were listening for your mother's high-pitched voice and simply didn't hear his much lower pitched voice all the way from the basement. (If he doesn't believe you, you can always show him this discussion.) There is lots of evidence that detection of

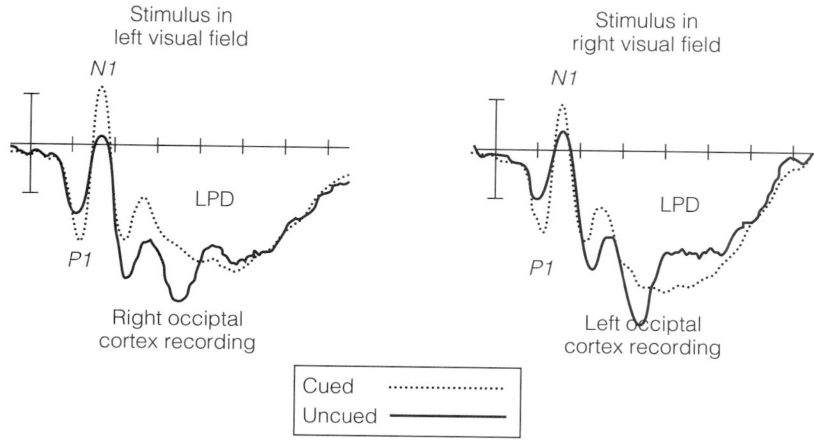

FIGURE 13.16 Event-related potentials measured in the experiment diagrammed in Figure 13.15. Results are displayed separately for targets in the left and right visual fields (LVF and RVF, respectively) and show enhanced P1 and N1 components for targets at expected locations (after Mangun & Hillyard, 1991).

sounds is more difficult when they are of uncertain frequency; that is, there is a cost of not attending to the appropriate frequency region (e.g., Scharf, Quigley, Aoki, Peachy, & Reeves, 1987; Swets, 1963). However, if observers are told which frequency to listen for by a nonauditory symbolic cue, their detection of the sound (Hafter & Schlauch, 1991) and discrimination of its intensity (Ward & Mori, 1996) are improved. Thus, preparation can help us to "tune in" or "tune out" an auditory stimulus by allowing us to select a frequency region to which to orient our attention.

The Neurophysiology of Preparing

In addition to the effects that attentional preparation has on behavior, such as allowing us to respond more rapidly to stimuli for which we are prepared, researchers have found preparation to be reflected in patterns of brain activity. There is an intriguing finding from measurements of event-related potentials related to preparation: When an observer sees a target at an expected location, some components of the event-related brain potential are larger than when the same target falls on the same retinal location but is unexpected. One example is a careful study by Mangun and Hillyard (1991), in which a paradigm similar to that in Figure 13.15 was used. In their study, associated with the shorter reaction times to stimuli presented at an expected (cued) location, several components of the event-related potential were significantly larger for expected targets. Figure 13.16A shows what these event-related potentials looked like. You can see that the P1 and N1 waves recorded from the scalp over the occipital cortex are larger (depart more from the baseline) for the cued targets (dotted lines) than for uncued targets (solid lines) regardless of to which visual field the target was presented.

A more recent study of a related paradigm involved fMRI and distinguished between the brain's response to the cues and those to the targets (Hopfinger, Buonocore, & Mangun, 2000). Cues caused enhanced activity in frontal, parietal and temporal lobes, indicating that these areas are part of a network involved in decoding the cue and directing voluntary attention to an expected target location, whereas targets caused enhanced activity in visual cortex, indicating that preparing for the target enhanced processing when it appeared at the expected location. These and similar studies are revealing the mechanisms and consequences of the brain's voluntary preparation for particular stimuli.

THEORIES OF ATTENTION

Ever since the first studies of attention, investigators have attempted to construct a coherent theoretical account of the major phenomena. As you have seen in this chapter, however, the concept of attention can mean many different things, and it has been studied in many different ways. Therefore, the goal of a coherent and widely accepted theory is still out of reach. At present there are several approaches to understanding attention. We will try to give you the flavor of a few of them here, but you must remember that not one of these approaches is adequate to explain all of the data described earlier, let alone the vast array of other data we do not have space to describe. Moreover, the results we have described on the neurophysiology of attention are having great influence, and will surely form a part of any comprehensive theory.

All theories of attention attempt to explain its filtering aspect. Probably the oldest surviving theoretical approach is the group of **structural theories.** As pointed out by Kahneman and Treisman (1984), the studies of stimulus filtering that were popular in the 1950s and 1960s seemed to imply that perceptual attention is structurally limited. The notion was that there is a bottleneck or a filter somewhere in the information-processing system beyond which only one, or at most a few, stimulus input can pass at one time. The first studies suggested that this bottleneck occurs very early in the perceptual process, just after registration by the sensory system and before the meaning of an input can be determined (Broadbent, 1958). This **early selection** model is depicted schematically in Figure 13.17. Imagine that you are trying to listen to only one person in a room full of talking people. According to an early selection model, you would isolate that person's voice by means of the physical characteristics (such as frequency, intensity, and location) that distinguish it from the others, rather than by means of what the various speakers are saying. Although the physical qualities are registered for all of the voices, only the words associated with the particular physical characteristics admitted by this early filter (such as low frequency, very intense, and from over there) are processed for content and understanding.

Early selection models have difficulty with evidence that at least some analysis is done on information coming through unattended perceptual channels. This processing may affect our responses even if we are unaware of it (e.g., Merikle, Smilek, & Eastwood, 2001). A striking example is when someone, in a conversation that you are not paying direct attention to, mentions your name. In this instance you sometimes immediately become aware of that fact and may even switch your attention to that conversation (see our earlier discussion of filtering and Wood & Cowan, 1995b). This kind of evidence led to a set of structural theories that emphasized **late selection.** They hypothesized that *all* information entering sensory systems gets some preliminary analysis. The bottleneck is then believed to occur at a stage of more or less conscious processing, when material is being entered into a longer-lasting memory (e.g., Deutsch & Deutsch, 1963). A schematic representation of this kind of model is shown in Figure 13.17. The debate between early and late selection still rages and has spilled over onto other approaches as well (Pashler, 1996).

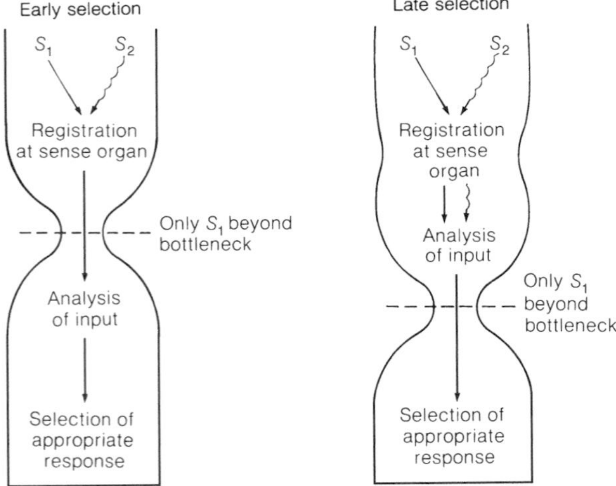

FIGURE 13.17 Bottleneck models of attention (stimuli are indicated by S_1 and S_2). Early selection models locate the bottleneck (the structural limitation on information processing) just after registration of the stimulus, whereas late selection models locate it after some amount of analysis.

A second general approach to attention has grown mostly from studies of search and preparation (Kahneman & Treisman, 1984), especially studies involving comparisons of focused and divided attention. The general finding that dividing attention between two tasks or searching for more than one target usually is more difficult than focusing on one task or target has led to the notion that there are **attentional resources** that can be "used up" by a task. If there is more demand than there are resources available, then performance suffers. The first theories of a limited attention capacity viewed attention as a single "pool" of capacity (e.g., Kahneman, 1973). A representation of such a model is shown in Figure 13.18. All of the available capacity is used for one task in Figure 13.18A, whereas in Figure 13.18B, involving divided attention, the capacity must be shared, leaving less processing resources for each task. This would predict that both of the processing tasks in a divided attention condition would be accomplished less efficiently because fewer resources are available to each.

In contrast to the usual situation, there have been some demonstrations of near-perfect division of attention, for instance, when an expert pianist sight-reads music and shadows a verbal message at the same time. This has led some theorists to suggest that there may be multiple resources, as shown in Figure 13.18C (e.g., Wickens, 1984). Some of these resources are probably specific to a particular sensory modality, whereas others may be attributable to an "executive" that monitors inputs from the various modalities and controls access to response selection. Whether attention to one task interferes with attention to another would then depend on the characteristics of the tasks and the processing required.

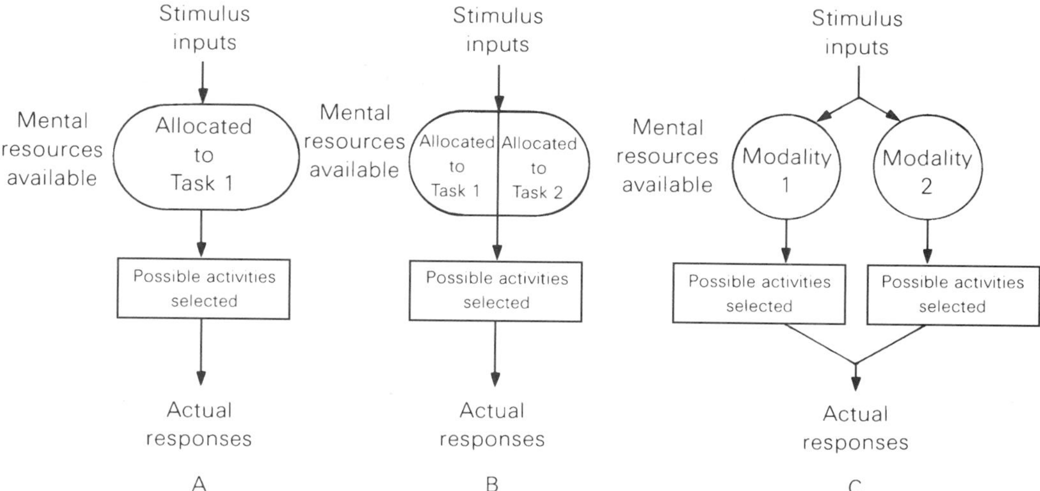

FIGURE 13.18 Attentional resource models. Parts A and B show a single resource model with either one (A) or two (B) tasks to accomplish simultaneously. In C separate resources are available for different sensory modalities or task types.

For example, monitoring and analyzing two prose passages read into the two ears probably require that the same set of resources and analyzers be utilized for each of the two tasks. This is like the situation of Figure 13.18B; hence these two tasks would interfere with each other. In contrast, drawing a picture or doodling while monitoring someone speaking probably involves different types of mental capacity, and one task will not compete with the other for mental resources (more like the situation in Figure 13.18C). Some research suggests that the bottleneck model and the capacity model can be combined, and it may make sense to think of selectivity and capacity limitations at both early and late processing stages (Dark, Johnston, Myles-Worsley, & Farah, 1985).

In addition to the models we have discussed, several newer types of attention theories have been proposed. These theories are based either on our growing knowledge of the neurophysiological underpinnings of attention and action (e.g., Parasuraman, 1998) or on a more abstract, often mathematical or computational, conceptualization of attention (e.g., Logan, 1996; Sperling & Weichselgartner, 1995). There have even been theories of how attention oscillates over time, and can be entrained to rhythmic events such as music (e.g., Large & Jones, 1999). These dynamic theories also tend to be mathematical, since the description of oscillators is. None of these theories has yet gained universal acceptance. Nonetheless, the rapid pace of attention research—and the novel approaches being proposed—promises that our understanding of this elusive yet ubiquitous phenomenon will continue to advance in the new millennium.

STUDY QUESTIONS

1. Describe each of the major varieties of attention and give an example of each.
2. What kinds of stimuli capture attention and why?
3. What do we know about the brain mechanisms of covert orienting?
4. How good is the attention filter? Give examples.
5. Describe the feature integration theory of visual search.
6. What evidence do we have that attention moves from item to item of a visual display during a difficult search?
7. What is automaticity and how does it affect visual search and the performance of dual tasks?
8. How does advance preparation affect the processing of a visual target?
9. What is the Yerkes-Dodson Law and how does it affect performance on tasks of different difficulty levels?
10. Describe the two major types of attention models and indicate how each would explain performance in a dual task situation when neither task is automatic.

CHAPTER 14

CONSCIOUSNESS

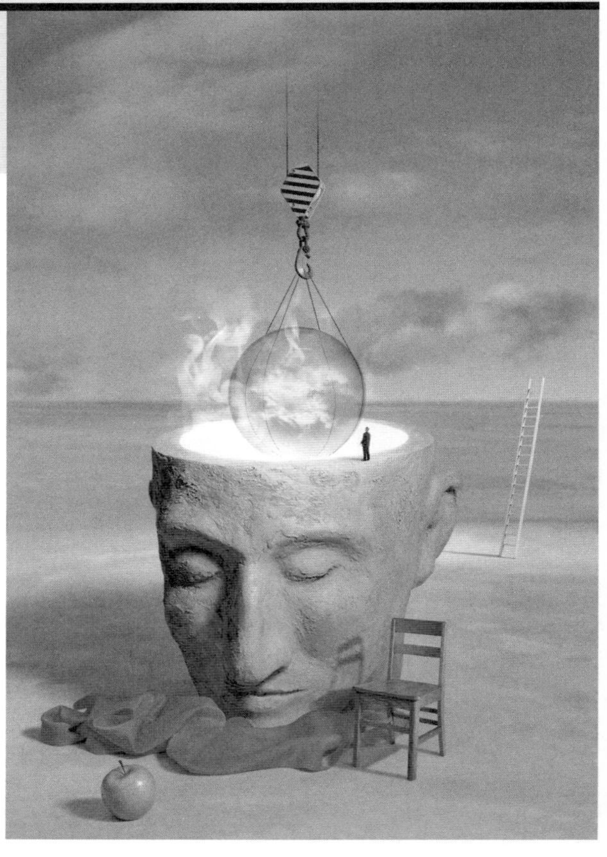

CHAPTER SUMMARY

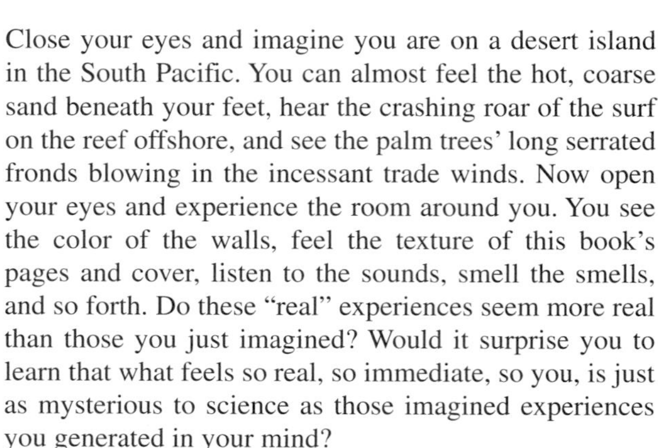

Close your eyes and imagine you are on a desert island in the South Pacific. You can almost feel the hot, coarse sand beneath your feet, hear the crashing roar of the surf on the reef offshore, and see the palm trees' long serrated fronds blowing in the incessant trade winds. Now open your eyes and experience the room around you. You see the color of the walls, feel the texture of this book's pages and cover, listen to the sounds, smell the smells, and so forth. Do these "real" experiences seem more real than those you just imagined? Would it surprise you to learn that what feels so real, so immediate, so you, is just as mysterious to science as those imagined experiences you generated in your mind?

We have just been asking some questions that asked you to report something about your state of consciousness. This book is about the scientific study of sensation and perception; and so it might be reasonable to ask why we seem to have gone astray into the realm of philosophers and poets to talk about consciousness. The reason is that consciousness is really a fundamental issue in the study of perception. What you experience at any moment of time is simply what is present in your consciousness; and much of that experience is generated by perception. When you tell people what you have perceived you are really telling them what you were consciously aware of. In some respects, your entire life as you know it is simply a series of sensations connected to different states of consciousness. Perhaps the author Henry James put it most eloquently when he noted, "Experience is never limited, and it is never complete; it is an immense sensibility, a kind of huge spider-web of the finest silken threads suspended in the chamber of consciousness, and catching every air-borne particle in its tissue" (James, 1884, *The Art of Fiction*).

Let us, however, put the more poetic statements aside, since there are some fundamental scientific questions that must be asked about consciousness if we are to understand perception in general. These questions would include the following:

1. How does perception give rise to consciousness?
2. Is consciousness really necessary for us to process and respond to sensory stimuli?
3. If unconscious perception is possible, what information comes in that way, and what do we do with it?
4. Does consciousness serve any real function? Presuming that the answer is yes, is that function sensory, perceptual, cognitive, or some means of linking perception to action?
5. Are there identifiable brain states, neural pathways, or locations in the brain that can give rise to conscious experience?

DEFINING CONSCIOUSNESS

Consciousness is notoriously hard to define, and some thinkers feel it is best left undefined. However, we must establish some guidelines as to what consciousness is, or is not, so that we can at least agree on what we are talking about. First we must distinguish between conscious and unconscious states. When you are in deep sleep, in a coma, or under a general anesthetic, we say you are unconscious. When you are awake and behaving normally, we say that you are in a conscious state. There are ambiguous states, like dreaming, sleepwalking, hypnosis, meditation, intoxication, and so forth. These states are difficult to classify and also might indicate problems with a simple categorization. We need to keep these questionable situations in mind as we proceed to learn about consciousness, but we need not delay our progress waiting for a complete understanding of these states.

Generally speaking, a working definition of consciousness might be that it includes everything that you can report about your world and your experience at any moment in time. The first experimental psychologists, working in the laboratory of Wilhelm Wundt in the 1870s, believed that the purpose of the science of psychology was simply to describe the contents and structure of consciousness. To that end observers were trained in the technique called **introspection,** from the Latin meaning "to look" (*spec*) "inside" (*intro*). This involved the careful description of the basic aspects of that individual's conscious and perceptual experiences at any instance. According to these researchers, anything that was not in consciousness could not affect the behavior of the individual.

Most people have heard of the great clinical psychologist Sigmund Freud. If you ask the average person why he was a controversial figure in psychological science, they will probably tell you that it was because he attributed sexual feelings to infants and young children. While that was indeed a point of controversy, the very basic aspect of Freud's theories that made them different from those that preceded him was his supposition that there was an active **unconscious,** that the events and activities that we are not conscious of can also affect our ongoing behaviors.

Freud's contention that unconscious factors can be significant has now come to be accepted doctrine. In fact, we now even refer to **preconscious** factors involving perceptual stimuli that are unconscious at this moment, but can easily be brought into consciousness, such as the weight of your body resting on your chair. That experience was not in consciousness until you turned the spotlight of your attention onto it, and then it leapt into your perceptual awareness. The technical term that tends to be used for our lack of consciousness for stimuli that we are not paying attention to is **inattentional blindness,** and it was discussed in Chapter 13. It applies not only to the touch sensation that we used in our example, but also to vision, hearing, tasting, smelling, and so forth.

One interesting aspect of this whole process is that we are not aware of how much we are not aware of. We feel we are aware of everything about the current scene and have an **illusion of complete perception.** Demonstration Box 14.1 provides a simple example of this. When we are looking for Waldo in the "Where's Waldo?" display, we feel we can see everything that is there, all the intricate details of the many other little people in the scene, their clothes, other props, landscape features, and so forth. Before we find Waldo, however, we are not "seeing" Waldo. Although we seem to be aware of everything in the scene, we are clearly not aware of Waldo. When, after much searching, we "find" him and are able to focus our attention on him, we can finally say we are aware of him.

It should be obvious that we are beginning to focus on a particular kind of consciousness that we can call **perceptual awareness.** When we are perceptually aware of something, we can report its presence, either verbally or by some prearranged signal; that will be our operational criterion for perceptual awareness (Frith, Perry, &

DEMONSTRATION BOX 14.1

WHERE'S WALDO? THE ILLUSION OF COMPLETE PERCEPTION

Look at the accompanying display. The usual task is to find Waldo, who is pictured at the top of this box, in this scene. Of course, this is not easy since the scene is complicated, and there are many visual objects that have similar features to Waldo. Waldo will not simply "pop out" (see Chapter 13). However, before you search for Waldo, let's do a little elementary phenomenological analysis. Look at the display. Pay attention to what you are experiencing. Most people would say they "see" everything in the scene. However, are you aware of Waldo there? You certainly can't point him out to an observer, which would be a good criterion to use for awareness of him. Despite your impression of seeing everything, you don't know where Waldo is. There is something in the scene that you are not seeing, that you are not aware of, even though the information about it has certainly been processed by your visual system. Now find Waldo. Pay attention to your experience when you find him. Now you are aware of him and can point him out to an observer. What is the difference between your feeling of seeing everything before and after finding Waldo? If you're like us, not much. And yet there are surely other aspects of the scene that you are still blissfully unaware of, just like you were of Waldo before you found him. The illusion of complete perception is very compelling, and it seems to be an illusion of conscious awareness.

Lumer, 1999). We will assume that although such reports about awareness can be lies, they cannot be mistaken. That is, since they are about our own personal, inner, experiences, we cannot, by definition, possibly mistake them for someone else's experiences, or report our experience incorrectly by mistake, or have an awareness of an experience of which we are unaware. We will be careful, however, to corroborate such reports, since they could be "white" lies told to please the experimenter, or "denial" lies told to avoid embarrassment. How could we corroborate such reports of personal experiences? With great difficulty, and usually by building a network of associated reports and related empirical facts, like whether relevant stimuli are above an objectively defined threshold (see Chapter 2).

Philosophical Issues

To say that we recognize the difficulties associated with studying consciousness, but still think that it can be investigated scientifically, places psychologists in the philosophical position known as **monism.** This position asserts that whatever consciousness is, it is a phenomenon of the world just like any other, like life, gravity, nuclear fission, and so forth. Monists can be subdivided into two groups, **materialists** who believe that the material world is fundamental and that consciousness is simply another phenomenon of matter, albeit a pretty special one, and a more spiritual and mystical group called **mentalists,** who believe that consciousness is fundamental and that the physical world as we know it arises from consciousness itself. Perceptual researchers are mostly materialists who believe that a thorough understanding of the physical brain could eventually eliminate the need for the concept of consciousness as a scientific entity and might allow it to be replaced by description of the underlying neurological processes (e.g., Kurthen, Grunewald, & Elger, 1998). Of course, this would not make consciousness as a describable behavioral experience disappear.

Monism contrasts with **dualism,** the position that consciousness is a phenomenon of the mental world or even possibly of the spiritual world. Dualism asserts that consciousness actually depends on a different form of reality than the events in the material world. There are many forms of dualism, including especially **substance dualism,** which is the idea that consciousness is made up of mental "stuff" that is different from the physical "stuff" that makes up the material world. A form of dualism that has become more popular recently is **property dualism,** the idea that although everything that exists is made up of physical matter, some of that matter (especially consciousness and also perhaps life itself) is arranged in ways that give it special, nonphysical properties. In some cases these nonphysical properties are said to be **emergent,** like the experience of the wetness of water at room temperature. The important feature of

BIOGRAPHY BOX 14.1

THE STREAM OF CONSCIOUSNESS

William James (1842–1910) wrote the first and perhaps the greatest textbook of general psychology ever published, the two-volume *Principles of Psychology* (1890). Generations of psychology students used this as their "bible" of psychology, not only because of its scholarly authority on the entire range of psychological topics but also because it was beautifully written. It is still a joy to read and stands as an excellent introduction to nearly every topic in psychology. One testament to its enduring impact is the fact that various quotes and ideas from it pervade modern writings on many topics. In the field of consciousness studies James is most famous for coining the still-current metaphor of the stream of consciousness. His speculations on consciousness and attention are still studied today for their insights.

William James was not just a great psychologist, however. He received his M.D. degree in 1869 after years of ill health and depression. He was, fortuitously (for he was at loose ends and still living at home at the age of 30!), asked to teach physiology in the medical school by Harvard's president Charles Eliot (who just happened to be a friend of his father). After several years he began to teach physiological psychology, imparting wisdom learned at the feet of Helmholtz and others during his frequent trips to Europe while recovering from his depressions. He established the first laboratory of psychology in North America in 1875 at Harvard. In the next year he moved to the philosophy department, initially teaching psychology but then moving to philosophy. He is the popularizer of the philosophy of **pragmatism,** and among his many books of philosophy is the well-known *Varieties of Religious Experience* (1902). He was much concerned with moral reasoning, and his pragmatic (naturally) solutions to moral problems are still as useful today as when he created them.

emergent properties of a substance is that they cannot be found by an examination of the molecules themselves. The problem with most dualistic theories is that they place consciousness outside of the realm that can be studied by science. In some respects this was done because of religious and spiritualistic considerations. Thus for the French philosopher Rene Descartes (1642) consciousness was made up of the same stuff that makes up the soul, and although it might reside in a particular place in the brain, it acted on the body and the world through the same mystical means that God acts on the universe.

Many people still adopt some form of dualism in their thinking about consciousness, mainly because conscious experience does not seem to follow from any scientific laws or ideas that currently exist. In so doing they are thinking only about physical laws and are thus trying to put consciousness beyond science. Yet at one time this was the same state people wishing to study emotions found themselves in. However, after Charles Darwin's 1873 studies, which showed the basic aspects of emotional expressions in animals and humans and also began to describe the stimulus situations and environmental conditions that evoke particular emotions, the situation changed. Now we have coherent theories of emotions, physiological measures that determine the strength and type of emotion, and a broad base of experimental data about the nature and control of emotions. The study of consciousness is now moving in that direction. Scientists have adopted some form of monism simply because it allows them to proceed with their research. Once we believe that consciousness is as tangible as any other form of behavior it then makes sense to do things like trying to discover the neural signature or brain sites and states that give us our perceptual awareness.

Forms of Consciousness

In some ways it seems as if there are several forms of consciousness. William James (1890; see Biography Box 14.1) coined the metaphor of the **stream of consciousness** when he observed that his perceptions and thoughts seemed to be always changing and yet there was never any "dead time" in them, any time when nothing was happening consciously. The time when he fell asleep was joined seamlessly to the time when he awoke and he perceived nothing in between except his dreams, which seemed to be a form of consciousness as well. As a river or stream of water flows in its channel, so consciousness seems to flow without pause in our minds.

There were moments when the nature of conscious seemed to change, such as during **substantive states,** which are intervals of time when our consciousness is occupied with a particular perceptual object or thought, such as when you might carefully study a face to see if you remember the person. Continuing with his metaphor, these are like an eddy in the stream that circles but does not get anywhere. There here are also moments when our consciousness seems to be in a state of change, when we are aware of relationships between thoughts but of no particular thought. This is like a straight run of current in the stream from one place to another. James called these **transitive states** of consciousness, and an example might be when we are rushing to leave the house in the morning for work and are aware of our urgency and movement, but once we are well on our way we can't recall if we locked the door or turned out the lights.

James asserted that the stream of consciousness was made up of only the substantive and transitive components. He also argued that consciousness is a *process* and not a thing. This idea is consistent both with the metaphor of the stream and also with the idea that there is no dead time in our perceptual awareness. We are only perceptually aware when the process is operating and cannot be aware during any time during which it is not, such as when we are under a general anesthetic, in a coma, or in a deep sleep. Dreaming is a special case because the process seems to be operating in dreams but without any sensory input to anchor it to the world. Try Demonstration Box 14.2 to get a feeling both for this kind of phenomenological analysis of perceptual aware-

DEMONSTRATION BOX 14.2

DESCRIPTIVE EXPERIENCE SAMPLING

This demonstration uses a modern version of James's analysis of experience to obtain first-person reports about conscious experience that can be analyzed the same way that results of laboratory experiments can be analyzed. We have adapted Hurlburt's (e.g., 1990) method of descriptive experience sampling to our needs by leaving out the detailed questioning that typically follows within 24 hours after a person's brief notations of what he or she was experiencing when each of a random series of beeps sounded during his or her daily activities.

To do the demonstration you will need some kind of stopwatch that can be programmed to make a beep at regular intervals. Set the watch so that it beeps every 60 seconds. Then go about whatever you wish to do. You are going to record, on a piece of paper, what you are conscious of every time the beeper beeps. Do this briefly by jotting down a symbol, either "s" for substantive or "t" for transitive and a word or two indicating the contents of your perceptual or cognitive awareness. If, say, the beeper went off while you were watching a news program on TV and you were at that moment aware of an image of a wrecked car on the TV screen, you would write "s car wreck." If you felt yourself in transition between two substantive states when the beeper went off, then write "t car-people" or some such.

After you have done this for a while (the longer the better—an hour would be good), look back over your notes. Obtain the proportion of the time that you were in each type of state, substantive or transitive, by dividing the number of "s" entries and "t" entries by the total number of entries. Which type of state dominates your awareness? Were there any states that didn't fit into one or the other category? You can also look at the contents of your notations. How many were visual images? How many were instances of you talking to yourself? It might interest you to know that people differ considerably in the relative amounts of each they experience (Hurlburt & Heavey, 2001). What else can you conclude from your study of your notations concerning the contents of your consciousness over this small time period?

ness and to confirm (or deny) James's conclusions with respect to your own stream of consciousness.

There are, of course, other approaches to describing the various forms of consciousness. Block (1985) developed four definitions for discussing consciousness. The first is **access consciousness,** referring to the availability of mental contents for verbal report and other actions. Actions can either be cognitive (ideas) or behaviors (overt activities). The second was **phenomenal consciousness,** referring to the actual experience of stimuli such as the color red, the note high C, the pain of a pinch, and so on. **Monitoring consciousness** refers to thoughts about one's own experiences that are distinct from those experiences, such as thinking about the fact that you are thinking. Finally, **self-consciousness** refers to awareness of a "self" that is distinct from the rest of the world.

We are obviously most concerned with perceptual awareness, and that seems to come closest to access consciousness, although since this is usually also accompanied by phenomenal consciousness as well, any explanation of access consciousness might also give clues about phenomenal consciousness. At the very least, we wish to understand how it is that someone can report his or her perceptual or other mental experiences, and this does seem to be within the reach of the methods of experimental psychology and of cognitive neuroscience.

MULTISTABLE CONSCIOUSNESS

People not only have the illusory feeling that they are consciously aware of everything that is going on in their immediate environment, but they also have the feeling that their immediate conscious experience is the only possible way of sensing the world. If you ask a person looking at a picture that he or she identifies as being "a dog" and suggest that perhaps another person might not see that dog or might actually see a cat, or perhaps a dog and a cat alternating in their consciousness, the person might view you as perhaps a bit strange or even demented. However, it is possible to show that our perceptual awareness of a situation can change, even though there are no changes in the stimuli that are reaching our receptors.

Perhaps the most studied form of what we can call *multistable* or *alternating* conscious is **binocular rivalry.** This phenomenon will become more important later, when we try to find activity patterns in the brain that may form the basis for consciousness, because it gives us systematic periods of consciousness and unconsciousness for certain stimuli without ever changing the stimulus input.

As you learned in Chapter 9, the view from each eye is slightly different because the eyes are separated by a few centimeters and view the world from different angles. Typically, perceptual mechanisms act to integrate these two slightly different views, resulting in a single view in consciousness and in stereoscopic depth perception. There are, however, limits to our ability to fuse the images from the two eyes. If the two views are very different, say horizontal stripes to the left eye and vertical stripes to the right eye, the brain refuses to merge the two views (which could, theoretically, be fused to look like a sort of a plaid pattern). Instead the two eyes seem to fight for control of consciousness. First the view of one eye will be **dominant** and visible in consciousness while the other eye's view will be **suppressed,** then the view will switch and the other eye's view will take over consciousness. The two views will continue to alternate in this way. This phenomenon is called *binocular rivalry* because it was assumed that the two eyes' views are competing with, or rivaling, each other to gain control of what a person is seeing.

In the laboratory these sorts of unfuseable stimuli can be presented in a *stereoscope*. This device uses prism lenses to make the images appear to overlap in space, as shown in Figure 14.1. You can also experience binocular rivalry for yourself by trying Demonstration Box 14.3, where a simpler technique is used to expose your two eyes to the disparate patterns.

We can use binocular rivalry as an example of how we might begin to look for mechanisms that affect consciousness. Thus our first guess might be that the stimuli that make it into consciousness if there is a conflict will be only the strongest of the stimuli. Thus suppose that

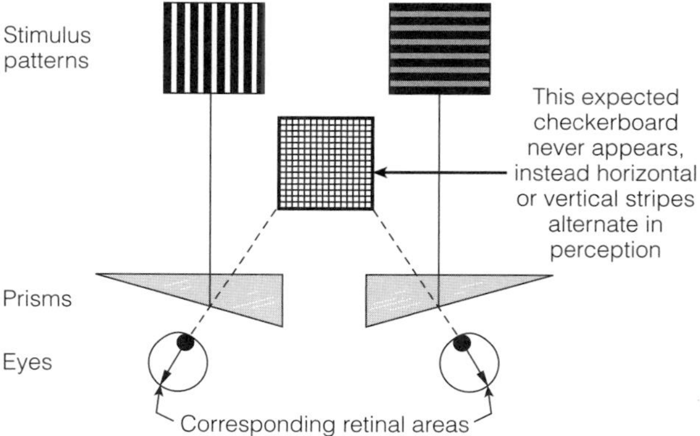

FIGURE 14.1 Typical optical setup used to produce binocular rivalry. Prism lenses make the two eyes' views appear to be in the same place in space.

DEMONSTRATION BOX 14.3

BINOCULAR RIVALRY

First obtain two bare toilet paper tubes. Then carefully draw a pattern of alternating black and white, approximately 1/2-cm-wide by 5-cm-long stripes on a piece of paper (use a ruler); you will need about 10 cm of these stripes. (You could also trace or photocopy the one or both of the stimuli in Figure 14.8.) Now cut the striped paper into two 5-cm-by-5-cm pieces. Place a black dot in the middle of each piece (on a white stripe). Tape each of the two striped pieces of paper over the end of one of the tubes. Now hold the tubes to your eyes aimed at an unpatterned, lighted surface (a lighted wall or window), with one tube oriented so that the stripes are vertical and the other so that the stripes are horizontal, and the far ends of the tubes point toward each other as much as possible. Try to see the black dots as one dot, and relax your eyes—this should gradually (it might take a minute or more) lead to fusion of the two eyes' views (you will see only one circle of lighted surface). However, instead of seeing a combination of the two striped fields, you should experience binocular rivalry: First you will see stripes in one direction and then, after a few seconds, stripes in the other direction, and so forth. Now try placing other types of patterns on the ends of the tubes and fusing the views, from simply rotating the stripes so they are in the same direction to pictures of different scenes, different types of line drawings, and so on. What types of scenes rival and what types of scenes blend? During rivalry, what is happening on the retina of each eye? Where in the brain do you think is the most central place where the suppressed eye's view is still represented?

the stimuli that we put into binocular conflict with each other differ in strength, perhaps because one has greater luminance contrast and thus is more easily seen. It would be reasonable to suggest that this would make that stimulus dominant for longer periods of time in consciousness. Actually, what happens is that stronger stimuli have the better ability to *fight off suppression* by the other eye, meaning that they are not visible for longer intervals, but rather are suppressed for shorter periods of time thus reducing the amount of time that we are conscious of the other eye's view (Blake, Fox, & McIntyre, 1971; Levelt, 1965). The amount of time that a stimulus is in view can also be affected by its psychological strength. Thus if we present faces that have strong emotions (especially strong negative emotions) to one eye, and a face that has neutral or weak emotions to the other eye, the face with the stronger emotions will be visible more of the time (Coren & Russell, 1992).

Binocular rivalry might also be used as an example of how we go about looking for neural explanations of conscious events. This can be done by modifying existing theoretical notions to fit the conscious phenomena that we are looking at. For example, since it appears that each monocular view pops in and out of consciousness, we could look for mechanisms that would support what can be called **eye rivalry.** Our search would then be oriented toward finding mechanisms to turn or suppress an entire eye's view. Here we might begin with the observation that in the cortical area V1 there are spatially separated bands of neurons that each receive inputs mainly from one eye. When adjacent strips of cortex from the two eyes differ, each monocular channel attempts to dominate consciousness. The idea is that each set of neurons tries to suppress the set of neurons representing the other eye's view by sending inhibition to them. This acts much like the lateral inhibition at the retinal level that causes brightness contrast (Chapter 4). Only here, what is suppressed is not the relative luminance response of a bit of the visual field, but rather one whole eye's view. Figure 14.2 is a schematic representation of this theory. One additional assumption is needed, namely that either the monocular band of neurons or the inhibitory pathways fatigue at some rate because of their high activity level. When they are fatigued enough, the formerly inhibited neurons can now begin to fire and begin to inhibit the neurons from the other eye, which will continue until they become tired and the other eye's neurons are rested enough to become dominant again. Obviously, what happens in VI will determine which eye's view becomes available to binocular neurons (which are responsive to input from both eyes) further along in the visual system. The activity of at least some of these binocular neurons is assumed to represent what the person is perceptually aware of (Blake, 1989; Kalarickal & Marshall, 2000). Several studies have used functional magnetic resonance imaging (fMRI, see Chapter 3) to record the activity from large groups of monocular neurons in Area V1; under some conditions the activity levels of the monocu-

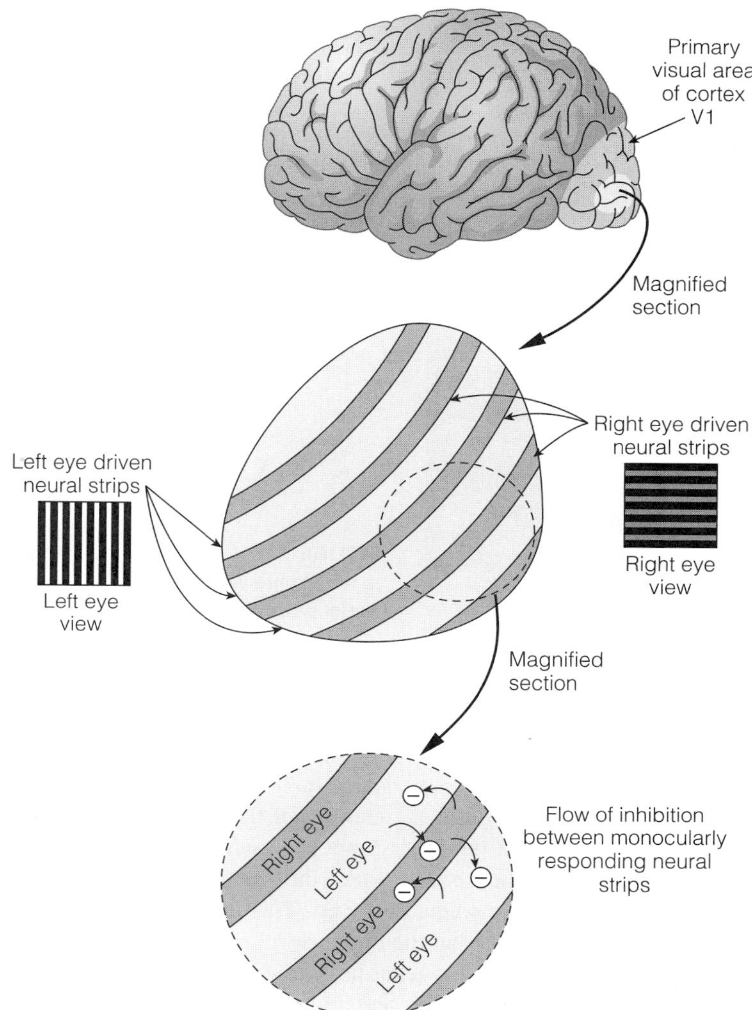

FIGURE 14.2 Eye rivalry is based on the assumption that the slabs of neurons that are driven by each eye in Area V1 of the cortex will inhibit one another as shown here.

lar neurons from the two eyes followed the stimulus alternations in consciousness (Tong & Engel, 2001), and these alternations could be tracked through higher levels in the brain (Polonsky, Blake, Braun, & Heeger, 2000). These findings indicate that area V1 could be the earliest, and controlling, site of binocular rivalry.

There is an alternative theory that deals with consciousness as if it contained the objects of some form of cognitive, categorical, or conceptual analysis, rather than the raw stuff of sensory inputs, such as might be represented by a single eye's input. At the neural level this might suggest that instead of an alternation between eyes occurring at an early level in the visual system, perhaps it is an alternation between groups of neurons tuned for specific patterns, and these inhibit each other as they vie for dominance. Thus we might have a rivalry situation where there is a face on one side and a set of vertical stripes on the other. When the neurons that register and respond to faces are most active, they inhibit the neurons that respond to vertical stripes and vice versa. The difference in this theory is that although our experience is of an alternation between eyes, it is really and alternation between stimulus configurations and thus it could be called **representation rivalry** or **pattern rivalry.**

Some evidence that representation rivalry is a possibility comes from the work of Logothetis and his colleagues (e.g., Leopold & Logothetis, 1996; Logothetis & Schall, 1989; Scheinberg & Logothetis, 1997). They used an experimental setup similar to that pictured in the top part of Figure 14.3 to investigate where in the visual pathways neural activity was correlated with the dominance periods in binocular rivalry. First they trained a

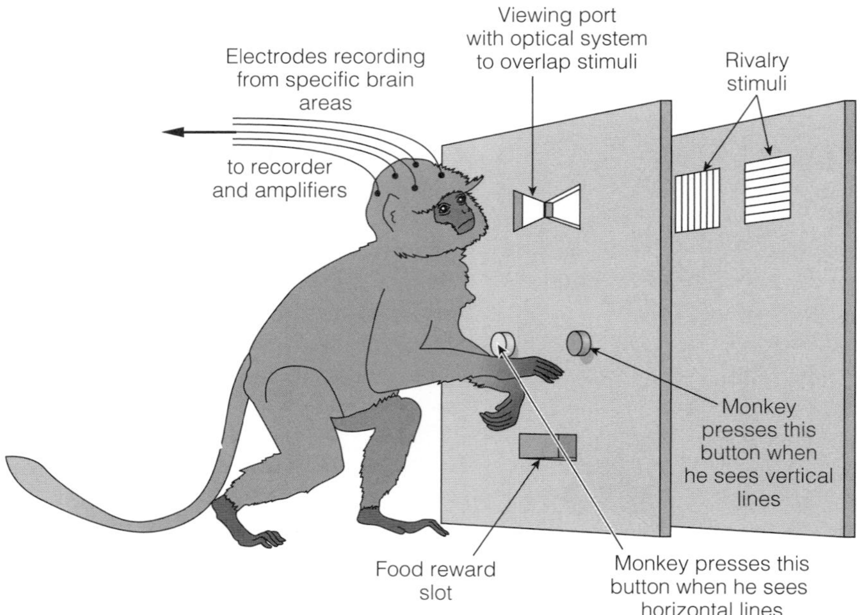

FIGURE 14.3 Experimental setup to determine where in the monkey's visual pathway binocular rivalry takes place.

laboratory monkey to make different responses depending on whether it was seeing vertical or horizontal stripes. This constituted a form of report by the animal as to what it was conscious of. Then they exposed the animal to either vertical stripes alone in one eye alternated with horizontal stripes alone in the other eye, or both stimuli simultaneously with one to each eye in a rivalry situation, while recording the activity of single neurons in V1 or V4.

For switches between the two patterns presented alone, many monocular neurons in Area V1 were found to change their activity as the stimulus changed. This is what you would expect since the input to VI was changing each time the stimulus changed. For the binocular rivalry stimuli, however, relatively few of the monocular neurons changed their activity when the dominant view switched suggesting that the alterations in visual consciousness were not due to activity at this location. However, when neurons in Area V4 were monitored in this way, many more of the binocular neurons located there were found to change their activity when the reported view changed during rivalry. Since Area V4 has mostly cells that accept inputs from both eyes simultaneously, these results are more consistent with representational rivalry occurring in binocular neurons in V4 or higher in the visual system.

Perhaps the strongest evidence for representation rivalry comes from a study that used a special presentation technique (Logothetis, Leopold, & Scheinberg, 1996). Patterns of differently oriented stripes were switched between the eyes at a rate of three times per second. Subjects appeared to be unaware of these rapid alternations and instead reported slowly alternating binocular rivalry very similar to that when the same patterns were not swapped between the eyes. This would be consistent with the idea that the higher-level neurons were registering the patterns, regardless of the eye used to receive them, and that representational rivalry occurred at those levels.

It seems likely that both forms of rivalry occur and that which appears depends on the nature of the stimuli used (Bonneh, Sagi, & Karni, 2001; Lee & Blake, 1999), the specific levels in the brain that are being measured (lower centers, such as V1 are more consistent with eye rivalry, with higher centers more consistent with representation rivalry), and perhaps even the cognitive task that the person is engaged in and the way in which his or her attention is being focused (e.g., Lumer, Friston, & Rees, 1998).

While the concept of representation rivalry might seem esoteric, it seems likely that this is one of the causes for fluctuations in consciousness that have nothing to do with binocular discrepancy of inputs. Consider, for example, Figure 14.4. Do you see the stylized saxophone player facing to the right? Most people do. However, if you look you will see emerging the face of a

FIGURE 14.4 A cartoonlike saxophone player is just one part of this multistable figure.

woman as well. Notice that when you see the woman's face you don't see the musician, and when you see the woman you don't see the saxophone player. These two representations will alternate in consciousness, much like the monocular views in binocular rivalry. This, however, cannot be something as simple as turning one eye on or off. Instead, you are turning a conscious representation of a pattern on or off in a form of representational rivalry. This suggests that consciousness might represent your ongoing hypothesis about what is out there in the world at any one moment. As your interpretation of the meaning of the stimuli changes, so does your conscious picture of the world. If this is true, then we should be looking for control centers in the brain that are removed from the basic sensory centers, and perhaps we should be looking for the coordination among several different neural processing centers.

IS THERE PERCEPTION WITHOUT AWARENESS?

In previous chapters, when talking about the perception of edges and also of sounds, we talked about the phenomenon known as **masking,** where the perception of one stimulus is blocked, or masked, by the introduction of another one. In the realm of vision this can easily be done by presenting a stimulus briefly, then following it immediately by another one that overlaps the spatial location of the first. A typical case might be to present a word, such as "cat," and then immediately following with a block of random lines, or X's and O's that overlap the place where "cat" appeared. The field of random lines would then represent the masking stimulus, and if the timing were correct, it can result in the original target word not appearing in consciousness. How such masking occurs is still a bit of a controversy, but it seems likely that the appearance of the second stimulus simply terminates the processing of the first stimulus and thus we never are aware of it.

Now if a stimulus is masked, and we are not conscious of it, then it should be the case that no information from that stimulus should be available to influence subsequent behaviors. However, this is not necessarily the case, as was shown in some classic studies by Marcel (1983a,b). In these studies an observer's task was simply to determine whether a letter string was a word (e.g., puppy, kitten) or not (uppyp, tnitek) as rapidly as he or she possibly could. Before the test string of letters, however, subjects were exposed to another word followed by a masking stimulus. The duration of the first word and the timing of the masking stimulus made the word virtually unidentifiable. The first stimulus was called a **prime stimulus** because the expectation was that it will serve to prepare the perceptual process for operation, such as in "priming a pump" or putting on an initial layer of paint to "prime" the surface so that the final coat will produce a more intense and even color. The actual sequence of exposure is shown in Figure 14.5.

The expectation that there would be some influence of the unconscious priming stimulus turned out to be true. When the prime word was meaningfully related to the target word (e.g., prime = dog, target = puppy), participants were able to identify a word more rapidly than when the prime word was unrelated in meaning (e.g., prime = sky, target = puppy). Because the effects depend on the meaning of the stimuli this is called **semantic priming.**

The importance of such masked priming experiments is that one knows that the stimulus did not reach consciousness because observers are not able to recognize it at above chance levels when given a number of possible alternatives, or in some cases observers even fail to notice that it was there, yet the unseen stimulus still has an effect on subsequent behaviors. Because this goes against the grain of the idea that perceptions must be conscious to have any influence on our actions, a number

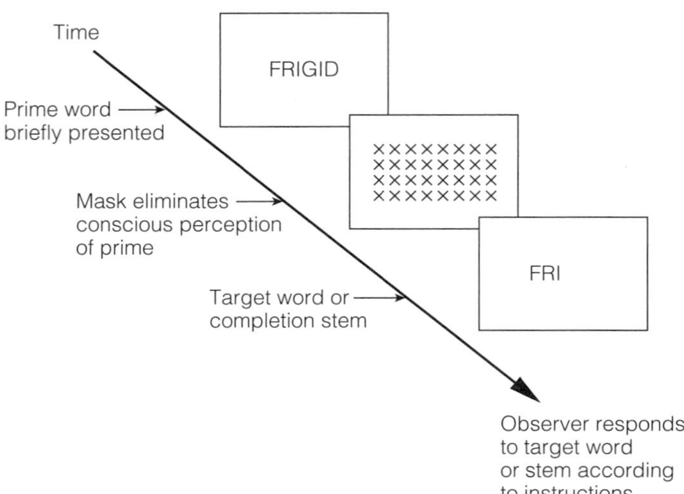

FIGURE 14.5 A sequence of stimuli used in a typical masked priming experiment.

of variations of such priming studies have been carried out to eliminate possible objections to the conclusion that there is "unconscious perception."

For example, in one variation of this technique, prime words were presented and followed by a mask after either 50 or 150 ms (Debner & Jacoby, 1994). Generally speaking, observers are virtually never consciously aware of the prime stimulus when the mask follows at 50 ms but often can identify it when there is a gap of 150 ms between the presentation of the prime and the mask. These researchers, however, used a subtle way of determining what the observers saw. Instead of just asking them to identify the prime stimulus, they asked subjects to complete a target stem of three letters, say FRI, with any word that came to mind *except the prime word*. In other words, if the priming word was "frigid," they were *not* to use that word to complete the FRI stem, but they could write FRINGE, FRIGHT, and so on. This means that the likelihood that they will complete the stem with the prime word should go down as the probability that they were consciously aware of the prime word goes up.

The data from this experiment are summarized in Figure 14.6. Observers completed the stem with the prime word (in violation of instructions) substantially more often in the 50-ms condition than they did in the 150-ms condition, which is what you would expect if the prime was having no effect. However, the picture becomes different when we compare the results to a baseline condition, with 50 ms between prime and mask but where the primes were completely unrelated to the test stems such

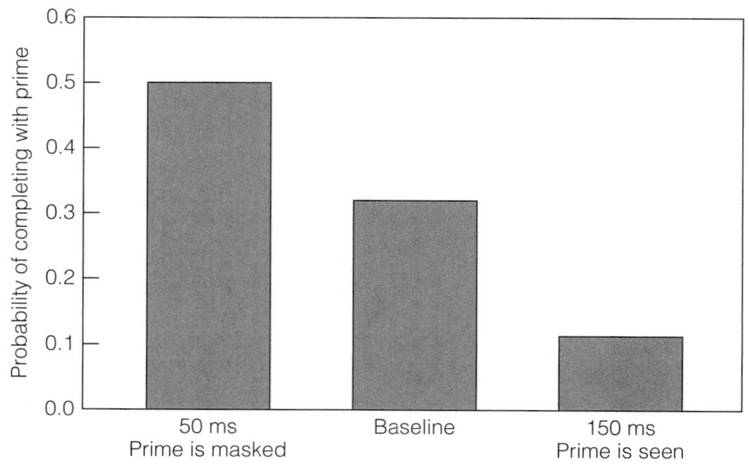

FIGURE 14.6 Results of masked priming experiments with manipulation of exposure duration. Baseline condition involved unrelated primes. The subject's task was to complete the test stem with anything except the prime.

as "elephant" and FRI. The probability of completing the stem with the prime used in the other conditions (e.g., "frigid" for the FRI stem) thus simply reflects the chance that an observer will randomly respond with the prime. Notice that subjects completed the stem with the prime *more often* in the 50-ms condition than in the baseline condition, which measures how available the prime words were as stem completion words when the stem was not "primed" with a stimulus related to the test stimulus. This means that the information from the stimulus that was not available in perceptual awareness was, nonetheless, influencing the observer's responses. Here the presence of the prime *increased* its likelihood of being used to complete the stem against instructions *not* to use it. Clearly, under conditions where we would expect the prime to be available more often to perceptual awareness, observers were able to avoid using it, as instructed, but the information from the "unseen" prime stimulus was making its way into the brain and influencing despite the fact that there was no conscious awareness of it.

ATTENTION AND CONSCIOUSNESS

We have already suggested that there might be some connection between attention and consciousness, and this becomes clearer as we look further into the data. Unseen priming stimuli influence us in a very similar way to stimuli that are not the focus of attention and therefore do not make it into consciousness. This can be seen in an experiment by Smith and Merikle (1999). In this experiment subjects were presented with computer displays that contained both a word and a cross at different locations. There is no prime stimulus and no mask involved here; rather, a stimulus will be kept out of conscious simply by directing the individual's attention away from it (this is inattentional blindness which we mentioned earlier). This is done by requiring observers to focus their attention on the word (*attended* condition) or to focus their attention on the cross (*unattended* condition, at least with respect to the word). Subjects were tested using the word and stem task similar to the previous (masking) experiment, with the instruction *not* to use the word that appeared in the previous display. There was also a baseline condition involving attention to crosses and unrelated words.

As you can see from Figure 14.7, the results of this experiment were much the same as those of Debner and Jacoby (1994). Obviously, the attended words were most often in consciousness, so observers completed the stems with attended words very rarely and less often than baseline. Subjects completed the stems with the words kept out of conscious because they were unattended, more often than baseline, which is similar to what happened when words were kept out of consciousness by masking. Thus inattentional blindness is not total blindness to the stimulus, and information is still available although we are not aware of it (see Mack & Rock, 1998). Studies such as these suggest that the gateway to consciousness is opened most reliably when we direct the focus of attention to a particular stimulus (e.g., Taylor, 2002).

It is interesting to note that what directs attention (and hence helps determine what is in consciousness) can, in fact, be a stimulus that never makes it into consciousness itself. Let's consider a fairly extreme case based on a clinical condition. For example, some patients with a lesion in the right parietal lobe can easily detect a stimulus in their left visual field when it is presented alone. However,

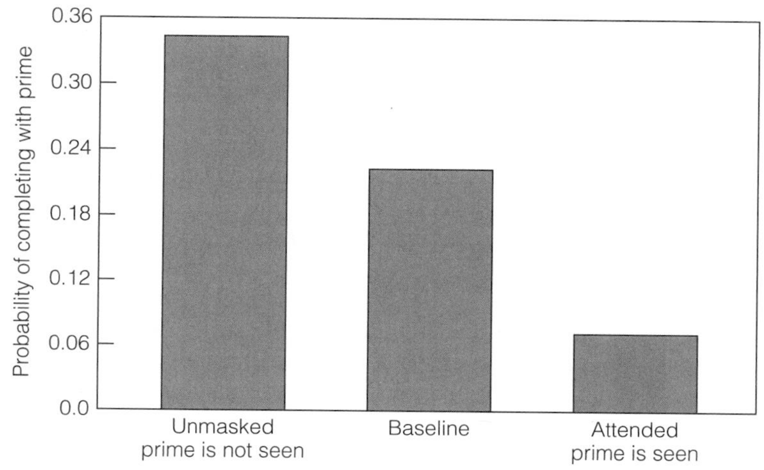

FIGURE 14.7 Manipulating attention produces results that are similar to masked priming. Baseline condition involved unrelated primes. The subject's task was to complete the test stem with anything except the prime.

if this stimulus is presented at the same time as another stimulus in their right visual field, they are no longer conscious of the stimulus in the left field. This phenomenon is called **visual extinction** (Merikle, Smilek, & Eastwood, 2001). In Chapter 13, we discussed a technique for studying the orienting of attention in which the subject was presented with a cue that would indicate which location (or which of several locations) a target would appear at. Although the cue was usually a valid indication of where the target would be, on some trials it was invalid. Usually observers could move their eyes and detect the target more quickly when there was a valid cue, but it could cost them some additional time if the cue was not valid and the target was in a different location. Now suppose that we present these patients with two cues one to each visual field, each suggesting a location where the target might appear. This is followed by a target alone to one of the two locations. Obviously, patients will claim to be unaware of the cue in the neglected visual field. Nonetheless, these they respond faster to a target presented at a previously cued location in the neglected visual field than they do when a target is presented in an uncued location in the same, neglected visual field (Danziger, Kingstone, & Rafal, 1998), *even though they were not consciously aware of the cue*. Thus the consciously unseen stimulus is still influencing their behaviors by directing the way that they orient their attention.

There is another way in which attention and consciousness can be seen as being linked. Look at Figure 14.8 and notice that it is a modernistic profile of a man looking toward your left. You can see his large eyes (is he wearing glasses?), his nose, and his pursed lips. Close your eyes and imagine what his hair and clothing might look like if they were drawn in.

If I stopped with the preceding description, you probably would have walked away with that image as your conscious representation of that picture; however, I now want you to look at it again. Look for a hand-written word that spells "Liar." Once this is pointed out to you, it becomes readily visible, and now we have another multistable or reversible figure, much like Figure 14.4 of the saxophone player and the woman, and these will rival with each other in consciousness. The important feature to note is that this figure was *not* ambiguous in your perception until the ambiguity was pointed out to you, thus causing you to redistribute your attention over the stimulus.

The research is clear on this issue. If individuals look at a stimulus and find that there is a consistent interpretation in consciousness, even though the figure is multistable, ambiguous, or reversible, there will be no

FIGURE 14.8 A modernistic, cursive drawing of the profile view of a man's face. Check the text to see what else you might be missing here.

fluctuations in consciousness. Why should there be? If consciousness has reached a reasonable conclusion as to what the stimulus represents, then no further investigation is needed. However, if an individual is informed that there is an alternative way of seeing the figure, then attention will begin to redistribute over the figure and the individual will begin to focus on new details and then the figure will begin to fluctuate in consciousness (Girgus, Rock, & Egatz, 1977; Rock & Mitchner, 1992). Furthermore, individuals who have more flexible control over their attentional processes are more likely to be able to achieve the perception of the alternate arrays. Thus university students have an easier time at such tasks than elderly individuals (e.g., Beer, Beer, Markley, & Camp, 1989) and some young children can't even achieve this when carefully prompted (Rock, Gopnik, & Hall, 1994).

There is an interesting implication from such findings. Since attention can be voluntarily directed toward stimuli, this suggests that what enters consciousness is, to some extent, under voluntary control. To see how this works, you might want to try Demonstration Box 14.4.

DEMONSTRATION BOX 14.4

ATTENTION AND CONSCIOUSNESS

The picture in this box is by M. C. Escher. In it you can see an array of many different animals, mythological or fantastic beings, and a few odd items. There are two sets of these figures that interlock to form a mosaic of sorts. When you see the light-colored figures you do not see the dark figures, and when you see the dark figures you do not see the light ones. Normally, these two sets of figures will rival with each other in your consciousness much like other multistable stimuli that we have looked at in this chapter.

Now, however, I want you to focus your attention on the light objects and try to keep it there. You might start this by looking at the guitar (lower right) and then shifting your attention to the female demon at the far right, then to the rooster to her left, then to the elephant to his left, then shift your attention down to the cat person, and so forth. During this whole long sequence of attentional shifts, you probably were only aware of the light-colored figures and the picture stopped alternating in consciousness.

To verify that this has nothing to do with the fact that we selected light-colored figures, you can now focus your attention on the dark-colored figures. Start with the Buddha-like figure in the center, shift your attention to the camel to his right, then down a bit to the fish, and further down to the flying demon, and so forth.

Your shifts in attention bias your analytic systems toward accepting either the dark or the light stimuli as being meaningful figures, and thus bias your consciousness toward the representation of these in awareness. The unattended to class of figures are thus much less likely to make their presence known in consciousness.

Previous research has found that the reversibility of ambiguous figures, or pictures that can be perceived in more ways than one, is unlikely for subjects who are unaware that the figure is ambiguous; in addition, reversals occur under certain conditions in which the subject is informed of the ambiguous figures possible alternatives (Girgus et al., 1977; Rock & Mitchener 1992).

Some experiments have explored the effect of age on the reversibility of ambiguous figures. Beer and colleagues tested a population of university students, young adults, and elderly people and found that more reversals occurred for the university students than the other age groups (1989). Rock and colleagues investigated the reversibility of ambiguous figures for three-year-olds and four-year-olds (1994). They found that none of the children reversed the ambiguous figures in the uninformed condition; more surprisingly, Rock and colleagues found that young children in the informed condition had the tendency not to reverse the ambiguous figures.

ACTIVE UNCONSCIOUSNESS

Before we consider more about the nature of consciousness and what its functions might be, it is also important to note that keeping something out of consciousness is sometimes useful and adaptive. In the studies considered previously, keeping extraneous stimuli out of consciousness by focusing our attention on stimuli of interest is probably useful, since attention and cognitive processing resources can then be used for the most relevant tasks.

There are other times when the relevance of consciousness for perceptual processing might be less valuable or even detrimental. Consider the simple situation where we are moving our eyes around the world to look at targets. One might theorize that continuous consciousness of the scene is not only useful but also necessary. However, this really is only true for certain varieties of eye movements, such as when you are tracking a continuously moving target. Under these conditions your eyes are making **smooth tracking movements.** If you swing your finger back and forth like a pendulum and have a friend follow it with his or her eyes, you can see these smooth tracking movements. You need to be continuously conscious of the target at all times or else it will drift off into the periphery.

There is another type of eye movement that we use when looking at the environment and these are called **saccades** (taken literally from the French *saccade* for twitch or jerk). These are quick jumpy movements that you can see if you now hold up one finger on each hand, about a foot or so apart, and ask your friend to look back and forth between them. Under these conditions our consciousness of the movement of our own eyes turns off during the actual movement period, a phenomenon known as **saccadic suppression.** Demonstration Box 14.5 shows the difference in the nature of consciousness between these two situations.

Why should consciousness be turned off during such eye movements? Part of the reason is that seeing the world slip by all of the time would be distracting and provide useless additional information for the brain to process. The eye movement system must make many

DEMONSTRATION BOX 14.5

CONSCIOUSNESS DURING EYE MOVEMENTS

During smooth tracking eye movements, when you are trying to keep your eye on a continuously moving target, you must have continuous consciousness. To show this, swing one finger back and forth at a moderate rate of speed and follow it with your eyes. Notice that the target is continuously visible. Now continue to track the target and notice the background. It is also continuously visible and can be seen slipping by in the opposite direction that the target is moving. (Paying continuous attention to both target and background for a prolonged period of time actually makes some people woozy, much like the initial effects of dizziness or seasickness.)

Next stand in front of a mirror and look at one of your eyes. Now, as quickly as you can, shift your gaze so that you are looking at your other eye. Do this several times, so that you are comfortable making eye movements of this nature. Notice that you never actually see your eyes move. You are only aware of your eyes at their starting point and at the end of the saccadic eye movement. Furthermore, you never have the image of your face (which forms the background here) swinging by in the direction opposite your eye movement. This is because of saccadic suppression, which has turned off consciousness during the 200 ms that the eye was moving.

computations about head, eye, and target positions to make accurate movements; however, it can simplify things using the **stable world assumption.** This simply assumes that most things in the world around us are standing still and do not have to be continuously monitored. This saves a lot of mental processing capacity that can be put to use interpreting the nature and identity of objects that we are looking at.

There are many other situations where information available to the visual system is systematically rendered unconscious. Let us give you another such situation. Look at a distance target, say a spot on the wall, and then, while keeping your eyes fixed on that target, point one finger at it and then let it drop out of sight. What did you see? Most of you will say that you saw your finger pointing at the target. Now repeat this exercise with your eyes still on the target, only now hold your hand in place. For most of you, after only a few seconds you will become aware of a double image of your pointing finger. We discussed where such double images come from in our treatment of binocular depth perception (Chapter 9). You were unaware of these double images because the information from the **sighting dominant eye** (the right eye in 70% of the population) is what gets into consciousness, while the nondominant eye's view is rendered unconscious. This is necessary because otherwise you could not successfully point at any object since you are trying to point to one object with two phenomenal fingers (see Coren, 1991, 1999).

Notice that in the case of the unconscious information from the nondominant eye it did eventually become conscious, suggesting that it was always available at some level. The same seems to be the situation for the unconscious information during saccadic suppression. This is useful because the stable world assumption may be wrong at any one moment in time, and we may need the information that things have changed if we are to adapt to our environment.

This can be seen in a variety of different experiments where things are changed during the time that the eye is moving and the world is momentarily not available in consciousness because of the saccadic suppression. In a typical experiment (Fecteau, Chua, Franks, & Enns, 2001) a person is asked to look at an illuminated target and then touch it with his hand. On some trials, the target is flashed on and then, just as the eye has begun to move, the target is displaced to another nearby location. Although in many cases the observer is consciously unaware of the fact that the target has been displaced, he is apt to make a very quick corrective eye movement, suggesting that some information was registered, but even more important, the arm movement took the target displacement into account and accurately reached the target, even though the observer was unaware that the target had jumped from one place to another.

Even when the target displacements are very large and the observer eventually notices them, there is evidence that identifying and localizing the targets are separate functions with different representations in consciousness. Take the experiment illustrated in Figure 14.9 (Castiello, Paulignan, & Jeannerod, 1991). Subjects sat at a table within easy reach of several target rods, any one of which could be illuminated at any moment. The task was to grasp the illuminated rod as quickly as possible after it was lit, and at the same time they had to utter the syllable "tah" to indicate the exact time that they became aware that the light on the rod went on.

The path of the subject's forefinger was tracked as the reaching motion was made. The thin lines between the subject's hand and the target rods, labeled 1, 2, and 3 in Figure 14.9A, shows the typical path of the forefinger. On 20% of the trials, however, when the center rod initially had been the illuminated target and just after the subject began to move toward that rod, it became dark and one of the outer rods was illuminated. On these trials subjects typically executed a smooth and rapid correction to grasp the new target rod. The heavy line in Figure 14.9 shows such a trial. The important manipulation here is that subjects had been instructed to say "tah" not only whenever they saw a target come on, but also as quickly as possible if they ever saw a shift in target location. Figure 14.9B shows a time line representing the average times at which these various events happened, beginning at the moment that the target rod changed (0 ms). As you can see, the start of the movement correction occurred on average about 100 ms after the target was changed and over 300 ms before the subject indicated that he or she was aware of the target change. Indeed, on average the moment of reported awareness of the change actually followed the moment of grasping the new target rod by a few msec. This means that much to the subject's surprise, they found themselves sometimes saying "tah" as they watched their hand already grasping the new target rod! Such data indicate that perceptual awareness seems to be quite slow in developing and that unconscious information was being processed much more quickly to help guide behavioral actions.

Another possible conclusion emerges from data like this. Perhaps perceptual processing treats certain attributes, such as location, differently than it does other attributes, such as object identification. If so, perhaps different levels of consciousness can be used for differ-

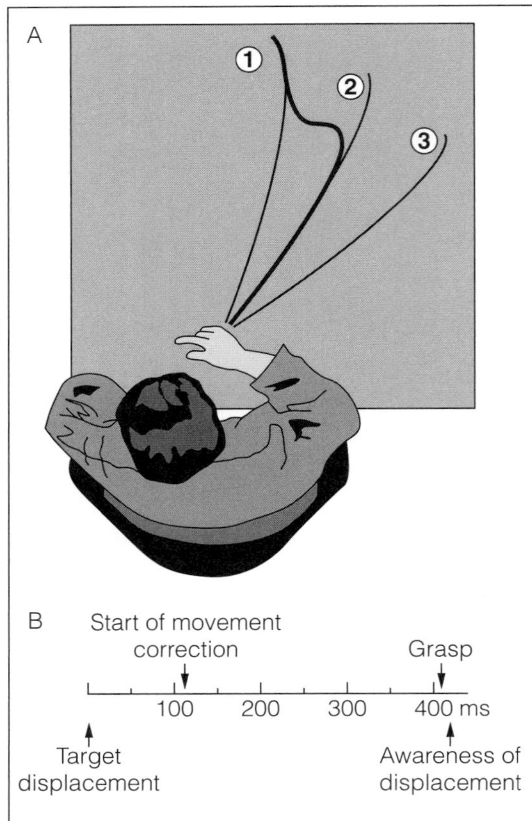

FIGURE 14.9 Experiment showing correction of movement well before awareness of the stimulus change that caused the correction. (A) The subject begins a movement toward a light target and then changes the movement when the target changes. (B) Time line showing when the movement correction began and when the subject reported awareness of the target change, relative to the time of the target change (0 ms) (from Frith, Perry & Lumer, 1999).

ent aspects of the stimulus environment. This sounds a bit strange, but clinical data suggest that it might be true.

PATHOLOGICAL CONSCIOUSNESS

There are some strange variations in perceptual awareness that are the result of certain pathological conditions. These are disturbances in very special and complex aspects of perception rather than simply causing a loss of sensitivity to a given stimulus modality. Some of these selectively affect parts of an individual's perceptual awareness, such as the ability to identify objects, or their specific properties, or to place them in space. In some cases they also may affect the ability to direct or distribute attention. In general, such conditions are called **agnosias,** from the Greek **a** meaning "not" and **gnosis** meaning "intuitive knowledge." People suffering from agnosias seem to be conscious of some aspects of the sensory world but often unaware of others. Such effects are often caused by severe toxic conditions, such as carbon monoxide poisoning (e.g., Patla & Goodale, 1996) as well as by diseases or injuries that damage or reduce the functioning in some parts of the brain, such as Alzheimer's disease (e.g., Kramer & Duffy, 1996) or strokes (Ramachandran, Altschuler, & Hillyer, 1997).

One of the most fascinating aspects of the agnosias is that they tend to break apart items that appear to be inseparable in consciousness. For example, when we look at an object it has a size, shape, color, orientation, and location in space that are part of its identity in our consciousness. Individuals with agnosias often fragment these aspects. Thus an individual who has **color agnosias** can still recognize colors and can also recognize objects, but when asked to describe the color of an object she cannot. When she looks at an object, it carries no color with it in consciousness.

Some agnosic patients can recognize objects if they are presented in familiar orientations, but not if they are presented from an unusual angle (e.g., Turnbull & McCarthy, 1996). The reverse of this occurs in some patients who can recognize the shape or form of an object—for instance, they can tell an X from an O—but they can't recognize its orientation. Thus, they can't discriminate between 6 and 9 (Turnbull, Beschin, & Della Sala, 1997). Even though shape and orientation appear to be part of the same thing in consciousness, they are clearly separately coded. In fact, we can create agnosic monkeys. Monkeys with lesions in the parietal cortex act like patients who can recognize shape but not orientation, whereas monkeys with lesions in the inferior temporal cortex cannot discriminate between different shapes but still can discriminate between shapes that differ only in orientation (Walsh & Butler, 1996).

What sort of underlying mechanisms are involved in these perceptual disturbances? As long ago as 1909, the Hungarian neurologist Balint made some observations that suggest a problem with the gateway to consciousness, attention. Thus, researchers find that such patients have a definite decrease in attention span, being able to hold only one object at a time in consciousness, regardless of its size (e.g., Rizzo & Robin, 1990). Such patients could not place a dot in the center of a circle because this would require paying attention to both the circle and the dot simultaneously. This type of patient is said to be suffering from **simultagnosia.** Thus, if a patient were shown a series of overlapping objects, such as those in Figure 14.10, she might report a single object, for example, the hammer, and deny that she can see any of the others (Williams, 1970). If such individuals are asked to copy a simple drawing, such as the one shown as the specimen in Figure 14.11, they depict only its individual

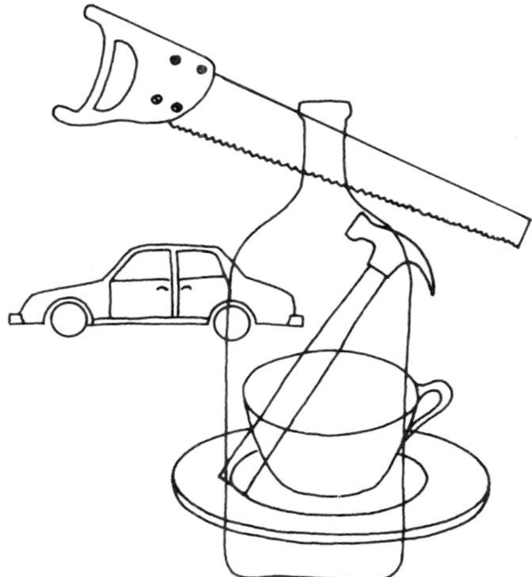

FIGURE 14.10 A test figure for simultagnosia.

Specimen

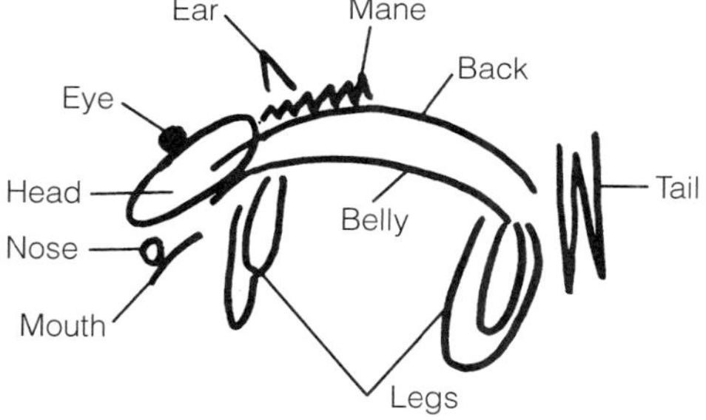

Copy

FIGURE 14.11 A target figure to be copied and a reproduction typical of a person suffering from visual integrative agnosia.

parts. Essentially, they give a visual list of most of the details. It appears as if by focusing on one part of the figure they lose the relative spatial location of the other parts of the figure which then makes it impossible to meld the parts into an integrated and unified figure in their consciousness (Goodale & Milner, 1991). Visual object agnosia and simultagnosia are often found in the same patients and are sometimes grouped together under the label **visual integrative agnosia** (e.g., Grailet & Seron, 1990). The attentional component of this problem is further suggested by the fact that a few patients have shown some improvement when given attentional training involving learning to look for certain cues and to organize the visual pattern (Perez, Tunkel, Lachmann, & Nagler, 1997).

There is an odd form of agnosia in which one side of the world and specific objects in the world drop out of consciousness. Such patients are said to be suffering from **visual hemineglect,** where the term **hemi** refers to "half" (see Chamorro & Sacco, 1990; Ladavas & Petronio, 1990). For example, if asked to draw symmetrical objects, they will usually produce some sort of distortion on one side. Thus, an individual with left-sided spatial agnosia would reproduce the copy shown in Figure 14.12. Although hemineglect has always been considered to be an esoteric and rare problem, recent evidence suggests that this is not so. In the Copenhagen Stroke Study, Pedersen, Jorgensen, Nakayama, Raaschou, and Olsen (1997) examined 602 consecutive stroke patients and found that 23% of them showed at least some symptoms of hemineglect.

Notice that many of these forms of agnosias seem to separate spatial characteristics from object characteristics. Agnosic patients often have difficulty consciously perceiving either the object qualities (e.g., color or shape) or the spatial aspects (e.g., location, orientation, or even that there is anything there on one side of the visual field) or difficulties putting spatial and object qualities together. This suggests that our consciousness of spatial and object characteristics might be the result of different mechanisms or subcomponents of the visual system. This seems to be confirmed by a series of intensive studies on a phenomenon called **blindsight,** in which a person could act appropriately toward visual objects even in the absence of perceptual awareness of important aspects of those objects or even of their existence. This phenomenon was named and described in detail by Lawrence Weiskrantz (e.g., 1986; see Biography Box 14.2). In studying several cases of blindsight, all of the patients had lesions, or areas of damage, somewhere in the visual processing areas of the brain in or near the occipital lobe (Areas V1, V2, and V3).

Probably the most extensively study case was a patient labeled DF whose injuries near the occipital lobe were the result of lack of oxygen in the brain (Wesikrantz, 1986). DF could not name objects nor verbally report their attributes such as orientation, size, or shape. By our criterion of requiring a report of some kind, outlined earlier, she was perceptually unaware of these things. When asked to perform **visually guided actions** toward the object, however, she could do so correctly—even though she claimed to be unaware of the perceptual basis for her action. Thus, if DF was asked to indicate the size of a block from a distance by using her thumb and forefinger to indicate its dimensions, her indicated dimensions were completely unrelated to the actual dimensions of the block. However, if asked to reach out and grasp the block, she was able to reach the correct

FIGURE 14.12 A target figure to be copied and a reproduction typical of a person with hemineglect.

BIOGRAPHY BOX 14.2

SEEING FOR ACTION WITHOUT AWARENESS

Lawrence Weiskrantz (1929–) is the neuropsychologist who discovered "blindsight," the ability to act correct toward an object without awareness of the relevant properties of that object or of its identity. He specializes in treating and understanding patients who have had brain injuries or disease. Such brain insults are usually accompanied by perceptual, cognitive, and behavioral problems such as agnosias. He has been studying such patients for many years and has contributed extensively to our knowledge of both the neural correlates of consciousness and of the effects of brain damage. In particular, he has shed light on the nature of information processing that takes place outside of awareness in such situations as blindsight and amnesia. Weiskrantz received his B.Sc. degree from Oxford University in 1950 and his Ph.D. from Harvard University in 1953 and is Emeritus Professor at Oxford University. He has also written books on animal intelligence and thought without language, and a textbook of neuropsychology emphasizing cognitive function.

distance and to position her thumb and fingers appropriately to pick it up. If she had used the dimensions she indicated from a distance she would have been unable to grasp the block, either hitting it with misplaced digits or simply waving the digits in the air near the block without touching it. Figure 14.13 illustrates this seeming paradox. Similarly, when asked to indicate the angle that a postcard would have to be placed in order to fit neatly into a "mail slot" in front of her, DF could not describe either verbally or by holding up an actual postcard how the card should be oriented. When asked to actually put the card in the slot, however, DF was able to put the card into the slot with the same ease as people who had no such brain damage. It should be clear why Weiskrantz named the visual phenomenon "blindsight." DF was reporting that she was "blind," or at least agnosic, to certain aspects of visual objects yet she was able to reach and grasp as if she could see those objects quite clearly. Similar phenomena have been reported in the other senses for patients with damage to the relevant brain areas: "deaf hearing" (Garde & Cowey, 2000), "numbsense" (Rossetti, Rode, & Boisson, 2002), and "blindsmell" (Schwartz, 2000).

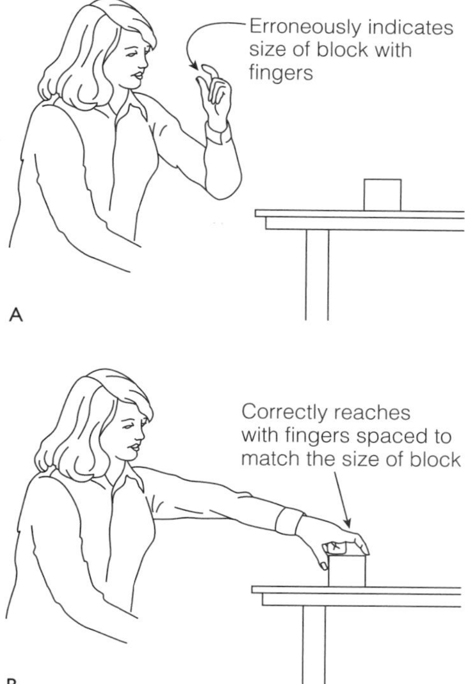

FIGURE 14.13 (A) DF incorrectly reports the dimensions of a block seen at a distance. (B) DF correctly positions her digits to grasp the same block.

TWO VISUAL SYSTEMS WITH DIFFERENT ACCESS TO CONSCIOUSNESS

While the agnosias are dramatic distortions of consciousness, there are other patients who appear to have even greater visual deficits. Those who have lesions in V1 seem to have localized blind regions in their visual field corresponding to the location of the damage to their primary visual cortex. These are called **scotomas** (from the Greek root *skoto* for dark). If a stimulus falls in the region of a scotoma, the patient cannot report even the *existence* of the relevant visual stimulus in consciousness. The surprise here is that many such individuals are still able to make appropriate eye movements to the location of the stimulus or are still able to reach out and touch the location of the stimulus (see Weiskrantz, 1996, for a review). What is going on here?

The data from neuropsychological disorders (and also from the pointing studies discussed earlier in normal individuals) suggest that the processes associated with identifying something in consciousness is different than the processes for localizing an object in space, and these processes can be separated. This suggests there may be two different visual systems as well with different access to consciousness. The first is for *perception,* which asks the question "What is out there?" and then displays that answer in consciousness. The second is for *action*, in the sense that it allows us to respond to the location of a stimulus in space, by reaching for it, hitting it, dodging it, or running away from it, and it asks the question "Where is it?"

These different forms of visual processing seem to have different evolutionary histories (Atkinson, 2000). The action system, which seems to be associated with the **dorsal processing stream,** which we discussed in Chapter 3, is older in an evolutionary sense, and we share it with all animals that have to use vision to guide action. This system is fast and seems to have direct connections to the brain centers that initiate body and eye movements. In order to grab, hit, or dodge something it is not important to know exactly what it is, what its color or texture are, or even to have more than a gross estimate of its size and shape. Since these are the kinds of details that we normally examine in consciousness, this system really doesn't need much if any perceptual awareness to operate efficiently.

It appears that it is the **ventral processing stream** that sustains the perception system. This is newer in evolutionary terms and seems to have been added to the larger brains of humans and other mammals along with the extra layers of cortical tissue that make up the **neocortex,** which allows more complex cognitive processes. The perception system is specially designed to categorize stimuli, and this requires analysis of color, texture, and fine-grained aspects of form, and finally assigning a name, function, and meaning to the stimulus. This is the system that we are using when we turn our attention to a stimulus, analyze our experience, think about our experiences, or try communicate aspects of what we have been aware of to others. In other words, this is the system that seems to construct our perceptual consciousness. As such it must take a bit more time and perhaps preprocess the material so that our picture of the world is as accurate as conditions allow.

Usually the perception and action systems are coordinated and complementary, but when brain damage to one of them is sustained, the other can act independently. In particular, when the ventral stream is so damaged that a person is no longer consciously aware of a visual stimulus or its perceptual properties, the dorsal stream can still guide appropriate actions toward that stimulus, sometimes to the surprise of the patient but it is not sufficient to produce conscious awareness. This has been confirmed in animal experiments involving monkeys (e.g., Cowey, Stoerig, & Le Mare, 1998). If the dorsal system is damaged and no longer functional, however, if a few remnants of the ventral system remain, these may be used to produce some visually guided actions—even if not enough of the ventral system is still functioning to produce a conscious experience (Wessinger, Fendrich, & Gazzaniga, 1997). This suggests that much of the information that the dorsal action system uses so quickly and efficiently is can also be passed on to the ventral perception system where it could be made available for further processing in consciousness. This makes good sense, since when we are scanning our conscious representation of the world, we are also aware of the location of the objects in space, both relative to our body and relative to each other, and this is the same kind of information that the action system used to guide its activities.

CONSCIOUS AND UNCONSCIOUS PROCESSING IN NORMAL INDIVIDUALS

If we are correct, and there are separate visual processing for perception and action, with consciousness only available to the perception system, then perhaps we could find situations where actions do not agree with the conscious experience of normal individuals. For this we will use some figures that produce systematic distortions in our perceptual awareness, namely **visual-geometric illusions.**

Visual illusions create surprising distortions of perceptual awareness (see Chapters 1, 10, and 16), but they seem to affect visually guided action less dramatically. Figure 14.14 shows some of the illusions that have been used in these experiments (Glover, 2002). In Figure 14.14A, called the Ebbinghaus illusion, the central circles are typically seen as different in size, although they are of equal diameter. In Figure 14.14B, the horizontal-vertical illusion, the vertical line is seen to be longer than the horizontal line, although they are the same. In Figure 14.14C, the tilt illusion, the central rectangles are seen to have different slants, although both are vertical. In Figure 14.14D, the Müller-Lyer illusion, the two horizontal

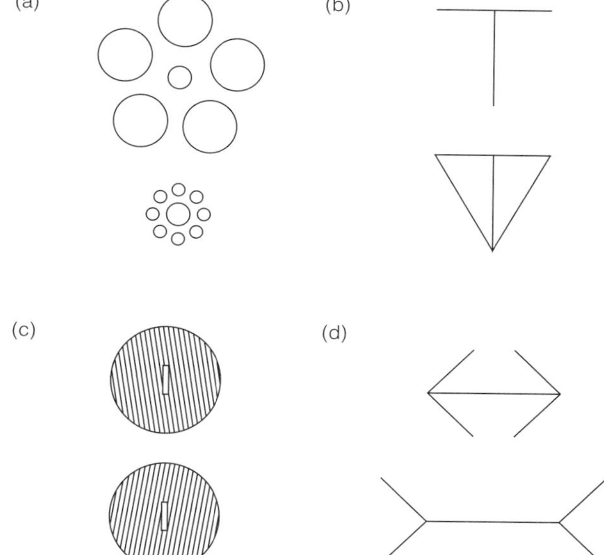

FIGURE 14.14 Some visual-geometric illusions that show greater magnitude when judged perceptually than when acted on.

lines are seen to have different lengths, although, again, they are the same (see Coren, 1997, or Coren & Girgus, 1978 for more on such illusions).

In all of these illusions, the global interpretation of the illusion configuration is at least partly responsible for the distortion. For example, misplaced size constancy, in which the horizontal line in the bottom part seems closer to the observer, and thus shorter, than does the identical horizontal line in the top part, is supposed to be partly responsible for the Müller-Lyer illusion (see Chapter 10). However, if instead of asking observers to estimate the length of the lines by using some matching technique we simply ask the observer to point to the ends of the lines with her finger (while we optically make the hand invisible), the observer accurately points to each line end, indicating that no illusion was present. Since the system responsible for visually guided action presumably does not participate in creating this global interpretation, perhaps it is not as susceptible to this distortion of perceptual awareness.

Another case where action and conscious perception dissociate comes from Aglioti, DeSouza, and Goodale (1995). They created an Ebbinghaus illusion (Figure 14.14A) out of circular "poker-chip" disks. In the perceptual awareness task, they varied the size of the central disks and asked subjects either to indicate when they appeared to be equal is size. Asking subjects to pick up one of the central disks by grasping it with their thumb and forefinger tested the action system. The space between these fingers as the subject goes to grasp the central disk is set by the action system and thus provides a measure of whether it is also affected by the illusion. Consistent with the idea of a dissociation between perceptual awareness and visually guided action systems, the perceptual judgments showed a relatively large illusion, about 8%, whereas the maximum grip aperture showed a reliably smaller illusion, about 5%. It is possible to adjust the size of the central disks so that the illusion is no longer present in consciousness. This involves making the central disk surrounded by larger circles physically larger than the disk surrounded by the smaller circles. When this is done, even though the central disks now appear to be the same size in consciousness, subjects still adjust their grip correctly so that the space between the fingers is larger when grasping the physically larger disk. In other words, subjects were matching their grip aperture to the actual size of the disks more closely than to the consciously perceived size. Thus the brain system responsible for visually guided action is less susceptible to the Ebbinghaus illusion than is the brain system that gives rise to our conscious impression of the size of the targets. Similar results have been found for all of the illusions shown in Figure 14.14 and several others as well. In each case, visually guided action is less susceptible to the perceptual distortions experienced in consciousness (Glover, 2002).

This pattern of results begins to tell us something that may help us understand the function of consciousness (Milner & Goodale, 1995). In Chapter 10 (see Figure 10-25) we spoke about global versus local processing. If, for example, we have a big letter H that is made up of small letter S's, our first impression (what gets into consciousness) is of the global configuration. Thus we "see" the letter H and might not even be aware that the components that made it up involved a collection of little letters. It takes extra effort to focus our attention on the smaller component letters. In a visual illusion, we respond to the global configuration, taking the elements that make up the context (for example the wings on the Müller-Lyer in 14.14D) into account to produce our interpretation of the pattern. Consciousness immediately displays the global products of the most sophisticated neural processes, including the gist, the layout, the meaning, and even the emotional value of a scene. It takes more effort to decompose the scene so that we become aware of the specific objects that are present, and it will take even more time and effort if we are trying to focus our attention so that we become aware of the specific details at individual points and edges. So consciousness is our best estimate of what is "out there" in the world, analyzed at the level that we need for **planning** our goal directed actions.

The action system does not need this global analysis. Processing more than the simple location of the line ends is unnecessary, and sometimes even counterproductive, to the process of reaching and grasping of specific objects. To interact physically with the stimulus depends on accurate information about the physical location and size of the objects being grasped so that information is processed in isolation. In many everyday instances the accuracy of the action system is assisted by **online control,** which simply refers to fact that movements can be monitored and corrected while they are being executed. Thus if the action system is monitoring the movement of the hand toward an object and notices that its current trajectory will cause it to miss the target, it can adjust the arm to put the hand back on target. Such behaviors are often seen for eye movements, where the initial movement is in the general direction of the target but it misses by some small amount, only to be immediately followed by a corrective flick that puts the eye on target.

NEURAL CORRELATES OF PERCEPTUAL AWARENESS

As scientists we begin with the assumption that consciousness is a function of the brain. If this is true, then we should be able to discover what aspects of brain activity are associated with perceptual awareness. This idea was given special significance in a paper by Crick and Koch (1990) in which they coined the phrase **neural correlates of consciousness.** They were referring to neural activity, perhaps in a specific brain area, which was closely associated with conscious awareness. Ideally, with enough experimentation and conceptual and theoretical analysis, we should be able to discover what brain is doing to produce our awareness. This would provide us with the neural signature of awareness. We already flirted with this idea when we discussed how brain processes and centers might be involved with binocular rivalry. Let us now look at this issue more generally.

There are several experimental situations in which we could profitably study brain activity and behavior that is relevant to this problem (Frith et al., 1999). The two main ones are as follows:

1. We can look for changes in brain activity under conditions in which *the observer's experience changes but the sensory stimulation does not* (as in binocular rivalry). Such experiments should allow us to determine where, and how, brain activity changes as our perceptual awareness changes.
2. The converse of the first situation would be to look at brain activity under conditions in which *the stimulus changes and so does the behavior, but experience does not* (as in masked priming). In this way we could learn what type of brain activity is involved in registering information that is used to guide action but does not make it to consciousness.

In some instance we can profitably use individuals with pathological conditions, such as blindsight or several of the specific agnosias, to achieve these conditions. Clinical cases can help us extend the research to see which pathways and brain centers have been damaged to produce the bizarre variants of conscious and unconscious processing that patients manifest.

Emotional and Arousing Stimuli

Certain biologically significant and emotionally arousing stimuli are capable of being processed without awareness. Examples of such stimuli are human faces, especially faces with intense emotional expressions. Research shows that even when individuals are not consciously aware that such an emotional stimulus has been presented, it is unconsciously processed and may produce emotional responses and autonomic nervous system arousal (e.g., Ellis, Young, & Koenken, 1993).

The amount of information extracted is even enough to support learning, despite the fact that the individual is not aware of the stimuli involved. This was shown using the familiar learning procedure called *classical conditioning*. When subjects are exposed several times to a picture of an angry face paired with a blast of 100-dB white noise, they react to later presentations of the face with an emotional response, which shows up as change in their galvanic skin response (GSR). This does not happen when they see a picture of an angry face that was not paired with the noise. This kind of emotional response can be conditioned even when the face that was paired with the noise is not consciously seen because it is masked by the subsequent presentation of another, neutral face that was not paired with noise (Öhman & Soares, 1994).

Emotional stimuli that are unconsciously processed provide a good example of how one might search for neural correlates of conscious and unconscious perception. There is now ample evidence that suggests that emotional responses, especially negative or fearful responses, are encoded in the amygdala, which is part of the limbic system of the brain (Davis, 1997; Whalen, 1998). Thus it should not be surprising to find that reactions to faces that have now been conditioned to a negative and arousing state produce responses in the amygdala as well. This has been confirmed using **positron emission tomography** (PET scans) as a brain imaging techniques (Morris, Öhman, & Dolan, 1998). An interesting variation on this theme involves a study that looked at war veterans who suffered from posttraumatic stress syndrome. They were shown faces with intense emotions in a masked priming task, and, even though they were not consciously aware of the faces, functional magnetic resonance imaging (fMRI) scans showed that their amygdalas were responding more vigorously than those of other war veterans who were not stress victims (Rauch et al., 2000).

A patient with blindsight also helps to round out the picture of the amygdala responding to unconscious stimuli. He was blind in most of his right visual field because of a lesion in his left striate cortex (V1). Nonetheless, he was able to make some discriminations among faces shown to his blind hemifield (where he said he could see no faces at all), and these discriminations were associated with activity in the amygdala, which was generally similar to that observed in normal subjects (Gelder, Vroomen, Pourtois, & Weiskrantz, 1999).

Up to now our working hypothesis has been that most of the unconscious processing has to do with the action system in the brain. Specifically, those centers that are most concerned with asking the question of where something is, rather than what it is. Is the amygdala, then, a counterexample of this? Not really. First, part of any action system would at least include determining whether a stimulus is positive (meaning you want to approach it) or negative (meaning you want to avoid it or run away), and this is very much what preliminary emotional processing is all about. Second, there is evidence that limbic system of the brain (which includes both the amygdala and the hippocampus) is involved with spatial learning and navigation (Wiener, Paul, & Eichnbaum, 1998) and some very specific aspects of egocentric localization such as head position and position of stimuli relative to the body (Knierim, Kudrimoti, & Mcnaughton, 1995). There is even the suggestion that one specific function of the amygdala is to assign a positive or negative value to a place in space to help you decide if you want to go there or not (Kashimori, Inoue, Kambara, & Uchiyama, 2001). Thus there are clearly action components associated with the unconscious process of the amygdalas.

It is important to note that the conscious processing of faces is not in the amygdala but appears to be in the temporal cortex, probably around the fusiform gyrus. This has been shown using binocular rivalry, by having subjects view nonfusable stimuli, where the stimulus to one eye is a face and the other is a field of lines or an object that is not a face. Under these conditions, when the individual becomes consciously aware of the face, there is a marked increase in neural activity in this region, which then decreases when the other stimulus becomes dominant in consciousness (e.g., Tong, Nakayama, Vaughan, & Kanwisher, 1998).

Neural Correlates of Masked Priming

Masked priming studies allow us to study the neural correlates of unconscious perceptual processing. For example, Leuthold and Kopp (1998) conducted a study in which subjects were asked to indicate the location of a target in a display consisting of two stimuli, a target and a distracter. Just before the target appeared, a priming display in which stimuli appeared in the locations that the target and the distracter would be shown with stimuli similar to the target or distracter. In this case the test display came so quickly after the priming stimulus that it acted as the masking stimulus and subjects were unable to say at which location the target-priming stimulus appeared. In fact, they were never conscious of the priming stimulus at all during the main target localization experiment. Nonetheless, subjects localized the target faster and more accurately when the target appeared at the same location as the unseen prime. This is, of course, the same kind of unconscious processing that we have described before. The difference is that in this instance physiological measures were taken of the brain's activity during the experiment.

Brain activity was measured by attaching electrodes to the scalp. This produces the familiar **electroencephalogram** or **EEG,** which measures the average activity of thousands of cells in a particular region. Locating a number of electrodes over various parts of the skull allows precise pinpointing of the areas of the brain that are most active (e.g., John, Prichep, Fridman, & Easton, 1988). Localized EEGs measured in response to brief sensory stimuli are called **event related potentials** or **ERPs.** We have been suggesting that conscious awareness is mostly handled by the ventral processing stream, and this is confirmed by the fact that no differences in the ventral stream were measured between trials, when the priming stimulus was a valid indicator or an invalid indicator of where the target would appear. This was the case for early events linked to the onset of the priming stimulus. Measures taken of later changes (when the observer was now consciously aware of the target that followed the prime) did show some differences. Thus it seems that the ventral stream is not much involved in processing the unseen prime stimulus.

Remember that we are assuming that unconscious processing is associated with the action system. This was confirmed by the fact that measures of activity that monitor readiness to respond by the motor cortex did discriminate between the two conditions. This result implies that each unseen prime directly activated the corresponding response pattern in the motor cortex and that this early activation speeded the response to the subsequent target. This happened even though the primes did not result in detectably different processing in the ventral stream, which is associated with awareness.

Change Blindness

Change blindness is a variety of inattentional blindness (e.g., Rensink, O'Regan, & Clark, 1997; see also Chapter 13). Typical change blindness experiments involve looking for a difference between two scenes. These are identical except for a single, nontrivial, change, such as when the engine of a Boeing 747 aircraft is missing in one but present in the other, or a girl's bathing suit is different in color. The two scenes are flicked back and forth, separated by a short blank period, until the subject correctly indicates the change. It may take many seconds of this alternating presentation before the observers detect the difference, even though it is readily obvious when pointed out. Until attention is focused on the change, it simply does not appear in consciousness (Rensink, et al., 1998).

A study of the change in brain activity as the observer goes from blindness of the change to awareness of the difference could help us determine the neural signature of consciousness. One study used an fMRI to record brain activity while observers viewed alternating visual displays that contained a difference (Beck, Rees, Frith, & Lavie, 2001). The observer was looking for differences between stimuli that contained pairs of faces or places. When a change was detected there was increased activity in the dorsal processing stream that was reflected in parietal and dorsolateral frontal cortex activity, regardless of the nature of the stimulus. However, there were different responses in other areas depending on whether the stimulus was a face or a place. When a face change was present but not detected, the ventral stream face area (but no others) did show more activation than when the face change was not present, indicating that the ventral stream registered the change in stimulus but without affecting awareness. Undetected place changes, however, elicited no special activity.

Earlier we noticed that in a patient who was missing the primary visual cortex (V1), there was no conscious awareness of stimuli, although unconscious processing could still take place. The full pattern of data suggests that V1 is necessary for visual awareness, but it is not sufficient. To have consciousness of the visual stimuli requires dorsal stream activation (including associated frontal areas of the brain) as well (Rees, Kreiman, & Koch, 2002). Figure 14.15 summarizes the places in the dorsal stream where activity has been shown to be correlated with visual awareness, including the areas mentioned when we discussed the study of Beck and colleagues (2001). That is not to say that ventral stream processing contributes nothing to awareness; it is just that ventral stream processing merely provides additional specific content that can be reviewed in consciousness once the dorsal stream has been activated and is supplying the general context and meaning of stimuli (Kanwisher, 2001). It appears that these two streams finally mix in the frontal cortical areas. Obviously, we are looking at findings that begin to suggest that there are many areas of the brain that are simultaneously active and may all contribute to the final conscious experience.

There is even some evidence suggesting that all of the neural correlates of perceptual awareness are not cortical, although the role that other areas play is not fully clear and may simply involve the transfer of information to the "centers of consciousness" in the brain. This conclusion comes from studies that have monitored the brain activity of people under general anesthetics. Such anesthetics abolish conscious awareness but not all brain activity. Different anesthetics have different effects on brain activity, but they are always widespread, which is consistent with the idea that the correlates of consciousness involve many centers in the brain (John, 2001). However, when brain activity is compared across different anesthetics, it seems that the only sites of action common to them all are the thalamus and the reticular activating system (Alkire, Haier, & Fallon, 2000). Both of these centers are subcortical (see Figure 13.3). The thalamus (in the midbrain) has been shown to play a role in focusing attention focusing, whereas the reticular activating system (in the

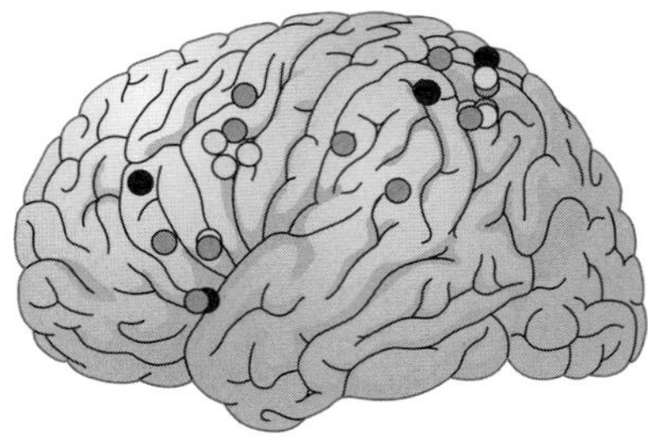

FIGURE 14.15 Some domain-general cortical areas implicated in perceptual awareness (from Rees et al., 2002).

BIOGRAPHY BOX 14.3

THE DYNAMIC CORE OF CONSCIOUSNESS

Gerald Maurice Edelman (1929–) began his scientific career studying the biochemistry of the vertebrate immune response. He helped elucidate the chemical structure and mode of action of the antibodies that attack invading cells. He shared the Nobel Prize in Medicine for this work in 1972. He also used fluorescence spectroscopy (finding out what atoms and molecules are present in a substance by observing what kinds of light they absorb or emit) to study the structure of proteins, and he developed new methods to separate both molecules and cells from mixtures so that they could be measured. After receiving the Nobel Prize, he became interested in neuroscience, in particular in understanding how the mind arises from the activity of the brain. To this end he founded the Neurosciences Institute and the Neurosciences Research Foundation, where this study has continued since 1981 among an exciting, ever-changing group of researchers. He published a series of books in the mid-1980s dealing first with *Neural Darwinism* (1987), the doctrine that a form of natural selection occurs among connections between neurons in the developing brain, pruning the initially multifarious connections to a lower number based on which ones have been functionally reinforced. In this book he also introduced the notion of "reentrant" neural processing, in which cortical areas that receive input from other areas send feedback to the originating area via so-called downward projections. This reentrant input then modifies the output of that area. This concept is discussed in several places in this textbook, especially in this chapter and in Chapter 10 when dealing with masking of one stimulus by another. It has become a workhorse concept in the field. More recently, Edelman has written several stimulating books on consciousness, including the one we refer to here, *A Universe of Consciousness* (2000, with Giulio Tononi), in which the concept of the dynamic core of consciousness is developed.

brainstem) is not only responsible for waking and sleeping states but also contains nuclei that generate a map of the surrounding space and seems to be involved in directing attention to particular locations (Edleman & Tononi, 2000). The thalamus is also the location of relay nuclei (like the lateral geniculate nucleus in the visual system) through which sensory messages pass on their way to the cortex. It has been proposed that general anesthetics may stop the thalamus from relaying information to the cortical centers that are also required for consciousness.

Consciousness seems to require the passing back and forth of a lot of neural information. First there is a **feed-forward sweep** of neural activity (from the retina to the lateral geniculate nucleus , to V1, V2, and on up), which is the analysis pathway that we are used to studying. However, it also appears that this later processing in higher brain centers (say the frontal cortex) can then feedback to the primary sensory areas needed for consciousness (say V1) and modify neural activity, and this is called **reentrant feedback** (Edelman, 1987; see Biography Box 14.3). We can observe this experimentally by noticing that the stimulus features that V1 responds to change over time after a pattern has been presented. For example, if a pattern like that in Figure 14.16 is presented to a monkey's eye, neurons in V1 can be seen to respond to orientation of the textures (a versus c) about 55 ms after the pattern is presented, to the boundary between

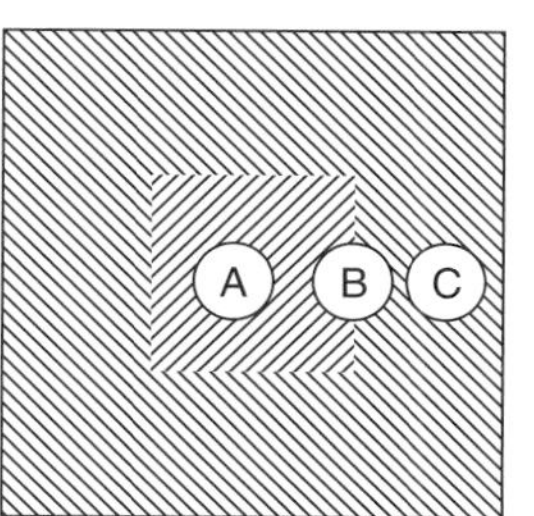

Test figure with object visible due to texture difference

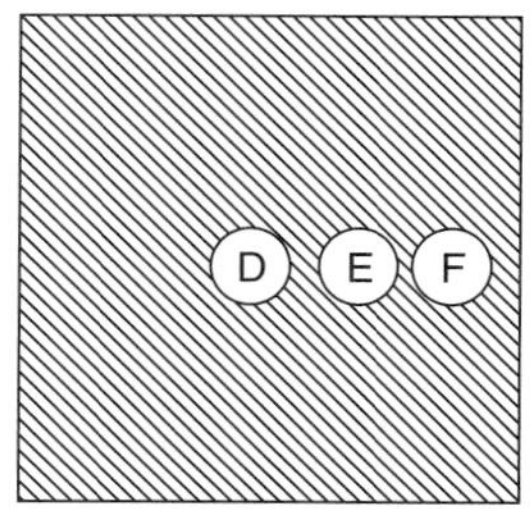

Comparison stimulus with no figure or texture difference

FIGURE 14.16 (Patterns used to show how V1 neuron tuning is changed by reentrant feedback (from Lamme & Roelfsema, 2000). The labeled circles represent locations on the figure to which a neuron's receptive field is exposed at different times during the experiment.

figure and ground (b versus a or c) after about 80 ms, and to whether their receptive field is wholly on the figure or wholly on the background (a versus d) about 100 ms after the presentation (Lamme & Roelfsema, 2000). The suggestion is that the way the neurons in V1 respond to the stimulus inputs is changing because of the reentrant feedback from the higher centers. It may even be the case that these feedforward and feedback loops are necessary for visual awareness to occur (Lamme, 2000).

DOES CONSCIOUSNESS HAVE A FUNCTION?

Before we go on with our search for the neural correlates of consciousness, it might be wise to stop and consider an important issue that may guide our search. Namely, what is the function of consciousness? It seems unlikely that such a complex process has evolved if it serves no function other than to fill our waking lives with some kind of mental picture show.

One purpose of consciousness seems to involve our ability to plan, to interpret the world, and to code information so that it can be entered into memory and processed by reasoning mechanisms. To that extent, consciousness seems to provide a working interpretation of the world around us. One explanation for the illusion of complete perception is that without it we would always have the suspicion that there were still things to sense and information that was unprocessed, and the resulting uncertainty would paralyze us and keep us from acting. In the case of perception the best motto seems to be "Sometimes wrong, but never in doubt."

The function of consciousness in this view is one of perceptual integration. In constructing a **global interpretation** of the perceptual world that we experience, consciousness allows many competing perceptual and cognitive processes to interact and influence each other. In this way reasoning can use consciousness to select actions. Figure 14.17 shows an example of how this might work in one case. The growl of the lion could signal the action "Run!" but the sight of the lion about to attack a gazelle, rather than the hunter, could be processed to conclude "Hang around and you might get some scraps." Integrating the various sights and sounds in a conscious interpretation of the lion hunting the gazelle allows the hunter to resolve the conflict between the perception-action systems and respond in a more adaptive way. He is able to wait nearby to pick up some leavings from the lion's kill at the same time that he is being watchful for any danger to himself from that or any other lion.

The integration processes in consciousness are more pervasive than this. We have already noted in earlier chapters that different parts of the brain are associated with the extraction of visual, auditory, tactile, and chemical stimulus information. Even within a single sensory modality, such as vision, the location of a stimulus, its color, the shape of its contour, and its state of movement are processed in different places in the brain. How, then, do all of these sensory qualities get "bound together"? It seems

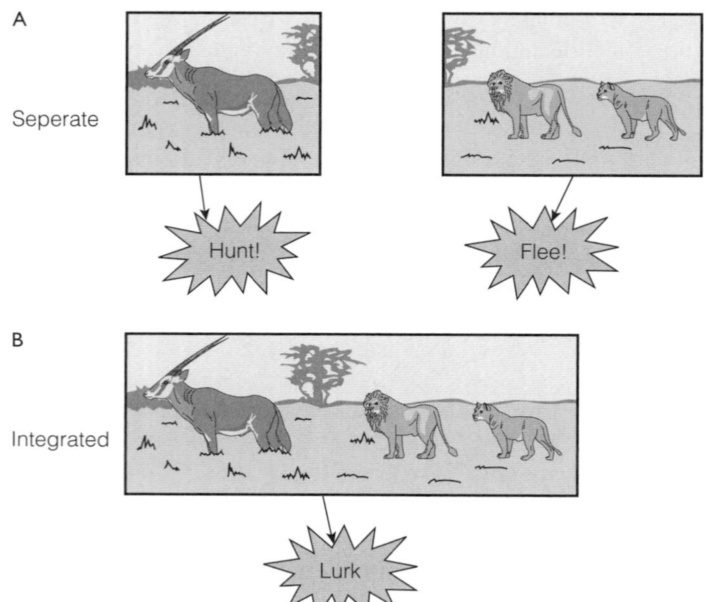

FIGURE 14.17 (A) Conflicting actions indicated by separate perception-action systems. (B) Integrated interpretation of the scene is the most adaptive.

likely that this is one of the main functions of consciousness. I do not see an isolated color, an odd shape, and some movement; instead I see a yellow taxicab passing me at a high rate of speed. Perhaps this is the true function of consciousness: to combine all of the information from the various sensory streams and various locations in the brain, to resolve the conflicts that might arise between the individual processes, and to form a global hypothesis as to what the objects and relationships among objects are, out there in the world (e.g., Baars, 1997). Our perceptual awareness is then that hypothesis. If this theory of the function of consciousness is true, then our search for the neural signature of consciousness is really the search for events and mechanisms that bind sensory qualities together.

The Dynamic Core

Even at the most basic levels of interpretation, such as our perception of a taxicab passing us on the road, we require the coordination of many higher-level brain processes. This daunting task most likely requires interactions between the parietal lobes, which encode the spatial positions of objects in the environment such as other cars on the road, and the frontal lobes, which interpret the object and also keep our attention focus on it rather than letting it drift to an observation of the sky; V4, which encodes color; V3 and V5, which encode movement; and so forth. Fortunately, research is providing some hints as to how processing among different brain areas is bound together in consciousness.

Studies examining the response patterns of single cells suggest that **synchronous neuronal firing** can bind the processing occurring in a number of discrete brain regions to create the larger functional unit that we are aware of in consciousness. Part of the "glue" that binds all of this activity together is timing. For example, neurons in different regions of the visual cortex fire in phase with one another if they are responding to the same object, but not if they are responding to different objects (Engel, Konig, Kreiter, Schillen, & Singer, 1992; Ward, 2003).

It is the synchrony, or coordination, of activity that seems to be most important in consciousness. A study involving binocular rivalry with cats as subjects provides an example (Figure 14.18). Rivalry was between displays of lines that were moving in opposite directions in the two eyes, and one can tell which one the cat is aware of by looking at which pattern the cat's eyes are tracking (optokinetic nystagmus). If only one pattern is visible (no rivalry), the neurons responding to a particular pattern were highly synchronous with each other, all firing at the same time (Figures 14.18B and 14.18D; the peak-to-peak size of the sine wave represents the degree of synchronization). When both patterns were presented simultaneously, however, both sets of neurons were responding at the same time. In this case the neurons responding to the "seen" pattern were much more highly synchronized (Figure 14.18C) than were those responding to the "unseen" pattern (Figure 14.18E). Thus, at least for cats, a neural correlate for perceptual awareness is synchronized neural activity in at least some brain areas. This conclusion can be extended to humans based on recordings of brain activity while human subjects viewed rivalrous patterns (Tononi, Russell, Srinivasan, & Edelman, 1998).

The necessity of synchronous firing for perceptual awareness is not limited to the binocular rivalry situation. For example, widespread synchronous brain activity was found in EEG records when subjects reported perceiving a face in an ambiguous figure but not when they reported a "meaningless shape" (Rodriquez et al., 1999). And a PET experiment found correlations among the activity level of different brain regions only when subjects were aware of the relationship between a visual event and an auditory event in an implicit learning task (McIntosh, Rajah, & Lobaugh, 1999). So synchronous neural activity over many brain regions seems to be strongly associated with perceptual and other forms of awareness.

Such findings have led researchers (e.g., Edelman & Tononi, 2000; Tononi and Edelman, 1998) to propose that the synchronous activity of neurons in different brain regions is both necessary and sufficient for perceptual awareness to occur. A large group of synchronously firing neurons forms the **dynamic core;** perceptual objects represented by neurons that are part of the dynamic core at any moment are in consciousness, whereas those represented by neurons not in the dynamic core are not in consciousness. This is how all aspects of perception get included in consciousness. In vision this would mean that both dorsal and ventral streams, the thalamus, amygdala, frontal and parietal lobes, and so on all fall into time-locked synchronous activity as we become consciously aware of the stimuli we are viewing.

There are, doubtless, other variables that are important. For example, it seems likely that synchronous neural activity must be sustained at some strength for some minimal time period in order to influence consciousness (see Rees et al., 2002). The new technologies that allow us to study the activities of the human brain (e.g., fMRI, ERP) will help to clarify the situation. It seems safe to say that our knowledge of consciousness may change a lot more quickly over the next few years than our knowledge in many of the other topics we have covered in this book. However, it does seem likely that consciousness is the "glue" that holds together the individual qualitative sensory "atoms" that make up our perceptual universe.

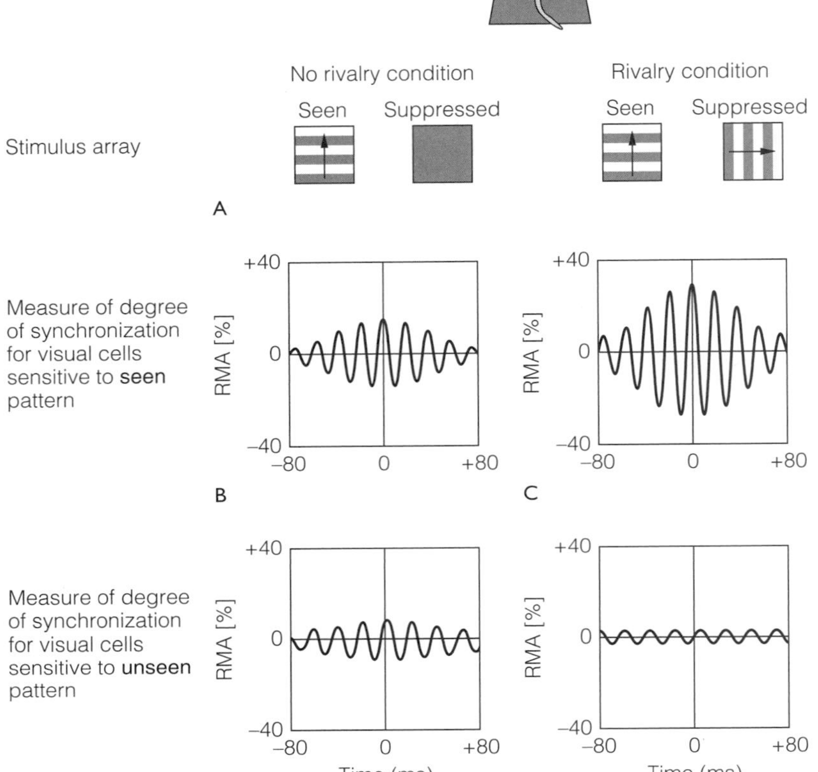

FIGURE 14.18 Measure of degree of synchronization for visual cells sensitive to unseen pattern (from Engels et al., 1999).

STUDY QUESTIONS

1. Distinguish between monism and dualism. Which position allows a scientific study of consciousness? Why?
2. What is saccadic suppression and why is it useful?
3. Discuss what functional role consciousness might serve in animal behavior that could have been selected for by evolution.
4. What is blindsight and why is it important to the study of perceptual awareness?
5. Summarize the evidence for the idea that visually guided reaching is controlled by a system that operates outside of perceptual awareness.
6. What do masked priming experiments reveal about the perceptual processing that occurs outside of perceptual awareness?
7. Describe eye rivalry and representation rivalry and discuss which is the better theory of binocular rivalry.
8. What are the agnosias and how can they help us understand consciousness?
9. What is the relationship between attention and consciousness?
10. Which brain areas have shown neural correlates of consciousness? Which of these are necessary for consciousness? Why?
11. What is the dynamic core and how does it explain perceptual awareness?

CHAPTER 15

DEVELOPMENT

CHAPTER SUMMARY

The camp counselor turned to the newest arrival and asked, "And how old are you, son?"

"Well," said the boy, "it all depends. According to my latest set of anatomical tests I'm 7. According to my physical dexterity test I'm 10. I've got a mental age of 11, a moral age of 9, and a social age of 10. If you are referring to my chronological age, though, that's 8, but nobody pays any attention to that these days."

Although you might not relish the thought of spending a summer with this child, his comments point out that there are significant changes in many of our physical and psychological characteristics as we age. Each of these changes has its own time course. Some changes represent physiological transformations occurring as the body matures (such as a person's anatomical age). Others represent patterns of behavior that are learned as the individual grows older (such as social or moral age). Still others may represent a combination of both learning and maturation (such as mental age). Although no one refers to a perceptual age, changes in perceptual characteristics also occur as an individual develops and matures. These changes are usually improvements producing perceptual experiences that more accurately represent the physical environment. However, there are also some perceptual capacities that deteriorate with age.

In considering how an individual's perceptual functioning changes, we can adopt two different perspectives. The first is long term, viewing people over their entire life

BIOGRAPHY BOX 15.1

EVERYTHING CHANGES WITH AGE

Alfred Binet (1857–1911) was born in Nice, France and later went to university in Paris. There he met the famous clinical psychologist Jean Charcot, who was studying hypnosis, and this caused Binet to become interested in higher mental processes. Often using his own daughters as experimental subjects he began to explore the way that their thinking changed as their age increased and they matured. The systematic emergence of their various cognitive skills gave him the idea that one could use the notion of "mental age" as a means of telling how far advanced a child was in its thinking and development. This would form the basis for the development of the first systematic psychological intelligence test, which was commissioned by the Minister of Instruction to determine how to sort children on the basis of their intelligence and educational needs.

Prior to his time, it was believed that children were born with fully functioning sensory and perceptual systems. Binet believed that since perception involved actions and interpretations by the mind, it would also change with age, just as every other mental ability does. He also felt that perception was the basis for all other mental activities and that there must be separate systems to interpret sensory inputs (thus we would have a visual memory, auditory memory and so forth). As an experimental psychologist he began to study perceptual changes using visual-geometric illusions and pattern perception. His data made it clear that the perceptual abilities and interpretations of young children were different from those of older children and adults. In this way he established the fact that perceptual abilities vary over the life span and thus justified the entire field of study that we know as *perceptual development.*

span. This is the **life span developmental approach,** which assumes that knowledge of a person's chronological age will allow us to predict many aspects of perceptual behavior. Biography Box 15.1 introduces you to one of the pioneers of this approach. The other approach is short term, viewing the changes that occur in perceptual responses as a result of a circumscribed set of experiences. This is the **perceptual learning approach.** It is based on the presumption that our interactions with the world can shape our percepts. These two approaches are not mutually exclusive; understanding the nature of perception often requires us to use both. Common to both approaches is the conclusion that, despite the fact that you may not be aware of it, your perceptual behavior is continually changing. Because the developmental and perceptual learning approaches use different techniques and often address somewhat different theoretical issues, we deal with these areas in separate chapters. Here we will begin with the developmental approach and then proceed to the effects of learning and experience in Chapter 16.

DEVELOPMENT OF THE NERVOUS SYSTEM

Research Challenges in Testing Infants

The perceptions of newborn infants (neonates) are difficult to assess. In the first few months of life, infants spend much of their time sleeping, and they do not respond to instructions or answer our questions in any direct fashion. They also produce only a limited range of observable behaviors. These challenges require experimenters to be quite creative in devising techniques to measure the perceptual abilities of the very young. Physiological measures are often preferred because they do not require much cooperation or sophistication on the part of the individual actually being measured. Of course, if the measurements are going to be invasive or might be protracted or uncomfortable, researchers are sometimes forced to use animal subjects rather than human infants. But this can create its own problems, because those aspects of such measures that are species specific are often unknown.

An alternative approach, which is rapidly increasing in popularity, is the use of brain imaging techniques such as **event-related potentials (ERPs)**. For example, we can determine how well the visual cortex of the infant is functioning by measuring event-related potentials in response to visual stimulation. The recordings are made by pasting electrodes (generally flat pieces of silver or tin) to the scalp and connecting them to very sensitive amplifiers. Plotting the output of these amplifiers over time reveals small changes in the electrical activity of the brain in response to stimulation and these are the ERPs or event-related potentials. When the stimuli are visual, these recordings are often called **visually evoked potentials (VEPs)**.

Other brain imaging techniques that work with infants include **positron emission tomography** (**PET** scans) and **functional magnetic resonance imaging** (**fMRI**), which we described briefly in Chapter 3. These techniques can be used to acquire pictures of infant brain activity that can be correlated with visual or auditory stimuli. Thus, we are able to determine whether the infant brain "sees" a stimulus pattern even though the infant cannot indicate this to us using any observable behavior (Poldrack, Pare-Blagoev, & Grant, 2002).

Almost all newborn infants (and even most premature infants) show brain responses to visual stimuli; however, these will differ from the adult to a greater or lesser degree depending on the stimulus pattern, size, and speed (Johnson & Mareschal, 2001). In general, the responses from subcortical regions of the brain are always present at birth, but the cortex is not very responsive in some areas. Over a period of about 3 to 6 months, the infant's electrical brain responses to visual stimuli come to look more and more like those of adults. It is generally agreed that during the first year of life the visual system matures rapidly and that, although it shows many adult capabilities by the end of the second year, some brain centers continue to develop until the child is 10 to 12 years of age or older (e.g., Johnston, Nishimura, Harum, Pekar, & Blue, 2001)

Patterns of Brain Change in Development

Before speaking about how perception changes as we develop and age, we must know something about the physiology of our sensory systems. What is our sensory apparatus capable of at birth, and how do these capacities change with age? Since the brain is involved in all aspects of perception, however, it is important that we understand something about its development in order to understand sensory systems.

Contrary to what you might be tempted to think at first, brain development does not primarily involve an increase in the number of neurons, nor does it involve even a systematic increase in the number of connections between neurons. In fact, the absolute number of cortical neurons for a well-defined brain region such as the primary visual cortex (Area V1) does not change very much from birth to about 10 years of age. During this first decade of life there is a slight increase in the gray matter in the brain; however, most of the changes in brain volume are due to a relative increase in the white matter in the brain, which reflects myelinization of neurons. Myelin is the fatty tissue that surrounds many neuronal axons and speeds the transmission of neural information. A number of brain imaging studies indicate that myelinization is complete in early infancy for the brain stem and midbrain, is completed in young childhood for the primary cortical sensory areas and parietal lobes, and is completed only in the early teen years for many other regions of the cortex (Paus, Collins, Evans, Leonard, Pike, & Zijdenbos, 2001). Since myelinization leads to faster neural interactions we should be looking for increasing perceptual speed during this period of development.

It comes as a surprise to most people to learn that loss of brain material is part of the normal developmental process. Although the developing brain does undergo some growth from the fetal period through about age 10, many more neurons and synaptic connections are available than are needed for later function. The mature brain actually is what remains after these excess building materials have been "sculpted" away." For example, mice lose up to 30% of their cortical neurons during development (Heumann & Leuba, 1983), and the monkey visual cortex loses 15% of its total cell population between birth and adulthood (O'Kusky & Colonnier, 1982).

For humans the issue is not so much one of losing neurons, but rather is closely tied to the loss of connections between neurons. This is referred to as **neuronal**

pruning by some researchers because under the microscope the connections look like "branches" from the axon of one neuron making contact with the dendritic "branches" of another neuron. Reducing the number of these branches can then be viewed as pruning of the neuronal tree. Figure 15.1 shows how the total number of synaptic connections in the visual cortex changes remarkably with age. The number of connections increases rapidly until about 8 months of age, after which it begins to decrease, declining to almost one half the maximum level between the ages of 8 months and 10 years. There is another smaller, but significant, decline in the number of connections in old age.

What is the possible importance of the inverted U-shaped trend in the number of connections that neurons are making with one another over development? One very promising theory is that the decline in the number of connections reflects the development of specialized pathways of information flow and specialized regions of cortex devoted to particular functions (e.g., Johnston, Nishimura, Harum, Pekar, & Blue, 2001). This theory proposes that in the young infant, different attributes of a visual stimulus, and even information from different sensory modalities, may be processed in a relatively diffuse and undifferentiated way. The emergence of specialized systems in development, through the loss of specific neuronal connections, results in information that is combined in early infancy being increasingly segregated or partitioned into relatively isolated modules as the child matures.

This theory makes some predictions that are interesting because they contrast with the general trend that perceptual functions tend to improve with development. For example, consider the development of the ocular dominance columns in Area V1 of the visual cortex. In humans these may take between 4 and 6 months to develop into their adultlike forms (Held, 1985; Hickey & Peduzzi, 1987). This implies that before the columns have become segregated, both eyes project to the same cells in the visual cortex. This leads to the interesting prediction that a young infant should have an integrated neural representation of some stimulus inputs that would not be possible for older infants. Support for this prediction was found in one experiment in which infants were shown vertical stripes in one eye and horizontal stripes in the other eye (Held, 1993). Infants under 4 months of age behaved in the same way as when they were shown a gridlike pattern in only one eye (the composite of the two striped patterns). Infants older than 4 months behaved toward the composite pattern as though it were a new stimulus.

Early Events

Since anything that affects the developing brain might be expected to affect the sensory systems, it should not be surprising to find that anything that disturbs the normal development of the nervous system and the brain might also lead to reductions in visual and auditory functions. The kinds of disruption that we are looking at are not major traumas that otherwise lead to reduced motor and cognitive functioning, but rather events that are taken as minor difficulties. For example, Harland and Coren (1996) studied a large sample of normally functioning university students, checking their medical history for any signs that they had had a difficult birth. Birth problems might be moderately serious, such as breathing difficulties, but could be relatively minor, such as a

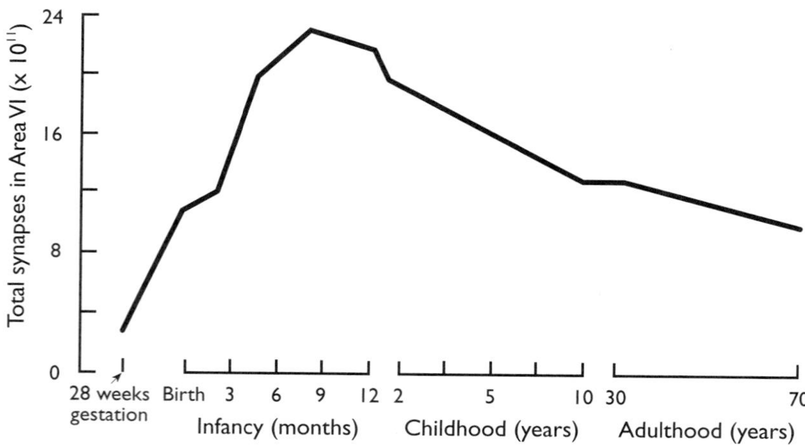

FIGURE 15.1 The estimated total number of synaptic connections in human brain Area V1 as a function of age. Drawn based on Huttenlocher (1990, p. 519).

prolonged labor, low birth weight, premature birth, being part of a twin pair, breech birth, or a birth that required instruments or surgery to deliver the infant. They found that university students with such events in their history were likely to have poorer visual acuity and binocular function and poorer auditory sensitivity as adults. Some of their findings were confirmed in a study of Danish army conscripts, where it was found that individuals who had a low birth weight (less than 3000 g or about 6.5 lb) were much more likely to have poor vision and hearing as adults (Olsen et al., 2001). It seems that such birth stressors may slow or moderately disrupt the development of the brain and nervous system, even if the individual appears to be otherwise normal.

Recently researchers have begun to look at events that might impact sensory function immediately following birth. One common individual difference in child rearing has to do with whether the infant is breast fed or fed using a baby formula. The major difference in these two nutritional sources is that human milk contains long-chain polyunsaturated fatty acids (specifically docosahexaenoic acid, or DHA) that are absent in most baby formulas. Because it is known that such nutrients are vital for the early formation of neural tissue, researchers began to look for possible sensory differences in breast- versus bottle-fed individuals. It is now becoming clear that bottle-fed children have somewhat poorer visual functioning later on in life, and they may also have moderate reductions in their hearing and speech discrimination abilities (e.g., Innis, Gilley, & Werker, 2001).

The Visual System

In comparison to the rest of the body, the size of the eye changes very little after birth. The body may increase in volume about twentyfold, but the eye increases in volume only about threefold, as a consequence of the length from the cornea to the retina growing from about 16 mm to about 24 mm (Hickey & Peduzzi, 1987). The infant's retina contains rods and cones, as does the adult's. Electrical measures indicate that these receptors are functioning from birth, although the responses may not yet exactly match those of older children or adults (Fulton & Hansen, 2000; Maurer, 1975). Anatomically, however, the retina is still immature at birth (Johnson, 1990). For instance, the region of the central fovea is not well defined in a 1-week-old infant—the cones in this region are stubby in appearance and much more sparsely packed than they will be eventually. Visual functioning of the retinal receptors is somewhat more developed at birth in the periphery of the eye than it is in the central region (Banks & Salapatek, 1983). Nonetheless, by perhaps as early as 3 months of age the rod and cone functions of the infant look much like those of an adult (Chien, Teller, & Palmer, 2000).

Until the recent rise of brain imaging techniques our knowledge of the status of the visual pathways in newborns and infants came mostly from animal studies, with the cat providing most of the data. If we measure the physiological functions of the various sites in the visual pathways of the cat at the time when the animal first opens its eyes, we get results like those in Table 15.1 (e.g., Atkinson, 2000). The table shows that a number of adultlike and immature response patterns coexist in the newborn cat. Thus, in the retinal ganglion cell, we find the expected center-surround arrangement of excitatory and inhibitory responses. However, the receptive fields differ in size from those of the adult, and there is a general sluggishness in the response.

In Chapter 3 we discussed two different visual pathways, one originating from the small ganglion cells in the retina, called the **parvocellular** pathway, and one originating from the larger ganglion cells, called the **magnocellular** pathway. These pathways appear to process different types of information in parallel, with the parvocellular pathway associated principally with color and detailed form vision and the magnocellular pathway specialized for movement and depth perception. These two systems are also characterized by response pattern differences—parvo cells give a sustained response, magno cells a transient response. In the cat and monkey, however, at the retinal level, these two response types are not well defined at birth.

Farther along in the visual pathways, at the lateral geniculate nucleus, we do find the adult division of two magnocellular layers and four parvocellular layers in the neonate. Here we also can observe the separation of the inputs from the two eyes into clearly defined layers that are interleaved. However, many of the neurons in the geniculate don't seem to respond to any sort of visual input, and the responses that can be measured are often slow and easily fatigued. The parvo neurons in the lateral geniculate reach their adult size first, whereas the magno neurons are much slower to develop. However, the relative maturity of the two systems seems to reverse itself by the time the child is 12 months of age. Despite the early differences that seem to favor the development of the parvocellular pathways, the functional brain imaging data suggest that it is actually the magnocellular pathway, which responds to the simpler visual dimensions of luminance and motion, that reaches its full functionality

TABLE 15.1 The Functional Condition of Various Sites in the Visual Pathways of the Newborn Cat

Adult-Like Responses	Immature Responses
Retinal Ganglion Cells	
Center-surround organization of receptive fields Adult percentage of on/off center	Low activity level Overly large receptive fields Slow responses to light and weak inhibition Parvo vs. magno responses not clear
Lateral Geniculate Nucleus	
Normal visual-field mapping Binocular separation of inputs	Low activity and silent areas Large receptive field diameter Slow, sluggish, fatigable responses
Superior Colliculus	
Normal visual-field mapping Center-surround receptive fields Adult percentage of on/off center	Slow, sluggish, fatigable responses Large receptive fields No movement direction sensitivtiy
Striate Cortex	
Normal visual-field mapping Adult separation of responses by eye of input	Sluggish, fatigable responses Many silent cells Fewer or absent orientation and direction-selective cells with broader tuning No binocular disparity cells

first, with adultlike responses by the age of 1 year. The parvocellular system, which responds to the more detailed and complex aspects of the visual stimulus, such as contour resolution, pattern perception, and color discrimination, continues to change in its responsiveness and actually does not make adult-like responses until the child has reached the age of 12 or 13 years (Madrid & Crognale, 2000).

The tectopulvinar system matures even faster. The superior colliculus shows the general organization of cell layers and the center-surround organization of receptive fields resembling those of an adult by 3 to 6 months. However, at birth the receptive field size of these neurons is much larger than that of adults, and the responses are relatively slow, weak, and not very sensitive to direction.

Finally, at the level of the primary visual cortex (V1), we find that the inputs from the two eyes are separated into the expected columnar arrangement discussed in Chapter 3 and that directional and orientation-sensitive neurons (both simple and complex) are present. In infant monkeys, single cell recordings show that some neurons are orientation selective, although they are fewer in number, and their responses are slow and easily fatigued. Within the primary visual cortex, the layers of cortex that receive inputs directly from the eye reach their mature size and complete the myelinization process before the layers that receive or send information from or to other brain centers. Also, even when neonatal neurons are relatively mature in appearance, their responses are slower and less vigorous than those of the adult. (Brown, 2001).

In human newborns, when behavioral measures are used, orientation selective responses have not been observed until 5 to 6 months of age (Braddick, Wattam-Bell, & Atkinson, 1986) and even then the responses are not adultlike (Candy, Skoczenski, & Norcia, 2001). In addition, binocular disparity-sensitive cells seem to be almost absent until several weeks of age in both monkeys and humans (Held, 1985). Overall, many of the characteristics of the adult system seem to be present in the newborn visual system, but the full adult pattern of response clearly is not present. Of course, many of these statements are species specific, and humans develop somewhat more slowly than do cats and monkeys. Thus, whereas those animals show separation of the two eyes into separate ocular dominance columns from birth, humans may take 4 to 6 months after birth to develop similar complex neural structures (Sanes, 2000). Taken together, these observations suggest that although most of the structures and mechanisms to sustain vision are present, the quality of information reaching the highest visual centers of the newborn's brain may be relatively poor, and different perceptual functions will emerge at different times during development.

PERCEPTION IN INFANTS

Behavioral Methods of Testing Infant Perception

Testing physiological functions in infants may be technologically complex, but trying to find out what infants actually perceive is even more complex. Methods of testing infants' capacities must be very carefully devised because we can't use verbal instructions or obtain verbal responses from them. The researcher's only recourse is to rely on observable behaviors, which for perception usually involve some form of reflex such as overt orienting. The **orienting reflex** involves eye movements, head turns, and visual following behavior in response to a stimulus that appears suddenly or is moving. The eliciting stimulus may be auditory, visual, or even tactile.

Given the limited response repertoire of a young infant, we can appreciate the methodological breakthrough made by Fantz (1961). His procedure, called **preferential looking,** involves first placing a young infant in a special chamber (either on its back or in an infant chair). Visual stimuli are then placed on the walls or the roof of the chamber. There is a tiny hole through which the experimenter can watch the infant looking at the stimuli. An apparatus similar to Fantz's is shown in Figure 15.2. When the infant views one of a pair of stimulus patterns placed in the chamber, the experimenter determines which one is being looked at by simply noting the side to which the eyes turn. A timer is used to record how long the infant views each of the two stimuli. If the infant looks at one target longer than the other, this is taken as indicating a preference for that target. The existence of a preference for a pattern implies that the infant can discriminate between the patterns. Unfortunately, this simple result does not tell us *why* the infant preferred to look at one stimulus rather than the other, nor can we be sure that the absence of a viewing preference means that the infant cannot discriminate between the two stimuli.

There have been many elaborations of this technique, such as the one called the **forced-choice preferential looking.** This procedure allows the study of stimulus detection as well as discrimination. Here, the infant is presented with only a single stimulus while its response is monitored by a hidden observer or TV camera. If, on the basis of the infant's head and eye movements alone, an observer can reliably determine whether the test target was presented to the left or to the right side of the screen, it is presumed that the information concerning the posi-

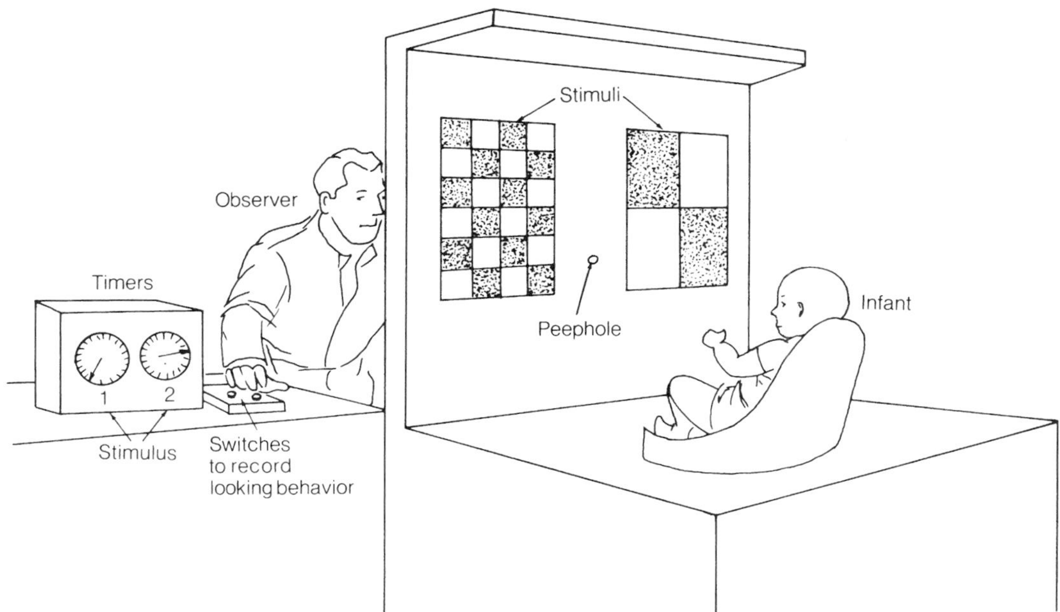

FIGURE 15.2 An apparatus for monitoring how long infants view particular stimuli.

BIOGRAPHY BOX 15.2

WHAT IS THE PERCEPTUAL EXPERIENCE OF A NEWBORN BABY?

Davida Y. Teller (1938–) has been asking this question for most of her adult life. Following the receipt of her Ph.D. degree from the University of California at Berkeley in 1965, Dr. Teller was appointed to the faculty at the University of Washington in Seattle, where she still supervises a very active research lab. The dilemma facing her was how to get information about the experience of an individual, in this case a newborn infant, who was unable to communicate in any of the ways that we usually think of. Her solution was elegant in its simplicity. Why not rely on behaviors that the infant does have under her control, such as where she chooses to look and how active her various muscles are? If a stimulus is having an influence on these behaviors of a baby, then information from the stimulus is moving through her sensory systems and affecting her actions.

Dr. Teller took this insight and turned it into a formal procedure for studying the sensory ability of newborns that we call **forced choice preferential looking.** This technique has a twist. Instead of treating the babies as "observers" who could make a report on a "stimulus," she treated the baby's behavior as the stimulus and employed adult observers of the babies. The idea is that if the baby responds differently enough to different stimuli so that observers looking at him can discriminate these differences, then he must be discriminating between the stimuli. In earlier years, to make the procedure even more rigorous, the adult observers often viewed the babies through a peephole, so that the babies could not see them and so that the adults themselves did not know which stimuli the babies had been given. The only response the adults were allowed to make was a guess as to which side of space the baby seemed to be looking. Although we now use more sophisticated versions of monitoring the babies' behaviors when viewing stimuli, the rationale remains the same. This approach is used by researchers all over the world to answer questions about newborn visual acuity, hearing, color vision, the ability to discriminate pictures, and even their preferences for particular kinds of faces.

---

tion of the target has been transmitted from the screen, through the infant's visual system and behavior, to the observer. At the minimum, this suggests that the infant can see the stimulus. Biography Box 15.2 introduces you to the scientist who invented and popularized this technique.

A further variation of this technique allows researchers to determine whether an infant can notice any difference between stimuli. Again, only one stimulus is presented, and the viewing behavior is monitored. At first the infant will spend a good deal of time looking at the stimulus, but as time passes it will begin to look at it less and less. Researchers often informally say that the infant is becoming "bored" with the stimulus. The technical name for this process is **habituation.** If a different stimulus is now presented, the baby will again look. This renewed interest in the stimulus suggests that the infant has recognized that something has changed and that the present stimulus is different from the former one. The technical name for the renewed interest in the stimulus is **dishabituation.** It is used by researchers as an indication that the infant has discriminated the current stimulus from the previous stimulus to which the infant had habituated.

Eye Movements and Attention

Over the past few decades we have seen a great increase in interest in the development of visual attention. The reason for this is that attention is seen as a necessary first step in perception. As you well know, it is possible to have an object in your visual field, and even to be looking directly at it, without really noticing it (Chapter 13). To be consciously aware of the object, your attention must be directed to it as well. In fact, the direction of attention toward a stimulus is often used as "proof" that the stimulus has been perceptually processed.

We can think of the visual attention of an infant as having three contributory components: alertness, spatial orienting, and attention to object features (e.g., Colombo, 2001). **Alertness** simply requires the infant to be aroused enough to process stimuli, and it seems to be under the control of whatever external stimulation is around the infant at the moment. For example, recognition of stimuli visible when the infant is feeding is considerably better than recognition of stimuli present at other times (Geva, Gardner, & Karmel, 1999). This is presumably because the act of feeding raises the arousal level, and in that more alert state infants can process information better. Over the first 3 months, however, the infant gradually becomes more alert under a broader range of circumstances and therefore a better perceptual processor.

Spatial orienting toward something usually involves turning the eyes and perhaps the head or body in its direction. There is evidence that this kind of orientating is handled by the tectopulvinar pathways, which, since they involve lower brain centers, are functioning reasonably well early in development. Spatial orienting by infants gives us evidence that they have the ability to perceive the direction of stimuli. Newborn infants can move their eyes so as to bring visual targets onto or close to their foveas. Thus, if we present a young infant (about 2 weeks of age) with a target that suddenly appears 20° from the fovea, it will slowly turn its eyes toward that target (e.g., Aslin, 1987). Furthermore, 3-month-old infants seem to be able to identify targets in the periphery of their visual field well enough to guide their eyes to selected or preferred stimuli (Maurer & Lewis, 1991).

Although infants will look at a target that suddenly appears or moves, infants' eye movements are not exactly like those of adults. Each of the two main types of voluntary eye movements takes some time to develop fully. The first type is **saccadic eye movements,** which are fast, ballistic movements from one target to another that occur when you direct your attention toward a target. In adults, a saccade will start the eye moving toward a target some distance from the current fixation point within 200 to 250 ms. The actual time taken by the movement itself can be as short as 4 to 10 ms. Saccades are also accurate in positioning the eye so that the new target is centered on the fovea. A typical long saccade would bring the eye to within 5 to 10% of the desired position. A representative adult eye movement to a target 30° from the current fixation point is shown in Figure 15.3. Infants are much slower to begin the saccade and tend to make a series of small saccades, often not reaching the target for well over a second, as also shown in Figure 15.3 (see Bronson, 1990). However, even the immature saccadic eye movements of infants can reveal something of their perceptual capacities. For example, expectation (see Chapter 13) can be studied in infants by showing them a light that either consistently alternates between two locations (so that its "next" location can be anticipated) or appears randomly at various locations. Newborn infants' eye movements are similar in both conditions, indicating that they probably are not able to anticipate where the light will be next even when it alternates consistently. By 3 to 4 months of age, however, infants move their eyes toward the "next" location when the light alternates consistently, indicating that they are expecting it to appear there (Haith, Hazan, & Goodman, 1988).

The other type of eye movements are called **smooth pursuit movements.** Here the eyes track a steadily mov-

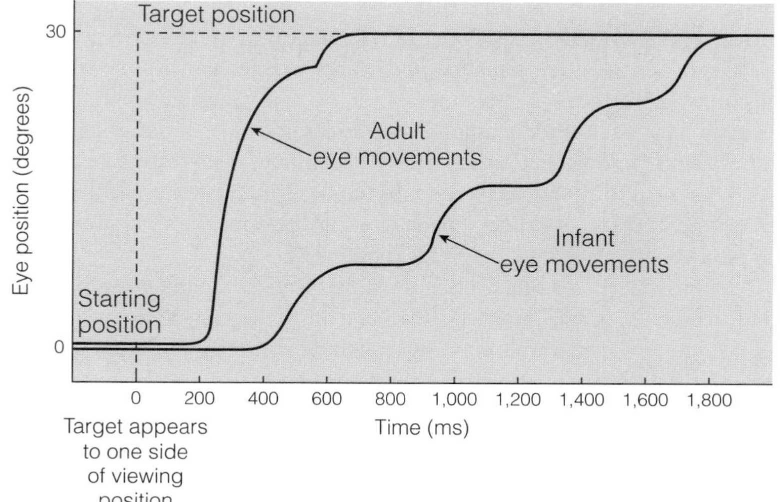

FIGURE 15.3 A typical adult eye movement to a target appearing 30 degrees to one side of fixation will involve a single, fast, large saccade and a small corrective flick, whereas an infant will have a longer delay before moving, and the movement will involve a series of shorter saccades.

ing object, such as a ball flying through the air or a person swinging on a swing, with a uniform and even motion. Smooth pursuit eye movements are possible in the newborn child, but they are not very efficient and the child only manages to hold the target on its fovea for about a third of the time (Lengyel, Weinacht, Charlier, & Gottlob, 1998). The rest of the time infants use short, jumpy saccadic eye movements to track even smoothly moving objects. Thus, rather than keep pace with the moving target, an infant grabs a glimpse of it, waits until it drifts from view, and then attempts to look at it again. As with saccades, newborns are unable to anticipate the path of an object that moves smoothly back and forth. Instead they seem always to be "catching up" with small stepwise movements that are the same size regardless of the speed of the object. This pattern does not simply reflect an immature motor system because infants can be shown to make much larger saccades under other circumstances (Aslin, 1981a). The adult pattern of smooth anticipatory movements begins to emerge at 8 to 10 weeks of age, and by 6 months of age infants can not only track with their eyes but also with their head and can make reaching movements that show they are predicting where the target will be next (von Hofsten, Vishton, Spelke, Feng, & Rosander, 1998).

The fact that infants move their eyes in response to moving or suddenly appearing stimuli can be used to measure other capacities in the newborn. For instance, if we show an adult observer a continuously moving pattern (such as a screen full of stripes all moving in one direction), we get a characteristic eye-movement pattern. The eye will smoothly track in the direction of the movement for a distance and then flick back in the opposite direction. After this return movement the observer's eyes fixate another stripe and follow it, and this process repeats itself while the observer views the array. This repetitive eye movement sequence in the presence of a moving pattern is called **optokinetic nystagmus.** A jerkier version of these eye movements is found in infants younger than 5 days. In fact, its appearance is so reliable that the absence of optokinetic nystagmus is used as an indication that there may be neurological problems. This eye-movement pattern seems to be automatic or reflexive in nature, rather than voluntary, and is probably controlled by the **tectopulvinar system,** which we described in Chapter 3 (see Richards & Hunter, 1998). If an infant cannot see a pattern of moving stripes (because they are not large enough or lack sufficient contrast), optokinetic nystagmus will be absent. This technique has been used to study brightness discrimination, visual acuity, and motion perception in infants (Banks & Salapatek, 1983).

Although newborns will move their eyes to suddenly appearing stimuli, they show a much more consistent response to stimuli in the **temporal visual field** (the peripheral portion of the visual field out toward the temples of the head) than to those in the **nasal visual field** (the central portion of the visual field, which is closer to the nose). By 2 months of age, this asymmetry has diminished greatly, although it can still be observed to some extent in adults (Posner, 1980). An interesting finding is that eye movements toward stimuli in the temporal visual field can be elicited by the superior colliculus, a part of the tectopulvinar system, without any contribution from the visual cortex. However, movements toward the nasal field require activation of the visual cortex in addition to the superior colliculus (Johnson, 1990). This suggests that the movement asymmetry found in infants arises from an immaturity in the control over eye movements exerted by the visual cortex (Maurer & Lewis, 1991).

The eye movements of young infants are also easily disrupted by the appearance of more than one stimulus in the visual field. "Competing" stimuli increase the time required to complete an eye movement and decrease the accuracy with which a saccade will cause a target to be fixated (Atkinson, Hood, Braddick, & Wattam-Bell, 1988). One very vivid demonstration of competition between brain regions in the infant occurs when an initial flashing light at the center of gaze is accompanied some time later by a light flashing in the visual periphery (Hood & Atkinson, 1993). The infant at first orients to the central flashing light. When the peripheral light begins to flash, the infant's head is drawn in the direction of the peripheral light, but the eyes appear to remain fixated on the central flashing light. A reasonable explanation of this behavior is that some reflexive neural mechanism is guiding the head to orient to the new light in the periphery, while another mechanism has "locked" the eye movement system onto the central light. This conflict is much less evident in 6- to 7-month-old infants than in 2- to 3-month-old infants, suggesting that these reflexes are gradually coming under the control of central, cortical mechanisms (Atkinson, Hood, Wattam-Bell, & Braddick, 1992; Johnson, 1995).

Another phenomenon of visual competition occurs when infants are faced with the choice between looking again at a previously fixated stimulus and at a new one. Infants up to 3 months of age tend to look again at the original stimulus, whereas 6- to 7-month-olds will choose to fixate the new stimulus instead (Hood & Atkinson, 1991; Johnson & Tucker, 1996). This is similar to the inhibition of return phenomenon seen in adults (see Chapter 13) in that it biases the older infant observer to take in new information. This bias toward the examination of objects in novel locations assists the infant in a full exploration of its visual world.

Visual Acuity

The visual acuity of infants is rather poor, especially in the periphery of the nasal visual field of each eye (Courage & Adams, 1996). This fact has been established in several ways. For instance, the optokinetic response that we described earlier can be used to test the visual acuity of infants. This is done by finding the narrowest width of stripes that will still produce the tracking response. Other ways, such as preferential looking procedures, can be used to measure infant visual acuity. Although the level of acuity found for infants varies with the technique and with the specific acuity stimulus used (Shimojo & Held, 1987; Skoczenski & Norcia, 1999), there is a general agreement that visual acuity is around 20/800 (6/240 in metric units) at birth. This is less acuity than is needed to see the single big E on a standard Snellen acuity chart (which is a Snellen acuity of 20/200).

Newborns also act as if they have limited ability to change focus through lens accommodation. They act as if their lenses are fixed in focus to see something about 20 cm away (White, 1971). This is about the distance of the mother's face for a nursing infant. However, the poor acuity and accommodative ability of the infant do not last for long. There is a rapid increase in visual acuity during the first 3 months of age and, as shown in Figure 15.4, the young child's acuity increases steadily with age. Some tests show, however, that the improvement continues for quite a while, and the child may not finally reach average adult levels until more than 7 years of age (Scharre, Cotter, Block, & Kelly, 1990). If you have access to a young infant, you can see the effect of this limited accommodation by trying Demonstration Box 15.1.

Brightness and Color

Several techniques have been used to assess the basic sensitivity of infants to brightness and color. One-month-old infants are about 1/50 as sensitive to light as are adults, whereas 3-month-old infants are 1/10 as sensitive to light both under dark-adapted (scotopic) and light-adapted (photopic) conditions (Powers, Schneck, & Teller, 1981). However, despite these differences infants are still very sensitive to light. For example, in Chapter 4 we found that an adult can detect as few as 6 quanta of light hitting anywhere in a patch of 1300 rod receptors. In comparison, a 3-month-old infant would need to receive about 60 quanta of light over the same region, and a 1-month-old infant would need about 300 quanta of light (Teller & Bornstein, 1987). Although that is substantially greater than that required by adults, it is still a very small amount of light.

Several studies show that despite differences in absolute sensitivity, the relative sensitivity of infants and adults to different wavelengths of light is about the same. Both are most sensitive to middle wavelengths and exhibit a gradual decrease in sensitivity to longer and shorter wavelengths. This does not mean, however, that infants have color vision equivalent to that of adults. In general, young infants do show some ability to discriminate between colors (e.g., Knobaluch, Vital-Durand, & Barbur, 2001). Infants have good color discrimination between the long and middle wavelengths of light (red and green), and, at least for large stimuli, this may be present as early as the first week of life. However, for the 1-month-old infant the short-wavelength (blue) discriminating mechanism

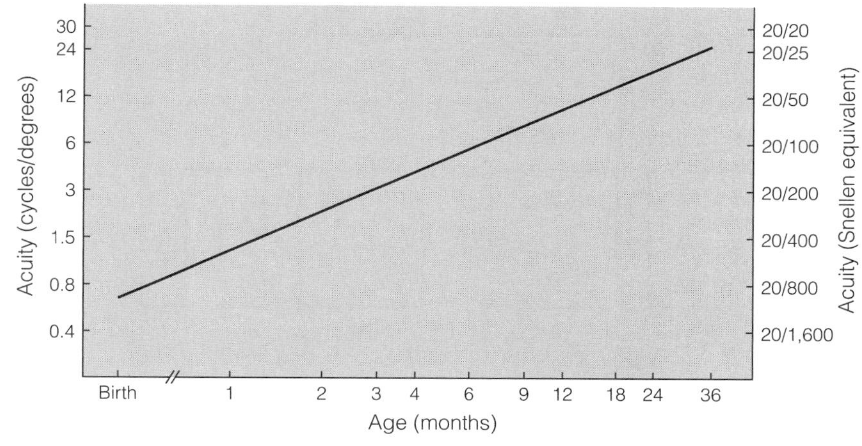

FIGURE 15.4 Steady improvement in visual acuity from birth to 3 years of age.

DEMONSTRATION BOX 15.1

INFANT ACCOMMODATION

To demonstrate that an infant's accommodation is limited to close objects, you will, of course, need an infant, preferably 2 months of age or younger. If you can find one, catch its attention and then slowly move a pencil from side to side near the infant's face. Use a distance of about 20 cm, or around 8 inches. Watch the child's head and eyes and notice that the infant will track, or at least try to track, the pencil. Now repeat this, but vary the distance to 1 m or 2 m away from the child. At this distance you should have exceeded the ability of the infant to accommodate, and you should notice that little, if any, tracking occurs.

seems to be still immature (Adams, 1995). Most 1-month-old infants have poor discrimination among the various short-wavelength stimuli. In fact, their discrimination appears to be much like that of tritanopic color-blind individuals (see Chapter 4). By the age of 2 months, however, most infants can make such short-wavelength discriminations (Adams & Courage, 1994).

Pattern Discrimination

The preferential looking technique has been used extensively to explore pattern perception in infants. Using this technique, it has been shown that even premature infants, born 1 to 2 months prior to a full-term gestation, often preferentially look at patterned stimuli rather than plain ones of equal average brightness and also sometimes discriminate between different patterns (Fantz & Miranda, 1977). This means that the optical and neural bases of pattern vision do not abruptly become functional at the end of the full term of pregnancy, which is the age at which infants ordinarily can first be observed. Rather, these mechanisms have already matured to a reasonable degree of function prior to the normal birth time.

Preferential looking studies have also shown that young infants can discriminate among a variety of different types of patterns. For instance, in one experiment newborn infants showed a clear preference for viewing patterns of stripes over a simple square and also preferred patterns with high contrast between the figures and the background. They showed a preference for larger patterns, indicating that they can discriminate size, and also preferred patterns containing many rather than few elements (see Slater & Johnson, 1998). In addition, they showed some ability to discriminate certain aspects defining contours, such as curvature, by preferring curved to straight-line elements. Figure 15.5 shows some

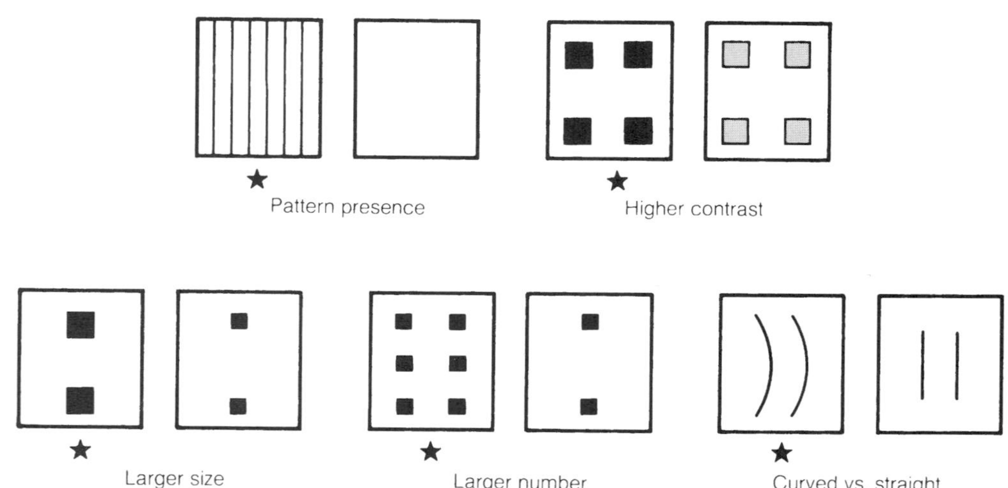

FIGURE 15.5 Patterns most looked at by newborns are indicated with a star for each pair of stimuli.

representative forms. In the figure, the star indicates those most preferred by newborns for each pair.

Generally, infants prefer moderately complex stimuli over those that are very simple or very complex, although preferences do change with age. Young infants prefer simple patterns with highly contrasting elements, whereas 5-month-olds can make more subtle distinctions in contrast and configuration. Banks and Salapatek (1983) suggested that pattern perception in infants reflects the developing ability to discriminate various spatial frequencies (see Chapter 9).

Preferences in viewing also show that some high-level aspects of pattern perception are possible for the young infant. Infants can discriminate the orientation of patterns within the first few weeks and perhaps even on the first day of life. Furthermore, they seem to be aware of certain forms of symmetry or its absence. Although infants respond to both the size and position of stimuli, at age 4 months they are relatively insensitive to certain subtle changes in sparsely defined configurations, such as patterns made up solely of a few dots (Dodwell, Humphrey, & Muir, 1987). Figure 15.6 summarizes the sensitivity of the 4-month-old infant to various aspects of visual patterns. It shows a pattern to which the infant is habituated and then some test patterns. The patterns with a plus sign exemplify changes that the infant would be expected to notice; the pattern with a minus sign exemplifies a change that the infant would not notice.

At only the age of 3 or 4 months infants seem to respond to the global aspects of figures and seem to be using the same kinds of Gestalt grouping principles (Chapter 9) that adults do, grouping objects on the basis of similarity and proximity (Slater, 2000). Infants can even be shown to be forming objects through the use of good continuation and closure. Thus if they are shown a pair of overlapping figures, such as Figure 15.7A, which adults see as a teardrop and a square, they will treat a variation of the figure that separates the components but keeps the figures formed by closure and good continuation intact (Figure 15.7B) as much more similar to the original than another stimulus such as Figure 15.7C, which still maintains all of the same elements but violates the Gestalt organizational principles (Quinn, Brown, & Streppa, 1997). Infants, however, are not as efficient at Gestalt grouping and sometimes fail if the display is complex or the organization cues are subtle, and they may require prior experience with the patterns before the normal adult pattern of grouping is found (Needham & Baillageron, 1998).

Object Perception

Certain meaningful patterns receive special attention, even from neonates. A number of researchers have studied the response of infants to targets that resemble the human face. One common procedure is to use some targets that are only head shaped, others containing only some facial features (such as a hairline or eyes), some containing scrambled facial features, and others that actually look like faces. Samples of such stimuli are shown in Figure 15.8. In general, it is found that very shortly after

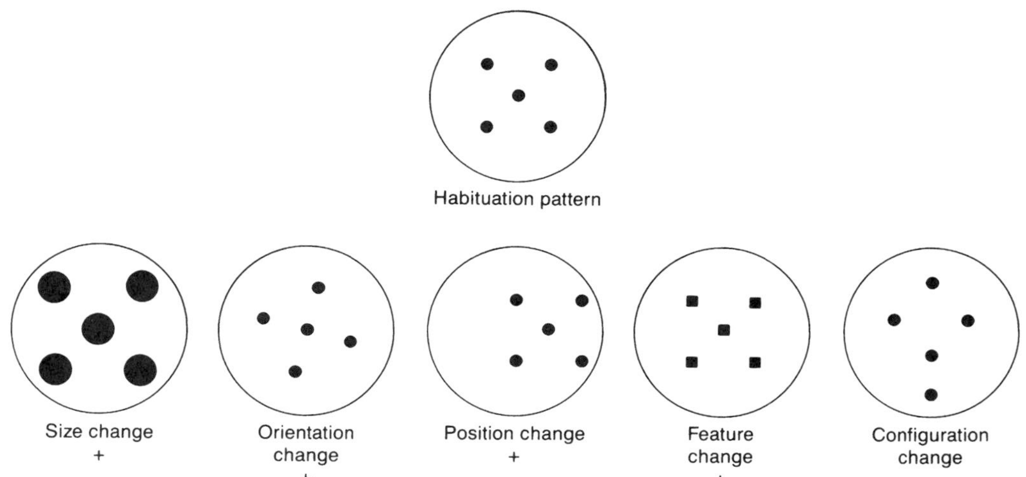

FIGURE 15.6 When 4-month-old infants habituate to the top pattern, they act as if they recognize changes in the pattern indicated by a plus (+) sign but do not recognize the change indicated by the minus (–) sign.

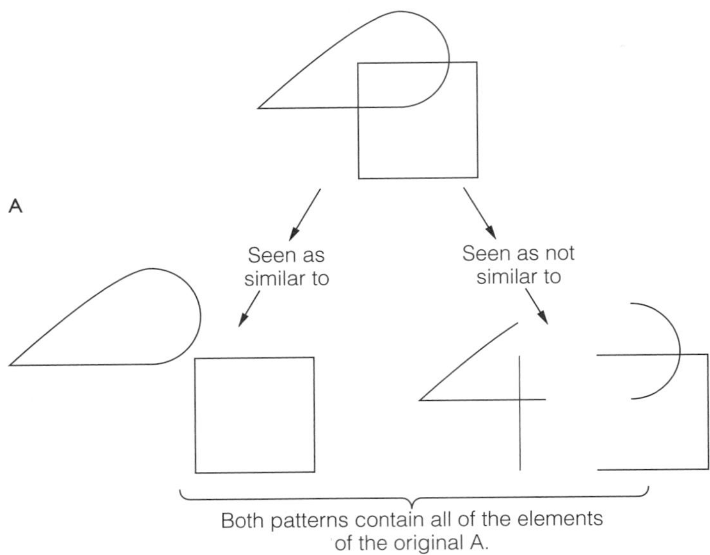

FIGURE 15.7 Infants respond to Figure A and Figure B as if they were very similar because they use the same gestalt grouping principles that adults do. Figure C has all of the elements of Figure A but breaks it up in a way that violates Gestalt principles and is seen as quite different by infants (based on Quinn, Brown, & Streppa, 1997).

birth infants begin to take special notice of the more face-like stimuli in preference to those with scrambled features (Valenza, Simion, Macchi-Cassia, & Umilta, 1996). Faces seem to be very special stimuli, in that they are recognized so early. Infants are specific in their facial recognition, preferring human faces over the faces of other primate species. All of this has led to speculation about the possibility that there might be specialization of parts of the brain for facial recognition (e.g., de-Haan, Pascalis, & Johnson, 2002). This is supported in part by the existence of a rare condition called **prosopagnosia.** Patients who suffer from this malady have difficulty perceiving and identifying human faces and in extreme cases may not be able to identify their own face in a mirror (Farah, Rabinowitz, Quinn, & Lui, 2000). It may also be supported by the observation that newborn infants, only 3 days old, prefer to look at faces that adults would judge to be attractive rather than at faces that adults would judge to be unattractive (Slater et al., 1998).

Between 1 month and 4 months of age, infants begin to take note of certain features in the facelike stimulus. The configurational and local features picked up by infants less than 1 month of age do seem to be sufficient to permit the infants to discriminate their own mother's face from that of a stranger, which suggests that young infants can discriminate among certain classes of fairly complex patterns. However, all features are not weighted equally. Changes in mouth and nose configurations can go unnoticed, but changes in the hairlines and eyes are critical. Thus simply covering the hairlines of women with a scarf makes it impossible for the young infant to discriminate his mother's face from that of a stranger (Pascalis, de Shonen, Morton, Deruelle, & Fabre-Grenet, 1995).

One group of researchers looked at the ability of infants to integrate fragments of an object that are physically separated from each other in the visual image, as, for instance, when a nearer object blocks part of a farther object from view. In one study 4-month-olds were repeat-

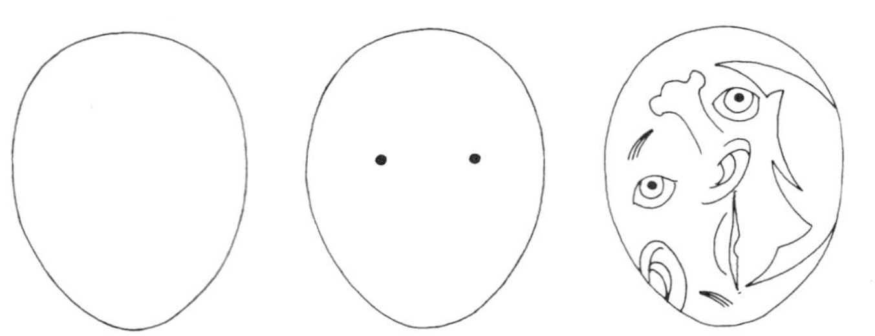

FIGURE 15.8 Schematic and scrambled facelike stimuli.

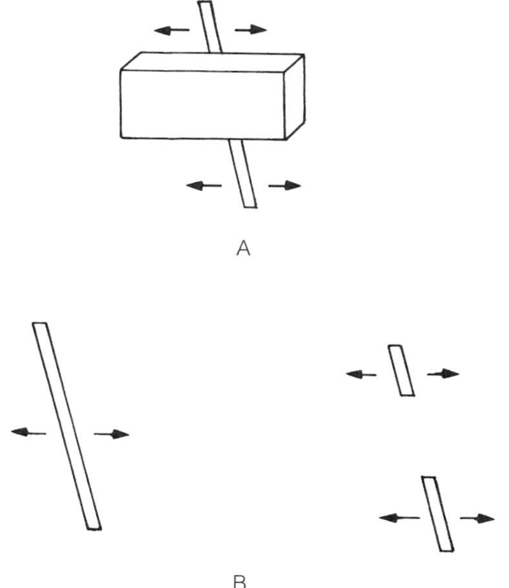

FIGURE 15.9 Stimuli to test whether objects are perceptually completed when they are partially obscured by other objects: (A) the original habituation stimulus; (B) two possible test stimuli.

edly shown a rod that moved back and forth but was partially occluded by a brick that lay in front of it. After the infants had habituated to this display, they were shown either a connected rod moving back and forth or two short rods that moved back and forth in synchrony. These displays are shown in Figure 15.9. The infants looked longer at the broken-rod display, indicating that they perceived this display as different from the occluded-rod display (Kellman & Spelke, 1983). This suggests that the infants were perceptually completing the object when it was partially occluded from sight. Infants can take into account certain shape distortions. This result has been shown under a number of conditions that occur when a moving object passes behind a nearer object (Craton & Yonas, 1990). Infants also seem to complete obstructed curved objects the same way that adults do (Johnson, Bremner, Slater, & Mason, 2000), although some infants have more difficulty than others in these tasks.

Figure 15.10 summarizes how the child's visual competence develops over the first few months of life.

Infant Hearing

The ears of infants are functional at birth, but the auditory cortex is still rather immature and continues to develop over the first year (Kuhl, 1987). Several studies have suggested that infants less than 6 months of age have higher absolute thresholds than adults have (e.g., Tharpe & Ashmead, 2001). An interesting feature of these data is that the differences are most noticeable in the frequency range below 10,000 Hz. The ability of adults to detect tones in this range is nearly twice as good as that of infants. At the higher frequencies, however, infants show more adultlike sensitivity.

Recently the development of magnetically based brain scanning techniques has permitted the investigation of the hearing ability of the fetus while still in its

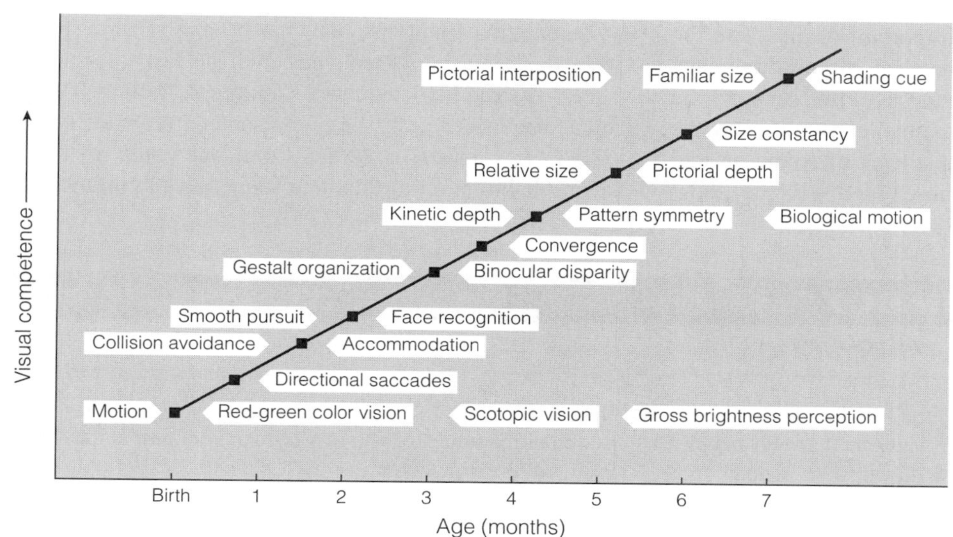

FIGURE 15.10 Various visual abilities, and sensitivity to various environmental or stimulus dimensions, appear at different ages.

mother's womb. Sounds in the environment of a pregnant woman can penetrate the tissues and fluids surrounding the developing fetus. Obviously, the air-based route of sound vibrations through the middle ear is not available to the fetus; however, it appears that sounds can be conveyed to the inner ear by bone conduction, passing the sounds directly through the skull, and brain responses to these stimuli can be detected perhaps as early as 20 weeks after conception (Sohmer, Perez, Sichel, Priner, & Freeman, 2001). Bone conduction works best for low-frequency sounds; the intensities of stimuli above 500 Hz are attenuated by around 50 dB. This means that the speech sounds available to the fetus will be mostly vowels, since consonants involve higher frequencies. Rhythmic patterns of music should also be heard. Not only are these sounds heard, but they are processed and registered by the fetus since there is evidence that just after birth the newborn child will show distinct preferences for his mother's voice, sometimes for his father's voice, and also for musical pieces that he was exposed to in the womb (Gerhardt & Abrams, 2000; Moon & Fifer, 2000). This proves not only the ability to hear, but also some perceptual learning ability in the fetus.

Once out of the womb, newborns demonstrate that they also can derive spatial information from sounds since they are able to localize the direction of a sound source by turning either their head or eyes toward the sound. This has been demonstrated as soon as 3 minutes after birth (Wertheimer, 1961). Long stimulus durations and frequent stimulus repetitions increase the likelihood of a head turn in the direction of the sound (Clarkson, Swain, Clifton, & Cohen, 1991).

Recall from Chapter 6 that there are several binaural cues that help to indicate the direction of a sound relative to the listener. The two most important of these are the time differences between the arrival of low-frequency sounds to the two ears (earlier to the closer ear) and the intensity differences between the two ears caused by the lack of bending of higher frequencies of sound around the head (more intense to the closer ear). Which of these cues is most effective for the infant? By directly controlling both the time differences between the ears and intensity of sound reaching the two ears, Clifton, Morrongiello, and Dowd (1984) demonstrated that newborn infants, and those up to about 9 weeks of age, respond to intensity differences between the two ears by turning in the direction of the sound. At these young ages, the more complex time discrimination cue is not adequate to induce the infant to turn its head in the appropriate direction. However, by age 5 months both cues are effective and cause the infant to look in the direction of the sound source (Muir, Clifton, & Clarkson, 1989). If you have access to an infant, Demonstration Box 15.2 will show you how to demonstrate auditory localization.

One of the more interesting biases that newborns exhibit is a preference to orient their head and eyes toward the location of a relatively high-pitched speaking voice. This bias seems to coincide conveniently with the tendency on the part of adults to speak in high-pitched and exaggerated voices to young infants. This kind of baby talk was once called **motherese** but is now referred to as **infant-directed talk** because it can be heard when men, women, and even young children speak to infants (Werker & McLeod, 1989). Infants of 4 to 6 months of age respond to such talk by increasing their smiling and vocalization (Fernald, 1985; Trehub & Trainor, 1990; Wolff, 1987) and by engaging in a "conversational" exchange of vowellike sounds (a sort of cooing) with the talker (Bloom, 1990).

There is now also growing evidence that infants perceptually group sounds in systematic ways, similar to the ways in which they (and adults) perceptually group visual patterns (Fernald, 2001). In one study infants of 6 to 9 months of age listened to sequences of tones separated by equal time intervals, in which the first three tones were the same high frequency and the last three tones were the same low frequency (Thorpe & Trehub, 1989). Such sequences can be represented graphically as *HHHLLL,* where *H* is the high tone and *L* the low. Following habituation to this tone sequence, the infants lis-

DEMONSTRATION BOX 15.2

AUDITORY LOCALIZATION IN INFANTS

If you have access to an infant, auditory localization is easily demonstrated. Simply look squarely at the child and then make a sharp sound near one ear. Good sound sources are a rattle, a snap of the fingers, or a toy "clicker." Watch the infant's head and eyes. You should see the eyes flick in the direction of the sound, or you may see the head turn in the direction of the stimulus.

tened to a modified tone sequence. In one such sequence there was a longer silent interval—indicated by an apostrophe (')—at the boundary between the two frequencies (*HHH'LLL*), which is the place where adults will tend to perceptually separate the series into two groups, and hence the silent pause seems "natural" in that position. This is the auditory equivalent of grouping based on the Gestalt law of similarity, which we discussed in Chapter 10. Alternatively, the silent interval could be placed in another place (e.g., *HHHL'LL*). This is an unexpected place for the silent pause, and it seems a bit strange perceptually, causing adults to pay a bit more attention to this stimulus sequence. In this study, infants also directed more attention to this sequence. This shows that the infants had also grouped the tones in the original sequence on the basis of their frequency similarity, much the way that adults do; hence the novel grouping was more surprising to them. Other studies have shown that this kind of **auditory grouping,** or perceptual organization of sounds on the basis of their temporal and frequency relationships, also occurs for infants' perceptions of classical music and lullabies (Jusczyk & Krumhansl, 1993; Trehub & Unyk, 1994).

Touch, Pain, Taste, and Smell

Touch sensitivity and heat sensitivity appear to be among the first sensory modalities to emerge during the course of fetal development (Hall & Oppenheim, 1987). This can be demonstrated through the reflexes of the infant, which show the ability to feel and to localize touch stimuli immediately after birth. For instance, there is the **rooting response,** in which an infant will reflexively turn its head in the direction of a touch to the cheek. This response helps the infant to locate its mother's breast for nursing. Demonstration Box 15.3 shows you how to elicit this directional response.

There has been a widespread belief among many clinicians and other investigators that because the cortex is not fully developed in the neonate, infants do not experience pain as severely as do adults, nor is its impact believed to persist as long. This has led to the practice of giving little treatment for pain to infants, even during or after major medical procedures and operations (see Liebeskind & Melzack, 1987). However, recent evidence suggests that this belief is wrong. Infants appear to be just as susceptible to the perception of pain as adults are and express it in similar ways in their facial muscle patterns (Craig & Hadjistavropoulos, 1994; Van Dijk et al., 2001). In fact, infants born prematurely only 23 weeks after conception have already developed a clear ability to sense and respond to pain (Morison, Grunau, Oberlander, & Whitfield, 2001). Even from birth there is already a noticeable sex difference in pain perception, with female newborns showing greater sensitivity than male newborns do (Guinsburg et al., 2000).

Taste receptors start to form early in fetal life and are apparent as early as 13 weeks after conception. In general, neonates appear to be as well equipped with taste receptors as are adults. Human infants, like the infants of most primates and particularly the great apes, show a strong positive response to sweet tastes such as sugar and a strong negative response to bitter tastes such as quinine (Steiner, Glaser, Hawilo, & Berridge, 2001). Even small differences in the concentration of sweetness produce differences in neonatal reactions. This appears to be an adaptive evolutionary mechanism, since things that taste sweet usually have nutritional value. In fact, reduced sensitivity to sweet-tasting stimuli has been associated with infants who fail to thrive, often because they simply do not eat sufficiently to fulfill their nutritional needs (Kasese, Drewett, & Wright, 2001). This can be contrasted to the fact that infants less than about 4 months of age seem to be insensitive to the taste of salt (Beauchamp & Cowart, 1985). It is interesting to note that the infant's early experiences with tastes, such as the baby formula that she is given if she is bottle fed, seem to determine taste

DEMONSTRATION BOX 15.3

THE ROOTING RESPONSE

The easiest method to show tactile sensitivity and localization in infants is to elicit the reflex called the rooting response. To see how early this response exists, a very young baby of less than 2 months of age should be used (although the response can be elicited in older infants). To demonstrate tactile localization ability, you should stroke the infant's cheek lightly with your finger. If you stroke the right cheek, the infant should turn to the right. If you stroke the left cheek, the infant should turn to the left.

preferences much later in childhood (Mennella & Beauchamp, 2002).

Much work on infant olfactory ability has involved presenting newborns with cotton swabs saturated with various smell stimuli. A swab is placed under a newborn's nose, and responses such as heart rate, respiration, and general bodily activity are monitored using a polygraph. These studies have shown that infants can detect a number of strong odorants, such as anise oil, asafoetida (rotten smell), alcohol, and vinegar. Moreover, even newborn infants turn away from noxious odors and toward pleasant ones (see Werner & Bernstein, 2001). This turning response has been used to show that infants respond to odorants of human body origin. There is even the suggestion that, in contrast to some of the limitations on infant sensory capacities, children actually may be more responsive than adults to human body odors (Filsinger & Fabes, 1985). Children are not only capable of making fine olfactory discriminations but they appear to be learning the significance of certain smells. Infants less than 2 weeks old will orient toward an object carrying their mother's scent, such as a breast pad (Cernoch & Porter, 1985). There is even evidence that such olfactory learning is taking place in the womb, since newborn children will selectively turn toward items that have been marked with their mothers' amniotic fluid, the same fluid their nose was full of prior to their birth (Schaal, Marlier, & Soussignan, 1998).

PERCEPTUAL CHANGE THROUGH CHILDHOOD

Throughout childhood there is a general improvement in perceptual discrimination, identification, and information processing. Many of these improvements occur fairly rapidly within the first year or two of life, whereas others continue over much longer time spans. The most dramatic changes seem to occur at around the age of 2 to 3 months, when there is a sudden improvement in the infant's visual abilities. Acuity increases markedly, tracking behavior becomes more adultlike, the ability to recognize individual elements surrounded by an enclosing contour appears, and infants begin to show more adultlike eye-movement patterns when viewing figures (see Courage & Adams, 1990; Gwiazada & Birch, 2001). By 3 to 4 months of age stereoscopic depth perception appears, and this ability continues to improve over the first 2 years (Fox, Aslin, Shea, & Dumais, 1980; Held, 1985). Although the most rapid period of improvement in the ability to discriminate depth based on binocular disparity seems to have been completed by about 30 months of age (Ciner, Schanel-Klitsch, & Scheiman, 1991), binocular depth perception continues to improve throughout childhood and into early adolescence.

Other basic visual processes also seem to develop rapidly over the first 2 years. Thus, visual acuity, which is originally poor, improves steadily into early childhood, and early astigmatic problems (lens flattening), which lower visual resolution in infants, also disappear. By 5 years of age children seem to have fully developed scotopic and photopic visual systems, which show adaptation effects and sensitivities equivalent to those of adults (Atkinson, 2000).

A similar pattern is found for the other senses. Consider hearing as an example. Infants begin with a substantial low-frequency hearing deficit and a lesser high-frequency deficit. Over the first 2 years hearing improves quickly, especially for the low frequencies, and the improvement then continues more gradually until about 10 years of age (Werner, 1996). Measurement of evoked cortical responses suggest that auditory processing ability takes a long time to develop into the adult pattern. Remarkably, the adult electrical waveform in the auditory regions of the brain does not reliably appear until the child is 14 to 16 years of age (Pasman, Rotteveel, Maassen, & Visco, 1999).

Eye Movements and Attention

In addition to changes in basic sensory processes, there appear to be changes in the patterns of attention and information encoding, which appear as developmental changes in perception. Theorists such as Hochberg (1981, 1982) have suggested that the way in which information is integrated over time changes as the child develops. The notion of **integration** involves the child's constructing mental models (like pictures or images), called **schemata,** to help make sense of the perceptual information available in a given situation. In addition, integration involves the child's selecting new information from the perceptual array through the process of **encoding.** After it is encoded, information has been modified into a form suitable for remembering. In this form it can be compared to other new information as well as to information from the existing schemata. This means that attention and memory are playing a major role in the perceptual process.

As we learned in Chapter 13, one of the ways by which we can observe the pattern of overt attention is by monitoring eye movements. Classically, developmental theorists, such as Piaget (1969), have argued that patterns of eye movements provide some clues as to which stimuli are being selected and compared by individuals of different ages. For instance, we know that adults display a strong tendency to look at forms that are informative, unusual, or of particular functional value. Thus, by monitoring eye-movement patterns in children, we can observe the **search** component of visual attention. Information about search should be helpful in determining how children are viewing, and hence constructing, their visual world (Kellman & Arterberry, 1998).

We have already seen that infants from birth to 2 months of age do make a variety of eye movements (such as fixating stationary stimuli, tracking moving stimuli, or moving their eyes toward stimuli in the periphery of the visual field), although not as precisely as adults do. More important, they often do not move their eyes to the most informative parts of the stimulus, at least by adult standards. Rather, they seem to view only limited parts of the stimulus, usually around a border or corner. For instance, when there is a distinct contour within the visual field of an infant, its eye is drawn toward it. In the 1970s it was first noticed that infants of around 1 month of age tend to direct their eyes toward one distinctive feature of a visual stimulus, such as the corner of a triangle. Their eyes seem to be "captured" by the feature because they dwell on it for prolonged periods (Salapatek & Kessen, 1973). Because the gaze of a 1-month-old infant is caught by the first contour encountered, most of the viewing time is spent focused on the external contours of a form. If the stimulus has internal features, they are ignored or missed. This changes by the age of 2 months. Now the infant scans the contours a little more, and shorter periods are spent on each feature. In addition, the 2-month-old dwells almost exclusively on the internal features of the stimulus, seemingly ignoring the overall pattern. These differences are shown in Figure 15.11.

We now understand that there are two aspects in the development of visual scanning. The first is a problem we might call "sticky saccades," which refers to the fact that once an infant has apprehended a stimulus he finds it difficult to disengage his attention and move on to the next target (Hood, 1995). Sometime between 2 and 4 months of age the infant begins to be able to disengage his eye quickly after briefly viewing a stimulus and then move on to the next target (Frick, Columbo, & Saxon, 1999). Shorter look durations and faster shifts to new targets are associated with more efficient visual information processing and better pattern recognition in infants (Rose, Feldman, & Jankowski, 2001).

The second problem that infants have is with "intelligent scanning," which means planned and efficient eye movements to pick up the most information as quickly as possible. In very young infants the eye is often inefficiently directed, does not adequately follow targets, spends time dwelling in regions that contain little target information, or "gets stuck" on one of many targets (Bronson, 1990). As the infant grows into a child, eye-movement patterns become more efficient, although the process is rather slow (Atkinson, 2000). The eye-movement patterns of 3- and 4-year-olds are similar to those of 2-month-olds. Children of this age spend most of their time dwelling on the internal details of a figure, with only an occasional eye movement beyond the contour boundary. The 4- or 5-year-old child begins to make eye-movement excursions toward the surrounding contour. At 6 and 7 years of age, there is a systematic scan of the outer portions of the stimulus with occasional eye movements into the interior. A typical sequence of eye movement pattern changes for a variety of stimuli is shown in Figure 15.12.

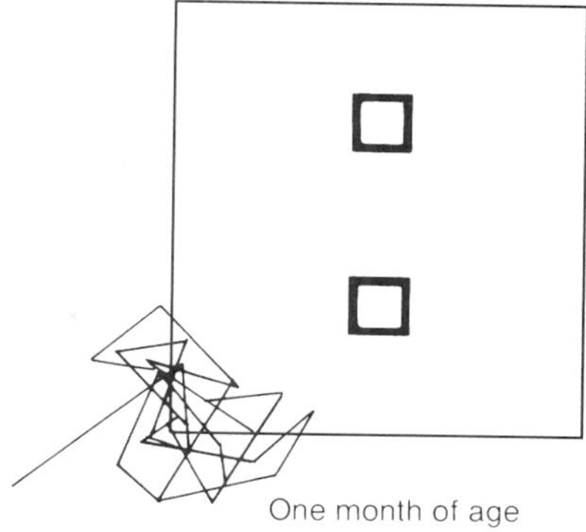

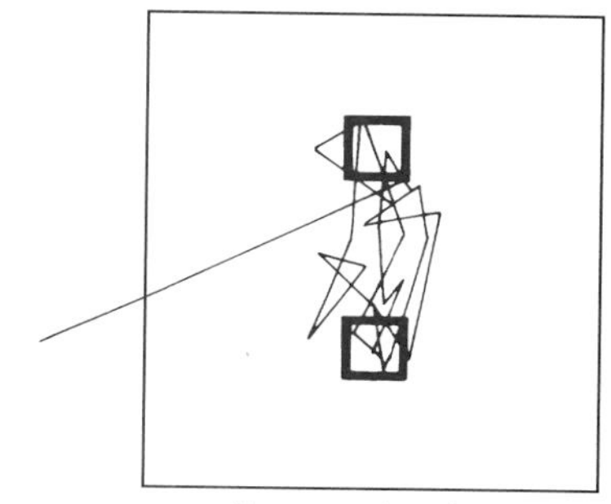

FIGURE 15.11 Eye movements typical of 1- and 2-month-old infants.

Eye-movement patterns have important consequences for certain perceptual discrimination tasks. In a now classic study, Vurpillot (1968) monitored the eye move-

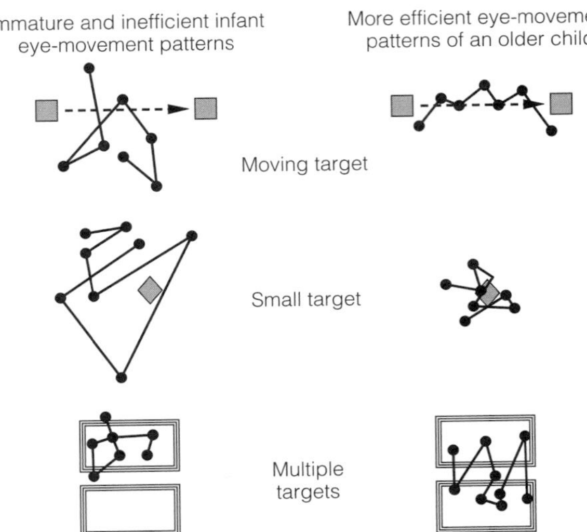

FIGURE 15.12 As children grow older, their eye movements become more appropriate for the stimuli they are looking at and more precise in their ability to stay on target, scan intelligently, and pick up relevant information. Dots represent fixations and lines between them represent eye movements.

FIGURE 15.13 A vegetable-fruit-bird figure used to measure part-versus-whole perception in children.

ments of children between the ages of 2 and 9 years. They were presented with pictures of houses with different kinds of windows and were asked to indicate whether or not the houses appeared to be the same, a task that required systematic comparison of the windows. She found that the youngest children did not conduct a systematic search. Rather, they often continued searching through the houses even after looking at two windows that were different. This lack of systematic viewing was accompanied by a low degree of accuracy in the discrimination judgments of the younger children. Older children, with more regular and systematic viewing patterns, were much more accurate. Other research suggests that younger children presented with figure matching tasks take longer to decide where to move their eyes than adults do in the same task. In addition, they make more eye movements and are less likely than adults are to look directly at the matching target in their first eye movements (Kellman & Arterberry, 1998). It is likely that these differences reflect differences in strategies of attention and information pickup rather than differences in visual capacity because eye movements seem to be strongly affected by task demands, meaning, context, and expectations (e.g., Colombo, 2001).

Such differences in observing strategy may explain why, as she becomes older, there is a gradual change in the way a child comes to view patterns and the elements that make them up (Elkind, 1978). For instance, consider Figure 15.13. It consists of several objects (fruits and vegetables) that are organized into a larger figure (a bird). Children 4 and 5 years old report seeing only the parts ("carrots and a pear and an orange"). By the age of 7, children report seeing both the parts and the global organization ("fruits and carrots and a bird"). By 8 or 9 years of age, most children show awareness of the relation between the parts and the global organization ("a bird made of fruits and vegetables"). This shift in the tendency to pay attention to the organized global arrangement, as a separate aspect of the parts that make up the picture, is a slow process. It does not appear to have reached the adult style of pattern perception until the ages of 15 to 16 years (Davidoff & Roberson, 2002).

Orienting and Filtering

Attention involves more than simply searching for targets and scanning the environment with eye movements. Several of these other aspects have also been shown to change systematically with age (Enns, 1990a; Enns & Cameron, 1987). For instance, the aspect we called **covert orienting** in Chapter 13 (a shift in attention without accompanying physical movement of the eye) shows changes with age for both **direct** and **information** cues. It is possible to measure covert orienting in response to a stimulus that suddenly appears in the visual periphery in children as young as 3 and 4 years of age (Enns, 1990a). However, when this ability has been studied systematically in 6- to 7-year-olds, it is apparent that these children do not shift their visual attention as efficiently as adults do (Akhtar & Enns, 1989; Brodeur & Enns, 1997; Enns & Brodeur, 1989). Even larger developmental differences can be seen when attention must be reoriented voluntarily by a child in response to an information cue. Children as old as 11 years of age require more time than adults do to shift their attention between information from two visual locations (Pearson & Lane, 1991b) or to shift between their information pickup between the two ears (Pearson & Lane, 1991a).

Selective attention also involves the component we called **filtering** in Chapter 13. This refers to the ability to ignore irrelevant stimuli in the environment while more task-relevant stimuli are being processed. Several studies have shown that children are more easily distracted by irrelevant stimuli (e.g., Day & Stone, 1980). Thus, in a card-sorting task where information from the pattern on each card is used to determine which pile it will be placed in, both children and adults show poorer performance if there are irrelevant as well as relevant features present in the patterns on the cards; however, children show a much greater reduction in efficiency than adults do (Well, Lorch, & Anderson, 1980).

There is an interesting set of phenomena that may show age changes in stimulus filtering more graphically. These are responses to **visual-geometric illusions,** which are simple line drawings in which the actual size, shape, or direction of some elements differs from the perceived size, shape, or direction (see Coren & Girgus, 1978). We have already encountered some of these illusions in Chapters 1, 10, and 14; two of them are shown in Figure 15.14. Figure 15.14A shows the **Mueller-Lyer illusion,** in which the line marked *x* appears to be longer than the line marked *y*. Figure 15.14B shows the **Ponzo illusion,** in which the line marked *w* appears to be longer than the line marked *z*. This is the case in spite of the fact that *x* and *y* are physically equal in length, and *w* and *z* are also physically equal to each other.

One explanation for certain visual-geometric illusions is that the lines that induce the illusion become confused with the test lines, thus causing the distortion (Coren, 1997). For instance, in the Mueller-Lyer illusion (Figure 15.14A), the upper figure *is* longer if you measure from wing tip to wing tip. Thus, confusing the wings with the horizontal line might add to the distortion. This explanation is supported by the fact that focusing attention on the lines, and ignoring the wings, reduces the strength of the illusion (Coren, 1999), whereas directing attention to certain parts of other figures can produce illusions (Coren & Porac, 1983a). If we accept this explanation and if children are poorer at filtering out extraneous stimuli, then we should expect that children will show stronger visual illusions than will adults. In general, we do find that visual illusions are stronger for children and decrease with age, suggesting that children are less able

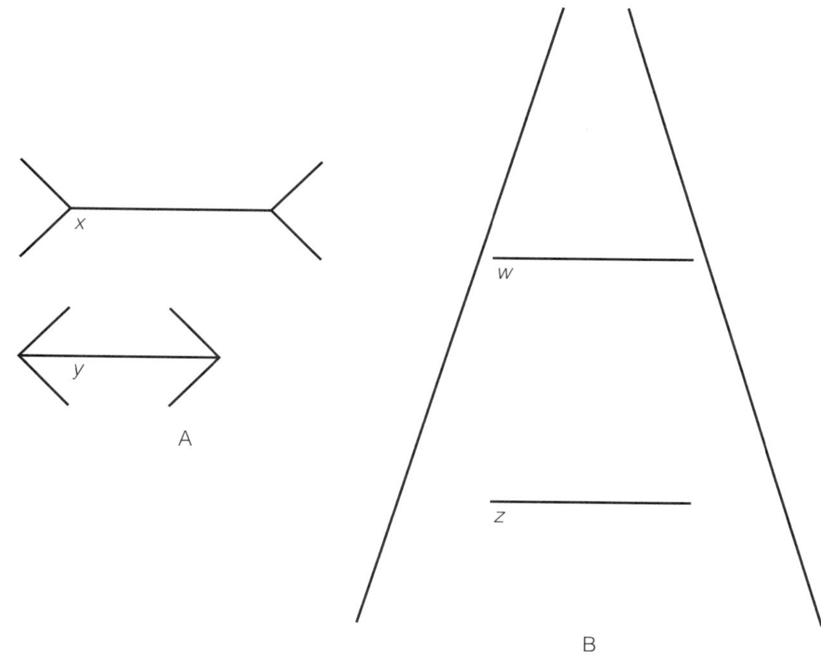

FIGURE 15.14 Two illusions that show age-related differences in their perception: (A) the Mueller-Lyer; (B) the Ponzo.

to ignore the inducing lines when making their judgments (Coren & Girgus, 1978; Enns & Girgus, 1985). In one study, illusion magnitude was found to decrease until about the age of 25 years, after which it didn't change further (Porac & Coren, 1981).

Encoding and Memory

Another factor that can affect perceptual development is the change in **encoding** ability. For a child to integrate and compare stimuli, he or she must first have the ability to register the information obtained in a glance, as well as the ability to remember information from other glances and the schemata associated with a particular class of stimuli. Thus, it is not surprising that several studies have shown that the ability to discriminate between visual patterns improves with age (e.g., Johnson, & Mareschal, 2001).

Studies that have directly compared the ability of children to encode versus to remember visual stimuli indicate that the largest developmental changes lie in the memory component. For instance, when children are presented with a brief (100 ms) visual display of eight items arranged in an imaginary circle, they can report the identity of the items with adult-like accuracy under some conditions (Morrison, Holmes, & Haith, 1974; Sheingold, 1973). Specifically, this is possible when a stimulus marker, indicating the item to be reported, appears within 50 to 200 ms of the onset of the display. When the delay between the display and the marker is longer than 200 ms, the children's accuracy is worse than adults'. This suggests that children are different from adults mainly in the memory processes associated with object identification, not in the initial stimulus encoding processes. Other studies have come to this same conclusion by varying the spatial and temporal distance between pieces of information that must be integrated before a response can be made (Enns & Girgus, 1986; Enns & King, 1990) and by varying the degree of symmetry in patterns that must be encoded only versus those that must be both encoded and remembered (Enns, 1987).

The Other Senses

As with visual abilities of children, care must be taken in studying the other senses to separate developmental changes in the early perceptual registration process from changes in the conceptual processes that are important in perception. One study of odor perception examined both odor sensitivity and odor identification in children 8 to 14 years of age (Cain & Stevens, 1995). Although children and young adults were equally able to discriminate various odors, the children performed poorly in being able to name the odors. This was true even though naming the same objects on the basis of visual cues was equally accurate at all ages. It therefore appears that the learning of associations between odors and specific objects is the aspect of odor perception that is slow to develop in childhood. An interesting aside is that adults are quite accurate in identifying the degree of pleasantness versus unpleasantness in odors simply by viewing videotapes of the faces of children who have been exposed to the odors (Soussignan & Schall, 1996).

PERCEPTUAL CHANGE IN ADULTS

Perceptual and sensory functions continue to change throughout the life span, although the rate of change is usually slower during adulthood than during infancy and childhood. Also, the earlier changes are toward increased efficiency in perceptual processing, whereas the later changes, beginning around age 40, are toward decreased functioning, as sensory receptors age and neural efficiency drops (Werner, Peterzell, & Scheetz, 1990).

It is important to recognize that there is a subtle interaction between perception and all aspects of an individual's life. For example, events happening at or near birth can influence the perceptual ability of an individual through their entire lifetime (e.g., Harland & Coren, 1996). The perceptual ability of the individual will then, in turn, influence all other aspects of their behavior. For example, relatively small deficiencies in vision or hearing can produce noticeable differences in the personality of an individual, and these differences will persist through adulthood (Coren & Harland, 1995). In fact, small variations in perceptual ability will have an impact on the measured intelligence and creativity of adults (Coren & Harland, 2001).

Some of the changes that occur in perception occur because of changes in the aging brain (Mendelson & Wells, 2002). There is a loss of the white matter in the brain, which is made up of nerve axons with myelin sheathing (Double et al., 1996). Since the myelin-covered axons carry information much more quickly than unmyelinated axons do, the loss of these fibers deep in the visual cortex could result in older individuals having slower visual responses (Peters, Moss, & Sethares, 2000). This is consistent with the findings that, at least in rats, aging results in a loss of neurons in the visual cortex that can accurately respond to rapidly moving or flickering targets (Mendelson & Wells, 2002). The presence of neural changes means that such visual losses can't sim-

BIOGRAPHY BOX 15.3

SENSATIONS AS THE BUILDING BLOCKS OF INTELLIGENCE

Jean Piaget (1896–1980) was born in Neuchâtel, Switzerland, and his father, who was a professor at the university there, encouraged his interest in science. Piaget published his first scientific paper at age 10 (concerning the sighting of an albino sparrow) and before he finished high school he had published several more papers on the biology of mollusks. After completing his Doctorate in Science at the same university where his father taught, he worked for a year at psychology labs in Zurich, where he met the clinical psychologist Eugen Bleulers and through him was introduced to the works of Freud and Jung. The next year he met Theodore Simon, who had worked with Binet on developing intelligence tests, and his interest in cognitive and perceptual development began.

Virtually at the same time that he took a position at the Rousseau Institute in Geneva, he published his first book on child intelligence, in which he suggested that there is no way to separate perception and intelligence. This is a theme that he would return to many times as he studied the intellectual development of children (often using his own children as subjects). Although best known outside of perception for his theory of stages of cognitive development, he never left perceptual research. He was the first person to suggest that eye movements could be used as a measure of visual attention and the first to notice how the patterns of eye movements changed as the child grew older and his perceptual abilities improved. He also followed up on Binet's suggestions that studying changes in perception of visual illusions with age could inform us about perceptual development. For Piaget there was no separation between cognitive, intellectual, personality, and perceptual development. Recent research indicating that small variations in sensory abilities early in life can have noticeable effects on thinking ability, creativity, and personality seems to confirm his conclusions.

ply be corrected using glasses, contact lenses or other measures that only affect the optics of the eye.

Visual Function and Aging

We have all seen individuals who, on reaching their mid- to late 40s, suddenly begin to wear reading glasses or bifocals in order to see the details of objects within arm's reach. This reduction in the accommodative range of the eye is called **presbyopia** and was discussed in Chapter 3. However, there are a number of other, less obvious, changes that occur in aging individuals and reduce their visual sensitivity. For instance, the aged eye generally has a smaller pupil size; hence less light enters the eye. The optics of the eye also become less efficient with increasing age because the crystalline lens continues to become yellower and darker, and the cornea also yellows somewhat (Artal, Berrio, Guirao, & Piers, 2002; Coren, 1987). Of course, we would expect a decrease in sensitivity because of the resulting decrease in the amount of light reaching the retina. Between 20 and 70 years of age, we find a consistent increase in threshold sensitivities for the detection of spots of light and patterns defined only by brightness changes (e.g., Sara & Faubert, 2000). This is particularly evident in dark adaptation. Although the time to reach minimum threshold remains the

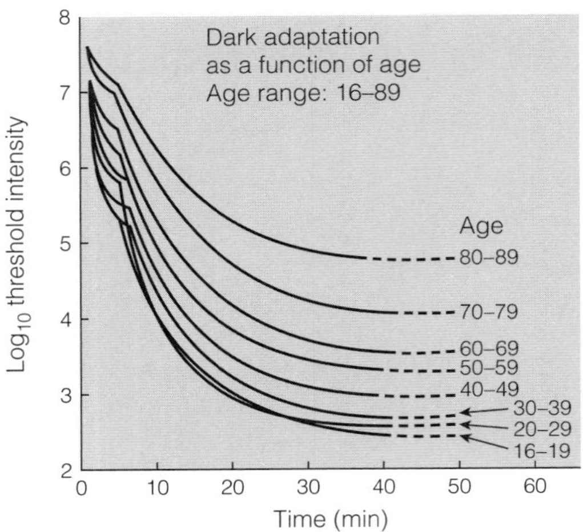

FIGURE 15.15 Age changes in dark adaptation.

same, the maximum sensitivity eventually achieved decreases with age. This is shown in Figure 15.15 (Jackson & Owsley, 2000).

Many studies have shown that visual acuity decreases with age; at age 40 nearly 94% of individuals have 20/20 visual acuity or better, whereas by age 80 only 6% have this level of acuity (see Birren & Schaie, 2001). The relationship between age and visual acuity can be seen in Figure 15.16.

The pattern of the acuity loss with age is interesting. Elder observers are still able to resolve visual details; however, the light level necessary for them to do so is greatly increased. In terms of our discussion in Chapter 4, we would say that the contrast threshold is higher for the elder observers (Crassini, Brown, & Bowman, 1988). There is a very large loss in binocular depth perception in the older individual, and while much of this might be due to optical factors (Schneck, Haegerstrom-Portnoy, Lott, & Brabyn 2000), it appears that the neural system that processes depth and movement information, the **magnocellular** pathway discussed in Chapter 3, might be more susceptible to aging effects than the **parvocellular** pathway, which is concerned with detail and color (Norman, Dawson, & Butler, 2000). These findings suggest that in tasks such as night driving—where good acuity and responses to relatively fast-moving stimuli are required, yet illumination conditions are low—elderly individuals might be inefficient and may even be at risk.

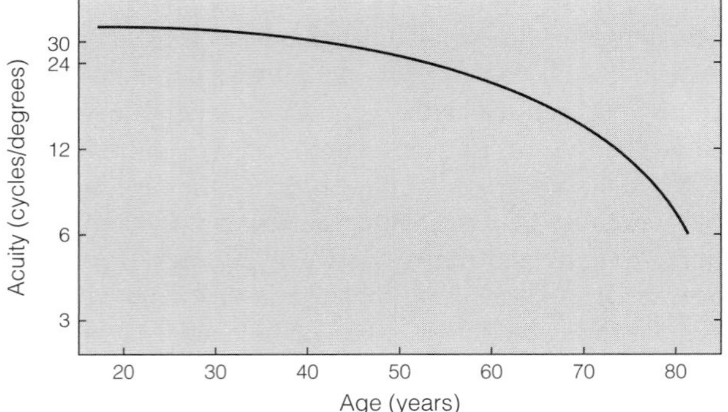

FIGURE 15.16 Age-related decrease in visual acuity.

Aging, Physical Conditions, and Color Vision

An individual may have normal color vision when tested at one stage in the life span but may show color discrimination defects when tested at a later stage. Color vision changes over the life span, and these changes can be dramatic in old age (Adams & Courage, 1994; Mercer, Courage, & Adams, 1991). Perhaps this is because the crystalline lens of the eye grows more yellow as we age; hence we look through a gradually darkening yellow filter (Coren, 1987; Coren & Girgus, 1972a). Other effects, such as the loss of cone pigment with age (Kilbride, Hutman, Fishman, & Read, 1986), may also account for changes in color vision. Generally speaking, aging seems to bring about a faster deterioration of blue vision (Schefrin & Werner, 1990). The blue system may be particularly susceptible to damage because there are relatively speaking many fewer S cones than either L or M cones. Most individuals are unaware of such perceptual changes because the onset is slow; however, the effect gradually accumulates.

Physical conditions can also result in losses in the ability to discriminate colors. Such acquired color vision losses are called dyschromatopsias. There are several diseases or physical conditions that lead to such dyschromatopsias. One typical cause for loss of color vision is exposure to certain solvents and neurotoxins (Campagna et al., 2001; Mergler, Bowler, & Cone, 1990). As in the case of aging, the most commonly observed losses are for sensitivity to blue (see Pokorny & Smith, 1986). Blue dyschromatopsias are observed in diabetics (Lakowski, Aspinall, & Kinnear, 1972), individuals with glaucoma (Lakowski & Drance, 1979), individuals with Parkinson's disease (Haug & Kolle, 1995), and alcoholics (Reynolds, 1979). These color vision losses can be aggravated by a number of factors. For instance, diabetic women who take oral contraceptives show significantly greater discrimination losses in the blue range (Lakowski & Morton, 1977). Acquired problems with the red-green system are rarer and usually are associated with cone degeneration or optic nerve diseases (Pinkers & Marre, 1983). Certain other physical conditions, such as coronary artery disease, produce a generalized loss of color vision rather than one affecting only the red-green or blue-yellow systems (Erb, Voelker, Adler, Wohlrab, & Zrenner, 2001). Perhaps by studying the patterns of color vision losses it may someday be possible to use subtle changes in perceptual ability to predict the onset of disease states before other symptoms appear, thus providing an earlier means of intervening to help the patient.

Aging and Attention

How do healthy older adults perform on the standard tests used to assess aspects of attention? On tests of covert orienting, filtering, and rapid enumeration, they often perform in a very similar way to college-age adults (e.g., Trick, Enns, & Brodeur, 1996). Like the children we discussed earlier, they tend to diverge from the performance of college-age adults on orienting tasks that involve informational cues. As long as the situation involves automatic, involuntary shifts, such as when a target suddenly appears in the visual field, attention shifts are efficient (Madden, 1986). However, if the cue is informational only, thus requiring a voluntary effort to reorient attention, shifts in visual orientation can be slow for elderly adults (e.g., Hartley, Keiley, & Slabach, 1990; Nissen & Corkin, 1985). On tests of visual filtering, elderly observers also perform similarly to college-age observers (D'Aloisio & Klein, 1990), as long as there is no uncertainty about where the to-be-identified target will appear (Plude & Hoyer, 1986) and stimuli are not presented too far into the visual periphery (Ceralla, 1985). Under these more taxing conditions performance drops in the elderly.

The attentional aspect in which older adults do show a consistent and substantial performance difference from younger adults is that of visual search or searching for specific object features (D'Aloisio & Klein, 1990; Plude, 1990). One possible explanation for this result is that the visual field of older observers might be smaller because of loss of acuity in the periphery of the retina, where there are fewer receptors. Although this is certainly true at the farthest edges of the visual field, within approximately 70° on either side of the center of gaze the acuity variation with age is not as pronounced (Scialfa, 1990). Because all visual search tasks involve displays that fall well within this range, the loss in peripheral acuity would not seem to be the major cause of the poorer performance. Moreover, older observers do not appear to have any difficulty identifying or counting isolated stimuli in the peripheral visual field (e.g., Sekuler & Ball, 1986). Thus, the difficulty must be with the search process itself.

Another possible explanation for poorer search performance with age is that elderly observers use inefficient viewing strategies. For example, it appears that older observers are more likely to be captured by the global aspects of the stimulus pattern and may miss local features, much like younger children (Roux & Ceccaldi, 2001). In addition, older observers seem to have more difficulty ignoring certain Gestalt organization aspects of a pattern, such as proximity or similarity, and thus are more likely to search inefficiently (Humphrey & Kramer, 1999).

In order to distinguish these attentional aging effects from receptor-related, acuity, eye-movement, and visual field effects, some researchers refer to the **useful field of view** (or simply **UFOV**) in their descriptions of aging (Ball, Roenker, & Bruni, 1990). The UFOV is defined as the area of the visual field that is functional for an observer at a given time and for a given task. Thus, for the tasks involving the detection of bright light flashes and the identification of briefly presented targets, we can say that the UFOV does not differ a great deal between younger and older adults. In contrast, for the task of finding a specific target amid many distracters, the UFOV is much smaller for older observers and they are much less efficient in their searching (Owsley, Burton-Danner, & Jackson, 2000). It is of interest, then, that studies looking for relations between traffic accident records and the UFOV indicate that there is no relation between the two when the UFOV is measured with tasks involving simple detection and identification. There is a significant relation between the number of traffic accidents that people have and the size of their UFOV, however, when UFOV is measured in a situation where they must identify targets in the presence of visual distracters (Avolio, Kroeck, & Panek, 1986).

Age Effects on Hearing

Hearing ability declines with age. As in the case of vision, changes occur in the brain. For example, neurons recorded from the auditory cortex of older rats did not respond as well to rapidly changing sound frequencies as do those of younger rats, suggesting, as in vision, that the auditory system is literally slowing down as the rats age (Mendelson & Ricketts, 2001). Generally speaking, hearing impairments begin to appear during middle age and occur with increasing frequency after age 60 (Weinstein, 2000). About 15% of all people over 65 could be classified as hearing impaired, and as many as 75% of all 70-year-olds have some hearing problems. The loss of

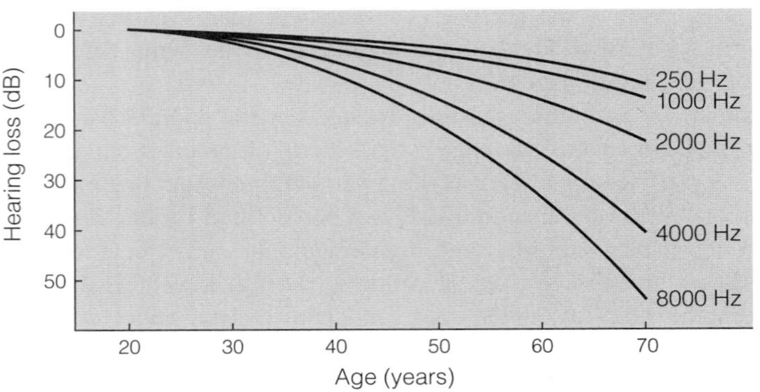

FIGURE 15.17 Age-related decrease in auditory sensitivity is particularly noticeable for the high frequencies.

hearing ability is much more marked for high-frequency stimuli. As can be seen from Figure 15.17, at age 70 there is still very little decrease in threshold sensitivity for a 1000-Hz tone, but for an 8000-Hz tone there is a reduction in threshold sensitivity of nearly 50 dB. The most handicapping aspect of hearing loss in the elderly is the inability to recognize speech, and the amount of loss of speech recognition can be directly predicted from the losses in pure tone hearing sensitivity (e.g., Coren & Hakstian, 1994). In terms of overall hearing ability, a loss of sensitivity of 25 dB represents a **slight hearing handicap.** This will produce a small but measurable effect on behavior, particularly with faint speech. At 55 dB of hearing loss, we have **marked hearing handicap,** where the individual has difficulty understanding loud speech. This level corresponds to a 45% hearing loss for speech range sounds.

It is possible to estimate a person's hearing sensitivity without using any audiometric equipment. This is done by simply asking people about their everyday experiences with sounds in the world. Because we normally use both ears, and our ability to hear a sound will depend on the ear with the better sensitivity, such an estimate will really be of our "better ear" sensitivity. Coren and Hakstian (1992) developed such a hearing screening inventory that correlates 0.81 with laboratory measures of pure tone hearing thresholds in the better ear. You can test yourself with it, using Demonstration Box 15.4. Using yourself, some friends, and some older family members such as your parents or grandparents, you can easily observe the age-related deterioration in hearing (and get a good idea of your own hearing sensitivity at the moment).

Much of the hearing loss in older people seems to be due to simple mechanical factors, such as decreasing flexibility of the inner ear mechanisms and loss or damage of the hair cells in the cochlea that are used to transduce the fluid vibrations into neural impulses (e.g., Rauch, Velazquez-Villasenor, Dimitri, & Merchant, 2001). However, there is also a general slowing in the auditory neural pathways that makes it difficult to follow rapidly changing stimuli (Burkard & Sims, 2001), and there are also losses in the efficiency of the auditory cortex that doubtless play a role as well (Mendelson & Ricketts, 2001).

Age Effects on the Other Senses

Absolute sensitivity in other modalities also decreases with advancing age. For example, detection thresholds for vibrating stimuli applied to the hand (Gesheider & Bolanowski, 1994) and foot (Walls, Ward, Chua, & Inglis, 2003) increase with age, indicating reduced touch sensitivity. This reduction becomes even greater after 65 years of age and seems to be substantially greater in the signals carried by the Pacinian corpuscles than in the NP I or NP II fibers (see Chapter 8, on touch). Further, although older observers show lower sensitivity to touch, the decrease in their sensitivity to pain is not as great and is selective. For instance, the sensation of pain induced by strong mechanical pressure is somewhat reduced while the pain due to the application of a very hot stimulus is not much different than that of younger adults (Pickering, Jourdan, Eschalier, & Dubray, 2002).

Some of the most noticeable changes with age occur in the realms of taste and smell. Odor sensitivity is greatly diminished, although the reduction is not uniform across all stimuli or individuals (Cain & Stevens, 1989). For instance, elderly subjects seem best able to discriminate among fruity odors, as compared to other classes of scents. However, they adapt more quickly than younger adults to a particular odor and, once adapted, require considerably more time to return to their original level of sensitivity (Stevens, Cain, Shiet, & Oatley, 1989). Odor memory also shows large age differences in adulthood. In one study many of the younger adults tested were able to recognize odors they had smelled one week earlier,

DEMONSTRATION BOX 15.4

HEARING SCREENING INVENTORY

It is easy to get an estimate of your own better ear hearing sensitivity using this test, which is called the **Hearing Screening Inventory*** (Coren & Hakstian, 1992). The inventory deals with a number of common situations. For the first eight items, you should select the response that best describes you and your behaviors from among these response alternatives: Never (or almost never), Seldom, Occasionally, Frequently, Always (or almost always). Simply circle the letter that corresponds to the first letter of your choice. (If you normally use a hearing aid, answer as if you were not wearing it.)

1. Are you ever bothered by feelings that your hearing is poor? N S O F A
2. Is your reading or studying easily interrupted by noises in nearby rooms? N S O F A
3. Can you hear the telephone ring when you are in the same room in which it is located? N S O F A
4. Can you hear the telephone ring when you are in the room next door? N S O F A
5. Do you find it difficult to make out the words in recordings of popular songs? N S O F A
6. When several people are talking in a room, do you have difficulty hearing an individual conversation? N S O F A
7. Can you hear the water boiling in a pot when you are in the kitchen? N S O F A
8. Can you follow the conversation when you are at a large dinner table? N S O F A

For the remaining four items answer with these response alternatives: Good, Average, Slightly Below Average, Poor, or Very Poor. Again, simply circle the letter that corresponds to the first letter of your choice.

9. Overall I would judge my hearing in my **right** ear to be G A S P V
10. Overall I would judge my hearing in my **left** ear to be G A S P V
11. Overall I would judge my ability to make out speech or conversations to be G A S P V
12. Overall I would judge my ability to judge the location of things by the sound they are making alone to be G A S P V

Scoring Instructions

Items 1, 5, and 6 are scored 1 for "Never," 2 for "Seldom," 3 for "Occasionally," 4 for "Frequently," and 5 for "Always." Items 2, 3, 4, 7, and 8 are reverse scored, with 1 for "Always" up to 5 for "Never." For Items 9 through 12, scoring goes from 1 for "Good" to 5 for "Very Poor." Your hearing sensitivity score is simply the sum of the 12 responses.

The higher the score, the poorer the hearing is in the better ear. A score of 27 or higher indicates a slight hearing handicap with 25 dB or more of hearing loss. A score of 37 or higher indicates a marked hearing handicap with a loss of 55 dB or more in the better ear. Now that you have your own scores, and maybe those of a couple of friends, give this test to some older relatives or acquaintances. In general, the older the individual, the higher the score that you will get, with some of the older individuals perhaps showing even marked hearing loss with scores of 37 or more.

whereas many of the elder adults failed to recognize such odors only minutes after the initial exposure (Stevens, Cain, & Demarque, 1990).

Diminished sensitivity to odor and taste in the elderly seem to be correlated, meaning that individuals who show large losses on one of these abilities are apt also to show large loses on the other (Kaneda et al., 2000). This combination of losses can reduce their ability to identify foods, especially when blended or pureed so that they are not identifiable by sight or texture in the mouth (Stevens, Cain, Demarque, & Ruthruff, 1991). This has the potential of putting the elderly at risk for ingesting dangerous or spoiled substances and overlooking important ingredients in their diet. Just how large this deficit in identification is can be seen by comparing the performance of a group of 20-year-olds at identifying foods by taste and smell alone with a group of adults whose average age is 73 years. As can be seen in Table 15.2, in most instances the younger individuals do twice as well as the elderly, although on some common items, such as coffee, performance is about the same for both age groups.

The loss of taste and smell is significant in terms of the health of the elderly since these factors have a large effect on appetite (Schiffman & Graham, 2000). The resulting loss in appetite results in diminished food intake in older people, and this is an important factor that often compromises the health of the aging person (Morley, 2001).

Global Changes in Perceptual Performance

Two types of change seem to occur with the aging of all the sensory modalities. The most important of these is a

TABLE 15.2 The Percentage fo 20-Year Olds Versus the Percentage of Elderly Individuals (Mean Age of 73 Years) Correctly Identifying Some Common Foods in Pureed Form (Based on Schiffman, 1977)

FOOD	20-YEAR-OLDS	ELDERLY
Apple	81	55
Lemon	52	24
Strawberry	78	33
Broccoli	30	0
Carrot	63	7
Corn	67	38
Beef	41	28
Coffee	89	70
Sugar	63	57

general slowing of neural responses, accompanied by an increasing persistence of the stimulus (actually slower recovery or clearing time) in the neural representation (Salthouse, 1996a, 1996b). This means that older individuals have more trouble with briefly presented stimuli and show slower reaction times to stimulus onsets and changes (e.g., Hultsch, MacDonald, & Dixon, 2002). They also have more difficulty identifying stimuli arriving in a rapid sequence and retrieve information more slowly from memory. This slowing of processing in the elderly individual becomes most apparent when the perceptual tasks are complex (see Cavanaugh, 2002).

A second general change that accompanies aging involves control over the information that enters and is sustained in short-term or working memory. In perceptual tasks this means that a working memory trace of the stimulus is not available for processing in consciousness long enough to have adequate information extracted from it to be useful (Gulya et al., 2002).

The problem here is not only maintaining working memory but also controlling what gets into and out of it. Because working memory is likely an important mechanism for consciousness, having a reduced ability to guide and control these contents can have serious effects on perception. One of the more noticeable effects of aging on everyday behavior is a reduced ability to prevent nonrelevant material from being processed and coming to consciousness (Carlson & Hasher, 1995; Hasher & Quig, 1997). For instance, elderly people are more likely to engage in sudden switches in conversation (Gold, Andres, Arbuckle, & Schwartzman, 1988) and they will momentarily activate a broader range of ideas in processing a sentence (Hamm & Hasher, 1992; Stolzfus, 1992). This failure to control the contents of working memory often persists much longer for them than for younger adults, sometimes long after the idea has served its purpose (Hamm & Hasher, 1992; Hartman & Hasher, 1991).

It is important to recognize that these effects can influence the processing of perceptual information in elderly individuals in each of the sensory systems. Such effects probably reflect the reorganization of the brain that is occurring as part of the normal aging process (Bennett, Sekuler, McIntosh, & Della-Maggiore, 2001). Once again, we are reminded that virtually anything that affects the brain has the potential to have an impact on perceptual functioning.

STUDY QUESTIONS

1. Which aspects of the development of the brain and neural system of an infant are most likely to result in perceptual changes during early infancy and childhood?
2. What perceptual capacities does a newborn human child have?
3. Describe some experimental methods that can be used to determine what infants perceive based on physiological measures. What are the strengths and weaknesses of each?
4. Describe some experimental methods that are based on observable behavior and can tell us what an infant can perceive. What are the strengths and weaknesses of each?
5. Which aspects of development can eye movements be used to study?
6. Describe some special patterns or pattern elements that infants and young children respond to. What do you think is the adaptive or evolutionary significance of these?
7. What are the major changes in perception that occur through childhood?
8. What are the major factors that influence the effect of aging on visual ability? Which aspects of vision are most affected?
9. What are the major factors that influence the deterioration of hearing with age? Which aspects of hearing are most affected?
10. Which sensory modalities are most sensitive to the aging process?
11. Describe some factors associated with aging that might affect perception in all of the sensory modalities.
12. Should older automobile drivers have their vision retested? Which aspects of vision should be tested? At what age? Why?

CHAPTER 16

LEARNING AND EXPERIENCE

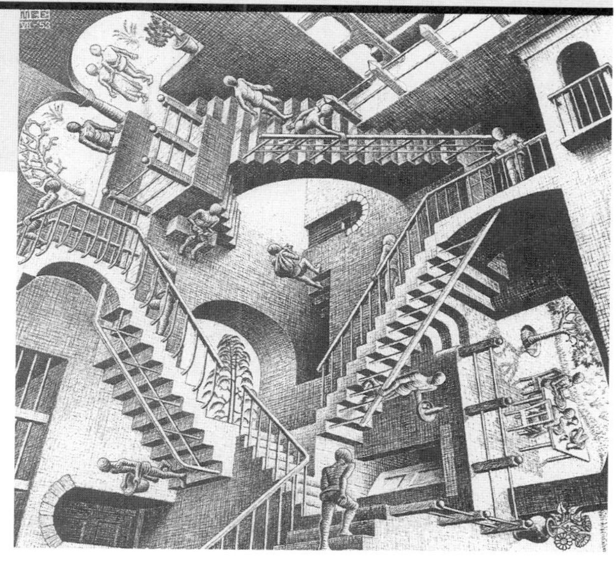

CHAPTER SUMMARY

An article in the *New York Times* spoke of a tea expert who was called in to determine the components of a blend of tea that an American company was about to market. A small cup of it was poured for him. He sniffed it gently, sipped a bit, swished it around in his mouth a little, and then looked up.

"I detect," he said crisply, "a rather good Assam, a run-of-the-mill Darjeeling, a mediocre Ceylon, and, of course, the tea bag" (Root, 1974).

Although we might be amazed at performances such as these, or similar ones of expert wine tasters, we must realize that this degree of perceptual discrimination has come about through years of training and experience. Such experts do not have some incredible native sensitivity and especially low thresholds for tastes and odors (e.g., Bende & Nordin, 1997). In other words, such experts have simply *learned* to taste, smell, and identify these flavors, by finding specific dimensions in the complex stimulus that permit them to make taste discriminations that seem astonishing to an untrained person (e.g., Brochet & Dubourdieu, 2001).

In some of the previous chapters we have mentioned some ways in which our history, experience, knowledge, and hypotheses affect our perception. Most people are willing to admit that some aspects of perception may be susceptible to the influences of experience, but they are often unaware of the magnitude of these influences. In fact, our past can influence even whether we perceive anything at all in certain circumstances. For example, suppose we briefly flash a visual stimulus (such as a word) in front of you. If we have chosen the duration and intensity of the stimulus carefully, you may be unaware of any aspect of the stimulus. If we flash the same stimulus again, we would expect that, again, you would see nothing. However, with repeated presentations something about its appearance will begin to change. Soon you will be able to make out fragments of this stimulus, and after a while these fragments will become more complex. Eventually the entire stimulus pattern will be identified on every trial (i.e., you can read the word), even though the luminance and exposure durations are the same as for the very first trials when you saw and identified nothing (Uhlarik & Johnson, 1978)! Your prior experience with this stimulus has changed your perceptual abilities in some manner, and now you can see what was formerly invisible. If we define perceptual learning as any relatively long-lasting change in perception that results from experience, then we must say that during the course of this experiment you have *learned* to see this pattern.

EXPERIENCE AND DEVELOPMENT

As an organism develops, its nervous system matures, and over the years many changes in physiology and perceptual ability also come about simply due to physiological maturation. Of course, as the months and years roll by, the organism is also accumulating new experiences with the environment and is encountering many chances to learn new perceptual coordinations. It is important for us to understand how the natural course of development interacts with an individual's life history to shape that individual's perception of the world.

Experience can affect the development of the individual's perceptual processes in several ways, as can be seen in Figure 16.1. The strongest form of interaction between experience and development is **induction.** Here, the presence of some sort of relevant experience actually determines both the presence and final level of the ability (Figure 16.1A). The weakest form of interaction effect we will call **maturation.** This actually represents no interaction at all, and the ability might be expected to develop regardless of the individual's experience or lack of it (Figure 16.1B). Another possible interaction is **enhancement.** Here the final level of an ability, which is already present or developing, is improved because of experiential factors (Figure 16.1C). **Facilitation** increases the rate at which an ability develops, but not its final level. Thus it provides earlier acquisition of the skill but not greater proficiency (Figure 16.1D). Finally, **maintenance** serves to stabilize, or to keep, an ability that is already present (Figure 16.1E). Of course, different mechanisms might be expected to produce each of these patterns of interaction between development and experience.

VARIETIES OF PERCEPTUAL LEARNING

It is important to recognize that there are several different types of perceptual learning (c.f. Goldstone, 1998). The most obvious is **attentional weighting.** This refers to the fact that our perceptual mechanisms adapt to the tasks and environments that they are presented with by increasing the amount of attention they pay to important stimulus dimensions and features. Conversely there is a decrease in the amount of attention paid to those dimensions and features of the stimulus that are irrelevant. In this case a **feature** refers to a single stimulus element while a **dimension** refers to a variable aspect of the stimulus. Thus "green" or "2 centimeters" are features while color or length are dimensions. Such attentional weighting can provide real benefits for perceptual processing by making perceptual searches more efficient (e.g., Greene & Rayner, 2001) and less susceptible to errors caused by distracting stimuli. This should, in turn, speed recognition and other perceptual decision-making tasks. The stimulus aspects that are selectively attended to can be simple or complex. Thus individuals show learning effects not just when trying to find individual features but also when searching for combinations or conjunctions of features (e.g., Sireteanu & Rettenbach, 2000). Even pigeons can learn to attend selectively to the complex feature "contains a human being" in photographs (Herrnstein, 1990).

Another, very important, form of perceptual learning is **differentiation,** which refers to the fact that stimuli that were once seen as being the same now become distinguishable (c.f. Gibson, 2000). This seems to be the reason why people are better able to identify faces belonging to races that they are most familiar with. For example, American Caucasians are much better at identifying individual Caucasian faces than those of African-Americans (e.g., Meissner & Brigham, 2001). Thus people learn to detect the features that are most useful in distinguishing between the class of faces that they most commonly see (O'Toole, Peterson, & Deffenbacher, 1996). An interesting aspect of learning to differentiate based on features is that when you have done so it becomes more difficult to ignore those learned differences when you have to categorize stimuli. Thus when observers have to classify individuals by race, Cau-

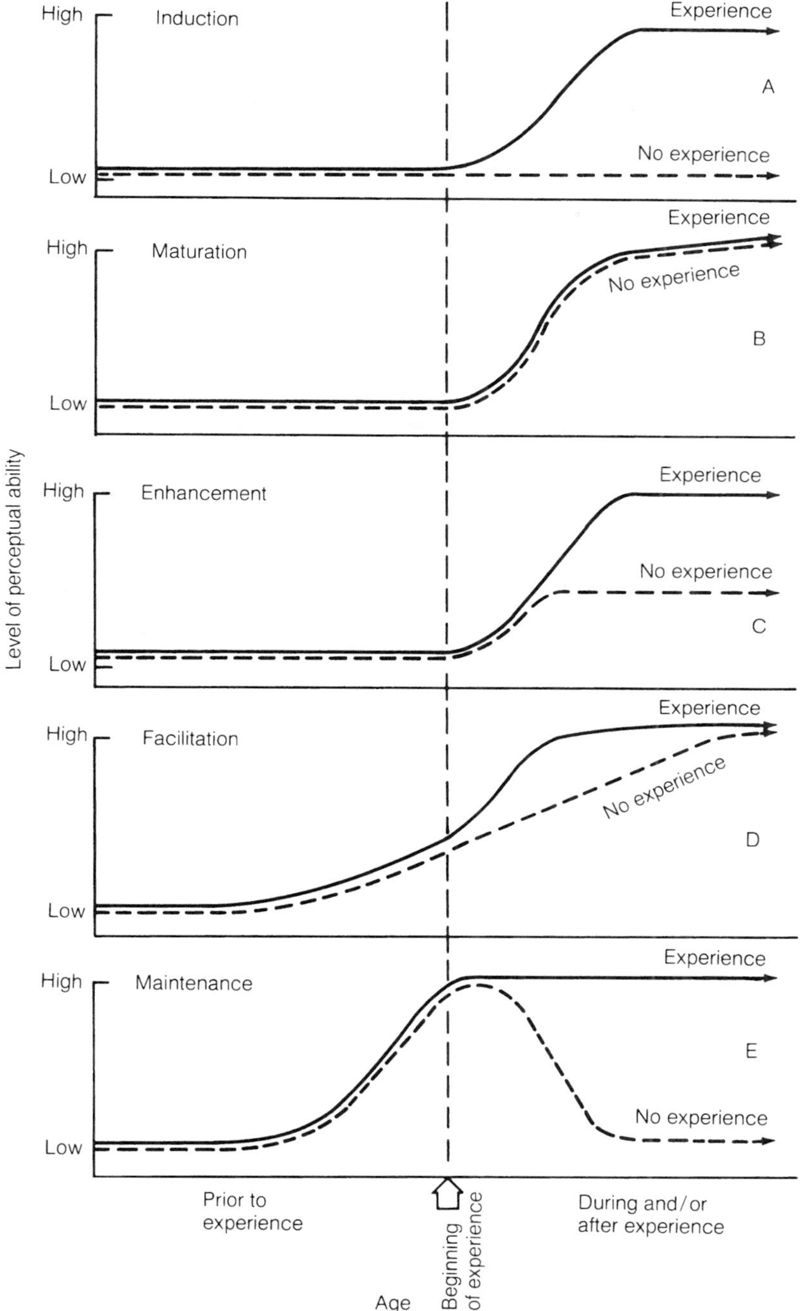

FIGURE 16.1 Various ways in which experience can interact with the development of perceptual abilities.

casians are faster at categorizing African-Americans (as African-Americans) than they are at classifying Caucasians (as Caucasians) (Valentine, 1991). The reason for this is that each of the familiar Caucasian faces is seen as different from each other, which makes it difficult, in this two-category discrimination task, to treat them as being equivalent.

One interesting aspect of perceptual learning based on differentiation is that in some circumstances it can be formally taught like other skills. For example, determining the sex of day-old chickens is difficult because the genitalia are not easily seen or well differentiated. This task, however, is important to poultry farmers because the egg-laying females are more economically valuable. For this reason expert chicken sorters are used to make the discrimination. In one study (Biederman & Shiffrar, 1987) a group of college students with no experience was taught to sort photographs of chickens. If the students were given a short page of instructions describing the shape differences between male and female chickens, they quickly achieved a sorting accuracy that was nearly as good as the experts. Thus they had been explicitly *taught* to differentiate among the stimuli. Some perceptual theorists, such as Eleanor J. Gibson (2000), maintain that virtually all of the phenomena that we call perceptual learning can be interpreted as some form of differentiation. She is discussed further in Biography Box 16.1.

There is another form of perceptual learning that might be considered to be the reverse of differentiation, and we can call this **unitization.** It involves treating a complex stimulus configuration as a single functional unit in consciousness. Thus, because of unitization, per-

BIOGRAPHY BOX 16.1

DISTINCTIONS AND ELABORATIONS

Eleanor J. Gibson (1910–) was educated at Cornell and at Yale, specializing in developmental psychology. At Cornell she met James J. Gibson (see Biography Box 9.1), who she later married. He was an important influence on her thinking, and they collaborated on several research projects. Perhaps her single greatest contribution to the study of perceptual development was the invention of the visual cliff (see Chapter 9) and the series of studies of infant depth perception conducted with Richard Walk using this device. Her studies of perceptual development led her to consider what caused perception to change over the life span. Ultimately she concluded that there was a vast amount of learning that was taking place, and this accounted for many developmental differences. There were two dominant viewpoints at that time, and although the labels had not yet been invented, they were analogous to what we have called *top-down* versus *bottom-up* processing. Top-down theorists, such as Helmholtz and later the transactional psychologists, suggested that we bring our experience, biases, hypotheses, and knowledge into the perceptual situation, and then *elaborate* our perceptual experience by adding these to our interpretation of the stimuli. Bottom-up theorists basically said that all that we have is the sensory data, and experience only allows us to discriminate better using the data at hand. This was close to the viewpoint of James J. Gibson as well, but what Eleanor provided was the theoretical framework based on *differentiation.* The idea was that we learn to attend to new features and stimulus dimensions and this is what improves our perceptual abilities. Using a methodology that anticipated some of the procedures used by computational and information-processing psychologists, she was able to show that each letter in the alphabet has unique features that distinguish it from the next. By indexing these features she created "confusion matrices" based on the similarities of features and was able to show that this predicted the percep-

tual errors that children made when trying to identify letters. This work paved the way for a number of educational improvements in reading instruction. For her work on perceptual development and learning she was given the U.S. National Medal of Science and is one of only 10 psychologists ever to receive this award.

ceptual task that required the detection of several parts can be accomplished by detecting a unified whole. An example of this comes from chess experts, who are much more likely to see patterns on the chessboard rather than analyzing them into individual pieces (e.g., Reingold, Charness, Schultetus, & Stampe, 2001). They are also less likely to be distracted by pieces that "don't matter" because they are not part of the pattern. This same process can be observed in many other settings, such as when weather experts learn to see the patterns in satellite images used to predict weather (Mogil, 2001). Actually learning to treat a complex collection of stimuli as a single pattern can also impair perceptual performance in some cases. For example, it is more difficult to recognize a picture if it is turned upside down; however, difficulty is greatly *increased* if we are *familiar* with the object in the picture (Diamond & Carey, 1986). For instance, a large difference between recognizing upright and inverted figures is found when people are asked to recognize dog breeds, but only for dog experts!

Perhaps the most surprising way in which perceptual learning occurs is through **stimulus imprinting.** The reason that imprinting is surprising is that it involves an actual change in the neural receptors that comes about through interaction with the environment. The term *imprinting* is metaphorical and is designed to capture the idea that a stimulus "shapes" the response of a receptor, much the way that pressing an object on wet clay leaves an imprint of that object, and when the clay dries into a hard slab it is now "specialized" to accept objects of that size and shape. The advantage of tuning neural receptors in the same way is that, for stimuli that are often repeated, such "shaped" receptors can increase the speed and accuracy with which such stimuli are processed. Such imprinting comes about simply because the stimulus is processed many times and has behavioral significance. An example of this is that cells in the auditory cortex become tuned to the frequency of often-repeated tones (Weinberger, 1993). It is likely that this is the way in which people develop the ability to recognize sounds that are specific to a language (Onishi, Chambers, & Fisher, 2002).

Restricted and Selective Rearing

The most direct method for assessing the relationship between development and experience is to deprive the observer of the opportunity to use a particular sensory modality from the moment of birth. At the very least this will prevent any perceptual learning from occurring through stimulus imprinting. After the observer has fully matured, we test the perceptual capacities in the deprived modality. If they have developed poorly, we would have demonstrated the need for experience in the development of normal functions. This technique is called **restricted rearing.** A somewhat more elegant technique involves deliberately altering the pattern of experience to which the developing organism is exposed from birth, thus biasing the opportunities for stimulus imprinting. For example, an animal may be exposed to only diffuse light, vertical stripes, the color red, and so forth. Such a technique should selectively bias, rather than eliminate, certain perceptual abilities if experience plays a role in their development. This technique is known as **selective rearing.**

Restricted rearing studies have demonstrated how important experience is for the normal development of neural receptors (see Brown, 2001). Let us consider what happens if we completely deprive an animal of any visual input by rearing it in the dark from birth. This animal will have a visual cortex that shows reduced overall responsiveness to visual stimuli when tested using the electrode implantation techniques discussed in Chapter 3. Furthermore, those neurons that are found to be responsive will not show the usual degree of orientation and movement selectivity, contrast sensitivity will be reduced, and the usual separation of responses according to eye of input will not be as clear (see Atkinson, 2000). Overall, the visual cortex of such animals appears to be very immature because of the absence of the usual history of visual experience (Fagiolini, Pizzorusso, Berardi, Domenici, & Maffei, 1994). Restricting sensory experience seems to disrupt the normal development of cortical centers responding for *any* sensory modality; thus rats deprived of normal smell inputs show abnormalities in their olfactory processing centers (Cummings & Brunjes, 1997).

Returning to the visual system, we find that the neurophysiological disruption caused by the absence of visual experience can be found all along the visual pathways. Some effects are seen in the processing done by the retina, but they also appear in other places such as the superior colliculus, the lateral geniculate nucleus, and the visual cortex (e.g., Binns & Salt, 1997). Different aspects of the visual pathways seem to be more or less susceptible to such damage. Thus, we find that parvonuclear ganglion cells are relatively unaffected by rearing animals in the dark, whereas magnonuclear ganglion cells are readily lost if no visual experience is available. Dark rearing can affect senses other than vision. For instance, in some animals, such as the guinea pig, restricting visual stimulation can also delay or disrupt development of the normal *auditory* maps in the brain, suggesting that the coordination of visual and auditory sensations requires simultaneous experiences (Withington, Binns, Ingham, & Thornton, 1994).

One common technique for studying the effects of experience on vision involves restricting the input to only one eye. This allows use of the other eye as a comparison. If the restriction of inputs involves only one eye, then the major disruption is found for cells that are normally driven by that eye and cells that normally respond to both eyes (Katz & Crowley, 2002). The degree of disruption of normal functioning seems to depend on when the period of deprivation begins. If the animal is deprived of binocular viewing during the period of 3 weeks to 3 months after birth, large disruptions of the normal pattern of binocular response occur. However, if the monocular viewing period is instituted after 3 months of age, even for periods of up to a year, virtually no effect is found. This means that there is a particular time period during which the visual experience is most required and most effective. Such an interval is called a **critical period,** and it characterizes many aspects of the interaction between experience and development (Aslin, 1985; Mitchell, 1981). Critical periods may correspond to periods of maximal growth and development in the nervous system. Any disruption of normal visual experience during the critical period, even for short periods, can affect final functioning. Unfortunately there is not one single critical period for each modality, but rather specific aspects of perceptual functioning and specific areas of the brain that control them seem to have different critical periods (e.g., Beaver, Ji, & Daw, 2001).

Perhaps the most subtle form of selective rearing involves limiting an animal to a world containing only a biased sample of stimuli, such as contours oriented in only one direction. Thus, an animal might be exposed to only vertically oriented lines from birth. This is accomplished by either using goggles that contain only lines of one orientation or by giving the animal experience for a few hours each day in an apparatus similar to that shown in Figure 16.2. This is simply a large cylinder containing nothing but vertical stripes and a clear plastic floor on which the animal stands. Notice that the animal is wearing a special collar that prevents it from seeing its own limbs.

What happens in the nervous system after exposure to this kind of selective rearing and stimulation might be called **environmental surgery.** Such surgery drastically alters the response characteristics of neurons in the visual cortex. Normally, when we insert an electrode into the visual cortex in order to map receptive fields, we find large numbers of neurons that respond most strongly to lines in a particular orientation, as we saw in Chapter 3, and the particular preferred orientations are rather evenly distributed. The left side of Figure 16.3 depicts this distribution as a set of lines each of which represents a neuron responding best to that orientation. However, recording from an animal that has never seen horizontal stripes produces a different result. In this animal, virtually no neurons are responsive to horizontally oriented lines, resulting in a distribution of preferred stimulus orientations much like that shown on the right in Figure 16.3 (Hirsch & Spinelli, 1970; Movshon & Van Sluyters, 1981). It is as if the absence of horizontally oriented stimuli in the environment has served as a (figurative)

FIGURE 16.2 An apparatus for selectively rearing a kitten so that its only visual experience will be with vertical lines.

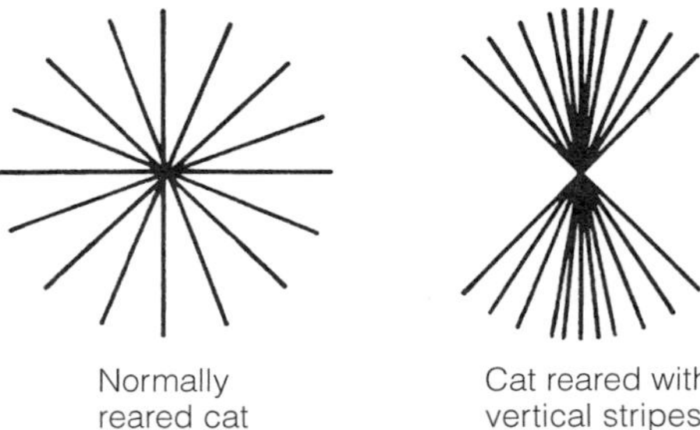

FIGURE 16.3 Distribution of the preferred orientation of cortical receptive fields in a normally reared cat versus that in a cat reared with selective exposure to vertical lines. Each line indicates the preferred orientation of one cell.

scalpel that has systematically cut off any response to stimuli other than the vertical stripes to which the animal was exposed.

If you recall our discussion of *stimulus imprinting,* an explanation for results such as these might be that the absence of the normal varied stimulus inputs has prevented the appropriate neural receptors from being imprinted. The flip side of this argument is that individuals who are frequently exposed to a certain set of stimuli should develop a set of tuned neural cells in the brain that respond to these inputs. For example, the organization of the primary auditory cortex is altered by experience with particular sound frequencies, with more cortical neurons more sharply tuned to the particular frequencies that have been frequently experienced (Recanzone, Schreiner, & Merzenich, 1993). Just how specific such neurons can be has been shown using functional magnetic resonance imaging of the brain. Subjects viewed strings of letters, numbers, and shapes, and it was found that one region of the brain (the left fusiform gyrus) seems to be tuned to respond more vigorously to letters than to either digits or shapes (Polk, et al., 2002). This is a remarkable form of tuning of neural responses, since letters and digits are culturally defined stimuli. It could lead to the speculation that the brains of individuals of different cultures, or even of different levels of education, might actually be tuned in such a way that these varied groups of people might actually see the world differently.

Perceptual Effects

Exactly what effects do these unusual environmental experiences have on perception? Several studies have looked at the long-term effects of restricted rearing on various species. In general, they all have similar results. For example, a kitten reared in total darkness until the age of 6 months would at first appear to be completely blind when brought into the light. Within about 48 hours, however, responses to visual stimulation would begin to appear in a piecemeal fashion. After about 2 months of normal experience, a great deal of visual function would have been recovered. Still, there will be measurable deficits in many visual tasks, including obstacle avoidance, tracking, jumping under visual guidance, and eye blinks to oncoming objects, even after 2 years of normal experience (see Atkinson, 2000). Dark-reared animals also seem less responsive to visual information and use it less efficiently in other tasks, such as maze or spatial learning (Tees & Buhrmann, 1990).

There is a human analog to restricted rearing, and it occurs when individuals develop cataracts in infancy. Generally these opaque formations on the cornea or lens of the eye will let some light through, but patterns are not visible and all is a great blur. After such patients have had their cataracts removed, vision returns, but like the cats with restricted rearing, there are deficits. After their operations patients can generally identify motion, color, and the direction (right, left, up or down) that a target appears. They can also make crude size judgments. However, the recognition of visual shape is greatly impaired. These adults are often unable to identify familiar objects by sight, although they are capable of identifying them if they are allowed to touch the objects. When asked to discriminate between a square and a triangle, they have to seek out and count the corners of the figure before the forms can be distinguished from each other (e.g., Sasaki, 1996; Senden, 1960). The deficits in form and pattern perception appear to persist. Even after 9 years of normal visual experience, former cataract patients still show deficits in their ability to recognize faces when compared to individuals whose vision developed normally (Le Grand, Mondloch, Maurer, & Brent, 2001). In most cases visual acuity never fully recovers to normal levels and there is a loss of contrast sensitivity at the higher spatial frequencies (Ellemberg, Lewis, Maurer, Lui, & Brent, 1999). There are also some more subtle effects of this form of restricted visual experience. One of these is on the distribution of visual attention. Individuals who had early cataracts are more likely to be affected by the presence of irrelevant distracting visual stimuli, and their responses to cues indicating where targets would appear are also abnormal (Goldberg, Maurer, Lewis, & Brent, 2001).

If an individual has a cataract that limits vision for only one eye, that is the human equivalent of monocular restricted rearing. The physiological data in cats suggested that there were fewer neurons driven by the eye with restricted vision. This would suggest poor visual acuity in the restricted eye, which is what is normally found (Ellemberg, Maurer, & Brent, 2000). The fact that binocularly driven neurons are seldom found in animals tested after monocular restriction would suggest that stereoscopic depth ability would be disrupted. This is what is usually observed in such human patients, although stereoscopic vision may show some improvement with appropriate controlled stimulus exposure treatment programs (Brown, Archer, & Del Monte, 1999).

Restricted rearing can have some less obvious effects on aspects of perception such as the visual field. **Visual**

field refers to the region of the outside world to which an eye will respond, measured in degrees around the head. For instance, Figure 16.4 shows the visual fields for the right and left eyes of a cat. There is a rather large region of overlap between the two eyes in the frontal part of the field. This is the region of binocular vision, where either or both eyes of the cat should be able to see an object. Generally, if an interesting stimulus appears in the visual field of a cat, it will immediately turn its eyes and head toward it, displaying an orienting response (see Chapter 13). We can use this response to measure the effectiveness of stimuli in the visual field of the cat, and if we cover one eye at a time, we can measure each visual field separately.

Let us first consider an animal that has been completely dark reared. This animal shows a severe loss of response in the region of binocular overlap. Each eye seems to respond only to objects on its side of the head, as shown in the middle view of Figure 16.4. An animal reared with one eye occluded also does not show a binocularly responsive region of the visual field. The eye that had normal visual experience shows a normal visual field, overlapping well to the opposite side. However, the eye that did not receive visual experience acts as if it responds only to targets that are far to the side of the head and excludes all of the visual field that the normal eye covers, as shown in the bottom view of Figure 16.4 (Sherman, 1973).

A similar effect has been reported in humans. A young man was born with a cataract that prevented any patterned vision in his left eye; thus his visual experience was similar to the monocularly reared animals we have been discussing. When this cataract was removed at age 19, the normal eye had its usual visual field size, but the patient simply could not detect any stimuli in a large portion of the region where the two eyes' views overlapped (the binocular region) with the deprived (cataract) eye. Although there was some recovery over the next 10 months, the visual field of the deprived eye never became as large as that of the normal eye (Moran & Gordon, 1982). It is possible that depriving one eye of visual input may also reduce the visual field of the undeprived eye (Maire-Lepoivre & Przybyslawski, 1988).

The other form of selective rearing, in which an animal is reared under conditions of exposure to horizontal or vertical stripes alone, also produces a behavioral deficit in addition to the change in the distribution of cortical neurons with a specific set of preferred orientations. Here the results are not as dramatic as one might expect. Animals that have been reared only with vertical stripes are not blind to horizontal stripes; rather, they have measurably lower visual acuity for stripes in an orientation never seen during their rearing (Blasdel, Mitchell, Muir, & Pettigrew, 1977).

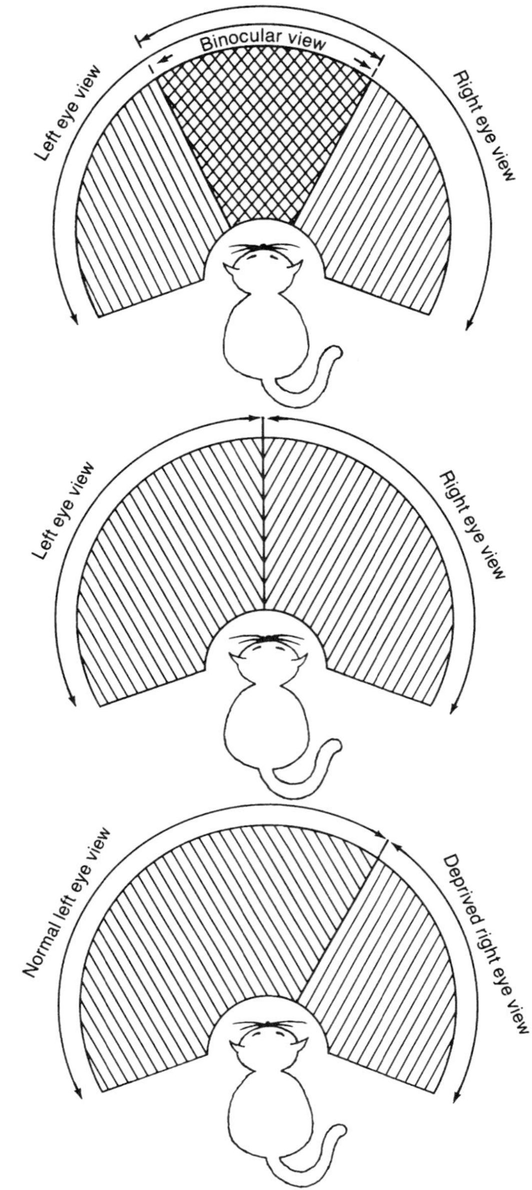

FIGURE 16.4 Regions of the visual field in which a cat will respond to visual stimuli presented to the right or left eye are altered by depriving one or both eyes of visual experience from birth (based on Sherman, 1973).

There is an interesting naturally occurring situation in humans that mimics the selective rearing of animals with contours in a single orientation. This arises from a common visual problem known as **astigmatism.** Astigmatism usually occurs if the cornea of the eye is not perfectly spherical, being flatter in some places and more curved in others. This deviation from perfect sphericity brings contours of some orientations into sharper focus than those of other orientations. Thus, with a vertical astigmatism, horizontal lines will be clear but vertical lines will be blurry, and so forth. The fact that this condition can mimic selective-rearing effects was shown by Freeman and Pettigrew (1973), who reared cats wearing cylindrical lenses that artificially created an astigmatism. They were able to show that such selective rearing can also alter the distribution of preferred orientations of visual cortical neurons, causing a reduction of the number of cells preferring the blurred orientation. Severe astigmatism at an early age in humans results in a permanent loss of visual acuity in the direction of the astigmatism. This is an acuity loss due to neural changes because it remains even after correcting for any optical errors and is probably the result of selective restriction of exposure to contours in the astigmatic direction (Mitchell, 1980).

Living in an urbanized environment causes a variation of this same selective-rearing effect. The nature of our carpentered cities means that we are frequently exposed to vertical lines (defining walls, corners, furniture legs, etc.) and to horizontal lines (defining floors, ceilings, table edges, etc.). Proportionally, we have much less exposure to oblique lines. Therefore, as inhabitants of such a selectively stimulating environment, we might be expected to show reduced acuity for diagonal lines relative to horizontal and vertical lines. In fact, the human visual system is **anisotropic,** meaning that it often reacts differently to stimuli depending on their orientation. In general, the normal visual system shows a slight, but well-defined, preference for horizontal or vertical stimuli over diagonal stimuli (Vogels & Orban, 1986). This is demonstrated in a number of acuity-related tasks, where resolution acuity and vernier acuity are poorer for stimuli oriented diagonally (Saarinen, & Levi, 1995), and has been shown even for moving stimuli (Coletta & Segu, 1993). This phenomenon is known as the **oblique effect** and can easily be demonstrated using Demonstration Box 16.1.

Some investigators feel that at least part of the oblique effect arises from genetic factors (Leehey, Moskowitz-Cook, Brill, & Held, 1975; Timney & Muir, 1976). There is, however, some interesting support for selective environmental effects. This came about from comparison of acuity for different line orientations between students from Queens University in Kingston, Ontario, and a group of Cree Indians from James Bay, Quebec (Annis & Frost 1973). The students had all grown up in typical North American buildings. The Cree Indians, however, were among the last to be raised in traditional housing consisting of a cook tent (or **meechwop**) in summer and a winter lodge (or **matoocan**) during the rest of the year. Both the insides and outsides of these structures consist of a rich array of contours, with no obvious preponderance of verticals and horizontals. In addition, the natural environment of the Cree shows no excesses of verticals and horizontals, in contrast to the urbanized environment of the students. In line with the selective exposure hypothesis, the students showed the expected reduction in acuity for obliquely oriented contours, whereas the Cree, without this selective exposure, did not. In the laboratory a learning factor has been shown for the oblique effect. Prolonged training (15 to 20 days) can improve our ability to see

DEMONSTRATION BOX 16.1

THE OBLIQUE EFFECT

To demonstrate that visual acuity is better for horizontal or vertical stimuli than for obliquely oriented stimuli, prop this book up on a table so you can see the three stimulus patterns. Now slowly walk backward from the book until you can no longer resolve clearly the oblique lines in the center circle. It will appear uniform gray at this point, as your resolution acuity fails. Notice, however, that at this distance you still can see that the left circle contains vertical lines and the right contains horizontal lines, thus indicating your greater visual acuity for these orientations.

obliquely oriented stimuli (Schoups, Vogels, & Orban, 1995).

Many of these restricted rearing and selective rearing effects show evidence of a critical period, which, as we noted earlier, is an age-related window of time, during which the organism is most sensitive to environmental effects (e.g., Desai, Cudmore, Nelson, & Turrigiano, 2002; Zhang, Bao, & Merzenich, 2002). This has implications for a number of common clinical conditions in humans. For example, children who suffer from **strabismus** (which is misaligned or crossed eyes) are deprived of the coördinated binocular experiences that normal individuals have. This may result in a complete loss of any stereoscopic perception, or even the complete suppression of vision in one eye (known as **amblyopia ex anopsia).** There is a critical period, however, in which surgery to align the eyes can be successful and avoid any loss of perceptual ability (Daw, 1998). Research suggests that this critical period for correction is the first 24 months of life (Birch, Fawcett, & Stager, 2000).

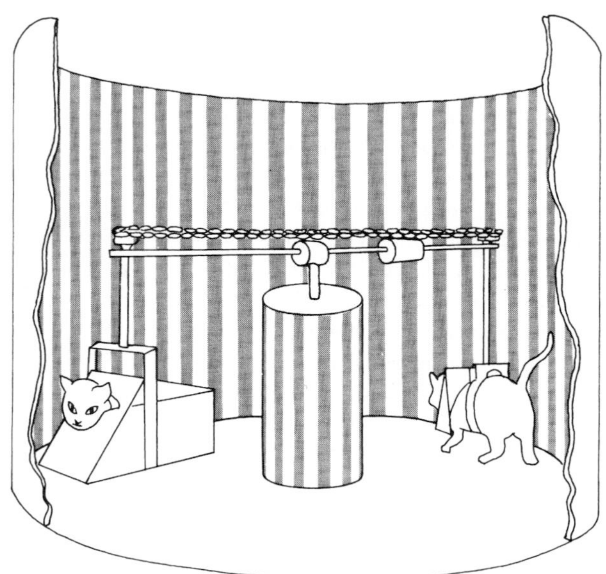

FIGURE 16.5 Kitten carousel for active or passive exposure to visual stimulation. (From R. Held & A. Hein, 1963, *Journal of Comparative and Physiological Psychology,* 56. Copyright 1963 by the American Psychological Association. Reprinted by permission.)

SENSORY-MOTOR LEARNING

One variable that seems to be essential for the development of normal visual functioning involves not only the eyes but also the entire body. It seems that normal perceptual development depends on active bodily movement under visual guidance. Holst and Mittelstäedt (1950) offered a distinction between stimulation that acts on a passive observer, which they called **exafference,** and stimulation that changes as a result of an individual's own movements, called **reafference.**

Reafference was shown to be necessary for the development of accurate visually guided spatial behavior in a classic series of experiments by Richard Held and Alan Hein. In one study they reared kittens in the dark until they were 8 to 12 weeks of age (Held & Hein, 1963). From that age on, the kittens received 3-hours of patterned visual exposure in a "carousel" apparatus, shown in Figure 16.5. As you can see from the figure, one of the animals is active and can walk around freely. The other animal is passive and is carried around in a gondola that moves in exactly the same direction and at exactly the same speed as the movements of the active animal. Thus, the moving animal experiences changing visual stimuli as a result of its own movements (reafference), whereas the passive animal experiences the same stimulation as exafference.

Both animals in each pair were later tested on a series of behaviors involving depth perception. These included dodging or blinking when presented with a rapidly approaching object and avoiding the deep side of the visual cliff (see Chapter 10). They were also tested for the visual placing response, a paw extension (as if to avoid collision) when the animals were moved quickly toward a surface. In all three measures, the active animals performed like normal kittens, and the passive animals showed little evidence of depth perception. It is interesting to note that if one eye receives active exposure and the other does not, only the actively exposed eye shows normal depth perception (Hein, Held, & Gower, 1970), indicating that the effects of experience are quite specific.

How much of the development of our visually guided behavior requires practice and exposure? Consider the simple tasks of reaching toward and picking up an object with one hand. These involve not only the accurate assessment of the distance and the size of the object but also the ability to guide your limb on the basis of the perceptual information. Held and Hein (1967) reared kittens in the dark until they were 4 weeks old. After this period, they were allowed 6 hours of free movement each day in a lighted and patterned environment. However, during the time when the kittens received their exposure to patterned stimuli, they wore lightweight opaque collars that prevented them from seeing their bodies or paws while

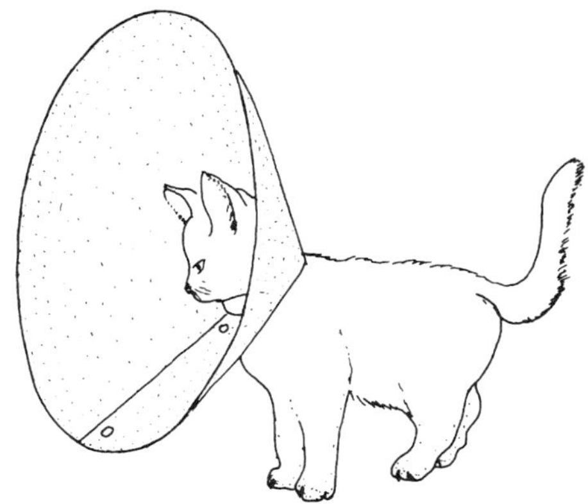

FIGURE 16.6 Kitten in a collar that prevents view of paws. (From A. Hein & R. Held, 1967, *Science*, 158, 390–392. Copyright 1967 by the American Association for the Advancement of Science.)

they moved about (see Figure 16.6). The remainder of the time, the kittens were placed in a dark room. After 12 days of such exposure, these animals showed normal depth perception, but their ability to accurately place their paws by visually directing them toward targets was poor. Nonetheless, after 18 hours of free movement in a lighted environment, with their paws visible, all directional confusions seemed to have disappeared. Similar effects were found in monkeys (Held & Bauer, 1967).

It is likely that human infants need experience to develop normal reaching behaviors. After the first month of life infants spend many hours watching their hands. Their reaching is inaccurate at first but improves steadily. Active practice seems to speed up this process. If conditions are arranged so that there are many objects to reach for and to play with, infants develop accurate reaching behavior several weeks earlier than do children who have not received this type of enriched experience. There is now evidence that in humans, experience with the sight of actively moving parts of the body is also necessary for the successful development of many sensory-motor coordinations. While this work was done on young organisms, visual feedback of this sort becomes even more important for sensory motor learning as individuals age (Wishart, Lee, Cunningham, & Murdoch, 2002).

PERCEPTUAL REARRANGEMENT

It is difficult to determine exactly how learning affected our perception when we first encountered the world; however, we can create an experimental analogy by, in effect, creating a new world of stimulus relationships and watching how we adapt to it. This was first done in 1896 by George Stratton (Stratton, 1897a, 1897b) who is discussed in Biography Box 16.2. Stratton's technique

BIOGRAPHY BOX 16.2

TURNING THE WORLD UPSIDE DOWN

George Malcolm Stratton (1865–1957) got his undergraduate degree at the University of California at Berkeley, then studied at Leipzig under Wilhelm Wundt and, in 1896, returned to Berkeley with his Ph.D. He also brought with him a large array of gleaming brass instruments to establish Berkeley's first psychological laboratory (in the Department of Philosophy). During his graduate studies one of the main controversies in psychology was the dispute between Helmholtz, who maintained that our accurate perception of the world depended to a great degree on learning, and his frequent opponent, Hering, who maintained that most perceptual processing was based on biologically programmed mechanisms. Stratton plunged directly into the controversy. His method of testing this was to provide a whole new world of perceptual relationships, namely by optically turning his world upside down, to see if he could adapt to the new arrangements. After wearing the inverting goggles for 8 days, Stratton was getting around the world quite well, and, unless he deliberately thought about the situation, the world looked "normal." When the goggles were removed there were disorienting aftereffects, and the world once again seemed strange for several hours. This led Stratton to conclude that if this new optical arrangement could be learned, then perhaps our original perception of the world was based on similar, but early, learning. Stratton went on to do further research in perception, including other methods of "rearranging" stimulus relationships, such as breaking the normal coordination between vision and touch and reversing the views of the two eyes. In addition, he contributed to the study of the history of psychology with his work on sensory and physiological psychology as it was understood before the time of Aristotle. He was also honored by being elected the seventeenth President of the American Psychological Association in 1908.

was rediscovered in the mid-1960s by Kohler (1962, 1964). The procedure involves optical **rearrangement** of spatial relations in the world using distorting lenses set in spectacles. The earliest procedures involved a massive distortion, literally turning the image of the world upside down. Observers wore these devices for several weeks, reporting that at first the world seemed very unstable, the visual field appeared to swing as the head was turned, there was difficulty walking, and they needed help to perform very simple tasks. However, after about 3 days one observer was able to ride a bicycle, and after only a few weeks he was able to ski. The observers reported that they sporadically experienced the world as being upright. If they observed common events that have definite directional components, such as smoke rising from a cigarette or water pouring from a pitcher, they reported that the world appeared to be upright. This suggests that their ability to adapt to the optically rearranged visual input was facilitated by the notion of gravitational direction along with interaction with familiar events and objects. It seems likely that a real perceptual change had taken place because when the inverting lenses were removed, observers experienced a sense of discomfort, and now, without the lenses, the world suddenly appeared to be inverted again, and they had difficulty moving about. However, the readaptation to the normal upright world was accomplished within a period of about 1 hour. Demonstration Box 16.2 shows how you can experience this inverted visual stimulation.

Most rearrangement studies involve a less dramatic change of optical input. A common technique is to use a wedge prism, which is a wedge-shaped piece of glass that bends, or refracts, light, shifting the appearance of objects a few degrees to one side. If an observer viewed the world through goggles containing such prisms and reached for an object, she would find herself missing it at first. After only a few minutes of practice, however, the observer's reaching would become accurate. We would say that she has adapted to the prismatic distortion; in other words, she has compensated for the optical distortion. If the observer is consciously correcting for the distortion (e.g., saying to herself, "I must reach 10 degrees to the right of where the object appears"), when the goggles were removed she would, of course, know

DEMONSTRATION BOX 16.2

OPTICAL INVERSION

You can experience some of the effects associated with inverted optical stimulation by holding a mirror as shown in the accompanying figure. Walk around and view the world by looking up at the mirror. Notice that the world seems inverted, and also notice how the world swings as you turn. Now pour some water from a glass. Does the water pour up or down? Are you sure?

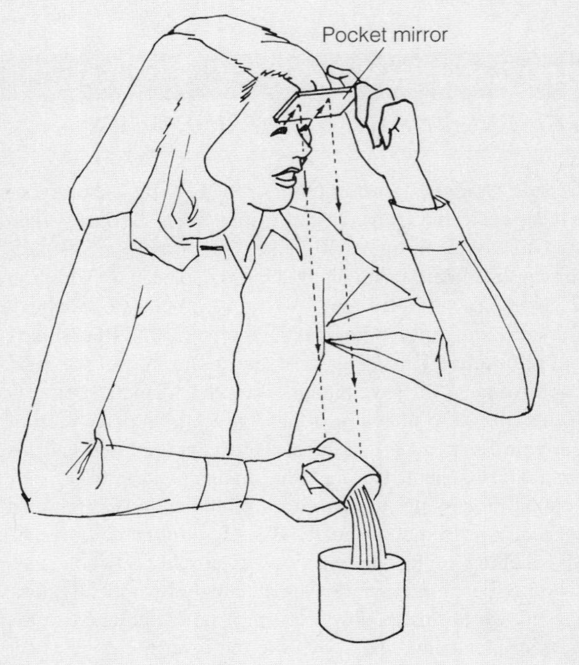

that the distortion is no longer present. Being rational, she should then drop this conscious correction and reach for seen stimuli with her usual accuracy. However, suppose that some perceptual change has occurred. In this case we would expect that when the distorting prism is removed, the visual world would now appear to be shifted several degrees to the side. When reaching for an object the observer should err in the direction *opposite* to that of the initial distortion. This is what actually does occur. These errors are called **aftereffects.** The occurrence of aftereffects in prism adaptation is evidence that some perceptual rearrangement has occurred (e.g., Redding & Wallace, 1997). This process is outlined in Figure 16.7.

Learning to adapt to the rearranged stimulation requires active movement. One early study used conditions similar to the kitten carousel discussed earlier. Observers wearing displacing prism goggles either walked around for about 1 hour (active exposure) or were wheeled around in a wheelchair over the same path for about 1 hour (passive exposure). They were then measured to see if any perceptual change had taken place. Adaptation to the prismatic distortion occurred in the active-exposure condition but not in the passive-exposure condition (Mikaelian & Held, 1964).

One important aspect of active movement under optically distorted conditions seems to be that it provides observers with some sort of error feedback, which informs them of the direction and the extent of the distortion. This information provides a basis for learning a new correlation between the incoming stimuli and the conscious percept. The more information we give observers about the nature of their errors, the greater is the adaptation to the distortion (Coren, 1966; Welch, 1971). The timing and amount of information from feedback are important factors in adaptation (Redding & Wallace, 1990). For instance, not being able to see the starting position of your hand before you begin to point to the target can slow the rate of adaptation (Redding & Wallace, 1997). Simply delaying, by a mere 50 ms, individuals' ability to see how accurate their hand movements are can also slow the rate of adaptation by a marked amount (Kitazawa & Kohno, 1995). The more "natural" and realistic the visual feedback, the faster the adaptation is as well. Thus

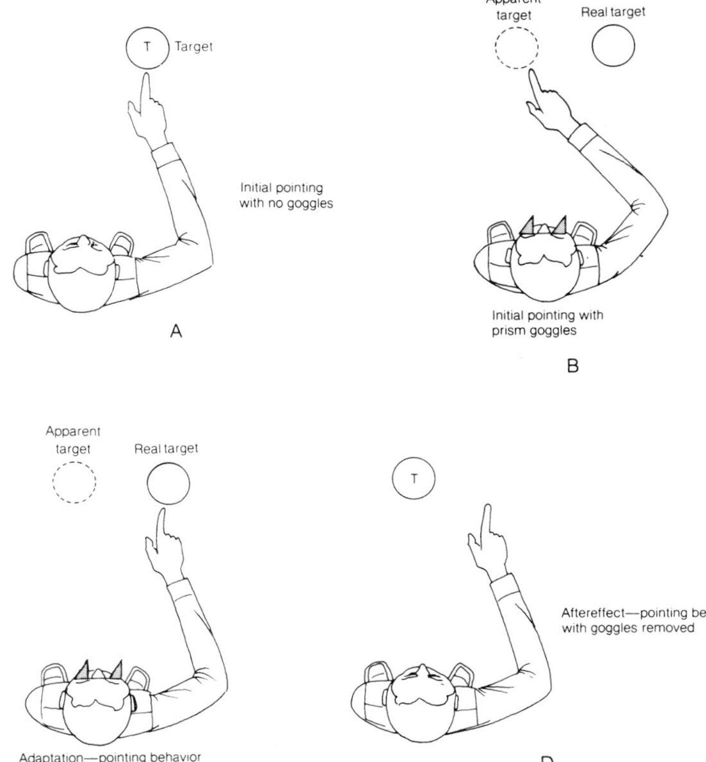

FIGURE 16.7 Prism adaptation and aftereffect.

actually seeing your hand reaching and missing is better then seeing a real-time video image of your hand and far better than a schematic, animated, or diagrammatic representation of your reaching movements (e.g., Norris, Greger, Martin, & Thach, 2001).

Under special circumstances information about the nature of the distortion can be obtained in ways other than active movement, and this information can support adaptation to perceptual rearrangement. For example, watching an object approach, which although it appears as though it will pass by instead makes contact with your face, is good evidence that there is a perceptual distortion, and this may produce some adaptation (e.g., Howard, Craske, & Templeton, 1965). Such passively obtained data, however, must be very convincing to produce perceptual change. For example, O'Leary and McMahon (1991) used a more subtle distortion, namely lenses that made stimuli appear too wide or too tall. When observers viewed photographs of faces distorted in this way, even though no active movement was engaged in, they still showed some adaptation to the distortion. When they viewed line drawings of simple figures (e.g., circles or squares), no adaptation occurred. Presumably, their familiarity with the normal dimensions of faces provided the cue that there was a distortion present and triggered the perceptual recalibration, while drawings, which may be easily distorted, did not produce sufficiently strong evidence of a change in the nature of the stimulus world to support perceptual change.

What actually changes during the adaptation process? Not just vision, but several perceptual systems seem to be affected, and the rate of adaptation may be different for different aspects of this perceptual recalibration (Redding & Wallace, 2002). One aspect of this adaptation is the position at which the observer feels various parts of his body to be located. Thus after prism adaptation, when observers are asked to point to a straight-ahead position (by feel alone), they tend to point off to the side indicating that there is some proprioceptive or "felt" component in the adaptation process (Harris, 1980). There are also purely visual recalibrations, however, and it is even possible to have adaptation to different patterns of distortion in each eye simultaneously (Foley, 1974; Redding & Wallace, 1997).

Illusion Decrement

There is another form of perceptual learning that is similar to rearrangement in that it involves learning to compensate for a perceptual error. It differs from the situations we have been discussing in that the error is not optical in nature, and the observer usually is not conscious either of the erroneous perception or of any perceptual change. The situation involves visual-geometric illusions, which are simple line drawings that evoke percepts differing in size or shape from those expected on the basis of physical measurements of the stimuli. We have encountered several of these already, in Chapters 1, 11, 14, and 15, including the Mueller-Lyer illusion (Figure 16.8), in which the horizontal line with the outward-turned wings (A) appears longer than the line with the inward-turned wings (B), despite the fact that the lines are physically equal in length. Suppose we pre-

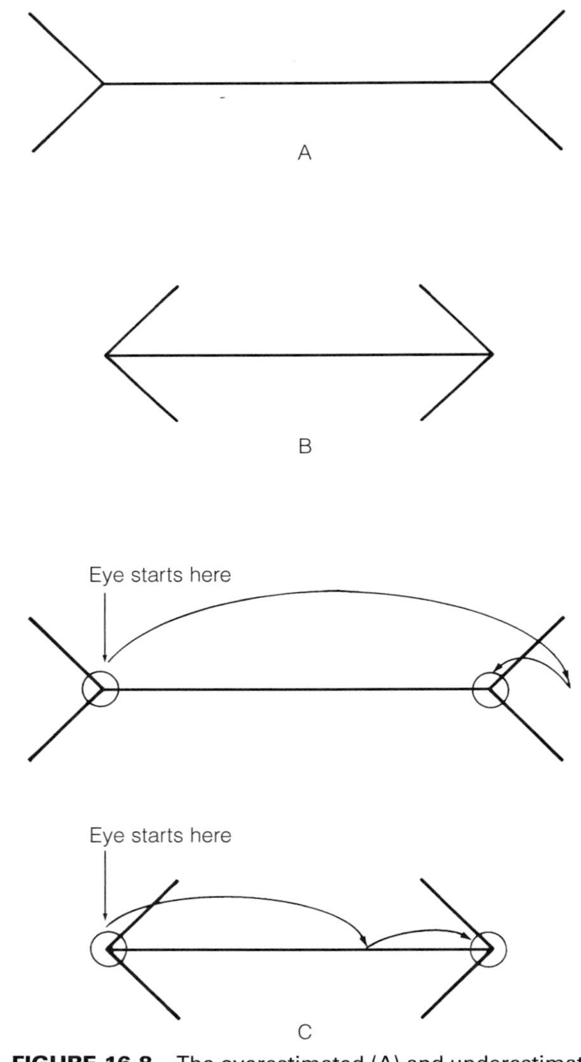

FIGURE 16.8 The overestimated (A) and underestimated (B) portions of the Mueller-Lyer illusion and (C) typical eye movements obtained when viewing them.

sent the Mueller-Lyer figure to an observer and measure her susceptibility to the line-length distortion. Next we instruct her to begin moving her eyes across the figure, scanning from one end of the horizontal line to the other on both portions of the figure. We ask her to be as accurate as possible with her eye movements. At 1-minute intervals we stop the scanning process and take measurements of illusion magnitude until a total of 5 minutes of viewing time has elapsed. This simple process of inspection leads to a 40% reduction in the original illusion magnitude (Coren & Porac, 1984). This decrease, known as **illusion decrement,** has been demonstrated many times and for many different types of illusions, not just the Mueller-Lyer illusion (e.g., Beckett, 1989; Glaser & Slotnick, 1995; Porac & Coren, 1985; Predebon, 1990).

What is happening in this situation? Some researchers have suggested that continuously inspecting the illusion figure fatigues or adapts some of the neural units that register or distort the pattern, and this is what accounts for a weakening of the illusion (Long, 1988; Porac, 1989). Although this may contribute to the process, it can't be a full explanation because inspection of fields of lines that have been designed to fatigue the same neural units does not result in a reduction of the illusion when the figure is viewed afterward (Coren, Girgus, & Schiano, 1986; Schiano & Jordan, 1990). If neural fatigue is not the answer, then it seems likely that we are looking at a form of perceptual learning (Coren, 1999; Long, 1988).

Perceptual learning requires some information processing that will later affect how a stimulus is perceived. In this situation observers must somehow learn that there is an illusion present so that they can begin to correct their perception and eliminate the illusory distortion. Observers get this information not via rulers or measuring tapes but, rather, via information from their eye movements (see Coren, 1986). If we measure the pattern of eye movements an observer makes over an illusion figure, we find that the eyes are directed to move as if the distorted percept were actually correct. In other words, if the eyes were resting on the end of the line in the perceptually elongated portion of the Mueller-Lyer figure (Figure 16.8A), an attempt to look at the far end of the line would produce an eye movement that is too long. This eye-movement error is in agreement with the percept, which tends to overestimate the length of the line. A corrective adjustment in the eye movement must be made if the fovea is to come to rest on the exact end of the line. The opposite happens for the underestimated portion of the Mueller-Lyer figure (Figure 16.8B). Here the eye movements are too short (again in agreement with the perceptual underestimation of the line length), and a corrective adjustment must be made. The eye-movement patterns over the two portions of the figure are shown in Figure 16.8C.

In Chapters 13 and 15 we saw instances where patterns of eye movements could be used to tell us something about the information-processing abilities of an observer. The same reasoning can be applied to the study of eye-movement patterns across illusion configurations. As the observer views the illusory array, eye movements and eye-movement errors provide information about the existence (as well as the direction and the strength) of the illusory distortion. This error information can be used by the observer to correct the percept. This point of view is supported by the fact that an illusion decrement does not occur unless the observer is allowed to scan the figure (Coren, Girgus, & Schiano, 1986), and the amount of decrement depends on the amount of time that the observer has had to actively explore the figure with his eyes (Predebon, 1998).

The phenomenon of illusion decrement implies that perceptual learning is taking place (Brosvic, Walker, Perry, Degnan, & Dihoff, 1997; Coren, 1997). The information obtained from the eye movements is being used to reduce a perceptual error, and the direction of this change (from greater to lesser illusion susceptibility) mimics that associated with perceptual rearrangement studies (see also Brosvic & Farrelly, 1993). The most interesting aspect of this form of perceptual adjustment, however, is the fact that nothing about it appears to be available to consciousness. Unless provided with a ruler or a direct explanation, the observer does not consciously know that the perception is in error, nor does he know that illusory error has been reduced as a result of his active interactions with the illusion figure! The percept simply becomes more accurate with no change in the observer's own awareness.

CONTEXT AND MEANING

Basically, all percepts are potentially ambiguous. Consider a target that casts a square image on the retinal surface. The object the image represents could actually be one of an infinite number of different shapes at any distance or inclination relative to the observer, as is shown in Figure 16.9. Because any retinal image can be caused by a variety of different physical targets in the world, it is surprising that our normal perceptual experiences are generally so unambiguous. What we perceive seems to

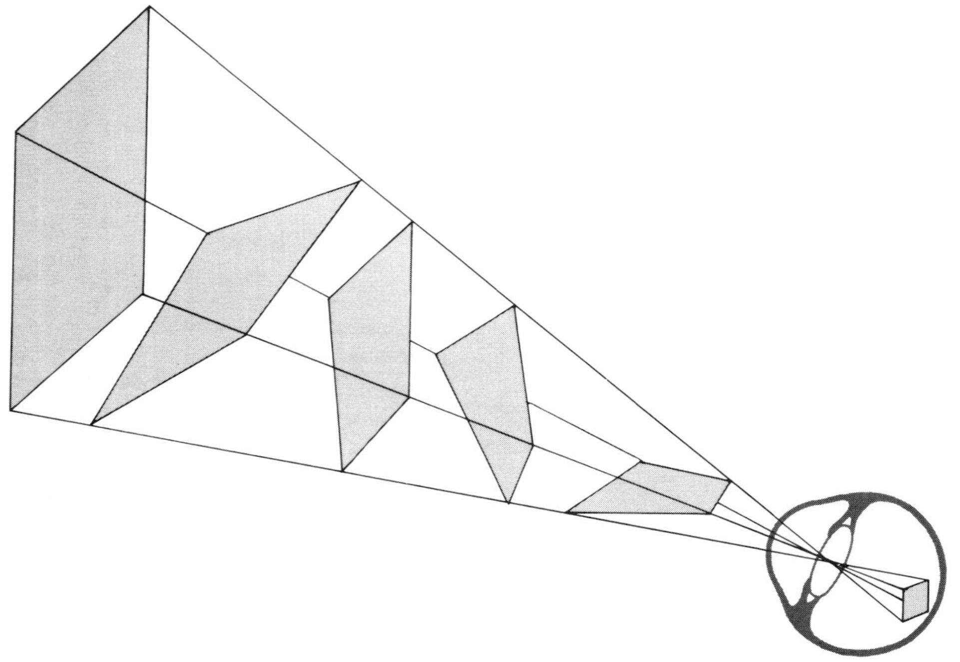

FIGURE 16.9 Many different objects at different distances and slants, all of which cast the same square retinal image (from Coren & Girgus, 1978).

be the result of a decision-making process in which we deduce, on the basis of all available information, what the stimulus object is. **This transactional viewpoint** was popularized by the classic work of Ames (1951) and Brunswick (1955). It maintains that any current perceptual experience consists of a complex evaluation of the significance of the stimuli reaching our receptors. Through our life experience we learn that certain objects or conditions have a high probability of being related to each other. On this basis we derive our "best bet" as to what we are viewing. In a sense, the world we are experiencing is more the *result* of perceptual processing than the *cause* of the perception (Coren, 1984). The transactional viewpoint implies that if our expectations change or our analysis of the situation changes, then our perceptual experience will also change. A similar viewpoint was offered by Irvin Rock (see Biography Box 16.3), who called this **indirect perception** (e.g., Rock, 1997). The reason that it is called "indirect" is because perception is not an automatic process of registering stimuli but rather one that requires extensive computation and intelligence to succeed. Fortunately, this computation takes place quickly and effortlessly, but it is complex and sophisticated nevertheless, as it draws inferences, makes guesses based on experience, and bases one perception on those that have preceded it. A simple example of the effect of context and expectations can be seen in Demonstration Box 16.3.

Most of our percepts are constructed from incomplete stimuli. Look at Figure 16.10A. It is clear that this represents a dog, yet it should also be clear that there is no dog present. The figure is completely constructed in the mind's eye of the observer. The elephant in Figure 16.10B will probably be somewhat more difficult to identify. The less familiar the object, the more difficult is the identification. Furthermore, you must begin with the initial hypothesis that there is some object there in the first place; otherwise you may never see any pattern at all (Reynolds, 1985). However, after you have seen (or "constructed") the figure, the meaningful organization will be apparent immediately when you look at it again. Our ability to perceive these stimuli as objects depends on our prior experience. This was shown by Steinfield (1967), who found that when observers were told a story about an ocean cruise, they identified Figure 16.10C as a steamship in less than 5 seconds. Observers who were told an irrelevant story took six times longer to identify the figure.

To understand what is going on in these situations you must first realize the difference between stimuli that are **registered** and those that are **apprehended** (Coren, 1989). Apprehended stimuli are present in our conscious experience, whereas registered stimuli have sufficient impact to trigger some form of perceptual processing without actually being strong enough to make us *consciously aware* of their presence (e.g., Mack & Rock, 1998). This means that some of the experiences that affect perception may take place without any conscious awareness. For instance, earlier in the chapter we spoke

BIOGRAPHY BOX 16.3

INTELLIGENT PERCEPTION

Irvin Rock (1922–1995) was educated first at the City College of New York and then went on to earn his doctorate with Hans Wallach at the New School for Social Research. He spent much of his active research life at Rutgers University. His early work on the moon illusion, done with Lloyd Kaufman, demonstrated his interest in the way that context influences perception. This research demonstrated that the moon illusion is a logical outcome of the rules by which the visual system processes size and distance in general (see also Chapter 10). Several of those experiments were conducted on the rooftop of a New York City building, with an artificial moon that could be projected to appear anywhere in the sky. A number of Rock's theoretical ideas foreshadowed important problems in computational vision. For instance, the perception of shapes is very much influenced by our internal description and coding of that shape and also the context in which that shape occurs. Thus, in some ways, he became the leading modern advocate of the position suggested by Helmholtz, namely that visual perception is based on unconscious inferences. To the consternation of the bottom-up theorists, Rock repeatedly showed the thoughtlike character of perception and the difficulty of reducing it to the processing of relatively local stimulus information and the simple piecing together and synthesis that can be provided by automatic, unintelligent, or simply programmed mechanisms. Thus he delighted in pointing out that the performances of the most sophisticated computers and modern programming are dwarfed by the perceptual feats of every three-year-old when it comes to recognizing objects and surfaces in complex environments. Furthermore, the simple act of turning some figures upside down can completely change their perceptual meaning, although no local stimuli have been altered at all. For Rock the very same processes that are involved in thinking and learning are fundamental to our perception of the world. In recognition of his research and theoretical contributions, Rock was an elected to the Society of Experimental Psychologists and was twice given the Research Scientist Award from the U.S. Public Health Service.

of an experiment in which researchers presented a word for so brief a time that it could not be identified. They found that if the word was presented several times, even though the length of time of each presentation was not increased, the word was eventually identified. What was going on in that instance is analogous to **perceptual priming,** which we spoke about in Chapter 14. In terms of the effects of experience on perception, a prime can be seen as a registered stimulus which is strong enough to activate hypotheses as to what the object might be, and

DEMONSTRATION BOX 16.3

A CONTEXT EFFECT ON PERCEPTION

Read the accompanying handwritten message. You probably read it as "My phone number is area code 604, 876-1569. Please call!" If you did, you were being affected by several contextual influences on perception. Go back to the message and look carefully at the script. You will see that the two pairs of characters you read as the word **is** and the number 15 are identical. In addition, the **h** in the word **phone** and the **b** in the word **number** are identical, as are the **d** in the word **code** and the **l** in the word **please**. You saw each letter or number within a context when you first read the message, and this context determined how you interpreted the script character.

My phone number 15 area
code 604, 876-1569. Please call!

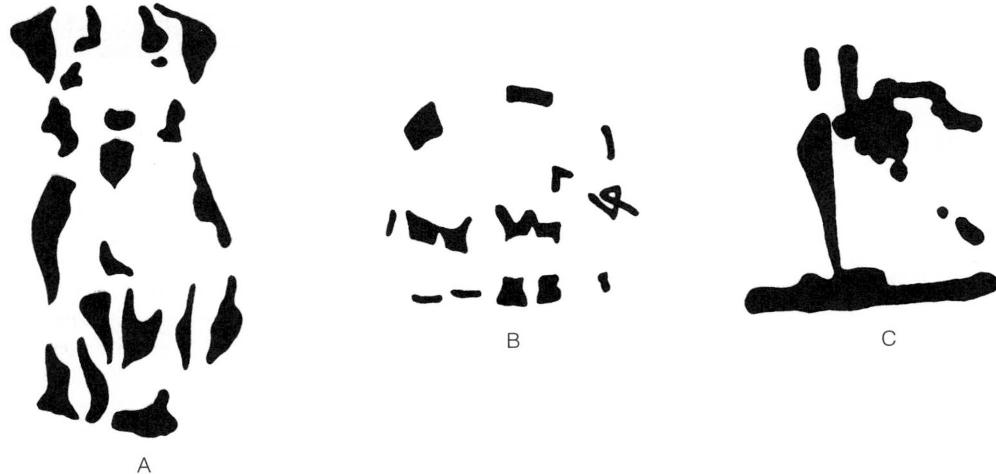

FIGURE 16.10 Some degraded stimuli that may be seen as objects (based on Street, 1931).

as the information extraction from incoming stimuli continues, these hypotheses are evaluated until the stimulus appears to make sense. At this point, the conscious identification response may take place.

The same perceptual hypotheses, allowing us eventually to formulate a percept from minimal or degraded input, can also modify our perception so that it no longer accurately represents the stimulus. For example, Ross and Schilder (1934) presented observers with a series of briefly flashed line drawings. Some of the drawings were incomplete or distorted, such as three-armed people and faces with a mouth missing. A look at some of the observers' comments is informative. When presented with the side view of a dog with the left hind leg missing, an observer reported, "It's a dog, a wolf, two ears stand upright, a round mouth, a long tail." The experimenter then instructed the observer: "Look at his legs." Observer: "He has five toes on each leg." Experimenter: "Look at the hind legs." Observer: "I saw two; the tail goes up."

Despite continued pressure from the experimenter, the observer continued to correct the percept, filling in the missing leg on the hypothesis that dogs have four legs.

These researchers also used a drawing of a woman's head facing forward. She had two large eyes as well as a large third eye on her forehead. One observer described the drawing as "a woman with long hair, black, two eyes, one nose, one mouth, two ears." The stimulus was presented again briefly, and the observer was asked if the forehead was in order, to which he replied, "Yes." After several other stimuli were presented again, the observer now reported, "The same woman I saw before. She is funny—big eyes, a big nose, and a big mouth." Experimenter: "Look at the forehead." Observer: "She has a small curl in the middle."

Even with more brief presentations, this observer still insisted that all that appeared on the forehead was a curl of hair. Third eyes do not occur normally, so we apparently correct our percept on the basis of our expectations—we see extra hair, not extra eyes. You may see how our expectations alter our perceptions in Demonstration box 16.4.

It is interesting to note that even the perceptual comparisons that lead to various illusions and systematic distortions require a consideration of the context and

DEMONSTRATION BOX 16.4

AN EXPECTANCY EFFECT ON PERCEPTION

Turn to Color Plate 9 and *quickly* count the number of aces of spades you see. Then return to this demonstration box. Although you probably saw only two aces of spades, three are actually there. One of the aces of spades is printed in red ink rather than black. The red spade is also upside down. Because you "expect" spades to be black and right-side-up, your identification process for incongruent or unexpected stimuli is impaired.

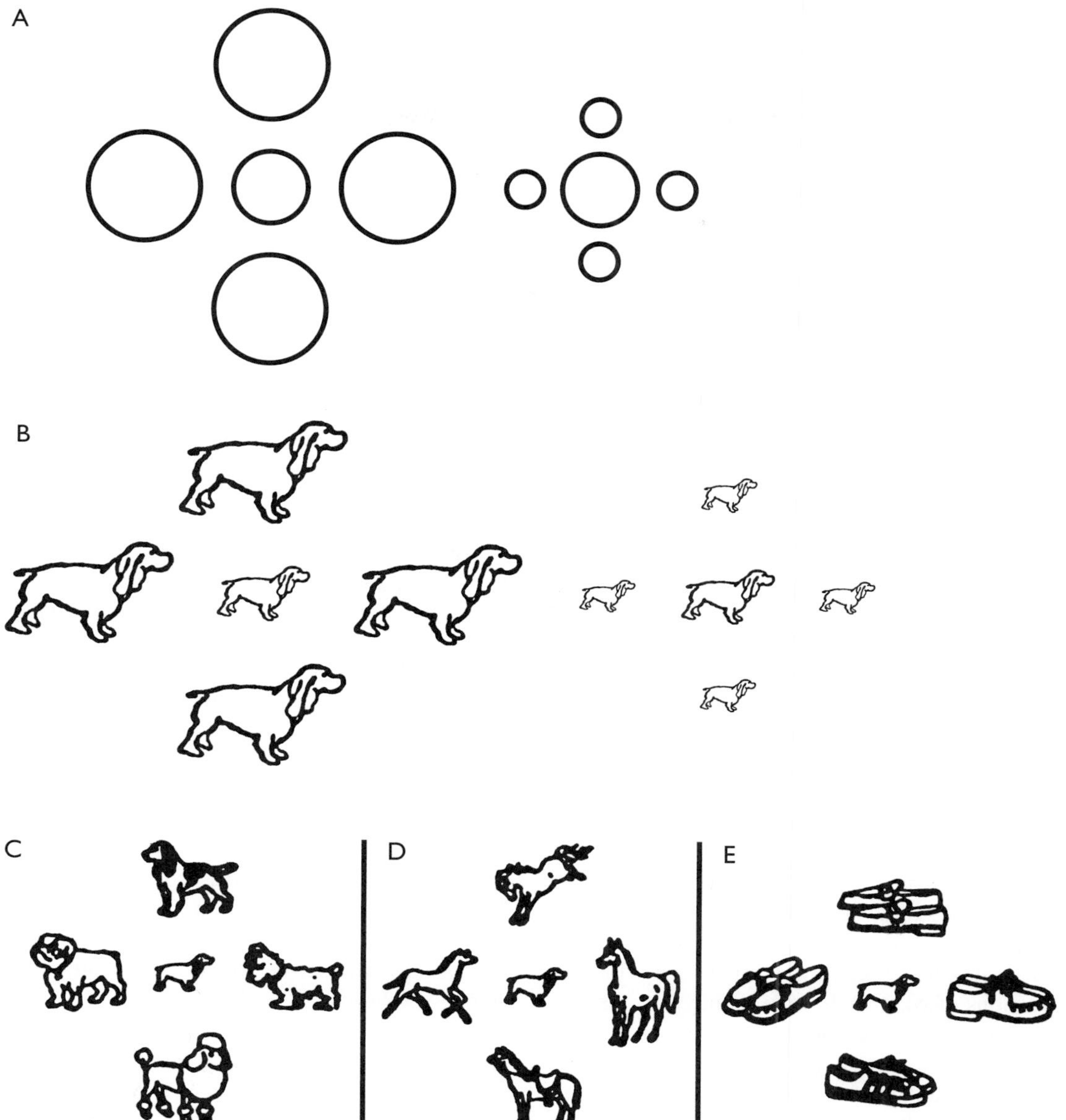

FIGURE 16.11 (A) The Ebbinghaus illusion, where the central item surrounded by large inducers is seen as smaller than that surrounded by small inducers, also occurs in meaningful objects (B). The strength of the illusion diminishes as we go from illusion variants with test and surrounding stimuli drawn from the same class but not identical in form (C), a conceptually near class of stimuli (D), or obviously different classes of objects (E) (after Coren & Enns, 1993).

meaning of the stimuli. Consider the familiar Ebbinghaus illusion that is shown in Figure 16.11A. In this illusion the central circle surrounded by large circles is seen as smaller than the circle surrounded by small circles even though both are the same size. This same illusion occurs if we use meaningful objects rather than circles, as in Figure 16.11B, where the dog surrounded by large dogs appears to be smaller than the dog surrounded by small dogs. It is important to note, however, that the conceptual nature or identity of the objects surrounding the test stimuli is important in determining the strength of this illusion. Coren and Enns (1993) showed that the illusion was strongest when the objects surrounding the test figures were absolutely identical to test objects, as in

Figure 16.11B. If the objects were drawn from the same class of stimuli as the test object (such as dogs) but were visually dissimilar (as in Figure 16.11C, which shows only the large surround half of the illusion), the size of the distortion was reduced. It was reduced further if the surrounding figures were drawn from a near, but dissimilar, conceptual class (e.g., four-footed animals such as horses, as in Figure 16.11D). The illusion virtually disappeared when surrounding objects were drawn from a distant and irrelevant class of items, such as shoes (as in Figure 16.11E). Thus, it is clear that we first classify and identify items that form the context for the stimuli at which we are looking. Our final conscious perception of the stimulus (whether correct or distorted) will be strongly affected by our experience with such classes of stimuli and the way in which we identify and categorize them.

Eyewitness Testimony

Language and expectation can also serve to modify our reports of what we have seen. In a classic experiment Carmichael, Hogan, and Walter (1932) presented observers with simple line drawings and associated each with a label. Observers were then asked to reproduce these drawings. In general, their reproductions were biased in the direction of the verbal label. When presented with Figure 16.12A and told that it was a broom, observers tended to reproduce patterns similar to Figure 16.12B. When told that it was a rifle, observers tended to reproduce patterns similar to Figure 16.12C. In this experiment the reproductions occurred only a few moments after the stimulus was taken away. Such distortions in our recollections of what we have seen may have important consequences for many behaviors. Our memory of scientific data presented in a graph or our ability to reproduce contours drawn on a map may be distorted by the context provided from someone's verbal description of it (Tversky & Schiano, 1989). It also may explain why eyewitness reports of events that occurred during a crime tend to be remarkably unreliable, even when obtained immediately after the event. Observers have a tendency to include details that they could not have seen. Such details are often provided on the basis of an observer's expectations or biases (e.g., Cutler & Penrod, 1995).

Information received after a stimulus is seen can distort the way that it is encoded (Zaragoza & Lane, 1994). In one often-cited experiment Loftus (1974) showed observers a brief videotape of an automobile accident and then asked them some questions about what they had just observed. For one group of observers one of the questions was, "How fast was the white sports car going while traveling along the country road?" For the other group the question was, "How fast was the white sports car going when it passed the barn while traveling along the country road?" In fact, there was no barn present. Yet when questioned about the incident a week later, more than 17% of the group exposed to the false suggestion about a barn answered the question "Did you see a barn?" by saying "Yes," as opposed to only 3% of the group that did not get such a suggestion.

There are limitations to how much a perception (or a remembered perception) can be affected by later inputs (see Haber & Haber, 2000). For instance, some data suggest that when we have clearly perceived something, the perceptual memory resists any later change. It seems that the suggestions from later (possibly false) context provided after the actual perceptual event act only to fill in gaps in the perception (Ross, Read, & Toglia, 1994). This is much like the observer's expectation that dogs have four legs, which caused the missing leg to be added perceptually in the experiment discussed earlier. This can lead to some problems, especially with eyewitness identifications made by children. Children seem to have the same accuracy as adults in identifying a person whom they saw before when that person is present in a lineup. However, if the lineup does not contain the person being sought, children are much more likely to misidentify a person whom they have never seen before (Dekle & Beal, 1996; Gross & Hayne, 1996). This may well be due to the expectation that the guilty party must be present, which then provides pressure for an erroneous identification.

One of the most fascinating aspects of eyewitness identifications is that our feeling of certainty (namely, how certain we are that our identification is correct) is

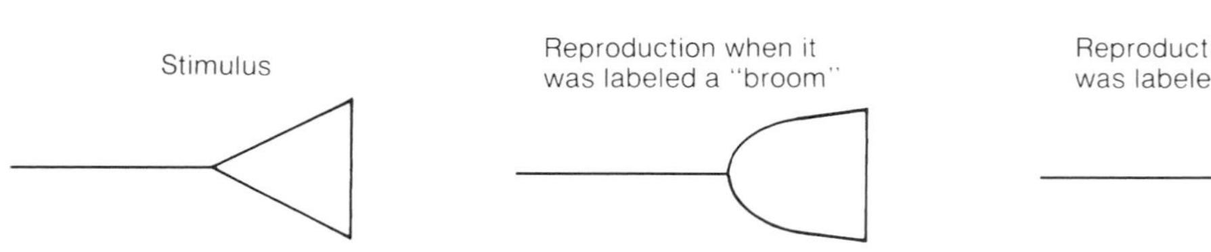

FIGURE 16.12 The effects of labels on later perceptual recall.

not a reasonable predictor of how accurate our description is of what we saw actually (Brewer, Keast, & Rishworth, 2002; Juslin & Olsson, 1996). Even though in trials juries tend to be swayed toward believing individuals who are very certain that they saw something and toward disbelieving individuals who are uncertain, both are equally likely to be correct or incorrect in their recollections. Asking observers to focus on details does not help accuracy and may even be counterproductive (Lane, Mather, Villa, & Morita, 2001). However, to a limited extent, structuring the questioning to fit the actual sequence of events may help to prevent some eyewitness errors, perhaps by restoring the original context that was present during the actual viewing of the events (Eisen, Quas, & Goodman, 2002).

ENVIRONMENTAL AND LIFE HISTORY DIFFERENCES

We have seen what effect the availability, or nonavailability, of particular environmental stimuli can have on the development of sensory systems and hence on the observer's later perceptual abilities. There also are aspects of our environment and culture that may teach us different perceptual strategies and may alter the internal set of expectations and analyses that we bring to each new perceptual situation. Thus, if we live in the desert or on the pampas or the plains, we are exposed to broad vistas of open space that are never experienced by a forest dweller. If we live in a technologically advanced country, we are exposed to sets of visual stimuli (such as photographs and television) that are usually not available to aboriginals dwelling in the African bush or the Australian outback. Such differences, especially when experienced over an entire lifetime, may have dramatic consequences for perceptual processes.

Picture Perception

In our civilized, urbanized, and media-intensive culture, we are inundated with images—not just the images of our immediate environment, but also images representing environments or objects that are not present. Some of these latter images are in the form of patterns of color or black and white shown on televisions and in cinemas. There are also photographs in magazines and newspapers, where we might "see" a baby elephant peaceably grazing a few feet in front of its gigantic mother, all in a 5-cm-square smudge of black ink on a perfectly flat surface. If you have some artistic talent, you may be able to represent such a scene with a few strokes of a pen on a sheet of paper and thus be able to let your friends "see for themselves" what you have seen. This seems like a perfectly natural fact of life.

Pictures of the sort we encounter daily are often viewed as simply "windows" through which we see other worlds, but this is not really the case. Certainly these images must follow many of the same optical laws as the real world, and observers must be aware of these laws to interpret pictorial stimuli. Pictures do contain much information that mimics the optical patterns encountered in natural viewing (Sedgwick, 1980), but there are many discrepancies between the two-dimensional pictured image and the three-dimensional real image and even some things that simply cannot be reproduced in the flat picture (e.g., Ono, Wade, & Lillakas, 2002). For instance, the actual sizes of the images are usually too large or too small, which in turn ruins the geometrical correspondence between the image and the actual scene (Lumsden, 1980). Furthermore, even if we could make the geometry of perspective perfect, it would be correct only for one viewing angle, and viewing any pictured image from a vantage point other than the viewpoint adopted by the camera or artist who produced the picture ought to lead to distorted percepts (Kennedy & Ostry, 1976). However, such distortions do not appear (Rosinski & Farber, 1980). We could enlarge this list of discrepancies between the real scene and a picture of it that should distort our perception. For instance, although the world is three dimensional, not only is the picture flat but there is a visible texture confirming its flatness, which should affect our perception (Yang & Kubovy, 1999). Furthermore, the picture is interpreted correctly even if its colors are all wrong, or even if there are no colors at all; and so forth. Such considerations have led some theorists to conclude that pictures may be statements in a sort of visual language that are created and interpreted according to the agreed-on set of conventions in any given culture. Thus, they are not simply representations of reality at all (Gombrich, 1972). At the very least, they must be interpreted as hypotheses shared among individuals growing up with a common heritage (Deregowski, 1999). By either of these two theories, however, the perception of pictures must be learned in some manner.

Before we investigate whether we must learn to interpret pictures, it is important for us to specify that we are really talking about two separate skills. The first is the ability to identify objects depicted in a picture, and the second is the ability to interpret the three-dimensional arrangement implied in the flat image.

Hochberg and Brooks (1962) conducted an heroic experiment, using one of their children as the subject. The child was reared to the age of 19 months carefully shielded from any sort of pictorial representation. This meant that the television was never used in the child's presence, nor were there magazines or picture books. Even the labels on cans and boxes of food were removed or covered. When the child was tested after this restricted rearing, he had no difficulty identifying pictures of common items. This implies that we need not learn to interpret patterns or drawings as representations of real-world objects.

Although there is anecdotal evidence suggesting that color photos are interpreted readily when shown to individuals who have lived in cultures where they have never experienced pictures, which would support the fact that learning is not needed, these findings are contradicted by animal studies that clearly show that pictures of objects are not spontaneously treated as being equivalent to real objects (Fagot, Martin, & Depy, 2000). The more common event, especially when black-and-white photos or drawings are used, is that individuals reared in isolated cultures with no exposure to pictures actually have difficulties interpreting graphic images. Deregowski (1980) collected a number of such reports, including one from a Scottish missionary working in Malawi (a country in southwestern Africa between northern Rhodesia and Mozambique) nearly 75 years ago:

> *Take a picture in black and white, and the natives cannot see it. You may tell the natives: "This is a picture of an ox and a dog"; and the people will look at it and look at you, and that look says that they consider you a liar. Perhaps you say again, "Yes, this is a picture of an ox and a dog. Look at the horn of the ox, and there is his tail!" And the boy will say, "Oh, yes and there is the dog's nose and eyes and ears!" Then the old people will look again and clap their hands and say, "Oh yes, it is a dog."*

Clearly, such a report indicates that the individuals involved did not respond to the photo with the immediate spontaneous object identification characteristic of our viewing of pictures. Still, when the individuals had their attention directed to the relevant aspects of the pattern, they did have an "Aha!" experience, indicating that the ability to identify the pattern was there, although they lacked training to direct their attention appropriately.

Although there may be a general ability to identify objects depicted in pictures, interpreting the implied spatial relationships seems to be more subject to cultural and educational influences. Identifying depth in a flat image requires a certain amount of selection among the perceptual cues available. For instance, a picture might include such cues for depth as **linear perspective, interposition,** and **texture gradients,** among others mentioned in Chapter 10. However, there are also cues indicating that the picture is flat; there is no **binocular disparity** between items in the picture, and all of the elements in the picture require the same degree of **accommodation** and **convergence** and there is an overlying visible texture indicating the surface (see Chapter 9). Thus, to see a drawing or a photograph as representing an arrangement of objects in three dimensions, rather than as a flat surface with different shadings of dark and light, you must attend to some depth cues and ignore others (Pick, 1987, Yang, & Kubovy, 1999). An observer's particular perceptual strategy may depend on her life history and the relative frequency with which certain cues are encountered in the immediate environment.

Hudson (1962) attempted to separate cultural factors associated with the use of pictorial depth information. His technique consisted of using a series of pictures that depicted certain combinations of pictorial depth cues. Figure 16.13 shows one picture similar to those used by Hudson; as you can see, it depicts a hunting scene containing two pictorial depth cues. The first is **interposition,** in which objects close to the observer block the view of portions of more distant objects. Because the hunter and the antelope are covering portions of the rocks, they appear to be closer to the observer than are the rocks.

The second pictorial depth cue contained in this picture is **familiar size.** We know the relative sizes of familiar objects; therefore, if an object is depicted as relatively small or large, we will judge its distance from us in a way consistent with our expectations based on its known size. For example, an elephant is a very large animal. However, in Figure 16.13 the elephant is one of the smallest items in the picture. If we are responding to the cue of familiar size, we would tend to see the elephant as being the most distant object in this hunting scene. When something as large as an elephant casts a smaller image than an antelope, the elephant must be farther away because we know it is physically larger than the antelope.

Hudson used these stimuli because they are uniquely constructed to allow for both **two-dimensional** (no use of pictorial depth) and **three-dimensional** (full use of pictorial depth) types of responses. Suppose we asked an observer to describe what she saw in this picture. First we would expect her to identify correctly all of the component objects in the picture. However, suppose we also asked her to describe the actions taking place. A correct three-dimensional response would indicate that the hunter is attempting to spear the antelope (which is, of course, nearer to him than is the elephant if pictorial depth is perceived). A two-dimensional response would state that the hunter is attempting to spear the elephant,

FIGURE 16.13 A figure used to test ability to respond to pictorial depth cues (based on Hudson, 1962).

which is actually physically closer to the tip of the spear in the picture. Such a response would indicate that the observer had not responded to either the interposition cue or the familiar-size cue, both of which place the elephant at a greater distance from the hunter than is the antelope.

Stimuli similar to these have been used in a number of studies conducted throughout Africa to test observers from a number of tribal and linguistic groups. The results indicate that compared to Western observers the African observers have difficulty seeing pictorial depth in these pictures, a fact that has been verified using other types of pictures (see Deregowski, 1999). Presumably this is because African observers have been relatively isolated from the sort of formal exposure and training with drawings that Western-style education and exposure to the mass media provide. The ability to perceive three-dimensionality in pictures seems to be improved if more depth cues are added or if formal education, involving the use of picture books, drawings, and so forth, has been experienced (see Parks, 2001). This has also been confirmed using animals, namely birds and primates, where both the number of cues and specific training factors have been manipulated (see Fagot, 2000). Use of some depth cues is more easily learned than that of others; thus use of height in the picture plane is acquired before that of differences in relative size when viewing or drawing pictures (c.f. Cox & Perara, 2001). You can explore your own tendencies to use certain depth cues but not others by trying Demonstration Box 16.5.

DEMONSTRATION BOX 16.5

CROSS-CULTURAL DIFFERENCES IN PERCEPTION

The figure accompanying this box is sometimes called the "devil's tuning fork." Look at the figure for about 30 seconds or so; then close the book and try to draw it from memory. Return to this box when you have done this.

Most of you probably found this task to be difficult. The source of your difficulty comes from the fact that your cultural experience with graphic representations has caused you to interpret this two-dimensional stimulus as a three-dimensional object. Unfortunately, such an interpretation leads to problems because the depth cues implied in this figure are ambiguous. It is interesting to note that Africans who have not received formal education have no difficulty reproducing the figure. Because they do not interpret the figure as three-dimensional, they merely see a pattern of flat lines, which is easy to reproduce.

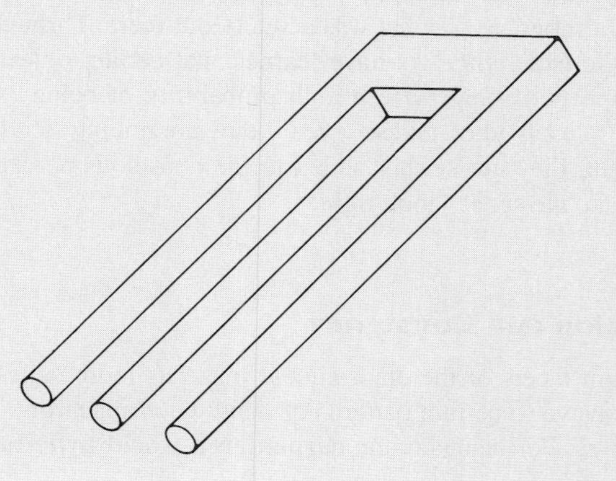

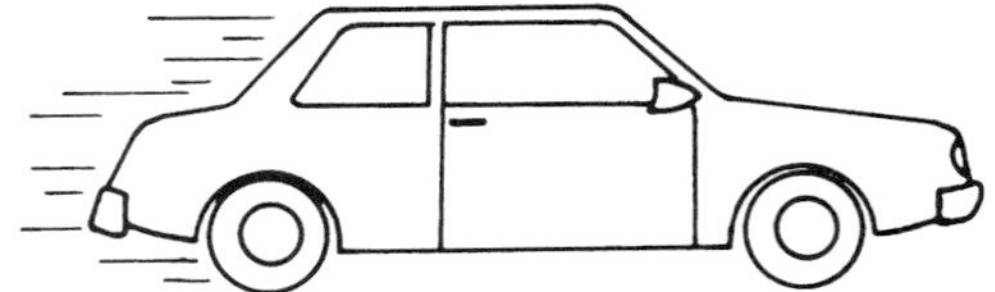

FIGURE 16.14 Scenes conventionally recognized as depicting motion by Western observers but not necessarily by non-Western observers.

Culturally determined conventions associated with the interpretation of pictures can be shown best in situations where the flat, stationary picture is supposed to depict not only three-dimensionality but also motion. For instance, Figure 16.14 depicts a scene in which there are three different forms of motion. From left to right, we see a speeding car, a boy rapidly whipping his head around, and a dog wagging its tail. Of course, there is no actual motion, yet we "read" such motion into the pictures. Within Western cultures, such interpretation of motion in pictorial arrays may appear as early as 4 years of age (Friedman & Stevenson, 1975). Non-Western cultures without pictorial experience, however, virtually never "see" movement in such representations. The likelihood that movement will be seen in such representations increases with education, urbanization, and exposure to pictorial materials (Friedman & Stevenson, 1980).

An interesting feature of picture perception is that after we have learned to "see" pictures, we actually end up seeing more than is physically present. First, remember that any picture is just a small sample of information that would be present if we were actually looking at the actual scene in the real world. When we look at a photograph and are later asked to recall or to draw what we saw, we tend to remember seeing information that was not really in the picture but was likely to have existed just outside the camera's field of view. This tendency is called **boundary extension** (Intraub & Berkowits, 1996; Intraub & Gottesman, 1996). This is another example of the fact that our current perceptual experience consists of the "best bet" as to what was actually out there. Through our life experience we have learned that certain objects or aspects of view have a high probability of being related to each other, and so, even if they are not physically present, they are simply added to the conscious percept to make the scene "look right."

Illusion and Constancy

Certain facets of the environment make us more or less responsive to certain patterns of depth cues appearing in pictures. For instance, the **carpentered world hypothesis** begins with the observation that in the urbanized Western world, rooms and buildings are usually rectangular, many objects in the environment have right-angled corners, city streets have straight sides, and so forth. Surrounded by such an environment, we may learn to depend more heavily on depth cues based on linear perspective than would people who live in less "carpentered" and more rural environments (Coren & Girgus, 1978). For example, rural, isolated Zulus have been described as surrounded by a circular culture. They live in round huts with round doors. They do not plow their land in straight furrows but instead tend to use curved furrows. Individuals living in such a world would not be expected to rely on linear perspective as heavily as do those of us living in a more linear environment.

In a classic study Segall, Campbell, and Herskovits (1966) compared the responsiveness of individuals in carpentered versus noncarpentered environments to certain types of depth cues. However, instead of using pictures like those that Hudson used, as stimulus materials they chose a more subtle class of patterns, namely the visual-geometric illusions. Some of these configurations were discussed in Chapter 10, where we pointed out how susceptibility to size distortions in some figures, such as the Mueller-Lyer illusion, may be dependent on a three-dimensional interpretation of the pattern (to refresh your memory, refer back to Figure 10-13). As we discussed then, the apparently longer portion of the Mueller-Lyer figure may be interpreted as a corner of a room receding in depth because the wings of the illusion act as linear perspective cues. The inappropriate application of size constancy based on this interpretation of the wings of the figure as perspective cues results in our overestimation of the size of this segment of the figure relative to the segment with the inward-turned wings. Because pictorial depth information is thought to play a role in the formation of these illusory percepts, these types of configurations are well suited to an exploration of the carpentered world hypothesis.

Segall and colleagues gathered data from throughout Africa and also from several groups of people living in Evanston, Illinois. Although there are variations within the noncarpentered samples, the average Mueller-Lyer illusion was greater for the more urban groups. Similar results have been reported for other perspective-related illusions (Coren & Girgus, 1978).

Although the observed differences in illusion susceptibility for different cultural groups may be partially caused by factors other than experience with a carpentered world, there is ample evidence that the absence of experience with certain types of depth cues impairs other perceptual functions (such as size constancy) that are dependent on depth perception. One of the most striking examples of this was provided by the anthropologist Turnbull (1961). He observed the behavior of the Bambuti Pygmies, who live in the Ituri forest in the Congo. Because they live in the dense rain forest, their vision is generally limited to short distances, with vistas that extend for, at most, only 30 m. Therefore, their life history seems to lack the visual experience needed to learn to use the depth cues responsible for the maintenance of size constancy at greater viewing distances. Turnbull noted one instance when he had taken his Bambuti guide, Kenge, out of the forest for the first time in his life. They were crossing a broad plain and happened to spot a herd of buffalo:

> *Kenge looked over the plains and down to where a herd of about a hundred buffalo was grazing some miles away. He asked me what kind of insects they were, and I told him they were buffalo, twice as big as the forest buffalo known to him. He laughed loudly and told me not to tell such stupid stories. . . . We got into the car and drove down to where the animals were grazing. He watched them getting larger and larger, and though he was as courageous as any Pygmy, he moved over and sat close to me and muttered that it was witchcraft. . . . Finally, when he realized that they were real buffalo he was no longer afraid, but what puzzled him still was why they had been so small, and whether they really had been small and suddenly grown larger, or whether it had been some kind of trickery. (From C. Turnbull,* American Journal of Psychology, *74. Copyright 1961 The University of Illinois Press.)*

Turnbull's description of Kenge's perceptual impressions suggests that our experience with particular stimuli prevalent in our immediate environment can result in differences in how we perceive new stimuli and new situations. It seems that we learn to utilize stimulus information that we encounter frequently, but we fail to learn to utilize stimulus information that is rare. This holds for the auditory as well as the visual environment.

Speech

The most dominant feature in our auditory environment is the constant flow of language sounds that surrounds us. As discussed in Chapter 6, each language uses a small set of word-differentiating **phonemes,** which are the functionally characteristic sounds of that language. Because different languages use different subsets and combinations of these phonemes, experiments on people reared in different linguistic settings offer a unique opportunity to observe the effects of specific kinds of experience on perception (see Kuhl, Tsao, Liu, Zhang, & De Boer, 2001). Because some sounds may be treated as distinctively different in some languages and not in others—for instance, the sounds "r" as in **rope** and "l" as in **lope** are different phonemes in English, but not in Japanese—we would expect a bias in the auditory experience of individuals brought up surrounded by one or the other of these two languages. Numerous studies have shown that adults who have grown up with exposure to only one language often have difficulty discriminating certain linguistic contrasts characteristic of other languages (e.g., Harnsberger, 2001). This type of difficulty may persist even if the adults have learned the other language and appear to be fluent in it. An early demonstration of this comes from Goto (1971), who recorded pairs of words that contrasted the "r" and "l" sounds (such as **lead** versus **read** or **play** versus **pray**). Several native Japanese speakers, who were bilingual in Japanese and English, could produce these sounds so that native English-speaking listeners could differentiate them without error. However, this seems to be a learned ability to **produce** rather than to perceive the phonemic difference because, when asked to listen to recordings of pairs of words that contrasted these phonemes, the native Japanese speakers could not perceive the difference, *even when listening to their own speech productions!*

The mechanism responsible for our ability to discriminate some speech sounds but not others is still somewhat mysterious, but it seems to be a form of template learning as we discussed previously. In addition, it seems to have a critical period, with early learning being important. Thus it appears that babies are born with the ability to discriminate certain sound pairs not used in their native tongue, and they appear to lose this ability as adults (see Werker & Desjardins, 2001). A striking example was provided by Werker, Gilbert, Humphrey, and Tees (1981), who presented English-speaking and Hindi-speaking adults with pairs of sounds that are different phonemes in Hindi but not in English. As we might expect, the adult Hindi speakers could make the discrimination, but the adult English speakers could not. The interesting result, however, is that 6-month-old infants from English-speaking homes could make the discrimination. It seems that at some time during the first year of exposure to the language, infants begin to respond selectively to certain aspects in their linguistic environment and to lose selectively their ability to respond to phonemic distinctions not used in their native language.

This is not to say that one cannot learn to make certain phonemic distinctions. Evidence suggests that learning through exposure and experience plays a role in the ability to discriminate between various linguistic sounds, and some linguistic discriminations seem to be learned during the childhood years (Bosch & Sebastian-Galles, 2001). However, this appears to be limited to certain dimensions of the sounds. Tees and Werker (1984) showed that short-term intensive training improved the ability of native English speakers to make certain nonnative (Hindi) speech discriminations, although after 5 years of language study the ability to make these discriminations was already apparent. An interesting additional finding pertained to individuals who spent their early years in a setting where Hindi was spoken (perhaps by a live-in relative). Even though these individuals had never studied the language and as adults were unable to speak, understand, or write more than a few words of Hindi, it was found that they could make the phonemic discriminations that nonnative Hindi speakers found impossible. Thus, their early experience seems to have "tuned" their speech-sound decoding capacity for certain phonemes even though they were not actually speaking the language.

In terms of our earlier discussion about the relationship between experience and development, these results suggest that different aspects of the perception of speechlike sounds follow different courses. Whereas some auditory discriminations are facilitated through contact with particular sounds in the linguistic environment, others are lost through their absence or rarity, thus showing that experience is necessary for their maintenance (cf. Jusczyk & Luce, 2002). Obviously, if some clinical condition, such as selective hearing loss, affects our auditory environment during the early critical period, it may also greatly affect our ability to discriminate language sounds, even if some hearing is restored through something like cochlear implants at a later time (e.g., Clark, 2002).

It is important to note that although human infants seem to be particularly tuned to build and modify phonemic templates that will allow them to perceive their native language better, this is not an exclusively human characteristic. Some of these same learning patterns have been shown in tamarin monkeys as well (Ramus, Hauser, Miller, Morris, & Mehler, 2001). Overall, this confirms that much of what we perceive and many of the perceptual distinctions we make are strongly influenced by the environment in which we were reared and to the extent that our cultural heritage influences that environment, our perceptual abilities are also affected by our cultures.

Effects of Occupation

Even within a given culture there is selective exposure to different sets of environmental stimuli. You are exposed to your occupational setting for about one half of your adult working life, and specific sets of occupational experiences can affect your perceptual abilities both at the physiological and at higher cognitive levels. One aspect of an occupation that may have physiological effects on a sensory system is the magnitude of sound, light, or chemical stimulation to which you are exposed.

Consider, for example, the amount of auditory input that bombards you in your occupational setting. Some work environments are relatively quiet (such as offices and small stores); others are associated with continuous high-intensity noise (e.g., factories, mills, or rock music bands). Figure 16.15 illustrates the effects of noise on hearing for different occupations. The horizontal axis represents the frequencies at which hearing was tested in a sample of male office, farm, and factory workers. The 0-dB point on the vertical axis represents the average minimum threshold for young adults of an auditory experience. The three curves on the graph plot the average threshold sound intensity at each of the frequencies used in the test. As you can see, the group of factory workers has a lowered sensitivity (higher average thresholds).

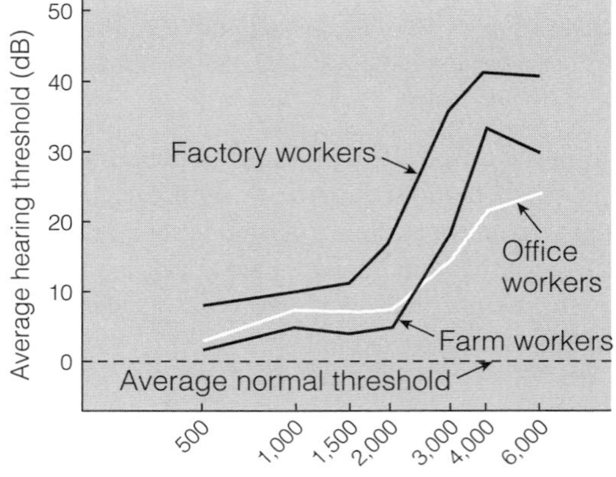

FIGURE 16.15 The effect of occupation on hearing (based on Glorig, Wheeler, Quigle, Grings, & Summerfield, 1970).

TABLE 16.1 Hearing Loss and Noise Level

Duration in Hours per Day	DeciBels	Some Typical Examples of Noise Sources
10 hours or more	Less than 85 dB	Busy truck traffic
8	85	Blender with ice Electric razor
4	88	Motor cycle
2	91	Gas lawnmower Truck with muffler
1	94	Chainsaw
30 minutes	97	Walkman at maximum
15 minutes	100	Car horn at 5 meters

Hearing loss depends on both the noise level and the amount of time that an individual is exposed to it. This table indicates the permissible duration of noise before damage occurs in a typical person.

To give you an idea of how sensitive the ear is to noise damage, if an individual is exposed to occupational noise levels during the working day that are 80 dB or less, then 5% of them will develop significant hearing losses. This number increases to a range of 5 to 15% if the average daily noise level is 85 dB, and to 15 to 25% if the average daily noise level is 90 dB (e.g., Prince, 2002). The impact of noise is greater for men than for women and increases with age (e.g., Palmer et al., 2002). The greatest losses appear to be in the higher frequencies. Table 16.1 gives the permissible noise durations for common occupational sound levels.

The number of occupational and recreational settings that are associated with levels of sound that reliably cause hearing damage is remarkably large. For example, individuals who use firearms recreationally show marked losses in hearing (Stewart, Pankiw, Lehman, & Simpson, 2002). Even astronauts suffer occupationally related hearing losses from the sounds of the rocket engines during space flight and the continuous noise of the equipment in the space stations (e.g., Buckley et al., 2001). Perhaps of particular interest to young people is the fact that performers of rock music may also suffer hearing losses. In Figure 16.16 average auditory thresholds are again plotted for various test frequencies. The lowest curve represents the thresholds of the control group of nonperformers. Notice that relative to nonperformers of the same age, the rock performers have elevated auditory thresholds (lower sensitivity). At 4000 Hz there is approximately 20 dB difference between the thresholds of the performers and the controls. To give you a reference point, a 20-dB difference would be roughly equivalent to being able to hear a normal conversational tone as opposed to a shout. Figure 16.16 also shows the immediate effects of prolonged exposure to very loud sounds. The top curve on this graph plots the measured thresholds immediately after 85 minutes of exposure to very loud music; as you can see, the threshold at 4000 Hz has risen to 25 dB. More recently it has been shown that university students who work in recreational venues where loud music is played suffer from similar long-term hearing losses (Sadhra, Jackson, Ryder, & Brown, 2002).

In a similar vein, there are occupations that expose the eyes to high-intensity lights (such as welding arcs and furnace blazes). In the same manner that prolonged exposure to high-intensity sound can permanently impair

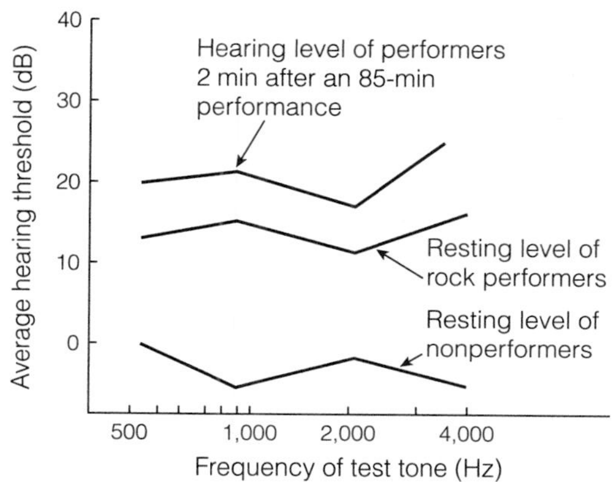

FIGURE 16.16 A comparison of the hearing of rock performers to that of nonperformers (based on Rice et al., 1968).

hearing, prolonged exposure to high-intensity light can permanently impair vision (Noell, 1980).

Perhaps the most interesting occupational effect on vision pertains to **myopia** (nearsightedness). Physiologically this is a condition where the length of the eye is somewhat too great, and the parallel rays of light from distant objects come to a focus in front of the retina, resulting in poor distance acuity. Myopia is actually the most prevalent visual disorder in the world, affecting over 2 billion individuals. Over the past 40 years a number of studies have established that one of the major causes of myopia has to do with a life history of exposure to "near work," which would include reading and other activities restricted to close distances (see Grosvenor & Flom, 1991; Lundervold, Lewin, & Irvin, 1987). It is believed that trying hard to see leads to overaccommodation of the crystalline lens and some increased internal pressure in the eye. Over a long period of time this may actually lengthen the eye and lead to myopia (Freidman, 1981). It has been demonstrated that after only a short span of near work (such as 3 hours of editing text on a visual display terminal), a person may become temporarily myopic (Jaschinski-Kruza, 1984). It is also possible to induce myopia in animals by using certain environmental and visual exposure conditions (e.g., Sivak, et al., 1990). In monkeys this has been done by rearing them under conditions where for extended periods the maximum visual distance that they could see was around 50 cm (e.g., Young, 1981).

The most common way to correct for myopia is, of course, to prescribe eyeglasses. In fact, with the high prevalence of myopia, we are very used to seeing people with glasses. It is so common that we seldom think about glasses, which must have been the case with the artist who depicted the circumcision of Jesus in the painting shown in Figure 16.17. Notice that one of the rabbis in the picture is using **pince-nez** or "nose clip" eyeglasses that permit the use of both hands, even those these were not to be invented for another 1500 years!

Glasses, however, are not the only solution to myopia that has been suggested. One attempted remedy is based on the assumption that if myopia comes about through a particular pattern of eye use, then it should be possible to develop a set of exercises that might reverse the process that is causing nearsightedness. Vision training to correct myopia has been discussed and debated extensively ever since 1920, when William Bates wrote his controversial book titled *Better Eyesight without Glasses.* He and his successors emphasized certain eye exercises and discouraged the use of corrective spectacles. Since that time a number of different training techniques have been developed. Some use recognition training, some use focus exercises to accommodate to more distant targets, and some have used even biofeedback techniques, where complex oculometers monitor the individual's state of lens accommodation (Kaplan, 1995; Woo & Wilson, 1990).

How well does vision training work for myopia or any other form of visual difficulty? There have been some reports of success, with at least some individuals showing measurable improvement in their ability to recognize familiar targets and letters (e.g., Lundervold, Lewin, & Irvin, 1987). Unfortunately, this success seems to be due to attentional changes, which allow individuals to recognize blurred stimuli better, rather than to any actual improvement in the refractive state of the eye (Goodson & Rahe, 1981). Most studies have shown that the vision training does not really change visual acuity at all (e.g., Long, 1994). It certainly does not allow individuals better distance vision in situations where the targets have few recognition clues when they are blurred or are much different from the ones that the individuals trained with (e.g., Koslowe, Spierer, Rosner, & Belkin, 1991). A series of studies by Fahle and associates (e.g., Fahle, 1997; Herzog & Fahle, 1997) makes it clear why this is the case. Using tasks involving vernier acuity (see Chapter 4), they found that there was rapid improvement in acuity with practice, especially with appropriate feedback about errors. Unfortunately, the learning was specific for the stimuli used. If a stimulus is rotated, say, from horizontal to vertical, if the pattern is altered in any visible way, or even if it is moved to a different location on the retina, then all of the training effects are lost. This lack of transfer from one set of learned discriminations to a new one is not unique to vision but also occurs in touch and other modalities (e.g., Sathian & Zangaladze, 1997). Thus, although an individual's viewing practices and near work habits are capable of causing myopia, simple training and exercise procedures do not seem to be able to reverse the condition after it has developed.

Perceptual Set

Experiences we have in an occupational or other setting may bias our perception and interpretation of various stimuli. This seems to be because specific past experiences produce a sensitization or predisposition to "see" a situation in a certain way, especially when several alternative perceptual experiences are possible (as when the stimulus is ambiguous or degraded because of poor viewing conditions). Technically, this is known as a **perceptual set,** and it refers specifically to the expectancies

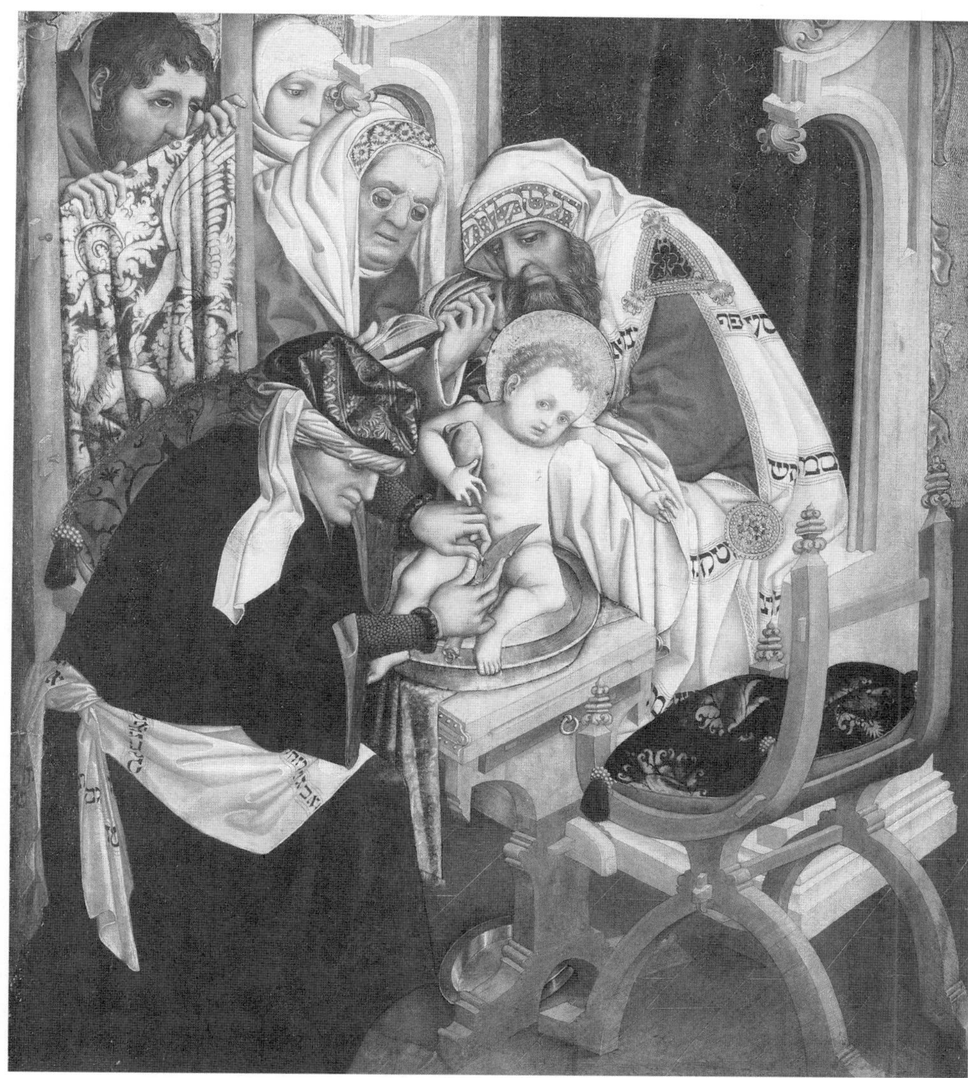

FIGURE 16.17 A painting depicting the circumcision of Jesus, with a rabbi wearing glasses, despite the fact that these were invented 1500 years *after* Jesus' birth.

or predispositions an observer brings to the perceptual situation (Coren, 1984). In many respects, set can be thought of as another example of selective attention (as we discussed in Chapter 13), in which the observer is set to process some but not all incoming information or to organize it in a specific manner. To get a better feeling for how set operates, you might try Demonstration Box 16.6.

As an example, let us consider police as observers and eyewitnesses because this is an occupation in which accurate observation is important. Some findings suggest that perceptual set may influence the observations of police in certain situations. In one study, police officers and civilians were shown films of a street scene over a period of several hours. Their task was to categorize the people who appeared as wanted (photos on display below the screen) or unwanted and to categorize the actions they engaged in as normal exchanges of goods or as thefts. The police tended to report more alleged thefts than did the nonpolice, although there was no significant difference between the police and civilians in their actual detection of people and actions that were to be categorized (Clifford & Bull, 1978).

A more subtle demonstration of this effect of set was provided by Toch and Schulte (1961), who studied perception of violence and crime in ambiguous visual scenes. They simultaneously presented different pictures to each eye in a stereoscope (see Chapter 9). One eye

DEMONSTRATION BOX 16.6

PERCEPTUAL SET

Something of the flavor of perceptual set can be experienced by simply reading the following set of words out loud:

MACBETH
MACARTHUR
MACWILLIAMS
MACNAMARA
MACDILLON
MACDONALD
MACMASTER
MACDOWELL
MACHINES
MACKENZIE

Now look back at the next-to-the-last word. Did you pronounce it as if it were organized as the name *Mac Hines,* or did you pronounce it as if it were organized as the more familiar and natural form that makes the common word *machines?* If you pronounced it as the name, organizing the prefix *Mac* into a separate unit, you were demonstrating the effects of perceptual set.

was shown a violent scene and the other a nonviolent scene, as in the pair of stimuli in Figure 16.18. If these two views are seen simultaneously by the two eyes, perceptual confusion should result. Observers tend to resolve this ambiguous situation in favor of one scene or the other; that scene then dominates the percept. Toch and Schulte were interested in exploring the notion that police students would be predisposed to interpret this particular ambiguous situation in terms of the violent as opposed to the nonviolent scene. They compared the performance of advanced police administration students with two control groups: beginning police students and university students. In general, they found that the advanced police students interpreted the stereograms as depicting violence approximately twice as many times as did the other two groups. Thus, their data provide some evidence that certain occupations, especially those requiring intensive training, may set an individual to interpret ambiguous stimulation in a particular way.

We are not singling out the police for scrutiny. Perceptual set associated with occupational training, experience, and education can affect all groups of individuals. An example of how our educational background can bias our perception can be seen by looking at Figure 16.19A. Most Western observers will see a complex pattern of black shapes, which, by some stretching of the imagina-

FIGURE 16.18 A stereogram used to test for occupational influences on the perception of violence (from H. H. Toch & R. Schulte, 1961, *British Journal of Psychology,* 52, 389–393).

A

B

FIGURE 16.19 Although (A) may appear to be a relatively random collection of black shapes, perhaps depicting some sort of boot, it is actually similar to (B) in that it contains the word **FLY** depicted in the white areas, but in (A) the word is in Chinese calligraphy.

tion, might appear to cohere into some sort of a boot. Conversely, Figure 16.19B is different. Here the white spaces clearly shape the word *FLY,* whereas the black spaces serve as the background. Our familiarity with the English language helps to focus our attention on this region of the figure, and we supply the missing contours, subjectively, to complete the percept (see Chapter 11). Actually, if you were an educated native Chinese, you might be more captured by Figure 16.19A because it outlines in the white spaces between the black shapes the calligraphic character for the Chinese word *FLY,* and Figure 16.19B might appear to be merely five meaningless black shapes (see Coren, Porac, & Theodor, 1987).

Another interesting example of perceptual set based on language (here written language) has been provided by Diener (1990). Look at the two words printed in Figure 16.20. Pay particular attention to the letter *P* in both. In the word on the left the letter *P* appears to be a lowercase letter, and on the right it appears to be an uppercase letter. Now look at the size of both of these letters. Notice that the uppercase *P* appears to be physically larger than its lowercase counterpart. Actually both are the same size. Your set and expectations based on your knowledge that uppercase letters are usually larger than lowercase letters have distorted your perception in this case.

Although we have singled out vision for most of our discussion, it is important to note that set effects can be found in all aspects of perception. For example, consider the case of the apparent intensity of an odor. It has been shown that a strawberry odor smells more intense when the solution in which it is presented is colored red than

apt APt

FIGURE 16.20 The letter *P* in the word on the right appears to be in uppercase and also appears to be larger than the letter on the left. The two letters, however, are physically identical (based on Diener, 1990).

when it is colorless (Zellner & Kautz, 1990). It is as if the brain were saying "Strawberries are red, so something that is red must have more strawberry quality than something that is colorless." A similar effect occurred when attempts were made to market clear, colorless cola drinks. The product failed because many people complained that these drinks had "washed out" or "weak" flavors. This is because we are set to see our carbonated cola drinks as brown.

Some set effects can even have potentially lethal consequences. Consider the case of **anorexia nervosa.** This is an eating disorder in which patients see themselves as being too fat, and in response to this perception they virtually starve themselves to death. Recent data suggest that one aspect of this problem involves the misperception of the individual's body size, and this is the result of a process analogous to perceptual set, where the influences come from cultural and media exposure to an ultra thin body size as the ideal (e.g., Epstein, et al., 2001). In summary, then, much of what you perceive is determined, not just by the stimuli that are "out there" in the environment, but by what your experience, culture, and education have set you to perceive.

STUDY QUESTIONS

1. List the various ways that learning and development can interact. How might you design an experiment to test for each of these?
2. List the varieties of perceptual learning and describe an example of each.
3. What is the difference between selective and restrictive rearing? Do they address the same questions? If not, what are the best uses of each?
4. What is the oblique effect? How is it related to perceptual learning?
5. In perceptual rearrangement studies, what is the real proof that perception has changed? What factors influence this perceptual change?
6. What is illusion decrement and how does it relate to perceptual learning?
7. What is the difference between registered and apprehended stimuli? Why is this concept important for perceptual learning?
8. Is perceptual learning necessary for correct interpretation of pictures? If so, which aspects of picture perception are most affected by learning and experience?
9. Describe some aspects of speech perception that are influenced by learning and experience. Give some examples of the "misinterpretations" or "mispronunciations" that might result from experiential effects.
10. Define "perceptual set" and give some examples of how it affects everyday interpretation of our world.

REFERENCES

Aaron, M. (1975). Effect of the menstrual cycle on subjective ratings of sweetness. *Perceptual and Motor Skills,* 40, 974.

Abraham, H. D., & Wolf, E. (1988). Visual function in past users of LSD: Psychophysical findings. *Journal of Abnormal Psychology,* 97, 443–447.

Adam, N., Rosner, B. S., Hosick, E. C., & Clark, D. L. (1971). Effect of anesthetic drugs on time production and alpha rhythm. *Perception & Psychophysics,* 10, 133–136.

Adams, A. S., Brown, B., Haegerstrom-Portnoy, G., & Flom, M. C. (1976). Evidence for acute effect of alcohol and marijuana on color discrimination. *Perception & Psychophysics,* 20, 119–124.

Adams, C. L., & Molfese, D. L. (1987). Electrophysiological correlates of categorical speech perception for voicing contrasts in dogs. *Developmental Neuropsychology,* 3, 175–189.

Adams, D. L., & Zeki, S. (2001). Functional organization of macaque V3 for stereoscopic depth. *Journal of Neurophysiology,* 86, 2195–2203.

Adams, D. L., & Zeki, S. (2001). Functional organization of macaque V3 for stereoscopic depth. *Journal of Neurophysiology,* 86, 2195–2203.

Adams, R. D. (1977). Intervening stimulus effects on category judgments of duration. *Perception & Psychophysics,* 21, 527–534.

Adams, R. J. (1995). Further exploration of human neonatal chromatic achromatic discrimination. *Journal of Experimental Child Psychology,* 60, 344–360.

Adams, R. J., & Courage, M. L. (1994). Systematic measurement of human neonatal color vision. *Vision Research,* 34, 1691–1701.

Aglioti, S. DeSouza, J. F. X., & Goodale, M. A. (1995). Size contrast illusions deceive the eye but not the hand. *Current Biology,* 5, 679–685.

Agostini, T., & Proffitt, D. R. (1993). Perceptual organization evokes simultaneous lightness contrast. *Perception,* 22, 263–272.

Aitkin, L., & Martin, R. (1990). Neurons in the inferior colliculus of cats sensitive to sound-source elevation. *Hearing Research,* 50, 97–106.

Akhtar, N., & Enns, J. T. (1989). Relations between covert orienting and filtering in the development of visual attention. *Journal of Experimental Child Psychology,* 48, 315–334.

Akil, H., & Watson S. J. (1980). The role of endogenous opiates in pain control. In H. W. Kosterlitz & L. Y. Terenius (Eds.), *Pain and Society* (pp. 201–222). Weinheim: Verlag Chemie Gmblt.

Alain, C., Arnott, S. R., & Picton, T. W. (2001). Bottom-up and top-down influences on auditory scene analysis: Evidence from event-related brain potentials. *Journal of Experimental Psychology: Human Perception and Performance,* 27, 1072–1089.

Alain, C., Arnott, S. R., Hevenor, S., Graham, S., & Grady, C. L. (2001). "What" and "where" in the human auditory system. *Proceedings of the National Academy of Science (USA),* 98, 12301–12306.

Alais, D., Blake, R., & Lee, S.-H. (1998). Features that vary together over time group together over space. *Nature Neuroscience,* 1, 160–164.

Albert, M. K. (2001). Surface perception and the generic view principle. *Trends in Cognitive Sciences,* 5(5), 197–203.

Albert, M. K., & Tse, P. (2000). The role of surface attachment in perceived volumetric shape. *Perception,* 29, 409–420.

Albright T. D., & Stoner G. R. (2002). Contextual influences on visual processing. *Annual Review of Neuroscience,* 25, 339–379.

Alexander, J. B., & Gudeman, H. E. (1965). Personal and interpersonal measures of field dependence. *Perceptual and Motor Skills,* 20, 70–86.

Algom, D., & Marks, L. E. (1990). Range and regression, loudness scales, and loudness processing: Toward a context-bound psychophysics. *Journal of Experimental Psychology: Human Perception and Performance,* 16, 706–727.

Algom, D., Ben-Aharon, B., & Cohen-Raz, L. (1989). Dichotic, diotic, and monaural summation of loudness: A comprehensive analysis of composition and psychophysical functions. *Perception & Psychophysics,* 46, 567–578.

Algom, D., Raphaeli, N., & Cohen-Raz, L. (1986). Integration of noxious stimulation across separate somatosensory communications systems: A functional theory of pain. *Journal of Experimental Psychology: Human Perception and Performance,* 12, 92–102.

Algom, D., Rubin, A., & Cohen-Raz, L. (1989). Binaural and temporal integration of the loudness of tones and noises. *Perception & Psychophysics,* 46, 155–166.

Alho, K., Teraniemi, M., Huotilainen, M., Lavikainen, J., Tiitinen, H., Ilmoniemi, R. J., Knuutila, J., & Näätänen, R. (1996). Processing of complex sounds in the human auditory cortex as revealed by magnetic brain responses. *Psychophysiology,* 33, 369–375.

Ali, M. R., & Amir, T. (1989). Effects of fasting on visual flicker fusion. *Perceptual and Motor Skills,* 69, 627–631.

Alkire, M. T., Haier, R. J., & Fallon, J. H. (2000). Toward a unified theory of narcosis: Brain imaging evidence for a thalamocortical switch as the neurophysiologic basis of anesthetic-induced unconsciousness. *Consciousness and Cognition,* 9, 370–386.

Allan, L. G., & Siegel, S. (1986). McCollough effects as conditioned responses: Reply to Skowbo. *Psychological Bulletin,* 100, 388–393.

Allen, J. R. (1985). Salicylate-induced musical perceptions. *New England Journal of Medicine,* 313, 642–643.

Allen, M. (1970). *Vision and Highway Safety.* Radnor, PA: Chilton Books.

Allison, A. C. (1953). The structure of the olfactory bulb and its relation to the olfactory pathways in the rabbit and the rat. *Journal of Comparative Neurology,* 98, 309–348.

Alpern, M. (1979). Lack of uniformity in color matching. *Journal of Physiology,* 288, 85–105.

Amanzio, M., Pollo, A., Maggi, G., & Benedetti, F. (2001). Response variability to analgesics: a role for non-specific activation of endogenous opioids. *Pain,* 90, 205–215.

Ames, A. Jr. (1951). Visual perception and the rotating trapezoid window. *Psychological Monographs,* 65 (14, Whole No. 324).

Ames, A. Jr. (1955). *The nature of our Perception, Apprehensions and Behavior.* Princeton, NJ: Princeton University Press.

Amoore, J. E. (1970). *Molecular Basis of Odor.* Springfield, IL: Thomas.

Amoore, J. E. (1975). Four primary odor modalities of man: Experimental evidence and possible significance. In D. A. Denton & J. P. Coghlan (Eds.), *Olfaction and Taste V* (pp. 283–289). New York: Academic Press.

Amoore, J. E., Pelosi, P., & Forrester, L. J. (1977). Specific anosmias to 5a-androst-16en-3one and w-penta-decalone: The urinous and musky odors. *Chemical Senses and Flavor,* 5, 401–425.

Amure, B. O. (1978). Nicotine and decay of the McCollough effect. *Vision Research,* 18, 1449–1451.

Andersen, G. J., & Braunstein, M. L. (1985). Induced self-motion in central vision. *Journal of Experimental Psychology: Human Perception and Performance,* 11, 122–132.

Anderson, N. H. (1975). On the role of context effects in psychophysical judgment. *Psychological Review,* 82, 462–482.

Anderson, N. H. (1992). Integration psychophysics and cognition. In D. Algom (Ed.), *Psychophysical Approaches to Cognition* (pp. 13–113). New York: North Holland.

Anderson, N. S., & Fitts, P. M. (1958). Amount of information gained during brief exposures of numerals and colors. *Journal of Experimental Psychology,* 56, 362–369.

Andreasen, N. C. (1988). Brain imaging: Applications in psychiatry. *Science,* 239, 1381–1388.

Annis, R. C., & Frost, B. (1973). Human visual ecology and orientation anisotropies in acuity. *Science,* 182, 729–731.

Anstis, S. M. (1975). What does visual perception tell us about visual coding? In M. S. Gazzaniga & C. Blakemore (Eds.), *Handbook of Psychobiology* (pp. 267–234). New York: Academic Press.

Anstis, S. M. (1978). Apparent movement. In R. Held, H. W. Leibowitz, & H. L. Teuber (Eds.), *Handbook of Sensory Physiology* (pp. 655–673). New York: Springer-Verlag.

Anstis, S. M., & Mather, G. (1985). Effects of luminance and contrast on direction of ambiguous motion. *Perception,* 14, 167–179.

Arend, L. E. (1993). Mesopic lightness, brightness and brightness contrast. *Perception & Psychophysics,* 54, 469–476.

Arend, L. E., & Spehar, B. (1993). Lightness, brightness and brightness contrast: 2. Reflectance variation. *Perception & Psychophysics,* 54, 457–468.

Arlin, M. (1986). The effects of quantity, complexity, and attentional demand on children's time perception. *Perception & Psychophysics,* 40, 177–182.

Artal, P., Berrio, E., Guirao, A., & Piers, P. (2002). Contribution of the cornea and internal surfaces to the change of ocular aberrations with age. *Journal of the Optical Society of America A,* 19, 137–143

Arterberry, M. (2001). Perceptual unit formation in infancy. In T. F. Shipley, & P. J. Kellman, (Eds.), *From Fragments to Objects: Segmentation and Grouping in Vision* (pp. 37–70). Amsterdam: Elsevier.

Arterberry, M., & Yonas, A. (1989). Self-produced locomotion and the development of responsiveness to linear perspective and texture gradients. *Developmental Psychology,* 25, 976–982.

Asano, F., Suzuki, Y., & Sone, T. (1990). Role of spectral cues in median plane localization. *Journal of the Acoustical Society of America,* 88, 159–168.

Aschersleben, G., Bachmann, T., & Muesseler, J (1999). Cognitive contributions to the perception of spatial and temporal events. Adv*ances in Psychology, 129.* Amsterdam, Netherlands: North-Holland/Elsevier Science Publishers.

Aschoff, J. (1979). Circadian rhythms: General features and endocrinological aspects. In D. T. Krieger (Ed.), *Endocrine Rhythms* (pp. 1–61). New York: Raven Press.

Aschoff, J. (1981). *Handbook of Behavioral Neurobiology,* Vol. 4. New York: Plenum Press.

Aschoff, J. (1984). Circadian timing. *Annals of the New York Academy of Sciences,* 423, 442–468.

Ashmead, D. H., Davis, D. L., & Northington, A. (1995). Contributions of listeners' approaching motion to auditory distance perception. *Journal of Experimental Psychology: Human Perception and Performance,* 21, 239–256.

Aslin, R. N. (1981a). Development of smooth pursuit in human infants. In D. Fisher, R. Monty, & J. Senders (Eds.), *Eye Movements: Cognition and Visual Perception* (pp. 31–52). Hillsdale, NJ: Erlbaum.

Aslin, R. N. (1981b). Experiential influences and sensitive periods in perceptual development: A unified model. In R. N. Aslin, J. R. Alberts, & M. R. Peterson (Eds.), *Development of Perception* (pp. 45–93). New York: Academic Press.

Aslin, R. N. (1985). Effects of experience on sensory and perceptual development: Implications for infant cognition. In J. Mehler & R. Fox (Eds.), *Neonate Cognition: Beyond the Blooming Buzzing Confusion* (pp. 157–184). Hillsdale, NJ: Erlbaum.

Aslin, R. N., & Dumais, S. (1980). Binocular vision in infants: A review and a theoretical framework. In H. Reese & L. Lipsett (Eds.), *Advances in Child Development and Behavior,* Vol. 15 (pp. 54–95). New York: Academic Press.

Aslin, R. N., & Smith, L. B. (1988). Perceptual development. *Annual Review of Psychology,* 39, 435–473.

ASVA 97. (1997). Proceedings of the International Symposium on Simulation, Visualization and Auralization for Acoustic Research and Education. Tokyo: Acoustical Society of Japan.

Atkinson, J. (2000). *The Developing Visual Brain.* New York: Oxford University Press.

Atkinson, J., Hood, B., Braddick, O. J., & Wattam-Bell, J. (1988). Infants' control of fixation shifts with single and competing targets: Mechanisms for shifting attention. *Perception,* 17, 367–368.

Atkinson, J., Hood, B., Wattam-Bell, J., & Braddick, O. (1992). Changes in infants' ability to switch visual attention in the first three months of life. *Perception,* 21, 643–653.

Attneave, F. (1954). Some informational aspects of visual perception. *Psychological Review,* 61, 183–193.

Attneave, F. (1955). Symmetry, information and memory for patterns. *American Journal of Psychology,* 68, 209–222.

Attneave, F. (1974). Multistability in perception. *Scientific American,* 225, 63–71.

Attwood, C. I., Harris, J. P., & Sullivan, G. D. (2001). Learning to search for visual targets defined by edges or by shading: Evidence for nonequivalence of line drawings and surface representations. *Visual Cognition,* 8, 751–767.

Atzori, M., Lei, S., Evans, D. I. P., Kanold, P. O., Phillips-Tansey, E., McIntyre, O., & McBain, C. J. (2001). Differential synaptic processing separates stationary from transient inputs to the auditory cortex. *Nature Neuroscience,* 4, 1230–1237.

Aubert, H. (1886). Die Bewegungsempfindung. *Archiv fuer die Gesamte Physiologie des Menschen and der Tiere,* 39, 347–370.

Augenstine, L. G. (1962). A model of how humans process information. *Biometrics,* 18, 420–421.

Avant, L. L. (1965). Vision in the Ganzfeld. *Psychological Bulletin,* 64, 246–258.

Avant, L. L., & Lyman, P. J. (1975). Stimulus familiarity modifies perceived duration in prerecognition visual processing. *Journal of Experimental Psychology: Human Perception and Performance,* 1, 205–213.

Avant, L. L., Lyman, P. J., & Antes, J. R. (1975). Effects of stimulus familiarity upon judged visual duration. *Perception & Psychophysics,* 17, 253–262.

Avolio, B., Kroeck, K., & Panek, P. (1986). Individual differences in information processing ability as a predictor of motor vehicle accidents. *Human Factors,* 27, 577–588.

Baars, B. J. (1997). In the theatre of consciousness: Global workspace theory, a rigorous scientific theory of consciousness. *Journal of Consciousness Studies,* 4, 292–309.

Bachman, T., & Allik, J. (1976). Integration and interruption in the masking of form by form. *Perception,* 5, 79–97.

Backus, B. T., Fleet, D. J., Parker, A.J., & Heeger, D.J. (2001). Human cortical activity correlates with stereoscopic depth perception. *Journal of Neurophysiology,* 86, 2054–2068.

Baddeley, A. D. (1966). Time estimation at reduced body temperature. *American Journal of Psychology,* 79, 475–479.

Baird, J. C. (1975). Psychophysical study of numbers: IV. Generalized preferred state theory. *Psychological Research,* 38, 175–187.

Baird, J. C., Green, D. M., & Luce, R. D. (1980). Variability and sequential effect in cross modality matching of area and loudness. *Journal of Experimental Psychology: Human Perception and Psychophysics,* 6, 277–289.

Bakalyar, H. A., & Reed, R. R. (1990). Identification of specialized adenylyl cyclase that may mediate odorant detection. *Science,* 250, 1403–1406.

Balint, R. (1909). Seelenlahmung des "Schauens," optische Ataxie, raumliche Storung der Aufmerksamkeit. Monatsschr. *Psychiatric Neurology,* 25, 51–81.

Ball, K. K., Roenker, D. L., & Bruni, J. R. (1990). Developmental changes in attention and visual search throughout adulthood. In J. T. Enns (Ed.), *The Development of Attention: Research and Theory* (pp. 489–508). Amsterdam: Elsevier.

Ballard, D. H., Hinton, G. E., & Sejnowski, T. J. (1983). Parallel visual computation. *Nature,* 306, 21–26.

Ballas, J. A. (1993). Common factors in the identification of an assortment of brief everyday sounds. *Journal of Experimental Psychology: Human Perception and Performance,* 19, 250–267.

Balogh, R. D., & Porter, R. H. (1986). Olfactory preferences resulting from mere exposure in human neonates. *Infant Behavior and Development,* 9, 395–401.

Baltes, P. B., & Lindenberger, U. (1997). Emergence of a powerful connection between sensory and cognitive functions across the adult life span: A new window to the study of cognitive aging? *Psychology and Aging,* 12, 12–21.

Banks, M. S., & Ehrlich, S. M. (1996). Estimating heading during real and simulated eye movements. *Vision Research,* 36, 431–443.

Barac-Cikoja, D., & Turvey, M. T. (1993). Haptically perceiving size at a distance. *Journal of Experimental Psychology: General,* 122, 331–346.

Barac-Cikoja, D., & Turvey, M. T. (1995). Does perceived size depend on perceived distance? An argument from extended haptic perception. *Perception & Psychophysics,* 57, 216–224.

Barbeito, R. (1981). Sighting dominance: An explanation based on the processing of visual direction in tests of sighting dominance. *Vision Research,* 21, 855–860.

Barbet I & Fagot J. (2002). Perception of the corridor illusion by baboons (Papio papio). *Behavior and Brain Research,* 132, 111–115.

Barkley, R. A, Murphy, K. R., & Bush, T. (2001). Time perception and reproduction in young adults with attention deficit hyperactivity disorder. *Neuropsychology,* 15. 351–360.

Barlow, H. B. (1985). The role of single neurons in the psychology of perception. *Quarterly Journal of Experimental Psychology,* 37A, 121–145.

Barrick, C. B., Taylor, D., & Correa, E. I. (2002). Color sensitivity and mood disorders: Biology or metaphor? *Journal of Affective Disorders,* 68, 67–71.

Bartels, A., & Zeki, S. (2002). The architecture of the color center in the human visual brain: New results and a review. *European Journal of Neuroscience,* 12, 172–193.

Bartoshuk, L. M. (1978). Gustatory system. In R. B. Masterton (Ed.), *Handbook of Behavioral Neurobiology,* Vol. I: *Sensory Integration* (pp. 503–567). New York: Plenum Press.

Bartoshuk, L. M. (1974). Taste illusions: Some demonstrations. *Annals of the New York Academy of Sciences,* 237, 279–285.

Bartoshuk, L. M. (1988). Clinical psychophysics of taste. *Gerodontics,* 4, 249–255.

Bartoshuk, L. M. (1990). Distinctions between taste and smell relevant to the role of experience. In E. Capaldi & T. L. Powley (Eds.), *Taste, Experience, and Feeding* (pp. 62–72). Washington, DC: American Psychological Association.

Bartoshuk, L. M. (1993). Genetic and pathological taste variation: What can we learn from animal models and human disease? In D. Chadwick, J. Marsh, & J. Goode (Eds.), *The Molecular Basis of Smell and Taste Transduction* (pp. 251–267). New York: Wiley.

Bartoshuk, L. M., Rifkin, B., Marks, L. E., & Hooper, J. E. (1988). Bitterness of KCl and benzoate: Related to genetic status for sensitivity to PTC/PROP. *Chemical Senses,* 13, 517–528.

Bashford, J. A., Warren, R. M., & Brown, C. A. (1996). Use of speech-modulated noise adds strong "bottom-up" cues for phonemic restoration. *Perception & Psychophysics,* 58, 342–350.

Basnyat, B., & Litch, J. A. (1997). Medical problems of porters and trekkers in the Nepal Himalaya. *Wilderness and Environmental Medicine,* 8, 78–81.

Bates, M. E. (1989). The effect of repeated occasions of alcohol intoxication on two processes involved in the visual discrimination of movement. *Journal of Studies on Alcohol,* 50, 143–154.

Batteau, D. W. (1967). The role of the pinna in human localization. *Proceedings of the Royal Society of London, Series B,* 168, 158–180.

Baumgat, F., Gaschler-Markefski, B., Woldorff, M., Heinz, H-J., & Scheich, H. (1999). A movement-sensitive area in auditory cortex. *Nature,* 400, 724–726.

Baylis, G. C. & Driver, J. (1995). One-sided edge-assignment in vision: 1. Figure-ground segmentation and attention to objects. *Current Directions in Psychological Science,* 4, 201–206.

Baylis, G. C., & Cale, E. M. (2001). The figure has a shape, but the ground does not: Evidence from a planning paradigm. *Journal of Experimental Psychology: Human Perception and Performance,* 27, 633–643

Baylis, G. C., & Driver, J. (2001). Perception of symmetry and repetition within and across visual shapes: Part descriptions and object based attention. *Visual Cognition,* 8, 163–196.

Beauchamp, G. K., & Cowart, B. J. (1985). Congenital and experiential factors in the development of human flavor preferences. *Appetite,* 6, 357–372.

Beaver, C. J., Ji, Q., & Daw, N. W. (2001). Layer differences in the effect of monocular vision in light- and dark-reared kittens. *Visual Neuroscience,* 18, 811–820

Beck, D. M., Rees, G., Frith, C. D., & Lavie, N. (2001). Neural correlates of change detection and change blindness. *Nature Neuroscience,* 4, 645–650.

Beck, J., & Rosenfeld, A. (1989). Line segregation. *Spatial Vision,* 4, 75–101.

Beck, J., & Schwartz, T. (1979). Vernier acuity with dot test objects. *Vision Research,* 19, 313–319.

Beck, N. C., & Siegel, L. J. (1980). Preparation for childbirth and contemporary research on pain, anxiety, and stress reduction: A review and critique. *Psychosomatic Medicine,* 42, 429–447.

Becker, W., & Saglam, H. (2001). Perception of angular head position during attempted alignment with eccentric visual objects. *Experimental Brain Research,* 138, 185–192.

Beckett, P. A. (1989). Illusion decrement and transfer of illusion decrement in real- and subjective-contour Poggendorff figures. *Perception & Psychophysics,* 45, 550–556.

Beer, J., Beer, J., Markley, R. P., & Camp, C. J. (1989). Age and living conditions as related to perceptions of ambiguous figures. *Psychological Reports,* 64, 1027–1033.

Begeson, T. R., & Trehub, S. E. (2002). Absolute pitch and tempo in mothers' songs to infants. *Psychological Science,* 13, 72–75.

Begleiter, H., Porjesz, B., & Chou, C. L. (1981). Auditory brain-stem potentials in chronic alcoholics. *Science,* 211, 1064–1066.

Beidler, L. M., & Smallman, R. L. (1965). Renewal of cells within taste buds. *Journal of Cell Biology,* 27, 263–272.

Bekesy, G. von. (1947). A new audiometer. *Acta otolaryngologica,* 35, 411–422.

Bekesy, G. von. (1959). Synchronism of neural discharges and their demultiplication in pitch perception on the skin and in learning. *Journal of the Acoustical Society of America,* 31, 338–349.

Bekesy, G. von. (1960). *Experiments in Hearing.* New York: McGraw-Hill.

Bekesy, G. von. (1967). *Sensory Inhibition.* Princeton, NJ: Princeton University Press.

Belin, P., Zatorre, R.J., Lafaille, P., Ahad, P., & Pike, B. (2000). Voice selective areas in human auditory cortex. *Nature,* 403, 309–312.

Belliveau, J. W., Kennedy, D. N., McKinstry, R. C., Buchbinder, R. R., Weisskopff, R. M., Cohen, M. S., Vevea, J. M., Brady, T. J., & Rosen, B. R. (1991). Functional mapping of the human visual cortex by magnetic resonance imaging. *Science,* 254, 716–719.

Belluscio, L., Lodovichi, C., Feinstein, P., Mombaerts, P., & Katz, L. C. (2002). Odorant receptors instruct functional circuitry in the mouse olfactory bulb. *Nature,* 419, 296–300.

Bem, S. L. (1981). Gender schema theory: A cognitive account of sex typing. *Psychological Review,* 88, 354–364.

Bende, M., & Nordin, S. (1997). Perceptual learning in olfaction: Professional wine tasters versus controls. *Physiology & Behavior,* 62, 1065–1070.

Benedetti, F. (1985). Processing of tactile spatial information with crossed fingers. *Journal of Experimental Psychology: Human Perception and Performance,* 11, 517–525.

Bennett, P. J., Sekuler, A. B., McIntosh, A. R., Della-Maggiore, V. (2001). The effects of aging on visual memory: evidence for functional reorganization of cortical networks. *Acta Psychologica,* 107, 249–273.

Bennett, T. L., & Morgan, R. J. (1978). Temporary threshold shifts in auditory sensitivity produced by the combined effects of noise and sodium salicylate. *Bulletin of the Psychonomic Society,* 12, 95–98.

Bentham, J. van (1985). Semantics of time. In J. A. Michon & J. L. Jackson (Eds.), *Time, Mind and Behavior* (pp. 266–278). Berlin: Springer-Verlag.

Berbaum, K., & Lenel, J. C. (1983). Objects in the path of apparent motion. *American Journal of Psychology,* 96, 491–501.

Berbaum, K., Bever, T., & Chung, C. S. (1983). Light source position in the perception of object shape. *Perception,* 12, 411–416.

Berg, B. G., & Green, D. M. (1990). Spectral weights in profile listening. *Journal of the Acoustical Society of America,* 88, 758–766.

Bergeijk, W. A. van. (1967). The evolution of vertebrate hearing. In W. D. Neff (Ed.), *Contributions to Sensory Physiology,* Vol. 2 (pp. 1–49). New York: Academic Press.

Berger, G. O. (1896). Uber den Einfluss der Reizstarke auf die Dauer einfacher psychischer Vorgange mit besonderer Rucksicht auf Lichtreize. *Philosophische Studien* (Wundt), 3, 38–93.

Berglund, B., Hogman, L., & Johansson, I. (1988). *Reliability of Odor Measurements Near Threshold. Reports from the Department of Psychology.* Stockholm: The University of Stockholm.

Berglund, M. B. (1991). Quality assurance in environmental psychophysics. In S. J. Bolanowski & G. A. Gescheider (Eds.), *Ratio Scaling of Psychological Magnitude* (pp. 140–162). Hillsdale, NJ: Erlbaum.

Berkley, M. A. (1982). Neural substrates of the visual perception of movement. In A. H. Wertheim, W. A. Wagenaar, & H. W. Leibowitz (Eds.), *Tutorials on Motion Perception* (pp. 201–229). New York: Plenum Press.

Berman, E. R. (1991). *Biochemistry of the Eye.* New York: Plenum Press.

Berman, K. F., Zec, R. F., & Weinberger, D. R. (1986). Physiologic dysfunction of dorsolateral prefrontal cortex in schizophrenia: II. Role of neuroleptic treatment, attention and mental effort. *Archives of General Psychiatry,* 43, 126–135.

Berndt, R. S., & Mitchum, C. C. (1997). Lexical-semantic organization: Evidence from aphasia. *Clinical Neuroscience,* 4, 57–63.

Bernstein, I. H., Bissonnette, V., Vyas, A., & Barclay, P. (1989). Semantic priming: Subliminal perception or context. *Perception & Psychophysics,* 45, 153–161.

Besser, G. (1966). Centrally acting drugs and auditory flutter. In A. Herxheimer (Ed.), *Proceedings of the Symposium on Drugs and Sensory Functions* (pp. 199–200). London: SS Churchill, Ltd.

Besson, M., & Faita, F. (1995). An event-related potential (ERP) study of musical expectancy: Comparison of musicians with nonmusicians. *Journal of Experimental Psychology: Human Perception and Performance,* 21, 1278–1296.

Best, C. T. (1994). The emergence of language-specific phonemic influences in infant speech perception. In J. Goodman & H. C. Nusbaum (Eds.), *Speech Perception and Word Recognition.* (pp. 167–224). Cambridge, MA: MIT Press.

Betke, K. (1991). New hearing threshold measurements for pure tones under free-field listening conditions. *Journal of the Acoustical Society of America,* 89, 2400–2403.

Bharucha, J. J. (1996). Melodic anchoring. *Music Perception,* 13, 383–400.

Bhatia, B. (1975). Minimum separable as function of speed of a moving object. *Vision Research,* 15, 23–33.

Bhatt R. S., & Bertin, E. (2001). Pictorial cues and three-dimensional information processing in early infancy. *Journal of Experimental Child Psychology,* 80, 315–332.

Biederman, I., & Shiffrar, M. M. (1987). Sexing dayold chicks: a case study and expert systems analysis of a difficult perceptual-learning task. *Journal of Experimental Psychology: Learning, Memory & Cognition,* 13, 640–645.

Biederman, I. (1987). Recognition-by-components: A theory of human image understanding. *Psychological Review,* 94, 115–147.

Biederman, I., Glass, A. L., & Stacey, E. W. Jr. (1973). Searching for objects in real-world scenes. *Journal of Experimental Psychology,* 97, 22–27.

Bigand, E. (1997). Perceiving musical stability: The effect of tonal structure, rhythm, and musical expertise. *Journal of Experimental Psychology: Human Perception and Performance,* 23, 808–822.

Bigand, E., Parncutt, R., & Lerdahl, F. (1996). Perception of musical tension in short chord sequences: The influence of harmonic function, sensory dissonance, horizontal motion, and musical training. *Perception & Psychophysics,* 58, 125–141.

Billings, B. L., & Stokinger, T. E. (1977). Investigation of several aspects of low-frequency (200 Hz). central masking. *Journal of the Acoustical Society of America,* 61, 1260–1263.

Binns, K. E., & Salt, T. E. (1997). Post eye-opening maturation of visual receptive field diameters in the superior colliculus of normal- and dark-reared rats. *Brain Research: Developmental Brain Research,* 99, 263–266.

Birch, E. E., Shimojo, S., & Held, R. (1985). Preferential-looking assessment of fusion and stereopsis in infants aged 1–6 months. *Investigative Ophthalmology and Visual Science,* 26, 366–370.

Birch, E. E., Fawcett, S., & Stager, D. R. (2000). Why does early surgical alignment improve stereoacuity outcomes in infantile esotropia? *Journal of Aapos: American Association for Pediatric Ophthalmology & Strabismus,* 4, 10–14.

Birren, J. E., Casperson, R. C., & Botwinick, J. (1950). Age changes in pupil size. *Journal of Gerontology,* 5, 267–271.

Birren, J. E., & Schaie, E. W. (2001). *Handbook of the Psychology of Aging.* (5th ed). San Diego: Academic Press.

Bishop, P .O. (1981). Binocular vision. In R. A. Moses (Ed.), *Adler's Physiology of the Eye: Clinical Applications* (7th ed.). (pp. 575–649). St. Louis, MO: Mosby.

Bishop, P. O., & Pettigrew, J. D. (1986). Neural mechanisms of binocular vision. *Vision Research,* 26, 1587–1600.

Blake, R. (1989). A neural theory of binocular rivalry. *Psychological Review,* 96, 145–167.

Blake, R., Fox, R., & McIntyre, C. (1971). Stochastic properties of stabilized-image binocular rivalry alternations. *Journal of Experimental Psychology,* 88, 327–332.

Blakemore, C., & Nachmias, J. (1971). Orientation specificity on two visual aftereffects. *Journal of Physiology,* 171, 286–288.

Blakeslee, A. F., & Salmon, T. H. (1935). Genetics of sensory thresholds: Individual taste reactions for different substances. *Proceedings of the National Academy of Sciences of the U.S.A.,* 21, 84–90.

Blasdel, G. G., Mitchell, D. E., Muir, D. W., & Pettigrew, J. D. (1977). A combined physiological and behavioral study of the effect of early visual experience with contours of a single orientation. *Journal of Physiology,* 265, 615–636.

Blazynski, C., & Ostroy, S. E. (1981). Dual pathways in the photolysis of rhodopsin: Studies using a direct chemical method. *Vision Research,* 21, 833–841.

Bleeker, M. L., & Bolla-Wilson, K. (1987). Simple visual reaction time: Sex and age differences. *Developmental Neuropsychology,* 3, 165–172.

Bliss, J. C., Katcher, M. H., Rogers, C. H., & Shepard, R. P. (1970). Optical-to-tactile image conversion for the blind. *IEEE Transactions on ManMachine Systems,* 11, 58–65.

Block, N. (1995). On a confusion about a function of consciousness. *Behavioral and Brain Science,* 18, 227–287.

Block, R. A. (1974). Memory and the experience of duration in retrospect. *Memory and Cognition,* 2, 153–160.

Block, R. A. (1978). Remembered duration: Effects of event and sequence complexity. *Memory and Cognition,* 6, 320–326.

Block, R. A., George, E. J., & Reed, M. A. (1980). A watched pot sometimes boils: A study of duration experience. *Acta Psychologica,* 46, 81–94.

Bloom, K. (1990). Selectivity and early infant vocalization. In J. T. Enns (Ed.), *The Development of Attention: Research and Theory* (pp. 121–136). Amsterdam: Elsevier.

Blough, P. M., & Slavin, K. (1987). Reaction time assessments of gender differences in visual-spatial performance. *Perception & Psychophysics,* 41, 276–281.

Bolton, T. L. (1894). Rhythm. *American Journal of Psychology,* 6, 145–238.

Bonneh, Y., Sagi, D., & Karni, A. (2001). A transition between eye and object rivalry determined by stimulus coherence. *Vision Research,* 41, 981–989.

Bonnel, A.-M., & Hafter, E. R. (1998). Divided attention between simultaneous auditory and visual signals. *Perception & Psychophysics,* 60, 179–190.

Bonnel, A.-M., & Prinzmetal, W. (1998). Dividing attention between the color and the shape of objects. *Perception & Psychophysics,* 60, 113–124.

Bonnet, C. (1984). Discrimination of velocities and mechanisms of motion perception. *Perception,* 13, 275–282.

Bootsma, R. J., & Oudejans, R. (1993). Visual information about time to collision between two objects. *Journal of Experimental Psychology: Human Perception and Performance,* 19, 1041–1052.

Borg, G. A. V. (1982). Psychophysical bases of perceived exertion. *Medicine and Science in Sports and Exercise,* 14, 377–381.

Borg, G., Diamant, H., Oakley, B., Strom, L., & Zotterman, Y. (1967). A comparative study of neural and psychophysical responses to gustatory stimuli. In T. Hayashi (Ed.), *Olfaction and Taste II* (pp. 253–264). Oxford: Pergamon Press.

Bornstein, M. H., Kessen, W., & Weiskopf, S. (1976). Color vision and hue categorization in young human infants. *Journal of Experimental Psychology: Human Perception and Performance,* 2,115–129.

Bosch, L., & Sebastian-Galles, N. (2001). Early language differentiation in bilingual infants. In J. Cenoz, & F. Genesee (Eds.), *Trends in Bilingual Acquisition. Trends in Language Acquisition Research,* Vol. 1. (pp. 71–93). Amsterdam: John Benjamins Publishing Company.

Botstein, D. (1986). The molecular biology of color vision. *Science,* 232, 142–143.

Bouma, H. (1970). Interaction effects in parafoveal letter recognition. *Nature,* 226, 177–178.

Bowmaker, J. K., & Dartnall, H. J. A. (1980). Visual pigments of rods and cones in a human retina. *Journal of Physiology,* 298, 501–511.

Boycott, B. B., & Waessle, H. (1974). The morphological types of ganglion cells of the domestic cat's retina. *Journal of Physiology,* 240, 397–419.

Boynton, R. M. (1971). Color vision. In J. W. King & L. A. Riggs (Eds.), *Woodworth and Schlossberg's Experimental Psychology* (3rd ed.; pp. 315–368). New York: Holt, Rinehart and Winston.

Boynton, R. M. (1979). *Human Color Vision.* New York: Holt, Rinehart and Winston.

Boynton, R. M., & Gordon, J. (1965). Bezold-Brucke hue shift measured by color-naming technique. *Journal of the Optical Society of America,* 55, 78–86.

Brabyn, L. B., & McGuinness, D. (1979). Gender differences in response to spatial frequency and stimulus orientation. *Perception & Psychophysics,* 26, 319–324.

Braddick, O. (1974). A short-range process in apparent motion. *Vision Research,* 14, 519–527.

Braddick, O. J. (1980). Low-level and high-level processes in apparent motion. *Philosophical Transactions of the Royal Society of London, Series B,* 290, 137–151.

Bradshaw, M. F., Parton, A. D., & Glennerster, A. (2000). The task dependent use of binocular disparity and motion parallax information. *Vision Research,* 40, 3725–3734.

Braff, D. L., Silverton, L., Saccuzzo, D. P., & Janowsky, D. S. (1981). Impaired speed of visual information processing in marihuana intoxication. *American Journal of Psychiatry,* 138(5), 613–617.

Brainard, D. H., Wandell, B. A., & Chichilnisky, E. (1993). Color constancy: From physics to appearance. *Current Directions in Psychological Science,* 2, 365–370.

Braine L. G., Plastow, E., & Greene, S. I. (1987). Judgments of shape orientation: A matter of contrasts. *Perception & Psychophysics,* 41, 335–344.

Branka, S. (2002). The role of contrast polarity in perceptual closure. *Vision Research,* 42, 343–350.

Brass, D., & Kemp, D. T. (1993). Suppression of stimulus frequency otoacoustic emissions. *Journal of the Acoustical Society of America,* 93, 920–939.

Braunstein, M. L., & Liter, J. C. (1993). Recovering three-dimensional shape from perspective translations and orthographic rotations. *Journal of Experimental Psychology: Human Perception and Performance,* 19, 598–614.

Bregman, A. S. (1978). Auditory streaming: Competition among alternative organizations. *Perception & Psychophysics,* 23, 391–398.

Bregman, A. S. (1981). Asking the "What for?" question in auditory perception. In M. Kubovy & J. R. Pometrantz (Eds.), *Perceptual Organization* (pp. 99–118). Hillsdale, NJ: Erlbaum.

Bregman, A. S. (1990). *Auditory Scene Analysis.* Cambridge, MA: Bradford/MIT Press.

Bregman, A. S., & Ahad, P.A. (1996). *Demonstrations of Auditory Scene Analysis: The Perceptual Organization of Sound.* Compact disk distributed by MIT Press, Cambridge, MA.

Breitmeyer, B. G. (1984). *Visual Masking: An Integrative Approach.* New York: Oxford University Press.

Breitmeyer, B. G. (1989). A visually based deficit in specific reading disability. *Irish Journal of Psychology,* 10, 534–541.

Breitmeyer, B. G., & Ogmen, H. (2000). Recent models and findings in visual backward masking: A comparison, review, and update. *Perception and Psychophysics,* 62, 1572–1595.

Brennan, P., Kaba, H., & Keverne, E. B. (1990). Olfactory recognition: A simple memory system. *Science,* 250, 1223–1226.

Brenner, E., & Cornelissen F. W. (2000). Separate simultaneous processing of egocentric and relative positions. *Vision Research,* 40, 2557–2563.

Brenner, E., & Cornelissen F. W. (2002). The influence of chromatic and achromatic variability on chromatic induction and perceived colour. *Perception,* 31, 225–232.

Brenowitz, E. A. (1991). Altered perceptions of species-specific song by female birds after lesions of a forebrain nucleus. *Science,* 251, 303–305.

Breslin, P. A. S., Beauchamp, G. K., & Pugh, A. N. Jr. (1996). Monogeusia for fructose, glucose, sucrose and maltose. *Perception & Psychophysics,* 58, 327–341.

Brewer, N., Keast, A., & Rishworth, A. (2002). The confidence accuracy relationship in eyewitness identification: The effects of reflection and disconfirmation on correlation and calibration. *Journal of Experimental Psychology: Applied,* 8, 44–56.

Bridgeman, B., Graziano, J. A. (1989). Effect of context and efference copy on visual straight ahead. *Vision Research,* 29, 1729–1736.

Bridges, C. D. B. (1986). Biochemistry of vision-A perspective. *Vision Research,* 26, 1317–1337.

Brillat-Savarin, J. A. (1971). The physiology of taste: Or meditations on transcendental gastronomy (M. K. F. Fisher, Trans.). New York: Knopf. (Original work published 1825)

Broadbent, D. (1958). *Perception and Communication.* Oxford: Pergamon.

Broadbent, D. E., & Gregory, M. (1963). Vigilance considered as a statistical decision. *British Journal of Psychology,* 54, 309–323.

Brochet, F., & Dubourdieu, D. (2001). Wine descriptive language supports cognitive specificity of chemical senses. *Brain and Language,* 77, 187–196.

Brodeur, D. A., & Enns, J. T. (1997). Lifespan differences in covert visual orienting. *Canadian Journal of Experimental Psychology,* 51, 20–35.

Brodmann, K. (1914). Physiologie des gehirng. In F. Krause (Ed.), *Allsemaie chirurgie der gehirnkankheiten.* Stuttgart: F. Enke.

Bronkhorst, A. W., Bosman, A. J., & Smoorenburg, G. F. (1993). A model for context effects in speech recognition. *Journal of the Acoustical Society of America,* 93, 499–509.

Bronkhurst, A. W. (1995). Localization of real and virtual sound sources. *Journal of the Acoustical Society of America,* 98, 2542–2553.

Bronson, G. W. (1990). Changes in infants' scanning across the 2– to 14–week age period. *Journal of Experimental Child Psychology,* 49, 101–125.

Brooks, P. L., & Frost, B. J. (1983). Evaluation of a tactile vocoder for word recognition. *Journal of the Acoustical Society of America,* 74, 34–39.

Brooks, R. A. (1981). Symbolic reasoning among 3–D models and 2–D images. *Artificial Intelligence,* 17, 205–244.

Brosvic, G. M., & Farrelly, M. (1993). Nonequivalent roles for motor and visual feedback in the Mueller Lyer and horizontal-vertical illusions. *Bulletin of the Psychonomic Society,* 31, 42–44.

Brosvic, G. M., Walker, M. A., Perry, N., Degnan, S., & Dihoff, R. E. (1997). Illusion decrement as a function of duration of inspection and figure type. *Perceptual & Motor Skills,* 84, 779–783.

Brown, A. C., Beeler, W. J., Kloka, A. C., & Fields, R. W. (1985). Spatial summation of pre-pain and pain in human teeth. *Pain,* 21, 1–16.

Brown, B. (1972). Resolution thresholds for moving targets at the fovea and in the peripheral retina. *Vision Research,* 12, 293–304.

Brown, J. M., & Koch, C. J. (1991). *Influences of Closure and Occlusion on the Perception of Fragmented Pictures.* Paper presented at Association for Research in Vision and Opthalmology (ARVO), May 1991, Sarasota, FL.

Brown, J. W. (1990). Psychology of time awareness. *Brain and Cognition,* 14, 144–164.

Brown, L. G. (1996). Additional rules for the transformed up-down method in psychophysics. *Perception & Psychophysics,* 58, 959–962.

Brown, M. (2001). *The Developing Brain.* New York : Oxford University Press.

Brown, P. K., & Wald, G. (1964). Visual pigments in single rods and cones of the human retina. *Science,* 144, 45–52.

Brown, S. W. (1985). Time perception and attention: The effects of prospective versus retrospective paradigms and task demands on perceived duration. *Perception & Psychophysics,* 38, 115–124.

Brown, S. M. Archer, S., & Del Monte, M. A. (1999). Stereopsis and binocular vision after surgery for unilateral infantile cataract. *Journal of Aapos: American Association for Pediatric Ophthalmology & Strabismus.* 3, 109–113.

Brown, S. W., & Boltz, M. G. (2002). Attentional processes in time perception: Effects of mental workload and event structure. *Journal of Experimental Psychology: Human Perception and Performance,* 28, 600–615.

Brown, T. S. (1975). General biology of sensory systems. In B. Scharf (Ed.), *Experimental Sensory Psychology* (pp. 69–111). Glenview, IL: Scott-Foresman.

Brown, W. (1910). The judgment of difference. University of California, Berkeley, *Publications in Psychology,* 1, 1–71.

Brownell, W. E., Bader, C. R., Bertrand, D., & de Ribaupierre, Y. (1985). Evoked mechanical responses of isolated cochlear outer hair cells. *Science,* 227, 194–196.

Bruce, C., Desimone, R., & Gross, C. G. (1981). Visual properties of neurons in a polysensory area in superior temporal sulcus of the macaque. *Journal of Neurophysiology,* 46, 369–384.

Bruno, N., & Bertamini, M. (1997). Amodal completion of partly occluded surfaces: Is there a mosaic stage? *Journal of Experimental Psychology: Human Perception and Performance,* 23, 1412–1426.

Bruno, N., & Cutting, J. E. (1988). Minimodularity and the perception of layout. *Journal of Experimental Psychology: General,* 117, 161–170.

Brussell, E. M., & Festinger, L. (1973). The Gelb effect: Brightness contrast plus attention. *American Journal of Psychology,* 86, 225–235.

Bryden, M. P., & George, J. (1990). Sex differences and the role of figural complexity in determining the rate of mental rotation. *Perceptual and Motor Skills,* 70, 467–477.

Buchtel, H. A., & Stewart, J. D. (1989). Auditory agnosia: Apperceptive or associative disorder? *Brain and Language,* 37, 12–25.

Buck, S. L. (2001). What is the hue of rod vision? *Color Research and Application,* 26 (supplement), S57–S59.

Buckey, J. C. Jr., Musiek, F. E., Kline-Schoder, R., Clark, J. C., Hart, S., & Havelka, J. (2001). Hearing loss in space. *Aviation, Space & Environmental Medicine,* 72, 1121–1124

Bujas, Z., Szabo, S., Ajdukovic, D., & Mayer, D. (1991). Time course of recovery from gustatory adaptation to NaCl. *Perception & Psychophysics,* 49, 517–521.

Bullier J. (2001). Integrated model of visual processing. *Brain Research Reviews,* 36, 96–107.

Burg, A. (1968). Lateral visual field as related to age and sex. *Journal of Applied Psychology,* 52, 10–15.

Burkard, R. F., & Sims, D. (2001). The human auditory brainstem response to high click rates: aging effects. *American Journal of Audiology,* 10, 53–61.

Burr, D. C., Ross, J., & Morrone, M. C. (1986). Smooth and sampled motion. *Vision Research,* 26, 643–652.

Burr, D. C., & Corsale, B. (2001). Dependency of reaction times to motion onset on luminance and chromatic contrast. *Vision Research,* 41, 1039–1048.

Burt, P., & Julesz, B. (1980). A disparity gradient limit for binocular fusion. *Science,* 208, 615–617.

Burt, P., & Sperling, G. (1981). Time, distance and feature trade-offs in visual apparent motion. *Psychological Review,* 88, 137–151.

Burton, G., Turvey, M. T., & Solomon, H. Y. (1990). Can shape be perceived by dynamic touch? *Perception & Psychophysics,* 48, 477–487.

Burton, H., & Sinclair, R. (1996). Somatosensory cortex and tactile perceptions. In L. Kruger (Ed.), *Pain and Touch* (pp. 105–177). San Diego: Academic Press.

Bushnell, M. C., & Duncan, G. H. (1989). Sensory and affective aspects of pain perception: Is medial thalamus restricted to emotional issues? *Experimental Brain Research,* 78, 415–418.

Butler, D. L., & Kring, A. M. (1987). Integration of features in depictions as a function of size. *Perception & Psychophysics,* 41, 159–164.

Butler, R. A. (1987). An analysis of the monaural displacement of sound in space. *Perception & Psychophysics,* 41, 1–7.

Butler, R. A., Levy, E. T., & Neff, W. D. (1980). Apparent distance of sounds recorded in echoic and anechoic chambers. *Journal of Experimental Psychology: Human Perception and Physiology,* 6, 745–750.

Butters, N., Barton, M., & Brody, B. A. (1970). Right parietal lobe and crossmodel associations. *Cortex,* 6, 19–46.

Caelli, T. (1982). On discriminating visual textures and images. *Perception & Psychophysics,* 31, 149–159.

Caelli, T. (1988). An adaptive computational model for texture segregation. *IEEE Transactions on Systems, Man, and Cybernetics,* 18, 9–17.

Cahoon, D., & Edmonds, E. M. (1980). The watched pot still won't boil: Expectancy as a variable in estimating the passage of time. *Bulletin of the Psychonomic Society,* 16, 115–116.

Cain, W. S. (1969). Odor intensity: Differences in the exponent of the psychophysical function. *Perception & Psychophysics,* 6, 349–354.

Cain, W. S. (1977). Differential sensitivity for smell: "Noise" at the nose. *Science,* 195, 796–798.

Cain, W. S., & Engen, T. (1969). Olfactory adaptation and the scaling of odor intensity. In C. Pfaffman (Ed.), *Olfaction and Taste III* (pp. 127–141). New York: Rockefeller University Press.

Cain, W. S., & Johnson, F. Jr. (1978). Lability of odor pleasantness: Influence of mere exposure. *Perception,* 7, 459–465.

Cain, W. S., & Stevens, J. C. (1989). Uniformity of olfactory loss in aging. *Annals of the New York Academy of Sciences,* 561, 29–38.

Cain, W. S., & Stevens, J. C. (1995). Life-span development of odor identification, learning, and olfactory sensitivity. *Perception,* 24, 1457–1472.

Cajal, S. R. (1893). La retine des vertebres. Cellule, 9, 17–257.

Calis, G., & Leeuwenberg, E. (1981). Grounding the figure. *Journal of Experimental Psychology: Human Perception and Performance,* 7, 1386–1397.

Callaghan, T. C. (1989). Interference and dominance in texture segregation: Hue, geometric form, and line orientation. *Perception & Psychophysics,* 46, 299–311.

Calloway, S. L., Lloyd, I. C., & Henson, D. B. (2001). A clinical evaluation of random dot stereoacuity cards in infants. *Eye,* 15, 629–634

Campagna, D., Stengel, B., Mergler, D., Limasset, J. C., Diebold, F., & Michard, D. (2001). Color vision and occupational toluene exposure. *Neurotoxicology and Teratology,* 23, 473–480.

Campbell, F. W., & Maffei, L. (1981). The influence of spatial frequency and contrast on the perception of moving patterns. *Vision Research,* 21, 713–721.

Campbell, K. B., Baribeau-Braun, J., & Braun, C. (1981). Neuroanatomical and physiological foundations of extraversion. *Psychophysiology,* 18, 263–267.

Campbell, S. S., Murphy, P. J., & Boothroyd, C. E. (2001). Long term time estimation is influenced by circadian phase. *Physiology and Behavior,* 72, 589–593

Candy, T. R., Skoczenski, A. M., & Norcia, A. M. (2001). Normalization models applied to orientation masking in the human infant. *Journal of Neuroscience,* 21, 4530–4541

Canévet, G., Hellman, R., & Scharf, B. (1986). Group estimation of loudness in sound fields. *Acustica,* 60, 277–282.

Cannon, M. W. Jr. (1983). Contrast sensitivity: Psychophysical and evoked potential methods compared. *Vision Research,* 23, 87–95.

Cansino, S., Williamson, S. J., & Karron, D. (1994). Tonotopic organization of human auditory association cortex. *Brain Research,* 663, 38–50.

Carlson, M. C., & Hasher, L. (1995). Aging, distraction, and the benefits of predictable location. *Psychology & Aging,* 10, 427–436.

Carlson, V. R. (1977). Instructions and perceptual constancy judgments. In W. Epstein (Ed.), *Stability and Constancy in Visual Perception: Mechanisms and Processes* (pp. 217–254). New York: Wiley.

Carlyon, R. P. (1988). The development and decline of forward masking. *Hearing Research,* 32, 65–80.

Carmichael, L., Hogan, H. P., & Walter, A. A. (1932). An experimental study of the effect of language on the reproduction of visually perceived forms. *Journal of Experimental Psychology,* 15, 73–86.

Carpenter, D. L., & Dugan, M. P. (1983). Motion parallax information for direction of rotation in depth: Order and direction components. *Perception,* 12, 559–569.

Carver, R. A., & Brown, V. (1997). Effects of amount of attention allocated to the location of visual stimulus pairs on perception of simultaneity. *Perception and Psychophysics,* 59, 534–542

Casagrande, V. A., Xu, X., & Sary, G. (2002). Static and dynamic views of visual cortical organization. *Progress in Brain Research,* 36, 389–408.

Casanova, C., Merabet, L., Desautels, A., & Minville, K. (2001). Higher-order motion processing in the pulvinar. *Progress in Brain Research,* 134, 71–82.

Cassone, V. M. (1990). Effects of melatonin on vertebrate circadian systems. *Trends in Neurosciences,* 13, 457–464.

Castiello, U. (2001). Implicit processing of shadows. *Vision Research,* 41, 2305–2309.

Castiello, U., Paulignan, Y., & Jeannerod, M. (1991). Temporal dissociation of motor responses and subjective awareness. *Brain,* 114, 2639–2655.

Cattell, J. M. (1886). The influence of the intensity of the stimulus on the length of the reaction time. *Brain,* 9, 512–514.

Caudek, C., Domini, F., & Di Luca, M. (2002). Short term temporal recruitment in structure from motion. *Vision Research,* 42, 1213–1223.

Cavanagh, P., & Leclerc, Y. G. (1989). Shape from shadows. *Journal of Experimental Psychology: Human Perception and Performance,* 15, 3–27.

Cavanagh, P., & Mather, G. (1989). Motion: The long and short of it. *Spatial Vision,* 4, 103–129.

Cavanagh, P., Tyler, C. W., & Favreau, O. E. (1984). Perceived velocity of moving chromatic gratings. *Journal of the Optical Society of America A,* 1, 893–899.

Cavanaugh, J. C. (2002). *Adult Development and Aging* (4th ed.) Belmont, CA: Wadsworth Thomson Learning.

Cegalis, J. A., & Deptula, D. (1981). Attention in schizophrenia: Signal detection in the visual periphery. *Journal of Nervous and Mental Health Diseases,* 169, 751–760.

Ceralla, J. (1985). Age-related decline in extra-foveal letter perception. *Journal of Gerontology,* 40, 727–736.

Cernoch, J. M., & Porter, R. H. (1985). Recognition of maternal axillary odors by infants. *Child Development,* 56, 1593–1598.

Chalmers, D. (1996). *The Conscious Mind: In Search of a Fundamental Theory.* New York: Oxford University Press.

Chamorro, A., & Sacco, R. L. (1990). Visual hemineglect and hemihallucinations in a patient with subcortical infarction. *Neurology,* 40, 1463–1464.

Cheeseman, J., & Merikle, P. M. (1984). Priming with and without awareness. *Perception & Psychophysics,* 36, 387–395.

Cheng, P. W. (1985). Restructuring versus automaticity: Alternative accounts of skill acquisition. *Psychological Review,* 92, 414–423.

Cheour-Luhtanen, M., Alho, K., Saino, K., Rinne, T., Reinikainen, K, Pohjavouri, M., Renlund, M., Aaltonen, O., Eerola, O., & Näätänen, R. (1996). The ontogenetically earliest discriminative response of the human brain. *Psychophysiology,* 33, 478–481.

Cherry, E. C. (1953). Some experiments on the recognition of speech, with one and with two ears. *Journal of the Acoustical Society of America,* 25, 975–979.

Chien, S. H., Teller, D. Y., & Palmer, J. (2000). The transistion from scotopic to photopic vision in 3–month-old infants and adults: an evaluation of the rod dominance hypothesis. *Vision Research,* 40, 3853–3871.

Chocolle, R. (1940). Variations des temps de réaction auditifs en fonction de l'intensité à diverses frequences. *Année Psychologique,* 41, 65–124.

Chocolle, R. (1962). Les effets des interactions interaurales dans l'audition. *Journale de Psychologie,* 3, 255–282.

Cholewiak, R. W., & Collins, A. A. (1997). Individual differences in the vibrotactile perception of a "simple" pattern set. Pe*rception & Psychophysics,* 59, 850–866.

Cholewiak, R. W., & Craig, J. C. (1984). Vibrotactile pattern recognition and discrimination at several body sites. *Perception & Psychophysics,* 35, 503–514.

Chomsky, N., & Miller, G. A. (1963). Introduction to the formal analysis of natural languages. In R. D. Luce, R. Bush, & E. Galanter (Eds.), *Handbook of Mathematical Psychology,* Vol. 2 (pp. 269–231). New York: Wiley.

Choudhurt, B. P., & Crossey, A. D. (1981). Slow-movement sensitivity in the human field of vision. *Physiology and Behavior,* 26, 125–128.

Chun, M. M., & Jiang, Y. (1998). Contextual cueing: Implicit learning and memory of visual context guides spatial attention. *Cognitive Psychology,* 36, 28–71.

Chun, M. M., & Potter, M. C. (1993). A two-stage model for multiple-target detection in rapid serial visual presentation. *Journal of Experimental Psychology: Human Perception & Performance,* 21(1), 109–127.

Ciner, E. B., Schanel-Klitsch, E., & Scheiman, M. (1991). Stereoacuity development in young children. *Optometry & Vision Science,* 68, 533–536.

Clark, A. A., Troscianko, T., Campbell N. W., & Thomas, B. T. (2000). A comparison between human and machine labelling of image regions. *Perception,* 29, 1127–1138.

Clark, H. H., & Clark, E. V. (1977). *Psychology and Language: An Introduction to Psycholinguistics.* New York: Harcourt.

Clark, G. M. (2002). Learning to understand speech with the cochlear implant. In M. Fahle & T. Poggio (Eds.), *Perceptual Learning.* (pp. 147–160). Cambridge, MA: MIT Press.

Clarke, S., Thiran, A. B., Maeder, P., Adriani, M., Vernet, O., Regli, L., Cuisenaire, O., & Thiran, J-P. (2002). What and where in human audition: Selective deficits following focal hemispheric lesions. *Experimental Brain Research,* 147, 8–15.

Clarkson, M. G., Swain, I. U., Clifton, R. K., & Cohen, K. (1991). Newborns' head orientation toward trains of brief sounds. *Journal of the Acoustical Society of America,* 89, 2411–2420.

Clarkson-Smith, L., & Halpern, D. F. (1983). Can age-related deficits in spatial memory be attenuated through the use of verbal coding? *Experimental Aging Research,* 9, 179–184.

Clifford, B. R., & Bull, R. (1978). *The psychology of Person Identification.* London: Routledge & Kegan Paul.

Clifton, R. K., Morrongiello, B. A., & Dowd, J. M. (1984). A developmental look at an auditory illusion: The precedence effect. *Developmental Biology,* 17, 519–536.

Cogan, R., & Spinnato, J. A. (1986). Pain and discomfort thresholds in late pregnancy. *Pain,* 27, 63–68.

Coghill, R. C., Talbot, J. D., Evans, A. C., Meyer, E., Gjedde, A., Bushnell, M. C., & Duncan, G. H. (1994). Distributed processing of pain and vibration by the human brain. *Journal of Neuroscience,* 14, 4095–4108.

Cohen, J. D., Noll, D. C., & Schneider, W. (1993). Functional magnetic resonance imaging: Overview and methods for psychological research. *Behavior Research Methods, Instruments & Computers,* 25, 101–113.

Cohen, W. (1958). Color-perception in the chromatic Ganzfeld. *American Journal of Psychology,* 71, 390–394.

Coles, M. G., Gale, A., & Kline, P. (1971). Personality and habituation of the orienting reaction: Tonic and response measures of electrodermal activity. *Psychophysiology,* 8, 54–63.

Coletta, N. J., & Segu, P. (1993). An oblique effect in parafoveal motion perception. *Vision Research,* 33, 2747–2756.

Collett, T. S., & Parker, A. J. (1998). Depth constancy. In V. Walsh, & J. Kulikowski (Eds.), *Perceptual Constancy: Why Things Look as They Do* (pp. 409–435). New York: Cambridge University Press.

Collings, V. B. (1974). Human taste response as a function of locus of stimulation on the tongue and soft palate. *Perception & Psychophysics,* 16, 169–174.

Collins, A. A., & Cholewiak, R. W. (1994). The shape of the vibrotactile loudness function: The effect of stimulus repetition and skin-contactor coupling. *Perception & Psychophysics,* 55, 465–472.

Collins, D. W., & Kimura, D. (1997). A large sex difference on a two-dimensional mental rotation task. *Behavioral Neuroscience,* 111, 845–849.

Colombo, J. (2001). The development of visual attention in infancy. *Annual Review of Psychology,* 52, 337–367.

Comfort, A. (1971). Likelihood of human pheromones. *Nature,* 230, 432–433.

Condon, W. S., & Sander, L. W. (1974). Neonate movement is synchronized with adult speech: Interactional participation and language acquisition. *Science,* 183, 99–101.

Cook, P. R. (Ed.). (1999). *Music, Cognition and Computerized Sound: An Introduction to Psychoacoustics* (with accompanying CD). Cambridge, MA: MIT Press.

Cooke, N. M., Breen, T. J., & Schvaneveldt, R. W. (1987). Is consistent mapping necessary for high-speed search? *Journal of Experimental Psychology: Learning, Memory, and Cognition,* 13, 223–229.

Corbetta, M., Miezin, F. M., Dobmeyer, S., Shulman, G. L., & Petersen, S. E. (1991). Selective and divided attention during visual discrimination of shape, color, and speed: Functional anatomy by positron emission tomography. *Journal of Neuroscience,* 11, 2383–2402.

Coren, S. (1966). Adaptation to prismatic displacement as a function of the amount of available information. *Psychonomic Science,* 4, 407–408.

Coren, S. (1969). Brightness contrast as a function of figure-ground relations. *Journal of Experimental Psychology,* 80, 517–524.

Coren, S. (1972). Subjective contours and apparent depth. *Psychological Review,* 79, 359–367.

Coren, S. (1986). An efferent component in the visual perception of direction and extent. *Psychological Review,* 93, 391–410.

Coren, S. (1987). In vivo measures of the density of human lens pigmentation: A rapid and simple psychophysical procedure. *Acta Ophthalmologica,* 65, 575–578.

Coren, S. (1989). The many moon illusions: An integration through analysis. In M. Hershenson (Ed.), The moon illusion (pp. 351–370). Hillsdale, NJ: Erlbaum.

Coren, S. (1991). Retinal mechanisms in the perception of subjective contours: The contribution of lateral inhibition. *Perception,* 20, 181–191.

Coren, S. (1992). Psychophysical scaling: Context & illusion. *Behavioral and Brain Sciences,* 15, 563–564.

Coren, S. (1992). The left-hander syndrome: The causes and consequences of left-handedness. New York: Free Press/ Macmillan (pp. i-x, 1–308). [North American Edition]

Coren, S. (1992). The moon illusion: A different view through the legs. *Perceptual and Motor Skills,* 75, 827–831.

Coren, S. (1993). The left-hander syndrome: The causes and consequences of left-handedness (pp. i-x, 1–317). New York: Vintage Books.

Coren, S. (1994). Constraints on context effects in perception: Evidence from visual illusions. In L. M. Ward (Ed.), *Fechner Day 94. Proceedings of the International Society for Psychophysics* (pp. 54–61). Vancouver, Canada: The International Society of Psychophysics.

Coren, S. (1997). *Sleep Thieves.* New York: Free Press.

Coren, S. (1997). Visual illusions. In R. Dulbecco (Ed.), *Encyclopedia of Human Biology,* 2nd ed., Vol. 8 (pp. 717–721). Orlando, FL: Academic Press.

Coren, S. (1999). La percezione delle illusioni visve [The Perception of Visual Illusions]. In F. Purghe', N. Stucchi, & T. Costa (Eds.), *La Percezione Visiva [Visual Perception]* (pp. 369–389). Milan: UTET Libreria Srl.

Coren, S. (1999). Sensory motor performance as a function of eye dominance and handedness. *Perceptual and Motor Skills,* 88, 424–426.

Coren, S., & Aks, D. J. (1990). Moon illusion in pictures: A multimechanism approach. *Journal of Experimental Psychology: Human Perception and Performance,* 16, 365–380.

Coren, S., & Enns, J. T. (1993). Size contrast as a function of conceptual similarity between test and inducers. *Perception & Psychophysics,* 54, 579–588.

Coren, S., & Girgus, J. S. (1977). Illusions and constancies. In W. Epstein (Ed.), Stability and constancy in visual perception: Mechanisms and processes (pp. 255–284). New York: Wiley.

Coren, S., & Girgus, J. S. (1978). *Seeing is Deceiving: The Psychology of Visual Illusions.* Hillsdale, NJ: Erlbaum.

Coren, S., & Girgus, J. S. (1980). Principles of perceptual organization and spatial distortion: The Gestalt illusions. *Journal of Experimental Psychology: Human Perception and Performance,* 6, 404–412.

Coren, S., & Hakstian, A. R. (1987). Visual screening without the use of technical equipment: Preliminary development of a behaviorally validated questionnaire. *Applied Optics,* 26, 1468–1472.

Coren, S., & Hakstian, A. R. (1988). Color vision screening without the use of technical equipment: Scale development and cross-validation. *Perception & Psychophysics,* 43, 115–120.

Coren, S., & Hakstian, A. R. (1989). A behaviorally validated self-report inventory of the measurement of visual acuity. *International Journal of Epidemiology,* 18, 451–456.

Coren, S., & Hakstian, A. R. (1992). The development and cross-validation of a self-report inventory to assess pure tone threshold hearing sensitivity. *Journal of Speech and Hearing Research,* 35, 921–928.

Coren, S., & Hakstian, A. R. (1994). Predicting speech recognition thresholds from pure tone hearing thresholds. *Perceptual and Motor Skills,* 79, 1003–1008.

Coren, S., & Hakstian, A. R. (1995). Testing color discrimination without the use of special stimuli or technical equipment. *Perceptual and Motor Skills,* 81, 931–938.

Coren, S., & Hakstian, A. R. (1996). Screening for stereopsis without the use of technical equipment: Scale development and cross-validation. *International Journal of Epidemiology,* 25, 146–152.

Coren, S., & Harland, R. E. (1994). Subjective contours and visual-geometric illusions: Do they share common mechanisms? *Italian Journal of Psychology* [Giornale Italiano di Psicologia], 20, 709–730.

Coren, S., & Harland, R. E. (1995). Personality correlates of variations in visual and auditory abilities. *Personality and Individual Differences,* 18, 15–25.

Coren, S. & Harland, R. E. (2001).

Coren, S., & Keith, B. (1970). Bezold-Brucke effect: Pigment or neural locus? *Journal of the Optical Society of America,* 60, 559–562.

Coren, S., & Komoda, M. K. (1973). Apparent lightness as a function of perceived direction of incident illumination. *American Journal of Psychology,* 86, 345–349.

Coren, S., & Porac, C. (1978). Iris pigmentation and visual-geometric illusions. *Perception,* 7, 473–478.

Coren, S., & Porac, C. (1983a). The creation and reversal of the Mueller-Lyer illusion through attentional manipulation. *Perception,* 12, 49–54.

Coren, S., & Porac, C. (1983b). Subjective contours and apparent depth: A direct test. *Perception & Psychophysics,* 33, 197–200.

Coren, S., & Porac, C. (1984). Structural and cognitive components in the Mueller-Lyer illusion assessed via cyclopean presentation. *Perception & Psychophysics,* 35, 313–318.

Coren, S., & Porac, C. (1987). Individual differences in visual-geometric illusions: Predictions from measures of spatial cognitive abilities. *Perception & Psychophysics,* 41, 211–219.

Coren, S., & Russell, J. A. (1992). The relative dominance of different facial expressions of emotion under conditions of perceptual ambiguity. *Cognition and Emotion,* 6, 339–356.

Coren, S., Bradley, D. R., Hoenig, P., & Girgus, J. S. (1975). The effect of smooth tracking and saccadic eye movements on the perception of SIE: The shrinking circle illusion. *Vision Research,* 15, 49–55.

Coren, S., Girgus, J. S., & Schiano, D. (1986). Is adaptation of orientation-specific cortical cells a possible explanation of illusion decrement? *Bulletin of the Psychonomic Society,* 24, 207–210.

Coren, S., Porac C., & Duncan, P. (1981). Lateral preference in pre-school children and young adults. *Child Development,* 52, 443–450.

Coren, S., Porac, C., & Theodor, L. H. (1987). Set and subjective contour. In S. Petry & G. E. Meyer (Eds.), *The Perception of Illusory Contours* (pp. 237–245). New York: Springer-Verlag.

Coren, S., Porac, C., Aks, D. J., & Morikawa, K. (1988). A method to assess the relative contribution of lateral inhibition to the magnitude of visual-geometric illusions. *Perception & Psychophysics,* 43, 551–558.

Coren, S., Whitehead, L. A., Baca, M. J., & Patten, R. (1995). Navigational range lights: The effect of stimulus configuration on alignment accuracy. *Ergonomics,* 38, 1360–1367.

Cormack, R. H. (1984). Stereoscopic depth perception at far viewing distances. *Perception & Psychophysics,* 35, 423–428.

Cornsweet, T. N. (1956). Determination of the stimuli for involuntary drifts and saccadic eye movements. *Journal of the Optical Society of America,* 46, 987–993.

Cornsweet, T. N. (1962). The staircase-method in psychophysics. *American Journal of Psychology,* 75, 485–491.

Cornsweet, T. N. (1970). *Visual Perception.* New York: Academic Press.

Correia, M. J., & Guedry, F. E. (1978). The vestibular system: Basic biophysical and physiological mechanisms. In R. B. Masterton (Ed.), *Handbook of sensory neurobiology,* Vol. I, *Sensory Integration.* New York: Plenum Press.

Corso, J. F. (1959). Age and sex differences in thresholds. *Journal of the Acoustical Society of America,* 31, 498–509.

Corthout, E., Uttl, B., Walsh, V., Hallett, M., & Cowey, A. (1999). Timing of activity in early visual cortex as revealed by transcranial magnetic stimulation. *Neuroreport,* 10, 2631–2634.

Corthout, E., Uttl, B., Ziemann, U., Cowey, A., & Hallett, M. (1999). Two periods of processing in the (circum)striate visual cortex as revealed by transcranial magnetic stimulation. *Neuropsychologia,* 37, 137–145.

Courage, M. L., & Adams, J. (1990). The early development of visual acuity in the binocular and monocular peripheral fields. *Infant Behavioral Development,* 13, 123–128.

Courage, M. L., & Adams, R. J. (1996). Infant peripheral vision: The development of monocular visual acuity in the first 3 months of postnatal life. *Vision Research,* 36, 1207–1215.

Cowan, R. S. C., Alcantara, J. I., Blamey, P. J., & Clark, G. M. (1988). Preliminary evaluation of a multichannel electrotactile speech processor. *Journal of the Acoustical Society of America,* 83, 2328–2338.

Cowley, J. J., & Broolsbank, B. W. L. (1991). Human exposure to putative pheromones and changes in aspects of social behavior. *Journal of Steroid Biochemistry and Molecular Biology,* 39, 647–659.

Cowley, J. J., Johnson, A. L., & Brooksbank, B. W. L. (1977). The effect of two odorous compounds on performance in an assessment-of-people test. *Psychoneuroendocrinology,* 2, 159–172.

Cox, M. V., & Perara, J. (2001). Children's use of the height and size cues to depict a projective depth relationship in their pictures. *Psychologia: An International Journal of Psychology in the Orient,* 44, 99–110.

Craig, J. C. (1978). Vibrotactile pattern recognition and masking. In G. Gordon (Ed.), *Active Touch: The Mechanism of Recognition of Objects by Manipulation* (pp. 229–242). Oxford: Pergamon Press.

Craig, J. C. (1983). The role of onset in the perception of sequentially presented vibrotactile patterns. *Perception & Psychophysics,* 34, 421–432.

Craig, J. C. (1989). Interference in localizing tactile stimuli. *Perception & Psychophysics,* 45, 343–355.

Craig, J. C. (1995). Vibrotactile masking: The role of response competition. *Perception & Psychophysics,* 57, 1190–1200.

Craig, J. C., & Evans, P. M. (1987). Vibrotactile masking and the persistence of tactual features. *Perception & Psychophysics,* 42, 309–317.

Craig, K. D., & Coren, S. (1975). Signal detection analysis of social modelling influences on pain expressions. *Journal of Psychosomatic Research,* 19, 105–112.

Craig, K. D., & Hadjistavropoulos, H. D. (1994). A comparison of two measures of facial activity during pain in the newborn child. *Journal of Pediatric Psychology,* 19, 305–318.

Craig, K. D., & Prkachin, K. M. (1978). Social modeling influences on sensory decision theory and psychophysiological indexes of pain. *Journal of Personality and Social Psychology,* 36, 805–815.

Craig, K. D., Best, H., & Ward, L. M. (1975). Social modelling influences on psychophysical judgments of electrical stimulation. *Journal of Abnormal Psychology,* 84, 366–373.

Crassini, B., Brown, B., & Bowman, K. (1988). Age-related changes in contrast sensitivity in central and peripheral retina. *Perception,* 17, 315–332.

Craton, L. G., & Yonas, A. (1990). The role of motion in infants' perception of occlusion. In J. T. Enns (Ed.), *The Development of Attention: Research and Theory* (pp. 21–46). Amsterdam: Elsevier.

Crawley, E. J., Acker-Mills, B. E., Pastore, R. E., & Weil, S. (2002). Change detection in multi-voice music: The role of musical structure, musical training, and task demands. *Journal of Experimental Psychology: Human Perception and Performance,* 28, 367–378.

Crick, F. (1994). *The Astonishing Hypothesis.* New York: Simon & Schuster.

Crick, F., & Koch, C. (1990). Some reflections on visual awareness. *Cold Spring Harbor Symposia in Quantitative Biology,* 55, 953–962.

Cronly-Dillon, J., & Gregory, R. L. (1991). *Evolution of the Eye and Visual System.* Boca Raton, FL: CRC Press.

Crowley, J. C., & Katz, L. C. (2002). Ocular dominance development revisited. *Current Opinion in Neurobiology,* 12, 10410–10419.

Crutchfield, R. S., Woodworth, D. G., & Albrecht, R. E. (1958). *Perceptual Performance and the Effective Person* (WADC-TN-58–60). Lackland Air Force Base, TX: Wright Air Development Center (NTIS No. AD-151–039).

Cruz, A., & Green, B.G. (2000). Thermal stimulation of taste. *Nature,* 403, 889–892.

Csibra, G. (2001). Illusory contour figures are perceived as occluding surfaces by 8-month-old infants. *Developmental Science,* 4, F7–F11.

Cuddy, L. L., Cohen, A. J., & Mewhort, D. J. K. (1981). Perception of structure in short melodic sequences. *Journal of Experimental Psychology: Human Perception and Performance,* 7, 869–883.

Cummings D. M., Brunjes, P. C. (1997). The effects of variable periods of functional deprivation on olfactory bulb development in rats. *Experimental Neurology,*148, 360–366.

Cummings, B. G., & Parker, A. J. (2000). Local disparity not perceived depth is signaled by binocular neurons in cortical area V1 of the macaque. *Journal of Neuroscience,* 20, 4758–4767.

Curcio, C. A., Sloan, K. R., Packer, O., Hendrickson, A. E., & Kalina, R. E. (1987). Distribution of cones in human and monkey retina: Individual variability and radial asymmetry. *Science,* 236, 579–582.

Cutler, B. L., & Penrod, S. D. (1995). *Mistaken Identification: The Eyewitness, Psychology and the Law.* New York: University of Cambridge Press.

Cutler, W. B., Preti, G., Krieger, A., Huggins, G. R., Garcia, C. R., & Lawley, H. J. (1986). Human axillary secretions influence women's menstrual cycles: The role of donor extract from men. *Hormones and Behavior,* 20, 463–473.

Cutting, J. E. (1976). Auditory and linguistic processes in speech perception: Inferences from six fusions in dichotic listening. *Psychological Review,* 83, 114–140.

Cutting, J. E. (1987). Perception and information. *Annual Review of Psychology,* 38, 61–90.

Cutting, J. E., & Kozlowski, L. T. (1977). Recognizing friends by their walk: Gait perception without familiarity cues. *Bulletin of the Psychonomic Society,* 9, 353–356.

Cutting, J. E., & Vishton, P. M. (1997). Heading and path information from retinal flow in naturalistic environments. *Perception & Psychophysics,* 59, 426–441.

Cutting, J. E., Proffitt, D. R. (1981). Gait perception as an example of how we may perceive events. In R. Walk & H. L. Pick Jr. (Eds.), *Intersensory Perception and Sensory Integration* (pp. 249–273). New York: Plenum Press.

Cutting, J. E., Proffitt, D. R., & Kozlowski, L. T. (1978). A biomechanical invariant for gait perception. *Journal of Experimental Psychology: Human Perception and Performance,* 4, 357–372.

Cynader, M., & Regan, D. (1978). Neurons in cat parastriate cortex sensitive to the direction of motion in three-dimensional space. *Journal of Physiology,* 274, 549–569.

Daan, S., Beersma, D. G. M., & Borbely, A. A. (1984). Timing of human sleep: Recovery process gated by a circadian pacemaker. *American Journal of Physiology,* 246, 161–178.

Dacey, D. M. (2000). Parallel pathways for spectral coding in primate retina. *Annual Review of Neuroscience,* 23, 743–775.

Dacey, D. M. (1988). Dopamine-accumulating retinal neurons revealed by in vitro fluorescence display a unique morphology. *Science,* 240, 1196–1198.

Dallenbach, K. M. (1939). Pain: History and present status. *American Journal of Psychology,* 52, 331–347.

Dallos, P., Santos-Sacchi, J., & Flock, A. (1982). Intracellular recordings from cochlear outer hair cells. *Science,* 18, 582–584.

Dalton, K. (1964). *The Premenstrual Syndrome.* Springfield, IL: Thomas.

Dalziel, C. C., & Egan, D. J. (1982). Crystalline lens thickness changes as observed by pachometry. *American Journal of Optometry and Physiological Optics,* 59, 442–447.

Damasio, A. R. (1994). *Descartes' Error.* New York: Putnam.

Damasio, A. R., & Tranel, D. (1990). Face agnosia and the neural substrates of memory. *Annual Review of Neuroscience,* 13, 89–109.

Dannemiller, J. L. (1989). Computational approaches to color constancy: Adaptive and ontogenetic considerations. *Psychological Review,* 96, 225–266.

Dannemiller, J. L., & Freedland, R. L. (1991). Detection of relative motion by human infants. *Developmental Psychology,* 27, 67–78.

Danziger, S., Kingstone, A., & Rafal, R. D. (1998). Orienting to extinguished signals in hemispatial neglect. *Psychological Science,* 9, 119–123.

Darian-Smith, I., Sugitani, M., Heywood, J., Karita, K., & Goodwin, A. (1982). Touching textured surfaces: Cells in somatosensory cortex respond both to finger movement and to surface features. *Science,* 218, 906–909.

Dark, V. J. (1988). Semantic priming, prime reportability, and retroactive priming are interdependent. *Memory and Cognition,* 16, 299–308.

Dark, V., Johnston, W., Myles-Worsley, M., & Farah, M. (1985). Levels of selection and capacity limits. *Journal of Experimental Psychology: General,* 114, 472–497.

Dartnall, H. M. A. (1957). *The Visual Pigments.* London: Methuen.

Daugman, J. G. (1980). Two-dimensional spectral analysis of cortical receptive field profiles. *Vision Research,* 20, 847–856.

Davidoff, J., & Roberson, D. (2001). Development of anaimal recognition: A difference between parts and wholes. *Journal of Experimental Child Psychology,* 81, 217–234.

Davidoff, J. B. (1975). *Differences in Visual Perception: The Individual Eye.* New York: Academic Press.

Davis, M. (1997): The neurobiology of fear responses: The role of the amygdala. *Journal of Neuropsychiatry and Clinical Neuroscience,* 9, 382–402 .

Daw, N.W. (1998). Critical periods and amblyopia. *Archives of Ophthalmology,* 116, 502–505.

Dawkins, R. (1996). *Climbing Mount Improbable.* New York: Random House.

Dawson, J. L. (1967). Cultural and physiological influences upon spatial processes in West Africa: I. *International Journal of Psychology,* 2, 115–128.

Dawson, M. R. W. (1991). The how and why of what went where in apparent motion: Modelling solutions to the motion correspondence problem. *Psychological Review,* 98, 569–603.

Dawson, M. R. W., & Di Lollo, V. (1990). Effects of adapting luminance and stimulus contrast on the temporal and spatial limits of short-range motion. *Vision Research,* 30, 415–429.

Dawson, M. R. W., & Pylyshyn, Z. W. (1988). Natural constraints on apparent motion. In Z. W. Pylyshyn (Ed.), *Computational Processes in Human Vision* (pp. 99–120). Norwood, NJ: Ablex.

Day, M. C., & Stone, C. A. (1980). Children's use of perceptual set. *Journal of Experimental Child Psychology,* 29, 428–445.

Day, R. S. (1968). *Fusion in Dichotic Listening.* Unpublished doctoral dissertation, Stanford University, Stanford, CA.

Day, R. S. (1970). Temporal order judgments in speech: Are individuals language-bound or stimulus-bound? *Haskins Laboratories Status Report* (SR-21/22), 71–87.

de Gelder, B., Vroomen, J., Pourtois, G., & Weiskrantz L. (1999). Non-conscious recognition of affect in the absence of striate cortex. *NeuroReport,* 10, 3759–3763.

De Monasterio, F. M. (1978). Center and surround mechanisms of opponent-color X and Y ganglion cells of retina of macaques. *Journal of Neurophysiology,* 41, 1418–1434.

De Renzi, D. E. (1982). *Disorders of Space Exploration and Cognition.* New York: Wiley.

De Valois, R. L., Cottaris, N. P., Elfar, S. D., Mahon, L. E., & Wilson, J. A. (2000). Some transformations of color information from lateral geniculate nucleus to striate cortex. *Proceedings of the National Academy of Science, USA,* 97, 4997–5002.

De Vries, H., & Stuiver, M. (1961). The absolute sensitivity of the human sense of smell. In W. A. Rosenblith (Ed.), *Communication Processes* (pp. 159–167). New York: Wiley.

De Vries, J. V. (1968). *Perspective.* New York: Dover. (Original work published 1604)

Debner, J. A., & Jacoby, L.L. (1994). Unconscious perception:attention, awareness, and control. *Journal of Experimental Psychology: Learning, Memory and Cognition,* 20, 304–317.

DeGangi, G. A., & Greenspan, S. I. (1988). The development of sensory functions in infants. *Physical & Occupational Therapy in Pediatrics,* 8, 21–33.

de-Haan, M., Pascalis, O., & Johnson, M. H. (2002). Specialization of neural mechanisms underlying face recognition in human infants. *Journal of Cognitive Neuroscience,* 14, 199–209.

Dekle, D. J., & Beal, C. R. (1996). Children as witnesses: A comparison of lineup versus showup identification methods. *Applied Cognitive Psychology,* 10, 1–12.

Del Punta, K., Leinders-Zufall, T., Rodriguez, I., Jukam, D., Wysocki, C. J., Ogawa, S., Zufall, F., & Mombaerts, P. (2002). Deficient pheromone responses in mice lacking a cluster of vomeronasal receptor genes. *Nature,* 419, 70–74.

Deliege, I., & Melen, M. (1996). Musical schemata in real-time listening to a piece of music. *Music Perception,* 14, 117–160.

Delorne, A., & Martin, C. (1986). Roles of retinal periphery and depth periphery in linear vection and visual control of standing in humans. *Canadian Journal of Psychology,* 40, 176–187.

Demer, J. L., & Crane, B. T. (2001). Ocular compensation due to labyrinthine input during natural motion. In J. Goebel, & S. M. Highstein. (Eds.). *The Vestibular Labyrinth in Health and Disease.* Annals of the New York Academy of Sciences,

Vol. 942 (pp. 148–161). New York: New York Academy of Sciences.

Dennett, D.C. (1991). Consciousness Explained. Boston: Little, Brown & Company.

Deregowski, J. (1980). *Illusions, Patterns and Pictures: A Cross-Cultural Perspective.* London: Academic Press.

Deregowski, J. B. (1999). Pictorial perception: Individual and group differences within the human species. *Cahiers de Psychologie Cognitive/Current Psychology of Cognition,* 18, 1031–1063.

Desai, N. S., Cudmore, R. H., Nelson, S. B., Turrigiano, G. G. (2002). Critical periods for experience-dependent synaptic scaling in visual cortex. *Nature Neuroscience,* 5, 712–714.

Descartes, R. (1642). *Meditationes de prima Philosophia in quibus Dei Existencia, & animae humanae à corpore distinctio, demonstrantur.* Amstelodami: Apud Danielem Elsevirium.

Desimone, R., Schein, S. J., Moran, J., & Ungerleider, L. G. (1985). Contour, color and shape analysis beyond the striate cortex. *Vision Research,* 25, 441–452.

Desjardins, R. N., Rogers, J., & Werker, J. F. (1997). An exploration of why preschoolers perform differently than do adults in audiovisual speech perception tasks. *Journal of Experimental Child Psychology,* 66, 85–110.

Deubel, H., Bridgeman, B., & Schneider, W. X. (1998). Immediate post-saccadic information mediates space constancy. *Vision Research,* 38, 3147–3159.

Deutsch, D. (1978). The psychology of music. In E. C. Carterette & M. P. Friedman (Eds.), *Handbook of perception,* Vol. X, *Perceptual Ecology* (pp. 191–224). New York: Academic Press.

Deutsch, D. (1995). *Musical Illusions and Paradoxes.* La Jolla, CA: Philomel Records, Inc.

Deutsch, D. (Ed.). (1998). *The Psychology of Music* (2nd ed.). New York: Academic Press.

Deutsch, D. (Ed.). (1982). *The Psychology of Music.* New York: Academic Press.

Deutsch, D., & Feroe, J. (1981). The internal representation of pitch sequences in tonal music. *Psychological Review,* 88, 503–522.

Deutsch, J. A., & Deutsch, D. (1963). Attention: Some theoretical considerations. *Psychological Review,* 70, 80–90.

DeValois, R. L., & DeValois, K. K. (1980). Spatial vision. *Annual Review of Psychology,* 31, 309–341.

DeValois, R. L., & DeValois, K. K. (1991). Vernier acuity with stationary moving Gabors. *Vision Research,* 31, 1619–1626.

DeValois, R. L., & DeValois, K. K. (1975). Neural coding of color. In E. C. Carterette & M. P. Friedman (Eds.), *Handbook of Perception,* Vol. V, *Seeing* (pp. 117–168). New York: Academic Press.

DeWitt, L. A., & Samuel, A. G. (1990). The role of knowledge-based expectations in music perception: Evidence from musical restoration. *Journal of Memory & Language,* 26, 36–56.

DeYoe, E. A., & van Essen, D. C. (1988). Concurrent processing streams in monkey visual cortex. *Trends in Neuroscience,* 11, 219–226.

Di Lollo, V. (1980). Temporal integration in visual memory. *Journal of Experimental Psychology: General,* 109, 75–97.

Di Lollo, V. (1984). On the relationship between stimulus intensity and duration of visible persistence. *Journal of Experimental Psychology: Human Perception & Performance,* 10, 144–151.

Di Lollo, V., & Bischof, W. F. (1995). Inverse-intensity effect in duration of visible persistence. *Psychological Bulletin,* 118, 223–237.

Di Marzo, V., Blumberg, P. M., & Szallasi, A. (2002). Endovanilloid signaling in pain. *Current Opinion in Neurobiology,* 12, 372–379.

Diamant, H., Funakoshi, M., Strom, L., & Zotterman, Y. (1963). Electrophysiological studies on human taste nerves. In Y. Zotterman (Ed.), *Olfaction and Taste* (pp. 191–203). Oxford: Pergamon Press.

Diamond, R., & Carey, S. (1986). Why faces are and are not special: an effect of expertise. *Journal of Experimental Psychology: General,* 115, 107–117.

DiCarlo, L. T., & Cross, D. V. (1990). Sequential effects in magnitude scaling: Models and theory. *Journal of Experimental Psychology: General,* 119, 375–396.

Dichgans, J., & Brandt, T. (1978). Visual-vestibular interaction: Effects on self-motion perception and postural control. In R. Held, H. W. Leibowitz, & H. L. Teuber (Eds.), *Handbook of Sensory Physiology,* Vol. 7, *Perception* (pp. 755–804). New York: Springer-Verlag.

Diener, D. (1990). The P&P illusion. *Perception & Psychophysics,* 47, 65–67.

Ditchburn, R. W. (1973). *Eye Movements and Perception.* Oxford: Clarendon Press.

DiZio, P. A., & Lackner, J. R. (1986). Perceived orientation, motion, and configuration of the body during viewing of an off-vertical rotating surface. *Perception & Psychophysics,* 39, 39–46.

Dobson, V., & Teller, D. Y. (1978). Visual acuity in human infants: A review and comparison of behavioral and electrophysiological studies. *Vision Research,* 18, 1469–1483.

Dodwell, P. C., & Humphrey, G. K. (1990). A functional theory of the McCollough effect. *Psychological Review,* 97, 78–89.

Dodwell, P. C., Humphrey, G. K., & Muir, D. W. (1987). Shape and pattern perception. In P. Salapatek & L. Cohen (Eds.), *Handbook of Infant Perception,* Vol. 2, *From Perception to Cognition* (pp. 1–80). Orlando: Academic Press.

Doetsch, G. S., Ganchrow, J. J., Nelson, L. M., & Erickson, R. P. (1969). Information processing in the taste system of the rat. In C. Pfaffman (Ed.), *Olfaction and Taste III* (pp. 492–511). New York: Rockefeller University Press.

Doherty, M. E., & Keeley, S. M. (1972). On the identification of repeatedly presented visual stimuli. *Psychological Bulletin,* 78, 142–154.

Domini, F., Blaser, E., & Cicerone, C. M. (2000). Color specific depth mechanisms revealed by a color contingent depth aftereffect. *Vision Research,* 40, 359–364.

Donaldson, I. M. (2000). The functions of the proprioceptors of the eye muscles. *Philosophical Transactions of the Royal Society of London, Series B: Biological Sciences,* 355, 1685–1754.

Donaldson, I. M. L., & Long, A. C. (1980). Interactions between extraocular proprioceptive and visual signals in the superior colliculus of the cat. *Journal of Physiology,* 298, 85–110.

Doner, J., Lappin, J. S., & Perfetto, G. (1984). Detection of three-dimensional structure in moving optical patterns. *Journal of Experimental Psychology: Human Perception and Performance,* 10, 1–11.

Doorschot, P. C., Kappers A. M., & Koenderink, J. J. (2001). The combined influence of binocular disparity and shading on pictorial shape. *Perception and Psychophysics,* 63, 1038–1047.

Dorr, S., & Neumeyer, C. (1996). The goldfish-A colour-constant animal. *Perception,* 25, 243–250.

Doty, R. L. (1985). The primates: III. Humans. In R. E. Brown & D. W. MacDonald (Eds.), *Social Odours in Mammals,* Vol. 2 (pp. 804–832). Oxford: Clarendon Press.

Doty, R. L. (2001). Olfaction. *Annual Review of Psychology,* 52, 423–452.

Doty, R. L., Applebaum, S., Zusho, H., & Settle, R. G. (1985). Sex differences in odor identification ability: A cross-cultural analysis. *Neuropsychologia,* 23, 667–672.

Doty, R. L., Green, P. A., Ram, C., & Yankell, S. L. (1982). Communication of gender from human breath odors: Relationship to perceived intensity and pleasantness. *Hormones and Behavior,* 16, 13–22.

Doty, R. L., Shaman, P., & Applebaum, S. L. (1984). Smell identification ability: Changes with age. *Science,* 226, 1441–1443.

Doty, R. L., Yousem, D. M., Pham, L. T., Kreshak, A. A., Geckle, R., & Lee, W. W. (1997). Olfactory dysfunction in patients with head trauma. *Archives of Neurology,* 54, 1131–1140.

Double, K. L., Halliday, G. M., Kril, J. J., Harasty, J. A., Cullen, K., Brooks, W. S., Creasey, H., & Broe, G. A. (1996). Topography of brain atrophy during normal aging and Alzheimer's disease. *Neurobiology of Aging,* 17, 513–521.

Dowling, W. J., & Carterette, E. C. (Eds.). (1987). The understanding of melody and rhythm [Special issue]. *Perception & Psychophysics,* 41, 482–656.

Dowling, W. J., & Harwood, D. L. (1986). *Music Cognition.* Orlando: Academic Press.

Dowling, W. J., Kwak, S., & Andrews, M. W. (1995). The time course of recognition of novel melodies. *Perception & Psychophysics,* 57, 134–139.

Downing, C. J. (1988). Expectancy and visual-spatial attention: Effects on perceptual quality. *Journal of Experimental Psychology: Human Perception and Performance,* 14, 188–202.

Drayna, D., Manichaikul, A., de lange, M., Sneider, H., & Spector, T. (2001). Genetic correlates of musical pitch recognition in humans. *Science,* 291, 1969–1972.

Dresp B., & Grossberg S. (1999). Spatial facilitation by color and luminance edges: Boundary, surface, and attentional factors. *Vision Research,* 39, 3431–3443.

Driver, J. (1996). Enhancement of selective listening by illusory mislocation of speech sounds due to lip-reading. *Nature,* 381, 66–68.

Droit-Volet, S., & Wearden, J. (2001). Speeding up an internal clock in children? Effects of visual flicker on subjective duration. *Quarterly Journal of Experimental Psychology: Comparative and Physiological Psychology,* 55B, 193–211.

Droscher, V. B. (1971). *The Magic of the Senses: New Discoveries in Animal Perception.* New York: Harper.

Drum, B. (1980). Relation of brightness to threshold for light-adapted and dark-adapted rods and cones: Effects of retinal eccentricity and target size. *Perception,* 9, 633–650.

Drum, B. (1981). Brightness interactions between rods and cones. *Perception & Psychophysics,* 29, 505–510.

Dulac, C. (2000). Sensory coding of pheromone signals in mammals. *Current Opinion in Neurobiology,* 10, 511–518.

Duncan, J. (1984). Selective attention and the organization of visual information. *Journal of Experimental Psychology: General,* 113, 501–517.

Duncan, J., & Humphreys, G. W. (1989). Visual search and stimulus similarity. *Psychological Review,* 96, 433–458.

Duncker, K. (1929). Uber induzierte Bewegung (ein Beitrag zur Theorie optisch warigenommener Bewegung). *Psychologische Forschung,* 2, 180–259.

Durlach, N. I., Delhorne, L. A., Wong, A., Ko, W. Y., Rabinowitz, W. M., & Hollerbach, J. (1989). Manual discrimination and identification of length by the finger-span method. *Perception & Psychophysics,* 46, 29–38.

Easterbrook, J. A. (1959). The effect of emotion on cue utilization and the organization of behavior. *Psychological Review,* 66, 183–201.

Easton, R. D., & Basala, M. (1982). Perceptual dominance during lipreading. *Perception & Psychophysics,* 32, 562–570.

Ebrahimi, F. A. W., & Chess, A. (1998). The specification of olfactory neurons. *Current Opinion in Neurobiology,* 8, 453–457.

Edelman, G. M. (1987). *Neural Darwinism: The Theory of Neuronal Group Selection.* New York: Basic Books.

Edelman, G. M., & Tononi, G. (2000). *A Universe of Consciousness.* New York: Basic Books.

Edelman, S., & Intrator, N. (2002). Models of perceptual learning. In M. Fahle & T. Poggio (Eds.), *Perceptual Learning* (pp. 337–353). Cambridge, MA: MIT Press.

Edwards, A., & Cohen, S. (1961). Visual illusions, tactile sensibility and reaction time under LSD-25. *Psychopharmacologia,* 2, 297–303.

Efron, R. (1967). The duration of the present. *Annals of the New York Academy of Sciences,* 138, 713–729.

Efron, R. (1973). Conservation of temporal information by perceptual systems. *Perception & Psychophysics,* 14, 518–530.

Egan, J. P. (1975). *Signal Detection Theory and ROC-Analysis.* New York: Academic Press.

Egeth, H. E., & Yantis, S. (1997). Visual attention: Control, representation, and time course. *Annual Review of Psychology,* 48, 269–297.

Egeth, H. E., Virzi, R. A., & Garbart, H. (1984). Searching for conjunctively defined targets. *Journal of Experimental Psychology: Human Perception and Performance,* 10, 32–39.

Eggermont, J. J. (1995). Representation of a voice onset time continuum in primary auditory cortex of the cat. *Journal of the Acoustical Society of America,* 98, 911–920.

Eggert, T., Ditterich, J., & Straube, A. (2001). Mislocalization of peripheral targets during fixation. *Vision Research,* 41, 343–352.

Egly, R., Driver, J., & Rafal, R. D. (1994). Shifting visual attention between objects and locations: Evidence from normal and parietal lesion subjects. *Journal of Experimental Psychology: General,* 123, 161–177.

Egly, R., Driver, J., & Rafal, R. D. (1994). Shifting visual attention between objects and locations: Evidence from normal and parietal lesion subjects. *Journal of Experimental Psychology: General,* 123, 161–177.

Eichengreen, J. M., Coren, S., & Nachmias, J. (1966). Visual-cliff preference by infant rats: Effects of rearing and test conditions. *Science,* 151, 830–831.

Eimas, P. D., & Miller, J. D. (1980). Contextual effects in infant speech perception. *Science,* 209, 1140–1141.

Eimas, P. D., Siqueland, E. R., Jusczyk, P., & Vigorito, J. (1971). Speech perception in infants. *Science,* 171, 303–306.

Einstein, A., & Besso, M. (1972). *Correspondence 1903–1955.* Paris: Hermann.

Eisen, M. L., Quas, J. A., & Goodman, G. S. (2002). *Memory and Suggestibility in the Forensic Interview.* (Personality and Clinical Psychology Series). Mahwah, NJ: Erlbaum.

Elder, J., & Zucker, S. (1993). The effect of contour closure on the rapid discrimination of two-dimensional shapes. *Vision Research,* 33, 981–991.

Elder, J., & Zucker, S. (1994). A measure of closure. *Vision Research,* 34, 3361–3369.

Elkind, D. (1978). *The Child's Reality: Three Developmental Themes.* Hillsdale, NJ: Erlbaum.

Ellemberg, D., Lewis, T. L., Maurer, D., Lui, C. H., & Brent, H. P. (1999). Spatial and temporal vision in patients treated for bilateral congenital cataracts. *Vision Research,* 39, 3480–3489.

Ellemberg, D., Hammarrenger, B., Lepore, F., Roy, M. S., & Guillemot, J. P. (2002). Contrast dependency of VEPs as a function of spatial frequency: The parvocellular and magnocellular contributions to human VEPs. *Spatial Vision,* 15, 99–111.

Ellemberg, D., Maurer, D., & Brent, H. P. (2000). Influence of monocular deprivation during infancy on the later development of spatial and temporal vision. *Vision Research,* 40, 3283–3295.

Ellermeier, W., & Westphal, W. (1995). Gender differences in pain ratings and pupil reactions to painful pressure stimuli. *Pain,* 61, 435–439.

Ellis, H. (1905). *Sexual Selection in Man.* New York: Davis.

Ellis, H. D., & Young, A. W. (1988). Training in face-processing skills for a child with acquired prosopagnosia. *Developmental Neuropsychology,* 4, 283–294.

Ellis, H. D., Young, A. W., & Koenken, G. 1993. Covert face recognition without prosopagnosia. *Behavioral Neurology,* 6, 27–32.

Emmerson, P. G., & Ross, H. E. (1986). The effect of brightness on colour recognition under water. *Ergonomics,* 29, 1647–1658.

Engel, A. K., Konig, P., Kreiter, A. K., & Singer, W. (1991). Interhemispheric synchronization of oscillatory neural responses in cat visual cortex. *Science,* 252, 1177–1179.

Engel, A. K., König, P., Kreiter, A. K., Schillen, T. B., & Singer, W. (1992). Temporal coding in the visual cortex: new vistas on integration in the nervous system. *Trends in Neurosciences,* 15, 218–226.

Engel, A. K., Fries, P., König, P., Brecht, M., & Singer, W. (1999). Temporal binding, binocular rivalry, and consciousness. *Consciousness and Cognition,* 8, 128–151.

Engelien, A., Yang, Y., Engelien, W., Zonana, J., Stern, E., & Silbersweig, D. A. (2002). Physiological mapping of human auditory cortices with a silent event-related fMRI technique. *Neuroimage,* 16, 944–953.

Engen, T. (1982). *Perception of Odors.* New York: Academic Press.

Enns, J. T. (1986). Seeing textons in context. *Perception & Psychophysics,* 39, 143–147.

Enns, J. T. (1987). A developmental look at pattern symmetry in perception and memory. *Developmental Psychology,* 23, 839–850.

Enns, J. T. (1990a). Relations between components of visual attention. In J. T. Enns (Ed.), *The Development of Attention: Research and Theory* (pp. 447–466). Amsterdam: Elsevier.

Enns, J. T. (1990b). Three dimensional features that pop out in visual search. In D. Brogan (Ed.), *Visual Search* (pp. 37–45). London: Taylor & Francis.

Enns, J. T. (1992). Sensitivity of early human vision to 3-D orientation in line-drawings. *Canadian Journal of Psychology,* 46, 143–169.

Enns, J. T., & Brodeur, D. A. (1989). A developmental study of covert orienting to peripheral visual cues. *Journal of Experimental Child Psychology,* 48, 171–189.

Enns, J. T., & Cameron, S. (1987). Selective attention in young children: The relations between visual search, filtering and priming. *Journal of Experimental Child Psychology,* 44, 38–63.

Enns, J. T., & Coren, S. (1995). The Box Alignment Illusion: An orientation illusion induced by pictorial depth. *Perception & Psychophysics,* 57, 1163–1174.

Enns, J. T., & Di Lollo, V. (1997). Object substitution: A new form of visual masking in unattended visual locations. *Psychological Science,* 8, 135–139.

Enns, J. T., & Di Lollo, V. (2000). What's new in visual masking? *Trends in Cognitive Sciences,* 4, 345–352.

Enns, J. T., & Girgus, J. S. (1985). Perceptual grouping and spatial distortion: A developmental study. *Developmental Psychology,* 21, 241–246.

Enns, J. T., & Girgus, J. S. (1986). A developmental study of shape integration over space and time. *Developmental Psychology,* 22, 491–499.

Enns, J. T., & King, K. A. (1990). Components of line-drawing interpretation: A developmental study. *Developmental Psychology,* 26, 469–479.

Enns, J. T., & Kingstone, A. (1995). Access to global and local properties in visual search for compound stimuli. *Psychological Science,* 5, 283–291.

Enns, J. T., & Prinzmetal, W. (1984). The role of redundancy in the object-line effect. *Perception & Psychophysics,* 35, 22–32.

Enns, J. T., & Rensink, R. A. (1990). Influence of scene-based properties on visual search. *Science,* 247, 721–723.

Enns, J. T., Brehaut, J., & Shore, D. I. (1999). The duration of a brief event in the mind's eye. *Journal of General Psychology,* 126, 355–372.

Enns, J. T., Austen, E. L., Di Lollo, V., Rauschenberger, R., & Yantis, S. (2001). New objects dominate luminance transients in attentional priority setting. *Journal of Experimental Psychology: Human Perception & Performance,* 27, 1287–1302.

Enns, J. T. (2002). Visual binding in the standing wave illusion. *Psychonomic Bulletin and Review,* 9, 489–496.

Enright, J. T. (1987a). Art and the oculomotor system: Perspective illustrations evoke vergence changes. *Perception,* 16, 731–746.

Enright, J. T. (1987b). Perspective vergence: Oculomotor responses to line drawings. *Vision Research,* 27, 1513–1526.

Epstein, J. W., Wiseman, C. V., Sunday, S. R., Klapper, F., Alkalay, L., & Halmi, K. A. (2001). Neurocognitive evidence favors "top down" over "bottom up" mechanisms in the pathogenesis of body size distortions in anorexia nervosa. *Eating and Weight Disorders,* 6, 140–147.

Epstein, W., & Park, J. N. (1964). Shape constancy: Functional relationships and theoretical formulations. *Psychological Bulletin,* 62, 180–196.

Epstein, W., Hatfield, G., & Muise, G. (1977). Perceived shape at a slant as a function of processing time and processing load. *Journal of Experimental Psychology: Human Perception and Performance,* 3, 473–483.

Erb, C., Voelker, W. A., Wohlrab, M., & Zrenner, E. (2001).Color-vision disturbances in patients with coronary artery disease. *Color Research and Application,* 26(Suppl.), S288–S291.

Erickson, R. P. (1963). Sensory neural patterns and gustation. In Y. Zotterman (Ed.), *Olfaction and Taste* (pp. 205–213). Oxford: Pergamon Press.

Eriksen, C. W., & Collins, J. F. (1968). Sensory traces versus the psychological movement in the temporal organization of form. *Journal of Experimental Psychology,* 77, 376–382.

Eriksen, C. W., & Hake, H. W. (1955). Absolute judgments as a function of stimulus range and number of stimulus and response categories. *Journal of Experimental Psychology,* 49, 323–332.

Eriksen, C. W., & Hoffman, J. E. (1972). Some characteristics of selective attention in visual perception determined by vocal reaction time. *Perception & Psychophysics,* 11, 169–171.

Eriksen, C. W., & St. James, J. D. (1986). Visual attention within and around the field of focal attention: A zoom lens model. *Perception & Psychophysics,* 40, 225–240.

Ernst, M., Lee, M. H. M., Dworkin, B., & Zaretsky, H. H. (1986). Pain perception decrement produced through repeated stimulation. *Pain,* 26, 221–231.

Evans, E. F. (1975). Cochlear nerve and cochlear nucleus. In W. D. Keidel & W. D. Neff (Eds.), *Handbook of Sensory Physiology,* Vol. V/2. *Auditory system: Physiology (CNS). Behavioral Studies. Psychoacoustics* (pp. 1–108). New York: Springer-Verlag.

Evans, P. M. (1987). Vibrotactile masking: Temporal integration, persistence, and strengths of representation. *Perception & Psychophysics,* 42, 515–525.

Evers, S., & Suhr, B. (2000). Changes of the neurotransmitter serotonin but not of hormones during short time music perception. *European Archives of Psychiatry and Clinical Neuroscience,* 250, 144–147.

Evers, S., Dannert, J., Roedding, D., Roetter, G., & Ringlestein, E.B. (1999). The cerebra haemodynamics of music perception: A transcranial Doppler sonography study. *Brain,* 122, 75–85.

Eysenck, H. J. (1967). *The Biological Basis of Personality.* Springfield, IL: Thomas.

Fagen, D., & Swift, C. G. (1988). Effects of caffeine on vigilance and other performance tests in normal subjects. *Journal of Psychopharmacology,* 2, 19–25.

Fagiolini, M., Pizzorusso, T., Berardi, N., Domenici, L., & Maffei, L. (1994). Functional postnatal development of the rat primary visual cortex and the role of visual experience: Dark rearing and monocular deprivation. *Vision Research,* 34, 709–720.

Fagot, J., Martin, M. J., & Depy, D. (2000). What is the evidence for an equivalence between objects and pictures in birds and nonhuman primates? In Fagot, J. (Ed.), *Picture Perception in Animals* (pp. 295–320). Philadelphia: Psychology Press.

Fagot, J. (2000). *Picture Perception in Animals.* Philadelphia: Psychology Press.

Fahle, M. (1997). Specificity of learning curvature, orientation, and vernier discriminations. *Vision Research,* 37, 1885–1895.

Fahle, M., & Poggio, T. (Eds). (2002). *Perceptual Learning.* Cambridge, MA: MIT Press.

Fant, G. (1967). Auditory patterns of speech. In W. Wathen-Dunn (Ed.), *Models for the Perception of Speech and Visual Form* (pp. 111–125). Cambridge, MA: MIT Press.

Fantz, R. L. (1961). The origin of form perception. *Scientific American,* 204, 66–72.

Fantz, R. L. (1965). Ontogeny of perception. In A. M. Schrier, H. F. Harlow, & F. Stollnitz (Eds.), *Behavior of Nonhuman Primates* (Vol. 2, pp. 365–403). New York: Academic Press.

Fantz, R. L., & Miranda, S. B. (1977). Visual processing in the newborn preterm, and mentally high-risk infant. In L. Gluck (Ed.), *Intrauterine Asphyxia and the Developing Fetal Brain* (pp. 453–471). Chicago: Year Book Medical Publishers.

Farah, M. J., Rabinowitz, C., Quinn, G. E., & Lui, G. T. (2000). Early commitment of neural substrates for face recognition. *Journal of Cognitive Neuropsychology,* 17, 117–123.`

Farrell, J. E. (1983). Visual transformations underlying apparent movement. *Perception & Psychophysics,* 33, 85–92.

Farrimond, T. (1990). Effect of alcohol on visual constancy values and possible relation to driving performance. *Perceptual and Motor Skills,* 70, 291–295.

Fechner, G. T. (1966). Elements of psychophysics. (H. E. Alder, Trans.). New York: Holt, Rinehart and Winston. (Original work published 1860)

Fecteau, J. H., Chua, R., Franks, I., & Enns, J. T. (2001). Visual awareness and the on-line modification of action. *Canadian Journal of Experimental Psychology,* 55, 106–112.

Feeney, J. J, Howard, J. H. R., & Howard, D. V. (2002). Implicit learning of higher order sequences in middle age. *Psychology and Aging,* 17, 351–355.

Feldman, J. (2000). Bias toward regular form in mental shape spaces. *Journal of Experimental Psychology: Human Perception and Performance,* 26, 152–165.

Fender, D. H. (1971). Time delays in the human eye-tracking system. In P. Bach-y-Rita, C. C. Collins, & J. E. Hyde (Eds.), *The Control of Eye Movements* (pp. 539–543). New York: Academic Press.

Fernald, A. (1985). Four-month-old infants prefer to listen to motherese. *Infant Behavior and Development,* 8, 181–195.

Fernald, A. (2001). Hearing, listening, and understanding: Auditory development in infancy. In G. Bremner & A. Fogel (Eds.), *Blackwell Handbook of Infant Development.* Handbooks of Developmental Psychology. (pp. 35–70). Malden, MA: Blackwell Publishers.

Festinger, L., Allyn, M. R., & White, C. W. (1971). The perception of color with achromatic stimulation. *Vision Research,* 11, 591–612.

Festinger, L., Coren, S., & Rivers, G. (1970). The effect of attention on brightness contrast and assimilation. *American Journal of Psychology,* 83, 189–207.

Field, D. J., & Hayes, A. (1993). Contour integration by the human visual system: Evidence for a local "association field." *Vision Research,* 33, 173–193.

Fiez, J. A., & Raichle, M. E. (1995). PET studies of auditory and phonological processing: Effects of stimulus characteristics and task demands. *Journal of Cognitive Neuroscience,* 7, 357–375.

Filsinger, E. E., & Fabes, R. A. (1985). Odor communication, pheromones, and human families. *Journal of Marriage and the Family,* 47, 349–360.

Fine, B. J., & Kobrick, J. L. (1987). Cigarette smoking, field-dependence and contrast sensitivity. *Aviation, Space and Environmental Medicine,* 58, 777–782.

Fiorani, M. Jr, Rosa, M. G. P., Gattass, R., & Rocha-Miranda, C. E. (1992). Dynamic surrounds of receptive fields in primate striate cortex: A physiological basis for perceptual completion? *Proceedings of the National Academy of Science,* 89, 8547–8551.

Firestein, S., & Werblin, F. (1989). Odor-induced membrane currents in vertebrate-olfactory receptor neurons. *Science,* 244, 79–82.

Fisher, R. (1967). The biological fabric of time. In *Interdisciplinary Perspectives of Time, Annals of the New York Academy of Sciences,* 138, 451–465.

Fisk, A. D., & Schneider, W. (1981). Control and automatic processing during tasks requiring sustained attention: A new approach to vigilance. *Human Factors,* 23, 737–750.

Fitzpatrick, V., Pasnak, R., & Tyer, Z. E. (1982). The effect of familiar size at familiar distances. *Perception,* 11, 85–91.

Flandrin, J. M., & Jeannerod, M. (1981). Effects of unilateral superior colliculus ablation on oculomotor and vistibulo-ocular responses in the cat. *Experimental Brain Research,* 42, 73–80.

Flock, H. R., & Nusinowitz, S. (1984). Visual structures for achromatic color perceptions. *Perception & Psychophysics,* 36, 111–130.

Flom, M. C., Brown, B., Adams, A. J., & Jones, R. T. (1976). Alcohol and marihuana effects on ocular tracking. *American Journal of Optometry and Physiological Optics,* 53, 764–773.

Florentine, M. (1986). Level discrimination of tones as a function of duration. *Journal of the Acoustical Society of America,* 79, 792–798.

Florentine, M., Buus, S., & Mason, C. R. (1987). Level discrimination as a function of level for tones from 0.25 to 16 kHz. *Journal of the Acoustical Society of America,* 81, 1528–1541.

Fodor, J. A. (1983). *Modularity of Mind: An Essay on Faculty Psychology.* Cambridge, MA: MIT Press.

Foley, J. E. (1974). Factors governing interocular transfer of prism adaptation. *Psychological Review,* 81, 183–186.

Folk, C. L., Remington, R. W., & Johnston, J. C. (1992). Involuntary covert orienting is contingent on attentional control settings. *Journal of Experimental Psychology: Human Perception and Performance,* 18, 1030–1044.

Forrester, J. V. (2002). *The Eye: Basic Sciences in Practice* (2nd ed.). New York: W. B. Saunders.

Foulke, E., & Sticht, T. (1969). Review of research on the intelligibility and comprehension of accelerated speech. *Psychological Bulletin,* 72, 50–62.

Fowler, C. A. (1996). Listeners do hear sounds, not tongues. *Journal of the Acoustical Society of America,* 99, 1730–1741.

Fox, K., Glazewski, S., & Schulze, S. (2000). Plasticity and stability of somatosensory maps in thalamus and cortex. *Current Opinion in Neurobiology,* 10, 494–497.

Fox, P. T., Mintun, M. A., Reiman, E. M., & Raichle, M. E. (1988). Enhanced detection of focal brain responses using intersubject averaging and change-distribution analysis of subtracted PET images. *Journal of Cerebral Blood Flow and Metabolism,* 8, 642–653.

Fox, R., & McDaniel, C. (1982). The perception of biological motion by human infants. *Science,* 486–487.

Fox, R., Aslin, R. N., Shea, S. L., & Dumais, S. T. (1980). Stereopsis in infants. *Science,* 207, 323–324.

Fraisse, P. (1963). *The Psychology of Time.* New York: Harper & Row.

Frankenhauser, M. (1959). *The Estimation of Time.* Stockholm: Almqvist & Wiksell.

Fraser, J. (1908). A new illusion of direction. *British Journal of Psychology,* 8, 49–54.

Frederick, D. L., Gillam, M. P., Lensing, S., & Paule, M. G. (1997). Acute effects of LSD on rhesus monkey operant test battery performance. *Pharmacology, Biochemistry & Behavior,* 57, 633–641.

Freeman, R., & Pettigrew, J. (1973). Alteration of visual cortex from environmental asymmetries. *Nature,* 246, 359–360.

Freeman, T. C. A. (2002). Transducer models of head centred motion perception. *Vision Research,* 41, 2741–2755

Freud, S. (1953). *On Aphasia.* London: Imago.

Frey, M. von, & Goldman, A. (1915). Der zeitliche Verlauf det Einstellung bei den Druckempfindungen. *Zeitschrift feur Biologie,* 65, 183–202.

Frey, M. von, & Kiesow, F. (1899). Uber die Function der Tastkorperchen. *Zeitschrift feur Psychologie,* 20, 126–163.

Freyd, J., & Tversky, B. (1984). Force of symmetry in form perception. *American Journal of Psychology,* 97, 109–126.

Friberg, T. R., & Borrero, G. (2000). Diminished perception of ambient light: A symptom of clinical depression? *Journal of Affective Disorders,* 61, 113–118.

Frick, J. E., Colombo, J., & Saxon, T. F. (1999). Individual and developmental differences in disengagement of fixation in early infancy. *Child Development,* 70, 537–548.

Friedman, A. (1979). Framing pictures: The role of knowledge in automatized encoding and memory for gist. *Journal of Experimental Psychology: General,* 108, 316–355.

Friedman, S. L., & Stevenson, M. (1975). Developmental changes in the understanding of implied motion in two-dimensional pictures. *Child Development,* 46, 773–778.

Friedman, S. L., & Stevenson, M. (1980). Perception of movements in pictures. In M. Hagen (Ed.), *Perception of Pictures,* Vol. I, *Alberti's Window: The Projective Model of Pictural Information* (pp. 225–255). New York: Academic Press.

Fries, P., Roelfsema, P. R., Engel, A. K., König, P., & Singer, W. (1997). Synchronization of oscillatory responses in visual cortex correlates with perception in interocular rivalry. *Proceedings of the National Academy of Sciences USA,* 94, 12699–12704.

Friesen, C. K., & Kingstone, A. (1998). The eyes have it! Reflexive orienting is triggered by nonpredictive gaze. *Psychonomic Bulletin & Review,* 5, 490–495.

Frisby, J. P. (1980). *Seeing: Illusion, Brain and Mind.* Oxford: Oxford University Press.

Frishman, L. J. (2001). Basic visual processes. In E. B. Goldstein (ed.), *Blackwell Handbook of Perception,* (pp. 53–91). Malden, MA: Blackwell Pubishers.

Frith, C., Perry, R., & Lumer, E. (1999). The neural correlates of conscious experience: An experimental framework. *Trends in Cognitive Sciences,* 3, 105–114.

Fuld, K., Wooten, B. R., & Whalen, J. J. (1981). The elemental hues of short-wave and extraspectral lights. *Perception & Psychophysics,* 29, 317–322.

Fuller, C. A., Lydic, R., Sulzman, F. M., Albers, H. E., Tepper, B., & Moore-Ede, M. C. (1981). Circadian rhythm of body temperature persists after suprachiamatic lesions in the squirrel monkey. *American Journal of Physiology,* 241, R385–R391.

Fulton A. B., & Hansen, R. M. (2000). The development of scotopic sensitivity. *Investigative Ophthalmology & Visual Science,* 41, 1588–1596.

Fulton, J. F., & Bailey, P. (1929). Tumors in the region of the third ventricle: Their diagnosis and relation to pathological sleep. *Journal of Nervous and Mental Disorders,* 69, 1–25,145–164, 261–277.

Funkenstein, H. H., Nelson, P. G., Winter, P. L., Wolberg, Z., & Newman, J. D. (1971). Unit responses in auditory cortex of awake squirrel monkeys to vocal stimulation. In M. B. Saschs (Ed.), *Physiology of the Auditory System* (pp. 307–326). Baltimore: National Educational Consultants, Inc.

Gagne, J. P. (1988). Excess masking among listeners with a sensorineural hearing loss. *Journal of the Acoustical Society of America,* 83, 2311–2321.

Gaik, W. (1993). Combined evaluation of interaural time and intensity differences: Psychoacoustic results and computer modelling. *Journal of the Acoustical Society of America,* 94, 98–110.

Galati, G., Lobel, E., Valla, G., Berthoz, A., Pizzamiglio, L., & Le Bihan, D. (2000). The neural basis of egocentric and allocentric coding of space in humans: A functional magnetic resonance study. *Experimental Brain Research,* 133, 156–164.

Gallant, J. L., Shoup, R. E., & Mazer, J. A. (2000). A human extrastriate area functionally homologous to macaque V4. *Neuron.* 27, 227–235.

Garbin, C. P. (1988). Visual-haptic perceptual nonequivalence for shape information and its impact upon cross-modal performance. *Journal of Experimental Psychology: Human Perception and Performance,* 14, 547–553.

Garner, W. R. (1953). An informational analysis of absolute judgments of loudness. *Journal of Experimental Psychology,* 46, 373–380.

Garner, W. R. (1962). *Uncertainty and Structure as Psychological Concepts.* New York: Wiley.

Garner, W. R. (1978). Aspects of a stimulus: Features, dimensions and configurations. In E. H. Rosch & B. B. Lloyd (Eds.), *Cognition and Categorization* (pp. 99–139). Hillsdale, NJ: Erlbaum.

Geisler, C. D., Yates, G. K., Patuzzi, R. B., & Johnstone, B. M. (1990). Saturation of outer hair cell receptor currents causes two-tone suppression. *Hearing Research,* 44, 241–256.

Gelb, A. (1929). Die "Farbenkonstanz" der Sehdinge. *Handbuch der normalen und pathologische physiologie,* 12, 549–678.

Geldard, F. A. (1972). *The Human Senses* (2nd ed.). New York: Wiley.

Gent, J. F. (1979). An exponential model for adaptation in taste. *Sensory Processes,* 3, 303–316.

Gerbino, W., & Salmaso, D. (1987). The effect of amodal completion on visual matching. *Acta Psychologia,* 65, 25–46.

Gerbrandt, L. K., Spinelli, D. N., & Pribram, K. H. (1970). Interaction of visual attention and temporal cortex stimulation on electrical activity evoked in striate cortex. *Electroencephalography and Clinical Neurology,* 29, 146.

Gerhardt, K. J., & Abrams, R. M. (2000). Fetal exposures to sound and vibroacoustic stimulation. *Journal of Perinatology,* 20, S21–30.

Gerkema, M. P., & Groos, G. A. (1990). Differential elimination of circadian and ultradian rhythmicity by hypothalamic lesions in the common vole, Microtus arvalis. *Journal of Biological Rhythms,* 5, 81–95.

Gescheider, G. A. (1988). Psychophysical scaling. *Annual Review of Psychology,* 39, 169–200.

Gescheider, G. A. (1997). *Psychophysics, the Fundamentals.* Mahwah, NJ: Erlbaum.

Gescheider, G. A., & Bolanowski, S. J. (1994). The effects of aging on information-processing channels in the sense of touch: I. Absolute sensitivity. *Somatosensory and Motor Research,* 11, 345–357.

Gescheider, G. A., Bolanowski, S. J. Jr., & Verrillo, R. T. (1989). Vibrotactile masking: Effects of stimulus onset asynchrony and stimulus frequency. *Journal of the Acoustical Society of America,* 85, 2059–2064.

Gescheider, G. A., Bolanowski, S. J., Verrillo, R. T., Arpajian, D. J., & Ryan, T. F. (1990). Vibrotadile intensity discrimination measured by three methods. *Journal of the Acoustical Society of America,* 87, 330–338.

Gesteland, R. C., Lettvin, J. Y., Pitts, W. H., & Rojas, A. (1963). Odor specificities of the frog's olfactory receptors. In Y. Zotterman (Ed.), *Olfaction and Taste* (pp. 19–34). Oxford: Pergamon Press.

Geva, R., Gardner, J. M., & Karmel, B. Z. (1999). Feeding-based arousal effects on visual recognition memory in early infancy. *Developmental Psychology,* 35, 640–650.

Gfeller, K., Witt, S. A., Kim, K. H., Adamek, M., & Coffman, D. (2000). Preliminary report of a computerized music training program for adult cochlear implant recipients. *Journal of the Academy of Rehabilitative Audiology,* 1999, 32, 11–27.

Gibson, E. J. (2000). Perceptual learning in development: Some basic concepts. *Ecological Psychology,* 12, 295–302.

Gibson, J. J. (1966). *The Senses Considered as Perceptual Systems.* Boston: Houghton Mifflin.

Gilbert, A. N., & Martin, R. (1996). Cross-modal correspondence between vision and olfaction: The color of smells. *American Journal of Psychology,* 109, 335–351.

Gilbertson, T. A. (1998). Gustatory mechanisms for the detection of fat. *Current Opinion in Neurobiology,* 8, 447–452.

Gilbertson, T. A., Damak, S., & Margolskee, R. F. (2000). The molecular physiology of taste transduction. *Current Opinion in Neurobiology,* 10, 519–527.

Gilchrist, A., Kossyfidis, C., Bonato, F., Agostini, T., Cataliotti, J., Li, X., Spehar, B., Annan, V., & Economou, E. (1999). An anchoring theory of lightness perception. *Psychological Review,* 106, 795–834.

Gilchrist, A. L. (1988). Lightness contrast and failures of constancy: A common explanation. *Perception & Psychophysics,* 43, 415–424.

Gilchrist, A. L., Delman, S., & Jacobsen, A. (1983). The classification and integration of edges as critical to the perception of reflectance and illumination. *Perception & Psychophysics,* 33, 425–436.

Gilchrist, A. L., & Annan, V. Jr. (2002). Articulation effects in lightness: Historical background and theoretical implications. *Perception,* 31, 141–150.

Gilger, J. W., & Ho, H. (1989). Gender differences in adult spatial information processing: Their relationship to pubertal timing, adolescent activities and sex-typing of personality. *Cognitive Development,* 4, 197–214.

Gillam, B., & Nakayama, K. (2002). Subjective contours at line terminations depend on scene layout analysis, not image processing. *Journal of Experimental Psychology: Human Perception and Performance,* 28, 43–53.

Gillam, B. (1980). Geometrical illusions. *Scientific American,* 242, 102–111.

Gillam, B. (2002). Varieties of grouping and its role in determining surface layout. In T. F. Shipley, & P. J. Kellman (Eds.), *From Fragments to Objects: Segmentation and Grouping in Vision* (pp. 247–264). Amsterdam: Elsevier.

Gillam, B., & Nakayama, K. (2002). Subjective contours at line terminations depend on scene layout analysis, not image processing. *Journal of Experimental Psychology: Human Perception and Performance,* 28, 43–53.

Gilmore, M. M., & Murphy, C. (1989). Aging is associated with increased Weber ratios for caffeine, but not for sucrose. *Perception & Psychophysics,* 46, 555–559.

Gintzler, A. R. (1980). Endorphin-mediated increases in pain threshold during pregnancy. *Science,* 210, 193–195.

Girgus, J. J., Rock, I., & Egatz, R. (1977). The effect of knowledge of reversibility on the reversibility of ambiguous figures. *Perception & Psychophysics,* 22 (6), 550–556.

Girgus, J. S., & Coren, S. (1987). The interaction between stimulus variations and age trends in the Poggendorff illusion. *Perception & Psychophysics,* 41, 60–66.

Glaser, A. L., & Slotnick, B. M. (1995). Visual inspection alone produces a decrement in the horizontal vertical illusion. *Perceptual & Motor Skills,* 81, 323–330.

Glass, A. L., & Holyoak, K. J. (1986). *Cognition.* New York: Random House.

Gliner, J. A., Horvath, S. M., & Mihevic, P. M. (1983). Carbon monoxide and human performance in a single and dual task methodology. *Aviation, Space and Environmental Medicine,* 54, 714–717.

Glorig, A., Wheeler, D., Quigle, R., Grings, W., & Summerfield, A. (1970). 1954 Wisconsin State Fair hearing survey: Statistical treatment of clinical and audiometric data. Cited in D. D. Kryter, *The Effects of Noise on Man* (p. 116). New York: Academic Press.

Glover, S. (2002). Visual illusions affect planning but not control. *Trends in Cognitive Sciences,* 6, 288–292.

Goebel, J., & Highstein, S. M. (2002). The vestibular labyrinth in health and disease. *Annals of the New York Academy of Sciences,* vol. 942. New York: New York Academy of Sciences.

Gogel, W. C., & Koslow, M. (1972). The adjacency principle and induced movement. *Perception & Psychophysics,* 11, 309–324.

Gold, D., Andres, D., Arbuckle, T., & Schwartzman, A. (1988). Measurement and correlates of verbosity in elderly people. *Journal of Gerontology: Psychological Sciences,* 43, P27–P33.

Goldberg, M. C., Maurer, D., Lewis, T. L., & Brent, H. P. (2001). The influence of binocular visual deprivation on the development of visual-spatial attention. *Developmental Neuropsychology,* 19, 53–81.

Goldfoot, D. A. (1981). Olfaction, sexual behavior and the pheromone hypothesis in the rhesus monkey: A critique. *American Zoologist,* 21, 153–164.

Goldstein, E. B. (1980). *Sensation and Perception.* Belmont, CA: Wadsworth.

Goldstein, J. L. (1973). An optimum processor theory for the central formation of the pitch of complex tones. *Journal of the Acoustical Society of America,* 54, 1496–1516.

Goldstone, R. L. (1998). Perceptual learning. *Annual Review of Psychology,* 49, 585–612.

Goldstone, S., Boardman, W. K., & Lhamon, W. T. (1958). Effect of quinal barbitone dextro-amphetamine, and placebo on apparent time. *British Journal of Psychology,* 49, 324–328.

Gombrich, E. H. (1972). The mask and the face: The perception of physiognomic likeness in life and in art. In E. H. Gombrich, J. Hochberg, & M. Black (Eds.), *Art, Perception and Reality* (pp. 1–46). Baltimore: Johns Hopkins Press.

Goodale, M. A. (2001). Different spaces and different times for perception and action. *Progress in Brain Research,* 134, 313–331.

Goodale, M. A., & Milner, A. D. (1991). A neurological dissociation between perceiving objects and grasping them. *Nature,* 349, 154–156.

Goodman, L., & Gilman, A. (Eds.). (1965). *The Pharmacological Basis of Therapeutics.* New York: Macmillan.

Goodson, R., & Rahe, A. (1981). Visual training effects on normal vision. *American Journal of Optometry and Physiological Optics,* 58, 787–791.

Goodwin, M., Gooding, K. M., & Regnier, F. (1979). Sex pheromone in the dog. *Science,* 203, 559–561.

Goolkasian, P. (1980). Cyclic changes in pain perception: A ROC analysis. *Perception & Psychophysics,* 27, 499–504.

Gordon, J., & Abramov, I. (2001). Color vision. In E. B. Goldstein (Ed.), *Blackwell Handbook of Perception,* (pp. 92–127). Malden, MA: Blackwell Pubishers.

Gordon, J., Abramov, I, & Chan, H. (1994). Describing color appearance: hue and saturation scaling. *Perception and Psychophysics,* 56, 27–41.

Gosselin, F., & Schyns, P. G. (2001). Why do we SLIP to the basic level? Computational constraints and their implementation. *Psychological Review,* 108, 735–758.

Goto, H. (1971). Auditory perception by normal Japanese adults of the sounds "L" or "R." *Neuropsychologia,* 9, 317–323.

Gottleib, M. D., Kietzman, M. I., & Bernhaus, I. J. (1985). Two-pulse measures of temporal integration in the fovea and peripheral retina. *Perception & Psychophysics,* 37, 135–138.

Gouras, P., & Zrenner, E. (1981). Color coding in primate retina. *Vision Research,* 21, 1591–1598.

Gracely, R. H., & Naliboff, B. D. (1996). Measurement of pain sensation. In L. Kruger (Ed.), *Pain and Touch* (pp. 243–313). San Diego: Academic Press.

Graham, C. H., & Hisa, Y. (1958). Color defect and color theory. *Science,* 127, 657–682.

Graham, N. (1980). Spatial-frequency channels in human vision: Detecting edges without edge detectors. In C. S. Harris (Ed.), *Visual Coding and Adaptability* (pp. 215–262). Hillsdale, NJ: Erlbaum.

Graham, N. (1981). Psychophysics of spatial-frequency channels. In M. Kubovy & J. Pomerantz (Eds.), *Perceptual Organization* (pp. 1–26). Hillsdale, NJ: Erlbaum.

Graham, N. V. S. (1989). *Vision Pattern Analyzers.* New York: Oxford University Press.

Grailet, J. M., & Seron, X. (1990). Case report of a visual integrative agnosia. *Cognitive Neuropsychology,* 7, 275–309.

Granger, G. W., & Ikeda, H. (1976). Drugs and visual thresholds. In A. Herxheimer (Ed.), *Drugs and sensory functions* (pp. 299–344). London: Churchill.

Granrud, C. E., & Yonas, A. (1985). Infants' sensitivity to the depth cue of shading. *Perception & Psychophysics, 37*, 415–419.

Granrud, C. E., Haake, R. J., & Yonas, A. (1985). Infants' sensitivity to familiar size: The effect of memory on spatial perception. *Perception & Psychophysics, 37*, 459–466.

Grau, J. W., & Nelson, D. G. K. (1988). The distinction between integral and separable dimensions: Evidence for the integrality of pitch and loudness. *Journal of Experimental Psychology: General, 117*, 347–370.

Gray, C. M., Konig, P., Engel, A. K., & Singer, W. (1989). Oscillatory responses in cat visual cortex exhibit intercolumnar synchronization which reflects global stimulus properties. *Nature, 338*, 334–337.

Gray, C. M., & Singer, W. (1989). Stimulus-specific neuronal oscillations in orientation columns of cat visual cortex. *Proceedings of the National Academy of Sciences USA, 91*, 6339–6343.

Green, B. G. (1985). Heat pain thresholds in the oral-facial region. *Perception & Psychophysics, 38*, 110–114.

Green, B. G. (1987). The effect of cooling on the vibrotactile sensitivity of the tongue. *Perception & Psychophysics, 42*, 423–430.

Green, D. G., & Powers, M. K. (1982). Mechanisms of light adaptation in rat retina. *Vision Research, 22*, 209–216.

Green, D. M. (1987). *Profile Analysis: Auditory Intensity Discrimination.* New York: Oxford University Press.

Green, D. M., & Swets, J. A. (1974). *Signal Detection Theory and Psychophysics* (reprint). New York: Krieger. (Original work published 1966)

Green, P. R., & Davies, I. B. (1993). Interaction of visual and tactile information in the control of chicks' locomotion in the visual cliff. *Perception, 22*, 1319–1331.

Greenberg, M. J. (1981). The dependence of odor intensity on the hydrophobic properties of molecules. In H. R. Moskowitz & C. B. Warren (Eds.), *Odor Quality and Chemical Structure* (pp. 177–194). Washington, DC: American Chemical Society.

Greene, H. A., & Madden, D. J. (1987). Adult age differences in visual acuity, stereopsis, and contrast sensitivity. *American Journal of Optometry and Physiological Optics, 64*, 749–753.

Greene, H. H., & Rayner, K. (2001). Eye movements and familiarity effects in visual search. *Vision Research, 41*, 3763–3773.

Greenspan, J. D., & Bolanowski, S. J. (1996). The psychophysics of tactile perception and its physiological basis. In L. Kruger (Ed.), *Pain and Touch* (pp. 25–103). San Diego: Academic Press.

Greenwood, D. D. (1990). A cochlear frequency-position function for several species—29 years later. *Journal of the Acoustical Society of America, 87*, 2592–2605.

Gregory, R. L. (1978). *Eye and Brain* (3rd ed.). New York: McGraw-Hill.

Grice, G. R., Nullmeyer, R., & Schnizlein, J. M. (1979). Variable criterion analysis of brightness effects in simple reaction time. *Journal of Experimental Psychology: Human Performance and Perception, 5*, 303–314.

Grondin, S. (2001). From physical time to the first and second moments of psychological time. *Psychological Bulletin, 127*, 22–44.

Groos, G., & Daan, S. (1985). The use of the biological clocks in time perception. In J. A. Michon & J. L. Jackson (Eds.), *Time, Mind and Behavior* (pp. 65–74). Berlin: Springer-Verlag.

Groos, G., & Meijer, J. H. (1985). The effects of illumination on suprachiasmatic nucleus electrical discharge. *Annals of the New York Academy of Sciences, 453*, 134–146.

Gross, C. G., Rocha-Miranda, E. C., & Bender, D. B. (1972). Visual properties of neurons in inferotemporal cortex of the macaque. *Journal of Neurophysiology, 35*, 96–111.

Gross, J., & Hayne, H. (1996). Eyewitness identification by 5- to 6-year-old children. *Law & Human Behavior, 20*, 359–373.

Grossberg, S., Hwang, S., & Mingolla, E. (2002). Thalamocortical dynamics of the McCollough effect: boundary-surface alignment through perceptual learning. *Vision Research, 42*, 1259–1286.

Grossberg, S., & Kelly, F. (1999). Neural dynamics of binocular brightness perception. *Vision Research, 39*, 3796–3816.

Grossberg, J. M., & Grant, B. F. (1978). Clinical psychophysics. *Psychological Bulletin, 85*, 1154–1176.

Grossberg, S. (1983). The quantized geometry of visual space: The coherent computation of depth, form, and lightness. *Behavioral and Brain Sciences, 6*, 625–692.

Grossberg, S. (1995). The attentive brain. *American Scientist, 83*, 438–449.

Grosvenor, T., & Flom, M. C. (Eds.). (1991). *Refractive Anomalies: Research and Clinical Applications.* Boston: Butterworth-Heineman.

Guenther, F. H., & Gjaja, M. N. (1996). The perceptual magnet effect as an emergent property of neural map formation. *Journal of the Acoustical Society of America, 100*, 1111–1121.

Guillery, R. W., Feig, S. L., & Lozsádi, D. A. (1998). Paying attention to the thalamic reticular nucleus. *Trends in Neuroscience, 21*, 28–32.

Guinsburg, R., de Araujo, P. C., Branco, M. F, Xavier, B. R., Berenguel, R. C., Tonelotto, J., & Kopelman, B. I. (2000). Differences in pain expression between male and female newborn infants. *Pain, 85*, 127–133.

Guirao, M. (1991). A single scale based on ratio and partition estimates. In S. J. Bolanowski & G. A. Gescheider (Eds.), *Ratio Scaling of Psychological Magnitude* (pp. 59–78). Hillsdale, NJ: Erlbaum.

Guitton, D., Crommelink, M., & Roucoux, A. (1980). Stimulation of the superior colliculus in the alert cat: Eye movement and neck EMG activity evoked when the head is restrained. *Experimental Brain Research, 39*, 63–74.

Gulya, M., Rossi-George, A., Hartshorn, K., Vieira, A., Rovee-Collier, C., Johnson, M. K., & Chalfonte, B. L. (2002). The development of explicit memory for basic perceptual features. *Journal of Experimental Child Psychology,* 81, 276–297.

Gurnsey, R., & Fleet, D. J. (2001). Texture space. *Vision Research,* 41, 745–757.

Gurnsey R., Sally, S. L., Potechin, C., Mancini, S. (2002). Optimising the Pinna-Brelstaff illusion. *Perception,* 31, 1275–1280.

Gustafson, R. (1986). Effect of moderate doses of alcohol on simple auditory reaction time in a vigilance setting. *Perceptual and Motor Skills,* 62, 683–690.

Gwiazda, J., & Birch, E. E. (2001). Perceptual development: vision. In E. B. Goldstein (Ed.), *Blackwell Handbook of Perception.* Handbook of Experimental Psychology Series. (pp. 637–668). Oxford: Blackwell.

Haber, R.N. (1970). How we remember what we see. *Scientific American,* 222(5), 104–112.

Haber, R. N., & Haber, L. (2000). Experiencing, remembering and reporting events. *Psychology, Public Policy, and Law,* 6, 1057–1097.

Hafter, E. R., & Buell, T. (1990). Restarting the adapted binaural system. *Journal of the Acoustical Society of America,* 88, 806–812.

Hafter, E. R., & Schlauch, R. S. (1991). Cognitive factors and selection of auditory listening bands. In A. L. Dancer, D. Henderson, R. J. Salvi, & R. P. Hammernik (Eds.), *Noise Induced Hearing Loss* (pp. 303–310). Philadelphia: B. C. Decker.

Hahn, H. (1934). Die Adaptation des Geschmackssinnes. *Zeitschrift fuer Sinnesphysiologie,* 65, 105–145.

Haith, M. M., Hazan, C., & Goodman, G. S. (1988). Expectation and anticipation of dynamic visual events by 3.5-month-old babies. *Child Development,* 59, 467–479.

Hall, M. J., Bartoshuk, L. M., Cain, W. S., & Stevens, J. C. (1975). PTC taste blindness and the taste of caffeine. *Nature* (London), 253, 442–443.

Hall, W. G., & Oppenheim, R. W. (1987). Developmental psychobiology: Prenatal, perinatal and early postnatal aspects of behavioral development. *Annual Review of Psychology,* 38, 91–128.

Halpern, D. F. (1992). *Sex Differences in Cognitive Ability.* Hillsdale, NJ: Erlbaum.

Halpern, D. L., Blake, R., & Hillenbrand, J. (1986). Psychoacoustics of a chilling sound. *Perception & Psychophysics,* 39, 77–80.

Halsam, D. (1967). Individual differences in pain threshold and level of arousal. *British Journal of Psychology,* 58, 139–142.

Hamalainen, H., & Jarvilehto, T. (1981). Peripheral neural basis of tactile sensations in man: I. Effect of frequency and probe area on sensations elicited by single mechanical pulses on hairy and glabrous skin of the hand. *Brain Research,* 219, 1–12.

Hamm, V. P., & Hasher, L. (1992). Age and the availablity of inferences. *Psychology & Aging,* 7, 56–64.

Hanazawa, A., & Komatsu, H. (2001). Influence of the direction of elemental luminance gradients on the responses of V4 cells to textured surfaces. *Journal of Neuroscience,* 21, 4490–4497.

Handel, S., & Oshinsky, J. S. (1981). The meter of syncopated auditory polyrhythms. *Perception & Psychophysics,* 30, 1–9.

Hantz, E. C., & Kreilick, K. G. (1995). Effects of musical training and absolute pitch on a pitch memory task: An event-related potential study. *Psychomusicology,* 14, 53–76.

Hardie, R. C., & Kirschfeld, K. (1983). Ultraviolet sensitivity of fly photoreceptors R7 and R8: Evidence for a sensitizing function. *Biophysics of Structure and Mechanism,* 9, 171–180.

Hardy, J. D., Stolwijk, J. A. J., & Hoffman, D. (1968). Pain following step increase in skin temperature. In D. R. Kenshalo (Ed.), *The Skin Senses* (pp. 444–457). Springfield, IL: Thomas.

Hardy, J. D., Wolff, H. G., & Goodell, B. S. (1943). The pain threshold in man. *Research Publications Association for Research in Nervous and Mental Disease,* 23, 1–15.

Hardy, J. D., Wolff, H. G., & Goodell, H. (1947). Studies on pain: Discrimination of differences in intensity of a pain stimulus as a basis of a scale of pain intensity. *Journal of Clinical Investigation,* 26, 1152–1158.

Hari, R. (1994). Human cortical functions revealed by magnetoencephalography. *Progress in Brain Research,* 100, 163–168.

Harkins, S., & Green, R. G. (1975). Discriminability and criterion differences between extraverts and introverts during vigilance. *Journal of Research in Personality,* 9, 335–340.

Harland, R.E., & Coren, S. (2001). Individual differences in divergent thinking as a function of variations in sensory status. *Creativity Research Journal,* 13, 383–389.

Harland, R. E., & Coren, S. (1996). Adult sensory capacities as a function of birth risk factors. *Journal of Clinical and Experimental Neuropsychology,* 18, 394–405.

Harlow, H. (1959, June). Love in infant monkeys. *Scientific American,* 200, 68–79.

Harmon, L. D. (1973). The recognition of faces. *Scientific American,* 229, 70–82.

Harmon, L. D., & Julesz, B. (1973). Masking in visual recognition: Effects of two dimensional filtered noise. *Science,* 180, 1194–1197.

Harnsberger, JD (2001). The perception of Malayalam nasal consonants by Marathi, Punjabi, Tamil, Oriya, Bengali, and American English listeners: A multidimensional scaling analysis. *Journal of Phonetics,* 29, 303–327.

Harris, C. S. (1980). Insight or out of sight?: Two examples of perceptual plasticity in the human adult. In C. S. Harris (Ed.), *Visual Coding and Adaptability* (pp. 95–149). Hillsdale, NJ: Erlbaum.

Harris, L. J. (1981). Sex related variations in spatial skill. In L. S. Liben, A. H. Patterson, & N. Newcombe (Eds.), *Spatial*

Representation and Behavior across the Lifespan: Theory and Application (pp. 83–128). New York: Academic Press.

Harrison, W. A., & Burns, E. M. (1993). Effects of contralateral acoustic stimulation on spontaneous otoacoustic emissions. *Journal of the Acoustical Society of America, 94*, 2649–2658.

Hartley, A. A., Keiley, J. M., & Slabach, E. H. (1990). Age differences and similarities in the effects of cues and prompts. *Journal of Experimental Psychology: Human Perception and Performance, 16*, 523–537.

Hartley, D. E. H., Wright, B. A., Hogan, S. C., & Moore, D. R. (2000). Age related improvements in auditory backward and simultaneous masking in 6 to 10 year old children. *Journal of Speech, Language, and Hearing Research, 43*, 1402–1415.

Hartline, H. K. (1940). The receptive fields of optic nerve fibers. *American Journal of Physiology, 130*, 690–699.

Hartline, H. K., & Ratliff, F. (1957). Inhibitory interaction of receptor units in the eye of Limulus. *Journal of General Physiology, 40*, 357–376.

Hartman, A., & Hollister, L. (1963). Effect of mescaline, lysergic acid diethylamide and psilocybin on color perception. *Psychopharmacologia, 4*, 441–451.

Hartman, M., & Hasher, L. (1991). Aging and suppression: Memory for previously relevant information. *Psychology & Aging, 6*, 587–594.

Hasher, L., & Quig, M. B. (1997). Inhibitory control over no longer relevant information: Adult age differences. *Memory and Cognition, 25*, 286–295.

Hashimoto, H. (1966). A phenomenal analysis of social perception. *Child Development. 2*, 3–26.

Haug, B. A., & Kolle, R. U. (1995). Predominant affection of the blue cone pathway in Parkinson's disease. *Brain, 118*, 771–778.

Hausen, K. (1982). Movement sensitive interneurons in the optomotor system of the fly. II. The horizontal cells: Receptive field organization and response characteristics. *Biological Cybernetics, 46*, 67–79.

Hautzel, H., Taylor, J. G., Krause, B. J., Schmitz, N., Tellman, L., Ziemons, K., Shah, N. J., Herzog, H., & Mueller-Gaertner, H. W. (2001). The motion aftereffect: More than area V5/MT? Evidence from sup 1 sup 5O butanol PET studies. *Brain Research, 892*, 281–292.

He, J., Hashikawa, T., Ojima, H., & Kinouchi, Y. (1997). Temporal integration and duration tuning in the dorsal zone of cat auditory cortex. *The Journal of Neuroscience, 17*, 2615–2625.

He, L. (1987). Involvement of endogenous opioid peptides in acupuncture analgesia. *Pain, 31*, 99–122.

He, S., & Davis, W. L. (2001). Filling-in at the natural blind spot contributes to binocular rivalry. *Vision Research, 41*, 835–840.

He, S., Cavanagh, P., & Intriligator, J. (1996). Attentional resolution and the locus of visual awareness. *Nature, 383*, 334–337.

He, Z. J., & Nakayama, K. (1992). Surfaces versus features in visual search. *Nature, 359*, 231–233.

Head, H. (1920). *Studies in Neurology.* London & New York: Oxford University Press.

Heaps, C., & Handel, S. (1999). Similarity and features of natural textures. *Journal of Experimental Psychology: Human Perception and Performance, 25*, 299–320.

Heaton, J. M. (1968). *The Eye: Phenomenology and Psychology of Function and Disorder.* London: Tavistock.

Hecht, H., & Proffitt, D. (1991). Apparent extended body motions in depth. *Journal of Experimental Psychology: Human Perception and Performance, 17*, 1090–1103.

Hecht, S., & Mandelbaum, M. (1938). Rod-cone dark adaptation and vitamin A. *Science, 88*, 219–221.

Hecht, S., Shlaer, S., & Pirenne, M. H. (1942). Energy quanta and vision. *Journal of General Physiology, 25*, 819–840.

Heckmann, T., Post, R. B., & Deering, L. (1991). Induced motion of a fixated target: Influence of voluntary eye deviation. *Perception & Psychophysics, 50*, 230–236.

Heffner, H. E., & Heffner, R. S. (1984). Temporal lobe lesions and perception of species-specific vocalizations by macaques. *Science, 226*, 75–76.

Heggelund, P. (1981). Receptive field organization of simple cells in cat striate cortex. *Experimental Brain Research, 42*, 89–98.

Heider, B., Spillmann, L., & Peterhans, E. (2002). Stereoscopic illusory contours: Cortical neuron responses and human perception. *Journal of Cognitive Neuroscience, 14*, 1018–1029.

Heider, F., & Simmel, M. (1944). An experimental study of apparent behavior. *American Journal of Psychology, 57*, 243–249.

Hein, A., & Diamond, R. M. (1971). Contrasting development of visually triggered and guided movements in kittens with respect to interocular and interline equivalence. *Journal of Comparative and Physiological Psychology, 76*, 219–224.

Hein, A., & Held, R. (1967). Dissociation of the visual placing response into elicited and guided components. *Science, 158*, 390–392.

Hein, A., Held, R., & Gower, E. C. (1970). Development and segmentation of visually controlled movement by selective exposure during rearing. *Journal of Comparative and Physiological Psychology, 73*, 181–187.

Heinemann, E. G., & Chase, S. (1995). A quantitative model for simultaneous brightness induction. *Vision Research, 35*, 2007–2020.

Held, R. (1993). Binocular vision-Behavioral and neuronal development. In M. H. Johnson (Ed.), *Brain Development and Cognition: A Reader* (pp. 152–166). Oxford, UK: Blackwell.

Held, R., & Bauer, J. A. (1967). Visually guided reaching in infant monkeys after restricted rearing. *Science, 155*, 718–720.

Held, R., & Hein, A. (1963). Movement-produced stimulation in the development of visually guided behavior. *Journal of Comparative and Physiological Psychology, 56*, 872–876.

Held, R., & Hein, A. (1967). On the modifiability of form perception. In W. Wathen-Dunn (Ed.), *Models for the Perception of Speech and Visual Form* (pp. 296–304). Cambridge, MA: MIT Press.

Hellekant, G. (1965). Electrophysiological investigation of the gustatory effect of ethyl alcohol: The summated response of the chorda tympani in the cat, dog and rat. *Acta Physiologica Scandinavica,* 64, 392–397.

Heller, M. A. (1989). Texture perception in sighted and blind observers. *Perception & Psychophysics,* 45, 49–54.

Heller, M. A., Calcaterra, J. A., Burson, L. L., & Green, S. L. (1997). The tactual-horizontal-vertical illusion depends on radial motion of the entire arm. *Perception & Psychophysics,* 59, 1297–1311.

Hellman, R. P., & Zwislocki, J. J. (1968). Loudness determination at low sound frequencies. *Journal of the Acoustical Society of America,* 43, 60–64.

Helmholtz, H. E. F. von (1930). *The Sensations of Tone* (A. J. Ellis, Trans.). New York: Longmans, Green. (Original work published 1863)

Helson, H. (1964). *Adaptation Level Theory: An Experimental and Systematic Approach To Behavior.* New York: Harper.

Henderson, J. M., & Hollingworth, A. (2002). Eye movements, visual memory, and scene representation. In M. A. Peterson & G. Rhodes (Eds.), *Analytic and Holistic Processes in the Perception of Faces, Objects, and Scenes.* New York: JAI/Ablex.

Hendry, S. H. C., & Reid, R. C. (2000). The koniocellular pathway in primate vision. *Annual Review of Neuroscience,* 23, 127–153.

Henmon, V. A. C. (1906). The time of perception as a measure of differences in sensations. *Archives of Philosophy, Psychology and Scientific Methods,* No. 8.

Henn, V., Cohen, B., & Young, L. (1980). Visual-vestibular interaction in motion perception and the generation of nystagmus. *Neurosciences Research Program Bulletin,* 18, 459–651.

Henning, H. (1916). Die Qualitatenreihe des Geschmaks. *Zeitschrift fuer Psychologie,* 74, 203–219.

Hensel, H. (1981). *Thermoreception and Temperature Regulation.* New York: Academic Press.

Hermes, D. J. (1990). Vowel-onset detection. *Journal of the Acoustical Society of America,* 87, 866–873.

Hernandez-Peon, R. (1964). Psychiatric implications of neurophysiological research. *Bulletin of the Meninger Clinic,* 28, 165–185.

Herrnstein, R. J. 1990. Levels of stimulus control: a functional approach. *Cognition,* 37, 133–166.

Hershberger, W. (1987). Saccadic eye movements and the perception of visual direction. *Perception & Psychophysics,* 41, 35–44.

Hershberger, W. A., & Misceo, G. F. (1996). Touch dominates haptic estimates of discordant visual-haptic size. *Perception & Psychophysics,* 58, 1124–1132.

Hershenson, M. (1989). *The Moon Illusion.* Hillsdale, NJ: Erlbaum.

Hershenson, M., & Bader, P. (1990). Development of the spiral aftereffect. *Bulletin of the Psychonomic Society,* 28, 300–301.

Herz, R. S., & Engen, T. (1996). Odor memory: Review and analysis. *Psychonomic Bulletin & Review,* 3, 300–313.

Herzog, M. H., & Fahle M. (1997). The role of feedback in learning a vernier discrimination task. *Vision Research,* 37, 2133–2141.

Hess, E. H. (1950). Development of the chick's response to light and shade cues of depth. *Journal of Comparative and Physiological Psychology,* 43, 112–122.

Hess, R. H., Baker, C. L., & Zihl, J. (1989). The "motion-blind" patient: Low-level spatial and temporal filters. *Journal of Neuroscience,* 9, 1628–1640.

Hettinger, L. J. (2002). Illusory self motion in virtual environments. In K. M. Stanney (Ed.), *Handbook of Virtual Environments: Design, Implementation, and Applications. Human Factors and Ergonomics.* (pp. 471–491). Mahwah, NJ: Erlbaum.

Heumann, D., & Leuba, G. (1983). Neuronal death in the development and aging of the cerebral cortex of the mouse. *Neuropathology and Applied Neurobiology,* 9, 297–311.

Heywood, C. A., & Cowey, A. (1987). On the role of cortical area V4 in the discrimination of hue and pattern in macaque monkeys. *Journal of Neuroscience,* 7, 2601–2617.

Hick, W. E. (1952). On the rate of gain of information. *Quarterly Journal of Experimental Psychology,* 4, 11–26.

Hickey, T. L., & Peduzzi, J. D. (1987). Structure and development of the visual system. In P. Salapatek & L. Cohen (Eds.), *Handbook of Infant Perception: Vol. 1. From Sensation to Perception* (pp. 1–43). Orlando: Academic Press.

Hicks, R. E., Miller, G. W., & Kinsbourne, M. (1976). Prospective and retrospective judgments of time as a function of amount of information processed. *American Journal of Psychology,* 89, 719–730.

Hicks, R. E., Miller, G. W., Gaes, G., & Bierman, K. (1977). Concurrent processing demands and the experience of time in passing. *American Journal of Psychology,* 90, 431–446.

Hicks, T. P., Molotchnikoff, S., & Ono, T. (1993). *The Visually Responsive Neuron: From Basic Neurophysiology to Behavior.* New York: Elsevier.

Hier, D. B., & Crowley, W. F. Jr. (1982). Spatial ability in androgen-deficient men. *New England Journal of Medicine,* 306, 1202–1205.

Higgins, S. T., & Bickel, W. K. (1990). Effects of intranasal cocaine on human learning, performance and physiology. *Psychopharmacology,* 102, 451–458.

Hilgetag, C. C., Theoret, H., & Pascual-Leone, A. (2001). Enhanced visual spatial attention ipsilateral to rTMS-induced 'virtual lesions' of human parietal cortex. *Nature Neuroscience,* 4, 953–957.

Hillyard, S. A., Hink, R. F., Schwent, V. L., & Picton, T. W. (1973). Electrical signs of selective attention in the human brain. *Science,* 12, 177–180.

Hirsch, H. V., & Spinelli, D. N. (1970). Visual experience modifies distribution of horizontally and vertically oriented receptive fields in cats. *Science,* 168, 869–871.

Hoagland, H. (1933). The physiological control of judgment of duration: Evidence for a chemical clock. *Journal of General Psychology,* 9, 267–287.

Hochberg, J. (1981). On cognition in perception: Perceptual coupling and unconscious inference. *Cognition,* 10, 127–134.

Hochberg, J. (1982). How big is a stimulus? In J. Beck (Ed.), *Organization and Representation in Perception* (pp. 191–218). Hillsdale, NJ: Erlbaum.

Hochberg, J., & Brooks, V. (1960). The psychophysics of form: Reversible-perspective drawings of spatial objects. *American Journal of Psychology,* 73, 337–354.

Hochberg, J., & Brooks, V. (1962). Pictorial recognition as an unlearned ability: A study of one child's performance. *American Journal of Psychology,* 75, 624–628.

Hoffer, A., & Osmond, H. (1967). *The Hallucinogens.* New York: Academic Press.

Hoffman, D. D. (1998). *Visual Intelligence: How We Create What We See.* New York: W. W. Norton & Company.

Hoffman, D. D. , & Richards, W. A. (1984). Parts of recognition. *Cognition,* 18, 65–96.

Hogben, J. H., & Di Lollo, V. (1985). Suppression of visible persistence in apparent motion. *Perception & Psychophysics,* 38, 450–460.

Hogervorst, M. A., & Eagle, R. A. (2000). The role of perspective effects and accelerations in perceived three dimensional structure-from-motion. *Journal of Experimental Psychology: Human Perception and Performance,* 26, 934–955.

Holland, H. (1960). Drugs and personality: XII. A comparison of several drugs by the flicker-fusion method. *Journal of Mental Science,* 106, 858–861.

Holst, E. von, & Mittelstaedt, H. (1950). Das Reafferenzprincip (wechselwirkungen zeischen zentral Nervensystem und Peripherie). *Naturwissenschaften,* 37, 464–476.

Hood, B. M. (1993). Inhibition of return produced by covert shifts of visual attention in 6-month-old infants. *Infant Behavior and Development,* 16, 245–254.

Hood, B. M., & Atkinson, J. (1991). Sensory visual loss and cognitive deficits in the selective attentional system of normal infants and neurologically impaired children. *Developmental Medicine and Child Neurology,* 32, 1067–1077.

Hood, B. M., & Atkinson, J. (1993). Disengaging visual attention in the infant and adult. *Infant Behavior & Development,* 16, 405–422.

Hood, B. M. (1993). Shifts of visual attention in the infant. In C. Rovee-Collier & L. Lipsitt (Eds.), *Advances in Infancy Research* (pp. 163–216). Norwood NJ: Ablex.

Hood, D.C. (1998). Lower level processing and models of light adaptation. *Annual Review of Psychology,* 49, 503–535.

Hopfinger, J. B., Buonocore, M. H., & Mangun, G. R. (2000). The neural mechanisms of top-down attentional control. *Nature Neuroscience,* 3, 284–291.

Horner, D. T. (1991). The effects of complexity on the perception of vibrotactile patterns. *Perception & Psychophysics,* 49, 551–562.

Horner, D. T. (1997). The effect of shape and location on temporal masking of spatial vibrotactile patterns. *Perception & Psychophysics,* 59, 1255–1265.

Howard, C. M., Tregear, S. J., & Werner, J. S. (2000). Time course of early mesopic adaptation to luminance decrements and recovery of spatial resolution. *Vision Research,* 40. 3059–3064.

Howard, I. P. (2002). Depth perception. In H. Pashler & S. Yantis (Eds.), *Steven's Handbook of Experimental Psychology* (3rd ed.), Vol. 1: *Sensation and Perception* (pp. 77–120). New York: Wiley.

Howard, I. P., Bergstrom, S. S., & Ohmi, M. (1990). Shape from shading in different frames of reference. *Perception,* 19, 523–530.

Howard, I. P., Craske, B., & Templeton, W. B. (1965). Visuomotor adaptation to discordant exafferent stimulation. *Journal of Experimental Psychology,* 70, 189–191.

Hoyle, F. (1959). *The Black Cloud.* New York: Signet.

Hu, S., Grant, W. F., Stern, R. M., & Koch, K. (1991). Motion sickness severity and physiological correlates during repeated exposures to a rotating optokinetic drum. *Aviation, Space and Environmental Medicine,* 62, 308–314.

Huang, L., & Pashler, H. (2002). Symmetry detection and visual attention: A "binary map" hypothesis. *Vision Research,* 42, 1421–1430.

Hubel, D. H., & Wiesel, T. N. (1962). Receptive fields, binocular interaction and functional architecture in the cat's visual cortex. *Journal of Physiology* (London), 160, 106–154.

Hudson, W. (1962). Pictorial perception and educational adaptation in Africa. *Psychologia, Africana,* 9, 226–239.

Hudspeth, A. J. (1985). The cellular basis of hearing: The biophysics of hair cells. *Science,* 230, 745–752.

Hughes, H. C. (1986). Asymmetric interference between components of suprathreshold compound gratings. *Perception & Psychophysics,* 40, 241–250.

Hukin, R. W., & Darwin, C. J. (1995). Comparison of the effect of onset asynchrony on auditory grouping in pitch matching and vowel identification. *Perception & Psychophysics,* 57, 191–196.

Hulse, S. H., & Page, S. C. (1988). Toward a comparative psychology of music perception. *Music Perception,* 5, 427–452.

Hultsch D. F., MacDonald, S. W., & Dixon, R. A. (2002). Variability in reaction time performance of younger and older adults. *Journal of Gerontology B,* 57, P101–115.

Hummel, J. E., & Biederman, I. (1992). Dynamic binding in a neural network for shape recognition. *Psychological Review,* 99, 480–517.

Humphrey D. G., Kramer, A. F. (1999). Age-related differences in perceptual organization and selective attention: implications for display segmentation and recall performance. *Experimental Aging Research,* 25, 1–26.

Humphreys, G. W. (1984). Shape constancy: The effects of changing shape orientation and the effects of changing the position of focal features. *Perception & Psychophysics,* 36, 50–64.

Humphries, S. A., Johnson, M. H., & Long, N. R. (1996). An investigation of the gate control theory of pain using the experimental pain stimulus of potassium iontophoresis. *Perception & Psychophysics,* 58, 693–703.

Hung, P., & Berns, R. S. (1995). Determination of constant hue loci for a CRT gamut and their predictions using color appearance spaces. *Color Research & Application,* 20, 285–295.

Hunzelmann, N., & Spillman, L. (1984). Movement adaptation in the peripheral retina. *Vision Research,* 24, 1765–1769.

Hurlbert, A. (2000). Visual perception: Learning to see through noise. *Current Biology,* 10, R231–R233.

Hurlbert, A. C., & Poggio, T. A. (1988). Synthesizing a color algorithm from examples. *Science,* 239, 482–485.

Hurlburt, R. T. (1990). *Sampling Normal and Schizophrenic Inner Experience.* NY: Plenum Press.

Hurlburt, R. T., & Heavey, C. L. (2001). Telling what we know: describing inner experience. *Trends in Cognitive Sciences,* 5, 400–403.

Hurvich, L. M., & Jameson, D. (1974). Opponent processes as a model of neural organization. *American Psychologist,* 29, 88–102.

Husain M., & Jackson, S. R. (2001). Vision: Visual space is not what it appears to be. *Current Biology,* 11, R753–755.

Huttenlocher, P. R. (1990). Morphometric study of human cerebral cortex development. *Neuropsychologia,* 28, 517–527.

Huxley, A. (1963). *The Doors of Perception and Heaven and Hell.* New York: Harper.

Iacono, W. G., Pelouqin, L. J., Lumry, A. E., Valentine, R. H., & Tuason, V. B. (1982). Eye tracking in patients with unipolar and bipolar affective disorders in remission. *Journal of Abnormal Psychology,* 91, 35–44.

Iadecola, C. (1993). Regulation of cerebral microcirculation during neural activity: Is nitric oxide the missing link? *Trends in Neurosciences,* 16, 206–214.

Innis, S. M., Gilley, J., & Werker, J. (2001). Are human milk long-chain polyunsaturated fatty acids related to visual and neural development in breast-fed term infants? *Journal of Pediatrics,* 139, 532–538.

Intraub, H. (1985). Visual dissociation: An illusory conjunction of pictures and forms. *Journal of Experimental Psychology: Human Perception and Performance,* 11, 431–442.

Intraub, H. (1997). The representation of visual scenes. *Trends in Cognitive Science,* 1, 217–222.

Intraub, H., & Berkowits, D. (1996). Beyond the edges of a picture. *American Journal of Psychology,* 109, 581–598.

Intraub, H., & Gottesman, C. V. (1996). Boundary extension for briefly glimpsed photographs: Do common perceptual processes result in unexpected memory distortions? *Journal of Memory & Language,* 35, 118–134.

Ippolitov, F. W. (1973). Interanalyzer differences in the sensitivity-strength parameter for vision, hearing and cutaneous modalities. In V. D. Nebylitsyn & J. A. Gray (Eds.), *Biological Bases of Individual Behavior* (pp. 43–61). New York: Academic Press.

Irwin, R. J., Hautus, M. J., Dawson, N. J., Welch, D., & Bayly, M. F. (1994). Discriminability of electrocutaneous stimuli after topical anesthesia: Detection-theory measurement of sensitivity to painful stimuli. *Perception & Psychophysics,* 55, 125–132.

Ittelson, W. H. (1960). *Visual Space Perception.* Berlin and New York: Springer-Verlag.

Ittelson, W. H. (1962). Perception and transactional psychology. In S. Koch (Ed.), *Psychology: A Study of a Science,* Vol. 4 (pp. 660–704). New York: McGraw-Hill.

Iverson, P. (1995). Auditory stream segregation by musical timbre: Effects of static and dynamic acoustic attributes. *Journal of Experimental Psychology: Human Perception and Performance,* 21, 751–763.

Iwamura, Y. (1998). Hierarchical somatosensory processing. *Current Opinion in Neurobiology,* 8, 522–528.

Jackson, G. R., & Owsley, C. (2000). Scotopic sensitivity during adulthood. *Vision Research,* 40, 2467–2473.

Jacobs, G. H. (1976). Color vision. *Annual Review of Psychology,* 27, 63–89.

Jacobs, G. H. (1986). Cones and opponency. *Vision Research,* 26, 1533–1541.

Jacobs, G. H. (1993). The distribution and nature of colour vision among the mammals. *Biological Reviews,* 68, 413–471.

Jacobs, R. A., & Fine, I. (1999). Experience dependent integration of texture and motion cues to depth. *Vision Research,* 39, 4062–4075.

Jacobs, R. A. (2002). What determines visual cue reliability? *Trends in Cognitive Sciences,* 6, 345–350.

Jacobsen, A., & Gilchrist, A. (1988). The ratio principle holds over a million-to-one range of illumination. *Perception & Psychophysics,* 43, 1–6.

James, W. (1890). *The Principles of Psychology.* New York: Holt.

Jameson, D., & Hurvich, L. M. (1989). Essay concerning color constancy. *Annual Review of Psychology,* 40, 1–22.

Jameson, K. A., Highnote, S. M., & Wasserman, L. M. (2001). Richer color experiences in observers with multiple photopigment opsin genes. *Psychonomic Bulletin & Review,* 8, 244–261.

Janal, M. N., Clark, W. C., & Carroll, J. D. (1991). Multidimensional scaling of painful and innocuous electrocutaneous stimuli: Reliability and individual differences. *Perception & Psychophysics,* 50, 108–116.

Jansson, G., Bergstrom, S. S., & Epstein, W. (Eds.). (1994). *Perceiving Events and Objects.* Hillsdale, NJ: Erlbaum.

Jaschinski-Kruza, W. (1984). Transient myopia after visual work. *Ergonomics,* 27, 1181–1189.

Javel, E. (1996). Long-term adaptation in cat auditory nerve fiber responses. *Journal of the Acoustical Society of America,* 99, 1040–1052.

Javitt, J. C., & Taylor, H. R. (1994). Cataract and latitude. *Documenta Ophthalmologica,* 88, 307–325.

Jeffery, G. (2001). Architecture of the optic chiasm and the mechanisms that sculpt its development. *Physiological Reviews,* 81, 1393–1414.

Jeka, J. J., Easton, R. D., Bentzen, B. L., & Lackner, J. R. (1996). Haptic cues for orientation and postural control in sighted and blind individuals. *Perception & Psychophysics,* 58, 409–423.

Jenness, J. W., & Shevell, S. K. (1995). Color appearance with sparse chromatic context. *Vision Research,* 35, 797–805.

Jesteadt, W., & Wier, C. C. (1977). Comparison of monaural and binaural discrimination of intensity and frequency. *Journal of the Acoustical Society of America,* 61, 1599–1603.

Jin, E. W., & Shevell, S. K. (1996). Color memory and color constancy. *Journal of the Optical Society of America A-Optics & Image Science,* 13, 1981–1991.

Johansson, G. (1976a). Visual motion perception. In R. Held & W. Richards (Eds.), *Recent progress in perception: Readings from Scientific American* (pp. 67–75). San Francisco: Freeman.

Johansson, G. (1976b). Spatio-temporal differentiation and integration in visual motion perception. *Psychological Research,* 38, 379–393.

Johansson, G., von Hofsten, C., & Jansson, G. (1980). Event perception. *Annual Review of Psychology,* 31, 27–63.

John, E. R. (2001). A field theory of consciousness. *Consciousness and Cognition,* 10, 184–213.

John, E. R., Prichep, L. S., Fridman, J., & Easton, P. (1988). Neurometrics: Computer-assisted differential diagnosis of brain dysfunctions. *Science,* 239, 162–169.

Johnson, C. H., & Hastings, J. W. (1986). The elusive mechanism of the circadian clock. *American Scientist,* 74(1), 29–36.

Johnson, D. H. (1980). The relationship between spike rate and synchrony in responses of auditory-nerve fibers to single tones. *Journal of the Acoustical Society of America,* 68, 1115–1122.

Johnson, E. S., & Meade, A. C. (1987). Developmental patterns of spatial ability: An early sex difference. *Child Development,* 58, 725–740.

Johnson, K. O. (2001). The roles and functions of cutaneous mechanoreceptors. *Current Opinion in Neurobiology,* 11, 455–461.

Johnson, M. A. (1986). Color vision in the peripheral retina. *American Journal of Optometry and Physiological Optics,* 63, 97–103.

Johnson, M. H. (1995). The inhibition of automatic saccades in early infancy. *Developmental Psychobiology,* 28, 281–291.

Johnson, M. H. (2001). Functional brain development during infancy. In, G. Bremner & A. Fogel (Eds.), *Blackwell Handbook of Infant Development.* Handbooks of Developmental Psychology (pp. 169–190). Malden, MA: Blackwell Publishers.

Johnson, M. H., & Mareschal, D. (2001). Cognitive and perceptual development during infancy. *Current Opinion in Neurobiology,* 11, 213–218.

Johnson, M. H., & Tucker, L. A. (1996). The development and temporal dynamics of spatial orienting in infants. *Journal of Experimental Child Psychology,* 63, 171–188.

Johnson, S. P., Bremner, J. G., Slater, A. M., & Mason, U. C. (2000). The role of good form in young infants' perception of partly occluded objects. *Journal of Experimental Child Psychology,* 76, 1–25.

Johnston, M. V., Nishimura, A., Harum, K., Pekar, J., & Blue, M. E. (2001). Sculpting the developing brain. *Advances in Pediatrics,* 48, 1–38.

Jones, D. T., & Reed, R. R. (1989). Golf: An olfactory neuron specific-G protein involved in odorant signal transduction. *Science,* 244, 790–795.

Jones, M. B., Chronister, J. L., & Kennedy, R. S. (1998). Effects of alcohol on perceptual speed. *Perceptual and Motor Skills,* 87, 1247–1255.

Jonides, J. (1980). Towards a model of the mind's eye's movements. *Canadian Journal of Psychology,* 34, 103–112.

Jonides, J., & Yantis, S. (1988). Uniqueness of abrupt visual onset in capturing attention. *Perception & Psychophysics,* 43, 346–355.

Joubert, C. E. (1983). Subjective acceleration of time: Death anxiety and sex differences. *Perceptual and Motor Skills,* 57, 49–50.

Joubert, C. E. (1990). Subjective expectations of the acceleration of time with aging. *Perceptual and Motor Skills,* 70, 334.

Jourdain, R. (1997). *Music, The Brain, and Ecstasy.* New York: Avon.

Julesz, B. (1964). Binocular depth perception without familiarity cues. *Science,* 145, 356–362.

Julesz, B. (1971). *Foundations of Cyclopean Perception.* Chicago: University of Chicago Press.

Julesz, B. (1978). Perceptual limits of texture discrimination and their implications to figure-ground separation. In E. Leeuwenberg & H. Buffart (Eds.), *Formal Theories of Perception* (pp. 205–216). New York: Wiley.

Julesz, B. (1980). Spatial nonlinearities in the instantaneous perception of textures with identical power spectra. In C. Longuet-Higgins & N. S. Sutherland (Eds.), *The Psychology of Vision.* Philosophical Transactions of the Royal Society, London, 290, 83–94.

Julesz, B. (1984). A brief outline of the texton theory of human vision. *Trends in Neuroscience,* 7, 41–45.

Julesz, B., & Schumer, R. A. (1981). Early visual perception. *Annual Review of Psychology,* 32, 575–627.

Jusczyk, P. W. (1986). Toward a model of the development of speech perception. In J. S. Perkell & D. H. Klatt (Eds.), Invariance and variability in speech processes (pp. 1–19). Hillsdale, NJ: Erlbaum.

Jusczyk, P. W., & Krumhansl, C. L. (1993). Pitch and rhythmic patterns affecting infants' sensitivity to musical phrase structure. *Journal of Experimental Psychology: Human Perception and Performance,* 19, 627–640.

Jusczyk, P. W., & Luce, P. A. (2002). Speech perception. In H. Pashler & S. Yantis (Eds.), *Stevens Handbook of Experimental Psychology* (3rd ed.), Vol. 1: *Sensation and Perception* (pp. 493–536). New York: Wiley.

Juslin, P., & Olsson, N. (1996). Calibration and diagnosticity of confidence in eyewitness identification: Comments on what can be inferred from the low confidence-accuracy correlation. *Journal of Experimental Psychology: Learning, Memory, and Cognition,* 22, 1304–1316.

Kaas, J. H., & Lyon, D. C. (2001). Visual cortex organization in primates: Theories of V3 and adjoining visual areas. *Progress in Brain Research,* 134, 285–295.

Kaas, J. H. (1983). The organization of somatosensory cortex in primates and other mammals. In C. von Euler, O. Franzen, U. Lindblom, & D. Ottoson (Eds.), *Somatosensory Mechanisms* (pp. 51–60). New York: Plenum Press.

Kable, J. W., Lease-Spellmeyer, J., & Chatterjee, A. (2002). Neural substrates of action event knowledge. Journal of *Cognitive Neuroscience,* 14, 795–805.

Kaernbach, C. (1991). Simple adaptive testing with the weighted up-down method. *Perception & Psychophysics,* 49, 227–229.

Kahneman, D. (1967). An onset-onset law for one case of apparent motion and metacontrast. *Perception & Psychophysics,* 2, 577–584.

Kahneman, D. (1968). Method, findings, and theory in studies of visual masking. *Psychological Bulletin,* 70, 404–425.

Kahneman, D. (1973). *Attention and Effort.* Englewood Cliffs, NJ: Prentice Hall.

Kahneman, D., & Treisman, A. (1984). Changing views of attention and automaticity. In R. Parasuraman & D. R. Davies (Eds.), *Varieties of Attention* (pp. 29–61). Orlando: Academic Press.

Kahneman, D., Norman, J., & Kubovy, M. (1967). Critical duration for the resolution of form: Centrally or peripherally determined? *Journal of Experimental Psychology,* 73, 323–327.

Kaiser, M., & Calderone, J. B. (1991). Factors influencing perceived angular velocity. *Perception & Psychophysics,* 50, 428–434.

Kaiser, P. K., & Boynton, R. M. (1985). Role of the blue mechanism in wavelength discrimination. *Vision Research,* 25, 523–529.

Kalarickal, G. J., & Marshall, J. A. (2000). Neural model of temporal and stochastic properties of binocular rivalry. *Neurocomputing,* 32–33, 843–853.

Kaneda, H., Maeshima, K., Goto, N., Kobayakawa, T., Ayabe-Kanamura, S., & Saito, S. (2000). Decline in taste and odor discrimination abilities with age, and relationship between gustation and olfaction. *Chemical Senses,* 25, 331–337.

Kanisza, G. (1979). *Organization in Vision: Essays on Gestalt Perception.* New York: Praeger.

Kanizsa, G., Renzi, P., Conte, S., Compostela, C., & Guerani, L. (1993). Amodal completion in mouse vision. *Perception,* 22, 713–721.

Kanwisher, N. (2001). Neural events and perceptual awareness. *Cognition,* 79, 89–113.

Kaplan, A., & Glanville, E. (1964). Taste thresholds for bitterness and cigarette smoking. *Nature* (London), 202, 1366.

Kaplan, R-M. (1995). *The Power Behind Your Eyes: Improving Your Eye Sight with Integrated Vision Therapy.* Rochester, VT: Healing Arts Press.

Kaptein, N. A., Theeuwes, J., & van der Heijden, A. H. C. (1995). Search for a conjunctively defined target can be selectively limited to a color-defined subset of elements. *Journal of Experimental Psychology: Human Perception and Performance,* 21, 1053–1069.

Kasese, H. M., Drewett, R., & Wright, C. (2001). Sweetness preferences in 1–year-old children who fail to thrive. *Journal of Reproductive and Infant Psychology,* 19, 253–257.

Kashimori, Y., Inoue, S., Kambara, T., & Uchiyama, M. (2001). A neural model of amygdala playing an essential role in formation of brain maps for accomplishing spatial tasks. *Neurocomputing: An International Journal,* 38, 705–712.

Kastner, S., de Weerd, P., & Ungerleider, L. G. (2000). Texture segregation in the human visual cortex: A functional MRI study. *Journal of Neurophysiology,* 83, 2453–2457.

Katz, L. C., & Crowley, J. C. (2002). Development of cortical circuits: lessons from ocular dominance columns. *Nature Review of Neuroscience,* 3, 34–42.

Katz, D. B., Nicolelis, M. A. L., & Simon, S. A. (2002). Gustatory processing is dynamic and distributed. *Current Opinion in Neurobiology,* 12, 448–454.

Kauer, J. S. (1987). Coding in the olfactory system. In T. E. Finger & W. L. Silver (Eds.), *Neurobiology of Taste and Smell* (pp. 205–232). New York: Wiley.

Kaufman, L., & Kaufman, J. H. (2000). Explaining the moon illusion. *Proceedings of the National Academy of Science, U.S.A.,* 97, 500–555.

Kaufman, L. (1974). *Sight and Mind: An Introduction to Visual Perception.* London and New York: Oxford University Press.

Kaufman, L., & Rock, I. (1989). The moon illusion thirty years later. In M. Hershenson (Ed.), *The Moon Illusion* (pp. 193–234). Hillsdale, NJ: Erlbaum.

Kaye, M., Mitchell, D. E., & Cynader, M. (1982). Depth perception, eye dominance and cortical binocularity of dark-reared cats. *Developmental Brain Research,* 2, 37–53.

Kellman, P. J. (1984). Perception of three-dimensional form by human infants. *Perception & Psychophysics,* 36, 353–358.

Kellman, P. J. (2000). An update on Gestalt psychology. In B. Landau & J. Sabini et al. (Eds.), *Perception, Cognition, and Language: Essays in Honor of Henry and Lila Gleitman* (pp. 157–190). Cambridge, MA: MIT Press.

Kellman, P. J., & Shipley, T. F. (1990). A theory of visual interpolation in object perception. *Cognition,* 23, 141–221.

Kellman, P. J., & Arterberry, M. E. (1998). *The Cradle of Knowledge: Development of Perception in Infancy.* Cambridge, MA: MIT Press.

Kellman, P. J., Guttman, S. E., & Wickens, T. D. (2001). Geometric and neural models of object perception. In T. F. Shipley & P. J. Kellman (Eds.), *From Fragments to Objects: Segmentation and Grouping in Vision.* (pp. 183–246). Amsterdam: Elsevier.

Kemp, D. T. (1978). Stimulated acoustic emissions from within the human auditory system. *Journal of the Acoustical Society of America,* 64, 1386–1391.

Kendrick, K. M., & Baldwin, B. A. (1987). Cells in the temporal cortex of conscious sheep can respond preferentially to the sight of faces. *Science,* 236, 448–450.

Kennedy, J. M., & Domander, R. (1985). Shape and contour: The points of maximum change least useful for recognition. *Perception,* 14, 367–370.

Kennedy, J. M., & Ostry, D. (1976). Approaches to picture perception: Perceptual experience and ecological optics. *Canadian Journal of Psychology,* 30, 90–98.

Kenshalo, D. R., & Isensee, O. (1983). Responses of primate SI cortical neurons to noxious stimuli. *Journal of Neurophysiology,* 50, 1479–1496.

Kersten, D., & Knill, D. C. (1996). Illusory motion from shadows. *Nature,* 379, 31.

Khan, A. Z., & Crawford, J. D. (2001). Ocular dominance reverses as a function of horizontal gaze angle. *Vision Research,* 41, 1743–1748.

Kiang, K. Y. S., Rho, J. M., Northrop, C. C., Liberman, M. C., & Ryugo, D. K. (1982). Hair-cell innervation by spiral ganglion cells in adult cats. *Science,* 217, 175–177.

Kilbride, P. E., Hutman, L. P., Fishman, M., & Read, J. S. (1986). Foveal cone pigment density difference in the aging human eye. *Vision Research,* 26, 321–325.

Kim, M-S., & Cave, K. R. (1995). Spatial attention in visual search for features and feature conjunctions. *Psychological Science,* 6, 376–380.

Kimchi, R. (1992). Primacy of wholistic processing and global/local paradigm: A critical review. *Psychological Bulletin,* 112, 24–38.

Kimura, K., & Beidler, L. M. (1961). Microelectrode study of taste receptors of rat and hamster. *Journal of Cellular and Comparative Physiology,* 58, 131–140.

Kinchla, R. A., & Wolfe, J. (1979). The order of visual processing: "Top-down," "bottom-up," or "middle-out." *Perception & Psychophysics,* 25, 225–231.

King, M. C., & Lockhead, G. R. (1981). Response scales and sequential effects in judgment. *Perception & Psychophysics,* 30, 599–603.

King, J. W., & Riggs, L. A. (Eds.), *Woodworth and Schlossberg's Experimental Psychology* (3rd ed., pp. 315–368). New York: Holt, Rinehart and Winston.

Kingstone, A., Enns, J. T., Mangun, G. R., & Gazzaniga, M. S. (1995). Guided visual search is a left-hemisphere process in split-brain patients. *Psychological Science,* 6, 118–121.

Kirk-Smith, M. D., & Booth, D. A. (1980). Effects of androstenone on choice of location in other's presence. In H. van der Starre (Ed.), *Olfaction and Taste* VII (pp. 397–400). London: IRL Press.

Kirk-Smith, M. D., Booth, D. A., Caroll, D., & Davies, P. (1978). Human social attitudes affected by androstenol. *Research Communications in Psychology, Psychiatry and Behavior,* 3, 379–384.

Kitazawa, S., & Kohno, T. (1995). Effects of delayed visual information on the rate and amount of prism adaptation in the human. *Journal of Neuroscience,* 15, 7644–7652.

Kitzes, L. M., Gibson, M. M., Rose, J. E., & Hind, J. E. (1978). Initial discharge latency and threshold considerations for some neurons in cochlear nucleus complex of the cat. *Journal of Neurophysiology,* 41, 1165–1182.

Klatt, D. H. (1980). Speech perception: A model of acoustic-phonetic analysis and lexical access. In R. Cole (Ed.), *Perception and Production of Fluent Speech* (pp. 243–288). Hillsdale, NJ: Erlbaum.

Klatzky, R. L., & Lederman, S. J. (1995). Identifying objects from a haptic glance. *Perception & Psychophysics,* 57, 1111–1123.

Klatzky, R. L., Lederman S. J., & Metzger, V. A. (1985). Identifying objects by touch: An "expert system." *Perception & Psychophysics,* 37, 299–302.

Klatzky, R. L., Lederman, S. J., & Matula, D. E. (1993). Haptic exploration in the presence of vision. *Journal of Experimental Psychology: Human Perception & Performance,* 19, 726–743.

Klatzky, R. L., Lederman, S. J., & Reed, C. (1987). There's more to touch than meets the eye: The salience of object attributes for haptics with and without vision. *Journal of Experimental Psychology: General,* 116, 356–369.

Klatzky, R. L., Lederman, S. J., & Reed, C. (1989). Haptic integration of object properties: Texture, hardness and planar contour. *Journal of Experimental Psychology: Human Perception and Performance,* 15, 45–57.

Klein, G. S. (1970). *Perception, Motives and Personality.* New York: Knopf.

Klein, R. (1980). Does oculomotor readiness mediate cognitive control of visual attention? In R. S. Nickerson (Ed.), *Attention and Performance* VIII (pp. 259–276). Hillsdale, NJ: Erlbaum.

Klein, R. (1988). Inhibitory tagging system facilitates visual search. *Nature,* 334, 430–431.

Klein, R. M. (2000). Inhibition of return. *Trends in Cognitive Sciences,* 4, 138–147.

Klein, S. A., & Levi, D. M. (1985). Hyperacuity threshold of 1.0 second: Theoretical predictions and empirical validation. *Journal of the Optical Society of America,* A2, 1170–1190.

Kleiser, R., Skrandies, W. (2000). Neural correlates of reafference: evoked brain activity during motion perception and saccadic eye movements. *Experimental Brain Research,* 133, 312–320.

Kluender, K. R., & Jenison, R. L. (1992). Effects of glide slope, noise intensity, and noise duration on the extrapolation of FM glides through noise. *Perception & Psychophysics,* 51, 231–238.

Kluender, K. R., & Lotto, A. J. (1994). Effects of first formant onset frequency on [-voice] judgments results from auditory processes not specific to humans. *Journal of the Acoustical Society of America,* 95, 1044–1052.

Kluender, K. R., Diehl, R. L., & Killeen, P. R. (1987). Japanese quail can learn phonetic categories. *Science,* 237, 1195–1197.

Klutky, N. (1990). Geschlechtsunterschiede in der Gedachtnisleistung fur Geruche, Tonfolgen und Farben. *Zeitschrift fur Experimentelle und Angewandte Psychologie,* 37, 437–446.

Kluver, H., & Bucy, P. C. (1937). "Psychic blindness" and other symptoms following bilateral temporal lobectomy in rhesus monkeys. *American Journal of Physiology,* 119, 352–353.

Klymenko, V., & Weisstein, N. (1986). Spatial frequency differences can determine figure-ground organization. *Journal of Experimental Psychology: Human Perception and Performance,* 12, 324–330.

Knau, H. (2000). Thresholds for detecting slowly changing Ganzfeld luminances. *Journal of the Optical Society of America A: Optics and Image Science,* 17, 1382–1387.

Knierim, J. J., Kudrimoti, H. S., & Mcnaughton, B. L. (1995). Place cells, head direction cells, and the learning of landmark stability. *Journal of Neuroscience,* 15, 1648–1659.

Knoblauch, K., Vital-Durand, F., & Barbur, J. L. (2001). Variation of chromatic sensitivity across the life span. *Vision Research,* 41, 23–26.

Knudsen, E. I., & Brainard, M. S. (1991). Visual instruction of the neural map of auditory space in the developing optic tectum. *Science,* 253, 85–87.

Knudsen, E. I., & Knudsen, P. F. (1989). Vision calibrates sound localization in developing barn owls. *The Journal of Neuroscience,* 9, 3306–3313.

Koffka, K. (1935). *Principles of Gestalt Psychology.* New York: Harcourt, Brace & World.

Kohl, J. V., & Francoeur, R. T. (1995). *The Scent of Eros.* New York: Continuum.

Kohler, I. (1962). Experiments with goggles. *Scientific American,* 206, 62–86.

Kohler, I. (1964). The formation and transformation of the perceptual world. *Psychological Issues,* 3 (Whole No. 4).

Kohler, W. (1923). Zur Theories des Sukzessivvergleichs und der Zeitfehler. *Psychologische Forschung,* 4, 115–175.

Kolb, B., & Whishaw, I. Q. (2003). *Fundamentals of Human Neuropsychology* (5th Ed.) NY: Worth Publishers.

Kolers, P. A., & Brewster, J. M. (1985). Rhythms and responses. *Journal of Experimental Psychology: Human Perception and Performance,* 11, 150–167.

Kolers, P. A., & von Grunau, M. (1976). Shape and color in apparent motion. *Vision Research,* 16, 329–335.

Konstadt, N., & Forman, E. (1965). Field dependence and external directedness. *Journal of Personality and Social Psychology,* 1, 490–493.

Korsching, S. (2002). Olfactory maps and odor images. *Current Opinion in Neurobiology,* 12, 387–392.

Koslowe, K. C., Spierer, A., Rosner, M., & Belkin, M. (1991). Evaluation of accommotrac biofeedback training for myopia control. *Optometry and Vision Science,* 68, 338–343.

Kral, A. (2000). Temporal code and speech recognition. *Acta-Oto-Laryngologica,* 120, 529–530.

Kramer, J. H., & Duffy, J. M. (1996). Aphasia, apraxia, and agnosia in the diagnosis of dementia. *Dementia,* 7, 23–26.

Krauskopf, J., & Reeves, A. (1980). Measurement of the effect of photon noise on detection. *Vision Research,* 20, 193–196.

Kreiman, G., Koch, C., & Fried, I. (2000). Imagery neurons in the human brain. *Nature,* 408, 357–361.

Kremenitzer, J. P., Vaughan, H. G., Kurtzberg, D., & Dowling, K. (1979). Smooth-pursuit eye movements in the newborn infant. *Child Development,* 50, 442–448.

Kries, J. von. (1895). Uber die Natur gewisser mit den spychischen Vorgangen verknupfter Ghirnzustande. *Zeitschrift fur Psychologie,* 8, 1–33.

Krueger, L. E. (1991). Toward a unified psychophysical law and beyond. In S. J. Bolanowski Jr. & G. A. Gescheider (Eds.), *Ratio Scaling of Psychological Magnitude* (pp. 101–114). Hillsdale, NJ: Erlbaum.

Kruger, J. (1981). The difference between x- and y-type responses in ganglion cells of the cat's retina. *Vision Research,* 21, 1685–1687.

Krumhansl, C. L. (1985). Perceiving tonal structure in music. *American Scientist,* 73, 371–378.

Krumhansl, C. L. (1990). *Cognitive Foundations of Musical Pitch.* Oxford: Oxford University Press.

Krumhansl, C. L. (2000). Rhythm and pitch in music cognition. *Psychological Bulletin,* 126, 159–179.

Krumhansl, C. L., & Shepard, R. N. (1979). Quantification of the hierarchy of tonal functions within a diatonic context. *Journal of Experimental Psychology: Human Perception and Performance,* 5, 579–594.

Krumhansl, C. L., Bharucha, J. J., & Kessler, E. J. (1982). Perceived harmonic structure of chords in three related musical keys. *Journal of Experimental Psychology: Human Perception and Performance,* 8, 24–36.

Krummenacher, J. M., Hermann, J., & Heller, D. (2002). Visual search for dimensionally redundant pop out targets: Redundancy gains in compound tasks. *Visual Cognition,* 9, 801–837.

Krupinski, E., Roehrig, H., & Furukawa, T. (1999). Influence of film and monitor display luminance on observer performance and visual search. *Academic Radiology,* 6(7), 411–418.

Kryter, K. D. (1985). *The Effects of Noise on Man* (2nd ed.). Orlando: Academic Press.

Kubovy, M., & Wagemans, J. (1995). Grouping by proximity and multistability in dot lattices: A quantitative Gestalt theory. *Psychological Science,* 6, 225–234.

Kuffler, S. W. (1953). Discharge patterns and functional organization of mammalian retina. *Journal of Neurophysiology,* 16, 37–68.

Kuhl, P. K. (1991). Human adults and human infants show a "perceptual magnet effect" for prototypes of speech categories, monkeys do not. *Perception & Psychophysics,* 50, 93–107.

Kuhl, P. K., & Meltzoff, A. N. (1982). The bimodal perception of speech in infancy. *Science,* 218, 1138–1141.

Kuhl, P. K., & Padden, D. M. (1983). Enhanced discriminability at the phonetic boundaries for the place feature in macaques. *Journal of the Acoustical Society of America,* 73, 1003–1010.

Kuhl, P. K., Williams, K. A., Lacerda, F., Stevens, K. N., & Lindbloom, B. (1992). Linguistic experience alters phonetic perception in infants by 6 months of age. *Science,* 255, 606–608.

Kuhl, PK, Tsao, FM, Liu, HM, Zhang, Y., & De Boer, B. (2001). Language/culture/mind/brain: Progress at the margins between disciplines. In A. R. Damasio & A. Harrington et al. (Eds.), *Unity of Knowledge: The Convergence of Natural and Human Science.* Annals of the New York Academy of Sciences, vol. 935 (pp. 136–174). New York: New York Academy of Sciences.

Kulikowski, J. J., Walsh, V., McKeefry, D., Butler, S. R., & Carden, D. (1994). The electrophysiological basis of colour processing in macaques with V4 lesions. *Behavioural Brain Research,* 60, 73–78.

Kuriki, I., & Uchikawa, K. (1996). Limitations of surface-color and apparent-color constancy. *Journal of the Optical Society of America A-Optics & Image Science,* 13, 1622–1636.

Kurthen, M., Grunewald, T., & Elger, C.E. (1998). Will there be a scientific theory of consciousness? *Trends in Cognitive Sciences,* 2, 229–234.

Kurtz, D., & Butter, C. M. (1980). Impairments in visual discrimination performance and gaze shifts in monkeys with superior colliculus lesions. *Brain Research,* 196, 109–124.

Kuyk, T., Veres, J. G. III, Lahey, M. A., & Clark, D. J. (1986). The ability of protan color defectives to perform color-dependent air traffic control tasks. *American Journal of Optometry and Physiological Optics,* 63, 582–586.

LaBerge, D. (1995). *Attentional Processing: The Brain's Art of Mindfulness.* Cambridge, MA: Harvard University Press.

LaBerge, D., & Brown, V. (1989). Theory of attentional operations in shape identification. *Psychological Review,* 96, 101–124.

Lability of odor pleasantness: Influence of mere exposure. *Perception,* 7, 459–465.

Ladavas, E., & Petronio, A. (1990). The deployment of visual attention in the intact field of hemineglect patients. *Cortex,* 26, 307–317.

Ladefoged, P. (1975). *A Course in Phonetics.* New York: Harcourt Brace Jovanovich.

Lakotos, S., McAdams, S., & Caussé, R. (1997). The representation of auditory source characteristics: Simple geometric form. *Perception & Psychophysics,* 59, 1180–1190.

Lakowski, R., & Drance, S. M. (1979). Acquired dyschromatopsias: The earliest functional losses in glaucoma. *Documenta Ophthalmologica,* Proceedings Series 19, 159–165.

Lakowski, R., & Morton, B. A. (1977). The effect of oral contraceptives on colour vision in diabetic women. *Canadian Journal of Ophthalmology,* 12, 89–97.

Lakowski, R., Aspinall, P. A., & Kinnear, P. R. (1972). Association between colour vision losses and diabetes mellitus. *Ophthalmic Research,* 4, 145–159.

Lamb, M. R., & Yund, E. W. (1996). Spatial frequency and attention: Effects of level-, target-, and location-repetition on the processing of global and local forms. *Perception & Psychophysics,* 58, 363–373.

Lamme, V. A. F. (2000). Neural mechanisms of visual awareness: A linking proposition. *Brain and Mind,* 1, 385–406.

Lamme, V. A. F. (2003). Why visual attention and awareness are different. *Trends in Cognitive Sciences,* 7, 12–18.

Lamme, V. A. F., & Roelfsema, P.R. (2000). The distinct modes of vision offered by feedforward and recurrent processing. *Trends in Neurosciences,* 23, 571–579.

Lamour, Y., Willer, J. C., & Guilbaud, G. (1983). Rat somatosensory (SmI). cortex: I. Characteristics of neuronal responses to noxious stimulation and comparison with responses to non-noxious stimulation. *Experimental Brain Research,* 49, 35–45.

Land, E. H. (1986). Recent advances in retinex theory. *Vision Research,* 26, 7–21.

Landis T. (2000). Disruption of space perception due to cortical lesions. *Spatial Vision,* 13, 179–191.

Landolt, E. (1889). Tableau d'optotypes pour la determination de l'acuité visuelle. *Societé Francais d'Ophthalmologie,* 1, 385ff.

Lane, S. M., Mather, M., Villa, D., & Morita, S. K. (2001). How events are reviewed matters: Effects of varied focus on eyewitness suggestibility. *Memory and Cognition,* 29, 940–947.

Lappin, J. S., Donnelly, M. P., & Kojima, H. (2001). Coherence of early motion signals. *Vision Research,* 41, 1631–1644.

Large, E. W., & Jones, M. R. (1999). The dynamics of attending: How people track time-varying events. *Psychological Review,* 106, 119–159.

Larish, J. F., & Flach, J. M. (1990). Sources of optical information useful for the perception of speed of rectilinear selfmotion. *Journal of Experimental Psychology: Human Perception and Performance,* 16, 295–302.

Lawless, H. T., & Stevens, D. A. (1988). Responses by humans to oral chemical irritants as a function of locus of stimulation. *Perception & Psychophysics,* 43, 72–78.

Le Grand, R., Mondloch, C.J. Maurer, D & Brent, H.P. (2001). Early visual experience and face processing. *Nature,* 410, 890.

Le Rohellec, J., & Viénot, F.(2001). of luminance and spectral adaptation upon Benham subjective colours. *Color Research and Application,* 26(Suppl.), S174–S179.

Lea, S. E. G. (1984). *Instinct, Environment, and Behaviour.* London: Methuen.

Lederman, S. J., Browse, R. A., & Klatzky, R. L. (1988). Haptic processing of spatially distributed information. *Perception & Psychophysics,* 44, 222–232.

Lee, D. N. (1976). A theory of the visual control of braking based on information about time-to-collision. *Perception* 5, 437–459

Lee, D. S., Lee, J. S., Oh, S. H., Kim, S-K., Kim, J-W., Chung, J-K., Lee, M. C., & Kim, C. S. (2001). Cross-modal plasticity and cochlear implants. *Nature,* 409, 149–150.

Lee, S., & Blake, R. (1999). Rival ideas about binocular rivalry. *Vision Research,* 39, 1447–1454.

Leehey, S. C., Moskowitz-Cook, A., Brill, S., & Held, R. (1975). Orientational anisotropy in infant vision. *Science,* 190, 900–902.

Leek, M. R., Hanna, T. E., & Marshall, L. (1992). Estimation of psychometric functions from adaptive tracking procedures. *Perception & Psychophysics,* 51, 247–256.

Leeuwenberg, E. L. J. (1988). *On Geon and Global Precedence in Form Perception.* Paper presented at the meetings of the Psychonomic Society, Chicago.

Lefton, L. A. (1973). Metacontrast: A review. *Perception & Psychophysics,* 13, 161–171.

Lehmkuhle, S., & Fox, R. (1980). Effect of depth separation of metacontrast masking. *Journal of Experimental Psychology: Human Perception and Performance,* 6, 605–621.

Lehmkuhle, S., Kratz, K. E., & Sherman, S. M. (1982). Spatial and temporal sensitivity of normal and amblyopic cats. *Journal of Neurophysiology,* 48, 372–387.

Leibowitz, H. W., & Moore, D. (1966). Role of changes in accommodations and convergence in the perception of size. *Journal of the Optical Society of America,* 56, 1120–1123.

Leibowitz, H. W., Post, R. B., Brandt, T., & Dichgans, J. (1982). Implications of recent developments in dynamic spatial orientation and visual resolution for vehicle guidance. In A. H. Wertheim, W. A. Wagenaar, & H. W. Leibowitz (Eds.), *Tutorials on Motion Perception* (pp. 231–260). New York: Plenum Press.

Leibowitz, H. W., Shupert, C. L., Post, R. B., & Dichgans, J. (1983). Autokinetic drifts and gaze deviation. *Perception & Psychophysics,* 33, 455–459.

Leinonen, L. (1983). Integration of somatosensory events in the posterior parietal cortex of the monkey. In C. von Euler, O. Franzen, U. Lindblom, & D. Ottoson (Eds.), *Somatosensory Mechanisms* (pp. 113–124). New York: Plenum Press.

Lemlich, R. N. (1975). Subjective acceleration of time with aging. *Perceptual and Motor Skills,* 41, 235–238.

Lengyel, D., Weinacht, S., Charlier, J., & Gottlob I. (1998). The development of visual pursuit during the first months of life. *Graefes Archive for Clinical & Experimental Ophthalmology,* 236, 440–444.

Lenhoff, H. M., Perales, O., & Hickok, G. (2001). Absolute pitch in Williams Syndrome. *Music Perception,* 18, 491–503.

Lenneberg, E. H. (1967). *Biological Foundations of Language.* New York: Wiley.

Lenneberg, & Lenneberg, E. H. (Eds.). (1975). *Foundations of Language and Development: A Multidisciplinary Approach* (pp. 121–135). New York: Academic Press.

Lennie, P., Trevarthen, C., Van Essen, D., & Waessle, H. (1990). Parallel processing of visual information. In L. Spillman & J. S. Werner (Eds.), *Visual Perception: The Neurophysiological Foundations* (pp. 103–128). Orlando: Academic Press.

Leonards, U., & Singer, W. (1997). Selective temporal interactions between processing streams with differential sensitivity for colour and luminance contrast. *Vision Research,* 37, 1129–1140.

Leopold, D. A., & Logothetis, N. K. (1996). Activity changes in early visual cortex reflect monkeys' percept during binocular rivalry. *Nature,* 379, 549–552.

LePage, E. L. (1987). A spatial template for the shape of tuning curves in the mammalian cochlea. *Journal of the Acoustical Society of America,* 82, 155–164.

LePage, E. L. (1989). Functional role of the olivo-cochlear bundle: A motor unit control system in the mammalian cochlea. *Hearing Research,* 38, 177–198.

Lerdahl, F., & Jackendoff, R. (1983). *A Generative Theory of Tonal Music.* Cambridge, MA: MIT Press.

Leslie, A. M. (1986). Getting development off the ground. In P. Geert (Ed.), *Modularity and the Infant's Perception of Causality* (pp. 406–437). Amsterdam: North Holland.

Leuthold, H., & Kopp, B. (1998). Mechanisms of priming by masked stimuli: Inferences from event-related brain potentials. *Psychological Science,* 9, 263–269.

Levelt, W. J. M., Riemersma, J. B., & Bunt, A. A. (1972). Binaural additivity of loudness. *British Journal of Mathematical and Statistical Psychology,* 25, 51–68.

Levelt, W. J. M. (1965). *On Binocular Rivalry.* The Hague: Mouton.

Levi, D. M., McGraw, P. V., & Klein, S. A. (2000). Vernier and contrast discrimination in central and peripheral vision. *Vision Research,* 40, 973–988.

Levin, A., Lipton, R. B., & Holzman, P. S. (1981). Pursuit eye movements in psychopathology: Effects of target characteristics. *Biological Psychiatry,* 16, 255–267.

Levine, D. N., & Calvanio, R. (1989). Prosopagnosia: A defect in visual configural processing. *Brain and Cognition,* 10, 149–170.

Levine, M. W., & Shefner, J. M. (1981). *Fundamentals of Sensation and Perception.* Reading, MA: Addison-Wesley.

Levitin, D. J., & Cook, P. R. (1996). Memory for musical tempo: Additional evidence that auditory memory is absolute. *Perception & Psychophysics,* 58, 927–935.

Levitt, H. (1971). Transformed up-down methods in psychoacoustics. *Journal of the Acoustical Society of America,* 49, 467–477.

Levy, D. L., Lipton, R. B., & Holzman, P. S. (1981). Smooth pursuit eye movements: Effects of alcohol and chloral hydrate. *Journal of Psychiatric Research,* 16, 1–11.

Lewis, J. W., Terman, G. W., Shavit, Y., Nelson, L. R., & Liebeskind, J. C. (1984). Neural, neurochemical, and hormonal bases of stress-induced analgesia. In L. Kruger & J. C.

Liebeskind (Eds.), *Neural Mechanisms of Pain* (pp. 277–288). New York: Raven Press.

Lewis, P. A., & Walsh, V. (2002). Neuropsychology: Time out of mind. *Current Biology,* 12, R9–R11

Li, A., & Zaidi Q. (2000). Perception of three-dimensional shape from texture is based on patterns of oriented energy. *Vision Research,* 40, 217–242.

Liberman, A. M. (1982). On finding that speech is special. *American Psychologist,* 37, 148–167.

Liberman, A. M., & Mattingly, I. G. (1985). The motor theory of speech perception revised. *Cognition,* 21, 1–36.

Liberman, A. M., Cooper, F. S., Shankweiler, D. P., & Studdert-Kennedy, M. (1967). Perception of the speech code. *Psychological Review,* 74, 431–461.

Liberman, A. M., Harris, K. S., Hoffman, H. A., & Griffith, B. C. (1957). The discrimination of sounds within and across phoneme boundaries. *Journal of Experimental Psychology,* 54, 358–368.

Liberman, M. C. (1982). Single-neuron labeling in the cat auditory nerve. *Science,* 216, 1239–1241.

Liberman, M. C., Gao, J., He, D. Z. Z., Wu, X., Jia, S., & Zuo, J. (2002). Prestin is required for electromotility of the outer hair cell and for the cochlear amplifier. *Nature,* 419, 300–304.

Liberman,-Alvin-Meyer (Ed.). (1996). *Speech: A Special Code.* Cambridge, MA: The MIT Press.

Libet, B. (1999). How does conscious experience arise? The neural time factor. *Brain Research Buletin,* 56, 339–340.

Libet, B. (2002). The timing of mental events: Libet's experimental findings and their implications. *Consciousness and Cognition,* 11, 291–299.

Libet, B., Gleason, C. A., Wright, E. W., & Pearl, D. K. (1983). Time of conscious intention to act in relation to onset of cerebral activity (readiness potential): The unconscious initiation of a freely voluntary act. *Brain,* 106, 623–642.

Libet, B., Wright, E. W., Feinstein, B., & Pearl, D. K. (1979). Subjective referral of the timing for a conscious sensory experience: A functional role for the somatosensory specific projection system in man. *Brain,* 102, 193–224.

Libet, B., Wright, E. W., Feinstein, B., & Pearl, D. K. (1992). Retroactive enhancement of a skin sensation by a delayed cortical stimulus in man: Evidence for delay of a conscious sensory experience. *Consciousness and Cognition,* 1, 365–375.

Liebeskind, J. C., & Melzack, R. (1987). The International Pain Foundation: Meeting a need for education in pain management. *Pain,* 30, 1.

Liegois-Chauvel, C., Giraud, K., Badier, J-M., Marquis, P., & Chauvel, P. (2001). Intracerebral evoked potentials in pitch perception reveal a functional asymmetry of the human auditory cortex. In R. J. Zatorre & I. Peretz (Eds.), *The Biological Foundations of Music* (pp. 117–132). Annals of the New York Academy of Sciences, Vol. 930. New York: The New York Academy of Sciences.

Light, A. R. (1992). *The Initial Processing of Pain and Its Descending Control: Spinal and Trigeminal Systems.* Basel: Karger.

Lim, D. J. (1980). Cochlear anatomy related to cochlear micromechanics: A review. *Journal of the Acoustical Society of America,* 67, 1686–1695.

Linberg, K., Cuenca, N., Ahnelt, P., Fisher, S., & Kolb, H. (2001). Comparative anatomy of major retinal pathways in the eyes of nocturnal and diurnal mammals. *Progress in Brain Research,* 131, 27–52.

Lindblom, B. (1996). Role of articulation in speech perception: Clues from production. *Journal of the Acoustical Society of America,* 99, 1683–1692.

Lindner, A., Schwarz, U., & Ilg, U. J. (2001). Cancellation of self induced retinal image motion during smooth pursuit eye movements. *Vision Research,* 41, 1685–1694.

Lindsay, P. H., & Norman, D. A. (1977). *Human Information Processing* (2nd ed.). New York: Academic Press.

Lindsey, D. T., & Teller, D. Y. (1990). Motion at isoluminance: Discrimination detection ratios for moving isoluminant gratings. *Vision Research,* 30, 1751–1761.

Lindsey, D. T., & Brown, A. M. (2002). Color naming and the phototoxic effects of sunlight on the eye. *Psychological Science,* 13, 506–512.

Link, S. (1993). *The Wave Theory of Similarity and Difference.* Mahwah, NJ: Erlbaum.

Linton, H., & Graham, E. (1959). Personality correlates of persuasibility. In I. Janis (Ed.), *Personality and Persuasibility* (pp. 69–101). New Haven, CT: Yale University Press.

Liotti, M., Fox, P. T., & LaBerge, D. (1994). PET measurements of attention to closely spaced visual shapes. *Society for Neurosciences Abstracts,* 20, 354.

Liu, L-C., Gaetz, W.C., Bosnyak, D.J., & Roberts, L.E. (2000). Evidence for fusion and segregation induced by 12 Hz multiple-digit stimulation in humans. *Neuroreport,* 11, 2313–2318.

Livingstone, M. S., & Hubel, D. H. (1988). Segregation of form, color, movement and depth: Anatomy, physiology, and perception. *Science,* 240, 740–749.

Locke, J. L. (1983). *Phonological Acquisition and Change.* New York: Academic Press.

Lockhead, G. R. (1966). Effects of dimensional redundancy on visual discrimination. *Journal of Experimental Psychology,* 72, 95–104.

Lockhead, G. R., & Byrd, R. (1981). Practically perfect pitch. *Journal of the Acoustical Society of America,* 70, 387–389.

Loewenstein, W. R. (1960). Biological transducers. *Scientific American,* 203, 98–108.

Loftus, E. (1974). Reconstructing memory: The incredible eye witness. *Psychology Today,* 8, 116–119.

Logan, G. D. (1988). Toward an instance theory of automatization. *Psychological Review,* 95, 492–527.

Logan, G. D. (1996). The CODE theory of visual attention: An integration of space-based and object-based attention. *Psychological Review,* 103, 603–649.

Logothetis, N. K., & Schall, J. D. (1989). Neuronal correlates of subjective visual perception. *Science* 245, 761–763.

Logothetis, N. K., Leopold, D. A., & Scheinberg, D. L. (1996). What is rivaling during binocular rivalry? *Nature,* 380, 621–624.

Lohman, D. F. (1986). The effect of speed-accuracy tradeoff on sex differences in mental rotation. *Perception & Psychophysics,* 39, 427–436.

Long, G. M. (1988). Selective adaptation vs. transfer of decrement: The conjoint effects of neural fatigue and perceptual learning. *Perception & Psychophysics,* 43, 207–209.

Long, G. M. (1994). Exercises for training vision and dynamic visual acuity among college students. *Perceptual & Motor Skills,* 78, 1049–1050.

Lonsbury-Martin, B. L., Harris, F. P., Stagner, B. B., Hawkins, M. D., & Martin, G. K. (1990). Distortion product emissions in humans: I. Basic properties in normally hearing subjects. *Annals of Otology, Rhinology and Laryngology,* 99, 3–14.

Loomis, J. M. (1978). Lateral masking in foveal and eccentric vision. *Vision Research,* 18, 335–338.

Loop, M. S. (1984). Effect of duration on detection by the chromatic and achromatic systems. *Perception & Psychophysics,* 36, 65–67.

Loosen, F. (1995). The effect of musical experience on the conception of accurate tuning. *Music Perception,* 12, 291–306.

Lorist, M. M., & Snel, J. (1997). Caffeine effects on perceptual and motor processes. *Electroencephalography & Clinical Neurophysiology,* 102, 401–413.

Lovegrove, W. J., & Over, R. (1973). Color selectivity in orientation masking and aftereffect. *Vision Research,* 13, 895–902.

Lowe, D. (1987). Three-dimensional object recognition from single two-dimensional images. *Artificial Intelligence,* 31, 355–395.

Lowenstein, O., & Sand, A. (1940). The mechanism of the semicircular canal: A study of the responses of single-fibre preparations to angular accelerations and to rotation at constant speed. *Proceedings of the Royal Society of London, Series B,* 129, 256–275.

Lu, T., Liang, L., & Wang, X. (2001). Temporal and rate representations of time-varying signals in the auditory cortex of awake primates. *Nature Neuroscience,* 4, 1131–1138.

Luce, R. D. (1990). "On the possible psychophysical laws" revisited: Remarks on cross-modality matching. *Psychological Review,* 97, 66–77.

Luce, R. D., & Mo, S. S. (1965). Magnitude estimation of heaviness and loudness by individual observers: A test of a probabilistic response theory. *The British Journal of Mathematical and Statistical Psychology,* 18, 159–174.

Luck, S. J., & Hillyard, S. A. (1994). Spatial filtering during visual search: Evidence from human electrophysiology. *Journal of Experimental Psychology: Human Perception and Performance,* 20, 1000–1114.

Lumer, E. D., Friston, K. J., & Rees, G. (1998). Neural correlates of perceptual rivalry in the human brain. *Science,* 280, 1930–1934.

Lumsden, E. (1980). Problems of magnification and minification: An explanation of the distortions of distance, slant, shape, and velocity. In M. Hagen (Ed.), *Perception of Pictures: Vol. I, Alberti's Window: The Projective Model of Pictorial Information* (pp. 91–135). New York: Academic Press.

Lunch, E. D., Lee, M. K., Morrow, J. E., Welsch, P. L., León, P. E., & King, M-C. (1997). Nonsyndromic deafness DFNA1 associated with muta-tion of a human homolog of the Drosophila gene diaphanous. *Science,* 278, 1315–1318.

Lundervold, D., Lewin, L. M., & Irvin, L. K. (1987). Rehabilitation of visual impairments: A critical review. *Clinical Psychology Review,* 7, 169–185.

Luria, A. R. (1973). *The Working Brain.* London: Penguin.

Lustig, C & Meck, W. H. (2001). Paying attention to time as one gets older. *Psychological Science,* 12, 478–484.

Lynch, M. P., & Eilers, R. E. (1990). Innateness, experience, and music perception. *Psychological Science,* 1, 272–276.

Lynn, P. A., & Sayers, B. M. A. (1970). Cochlear innervation, signal processing, and their relation to auditory timeintensity effects. *Journal of the Acoustical Society of America,* 47, 523–533.

Macaluso, E., Frith, C., & Driver, J. (2000). Modulation of human visual cortex by crossmodal spatial attention. *Science,* 289, 1206–1208.

MacArthur, R. O., & Sekuler, R. (1982). Alcohol and motion perception. *Perception & Psychophysics,* 31, 502–505.

MacDonald, D. W., & Brown, R. E. (1985). Introduction: The pheromone concept in mammalian chemical communication. In R. E. Brown & D. W. MacDonald (Eds.), *Social Odours in Mammals,* Vol. 1 (pp. 1–18). Oxford: Clarendon Press.

MacEvoy, S. P., Paradiso, M. A. (2001). Lightness constancy in primary visual cortex. *Proceedings of the National Academy of Science, U.S.A.,* 98, 8827–8831.

MacFarlane, A. (1975). Olfaction in the development of social preferences in the human neonate. In *Ciba Foundation Symposium 33: The Human Neonate in Parent-Infant Interaction* (pp. 103–177). Amsterdam: Elsevier.

Mach, E. (1959). *The Analysis of Sensations and the Relation of the Physical to the Psychical.* New York: Dover. (Originally published 1886)

Mack, A., & Rock, I. (1998). *Inattentional Blindness: Perception without Attention.* Cambridge, MA: The MIT Press.

Mack, A., Heuer, F., Fendrich, R., Vilardi, K., & Chambers, D. (1985). Induced motion and oculomotor capture. *Journal of Experimental Psychology: Human Perception and Performance,* 11, 329–345.

MacKain, K., Studdert-Kennedy, M., Spieker, S., & Stern, D. (1983). Infant intermodal speech perception is a left hemisphere function. *Science,* 219, 1347–1349.

Mackworth, N. H. (1948). The breakdown of vigilance during prolonged visual search. *Quarterly Journal of Experimental Psychology,* 1, 6–21.

MacLeod, D. I. (1978). Visual sensitivity. *Annual Review of Psychology,* 29, 613–645.

MacLeod, P. (1971). An experimental approach to the peripheral mechanisms of olfactory discrimination. In G. Ohloff & A. F. Thomas (Eds.), *Gustation and Olfaction* (pp. 28–44). New York: Academic Press.

Macmillan, N. A., & Creelman, C. D. (1991). *Detection Theory: A User's Guide.* Cambridge: Cambridge University Press.

Macmillan, N. A. (Ed.). (2002). Psychometric functions and adaptive methods. *Perception & Psychophysics,* 63, No. 8.

MacNichol, E. F. Jr. (1986). A unifying presentation of photopigment spectra. *Vision Research,* 29, 543–546.

Macpherson, E. A., & Middlebrooks, J. C. (2002). Listener weighting of cues for lateral angle: the duplex theory of sound localization revisited. *Journal of the Acoustical Society of America,* 111, 2219–2236.

Madden, D. J. (1986). Adult age differences in the attentional capacity demands of visual search. *Cognitive Development,* 2, 100–107.

Maddox, W. T. (2001). Separating perceptual processes from decisional processes in identification and categorization. *Perception & Psychophysics,* 63, 1183–200.

Madison, C., Thompson, W., Kersten, D., Shirley, P., & Smits, B. (2001). Use of interreflection and shadow for surface contact. *Perception and Psychophysics,* 63, 187–194.

Madrid, M., & Crognale, M. A. (2000). Long-term maturation of visual pathways. *Visual Neuroscience,* 17,831–837.

Mair, R. G., Bouffard, J. A., Engen, T., & Morton, T. (1978). Olfactory sensitivity during the menstrual cycle. *Sensory Process,* 2, 90–98.

Maire-Lepoivre, E., & Przybyslawski, J. (1988). Visual field in dark-reared cats after an extended period of recovery. *Behavioural Brain Research,* 28, 245–251.

Makous, J. C., & Middlebrooks, J. C. (1990).Two-dimensional sound localization by human listeners. *Journal of the Acoustical Society of America,* 87, 2188–2200.

Mallot, H. A. (2000). *Computational Vision: Information Processing in Perception and Visual Behavior.* Cambridge, MA: MIT Press.

Mamassian, P., & Landy, M.S. (2001). Interaction of visual prior constraints. *Vision Research,* 41, 2653–2668.

Mamtani, R., & Cimino, A. (2002). A primer of complementary and alternative medicine and its relevance in the treatment of mental health problems. *Psychiatric Quarterly,* 73, 367–381.

Mandler, G. (1980). Recognizing: The judgment of previous occurrence. *Psychological Review,* 87, 252–271.

Mangun, G. R., & Hillyard, S. A. (1991). Modulation of sensory-evoked brain potentials indicate changes in perceptual processing during visual-spatial priming. *Journal of Experimental Psychology: Human Perception and Performance,* 17, 1057–1074.

Manjeshwar, R. M., & Wilson, D. L. (2001). Hyperefficient detection of targets in noisy images. *Journal of the Optical Society of America A: Optics, Image Science and Vision,* 18, 507–513.

Manley, G. A., & Köpp, C. (1998). Phylogenetic development of the cochlea and its innervation. *Current Opinion in Neurobiology,* 8, 468–474.

Marcel, A. J. (1983a). Conscious and unconscious perception: Experiments on visual masking and recognition. *Cognitive Psychology,* 15, 197–237.

Marcel, A. J. (1983b). Conscious and unconscious perception: An approach to the relations between phenomenal experience and perceptual processes. *Cognitive Psychology,* 15: 238–300.

Marks, L. E. (1979). Summation of vibrotactile intensity: An analogy to auditory critical bands? *Sensory Processes,* 3, 188–203.

Marks, L. E. (1988). Magnitude estimation and sensory matching. *Perception & Psychophysics,* 43, 511–525.

Marks, L. E., Galanter, E., & Baird, J. C. (1995). Binaural summation after learning psychophysical functions for loudness. *Perception & Psychophysics,* 57, 1209–1216.

Marks, L. E., Szczesiul, R., & Ohlott, P. (1986). On the cross-modal perception of intensity. *Journal of Experimental Psychology: Human Perception and Performance,* 12, 517–534.

Marks, W. B., Dobelle, W. H., & MacNichol, E. F. (1964). Visual pigments of single primate cones. *Science,* 143, 1181–1183.

Marotta, J. J., & Goodale, M. A. (2001). The role of familiar size in the control of grasping. *Journal of Cognitive Neuroscience,* 13, 8–17.

Marr, D. (1982). *Vision.* San Francisco: W. H. Freeman.

Marr, D., & Poggio, T. (1979). A computational theory of human stereo vision. *Proceedings of the Royal Society (London), Series B,* 204, 301–328.

Marr, D., & Ullman, S. (1981). Directional selectivity and its use in early visual processing. *Proceedings of the Royal Society of London, Series B,* 211, 151–180.

Marshall, D. A., & Moulton, D. G. (1981). Olfactory sensitivity to a-ionine in humans and dogs. *Chemical Senses,* 6, 53–61.

Marslen-Wilson, W. (1989). Access and integration: Projecting sound onto meaning. In W. Marslen-Wilson (Ed.), *Lexical Representation and Process* (pp. 3–24). Cambridge, MA: MIT Press.

Marslen-Wilson, W. D. (1980). Speech understanding as a psychological process. In J. C. Simon (Ed.), *Spoken Language Generation and Understanding* (pp. 39–67). Dordrecht, Netherlands: Reidel.

Martin P., Hudspeth A. J., Jülicher, F. (2001). Comparison of a hair bundle's spontaneous oscillations with its response to mechanical stimulation reveals the underlying active process. *Proceedings of the National Academy of Science (USA),* 98, 14380–14385.

Martin, D. K., & Holden, B. A. (1982). A new method for measuring the diameter of the in vivo human cornea. *American Journal of Optometry and Physiological Optics,* 59, 436–441.

Martin, G. K., Lonsbury-Martin, B. L., Probst, R., & Coats, A. C. (1988). Spontaneous otoacoustic emissions in a nonhuman primate: I. Basic features and relations to other emissions. *Hearing Research,* 33, 49–68.

Martin, M. (1979). Local and global processing: The role of sparsity. *Memory and Cognition,* 7, 476–484.

Martin, R. L., Webster, W. R., & Service, J. (1988). The frequency organization of the inferior colliculus of the guinea pig: A [14C]-2–deoxyglucose study. *Hearing Research,* 33, 245–256.

Masica, D. N., Money, J., Ehrhardt, A. A., & Lewis, V. G. (1969). IQ, fetal sex hormones and cognitive patterns studies in testicular feminizing syndrome of androgen insensitivity. *Johns Hopkins Medical Journal,* 124, 34.

Masland, R. H. (2001). The fundamental plan of the retina. *Nature Neuroscience,* 4, 877–886.

Masland, R. H. (1986). The functional architecture of the retina. *Scientific American,* 255, 102–111.

Massaro, D. (1988). Ambiguity in perception and experimentation. *Journal of Experimental Psychology: General,* 117, 417–421.

Massaro, D. W. (1987). *Speech Perception by Ear and Eye: A Paradigm for Psychological Inquiry.* Hillsdale, NJ: Erlbaum.

Masters, M. S., & Sanders, B. (1993). Is the gender difference in mental rotation disappearing? *Behavior Genetics,* 23, 337–341.

Mather, G., & Smith, D. R. R. (2000). Depth cue integration: Stereopsis and image blur. *Vision Research,* 40, 3501–3506.

Mather, J. A., & Fisk, J. D. (1985). Orienting to targets by looking and pointing: Parallels and interactions in ocular and manual performance. *Quarterly Journal of Experimental Psychology,* 37A, 315–338.

Matin, L., & MacKinnon, G. E. (1964). Autokinetic movement: Selective manipulation of directional components by image stabilization. *Science,* 143, 147–148.

Maturana, H. R., Lettvin, J. Y., McCulloch, W. S., & Pitts, W. H. (1960). Anatomy and physiology of vision in the frog (Rana pipins). *Journal of General Physiology,* 43(Suppl. 2), 129–171.

Maunsell, J. H. R., & Newsome, W. T. (1987). Visual processing in monkey extrastriate cortex. *Annual Review of Neuroscience,* 10, 363–401.

Maunsell, J. H. R., & Van Essen, D. C. (1983). Functional properties of neurons in middle temporal visual area of the macaque monkey: I. Selectivity for stimulus direction, speed, and orientation. *Journal of Neurophysiology,* 49, 1127–1147.

Maurer, D. (1975). Infant visual perception: Methods of study. In L. B. Cohen & P. Salapatek (Eds.), *Infant Perception: From Sensation to Cognition, Basic Visual Processes,* Vol. 1 (pp. 1–77). New York: Academic Press.

Maurer, D., & Lewis, T. L. (1991). The development of peripheral vision and its physiological underpinnings. In M. J. Weiss & P. R. Zelazo (Eds.), *Newborn Attention* (pp. 218–255). Norwood, NJ: Ablex.

Maxwell, J. C. (1873). *Treatise on Electricity and Magnetism.* Oxford: Clarendon Press.

May, B., & Moody, D. B. (1989). Categorical perception of conspecific communication sounds by Japanese macaques, Macaca fuscata. *Journal of the Acoustical Society of America,* 85, 837–847.

Mayhew, J. E. W., & Frisby, J. P. (1979). Convergent disparity discriminations in narrow-band-filtered random-dot stereograms. *Vision Research,* 19, 63–71.

Mayhew, J. E. W., & Frisby, J. P. (1980). The computation of binocular edges. *Perception,* 9, 69–86.

Maylor, E. A., & Hockey, R. (1985). Inhibitory component of externally controlled covert orienting in visual space. *Journal of Experimental Psychology: Human Perception and Performance,* 11, 777–787.

McAdams, S., Winsberg, S., Donna-dieu, S., De Soete, G., & Krimphoff, J. (1995). Perceptual scaling of synthesized musical timbres: Common dimensions, specificities, and latent subject classes. *Psychological Research,* 58, 177–192.

McAlpine, D., Jiang, D., & Palmer, A.R. (2001). A neural code for low-frequency sound localization in mammals. *Nature Neuroscience,* 4, 396–401.

McBeath, M. K., Shaffer, D. M., & Kaiser, M. K. (28 April 1995). How baseball outfielders determine where to run to catch fly balls. *Science,* 268, 569–573.

McBride, R. L. (1993). Three models for taste mixtures. In D. G. Laing, W. S. Cain, R. L. McBride, & B. W. Ache (Eds.), *Perception of Complex Smells and Tastes* (pp. 265–282). New York: Academic Press.

McBurney, D. H. (1969). Effects of adaptation on human taste function. In C. Pfaffman (Ed.), *Olfaction and Taste III* (pp. 407–419). New York: Rockefeller University Press.

McBurney, D. H., Levine, J. M., & Cavanaugh, P. H. (1977). Psychophysical and social ratings of human body odor. *Personality and Social Psychology Bulletin,* 3, 135–138.

McCamy, C.S. (1998). On the number of discernable colors. *Color Research and Application,* 23, 337.

McClain, L. (1983). Interval estimation: Effect of processing demands on prospective and retrospective reports. *Perception & Psychophysics,* 34, 185–189.

McClellan, P. G., & Bernstein, I. H. (1984). What makes the Mueller a liar: A multiple-cue approach. *Perception & Psychophysics,* 36, 234–244.

McClelland, J. L., & Elman, J. L. (1986). The TRACE model of speech perception. *Cognitive Psychology,* 18, 1–86.

McClintock, M. K. (1971). Menstrual synchrony and suppression. *Nature* (London), 229, 244–245.

McDonald, J. J., & Ward, L. M. (1999). Spatial relevance determines facilitatory and inhibitory effects of auditory covert spatial orienting. *Journal of Experimental Psychology: Human Perception and Performance,* 25, 1234–1252.

McDonald, J. J., Teder-Salejarvi, W. A., & Hillyard, S. A. (2000). Involuntary orienting to sound improves visual perception. *Nature,* 407, 906–908.

McDonald, J. J., Teder-Salejarvi, W. A., & Ward, L. M. (2001). Multisensory integration and crossmodal attention effects in the human brain. *Science,* 298, 1791a (online).

McDonald, J. J., Teder-Sälejärvi, W. A., Heraldez, D., & Hillyard, S. A. (2001). Electrophysiological evidence for the "missing link" in crossmodal attention. *Canadian Journal of Experimental Psychology,* 55, 141–149.

McDonald, J. J., Ward, L. M., & Kiehl, K. A. (1999). An event-related brain potential study of inhibition of return. *Perception & Psychophysics,* 61, 1411–1423.

McFadden, D., & Pasanen, E. G. (1994). Otoacoustic emissions and quinine sulfate. *Journal of the Acoustical Society of America,* 95, 3460–3474.

McGee, M. G. (1979). Human spatial abilities: Psychometric studies and environmental, genetic, hormonal, and neurological influences. *Psychological Bulletin,* 86, 889–918.

McGlone, J. (1981). Sexual variations in behavior during spatial and verbal tasks. *Canadian Journal of Psychology,* 35, 277–282.

McGuinness, D. (1972). Hearing: Individual differences in perceiving. *Perception,* 1, 465–473.

McGuinness, D. (1976a). Away from a unisex psychology: Individual differences in visual sensory and perceptual processes. *Perception,* 5, 279–294.

McGuinness, D. (1976b). Sex differences in the organization of perception and cognition. In B. Lloyd & U. Archer (Eds.), *Exploring Sex Differences* (pp. 123–156). New York: Academic Press.

McGuinness, D., & Lewis, I. (1976). Sex differences in visual persistence: Experiments on the Ganzfeld and the afterimage. *Perception,* 5, 295–301.

McGurk, H., & MacDonald, J. (1976). Hearing lips and seeing voices. *Nature,* 264, 746–748.

McIlwain, J. T. (1996). *An Introduction to the Biology of Vision.* New York: Cambridge University Press.

McIntosh, A. R., Rajah, M. N., & Lobaugh, N. J. (1999). Interactions of prefrontal cortex in relation to awareness in sensory learning. *Science,* 284, 1531–1533.

McKeefry, D. J. (2001). Chromatic visual evoked potentials elicited by fast and slow motion onset. *Color Research and Application*, 26(Suppl.): S145–S149.

Mechler F., & Ringach DL.(2002). On the classification of simple and complex cells. *Vision Research,* 42, 1017–1033.

Meck, W. H., & Benson, A. M. (2002). Dissecting the brain's internal clock: How frontal-striatal circuitry keeps time and shifts attention. *Brain and Cognition,* 48, 195–211.

Meddis, R. (1988). Simulation of auditory-neural transduction: Further studies. *Journal of the Acoustical Society of America,* 83, 1056–1063.

Meehan, J. W. (1993). Apparent minification in an imaging display under reduced viewing conditions. *Perception,* 22, 1075–1084.

Meese, T. S. (1995). Using the standard staircase to measure the point of subjective equality: A guide based on computer simulations. *Perception & Psychophysics,* 57, 267–281.

Meiselman, H. L., Bose, H. E., & Nykvist, W. F. (1972). Magnitude production and magnitude estimation of taste intensity. *Perception & Psychophysics,* 12, 249–252.

Meissner, C.A., & Brigham, J.C. (2001). Thirty years of investigating the own race bias in memory for faces: A meta analytic review. *Psychology, Public Policy, and Law,* 7, 3–35.

Melara, R. D., & Marks, L. E. (1990). Interaction among auditory dimensions: Timbre, pitch, and loudness. *Perception & Psychophysics,* 48, 169–178.

Melzack, R., & Casey, K. L. (1968). Sensory, motivational, and central control determinants of pain. In D. R. Kenshalo (Ed.), *The Skin Senses* (pp. 423–443). Springfield, IL: Thomas.

Melzack, R., & Wall, P. D. (1965). Pain mechanisms: A new theory. *Science,* 150, 971–979.

Melzack, R., & Wall, P. D. (1988). *The Challenge of Pain* (2nd ed.). London: Penguin.

Melzack, R., Wall, P. D., & Ty, T. C. (1982). Acute pain in an emergency clinic: Latency of onset and descriptor patterns related to different injuries. *Pain,* 14, 33–43.

Mendelson, J. R., Ricketts, C. (2001). Age-related temporal processing speed deterioration in auditory cortex. *Hearing Research,* 158, 84–94.

Mendelson, J. R., Wells, E. F. (2002). Age-related changes in the visual cortex. *Vision Research,* 42, 695–703.

Menini, A. (1999). Calcium signaling and regulation in olfactory neurons. *Current Opinion in Neurobiology,* 9, 419–426.

Mennella, J. A., & Beauchamp, G. K., (2002). Flavor experiences during formula feeding are related to preferences during childhood, *Early Human Development,* 68, 71–82.

Menning, H., Roberts, L.E., & Pantev, C. (2000). Plastic changes in the auditory cortex induced by intensive frequency discrimination training. *Neuroreport,* 11, 817–822.

Mercer, M. E., Courage, M. L., & Adams, R. J. (1991). Contrast/color card procedure: A new test of young infants' color vision. *Optometry and Vision Science,* 68, 522–532.

Mergler, D., Bowler, R., & Cone, J. (1990). Colour vision loss among disabled workers with neuropsychological impairment. *Neurotoxicology and Teratology,* 12, 669–672.

Mergner, T., Anastasopoulos, D., Becker, W., & Deecke, L. (1981). Discrimination between trunk and head rotation: A study comparing neuronal data from the cat with human psychophysics. *Acta Psychologica,* 48, 291–302.

Merikle, P. M., Smilek, D., & Eastwood, J. D. (2001). Perception without awareness: Perspectives from cognitive psychlogy. *Cognition,* 79, 115–134.

Merkel, J. (1885). Die zeitlichen Verhaltnisse der Willensthatigkeit. *Philosophische Studien* (Wundt), 2, 73–127.

Mershon, D. H., Ballenger, W. L., Little, A. D., McMurtry, P. L., & Buchanan, J. L. (1989). Effects of room reflectance and background noise on perceived auditory distance. *Perception,* 18, 403–416.

Mershon, D. H., Desaulniers, D. H., & Amerson, T. L. Jr. (1980). Visual capture in auditory distance perception: Proximity image effect reconsidered. *Journal of Auditory Research,* 20, 129–136.

Mershon, D. H., Desaulniers, D. H., Kiefer, S. A., & Amerson, T. L. Jr. (1981). Perceived loudness and visually determined auditory distance. *Perception,* 10, 531–543.

Metzler, D. E., & Harris, C. M. (1978). Shapes of spectral bands of visual pigments. *Vision Research,* 18, 1417–1420.

Miceli, G., Fouch, E., Capasso, R., Shelton, J. R., Tomaiuolo, F., & Caramazza, A. (2001). The dissociation of color from form and function knowledge. *Nature Neuroscience,* 4, 662–667.

Michael, R. P., Keverne, E. B., & Bonsall, R. W. (1971). Pheromones: Isolation of male sex attractants from a female primate. *Science,* 172, 964–966.

Michael, S., & Sherrick, M. F. (1986). Perception of induced visual motion: Effects of relative position, shape and size of the surround. *Canadian Journal of Psychology,* 40, 122–125.

Michaels, C. F., & Turvey, M. T. (1979). Central sources of masking: Indexing structures supporting seeing at a single, brief glance. *Psychological Research,* 41, 1–61.

Michell, J. (1986). Measurement scales and statistics: A clash of paradigms. *Psychological Bulletin,* 100, 398–407.

Michon, J. (1985). The compleat time experiencer. In J. A. Michon & J. L. Jackson (Eds.), *Time, Mind and Behavior* (pp. 20–52). Berlin: Springer-Verlag.

Middlebrooks, J. C., Clock, A. C., Xu, L., & Green, D. M. (1994). A panoramic code for sound location by cortical neurons. *Science,* 264, 842–844.

Mikaelian, H., & Held, R. (1964). Two types of adaptation to an optically-rotated visual field. *American Journal of Psychology,* 77, 257–263.

Miles, F. A., & Fuller, J. E. (1975). Visual tracking and the primate flocculus. *Science,* 189, 1000–1002.

Mill, J. (1829). *Analysis of the Phenomena of the Human Mind.* London: Baldwin and Cradock.

Miller, D. L., Moore, R. K., & Wooten, B. R. (1984). When push comes to pull: Impressions of visual direction. *Perception & Psychophysics,* 36, 396–397.

Miller, G. A. (1956). The magical number seven, plus or minus two: Some limits on our capacity for processing information. *Psychological Review,* 63, 81–97.

Miller, G. W., Hicks, R. E., & Willette, M. (1978). Effects of concurrent verbal rehearsal and temporal set upon judgments of temporal duration. *Acta Psychologica,* 42, 173–179.

Miller, J. (1982). Divided attention: Evidence for coactivation with redundant signals. *Cognitive Psychology,* 14, 247–279.

Miller, J. L., & Eimas, P. D. (1995). Speech perception: From signal to word. *Annual Review of Psychology,* 46, 467–492.

Miller, J. L., & Liberman, A. M. (1979). Some effects of later-occurring information on the perception of stop consonants and semivowel. *Perception & Psychophysics,* 25, 457–465.

Miller, R. J. (1991). The effect of ingested alcohol on fusion latency at various viewing distances. *Perception & Psychophysics,* 50, 575–583.

Miller, R. J. (1999). The cumulative influence of depth and flatness information on the perception of size in pictorial representations. *Empirical Studies of the Arts,* 17, 37–57.

Miller, R. J., Pigion, R. G., & Martin, K. D. (1985). The effects of ingested alcohol on accommodation. *Perception & Psychophysics,* 37, 407–414.

Mills, A. W. (1958). On the minimum audible angle. *Journal of the Acoustical Society of America,* 30, 127–246.

Mills, A. W. (1960). Lateralization of high-frequency tones. *Journal of the Acoustical Society of America,* 32, 132–134.

Milne, J., & Milne, M. (1967). *The Senses of Animals and Men.* New York: Atheneum.

Milner, A. D., & Goodale, M.A. (1995). *The Visual Brain in Action.* Oxford: Oxford University Press.

Miron, D., Duncan, G. H., & Bushnell, M. C. (1989). Effects of attention on the intensity and unpleasantness of thermal pain. *Pain,* 39, 345–352.

Mishkin, M., & Lewis, M. E. (1982). Equivalence of parieto-preoccipital subareas for visuospatial ability in monkeys. *Journal of Brain and Behavioral Sciences,* 6, 41–55.

Mitchell, D. (1978). Effect of early visual experience on the development of certain perceptual abilities in animals and man. In R. Walk & H. Pick (Eds.), *Perception and Experience.* New York: Plenum Press.

Mitchell, D. (1980). The influence of early visual experience on visual perception. In C. Harris (Ed.), *Visual coding and adaptability* (pp. 1–50). Hillsdale, NJ: Erlbaum.

Mitchell, D. (1981). Sensitive periods in visual development. In R. Aslin, J. Alberts, & M. Petersen (Eds.), *Development of Perception* (pp. 1–43). New York: Academic Press.

Miyazaki, K. (1995). Perception of relative pitch with different references: Some absolute-pitch listeners cannot tell musical interval names. *Perception & Psychophysics,* 57, 962–970.

Mogil, H. M. (2001) The skilled interpretation of weather satellite images: Learning to see patterns and not just cues. In R. R. Hoffman & A. B. Markman (Eds.), *Interpreting Remote Sensing Imagery: Human Factors* (pp. 235–272). NY: Lewis Publishers.

Moller, A. R. (1999). Review of the roles of temporal and place coding of frequency in speech discrimination. *Acta-Oto-Laryngologica,* 119, 424–430.

Mollon, J. (1995). Seeing colour. In T. Lamb & J. Bourriau (Eds.), *Colour: Art & Science* (pp. 127–150). Cambridge, England: Cambridge University Press.

Moncrieff, R. W. (1956). Olfactory adaptation and colour likeness. *Journal of Physiology* (London), 133, 301–316.

Money, J. (1965). Psychosexual differentiation. In J. Money (Ed.), *Sex Research: New Developments* (pp. 3–23). New York: Holt.

Monmayeur, J-P., & Matsunami, H. (2002). Receptors for bitter and sweet taste. *Current Opinion in Neurobiology,* 12, 366–371.

Montellese, S., Sharpe, L. T., & Brown, J. L. (1979). Changes in critical duration during dark-adaptation. *Vision Research,* 19, 1147–1153.

Montgomery, J. C., & MacDonald, J. A. (1987). Sensory tuning of lateral line receptors in Antarctic fish to the movements of planktonic prey. *Science,* 235, 195–196.

Mon-Williams, M., & Tresilian, J. R. (2000). Ordinal depth information from accommodation? *Ergonomics,* 43, 391–404.

Moon, C. M., & Fifer W. P. (2000). Evidence of transnatal auditory learning. *Journal of Perinatology,* 20, S37–44.

Moonen, C. T. W., van Zijl, P. C. M., Frank, J. A., Le Bihan, D., & Becker, E. D. (1990). Functional magnetic resonance imaging in medicine and physiology. *Science,* 250, 53–61.

Moore, B. C. J. (2001). Basic auditory processes. In E. B. Goldstein (Ed.), *Blackwell Handbook of Perception,* (pp. 379–407). Malden, MA: Blackwell Publishers.

Moore, C., Yantis, S., & Vaughan, B. (1998). Object-based visual selection: Evidence from perceptual completion. *Psychological Science,* 9, 104–110.

Moran, J., & Desimone, R. (1985). Selective attention gates visual processing in the extrastriate cortex. *Science,* 229, 782–784.

Moran, J., & Gordon, B. (1982). Long term visual deprivation in a human. *Vision Research,* 22, 27–36.

Moray, N. (1959). Attention in dichotic listening: Affective cues and the influence of instructions. *Quarterly Journal of Experimental Psychology,* 11, 56–60.

Moray, N. (1969). *Attention: Selective Processes in Vision and Hearing.* London: Hutchinson Educational.

Mori, S., & Ward, L. M. (1991). *Listening versus Hearing: Attentional Effects on Intensity Discrimination.* Technical Report on Hearing: The Acoustical Society of Japan, No. H-91–36.

Mori, S., & Ward, L. M. (1992). *Listening versus Hearing II: Attentional Effects on Intensity Discrimination by Musicians.* Technical Report on Hearing: The Acoustical Society of Japan, No. H-92–48.

Morimoto, M. (2001). The contribution of the two ears to the perception of vertical angle in sagittal planes. *Journal of the Acoustical Society of America,* 109, 1596–1603.

Morison, S. J., Grunau, R. E., Oberlander, T. F., & Whitfield, M. F. (2001). Relations between behavioral and cardiac autonomic reactivity to acute pain in preterm neonates. *Clinical Journal of Pain,* 17, 350–358.

Morley J. E. (2001). Decreased food intake with aging. *Journal of Gerontology A,* 56 Spec., No. 2, 81–88.

Morris, J. S., Öhman, A., & Dolan, R. J. (1998). Conscious and unconscious emotional learning in the human amygdala. *Nature,* 393, 467–470.

Morris, M. W. & Peng, K. (1994). Culture and cause: American and Chinese attributions for social and physical events. *Journal of Personality and Social Psychology,* 67, 949–971.

Morrison, F. J., Holmes, D. L., & Haith, M. M. (1974). A developmental study of the effect of familiarity on short-term visual memory. *Journal of Experimental Child Psychology,* 18, 412–425.

Morrison, J. D., & Whiteside, T. C. D. (1984). Binocular cues in the perception of distance of a point source of light. *Perception,* 13, 555–566.

Morse, P. A., & Molfese, D. L. (1987). Categorical perception for voicing contrasts in normal and lead-treated rhesus monkeys: Electrophysiological indices. *Brain and Language,* 30, 63–80.

Morse, R. P., & Evans, E. F. (1996). Enhancement of vowel coding for cochlear implants by the addition of noise. *Nature Medicine,* 2, 928–932.

Moskowitz, H., Sharma, S., & McGlothlin, W. (1972). Effect of marijuana upon peripheral vision as a function of the information processing demands in central vision. *Perceptual and Motor Skills,* 35, 875.

Mountcastle, V. B., Motter, B. C., Steinmetz, M. A., & Sestokas, A. K. (1987). Common and differential effects of attentive fixation on the excitability of parietal and prestriate (V4). Cortical visual neurons in the macaque monkey. *Journal of Neuroscience,* 7, 2239–2255.

Movshon, J. A., & Newsome, W. T. (1992). Neural foundations of visual motion perception. *Current Directions in Psychological Science,* 1, 35–39.

Movshon, J. A., Adelson, E. H., Gizzi, M. S., & Newsome, W. T. (1985). The analysis of moving visual patterns. In C. Chagas, R. Gattass, & C. Gross (Eds.), *Pattern Recognition Mechanisms* (pp. 117–151). Rome: Vatican Press.

Mozel, M. M., Smith, B., Smith, P., Sullivan, R., & Swender, P. (1969). Nasal chemoreception in flavor identification. *Archives of Otolaryngology,* 90, 367–373.

Muckli, L., Kiregeskorte, N., Lanfermann, H., Zanella, F. E., Singer, W., & Goebel, R. (2002). Apparent motion: Event related functional magnetic resonance imaging of perceptual switches and states. *Journal of Neuroscience,* 22, 3342–3444.

Muir, D. W., Clifton, R. K., & Clarkson, M. G. (1989). The development of a human auditory localization response: A U-shaped function. *Canadian Journal of Psychology,* 43, 199–216.

Mullen, K. T. (1990). The chromatic coding of space. In C. Blakemore (Ed.), *Vision: Coding and Efficiency* (pp. 150–158). New York: Cambridge University Press.

Muller, H. J., & Rabbitt, P. M. A. (1989). Reflexive and voluntary orienting of visual attention: Time course of activation and resistance to interruption. *Journal of Experimental Psychology: Human Perception and Performance,* 15, 315–330.

Mulligan, R. M., & Schiffman, H. R. (1979). Temporal experience as a function of organization in memory. *Bulletin of the Psychonomic Society,* 14, 417–420.

Munoz, D. P., & Wurtz, R. H. (1993). Fixation cells in monkey superior colliculus: I: Characteristics of cell discharge. *Journal of Neurophysiology,* 70, 559–575.

Munoz, D. P., & Wurtz, R. H. (1995). Saccade-related activity in monkey superior colliculus: I: Characteristics of burst and buildup neurons. *Journal of Neurophysiology,* 73, 2313–2333.

Munsell, A. H. (1915). *Atlas of the Munsell Color System.* Maldin, MA: Wadsworth, Howland.

Murphy, C., & Cain, W. S. (1980). Taste and olfaction: Independence vs. interaction. *Physiology and Behavior,* 24, 601–605.

Murray, J. B. (1986). Marijuana's effects on human cognitive functions, psychomotor functions, and personality. *Journal of General Psychology,* 113, 23–55.

Murray, R. F., Sekuler, A. B., & Bennett, P. J. (2001). Time course of amodal completion revealed by a shape discrimination task. *Psychonomic Bulletin & Review,* 8, 713–720.

Mustillo, P. (1985). Binocular mechanisms mediating crossed and uncrossed stereopsis. *Psychological Bulletin,* 97, 187–201.

Myers, A. K. (1982). Psychophysical scaling and scales of physical stimulus measurement. *Psychological Bulletin,* 92, 203–214.

Näätänen, R. (1992). *Attention and Brain Function.* Hillsdale, NJ: Lawrence Erlbaum.

Näätänen, R., Lehtokoski, A., Lennes, M., Cheour, M., Houtilainen, M., Ilvonen, A., Vainlo, M., Alkus, P., Ilmoniemi, Luuk, A., Allik, J., Sinkkonen, J., & Alho, K. (1997). Language-specific phoneme representations revealed by electric and magnetic brain responses. *Nature,* 385, 432–434.

Nagy, A. L. (1980). Short-flash Bezold-Brucke hue shifts. *Vision Research,* 20, 361–368.

Nakayama, K. (1985). Biological image motion processing: A review. *Vision Research,* 25, 625–660.

Nakayama, K. (2001). Modularity in perception, its relation to cognition and knowledge. In E. B. Goldstein (Ed.), *Blackwell Handbook of Perception* (pp. 737–759). Malden, MA: Blackwell Publishers.

Nathans, J. (1987). Molecular biology of visual pigments. *Annual Review of Neuroscience,* 10, 163–164.

Nathans, J., Piantanida, T. P., Eddy, R. L., Shows, T. B., & Hogness, D. S. (1986). Molecular genetics of inherited variation in human color vision. *Science,* 232, 203–210.

Navon, D. (1977). Forest before trees: The precedence of global features in visual perception. *Cognitive Psychology,* 9, 353–383.

Navon, D., & Norman, J. (1983). Does global precedence really depend on visual angle? *Journal of Experimental Psychology: Human Perception and Performance,* 9, 955–965.

Needham, A., & Baillargeon, R. (1998). Effects of prior experience on 4.5-month-old infants' object segregation. *Infant Behavior and Development,* 21, 1–24.

Neisser, U. (1976). *Cognition and Reality: Principles and Implications of Cognitive Psychology.* San Francisco: Freeman.

Neisser, U., & Becklin, R. (1975). Selective looking: Attending to visually specified events. *Cognitive Psychology,* 7, 480–494.

Neitz, J., & Jacobs, G. H. (1986). Polymorphism of the long-wavelength cone in normal human colour vision. *Nature,* 323, 623–625.

Nelson, G., Chandrashekar, J., Hoon, M. A., Feng, L., Zhao, G., Ryba, N. J. P., & Zuker, C. S. (2002). An amino-acid taste receptor. *Nature,* 416, 199–202.

Nelson, R., Kolb, H., Robinson, M. M., & Mariani, A. P. (1981). Neural circuitry of the cat retina: Cone pathways to ganglion cells. *Vision Research,* 21, 1527–1537.

Neumann, H., Pessoa, L., Hansen, T. (2001). Visual filling-in for computing perceptual surface properties. *Biological Cybernetics,* 85, 355–369.

Neumann, R., & Strack, F. (2000). Experiential and nonexperiential routes of motor influence on affect and evaluation. In H. Bless & J. P. Forgas (Eds.), *The Message Within: The Role of Subjective Experience in Social Cognition and Behavior* (pp. 52–68). Philadelphia: Psychology Press.

Neumeyer, C. (1998). Comparative aspects of color constancy. In V. Walsh & J. Kulikowski (Eds.), *Perceptual Constancy: Why Things Look as They Do* (pp. 323–351). New York: Cambridge University Press.

Newhall, S. M., Burnham, R. W., & Clark, J. R. (1957). Comparison of successive with simultaneous color matching. *Journal of the Optical Society of America,* 47, 43–56.

Newhall, S. M., Nickerson, D., & Judd, D. B. (1943). Final report of the O.S.A. subcommittee on spacing of the Munsell colors. *Journal of the Optical Society of America,* 33, 385–418.

Newsome, W. T., & Pare, E. B. (1988). A selective impairment of motion processing following lesions of the middle temporal visual area (MT). *Journal of Neuroscience,* 8, 2201–2211.

Newsome, W. T., Britten, K. H., & Movshon, J. A. (1989). Neuronal correlates of a perceptual decision. *Nature,* 341, 52–54.

Niall, K. K. (1990). Projective invariance and picture perception. *Perception,* 19, 637–660.

Nickell, W. T. (1997). Basic anatomy and physiology of olfaction. In A. M. Seiden (Ed.), *Taste and Smell Disorders* (pp. 20–37). New York: Thieme.

Nihjawan, R. (1994). Motion extrapolation in catching. *Nature,* 370, 256–257.

Nijhawan, R. (1991). Three-dimensional Mueller-Lyer illusion. *Perception & Psychophysics,* 49, 333–341.

Nilsen, K. E., & Russell, I. J. (1999). Timing of cochlear feedback: Spatial and temporal representation of a tone across the basilar membrane. *Nature Neuroscience,* 2, 642–648.

Nishiike, S., Nakagawa, S., Tonoike, M., Takeda, N., & Kubo, T. (2001). Information processing of visually induced apparent self motion in the cortex of humans: Analysis with magnetoencephalography. *Acta Oto-Laryngologica,* 121, 113–115.

Nishiike, S., Nakagawa, S., Tonoike, M., Takeda, N., & Kubo, T. (2001). Information processing of visually induced apparent self motion in the cortex of humans: Analysis with magnetoencephalography. *Acta Oto-Laryngologica,* 121(Suppl. 545), 113–115.

Nisson, M. J., & Corkin, S. (1985). Effectiveness of attentional cueing in older and younger adults. *Journal of Gerontology,* 40, 185–191.

Noell, W. (1980). Possible mechanisms of photoreceptor damage by light in mammalian eyes. *Vision Research,* 20, 1163–1172.

Norman, J. F., Dawson, T. E., & Butler, A. K. (2000). The effects of age upon the perception of depth and 3–D shape from differential motion and binocular disparity. *Perception,* 29, 1335–1359.

Norman, D. A. (1969). Memory while shadowing. *Quarterly Journal of Experimental Psychology,* 21, 85–93.

Norman, D. A., Rumelhart, D. E., and the LNR Research Group. (1975). *Explorations in Cognition.* San Francisco: Freeman.

Norris, S. A., Greger, B. E., Martin, T. A., & Thach, W. T. (2001). Prism adaptation of reaching is dependent on the type of visual feedback of hand and target position. *Brain Research,* 905, 207–219.

Norton, S. J., Schultz, M. C., Reed, C. M., Braida, L. D., Durlach, N. I., Rabinowitz, W. M., & Chomsky, C. (1977). Analytic study of the Tadoma method: Background and preliminary results. *Journal of Speech and Hearing Research,* 20, 574–595.

Norton, T. T. (1981). Geniculate and extrageniculate visual systems in the tree shrew. In A. R. Morrison & P. L. Strick (Eds.), *Changing Concepts of the Nervous System* (pp. 377–410). New York: Academic Press.

Norwich, K. H. (1983). To perceive is to doubt: The relativity of perception. *Journal of Theoretical Biology,* 102, 175–190.

Norwich, K. H. (1984). The psychophysics of taste from the entropy of the stimulus. *Perception & Psychophysics,* 35, 269–278.

Norwich, K. N. (1993). *Information, Sensation and Perception.* Orlando: Academic Press.

Nothdurft, H. C., Gallant, J. L., & Van Essen, D. C. (2000). Response profiles to texture border patterns in area V1. *Visual Neuroscience,* 17, 421–436.

Nusbaum, H. C., & Schwab, E. C. (1986). The role of attention and active processing in speech perception. In E. C. Schwab & H. C. Nusbaum (Eds.), *Pattern Recognition by Humans and Machines,* Vol. 1. *Speech Perception* (pp. 113–157). Orlando: Academic Press.

O'Brien, J., & Johnston, A. (2000). When texture takes precedence over motion in depth perception. *Perception,* 29, 437–452.

Ogasawara, K., McHaftie, J. G., & Stein, B. E. (1984). Two visual corticotectal systems in the cat. *Journal of Neurophysiology,* 52, 1226–1245.

Ohala, J. J. (1986). Phonological evidence for top-down processing in speech perception. In J. S. Perkell and D. H. Klatt (Eds.), *Invariance and Variability in Speech Processes* (pp. 386–397). Hillsdale, NJ: Erlbaum.

Ohala, J. J. (1996). Speech perception is hearing sounds, not tongues. *Journal of the Acoustical Society of America,* 99, 1718–1725.

Öhman, A., & Soares, J. J. F. (1994). "Unconscious anxiety": Phobic responses to masked stimuli. *Journal of Abnormal Psychology,* 103, 231–240.

O'Kusky, J., & Colonnier, M. (1982). Postnatal changes in the number of neurons and synapses in the visual cortex (A17). of the macaque monkey. *Journal of Comparative Neurology,* 210, 291–296.

Olausson, H., Lamarre, Y., Backlund, H., Morin, C., Wallin, B. G., Starck, G., Ekholm, S., Strigo, I., Worsley, K., Vallbo, A. B., & Bushnell, M. C. (2002). Unmyelinated tactile afferents signal touch and project to insular cortex. *Nature Neuroscience,* 5, 900–904.

O'Leary, A., & McMahon, M. (1991). Adaptation to form distortion of a familiar shape. *Perception & Psychophysics,* 49, 328–332.

Olsen, J., Sorensen, H. T., Steffensen, F. H. Sabroe S., Gillman, M. W., Fischer, P. R., & Rothman, K. J. (2001). The association of indicators of fetal growth with visual acuity and hearing among conscripts. *Epidemiology,* 12, 235–238.

Olson, E. S. (1999). Direct measurement of intra-cochlear pressure waves. *Nature,* 402, 525–529.

Olzak, L. (1986). Widely separated spatial frequencies: Mechanism interactions. *Vision Research,* 26, 1143–1154.

Onishi, K. H., Chambers, K. E., & Fisher, C. (2002). Learning phonotactic constraints from brief auditory experience. *Cognition,* 83, B13–B23.

Ono, H., Wade, N. J., Lillakas, L. (2002). The pursuit of Leonardo's constraint. *Perception,* 31, 83–102.

Ono, H., & Rogers, B. J. (1988). Dynamic occlusion and motion parallax in depth perception. *Perception,* 17, 255–256.

Ono, H., & Weber, E. U. (1981). Nonveridical visual direction produced by monocular viewing. *Journal of Experimental Psychology: Human Perception and Performance,* 7, 937–947.

Orban, G. A., Kennedy, H., & Maes, H. (1981a). Response to movement of neurons in areas 17 and 18 of the cat: Velocity sensitivity. *Journal of Neurophysiology,* 45, 1043–1058.

O'Regan, J. K., & Noe, A.. (2001). A sensorimotor account of vision and visual consciousness. *Behavioral and Brain Sciences,* 24, 939–1031.

Ornstein, R. E. (1969). *On the Experience of Time.* London: Penguin.

Osaka, N. (1981). Brightness exponent as a function of flash duration and retinal eccentricity. *Perception & Psychophysics,* 30, 144–148.

Osborne, M. P., Comis, S. D., & Pickles, J. O. (1988). Further observations on the fine structure of tip links between stereocilia of the guinea pig cochlea. *Hearing Research,* 35, 99–108.

O'Shaughnessy, D. (1996). Critique: Speech perception: Acoustic or articulatory? *Journal of the Acoustical Society of America,* 99, 1726–1729.

Osterberg, G. (1935). Topography of the layer of rods and cones in the human retina. *Acta Ophthalmologica* (Suppl. 6).

Ostfeld, A. (1961). Effects of LSD-25 and JB318 on tests of visual and perceptual functions in man. *Federation Proceedings, Federation of American Societies for Experimental Biology,* 20, 876–883.

O'Toole, A. J., Peterson, J., & Deffenbacher, K. A. (1996). An other-race effect for categorizing faces by sex. *Perception,* 25, 669–676.

Owsley, C. (1983). The role of motion in infants' perception of solid shape. *Perception,* 12, 707–717.

Owsley, C., Burton-Danner, K., & Jackson, G. R. (2000). Aging and spatial localization during feature search. *Gerontology,* 46, 300–305.

Owsley, C. J., Sekuler, R., & Siemensen, D. (1983). Contrast sensitivity throughout adulthood. *Vision Research,* 23, 689–699.

Oyama, T. (1968). A behavioristic analysis of Stevens's magnitude estimation method. *Perception & Psychophysics,* 31, 317–320.

Oyama, T. (1986). The effect of stimulus organization on numerosity discrimination. *Japanese Psychological Research,* 28, 77–86.

Pagano, C. C., Kinsella-Shaw, J. M., Cassidy, P. E., & Turvey, M. T. (1994). Role of the inertia tensor in haptically perceiving where an object is grasped. *Journal of Experimental Psychology: Human Perception & Performance,* 20, 276–285.

Palmer, K. T., Griffin, M. J., Syddall, H. E., Davis, A., Pannett, B., & Coggon, D. (2002). Occupational exposure to noise and the attributable burden of hearingn difficulties in Great Britain. *Occupational and Environmental Medicine,* 59, 634–639.

Palmer, A. R., Winter, I. M., & Darwin, C. J. (1986). The representation of steady-state vowel sounds in the temporal discharge pattern of the guinea pig cochlear nerve and primarylike cochlear nucleus neurons. *Journal of the Acoustical Society of America,* 79, 100–113.

Palmer, J. (1986). Mechanisms of displacement discrimination with and without perceived movement. *Journal of Experimental Psychology: Human Perception and Performance,* 12, 411–421.

Palmer, S. E. (1975a). The effects of contextual scenes on the identification of objects. *Memory and Cognition,* 3, 519–526.

Palmer, S. E. (1975b). Visual perception and world knowledge: Notes on a model of sensory-cognitive interaction. In D. A. Norman & D. E. Rumelhart (Eds.), *Explorations in Cognition* (pp. 297–307). San Francisco: Freeman.

Palmer, S. E., & Rock, I. (1994). Rethinking perceptual organization: The role of uniform connectedness. *Psychonomic Bulletin & Review,* 1, 29–55.

Palmer, S. E., Neff, J., & Beck, D. (1996). Late influences on perceptual grouping: Amodal completion. *Psychonomic Bulletin & Review,* 3, 75–80.

Palmer, S. E. (1999). *Vision Science: Photons to Phenomenology.* Cambridge, MA : MIT Press.

Palmer, S. E. (2002). Perceptual organization in vision. In H. Pashler & S. Yantis (Eds.), *Stevens Handbook of Experimental Psychology* (3rd ed.), Vol. 1: *Sensation and Perception* (pp. 177–234). New York: Wiley.

Palmisano, S. (2002). Consistent stereoscopic information increases the perceived speed of vection in depth. *Perception,* 31, 463–480.

Pantev, C., Hoke, M., Lutkenhoner, B., & Lehnertz, K. (1989). Tonotopic organization of the auditory cortex: Pitch versus frequency representation. *Science,* 246, 486–488.

Paramei, G. V. (1996). Color space of normally sighted and color deficient observers reconstructed from color naming. *Psychological Science,* 7, 311–317.

Parasuraman, R. (1984). Sustained attention in detection and discrimination. In R. Parasuraman & D. R. Davies (Eds.), *Varieties of Attention* (pp. 243–271). Orlando: Academic Press.

Parasuraman, R. (1998). *The Attentive Brain.* Cambridge, MA: The MIT Press.

Parducci, A. (1965). Category judgment: A range-frequency model. *Psychological Review,* 72, 407–418.

Parker, D. E. (1980). The vestibular apparatus. *Scientific American,* 243, 118–135.

Parks, T. E. (1965). Post-retinal visual storage. *American Journal of Psychology,* 78, 145–147.

Parks, T. E. (2001). *Looking at Looking: An Introduction to the Intelligence of Vision.* Thousand Oaks, CA: Sage Publications.

Parlee, M. B. (1983). Menstrual rhythms in sensory processes: A review of fluctuations in vision, olfaction, audition, taste and touch. *Psychological Bulletin,* 93, 539–548.

Parrott, A. C. (1988). Transdermal scopolamine: Effects upon psychological performance and visual functioning at sea. *Human Psychopharmacology Clinical & Experimental,* 3, 119–125.

Pascalis, O., de Schonen, S., Morton, J., Deruelle, C., & Fabre-Grenet, M. (1995). Mother's face recognition by neonates: A replication and an extension. *Infant Behavior and Development,* 18, 79–85.

Pashler, H. (1987). Detecting conjunctions of color and form: Reassessing the serial search hypothesis. *Perception & Psychophysics,* 41, 191–201.

Pashler, H. (1996). *The Psychology of Attention.* Cambridge, MA: MIT Press.

Pashler, H., Johnston, J. C., & Ruthruff, E. (2001). Attention and performance. *Annual Review of Psychology,* 52, 629–651.

Pasman, J. W., Rotteveel, J. J., Maassen, B., & Visco, Y. M. (1999). The maturation of auditory cortical evoked responses between (preterm). Birth and 14 years of age. *European Journal of Paediatric Neurology,* 3, 79–82.

Pastore, R. E., & Li, X. F. (1990). Categorical perception of nonspeech chirps and bleats. *Perception & Psychophysics,* 48, 151–156.

Patla, A. E., & Goodale, M. A. (1996). Obstacle avoidance during locomotion is unaffected in a patient with visual form agnosia. *Neuroreport,* 8, 165–168.

Patterson, R. D. (1969). Noise masking of a change in residue pitch. *Journal of the Acoustical Society of America,* 45, 1520–1524.

Paus T., Collins, D. L., Evans, A. C., Leonard, G., Pike, B., & Zijdenbos, A. (2001). Maturation of white matter in the human brain: a review of magnetic resonance studies. *Brain Research Bulletin,* 54, 255–266.

Paus, T., Zatorre, R. J., Hofle, N., Caramanos, Z., Gotman, J., Petrides, M., & Evans, A. C. (1997). Time-related changes in neural systems underlying attention and arousal during the performance of an auditory vigilance task. *Journal of Cognitive Neuroscience,* 9, 392–408.

Pavlova, M., Stoudt, M., Sokolov, A., Birbaumer, N. & Krägeloh-Mann, I. (2003). Perception and production of biological movement in patients with early periventricular brain lesions. *Brain,* 126, 692–701.

Pearson, D. A., & Lane, D. M. (1991a). Auditory attention switching: A developmental study. *Journal of Experimental Child Psychology,* 51, 320–334.

Pearson, D. A., & Lane, D. M. (1991b). Visual attention movements: A developmental study. *Child Development,* 61, 1779–1795.

Pedersen, P. M., Jorgensen, H. S., Nakayama, H., Raaschou, H. O., & Olsen, T. S. (1997). Hemineglect in acute stroke-incidence and prognostic implications. The Copenhagen Stroke Study. *American Journal of Physical Medicine & Rehabilitation,* 76, 122–127.

Pelosi, P., & Tirindelli, R. (1989). Structure/activity studies and characterization of an odorant-binding protein. In J. G. Brand, J. H. Teeter, R. H. Cagan, & M. R. Kare (Eds.), *Chemical Senses,* Vol. 1: *Receptor Events and Transduction in Taste and Olfaction* (pp. 207–226). New York: Marcel Dekker, Inc.

Penfield, W., & Rasmussen, T. (1950). *The Cerebral Cortex of Man.* New York: Macmillan.

Pentland, A. P. (1986). Perceptual organization and the representation of natural form. *Artificial Intelligence,* 28, 293–331.

Perez, F. M., Tunkel, R. S., Lachmann, E. A., & Nagler, W. (1997). Balint's syndrome arising from bilateral posterior cortical atrophy or infarction: Rehabilitation strategies and their limitation. *Disability & Rehabilitation,* 18, 300–304.

Perkell, J. S., & Klatt, D. H. (Eds.). (1986). *Invariance and Variability in Speech Processes.* Hillsdale, NJ: Erlbaum.

Perl, E. R. (1984). Characterization of nociceptors and their activation of neurons in the superficial dorsal horn: First steps for the sensation of pain. In L. Kruger & J. C. Liebeskind (Eds.), *Neural Mechanisms of Pain* (pp. 23–52). New York: Raven Press.

Perlman, M., & Krumhansl, C. L. (1996). An experimental study of interval standards in Javanese and Western musicians. *Music Perception,* 14, 95–116.

Perrett, D. I., & Mistlin, A. M. (1987). Visual neurones responsive to faces. *Trends in Neuroscience,* 10, 358–364.

Perrett, S., & Noble, W. (1995). Available response choices affect localization of sound. *Perception & Psychophysics,* 57, 150–158.

Perrone, J. A., & Thiele, A. (2002). A model of speed tuning in MT neurons. *Vision Research,* 42, 1035–1051.

Perrott, D. R., & Saberi, K. (1990). Minimum audible angle thresholds for sources varying in both elevation and azimuth. *Journal of the Acoustical Society of America,* 87, 1728–1731.

Perry, C., & Ziegler, J. C. (2002). On the nature of phonological assembly: Evidence from backward masking. *Language and Cognitive Processes,* 17, 31–59.

Peters, A., Moss, M. B., & Sethares, C. (2000). Effects of aging on myelinated nerve fibers in monkey primary visual cortex. *Journal of Comparative Neurology,* 419, 364–376.

Petersen, A. C., & Crockett, L. (1985, August). Factors influencing sex differences in spatial ability during adolescence. In S. L. Willis (Chair), *Sex Differences in Spatial Ability Across the Lifespan.* Symposium conducted at the Ninety-Third Annual Convention of the American Psychological Association, Los Angeles, CA.

Petersen, R. S., Panzeri, S., & Diamond, M. E. (2002). Population coding in somatosensory cortex. *Current Opinion in Neurobiology,* 12, 441–447.

Petersik, J. T. (1989). The two-process distinction in apparent motion. *Psychological Bulletin,* 106, 107–127.

Peterson (Eds.), *Development of Perception* (pp. 45–93). New York: Academic Press.

Peterson, A. C. (1976). Physical androgyny and cognitive functioning in adolescence. *Developmental Psychology,* 12, 524–533.

Peterson, M. A. Object perception. (2000). In E. B. Goldstein (Ed.), *Blackwell Handbook of Perception,* Chapter 6. London: Blackwell Publishers.

Peterson, M. A., de Gelder, B., Rapcsak, S. Z., Gerhardstein, P. C., and Bachoud-Lévi, A.-C. (2000). Object memory effects on figure assignment: Conscious object recognition is not necessary or sufficient. *Vision Research,* 40, 1549–1567.

Petitto, L. A., & Marentette, P. F. (1991). Babbling in the manual mode: Evidence for the ontogeny of language. *Science,* 251, 1493–1496.

Petrovic, P., Kalso, E., Petersson, K. M., & Ingvar, M. (2002). Placebo and opioid analgesia: Imaging a shared neuronal network. *Science,* 295, 1737–1740.

Petry, S., & Meyer, G. E. (1987). The perception of illusory contours. New York: Springer-Verlag.

Peuskens, H., Sunaert, S., Dupont, P., Van Hecke, P., & Orban, G. A. (2001). Human brain regions involved in heading estimation. *Journal of Neuroscience,* 21, 2451–2461.

Pfaff, D. (1968). Effects of temperature and time of day on judgment. *Journal of Experimental Psychology,* 76, 419–422.

Pfaff, D. W. (Ed.). (1985). *Taste, Olfaction, and the Central Nervous System: A Festschrift in Honor of Carl Pfaffman.* New York: The Rockefeller University Press.

Pfaffman, C. (1955). Gustatory nerve impulses in rat, cat, and rabbit. *Journal of Neurophysiology,* 18, 429–440.

Pfaffman, C. (1974). Specificity of the sweet receptors of the squirrel monkey. *Chemical Senses and Flavor,* 1, 61–67.

Pfaffman, C., Bartoshuk, L., & McBurney, D. H. (1971). Taste psychophysics. *Handbook of Sensory Physiology,* 1, 75–101.

Pfeiffer, R. R. (1966). Classification of response patterns of spike discharges for units in the cochlear nucleus: Tone-burst stimulation. *Experimental Brain Research,* 1, 220–235.

Philbeck, J. W., & Mershon, D. H. (2002). Knowledge about typical source output influences perceived auditory distance. *Journal of the Acoustical Society of America,* 111, 1980–1983.

Phillips, C. G., Zeki, S., & Barlow, H. B. (1984). Localization of function in the cerebral cortex. *Brain,* 107, 328–360.

Phillipson, O. T., & Harris, J. P. (1984). Effects of chloropromazine and promazine on the perception of some multi-stable visual figures. *Quarterly Journal of Experimental Psychology,* 36A, 291–308.

Phillipson, O. T., & Harris, J. P. (1985). Perceptual changes in schizophrenia: A questionnaire survey. *Psychological Medicine,* 15, 859–866.

Piaget, J. (1969). *The Mechanisms of Perception* (G. N. Seagrine, Trans.). New York: Oxford University Press.

Pick, H. L. Jr. (1992). Eleanor J. Gibson: Learning to perceive and perceiving to learn. *Developmental Psychology,* 28, 787–794.

Pickering, G., Jourdan, D., Eschalier, A., & Dubray, C. (2002). Impact of age, gender and cognitive functioning on pain perception. *Gerontology,* 48, 112–118.

Pickles, J. O. (1988). *An Introduction to the Physiology of Hearing* (2nd ed.). San Diego: Academic Press.

Pickles, J. O., Comis, S. D., & Osborne, M. P. (1984). Cross-links between stereocilia in the guinea pig organ of Corti, and their possible relation to sensory transduction. *Hearing Research,* 15, 103–112.

Pickles, J. O., Osborne, M. P., Comis, S. D., Köppl, C., Gleich, O., Brix, J., & Manley, G. A. (1989). Tip-link organization in relation to the structure and orientation of stereovillar bundles. In J. P. Wilson & D. T. Kemp (Eds.), *Cochlear Mechanisms: Structure, Function and Models.* (pp. 37–44). New York: Plenum Press.

Piehler, O., & Pantle, A.J. (2001). Direction specific changes of sensitivity after brief apparent motion stimuli. *Vision Research,* 41, 2195–2205.

Pierce, J. D. Jr., & Wysocki, C. J. (1996). The role of perceptual and structural similarity in cross adaptation. *Chemical Senses,* 21, 223–237.

Pind, J. (1995). Speaking rate, voice-onset time, and quantity: The search for higher-order invariants for two Icelandic speech cues. *Perception & Psychophysics,* 57, 291–304.

Pinker, S. (1997). *How the Mind Works.* New York: W. W. Norton.

Pinkers, A., & Marre, M. (1983). Basic phenomena in acquired colour vision deficiency. *Documenta Ophthalmologica,* 55, 251–271.

Pinna, B., & Brelstaff, G. J. (2000). A new visual illusion of relative motion. *Vision Research,* 40 (16), 2091–2096.

Pirozzolo, F. J. (1978). *The Neuropsychology of Developmental Reading Disorders.* New York: Praeger.

Pisoni, D. B. (1973). Auditory and phonetic codes in the discrimination of consonants and vowels. *Perception & Psychophysics,* 13, 253–260.

Pisoni, D. B., & Luce, P. A. (1986). Speech perception: Research, theory, and the principal issues. In E. C. Schwab & H. C. Nusbaum (Eds.), *Pattern Recognition by Humans and Machines,* Vol. 1. *Speech Perception* (pp. 1–50). Orlando: Academic Press.

Plateau, M. H. (1872). Sur la mesure des sensations physiques, et sur la loi qui lie l'intensité de la cause excitante. *Bulletin de l'Academie Royale de Belgique,* 33, 376–388.

Plude, D. J. (1990). Aging, feature integration, and visual attention. In J. T. Enns (Ed.), *The Development of Attention: Research and Theory* (pp. 467–487). Amsterdam: Elsevier.

Poggio, G. F., & Poggio, T. (1984). The analysis of stereopsis. *Annual Review of Neuroscience,* 7, 379–412.

Poggio, G. F., & Talbot, W. H. (1981). Mechanisms of static and dynamic stereopsis in foveal cortex of rhesus monkey. *Journal of Physiology,* 315, 469–492.

Pointer, M. R. (1998). On the number of discernable colors. *Color Research and Application,* 23, 337.

Pokorny, J., & Smith, V. C. (1986). Eye disease and color defects. *Vision Research,* 26, 1573–1584.

Pola, J., & Wyatt, H. J. (1989). The perception of target motion during smooth pursuit eye movements in the open-loop condition: Characteristics of retinal and extraretinal signals. *Vision Research,* 29, 471–483.

Poldrack, R. A., Pare-Blagoev, E. J. & Grant, P. E. (2002). Pediatric functional magnetic resonance imaging: progress and challenges. *Topics in Magnetic Resonance Imaging,* 13, 61–70.

Polk, T. A., Stallcup, M., Aguirre, G. K., Alsop, D. C., D'Esposito, M., Detre, J. A. & Farah, M. J. (2002). Neural specialization for letter recognition. *Journal of Cognitive Neuroscience,* 14, 145–159.

Polka, L., & Werker, J. F. (1994). Developmental changes in perception of nonnative vowel contrasts. *Journal of Experimental Psychology: Human Perception and Performance,* 20, 421–435.

Pollack, I. (1952). The information of elementary auditory displays. *Journal of the Acoustical Society of America,* 24, 745–749.

Pollack, I. (1953). The information of elementary auditory displays: II. *Journal of the Acoustical Society of America,* 25, 765–769.

Pollack, I., & Pickett, J. M. (1964). Intelligibility of excerpts from fluent speech: Auditory vs. structural context. *Journal of Verbal Learning and Verbal Behavior,* 3, 79–84.

Polonsky, A., Blake, R., Braun, J., & Heeger, D.J. (2000). Neuronal activity in human primary visual cortex correaltes with perception during binocular rivalry. *Nature Neuroscience,* 3, 153–1159.

Polster, M. R., & Rapcsak, S. Z. (1996). Representations in learning new faces: Evidence from prosopagnosia. *Journal of the International Neuropsychological Society,* 2, 240–248.

Poltrock, S. E., Lansman, M., & Hunt, E. (1982). Automatic and controlled attention processes in auditory target detection. *Journal of Experimental Psychology: Human Perception and Performance,* 8, 37–45.

Pomerantz, J. R. (1983). Global and local precedence: Selective attention in form and motion perception. *Journal of Experimental Psychology: General,* 112, 511–535.

Pomerantz, J. R., Goldberg, D., Golder, P., & Tetewsky, S. (1981). Subjective contours can facilitate performance in a reaction-time task. *Perception & Psychophysics,* 29, 605–611.

Pons, T. P., Garraghty, P. E., Friedman, D. P., & Mishkin, M. (1987). Physiological evidence for serial processing in somatosensory cortex. *Science,* 237, 417–420.

Pons, T. P., Garraghty, P. E., Ommaya, A. K., Kaas, J. H., Taub, E., & Mishkin, M. (1991). Massive cortical reorganization after sensory deafferentation in adult macaques. *Science,* 252, 1857–1860.

Pont, S. C., Kappers, A. M. L., & Koenderink, J. J. (1997). Haptic curvature discrimination at several regions of the hand. *Perception & Psychophysics,* 59, 1225–1240.

Poom, L. (2001). Visual summation of luminance lines and illusory contours induced by pictorial, motion, and disparity cues. *Vision Research,* 41, 3805–3816.

Poppel, E. (1978). Time perception. In R. Held, H. W. Leibowitz, & H. L. Teuber (Eds.), *Handbook of Sensory Physiology,* Vol. VIII. *Perception* (pp. 713–729). New York: Springer-Verlag.

Poppel, E. (1997). A hierarchical model of temporal perception. *Trends in Cognitive Science,* 1, 56–61.

Popper, R., Parker, S., & Galanter, E. (1986). Dual loudness scales in individual subjects. *Journal of Experimental Psychology: Human Perception and Performance,* 12, 61–69.

Porac, C. (1989). Is visual illusion decrement based on selective adaptation? *Perception & Psychophysics,* 46, 279–283.

Porac, C., & Coren, S. (1976). The dominant eye. *Psychological Bulletin,* 83, 880–897.

Porac, C., & Coren, S. (1981). Life-span age trends in the perception of the Mueller-Lyer: An additional evidence for the existence of two illusions. *Canadian Journal of Psychology,* 35, 58–62.

Porac, C., & Coren, S. (1985). Transfer of illusion decrement: The effects of global versus local figural variations. *Perception & Psychophysics,* 37, 515–522.

Porac, C., & Coren, S. (1986). Sighting dominance and egocentric localization. *Vision Research,* 26, 1709–1713.

Porter, R. H., Balogh, R. D., Cernoch, J. M., & Franchi, C. (1986). Recognition of kin through characteristic body odors. *Chemical Senses,* 11, 389–395.

Posner, M. I. (1978). *Chronometric Exploration of Mind.* Hillsdale, NJ: Erlbaum.

Posner, M. I. (1980). Orienting of attention. *Quarterly Journal of Experimental Psychology,* 32, 3–25.

Posner, M. I., & Cohen, Y. (1984). Components of visual attention. In H. Bouma & D. G. Bouhuis (Eds.), *Attention and Performance X* (pp. 531–556). Hillsdale, NJ: Erlbaum.

Posner, M. I., & Petersen, S. E. (1990). The attention system of the human brain. *Annual Review of Neuroscience,* 13, 25–42.

Posner, M. I., & Raichle, M. E. (1994). *Images of the Mind.* New York: Scientific American Library.

Posner, M. I., Rafal, R. D., Choate, L. S., & Vaughan, J. (1985). Inhibition of return: Neural basis and function. *Cognitive Neuropsychology,* 2, 211–228.

Posner, M. I., Walker, J. A., Friedrich, F. J., & Rafal, R. D. (1984). Effects of parietal injury on covert orienting of attention. *Journal of Neuroscience,* 4, 1863–1874.

Post, B., & Leibowitz, H. W. (1985). A revised analysis of the role of efference in motion perception. *Perception,* 14, 631–643.

Potter, M. C. (1993). Very short-term conceptual memory. *Memory & Cognition,* 21(2), 156–161.

Potter, M. C. (1999). Understanding sentences and scenes: The role of conceptual short term memory. In V. Coltheart (Ed)., *Fleeting Memories* (pp. 13–46). Cambridge, MA: MIT Press.

Potter, M. C., O'Connor, D. H., & Oliva, A. (2002). *Remember Rooms But Not Viewpoints.* Poster presented at Vision Sciences Society, Sarasota, FL.

Poulton, E. C. (1989). *Bias in Quantifying Judgments.* Hillsdale, NJ: Erlbaum.

Powers, M. K., Schneck, M., & Teller, D. Y. (1981). Spectral sensitivity of human infants at absolute visual threshold. *Vision Research,* 21, 1005–1016.

Poynter, W. D., & Holma, D. (1985). Duration judgment and the experience of change. *Perception & Psychophysics,* 33, 548–560.

Predebon, J. (1990). Illusion decrement and transfer of illusion decrement in obtuse- and acute-angle variants of the Poggendorff illusion. *Perception & Psychophysics,* 48, 467–476.

Predebon, J. (1998). Decrement of the Brentano Mueller-Lyer illusion as a function of inspection time. *Perception,* 27, 183–192.

Preti, G., Cutler, W. B., Garcia, C. R., Huggins, G. R., & Lawley, H. J. (1986). Human axillary secretions influence women's menstrual cycles: The role of donor extract of females. *Hormones and Behavior,* 20, 474–482.

Previc, F. H. (1994). The relationship between eye dominance and head tilt in humans. *Neuropsychologia,* 32, 1297–1303.

Prime, D. J., Tata, M. S., & Ward, L. M. (in press). Event-related potential evidence for attentional inhibition of return in audition. *NeuroReport,* 14.

Prince, M. M. (2002). Distribution of risk factors for hearing loss: implications for evaluating risk of occupational noise-induced hearing loss. *Journal of the Acoustical Society of America,* 112, 557–567.

Prinzmetal, W. (1981). Principles of feature integration in visual perception. *Perception & Psychophysics,* 30, 330–340.

Prinzmetal, W., & Millis-Wright, M. (1984). Cognitive and linguistic factors affect visual feature integration. *Cognitive Psychology,* 16, 305–340.

Prinzmetal, W., Henderson, D., & Ivry, R. (1995). Loosening the constraints on illusory conjunctions: Assessing the roles of exposure duration and attention. *Journal of Experimental Psychology: Human Perception and Performance,* 21, 1362–1375.

Pritchard, R. M., Heron, W., & Hebb, D. O. (1960). Visual perception approached by the method of stabilized images. *Canadian Journal of Psychology,* 14, 67–77.

Prophet, W. D., Hoffman, D. D., & Cicerone, C. M. (2001). Contours from apparent motion: a computational theory. In T. F. Shipley & P. J. Kellman (Eds.), *From Fragments to Objects: Segmentation and Grouping in Vision.* (pp. 509–529). Amsterdam: Elsevier.

Puckett, J. de W., & Steinman, R. M. (1969). Tracking eye movements with and without saccadic correction. *Vision Research,* 9, 295–303.

Puel, J. L., Bobbin, R. P., & Fallon, M. (1988). An ipsilateral cochlear efferent loop protects the cochlea during intense sound exposure. *Hearing Research,* 37, 65–70.

Purghé, F., & Coren, S. (1992). Subjective contours 1900–1990: Research trends and bibliography. *Perception & Psychophysics,* 51, 291–304.

Quinn P. C., Brown, C. R., & Streppa, M. L. (1997). Perceptual organization of complex visual configurations by young infants. *Infant Behavior and Development,* 20, 35–46.

Quinn, P. C., Wooten, B. R., & Ludman, E. J. (1985). Achromatic color categories. *Perception & Psychophysics,* 37, 198–204.

Raab, E. (1980). Cortical binocularity in infants. *Nature,* 288, 363–385.

Rabbitt, P. M. A. (1984). The control of attention in visual search. In R. Parasuraman & D. R. Davies (Eds.), *Varieties of Attention* (pp. 273–291). Orlando: Academic Press.

Rabbitt, R. D. (1990). A hierarchy of examples illustrating the acoustic coupling of the eardrum. *Journal of the Acoustical Society of America,* 87, 2566–2582.

Rabinowitz, W. M., Houtsma, A. J. M., Durlach, N. I., & Delhorne, L. A. (1987). Multidimensional tactile displays: Identification of vibratory intensity, frequency, and contactor area. *Journal of the Acoustical Society of America,* 82, 1243–1252.

Rader, N.V. (1997). Change and variation in responses to perceptual information. In C. Dent-Read & P. Zukow-Goldring (Eds.), *Evolving Explanations of Development: Ecological Approaches to Organism-Environment Systems* (pp. 129–157). Washington, DC: American Psychological Association.

Raftenberg, M. N. (1990). Flow of endolymph in the inner spiral sulcus and the subtectorial space. *Journal of the Acoustical Society of America,* 87, 2606–2620.

Ramachandran, V. S. (1986). Capture of stereopsis and apparent motion by illusory contours. *Perception & Psychophysics,* 39, 361–373.

Ramachandran, V. S. (1988). Perceiving shape from shading. *Scientific American,* 259, 76–83.

Ramachandran, V. S., & Anstis, S. M. (1986). The perception of apparent motion. *Scientific American,* 254, 80–87.

Ramachandran, V. S., Altschuler, E. L., & Hillyer, S. (1997). Mirror agnosia. *Proceedings of the Royal Society of London—Series B: Biological Sciences,* 264, 645–647.

Ramesh, R. (2000). Centrifugal pathways protect hearing sensitivity at the cochlea in noisy environments that exacerbate the damage induced by loud sound. *Journal of Neuroscience,* 20, 6684–6693.

Rammsayer, T., & Lustnauer, S. (1989). Sex differences in time perception. *Perceptual and Motor Skills,* 68, 195–198.

Ramus, F. H., Hauser, M. D., Miller, C., Morris, D., & Mehler, J. (2001). Language discrimination by human newborns and by cotton-top tamarin monkeys. In M. Tomasello & E. Bates (Eds.). *Language Development: The Essential Readings. Essential Readings in Developmental Psychology* (pp. 34–41). Malden, MA: Blackwell Publishers.

Rao, R. P. N., Olshausen, B. A., & Lewicki, M. S. (Eds.) (2002). *Probabilistic Models of the Brain: Perception and Neural Function.* Cambridge, MA: MIT Press.

Ratliff, F. (1965). *Mach Bands: Quantitative Studies on Neural Networks in the Retina.* San Francisco: Holden-Day.

Rauch, S. D., Velazquez-Villasenor, L., Dimitri, P. S., Merchant, S. N. (2001). Decreasing hair cell counts in aging humans. *Annals of the New York Academy of Science,* 942, 220–227.

Rauch S. L., Whalen, P. J., Shin, L. M., McInerney, S. C., Macklin, M. L., Lasko, N. B., Orr, S. P., & Pitman R. K. (2000). Exaggerated amygdala response to masked facial stimuli in posttraumatic stress disorder: A functional MRI study. *Biological Psychiatry,* 47, 769–776.

Rauschecker, J. P., & Tian, B. (2000). Mechanisms and streams for processing of "what" and "where" in auditory cortex. *Proceedings of the National Academy of Science (USA),* 97, 11800–11806.

Rayleigh, L. (1907). On our perception of sound direction. *Philosophical Magazine,* 13(6), 214–232.

Raymond, J. E., Shapiro, K. L., & Rose, D. J. (1984). Optokinetic backgrounds affect perceived velocity during ocular tracking. *Perception & Psychophysics,* 36, 221–224.

Rea, M. M., & Sweeney, J. A. (1989). Changes in eye tracking during clinical stabilization in schizophrenia. *Psychiatry Research,* 28, 31–39.

Reason, J. (1984). Lapses of attention in everyday life. In R. Parasuraman & D. R. Davies (Eds.), *Varieties of Attention* (pp. 515–549). Orlando: Academic Press.

Redding, G. M., & Wallace, B. (1990). Effects on prism adaptation of duration and timing of visual feedback during pointing. *Journal of Motor Behavior,* 22, 209–224.

Redding, G. M., & Wallace, B. (1997). Prism adaptation during target pointing from visible and nonvisible starting locations. *Journal of Motor Behavior,* 29, 119–130.

Redding, G. M., & Wallace, B. (2002). Strategic calibration and spatial alignment: A model from prism adaptation. *Journal of Motor Behavior,* 34, 126–138.

Redding, G. M., & Wallace, B. (1997). *Adaptive Spatial Alignment.* Hillsdale, NJ: Erlbaum.

Reddy, D. R. (1976). Speech recognition by machine: A review. *Proceedings of the IEEE,* 64, 501–531.

Rees, G., Kreiman, G., & Koch, C. (2002). Neural correlates of consciousness in humans. *Nature Reviews: Neuroscience,* 3, 261–270.

Regan, B. C., Julliot, C. Simmen, B., Vienot, F., Charles-Dominique, P., & Mollon, J. D. (2001). Fruits, foliage and the evolution of primate colour vision. *Philosophical Transactions of the Royal Society of London, Series B: Biological Sciences,* 356, 229–283.

Regan, D. M., & Beverly, K. (1982). How do we avoid confounding the direction we are looking and the direction we are moving? *Science,* 215, 194–196.

Regan, D. M., & Gray, R. (2000). Visually guided collision avoidance and collision achievement. *Trends in Cognitive Sciences,* 4, 99–107.

Regolin, L., & Vallortigara, G. (1995). Perception of partly occluded objects by young chicks. *Perception & Psychophysics,* 57, 971–976.

Rehn, T. (1978). Perceived odor intensity as a function of airflow through the nose. *Sensory Processes,* 2, 198–205.

Reichardt, W. (1961). Autocorrelation: A principle for the evaluation of sensory information by the central nervous system. In W. A. Rosenblith (Ed.), *Principles of Sensory Communication* (pp. 303–317). New York: Wiley.

Reichardt, W., & Poggio, T. (1979). Figure-ground discrimination by relative movement in the visual system of the fly. *Biological Cybernetics,* 35, 81–100.

Reingold, E. M., Charness, N., Schultetus, R. S., & Stampe, D. M. (2001). Perceptual automaticity in expert chess players: Parallel encoding of chess relations. *Psychonomic Bulletin and Review,* 8, 504–510.

Reisberg, D., & O'Shaughnessy, M. (1984). Diverting subjects' concentration slows figural reversals. *Perception,* 13, 461–468.

Remez, R. E. (1996). Critique: Auditory form and gestural topology in the perception of speech. *Journal of the Acoustical Society of America,* 99, 1695–1698.

Remez, R. E., Rubin, P. E., Pisoni, D. B., & Carrell, T. D. (1981). Speech perception without traditional speech cues. *Science,* 212, 947–950.

Remington, R. (1980). Attention and saccadic eye movements. *Journal of Experimental Psychology: Human Perception and Performance,* 6, 726–744.

Rencanzone, G. H., Schreiner, C. E., & Merzenich, M. M. (1993). Plasticity in the frequency representation of primary auditory cortex following discrimination training in adult owl monkeys. *The Journal of Neuroscience,* 13, 87–103.

Rensink, R. A. (2002). Change detection. *Annual Review of Psychology,* 53, 245–277.

Rensink, R. A., O'Regan, K., & Clark, J. J. (1997). To see or not to see: The need for attention to perceive changes in scenes. *Psychological Science,* 8, 368–373.

Repp, B. H. (1987). The sound of two hands clapping: An exploratory study. *Journal of the Acoustical Society of America,* 81, 1100–1109.

Reynolds, D. C. (1979). A visual profile of the alcoholic driver. *American Journal of Optometry and Physiological Optics,* 56, 241–251.

Reynolds, R. I. (1985). The role of object-hypotheses in the organization of fragmented figures. *Perception,* 14, 49–52.

Rhee, K., Kim, D., & Kim, Y. (1965). *The Effects of Smoking on Night Vision.* 14th Pacific Medical Conference (Professional Papers).

Rhode, W. S., & Greenberg, S. (1994). Encoding of amplitude modulation in the cochlear nucleus of the cat. *Journal of Neurophysiology,* 71, 1797–1825.

Rhodes, G., Yoshikawa, S., Clark, A., Lee, K., McKay, R., & Akamatsu, S. (2001). Attractiveness of facial averageness and symmetry in non Western cultures: In search of biologically based standards of beauty. *Perception,* 30, 611–625.

Rhodes, G. (1987). Auditory attention and the representation of spatial information. *Perception & Psychophysics,* 42, 1–14.

Ricci, C., & Blundo, C. (1990). Perception of ambiguous figures after focal brain lesions. *Neuropsychologia,* 28, 1163–1173.

Rice, C. G., Ayley, J. B., Bartlett, B., Bedford, W., Gregory, W., & Hallum, G. (1968). A pilot study on the effects of pop group music on hearing. Cited in K. D. Kryter (1970). *The Effects of Noise on Man* (p. 203). New York: Academic Press.

Richards, J. E., & Hunter, S. K. (1998). Attention and eye movement in young infants:neural control and development. In J. E. Richards (Ed.), *Cognitive Neuroscience of Attention: A Developmental Perspective* (pp. 131–162). Mahwah, NJ: Erlbaum.

Ridder W. H., McCulloch, D., & Herbert, A. M. (1998). Stimulus duration, neural adaptation, and sweep visual evoked potential acuity estimates. *Investigative Ophthalmology & Visual Science,* 39. 2759–2768.

Riesenhuber, M., & Poggio, T. (2000). Models of object recognition. *Nature Neuroscience,* 3 (Suppl), 1199–1204.

Riesz, R. R. (1928). Differential intensity sensitivity of the ear for pure tones. *Physical Review,* 31, 867–875.

Riggs, L. A., Ratliff, F., Cornsweet, J. C., & Cornsweet, T. N. (1953). The disappearance of steadily fixated visual test objects. *Journal of the Optical Society of America,* 43, 495–501.

Rijnsdorp, A., Daan, S., & Dijkstra, C. (1981). Hunting in the kestrel (Falco tinnunculus) and the adaptive significance of daily habits. *Oecologia,* 50, 391–406.

Rivest, J., & Ono, H. (1989). The roles of convergence and apparent distance in depth constancy with motion parallax. *Perception & Psychophysics,* 46, 401–408.

Rizzo, M., & Robin, D. (1990). Simultagnosia: A defect of sustained attention yields insights on visual information processing. *Neurology,* 40, 447–455.

Roberts, M., & Summerfield, A. Q. (1981). Audio-visual adaptation in speech perception. *Perception & Psychophysics,* 30, 309–314.

Robinson, D. L., & Kertzman, C. (1995). Covert orienting of attention in macaques. III. Contributions of the superior colliculus. *Journal of Neurophysiology,* 74, 713–721.

Robinson, D. L., Bowman, E. M., & Kertzman, C. (1995). Covert orienting of attention in macaques. II. Contributions of parietal cortex. *Journal of Neurophysiology,* 74, 698–712.

Robinson, D. W., & Dadson, R. S. (1956). A redetermination of the equal-loudness relations for pure tones. *British Journal of Applied Physics,* 7, 166–181.

Robinson, K., & Patterson, R. D. (1996). The stimulus duration required to identify vowels, their octave, and their pitch chroma. *Journal of the Acoustical Society of America,* 98, 1858–1865.

Rock, I. (1997). *Indirect Perception.* Cambridge, MA: MIT Press.

Rock, I., & Brosgole, L. (1964). Grouping based on phenomenal proximity. *Journal of Experimental Psychology,* 67, 531–538.

Rock, I., & Guttman, D. (1981). The effect of inattention on form perception. *Journal of Experimental Psychology: Human Perception and Performance,* 7, 275–285.

Rock, I., & Halper, F. (1969). Form perception without a retinal image. *American Journal of Psychology,* 82, 425–440.

Rock, I., & Mitchener, K. (1992). Further evidence of failure of reversal of ambiguous figures by uninformed subjects. *Perception,* 21, 39–45.

Rock, I., Gopnik, A., & Hall, S. (1994). Do young children reverse ambiguous figures? *Perception,* 23, 635–644.

Rock, I., Nijhawan, R., Palmer, S. E., & Tudor, L. (1992). Grouping based on phenomenal similarity of achromatic color. *Perception,* 21, 779–789.

Rodieck, R. W. (1965). Quantitative analysis of the cat retinal ganglion cell response to visual stimuli. *Vision Research,* 5, 583–601.

Rodieck, R. W. (1973). *The Vertebrate Retina: Principles of Structure and Function.* San Francisco: Freeman.

Rodieck, R. W. (1979). Visual pathways. *Annual Review of Neuroscience,* 2, 193–226.

Rodieck, R.W. (1998). *The First Steps in Seeing.* Sunderland, MA: Sinauer.

Rodriguez, E., George, N., Lachaux, J-P., Martinerie, J., Renault, B., & Varela, F. J. (1999). Perception's shadow: Long-distance synchronization of human brain activity. *Nature,* 397, 430–433.

Roeckelein, J. E. (2000). *The Concept of Time in Psychology: A Resource Book and Annotated Bibliography.* Westport, CT: Greenwood Press.

Roelofs, C. O. (1935). Optische Lokalisation. *Archiv fuer Augenheilkunde,* 109, 395–415.

Rogel, M. J. (1978). A critical evaluation of the possibility of higher primate reproductive and sexual pheromones. *Psychological Bulletin,* 85, 810–830.

Rogers, B. J., & Collett, T. S. (1989). The appearance of surfaces specified by motion parallax and binocular disparity. *Quarterly Journal of Experimental Psychology: Human Experimental Psychology,* 41, 697–717.

Rohaly, A.M., & Wilson, H.R. (1999). The effects of contrast on perceived depth and depth discrimination. *Vision Research,* 39, 9–18.

Rohrbaugh, J. W. (1984). The orienting reflex: Performance and central nervous system manifestations. In R. Parasuraman & D. R. Davies (Eds.), *Varieties of Attention* (pp. 323–373). Orlando: Academic Press.

Rollman, G. B., & Harris, G. (1987). The detectability, discriminability, and perceived magnitude of painful electric shock. *Perception & Psychophysics,* 42, 257–268.

Rolls, E. T., & Deco, G (2002). *Computational Neuroscience of Vision.* London: Oxford University Press.

Romani, G. L., Williamson, S. J., & Kaufman, L. (1982). Tonotopic organization of the human auditory cortex. *Science,* 216, 1339–1340.

Romanski, L. M., Tian, B., Fritz, P. S., Goldman-Rakic, & J. P. Rauschecker (1999). Dual streams of auditory afferants targte multiple domains in the prefrontal cortex. *Nature Neuroscience,* 2, 1131–1136.

Roorda, A., & Williams, D. R. (1999). The arrangement of the three cone classes in the living human eye. *Nature,* 397, 520–522.

Root, W. (1974, December 22). Of wine and noses. *New York Times Magazine,* pp. 14 et seq.

Roscoe, S. N. (1989). The zoom-lens hypothesis. In M. Hershenson (Ed.), *The Moon Illusion* (pp. 31–58). Hillsdale, NJ: Erlbaum.

Rose, J. E., Brugge, J. F., Anderson, D. J., & Hind, J. E. (1967). Phase-locked response to low frequency tones in single auditory nerve fibers of the squirrel monkey. *Journal of Neurophysiology,* 30, 769–793.

Rose, J. E., Galambos, R., & Hughes, J. (1959). Microelectrode studies of the cochlear nuclei of the cat. *Johns Hopkins Hospital Bulletin,* 14, 211–251.

Rose, J. E., Galambos, R., & Hughes, J. (1960). Organization of frequency sensitive neurons in the cochlear nuclear complex of the cat. In G. L. Rasmussen & W. F. Windle (Eds.), *Neural Mechanisms of the Auditory and Vestibular Systems* (pp. 116–136). Springfield, IL: Thomas.

Rose, S. A, Feldman, J. F., & Jankowski, J. J. (2001). Attention and recognition memory in the 1st year of life: A longitudinal study of preterm and full-term infants. *Developmental Psychology,* 37, 135–151.

Rosinski, R., & Farber, J. (1980). Compensation for viewing point in the perception of pictured space. In M. Hagen (Ed.), *Perception of Pictures,* Vol. 1. *Albert's Window: The Projective Model of Pictorial Information.* (pp. 137–176). New York: Academic Press.

Ross, D. F., Read, J. D., & Toglia, M. P. (1994). *Adult Eyewitness Testimony: Current Trends and Developments.* New York: University of Cambridge Press.

Ross, H. (1975, June 19). Mist, murk and visual perception. *New Scientist,* 66, pp. 658–660.

Ross, H. E., & Plug, C. (1998). The history of size constancy and size illusions. In V. Walsh & J. Kulikowski (Eds.), *Perceptual Constancy: Why Things Look as They Do.* (pp. 499–528). New York: Cambridge University Press.

Ross, H. E. & Plug, C. (2002). The *Mystery of the Moon Illusion: Exploring Size Perception.* Oxford: Oxford University Press.

Ross, J., Morrone, M. C., Goldberg, M. C., & Burr, D. C. (2001). Changes in visual perception at the time of saccades. *Trends in Cognitive Science,* 24(2), 113–121.

Ross, N., & Schilder, P. (1934). Tachistoscopic experiments on the perception of the human figure. *Journal of General Psychology,* 10, 152–172.

Rossi, A. F., Rittenhouse, C. D., & Paradiso, M. A. (1996). The representation of brightness in primary visual cortex. *Science,* 273, 1104–1107.

Rothbart, M. K., Posner, M. I., & Boylan, A. (1990). Regulatory mechanisms in infant development. In J. T. Enns (Ed.), *The Development of Attention: Research and Theory* (pp. 47–66). Amsterdam: Elsevier.

Rouder, J. N. (2001). Absolute identification with simple and complex stimuli. *Psychological Science,* 12, 318–322.

Rouiller, E. M., Rodrigues-Dagaeff, C., Simm, G., De Ribaupierre, Y., Villa, A., & De Ribaupierre, F. (1989). Functional organization of the medial division of the medial geniculate body of the cat: Tonotopic organization, spatial distribution of response properties and cortical connections. *Hearing Research,* 39, 127–142.

Roux, F., Ceccaldi, M. (2001). Does aging affect the allocation of visual attention in global and local information processing? *Brain and Cognition,* 46, 383–396.

Royden, C. S., & Hildreth, E. C. (1996). Human heading judgments in the presence of moving objects. *Perception & Psychophysics,* 58, 836–856.

Royster, L. H., Royster, J. D., & Thomas, W. G. (1980). Representative hearing levels by race and sex in North Carolina industry. *Journal of the Acoustical Society of America,* 68, 551–566.

Rozin, P. (1978). The use of characteristic flavorings in human culinary practice. In C. M. Apt (Ed.), *Flavor: Its Chemical, Behavioral, and Commercial Aspects* (pp. 101–127). Boulder, CO: Westview Press.

Rubin, E. (1915). *Synoplevede figuren.* Copenhagen: Gyldendalske.

Rubin, E. (1921). *Visuell wahrgenommene figuren.* Copenhagen: Gyldendalske.

Rubin, N. (2001). The role of junctions in surface completion and contour matching. *Perception,* 30, 339–366.

Ruble, D. N., & Nakamura, C. Y. (1972). Task orientation versus social orientation in young children and their attention to relevant social cues. *Child Development,* 43, 471–480.

Ruggieri, V., Cei, A., Ceridono, D., & Bergerone, C. (1980). Dimensional approach to the study of sighting dominance. *Perceptual and Motor Skills,* 51, 247–251.

Rusak, B., & Groos, G. (1982). Suprachiasmatic stimulation phase shifts rodent circadian rhythms. *Science,* 215, 1407–1409.

Rusak, B., & Zucker, I. (1979). Neural regulation of circadian rhythms. *Physiological Review,* 59, 449–526.

Rushton, S. K., & Wann, J. P. (1999). Weighted combination of size and disparity: A computational model for timing a ball catch. *Nature Neuroscience,* 2, 186–190.

Ruttiger, L., & Lee, B. B. (2000). Chromatic and luminance contributions to a hyperacuity task. *Vision Research,* 40, 817–232.

Saarinen, J., & Levi, D. M. (1995). Orientation anisotropy in vernier acuity. *Vision Research,* 35, 1449–1461.

Sachs, M. B., & Kiang, N. Y. S. (1968). Two-tone inhibition in auditory nerve fibers. *Journal of the Acoustical Society of America,* 43, 1120–1128.

Sacks, O. (1987). *The Man Who Mistook His Wife for a Hat.* New York: Summit.

Sacks, O. (1997). *The Island of the Colorblind.* New York: Random House.

Sadhra, S., Jackson, C. A., Ryder, T., & Brown, M. J. (2002). Noise exposure and hearing loss among student employees working in university entertainment venues. *Annals of Occupational Hygiene,* 46, 455–463.

Sahley, T. L., Nodar, R. H., & Musiek, F. E. (1997). *Efferent Auditory System: Structure and Function.* San Diego: Singular Publishing Group.

Sala, S. D., Kinnear, P., Spinnler, H., & Stangalino, C. (2000). Color-to-figure matching in Alzheimer's disease. *Archives of Clinical Neuropsychology,* 15, 571–585.

Salapatek, P., & Kessen, W. (1973). Prolonged investigation of a plane geometric triangle by the human newborn. *Journal of Experimental Child Psychology,* 15, 22–29.

Salmelin, R., Hari, R., Lounasmaa, O. V., & Sams, M. (1994). Dynamics of brain activation during picture naming. *Nature,* 368, 463–465.

Salthouse, T. A. (1996a). The processing-speed theory of adult age differences in cognition. *Psychological Review,* 103, 403–428.

Salthouse, T. A. (1996b). Constraints on theories of cognitive aging. *Psychonomic Bulletin & Review,* 3, 287–299.

Samuel, A. G. (1996). Phoneme restoration. *Language and Cognitive Processes,* 11, 647–653.

Samuel, A. G. (1997). Lexical activation produces potent phonemic percepts. *Cognitive Psychology,* 32, 97–127.

Samuel, A. G., & Kat, D. (1996). Early levels of analysis of speech. *Journal of Experimental Psychology: Human Perception and Performance,* 22, 676–694.

Sanders, B., Soares, M. P., & D'Aquila, J. M. (1982). Sex difference on one test of spatial visualization: A nontrivial difference. *Child Development,* 53, 1106–1110.

Sanders, G., & Ross-Field, L. (1986). Sexual orientation and visuospatial ability. *Brain and Cognition,* 5, 280–290.

Sanes, D. H. (2000). *Development of the Nervous System.* San Diego: Academic Press.

Sanford, E. C. (1898). *A Course in Experimental Psychology: Part I, Sensation and Perception.* Boston: Heath.

Sara, M., & Faubert, J. (2000). Aging, perception, and visual short-term memory for luminance-defined form. *Ophthalmic Physiology & Optics,* 20, 314–322.

Sasaki, K., & Hockwin, O. (2002). *Progress in Lens and Cataract Research: In Honour of Professor Kazuyuki Sasaki.* New York: Karger.

Sasaki, M. (1996). Characteristics and the internal system of visual and tactual form perception, following a congenital cataract operation. *Japanese Journal of Developmental Psychology,* 7, 180–189.

Sathian, K., & Zangaladze, A. (1997). Tactile learning is task specific but transfers between fingers. *Perception & Psychophysics,* 59, 119–128.

Saumier, D., Arguin, M., Lefebvre, C., & Lassonde, M. (2002). Visual object agnosia as a problem in integrating parts and part relations. *Brain & Cognition,* 48, 531–537.

Savic, I. (2002). Imaging of brain activation by odorants in humans. *Current Opinion in Neurobiology,* 12, 455–461.

Savic, I., Berglund, H., Gulyas, B., & Roland, P. (2001). Smelling of odorous sex hormone-like compounds causes sex-differentiated hypothalamic activations in humans. *Neuron,* 31, 661–668.

Sawusch, J. R., & Gagnon, D. A. (1995). Auditory coding, cues, and coherence in phonetic perception. *Journal of Experimental Psychology: Human Perception and Performance,* 21, 635–652.

Schaal, B., Marlier, L., & Soussignan, R. (1998). Olfactory function in the human fetus: Evidence from selective neonatal responsiveness to the odor of amniotic fluid. *Behavioral Neuroscience,* 112, 1438–1449.

Schab, F. R. (1991). Odor memory: Taking stock. Psychological Bulletin, 109, 242–251.

Schall, J. D., & Thompson, K. G. (1999). Neural selection and control of visually guided eye movements. *Annual Review of Neuroscience,* 22, 241–259.

Scharf, B. (1964). Partial masking. *Acustica,* 14, 16–23.

Scharf, B. (1975). Audition. In B. Scharf (Ed.), *Experimental Sensory Psychology* (pp. 112–149). Glenview, IL: Scott, Foresman.

Scharf, B. (1978). Loudness. In E. C. Carterette & M. P. Friedman (Eds.), *Handbook of Perception,* Vol. IV. *Hearing.* (pp. 187–242). New York: Academic Press.

Scharf, B. (1989). Spectral specificity in auditory detection: The effect of listening on hearing. *Journal of the Acoustical Society of Japan,* 10, 309–317.

Scharf, B., Quigley, S., Aoki, C., Peachey, N., & Reeves, A. (1987). Focused auditory attention and frequency selectivity. *Perception & Psychophysics,* 42, 215–223.

Scharre, J. E., Cotter, S. A., Block, S. S., & Kelly, S. A. (1990). Normative contrast sensitivity data for young children. *Optometry and Vision Science,* 67, 826–832.

Schefrin, B. E., & Werner, J. S. (1990). Loci of spectral unique hues throughout the life span. *Journal of the Optical Society of America A,* 7, 305–311.

Scheinberg, D. L., & Logothetis, N. K. (1997). The role of temporal cortical areas in perceptual organization. *Proceedings of the National Academy of Science USA,* 94, 3408–3413.

Schellenberg, E. G., & Trehub, S. E. (in press). Accurate pitch memory is widespread. *Psychological Science,* 14.

Schenkel, K. D. (1967). Die beidohrigen Mithorschoellen von Impulsen. *Acustica,* 18, 38–46.

Scher, D., Pionk, M., & Purcell, D. G. (1981). Visual sensitivity fluctuations during the menstrual cycle under dark and light adaptation. *Bulletin of the Psychonomic Society,* 18, 159–160.

Schiano, D. J., & Jordan, K. (1990). Mueller-Lyer decrement: Practice or prolonged inspection? *Perception,* 19, 307–316.

Schiff, W., & Oldak, R. (1990). Accuracy of judging time to arrival: Effects of modality, trajectory, and gender. *Journal of Experimental Psychology: Human Perception and Performance,* 16, 303–316.

Schiffman, S. S. (1974). Physiochemical correlates of olfactory quality. *Science,* 185, 112–117.

Schiffman S. S., & Graham B. G. (2000). Taste and smell perception affect appetite and immunity in the elderly. *European Journal of Clinical Nutrition,* 54 (Suppl. 3), S54–63.

Schiller, P. H. (1986). The central visual system. *Vision Research,* 26, 1351–1386.

Schindler, R. A., & Merzenich, M. M. (Eds.). (1985). *Cochlear Implants.* New York: Raven Press.

Schirillo, J. A., & Arend, L. E. (1995). Illumination change at a depth edge can reduce lightness constancy. *Perception & Psychophysics,* 57, 225–230.

Schlaug, G., & Jäncke, L. (1995). In vivo evidence of structural brain asymmetry in musicians. *Science,* 267, 699–701.

Schlaug, G., Jäncke, L., Huang, Y., Staiger, J. F., & Steinmetz, H. (1995). Increased corpus callosum size in musicians. *Neuropsychologia,* 33, 1047–1055.

Schlottmann, A. (1999). Seeing it happen and knowing how it works: how children understand the relation between perceptual causality and underlying mechanism. *Developmental Psychology,* 35, 303–317.

Schmiedt, R. A., Zwislocki, J. J., & Hamernik, R. P. (1980). Effects of hair cell lesions on responses of cochlear nerve fibers: I. Lesions, tuning curves, two-tone inhibition, and responses to trapezoidal-wave patterns. *Journal of Neurophysiology,* 43, 1367–1389.

Schnapf, J. L., & Baylor, D. A. (1987). How photoreceptor cells respond to light. *Scientific American,* 256, 40–47.

Schneck, M. E., Haegerstrom-Portnoy, G., Lott, L. A., & Brabyn, J. A. (2000). Ocular contributions to age-related loss in coarse stereopsis. *Optometry and Vision Science,* 77, 531–536.

Schneider, B. A., & Cohen, A. J. (1997). Binaural additivity of loudness in children and adults. *Perception & Psychophysics,* 59, 655–664.

Schneider, B., & Parker, S. (1990). Does stimulus context affect loudness or only loudness judgments? *Perception & Psychophysics,* 48, 409–418.

Schneider, D. (1969). Insect olfaction: Deciphering system for chemical messages. *Science,* 163, 1031–1037.

Schneider, G. E. (1969). Two visual systems. *Science,* 163, 895–902.

Schneider, R., Costiloe, J., Howard, R., & Wolf, S. (1958). Olfactory perception thresholds in hypogonadal women: Changes accompanying administration of androgen and estrogen. *Journal of Clinical Endocrinology,* 18, 379–390.

Schneider, W., & Schiffrin, R. M. (1977). Controlled and automatic human information processing: I. Detection, search and attention. *Psychological Review,* 84, 1–66.

Schneider, W., Dumais, S. T., & Shiffrin, R. M. (1984). Automatic and control processing and attention. In R. Parasuraman & D. R. Davies (Eds.), *Varieties of Attention* (pp. 1–27). Orlando: Academic Press.

Schnupp, J. W. H., Mrsic-Flogel, T. D., & King, A. J. (2001). Linear processing of spatial cues in primary auditory cortex. *Nature,* 414, 200–204.

Scholl, B.J., & Nakayama, K. (2002). Causal capture: Contextual effects on the perception of collision events. *Psychological Science,* 13, 493–498.

Scholl, B. J., & Tremoulet, P. D. (2000). Perceptual causality and animacy. *Trends in Cognitive Science,* 1, 56–61.

Scholz, J., & Woolf, C. J. (2002). Can we conquer pain? *Nature Neuroscience* (Suppl.), 5, 1062–1067.

Schoups, A. A., Vogels, R., & Orban, G. A. (1995). Human perceptual learning in identifying the oblique orientation: Retinotopy, orientation specificity and monocularity. *Journal of Physiology,* 483, 797–810.

Schouten, M. E. H. (1980). The case against a speech mode of perception. *Acta Psychologica,* 44, 71–98.

Schubert, E. D. (1978). History of research on hearing. In E. C. Carterette & M. P. Friedman (Eds.), *Handbook of Perception,* Vol. IV. *Hearing* (pp. 41–80). New York: Academic Press.

Schull, J., Kaplan, H., & O'Brien, C. P. (1981). Naloxone can alter experimental pain and mood in humans. *Physiological Psychology,* 9, 245–250.

Schulman, P. H. (1979). Eye movements do not cause induced motion. *Perception & Psychophysics,* 26, 381–383.

Schultz, D., & Schultz, S. (1996). *A History of Modern Psychology* (5th ed.). Ft. Worth, TX: Harcourt Brace Jovanovich.

Schulze, H. H. (1989). Categorical perception of rhythmic patterns. *Psychological Research,* 51, 10–15.

Schwartz, S. H., & Loop, M. S. (1984). Effect of duration on detection by the chromatic and achromatic systems. *Perception & Psychophysics,* 36, 65–67.

Scialfa, C. T. (1990). Adult age differences in visual search: The role of non-attentional processes. In J. T. Enns (Ed.), *The Development of Attention: Research and Theory* (pp. 509–526). Amsterdam: Elsevier.

Scott, T. R. (1990). The effect of physiological need on taste. In E. Capaldi & L. T. Powley (Eds.), *Taste, Experience, and Feeding* (pp. 45–61). Washington, DC: American Psychological Association.

Sedgwick, H. (1980). The geometry of spatial layout in pictorial representation. In M. Hagen (Ed.), *Perception of Pictures,* Vol. I. *Alberti's Window: The Projective Model of Pictorial Information* (pp. 33–90). New York: Academic Press.

Sedgwick, H. A. (2001). Visual space perception. In E. B. Goldstein, (Ed.), *Blackwell Handbook of Perception,* (pp. 128–167). Malden, MA: Blackwell Publishers.

See, J. E., Howe, S. R., Warm, J. S., & Dember, W. N. (1995). Meta-analysis of the sensitivity decrement in vigilance. *Psychological Bulletin,* 117, 230–249.

Segall, M. H., Campbell, D. T., & Herskovits, M. J. (1966). *The Influence of Culture on Visual Perception.* Indianapolis: Bobbs-Merrill.

Seggie, J., & Canny, C. (1989). Antidepressant medication reverses increased sensitivity to light in depression: Preliminary report. *Progress in Neuro-Psychopharmacology and Biological Psychiatry,* 13, 537–541.

Seifritz, E., Esposito, F., Hennel, F., Mustovic, H., Neuhoff, J. G., Bilecen, D., Tedeschi, G., Scheffler, K., & Di Salle, F. (2002). Spatiotemporal pattern of neural processing in the human auditory cortex. *Science,* 297, 1706–1708.

Sekuler, A. B. (1996). Axis of elongation can determine reference frames for object perception. *Canadian Journal of Experimental Psychology,* 50, 270–279.

Sekuler, A. B., & Lee, J. A. J. (1996). Pigeons do not complete partly occluded figures. *Perception,* 25, 1109–1120.

Sekuler, A. B., & Palmer, S. E. (1992). Perception of partly occluded objects: A microgenetic analysis. *Journal of Experimental Psychology: General,* 121, 95–111.

Sekuler, A., & Murray, R. F. (2001). Amodal Completion: A case study in grouping. In T. F. Shipley, & P. J. Kellman, (Eds.), *From Fragments to Objects: Segmentation and Grouping in Vision* (pp. 265–294). Amsterdam: Elsevier.

Sekuler, R., & Ball, K. (1986). Visual localization: Age and practice. *Journal of the Optical Society of America A,* 3, 864–867.

Sekuler, R., Ball, K., Tynan, P., & Machmer, J. (1982). Psychophysics of motion perception. In A. H. Wertheim, W. A. Wagenaar, & H. W. Leibowitz (Eds.), *Tutorials on Motion Perception* (pp. 81–100). New York: Plenum Press.

Selfridge, O. G. (1959). Pandemonium: A paradigm for learning. In D. V. Blake & A. M. Uttley (Eds.), *Proceedings of the Symposium on the Mechanisation of Thought Processes* (pp. 511–529). London: HM Stationery Office.

Semenza, C. (1988). Impairment in localization of body parts. *Cortex,* 24, 443–449.

Semple, M. N., & Kitzes, L. M. (1987). Binaural processing of sound pressure level in the inferior colliculus. Journal of *Neurophysiology,* 57, 1130–1147.

Senden, M. von. (1960). *Space and Sight: The Perception of Space and Shape in Congenitally Blind Patients Before and After Operation.* London: Methuen.

Serafine, M. L., & Glassman, N. (1989). The cognitive reality of hierarchic structure in music. *Music Perception,* 6, 397–430.

Serafini, S. (1995). Timbre judgments of Javanese gamelan instruments by trained and untrained adults. *Psychomusicology,* 14, 137–153.

Servos, P., Osu, R., Santi, A., & Kawato, M (2002). The neural substrates of biological motion perception: An fMRI study. *Cerebral Cortex,* 12, 772–782.

Seymoure, P., & Juraska, J. M. (1997). Vernier and grating acuity in adult hooded rats: The influence of sex. *Behavioral Neuroscience,* 111, 792–800.

Shaffer, D. M., & McBeath, M. K. (2002). Baseball Outfielders Maintain a Linear Optical Trajectory when Tracking Uncatchable Fly Balls. *Journal of Experimental Psychology: Human Perception and Performance,* 28, 335–348.

Shaffer, H. L. (1975). Multiple attention in continuous verbal tasks. In P. M. A. Rabbitt & S. Dornic (Eds.), *Attention and Performance* (pp. 157–167). V. London: Academic Press.

Shaffer, L. H. (1985). Timing in action. In J. A. Michon & J. L. Jackson (Eds.), *Time, Mind and Behavior* (pp. 226–242). Berlin: Springer-Verlag.

Shallice, T., & Vickers, D. (1964). Theories and experiments on discrimination times. *Ergonomics,* 7, 37–49.

Shamma, S. (2001). On the role of space and time in auditory processing. *Trends in Cognitive Sciences,* 5, 340–348.

Shannon, C. E., & Weaver, W. (1949). *The Mathematical Theory of Communication.* Urbana: University of Illinois Press.

Shannon, R. V., & Otto, S. R. (1990). Psychophysical measures from electrical stimulation of the human cochlear nucleus. *Hearing Research,* 47, 159–168.

Shapiro, K. L., & Egerman, B. (1984). Effects of arousal on human visual dominance. *Perception & Psychophysics,* 35, 547–552.

Shapiro, K. L., & Johnson, T. L. (1987). Effects of arousal on attention to central and peripheral visual stimuli. *Acta Psychologica,* 66, 157–172.

Shapiro, K. L., & Lim, A. (1989). The impact of anxiety on visual attention to central and peripheral events. *Behaviour Research & Therapy,* 27, 345–351.

Shapley, R. (1986). The importance of contrast for the activity of single neurons, the VEP and perception. *Vision Research,* 26, 45–61.

Shapley, R. (1990). Visual sensitivity and parallel retino-cortical channels. *Annual Review of Psychology,* 41, 635–658.

Shapley, R., & Enroth-Cugell, C. (1984). Visual adaptation and retinal gain controls. *Progress in Retinal Research,* 3, 263–346.

Shapley, R., & Kaplan, E. (1989). Responses of magnocellular LGN neurons and M retinal ganglion cells to drifting heterochromatic gratings. *Investigative Ophthalmology and Visual Science,* 30 (Suppl.), 323.

Shapley, R., & Reid, R. C. (1985). Contrast and assimilation in the perception of brightness. *Proceedings of the National Academy of Science, USA,* 82, 5983–5986.

Sharma, S., & Moskowitz, H. (1972). Effect of marijuana on the visual autokinetic phenomenon. *Perceptual and Motor Skills,* 35, 891.

Sharpe, L. T., & Nordby, K. (1989). Total color-blindness: An introduction. In R. F. Hess, L. T. Sharpe, & K. Nordby (Eds.), *Night Vision: Basic, Clinical and Applied Aspects.* (pp. 253–269). Cambridge: Cambridge University Press.

Sharpe, L. T., & Jägle, H. (2001). I used to be color blind. *Color Research and Application,* 26 (Suppl.), S269–S271.

Shebilske, W. L. (1977). Visuomotor coordination in visual direction and position constancies. In W. Epstein (Ed.), *Stability and Constancy in Visual Perception: Mechanisms and Processes* (pp. 23–70). New York: Wiley.

Sheedy, J. E., Bailey, I. L., Buri, M., & Bass, E. (1986). Binocular vs. monocular task performance. *American Journal of Optometry and Physiological Optics,* 63, 839–846.

Sheingold, K. (1973). Developmental differences in the uptake and storage of visual information. *Journal of Experimental Child Psychology,* 16, 1–11.

Shepard, M., & Muller, H. J. (1989). Movement versus focusing of attention. *Perception & Psychophysics,* 46, 146–154.

Shepard, R. N. (1982). Geometrical approximations to the structure of musical pitch. *Psychological Review,* 89, 305–333.

Shepard, R. N., & Zare, S. L. (1983). Path-guided apparent motion. *Science,* 220, 632–634.

Shera, C. A., & Zweig, G. (1991). Asymmetry suppresses the cochlear catastrophe. *Journal of the Acoustical Society of America,* 89, 1276–1289.

Shera, C. A., Guinan, J. J., & Oxenham, A. J. (2002). Revised estimates of human cochlear tuning from otoacoustic and behavioral measurements. *Proceedings of the National Academy of Science (USA),* 99, 3318–3323.

Sherman, S. M. (1973). Visual field defects in monocularly and binocularly deprived cats. *Brain Research,* 49, 25–45.

Sherman, S. M. (1985). Parallel W-, X- and Y-cell pathways in the cat: A model for visual function. In D. Rose & V. G. Dobson (Eds.), *Models of the Visual Cortex* (pp. 71–84). Chichester: Wiley.

Sherman, S. M. (2001). Thalamic relay functions. *Progress in Brain Research,* 134, 51–69.

Sherrington, C. S. (1906). *Integrative Action of the Nervous System.* New Haven, CT: Yale University Press.

Sheth, B., Nijhawan, R., & Shimojo, S. (2000). Changing objects lead briefly flashed ones. *Nature Neuroscience,* 3, 489–495.

Shevell, S. K., & Wei, J. (2000). A central mechanism of chromatic contrast. *Vision Research,* 40, 3173–3180.

Shevell, S. K. (2001). The time course of chromatic adaptation. *Color Research and Application,* 26(Suppl.), S170–S173.

Shiffrin, R. M., & Schneider, W. (1977). Controlled and automatic human information processing: II. Perceptual learning, automatic attending and a general theory. *Psychological Review,* 84, 127–190.

Shimojo, S., & Held, R. (1987). Vernier acuity is less than grating acuity in 2- and 3-month olds. *Vision Research,* 27, 77–86.

Shimojo, S., & Richards, W. (1986). "Seeing" shapes that are almost totally occluded: A new look at Park's camel. *Perception & Psychophysics,* 39, 418–426.

Shinn-Cunningham, B. G., Zurek, P. M., Durlach, N. I., & Clifton, R. K. (1995). Cross-frequency interactions in the precedence effect. *Journal of the Acoustical Society of America,* 98, 164–171.

Shipley, T. F., & Kellman, P. J. (1994). Spatiotemporal boundary formation: Boundary, form, and motion perception from transformations of surface elements. *Journal of Experimental Psychology: General,* 123, 3–20.

Shirillo, J. A. (2001). Tutorial on the importance of color in language and culture. *Color Research and Application,* 26, 179–192.

Shockey, L., & Reddy, R. (1974, August). *Quantitative Analysis of Speech Perception: Results from Transcription of Connected Speech from Unfamiliar Languages.* Paper presented at the Speech Communications Seminar, Stockholm.

Shore, D. I., & Enns, J. T. (1997). Shape completion time depends on the size of the occluded region. *Journal of Experimental Psychology: Human Perception & Performance,* 23, 980–998.

Shostak, Y., Ding, Y., Mavity-Hudson, J., & Casagrande, V. A. (2002). Cortical synaptic arrangements of the third visual pathway in three primate species: Macaca mulatta, Saimiri sciureus, and Aotus trivirgatus. *Journal of Neuroscience,* 22, 2885–2893.

Shower, E. G., & Biddulph, R. (1931). Differential pitch sensitivity of the ear. *Journal of Acoustical Society of America,* 3, 275–287.

Shulman, G. L., Wilson, J., & Sheehy, J. B. (1985). Spatial determinants of the distribution of attention. *Perception & Psychophysics,* 37, 59–65.

Shurtleff, D., Raslear, T. G., & Simmons, L. (1990). Circadian variations in time perception in rats. *Physiology and Behavior,* 47, 931–939.

Sibony, P. A., Evinger, C., & Manning, K. A. (1987). Effects of tobacco on pursuit eye movements and blinks. *Investigative Ophthalmology and Visual Science,* 28, 316.

Siddle, D. A., Morish, R. B., White, K. D., & Mangen, G. L. (1969). Relation of visual sensitivity to extraversion. *Journal of Experimental Research in Personality,* 3, 264–267.

Sillito, A. M., Jones, H. E., Gerstein, G. L., & West, D. C. (1994). Feature-linked synchronization of thalamic relay cell firing induced by feedback from the visual cortex. *Nature,* 369, 479–482.

Simons, D. J., & Chabris, C. F. (1999). Gorillas in our midst: Sustained inattentional blindness for dynamic events. *Perception,* 28, 1059–1074.

Simpson, W. A. (1988). The method of constant stimuli is efficient. *Perception & Psychophysics,* 44, 433–436.

Sincich, L. C., & Horton, J. C. (2002). Divided by cytochrome oxidase: a map of the projections from V1 to V2 in macaques. *Science,* 295, 1734–1737.

Sinclair, D. C., & Stokes, B. A. R. (1964). The production and characteristics of "second pain." *Brain,* 87, 609–618.

Singh, M., & Hoffman, D. D. (2001). Part-based representations of visual shape and implications for visual cognition. In T. F. Shipley & P. J. Kellman (Eds.). *From Fragments to Objects: Segmentation and Grouping in Vision* (pp. 401–459). Amsterdam: Elsevier.

Sinnot, J., & Rauth, J. (1937). Effect of smoking on taste thresholds. *Journal of General Psychology,* 17, 155–162.

Sinnott, J. M., Brown, C. H., Malik, W. T., & Kressley, R. A. (1997). A multidimensional analysis of vowel discrimination in humans and monkeys. *Perception & Psychophysics,* 59, 1214–1224.

Sireteanu, R., & Rettenbach, R. (2000). Perceptual learning in visual search generalizes over tasks, locations, and eyes. *Vision Research,* 40, 2925–2949.

Sivak, J. G., Barrie, D. L., Callender, M. G., Doughty, M. J., Seltner, R. L., & West, J. A. (1990). Optical causes of experimental myopia. In *Myopia and the Control of Eye Growth.* Ciba Foundation Symposium 155 (pp. 160–177). Chichester: Wiley.

Sivian, L. S., & White, S. D. (1933). On minimum audible sound fields. *Journal of the Acoustical Society of America,* 4, 288–321.

Skoczenski, A. M., & Norcia, A. M. (1999). Development of VEP Vernier acuity and grating acuity in human infants. *Investigative Opthalmology and Vision Science,* 40, 2411–2417.

Skottun, B. C. (2000). Hyperacuity and the estimated positional accuracy of a theoretical simple cell. *Vision Research,* 40, 3117–3120.

Skowbo, D. (1984). Are McCollough effects conditioned responses? *Psychological Bulletin,* 96, 215–226.

Slater, A., & Johnson, S.P. (1998). Visual sensory and perceptual abilities of the newborn: beyond the blooming, buzzing confusion. In F. Simion & G. Butterworth (Eds.), *The Development of Sensory, Motor and Cognitive Capacities in Early Infancy: From Perception to Cognition,* (pp 121–141). East Sussex: Psychology Press.

Slater, A. (2000). Visual perception in the young infant: early organization and rapid learning. In D. Muir & A. Slater (Eds.), *Infant Development: The Essential Readings* (pp. 95–116). Oxford: Blackwell Publishing.

Slater, A., von der Shulenburg, C., Brown, E., Badenoch, M., Butterworth, G., Parsons, S., & Samuels, C. (1998). Newborn infants prefer attractive faces. *Infant Behavior and Development,* 21, 345–354.

Slaughter, M. M., & Miller, R. F. (1981). 2-Amino-4-phosphonobutyric acid: A new pharmacological tool for retina research. *Science,* 211, 182–184.

Sloane, M. E., Ost, J. W., Etheredge, D. B., & Henderlite, S. E. (1989). Overprediction and blocking in the McCollough effect. *Perception & Psychophysics,* 45, 110–120.

Sloane, S. A., Shea, S. L., Proctor, M. M., & Dewsbury, D. A. (1978). Visual cliff performance in 10 species of muroid rodents. *Animal Learning and Behavior,* 6, 244–248.

Small, L. H., & Bond, Z. S. (1986). Distortions and deletions: Word-initial consonant specificity in fluent speech. *Perception & Psychophysics,* 40, 20–26.

Smith, A., & Over, R. (1979). Motor aftereffect with subjective contours. *Perception & Psychophysics,* 25, 95–98.

Smith, D. V., & St. John, S. J. (1999). Neural coding of gustatory information. *Current Opinion in Neurobiology,* 9, 427–435.

Smith, S. D., & Merikle, P. M. (1999, June). *Assessing the Duration of Memory for Information Perceived without Awareness.* Meeting of the Association for the Scientific Study of Consciousness, London, Canada.

Smith, T. C., & Jahr, C. E. (2002). Self-inhibition of olfactory bulb neurons. *Nature Neuroscience,* 5, 760–766.

Smith, V. C., Jin, P. Q., & Pokorny, J. (2001). The role of spatial frequency in color induction. *Vision Research,* 41, 1007–1021.

Smith, W. S., Frazier, N. I., Ward, S., & Webb, F. (1983). Early adolescent girls' and boys' learning of spatial visualization skill-replications. *Journal of Education,* 67, 239–243.

Smith, Z. M., Delgutte, B., & Oxenham, A. J. (2002). Chimaeric sounds reveal dichotomies in auditory perception. *Nature,* 416, 87–90.

Snellen, H. (1862). *Probebuchstaben zur Bestimmung der Sehscharfe.* Utrecht: Weijer.

Snodgrass, J. G., & Corwin, J. (1988). Pragmatics of measuring recognition memory: Applications to dementia and amnesia. *Journal of Experimental Psychology: Human Perception and Performance,* 117, 34–50.

Söderfeldt, B., Ingvar, M., Rönnberg, J., Eriksson, L., Serrander, M., & Stone-Elander, S. (1997). Signed and spoken language perception studied by positron emission tomography. *Neurology,* 49, 82–87.

Soechting, J. F., Engel, K. C., & Flanders, M. (2001). The Duncker illusion and eye hand coordination. *Journal of Neurophysiology,* 85, 843–854.

Sohmer, H., Perez, R., Sichel, J. Y., Priner R., & Freeman S. (2001).The pathway enabling external sounds to reach and excite the fetal inner ear. *Audiology & Neuro-Otology,* 6, 109–116.

Sokolov, E. N. (1975). The neuronal mechanisms of the orienting reflex. In E. N. Sokolov & O. S. Vinogradova (Eds.), *Neuronal Mechanisms of the Orienting Reflex* (pp. 217–238). New York: Wiley.

Soussignan, R., & Schall, B. (1996). Children's facial responsiveness to odors: Influences of hedonic valence of odor, gender, age, and social presence. *Developmental Psychology,* 32, 367–379.

Spence, C. J., & Driver, J. (1994). Covert spatial orienting in audition: Exogenous and endogenous mechanisms facilitate sound localization. *Journal of Experimental Psychology: Human Perception and Performance,* 20, 555–574.

Spence, C. J., & Driver, J. (1997). Audiovisual links in exogenous covert spatial orienting. *Perception & Psychophysics,* 59, 1–22.

Spence, C. J., & Driver, J. (1998). Auditory and audiovisual inhibition of return. *Perception & Psychophysics,* 60, 125–139.

Spence, C., & Driver, J. (1997). Audiovisual links in exogenous covert spatial orienting. *Perception & Psychophysics,* 59, 1–22.

Sperling, G., & Weichselgartner, E. (1995). Episodic theory of the dynamics of spatial attention. *Psychological Review,* 102, 503–532.

Sperry, R. W. (1943). Effect of 180 degree rotation of the retinal field on visuomotor coordination. *Journal of Experimental Zoology,* 92, 263–277.

Spitzer, M. W., & Semple, M. N. (1991). Interaural phase coding in auditory midbrain: Influence of dynamic stimulus features. *Science,* 254, 721–724.

Spoendlin, H. H. (1978). The afferent innervation of the cochlea. In R. F. Naunton & C. Fernandey (Eds.), *Evoked Electrical Activity in the Auditory Nervous System* (pp. 21–42). New York: Academic Press.

Spoendlin, H. H., & Schrott, A. (1989). Analysis of the human auditory nerve. *Hearing Research,* 43, 25–38.

Sprafkin, C., Serbin, L. A., Denier, C., & Conner, J. M. (1983). Sex-differentiated play: Cognitive consequences and early interventions. In M. B. Liss (Ed.), *Social and Cognitive Skills* (pp. 167–192). New York: Academic Press.

Staecker, H., & Van De Water, T.R. (1998). Factors controlling hair-cell regeneration/repair in the inner ear. *Current Opinion in Neurobiology,* 8, 480–487.

Standing, L. (1973). Learning 10,000 pictures. *Quarterly Journal of Experimental Psychology,* 25, 207–222.

Stebbins, W. C. (1980). The evolution of hearing in the mammals. In A. N. Popper & R. R. Fay (Eds.), *Comparative Studies of Hearing in Vertebrates* (pp. 421–436). New York: Springer-Verlag.

Stein, B. E., & Meredith, M. A. (1993). *The Merging of the Senses.* Cambridge, MA: MIT Press.

Steinberg, A. (1955). Changes in time perception induced by an anaesthetic drug. *British Journal of Psychology,* 46, 273–279.

Steiner, J. E., Glaser, D., Hawilo, M. E., & Berridge, K. C. (2001). Comparative expression of hedonic impact: Affective reactions to taste by human infants and other primates. *Neuroscience and Biobehavioral Reviews,* 25, 53–74.

Steinfield, G. J. (1967). Concepts of set and availability and their relation to the reorganization of ambiguous pictorial stimuli. *Psychological Review,* 74, 505–525.

Steinschneider, M., Schroeder, C. E., Arezzo, J. C., & Vaughan, H. G. Jr. (1995). Physiologic correlates of the voice onset time boundary in primary auditory cortex (A1) of the awake monkey: Temporal response patterns. *Brain and Language,* 48, 326–340.

Stelmach, L. B., & Herdman, C. M. (1991). Directed attention and perception of temporal order. *Journal of Experimental Psychology: Human Perception & Performance,* 17, 539–550.

Stelmack, R. M., & Campbell, K. B. (1974). Extraversion and auditory sensitivity to high and low frequency. *Perceptual and Motor Skills,* 38, 875–879.

Stelmack, R. M., Achorn, E., & Michaud, A. (1977). Extravision and individual differences in auditory evoked response. *Psychophysiology,* 14, 368–374.

Stephan, F. K., & Nunez, A. A. (1977). Elimination of circadian rhythms in drinking activity, sleep, and temperature by isolation of suprachiasmatic nuclei. *Behavioral Biology,* 20, 1–16.

Stephens, P. R., & Young, J. Z. (1982). The stacocyst of the squid Loligo. *Journal of Zoology,* London, 197, 241–266.

Stern, K., & McClintock, M. K. (1998). Regulation of ovulation by human pheromones. *Nature,* 392, 177–179.

Stern, R. M., Koch, K. L., Leibowitz, H. W., Lindblad, I. M., Shupert, C. L., & Stewart, W. R. (1985). Tachygastria and motion sickness. *Aviation, Space and Environmental Medicine,* 56, 1074–1077.

Sternbach, R. A. (1963). Congenital insensitivity to pain: A review. *Psychological Bulletin,* 60, 252–264.

Sternberg, S. (1975). Memory scanning: New findings and current controversies. *Quarterly Journal of Experimental Psychology,* 27, 1–32.

Stevens, D. A., & Lawless, H. T. (1986). Putting out the fire: Effects of tastants on oral chemical irritation. *Perception & Psychophysics,* 39, 346–350.

Stevens, J. C. (1990). Perceived roughness as a function of body locus. *Perception & Psychophysics,* 47, 298–304.

Stevens, J. C., & Cain, W. S. (1986). Smelling via the mouth: Effects of aging. *Perception & Psychophysics,* 40, 142–146.

Stevens, J. C., Cain, W. S., & Burke, R. J. (1988). Variability of olfactory thresholds. *Chemical Senses,* 13, 643–653.

Stevens, J. C., Cain, W. S., & Demarque, A. (1990). Memory and identification of simulated odors in elderly and young persons. *Bulletin of the Psychonomic Society,* 28, 293–296.

Stevens, J. C., Cain, W. S., Demarque, A., & Ruthruff, A. M. (1991). On the discrimination of missing ingredients: Aging and salt flavor. *Appetite,* 16, 129–140.

Stevens, J. C., Cain, W. S., Shiet, F. T., & Oatley, M. W. (1989). Olfactory adaptation and recovery in old age. *Perception,* 18, 265–276.

Stevens, K. N. (1996). Critique: Articulatory-acoustic relations and their role in speech perception. *Journal of the Acoustical Society of America,* 99, 1693–1694.

Stevens, K. N., & House, A. S. (1972). Speech perception. In J. V. Tobias (Ed.), *Foundations of Modern Auditory Theory,* Vol. 2 (pp. 3–62). New York: Academic Press.

Stevens, S. S. (1935). The relation of pitch to intensity. *Journal of the Acoustical Society of America,* 6, 150–154.

Stevens, S. S. (1956). The direct estimation of sensory magnitudes-loudness. *American Journal of Psychology,* 69, 1–25.

Stevens, S. S. (1959). Tactile vibration: Dynamics of sensory intensity. *Journal of Experimental Psychology,* 57, 210–218.

Stevens, S. S. (1961). The psychophysics of sensory function. In W. A. Rosenblith (Ed.), *Sensory Communication* (pp. 1–33). Cambridge, MA: MIT Press.

Stevens, S. S. (1975). *Psychophysics: Introduction to Its Perceptual, Neural, and Social Prospects.* New York: Wiley.

Stevens, S. S., & Galanter, E. (1957). Ratio scales and category scales for a dozen perceptual continua. *Journal of Experimental Psychology,* 54, 377–411.

Stevens, S. S., & Newman, E. B. (1934). The localization of pure tones. *Proceedings of the National Academy of Sciences (USA),* 20, 593–596.

Stevens, S. S., & Warshovsky, F. (1965). *Sound and Hearing.* New York: Time-Life Books.

Stevens, S. S., Volkman, J., & Newman, E. B. (1937). A scale for the measurement of the psychological magnitude of pitch. *Journal of the Acoustical Society of America,* 8, 185–190.

Stewart, C. E., & Hudspeth, A. J. (2000). Effects of salicylates and aminoglycosides on spontaneous otoacoustic emissions in the Tokay gecko. *Proceedings of the National Academy of Science (USA),* 97, 454–459.

Stewart, M., Pankiw, R., Lehman, M. E., Simpson, T. H. (2002). Hearing loss and hearing handicap in users of recreational firearms. *Journal of the American Academy of Audiology,* 13, 160–168.

Stinson, M. R., & Khanna, S. M. (1989). Sound propagation in the ear canal and coupling to the eardrum, with measurements on model systems. *Journal of the Acoustical Society of America,* 85, 2481–2491.

Stoffregen, T. A. (1985). Flow structure versus retinal location in the optical control of stance. *Journal of Experimental Psychology: Human Perception and Performance,* 11, 554–565.

Stolzfus, E. R. (1992). *Aging and Breadth of Availability during Language Processing.* Unpublished doctoral dissertation, Duke University.

Stone, L. S. (1960). Polarization of the retina and development of vision. *Journal of Experimental Zoology,* 145, 85–93.

Strassmaier, M., & Gillespie, P.G. (2002). The hair cell's transduction channel. *Current Opinion in Neurobiology,* 12, 380–386.

Stratton, G. M. (1896). Some preliminary experiments on vision without inversion of the retinal image. *Psychological Review,* 3, 611–617.

Stratton, G. M. (1897a). Upright vision and the retinal image. *Psychological Review,* 4, 182–187.

Stratton, G. M. (1897b). Vision without inversion of the retinal image. *Psychological Review,* 4, 341–360.

Street, R. F. (1931). *A Gestalt Completion Test: A Study of a Cross Section of Intellect.* New York: Bureau of Publication, Columbia University.

Stromeyer, C. F., III. (1978). Form-color aftereffects in human vision. In R. Held, H. Leibowitz, & H. L. Teuber (Eds.), *Handbook of Sensory Physiology,* Vol. 8 (pp. 97–142). New York: Springer-Verlag.

Stroop, J. (1935). Studies of interference in serial verbal reactions. *Journal of Experimental Psychology,* 18, 624–643.

Stroud, J. M. (1955). The fine structure of psychological time. In H. Quastler (Ed.), *Information Theory in Psychology: Problems and Methods* (pp. 174–207). Glencoe, IL: Free Press.

Stuart, G. W., & Day, R. H. (1988). The Fraser illusion: Simple figures. *Perception & Psychophysics,* 44, 409–420.

Sturzel F., & Spillmann L. (2001). Texture fading correlates with stimulus salience. *Vision Research,* 41, 2969–2977.

Suedfeld, P. (1980). *Restricted Environmental Stimulation: Research and Clinical Applications.* New York: Wiley.

Sugihara, H., Murakami, I., Shenoy, K. V., Andersen, R. A., & Komatsu, H. (2002). Response of MSTd Neurons to simulated 3D orientation of rotating planes. *Journal of Neurophysiology,* 87, 273–285.

Sun, J., & Perona, P. (1998). Where is the sun? *Nature Neuroscience,* 1, 183–184.

Sussman, H. M. (1991a). The representation of stop consonants in three-dimensional acoustic space. *Phonetica,* 48, 18–31.

Sussman, H. M. (1991b). An investigation of locus equations as a source of relational invariance for stop place categorization. *Journal of the Acoustical Society of America,* 90, 1309–1325.

Svaetichin, G. (1956). Spectral response curves of single cones. *Acta Physiologica Scandinavica,* 1, 93–101.

Svaetichin, G., & MacNichol, E. F. Jr. (1958). Retinal mechanisms for achromatic vision. *Annals of the New York Academy of Sciences,* 74, 385–404.

Swarbrick, L., & Whitfield, I. C. (1972). Auditory cortical units selectively responsive to stimulus "shape." *Journal of Physiology* (London), 224, 68–69.

Swensson, R. G. (1980). A two-stage detection model applied to skilled visual search by radiologists. *Perception & Psychophysics,* 27, 11–16.

Swets, J. A. (1963). Central factors in auditory frequency selectivity. *Psychological Bulletin,* 60, 429–441.

Swift, C. G., & Tiplady, B. (1988). The effects of age on the response to caffeine. *Psychopharmacology,* 94, 29–31.

Swindale N. (2001). Cortical cartography: what's in a map? *Current Biology,* 11, R764–767.

Swindale, N. V., & Cynader, M. S. (1986). Vernier acuity of neurones in cat visual cortex. *Nature,* 319, 591–593.

Szabo, S., Bujas, Z., Ajdukovic, D., Mayer, D., & Vodanovic, M. (1997). Influence of the intensity of NaCl solutions on adaptation degree and recovery time course. *Perception & Psychophysics,* 59, 180–186.

Szentagothai, J. (1950). The elementary vestibulo-ocular reflex arc. *Journal of Neurophysiology,* 13, 395–407.

Takeda, T., Hashimoto, K., Hiruma, N., & Fukui, Y. (1999). Characteristics of accommodation toward apparent depth. *Vision Research,* 39, 2087–2097.

Talwar, S. K., & Gerstein, G. L. (2001). Reorganization in awake rat auditory cortex by local microstimulation and its effect on frequency-discrimination behavior. *Journal of Neurophysiology,* 86, 1555–1572.

Tam, W. J., & Stelmach, L. B. (1998). Display duration and stereoscopic depth discrimination. *Canadian Journal of Experimental Psychology,* 52, 56–61.

Tan, H. Z., Rabinowitz, W. M., & Durlach, N. I. (1989). Analysis of a synthetic Tadoma system as a multidimensional tactile display. *Journal of the Acoustical Society of America,* 86, 981–988.

Tanaka K. (1996). Inferotemporal cortex and object vision. *Annual Review of Neuroscience,* 19, 109–139.

Tarr, M. J., & Bülthoff, H. H. (1998). Image-based object recognition in man, monkey, and machine. *Cognition,* 67(1–2), 1–20.

Tart, C. (1971). *On Being Stoned.* Palo Alto: Science and Behavior Books.

Tassinari, G., Campara, D., Balercia, G., Chilosi, M., Martignoni, G., & Marzi, C. A. (1994). Magnocellular and parvocellular pathways are segregated in the human optic tract. *Neuroreport,* 5, 1425–1428.

Taylor, J. G. (2002). Paying attention to consciousness. *Trends in Cognitive Sciences,* 6, 206–210.

Taylor, S. P., & Woodhouse, J. M. (1980). A new illusion and possible links with the Munsterberg and Fraser illions of direction. *Perception & Psychophysics,* 9, 479–481.

Tedford, W. H., Warren, D. E., & Flynn, W. E. (1977). Alternation of shock aversion thresholds during menstrual cycle. *Perception & Psychophysics,* 21, 193–196.

Tees, R. C. (1974). Effect of visual deprivation on development of depth perception in the rat. *Journal of Comparative and Physiological Psychology,* 86, 300–308.

Tees, R. C., & Buhrmann, K. (1990). The effect of early experience on water maze spatial learning and memory in rats. *Developmental Psychobiology,* 23, 427–439.

Tees, R. C., & Midgley, G. (1978). Extent of recovery of function after early sensory deprivation in the rat. *Journal of Comparative and Physiological Psychology,* 92, 768–777.

Tees, R. C., & Werker, J. F. (1984). Perceptual flexibility: Maintenance or recovery of the ability to discriminate nonnative speech sounds. *Canadian Journal of Psychology,* 38, 579–590.

Teghtsoonian, M., & Teghtsoonian, R. (1983). Consistency of individual exponents in cross-modality matching. *Perception & Psychophysics,* 33, 203–214.

Teghtsoonian, R. (1971). On the exponents in Stevens' law and the constant in Ekman's law. *Psychological Review,* 78, 71–80.

Teghtsoonian, R., Teghtsoonian, M., Bergulund, B., & Berglund, U. (1978). Invariance of odor strength with sniff vigor: An olfactory analogue to size constancy. *Journal of Experimental Psychology: Human Perception and Performance,* 4, 144–152.

Telford, L., & Howard, I. P. (1996). Role of optical flow field asymmetry in the perception of heading during linear motion. *Perception & Psychophysics,* 58, 283–288.

Teller, D. Y., & Bornstein, M. H. (1987). Infant color vision and color perception. In P. Salapatek & L. Cohen (Eds.), *Handbook of Infant Perception,* Vol. 1. *From Sensation to Perception* (pp. 185–237). Orlando: Academic Press.

Teller, D. Y., Morse, R., Borton, R., & Regal, D. (1974). Visual acuity for vertical and diagonal gratings in human infants. *Vision Research,* 14: 1433–1439.

Tharpe, A. M., & Ashmead, D. H. (2001).A longitudinal investigation of infant auditory sensitivity. *American Journal of Audiology,* 10, 104–112.

Thomas, E. A. C., & Weaver, W. B. (1975). Cognitive processing and time perception. *Perception & Psychophysics,* 17, 363–367.

Thomas, G., Goldberg, J. H., Cannon, D. J., & Hillis, S. L. (2002). Surface textures improve the robustness of stereoscopic depth cues. *Human Factors,* 44, 157–170.

Thomas, H., Jamison, W., & Hammel, D. D. (1973). Observation is insufficient for discovering that the surface of still water is invariantly horizontal. *Science,* 181, 173–174.

Thorpe, L. A., & Trehub, S. E. (1989). Duration illusion and auditory grouping in infancy. *Developmental Psychology,* 24, 484–491.

Tian, B., Reser, D., Durham, A., Kustov, A., & Rauschecker, J.P. (2001). Functional specialization in Rhesus monkey auditory cortex. *Science,* 292, 290–293.

Timney, B. (1985). Visual experience and the development of depth perception. In D. J. Ingle, M. Jeannerod, & D. N. Lee (Eds.), *Brain Mechanisms and Spatial Vision* (pp. 147–174). Dordrecht: Martinus Nijhoff.

Timney, B., & Muir, D. W. (1976). Orientation anisotropy: Incidence and magnitude in Caucasian & Chinese subjects. *Science,* 193, 699–700.

Tipper, S. P., Weaver, B., Jerreat, L. M., & Burak, A. L. (1994). Object-based and environment-based inhibition of return of visual attention. *Journal of Experimental Psychology: Human Perception and Performance,* 20, 478–499.

Toch, H. H., & Schulte, R. (1961). Readiness to perceive violence as a result of police training. *British Journal of Psychology,* 52, 389–393.

Todd, J. T., & Akerstrom, R. A. (1987). Perception of three-dimensional form from patterns of optical texture. *Journal of Experimental Psychology: Human Perception and Performance,* 13, 242–255.

Toet, A., & Levi, D. M. (1992). The two-dimensional shape of spatial interaction zones in the parafovea. *Vision Research,* 32, 1349–1357.

Tollin, D. J., & Yin, T. C. T. (2002a). The coding of spatial location by single units in the lateral superior olive of the cat: I. Spatial receptive fields in azimuth. *Journal of Neuroscience,* 22, 1454–1467.

Tollin, D. J., & Yin, T. C. T. (2002b). The coding of spatial location by single units in the lateral superior olive of the cat: II. The determinants of spatial receptive fields in azimuth. *Journal of Neuroscience,* 22, 1468–1479.

Tomlinson, R. W. W., & Schwarz, D. W. F. (1988). Perception of the missing fundamental in nonhuman primates. *Journal of the Acoustical Society of America,* 84, 560–565.

Tong, F., & Engel, S. A. (2001). Interocular rivalry revealed in the human cortical blind-spot representation. *Nature,* 411, 195–198.

Tong, F., Nakayama, K., Vaughan, J. T., & Kanwisher, N. 1998. Binocular rivalry and visual awareness in human extrastriate cortex. *Neuron,* 21, 753–759.

Tononi, G., & Edelman, G. M. (1998). Consciousness and complexity. *Science,* 282, 1846–1851.

Tononi, G., Srivinivasan, R., Russell, D. P., & Edelman, G. M. (1998). Investigating neural correlates of conscious perception by frequency-tagged neuromagnetic responses. *Proceedings of the National Academy of Sciences (USA),* 95, 3198–3203.

Torgerson, W. S. (1961). Distances and ratios in psychophysical scaling. *Acta Psychologica,* 19, 201–205.

Trainor, L. J., & Trehub, S. E. (1994). Key membership and implied harmony in Western tonal music: Developmental perspectives. *Perception & Psychophysics,* 56, 125–132.

Trehub, S. E., & Unyk, A. M. (1994). Children's songs to infant siblings: Parallels with speech. *Journal of Child Language,* 21, 735–744.

Treisman, A. M. (1982). Perceptual groupings and attention in visual search for features and for objects. *Journal of Experimental Psychology: Human Perception and Performance,* 8, 194–214.

Treisman, A. M. (1986a). Features and objects in visual processing. *Scientific American,* 255, 114B-125.

Treisman, A. M. (1986b). Properties, parts, and objects. In K. R. Boff, L. Kaufman, & J. P. Thomas (Eds.), *Handbook of Perception and Human Performance* (pp. 351–357). New York: Wiley.

Treisman, A. M., & Davies, A. (1972). Divided attention to ear and eye. In S. Kornblum (Ed.), *Attention and Performance* IV (pp. 101–118). New York: Academic Press.

Treisman, A. M., & Gelade, G. (1980). A feature-integration theory of attention. *Cognitive Psychology,* 12, 97–136.

Treisman, A. M., & Gormican, S. (1988). Feature analysis in early vision: Evidence from search asymmetries. *Psychological Review,* 95, 15–48.

Treisman, A. M., Cavanagh, P., Fischer, B., Ramachandran, V. S., & von der Heydt, R. (1990). Form perception and attention: Striate cortex and beyond. In L. Spillman & J. S. Werner (Eds.), *Visual Perception* (pp. 273–316). New York: Academic Press.

Treisman, M. (1963). Temporal discrimination and the indifference interval: Implications for the model of an internal clock. *Psychological Monographs,* 77 (1–31, Whole No. 576).

Treisman, M. (1976). On the use and misuse of psychophysical terms. *Psychological Review,* 83, 246–256.

Tresilian, J. R. (1993). Four questions of time-to-contact: an analysis of research in interceptive timing. *Perception,* 22, 653–680.

Tresilian, J. R. (1994). Approximate information sources and perceptual variables in interceptive timing. *Journal of Experimental Psychology: Human Perception and Performance,* 20, 154–173.

Tresilian, J. R. (1999). Visually timed action: Time-out for 'tau'? *Trends in Cognitive Sciences,* 3, 301–310.

Tresilian, J. R., & Mon-Williams, M. (2000). Getting the measure of vergence weight in nearness perception. *Experimental Brain Research,* 132, 362–368.

Tress, K. H., & Kugler, B. T. (1979). Interocular transfer of movement after-effects in schizophrenia. *British Journal of Psychology,* 70, 389–392.

Trick, L., Enns, J. T., & Brodeur, D. A. (1996). Lifespan changes in visual enumeration: The number discrimination task. *Developmental Psychology,* 32, 925–932.

Tronick, E. (1972). Stimulus control and the growth of the infant's effective visual field. *Perception & Psychophysics,* 11, 373–376.

Troscianko, T., & Fahle, M. (1988). Why do isoluminant stimuli appear slower? *Journal of the Optical Society of America A,* 5, 871–880.

Trout, J. D., & Poser, W. J. (1990). Auditory and phonemic influences on phonemic restoration. *Language & Speech,* 33, 121–135.

Tsal, Y. (1983). Movements of attention across the visual field. *Journal of Experimental Psychology: Human Perception and Performance,* 9, 523–530.

Tuck, J. P., & Long, G. M. (1990). The role of small-field tritanopia in two measures of color vision. *Ophthalmic and Physiological Optics,* 10, 195–199.

Tulunay, K. U., & Olson, J. D. (1996). Brightness of uniform stabilized fields. *Vision Research,* 36, 351–359.

Turnbull, C. (1961). Some observations regarding the experiences and behavior of the Bambuti Pygmies. *American Journal of Psychology,* 74, 304–308.

Turnbull, O. H., Beschin, N., & Della Sala, S. (1997). Agnosia for object orientation: Implications for theories of object recognition. *Neuropsychologia,* 35, 153–163.

Turnbull, O. H., & McCarthy, R. A. (1996). When is a view unusual? A single case study of orientation-dependent visual agnosia. *Brain Research Bulletin,* 40, 497–502.

Turner, P. (1968). Amphetamines and smell threshold in man. In A. Herxheimer (Ed.), *Drugs and Sensory Functions* (pp. 91–100). Boston: Little, Brown.

Turvey, M. T., Burton, G., Pagano, C. C., Solomon, H. Y., & Runeson, S. (1992). Role of the inertia tensor in perceiving object orientation by dynamic touch. *Journal of Experimental Psychology: Human Perception & Performance,* 18, 714–727.

Tversky, B., & Schiano, D. J. (1989). Perceptual and conceptual factors in distortions in memory for graphs and maps. *Journal of Experimental Psychology: General,* 118, 387–398.

Tyler, C. W. (2002). *Human Symmetry Perception and Its Computational Analysis.* Mahwah, NJ: Erlbaum.

Uchikawa, K., Uchicawa, H., & Boynton, R. M. (1989). Partial color constancy of isolated surface colors examined by a color-naming method. *Perception,* 18, 83–91.

Uhlarik, J., & Johnson, R. (1978). Development of form perception in repeated brief exposures to visual stimuli. In R. Walk & L. Pick Jr. (Eds.), *Perception and Experience.* New York: Plenum.

Ujike, H., & Ono, H. (2001). Depth thresholds of motion parallax as a function of head movement velocity. *Vision Research,* 41, 2835–2843.

Ullman, S. (1979). The interpretation of structure from motion. *Proceedings of the Royal Society of London, Series B,* 203, 405–426.

Ulrich, R. (1987). Threshold models of temporal-order judgments evaluated by a ternary response task. *Perception & Psychophysics,* 42, 224–239.

Ungerleider, L. G., & Mishkin, M. (1982). Two cortical visual systems. In D. J. Ingle, M. A. Goodale, & R. J. W. Mansfield (Eds.), *Analysis of Visual Behavior* (pp. 549–586). Cambridge, MA: MIT Press.

Usher M., & McClelland J. L. (2001). The time course of perceptual choice: the leaky, competing accumulator model. *Psychological Review,* 108, 550–592.

Usher, M., & Donnelly, N. (1998). Visual synchrony affects binding and segmentation in perception. *Nature,* 394, 179–182.

Valentine, T. (1991). A unified account of the effects of distinctiveness, inversion, and race in face recognition. *Quarterly Journal of Experimental Psychology: Human Experimental Psychology,* 43, 161–204.

Vallbo, A. B. (1981). Sensations evoked from the glabrous skin of the human hand by electrical stimulation of unitary mechano-sensitive afferents. *British Research,* 215, 359–363.

Vallbo, A. B. (1983). Tactile sensation related to activity in primary afferents with special reference to detection problems. In C. von Euler, O. Franzen, U. Lindblom, & D. Ottoson (Eds.), *Somatosensory Mechanisms* (pp. 163–172). New York, Plenum Press.

Van Beers, R. J., Wolpert, D. M., & Haggard, P. (2001). Sensorimotor integration compensates for visual localization errors during smooth pursuit eye movements. *Journal of Neurophysiology,* 85, 1914–1922.

Van Dijk, M., de Boer, J., Koot, H. M., Duivenvoorden, H. J., Passchier, J., Bouwmeester, N., & Tibboel, D. (2001). The association between physiological and behavioral pain measures in 0– to 3–year-old infants after major surgery. *Journal of Pain and Symptom Management,* 22(1), 600–609.

Van Doren, C. L. (1989). A model of spatiotemporal sensitivity linking psychophysics to tissue mechanics. *Journal of the Acoustical Society of America,* 85, 2065–2080.

Van Essen, D. C. (1984). Functional organization of primate visual cortex. In A. Peters & E. G. Jones (Eds.), *Cerebral Cortex,* Vol. 3 (pp. 259–329). New York: Plenum Press.

Van Essen, D. C., Anderson, C. H., & Felleman, D. J. (1992). Information processing in the primate visual system: An integrated systems perspective. *Science,* 255, 419–423.

Van Lancker, D. R., & Kreiman, J. (1989). Voice perception deficits: Neuroanatomical correlates of phonagnosia. *Journal of Clinical and Experimental Neuropsychology,* 11, 665–674.

Van Lier, R. (2001). Simplicity, regularity, and perceptual interpretations: A structural information approach. In T. F. Shipley & P. J. Kellman (Eds.), *From Fragments to Objects: Segmentation and Grouping in Vision.* (pp. 231–252). Amsterdam: Elsevier.

van Santen, J. P. H., & Sperling, G. (1985). Elaborated Reichardt detectors. *Journal of the Optical Society of America A,* 2, 300–321.

van Tonder, G.J., & Ejima Y. (2000a). From image segmentation to anti-textons. *Perception,* 29, 1231–1247.

van Tonder, G. J., & Ejima, Y. (2000b). The patchwork engine: Image segmentation from shape symmetries. *Neural Networks,* 13, 291–303.

Vanduffel, W., Tootell, R. B., Schoups, A. A., & Orban, G. A. (2002). The organization of orientation selectivity throughout macaque visual cortex. *Cerebral Cortex,* 12, 647–662.

Varma, V. K., & Malhotra, A. K. (1988). Cannabis and cognitive functions: A prospective study. *Drug & Alcohol Dependence,* 21, 147–152.

Vecera, S. P., Vogel, E. K., & Woodman, G. F. (2002). Lower region: A new cue for figure ground assignment. *Journal of Experimental Psychology: General,* 131, 194–205.

Velle, W. (1987). Sex differences in sensory functions. *Perspectives in Biology and Medicine,* 30, 490–522.

Verhey, J. L., & Kollmeir, B. (2002). Spectral loudness summation as a function of duration. *Journal of the Acoustical Society of America,* 111, 1349–1358.

Verrey, L. (1888). Hemiachromatopsie droite absolue. *Archives of Ophthalmology (Paris),* 8, 289–301.

Verrillo, R. T. (1968). A duplex mechanism of mechanoreception. In D. R. Kenshalo (Ed.), *The Skin Senses* (pp. 139–159). Springfield, IL: Thomas.

Verrillo, R. T., & Bolanowski, S. J. Jr. (1986). The effects of skin temperature on the psychophysical responses to vibration on glabrous and hairy skin. *Journal of the Acoustical Society of America,* 80, 528–532.

Verrillo, R. T., Fraioli, A. J., & Smith, R. L. (1969). Sensation magnitude of vibrotactile stimuli. *Perception & Psychophysics,* 6, 366–372.

Viemeister, N. F. (1988). Intensity coding and the dynamic range problem. *Hearing Research,* 34, 267–274.

Vierck, C. (1978). Somatosensory system. In R. B. Masterston (Ed.), *Handbook of Sensory Neurobiology,* Vol. I. *Sensory Integration* (pp. 249–310). New York: Plenum Press.

Vimal, R. L. P., Pokorny, J., & Smith, V. C. (1987). Appearance of steadily viewed lights. *Vision Research,* 27, 1309–1318.

Vogels, R., & Orban, G. A. (1986). Decision factors affecting line orientation judgments in the method of single stimuli. *Perception & Psychophysics,* 40, 74–84.

von Hofsten, C., Vishton, P., Spelke, E. S., Feng, Q., & Rosander, K. (1998). Predictive action in infancy: tracking and reaching for moving objects. *Cognition,* 67, 255–285.

Von Hofsten, C. (1983). Catching skills in infancy. *Journal of Experimental Psychology: Human Perception and Performance,* 9, 75–85.

Vroomen, J., Bertelson, P., & de Gelder, B. (2001). The ventriloquist effect does not depend on the direction of automatic visual attention. *Perception & Psychophysics,* 63, 651–659.

Vurpillot, E. (1968). The development of scanning strategies and their relation to visual differentiation. *Journal of Experimental Child Psychology,* 6, 632–650.

W. Epstein (Ed.), *Stability and Constancy in Visual Perception: Mechanisms and Processes* (pp. 217–254). New York: Wiley.

Waber, D. P. (1976). Sex differences in cognition: A function of maturation rate? *Science,* 192, 572–574.

Waber, D. P. (1977). Sex differences in mental abilities, hemispheric lateralization and rate of physical growth at adolescence. *Developmental Psychology,* 13, 29–38.

Wacholtz, E. (1996). Can we learn from the clinically significant face processing deficits, prosopagnosia and Capgras delusion? *Neuropsychology Review,* 6, 203–257.

Wade, N. J. (1984). *Brewster & Wheatstone on Vision.* New York: Academic Press.

Wade, N. J., & Brozek, J. (2001). *Purkinje's Vision: The Dawning of Neuroscience.* Mahwah, NJ: Erlbaum.

Waespe, W., & Henn, V. (1977). Neuronal activity in the vestibular nuclei of the alert monkey during vestibular and optokinetic stimulation. *Experimental Brain Research,* 27, 523–538.

Wahl, O. F., & Sieg, D. (1980). Time estimation among schizophrenics. *Perceptual and Motor Skills,* 50, 535–541.

Wald, G. (1968). The molecular basis of visual excitation. *Nature* (London), 219, 800–807.

Walk, R. D., & Gibson, E. J. (1961). A comparative and analytic study of visual depth perception. *Psychological Monographs,* 75, 1–44.

Walker, J. L. (1977). Time estimation and total subjective time. *Perceptual and Motor Skills,* 44, 527–532.

Wall, P. D. (1979). On the relation of injury to pain. *Pain,* 6, 253–264.

Wallace, B., & Priebe, F. A. (1985). Hypnotic susceptibility, interference and alternation frequency to the Necker cube illusion. *Journal of General Psychology,* 112, 271–277.

Wallace, P. (1977). Individual discrimination of humans by odor. *Physiology and Behavior,* 19, 577–579.

Wallach, H. (1972). The perception of neutral colors. In R. Held & W. Richards (Eds.), *Perception: Mechanisms and Models: Readings from Scientific American* (pp. 278–285). San Francisco: Freeman. (Originally published in Scientific American, 1963).

Wallach, H. (1987). Perceiving a stable environment when one moves. *Annual Review of Psychology,* 38, 1–27.

Wallach, H., & Becklen, R. (1983). An effect of speed on induced motion. *Perception & Psychophysics,* 34, 237–242.

Wallach, H., Becklen, R., & Nitzberg, D. (1985). Vector analysis and process combination in motion perception. *Journal of Experimental Psychology: Human Perception and Performance,* 11, 93–102.

Wallach, H., Newman, E. B., & Rosenzweig, M. R. (1949). The precedence effect in sound localization. *American Journal of Psychology,* 62, 315–336.

Walls, G. L. (1951). A theory of ocular dominance. *AMA Archives of Ophthalmology,* 45, 387–412.

Walsh, V., & Butler, S. R. (1996). The effects of visual cortex lesions on the perception of rotated shapes. *Behavioural Brain Research,* 76, 127–142.

Wandell, B. A. (1995). *Foundations of Vision.* Sunderland, MA: Sinauer Associates.

Wang, M. Q., & Taylor-Nicholson, M. E. (1992). Psychomotor and visual performance under the time-course effect of alcohol. *Perceptual and Motor Skills,* 75, 1095–1106.

Warchol, M. E., Lambert, P. R., Goldstein, B. J., Forge, A., & Corwin, J. T. (1993). Regenerative proliferation in inner ear sensory epithelia from adult guinea pigs and humans. *Science,* 259, 1619–1622.

Ward, L. M. (1973). Repeated magnitude estimations with a variable standard: Sequential effects and other properties. *Perception & Psychophysics,* 13, 193–200.

Ward, L. M. (1974). Power functions for category judgments of duration and line length. *Perceptual and Motor Skills,* 38, 1182.

Ward, L. M. (1975). Sequential dependencies and response range in cross-modality matches of duration to loudness. *Perception & Psychophysics,* 18, 217–223.

Ward, L. M. (1983). On processing dominance: Comment on Pomerantz. *Journal of Experimental Psychology: General,* 112, 541–546.

Ward, L. M. (1985). Covert focussing of the attentional gaze. *Canadian Journal of Psychology,* 39, 546–563.

Ward, L. M. (1987). Remembrance of sounds past: Memory and psychophysical scaling. *Journal of Experimental Psychology: Human Perception and Performance,* 13, 216–227.

Ward, L. M. (1990). Critical bands and mixed-frequency scaling: Sequential dependencies, equal-loudness contours, and power function exponents. *Perception & Psychophysics,* 47, 551–562.

Ward, L. M. (1992). Mind in psychophysics. In D. Algom (Ed.), *Psychophysical Approaches to Cognition* (pp. 187–249). Amsterdam: North-Holland (Elsevier).

Ward, L. M. (1994). Supramodal and modality-specific mechanisms for stimulus-driven shifts of auditory and visual attention. *Canadian Journal of Experimental Psychology,* 48, 242–259.

Ward, L. M. (1997). Involuntary listen-ing aids hearing. *Psychological Science,* 8, 112–118.

Ward, L. M. (2002). *Dynamical Cognitive Science.* Cambridge, MA: MIT Press.

Ward, L. M. (2003). Oscillations and synchrony in cognition. In V. Jirsa & J.A.S. Kelso (Eds.), *Coordination Dynamics: Issues and Trends* (pp. xx-yy). New York: Springer Verlag.

Ward, L. M., & Davidson, K. P. (1993). Where the action is: Weber fractions as a function of sound pressure at low frequencies. *Journal of the Acoustical Society of America,* 94, 2587–2594.

Ward, L. M., & Lockhead, G. R. (1970). Sequential effects and memory in category judgments. *Journal of Experimental Psychology,* 854, 27–34.

Ward, L. M., & Mori, S. (1996). Attention cueing aids auditory intensity resolution. *Journal of the Acoustical Society of America,* 100, 1722–1727.

Ward, L. M., Armstrong, J., & Golestani, N. (1996). Intensity resolution and subjective magnitude in psychophysical scaling. *Perception & Psychophysics,* 58, 793–801.

Ward, L. M., McDonald, J. J., & Golestani, N. (1998). Cross-modal control of attention shifts. In R. D. Wright (Ed.), *Visual Attention* (pp. 232–268). New York: Oxford University Press.

Ward, L. M., Porac, P., Coren, S., & Girgus, J. S. (1977). The case for misapplied constancy scaling: Depth associations elicited by illusion configurations. *American Journal of Psychology,* 90, 609–620.

Ward, T. B. (1985). Individual differences in processing stimulus dimensions: Relation to selective processing ability. *Perception & Psychophysics,* 37, 471–482.

Ward, W. D. (1999). Absolute pitch. In D. Deutsch (Ed.), *The Psychology of Music* (2nd ed.). (pp. 265–298). New York: Academic Press.

Ware, C. (1981). Subjective contours independent of subjective brighteners. *Perception & Psychophysics,* 29, 500–504.

Warm, J. S., & McCray, R. E. (1969). Influence of word frequency and length on the apparent duration of tachistoscopic presentations. *Journal of Experimental Psychology,* 79, 56–58.

Warren, R. M. (1970). Perceptual restoration of missing speech sounds. *Science,* 167, 392–393.

Warren, R. M. (1984). Perceptual restoration of obliterated sounds. *Psychological Bulletin,* 96, 371–383.

Warren, R. M., Obusek, C. J., Farmer, R. M., & Warren, R. P. (1969). Auditory sequence: Confusion of patterns other than speech or music. *Science,* 164, 586–587.

Warren, R. M., Reiner, K. R., Bashford, J. A. Jr., & Brubaker, B. S. (1995). Spectral redundancy: Intelligibility of sentences heard through narrow spectral slits. *Perception & Psychophysics,* 57, 175–182.

Warren, W. H., & Hannon, D. J. (1988). Direction of self-motion is perceived from optical flow. *Nature,* 336, 162–163.

Washburn, D., & Humphrey, D (2001). Symmetries in the mind: Production, perception, and preference for seven one dimensional patterns. *Visual Arts Research,* 27, 57–68

Watanabe, T., & Katsuki, Y. (1974). Response patterns of single auditory neurons of the cat to species-specific vocalization. *Japanese Journal of Physiology,* 24, 135–155.

Watkins, L. R., & Mayer, D. J. (1982). Organization of endogenous opiate and nonopiate pain control systems. *Science,* 216, 1185–1192.

Watson, A. B. (1983). Detection and recognition of simple spatial forms. In O. J. Braddick & A. C. Sleigh (Eds.), *Physical and Biological Processing of Images* (pp. 100–114). New York: Springer-Verlag.

Watson, A. B., & Fitzhugh, A. (1990). The method of constant stimuli is inefficient. *Perception & Psychophysics,* 47, 87–91.

Weber, E. H. (1834). *De pulen, resorptione, auditu et tactu: Annotationes anatomicae et physiologicae.* Leipzig: Koehler.

Webster, M. A., & Mollon, J. D. (1995). Colour constancy influenced by contrast adaptation. *Nature,* 373, 694–698.

Webster, M., & DeValois, R. (1985). Relationship between spatial frequency and orientation tuning of striate cortex cells. *Journal of the Optical Society of America A,* 2, 1124–1132.

Webster, M. A., Miyahara, E., Malkoc, G., & Raker, W. E. (2000). Variations in normal color vision: II. Unique hues. *Journal of the Optical Society of America A: Optics and Image Science,* 17, 1545–1555.

Webster, W. R., & Atkin, L. M. (1975). Central auditory processing. In M. S. Gazzaniga & C. Blakemore (Eds.), *Handbook of Sensory Psychobiology* (pp. 325–364). New York: Academic Press.

Weeks, R. A., Aziz-Sultan, A., Bushara, K. O., Tian, B., Wessinger, C. M., Dang, N., Rauschecker, J. P., & Hallett, M. (1999). A PET study of human auditory spatial processing. *Neuroscience Letters,* 262, 155–158.

Wegner, A. J. & Fahle, M. (1999). Alcohol and visual performance. *Progress in Neuro Psychopharmacology and Biological Psychiatry,* 23, 465–482.

Weiffenbach, J. M., Baum, B. J., & Burghauser, B. (1982). Taste thresholds: Quality specific variation with human aging. *Journal of Gerontology,* 37, 372–377.

Weil, A. T., Zinberg, E., & Nelson, J. N. (1968). Clinical and psychological effects of marijuana in man. *Science,* 162, 1234–1242.

Weinberger, N. M. (1993). Learning-induced changes of auditory receptive fields. *Current Opinion in Neurobiology,* 3, 570–577.

Weinstein, B. E. (2000). *Geriatric Audiology.* New York: Thieme.

Weinstein, E. A., Cole, M., Mitchell, M. S., & Lyerly, O. G. (1964). Anosagnosia and aphasia. *Archives of Neurology,* 10, 376–386.

Weinstein, S. (1968). Intensive and extensive aspects of tactile sensitivity as a function of body part, sex, and laterality. In D. R. Kenshalo (Ed.), *The Skin Senses* (pp. 195–218). Springfield, IL: Thomas.

Weinstein, S., & Sersen, E. A. (1961). Tactual sensitivity as a function of handedness and laterality. *Journal of Comparative and Physiological Psychology,* 54, 665–669.

Weisenberger, J. M., Broadstone, S. M., & Saunders, F. A. (1989). Evaluation of two multichannel tactile aids for the hearing impaired. *Journal of the Acoustical Society of America,* 86, 1764–1775.

Weiskrantz, L. (1986). *Blindsight*: A Case Study and Implications. Oxford: Oxford University Press.

Weiskrantz, L. (1997). *Consciousness Lost and Found: A Neuropsychological Exploration.* Oxford: Oxford University Press.

Weisstein, N. A. (1968). Rashevsky-Landahl neural net: Simulation of metacontrast. *Psychological Review,* 75, 494–521.

Weisstein, N. A. (1980). Tutorial: The joy of Fourier analysis. In C. S. Harris (Ed.), *Visual Coding and Adaptability* (pp. 365–380). Hillsdale, NJ: Erlbaum.

Weisstein, N. A., & Wong, E. (1986). Figure-ground organization and the spatial and temporal responses of the visual system. In E. C. Schwab & H. C. Nusbaum (Eds.), *Pattern Recognition by Humans and Machines,* Vol. 2. *Visual Perception* (pp. 31–64). Orlando: Academic Press.

Weisstein, N. A., Harris, C., Berbaum, K., Tangney, J., & Williams, A. (1977). Contrast reduction by small localized stimuli: Extensive spatial spread of above-threshold orientation-selective masking. *Vision Research,* 17, 341–350.

Weisstein, N. A., Matthews, M., & Berbaum, K. (1974, November). *Illusory Contours Can Mask Real Contours.* Paper presented at the meeting of the Psychonomic Society, Boston.

Weisstein, N. A., Ozog, G., & Szoc, R. (1975). A comparison and elaboration of two models of metacontrast. *Psychological Review,* 82, 325–343.

Welch, R. B. (1971). Prism adaptation: The "target pointing effect" as a function of exposure trials. *Perception & Psychophysics,* 5, 102–104.

Welford, A. T. (1980). *Reaction Times.* London: Academic Press.

Well, A. D., Lorch, E. P., & Anderson, D. R. (1980). Developmental trends in distractability: Is absolute or proportional decrement the appropriate measure of interference? *Journal of Experimental Child Psychology,* 30, 109–124.

Wells, C., Ward, L. M., Chua, R. & Inglis, T. (2003). Regional variation and changes with ageing in vibrotactile sensitivity in the human footsole. *Journal of Gerontology: Biological Sciences.*

Wenzel, E. M., Arruda, M., Kistler, D. J., & Wightman, F. L. (1993). Localization using nonindividualized head-related transfer functions. *Journal of the Acoustical Society of America,* 94, 111–123.

Werker, J. F. (1989). Becoming a native listener. *American Scientist,* 77, 54–59.

Werker, J. F. (1992). Cross-language speech perception: Developmental change does not involve loss. In J. Goodman & H. C. Nusbaum (Eds.), *Speech Perception and Word Recognition.* Cambridge, MA: MIT Press.

Werker, J. F., & Logan, J. S. (1985), Cross-language evidence for three factors in speech perception. *Perception & Psychophysics,* 37, 35–44.

Werker, J. F., & McLeod, P. J. (1989). Infant preference for both male and female infant directed talk: A development of attention and affective responsiveness. *Canadian Journal of Psychology,* 43, 230–246.

Werker, J. F., Gilbert, J., Humphrey, K., & Tees, R. (1981). Developmental aspects of cross-language speech perception. *Child Development,* 52, 349–355.

Werker, J. F., & Desjardins, R. N. (2001). Listening to speech in the 1st year of life. In M. Tomasello, & E. Bates, (Eds.), *Language Development: The Essential Readings. Essential Readings in Developmental Psychology* (pp. 26–33). Malden, MA: Blackwell Publishers.

Werner, H. (1935). Studies on contour. *American Journal of Psychology,* 47, 40–64.

Werner, J. S., & Walraven, J. (1982). Effect of chromatic adaptation on the achromatic locus: The role of contrast, luminance and background color. *Vision Research,* 22, 929–943.

Werner, L. A., & Bernstein, I. L. (2001). Development of the auditory, gustatory, olfactory, and somatosensory systems. In E. B. Goldstein (Ed.), *Blackwell Handbook of Perception* (pp. 669–708). Handbook of Experimental Psychology Series. Oxford: Blackwell Publishers.

Werner, L. A. (1996). *Human Auditory Development.* Madison WI: Brown & Benchmark.

Wertheimer, M. (1912). Experimentelle Studien uber das Sehen von Bewegung. *Zeitschrift fur Psychologie,* 61, 161–265.

Wertheimer, M. (1923). Principles of perceptual organization (Abridged trans. by M. Wertheimer). In D. S. Beardslee & M. Wertheimer (Eds.), *Readings in Perception* (pp. 115–137). Princeton, NJ: Van Nostrand-Reinhold. (Original work published 1923, *Psychologishe Forschung,* 41, 301–350)

Wertheimer, M. (1961). Psychomotor coordination of auditory and visual space at birth. *Science,* 134, 1692.

Wessinger, C. M., Fendrich, R., & Gazzaniga, M. S. (1997). Islands of residual vision in hemianopic patients. *Journal of Cognitive Neuroscience,* 9, 203–221.

West, R. L., Ward., L. M., Khosla, R. (2000). Constrained scaling: The effect of learned psychophysical scales on idiosyncratic response bias. *Perception & Psychophysics,* 62, 137–151.

Westerman, L. A., & Smith, R. L. (1988). A diffusion model of the transient response of the cochlear inner hair cell synapse. *Journal of the Acoustical Society of America,* 83, 2266–2276.

Westerman, S. J. & Cribbin, T. (1998). Individual differences in the use of depth cues: Implications for computer and video based tasks. *Acta Psychologica,* 99, 293–310.

Westheimer, G. (1979). Spatial sense of the eye. Investigative *Ophthalmology and Visual Science,* 18, 893–912.

Wever, E. G. (1970). *Theory of Hearing.* New York: Wiley.

Wever, R. A. (1979). *The Circadian System of Man.* New York: Springer-Verlag.

Wever, R. A. (1989). Light effects on human circadian rhythms: A review of recent Andechs experiments. *Journal of Biological Rhythms*, 4, 161–185.

Wexler, M., Panerai, F., Lamouret, I., & Droulez, J. (2001). Self-motion and the perception of stationary objects. *Nature,* 409, 85–88.

Whalen, P. J. (1998): Fear, vigilance, and ambiguity: Initial neuro-imaging studies of the human amygdala. *Current Directions in Psychological Science,* 7:177–188.

White, B. W., Saunders, F. A., Scadden, L., Bach-y-Rita, P., & Collins, C. C. (1970). Seeing with the skin. *Perception & Psychophysics,* 7, 23–27.

White, C. (1963). Temporal numerosity and the psychological unit of duration. *Psychological Monographs,* 77 (1–37, Whole No. 575).

White, P. A., & Milne, A. (1997). Phenomenal causality: impressions of pulling in the visual perception of objects in motion. *American Journal of Psychology,* 110, 573–602.

White, P. A., & Milne, A. (1999). Impressions of enforced disintegration and bursting in the visual perception of collision events. *Journal of Experimental Psychology: General,* 128, 499–516.

Whitfield, I. C. (1967). *The Auditory Pathway.* London: Arnold.

Whitfield, I. C. (1968). The organiza-tion of the auditory pathways. *Journal of Sound and Vibration Research,* 8, 108–117.

Whitfield, I. C. (1978). The neural code. In E. C. Carterette & M. P. Friedman (Eds.), *Handbook of Perception,* Vol. IV. *Hearing* (pp. 163–183). New York: Academic Press.

Whitfield, I. C. (1980). Auditory cortex and the pitch of complex tones. *Journal of the Acoustical Society of America,* 67, 644–647.

Whitfield, I. C., & Evans, E. F. (1965). Responses of auditory cortical neurons to stimuli of changing frequency. *Journal of Neurophysiology,* 28, 655–672.

Whitsel, B. L., Dreyer, D. A., Hollins, M., & Young, M. G. (1979). The coding of direction of tactile stimulus movement: Correlative psychophysical and electrophysiological data. In D. R. Kenshalo (Ed.), *Sensory Functions of the Skin of Humans* (pp. 79–108). New York: Plenum Press.

Whytt, R. (1751). *An Essay on the Vital and Other Involuntary Motions of Animals.* Edinburgh: Balfour & Neill.

Wichmann, F. A., Sharpe, L. T., & Gegenfurtner, K. R. (2002). contributions of color to recognition memory for natural scenes. *Journal of Experimental Psychology: Learning, Memory & Cognition,* 28, 509–520.

Wickens, C. D. (1984). Processing resources in attention. In R. Parasuraman & D. R. Davies (Eds.), *Varieties of Attention* (pp. 63–101). Orlando: Academic Press.

Wiener, N. (1961). *Cybernetics* (2nd ed.). Cambridge, MA: MIT Press.

Wiener, S. I., Paul, C. A., & Eichnbaum, H. H. (1998). Spatial and behavioral correction of hippocampal neuronal activity. *Journal of Neuroscience,* 9, 2737–2763.

Wier, C. C., Jesteadt, W., & Green, D. M. (1977). Frequency discrimination as a function of frequency and sensation level. *Journal of the Acoustical Society of America,* 61, 178–184.

Wier, C. C., Pasanen, E. G., & McFadden, D. (1988). Partial dissociation of spontaneous otoacoustic emissions and distortion products during aspirin use. *Journal of the Acoustical Society of America,* 84, 230–237.

Wightman, F. L., & Kistler, D. J. (1989). Headphone simulation of free-field listening II: Psychophysical validation. *Journal of the Acoustical Society of America,* 85, 868–878.

Wilkinson, F., Wilson, H., R., & Ellemberg, D. (1997). Lateral interactions in peripherally viewed texture arrays. *Journal of the Optical Society of America,* 14, 2057–2068.

Willer, J. C., Dehen, H., & Cambier, J. (1981). Stress-induced analgesia in humans: Endogenous opioids and naloxone-reversible depression of pain reflexes. *Science,* 212, 689–690.

Williams, D. R., MacLeod, D. I. A., Hayhoe, M. M. (1981). Foveal tritanopia. *Vision Research,* 21, 1341–1356.

Williams, J. M. (1979). Distortions of vision and pain: Two functional facets of D-lysergic diethylamide. *Perceptual and Motor Skills,* 49, 499–528.

Williams, M. (1970). *Brain Damage and the Mind.* London: Penguin.

Willis, W. D. (1985). *The Pain System: The Neural Basis of Nociceptive Transmission in the Mammalian Nervous System.* Basel: Karger.

Wilson, E. O. (1971). *The Insect Societies.* Cambridge, MA: Harvard University Press.

Wilson, H. C. (1987). Female axillary secretions influence women's menstrual cycles: A critique. *Hormones and Behavior,* 21, 536–546.

Wilson, H. C. (1988). Male axillary secretions influence women's menstrual cycles: A critique. *Hormones and Behavior,* 22, 266–271.

Wilson, H. R., & Wilkinson, F. (2002). Symmetry perception: A novel approach for biological shapes. *Vision Research,* 42, 589–597.

Wilson, H. R., & Bergen, J. R. (1979). A four mechanism model for threshold spatial vision. *Vision Research,* 19, 19–32.

Wilson, H. R., & Gelb, D. J. (1984). Modified line element theory for spatial frequency and width discrimination. *Journal of the Optical Society of America A,* 1, 124–131.

Wilson, H. R., Levi, D., Maffei, L., Rovamo, J., DeValois, R. (1990). The perception of form: Retina to striate cortex. In L. Spillman & J. S. Werner (Eds.), *Visual Perception: The Neurophysiological Foundations* (pp. 231–272). New York: Academic Press.

Wilson, J. R., DeFries, J. C., McClearn, G. C., Vandenberg, S. G., Johnson, R. C., & Rashad, M. N. (1975). Cognitive abilities: Use of family data as a control to assess sex and age differences in two ethnic groups. *International Journal of Aging and Human Development,* 6, 261–275.

Wilson, M. (1957). Effects of circumscribed cortical lesions upon somesthetic and visual discrimination in the monkey. *Journal of Comparative and Physiological Psychology,* 50, 630–635.

Wishart, L. R., Lee, T. D., Cunningham, S. J., & Murdoch, J. E. (2002). Age-related differences and the role of augmented visual feedback in learning a bimanual coordination pattern. *Acta Psychologica,* 110, 247–263.

Withington Wray, D. J., Binns, K. E., Dhanjal, S. S., Brickley, S. G., & Keating, M. J. (1990). The maturation of the superior collicular map of auditory space in the guinea pig is disrupted by developmental auditory deprivation. *European Journal of Neuroscience,* 2, 693–703.

Withington, D. J., Binns, K. E., Ingham, N. J., & Thornton, S. K. (1994). Plasticity in the superior collicular auditory space map of adult guinea-pigs. *Experimental Physiology,* 79, 319–325.

Witkin, H. A., & Berry, J. W. (1975). Psychological differentiation in cross-cultural perspective. *Journal of Cross-Cultural Psychology, 6,* 4–87.

Wolfe, J. M. (1998). What can 1 million trials tell us about visual search? *Psychological Science,* 9, 33–39.

Wolfe, J. M., & O'Connell, K. M. (1986). Fatigue and structural change: Two consequences of visual pattern adaptation. *Investigative Ophthalmology and Visual Science,* 28, 173–212.

Wolff, H. G., & Goodell, B. S. (1943). The relation of attitude and suggestion to the perception of and reaction to pain. *Research Publications, Association for Research in Nervous and Mental Disease,* 23, 434–448.

Wolff, P. H. (1987). *The Development of Behavioral States and the Expression of Emotions in Early Infancy.* Chicago: University of Chicago Press.

Wolken, J. J. (1995). *Light Detectors, Photoreceptors, and Imaging Systems in Nature.* New York : Oxford University Press.

Wong, C., & Weisstein, N. (1982). A new perceptual context-superiority effect: Line segments are more visible against a figure than against a ground. *Science,* 218, 587–589.

Wong, E., & Weisstein, N. (1987). The effects of flicker on the perception of figure and ground. *Perception & Psychophysics,* 41, 440–448.

Wood, N. L., & Cowan, N. (1995a). The cocktail party phenomenon revisited: Attention and memory in the classic selective listening procedure of Cherry (1953). *Journal of Experimental Psychology: General,* 124, 243–262.

Wood, N. L., & Cowan, N. (1995b). The cocktail party phenomenon revisited: How frequent are attention shifts to one's name in an irrelevant auditory channel? *Journal of Experimental Psychology: Learning, Memory, and Cognition,* 21, 255–260.

Wood, R. W. (1985). The "haunted swing" illusion. *Psychological Review,* 2, 277–278.

Woodfield, R. L. (1984). Embedded figures test performance before and after childbirth. *British Journal of Psychology,* 75, 81–88.

Woodman, G. F., & Luck, S. J. (1999). Electrophysiological measurement of rapid shifts of attention during visual search. *Nature,* 400, 867–869.

Woodrow, H. (1951). Time perception. In S. S. Stevens (Ed.), *Handbook of Experimental Psychology* (pp. 1224–1236). New York: Wiley.

Woodworth, R. S. (1938). *Experimental Psychology.* New York: Holt, Rinehart and Winston.

Woolard, H. H., Weddell, G., & Harpman, J. A. (1940). Observations of the neuro-historical basis of cutaneous pain. *Journal of Anatomy,* 74, 413–440.

Worchel, P., & Dallenbach, K. M. (1947). "Facial vision": Perception of obstacles by the deaf-blind. *American Journal of Psychology,* 60, 502–553.

Wright, M. J., & Johnston, A. (1985). Invariant tuning of motion aftereffect. *Vision Research,* 25, 1947–1955.

Wright, N. H. (1964). Temporal summation and backward masking. *Journal of the Acoustical Society of America,* 36, 927–932.

Wright, R. D., & Richard, C. M. (1998). Inhibition-of-return is not reflexive. In R. D. Wright (Ed.), *Visual Attention* (pp. 330–347). New York: Oxford University Press.

Wright, R. D., & Ward, L. M. (1998). Control of visual attention. In R. D. Wright (Ed.), *Visual Attention* (pp. 132–186). New York: Oxford University Press.

Wulf, G., & Prinz,W (2001). Directing attention to movement effects enhances learning: A review. *Psychonomic Bulletin and Review,* 8, 648–660.

Wurtz, R. H. (1996). Vision for the control of movement. *Investigative Ophthalmology & Visual Science,* 37, 2131–2145.

Wurtz, R. H., Goldberg, M. E., & Robinson, D. L. (1980). Behavioral modulation of visual responses in monkeys. *Progress in Psychobiology and Physiological Psychology,* 9, 42–83.

Wyburn, G. M., Pickford, R. W., & Hurst, R. J. (1964). *Human Senses and Perception.* Toronto: University of Toronto Press.

Wysocki, C. J., & Meredith, M. (1987). *The Vomeronasal System.* New York: Wiley.

Wyszecki, G., & Stiles, W. S. (1967). *Color Science: Concepts and Methods, Quantitative Data and Formulas.* New York: Wiley.

Wyttenbach, R. A., & Hoy, R. R. (1993). Demonstration of the precedence effect in an insect. *Journal of the Acoustical Society of America,* 94, 777–784.

Wyttenbach, R. A., May, M. L., & Hoy, R. R. (1996). Categorical perception of sound frequency by crickets. *Science,* 273, 1542–1544.

Xiao, Z., & Suga, N. (2002). Modulation of cochlear hair cells by the auditory cortex in the mustached bat. *Nature Neuroscience,* 5, 57–63.

Xu, L., Furukawa, S., & Middlebrooks, J. C. (2000). Cortical mechanisms for auditory spatial illusions. *Acta Oto-Laryngologica,* 120, 263–266.

Yaksh, T. L. (1984). Multiple spinal opiate receptor systems in analgesia. In L. Kruger & J. C. Liebeskind (Eds.), *Neural Mechanisms of Pain* (pp. 197–216). New York: Raven Press.

Yang, T., & Kubovy, M. (1999). Weakening the robustness of perspective: Evidence for a modified theory of compensation in picture perception. *Perception and Psychophysics,* 61, 456–467.

Yantis, S. (1992). Multielement visual tracking: Attention and perceptual organization. *Cognitive Psychology,* 24, 295–340.

Yantis, S. (1995). Perceived continuity of occluded visual objects. *Psychological Science,* 6(3), 182–186.

Yantis, S., & Hillstrom, A. P. (1994). Stimulus-driven attentional capture: Evidence from equiluminant visual objects. *Journal of Experimental Psychology: Human Perception and Performance,* 20, 95–107.

Yantis, S., & Jonides, J. (1984). Abrupt onsets and selective attention: Evidence from visual search. *Journal of Experimental Psychology: Human Perception and Performance,* 10, 601–621.

Yantis, S., & Jonides, J. (1990). Abrupt visual onsets and selective attention: Voluntary versus automatic allocation. *Journal of Experimental Psychology: Human Perception and Performance,* 16, 121–134.

Yarbus, A. L. (1967). *Eye Movements and Vision.* New York: Plenum Press.

Yates, G., Robertson, D., & Johnstone, B. M. (1985). Very rapid adaptation in the guinea pig auditory nerve. *Hearing Research,* 17, 1–12.

Yen, W. (1975). Sex-linked major gene influence on selected types of spatial performance. *Behavior Genetics,* 5, 281–298.

Yendrikhovskij, S. N., Blommaert, F. J. J., & de-Ridder, H. (1999). Representation of memory prototype for an object color. *Color Research and Application,* 24, 393–410.

Yerkes, R. M., & Dodson, J. D. (1908). The relation of strength of stimulus to rapidity of habit formation. *Journal of Comparative Neurology and Psychology,* 18, 459–482.

Yin, C., Kellman, P. J., & Shipley, T. F. (2000). Surface integration influences depth discrimination. *Vision Research,* 40, 1969–1978.

Yonas, A. (1981). Infants' response to optical information for collision. In R. N. Aslin, J. R. Alberts, & M. R. Petersen (Eds.), *Development of Perception* (pp. 313–334). New York: Academic Press.

Yonas, A., & Craton, L. G. (1987). Relative motion: Kinetic information for the order of depth at an edge. *Perception & Psychophysics,* 41, 53–59.

Yonas, A., & Craton, L. G. (1990). Kinetic occlusion: Further studies of the boundary-flow cue. *Perception & Psychophysics,* 47, 169–179.

Yonas, A., & Granrud, C. E. (1985). The development of sensitivity to kinetic, binocular and pictorial depth information in human infants. In D. Ingle, D. Lee, & M. Jeannerod (Eds.), *Brain Mechanisms and Spatial Vision* (pp. 113–145). Dordrecht, Netherlands: Nijoff.

Yonas, A., & Granrud, C. E. (1986). Infants' distance perception from linear perspective and texture gradients. *Infant Behavior and Development,* 9, 247–256.

Yonas, A., Goldsmith, L. T., & Hallstrom, J. (1978). Development of sensitivity to information provided by cast shadows in pictures. *Perception,* 7, 333–341.

Yost, W. A. (2001). Auditory localization and scene perception. In E. B. Goldstein (Ed.), *Blackwell Handbook of Perception.* Oxford: Blackwell Publishers.

Young, F. A. (1981). Primate myopia. *American Journal of Optometry and Physiological Optics,* 58, 560–566.

Young, L. L., & Wilson, K. A. (1982). Effects of acetylsalicylic acid on speech discrimination. *Audiology,* 21, 342–349.

Young, L. R. (1971). Pursuit eye tracking movements. In P. Bachy-Rita, C. C. Collins, & J. E. Hyde (Eds.), *The Control of Eye Movements* (pp. 429–443). New York: Academic Press.

Young, R. A. (1977). Some observations on temporal coding of color vision: Psychophysical results. *Vision Research,* 17, 957–965.

Yund, E. W., Morgan, H., & Efron, R. (1983). The micropattern effect and visible persistence. *Perception & Psychophysics,* 34, 209–213.

Zadnik, K. (1997). *The Ocular Examination: Measurements and Findings.* Philadelphia : W.B. Saunders.

Zahorik, P., & Wightman, F. L. (2001). Loudness constancy with varying sound source distance. *Nature Neuroscience,* 4, 78–83.

Zakay, D., Nitzan, D., & Glicksohn, J. (1983). The influence of task difficulty and external tempo on subjective time estimation. *Perception & Psychophysics,* 34, 451–456.

Zaragoza, M. S., & Lane, S. M. (1994). Source misattributions and the suggestibility of eyewitness memory. *Journal of Experimental Psychology: Learning, Memory, and Cognition,* 20, 934–945.

Zatorre, R. J., & Jones-Gotman, M. (1990). Right-nostril advantage for discrimination of odors. *Perception & Psychophysics,* 47, 526–531.

Zatorre, R. J., Evans, A. C., Meyer, E., & Gjedde, A. (1992). Lateralization of phonetic and pitch discrimination in speech processing. *Science,* 256, 846–849.

Zatorre, R. J., Meyer, E., Gjede, A., & Evans, A. C. (1996). PET studies of phonetic processing of speech: Re-view, replication and reanalysis. *Cerebral Cortex,* 6, 21–30.

Zatorre, R. J., & Peretz, I. (2001). *The Biological Foundations of Music.* New York: New York Academy of Sciences.

Zatorre, R. J., Belin, P., & Penhune, V. B. (2002). Structure and function of auditory cortex: Music and speech. *Trends in Cognitive Sciences,* 6, 37–46.

Zatorre, R. J., Bouffard, M., Ahad, P., & Belin, P. (2002). Where is "where" in the human auditory cortex? *Nature Neuroscience,* 5, (pp. 905–909).

Zebrowitz, L. A., & Rhodes, G. (2002). Nature let a hundred flowers bloom: The multiple ways and wherefores of attractiveness. In G. I. Rhodes & L. A. Zebrowitz (Eds.), *Facial Attrativeness: Evolutionary, Cognitive, and Social perspectives. Advances in Visual Cognition,* Vol. 1 (pp. 261–293). Westport, CT: Ablex Publishing.

Zeki, S. (1990). A century of cerebral achromatopsia. *Brain,* 113, 1721–1777.

Zeki, S. (1991). Cerebral akinetopsia (cerebral visual motion blindness). *Brain,* 114, 811–824.

Zeki, S. (1993). *A Vision of the Brain.* Oxford: Blackwell.

Zeki, S., & Shipp, S. (1988). The functional logic of cortical connections. *Nature,* 335, 311–317.

Zeki, S., Aglioti, S., McKeefry, D., & Berlucchi, G. (1999). The neurological basis of conscious color perception in a blind patient. *Proceedings of the National Academy of Science,* 96(24), 14124–14129.

Zellner, D. (1991). How foods get to be liked: Some general mechanisms and some special cases. In R. C. Boles (Ed.), *The Hedonics of Taste* (pp. 199–217). Hillsdale, NJ: Erlbaum.

Zellner, D. A., & Kautz, M. A. (1990). Color affects perceived odor intensity. *Journal of Experimental Psychology: Human Perception and Performance,* 16, 391–397.

Zhang, L. I., Bao, S., & Merzenich, M. M. (2002). Disruption of primary auditory cortex by synchronous auditory inputs during a critical period. *Proceedings of the National Academy of Science, U.S.A.,* 99. 2309–2314.

Zhao, H-B., & Santos-Sacchi, J. (1999). Auditory collusion and a coupled couple of outer hair cells. *Nature,* 399, 359–362.

Zigler, M. J. (1932). Pressure adaptation time: A function of intensity and extensity. *American Journal of Psychology,* 44, 709–720.

Zihl, J., von Cramon, D., & Mai, N. (1983). Selective disturbance of movement vision after bilateral brain damage. *Brain,* 106, 313–340.

Zrenner, E., Abramov, I., Akita, M., Cowey, A., Livingstone, M., & Valberg, A. (1990). Color perception: Retina to cortex. In L. Spillman & J. Werner (Eds.), *Visual Perception: The Neurophysiological Foundations.* (pp. 163–204). New York: Academic Press.

Zucker, I., Wade, G., & Ziegler, R. (1972). Sexual and hormonal influences on eating, taste preferences, and body weight of hamsters. *Physiology and Behavior,* 8, 101–111.

Zucker, S. (1987). Early vision. In S. C. Shapiro (Ed.), *The Encyclopedia of Artificial Intelligence* (pp. 1131–1152). New York: Wiley.

Zuidema, P., Gresnight, A. M., Bouman, M. A., & Koenderink, J. J. (1978). A quanta coincidence model for absolute threshold vision incorporating deviations from Ricco's law. *Vision Research,* 18, 1685–1689.

Zurek, P. M. (1980). The precedence effect and its possible role in the avoidance of interaural ambiguities. *Journal of the Acoustical Society of America,* 67, 952–964.

Zwicker, E. (1958). Uber psychologische und methodosche Grundlagen der Lautheit. *Acustica,* 8, 237–258.

Zwiers, M. P., Van Opstal, A. J., & Cruysberg, J. R. M. (2001). Spatial hearing deficit in early-blind humans. *Journal of Neuroscience,* 21, 1–5.

Zwislocki, J. J. (1978). Masking: Experimental and theoretical aspects of simultaneous, forward, backward, and central masking. In E. C. Carterette & M. P. Friedman (Eds.), *Handbook of Perception,* Vol. IV. *Hearing* (pp. 283–336). New York: Academic Press.

Zwislocki, J. J. (2002). *Auditory Sound Transmission: An Autobiographical Perspective*. Mahwah, NJ: Erlbaum.

Zwislocki, J. J., Damianopoulos, E. N., Buining, E., & Glantz, J. (1967). Central masking: Some steady-state and transient effects. *Perception & Psychophysics,* 2, 59–64.

PHOTO CREDITS

Chapter 1

Page 1: PhotoDisc, Inc./Getty Images. Page 5: Corbis Digital Stock.

Chapter 2

Page 13: Mauro Fermariello/Photo Researchers. Page 15: Psychology Archives, The University of Akron.

Chapter 3

Page 43: D. Parker/Photo Researchers. Page 59: Bettmann/Corbis.

Chapter 4

Page 80: Photo Researchers. Pages 89 & 96: Bettmann/Corbis.

Chapter 5

Page 116: Digital Vision/Getty Images. Page 125: Corbis Images. Page 136: Bettmann/Corbis.

Chapter 6

Page 143: Royalty-free/Corbis Images. Page 162: Courtesy of Albert S. Bregman. Page 178: Courtesy of Bill Carter, Yale University.

Chapter 7

Page 179: Royalty-free/Corbis Images. Page 193: Courtesy of The University of Pennsylvania.

Chapter 8

Page 216: Stone/Getty Images. Page 241: Bettmann/Corbis.

Chapter 9

Page 256: Sandro Vannini/Corbis Images. Page 258: Walter Rohdich; Frank Lane Picture Agency/Corbis Images. Page 281: Reproduced by Courtesy of the Trustees of The British Museum. Page 285: Courtesy of Ian P. Howard.

Chapter 10

Page 291: Bryan Allen/Corbis Images. Page 311: Courtesy of Alan L. Gilchrist. Page 315: Courtesy of Julian Hochberg.

Chapter 11

Page 330: Royalty-free/Corbis Images. Page 339: Courtesy of Wolf Singer. Page 343: Reproduced by permission of Bruno Breitmeyer.

Chapter 12

Page 356: Royalty-free/Corbis Images. Page 373: Courtesy of Sverker Runeson, (c)1970 Sverker Runeson. Page 379: Copyright John Wiley & Sons, Inc.

Chapter 13

Page 388: Charles Gupton/Corbis Images. Pages 406 & 407: PhotoDisc, Inc./Getty Images. Page 408: Courtesy of Anne Treisman. Page 415: Courtesy of Michael Posner.

Chapter 14

Page 420: Photographer's Choice/Getty Images. Pages 423 & 445: Bettmann/Corbis.

Chapter 15

Page 449: Laura Dwight/Corbis Images. Page 450: Psychology Archives, The University of Akron. Page 456: Courtesy of Anthony Young (c)Anthony Young. Page 471: Bettmann/Corbis.

Chapter 16

Page 477: M.C. Escher's "Relativity" (c)2003 Cordon Art B.V.-Baarn Holland. All rights reserved. Page 480: Cornell University/(c)AP/Wide World Photos. Page 505: The Art Archive/Suermondt Museum Aachen/The Picture Desk.

Color Plate 3

Yellow fire engine: Philip James Corwin/Corbis Images.

Red fire engine: Joseph Sohm; ChromoSohmn Inc./Corbis Images.

Color Plate 7

Royalty-free/Corbis Images.

AUTHOR INDEX

AUTHOR INDEX

SUBJECT INDEX